The Encyclopedia of
WORLD AIR POWER

The Encyclopedia of
WORLD
AIR POWER

Consultant Editor: Bill Gunston

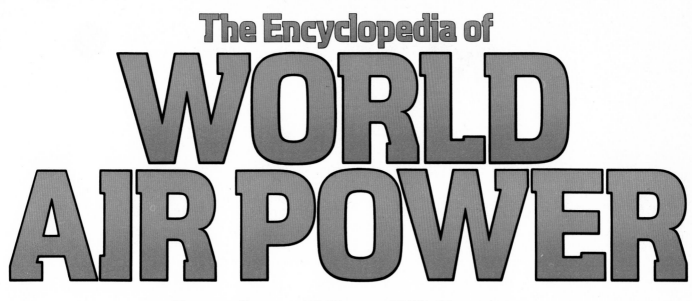

CRESCENT BOOKS
New York

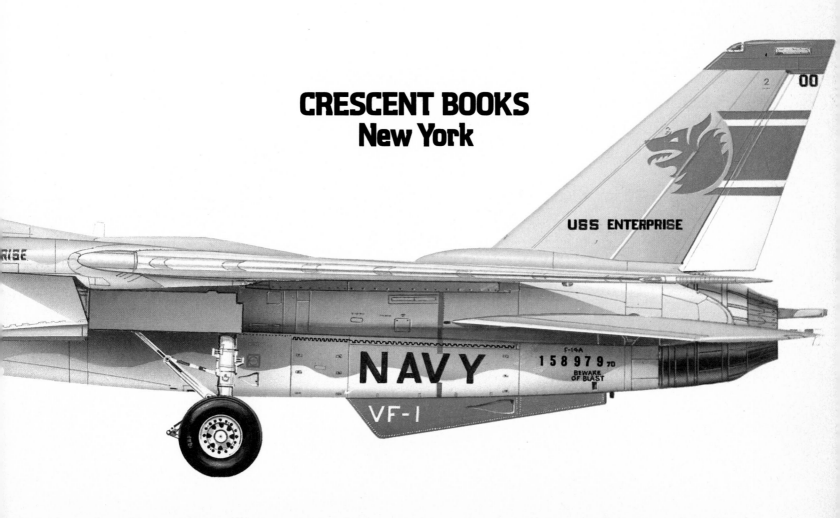

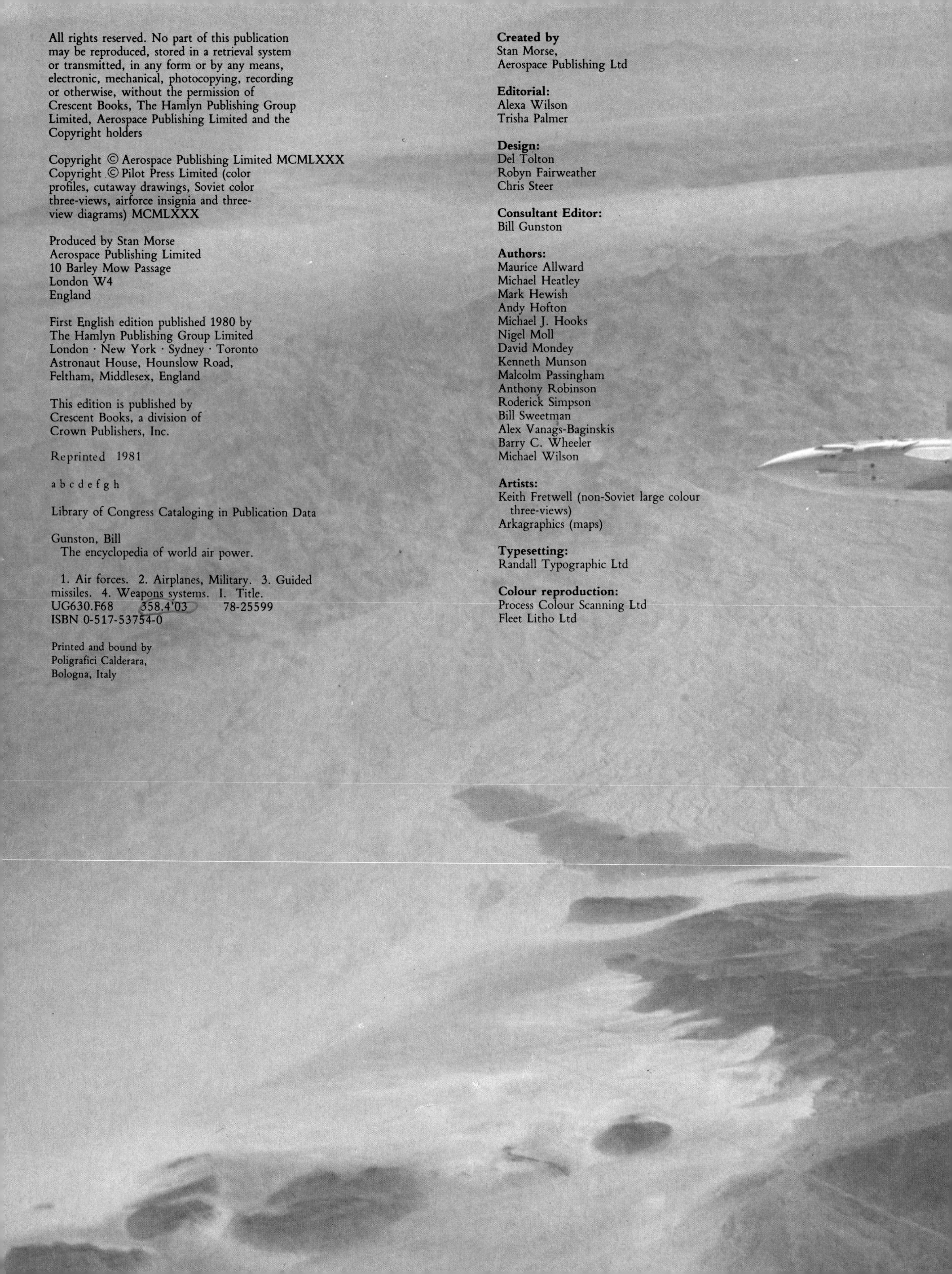

Copyright © Aerospace Publishing Limited MCMLXXX
Copyright © Pilot Press Limited (color
profiles, cutaway drawings, Soviet color
three-views, airforce insignia and three-
view diagrams) MCMLXXX

Produced by Stan Morse
Aerospace Publishing Limited
10 Barley Mow Passage
London W4
England

First English edition published 1980 by
The Hamlyn Publishing Group Limited
London · New York · Sydney · Toronto
Astronaut House, Hounslow Road,
Feltham, Middlesex, England

This edition is published by
Crescent Books, a division of
Crown Publishers, Inc.

Reprinted 1981

a b c d e f g h

Library of Congress Cataloging in Publication Data

Gunston, Bill
   The encyclopedia of world air power.

   1. Air forces. 2. Airplanes, Military. 3. Guided
missiles. 4. Weapons systems. I. Title.
UG630.F68   358.4'03   78-25599
ISBN 0-517-53754-0

Printed and bound by
Poligrafici Calderara,
Bologna, Italy

Created by
Stan Morse,
Aerospace Publishing Ltd

Editorial:
Alexa Wilson
Trisha Palmer

Design:
Del Tolton
Robyn Fairweather
Chris Steer

Consultant Editor:
Bill Gunston

Authors:
Maurice Allward
Michael Heatley
Mark Hewish
Andy Hofton
Michael J. Hooks
Nigel Moll
David Mondey
Kenneth Munson
Malcolm Passingham
Anthony Robinson
Roderick Simpson
Bill Sweetman
Alex Vanags-Baginskis
Barry C. Wheeler
Michael Wilson

Artists:
Keith Fretwell (non-Soviet large colour
   three-views)
Arkagraphics (maps)

Typesetting:
Randall Typographic Ltd

Colour reproduction:
Process Colour Scanning Ltd
Fleet Litho Ltd

Contents

The World's Air Forces

International noses belonging to some of the German-assembled Tornado IDS aircraft on the flight-line at Manching, one of the three Tornado flight-test bases.

Western Europe

After a dangerous period of near-neglect, NATO is modernising its air defences. Faced with ever-growing improvements in the Warsaw Pact air arms, the allies have embarked on several major re-equipment programmes. Most have agreed to increase defence spending by 3 per cent in real terms to offset recent inflation.

Two aircraft programmes dominate the European scene. Belgium, Denmark, Norway and the Netherlands have chosen the General Dynamics F-16 to replace ageing F-104Gs and will build the type on European assembly lines. Britain, Italy and West Germany will re-equip in the early 1980s with the Panavia Tornado fighter-bomber, an aircraft whose qualities are beginning to attract serious USAF interest.

Faced with the need to replace its delta-winged Mirage III fleet, France is pursuing its traditional course of dogged independence. Dassault's technicians have re-thought their delta-wing concept to produce the Mirage 2000 — Europe's only serious rival to the F-16. Development of the larger twin-engined Mirage 4000 continues despite the lack of an obvious customer.

Britain has at last decided that 70 interceptors hardly form a credible air defence and will boost its present F-4 and Lightning force with additional Lightnings withdrawn from reserve and armed Hawk trainers. In the longer term the Tornado F.2 interceptor will be deployed with the RAF from the mid-80s onwards.

Spain is likely to adopt either the F-16, F-18A, F-18L or Mirage 2000 as its next interceptor, while in Austria the decision between Northrop's F-5E and the Saab-Scania Viggen seems unlikely in the near future. The JA37 interceptor variant of Viggen will give the Royal Swedish Air Force a first-rate air-defence fighter but cancellation of the B3LA strike/trainer project has left a vital gap in Sweden's close-support plans.

At the other end of Europe, Turkey is desperately short of modern aircraft; lack of funds and the US arms embargo imposed after the 1974 invasion of Cyprus has left Turkey heavily dependent on veteran types such as the F-100 and F-102.

Austria	15	Italy	16
Belgium	11	Malta	17
Denmark	18	Netherlands	14
Finland	19	Norway	18
France	9	Portugal	8
Germany (West)	14	Spain	8
Great Britain	11	Sweden	18
Greece	17	Switzerland	15
Ireland (Eire)	13	Turkey	17

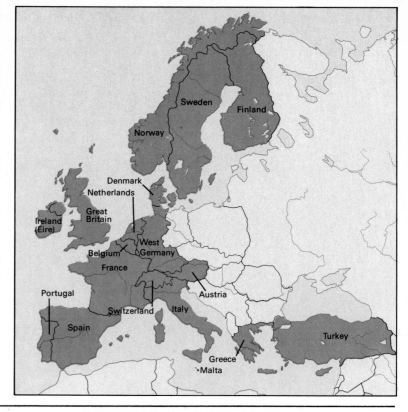

Portugal

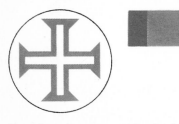

Forca Aerea Portuguesa: Although stabilising politically, Portugal still faces economic problems and her armed forces are having to forsake any extensive modernization. This is particularly true of the air force, whose only new purchase in recent months has been that of some C-130s; six Northrop T-38As, Portugal's first supersonic aircraft, have been purchased from USAF stocks. Front-line air defence is the task of Escuadra 201 with 20 North American F-86F Sabres based on the west coast at BA-5, Monte Real (FAP uses base designations but recently has begun to revert to squadron numbers). Farther south is BA-6 Montijo, which houses a ground-attack unit, No 301 Sqn, flying 18 ex-*Luftwaffe* Fiat G91R-4s of some 60 originally supplied, and six two-seat G91T-3s (from the same source) used for advanced training and conversion. Also at Montijo is a maritime reconnaissance unit, which until the end of 1977 was operating four ex-Royal Netherlands Navy

Lockheed SP-2E Neptunes attached to NATO. However, these machines have been withdrawn from service and a replacement is urgently needed; surplus USN Lockheed P-3A Orions have been mentioned. Until a decision is made, the five Lockheed C-130Hs have been tasked with providing SAR and fishery protection. BA-6 houses two helicopter units flying assault and transport duties, one equipped with 24 Aérospatiale (Sud) Alouette IIIs and the other with 12 SA.330 Pumas, of which four fly from BA-4, Lajes, in the Azores.

Long-range transport and government flights are flown by 10 Douglas DC-6A/Bs operated from Lisbon, reinforced in 1978 by five C-130H Hercules of No 501 Sqn. With the arrival of the Hercules, the DC-6s and the smaller Nord Noratlas are due to be phased out of service. Headquarters of the FAP transport element is at BA-3, Trancos, and types in use include 10 Noratlases of 30 originally acquired from French and German stocks, a few Douglas C-47s and the majority of 24 CASA Aviocars ordered in 1974 and currently flying from three bases (BA-1 Sintra, BA-3 Tancos and BA-4 Lajes).

A total of 32 Cessna/Reims F337s are in service for liaison and light communications work, having been delivered between 1974 and 1976. Sixteen are equipped to FTB.337G Milirole standard for COIN duties and eight operate in the photo-recce role. Less than a handful of Dornier Do 27s are still flying, but

Like nearly all the world's air forces the Forca Aerea Portuguesa has relied on the military DC-3 versions since World War II; now nearly all (with BA-1 and BA-3) have been replaced by the Spanish-built Casa C-212 Aviocar.

the FAP North American T-6 inventory still stands at nearly 20 in service. Thirty licence-built de Havilland Chipmunks are used for primary tuition from BA-2 Ota, while about 15 Cessna T-37Cs fly in the basic training role from BA-1 at Sintra. Advanced work is flown

on 11 Lockheed T-33As of No 103 Sqn at BA-1 and at BA-5, Monte Real. Delivered to the same base in 1977 were six ex-USAF Northrop T-38As. Helicopter training is performed on about 10 Alouette IIIs at BA-3, Tancos.

Spain

Ejercito del Aire: Spain is divided into three air regions: No 1 headquartered in Madrid, No 2 in Seville and No 3 in Zaragoza, with a fourth region covering the Canaries. Within these regions Air Defence Command operates two squadrons (known as *Escuadrones*), Nos 111 and 112 of the 11th Wing (known as *Ala*) at Manises, with 22 Dassault Mirage

IIIEEs and six IIIDE two-seaters; two squadrons, Nos 121 and 122, form the 12th Wing at Torrejón with 33 McDonnell Douglas F-4CR(S) Phantoms of 36 delivered. At Los Llanos in the south is No 14 Wing with No 141 Sqn, equipped with 14 Mirage F1-CEs. A further nine ordered in January 1977 are expected to equip the planned No 142 Sqn of the same wing; 48 more Mirages are on order comprising 42 F1-CE interceptors and six F1-BE trainers. An operational conversion group, Grupo 41, is attached to ADC at Zaragoza and equipped with more than 20 Lockheed T-33As.

Tactical Air Command has been reorganised and now comprises the 21st Wing based at Moron, with No 211 Sqn flying nine Northrop SF-5As, nine SRF-5As and SF-5Bs, and No 214 Sqn with 23 Hispano HA.220 Super

Saetas. Based in the Canary Islands at Gando for air support and reconnaissance is the 46th Wing, which is made up of four squadrons; Nos 461 Sqn with 12 CASA Aviocars, 462 Sqn with some 15 HA.200D Saetas, 463 with about 20 North American T-6Ds, and 464 Sqn with nine SRF-5As, eight SF-5As and two SF-5Bs flying in the tactical reconnaissance role. At La Parra No 221 Sqn, with two of three ex-USN Lockheed P-3A Orions delivered, operates in the ASW role manned by joint EdA/Navy crews. Three more Orions were delivered during 1979. Also attached to Tactical Command is a liaison flight at Tablada (Flight 407) with seven Cessna O-1E Bird Dogs and 12 Dornier Do 27s.

Air Transport Command has withdrawn from use its Douglas C-47s and C-54s and now enjoys a more modern inventory. The

35th Wing at Getafe is composed of two units: No 351 Sqn, re-equipping from 12 CASA Azor freighter/transports to nine CASA 212s; and No 352, flying CASA 212 Aviocars. (A recent re-order for Aviocars is understood to have taken total EdA procurement of the type to 71 aircraft.)

At Villanubla is the 37th Wing, whose No 372 Sqn flies 12 De Havilland Canada Caribous, while No 371 Sqn is expected to receive some Aviocars. Autonomous within the Command is No 301 Sqn, the Lockheed C-130 Hercules unit based at Zaragoza, which is equipped with four transport versions and three KC-130H tankers for flight refuelling of the F-4s. The 91st Group at Getafe has No 911 Sqn with four Aviocars and eight Azors, and No 912 Sqn with five Piper Aztec Es and a Piper Navajo, 61 North American

T-6s and five Beech Barons.

Within training command is No 791 Sqn at San Javier, whose task is basic training using 29 Beech F.33C Bonanzas and 25 Beech T-34As; No 792 Sqn has a dual role, some eight AISA I.115s operating in the basic role and five C-212EI Aviocars flying as crew trainers: No 793 Sqn has 37 North American T-6Gs, 30 T-6Ds and 62 Hispano HA.200s for conversion training. Jet conversion is done on 23 SF-5Bs of Nos 731 and 732 Sqns at Talavera la Real, while multi-engine training is performed by No 74 Sqn with eight Aviocars and No 742 Sqn with 24 F.33A Bonanzas, eight Beech King Air C90 instrument trainers and 18 Beech Baron twin trainers. A total of 60 CASA C-101 basic/advanced trainers are on order, with the first unit becoming operational in 1980. At Cuatro Vientos Nos 751 and 752 Sqns fly 24 Agusta AB 47Gs and three Bell UH-1Hs for helicopter training; 17 Hughes 300s have been ordered to replace the older types in use. Fourteen AB 205 helicopters operate on VIP and SAR duties as part of Servicio de Busqueda y Salvamento, operating alongside nine Grumman SA-16A Albatross, five Aérospatiale (Sud) Alouette IIIs, three AB 47Js and two Do 27s flying in three units (Nos 801, 802 and 803 Sqns) from Mallorca, the Canary Islands and Madrid respectively. Three Fokker F.27M Maritime SAR aircraft have been ordered for delivery in 1979 to replace the Albatross amphibians, and one will be based at each of the above bases. In addition there are 11 other units, tasked mainly with support and liaison duties and including No 401 Sqn with an ex-Iberia DC-8-52 and four Dassault Falcon 20s for VIP use, No 403 Sqn at Cuatro Vientos with five Do 27s, five Aviocars for photographic work, No 404 Sqn at Torrejón with seven Canadair CL-215 amphibians for fire-fighting and tactical duties, and No 721 Sqn at Alcanterilla with Aviocars for paratroop training.

A defence treaty signed in 1976 between Spain and the United States allows the latter continued use of the airfields at Torrejón, Zaragoza and Moron, together with the naval base at Rota. In return the Spanish air force is to receive more modern equipment, believed to include up to 72 General Dynamics F-16s for four 18-aircraft squadrons, and, as an interim measure, four more F-4Cs and four RF-4Cs to supplement the present force of F-4Cs currently in use; Spain has refused to accept the 42 F-4Es previously agreed to. Also purchased through the USAF is Spain's air-defence system known as Combat Grande. This consists of seven long-range radar sites supplying data round-the-clock to a central computer, from where the information is transmitted to the appropriate Air Sector; fully automatic operation of the system began in 1978.

Arma Aérea de la Armada: Spain's naval air arm operates the 15,890-ton helicopter carrier Dedalo (ex-USS Cabot), transferred in August 1967, which, with the acquisition of V/STOL BAe Matadors, has been reclassified as an aircraft-carrier. The six AV-8A Matadors (reduced to five following a crash in 1976) and two TAV-8A two-seat combat trainers, ordered via the United States in 1973, form No 008 Sqn. To increase the effectiveness of the force, a further five Matadors have been ordered and eventual deliveries could take the total to 24 aircraft. The remaining strength of the naval air arm is made up chiefly of helicopters operating in the ASW, SAR and transport roles.

The largest type in service is the Sikorsky SH-3D Sea King, which flies with No 005 Sqn at Rota naval base. Twelve aircraft are in service and detachments are periodically sent aboard Dedalo. No 001 Sqn has 12 Bell/AB 47s for pilot training and communications duties; a sister unit, No 002 Sqn, was disband-

Spain's EdA uses the comfortable Beech F.33C Bonanza, which it calls the E-24. These aircraft equip Training Command's No 791 Sqn, at San Javier. Other squadrons still use the T-6, while jet training is done on the HA-200.

ed in 1976. Four AB 212ASW anti-submarine helicopters delivered to the arm in 1974 equip No 003 Sqn, which also has on charge four AB 204B transport machines for Marine assault use. Another ASW unit is No 006 Sqn, flying 13 Hughes 500M (ASW)s received in 1972; detachments are regularly deployed aboard destroyers. For attack duties six Bell AH-1G HueyCobras of eight delivered form No 007 Sqn. Fixed-wing liaison duties are performed by No 004 Sqn, with two Piper Comanches and two Twin Comanches.

Fuerzas Aeromoviles del Ejército de Tierra (FAMET): Established in July 1965, this aviation branch of the Spanish army is a helicopter force with some 80 machines. The headquarters is at Los Remedios, Madrid, and the present establishment is made up of five

Helicopter Units or Unidades de Helicopteros. At the HQ base is Unidad 1, equipped with three Bell OH-58As, 16 Bell AB 205s and two Alouette IIIs for a variety of duties including close-support and liaison. Unidad II is at Virgen del Camino, with three Bell OH-58As and 12 Bell UH-1Hs; a similar establishment is flown by Unidad III at Agoncillo and Unidad IV at El Copero. FAMET's heavy transport flight is Unidad V at Los Remedios, equipped with six Boeing CH-47C Chinooks plus a further three for imminent delivery. In addition to the Chinooks, helicopter strength totals 52 Bell UH-1Hs, six UH-1Bs (used for training), 12 Bell OH-58As/AB 206s, six Bell 47Gs and 2 Alouette IIIs. A further 18 OH-58As and 8 UH-1Hs have been ordered.

France

L'Armee de l'Air: France's nuclear strike force of 50 Dassault Mirage IV strategic bombers is expected to remain in service until 1985, when silo-based S-3 missiles will form the country's strategic deterrent until the year 2000. A total of 62 Mirage IVs were originally delivered to the air force, and the 33 aircraft on call for service equip six squadrons in two wings (91 and 94 Escadres) dispersed among some six bases. Twelve Mirage IVAs have been converted for long-range reconnaissance at both high and low level. Three tanker squadrons support the bombers, each with four Boeing KC-135Fs, the 11 remaining aircraft being based at Istres. These aircraft are due to be re-engined with CFM56s.

The conventional air force has three main commands, Air Defence, Tactical and Air Transport, operating within four air regions (No 1 with headquarters at Metz, No 2 at Paris, No 3 at Bordeaux and No 4 at Aix-en-Provence). Approximately 500 combat aircraft are in service, of which 345 are Dassault Mirage IIIs, 5s and F1s, and there are another 1,000 transport and second-line types in the inventory.

Tactical Command, or Commandement Aérien Tactique, is divided into 1st and 2nd CATac and controls seven squadrons of Mirage IIIE fighter-bombers with a combined conventional/nuclear attack role (2nd Wing at Dijon with two squadrons and the Mirage OCU with IIIB/C/BEs; the 4th Wing at Luxeuil with two squadrons; 13th Wing at Colmar, which has three squadrons of Mirage IIIEs and the 5Fs relinquished by 3rd Wing at Nancy, which is now a SEPECAT Jaguar unit). The 33rd Wing at Strasbourg

Here seen without drop tanks, the Mirage IIIR, together with the doppler-equipped IIIRD, equips the French Armée de l'Air's No 33 Tac Recon Wing at Strasbourg.

comprises three squadrons with nearly 50 Mirage IIIR/RDs and a few Lockheed RT-33As. Jaguars continue to join the squadrons, the 7th Wing at Nancy having three units, the 11th Wing at Toul-Rosieres three more, and the 3rd Wing, also at Nancy, also three squadrons.

In 1980, when the last of 200 Jaguars is delivered to the air force, a total of ten squadrons in three wings will be operational. In addition, the 92nd Wing at Bordeaux with

two Dassault Vautour squadrons, was disbanded to be replaced on 1 January 1979 by a Jaguar unit with 20 aircraft. North American F-100D/F Super Sabres and Dassault Mystère IVAs previously flown by the air force have been flown to the UK for storage, having been supplied and purchased through the US Offshore Procurement programme. A training unit, the 8th Wing at Cazaux, is scheduled to continue flying Mystère IVs until the arrival of Dassault-Breguet/Dornier Alpha

Jets in 1982. The wing uses the aircraft in the jet conversion and weapon-training roles.

Air Defence Command or Commandement Air des Forces de Défense Aérienne (CAFDA), has an interceptor network linked to NATO's 'NADGE' chain and operating within the Strida air defence system. To extend radar range, a French AWACS is being developed, based on the A300 Airbus and scheduled for service in 1982. Six squadrons are now equipped with Mirage F1s (two in the 5th Wing at

continued

Orange, two in the 12th Wing at Cambrai and two in the 30th Wing at Reims) of a planned procurement of 231 aircraft for eight squadrons in four wings; initial order was for 105 F1s followed by a further 63 aircraft of a planned second batch of 109. At Creil, the 10th Wing operates two squadrons of Mirage IIICs and is due to receive F1s from 1980, the 1978 defence budget having set aside funds for 33 F1s for this unit. A third squadron in the three existing wings may be formed with the later production aircraft.

Air Transport Command, or *Commandement du Transport Aérien Militaire* (CoTAM), comprises the C.160 Transalls totalling some 46 aircraft in the 61st Wing with headquarters at Orleans, and four squadrons of Nord Noratlas totalling nearly 120 aircraft (two squadrons in the 62nd Wing at Reims and two squadrons in the 64th Wing at Evreux). Discussions among Aérospatiale, MBB and VFW-Fokker concerning the re-opening of the Transall production line were successfully concluded in 1977 and the first machines off the new line are due in 1980 to meet a French requirement for 25 aircraft to replace the Noratlas.

For long-range VIP work, one squadron of the 60th Wing at Roissy flies four McDonnell Douglas DC-8Fs, while a second squadron at Villacoublay operates a mixed fleet of VIP/liaison types including an Aérospatiale (Sud-Aviation) Caravelle, five Dassault Falcons, two Aérospatiale Pumas and three Cessna 411s. Nine Douglas DC-6A/Bs in a squadron of the 64th Wing at Evreux have recently been replaced by three ex-UTA Caravelle 11Rs for flights between France and her Pacific bases. The 65th Wing has two squadrons flying short-range liaison duties with Nord Frégates, Falcon 20s, Morane-Saulnier Paris and Holste Broussards. Five helicopter squadrons are concerned mainly with liaison and SAR duties and have about 50 Aérospatiale (Sud) Alouette II/IIIs and 10 Pumas. The training units will be steadily modernized over the next few years with the arrival of Alpha Jets, while twin conversion continues on 34 Dassault Flamants recently refurbished and expected to remain in service until at least 1980. Miscellaneous types include eight Cessna 310Ns, two 310Ks and two 310Ls. A large Potez-Air Fouga Magister training and liaison force totals some 300 aircraft. Overseas, the air force has conducted strike operation with Jaguars, supported by Transalls, against Polisario guerrillas from bases in Senegal and Mauritania. Other sup-

port elements operate from St Denis Réunion in the West Indies and from Papeete in the Pacific, mostly flying Alouette helicopters and Noratlas transports. Based at Noumea is ETOM 52 equipped with three Puma helicopters for support work.

The first of four government-ordered prototypes of the French air force Dassault Mirage 2000 programme made its first flight on 10 March 1978. The planned initial production order is for 127 aircraft, with deliveries due to begin in 1982. Total procurement is likely to reach 250-300 aircraft, replacing the present Mirage III force. Although specified as a multi-role aircraft, the 2000 will have a bias towards interception/air superiority but with a ground-attack capability. A twin-jet Super Mirage 4000 strike aircraft is under development as a private venture by the company, and first flight was made early in 1979. Delivery of the 200 Alpha Jet E1 trainers on order began during 1979, replacing Mystère IVAs and T-33As.

Aèronautique Navale: The French navy maintains two 27,300-ton aircraft carriers, *Clemenceau* and *Foch*, with a strike force of several units. In the strike role there are two squadrons, *Flottilles* 11F and 17F, with 36 Dassault Etendard IVMs and based at Landivisiau and Hyères respectively, and a reconnaissance squadron, *Flottille* 16F, based at Landivisiau, with 14 Etendard IVPs. For the interceptor role there are 32 Vought F-8E(FN) Crusaders in two squadrons based at Landivisiau, *Flottilles* 12F and 14F. A total of 71 Dassault Super Etendards are scheduled to be ordered to replace both the Etendards and the Crusaders from 1978. The first production Super Etendard flew in November 1977 and the first unit to become operational was deployed aboard *Clemenceau* in January 1979. Carrier-based fixed-wing ASW work is performed by two Breguet Alizé squadrons, *Flottilles* 4F and 6F, home-based at Lann-Bihoué and Nîmes-Garons respectively; a total of 46

aircraft remain on strength, of which 28 are being modernised with new radar and ESM, and are due for service from 1980 until 1990–92 when the two carriers are due for retirement. *Flottille* 32F supplements the Alizé units aboard the carriers, being equipped with 10 Aérospatiale (Sud) Super Frelon ASW helicopters and operating from Lanvéoc-Poulmic.

Maritime Patrol Command encompasses the shore-based MR units covering the Channel, Atlantic and Mediterranean areas. Thirty-five Breguet Atlantics equip four units (*Flottilles* 21F and 22F at Nîmes-Garons and 23F and 24F at Lann-Bihoué) and 14 Lockheed SP-2H Neptunes fly with *Flottille* 25F, also at Lann-Bihoué. An updated version of the Atlantic, known as the M4 or 'Atlantic *Nouvelle Génération*', is under development by Dassault-Breguet for service in early 1985. A total of 42 will be ordered. The 11,000-ton helicopter carrier *Jeanne d'Arc* is used as an officer training ship but can be operated in the ASW role with accommodation for some eight helicopters. A second vessel of 18,000 tons has been ordered, designated PH-75 and due for service in the 1980s. Helicopter-equipped units include *Flottille* 34F based at Lanvéoc-Poulmic, flying Aérospatiale (Sud) Alouette IIIs for shipboard detachment, *Flottille* 31F at St Mandrier with ten Westland Lynx, *Flottille* 33F at the same base with 16 HSS-1s replaced in 1979 by five Super Frelons; *Escadrilles* 22S and 23S (Alouette III units) fly communication duties and supply helicopters for planeguard work aboard the carriers. The *Aéronavale* Lynx order stands at 26 aircraft for ASW and surface strike, with deliveries beginning in October 1978 to replace ASW HSS-1s and Alouettes.

Second-line units include *Escadrille* 2S at Lann-Bihoué, flying three Piper Navajos and four Nord 262s of 21 supplied to the service; *Escadrille* 3S at Hyères with four 262s and five Navajo; *Escadrille* 20S at St Raphael, operating as a flight-test wing mainly equipped with helicopters; and *Escadrille* 12S, based in Papeete with three specially modified Neptunes. Fifteen SOCATA Rallye 100s are used for training, together with some Alizés and Fouga Zéphyrs.

Five Dassault Falcon 10MERS are used for radar training and fleet support at Landivisiau and Hyères, while nine Morane-Saulnier Paris operate from the former base as high-speed transports. Overseas, a number of units operate various second-line types, including *Escadrille* 9S with Neptunes, Douglas C-47s and Douglas C-54s on New Caledonia and some Alouette IIIs on Hao.

Aviation Légère de l'Armée de Terre (ALAT): Like many of the world's army aviation formations, France's ALAT is almost entirely helicopter-equipped and provides observation and liaison services for army ground forces. The force has, however, undergone a reorganisation from the traditional *Groupes d'Aviation Légère de Corps d'Armée* (Galca) and the *GAL de Division* (Galdiv) to *Regiments d'Helicoptères de Combat* (RHC). Of the planned total of six RHCs, all have formed or are about to form. Each regiment has seven *escadrilles* or squadrons, comprising two reconnaissance units equipped with Aérospatiale Gazelles, three anti-tank units equipped with Aérospatiale (Sud) Alouette IIIs armed with SS.11s and later Gazelles with HOT and two *escadrilles de manoeuvre* equipped with Aérospatiale Pumas.

Two of the regiments are being attached to each of the French army's two army corps, and the command of each regiment will be integrated with corps headquarters. The remaining two RHCs will be held in reserve. In addition, one *Groupe d'Helicoptères Légères* (GHL) composed of 30 Gazelles and Alouette IIs and IIIs will be attached to each of the army corps for utility work such as casevac, liaison and AOP. Another GHL of 20 light helicopters is attached to each of the six French military territorial regions. ALAT's helicopter inventory includes 140 Pumas, 220 Alouette IIs for the LOH role and 84 Alouette IIIs, many equipped with SS.11 missiles for anti-tank duties. A total of 170 Gazelles are being delivered, with more than half in service, replacing the Alouette IIs. ALAT intends to retain the SS.11-armed Alouette III force in service alongside the HOT-armed Gazelles for the foreseeable future. The first SA.341F/HOT unit is the 3rd *Regt. d'Heli* based at Etain, which formed in September 1978. A third-generation anti-tank helicopter is being considered but nothing firm has yet been announced.

Fixed-wing Cessna O-1s and Holste Broussards continue in service at the ALAT basic pilot training base of Dax in south-west France, to give pupils their initial air experience. Trainees then proceed to Alouette IIs and complete the course on Gazelles. Also in use are a few Piper Super Cubs and Tri-Pacers.

Dassault-Breguet persuaded the French Aéronavale that it would be better to buy the Super Etendard than the previously developed and more capable Jaguar. After some delays and a cut in numbers to 71 these aircraft entered service in 1979.

Belgium

Force Aérienne Belge: Belgium's combat units form part of NATO's 2nd ATAF along with the British, Dutch and German air forces based in Europe. In June 1975, the Belgian government announced the choice of the General Dynamics F-16 to replace the FAB's Starfighter force from 1979; a total of 116 aircraft (104 single-seat F-16As and 12 two-seat F-16Bs) are on order. The first of 18 F-16s was delivered in January 1979 from the Sabca/Fairey production lines at Gosselies, to be followed by 12 in 1980, 19 in 1981, 22 in 1982, 22 in 1983 and nine in 1984. The Lockheed F-104 Starfighter force due for replacement comprises the 10th Wing at Kleine Brogel with two squadrons or *Smaldeel* (Nos 23 and 31) each with 18 F-104Gs in the fighter-bomber role; and the 1st Wing at Beauvechain with Nos 349 and 350 Sqns, again each flying 18 F-104Gs and operating in the all-weather fighter-interceptor role. The first unit to convert to the F-16 is No 349 Sqn, which began conversion in 1979. Two-seat TF-104Gs are on the strength of each unit. A total of 100 single-seat and 12 two-seat Starfighters were originally delivered to the FAB, but attrition has reduced these numbers to a total in-service figure of 81 aircraft.

The Dassault Mirage force consists of the 2nd Tactical Wing, with No 2 Sqn flying 18 Mirage 5BAs in the fighter-bomber role and No 42 Sqn flying 18 tactical reconnaissance Mirage 5BRs from Florennes. The 3rd Tactical Wing, based at Bierset, is made up of No 1 Sqn with Mirage 5BA fighter-bombers and No 8 Sqn with two-seat 5BDs, the latter operating as an OCU while retaining its combat status. A total of 106 Mirages were originally procured, consisting of 63 5BAs, 27 5BRs and 16 5BD conversion trainers, but some 18 have been lost.

No 15 Transport and Communications

FB-01 of the Belgian Air Force, the first General Dynamics F-16 to be assembled in Europe, made its maiden flight in December 1978. A two-seat F-16B, it was very close to the final production standard, and is camouflaged in light grey.

Wing at Melsbroek comprises two squadrons, one of which, No 20 Sqn, is equipped with 12 Lockheed C-130H Hercules for heavy-lift and tactical work. The other unit is No 21 Sqn, equipped with a number of different types and flying liaison, communications and VIP duties. Two ex-Sabena Boeing 727QCs have replaced four long-serving Douglas DC-6Bs; six Swearingen Merlin IIIAs and two Dassault Falcon 20s cater for VIP and short-range liaison, while three BAe (Hawker Siddeley) HS 748s fitted with large freight doors are employed for transport duties.

Elementary training is flown on 33 SIAI-Marchetti SF.260MBs at Goetsenhoven of 36 originally delivered between 1969 and 1971. For basic training there are 40 Fouga Magisters in Nos 7 and 9 Sqns at Brustem, while advanced tuition is done on 12 Lockheed T-33As of No 11 Sqn at the same base. A total

of 33 Dassault-Breguet/Dornier Alpha Jet 1Bs are on order to replace the Magisters, with deliveries scheduled to begin early in 1979 and end by April 1980. A SAR flight, based at Coxyde and designated No 40 Sqn, flies five Westland Sea King Mk 48s delivered in December 1976, replacing 11 Sikorsky S-58s; one of the Sea Kings has a VIP interior for use by the Belgian royal family.

Force Navale Belge: The Belgian Navy operates one Sikorsky HSS-1 and three Aérospatiale Alouette IIIs on SAR and support duties in close co-operation with the Air Force's No 40 Sqn at Coxyde.

Force Terrestre Belge: The Belgian Army Air Corps flies almost 90 machines in four squadrons for liaison and AOP duties. Based at Brasschaat is the Light Aviation School (No 15

Sqn), equipped with seven Britten-Norman Defenders and 24 Aérospatiale Alouette IIs (Artouste- and Astazou-powered) of a total of 66 in service. Nos 16, 17 and 18 Sqns are based in Germany operating with NATO units, 16 Sqn flying Britten-Norman Defenders and 14 Alouette IIs from Cologne, and Nos 17 and 18 Sqns having approximately 18 Alouettes between them. The Defenders, based at Brasschaat and with No 16 Sqn, are used in the light transport, liaison and instrument training roles. Six Piper Super Cubs remain in the inventory for glider towing.

Gendarmerie: This small airborne arm of the Belgian police has an official strength of eight helicopters, comprising three Aérospatiale SA.330 Pumas and five Alouette IIs, based at Brasschaat and maintained by the Army Air Corps.

Great Britain

Royal Air Force: Since 1977 a number of steps have been taken to strengthen Britain's air arm. The infusion has been badly needed after nearly a decade of defence cuts which have left the RAF with a considerably reduced force operating in support of NATO and the defence of Great Britain. A long-standing requirement for a medium-lift helicopter is to be met with the announcement of an order for 33 Boeing CH-47 Chinooks. Costing $200 million, the aircraft are due for delivery beginning in July 1980. In 1978 it was revealed that a number of BAC VC10/Super VC10s would

Two Harrier GR.1s of the RAF over Belize during the crisis caused by the claim on the territory by Guatemala. No other combat aircraft could have provided such airpower in a distant region devoid of airfields or facilities.

continued

be converted into strategic tankers to supplement the RAF's present force of Handley Page Victor K.2s. The number due for conversion stands at five standard aircraft and four Super VC10s. BAe (HS) Hawk trainers continue to arrive at RAF Valley and at RAF Brawdy, while Westland Sea Kings have joined RAF SAR units following initial deployment late in 1978.

Strike Command's No 1 (Bomber) Group has six squadrons of HS (Avro) Vulcan B.2s totalling 85 aircraft (9, 35, 44, 50, 101 and 617 Sqns plus 230 OCU) and flying chiefly in the long-range low-level penetration role, and a fleet of 24 Victor K.2 tankers flying with 55 and 57 Sqns and 232 OCU based at Marham. Four Vulcan SR.2s equip 27 Strategic Reconnaissance Sqn at Scampton, and at Wyton 39 Sqn operates 17 BAC Canberra PR.9s in the high-altitude recconnaissance role alongside the electronic surveillance unit, 51 Sqn, which flies three BAe Nimrod R.1s and four Canberra B.6s. Also at Wyton is the Electronics Warfare School, the joint-services-operated 360 Sqn, with 17 ECM Canberra T.17s, and 13 Sqn with 14 Canberra PR.7s previously based in Malta until the withdrawal of British forces from the island in 1978. The Canberra training unit, 231 OCU, is currently based at Marham alongside the special target-facilities squadron, No 100, which operates Canberra B.2s, E.15s, T.19s and T.4s mainly in the high-altitude role; the other target-facilities unit is 7 Sqn, also Canberra-equipped with B.2s, T.4s and TT.18s and based at St Mawgan. The BAe (HS) Buccaneer S.2A/2B wing based at Honington has nearly 50 aircraft equipping 12 and 208 Sqns, the former equipped with Martel ASMs and currently assigned the maritime strike role. The Buccaneer OCU, No 237, is also on the base and a new unit, 216 Sqn, is due to form at Honington in early 1979, equipped with ex-RN S.2Bs. These aircraft were formerly flown by 809 Sqn on *Ark Royal* and the new unit will operate in the low-level strike role from Lossiemouth. Both the Buccaneers and the Vulcans will be replaced by 220 Panavia Tornado GR.1s of 385 planned for procurement starting in 1980. First base for Tornado will be Cottesmore, which will house an international OCU. The remaining 165 aircraft will be Tornado F.2s, planned to take over interceptor duties from the McDonnell Douglas F-4 Phantoms and BAe (BAC) Lightnings in the 1980s. One of the main weapons of the UK interceptor force in the future will be the advanced Sky Flash air-to-air missile, production examples of which are now being delivered. Also operated within No 1 Group is Brize Norton-based 115 Sqn, flying six BAe (HS) Andover E.3s on calibration duties having replaced Hawker Siddeley Argosies early in 1978.

Air defence is the responsibility of 11 Group, Strike Command, with headquarters at Bentley Priory. The BAC Lightning and McDonnell Douglas Phantom are currently the mainstay of the force. At Binbrook, 5 and 11 Sqns have nearly 40 Lightning F.3/F.6/T.5s, which are scheduled to remain operational until 1984 flying alongside the UK's chief air-defence aircraft, the Phantom. This interceptor in its FGR.2 form equips 23, 29, 56 and 111 Sqns and 228 OCU at Coningsby, Wattisham and Leuchars, while in its ex-naval FG.1 form it equips 43 Sqn at Leuchars in Scotland. Early-warning radar coverage of the UK is tied in the with the NATO Air Defence Ground Environment system, which operates in conjunction with three main radar units at Buchan, Boulmer and Neatishead. Missile protection is available at Leuchars by Rapier SAMs of 27 Sqn, RAF Regiment, with a second unit to be formed for the protection of Lossiemouth, while a Bloodhound 2 unit, 85 Sqn, has detachments at Bawdsey, North Coates and West Raynham, with a fourth base to be decided. Also under 11 Group is the early-warning Hawker Siddeley Shackleton AEW.2 squadron, No 8, based at Lossiemouth with 12 aircraft. These are due for replacement by 11 BAe Nimrod AEW.3s ordered in March 1977 for delivery in 1982 in preference to the Boeing E-3A AWACS after prolonged discussion with other NATO countries which examined a joint E-3A force. Eight aircraft are expected to be converted from the last production batch of Nimrods on the line at Woodford and three aircraft will come from the formerly Malta-based 203 Sqn, which has been disbanded.

No 18 (Maritime) Group has reponsibility for SAR and MR over the North Sea, Atlantic, and home waters. Four squadrons (42, 120, 201 and 206 Sqns plus 236 OCU) with 35 Nimrod MR.1s (total 46) operate from St Mawgan and Kinloss. A Nimrod updating programme is under way, Mk 1s being converted to Mk 2s by installation of Searchwater radar, extra sensors and improved navigational systems. Four aircraft are assigned to protecting North Sea oil and fishery interests. Helicopter SAR detachments are based around Britain from two squadrons equipped with Westland Whirlwind HAR.10s and Westland Wessex HC.2s. No 22 Sqn has five flights, one each at Chivenor (A Flt), Leuchars (B Flt), Valley (C Flt), Brawdy (D Flt) and Manston (E Flt); 202 Sqn operates four flights, one each at Boulmer (A Flt), Leconfield (B Flt), Coltishall (C Flt) and Lossiemouth (D Flt). To replace the Whirlwinds, additional Wessex and 15 Westland Sea King HAR Mk 3s joined the two squadrons during 1979.

No 38 Group is the RAF's tactical element and provides offensive support for the army, flying one squadron (No 1) and an OCU (No 233) of BAe Harrier GR.3s at Wittering, and a wing of three squadrons of SEPECAT Jaguar GR.1s (6, 41 and 54 Sqns) based at Coltishall. A total of 89 single- and 20 two-seat Harriers were procured for the RAF, but losses have taken these figures down to a total of around 80 aircraft, so in order to maintain the RAF's Harrier strength 24 more GR.3s are on order. The Jaguar force comprises 163 single-and 37 two-seaters, delivery of which is complete. The force is split into three units in the UK and five in Germany. Of the three units at Coltishall assigned to the UK Mobile Force, 41 Sqn is primarily a reconnaissance squadron, its aircraft equipped with BAC-built centreline reconnaissance pods, although the unit has a secondary ground-attack capability. At Odiham the 38 Group tactical helicopter force is made up of 72 Sqn, with 20 Wessex HC.2s, and 33 and 320 Sqns, which, with 240 OCU, have a total of some 36 Aérospatiale/Westland Puma HC.1s. A further 22 Pumas are required by the service and an order was officially placed early in 1979. The Chinooks are expected to replace the Wessex HC.2s in Germany and the UK. A detachment of six Harriers and some Puma support helicopters is based in Belize following the threat of invasion by Guatemala in July 1977.

In the long-range transport role and based at Brize Norton are 11 VC10s of 10 Sqn. At Lyneham is the Lockheed Hercules C.1 wing, comprising 24, 30, 47 and 70 Sqns and 242 OCU, and equipped with some 45 aircraft on tactical and strategic duties. The Hercules are undergoing a reconditioning programme at a cost of £25 million to maintain the force until the late 1980s and 30 aircraft will receive a 15-ft (4.57-in) fuselage stretch to increase their capacity. Two communications squadrons, 32 and 207 Sqn, fly Hunting Pembrokes, four HS.125-400s and two -600s, 13 de Havilland Devons and four Whirlwinds, while the Queen's Flight at Benson has three Andover CC.2s and two Wessex HCC.4s; 12 Andovers remain in RAF service, both C.1s and CC.2s. A Tactical Weapons Unit based at Brawdy is equipping with Hawk T.1 weapon trainers and nearly 80 Hawker Hunter Mk 6As in three 'shadow' squadrons, 63, 79 and 234 Sqns. A second TWU has been established at RAF Lossiemouth with the Hunters. This is to relieve congestion at Brawdy as increasing numbers of Hawks arrive.

RAF Germany's operational component is under the control of NATO's 2nd Allied Tactical Air Force and tasked with nuclear and conventional strike, support, reconnaissance and air defence. The Harrier force comprises two units, 3 and 4 Sqns based at Gutersloh, with aircraft from the former 20 Sqn increasing the establishment of the two units to some 36 machines. Jaguar strike operations centre on Brüggen, with 14, 17, 20 and 31 Sqns; the fifth Jaguar unit, 2 Sqn, flies tactical reconnaissance from the main PR base at Laarbruch. At the same base, 15 and 16 Sqns operate Buccaneer S.2s. Interception duties are performed by 19 and 92 Sqns at Wildenrath flying Phantom FGR.2s. Protecting the German bases are Rapier and Bloodhound units; RAF Regiment Rapier squadrons are 63 at Gutersloh, 16 at Wildenrath, 26 at Laarbruch and 37 at Brüggen. Three bases are covered by flights of Bloodhounds of 25 Sqn. At Wildenrath, about 12 Pembroke C.1s equip 60 Sqn providing communication flights throughout the command, and at Gutersloh are 15 Wessex HC.2s of 18 Sqn divided into three flights assigned to support I British Army Corps in Germany.

This echelon was formed by one Jaguar GR.1 from each of the five squadrons equipped with these fine aircraft based in Germany: Nos 2 (nearest camera, Laarbruch), 14 (Brüggen), 17 (Brüggen), 20 (Brüggen) and 31 (Brüggen).

The Malta-based Canberra PR unit, 13 Sqn, was moved to Wyton in 1978 when UK forces left the island. In Hong Kong is 28 Sqn with Wessex HC.2 helicopters, recently based at Kai Tak but now at Sek Kong; detachments of Hunters operate from Gibraltar for training purposes.

The training side of RAF Support Command has a strength of 180 BAC Jet Provost T.3/T.5s, 131 BAe (SA) Bulldogs, 19 HS. Dominies, 22 Hunters and 10 Aérospatiale/Westland Gazelles, although losses have reduced these numbers slightly. No 4 FTS Valley operates 20 Hunters and some of the 175 Hawks on order. The 50 Hawker Siddeley Gnat T.1s were retired from use in November 1978, their training work being taken over by the Hawks. Navigation training is performed by 6 FTS at Finningley on Dominies. A multi-engined training squadron based at Leeming uses eight Scottish Aviation Jetstreams, and at CFS Shawbury helicopter tuition is performed on the Gazelles. The Central Flying School is now based at RAF Leeming with Jet Provosts while 3 FTS, previously at Leeming and also with Jet Provosts, has moved to RAF Dishforth to prevent congestion at the former base. No 2 FTS at Church Fenton conducts primary flying grading on Bulldogs, while No 1 FTS at Linton-on-Ouse operates Jet Provosts in the basic phase.

Fleet Air Arm: A total of 34 BAe Sea Harrier FRS.1s are on order for operation from the anti-submarine cruisers HMS *Invincible* (19,500 tons), which was launched in May 1977, HMS *Illustrious*, launched in December 1978, and HMS *Ark Royal*. Deliveries of these aircraft began in 1979, and the air arm plans to carry one squadron of Sea Harriers and one of Westland Sea Kings in each of the new cruisers. The three units will be 800, 801 and 802 Sqns, with eight aircraft each. Shore base will be RNAS Yeovilton, where 700H Intensive Flying Trials Unit was formed in 1979. HMS *Invincible* will be commissioned in 1980 with a seven-degree bow ramp following successful Harrier trials on a 'ski-jump' at RAE Bedford. HMS *Hermes* has been converted to the ASW role and will operate 814 Sqn Sea Kings and a few Sea Harriers; she retains a secondary commando role. HMS *Bulwark* is to be restored to full operational status as an ASW carrier, while the navy's only strike carrier, HMS *Ark Royal*, was retired from service in December 1978. The McDonnell Douglas Phantom FG.1s of 892 Sqn and the BAe (HS) Buccaneer S.2s of 809 Sqn, previously part of *Ark Royal*'s air group, have been transferred to the RAF and the units disbanded. Also withdrawn from use is the Westland Gannet AEW.3 unit, 849 Sqn, home-based at Lossiemouth. The air group's Westland Sea King HAS.1 unit, 824 Sqn, is now the small ships squadron for the type. A Wessex HAS.3 drawn from 737 Sqn is assigned to each of the seven 'County' class guided-missile destroyers and the two cruisers, HMS *Blake* and *Tiger*, operate Sea Kings of 820 and 826 Sqns. The latter squadron was the first unit to receive the HAS.2 version of the Sea King late in 1977. Eight more Sea King HAS.2s were ordered and delivered in 1978, bringing the total RN orders for this type to 56 Mk 1s and 21 Mk 2s. One Westland Wasp HAS.1 from 829 Sqn is assigned to each of the 'Leander', 'Amazon', 'Sheffield', 'Tribal' and 'Rothesay' class ships, making 40 flights in total.

RNAS Yeovilton, shore HQ of the FAA, has two squadrons and a training unit of Commando/Wessex HU.5s (845, 846 and 707 Sqns) in addition to the Fleet Requirement and Air Direction Unit operated by Airwork Services Ltd, which has BAC Canberra T.22s and TT.18s and Hawker Hunter GA.11s. The two Wessex units will each receive four new Westland Sea King HU.4s from the 15 ordered in 1978. Also at the base is the first Westland Lynx Mk 2 squadron, No 702, which was commissioned in January 1978. This unit will supply flights to RN ships as well as train Lynx aircrew; HMS *Birmingham* has the first Lynx flight. A total of 88 SAR and ASW Lynx are on order, with later aircraft going to 'Leander' class and Type 42 ships. Other shore bases include Culdrose, where 750 Sqn flies eight Sea Prince T.1s for observer training. These were replaced during 1979 by the first of 16 BAe (SA) Jetstream T.2s procured from the original RAF order. At the same base is 705 Sqn, with Gazelle HT.2 pilot training helicopters; 706 Sqn, with 10 Sea Kings; and 771 Sqn SAR School, with Wessex 1s. At Lee-on-Solent, 781 Sqn, the navy's communications unit, flies four de Havilland Sea Herons and eight Sea Devons. Portland acts as a training and shore base for 703 and 829 Sqns, with Wasps; 737 Sqn, with

Wessex HAS.3s; and 772 Sqn fleet requirements unit, with Wessex HU.5s. Prestwick in Scotland houses the Sea King-equipped 819 Sqn. An air-experience flight of de Havilland Chipmunks is based at Roborough.

Army Air Corps: Army aviation is a corps in its own right within the British army and has a strength of about 38 fixed-wing aircraft and 400 helicopters. An AAC regiment comprises two squadrons in each army division, and each squadron can operate as a number of self-supporting flights. Aérospatiale/Westland Gazelle deliveries continue, with more than 130 of the 158 on order already in service. About half the Gazelles will be armed for the anti-tank role, the remainder being assigned to liaison and communication. Each of the four army divisions in Germany will receive one Gazelle LOH squadron and one TOW-armed Westland Lynx anti-tank squadron. All units in Germany and the UK previously flying Bell/Westland Sioux have been re-equipped with Gazelle. The Lynx Intensive Flying Trials Unit was disbanded in December 1978 at Middle Wallop and the first squadron in Germany, 654 Sqn at Minden, has now received Lynx AH.1s with more converting. A total of 100 Lynx AH.1s are on order to replace the AAC's 120 Westland Scouts, and all those deployed will be equipped with Tow missiles for the anti-tank role.

The recent reorganisation of the corps has seen an increase in the number of regiments in Germany to five, with a corresponding reduction in the UK-based force by one squadron. No 1 Wing, based at Detmold in Germany with BAOR, controls Nos 1, 2, 3, 4 and 9 Regiments. These regiments consist of the following squadrons: 651, 661, 652, 662, 653, 663, 654, 664, 659 and 669. No 2 Wing, AAC, UK Land Forces, based at Wilton, controls 5, 6, 7 and 8 Field Force embodying 655, 656, 657 and 658 Sqns, together with 7 Regiment, No 8 Flight at Netheravon. The Gazelles operated in Hong Kong by 11 Flight, previously 656 Sqn, have been replaced by Scouts with three of these aircraft operating in Brunei on detachment from Sek Kong, and there is a single Flight, No 16, based in Cyprus flying the eight remaining Aérospatiale (Sud) Alouette IIs. Units of DHC Beavers and Gazelles are assigned to Northern Ireland on four-month tours of anti-terrorist duties. About 14 Beavers and 24 de Havilland Chipmunks continue in army service for a variety of tasks including transport and training.

Pilot training is conducted at Middle Wallop on Bristow-operated Bell 47Gs at the basic stage, before moving to the advanced stage and Gazelle AH.1s.

British Aerospace Hawk T.1 of the RAF Tactical Weapons Unit at Brawdy, seen on a rocketing mission off the Welsh coast. Capable of carrying 6,500 lb (2948 kg) of weapons, the Hawk is a powerful tactical platform. By January 1980 the RAF had 160.

Ireland (Eire)

Irish Army Air Corps: The increased pressure of border operations and the advancing years of the equipment flown by the IAAC have prompted a re-equipment programme which is now nearing completion. To replace two remaining airworthy de Havilland Vampire T.55s, six Aérospatiale Super Magisters armed with 7.62-mm machine-guns and underwing rocket launchers have been delivered, the final two aircraft arriving in November 1976. These aircraft are primarily used for training. In the same month a Shorts Skyvan was demonstrated to the corps in response to a requirement for a de Havilland Dove replacement and a maritime patrol aircraft. Four aircraft would be required, but no

order has been forthcoming. Another type currently under evaluation is the Beech King Air 200, one of which has been leased for a three-year period of trial operations for evaluating surveillance equipment on maritime patrol duties.

The IAAC, headquartered at Casement Aerodrome, Baldonnel, is mainly employed on SAR, ambulance missions, border surveillance and reconnaissance, survey work and limited navaid checking. Three Doves, one equipped with survey cameras, are still flying but are about to be retired. Eight DHC Chipmunk trainers have been replaced by 10 SIAI-Marchetti SF.260WE Warriors, the first four of which were delivered in March 1978. While spares last, six of the retired Chipmunks will be used for liaison staff flying. The helicopter element comprises eight Aérospatiale Alouette IIIs of the Helicopter Rescue Service, which are also used for army co-operation duties. Seven of eight Cessna FR.172Hs with provision for underwing stores patrol the borders, flying from their base at Gormanston, County Meath. The four surviving Provosts were finally retired when the SF.260s arrived.

Most recent acquisition of the Irish Army Air Corps, ten SF.260WE Warriors provide economical multi-role and weapons capability well matched to the service's domestic needs. They are based mainly at the Casement HQ Airfield.

Netherlands

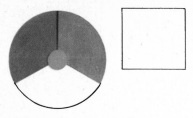

Koninklijke Luchtmacht: The Royal Netherlands Air Force forms part of NATO's 2nd ATAF and has two main commands: Tactical Air Command, controlling all combat elements, and Logistic and Training Command. A total of 120 Lockheed F-104G Starfighters and 18 two-seat TF-104Gs was originally procured by the KLu, though attrition has reduced the number in service to some 117 aircraft. Two interceptor squadrons, Nos 322 and 323 Sqns at Leeuwarden, operate within the NADGE air-defence system with 18 F-104Gs each plus six reserves. Supplementing these is the USAF's 32nd TFS at Soesterberg, flying 18 McDonnell Douglas F-15 Eagles under joint KLu/17th Air Force control. Two nuclear and conventional strike squadrons based at Volkel, Nos 311 and 312 Sqns, also fly F-104Gs. At the same base No 306 Sqn performs reconnaissance duties with Starfighters. The General Dynamics F-16 is replacing the F-104G force, the Netherlands order currently standing at 80 F-16As and 22 two-seat F-16Bs. First deliveries were made during 1979 to Nos 322 and 323 Sqns, with a

simultaneous change of role from interception to strike.

A total of 75 Canadair-built Northrop NF-5As and 30 NF-5Bs were delivered to the air force between 1969 and 1972. They equip three squadrons: Nos 314 at Eindhoven, 315 at Twenthe and 316 at Gilze Rijen; No 313 Sqn OCU training unit has two-seaters at Twenthe. Transport duties are undertaken by No 334 Sqn at Soesterberg, flying nine Fokker F.27M Troopships and three Mk 100 Friendships. Flown and operated by the air force on behalf of the army for AOP and liaison are 72 Aérospatiale (Sud) Alouette III helicopters of No 298 Sqn at Soesterberg and 299 Sqn at Deelen. No 300 Sqn also operates from Deelen, equipped with 30 MBB BO105Cs. KLu aircrew training begins in Canada, with students progressing from Beech Musketeers to Canadair Tutors and CF-5Bs. Operational jet conversion then takes place in Holland, using two-seat NF-5Bs and TF-104Gs.

Marine Luchtvaartdienst: The Royal Netherlands Naval Air Service is a small, compact maritime force of four squadrons, equipped with long-range maritime aircraft and helicopters. Seven Breguet SP-13H Atlantics, of nine originally ordered in 1968, equip No 321 Sqn at Valkenburg. On the same base are the 15 Lockheed SP-2H Neptunes of No 320 Sqn; both units are assigned to the ASW role. A Neptune replacement has been decided in favour of the Lockheed P-3C Orion, an order for 13 aircraft being placed in December 1978. A detachment of three Neptunes is based at

Standard tac-recon types of the KL (Royal Netherlands AF) are the RF-104G and Dutch/Canadian NF-5 Freedom Fighter. These are NF-5As with recon pods.

Curacao in the southern Caribbean. Two helicopter squadrons, Nos 7 Sqn and 860 Sqn at De Kooy, complete the force. The former unit has received six Westland UH-14A Lynx, which have replaced seven Agusta AB 204s in the SAR, VIP and ship-to-shore liaison role. A further 10 SH-14B Lynx entered service in 1979 with uprated engines and the ability to operate in the ASW role, equipped with dunking sonar for use from navy frigates. A further eight SH-14Cs were ordered in January 1978

in a deal worth £11.5 million. They will have MAD initially, with the possible later addition of sonar equipment. Still in use with No 860 Sqn are 10 Westland AH-12A Wasps. Twelve more Lynx are planned to replace the Wasps after 1983. Naval air training is carried out by the national training college for airline pilots on Cessna 150s and Saab Safirs, followed by the air force with F27s. Helicopter pilots train at Deelen on KLu Aérospatiale Alouette IIIs.

Germany (West)

Luftwaffe: The air arm of the Federal Republic of Germany is in the process of a major re-equipment and modernization programme which is planned to continue until the end of the 1970s. Fully committed to NATO's 2nd and 4th Allied Tactical Air Forces, the *Luftwaffe* and *Marineflieger* currently operate 600 aircraft, while the total strength for all three services is more than 2,100 aircraft. *Luftwaffe* manpower remains slightly above 100,000.

Main combat type now in full-scale service is the McDonnell Douglas F-4 Phantom, a total of 260 F-4F/RF-4Es of 273 delivered being in use. Equipping two fighter interceptor *Geschwader* are the F-4s flying with JG 71 at Wittmundhafen and JG 74 at Neuburg, assigned to the 2nd ATAF and the 4th ATAF respectively. Also flying F-4Fs are two fighter-bomber *Geschwader*: JaboG 35 at Pferdsfeld in the 4th ATAF, and JaboG 36 at Rheine-Hopsten in the 2nd ATAF. Eighty-eight RF-4Es equip two reconnaissance *Geschwader*, AG 51 at Bremgarten in the 4th ATAF and AG 52 at Leck in the 2nd ATAF. In February 1979 the second part of the re-equipment programme began with initial deliveries to the Fürstenfeldbruck base of the first of 175 Dassault-Breguet/Dornier Alpha Jet 1A light attack and tactical training aircraft. The first production Alpha Jet for the *Luftwaffe* made its first flight on 12 April 1978. The type will replace Fiat G.91s currently in service with *Waffenschule* 50. The third and final phase saw the first deliveries in 1979 of 324 Panavia Tornadoes to the *Luftwaffe* and *Marineflieger*. Present plans call for 212 Tornadoes to equip *Luftwaffe* units JaboG 31, 32, 33 and 34, and 112 for MFG 1 and 2 of the navy.

The Lockheed TF/F-104G Starfighter force of 430 aircraft is due to be replaced by Tornadoes and the current status of this type stands at four *Geschwader*: JaboG 31 at Noervenich (2nd ATAF), JaboG 32 at Lechfeld (4th ATAF), JaboG 33 at Buchel (2nd ATAF) and JaboG 34 at Memmingen

Now gradually becoming an important type in the West's armoury, the Tornado IDS is far more effective than any other aircraft of its size. This is No 13, a pre-production example, formating with speedbrakes open to kill speed.

(4th ATAF). The Starfighter OCU at Jever flies single and two-seaters. Of the 240 Fiat G.91R/3s on *Luftwaffe* charge, only about 100 remain fully operational. They fly in two attack wings, leKG 41 at Husum and leKG 43 at Oldenburg, both in the 2nd ATAF. When re-equipped with AlphaJets, leKG 41 and 43 will be redesignated fighter-bomber units, JaboG 41 and 43. About 55 two-seat G.91Ts fly with WS 50 at Fürstenfeldbruck for environmental training. When re-equipped with Alpha Jets the unit will be redesignated JaboG 49.

Two tactical transport wings — LTG 61 at Landsberg and LTG 63 at Hohn — operate 76 C.160D Transalls, while the Transall OCU at Wunsdorf has a further 14 of the type. A special government and VIP flight based at Köln-Wahn has four Boeing 707-320Cs, three Lockheed JetStars and four HFB 320 Hansa Jets. In April 1977 the first of three VFW 614s was delivered to the flight, the second arriving in June and the third aircraft in July. These replaced three Convair 440s. Based at Ahlhorn is the Helicopter Transport Wing

HTG 64, flying 105 Bell UH-1Ds. Every *Geschwader* has assigned to it four Dornier Skyservants for liaison and light transport duties. Three Bell 212s have been delivered for SAR work on Sardinia. Nine Hunting Pembrokes, three BAC Canberras, two Douglas C-47s and five Nord Noratlas remain in service on communications and special duties. Four Hansa Jets fly ECM sorties from Lechfeld. The Piaggio P.149D still flies with the Air Cadets Regiment in limited numbers for familiarisation flights. A replacement for these long-serving aircraft is currently being sought, types under consideration include the Beech T-34C, Pilatus PC-7 and the RFB Fantrainer. A total of 41 Northrop T-38s and 35 Cessna T-37Bs are stationed permanently in the United States for pilot training.

Marineflieger: The naval air arm of the *Bundeswehr* is scheduled to update its combat force of three fighter-bomber squadrons, currently flying 96 Lockheed F-104Gs, and its reconnaissance squadron with 25 RF-104Gs, with 112 Panavia Tornadoes from 1979. MFG

1 at Schleswig and MFG 2 at Eggebek are the two *Geschwader* involved. At Nordholz, MFG 3 operates 18 Breguet Atlantics on MR and ASW duties, and replacement of these aircraft has been deferred. Instead Dornier is to update them with modern equipment over the next few years. For SAR duties, 21 Westland Sea King Mk 41s equip MFG 5 at Kiel-Holtenau with detachments at Borkum, Heligoland and Sylt. Twenty Dornier Skyservants fly on communications and liaison with 2/MFG 5 together with 15 Sikorsky H-34G helicopters.

Heeresflieger: The army air corps provides liaison, communications and observation facilities for the *Bundeswehr* and operates about 550 helicopters. The German army is composed of three corps, each having its own Army Aviation Command. Each AAC has a squadron of 10 Aérospatiale (Sud) Alouette IIs, a light transport regiment with two *Staffeln* of 20 Bell UH-1Ds each and a medium transport regiment with two *Staffeln* of 16 Sikorsky CH-53Gs each. The main headquarters are at Munster in the north, Koblenz in the centre and Ulm in the south. A helicopter training centre at Buckeburg is equipped with all three major rotary-wing types. Dornier-built Bell UH-1Ds number 195, and there are 240 Alouette IIs, including about 50 Alouette-Astazous. A total of 110 CH-53Gs, built by VFW-Fokker, are in service with the three medium transport regiments, TR 15, TR 25 and TR 35. A total of 227 Messerschmitt-Bölkow-Blohm BO105M liaison and communications helicopters are planned to replace the Alouettes, and an initial order for 100 is now being met by MBB. In answer to the army's PAH-1 anti-tank helicopter requirement, orders have been placed for 212 BO105Ps each armed with six HOT ATGMs. Deliveries began during September 1979, with full entry into service in 1980, when a regiment of 56 PAH-1s will be attached to each German army corps and divided into flights of seven aircraft, which will in turn be attached to brigades or divisions. In answer to the army's other requirement (PAH-2, a specialized anti-tank helicopter) a number of companies are submitting bids.

The Federal German Marineflieger is a major operator of the Westland Sea King, with 21 of the Mk 41 species used for SAR (search and rescue) by MFG 5. This unit has its headquarters at Kiel-Holtenau, with Sea King detachments at readiness at Sylt, Borkum and Heligoland. A few H-34Gs also remain on duty.

Austria

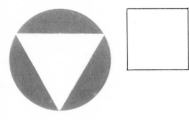

Oesterreichische Luftstreitkräfte: The Austrian Air Force is an integral part of the Federal Army and has a total strength of some 150 aircraft. The main strength of the OLk is made up of 36 Saab 105Ö fighter-bombers, most of which equip a Surveillance Wing or *Uberwachungsgeschwader* of *Fliegerregimenter* II and a Fighter-Bomber Wing or *Jagdbombergeschwader* of *Fliegerregimenter* III. Each of these wings comprises two Squadrons or *Staffeln*, each with seven or eight aircraft, based at Linz and Graz, one of the *Jagdbombergeschwader Staffeln* acting as a training unit. A light transport squadron, or *Flachflügelstaffel*, of *Fliegerregiment* I, operates two Short Skyvan 3Ms on supply work and aerial survey from Tulln, and at the end of 1976 it received 12

Pilatus PC-6 Turbo-Porters for operation on a variety of tasks including casevac, liaison and communication. Also on the strength of the unit are seven Cessna O-1E Bird Dog AOP aircraft and a single Saab *Safir*.

Because of the nature of the country, helicopters play an important role and the OLk has more than 60 in service, operating under the command of *Fliegerregiment* I at Linz. The machines equip three units: *Hubschraubergeschwader* (Helicopter Wing) I with 13 Agusta AB 204As flying mainly in the training role but having a SAR commitment, and a second *Staffel* with 12 Bell OH-58Bs delivered in 1975 – 76 for the AOP task; *Hubschraubergeschwader* II with two *Staffeln* flying 22 Aérospatiale Alouette IIIs on SAR missions; *Hubschraubergeschwader* III with 22 AB 204B utility helicopters, which are being replaced by 24 AB 212 twin-engined machines during 1979 – 80; and also in this unit are two Sikorsky S-65C-2 heavy-lift helicopters delivered in 1970. Approximately 20 Saab 91D Safirs equip *Fliegerregiment* II for basic pilot training at Tulln; some of the AB 206As are attached to the unit for helicopter training.

An announcement has been deferred on the choice of a new combat aircraft to re-equip the

These two Skyvan 3Ms are the main transport capability of the small OL, the Austrian air force. They equip the Flachflügelstaffel (light transport squadron) together with single-engined types including 12 new Pilatus Porters.

OLk's fighter-bomber units. A technical evaluation report is currently with the defence minister on the IAI Kfir C-2, Northrop F-5E and the Saab Viggen, with the choice likely to fall on the F-5E, with procurement expected in about 1980.

Switzerland

Swiss Air Force and Anti-Aircraft Command: This small country remains strongly neutral and has an air force of some 300 combat aircraft flying in a chiefly defensive role. A part of the army, the Swiss AF and Air Defence Corps has about 450,000 personnel, of which a large percentage are part-time militiamen. An efficient system of rock shelters and associated runways is operated to protect its aircraft and equipment in time of war. The force currently incorporates all the operational units into three regiments *(Fliegerregimenter)*, each consisting of between six and eight squadrons, or Fliegerstaffeln, with an establishment of some 18 aircraft each.

In 1979 the force phased into service the first new combat aircraft for some years when the initial batch of Northrop F-5E air-superiority fighters joins the front-line Surveillance Wing, which currently comprises five squadrons, two with Hawker Hunters, two with Dassault Mirages and the reconnaissance unit with Mirages and de Havilland Venoms. The F-5E was evaluated in 1974 and an order for 72 aircraft was finally placed in

1976. Deliveries to the air force are under way: 13 F-5Es and six two-seat F-5Fs have arrived from Northrop, while the remaining 53 aircraft, all Es, are being assembled at the Federal Aircraft Factory, Emmen, from components air-freighted from the USA. Four squadrons are scheduled to equip with these aircraft.

Just before selection of the F-5E and as an interim measure, the air force purchased a further 60 Hunters in 1974. These aircraft, Mk 58As and eight two-seat Mk 68s, together with existing machines, brought the Swiss Hunter inventory to 148. Armed with Sidewinder missiles and Saab BT9K bombing computers, the Hunters equip nine squadrons (Nos 1, 4, 5, 7, 8, 11, 18, 19 and 21 Sqns) in the ground-attack role, with two units, Nos 1 and 11 Sqns, assigned to the Surveillance Wing. Approximately 100 Venom F.4 fighter-bombers of 250 originally in service equip seven squadrons (Nos 2, 3, 6, 9, 13, 15 and 20 Sqns). A total of 36 Mirage IIIS interceptors and two two-seat IIIBS combat trainers equip two squadrons, Nos 16 and 17 Sqns at Ammen and Payerne, integrated into the Hughes Florida early-warning and air-defence system. Entering service in 1966, the 57 Mirages procured included 16 IIIRS tactical reconnaissance variants, and these fly in No 10 Sqn alongside eight camera-equipped Venoms.

A transport flight maintains three immaculate Junkers Ju 52/3m for both freight and paratroop training use. Three Beech Twin Bonanzas, six Dornier Do 27s, 11 Pilatus Porters and 24 Turbo-Porters form the fixed-

Still the most numerous and important Swiss combat aircraft until delivery of all the F-5Es, the Hunter equips Nos 1, 4, 5, 7, 8, 11, 18, 19 and 21 Staffeln in the ground-attack role. Most, including this example, are of the Mk 58A type.

wing element of seven light-aircraft squadrons (Nos 1-7 Sqns) flying liaison, communications and SAR duties. Also assigned to these units are 27 Aérospatiale (Sud) Alouette II and 80 Alouette III helicopters. A target-towing element has 23 F & W C-3605 turboprop-powered tugs introduced into service in the early 1970s. Training duties are performed by

some 120 Pilatus P-2/P-3s for multi-role and primary work respectively, with about 40 DH Vampire Mk 6s and 35 Vampire T.55s. flying in the advanced role. One regiment of 64 BAC Bloodhound 2s provides anti-aircraft defence alongside 19 light AA Battalions and 18 medium battalions equipped with 20-mm and 35-mm cannon respectively.

Italy

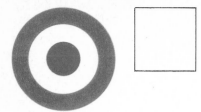

Aeronautica Militare Italiano: One of the original signatories of the North Atlantic Treaty, Italy plays an important role in Allied Forces Southern Europe, having some 19 squadrons assigned to 5th ATAF while retaining a small number of units for national defence. The current AMI force allocated to NATO is made up chiefly of Lockheed Starfighters, the F-104S version now predominating and having almost replaced the earlier F-104G. A total of 205 Aeritalia-built F-104S Starfighters were ordered and have been delivered, and these equip three interceptor wings or *Stormi* (the 4th Wing at Grosseto, the 9th at Grazzanise and the 53rd at Cameri), each with a squadron or *Gruppo* of 12 aircraft, 9, 10 and 21 Sqns respectively. Three further wings have a strike/interceptor role with the F-104S: the 5th Wing at Rimini-Miramare with 23 and 102 Sqns, the 36th Wing at Gioia del Colle with 12 and 156 Sqns, and the 51st Wing at Istrana (Treviso) with 22 and 155 Sqns. The 6th Wing at Ghedi, comprising 154 Sqn, flies F-104Gs in the bomber role, while the 3rd Wing at Verona-Villafranca, with 28 and 132 Sqns, operates F-104Ss and some 30 RF-104Gs in the tactical reconnaissance role. Twenty ex-AMI F-104Gs have been transferred to the Turkish air force. The remainder of the active Starfighter force is to be supplemented by the 100 Panavia Tornados on order, which are expected to replace the F-104Gs in the 6th Wing at Ghedi.

A fighter-bomber wing, the 8th at Cervia-San Giorgio with 101 Sqn, operates the twin-engined Aeritalia G.91Y, together with a further squadron, No 13, attached to the 32nd Wing at Brindisi. A total of 65 Ys were purchased. The AMI's remaining Fiat G.91R strike/reconnaissance element comprises the 2nd Wing at Treviso-San Angelo with 14 and 103 Sqns. The official Italian aerobatic team, *Frecce Tricolori*, operates G.91PANs in a dual combat/demonstration role as 313 Sqn at Rivolto. The team began to replace its ageing G.91s with the new Aermacchi MB339 during 1979.

Transport duties are performed by the 46th Brigade at Pisa, comprising 2 Sqn with 20 Fairchild C-119Gs, 50 Sqn with 13 Lockheed C-130H Hercules and 98 Sqn with Aeritalia G222s (15 aircraft). A total of 44 G 222s were delivered to replace the C-119s. A SAR wing, No 15 at Ciampino with 84 and 85 Sqns, is equipped with 12 Grumman HU-16A Albatross in the former unit and seven Agusta AB 47Js and 14 AB 204s in the latter. The helicopters are being replaced by 20 Agusta-built HH-3Fs, of which four have been delivered. The 14th Wing at Pratica di Mare near Rome is an ECM and radio calibration unit formed from 8 and 71 Sqns, and equipped with four Piaggio PD-808s, two Douglas EC-47s, two G 222s, and some Beech C-45s and Lockheed T-33As. Two squadrons, 92 and 306, form the 31st Wing, the former unit being equipped solely with two Agusta-built AS-61TS VIP helicopters and the latter squadron flying two Douglas DC-9-30s, two Douglas DC-6s and some PD-808s based at Ciampino. A total of 25 PD-808s are in AMI service, plus a number of helicopters including 90 AB 47Js, 60 AB 204Bs and 60 AB 206s.

Training begins on SIAI-Marchetti SF.260s, students graduating to MB326s in three squadrons or *Gruppi*, Nos 212, 213 and 214, at the basic training school at Lecce-Galatina. Advanced work is performed on approximately 100 G.91Ts of 201, 204 and 205 Sqns at Foggia-Amendola, and 28 two-seat TF-104Gs of 20 Sqn at Grosseto. Twenty SF.260AMs have replaced the Piaggio P.148s in 207 Sqn at Latina, and 100 of the new MB339s are scheduled to replace the 130 MB326s over the next few years. Liaison duties are performed by 51 Piaggio P.166Ms,

44 SIAI-Marchetti SM.208Ms and some of the PD-808s.

Three regional communication units are divided as follows: 1 Region at Milan flying Piaggio P.166Ms, North American T-6s, SM.208Ms, AB 47Js and AB 204Bs; 2 Region at Guidonia flying T-6s, P.166Ms, SM.208Ms, and C-47s; 3 Region at Bari-Palese flying AB 204Bs and P.166Ms.

Marinavia: Primarily a helicopter-equipped force, the *Marinavia* has an ASW element of 24 Agusta-built SH-3D Sea Kings in two units for deployment aboard Italian naval vessels. These will also equip the projected 10,000-ton helicopter carrier *Garibaldi*, ordered in 1977 for delivery to the Italian navy in 1982; it will carry 16 Sea Kings. Two further squadrons have 30 Agusta AB 204ASs, the latter being replaced by 48 AB 212ASW helicopters now being delivered. Five Agusta A 106 torpedo-carrying helicopters operate from 'Impavido' class ships.

For training/liaison duties, 12 AB 47G/Js are flown. The fixed-wing units comprise 86 Sqn, 30th Wing, at Cagliari Elmas with Breguet Atlantics, and 87 and 88 Sqns, 41st Wing, at Catania, flying 18 Grumman S-2F Trackers and the remainder of the 18 Breguet Atlantics originally delivered to the Service. These ASW units come under the command of the navy but are on the air force establishment.

Aviazione Leggera dell'Esercito (ALE): The army has a large helicopter force for liaison, AOP and anti-tank duties. More than 400 machines comprise 100 AB 47G/Js, 50 AB 204Bs, 138 AB 205s, and 142 AB 206s ordered

Pictured over Brindisi, its home town, the 32º Stormo (caccia-bombardieri-ricognitori) comprises the 13º Gruppo CBR with the Aeritalia G 91Y, some of which are seen here, and the 632ª Squadriglia Collegamenti with the G 91T.

This Agusta-built Sikorsky SH-3D is one of 24 (expected to be augmented) used in the ASW role from ships of the Italian fleet, with home basing at either La Spezia or Catania. Italy is expected to participate in the replacement WG.34.

for light observation duties. For heavy-lift work 26 Meridionali-built Boeing CH-47C Chinooks are being delivered, together with five Agusta A 109 Hirundos for TOW missile tests and an option on a further 60. Fixed-wing aircraft include some 110 Cessna O-1Es and Piper Super Cubs, and more than half of 80 SIAI-Marchetti SM.1019s on order to replace the older types.

Malta

Armed Forces of Malta: Headquartered at St Patrick's Barracks, Malta, this small air arm comprises a helicopter flight equipped with four Bell 47Gs originally donated by West Germany in 1971 and an Agusta AB 206 presented by Libya in 1973. Duties include general surveillance, transport and anti-smuggling patrols. The air arm's first fixed-wing equipment, two or three ex-West German Dornier Do 27s, has been received but with Malta's isolation following the withdrawal of British forces in 1978, Libya has stepped in as the country's main arms supplier. Three Aérospatiale (Sud) IIIs and a Super Frelon have been donated for SAR duties from Libyan air force stocks.

Greece

Elliniki Aeroporia: The Hellenic Air Force is organised into three main commands: Tactical Air, Training and Air Material. Within the 28th Tactical Air Command are six combat wings (*Pterighe*), each with up to three squadrons (*Mire*). No 110 Wing at Larissa flies strike/reconnaissance duties, with 345 Sqn operating 18 LTV A-7H Corsair IIs, and 348 and 349 Sqns each with 14 Northrop RF-5As. At Nea Ankhialos is No 111 Wing, which is assigned day interceptor duties with 337, 341 and 343 Sqns, each equipped with 15 Northrop F-5A/Bs. No 114 Wing is based at Tanagra and embraces two interceptor squadrons, 336 and 342, equipped with 40 Dassault Mirage F1CGs, delivery of which was completed in 1977. A further strike wing is No 115 at Souda Bay, comprising two units with A-7H Corsairs, 338 and 340 Sqns, while a fighter-bomber wing, No 116, is based at Araxos with nearly 30 Lockheed F-104G/TF-104Gs forming a single squadron, No 335. At Andravidha, No 117 Wing operates 18 McDonnell Douglas F-4E Phantoms in 339 Sqn and a second unit with a further 20 F-4Es. Eight RF-4Es equip a reconnaissance unit and 18 more F-4Es are being delivered to the following US government approval early in 1977, swelling the Greek Phantom inventory to 64 aircraft. The $259.2 million order for 60 LTV A-7Hs was completed in 1977 but a further order has been placed for five two-seat TA-7H trainers plus one two-seater conversion from an existing A-7H airframe; delivery of these is expected to be made in 1980. The 24 General Dynamics (Convair) F-102A/TF-102As previously operated by No 114 Wing have been withdrawn from use, as have the remaining Republic F-84F Thunderstreaks. Also within TAC is 363 Sqn at Eleusis equipped with eight ex-Norwegian Grumman HU-16B Albatross amphibians and flown under naval control for MR, ASW and SAR duties.

Air Material Command comprises two units, 355 and 356 Sqns, based at Eleusis and operating three main types. The heavy-lift and troop-transport fleet has 12 Lockheed C-130H Hercules, the last four having joined the fleet in 1977; nearly 40 ex-*Luftwaffe* Nord Noratlas, with a further 20 purchased from Israel in 1976; and 30 Douglas C-47s. A single Grumman Gulfstream I is used for VIP flights. Also based at Eleusis are three helicopter units: 357 Sqn with 10 Bell 47Gs; 359 Sqn with 12 Sikorsky H-19Ds; and 362 Sqn with 14 Agusta AB 205s. In 1977, 35 Bell UH-1 utility helicopters were delivered to Greece from the USA and are likely to replace the older types in Greek air force use. The air force may also to receive a small number of Boeing CH-47C heavy-lift helicopters from the USA.

Training Command has a National Air Academy at Dhekelia, where students undergo initial training on 20 Cessna T-41As. For basic jet instruction, 361 Sqn at Eleusis has 18 Cessna T-37Bs, with advanced tuition flown on 40 Rockwell T-2E Buckeyes operated by 360 Sqn at the same base. The T-2Es are replacing about 50 Lockheed T-33As used for some years and acquired from ex-*Luftwaffe* stocks. A number of T-33As have been converted by Dornier into target tugs.

When qualified, pilots proceed to the squadrons for operational conversion on to combat types via the two-seater variants, which include nine Northrop F-5Bs and four

Though Greece was not an original customer for the F-104G Starfighter its Elliniki Aeroporia has one fighter/bomber wing, No 116, equipped with the type. Some have been replaced by the A-7H, but still equip the wing's No 335 Sqn.

TF-104Gs. Eleven Canadair CL-215 water bombers are also in use.

The Greek navy has a helicopter force of four Aérospatiale (Sud) Alouette IIIs for liaison and communications duties, and is receiving between 12 and 16 AB.212 ASWs in an order announced in 1978. The army air component operates two Rockwell Commander 680s, 15 Piper L-21s and 25 Cessna U-17s. Helicopters include five Bell 47Gs, 40 AB 204/205s and 10 Bell UH-1Ds.

Relations between the United States and Greece, somewhat strained in recent years following the Cyprus debacle in 1974, warmed considerably in July 1977 with the signing of a new defence agreement between the two countries. The agreement guarantees Greece $410 million-worth of military aid over four years and in return allows the USA the use of some Greek military installations. It is also seen as an attempt to bolster the flagging southern flank of NATO and the 6th Allied Tactical Air Force, whose effectiveness has caused concern within the Alliance following the Greek-Turkish confrontation over Cyprus. Although withdrawn from NATO, Greece has indicated that in an emergency she would support the alliance.

Turkey

Turk Hava Kuvvetleri: The **Turkish air force** is divided into three main components under the overall direction of Air Forces Central Command. The combat squadron operates under the command of the First Tactical Air Force, Eskisehir Air Division, and the Third Tactical Air Force, Diyarbakir Air Division. The third component is Training Command, Izmir Air Division. From 12 air bases plus a further 17 smaller bases used in emergencies, the air force operates a total of 22 combat squadrons with more than 420 aircraft. Forty Italian-built Aeritalia F-104S Starfighter multi-role fighters equip two squadrons. The two strike squadrons fly 32 Lockheed F-104Gs and four TF-104Gs, and 20 ex-Italian air force F-104Gs were bought in 1976 to form a third unit. Forty McDonnell Douglas F-4E Phantoms equip two squadrons, with delivery of a further 32 Es and eight RF-4Es currently under way. Two interceptor squadrons operate 35 ex-USAF General Dynamics (Convair) F-102As and three TF-102As, and six ground-attack squadrons have 125 Northrop F-5As, 15 two-seat F-5Bs and seven ex-Libyan F-5As. A reconnaissance force of two squadrons has 36 RF-5As, and a further strike element of five squadrons has a total of 80 North American F-100D/F Super Sabres. Another 60 F-100Ds are in storage in central Anatolia.

The main transport base is Kayseri. This branch of the air force comes under general staff command. A total of four squadrons operate seven Lockheed C-130E Hercules, 20 C.160 Transalls, 14 Douglas C-47s, three C-54s, six Dornier Do 28s, and three Britten-Norman Islanders for survey work. Three BAC Viscounts are reported to have joined a support squadron at Etimesgut. Helicopters are used for liaison and support, and there are some 40 Agusta AB 205/205s in service.

Training Command, with a main base at Cigli in Izmir, has the following types in its inventory: 23 Cessna T-37B/Cs, 30 Lockheed T-33As, and five Beech T-42s. No 123 Sqn at Gumuavasi has 19 Cessna T-41Ds for basic training. A small number of Cessna 421Cs have been delivered to the service, the first arriving in 1977.

Turkey is a key member of NATO and her air force operates as part of the 6th Allied Tactical Air Force. In the view of many NATO allies, Turkey's continuing dispute with Greece seriously weakened the southern flank of the alliance. With Greece now virtually a member in name only, Turkey becomes even more important to Europe. Thus the American arms embargo, first imposed in 1975 after the Turkish invasion of Cyprus, was seen in many quarters as a foolhardy venture which was steadily undermining the USA's credibility within NATO. Before the lifting of the ban, limited US arms supplies had been granted to Turkey on a yearly basis. The country has since had to increase its defence spending, which has put serious strain on the Turkish economy. Turkey is still keen to establish its own aircraft industry (Tusas) and late in 1977 plans were announced for the licence manufacture of the Aermacchi

Seen on the flight line at Turin-Caselle before delivery from Aeritalia, these F-104S Starfighter all-weather interceptors are the most modern combat aircraft in the Turk Hava Kuvvetleri. A total of 40 were purchased, equipping two squadrons.

M.B.339 light jet trainer. However, the agreement does not appear to have gone very much further and the formal signing has since been postponed.

Turkish Army: The ground forces operate a variety of types, both fixed-wing and rotary-wing, divided into flights at divisional and corps level. Helicopters include 140 AB 204/204s, 16 AB 206s and 20 Bell 47Gs. A further 56 AB 205s are being delivered in two batches of 28 aircraft each. Fixed-wing types comprise nine Dornier Do 28 light transports, 16 Do 27 liaison aircraft, 18 Cessna 421Bs, five Beech Barons and seven Piper L-18 AOP aircraft.

Turkish Navy: In addition to eight ex-Dutch navy Grumman S-2As delivered in 1971, this service has received 12 S-2E Trackers and two TS-2A trainers from the USA for ASW and reconnaissance duties. Three AB 205s are used for liaison work and 12 AB 212ASWs are in service, with a further six 212s on option.

Denmark

Flyvevaabnet: Assigned to NATO's Allied Air Forces Northern Europe in a tactical role, the Royal Danish Air Force has two main operational commands, Air Tactical and Air Material Command. Under the former organisation, known as Tacden (Tactical Air Commander Denmark), a total of 51 Saab 35XD Drakens are allocated to No 725 Sqn at Karup, with 20 F.35XD fighter-bombers and three TF.35XD two-seaters; No 729 Sqn, at the same base operates 20 RF.35XDs and three TF.35XDs in a reconnaissance role. Two squadrons of North American F-100D/F Super Sabres (Nos 727 and 730 Sqns at Skrydstrup) also fly in a tactical role with approximately 24 single-seaters and 14 two-seat F-100Fs; the majority were acquired from ex-USAF stocks and recently refurbished to ex-

tend their useful lives. To replace the Super Sabres, Denmark has ordered GD F-16s: 46 F-16As and 12 two-seat F-16Bs, to equip No 727 Sqn in 1979, and No 730 Sqn in 1980.

A total of 47 Lockheed F-104G Starfighters are in the RDAF inventory, including 15 ex-Canadian AF CF-104Gs and seven two-seat CF-104Ds. Two interceptor units operate these machines, Nos 723 and 726 Sqns at Aalborg, with some of the two-seat Ds operating in the ECM role. At Vaerlose, No 721 Sqn forms the RDAF's transport element, operating eight Douglas C-47s and three Lockheed C-130H Hercules which have replaced five Douglas C-54s. At the same base, No 722 Sqn has an SAR role for which it is equipped with eight Sikorsky S-61As. Detachments of these helicopters are also based at Aalborg and Skrydstrup. It is expected that the service will order two more C-130Hs and two Boeing 737s.

Training, which was previously performed on 24 DHC Chipmunks (including five with station flights) at Avno, is now carried out on 21 of 32 Saab T-17 Supporters, the remaining nine aircraft operating with the Danish Army. After primary training on the T-17, students go to the United States for a course on USAF Cessna T-41s, progressing to Cessna T-37s

and Northrop T-38s before returning to Denmark for conversion to the two-seat TF-100Fs, TF-104Gs and TF.35s.

The nine Supporters are replacing the Danish Army's half-dozen KZ.VIIs and Piper Super Cubs in the observation role. The army aviation element has recently been renamed Army Flying Service and is headquartered at Vandel.

An army helicopter element flies 15 Hughes

500M LOHs delivered in 1971–1973. The Danish Navy has a small air element equipped with eight Aérospatiale Alouette IIIs for liaison duties; they are maintained at Vaerlose by the RDAF's No 722 Sqn. Late in 1977 the Danish Navy ordered eight Westland Lynx which were delivered in 1979. They will be used from frigates and shore bases on reconnaissance and fishery protection in Greenland, the Faroes and the North Sea.

Unlike most European nations the SAR Sea Kings of the Flyvevaabnet (Royal Danish AF) were built by Sikorsky. Eight equip No 722 Sqn at Vaerlose, with detached flights (usually of two aircraft each) at Skyrdstrup and Aalborg.

Norway

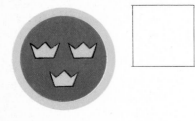

Royal Norwegian Air Force: A member of NATO, Norway has her forces assigned to Allied Forces Northern Europe. The choice of a Lockheed F-104 Starfighter and Northrop F-5 replacement has been made in favour of the General Dynamics F-16, and a contract was signed last year for 60 F-16As and 12 two-seat F-16Bs. Deliveries are due to begin in 1981. Current RNoAF combat strength comprises two fighter-bomber squadrons, Nos 336 Sqn at Rygge and 338 Sqn at Orland, each with 16 F-6As, and a third unit, No 718 Sqn at Sola, with 14 F-5Bs flying in the tactical training role. Also in the fighter-bomber role are 22 ex-Canadian CF-104D/G Starfighters of No 334 Sqn at Bodo. At the same base No 331 Sqn, flying most of the 27 F-104Gs and two TF-104Gs originally supplied in the

1960s, constitutes Norway's sole interceptor and all-weather fighter squadron. A tactical photo-reconnaissance squadron, No 717 at Rygge, operates 13 RF-5As. A maritime patrol unit, No 333 Sqn at Andoya, is equipped with five Lockheed P-3B Orions. Three more P-3s may be ordered in the near future.

One transport squadron, No 335 at Gardermoen, operates six Lockheed C-130H Hercules and two calibration and ECM-equipped Dassault Falcon 20Cs. A second unit, No 719 at Bodo, flies five DHC Twin Otters and eight Bell UH-1Bs on light transport and communications duties. The 24 UH-1Bs are divided between Nos 339 Sqn at Bardufoss for army support and 720 Sqn at Rygge flying SAR duties. Chief SAR squadron is No 330, flying 10 Westland Sea King Mk 43s delivered in 1972 and based at Bodo, with two aircraft each at Banak, Orland and Sola. The loss of one of the Sea Kings in April 1977 has prompted an order for a replacement. Six Westland Lynx, worth nearly £8 million, have been ordered for use from Norwegian Coastguard vessels. They will be uprated Lynx with deliveries planned to begin in 1981.

Basic training is performed on Saab Safirs at Vaernes and a further five ex-Swedish air force aircraft have recently been acquired. AOP and

Standard SAR (search and rescue) helicopter of the Royal Norwegian AF is the Westland Sea King 43, one of which is seen here. Ten are in use, with No 330 Sqn, based at Bodo as HQ and with two Sea Kings normally detached to Sola, Banak and Orland.

liaison duties are flown by 40 Cessna O-1E Bird Dogs and Piper L-18C Super Cubs crewed by army pilots and maintained by air force personnel.

Sweden

Flygvapen: This modern, efficient air arm is supported by a strong Swedish aircraft industry and continues with a steady modernisation and standardisation programme. The present Swedish air force has three main combat types in service: the Viggen, Draken and Saab -105, totalling just under 600 aircraft.

Current Swedish air force organisation is based on Flottiljer or Wings with two or three squadrons of about 18 aircraft each. Saab Viggens continue to join the service, replacing the Saab Draken fleet, and the Viggen force is expected eventually to run to almost 400 aircraft. Versions announced are the AJ37 all-weather attack aircraft, replacing Saab Lansens; SK37 two-seat trainer; SF37 reconnaissance aircraft; SH37 sea-surveillance and attack aircraft; and the JA37 interceptor, scheduled to equip at

J35F 'Filip' of the Swedish Flygvapen, with a Hughes-developed weapon system including an advanced radar (made by Ericsson), IR sensor (seen under the nose) and Swedish-made Falcon missiles.

least eight squadrons from this year onwards. More than 100 of 180 SK/AJ/SF/SH Viggens on order are now in service; 149 JA interceptors are on order, and the first production aircraft made its first flight in November 1977.

For attack and reconnaissance duties the Swedish air force has the following wings: F6, with two squadrons of AJ37 Viggens, recently replacing A32 Lansens at Karlsborg; F7, with two squadrons of AJ37 Viggens at Satenas;

F11, flying in the reconnaissance role with one squadron of S32C Lansens and one squadron of S35E Drakens at Nyköping; and F15, with one attack squadron of AJ37s and the Viggen conversion unit flying SK37s at Soderhamn.

Lansens were phased out of service as more Viggens are delivered.

For air defence 17 interceptor squadrons equipped with about 300 J35D/F Drakens are deployed throughout the country within six regional military districts incorporated into the Stril 60 air-defence system. They are: F1 at Vasteras, with two J35F squadrons; F4 at Ostersund, with three J35D squadrons; F10 at Angelholm, with three J35F squadrons; F12 at Kalmar, with one J35F squadron F13 at Norrköping, with one J35F squadron and a reconnaissance unit with SH/SF37 Viggens; F16 at Uppsala, with two J35/SK35 squadrons, including the Draken OCU; F17 at Ronneby, with one J35F squadron and an SH37 squadron and an SH37 squadron; and F21 at Lulea, with a reconnaissance squadron of S35Es, a fighter squadron flying J35Ds and a light-attack squadron with Saab Sk60Cs. As well as the single units in F13 and F17, SH37s will also equip one squadron in F21. In addition, a transport squadron is attached to F7 at Satenas, equipped with two Lockheed C-130Es, one C-130H and seven Douglas C-47s. Another unit flies two ex-SAS Sud Caravelles on high-speed transport and VIP duties from Malmslatt with F13M Wing.

Training is undertaken by F5 at Ljungbvhed FTS with Scottish Aviation SK-61 Bulldogs for basic training, followed by advanced work on SK-60s of the same unit. The Air Force College at Uppsala has SK-60s for tuition with F20, while F18 at Stockholm flies communications SK-60s plus some Safir liaison aircraft. A total of 58 Bulldogs have been delivered, and there are almost 150 Saab 105 (Sk60) trainers and 20 attack versions. F13M at Malmslatt has a squadron of 24 target-towing J32B Lansens, including about 12 for ECM work, and a few SK-60s.

Future defence plans announced in 1977 stated that the number of medium attack squadrons would remain at six, though the 17 fighter units at present in service will be reduced to 10 by 1982 and to nine by 1987. The eight reconnaissance units will be reduce to six by 1982.

Royal Swedish Navy: The helicopter force operated by the navy comprises two squadrons equipped with 10 Boeing/Kawasaki 107s, 10 Aérospatiale (Sud) Alouette IIs and 10 Agusta AB 206B JetRangers for ASW, minesweeping and rescue duties. The navy is understood to have taken over the air force rescue work, in-

Now in the early stages of operational service with Sweden's Flygvapen the Saab JA37 Viggen interceptor has outstanding all-round performance, advanced Ericsson pulse-doppler radar and Sky Flash medium-range missiles. Swedish AIM-9s are outboard.

corporating into its fleet the 10 ex-*Flygvapen* Boeing-Vertol 107s and six AB 204Bs.

Army Aviation Department: AOP duties and communications are the main roles of the Army air element. Types operated include five Dornier Do 27s, 12 Piper Super Cubs and 20 Bulldogs. Helicopters number 12 AB 204Bs, 40 AB 206As and six Alouette IIs.

Finland

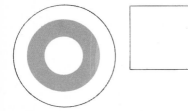

Ilmavoimat: Under the terms of the 1974 Treaty of Paris, the Finnish Air Force is limited to a strength of 60 combat aircraft and 3,000 personnel. The air arm, which in 1978 celebrated its 60th anniversary, is currently organised into three Air Defence Wings, each assigned to one of the three air-defence areas into which Finland is divided. The main Wing bases are at Rovaniemi, Tampere and Kuopio-Rissala, each with one front-line squadron together with the necessary support elements. Assigned the aerial defence of northern Finland is the Lapland Wing, made up of No 11 Sqn at Rovaniemi flying 27 Saab Drakens on all-weather fighter-bomber duties. The Draken force is made up of 12 J35Ss assembled by Valmet at Halli; six ex-Swedish AF J35BS aircraft originally leased to the Finns for training and subsequently purchased by them; and a further nine low-houred ex-Swedish AF aircraft comprising three two-seat S35C combat trainers and six J35F interceptors. Covering southern Finland is the Satakunta Wing with No 21 Sqn, equipped with armed Fouga Magisters for advanced and tactical training, while at Kuopio-Rissala is the

Amongst the oldest supersonic aircraft in service anywhere are about 15 MiG-21F fighters of 31 Sqn of the Kerelia Wing of the Ilmavoimat (Finnish AF), based normally at Kuopio-Rissala. The totally different 'MiG-21bis' is now also in service.

Karelia Wing, forming the defence of southeast Finland. The main unit in the Wing is No 31 Sqn, which flies approximately 18 Soviet-supplied Mikoyan-Gurevich MiG-21F day fighters and a conversion fight with three surviving MiG-21U two-seaters of four originally supplied. A replacement for these ageing aircraft led to an agreement with the Soviet Union for the acquisition of 30 late-model MiG-21*bis*. The first aircraft arrived in October 1978 and at least one two-seat model is included in the order.

Some 50–60 Valmet-built Magisters are still in service out of 80 originally acquired, and late in 1976 it was announced that the BAe (Hawker Siddeley) Hawk had been selected to replace these aircraft after a long evaluation of a number of types. An initial order for 50 was signed in December 1977 and delivery of the first four aircraft (designated Mk 51s) from the UK will begin in 1980, the remaining 46 being assembled under licence by Valmet; an eventual requirement exists for up to 100 Hawks. Also selected in 1976 was the indigenous Valmet Vinka to meet the air force's primary trainer requirement. Formerly known as the Leko-70, the Vinka began to replace 25 Saab Safirs at the Central Flying School, Kauhava, from April 1979, and a contract for 30 aircraft was signed in 1977. In return for the Hawk order, British Aerospace is expected to assist overseas sales of the Vinka when production gets under way.

Advanced construction training is perform-

ed by No 31 Sqn on the two-seat MiG-21Us and by No 11 Sqn on the two-seat Drakens (three MiG-15UTIs having recently been retired from service). A transport squadron at Utti operates both fixed-wing and helicopter types. Seven Douglas C-47s form the backbone of the unit, though a replacement for these aircraft is being actively sought. The two Ilyushin Il-28s used for some years for target-towing have been recently retired. The helicopter element has six Mil Mi-8s, three Mi-4s, one Agusta AB 206 JetRanger and one Hughes 500C. Two Cessna 402s and five Piper Cherokee Arrows have been leased by the air force and are flown on liaison duties from Tikkakoski.

Eastern Europe

"Quantity rather than quality" has been the traditional approach to weapon procurement followed by the Soviet Union and the rest of its Warsaw Pact allies. Rather than attempt to match the sophistication of Western hardware, Soviet designers concentrated on producing aircraft and weapons which could be mass-produced in large numbers for operation and maintenance by conscripts.

The 1970s has seen an ominous shift to a policy of "Quantity *and* quality" as aircraft of the MiG-19/Su-7/Tu-16 vintage have been replaced by more modern types. The Mach 3 performance of Mikoyan's MiG-25 Foxbat may grab the newspaper headlines, but this relatively specialized type would be of limited use in modern war. Far more disturbing to NATO is the same design bureau's MiG-23/27 Flogger — a good match for NATO's Phantoms and Jaguars.

During the SALT II negotiations, the Tupolev Backfire remained an issue of controversy. Independent performance analyses tend to confirm the Soviet claim that Backfire is not a strategic bomber but this news must come as cold comfort to the NATO allies of Western Europe against whose homelands the Tupolev bomber is presumably targeted.

If these programmes produced successful front-line aircraft, the same cannot be said for the Sukhoi Su-19 Fencer project. Deployment of this Soviet "mini-F-111" has been painfully slow and its appearance in East Germany is long overdue.

Reports of a 'MiG-29' fighter in the F-16 class have appeared at regular intervals in the last few years but hardware has yet to appear. Soviet aircraft in the same class as the US F-14, F-18 and A-10 have also been reported along with an improved two-seat Foxbat but none have been operationally deployed so far.

Most Warsaw Pact air forces simply accept whatever combat aircraft are made available by the Soviet Union, but Romania and Yugoslavia have collaborated on the Alpha Jet-sized Orao. Progress has been slow, showing just how difficult it is to switch from designing and building jet trainers to a fully-fledged combat type.

Albania and Yugoslavia follow independent defence and policies. Yugoslavian military aircraft have been purchased from East and West, but Albania must be wondering just where its next equipment will be coming from, having broken off relations with both the Soviet Union and China.

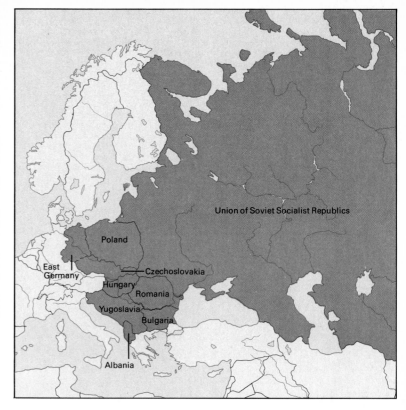

Albania **21**	Poland **20**
Bulgaria **21**	Romania **21**
Czechoslovakia **21**	USSR **22**
Germany (East) **20**	Yugoslavia **21**
Hungary **21**	

Germany (East)

Luftstreitkräfte und Luftverteidigung (LSK): A signatory of the Warsaw Pact, East Germany fields a mainly tactical air force and is the sole Pact country to make its force subordinate to the combined supreme command controlled from the USSR. Soviet units based in the country come under the command of the 16th Air Army and fly some 1,100 aircraft comprising Mikoyan-Gurevich MiG-21s, -23s, -25s, -27s, Sukhoi Su-17s, Mil Mi-8s and Mi-24s. The LSK is divided into two air-defence divisions: the Northern ADD with two fighter wings and three AA missile regiments; and the Southern ADD with four fighter wings and two AA missile regiments

(each wing comprises three squadrons). There is also a fighter training division.

All the interceptor and fighter-bomber units are now equipped with a total of some 280 MiG-21MFs/FLs, 80 Su-7s, and about 35 MiG-17s in a second-line role.

A few Ilyushin Il-28s remain in use for miscellaneous duties, while a transport force has 20 Il-14s, a similar number of Antonov An-24s, two Il-18s, three Tupolev Tu-124s and two Tu-134s, the last-mentioned types being for VIP and governmental use. Helicopters include about 80 Mi-4s and Mi-8s flying in two wings and a single naval helicopter wing. Trainers include Yakovlev Yak-11s and Zlin 226s for primary work, Czech Aero L-29s and MiG-15UTIs for advanced training, and Su-7Us and MiG-21Us for operational conversion.

Several of the Communist 'satellite countries' still use the piston-engined, but large and capable, Mi-4 transport helicopter; these examples belong to East Germany's LSK. The powerful Soviet helicopter force in East Germany is turbine-powered.

Poland

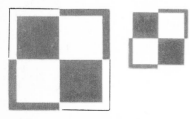

Polskie Wojska Lotnicze: With the largest air force among the Warsaw Pact countries, Poland has almost 900 aircraft, supplemented by a further 350 Soviet AF combat aircraft of the 37th Air Army based within her borders. Like other Pact air arms, the PWL has a strong tactical role, for which it operates about 200 Sukhoi Su-7s in five regiments, 60 indigenously-built Mikoyan-Gurevich MiG-17Fs (LIM-6) in one regiment and another regiment with 50 variable-geometry Su-20s replacing MiG-17s (approximately three squadrons form a regiment in the PWL). The interceptor force consists of some 36

squadrons in 10 regiments flying about 300 MiG-21s integrated into an interceptor/missile air-defence system. Some of the MiG-21 units are assigned the reconnaissance role. A few Ilyushin Il-28s continue in service for a variety of miscellaneous duties. Weapon-training and light-attack duties are carried out by a single-seat version of the Polish-developed WSK-Mielec TS-11 Iskra. About 45 Antonov An-12s, An-26s, Il-14s and An-2s equip transport units, and a communications and VIP element has two Tupolev Tu-134s and about five Yakovlev Yak-40s. A helicopter force numbering some 170 machines comprises Mil Mi-2 gunships, Mi-4s and Mi-8s. Short-range liaison is performed by indigenous CNPSL-PZL-Warszawa Wilgas, and training by TS-8s, TS-11s, MiG-21Us and Sukhoi Su-7Us. A shore-based naval air arm has a regiment of MiG-17Fs (LIM-6), some MiG-21s, a few Il-28s and a number of Mi-2/4/8s.

While the Soviet 16th Air Army in East Germany deploys the formidable Su-19 the Polish PWL has only the primitive and payload-restricted Su-7BM, shown here, and the directly derived Su-20, which is less powerful than the Soviet Su-17 version.

Czechoslovakia

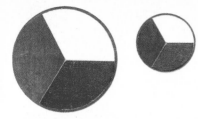

Ceskoslovenske Letectvo: A member of the Warsaw Pact, Czechoslovakia contributes a mainly tactical air force to the organisation, while having a defensive force of considerable strength. The air arm is made up of air regiments, each having up to three squadrons, and the interceptor force currently comprises some 18 squadrons in six regiments, flying 170 Mikoyan-Gurevich MiG-21s and 80 MiG-19s.

Twelve ground-support squadrons in four regiments have 70 Sukhoi Su-7s and about 100 MiG-17s. Six reconnaissance squadrons in two regiments operate some 80 MiG-21Rs for tactical use. A recent acquisition is a squadron of 12 MiG-23 'Floggers' based at Pardubice. The unit is likely to be expanded to regiment strength in the near future. Approximately 50 transport aircraft are in service, mainly Ilyushin Il-14s with a few Antonov An-24s and Il-18s plus a single Tupolev Tu-134 for VIP use. Helicopters include some 100 Mil Mi-4s and Mi-8s. The training fleet includes 150 Aero L-29s (with the new L-39 replacing them), MiG-15UTIs, Yakovlev Yak-11s, Zlin 326s and Il-28Us.

Now ready for retirement from operational service, though still available as a fuel-hungry trainer, the early Su-7B is still in wide use as a close-support and attack platform with the Czech CL. This one is starting the AL-7F engine.

Hungary

Hungarian Air Force: The smallest of the Warsaw Pact air arms, the Hungarian air force is closely supervised by the Soviet forces, and elements of the Soviet tactical air force are based in the country. In the interceptor role, two regiments with three squadrons each have about 116 Mikoyan-Gurevich MiG-21s, supported by a ground-attack regiment of three squadrons flying Sukhoi Su-7BMs. A number of MiG-17s are also on strength, together with some two-seat MiG-15UTI advanced trainers and a few Aero L-29 Delfins. Primary tuition is given on Zlin 42 trainers. Transports include Antonov An-2s, Ilyushin Il-14s, An-24s and a few of the more modern An-26s; two Tupolev Tu-134s operate in the VIP/government transport role. The helicopter elements have about 15 Mil Mi-4s and Mi-8s, together with some Kamov Ka-26s.

Romania

Fortele Aeriene ale Republicii Socialiste Romania: A member of the Warsaw Pact, Romania has an air arm which is small compared with those of other states in the bloc. Her modest aircraft manufacturing industry is involved in the Orao/IAR.93 light attack aircraft project in collaboration with SOKO in Yugoslavia (which has design leadership). Since the prototype made its first flight in 1974, development has been slow and the type has yet to enter service; Romania has a requirement for some 80 Oraos initially. The present combat force comprises five interceptor regiments encompassing some 16 squadrons with Mikoyan-Gurevich MiG-19s, more than 200 MiG-21s and a number of MiG-17s. Two ground-attack regiments, of three squadrons, each operated Sukhoi Su-7s and MiG-17s. Two transport squadrons are flying about 10 Antonov An-24s, two An-26s, An-30, 30 Ilyushin Il-14s and four VIP Il-18s. The helicopter force has 10 Mil Mi-4s, some Mi-2s and 20 Mi-8s. About 47 Aérospatiale (Sud) Alouette IIIs are armed for the anti-tank role. Training is performed on 60 IAR-823s, 60 Aero L29 Delfins and 55 MiG-15UTIs; operational conversion is flown on MiG-21Us and Sukhoi Su-7Us. A number of Let L-200 Morovas are used for communications duties.

Yugoslavia

Yugoslav Air Force: This progressive Communist country has an air force flying equipment from both East and West, although its more modern combat aircraft have been supplied by the Soviet Union. Eight interceptor squadrons have about 110 Mikoyan-Gurevich MiG-21F/PF/Ms and fewer that 50 North American F-86D/K Sabre all-weather fighters. For ground attack, 12 squadrons have 150 indigenous Soko Jastrebs, 30 Kraguj and about 15 remaining Republic F-84G Thunderjets. The new light strike trainer developed jointly with Romania and known as Orao (eagle) seems likely to replace most of the Yugoslavia's ground-attack fleet in the future, once production gets under way. Two reconnaissance squadrons have 15 Lockheed RT-33As and some Galeb/Jastrebs.

Two Gates Learjet 25Bs and a Boeing 727-200 are for Presidential use. Four Douglas DC-6Bs, 15 Douglas C-47s, 12 Antonov An-12s and 13 Ilyushin Il-14s form the fixed-wing transport force together with an Il-18 and three Yakovlev Yak-40s for governmental duties. Yugoslavia is receiving a number of An-26s from Russia to replace the fleet of C-47s. Helicopters include 10 Westland Whirlwinds, 18 Mil Mi-4s, 20 Aérospatiale (Sud) Alouette IIIs, 12 Mi-8s, some Agusta AB 205s and some of the 132 licence-built Aérospatiale/Westland Gazelles currently on order. For utility duties a substantial number of UTVA-66s are flown, and the training elements have 60 Galebs, 30 UTVA-75s, 30 T-33As and some MiG-15UTIs. The Yugoslav navy operates Mi-8s in the transport/assault roles, licence-built Gazelles and a few Kamov Ka-25 co-axial helicopters for ASW work.

Albania

Albanian People's Army Air Force: Relying on military equipment supplied by Communist China, before relations between the two countries ceased in mid-1978, the Albanian Air Force has a total combat strength of approximately 90 aircraft divided into two squadrons with 24 Shenyang F-2s (MiG-15s), two squadrons with 20 F-4s (MiG-17s), two squadrons with 36 F-6s (MiG-19s) and nearly 20 F-7s (MiG-21s). A transport unit has three Ilyushin Il-14s and some ten Antonov An-2s, plus nearly 30 Mil Mi-4s in a further two squadrons. Trainers include Yakovlev Yak-18s and Mikoyan-Gurevich MiG-15UTIs.

Bulgaria

Bulgarian Air Force: The air force of Bulgaria, a member of the Warsaw Pact, has a total strength of some 22,000 men and 250 combat aircraft. Four squadrons form a regiment with about 60 Mikoyan-Gurevich MiG-21 interceptors, and a further regiment has three squadrons of MiG-19s totalling some 36 aircraft. For fighter-bomber duties two regiments with six squadrons fly more than 70 MiG-17s, and a further MiG-17 equipped regiment operates in the fighter-reconnaissance role. A few Ilyushin Il-28s remain in use for second-line duties. Transports number approximately 30 and comprise Antonov An-2s, An-24s, Il-14s, four Il-18s and at least one Tupolev Tu-134. There are 40 Mil Mi-4 helicopters, and trainers include MiG-15UTIs and Aero L-29 Delfins. The Bulgarian Navy has about six Mi-4s and some Mi-2s.

Union of Soviet Socialist Republics

Soviet Military Aviation Forces: The heavy build-up of Russian military forces continues to cause concern in Western capitals. In Africa, Soviet expansionism has seen the Soviet air force demonstrate its massive capability over long distances, amply highlighted by the supply of arms to Ethiopia in 1977 and Afghanistan in 1979. The new breed of combat aircraft continues to replace older types, and it is estimated that Russia is manufacturing more than 1,000 advanced combat aircraft annually, the majority being of an offensive rather than defensive nature. New aircraft are under development for service in the 1980s, and reports have mentioned a smaller 'Foxbat'-type of ground-attack aircraft with fighter potential and a pure tank-buster à la Fairchild A-10.

The Soviet air force is made up of five separate major elements, each having a different role, command structure, and equipment: Long Range Aviation (*Aviatsiya Dal'nevo Deistviya*), Air Force of the Anti-Aircraft Defence of the Homeland (*Istrebitel'naya Aviatsiya P-VO Strany*), Frontal Aviation (*Frontovaya Aviatsiya*), Air Transport Aviation (*Voenno-transportnaya Aviatsiya*) and Naval Aviation (*Aviatsiya Voennomorskovo Flota*). The unit structure is based on divisions each comprising three or more regiments, which in turn consist of three squadrons each with 12 aircraft.

Long Range Aviation is divided into three groups, two in western Russia and one in the east, operating about 700 aircraft. Most modern type in service and the one that has caused much controversy in connection with the Strategic Arms Limitation Talks (SALT) is the variable-geometry Tupolev Tu-26 'Backfire-B' bomber. The Soviet Union has insisted the 'Backfire' is a tactical aircraft and so exempt from the SALT limitations, but intelligence sources have indicated that the aircraft has an unrefuelled combat radius of some 3,750 miles (6035 km) and is capable of carrying stand-off missiles, ending any doubt as to its strategic potential. The aircraft is believed to equip at least one air force regiment, with about 50 machines delivered. Production is believed to be running at between one and two aircraft a month. In addition there are about 110 Tu-95 'Bears' and 35 Myasishchev M-4 'Bison-Bs' and '-Cs' in the bombing role, plus 45 'Bison-As' and a number of Tu-16 'Badgers' employed in a flight-refuelling role. Approximately 140 Tu-22 'Blinders' and less than 300 older Tu-16 'Badgers' operate in the medium-range bomber role. These types are scheduled to be replaced by 'Backfires', possibly on a one-for-one basis. A tanker version of the Ilyushin Il-76 'Candid' transport is being developed to replace the 'Bisons'. Staging points are available to the strategic forces in the Arctic, the Mediterranean and some countries in Africa and the Far East.

Frontal Aviation is the Soviet Unions's tactical air force and, with 5,500 aircraft plus a further 3,000 second-line types, forms the bulk of Russia's aviation arm. Close support, interdiction and tactical strike are the main roles of the FA, and this force is currently undergoing a major re-equipment programme with new types replacing older aircraft. One of the most significant now in service is the variable-geometry Sukhoi Su-19 'Fencer' fighter-bomber, of which more than 250 are in use, some based in East Germany. Another variable-geometry aircraft now in use is the Mikoyan-Gurevich MiG-23 'Flogger', of which there are two main versions in FA service: the single-seat -23S 'Flogger-B' fighter

Far larger than the MiG-21, the Su-11 is still an important supersonic all-weather interceptor in the Soviet PVO, usually with an armament of two so-called 'Anab' AAMs, one radar-homing and the other with IR homing. Note jet blast deflectors, left.

and the two-seat -23U 'Flogger-C' trainer. A single-seat ground-attack version is known as 'Flogger-D' and designated MiG-27; 'Flogger' deliveries to the Soviet air force total about 1,000+ machines. It is expected that this type will eventually replace the 1,500+ MiG-21s now in service. About 400 Su-7s remain in use but their gradual withdrawal is under way, their place being taken by the variable-geometry Su-17 'Fitter-C'. About 200 MiG-17F 'Frescos' are operated in the ground-attack role and there are some units with MiG-25 'Foxbat-B' reconnaissance aircraft; there are also about 170 Yakovlev Yak-28 'Brewer-D' and '-E' reconnaissance and ECM aircraft. Two regiments of Mil

Mi-24 'Hind' helicopters are operational in East Germany, supported by a few hundred Mi-8 'Hip' assault helicopters. Revealed in 1977 was a new gunship version of the Mi-24 armed assault transport known as 'Hind-D' and equipped with a Gatling-type machine-gun in a turret under a modified nose.

Air Defence Forces of the Homeland as well as deploying numerous surface-to-air missiles, operate an interceptor force of some 3,300 aircraft, comprising about 1,000 Sukhoi Su-15 'Flagon-As', '-Ds' and '-Es', 1,500 MiG-23/25s, some 150 Tu-28P 'Fiddler' long-range interceptors, and some 700 Su-9/Su-11 'Fishpots'. There are also some Yak-28s, MiG-17s and a few Tu-22s, plus about 12

A frame from a Soviet propaganda film showing dusk takeoff of a Tu-22 supersonic reconnaissance platform of the Soviet naval air force (AV-MF). The sub-type cannot be identified but it is probably a so-called 'Blinder-C' with extensive cameras and other sensors and comprehensive ECM systems. Gross weight is 185,000 lb (83,900 kg).

Tu-126 'Moss' AWACS aircraft.

Military Transport Aviation has about 1,700 aircraft. There are 800 Antonov An-12 'Cubs', plus a smaller number of An-26s, An-24s, An-14s, Ilyushin Il-14s and Il-18s. About 30 An-22 'Cock' are in service for heavy-lift duties; the new Il-76 four-jet transport, which joined the ATA in 1975, continues to join the force in ever-increasing numbers and is expected to replace the fleet of An-12s. A new light jet transport, designated An-72, was revealed in 1977 and is being delivered to the air force to replace the An-24/26 series. A number of types are used for VIP/government tasks, including 600 used by the Frontal Aviation. Reliance is placed in the main on the Mi-8 but large numbers of Mi-4s are in use for a variety of tasks. Other types include about 500 Mi-1/s, some Mi-10 and Mi-12 heavy-lift helicopters, and Mi-6s and Mi-24s. Numerous liaison and communications aircraft are in service, while training types include the Yak-18 'Max' for primary duties, Aero L-29 'Mayas' for basic work (being replaced by the new Aero L-39) and MiG-15UTI 'Midgets' for advanced conversion. Operational conversion is flown on two-seat version of current combat types, including MiG-21U, MiG-23U, MiG-25U, Su-7U, Su-11U, Tu-22U and Yak-28U.

Naval Aviation has more than 1,250 aircraft, mostly based near the northwest and Black Sea coasts and organised into three regiments each with three squadrons at each base. The aircraft support four Soviet Fleets — the Baltic Red Banner Fleet, Northern Fleet, Black Sea Fleet and Far East Fleet. For long-range reconnaissance, approximately 45 Tu-95 'Bear-Ds' and 15 'Bear-Fs' are operated with 150 Tu-16 'Badger-C', '-D', '-E', and '-Fs', some of which are flown as tanker aircraft. About 275 Tu-16 'Badger-Gs' are used in the strike role equipped with one 'Kingfish', one 'Kipper' or two 'Kelt' ASMs, while nearly 50 Tu-22s fly on strike-reconnaissance, some with 'Kitchen' ASMs. A diminishing number

Still the standard shipboard ASW and missile-guidance helicopter of the Soviet naval air force, these Ka-25s are aboard the *Moskva*.

of Il-28 'Beagle' torpedo bombers, believed to be about 20, are still in service, together with a few M-4 'Bison-B/Cs' for long-range surveillance. Also with the naval air command is a small number of Tu-125 'Moss' AWACS aircraft and the first unit with about 50 'Backfire' bombers. Recently transferred to the Naval Aviation force were some variable-geometry Sukhoi Su-17 'Fitter-C' fighter-bombers, presumably for close-support duties in conjunction with Marine ground elements. For maritime reconnaissance and ASW duties there are 60 Il-38 'Mays' and about 100 Beriev M-12 'Mail' amphibians, together with a small number of elderly Be-6 'Madge' flying-boats for coastal patrol work. As well as some

200 miscellaneous types for support duties, there are 250 Mi-4, Mi-8 and Kamov Ka-25 'Hormone' helicopters. A new ASW version of the Mi-8 code-named 'Haze' employs MAD equipment and features a boat-shape hull.

Soviet Navy: Four 60,000-ton aircraft-carriers known as the 'Kiev' class are intended, with the first vessel, named *Kiev*, rejoining the Black Sea Fleet for operations in the Mediterranean. A second, named *Minsk*, is also in service and the *Kharkov* has still to be launched. The fourth, much larger ship, with more accommodation for aircraft, is under construction. *Kiev* carries about a dozen fixed-wing VTOL combat aircraft attributed to

Yakovlev and code-named 'Forger-A'. A two-seat trainer version, 'Forger-B', is also in use, and it is currently assumed that the other carriers will be equipped with these attack/recce aircraft or developed versions of them, as well as Kamov Ka-25 ASW helicopters. Also in service are two anti-submarine helicopter cruisers, the *Moskva* and *Leningrad*, each capable of accommodating up to 20 Ka-25 ASW helicopters. This type of helicopter has largely replaced the older Mi-4s used on ship and shore-based duties, a total of about 250 being in service.

Taxiing out for a night mission, this MiG-23S all-weather interceptor appears to be bright blue but is almost certainly a medium grey. The use of pictorial unit or individual badges or insignia, such as on the nose of this aircraft, has in recent years been very rare except in the case of record-breaking or special trials aircraft.

Mid East and North Africa

Two events have dominated the recent history of this area — the movement towards peace between Israel and Egypt and the collapse of the monarchy in Iran. Traditional hostility towards Israel has long been a unifying influence in the Arab world, but during actual hostilities the armed forces of Egypt have played a key role.

Starved of spare parts and support for its Soviet-supplied Air Force, Egypt must now look to the West for the new aircraft and weapons it needs to match the explosion of military strength which has taken place in Libya. Saudi Arabian funding for Egypt's F-5E deal has fallen through but the US is to supply about 30 F-4 Phantoms.

Syria, Iran and Libya remain favoured Soviet clients and the flow of advance weaponry to these countries continues. Libya is already reported to have received MiG-25 Foxbats and additional Tu-22 Blinders. All three nations have ordered French weapons or aircraft to lessen dependence on a single supplier.

New aircraft such as the F-15, E-2C Hawkeye and Kfir have greatly improved the combat effectiveness of the Israeli Air Force — a process which will continue as the F-16 and perhaps even the F-18 enter service.

Withdrawal of US technicians early in 1979 has badly hit the Iranian Air Force — now renamed the Islamic Iranian Air Force. Without US support the F-14 Tomcat fleet is effectively scrap metal and is being offered for sale. Iran should have no trouble keeping the relatively simple F-5 operational and has been using F-4s against Kurdish rebels. It remains to be seen for how long the Phantoms and helicopters can be kept operational without outside help, however.

Faced with the fall of the Shah of Iran, Saudi Arabia is determined to build up its own strength with US help without posing an obvious threat to its Israeli neighbours. The depth of US commitment to Saudi Arabia was demonstrated early in 1979 when USAF F-15s and E-3As were despatched on a visit to the kingdom.

Algeria	**24**	Morocco	**24**
Egypt	**25**	Oman	**27**
Iran	**30**	Qatar	**27**
Iraq	**28**	Saudi Arabia	**26**
Israel	**29**	South Yemen	**27**
Jordan	**26**	Syria	**28**
Kuwait	**28**	Tunisia	**24**
Lebanon	**28**	United Arab Emirates	**27**
Libya	**25**	Yemen	**27**

Morocco

Forces Armées Royales: The current FAR inventory comprises two fighter-bomber squadrons equipped with 15 Northrop F-5As and three F-5Bs, and two further ground-attack squadrons flying 24 Aérospatiale (Fouga) Magisters. All four units are committed to the anti-guerrilla war. For transport and supply duties, the FAR operates 12 Lockheed C-130H Hercules, delivered in two batches of six aircraft, the final one being delivered in 1977. These aircraft replace the fleet of 18 Fairchild C-119G Flying Boxcars originally supplied by the US, Canada and Italy. There are also six Beech King Air 100s used for staff and liaison transport, together with 12 Holste

MH.1521M Broussards. A helicopter element has 24 Agusta AB 205s delivered in 1970, at least eight AB 206s, five AB 212s, four Kaman HH-43B Huskies, four Aérospatiale (Sud) Alouette IIs, four Bell 47Gs, six Aérospatiale/Westland Gazelles and 40 Aérospatiale/Westland SA.330 Pumas. Six Meridionali-built Boeing CH-47C Chinooks were ordered in 1978 for heavy-lift duties and two further batches of six are likely to be ordered later. The training force has been modernized by the acquisition of 10 FFA AS.202 Bravo primary trainers, 12 Beech T-34C-1 Turbo-Mentors for the basic role and by the recent order for Dassault-Breguet/Dornier Alpha Jets for advanced work from 1980. Some of the 30 North American T-6s supplied by France in the 1960s remain in use, together with two Italian SIAI-Marchetti SF.260Ms. A single Dornier Skyservant is operated for the personal use of the King. Still in storage are 12 Mikoyan-Gurevich MiG-17s and two MiG-15UTIs.

A major re-equipment programme is currently under way, with the Moroccan defence budget allocating funds for new aircraft and

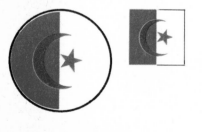

Morocco enjoys an up-to-date airlift capability with 12 C-130H Hercules.

equipment. The country is involved in a war in the Western Sahara against the Polisario guerrilla movement, which is being supported by Algeria and Libya. The conflict began when the former Spanish Sahara was divided up between Morocco and Mauritania. Among the new aircraft ordered for the air force are 50 Dassault Mirage F1-CH fighter-bombers, with a further 25 on option. Deliveries are underway and some two-seat F1-BH trainers

are understood to be included in the deal. Also from France, a total of 24 Alpha Jet E trainer/light strike aircraft have been ordered for delivery in 1980, while for airfield defence Morocco has purchased a number of Thomson-CSF Crotale low-level SAM systems. A request for 24 Rockwell OV-10 Bronco COIN aircraft and some Bell HueyCobra gunship helicopters from the USA has been agreed.

Algeria

Force Aérienne Algérienne: Established in 1962 in the wake of the French withdrawal from the country, the FAA has received substantial aid from the Soviet Union and Egypt, although in recent years orders have been placed with France and the USA. The most recent purchase has been that of six Beech T-34C Turbo-Mentors, to update the training element, which currently operates Aérospatiale Magisters. A defence agreement exists with Libya.

The current Algerian inventory comprises a

wing of three interceptor squadrons with 70 Mikoyan-Gurevich MiG-21Fs, three fighter-bomber squadrons with 60 MiG-17Fs, and two ground-attack squadrons flying 20 Sukhoi Su-7BMs. A second-line unit has 20 MiG-15s, while two bomber squadrons, of doubtful operational status, are equipped with 24 Ilyushin Il-28s. In 1971, 28 refurbished and armed Magister trainers were supplied by Aérospatiale for two squadrons, and at the same time five Aérospatiale SA.330 Pumas were bought for assault duties. Other

helicopters include six Hughes 269 trainers, 40 Mil Mi-4s, four Mi-6s and about 12 Mi-8s. Two transport squadrons fly four VIP Il-18s, eight Antonov An-12s and about six remaining Il-14s, plus six Fokker F.27s (five Mk 400s and one Mk 600). One Beech King Air is flown on navaid-calibration duties, while for liaison and training work there are three Super King Airs and three Queen Airs. An order for two Fokker-VFM F.28 Mk 3000Cs has been placed on behalf of the Algerian Navy.

Tunisia

Tunisian Republican Air Force: The Tunisian government has allowed to lapse the letter of offer for 16 Northrop F-5E fighter-bombers which it requested from the US Government in 1976. As a result, the single Tunisian air force combat squadron will continue to operate the survivors of 12 North American F-86F Sabres supplied by the USA in 1969 and now employed chiefly in the training role. The main strike potential in the Tunisian air force

is vested in eight Aermacchi M.B.326Bs bought in 1965 and flying in a dual strike/trainer squadron; supplementing these is a further batch of eight single-seat M.B.326KTs and four two-seat M.B.326LTs ordered in 1976. For basic training 12 SIAI-Marchetti SF.260WTs received in 1974, have replaced a similar number of Saab Safirs. Supplementing these are six SF.260C trainers delivered in 1978. Other types in use include 12 North

American T-7s, three Dassault Flamant transports, eight Aérospatiale (Sud) Alouette IIs, six Alouette IIIs and at least one Aérospatiale/Westland SA.330 Puma. Eighteen AB 205s were ordered in 1979 but no delivery date is known.

Libya

This Dassault-Breguet Mirage F1-A is one of the substantial force of A and all-weather E models for Libya.

Libyan Republic Air Force: Libya's long-standing arguments with Egypt erupted in July 1977 into a border conflict which saw both sides conducting air operations. El Adem, home base of a Mikoyan-Gurevich MiG-23 squadron and a Dassault-Breguet Mirage 5DR unit, was attacked by Egyptian aircraft, resulting in claims by Egypt of at least six aircraft destroyed on the ground. Libya claimed a total of two Tupolev Tu-16s, six Sukhoi Su-7/Su-22s, two MiG-21s and four Mirages shot down when the clash ended. Large stocks of Soviet-supplied military equipment have been received by Libya over the past few years, and many Russian advisers are working in the country. In a substantial arms deal signed between the two countries, the Libyan air force has been equipped with two squadrons of Soviet MiG-23 interceptors, MiG-27 strike aircraft and a few two-seat MiG-23Us totalling some 50 aircraft, a few Tu-16 bombers and a squadron of 12 Tu-22 'Blinders'. These last-mentioned aircraft are partially Soviet-crewed. A Soviet air force unit established itself at a Libyan base early in 1977,

flying five reconnaissance MiG-25s over the Mediterranean, having moved from its Syrian base in 1976. A two-seat MiG-25U was lost in the Mediterranean in November 1978. The USSR has operated regular long-range flights from bases in the country for some years, and the continuation of this accord is closely linked with the supply of arms to the country.

Total Mirage deliveries to the LRAF cover 60 Mirage 5D fighter-bombers in two squadrons and an OTU, 30 5DE interceptors in two further squadrons, 10 5DD trainers and 10 5DR reconnaissance aircraft. Joining this force are 38 Mirage F1s (plus 50 on option) comprising 16 F1-ADs, 16 F1-EDs and six two-seater F1-BDs. The transport arm of two squadrons remains largely Western-equipped, with eight Lockheed C-130H Hercules, nine Douglas C-47s, two Dassault-Breguet Falcon 20s and a

VIP Lockheed Jet-Star. A further eight C-130Hs remain embargoed in America, and despite Libyan requests there seems little likelihood of their being delivered. The lack of spares for the Hercules in LRAF service is causing operational problems and a replacement transport type has been decided. Twenty Tyne-engined Aeritalia G222s have been ordered for delivery in the early 1980s. Seemingly unopposed by the USA is the order currently being fulfilled by Meridionali in Italy for eight Boeing-Vertol CH-47C Chinook helicopters for the LRAF. A follow-on order for a further eight has been reported with an eventual total of 20 machines. The air force currently operates seven of nine Aérospatiale SA.321M Super Frelons for SAR and ASW duties, 12 Mil Mi-8s, three Bell 47s, Aérospatiale (Sud) Alouette IIIs, and three

Alouette IIs, two AB 212s with a single Agusta-built AS-61A-4 on order for VIP duties. Twelve ex-French air force Aérospatiale (Fouga) Magisters equip the training units, together with three Lockheed T-33As and two Dassault-Breguet Mystère 20 Mirage radar trainers. To update the training elements about 17 Yugoslav Soko Galebs have been delivered and negotiations have been concluded with SIAI-Marchetti for 250 SF.260WL primary trainers; 20 have already been delivered and the Italian company is setting up an assembly plant in Libya for SF.260 production.

The Libyan army has five AB 206 Jet-Rangers, four Alouette IIIs and six AB 47Gs, together with a few ex-Italian air force Cessna O-1s for liaison duties.

Egypt

Arab Republic of Egypt Air Force: The Egyptian Air Force currently operates much Russian equipment, but total numbers reflect aircraft acquired and not necessarily those operational. A bomber force has some 25 Tupolev Tu-16 'Badger-Gs', some armed with AS-5 'Kelt' ASMs, and a similar number of Ilyushin Il-28 light bombers. Fighter-bomber units are equipped with about 120 Sukhoi Su-7s, although some reports suggest a figure nearer 80, and nearly 150 Mikoyan-Gurevich MiG-17s, which also double in the low-level interceptor role. To help maintain the MiGs, China has provided spares and about 30 engines. Also in the strike role is a MiG-27 'Flogger-D' unit with 18 aircraft and some 48 Su-20 variable-geometry attack aircraft relinquished by the departing Russians. The border clash in July 1977 between Egypt and Libya resulted in claim and counter-claim, the Libyans announcing the destruction of two Tu-16s, six Sukhois, two MiG-21s and four Dassault Mirage IIIs; Egypt admitted losing two Su-20s but claimed the destruction of six Libyan aircraft at El Adem during a strike.

Interception missions are flown by some nine squadrons of the Air Defence Command equipped with 108 MiG-21MFs integrated into a Soviet-established air-defence system, which includes SAMs and radars. There are also about 150 MiG-21PFMs and about 100 MiG-21F attack aircraft; a few are equipped for reconnaissance. An agreement exists whereby UK companies are assisting the Egyptians in overhauling the MiGs and fitting them with Ferranti inertial navigation platforms and Smiths weapon-aiming HUDs. Supplementing the -21s are about 24 MiG-23 'Flogger-B' interceptors, six two-seat MiG-23U 'Flogger-C' combat trainers, and 52 Mirage IIIEEs, 38 of which were originally ordered by Saudi Arabia for operation by Egypt. A second batch of 14 Mirages was ordered in 1977. A few MiG-19s remain in service, but they are thought to have been relegated to second-line status.

Of the six Lockheed C-130 Hercules — four C-130Hs and two EC-130Hs delivered in 1977 — one was lost in Cyprus during an abortive commando raid and a further 14 have been delivered to replace the 25 Antonov An-12s in use. Other transports include 40 Ilyushin Il-14s and a VIP flight equipped with a Boeing 707, Boeing 737 and a Dassault Falcon 20. Helicopters are operated mainly by the army and navy and include a batch of Westland Commando assault aircraft comprising five Mk 1s and 23 Mk 2s, including two VIP machines. Four more Commando 2Es were delivered in 1979. From France, a further 12 Aérospatiale SA.342 Gazelles have been received to add to the 42 already in use, some being equipped with HOT missiles for anti-tank use and others flying in the light AOP role. Russian types include 70 Mil Mi-8s, many armed for assault work, 20 Mi-4s, and about 12 Mi-6 heavy-lift helicopters.

The Egyptian Navy, as well as operating

some Gazelles, also has a squadron of six Westland Sea King Mk 47s for ASW duties. Six Fournier RF4s are flown for AOP and Elint sorties with the air force. Training is performed on 100 Aero L-29 Delfins, although some are used in the ground-attack role. Other types include about 50 two-seat MiG-15UTIs, Su-7Us, MiG-21Us, Yakovlev Yak-11s, and some Il-14s used for navigation training. Of the 90 Al Kahira basic jet trainers built, a few survivors continue in use, and there are still 200 Gomhouria elementary trainers in service. No replacement for these types has yet been selected. A number of Polish (NPSL-PZL-Warszawa) Wilgas are also in use for liaison duties.

A partial answer to Egypt's critical re-equipment dilemma, following her severing of links with the Soviet Union, was announced in 1978 when the United States agreed to supply 42 Northrop F-5E fighter-bombers and eight F-5Fs. President Sadat had requested up

to 250 F-5s, and a re-order at a later date seems likely. Finance for the deal has come from Saudi Arabia, herself an F-5E operator, and in July 1977 it was announced that a five-year development plan for Egypt's armed forces would be paid for by Saudi money. Another firm commitment was announced in January 1978 when a £50 million order for 250 Westland Lynx helicopters and Rolls-Royce Gem engines was signed involving the manufacture of both items in Egypt for a number of Arab states. The first 20 Lynx will be built in the UK and knocked-down components will then be shipped out to Egypt for assembly, with total self-sufficiency eventually planned.

Long one of the world's largest users of Soviet equipment, the Egyptian AF appears still to be in receipt of such arms as witness this very new MiG-21bis (the current model with a new airframe including a large dorsal spine).

Jordan

Royal Jordanian Air Force: In the future Jordanian air force expansion programme, the front-line force will be increased to 176 fixed-wing aircraft, the Northrop F-5 element will be enlarged and the Lockheed F-104s will be withdrawn and replaced by 36 Dassault Mirage F1 interceptors. After protracted negotiations, a US air-defence system was ordered in 1976, involving Improved HAWKs, Vulcan guns and Redeye AA infantry missiles. Following the transfer of ex-Jordanian Hawker Hunters to Oman in 1975, Iran undertook to supply Jordan with 36 F-5A/Bs as new F-5Es arrived in Iran from America. The original order placed by Jordan for F-5Es covered 30 aircraft, but this has been increased to 44 F-5Es and two F-5Fs; yet another repeat order has taken the figure to 57 Es and six Fs. No 17 Squadron at Prince Hassan Air Base received the initial batch of 24 aircraft, and the others are understood to be joining 1 and 2 Sqn at King Hussein Air Base, Mafraq, which until recently have operated 30 F-5As for fighter-bomber duties. Four F-5Bs have provided two-seat training for all three squadrons. For interceptor work, F-5Es have replaced 9 Sqns 18 F-104As and four two-seat F-104Bs at Prince Hassan AB.

Based at King Abdullah Air Base, Amman, is the modest transport force of four Lockheed C-130B/H Hercules and four CASA C212-light transports replacing four Douglas C-47s; one of the C-212 Aviocars has an executive interior for government duties. Two Rockwell 75A Sabreliners are likely to be delivered for VIP use. A total of 15 Aérospatiale Alouette IIIs (six IIIs, six 316Bs and four 316C, although one has been lost) are based at Amman and are being supplemented by up to 12 Aérospatiale SA.342K Gazelles ordered in 1978 and four Sikorsky S-76s tentatively on order. At the Royal Jordanian Air Academy in Amman, 12 Scottish Aviation Bulldog elementary trainers are used for initial flying training; these aircraft have recently been transferred to the air force inventory. Students move on for advanced training to 6 Sqn at Mafraq, which operates 12 ex-USAF Cessna T-37Cs. At the personal disposal of King Hussein are a Riley Dove and a Boeing 727.

Saudi Arabia

Royal Saudi Air Force: The main interceptor force in the RSAF is composed of BAC Lightnings and Northrop F-5s. In September 1977, a further UK-Saudi defence contract was signed. Worth £500 million, it assures continuation of the long-standing agreement which involves the servicing of the Lightnings and Strikemasters and the training of Saudi nationals. A total of 31 BAC Lightning F.53s (32 delivered), two F.54s, three F.52s and five two-seat F.53s are operational with No 2 Sqn at Tabuk in the north on intercept duties; No 6 Sqn has been disbanded following its move from Khamis Mushayt. The remaining Lightnings operate from Dharan at the OCU.

Based at Taif and Khamis are four fighter-bomber squadrons including Nos 3 and 10, equipped with 70 Northrop F.5Es. These aircraft are equipped to carry Maverick guided bombs under a contract with Northrop, which also services and trains Saudi nationals on the aircraft. Two training units with a secondary strike potential are Nos 9 and 11 Sqns at Riyadh, which forms part of the King Faisal Air Academy. A total of 46 BAC Strikemaster Mk 80/80As have been bought by the RSAF; No 9 Sqn is a purely basic jet training unit, while No 11 Sqn operates in the weapon training role. Dharan-based No 7 Sqn, with 24 Northrop F-5F two-seat combat trainers, acts as the F-5 OCU, and its companion unit, No 15 Sqn, flies 20 older F-5B trainers, four of which have been transferred to the Yemeni air force.

Two transport squadrons, Nos 4 and 16 Sqns, are based at Jeddah and equipped with 10 Lockheed C-130Es, 25 C-130Hs and four KC-130H Hercules, the last for F-5 air refuelling. Based at Taif are Nos 12 and 14 Sqns, flying 16 Agusta AB 206 JetRangers used for helicopter training and 24 AB 205s on liaison, SAR and airfield crash rescue duties. A number of AB 212s have been recieved for coastal SAR work. No 8 Sqn at Riyadh, as part of the KFAA, is a primary training unit with an establishment of 13 Reims-built Cessna 172G/H/Ms. Forty CASA C-212 Aviocars have been ordered for light transport work from the Indonesian production line.

For general rescue duties the Saudi government has ordered six Kawasaki KV-107s (a further six are scheduled to follow) and the RSAF is expected to benefit from the Egyptian Lynx order when deliveries begin. Also in use are two Aérospatiale (Sud) Alouette IIIs and a Royal Flight, alias 1 Sqn, equipped with a single Boeing 707-320, two Lockheed JetStars, an AB 206 and two Agusta-built Sikorsky AS.61A-4 VIP helicopters delivered in 1977. On order for King Khaled is a specially equipped Boeing 747SP.

Future frontline combat re-equipment was assured in May 1978 when the United States

Soon to be replaced by F-15 Eagles, the Lightning F.53 has given good service with the RSAF. It is seen here armed with the Red Top missile.

Congress agreed to the sale of 60 McDonnell Douglas F-15 Eagles to Saudi Arabia to replace the force of BAC Lightnings currently in service. The F-15s are expected to be delivered between 1981 and 1984 and comprise 45 F-15As and 15 two-seat F-15B combat trainers. Saudi cash continues to finance not only her own military purchases but those of her Arab neighbours, and she was a major stockholder in the Cairo-based Arab Military Industries Organisation until the Egyptian-Israeli accord of spring 1979 led to the severing of Saudi-Egyptian links.

It had been announced in 1977 that Saudi Arabia would finance a five-year Egyptian arms-purchasing programme, with no repayments necessary; this was in addition to the procurement some years ago of Westland Sea Kings/Commandos and Dassault Mirages for Egypt.

Seen over the rugged territory of Saudi Arabia, the Strikemaster 80 and 80A have proved to be extremely cost-effective tactical aircraft, with the capability of sustained operations in the harshest environments. The RSAF has 46 of these machines, used mainly in training roles but with combat capability.

Yemen

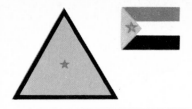

Yemen Arab Republic Air Force: In 1977 the US State Department approved the transfer of four Northrop F-5B trainers from Saudi Arabia to Yemen, a move highlighting North Yemen's closer ties with the Western world after many years in the Soviet sphere of influence. It was also suggested at the time of the F-5B agreement that Saudi Arabia may fund an order for 12 F-5E fighter-bombers for the Yemeni air force. This has now taken place and in addition two Saudi AF C-130 Hercules have also been supplied. Present combat inventory of the air arm comprises one squadron with 12 Mikoyan-Gurevich MiG-17s flying in the fighter-bomber role, and a second unit with 16 Il-28 light bombers. The transport force is made up two Short Skyvan 3Ms and a few Douglas C-47s and Ilyushin Il-14s, two AB 205s and some Mil Mi-4s.

South Yemen

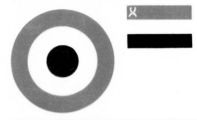

Air Force of the South Yemen People's Republic: Operating mostly Communist supplied aircraft, this air force has an interceptor squadron with 50 Mikoyan-Gurevich MiG-21s, a bomber squadron with six Ilyushin Il-28s, and a ground-attack unit with 40 MiG-17s. A transport squadron has four Il-14s, three Antonov An-24s and a few Douglas C-47s. About eight Mil Mi-8s and some Mi-4s are flying, and three MiG-14UTIs are used for training. A small detachment of Soviet Il-38 MR aircraft arrived at Aden in November 1978.

Oman

Sultan of Oman's Air Force: Formed with British assistance in 1958, this air arm has expanded rapidly since 1970 as the country's economy has developed. The 10-year Dhofar rebellion ended in 1976, and much of the tactical transport capacity used over that period has since been directed into civil aid and development. The force continues to be manned by a mixture of contract personnel, seconded RAF personnel and an increasing number of Omani nationals.

In 1974 an order worth some £47 million was placed with BAC for Rapier low-level SAMS, together with another order for 12 SEPECAT Jaguar International strike aircraft made up of 10 single-seaters and two trainers. A further order was placed in 1976 for an air-defence radar and communications system to be integrated with the Jaguars and Rapiers; it is based on Marconi S600 radars and a Marconi troposcatter communications system. Worth £25 million, this order has also been placed with BAC. The first two Jaguars were delivered in March 1977 and the last aircraft of the order has now been received. No 8 Sqn, the Jaguar unit, may receive another three machines if finance is available. The aircraft will complement rather than replace the Hawker Hunters of No 6 Sqn at the SOAF's Thumrayt main strike base. Of the 31 ex-Jordanian Hunter FGA.6s acquired in 1975, only about 15 are operational at any one time, the remainder being stored.

No 1 Sqn at Salalah has 12 BAC Strikemaster Mk 82/82As operating in the ground-attack and advanced training roles; a further two are in reserve. Five Strikemasters sold to Singapore were delivered at the beginning of 1977. Also at Salalah is No 3 Sqn, with 20 Agusta AB 205s, three AB 206s and five Bell 214B heavy-lift helicopters. Based at Seeb are Nos 2 Sqn, with 15 Short Skyvan 3Ms; 4 Sqn, with three BAC One-Eleven 475s; and 5 Sqn, with seven Britten-Norman Defenders. Detachments of Skyvans and Defenders are maintained at Salalah. The SOAF also has an Initial Aircrew Training School, a Technical Training School and a Flying Training School at the ex-RAF airfield at Masirah.

Two Pilatus Turbo-Porters and a single Gates Learjet 25B are operated by the Oman Police Air Wing; two Swearingen Metros were disposed of at the end of 1977 and the following year two DHC-5D Buffaloes were ordered for transport duties. The Royal Flight has two FFA AS.202 Bravos, an AB 212 and two Bell 212s.

Abu Dhabi (see United Arab Emirates)

Dubai (see United Arab Emirates)

United Arab Emirates

United Emirates Air Force: The air force of the United Arab Emirates was formed by the amalgamation of the three air units of Abu Dhabi (AD Air Force) and Dubai (Dubai Police Air Wing and the Union Air Force). Seven Gulf states make up the UAE federation — Abu Dhabi, Amman, Dubai, Fujairah, Ras al-Khaimah, Sharjah and Umm al-Qaiwain — and all contribute to the funding of the air force, which is headed by UAE President Sheikh Zayed of Abu Dhabi. The UEAF has its headquarters at Abu Dhabi but a Central Air Force Base has been establised at Dubai Airport, where a hangar, worshop and stores complex have been built.

Pakistani air force personnel continue to assist the air force in an advisory capacity following the non-renewal of the Airwork servicing contract in 1974; they are mainly concerned with the Dassault Mirage force.

At Abu Dhabi the UEAF has the nucleus of its combat force, a interceptor-strike wing of some 32 French-supplied Mirages. The first of these — 12 5AD strike fighters and two 5DAD combat trainers — arrived in 1974, but further deliveries in 1976-77 have taken the force to 26 Mirage 5ADs, three reconnaissance 5RADs and three 5DAD two-seaters flying in two squadrons. A ground-attack squadron, formed in 1970, operates eight BAe H.S. Hunter FGA.76s and two T.77 trainers from the base at Sharjah, and there are no plans at present to withdraw this unit from service.

The transport element is also based at Abu Dhabi and is equipped with two Lockheed C-130H Hercules delivered in 1975, three DHC Caribous (a fourth was damaged beyond repair in 1976), and four Britten-Norman Islanders. Four DHC-5D Buffaloes joined the force in 1978. The helicopter force has 10 Aérospatiale/Westland SA.330 Pumas, seven Aérospatiale (Sud) Alouette IIIs and some Agusta AB 205As, but this inventory is likely to be increased in the future when Egyptian Lynx deliveries begin, the UAE being one of the recipients of aircraft from the announced production agreement between Egypt and the UK. Also kept at the Abu Dhabi base is a Piper Pawnee Brave crop-spraying aircraft delivered in December 1975, and a Lake Buccaneer amphibian for the personal use of Sheikh Kalifa.

Dubai's Central Air Force Base is also the headquarters of the Police Air Wing, which has a small counter-insurgency force equipped with three armed single-seat Aermacchi M.B.326KDs and a two-seat M.B.326LD and a repeat order is being fulfilled for three more Ks and another two-seat L. For STOL transport duties, a single Aeritalia G222 was delivered in December 1976, and a second aircraft is on option. Also flown by the police are three Bell 206Bs and two Bell 205As, used for liaison and communications. There is also a Cessna 182 for training and an SIAI-Marchetti SF.260WD Warrior for armed training. The three ex-Abu Dhabi AB 206Bs which formed the basis of the Union Air Force in 1972 have since been joined at Dubai by four Bell 205As used for troop transport work, and three AB 212s.

Qatar

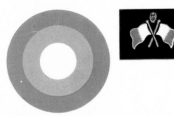

Qatar Emiri Air Force: The QEAF operates a small strike force of two Hawker Hunter FGA.78s (a third aircraft was lost in 1977) and a single two-seat T.79 from its main base at Doha on the Gulf. Flown and maintained by British personnel, the Hunters are used mainly on regular coastal patrols. Two Westland Whirlwind IIIs, supplied in 1968, are used for transport duties alongside three Westland Commando Mk 2As delivered in 1975. A fourth Mk 2C Commando is used for government and VIP transport. Three Westland Lynx HC.28 multi-role helicopters were ordered in 1976 and these have been delivered for joint use with the Qatar Police. The Qatar Police also operate two Aérospatiale/Westland SA.341 Gazelles in a dual civil/military role. Future procurement is reported to centre on some Dassault Mirage F1s to replace the Hunters.

This is half the strike force of the Qatar Emiri Air Force, the third of whose Hunter FGA.78s was shot down in 1977. British aircrew and ground staff predominate.

Kuwait

Kuwait Air Force: To protect the oilfields of this rich Arab state, all three Kuwaiti armed forces are being strengthened and new equipment phased into service. Kuwait has now received all the new aircraft it ordered during 1974 from the United States and France, and older types are being withdrawn from use. For strike duties there are two squadrons of McDonnell Douglas Skyhawks (30 A-4KUs and six two-seat TA-4KUs) based at one of two new airfields constructed by Yugoslav contractors to the south and west of the KAF's current main fighter base at Kuwait. Also delivered are 18 Dassault-Breguet Mirage F1 CK strike-fighters and two F1 BK two-seat combat trainers, which have replaced the squadron of 10 BAC F.53 Lightning interceptors and two T.67 two-seat trainers.

In service is a ground-attack squadron of nine BAC Mk 83 Strikemasters of 12 originally acquired in 1969 and 1971. Five Hawker Hunter T.67s complement these, but the four single-seat FGA.57s have been retired from use. To meet a pressing long-range transport requirement, two McDonnell Douglas DC-9-30 convertible passenger/cargo aircraft have been bought and are in service alongside two Lockheed L-100-20s delivered in 1971.

The helicopter force has also expanded and now operates 24 Aérospatiale/Westland SA.342 Gazelle AOP and liaison aircraft in two squadrons, one with an LOH role and the other with an anti-tank role, for which the Gazelles are equipped with HOT missiles. Twelve Aérospatiale/Westland SA.330 Pumas are used for troop carrying in a third helicopter squadron; two Agusta AB 206Bs and four AB 205s have been withdrawn from use and sold overseas.

Iraq

Iraqi Air Force: Over the past few years Iraq has received considerable supplies of arms from the Soviet Union and Iraqi bases have been regularly used by the Russian air force. At the beginning of 1979 a mutual defence agreement was signed between Iraq and Syria and tension continues between the two Arab states and Israel. However, talks were held in 1975 between Iraq and France, and further negotiations in June 1977 are reported to have included provisional agreement for the supply of 36 Dassault Mirage F1s, made up of 32 EQ interceptors and four BQ trainers. Presumably negotiated at the same time was an order for 10 Aérospatiale Super Frelon heavy-lift helicopters, delivered late in 1977. Forty Aérospatiale SA.342L Gazelle light helicopters have also been delivered.

Most modern type in the IAF's Support Command inventory is the Mikoyan-Gurevich MiG-23/27 'Flogger', with which two strike squadrons are equipped with a total of 40 aircraft, the − 23 predominating. Other types in service include more than 30 Hawker Hunter FGA.9/FR.10s in three strike squadrons out of 46 aircraft originally delivered, 30-plus MiG-17s in three fighter-bomber units, 12 Tupolev Tu-22 'Blinders' delivered from 1973 and equipping one bomber squadron, and a further unit with 10 Ilyushin Il-28s. Three strike squadrons fly 50 Sukhoi Su-7Bs, and a further two squadrons operate variable-geometry Sukhoi Su-22s delivered in 1974. For short-range COIN duties there are 16 BAC Jet Provost T.52s out of 20 delivered in 1964-65.

Though it relies mainly upon France for modern fighters, the air force of Iraq is chiefly Soviet supported and has an essentially all-Russian transport force in which are six of these An-12s. They will be supplemented by the much larger Il-76T.

Air Defence Command is made up of a ground-based early-warning system tied in with five squadrons of MiG-21PFMs, of which two have the MiG-21MF version. A mixed helicopter and transport force has seven of 12 Westland Wessex 52s, four Mil Mi-1s, 35 Mi-4s, 36 Mi-8s (two in VIP layout), 40 Aérospatiale (Sud) Alouette IIIs and a few Mi-6s, while one de Havilland Heron flies with 12 Antonov An-2s, six An-12s, 10 An-24s, at least two An-26s, 13 Il-14s and two Tu-124s for VIP use. Iraqi Airways have taken delivery of an Il-76 freighter, and presumably military versions are on the way to the IAF if not actually delivered. Trainers include Yakovlev Yak-11s, Mig-15UTIs, Aero L-29s, MiG-21Us and Hunter T.69s. The Aero L-39 is also in use for training and for secondary ground-attack work; the type is flown by the Air Force College at Tikret and a total of 24 are reportedly being delivered. For basic train-

ing the IAF has ordered 48 Swiss FFA Bravos for use by the air force and the Iraqi Flying Association. Two Britten-Norman Islanders are in service for light transport duties, and two Aérospatiale SA.330 Pumas and a Dassault Falcon 20 are used for VIP work. An order for 48 Pilatus PC-7s has been placed for basic training. Deliveries are likely to begin in late 1980.

Syria

Syrian Arab Air Force: Despite orders for second-line military aircraft from Western manufacturers, Syria continues to field a strong Soviet-supplied combat force, and the Syrian air force is generally regarded as one of the most efficient of the communist-backed Arab air arms. Backbone of the fighter/interceptor units are some 250 Mikoyan-Gurevich MiG-21PF/MF/bis equipping four regiments each having three squadrons. Some of these were used in 1979 in air battles over the Lebanon against Israeli McDonnell Douglas F-15s and a number were lost. There is also a regiment of three squadrons equipped with about 45 MiG-23/27 'Floggers', Syria being one of four Arab states to be supplied with these interceptor/ground-attack aircraft.

Doubling in the low-altitude intercept/strike role are some 50 MiG-17Fs, with a further 60 Sukhoi Su-7s and some Su-20 variable-geometry strike aircraft equipping the ground-attack elements. A small number of MiG-25 Foxbats have been acquired from Russia to help combat Israeli F-15 incursions into Syrian airspace.

The transport force has eight Ilyushin Il-14s, six Douglas C-47s, six Antonov An-12s, four Il-18s, and two Piper Navajos for survey and liaison work. At least nine Kamov Ka-25s are used for coastal ASW patrols, while as many as 50 Mil Mi-8s are used for assault and transport duties together with a lesser number of Mi-4s and Mi-6s. An order for Italian helicopters (six Meridionali-built Boeing CH-47C Chinooks, 12 Agusta SH-3D Sea Kings and 18 AB 212s) still awaits confirmation, but the purchase of at least 16 Aérospatiale/Westland SA.342L Gazelles, some armed with HOT missiles, took place in 1978. Trainers include Yakovlev Yak-11s, Yak-18s, Aero L-29 Delfins, and 48 CASA Flamingo basic trainers bought from Spain and Germany. Operational conversion is performed on two-seat versions of the front-line combat aircraft.

Lebanon

Force Aérienne Libanaise: The Lebanese air force continues to have on strength the single squadron of 10 Dassault-Breguet Mirage IIIEL interceptors and one IIIBL trainer, purchased in the late 1960s, although their utilisation is thought to be low. Main operational type is the Hawker Hunter: 17 F.70s (including a final batch of six ordered in 1975 to make up for losses) and two T.66 two-seaters in service. A de Havilland Dove 6 undertakes transport duties alongside a Rockwell Aero Commander, four Aérospatiale (Sud) Alouette IIs, 13 Alouette IIIs and six Agusta AB 212s. For basic training six BAe(SA) Bulldog 126s have replaced 10 DHC Chipmunks, while ad-

vanced tuition is performed on eight Fouga Super Magisters; three DH Vampire T.55s used for some years have been withdrawn from service.

Israel

Israel Defence Force/Air Force: American arms supplies to Israel continue, and following recent US Congressional approvals will extend to at least 1983. This timescale allows for the delivery of 30 more McDonnell Douglas F-15A/B Eagles to join the 25 already received. Approved at the same time was the purchase of 75 General Dynamics F-16A/B interceptors to balance arms supplies by the USA to Egypt and Saudi Arabia. The first IDF/AF Eagle squadron is operational and includes four refurbished development aircraft delivered in December 1976, although the remaining machines are new. Four Grumman E-2C Hawkeyes worth $170 million have also been received for electronic surveillance; deliveries were made in July/August 1978, and the country holds an option on two more.

The IDF/AF McDonnell Douglas Phantom force, in service since 1969, officially totals 204 F-4Es and 12 RF-4E reconnaissance aircraft in some seven strike/interceptor squadrons. Most of the F-4Es have been fitted with leading-edge slots to improve manoeuvrability. Included in the weaponry carried by the Phantoms and IAI Kfirs is the indigenous Luz air-to-surface missile for use against AA sites. More than 210 McDonnell Douglas A-4E/F/H/N Skyhawks, plus some 24 two-seat TA-4E/Hs, operate in the ground-attack role with six squadrons. Of the 72 Dassault Mirage IIICJs and five two-seat IIIBJs originally supplied by France before the 1967 war, perhaps as many as 40 aircraft survive in three interceptor squadrons, but this number is being increased by deliveries of the Kfir multi-role derivative of the Mirage with a J79 power-plant. Designed and built following France's embargo on the sale of Mirage 5s to Israel, the Kfir was officially revealed in 1975 and two main types are in use, one being the standard Kfir and the other the C-2 fitted with fore-planes. Interim-standard, Atar 9C-powered

Despite receipt of the F-15 Eagle the F-4 Phantom is still the most important combat type in the Heyl Ha'Avir inventory.

aircraft known as Neshers fought in the 1973 war, but early problems with the J79 installation prevented the Kfirs entering service in time for the conflict. A replacement for the Kfir, known as the Arye (Lion), is under development following a recommendation by the Knesset earlier in 1978.

For Elint and battlefield reconnaissance duties, the Israeli air force has two Grumman EV-1 Mohawks equipped with SLAR (side-looking airborne radar) pods and delivered in 1976. The air force has been steadily disposing of its older second-line French jet aircraft to a number of South American air arms. Honduras has purchased 12 Dassault Super Mystère B.2s in two batches, the aircraft being modified by Israel Aircraft Industries to take American J52 engines in place of the original French Atar 101s. Salvador has acquired 18 Dassault Ouragan fighter-bombers and six Potez-Air Fouga Magister trainers. Approx-

imately 80 IAI-built Magisters continue to fly in a dual strike/trainer role, and the postponement of a decision to replace them means that the type is to undergo a modification programme to extend useful life.

Transport wings of the Israeli air force operate 12 Lockheed C-130E, 12 C-130H Hercules and two KC-130H tankers; six Boeing C-97s flying as two-point tankers, ECM aircraft and transports; and 18 Douglas C-47s. The Boeing 707 fleet has expanded and now totals some 10 aircraft, including five ex-TWA machines converted by IAI to tanker/transports and some other change to command/control aircraft. The IDF/AF operates about 130 helicopters: eight Aérospatiale Super Frelons and 29 Sikorsky S-65/CH-53Ds for assault and transport, 45 Bell 205s (11 of these have been delivered to Rhodesia), 20 Bell 206 JetRangers for liaison and 12 Bell 212s. Late in 1978 the IAF/DF ordered 30 Hughes

500M attack helicopters armed with TOW anti-tank missiles. To ease spares and maintenance problems, Israeli air force technical teams have re-engined the Super Frelons with American powerplants in place of their Turboméca turboshafts.

For short-range utility and liaison work the force flies 14 Dornier Do 28s, 35 Do 27s, 28 Cessna U206C Super Skywagons and 16 Beech Queen Air 80s, together with eight to 10 Britten-Norman Islanders and one IAI Westwind 1123 for VIP duties. Some 20 Piper Super Cubs are still used for primary training and army liaison, and also on strength are two Cessna T-41D trainers and a single Cessna 180. A number of Ryan 124-1 Firebee reconnaissance drones and Northrop Chukar RPVs are in use with the air force. The Israeli navy operates three 1124N Sea Scan versions of the Westwind for MR and patrol duties, the aircraft being flown by air force crews.

Though its canards are not clearly visible, this flamboyantly demonstrated IAI Kfir is probably one of the standard C2 production models, carrying what appear to be two Shafrir AAMs and the largest size (1700-litre, 374 Imp gal) centreline drop tank. Buildings in the background are hardened against air attack.

Iran

Iranian Air Force: The current IAF strike-interceptor force has 10 squadrons of McDonnell Douglas Phantoms based at Shiraz, Tabriz and Tehran and equipped with 32 F-4Ds, 141 F-4Es and four RF-4Es, plus a further 12 RF-4Es and 36 F-4Es delivered between May 1976 and July 1977. The 141 Northrop F-5Es ordered some time ago are believed to have been delivered to some eight fighter-bomber squadrons based at Buskehr on the coast and at Tabriz. They replace the original F-5A force almost one-for-one. Redundant F-5As have been transferred to other air forces including those of Jordan, Greece, Pakistan and the original South Vietnamese air force. In all, 117 F-5A/RF-5As and 22 F-5Bs were supplied to the IAF. A batch of 28 two-seat F-5F combat trainers was recently delivered to Iran.

For maritime reconnaissance six Lockheed P-3F Orions have been delivered and are based at Bandar Abbas. To support the F-4/F-5/F-14 force, 13 Boeing 707-320C tanker/transports are in service, six equipped for three-point refuelling. Three of an order for nine ex-TWA Boeing 747s are being fitted with air-refuelling equipment. The loss of a 747 in Spain and the resale to TWA of two more have reduced the fleet to six but an order was announced in 1977 for four 747Fs, thus taking the fleet to 10 aircraft. The tactical transport element has 15 Lockheed C-130E and 49 C-130H Hercules and 13 Fokker F.27 Mk 400M Troopships, including two for aerial survey, and five F.27 Mk 600s, three of the latter for VIP use. Four C-130s were being converted for signal monitoring in connection with the Ibex intelligence-gathering network being installed along Iran's borders.

A helicopter element larger than many of the world's air arms has nearly 700 machines, although not all are in service; most will be flown by the Iranian army. One order recently

The Islamic Iranian AF remains the only one outside the USAF to operate a military version of the 747. Believed to number 11 aircraft, including four new 747-2J9Fs, some (but not this one) carry air-refuelling gear.

fulfilled was for 39 Bell 214C utility helicopters, worth $21.7 million, for SAR duties with the air force; deliveries began in December 1976 and were completed in February 1978. Six more Bell 214As are on order for government use at a cost of $4 million. In service are 10 Kaman HH-43F Huskies, 45 Agusta AB 205s, five AB 212s and 70 AB 206s. Two Italian Meridionali-built Boeing CH-47C Chinooks are in use with the air force, the remainder of these aircraft being operated by the army. Also in use are two Agusta-built Sikorsky S-61A-4 VIP helicopters. A major purchase which has been cancelled due to the recent crisis was an order for 350 Bell 214ST helicopters, the majority of them to be assembled at a new factory at Isfahan in Iran. Three Rockwell Aero Commander 690s and four Dassault Falcon 20s are used for liaison work, together with seven DHC Beavers. A total of 49 Beech Bonanzas (39 F.33Cs and 10 F.33As) are in service for training.

The political crisis in Iran at the beginning of 1979 resulted in the cancellation of many outstanding arms orders placed in the United

States and the UK. From America, Iran has cancelled the purchase of 160 General Dynamics F-16s, a second batch of 70 Grumman F-14s, 16 RF-4Es and seven Boeing E-3A Sentry AWACS. Bell Helicopters have ceased all work on its large contract for the local co-production of 400 Bell 214s, while the cancelled British orders mainly affect the Iranian army and involve Rapier missile units and Chieftain tanks.

The 80 Grumman F-14A Tomcats have all been delivered and fly from two bases, Khatami AFB at Isfahan where 50 are based, and Shiraz farther south with the remaining 30 aircraft.

Iranian Navy: Like the other two services, the navy air arm was expanded considerably during the mid-seventies and now operates 10 Agusta SH-3D Sea Kings for ASW work, plus another batch on order and believed to total 10 machines. Six Sikorsky RH-53Ds are currently being delivered. Other types in service include five Agusta AB 205s, 14 AB 206s, six AB 212s, six Rockwell Shrike Commanders for liaison, and two Fokker F.27 Mk 400Ms

and two Mk 600s for transport duties based at Mehrabad.

Iranian Army: One of the largest users of rotorcraft in the world, the army has procured numbers of helicopters, mainly from Italy and America. The largest type in use is the CH-47C Chinook, 20 of which have been received from Boeing and a further 20 from the Italian licensee, Meridionali. Yet another order for the type was announced in February 1977, this time for 50 more Italian-built aircraft plus spares and support worth about $425 million. These aircraft will be used in the tactical transport and assault roles. The Iranian army has a formidable anti-tank force comprising 202 Bell AH-1Js, many equipped with TOW missiles. For tactical and liaison duties, 287 Bell 214As have been delivered, the order completion date being February 1978.

The army also has a fixed-wing element operating about 40 Cessna 185s, 10 Cessna O-2s, six Cessna 310s, and two Fokker F.27 Friendships — one Mk 400M and one Mk 600 for transport and target-towing duties.

Though a formidable force on paper, the 200-odd Bell AH-1J SeaCobras of the Islamic Iranian Army Aviation are almost completely grounded through lack of spares and skilled service support, though small numbers have taken part in parades and ceremonial fly-pasts. Many were delivered with TOW capability, complete with missiles.

Africa

South Africa and Zimbabwe-Rhodesia field the largest and most effective air forces in sub-Saharan Africa. Most Black African air arms have less than 50 combat aircraft. Localised wars, nationalist guerilla movements and foreign intervention expeditions add to the pattern of African politics, ensuring that the area is never far from tomorrow's newspaper headlines.

United Nations arms embargoes against South Africa and Zimbabwe (Rhodesia) have had relatively little effect. SIAI-Marchetti SF-260 piston-engined strike trainers and Agusta 205 helicopters reached Zimbabwe during 1979 and the largely French-equipped South African air force seems to have little difficulty. As Zimbabwe, before the recent ceasefire agreement, tackled the twin problems of making the inevitable transition to majority rule while attempting to stem the flow of Nationalist guerilas across its borders, air strikes against guerilla bases in neighbouring nations showed the difficulty many small air forces have in policing large areas of air space.

Britain, France, Italy and the Soviet Union have been major suppliers of aircraft to Africa and the MiG-21 or Mirage has become a new status symbol among local air arms. For the Soviet Union, open warfare between two nations equipped with Soviet aircraft and missiles must have been somewhat of an embarrassment but the decision fully to back Ethiopia resulted in defeat for Somalia during a campaign which saw MiG-21s downed by SA-3 missiles.

Angola 35	Mali Republic 32
Benin 32	Mauritania 31
Botswana 37	Mozambique 36
Cameroun 35	Niger 33
Central African Empire 33	Nigeria 33
Chad 33	Rwanda 35
Congo Republic 33	Senegal 31
Ethiopia 34	Sierra Leone 31
Gabon 35	Somalia 34
Ghana 32	South Africa 37
Guinea Republic 31	Sudan 33
Haute-Volta 32	Tanzania 36
Ivory Coast 32	Togo 32
Kenya 34	Uganda 34
Liberia 32	Zaire 35
Malagasy Republic 36	Zambia 36
Malawi 36	Zimbabwe/Rhodesia 36

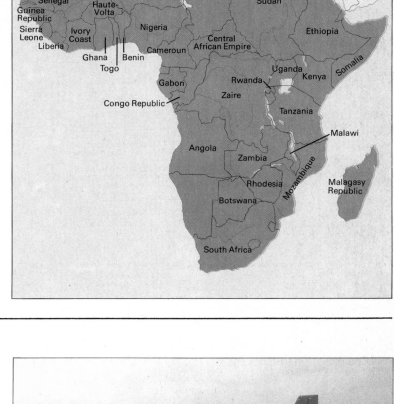

Mauritania

Mauritania Islamic Air Force: A limited modernization programme for this small air arm began in 1975 in an effort to combat the increasing activities of the Polisario guerrillas. Initially a transport arm, the air force subsequently acquired a small attack and counter-insurgency element in the form of six Britten-Norman Defenders. Equipped with a full range of underwing stores and gun-pods, these aircraft were delivered in 1976-77, but two have been lost on operations. A repeat order

for three Defenders was fulfilled last year to make up for attrition and to increase the size of the force.

Two DHC-5D Buffaloes have been delivered to expand the airlift capability of the air force. Operated jointly by the army and air force are two Short Skyvan 3M transports based at Nouakchott, along with two Holste MH.1521M Broussard liaison aircraft. Two Douglas DC-4s and a Sud Caravelle are used for long-range flights and four Reims F337 Super Skymasters are flown on FAC, training and COIN duties. An order for four more F337s is likely.

The versatile Defender has been found extremely useful by the Mauritania Islamic Defence Force, whose aircraft have carried various weapons including the Swiss SURA 80mm rocket in four five-tier rows. Seven are currently in use.

Senegal

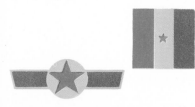

Armée de l'Air du Senegal: As with many ex-French colonies, Senegal has received a number of ex-Armée de l'Air aircraft and still benefits from a training agreement with France. In return French military units have been operating from bases in Senegal against Polisario Front guerrillas in Mauritania, eight SEPECAT Jaguar strike aircraft and some transports being involved in December 1977;

more recently two squadrons of Jaguars have been based at Dakar. The country's small air arm has a personnel strength of some 200 and is mainly concerned with internal policing, transport and liaison work. Two ex-French Fouga Magister jet trainers are in use alongside six Douglas C-47s, four Holste MH.1521M Broussards, two Aérospatiale (Sud) Alouette IIs, one Aérospatiale/Westland

Gazelle and a Reims F337 COIN aircraft. A single Boeing 707-200 is used for government and VIP flights and is based at Dakar. At the end of 1977 the first of six Fokker F27 Friendships was delivered to the air force, the others arriving in early 1979; the aircraft will operate between the airfields of Dakar, Ziguinchor and Tambacounda as well as other bases.

Guinea Republic

Force Aérienne de Guinea: This West African republic, for many years under the influence of the Soviet Union, is moving steadily into a more non-aligned position. Plans for a Soviet naval base to be constructed near the capital Conakry have been dropped, and for some time the use of refuelling facilities for Soviet long-range reconnaissance aircraft has been withdrawn. The air force, however, continues to operate the handful of Russian aircraft which it has used for some years and at

present there have been no moves to procure Western equipment. Eight Mikoyan-Gurevich MiG-17F fighter-bombers form the sole combat element in the force, of which only half may be operational. Other types include four Ilyushin Il-14s, four Antonov An-14s, two Il-18s for VIP use, one Bell 47G and a training element flying seven Yakovlev Yak-18s, a couple of MiG-15UTIs and some Czech Aero L-29 Delfins.

Sierra Leone

Sierra Leone Defence Force: Formed in 1973, this small air arm suffers from lack of finance. It operates a single BO105C

helicopter. All other aircraft (four Saab MFI-15 primary trainers and a Hughes 500 helicopter) have been sold.

Liberia

Liberian Army/Air Reconnaissance Unit: This airborne element of the 5,000-man Liberian army was established only in the mid-1970s. Largest type in use is the Douglas C-47, of which there are two. Also operated are a number of light aircraft including two Cessna 172s, one Cessna 185 and one Cessna 207. A few Cessna 337s have also been purchased.

Ivory Coast

Force Aérienne de Côte d'Ivoire: The air component of this ex-French colony operates in support of the Ivory Coast army, flying liaison and transport duties. However, the acquisition of a small combat element was announced in 1977 in the form of six Dassault-Breguet/Dornier Alpha Jets, with an option on a further six which has since been changed to a firm order. The 12 aircraft are to be equipped for a dual trainer/COIN role.

With headquarters at Abidjan, a government flight uses one Dassault Falcon 20, one Grumman Gulfstream II, one Fokker F27 Mk 600, two F.28 Mk 1000s and one Rockwell Aero Commander 500B. Currently in use are three Douglas C-47s, a Fokker F27 Mk 400M, three Reims F337s, three Aérospatiale SA.330 Pumas, three Aérospatiale (Sud) Alouette IIIs and two Alouette IIs. Two Reims-Cessna 150s provide basic training.

Mali Republic

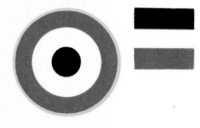

Force Aérienne du Mali: This former French colony has been courted by the Soviet Union and was supplied with a token combat force of five Mikoyan-Gurevich MiG-17s and one two-seat MiG-15UTI some years ago. For transport duties there are two Mil Mi-4 helicopters, two Antonov An-2 light transports, two Douglas C-47s and some Yakovlev trainers.

Haute-Volta

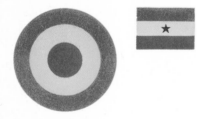

Force Aérienne de Haute-Volta: Receiving its independence from France in 1960, the Upper Volta Republic currently flies a selection of second-line types supplied by France. The aircraft include two Douglas C-47s, three Holste MH.1521M Broussards, a Rockwell Aero Commander 500 and a Reims Super Skymaster. Two Nord 262s are operated on VIP and transport duties. A single HS.748 was delivered in September 1977 for transport and supply work.

Ghana

Ghana Air Force: Established chiefly as a transport and internal policing force, the GAF recently underwent a re-equipment programme and now operates a variety of aircraft. Eight Britten-Norman Islanders are used for paratroop training, aerial survey and casevac duties, six Shorts Skyvan 3Ms are based at Takoradi and flown on tactical support, communications, coastal patrol and casualty duties, and three Fokker F.27 Mk 400Ms and two F.27 Mk 600s are operated on SAR and general transport work. A single Fokker F.28 Mk 3000 has replaced the HS.125 jet for VIP use. At Tamli in northern Ghana a squadron of seven Aermacchi MB326Fs bought in 1965 constitutes the air force's sole jet combat equipment. However, a repeat order for MB326s was placed in 1976 and is understood to total six single-seat KB aircraft; delivery of these is complete. Thirteen BAe (SA) Bulldog 120s ordered in two batches provides basic pilot training at Takoradi. A helicopter squadron has four Aérospatiale Alouette IIIs and two Bell 212s, the latter used for VIP and communications.

Togo

Force Aérienne Togolaise: This small African air arm, formed following independence from France in 1960, has expanded over the past few years from being a purely transport and supply force to one having a modest strike potential. This attack capability is based on three EMBRAER EMB-326GC Xavante two-seat strike/trainers bought from Brazil in 1976, plus a further three delivered late in 1978. In addition, five Dassault-Breguet/Dornier Alpha Jets have been ordered from France as a follow-on to five Aérospatiale Magister jet trainers purchased in 1975. Two DHC-5D Buffaloes from the reduced Zaïre order joined the transport force in 1976, other types in use being two Douglas C-47s, two Holste MH.1521M Broussards, two Reims Super Skymasters and an Aérospatiale (Sud) Alouette II helicopter. A single Lockheed L-100-20 is on order. An Aérospatiale/ Westland SA.330 Puma was delivered in 1975, as was a single Fokker F28 Mk 1000 for VIP duties.

Benin

Force Armée Populaire du Benin: Formerly known as Dahomey, this ex-French dependency changed its name in 1976, although there have been few reports of any change in the country's armed forces. The modest air arm acts as a supply and liaison force; it has three Douglas C-47s, a single Fokker F.27-600 received in 1978, a Cessna/Reims Super Skymaster and two or three Max Holste MH.1521M Broussards. There is also a Rockwell Aero Commander 500B for VIP use, a Bell 47G and an Aérospatiale Alouette II — almost all supplied from ex-French stocks. An Aérospatiale Corvette has been acquired for VIP duties.

Nigeria

Federal Nigerian Air Force: One of the more politically stable Black African states, Nigeria supports an air force that retains a non-aligned stance as far as equipment purchases are concerned. The front-line combat elements field Soviet-supplied types, while the support and training units are distinctly biased towards Western equipment. Late in 1975 an official announcement revealed that the NAF was undergoing a re-equipment programme, and this has given the force a more modern look. More than 20 Mikoyan-Gurevich MiG-21s including some two-seat MiG-21Us, have been supplied by the Soviet Union and these are based at Kano in the strike/interceptor role. Soviet aircraft have been flown by the NAF since the Biafran conflict, but it is believed that no more than four Ilyushin Il-28 bombers and about 12 of 41 MiG-17s original-

ly received are now airworthy.

The transport arm has six Lockheed C-130H Hercules, two Fokker F27 Mk 400s and a single F28 for VIP/government flights. Light transport and supply duties are flown by 20 Dornier Do 28D Skyservants, which also operate in the casevac and training roles. For liaison and communications there are 15 Do 27s, two Piper Navajos and a Navajo Chieftain, while short-range SAR missions are flown by four MBB BO-105Cs, six more of which have been ordered out of a requirement for 20. The helicopter force has been expanded with the addition of more Aérospatiale/Westland SA.330 Pumas to take the number in service to 10, joining three Westland Whirlwinds; 10 Aérospatiale (Sud) Alouette IIs are in storage. Primary training is performed on 20 Scottish Aviation Bulldog 123s delivered in 1973-74 plus a further batch of 12 aircraft received recently. Advanced flying is done on 10 Piaggio P.149Ds, four MiG-15UTIs, eight Aero L-29 Delfins and a couple of MiG-21Us. To replace the L-29s, the NAF has ordered 12 Dassault-Breguet/Dornier Alpha Jets from the Dornier production line and these aircraft will have full ground-attack capability.

One of the users of the F27 Friendship military versions (at one time called Troopships) is the Federal Nigerian Air Force, which has two Mk 400 passenger/cargo transports equipped for parachute troops or airdrops from side doors.

Chad

Escadrille Tchadienne: Under a re-negotiated defence treaty with France signed in 1976, the Chad government is receiving French help in resisting guerrilla activity by the National Liberation Front in the north of the country. Up to 1,000 French troops are stated to be in Chad, and in April 1978 some 10 *l'Armée de l'Air* SEPECAT Jaguar fighter-bombers, supported by Transall C-160 freighters, arrived in the capital, N'Djamena.

The small Chad air force benefits from French 'technical assistance' and currently operates only four ex-FAF Douglas A-1D Skyraiders in a ground-attack unit; at least one Skyraider has been lost to rebel ground-fire. Transport and supply duties are flown by three Douglas DC-4s, nine Douglas C-47s, some Nord Noratlas, and a single Aérospatiale Caravelle for the use of the President. Four Aérospatiale SA.330 Puma helicopters are used for tactical

troop transport work while for liaison there are about 10 Aérospatiale Alouette IIIs, two Max Holste MH.1521M Broussards, four Reims C337 Super Skymasters, and two Pilatus Turbo-Porters delivered in 1976.

Central African Empire

Force Aérienne Centrafricaine: This ex-French colony has been receiving aid from France since becoming independent in 1960. Current strength consists of 10 Aermacchi AL.60 light transports, an ex-Sterling Aérospatiale Caravelle and a Dassault Falcon 20 for VIP use, three Douglas C-47s, an ex-French AF Douglas DC-3, one Douglas DC-4, six Max Holste MH.1521M Broussards, an Aérospatiale Alouette II and a

few Sikorsky H-34 helicopters. Two Socata Rallye 235 light aircraft were delivered to the CAE in 1978 and may be under military command.

Niger

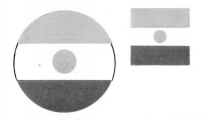

Force Aérienne du Niger: Formerly part of French West Africa, Niger still receives some aid from France. Its air arm currently operates a variety of transport and liaison aircraft, including a single ex-French Aéropostale Douglas C-54B, three ex-*Luftwaffe* Nord Noratlas, two Douglas C-47s, a Rockwell Aero Commander and two Reims Cessna F337s. For government flights there is a single Boeing 737. Two Lockheed C-130H Hercules

were ordered early in 1979, delivery being made towards the end of the year.

Sudan

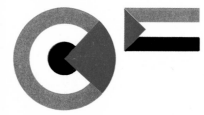

Sudanese Air Force: A major shift in policy by President Numeiry took place in 1978. Following an attempted coup against the President in 1971, allegedly with Soviet backing, relations between Russia and the Sudan deteriorated steadily until in May 1977 90 Soviet military advisers and some diplomatic staff were expelled. Thus the country has returned to the Western camp after nearly 10 years of Soviet dominance, a move undoubted-

ly helped by the promise of Arab money, particularly from Saudi Arabia, and the willingness of the USA to modernize the Sudanese armed forces. Initially the United States was reluctant to supply modern combat aircraft to the Sudan air force, so France was approached and orders were placed for batches of fighters and assault helicopters: more precisely, 14 Dassault Mirage 50 fighter-bombers and two Mirage trainers, 10 Aérospatiale/Westland SA.330 Puma troop-carrying helicopters. Following these orders, the USA announced that it would after all be willing to sell Northrop F-5Es to the Sudan and in February 1979 ten F-5Es and two F-5Fs were officially ordered. In March 1978, the Sudan air force received the first of six Lockheed C-130H Hercules (the 1,500th of the type built) ordered in April 1977, and the air force has also received four DHC-5D Buffaloes ordered around the same time. The present Sudanese

inventory comprises two combat squadrons, one flying some 20 Mikoyan-Gurevich MiG-21PF interceptors, and a fighter-bomber unit flying 12 Chinese-built MiG-17Fs (Shenyang F-4s). A transport squadron has six Antonov An-12s, five An-24s and the C-130Hs. Ten Mil Mi-8s are in use, but serviceability is thought to be low. A COIN squadron has three flyable BAC 145s of five supplied in the late 1960s, while the eight Jet Provost T.52s are reported to have been put into storage. Miscellaneous types include a single DHC Twin Otter Series 300 flown for survey work and eight Pilatus Turbo-Porters for light transport duties. A Beech King Air 90 is operated by the Police Air Wing, and 20 MBB BO-105s are on order.

33

Ethiopia

Ethiopian Air Force: Following some years of conflict with the Eritrean Liberation Army, the military government in Ethiopia found itself involved in a full-scale war with neighbouring Somalia in July 1977 over the disputed Ogaden desert region. A massive Soviet airlift of arms into Ethiopia followed early defeats of the Ethiopian Army at the hands of the Somalis. Influenced by Soviet and Cuban personnel and a flood of equipment, the Ogaden war reversed its course and ended in March 1978 with a ceasefire and the withdrawal of Somali troops from the area. Ethiopian Air Force flying was limited in the early stages of the war, but the advent of

Soviet-supplied Mikoyan-Gurevich MiG-21s, believed to total some 50 in number and flown by Cuban Air Force pilots, meant an increase in EAF involvement. By September 1977, at least 23 Somali MiGs were claimed as destroyed by Ethiopia, and reports stated later that both MiG-21s and 23s were being used for ground-attack sorties. Before the arrival of Soviet equipment, the EAF had an inventory of western aircraft, acquired over a number of years and mainly of American origin.

Four BAC Canberra B.52s were purchased in 1969 and the two survivors, together with about 12 Northrop F-5As, flew quite a number of sorties during the war; two F-5Bs are also on strength. A further fighter-bomber unit has 11 North American F-86F Sabres of doubtful operational status, and a COIN unit based at Dire-Dawa flies six North American T-28Ds. For transport work there are 12 Douglas C-47s, 12 Fairchild jet-augmented Packets, two Douglas C-54s, two de Havilland Doves, and an Ilyushin Il-14 donated by Russia some years ago. Trainers include 11 Lockheed T-28s. Five Aérospatiale Alouette IIIs, one SA.330 Puma, two Mil

This F-5A is one of 12 operated by the Ethiopian AF in the war against rebel forces in the Ogaden alongside a handful of other Western types and a much larger force of MiG-21 and MiG-23 tactical aircraft supplied by the Soviet Union.

Mi-8s and six Augusta AB 204Bs form the helicopter element.

The Ethiopian Army has a small support force flying six Bell UH-1Hs and four DHC Otters. Three DHC Twin Otters were delivered in 1977.

Somalia

Somalian Aeronautical Corps: In July 1977 the country became heavily involved in a war with neighbouring Ethiopia over the disputed Ogaden desert region. Initial Somali success

was followed by a total withdrawal after a massive Russian airlift of supplies into Ethiopia had turned the tide of the conflict. A ceasefire was agreed in March 1978 and although losses were inclined to be somewhat exaggerated, 23 Somali MiGs were claimed as destroyed by the Ethiopians. Paradoxically, before the war Somalia had been a major recipient of Soviet military and economic aid for some years and extensive port facilities had been built for the Soviet navy at Berbera and Kismayo in the south, while Russian long-range reconnaissance aircraft regularly operated from Somali bases. However, with the heavy Soviet involvement on the side of

Ethiopia, Somalia expelled all Soviet and Cuban advisers from the country late in 1977 and today Somalia faces critical serviceability problems in its armed forces, which are almost wholly Soviet equipped. The air force is reported to have received 25 Bell AH-1 HueyCobras and 70 Bell JetRangers from captured South Vietnamese stocks via private arms suppliers, but confirmation of this is still awaited. Reports at the beginning of 1979 spoke of Somalia's tentative approach to the Soviet Union following the lack of response of western countries to Somalia's requests for arms.

The front-line combat force before the war

comprised a squadron of 10 Mikoyan-Gurevich MiG-21s, two squadrons of some 40 MiG-17s and a bomber unit with 10 Ilyushin Il-28s based at Mogadishu. Transports include three Douglas C-47s, a Beech C-45, at least three Antonov An-24s and An-26s, and three An-2s. Eight Piaggio P.148s are used for primary training, together with at least one Cessna 150 Aerobat, plus 20 Yakovlev Yak-11s and a couple of MiG-15UTI advanced trainers. One helicopter squadron has Mil Mi-4s, Mi-8s and some Agusta AB 204s. Two Dornier Skyservants are flown by the Police Air Wing for liaison and supply duties. Four Aeritalia G.222s were ordered late in 1979.

Kenya

Kenya Air Force: Delivered during 1978 was the order worth $75 million for 10 Northrop F-5E fighter-bombers and two F-5F combat trainers placed in 1977. A single fighter-bomber squadron currently operates five Hawker Hunter FGA.9s delivered in 1974, and an attack/trainer unit has five BAC Mk 87 Strikemasters. To supplement and eventually replace the Strikemasters, the

Kenyan air force has ordered 12 British Aerospace Hawk Mk 52s which are expected to be equipped with weapon pylons for the dual strike/trainer role. Joining the two transport squadrons in 1978 were four DHC-5D Buffaloes, which operate alongside the existing force of six DHC Caribous, 15 DHC Beavers, one Rockwell Aero Commander 680F and a Piper Navajo Chieftain. Also in use are six Dornier Do 28 Skyservants for light STOL transport duties. A training element is equipped with 14 Scottish Aviation Bulldog 103s, the second batch, comprising nine machines, being delivered in 1977. Two Bell 47Gs and three Aérospatiale (Sud) Alouette IIs have been joined by two Aérospatiale/Westland SA.342K Gazelles for liaison duties and a batch of six Aérospatiale/Westland SA.330 Pumas is in service.

One of the numerous air forces to have bought the piston-engined STOL Dornier Skyservant is that of Kenya, which has six backing up a motley force of de Havilland Canada Beavers, Caribous and Buffaloes. France supplied Puma helicopters.

Uganda

Uganda Army Air Force: Since the destruction of half the Ugandan air force's combat force in the July 1976 Israeli commando raid on Entebbe, the Soviet Union has replaced the 11 MiGs lost, and the present Ugandan combat element now comprises two squadrons, one with 12 MiG-17Fs and the other with 10 MiG-21s. Supporting these units is a third assigned the light strike role and flying eight Israeli-supplied Fouga Magisters. For training there are at least two MiG-15UTIs and five Aero L-29 Delfins in the advanced role, while for basic tuition there are five Piaggio P.149s;

six primary FFA AS.202 Bravos have been received. A single Grumman Gulfstream II is in use for VIP flights, while transport duties are performed by the Police Air Wing, which has a DHC Twin Otter and a DHC Caribou. A helicopter element has six Agusta AB 205s and four AB 206s plus a number attached to the PAW. The Uganda army has about 10 Piper Super Cubs for liaison, training and spotting.

The effect of the 1979 invasion of Uganda by Tanzanian and exile forces has had an unspecified effect on Ugandan air strength, except to reduce its already weakened position by way of various ground losses.

Among the heterogenous assortment of aircraft in the Uganda Army Air Force are at least two Piper Aztecs used for liaison and VIP communications, supplementing the Gulfstream II favoured by the deposed former president.

Rwanda

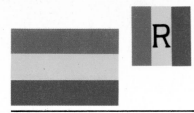

Rwanda Air Force: This small African state, originally administered by Belgium, gained its independence in 1962. Its modest air arm has undergone limited expansion over the past few years. Three Italian Aeritalia AM.3C AOP and liaison aircraft are in service alongside two Douglas C-47s for transport work, two Aérospatiale (Sud) Alouette IIIs and a Britten-Norman Islander. Three Fouga Magisters were acquired from France in 1975 for jet training, and in 1978 a Britten-Norman Defender was received.

Zaire

Force Aérienne Zaïroise: Just over a year after the last invasion of the southern state of Shaba by Katangese mercenaries, a second incursion occured in May 1978. President Mobuto once again appealed for aid to help combat the invasion, and France and Belgium responded with paratroops. Defeat of the mercenaries was swift but not before they had attacked a number of FAZ aircraft. These include at least six Aermacchi M.B.326 strike/trainers and two Aérospatiale/-Westland SA.330 Pumas.

The FAZ's Dassault Mirage force, for which orders were placed totalling 14 single-seat 5M fighter-bombers and three two-seat 5DM combat trainers, form part of the Combat Wing based at Kamina. Recent reports have suggested that no more than half the number ordered have been delivered due to severe financial problems and at least five have been lost in accidents. Two other squadrons of the three-squadron Combat Wing are ground-attack units equipped with about 10 surviving M.B.326GBs detached to Kamina and Kinshasa. Two M.B.326GBs have been ordered to replace losses and a further six, this time M.B.326K single-seat attack versions, are being delivered. Another unit has eight armed North American T-6Gs; 20 Reims Milirole COIN aircraft have been received recently.

A tactical transport squadron has two DHC Caribous and three DHC-5D Buffaloes, while two further transport units operate seven Lockheed C-130H Hercules, two Douglas DC-6s, 10 Douglas C-47s, two Curtiss C-46s and four Douglas C-54s. These units are normally based at Kinshasa and their equipment serviceability is doubtful. A helicopter element has 15 Aérospatiale (Sud) Alouette IIIs, seven Bell 47Gs and seven SA.330 Pumas, plus a single Super Frelon for the personal use of the President. At Kinshasa there are about 12 of 16 Cessna 150 Aerobats originally delivered for officer training. There are also 23 SIAI-Marchetti SF.260MZs and some T-6s for basic tuition. An order for a further ten SF.260s has been mooted but nothing firm has been decided.

Congo Republic

Congo Air Force: This ex-French colony has an air arm directed mainly at transport and communications work. Air force headquarters are in Brazzaville. Aircraft have been supplied by both France and the Soviet Union and include three Douglas C-47s, five Antonov An-24s, a Fokker-VFW F.28 Fellowship for VIP use, five Ilyushin Il-14s, three Max Holste MH.1521M Broussards and one Nord Frégate. Helicopters number three Aérospatiale Alouette IIs and an Alouette III.

Gabon

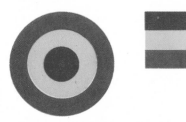

Force Aérienne Gabonaise: Formerly part of French Equatorial Africa, Gabon gained its independence in 1960 along with many other colonies, but it continues to maintain close ties with France. Announced in 1975 was an order for three Dassault Mirage 5Gs and two 5DGs, for the country's first combat squadron, and delivery of these has been made. Gabonais crews have undergone training in France. The transport force is composed of one Lockheed L-100-20, an L-100-30 and an Advanced C-130H, all being used chiefly for heavy engineering work within the country. A single VIP Grumman Gulfstream II, two NAMC YS-11As for joint civil/military use and a Dassault Falcon 20E also for VIP government use are also on strength. Other types include three Douglas C-47s, three Nord 262s, four Holste MH.1521M Broussards, one Reims C337, four Aérospatiale SA.330 Pumas and four Aérospatiale (Sud) Alouette IIJ helicopters.

Included in an order for six delta-wing Mirage 5s from the Force Aérienne Gabonaise was this dual-control 5DG on which Gabonese pilots trained in France before delivery. Only one runway in the country is available to the Mirages.

Cameroun

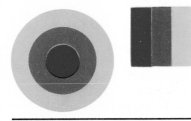

L'Armée de l'Air du Cameroun: Being an ex-French colony, this country has received aid from France since independence in 1960. In more recent years, however, the Cameroun Air Force has purchased equipment from other countries, as evidenced by an order placed in 1976 with Lockheed for two C-130H Hercules, delivery of which was made the following year. Two Hawker Siddeley HS 748s are in service, one of these being for Presidential use and based at Douala. For internal counter-insurgency work and training there are some four ex-French AF Fouga Magisters, while the transport arm is equipped with two DHC Caribous, four C-47s, two Dornier Do28s, a Beech Queen Air and seven Max Holste MH.1521M Broussards. Helicopters include an Aérospatiale SA.330 Puma for VIP use, two Aérospatiale Alouette IIs and an Alouette III.

Angola

Angolan Republic Air Force: This air arm, known as FAPA, was established by the Marxist MPLA government towards the end of the civil war in 1976. Soviet assistance provided FAPA with the nucleus of a combat element in the form of some Mikoyan-Gurevich MiG-21MFs, operated by Cuban-trained Portuguese mercenaries and Cubans. Twelve aircraft assembled at Luanda, Angola's capital, are believed still to be operational. In addition, eight MiG-17Fs were supplied, together with three MiG-15UTI two-seat trainers. The only other jet type in use is the Fiat G.91R-4, three ex-Portuguese Air Force examples of which were left behind when Portugal yielded the country to the Angolans. About 20 Aérospatiale Alouette IIIs from the same source are used for liaison duties, together with three Douglas C-47s. Six Antonov An-26 transports were delivered in 1977 but one was shot down in July that year by guerrilla forces. A number of ex-Portuguese-operated aircraft were left behind after the withdrawal, including Dornier Do 27s, North American T-6s and Portuguese OGMA-built Austers, and some are believed to be in FAPA service. Two Pilatus PC-6 Turbo-Porters were delivered in 1976. Although the western-backed FNLA and Unita parties continue to wage a guerrilla war against the MPLA, they are not thought to have the benefit of air power. Cuba continues to support Angola, with Soviet and limited East German assistance.

Zambia

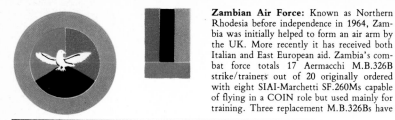

Zambian Air Force: Known as Northern Rhodesia before independence in 1964, Zambia was initially helped to form an air arm by the UK. More recently it has received both Italian and East European aid. Zambia's combat force totals 17 Aermacchi M.B.326B strike/trainers out of 20 originally ordered with eight SIAI-Marchetti SF.260Ms capable of flying in a COIN role but used mainly for training. Three replacement M.B.326Bs have been received to make up for losses. Four Yugoslav Soko Jastreb light attack aircraft and two Soko Galeb trainers are also on strength.

A transport unit has seven DHC-5D Buffalo STOL aircraft, 10 Douglas C-47s, five DHC Caribous, 10 Dornier Do 28 Skyservants and seven DHC Beavers. With the transport unit at Lusaka is a VIP flight operating one HS.748 and two Yakovlev Yak-40s. Still unconfirmed is the reported ac-quisition of some six Mil Mi-6 heavy-lift helicopters from Russia; they would comple-ment 25 Agusta AB 205As, 17 Bell 47Gs, one AB 212 and eight Aérospatiale (Sud) Alouette IIIs. For light attack and basic trainer duties, the air force has 20 Saab MFI-17 Safaris delivered in 1976-77. As part of an aid package China has supplied Zambia with a batch of Shenyang F-6 (MiG-19) fighters

Tanzania

Tanzanian People's Defence Force Air Wing: The combat element of the Tanzanian Air Wing is composed of three squadrons of Chinese-supplied jets totalling 16 Mikoyan-Gurevich MiG-21s (Shenyang F-8), eight MiG-19s (Shenyang F-6) and 10 MiG-17Fs (Shenyang F-4). Two MiG-15UTI trainers were also supplied. The transport force has shown the largest expansions in recent years, with orders being placed with British Aerospace for three HS.748s fitted with large freight doors, and with de Havilland Canada for four DHC-5D Buffaloes. The latter joined the force in 1978 and operate alongside 12 DHC Caribous, a single Antonov An-2 and six Cessna 310s (including two 310Qs). Five Piper Cherokee 140s operate in the training role and a Cherokee Six is also in service for liaison. For VIP flights there is a civilian-registered HS.748. The helicopter element has two Bell 47Gs and two Agusta AB 206s.

Madagascar

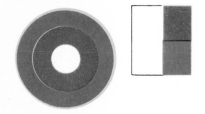

Armée de l'Air Madagascar: Previously known as Malagasy, this island republic has reverted to the name it used when it was a French colony. A small transport air arm was established by the French in the early 1960s but the country has recently formed a combat element with the help of North Korea, which has supplied the air arm with eight Mikoyan-Gurevich MiG-17 fighters. Other types in ser-vice total one Douglas C-53D, five C-47s, one Piper Aztec D and a Britten-Norman Defender operating alongside some aircraft delivered more recently, comprising three Reims Super Skymasters and four Cessna 172Ms for liaison and training respectively. A helicopter component consists of one Bell 47G, one Aérospatiale Alouette II and two Alouette IIIs.

Mozambique

Mozambique Air Arm: This ex-Portuguese colony has housed guerrilla bases for opera-tions against neighbouring Zimbabwe. With Soviet, Cuban and East European assistance it is steadily building an armed force which will incorporate an air arm. Two new air bases are being built, one near the port of Nacala and the other near Beira, and these are expected to accommodate the 35 Mikoyan-Gurevich MiG-21s delivered to the country early in 1978. It was reported that eight similar air-craft had arrived at Nacala in March 1977, all believed to have come from the Soviet Union. Also originating from this source and received in 1978 were three Mil Mi-8 helicopters. A number of ex-Portuguese air force aircraft, in-cluding some Nord Noratlas transports, are also flying in the country.

Malawi

Malawi Air Wing: Operating in support of the army and based at Blantyre is a small transport and liaison force equipped with six Dornier Do 28D-2 Skyservants, delivered in 1976 and 1978, and four Douglas C-47s. A further four Do 28s have been ordered for delivery in 1980 and these will join a single Aérospatiale/Westland SA.330L Puma and an Alouette III bought from France.

Zimbabwe (Rhodesia)

Zimbabwe Air Force: Anti-guerrilla opera-tions went on apace before the recent ceasefire. The Rhodesian air force has been involved in counter-insurgency work within the country on guerrilla bases in Mozambique, Botswana, Angola and Zambia. The war has taken a con-siderable toll of the country's resources, and defence spending has increased by nearly 44 per cent to £200 million, about 26 per cent of the total public spending. Still providing the long-range bomber-reconnaissance element in the air force is No 5 Sqn at Old Sarum, Salisbury, with about eight BAC Canberras, the survivors of 16 B.2s and three T.4s originally delivered to Rhodesia in the 1960s. The remaining aircraft have main-spar fatigue problems and are being progressively stripped to keep the others flying. Nos. 1 and 2 Sqns are based at Thornhill with nine Hawker Hunter FGA.9s and eight de Havilland Vam-

Despite considerable difficulties and shortages the Zimbabwe Air Force has managed to keep No 1 Squadron, with nominal strength of nine Hunter FGA.9s, continuously operational. French DEFA ammunition is standard.

pire FB.9s respectively; the latter unit also flies eight Vampire T.55s for OCU-type work, although occasionally it is assigned combat duties.

For obvious reasons, great stress is laid on the light attack elements in the Zimbabwe AF, and these comprise No 4 'Bush' Sqn and 7 Sqn. The former operates seven Aermacchi AL.60F5 Trojans of 12 originally supplied in 1967 and usually uses them for reconnaissance and FAC duties; a small number of Cessna 182s, and about 20 Cessna/Reims 337

Skymasters (known in Rhodesia as the Lynx) acquired via devious routes in 1976 and often flown in combat armed with SNEB rockets. No 7 Sqn is the sole helicopter unit and took the brunt of the 'search and destroy' missions, consequently suffering the heaviest loss rate in the air force. Flying Aérospatiale (Sud) Alouette IIIs, of which there are some 34 on strength (some reports have stated 66 Alouettes are in use), the unit co-operates closely with the army, particularly with elements known as Fireforce. For these COIN missions

the Alouettes act as troop transports as well as gunships armed with 20-mm and 0.303-in machine guns. Fireforce also uses the Douglas C-47s of No 3 Sqn for parachuting troops and supplies into difficult areas, and this squadron is thought to have at least eight aircraft on strength as well as three Britten-Norman Islanders for light transport duties. Revealed in 1978 was the acquisition from Israel of 11 Bell 205s currently employed on troop transport and gunship duties and attached to No 7 Sqn. Another new type in use is the

SIAI-Marchetti SF.260W Warrior, 22 of which were received via a Belgian distributor and ordered by the Comores. They are known as Genets and operate from Thornhill.

Basic training is performed on 13 BAC Provost T.52s of No 6 Sqn before pupils go to South Africa for conversion on to the Atlas-built Aermacchi M.B.326 Impala. These Impalas are believed to be owned by Rhodesia but have not been flown outside South Africa and are operated under the auspices of the SAAF.

Botswana

Botswana Defence Force: With increasing guerrilla activity along the border with Rhodesia, this small country has established a combined military unit for border patrol, casevac, communications and forward air control. Initial equipment for the airborne element of the BDF consists of two of three Britten-Norman Defenders procured, the third aircraft having been lost on operations in 1978. They are based at Gaberone Village and have provision for Sura rockets, Skyshout and

extra fuel tankage. Three more Defenders have been delivered, and to supplement these the Botswana government has received two Shorts Skyvan 3M utility transports delivered in 1979.

South Africa

South African Air Force: The ban by many countries on arms to South Africa has been expanded and endorsed by the UN, but the country is almost completely self-sufficient as far as arms are concerned. Aircraft licence production is firmly established, with the Atlas Aircraft Corporation currently building the single-seat Aermacchi M.B.326K or Impala II against initial SAAF orders for 50 aircraft, production of the two-seat Impala I having been completed with 151 built. Also being produced is the C.4M Kudu light transport, based on the AL-60 with the AM.3C wing and tailplane. Kudus are now in service with the Light Aircraft Command, and an initial order for 40 is being met. An even more important step by Atlas is the current assembly of Dassault Mirage F1-AZ strike aircraft, with eventual manufacture for a SAAF requirement that is expected to total some 100 aircraft. The air force is currently committed to a total of 48 F1s made up of 32 AZs and 16 CZs.

Strike Command, comprising five squadrons, has its headquarters at Waterkloof, which is also the SAAF's main Mirage F1 base. Having relinquished its Canadair Sabre 6s, No 1 Sqn is now flying a number of F1-AZ ground-attack aircraft. These share the airfield and support facilities with No 3 Sqn's 16 F1-CZ interceptors.

No 2 Sqn at Waterkloof fulfils both fighter-bomber and reconnaissance roles with a Dassault Mirage III complement of 16 IIICZs, four IIIRZs, four IIIR2Zs and three IIIBZs. Nos 12 and 24 Sqns, also based at Waterkloof, operate six BAC Canberra B(I).12s and three T.4s and eight HS Buccaneer S.50s respectively in the strike role. To increase the effectiveness of Strike Command, a new air base is being built at Hoedspruit in the northeast of the country.

Maritime Command operates from D.F. Malan Airport, Cape Town, with No 35 Sqn's seven Avro Shackleton MR.3s flying long-range maritime reconnaissance. These long-serving veterans are being re-sparred to extend their lives for another few years. At Ysterplaat Air Station, Cape Town, 27 Sqn operates 20 Piaggio P.166S Albatrosses for in-shore reconnaissance and liaison duties, with No 25 Sqn flying six Douglas C-47s in the fleet requirements role. Eleven Westland Wasps equip 22 Flight, serving aboard South African navy ships in the ASW and communication roles.

South Africa's seven Shackleton MR.3 ocean patrol aircraft have been rebuilt with new wing spars to extend their operational life to an estimated 30 years total, ending in the late 1980s. They equip No 35 Sqn at Daniel F Malan airport (named for a World War II ace fighter pilot of the Battle of Britain) at Cape Town. Their chief mission is the maintenance of unimpeded sea traffic round the Cape of Good Hope, the route taken by giant tankers between the Middle East and Europe.

Air Transport Command at Waterkloof has three squadrons. No 28 Sqn operates seven Lockheed C-130B Hercules and nine C.160Z Transalls from the Command HQ at Waterkloof. No 44 Sqn at Zwartkop has five Douglas DC-4s and 10 C-47s, while No 21 Sqn undertakes VIP duties with one Vickers Viscount 781, four HS.125s and five Swearingen Merlin IVAs. The last were delivered during 1975-76, and one is fitted out as an ambulance aircraft. Two further Merlin IVAs are civilian-registered for government use. Light Aircraft Command has its headquarters at Zwartkop. From Lanseria No 41 Sqn operates 20 Aeritalia AM.3C Bosboks and some Kudus. At Potechefstroom No 42 Sqn has a further 20 Bosboks, and No 11 Sqn flies 20 Cessna 185s. There are some Cessna 185s at Durban which are possibly operated by No 43

Sqn.

The helicopter element of the SAAF flies mostly French types. The 20 tactical Pumas of No 19 Sqn are divided into two flights at Zwartkop and Durban. Fourteen Aérospatiale Super Frelons for heavy lift and casevac duties equip No 15 Sqn at Zwartkop and Bloemspruit. There are two squadrons of Aérospatiale (Sud) Alouette IIIs; No 16 Sqn with 20 aircraft at Ysterplaat and Port Elizabeth, and No 17 Sqn with 10 aircraft at Zwartkop. Unconfirmed reports say that up to 20 more Pumas and a similar number of Alouettes were delivered to the helicopter force in 1975.

Training Command has nearly 100 North American Harvards at the Flying Training School at Dunnottar, and 80 Impala I/IIs at the FTS at Langebaanweg. There are three

Advanced Flying Schools: 86 AFS at Pietersberg with 12 ex-1 Sqn Sabre 6s, 16 Mirage IIIEZs, 10 IIID2Zs and three IIIDZs; 86 AFS at Bloemspruit with six C-47s; and 87 AFS has moved from Ysterplaat to Bloemspruit with 10 Alouette IIIs. The Active Citizen Force has almost changed over from Harvards to Impalas. The following units each have 15 aircraft: Nos 4 Sqn at Lanseria having moved from Waterkloof, 5 Sqn at Durban, 6 Sqn at Port Elizabeth, 8 Sqn at Bloemspruit and 7 Sqn at Ysterplaat. The only remaining Harvard unit is No 40 Sqn at Dunnottar, with 10 aircraft.

There are 13 Air Commando squadrons (101-112, plus 114 (Women's) ACS) under the control of the SAAF and equipped with civil light aircraft for use in emergencies.

Asia and Australasia

Two decades ago Western thinking on Asia and South-East Asia was preoccupied with the Domino Theory. This stated that as one nation became Communist, its neighbour was likely to follow, in time taking with it its own neighbour and so on. The reality has turned out to be less simple. China and the Soviet Union quarrelled in 1960, Vietnam, Laos and Cambodia became Communist and guerillas now threaten the stability of Thailand and Malaysia.

US support for South Vietnam and Cambodia was a spectacular failure. Socialist unity proved another chimera as Communist waged war on Communist in yet another round of South-East Asian war. The last five years has seen a Sino-Soviet-Vietnamese power struggle begin with the Soviet-backed Vietnamese invading China's ally Kampuchea (formerly Cambodia), then China in turn invading Vietnam.

Taiwan and South Korea are backed by the US, a commitment which is being phased out with growing detente between China and the West. China's air force is equipped by Soviet aircraft designs of mid to late 1950s origin. Even the F-6bis Fantan fighter is heavily dependent on MiG-19 technology but newer Chinese designs are on the drawing board and probably flying. North Korea and Vietnam are Soviet equipped but the latter also operates captured US types such as the F-5, A-37 and C-130.

Japan has produced its own planes but still relies on the US for advanced types such as the F-15 and P-3C. Australia's chronic shortage of funds has forced a stretchout of the Mirage IIIO's service life until a successor can be chosen. India finally selected Jaguar as its Deep Penetration Strike Aircraft, but allegations of bribery over the deal contributed to the collapse of Mr Charan Singh's government.

Afghanistan	**38**	Laos	**40**
Australia	**45**	Malaysia	**44**
Bangladesh	**40**	Mongolia	**41**
Brunei	**45**	Nepal	**39**
Burma	**40**	New Zealand	**46**
China	**40**	Pakistan	**38**
Hong Kong	**43**	Papua New Guinea	**45**
India	**39**	Philippines	**43**
Indonesia	**44**	Singapore	**44**
Japan	**41**	Sri Lanka	**39**
Kampuchea	**43**	Taiwan	**42**
Korea (North)	**41**	Thailand	**43**
Korea (South)	**41**	Vietnam	**43**

Afghanistan

Afghan Air Force: Following the Communist coup in April 1978, Russian military aid and assistance to Afghanistan has increased. The air force is wholly Russian-equipped and currently operates a fighter element of three squadrons of Mikoyan-Gurevich MiG-21s with approximately 40 aircraft, believed to be based at Pagram near Kabul. A wing of four squadrons with 50 MiG-17s, assigned the day interceptor role, operates from Mazar-i-Sharif in the north of the country. Two further squadrons operate 24 Sukhoi Su-7BMs, and another unit has 12 MiG-19s remaining of some 18 supplied in 1965. Three units are equipped with nearly 45 Ilyushin Il-28s flying in the light bomber role. Transports include two VIP Il-18Ds, 10 An-26s, 25 Il-14s and 10 Antonov An-2s. One helicopter squadron flies 18 Mil Mi-4s and a small number of Mi-8s from various bases.

Under Soviet guidance, training is performed on two-seat MiG-15UTIs, MiG-2IUs and Il-28Us, with a batch of Aero L-39 Albatross advanced trainers received during 1978.

Pakistan

Pakistan Air Force: The PAF Dassault Mirage force comprises four squadrons flying in the strike, interception and reconnaissance roles, equipped with 18 IIIEPs, five IIIDPs, 28 5PAs, and 13 IIIRPs including 10 delivered in 1977. Based at Masroor is No 7 Sqn, equipped with 15 surviving Martin B-57Bs of 26 originally supplied by the USA; they are operated mainly in the night attack role.

Seven interceptor squadrons, which also double in the fighter-bomber role, have about 140 Chinese-supplied and built Mikoyan-Gurevich MiG-19s (F-6s), some equipped with American Sidewinder missiles; all are being modified to accommodate British Martin-Baker ejection seats. Three ex-French *Aéronavale* Breguet Atlantics equip No 29 Sqn for long-range patrol and ASW duties, flying from a base near Karachi. A transport wing comprises No 6 Sqn, which flies six Lockheed C-130B Hercules, at least three C-130Es supplied by Iran and a single L-100 version, plus a Fokker F27 Mk 200 and a Dassault Falcon 20. Some Beech L-23s and a Rockwell Aero Commander are used for liaison work. Basic training is performed on the 45 Saab Supporters-which have replaced 30 North American T-6s; 30 Cessna T-37Cs and 12 Lockheed T-33As cater for advanced jet conversion before pilots transfer to operational squadrons via five MiG-

Three F-6 fighters of the Pakistan Air Force. About 140 of these extremely useful multi-role aircraft remain in use, updated by Martin-Baker seats, Ferranti nav/attack systems and early series Sidewinder air-to-air missiles.

15UTI two-seat trainers. Helicopters include 10 Kaman HH-43B Huskies, 14 Aérospatiale (Sud) Alouette IIIs, 12 Bell 47Gs and a single Aérospatiale/Westland SA.330 Puma for VIP use.

Little further news emerged on progress with the establishment of Pakistani Cessna T-41D primary-trainer and Hughes 500 helicopter assembly lines, a plan which was first announced in 1976. The PAF has a requirement for these aircraft, and 60 a year of the former and 60 a year of the latter were planned. More tangible was the commissioning in 1978 of a Mirage III/5 overhaul and repair facility, forming part of the Pakistan Aeronautical Complex, and situated at Kamra, near Rawalpindi. As well as catering for PAF Mirages, it is also expected to handle aircraft operated by other nations, notably the Mirage force flown by the United Arab Emirates and currently maintained by the Pakistanis.

Pakistan Navy: Six Westland Sea King Mk 45s bought in 1975 have replaced Sikorsky UH-19s in the ASW and SAR roles and are now equipped with Exocet anti-shipping missiles. Four Alouette IIIs are used for training and liaison duties.

Pakistan Army Aviation: The army operates about 12 Soviet-supplied Mil Mi-8s acquired in 1969, 20 Bell 47Gs and a similar number of Alouette IIIs. In 1977 an order was placed for 35 SA.330J Pumas for assault and transport duties. About 50 Cessna O-1s are in service for fixed-wing AOP and liaison.

Nepal

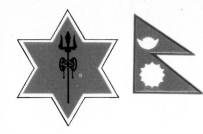

Royal Nepalese Army: The Air Wing of this small, efficient, British-trained army has two Short Skyvan 3Ms and three DHC Twin Otters for transport duties. The Royal Flight uses one of the Skyvans and an BAe H.S.748 Srs 2A delivered in 1975. Two Aérospatiale/Westland SA.330 Pumas are in service, one with the Royal Flight and the other with the Air Wing.

India

Indian Air Force: This large air arm has some 700 combat aircraft in 45 squadrons. A decision on the IAF requirement for a Deep Penetration Strike Aircraft to supplement and eventually replace the none-too-successful Sukhoi Su-7 was made in 1978 in favour of the SEPECAT Jaguar. The first 40 of an eventual 150 commenced delivery in mid-1979, the remainder being licence-built by Hindustan Aeronautics. To supplement the slow delivery of HAL Kiran trainers, an order for 50 Polish PZL TS-11 Iskra jet trainers was completed between October 1975 and March 1976; spinning and flameout problems with this type have yet to be fully solved and have already cost the force about five aircraft. However, the IAF training-programme restructuring has produced an embarrassing surplus of Kirans, and some of these are now going into storage. Deliveries of the unarmed Kiran Mk 1 are complete and deliveries of the Mk 1A began in 1978; Mk 2 development began in late 1979. The services's interceptor force operates Soviet equipment comprising 196 Hindustan-built Mikoyan-Gurevich MiG-21FLs, more than 50 Soviet-supplied examples, and some of the 150 MiG-21MFs now coming off the HAL assembly lines. These aircraft equip 11 units including Nos 1, 3, 4, 8, 28, 29, 30, 45, 47 and 108 Sqns and an OTU flying MiG-21U two-seat trainers. Some 150 Hawker Siddeley Gnat F.1s are in service with five squadrons (2, 15, 18, 22 and 23 Sqns) and deliveries of the first of 100 improved Mk 2 Gnat, Ajeet, have begun to 9 Sqn. A two-seat trainer version of the Ajeet is under development, and the prototype is due to fly in 1979, with production deliveries to the IAF planned for 1981.

Four ground-attack squadrons (14, 20, 27 and 37 Sqns) fly approximately 130 Hawker Hunter F.56/T.66s, and three further units have about 100 HAL HF-24 Marut Mk 1 strike aircraft, and a batch of 10 two-seat Mk ITs; production of this type has now ceased. Of the 150 Su-7B fighter-bombers delivered by the Soviet Union, some 130 remain in service with four squadrons (Nos 32, 101, 221 and 222), while 86 BAC Canberras (B[I].58s, B.74s, B[I].12s and T.13s) fly with three bomber units (Nos 5, 16 and 35). A photographic reconnaissance squadron, No 106, flies 12 Canberra PR.7s.

The IAF transport force is urgently seeking a new tactical transport to replace older aircraft in service, but despite favourable offers from Canada on the DHC Buffalo, no orders have been placed yet. The present inventory is made up of a heavy element of two units with 30 Antonov An-12s (25 and 44 Sqns); three medium transport units with 40 Fairchild

Though showing a complete absence of planning in their colour schemes, these HAL Type 77 (basically the MiG-21FL built under licence) fighter/bombers are tailored to the Indian AF's needs. Since 1973 HAL has built the later Type 96 and MiG-21bis.

C-119G jet-boosted Packets (12, 19 and 48 Sqns); and 11, 43 and 49 Sqns with 40 Douglas C-47s. STOL transport is provided by 33 Sqn's 20 DHC Caribous (including five ex-Ghanaian aircraft) and 41 and 59 Sqns' 29 DHC Otters, although the latter type is being phased out of service. One squadron, No 12, of HAL-built HS.748Ms is on strength, and six more 748s and one Tupolev Tu-124 fly for a Headquarters/VIP unit. A total of 71 HS.748s are in IAF service, including a further 10 freighter versions being built; 10 more ordered recently will take the Indian inventory to 81 aircraft. Some 200 helicopters include fewer than 100 Mil Mi-4s flying with six squadrons, although not all are operational and only three units may actually be flying the type; 35 Mi-8s equipping three units and 120 Aérospatiale (Sud) Alouette IIIs, also in three squadrons. Deliveries are under way of 100 licence-built Aérospatiale SA.315 Cheetahs to replace the 40-odd home-designed HAL Krishak fixed-wing AOPs and 20 Auster AOP.9s in a total of four liaison squadrons. A few Alouette IIIs also fly AOP duties. IAF Training Command, with HQ at Bangalore, requires some 130 Kirans, more than half of which have been delivered to the service; nearly 50 Polish Iskras are also being used for advanced training at the Fighter Training Wing at Hakimpet. Other types include nearly 70

HAL HT-2 primary trainers (scheduled to be replaced from 1981-82 by the Hindustan HPT-32 trainer, the prototype of which first flew in January 1977) flying from the EFS at Bidar; two-seat Hunter T.66s equip an OCU at Kalaikunda and there are Canberra T.13s, MiG-21Us and Su-7Us for operational conversion at squadron level. Multi-engine training is done on HS.748s at Yelahanka, near Bangalore, while seven HS.748s are used for navigation tuition.

Indian Navy: The navy operates the carrier INS *Vikrant* (ex-RN HMS *Hercules*, bought in 1957), which can accommodate 18 of 300 Sqn's 25 Hawker Siddeley Sea Hawks. A replacement for these aircraft is long overdue and, if the ever present credit problem can be resolved, an initial order for six single-seat BAe Sea Harriers and two trainer versions is to be placed. An eventual total of 25 Sea Harriers is envisaged. *Vikrant*, which is currently undergoing a refit, carries four Breguet Alizés and two Aérospatiale (Sud) Alouette III plane-guard helicopters from a total of 12 (310 Sqn) and 10 (321 Sqn) aircraft respectively. The navy planned to withdraw the Alizés in 1977 but is instead purchasing 12 refurbished ex-*Aéronavale* examples to make good attrition and increase the force to about 20 aircraft. A squadron (331) of eight torpedo-armed

Alouettes is deployed aboard 'Leander' class frigates. Two Westland Sea King Mk 42 squadrons, Nos 330 and 336 based at Cochin Naval Air Base, are operational on ASW duties with 12 aircraft; another three have been ordered. For fixed-wing training there are seven HAL Kirans, four de Havilland Vampire T.55s and four Sea Hawks with 551 Sqn. Fifteen Kirans are required by the navy, and deliveries continue slowly. No 550 Sqn at Cochin flies two de Havilland Devons for liaison work and five Britten-Norman Islanders for training and communications. The Islanders, delivered in 1977, are being modified for coastal-patrol duties with the addition of nose radar. Four Hughes 300s and some Alouettes are used for training with 561 Sqn. Now under naval command is 312 Sqn, a maritime reconnaissance unit based at Goa which will continue to use five MR Lockheed Super Constellations until 1981. Originally 6 Sqn IAF, the unit is supplemented by 315 Sqn at Dabolim, which operates three Soviet Ilyushin Il-38 'May' ASW aircraft delivered in 1977. A further three might be ordered in the future. Another order from Russia is one for five Kamov Ka-25 helicopters, which, it is reported, are to operate from the two 'Kashin' class destroyers due for delivery in 1978-79.

Sri Lanka

Sri Lanka Air Force: Five Soviet Mikoyan-Gurevich MiG-17F fighter-bombers supplied in 1971 form the equipment of Sri Lanka's only combat unit. A jet trainer squadron operates eight BAe Jet Provost T.51s and a MiG-15UTI. The transport force, which undertakes tourist flying in addition to its military tasks, is equipped with a Convair 440, five de Havilland Doves, two DH Herons, two Riley Herons, four Cessna Super Skymasters and two ex-Air Ceylon Douglas DC-3s. The helicopter fleet has recently been expanded with the purchase of two Aérospatiale SA.365 Dauphin IIs from France, and these join two Kamov Ka-26s, seven Bell JetRangers and six Bell 47Gs. Training is done on nine DHC Chipmunks and six Cessna 150s.

Bangladesh

Bangladesh Defence Force (Air Wing): Formerly East Pakistan, Bangladesh was established in 1971. A number of countries have provided military assistance to the armed forces, two of the more recent being Britain, which has a five-man officer team establishing a staff college in Dacca; and China, which has supplied 36 Shenyang F-6 (MiG-19S) day fighters. These are based at Tezgaon and Jessore with two squadrons. During an at-tempted coup in 1977 four MiG-19s were destroyed in ground fighting, together with a number of Russian-supplied Mikoyan-Gurevich MiG-21MF fighter-bombers. Of the 12 MiG-21s originally received, less than half remain in service. There are also two MiG-21U two-seat trainers. Several An-26s and a single An-24 constitute the fixed-wing transport element, while helicopters number four Aérospatiale Alouette IIIs, at least three Mil Mi-8s and six Bell 212s. For training, eight refurbished Magisters have been acquired from Aérospatiale.

Burma

Union of Burma Air Force: Main task of this small air arm continues to be internal security and counter-insurgency work. Operations have been conducted for some years against Communist guerillas in the north of the country. Modern equipment remains scarce in the UBAF, due to a relatively low annual defence budget, which in 1977 totalled $164 million. For strike duties there are some six armed Lockheed AT-33As from more than a dozen supplied by the USA in the late 1960s, and 10 SIAI-Marchetti SF.260MBs, which were delivered in 1976 and operate in the dual strike/trainer role. For advanced training the service has 12 Cessna T-37Cs and has received the first batch of 16 Pilatus PC-7 Turbo-Trainers, with a further 16 due for delivery in 1980.

Transport aircraft include some six Douglas C-47s, one Fokker F.27 Mk 100, four Pilatus Turbo-Porters and three Porters. It is also reported that the country has bought four ex-Allegheny Airlines Fairchild Hiller F.27s. Helicopters include nine Kaman HH-43B Huskies, 10 Kawasaki KV-107s, 13 Aérospatiale Alouette IIIs and 13 Kawasaki (Bell) 47Gs, although not all are believed to be serviceable. In 1975, 18 Bell UH-1s and at least one Bell 205 were supplied to Burma, initially for anti-narcotics patrols but now integrated into the UBAF for a variety of military work. For fixed-wing liaison there are about 10 Cessna 180s.

Laos

Air Force of the Liberation Army: Known before the communist takeover in April 1975 as the Royal Lao Air Force, the AFLA is believed still to be operating some US-supplied equipment, although spares difficulties must be limiting the effectiveness of the force. Late in 1977, the air force received its first super-sonic combat aircraft when 10 Mikoyan-Gurevich MiG-21s arrived at Vientiane's Wat-tay airport from the Soviet Union. American aircraft remaining in the country after the takeover included 63 North American T-28Ds and 10 Douglas AC-47 gunships for attack duties, four Cessna U-17As, one Rockwell Aero Commander 500 and a single DHC Beaver. The transport force has 18 Douglas C-47s, 42 Sikorsky UH-34s and six Aérospatiale (Sud) Alouette II/IIIs, the helicopters being used for rescue and army support work. Six Cessna T-41Ds are station-ed at a pilot training school. In 1977 the Soviet Union supplied the AFLA with a number of second-line types including some Mil Mi-8 helicopters, Autonov An-24 transports and a few An-2 liaison aircraft.

China (People's Republic of China)

Air Force of the People's Liberation Army: Mainland China has the world's third largest air force, with more than 4,500 aircraft in its inventory. The force is organised into air divisions, regiments and squadrons, three squadrons making one regiment and three regiments a division. Air defence districts protect the country, and the headquarters are in Peking.

Recent US estimates put the current AFPLA interceptor/fighter-bomber strength at some 4,100 home-produced MiG-17s (Shenyang F-4) and MiG-19s (Shenyang F-6) and only about 50 licence-built MiG-21F (Shenyang F-8) interceptors. Problems with the indigenous Shenyang F-9 design, which is based on the MiG-19 but with side intakes and a radar nose, have prevented large-scale production and only a small number of aircraft are believed to have been built. The supply and licence production of the Rolls-Royce Spey 202 turbofan, for which an agreement was signed in 1975, is thought to be intended for the later F-12 design. Little is known about this aircraft but it is understood to be single-engined and likely to embody a number of Western ideas and equipment. From France, China has received 13 Aérospatiale Super Frelon helicopters. Chinese interest in purchasing Harriers was reaffirmed in January 1979, and an initial order for 100, with the licence production of another 200, is a reported future outcome of any agreement. With the USA's recognition of China at the beginning of 1979, defence equipment orders between the two countries are likely.

A long-range bomber force is composed of 60 Tu-16 Badgers, a few Tu-4 Bulls and about 300 Il-28 Beagle light bombers. MR duties are performed by Beriev Be-6s, while a substantial transport arm has about 400 aircraft comprising An-2s, Li-2s, Il-14s and Il-18s. In an emergency the civil aviation fleet of airliners, which includes ten Boeing 707-320s, 38 HS Tridents, five Viscounts and five Il-62s, could be used. Helicopters total some 300 Mi-4s, and the training fleet comprises Yak 11s, Yak 18s and MiG-15UTIs.

Navy: Approximately 100 torpedo-carrying Il-28s are operated together with some 400 MiG-15/17/19 fighter-bombers integrated into the air force air-defence system. About 50 Mi-4s are also on strength.

Though widely considered obsolete by the mid-1960s, the MiG-19 was a superb basic design with extremely low wing-loading and plenty of thrust and gun power. From it the Chinese derived this F-6, a tactical fighter subjected to progressive improvement, and the redesigned and much heavier Fantan, which the West calls F-6bis.

Mongolia

Air Force of the Mongolian People's Republic: Over the past year there has been no known expansion of the air force of this Soviet satellite. One ground-attack squadron operates 10 Mikoyan-Gurevich MiG-15s in support of the army, and a transport force numbering some 30 aircraft flies Antonov An-2s, An-24s and Ilyushin Il-14s. Ten Mil Mi-1 and Mi-4 helicopters are operated, plus a few Yakovlev Yak-11 and -18 trainers.

Korea (North)

Korean People's Army Air Force: The combat strength of the KPAAF was increased in 1977 with additional Mikoyan-Gurevich MiG-21s supplied by the Soviet Union. There are currently nine units with about 170 aircraft forming the front-line force, and there is an additional interceptor element with some 50 MiG-19s. The establishment of a MiG-21 assembly line in the country was reported nearly three years ago, components being sup-plied in knocked-down form by the Soviet Union.

A large ground-attack force of more than a dozen squadrons operates about 350 MiG-17s and more than 30 Sukhoi Su-7s. A strike force has 70 Ilyushin Il-28s. About 40 transports include Antonov An-2s, Ilyushin Il-14s, two Il-18s and a Tupolev Tu-154B for VIP duties. A helicopter element totals about 20 Mil Mi-4s and a similar number of Mi-8s. Seventy Yakovlev Yak-18s and MiG-15UTIs, and a few two-seat MiG-21Us, are used for training.

Korea (South)

The **Republic of Korea** is a major user of Northrop F-5 fighters, having been supplied with 87 F-5A and 35 F-5B (of which this is one) followed by 126 F-5E and 20 F-5F Tiger IIs. The R.O.K. also uses F-4D and E Phantoms and has requested F-16s.

Republic of Korea Air Force: Current RoKAF strike force comprises three squadrons of McDonnell Douglas Phantoms made up of 18 F-4Ds and 19 F-4Es, with a further 18 Es due for delivery in 1979. Four squadrons with 126 Northrop F-5E fighter-bombers and nine F-5F trainers are replacing one-for-one the older force of 87 F-5As and 35 F-5Bs. Older types in use include two squadrons with nearly 50 North American F-86F Sabres fitted with AIM-9J Sidewinder missiles and an all-weather interceptor unit flying F-86Ds. A recon-naissance squadron operates 12 RF-5As.

To increase the effectiveness of the transport force, six Lockheed C-130H Hercules are being acquired shortly to supplement about 40 Curtiss C-46s, Douglas C-54s, Fairchild C-123Ks and Rockwell Aero Commanders; two HS.748s are used for Presidential flights and there is a Bell UH-1N for VIP use. The helicopter force flies six Sikorsky H-19s, five Bell UH-1Ds and two Bell 212s, these being used chiefly for SAR. Cessna O-1s and 12 O-2As fly forward-air-control duties, and a number of Cessna U-17s and DHC Beavers operate in the liaison role. The training ele-ment has 20 Cessna T-41Ds and 24 North American T-28Ds for basic instruction, and 30 Lockheed T-33As for advanced work. A number of two-seat F-5B/Fs are tasked with conversion flying.

This major Far Eastern air arm continues to be firmly based on American military support, and a steady modernization programme is being conducted to help strengthen the force. As well as having had major military overhaul facilities in the country for many years, an assembly line has been established for the Hughes 500M-D Defender multi-role heli-copter. Equipped with TOW for anti-tank use, 100 Defenders are being delivered to the South Korean armed forces. Like many US-supplied air arms, Korea has requested General Dynamics F-16s, 72 of them, but no deliveries are expected until 1981 when they are ex-pected to replace the F-4 Phantoms. In a fur-ther arms package announced in 1977, the RoKAF ordered 24 Rockwell OV-10Gs (worth $58.2 million) and 733 Sidewinder missiles. An order for about 50 Fairchild A-10As is reported to be a distinct possibility.

The ROK army has a variety of helicopters for liaison and spotting duties including Bell UH-1Ns and Hiller OH-23s.

The South Korean navy has a short-based ASW unit equipped with 20 Grumman S-2A/F Trackers and is to receive some ASW versions of the Hughes 500M-D Defender, which are being assembled in the country.

Japan

Japan Air Self-Defence Force: Economic problems and inflation continue to be reflected in military procurement, and the Fiscal Year 1978 approvals are still generally below those which the armed forces initially requested. For the JASDF, 56 of 96 aircraft requested are be-ing bought — 23 McDonnell Douglas F-15s, 15 Mitsubishi F-1s, three Mitsubishi T-2As, 14 Fuji T-3s (company designation KM-2B) and a Kawasaki-built KV-107-IIA. For FY79, the JASDF is to receive five F-1s, one Kawasaki C-1, four Grumman E-2C Hawkeyes, 11 T-2s, 12 T-3s, one Mitsubishi MU-2 and two KV-107-IIAs. The combat elements of the JASDF are assigned to three regional air commands, Northern, Central and Western, and Southwest Air Wing in Okinawa, all linked to the Base Air Defense Ground Environment (BADGE) system. Fourteen fighter squadrons operate in seven wings, the 2nd, 3rd, 5th, 6th, 7th, 8th, Southwest and General HQ. The 169 Mitsubishi-built Lockheed F-104Js equip six units, 202 to 207 Sqns, flying in the inter-ceptor role. A total of 185 North American F-86F Sabres still operate with the JASDF, fly-ing as advanced trainers in three squadrons (6, 8 and General HQ Sqns) and the 1st Air Wing of the Air Training command; most of the Sabres have been retired.

Five McDonnell Douglas F-4EJ squadrons totalling 140 aircraft are planned within five air wings, the 2nd, 6th, 7th, 8th and the Southwest, of which four have formed (301 to 304 Sqns); the fifth, No 305, was formed in 1978, replacing No 206 (F-104J) Sqn. A recon-naissance unit, 501 Sqn, is equipped with 14 RF-4EJs, a further 14 of which are required. In 1977, JASDF selected the McDonnell Douglas F-15 Eagle as a replacement for the F-104Js and requested procurement of 123 air-craft. The selection was approved by the Diet on April 4, 1978, but the number was de-creased to 100. The 100 F-15s, comprising single-seat F-15Cs and two-seat F-15Ds, are to be licence-built by Mitsubishi between 1980 and 1988, and JASDF hopes to acquire 23 more after the first production run to fill their initial request, forming five squadrons. A replacement for the Sabre force is the Mit-subishi F-1, orders for 59 of which have been placed. Several more will be required to equip a total of three squadrons. The first produc-tion F-1 has been completed and was delivered to the JASDF in September 1977. The first F-1 unit, No 3 Sqn of the 3rd Air Wing, was formed in late March 1978 with 18 aircraft. The JASDF had given up procurement of 10 to 15 Grumman E-2Cs in Fiscal 1978 due to the heavy expense of the F-15 programme, but it is to receive four machines in the Fiscal 1979 budget.

The Transport Wing of the JASDF com-prises three squadrons, Nos 1, 2 and 3, equip-ped with Kawasaki C-1s and NAMC YS-11As. Twenty-five of the 27 C-1s ordered are now in service, replacing Curtiss C-46Ds, and all should have been delivered by 1980. The last of the 48 C-46Ds was retired from service by March 1978. Four pre-series C-1s are also in use. There is an ECM training unit with a modified YS-11E and two Lockheed T-33As, and a flight check unit with two YS-11s, three MU-2Js and four T-33As. Five training wings are in operation: No 1, with some 50 G-86Fs and some 50 T-33As for advanced work; No 4, with 46 Mitsubishi T-2As; Nos 11 and 12, with some 80 Beech T-34As for primary train-ing; and the 13th Wing, with some 50 T-1A/Bs for intermediate duties. Sixty-six T-2As are being bought and the first and the second units, 21 and 22 Sqns, have been form-ed in the 4th Air Wing. Deliveries are scheduled to be completed by March 1981. The first 44 of 60 Fuji T-3s to replace the T-34As have been ordered so far.

The Air Rescue Wing has 21 Mitsubishi MU-2Ss, 28 KV-107-IIA helicopters and seven Sikorsky S-62As, with two more KV-107s ordered for delivery in FY79. Also the JASDF

continued

operates five Nike-J SAM groups. The Air SDF is seeking replacements for its Nike-Js and the BADGE system.

Japan Maritime Self-Defence Force: The JMSDF anti-submarine force comprises five shore-based air groups plus an independent unit assigned to the nation's Defence Fleet, and three independent smaller units controlled by each district command. Three (Nos 1, 2 and 4) of the five groups and the independent unit in Okinawa are equipped with 83 Kawasaki P-2Js, 13 Lockheed P-2Hs and 28 Grumman S-2As, while the fourth group (21st) and the other two independent units (Ohmura and Ohminato) are operating 83 Sikorsky SH-3As and the fifth group (31st) is flying 17 Shin Meiwa PS-1s. Of the 23 PS-1s delivered to date, four have been lost in accidents. Of the total, five P-2Hs and 21 S-2As are in storage; both types are due for retirement from service, in 1978 and 1982 respectively. Procurement of 45 Lockheed P-3C Orions requested by the JMSDF as a replacement for the P-2J/H force was approved by the Diet on April 4, 1978. The Orions for the JMSDF will be licence-produced by Kawasaki between 1981 and 1988. The JMSDF will form four squadrons with the 45 aircraft from 1982.

Fiscal Year 78 budget approvals cover eight P-3Cs, two Shin Meiwa US-1s, five KM-2s, a Beech King Air 90 and four SH-3As. FY79 budget approvals total one US-1, three KM-2s, two Beech King Airs, eight SH-3Bs, and two S-61As. The JMSDF is seeking a new helicopter to equip its frigates, and the type selected is expected to be the Sikorsky UH-60 following its selection for the USN's LAMPS programme. The current mine-sweeping unit, 111 Sqn, has 11 KV-107-IIAs. An air rescue unit, 71 Sqn, has three Shin Meiwa US-1s, three S-61As (used by the South Pole Observatory Group) and eight S-62As. Three more US-1s on order for the group are due to be delivered before 1980. No 61 Sqn has four YS-11s and an S-2A for transport duties. Four training groups have six YS-11Ts, five King Air 90s and 28 Queen Airs for instrument work, 26 KM-2s for intermediate training; a helicopter training element has three OH-6Js and eight Bell 47s.

Despite extreme budget pressures, small numbers of Mitsubishi T-2A supersonic trainers continue to be bought for the Japan air self-defence force. By late 1979 about 52 had reached the 4th Air Training Wing out of a planned total of 66.

Japan Ground Self-Defence Force: Sixteen aircraft are being purchased by the army's air arm in the FY 1978 budget. These comprise two Mitsubishi LR-1s (MU-2K), a KV-107-IIA, two Bell UH-1Hs, 10 Hughes OH-6Ds and one Bell AH-1S assault helicopter. The AH-1S is the second example of the type to be bought; the first vehicle was purchased in the last year for evaluation purposes in preparation for its acquisition by the army and possible licence-production in Japan. An initial order for some 32 AH-1Ss for two squadrons is plan-ned, and the eventual order will approach 80. FY79 budget approvals total 12 Hughes OH-6Ds, three UH-1Hs, one KV-107-IIA and three LR-1s. The current fixed-wing force comprises 13 LM-1/2, 27 O-1A/Es, and eight LR-1 (MU-2C/K) liaision and reconnaissance aircraft plus two T-34A trainers. The LM-1/2s and O-1A/Es are being withdrawn in favour of helicopters. This large rotary-wing force is planned to total 56 KV-107-IIAs, 54 UH-1Hs, 117 OH-6Js and 38 Hughes TH-55Js. In addition, there are 82 UH-1Bs in use. All combat units of the JGSDF's air element are assigned to the five district commands in 24 squadrons. Both KV-107-IIAs and UH-1H/Bs are used for transport duties, while the OH-6Js are operated in the liaison/LOH role. To replace the KV-107s, the JGSDF has selected the Boeing Chinook — up to 40 being required with two for test and evaluation by 1983 if government approval can be gained.

Taiwan (Republic of China)

Chinese Nationalist Air Force: The USA broke off diplomatic relations with Taiwan on 1 January 1979, but will honour outstanding arms agreements. A recipient of large-scale American aid, Taiwan has a powerful air force and has now established an aircraft manufacturing industry. Known as the Aero Industry Development Centre and situated at Taichung in central Taiwan, it is currently assembling an initial batch of 120 Northrop F-5Es for the CNAF against an air force requirement for some 300 to replace older types currently in service. A total of 162 F-5Es and 18 F-5F two-seaters are on order to date, 60 being supplied direct from the USA. A further 107 F-5s have been ordered, together with 500 Hughes Maverick ASMs. Three fighter-bomber squadrons make up the 1st Fighter Wing, flying 70 early Northrop F-5As, while the six squadrons of the 2nd and 3rd Wings are relinquishing nearly 100 North American F-86Fs for the new F-5Es. The 4th Fighter Wing has three squadrons with 90 North American F-100A/D Super Sabres, and the 5th Fighter Wing operates three interceptor squadrons equipped with 63 Lockheed F-104G Starfighters and a reconnaissance unit with eight RF-104Gs.

Nine Grumman S-2A Trackers are attached

Four of the 70-odd F-5A Freedom Fighters of the 1st Fighter Wing of the Taiwan (Chinese Nationalist) air force. The United States continues to send in equipment under previous agreements and the F-5E Tiger II is also being assembled locally.

to the navy for MR and ASW duties, while a rescue unit operates a few Grumman HU-16B Albatross. The single Air Transport Wing operates 40 Fairchild C-119G Packets, 10 Fairchild C-123 Providers, 30 Curtiss C-46 Commandos, 50 Douglas C-47s, at least five Douglas C-54s and a VIP Boeing 720B. Helicopters include six Hughes 500s, seven Sikorsky UH-19s, 10 Bell 47Gs and more than 60 AIDC-assembled Bell UH-1Hs. Also pro-duced by AIDC for the primary training role are 50 PL-1B Chienshou, with a further 30 locally developed T-CH-1B basic trainers to replace the force of North American T-6s and T-28s now in use. For jet training about 30 Northrop T-38s and some Lockheed T-33As are flown, while two-seat F-5Bs, TF-104Gs, F-100Fs, and F-5Fs are attached to the respective squadrons. Two Beech Super King Airs have been bought by the government for navaid calibration.

Chinese Nationalist Army: The air element of the CNA, engaged on support and liaison work, uses helicopters, including 50 locally produced Bell UH-1Hs delivered in 1974 – 75, two Kawaskai KH-4s and seven Sikorsky CH-34s.

Hong Kong

Royal Hong Kong Auxiliary Air Force: This policing and communications force, a department of the HK government, is based near RAF Kai Tak alongside the international airport. It is manned chiefly by part-time volunteers but operates full-time. Three Aérospatiale (Sud) Alouette III helicopters fly SAR, liaison and internal security sorties, and a single Britten-Norman Islander, delivered in 1972, is used for survey work and anti-smuggling patrols. Two Scottish Aviation Bulldog 128 trainers were delivered in 1977, and the single Beech Musketeer has been replaced by a Cessna 404 Titan.

Philippines

Philippine Air Force: At present the PAF has seven wings located at five main bases. The 5th Fighter Wing at Basa Air Base is made up of three Tactical Fighter Squadrons and a training unit: the 6th TFS has Northrop F-5A fighter-bombers and two-seat F-5B trainers, drawn from respective totals of 19 and three originally delivered; the 7th TFS has received the Vought F-8H Crusader and the 9th TFS has reverted to a training unit equipped with six North American F-86F Sabres and nearly 25 converted Beech T-34A Mentors; and the 105th Combat Crew Training Squadron flies some 10 Lockheed T-33As and reconnaissance RT-33As. To increase the effectiveness of the fighter elements, it was announced in 1977 that the PAF was to receive 35 F-8H Crusaders, purchased for $11.7 million, from the United States. Vought is overhauling 25 of the ex-USN F-8Hs under a $23 million contract, and deliveries have been made to the 7th TFS; the remaining 10 F-8Hs have been bought for spares.

The 15th Strike Wing has its headquarters at Sangley Point Station and operates two Attack Squadrons, the 16th and 25th, equipped with about 25 North American T-28Ds. A number of these aircraft, painted all-black for night operations, are based at Zamboanga for COIN missions against the Mindanao National Liberation Front. Also in the wing are the 17th Attack Sqn, flying 16 SIAI-Marchetti SF.260W Warrior light strike aircraft, and the 27th Search, Rescue and Reconnaissance Squadron, flying four Grumman HU-16B Albatross amphibians. Protection of Philippine airspace is organised under the 580th Aircraft Control and Warning Wing, which operates three squadrons manning radar sites at Paredes Air Station in the north, Gozar and Paranal.

There are two transport wings, the 205th and 220th. The 205th Airlift Wing is based at Nichols Air Base and operates the following units: the 204th Tactical Airlift Sqn, with eight Fokker F27 Mk 100s; the 206th and 207th Air Transport Sqns, with 30 Douglas C-47s; and the 505th Air Rescue Sqn, with 10 Bell UH-1Hs and some MBB BO-105s delivered in 1977. The 220th Heavy Airlift Wing at Mactan Air Base south of Manila is composed of the 221st Heavy Airlift Sqn, equipped with some 15 Fairchild C-123B/K Providers, including some ex-South Vietnamese AF machines; the 222nd HAS, with three Lockheed L-100-20s and six C-130H Hercules; and the 223rd Tactical Airlift Sqn, currently operating in 12 GAF Nomad light transports. The remaining transport element is the 700th Special Mission Wing stationed at Nichols Air Base, Pasay City. This formation embraces the 702nd Presidential Airlift Sqn, equipped with a few Bell UH-1Hs and UH-1Ns, two S-62As, one F27 Mk 200, four NAMC YS-11s, a BAC One-Eleven and a Boeing 707.

Divided between the Air Bases of Nichols and Sangley Point is the 240th Composite Wing, which comprises the 291st Special Air Mission Sqn, with DHC Beavers; the 303rd Air Recce Sqn, flying some Douglas AC-47s; the 601st Liaison Sqn, equipped with six Cessna U-17A/B Skywagons; and the 901st Weather Sqn, with Cessna 210 Centurions and C-47s. The 100th Training Wing is located at Fernando Air Base, Lipa City. Two squadrons make up the wing; the 101st equipped with about 12 Cessna T-41Ds, and the 102nd Pilot Training Sqn, flying 32 SF.260MPs, which replace T-34s and T-28s.

For many years a recipient of American aid under MAP, the Philippine air force is moving towards autonomy with the establishment of aircraft-production facilities. As part of the Philippines Aerospace Development Corporation, the Self-Reliance Development Wing of the PAF is planning production of the American Jet Industries Super Pinto jet trainer/COIN aircraft. Also to be produced is an indigenous basic piston-engined trainer design, designated XT-100 and first announced in 1976.

The Philippine navy has a small air element equipped with 10 Britten-Norman Defenders for SAR and anti-smuggling patrols, and at least three MBB BO-105 helicopters for liaison work.

Vietnam

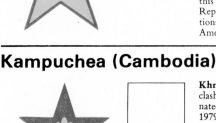

Vietnamese People's Air Force: The Vietnamese air force, originally the air arm of North Vietnam, now operates over what was South Vietnam, whose government collapsed in 1975. The communist Vietnamese regime has ideological and military differences with neighbouring Kampuchea's government and this resulted in the invasion of January 1979. Reports cited attacks on Kampuchean positions by Cessna A-37s, F-5Es and North American A-1 Skyraiders, presumably aircraft made serviceable from the 1,100 captured from the South Vietnamese air force in 1975. Camera-equipped Lockheed C-130 Hercules and Boeing Chinook helicopters are also reported in use. Vietnam has indicated unofficially that it is willing to sell off some of the war booty.

The Vietnamese air force has a strike force of 10 Ilyushin Il-28 light bombers, two interceptor squadrons with 30 Chinese-built Mikoyan-Gurevich MiG-19s (Shenyang F-6s), six fighter-bomber units with about 80 MiG-17s, two strike units with 30 Sukhoi Su-7s, and four interceptor squadrons with 70 MiG-21s. Transports include 20 Antonov An-2s, four An-24s, 12 Il-14s, 20 Lisunov Li-2s and a VIP Il-18. The helicopter element includes 12 Mil Mi-4s, five Mi-6 heavy-lift machines plus some nine Mi-8s. A further 10 Mi-4s fly under navy command for SAR duties.

Kampuchea (Cambodia)

Khmer Liberation Army: Fierce border clashes with neighbouring Vietnam culminated in the invasion of Kampuchea in January 1979. China supported the Khmer forces and supplied some 16 MiG-19s or F-6 day fighters but only six were uncrated at Kompong Chnang, 50 miles (80 km) north-east of the capital, and their use was believed to have been very limited. Guerilla resistance is continuing against the Vietnamese but the Khmer air force ceased to exist by February 1979. Types known to have been in the former Cambodian air force include Douglas AC-47 gunships, Fairchild C-123 and Douglas C-47 transports, Cessna O-1s, Bell UH-1H helicopters and North American T-28D attack/trainers.

Thailand

Royal Thai Air Force: The country's moderate attitude towards the neighbouring communist states has done nothing to lessen clashes along the Thai-Cambodia border nor the infiltration of communist-backed guerrillas in the north and along the border with Laos. To reduce the threat in the south, Thailand and Malaysia signed a co-operative agreement in March 1977 and joint operations have been conducted by the two countries' military forces. To increase the effectiveness of the RTAF, a $50 million order in 1976 for 17 Northrop F-5E fighter-bombers and three two-seat F-5F trainers is currently awaiting fulfilment. These will join the force of F-5As currently in Thai service, comprising No 13 Sqn at Don Muang, Bangkok, equipped with 24 F-5As, two F-5B trainers and four RF-5A reconnaissance aircraft. With No 13 Sqn in the 1st Combat Wing are No 11 Sqn, with 20 Lockheed T-33As and four RT-33As, and No 12 Sqn, with some of the 32 Rockwell OV-10C Broncos supplied to Thailand in two batches of 16 aircraft from 1971 onwards; a further six Broncos have been acquired via the US Department of Defense presumably to make up for attrition suffered by the earlier aircraft.

The 2nd Wing has at least six COIN squadrons (Nos 21, 22, 23, 53, 62 and 73 Sqns) equipped with the remainder of the OV-10Cs, 30 North American T-6Gs, 16 Cessna A-37Bs, 45 North American T-28Ds, and 31 Fairchild-Hiller AU-23A Peacemakers supplied in two batches of 11 and 20 aircraft. A single helicopter squadron, No 63, operates most of the RTAF rotary-wing force of 63 Bell UH-1Hs, 40 Sikorsky H-34Cs, 13 UH-19s and three Kaman HH-43B Huskies; 18 ex-US Army H-34s have been converted to S-58T standard by Thai-Am in Bangkok, with deliveries to the RTAF completed in 1978.

The transport units, Nos 61 and 62 Sqns, form part of the 6th Wing at Bangkok, operating between them 20 Douglas C-47s, at least 40 Fairchild C-123B/K Providers and five

One of the users of the versatile Rockwell OV-10 Bronco is the Royal Thai AF, which has 32 shared between the 1st and 2nd Air Combat Wings (with numerous other aircraft) and was in late 1979 receiving six more from US stocks to replace losses.

Beech C-45s. Two BAe HS.748s are attached to the Royal Flight at Bangkok, operating alongside one of two Swearingen Merlin IVAs delivered in December 1977 and in March 1978 (one crashed in November 1978). A further three Merlin IVs were ordered in 1978 for photographic reconnaissance duties. Training is centred at Korat Air Base, with basic work performed on 24 New Zealand Aerospace CT/4 Airtrainers, 12 SIAI-Marchetti SF.260MTs, at least four Cessna T-41Ds and 10 Continental-powered DHC Chipmunks.

Advanced training is done on 14 Cessna T-37Bs. A number of liaison types are also in service, including Helio U-10s, North American U-18Fs, and some Bell OH-13s.

Royal Thai Navy: the airborne arm of the navy has two Grumman HU-16B Albatross amphibians for SAR work, and about 10 Grumman S-2A Trackers delivered in 1966 for MR and ASW duties and based at Bangkok. Two Canadair CL-215s were received in 1978 for SAR duties.

Royal Thai Army: A variety of US-supplied fixed-wing and rotary-wing aircraft — including a force of some 90 Cessna O-1s for observation and liaison duties and a Beech 99 for transport work — are flown in support of the Thai army ground force. Helicopters include 16 Fairchild FH-1100s, three Bell 206s, six OH-23Fs and about 90 UH-1B/Ds; four Boeing CH-47As are flown on troop transport and supply duties. The **Thai Border Police** fly three DHC Caribous, three Short Skyvans, five Peacemakers and four Pilatus Porters,

three Dorner Skyservants and one CT/4 Airtainer. A helicopter element has 10 Bell 204Bs and 11 Bell 205s, plus two Bell 205As and four Bell 206Bs.

Malaysia

 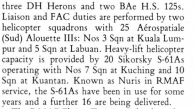

Royal Malaysian Air Force: With the acquisition of 14 Northrop F-5Es (two lost in accidents reducing the total to 12 aircraft) and two F-5B trainers, the RMAF has phased out the 16 ex-RAF Commonwealth Sabres which it has been flying since 1969. The F-5E/Bs now equip two Butterworth-based fighter-bomber squadrons: Nos 11 'Cobra' Sqn, previously with Sabres, and 12 'Tiger' Sqn. Two squadrons, Nos 6 and 9, operate 16 surviving Canadair CL-41G Tebuan armed trainers of 20 originally received, the former unit flying in the ground-attack role. The transport elements consist of 17 DHC Caribous divided between Nos 1 and 8 Sqns at Labuan, and six Lockheed C-130H Hercules newly delivered to 14 Sqn at Kuala Lumpur for heavy-lift and long-range transport work. Also at Kuala Lumpur is the VIP government unit, No 2 Sqn, equipped with two de Havilland Doves, two Fokker F.28 Mk 1000s,

three DH Herons and two BAe H.S. 125s. Liaison and FAC duties are performed by two helicopter squadrons with 25 Aérospatiale (Sud) Alouette IIIs: Nos 3 Sqn at Kuala Lumpur and 5 Sqn at Labuan. Heavy-lift helicopter capacity is provided by 20 Sikorsky S-61As operating with Nos 7 Sqn at Kuching and 10 Sqn at Kuantan. Known as Nuris in RMAF service, the S-61As have been in use for some years and a further 16 are being delivered.

The RMAF Flying Training School at Alor Star has 15 BAe (SA) Bulldog 102 primary trainers, and a helicopter FTS at Labuan has six Bell 47Gs and three ex-British army Bell Sioux. Also based at Alor Star are 12 Cessna 402Bs used for liaison, multi-engine training and survey work. Five Bell 206Bs and some Bell 212s have been received. Based at Butterworth are the two RAAF Dassault Mirage squadrons which form an important part of the five-power agreement involving Malaysia, Australia, New Zealand, Singapore and the UK. In 1977 a border agreement was signed with Thailand in an effort to reduce the communist guerrilla activity in the area. Joint operations have had limited success, the RMAF flying counter-insurgency (COIN) missions and supply flights in support of the armies.

Standard primary pilot trainer of the Royal Malaysian Air Force, the BAe Bulldog 102 equips the FTS at Alor Star in the north-west corner of the country north of Butterworth, the main F-5 base. Jet training is done on Tebuan (Wasp) CL-41Gs.

Singapore

Republic of Singapore Air Force: This small island nation officially established an Air Defence Command in September 1971 and subsequently renamed the arm the Republic of Singapore Air Force.

The current strike force comprises two

squadrons of BAe (H.S.) Hunter Mk 74s based at the main RSAF strike airfield of Tengah. These are No 140 (Osprey) Sqn, which also has four FR.74As on strength, and 141 (Merlin) Sqn. About 31 single-seat Hunters are in service, plus seven two-seat T.75s and the four reconnaissance FR.74As. At the same base are Nos 142 and 143 Sqns, equipped with 40 McDonnell Douglas A-4S Skyhawk fighter-bombers and six TA-4S two-seat trainers. These aircraft have been converted from ex-US Navy A-4Bs by Lockheed Aircraft Service Singapore (LASS). More than 100 modifications have been incorporated, including a new avionics fit and the installation of uprated 8,400-lb (3810-kg) J65 engines.

At Seletar, the RSAF's main training base,

No 130 (Eagle) Sqn operates about 16 BAC Strikemaster Mk 84s for basic jet and weapon training. To make up for attrition, a further five Strikemasters were acquired from Oman early in 1977. Another unit, No 150 (Falcon) Sqn, flies 14 SIAI-Marchetti SF.260MS basic trainers; some of these are being converted to Warrior standard for the carriage of underwing weapons. Replacing the seven Aérospatiale (Sud) Alouette III helicopters flown by No 120 (Condor) Sqn are 17 Bell UH-1Hs and three Bell 212s; they are used on liaison work and for plane-guard duties at Tengah. Transport duties are performed by No 121 Sqn, which has six Short Skyvan 3Ms used also for SAR and anti-smuggling duties around the island, and four second-hand

Lockheed C-130B Hercules delivered recently from Jordan and the USA.

The current combat element totals some 90 aircraft, but this figure increased early in 1979 when the first of 23 Northrop F-53/Fs arrived. Ordered in September 1976 at a cost of some $113 million, the 18 F-5Es and three two-seat F-5F combat trainers are assigned the interceptor role, for which they are equipped with AIM-9J Sidewinder missiles, 200 of which are included in the deal. The first aircraft arrived in February and delivery was completed by the end of 1979. Neighbouring Malaysia, with which Singapore has a defence agreement, also operates F-5Es, a factor which significantly influenced the RSAF's decision.

Indonesia

Tentara Nasional Indonesia Angkatan Udara: In April 1978, the Indonesian government signed a £25 million contract with British Aerospace for eight Hawk Mk 53 advanced trainers. An initial TNIAU requirement called for at least twice the number ordered, but finance problems limited the purchase; a repeat order is expected at a later date. The Hawks will replace 10 Lockheed T-33As currently in service, and the contract also covers the training of Indonesian pilots and engineers. Forming the front-line combat element of the TNIAU are three squadrons. One, based in East Java, flies 16 ex-RAAF Commonwealth Sabre fighters supplied in

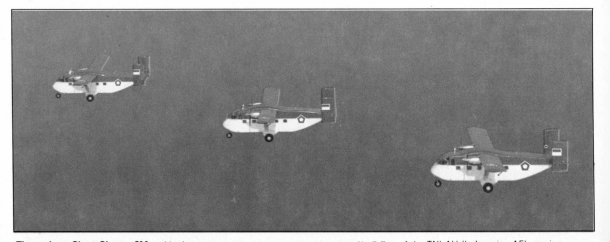

These three Short Skyvan 3M multi-role transports are part of the equipment on No 2 Sqn of the TNI-AU (Indonesian AF), serving alongside the growing fleet of locally assembled CASA C.212 Aviocars which have almost identical engines and similar cabin dimensions but cannot carry such a heavy payload. The C-130 serves as the heavy airlift aircraft.

1972 under an Indonesian/Australian aid agreement. A second squadron is equipped with 16 Rockwell OV-10F Bronco COIN aircraft supplied in 1976-77, while a third unit still operates 14 ground-attack North American F-51D Mustangs. To modernize the combat squadrons, the air force has ordered eight Northrop F-5E fighter-bombers and four F-5F trainers.

The transport element comprises a heavy-lift squadron, No 31, equipped with eight Lockheed C-130B Hercules, and a further unit, 2 Sqn, flying 12 Douglas C-47s and three Shorts Skyvans for short-range work. Eight Fokker F.27 Mk 400Ms have been received to modernize the force, plus the first of 25 Nurtanio-assembled CASA C-212 light transports. Three ex-Pakistani Lockheed L-1049G Super Constellations are reported to have been acquired. Under the aid agreement with Australia, the air force is getting six GAF Nomad Mission Masters. A Lockheed JetStar 6 is used for VIP transport, and a variety of smaller types are flown on liaison and communications work, including seven DHC Otters, five Cessna 401s, two Cessna 402s and five Cessna T207s. The helicopter fleet totals four Aérospatiale (Sud) Alouette IIIs, two Bell 204Bs, four Sikorsky H-34Ds and an S-61A. A batch of ex-Australian Bell 47Gs were received in 1978 and the air force has plans for the procurement of some Bell 205s. Nurtanio, the country's aircraft industrial concern, is to assemble SA.330 Pumas under licence from Aérospatiale, and an initial order was announced in 1978 for six machines for the TNIAU. Training is currently performed on some 15 Beech T-34As, but under a $10 million order 16 T-34C Turbo-Mentors have been delivered to replace the older aircraft; 10 T-33As will be replaced by eight Hawks. Soviet types in storage include 22 Tupolev Tu-16s, 10 Ilyushin Il-28s, 35 Mikoyan-Gurevich MiG-21s, 40 MiG-15/17s, 10 Il-14s, 10 Antonov An-12s, 20 Mil Mi-14s and nine Mi-6s.

Angatan Laut Republik Indonesia: Six GAF Nomad Search Master B utility aircraft are in service with the naval air arm, having been acquired under the aid agreement with Australia. They are used for coastal patrol and transport work from Surabaya in E. Java and are being joined by a second squadron of six Search Masters. Five Grumman HU-16B Albatross amphibians are still operated on SAR duties, while six Douglas C-47s fly in the support role. Helicopters used for liaison work include three Alouette IIs, three Alouette IIIs and four Bell 47Gs.

Tentara Nasional Indonesia Angatan Dorat: The air arm of the Indonesian army was formed in 1959 for liaison and support duties. Sixteen Bell 205A-1s received in 1978 from the United States for utility duties complement a variety of fixed-wing and helicopter types: two Douglas C-47s, two Rockwell Aero Commander 560s, one DHC Beaver and a Beech 18, seven Alouette IIIs and some Cessna 185s, O-1s, 310Ps and a number of licence-built Polish PZL Wilga 32s.

Brunei

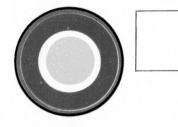

Royal Brunei Malay Regiment Air Wing: Formed in 1966 to support the Brunei Army and commanded by a seconded RAF officer, the Air Wing has standardised on types over the past few years and is now almost completely a helicopter force. The fleet consists of four Bell 212s, one fitted out for VIP use, three Bell 205As and three Bell JetRangers, the last being fitted with uprated engines to Model 206B standard for better tropical performance. For use by the Sultan but also operated as a transport by the wing is a single BAe (Hawker Siddeley) HS 748, which was delivered in 1971.

Papua-New Guinea

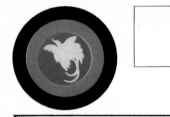

Papua-New Guinea Defence Force: The air element of the PNGDF comprises one Air Transport Squadron, which was formed in August 1975, shortly after the country's independence. The squadron operates four ex-Royal Australian Air Force Douglas C-47s and three GAF N22B Nomad utility aircraft. Personnel total 18 seconded Australian army and air force air and ground crew, including five pilots, and 57 PNG nationals, of whom 16 are pilots. Main roles of this small force are the support of the PNDGF, training and land and sea surveillance.

Australia

Royal Australian Air Force: The RAAF is organised into two main Commands, Operational Command controlling all flying elements except training, and Support Command encompassing Maintenance and Training Commands. Australia's strike force comprises Nos 1 and 6 Sqns equipped with 21 General Dynamics F-111Cs based at Amberley, Queensland, assigned both land and maritime long-range strike roles. Four aircraft have been fitted with sensors and reconnaissance equipment at a total cost of $A19million to increase the effectiveness of the force. A third squadron (No 2, also based at Amberley) operates eight Government Aircraft Factories Canberra B.20s in the PR and target-towing roles, plus four Canberra T.21s for training. Air defence is the task of three Dassault Mirage IIIO units; one of them, No 77 Sqn, is based at Williamtown, New South Wales, which forms the home base of the Mirage Wing. The two other squadrons, Nos 3 and 75, are based at Butterworth, Malaysia, as part of Australia's commitment to the five-power agreement involving Singapore, Malaysia, the UK, Australia and New Zealand. The RAAF acquired a total of 100 single-seat Dassault Mirage IIIOs and 16 two-seat IIIDOs. In addition to these aircraft, there is a reserve strike potential in 86 Aer-

Though the Royal Australian Air Force had to wait almost ten years longer than planned for it, the F-111C has since 1973 provided all-weather attack capability in 1 and 6 Sqns, based at Amberley, near Brisbane, plus a small reconnaissance force.

macchi/CAC M.B.326H attack/trainers which normally fly in the advanced training role as outlined overleaf.

Two maritime reconnaissance squadrons are operated: No 10 Sqn at Townsville, Queensland, flying 12 Lockheed SP-2H Neptunes; and No 11 Sqn at Edinburgh, South Australia, flying 10 Lockheed P-3B Orions. To replace the Neptunes, 10 new Lockheed P-3C Update II Orions delivered in 1978 – 79 at a cost of $A175million. The RAAF has a large transport force totalling five fixed-wing squadrons and three helicopter units. Backbone of the fleet are two squadrons of Lockheed Hercules: No 36 Sqn flying 12 C-130As and No 37 Sqn with 12 C-130Es, both based at Richmond, NSW. To replace the early A-series aircraft, 12 new C-130Hs are being delivered. Also at Richmond are two DHC Caribou-equipped units, Nos 35 and 38 Sqns, with a total of 23 aircraft. A replacement for these aircraft is needed but no selection has yet been made. Based at Fairbairn, Canberra, is 34 Sqn, which uses a variety of types for VIP duties, including two BAe (BAC) One-Elevens, three Dassault Mystère 20s and two BAe (Hawker Siddeley) HS 748s. The acquisition of two Boeing 727s for VIP duties is being considered. A sizeable force of Douglas C-47s remains in service, numbering some 17 aircraft, and these are likely to continue flying in various support roles until the end of 1980.

The two helicopter units, based at Fairbairn and Townsville, operate in the training role (No 5 Sqn with 31 Bell UH-1Bs) and on the support and SAR duties (No 9 Sqn with 16 UH-1D/Hs). A third unit, No 12 Sqn at Amberley, is equipped with 12 Boeing-Vertol CH-47C Chinooks for army support but budget restrictions have forced the temporary storage of at least some of these machines.

continued 45

New Zealand-built AESL CT/4 Airtrainers, totalling 31 aircraft, operate with No 1 FTS at Point Cook, and a further six aircraft at the Central Flying School at East Sale have replaced Commonwealth Aircraft CA-25 Winjeels. Six Airtrainers have been fitted with underwing hardpoints for use in training forward air controllers. Jet training is done at No 2 FTS Pearce, on 50 M.B.326s, while at East Sale the School of Air Navigation uses eight BAe (Hawker Siddeley) HS 748 T.2s for navigation training. Instructor training is performed at CFS East Sale on 15 M.B.326s.

The choice of a replacement for the Mirage IIIs in the Tactical Fighter Force has still to be decided. Requests for Proposals (RFP) are being assessed by the RAAF from submissions presented by European and American manufacturers. The types currently under evaluation are the GD F-16, McDonnell Douglas F-15 and F-18, Mirage 2000 and the Panavia Tornado. As a result of the high costs involved, the RAAF is having to restrict the number of aircraft to be purchased to a single squadron and the type chosen is likely to be more of a multi-role aircraft rather than a pure interceptor as originally envisaged. In the meantime, proposals are being studied for a programme to extend the useful lives of the Mirage IIIs into the late 1980s. A similar scheme is being undertaken by Hawker de Havilland for the large training force of M.B.326s. Initially thought to be a candidate for the new M.B.339, the RAAF seems to favour an extension of the service life of the well proven M.B.326 will take the aircraft into the 1990s.

Royal Australian Navy: The RAN's 20,000-ton light aircraft-carrier HMAS *Melbourne* (formerly HMS *Majestic*, bought in 1956) is scheduled to continue in service until the 1980s, and her Fleet Air Arm Air Group operates in the ASW, strike and ground-attack roles, as well as having an SAR capability. Three squadrons comprise the group: VF-805 with McDonnell Douglas A-4G Skyhawks, VS-816 with Grumman S-2G/E

Trackers and HS-817 with Westland Sea King Mk 50s. The carrier's aircraft complement totals 14 Skyhawks, six Trackers and six Sea Kings. The navy is known to be keen to replace *Melbourne* in the 1980s with a smaller carrier equipped for V/STOL aircraft and ASW helicopters. Shipbuilding firms have been asked to submit proposals, and when a firm decision has been made, probably not before the beginning of 1980, an order for BAe (Hawker Siddeley) Sea Harriers is sure to follow. The Tracker fleet is back up to strength following the disastrous hangar fire in December 1976, which all but destroyed the force; some 19 aircraft are now in service.

Other squadrons based at Nowra Naval Air Station, NSW, are HS-723, equipped with four Bell UH-1Bs, two Bell 206B-1 LOHs and four Westland Wessex HAS.31Bs flying in the fleet requirements, communications and SAR roles; VC-724, flying A-4G/TA-4G Skyhawks and eight M.B.326Hs on fixed-wing fighter ground-attack training, fleet requirements and trials duties; and VC-851, which operates two HS 748s modified for electronic warfare training. A total of 17 A-4G/TA-4G Skyhawks, eight Sea Kings and 28 other helicopters are in service.

Army Aviation: In 1968 the Australian Army Aviation Corps was created to organise and train the aviation units in the Australian Army. An Aviation Centre established at Oakey, Queensland, in 1971 accommodates the School of Army Aviation, 1st Aviation Regiment and No 5 Base Workshop Battalion, a major maintenance and repair facility. Helicopter squadrons are located with major field formations in Townsville, Queensland and Sydney, New South Wales. In addition to providing support for the army in Australia, aircraft are being used in Indonesia and Papua New Guinea.

Current fixed-wing equipment comprises 17 Pilatus PC-6 Turbo-Porters flying with the 171st Air Cavalry Flight at Holsworthy and 173rd Support Sqn at Oakey, and 11 GAF Nomad Mission Master utility aircraft delivered in 1977.

Dunking a sonobuoy, the Westland Sea King 50 is the standard ASW helicopter of the RAN's Fleet Air Arm Air Group, serving with HS-817 squadron. The Mk 50 was first of the uprated series of Westland Sea Kings.

New Zealand

Royal New Zealand Air Force: Economic restrictions continue to prevent any large-scale expansion of the RNZAF. Current personnel strength is some 4,300 and the service has an establishment of seven operational squadrons in the strike, transport and maritime roles under the command of Operations Group at Auckland. The other main element is Support Group, headquartered at Christchurch, which encompasses all units not concerned with front-line operational flying. Air force headquarters are in Wellington, alongside those of the army and navy and forming the country's tri-service defence organisation. An RNZAF unit is deployed in Singapore in support of the country's defence commitments in South-East Asia; the service also provides a small home defence force.

The present strike element is composed of nine McDonnell Douglas A-4K and four TA-4K Skyhawks flying with No 75 Sqn and based at Ohakea in North Island. Further north at Whenuapai, Auckland, No 5 Sqn operates in the maritime-reconnaissance role, flying five Lockheed P-3B Orions. Transport duties are undertaken from the same base by No 40 Sqn, which has an establishment of five Lockheed C-130H Hercules and a single BAe (H.S.) Devon; this unit is assigned the long-range transport task as well as doing heavy-lift logistical work. Also at Whenuapai is No 1 Sqn, flying troops and freight with six of the 10 HS Andover C.1s in use. These aircraft were purchased from the RAF in 1976 and

have replaced Douglas C-47s and Bristol Freighters in the short/medium-range transport role. The remaining four Andovers, plus two Devons, equip No 42 Sqn at Ohakea for a variety of tasks, including VIP work and twin continuation training. No 3 Sqn at Hobsonville forms the RNZAF's main helicopter unit, flying 10 Bell UH-1D and UH-1H Iroquois and six Bell 47Gs. Apart from air force work, the squadron is committed to army support. At Tengah in Singapore is the RNZAF Support Unit, equipped with four Bell UH-1H helicopters. Until recently these machines were part of No 41 Sqn, but in December 1977 this squadron relinquished its three remaining Bristol Mk 31 Freighters, the type having completed 26 years' sterling service with the New Zealand armed forces, and the unit was disbanded and the Support Unit established.

Operational strike training and jet conversion is performed by No 14 Sqn at Ohakea with 16 BAC Strikemaster Mk 88s. Pilot training begins on the 13 New Zealand Aerospace CT/4 Airtrainers at the FTS at Wigram, while four Bell 47Gs are used for helicopter training. New Zealand's long association with the North American Harvard came to an end in June 1977 when the type was retired from use at Wigram. A further six CT/4 airframes have been bought by the RNZAF for spares.

A token naval air component of two Westland Wasps comes under the wing of No 3 Sqn at Hobsonville when shore-based; deployed, they operate from the frigates HMNZS *Canterbury* and *Waikato*.

This fine portrait of a Strikemaster 88 shows a machine from RNZAF No 14 Squadron at Ohakea, which handles the service's jet conversion and operational strike training.

South America

Almost all the military aircraft operated by Latin American countries are of US, British, French or Italian origin. America's hold on the market was broken by US attempts to restrict the flow of advanced weaponry such as supersonic fighters to the area in order to prevent an arms race. As in any market, the customer is always right and in this case what the customer wanted was supersonic aircraft.

Mirage fighters have been sold to Argentina, Brazil, Colombia, Ecuador, Peru and Venezuela. Most nations regard the A-4 or Canberra as an effective bomber – refurbishment of the latter is a healthy source of business for British Aerospace. Ecuador adopted the Anglo/French Jaguar. Israel has attempted to market the Kfir, but the US has vetoed export of the J79 powerplant to South America. An Atar-powered variant known as Dagger may have been supplied to Argentina.

Soviet penetration of the area has been limited. The Cuban Air Force operates Soviet equipment and recently took delivery of 20 MiG-23 and MiG-27 Floggers. US reactions to this deployment seemed a little excessive since the limited tactical radius of the type would allow it to operate only over the state of Florida — an area whose air defences are already positioned to tackle intruders from Cuba. The tactical radius of Flogger is much less than that of the Il-28 Beagle bombers, withdrawal of which was negotiated during the 1962 Cuban missile crisis. Peru took delivery of 36 Su-22 Fitter fighter-bombers in 1977 but is reported to have found the avionics fitted to the aircraft rather more austere than was expected. Even the Sirena radar-warning receiver normally carried by the Su-20 export variant has been deleted.

Several countries have set up an aircraft-manufacturing industry. Brazil builds the Aermacchi MB-326 under licence as the Xavante while Argentina has designed and built a range of types including the IA58 Pucará counter-insurgency aircraft. An Argentinian two-seat jet trainer is also planned.

Argentina	52	Honduras	48
Bolivia	52	Jamaica	47
Brazil	50	Mexico	48
Chile	51	Nicaragua	48
Colombia	49	Panama	49
Cuba	47	Paraguay	52
Dominican Republic	47	Peru	50
Ecuador	49	Salvador	48
Guatemala	48	Uruguay	51
Guyana	49	Venezuela	49
Haiti	47		

Cuba

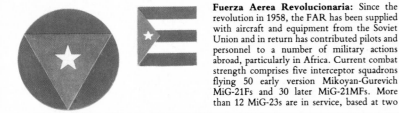

Fuerza Aerea Revolucionaria: Since the revolution in 1958, the FAR has been supplied with aircraft and equipment from the Soviet Union and in return has contributed pilots and personnel to a number of military actions abroad, particularly in Africa. Current combat strength comprises five interceptor squadrons flying 50 early version Mikoyan-Gurevich MiG-21Fs and 30 later MiG-21MFs. More than 12 MiG-23s are in service, based at two airfields, San Julian in the west and Guines near Havana, and Soviet Air Force pilots are regularly flying patrols in these aircraft as well as in the MiG-21s. Supplementing these units are two squadrons with 40 MiG-19s and four fighter-bomber squadrons equipped with 75 MiG-17s. A second-line training unit has 15 MiG-15s. The transport arm has some 50 aircraft made up of Antonov An-2 utility biplanes, Ilyushin Il-14s and An-24s, while the helicopter force has approximately 30 Mil Mi-1s and 24 Mi-4s. For training, two-seat MiG-15UTIs and Zlin 326s are used. Cuban bases are frequently used by Soviet long-range reconnaissance aircraft. For military transport duties to Africa, Cubana aircraft are used, usually supplemented by Soviet air force transports.

Jamaica

Jamaica Defence Force Air Wing: A transport force with additional SAR, liaison and police co-operation roles, the Air Wing is based at Up Park Camp, Kingston, and operates a variety of types. The fixed-wing element is made up of two Britten-Norman Islander transports, one DHC Twin Otter 300, one Beech King Air, a single Beech Duke and two Cessna 185 Skywagons. The helicopter flight operates four Bell 206B Jet-Rangers and three Bell 212 heavy-lifters.

Haiti

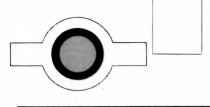

Haiti Air Corps: This small air arm has received limited American aid in recent years, but no modern combat aircraft are in service. The sole fighter-bomber squadron is reported to have retired its six long-serving North American F-51D Mustangs, the Air Corps replacing them with eight Cessna O-2A Super Skymasters equipped with underwing hardpoints for a dual liaison/COIN role. Other types include three Douglas C-47s, two Beech C-45s, a single Cessna 402, three DHC Beavers, four Sikorsky H-34s and five S-55s, mostly used for transport and supply work. Some training capacity was provided by three North American T-6 and three T-28s before their recent replacement by three Cessna 150s and a Cessna 172.

Dominican Republic

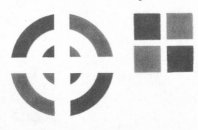

Fuerza Aerea Dominicana: This small country, situated in the Caribbean, operates a token air force under a central air command within which are some three active units. The fighter combat squadron equipped with more than a dozen North American F-51D Mustangs, acts mainly as a training unit. Seven Douglas B-26Ks form the bomber component, and the survivors of 10 de Havilland Vampire F.1/FB.50s constitute the country's sole jet equipment. For Coin duties approximately six North American T-28Ds are used, but these aircraft also fulfil a dual training commitment. With the country almost surrounded by water, the SAR and MR tasks assume considerable importance, although budget restrictions have not allowed for the replacement of the two Consolidated PBY-5A Catalinas in use. A transport squadron has six Douglas C-47s, six Curtiss C-46s and three DHC Beavers. Helicopters include three Aérospatiale Alouette II/IIIs, two Sikorsky H-19s, two Hiller UH-12Es and seven Hughes OH-6As. The training element has four Cessna 172s plus some North American T-6s and Beech T-11s.

Mexico

Fuerza Aerea Mexicana: Lack of finance is seen as the main reason why no new combat aircraft have been procured by the Mexican air force since the withdrawal from service of the 12 de Havilland Vampire F.3s. The present inventory comprises No 202 Sqn with 15 Lockheed AT-33 armed trainers, about 50 North American T-28s in four training squadrons (Nos 201, 205, 206 and 207 Sqns) and some 20 North American T-6s in Nos 203 and 204 Sqns, although not all the aircraft are operational. A light support unit, No 209 Sqn, uses 18 LASA-60s mainly for SAR duties, plus one Hiller 12E and nine Aérospatiales (Sud) Alouette IIIs.

A Heavy Transport Squadron is equipped with one Douglas DC-7, five C-54s and two C-118s, while a Light Transport Group has seven Douglas C-47s, one Short Skyvan, 20 Rockwell Aero Commander 500s, some Piper Aztecs, 12 Britten-Norman Islanders (government-operated) and 10 IAI Aravas. Based at Mexico City is a VIP and government squadron flying two Boeing 727-100QCs, an BAe H.S 125, a BAC One-Eleven and a Lockheed JetStar. The helicopter force stands at 14 Bell 47Gs, five Bell JetRangers, a Bell 212 and about 10 Bell 205s. Twenty aerobatic Beech Bonanza F33Cs have been delivered for

Though it is not the type of aircraft to equip whole squadrons the various species of Learjets are used by a surprising number of the world's armed forces as VIP transport and for many other duties. This Model 24D is operated by the Mexican Navy.

training, joining 20 Beech Musketeer Sports brought in 1970, and some Beech B55 Barons are used for twin training. The FAM has ordered 12 Pilatus PC-7 Turbo-Trainers to update the training syllabus at the basic stage, and these aircraft are expected to have provision for underwing armament, thus doubling in the COIN role; delivery is expected in 1979.

The Mexican navy operates four Grumman HU-16A Albatrosses for ASW and SAR duties, and another four are being bought from surplus ex-USN stocks. At least two Douglas C-47s, four Aérospatiale Alouette IIs and five Bell 47s are on strength. At least two Beech Bonanzas are used for twin training, and a VIP Gates Learjet 24D and Fairchild FH-227 are operated by the navy.

Guatemala

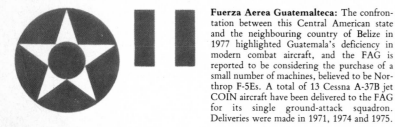

Fuerza Aerea Guatemalteca: The confrontation between this Central American state and the neighbouring country of Belize in 1977 highlighted Guatemala's deficiency in modern combat aircraft, and the FAG is reported to be considering the purchase of a small number of machines, believed to be Northrop F-5Es. A total of 13 Cessna A-37B jet COIN aircraft have been delivered to the FAG for its single ground-attack squadron. Deliveries were made in 1971, 1974 and 1975.

The other jet equipment operated by this Central American air arm comprises three Cessna T-37Cs, for conversion training, and five Lockheed T-33As, for advanced training. Both types were supplied by the United States under a military assistance agreement. The *Escuadron de Transporte* is headquartered at Guatemala City Airport and flies some nine Douglas C-47s, 10 Israeli-supplied IAI Arava light transports, one Douglas C-54 and one Douglas DC-6. Liaison missions are flown by

six Cessna 170s, three Cessna 180s, two Cessna U206Cs, six Bell UH-1Ds, three Sikorsky UH-19s and a Hiller OH-23G. For primary training 10 Aerotec T-23 Uirapurus have been bought from Brazil. Seven North American T-6s continue in use as basic trainers, and at least two Cessna 172s are operated.

Salvador

Fuerza Aerea Salvadorena: This small Central American republic has had frequent clashes with neighbouring Honduras over the past few years, and both countries have re-equipped with more modern combat aircraft. The FAS operates a squadron of 18 Dassault Ouragan fighter-bombers purchased from Israel in 1975, and from the same source came six Israeli-built Aérospatiale Magisters for strike/trainer duties. More recently, three ex-French AF Magisters have been delivered.

Supply and transport duties are performed by a squadron flying a mixed assortment of types including two Douglas DC-6s, 17 Douglas C-47s, and four IAI Arava light STOL aircraft. Helicopters include three Aérospatiale Lamas for SAR work, two Aérospatiale (Sud) Alouette IIIs and a single Hiller FH-1100. A training element operates a number of Cessna T-41Cs, 10 North American T-6s and three Beech T-34s.

Honduras

Fuerza Aerea Hondurena: To match the more modern jet equipment acquired by neighbouring El Salvador over the past few years, the Honduran air force took delivery in 1976 of 12 ex-Israeli air force Dassault Super Mystère B.2 fighter-bombers. Re-engined with Pratt & Whitney J52s to replace the original SNECMA Atars, these aircraft have given the country a marked combat ascendancy over adjoining air forces. The FAH is also equipped with a squadron of six Cessna A-37Bs, which

were delivered in three batches between June and November 1975.

Before this influx of jet equipment, the FAH had relied on a wing of World War II-vintage Vought F4U-5 Corsair fighter-bombers delivered in 1958 and 1959. Ten of these aircraft were based at Tocontin Airport near the Honduran capital. A reconnaissance/trainer unit based at San Pedro Sula air base is equipped with three Lockheed RT-33As.

Modern equipment was also phased into the

transport force when, in 1976, the first two IAI Arava light transports arrived. These now fly alongside five Douglas C-47s, two C-54s and a number of Beech C-45s. Four Cessna 180/185s fly liaison duties, while a basic training unit is equipped with five Cessna T-41As delivered in 1973, four North American T-28s and six T-6s; a further eight T-28As were acquired in August 1978 from ex-Moroccan stocks. The helicopter element is understood to be three Sikorsky H-19s.

Nicaragua

Fuerza Aerea de Nicaragua: This small air arm is chiefly committed to civilian duties but retains a token combat element for counter-insurgency work. This comprises a light strike element equipped with six Cessna O-2A Skymasters supplied by the USA. In 1979 these were used extensively by the Somoza regime to quell the guerrilla activities of the opposing Sandinistas. The Douglas B-26 Invaders totalling six in number are believed to

be grounded. There are also two ground-attack units with six Lockheed T-33As and six North American T-28Ds, all supplied by the United States. The transport arm has one IAI Arava light freighter, three Douglas C-47s, four Beech C-45s and 10 Cessna 180s. Five CASA C-212 Aviocars were delivered to the air force in 1977, the first arriving in June that year. A single BAe (H.S.) 125 flies VIP and liaison duties. Helicopters include one Hughes

269 for training, four Hughes OH-6As and three Sikorsky CH-34s. Piper Super Cubs and a few North American T-6s constitute the small training element.

Panama

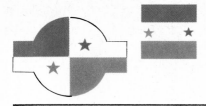

Fuerza Aerea Panamena: First formed in 1969 with American assistance, the FAP has no combat aircraft and operates mainly in the transport, liaison, coastguard and policing roles. When the United States relinquished control of the Panama Canal late in 1979, the FAP was to include patrols of this important seaway in its duties. The complete transfer of the zone to Panama is due on December 31, 1999.

Current FAP inventory comprises a single Lockheed Electra procured in 1975, four Douglas C-47s, two DHC Twin Otters, two DHC Otters and two Britten-Norman Islanders. The single IAI Westwind is no longer in service and liaison duties are performed by two Cessna U-17Bs and a Cessna 172. Helicopters total 12 Bell UH-1Bs delivered in 1977, two UH-1Ds, two UH-1Hs and one UH-1N. In 1978, the Panamanian government purchased a single Shorts Skyvan 3M.

Colombia

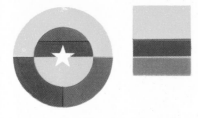

Fuerza Aerea Colombiana: This air force, in line with some others in South America, purchased Dassault Mirages in 1970 and currently operates 18 (14 Mirage 5COA fighter-bombers, two 5CORs for tactical reconnaissance and two 5COD trainers), which equip the single combat group at Germon Olana air base. A single bomber and reconnaissance squadron operates eight Douglas B-26Ks and RB-26Cs, and further combat potential is available from 10 Lockheed AT-33As usually flown in the advanced training role: 11 US and Canadian-supplied North American F-86 Sabres have been withdrawn.

The transport element comprises the military airline Satena, which operates services linking the capital Bogota with distant points around the country. Its fleet consists of two Douglas C-54s, seven Douglas DC-3s and three BAe (Hawker Siddeley) HS 748s. The air force Transport Command is equipped with one of three ex-Canadian Lockheed C-130B Hercules delivered in 1971, one Fokker-VFW F.28 Mk 1000 for VIP use, six Pilatus Porters and Turbo-Porters, 10 DHC Beavers, three C-54s, a few Beech C-45s and 16 Douglas C-47s. Ten Cessna T-37Cs, six Northrop T-38s delivered in 1978 from US surplus stocks, and 30 Cessna T-41Ds are used for training at Marco Fidel Suarez air base, Cali, and there are around 30 Beech T-34s for basic work including six acquired in 1977 from surplus American stocks. A large helicopter force has 27 Aérospatiale Lamas for SAR duties, 16 Bell 47Gs, 12 Hughes OH-6As, six Kaman HH-43 Huskies, six Sikorsky TH-55s, six Bell UH-1Bs and four Hiller H-23s; one Bell 212 is flown for Presidential use. Ten Hughes 500C/D Defenders have recently been delivered.

Venezuela

The Rockwell T-2D Buckeye is the standard advanced jet trainer of the Fuerza Aerea Venezolanas.

Fuerza Aerea Venezolanas: FAV has two combat groups, or *Grupos,* one encompassing the fighter squadrons, or *Escuadrones,* and the other the bomber squadrons. Grupo 12 administers three fighter squadrons: Escuadron 34, with 15 ex-Canadian Northrop CF-5As and four CF-5Bs; Escuadron 35, with 20 North American F-86K Sabres; and Escuadron 36, with nine Dassault Mirage IIIEVs, four 5Vs and two 5DVS. Grupo 13 has two bomber squadrons; Escuadron 39, with 29 BAe Canberras (18 B.2s, seven B[I].8s, two T.4s and two PR.3s) based at Maracay; and Escuadron 40, with 16 Rockwell OV-10E Broncos. The Canberras are undergoing a refurbishing programme in the UK and 'more than 20 aircraft are involved' according to British Aerospace.

Transport duties are performed by two units within the Grupo de Transporte based at Caracas: Escuadron 1, flying 20 Douglas C-47s and five Lockheed C-130H Hercules (a sixth aircraft was lost in September 1976); and Escuadron 2, with the survivors of 18 Fairchild C-123B Providers. Two HS.748s are in service, one for VIP duties and the other being an ex-LAV aircraft and attached to Esc 1. To supplement the VIP Boeing 737-200s the FAV has acquired a McDonnell Douglas DC-9.

A helicopter group which also flies fixed-wing types has 15 Aérospatiale (Sud) Alouette IIIs, 10 Sikorsky UH-19s and 12 Bell UH-1D/Hs operating alongside 12 Cessna 182Ns and some nine Beech Queen Airs. Training is the task of about 25 Beech T-34 Mentors and 12 Rockwell T-2D Buckeyes. A further 12 T-2Ds were delivered in 1977; these aircraft, which have a dual strike/trainer role, are destined to replace 12 BAe Jet Provost T.52 weapon trainers. Six Bell 206Bs and a single 206L were delivered in 1977, mainly for government use. An unconfirmed report has stated that the FAV has placed an order with Saab for up to 20 MFI-15/17 primary trainers.

The army has about 20 helicopters (Alouette IIIs and Bell 47Gs) for liaison duties with ground forces. Slightly smaller is the naval air component, which comprises six Grumman S-2E Trackers and four Grumman HU-16A Albatross amphibians for ASW and SAR duties, three C-47s, which are being replaced by a single ex-LAV HS.748 transport acquired in 1977, and two Bell 47Gs.

Guyana

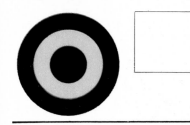

Guyana Defence Force Air Command: Formerly British Guiana, this independent Commonwealth country has a policing force, with headquarters in Georgetown, and operates eight Britten-Norman Islanders for transport duties. Two Helio Couriers have now been retired, and the force expanded with the purchase of a Beech King Air 200 in 1975 and a Cessna U206F delivered the following year for personnel transport. Helicopters total two Aérospatiale (Sud) Alouette IIIs, three Bell 212s and two Bell 206s.

Ecuador

Fuerza Aerea Ecuatoriana: Following America's veto on the sale to Ecuador of 24 Israeli Aircraft Industries Kfir fighter-bombers early in 1977, the FAE placed an order with Dassault for 16 Mirage F.1JEs and two F.1JB two-seat combat trainers; delivery was made in 1979. They will join the squadron of 12 BAC/Breguet Jaguar International strike aircraft delivered in 1977 under an order covering 10 single- and two two-seat trainers.

A bomber unit has three BAC Canberra B.6s of six originally delivered, and of the 16 BAC Srikemaster Mk 89s received, 14 survive to equip a strike/trainer unit. A counter-insurgency squadron was established in 1976 following the purchase of 12 Cessna A-37Bs from the USA. The Military Air Transport Group of the FAE has a variety of types including four Douglas DC-6s, two DHC-5D Buffalos delivered in 1976, and five BAe (Hawker Siddeley) HS 748s, two being Series 2A aircraft with a large freight door. Of these, two operate with TAME (*Transportes Aereos Nacionales Ecuatorianos*), the military airline branch of the FAE. Scheduled passenger and cargo flights are operated by this airline, which also has four Lockheed Electras and a single DHC Twin Otter. A further Twin Otter is in air force use together with one of two Lockheed C-130H Hercules delivered in 1977. The transport element makes occasional use of two Ecuatoriana Boeing 720s for long-range flights.

A helicopter element has two Aérospatiale SA.330 Pumas, four rescue Lamas, six Alouette IIIs, and some Bell 212s. A single Beech King Air 90 is in air force use for calibration work. The primary training element has 20 Cessna T-41s and 24 Cessna 150 Aerobats. To modernise the training force, 20 Beech T-34C Turbo-Mentors are on order to replace nine T-28s; 12 Lockheed T-33As are used for advanced work together with some of the Strikemasters. Twelve Italian SIAI-Marchetti SF.260 primary trainers were delivered to the FAE in 1977.

The Ecuadorean Army has a small support air arm equipped with a single Short Skyvan, three Pilatus Turbo-Porters and five IAI Aravas. For photo-survey work the army has a single Gates .Learjet 25D. The Ecuadorean Navy too has a liaison unit, equipped with two Aérospatiale Alouette III helicopters, one Arava, one Cessna 320E, one Cessna 177 and two Cessna T-41Ds.

Brazil

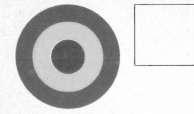

Forca Aerea Brasileira: The largest air arm in South America, the FAB is also one of the best equipped having recently undergone a modernisation programme. For pure interceptor duties, Brazil has a single squadron of 15 Dassault Mirages purchased from France in 1970 and currently based at Anapolis, near Brasilia. Designated 1st Air Defence Wing, the aircraft comprise 11 Mirage IIIEBRs plus four more ordered to make up for attrition, and four two-seat Mirage IIIDBRs; they form an important element of a French-installed computerised air-defence system known as DACTA I and II, which by the end of the 1980s will embrace the whole of Brazilian airspace. At Santa Cruz, the 1st Fighter Group, made up of two squadrons, has 36 Northrop F-5Es and six F-5B two-seat trainers, three of which have been lost. Also flying fighter duties are subsonic EMBRAER AT-26 Xavantes, which equip two squadrons of the 4th Fighter Group and a single squadron of the 14th FG. Xavantes perform a number of roles with the FAB, including ground-attack and training. Following the initial order for 112 aircraft, a contract for 40 was placed, followed by a second re-order for 20 aircraft which takes the FAB total to 172; the extra AT-26s should all have been delivered by the middle of 1980.

Reconnaissance and attack squadrons total five, three of which have AT-26s (Nos 3, 4 and 5) while the other two fly the indigenous armed version of the Neiva T-25 Universal (Nos 1 and 2 Sqns). Complementing these units are three liaison and observation squadrons equipped with Neiva L-42 Regentes, T-25s and Bell UH-1Hs. To make way for this updated equipment a number of aircraft are being withdrawn from use, including T-6s, Lockheed AT-33As, Douglas B-26Ks and Cessna T-37s.

Older aircraft continue in service with Maritime Command, however, even though an urgent need still exists to replace ageing types. All fixed-wing naval aircraft are operated under air force control, and within the Naval Command is the 1st Carrier-borne Aviation Group (*Grupo de Aviaco Embarcada*). This unit, based at Santa Cruz, flies eight ex-USN refurbished Grumman S-2E Trackers replacing a similar number of older S-2As now relegated to transport duties. Brazil's only aircraft-carrier, *Minas Gerais* (ex-HMS *Vengeance* and bought in 1957), normally accommodates six S-2s at any one time in addition to a helicopter component (see under *Forca Aeronaval*). A liaison unit operated by a FAB on behalf of the navy flies a few Pilatus P-3s and North American T-28s. The 7th GAv at Salvador has retired its seven Lockheed P-2E Neptunes and has received 12 EMB-111 maritime patrol versions of the Bandeirante transport, the first three of which were delivered in 1978. Designated P-95s in FAB service, all were delivered by the beginning of 1979. For long-range rescue work, the 6th GAv at Recife flies three Lockheed RC-130E Hercules. Two further SAR units are based at Florionapolis: No 2 Sqn, equipped with 13 Grumman SA-16A/B Albatross amphibians, and No 3 Sqn with six Bell SH-1Ds and a few Bell 47Gs.

For transport duties there are four units divided into the following: No 1 Sqn, I Group, equipped with seven C-130E, three C-130H and two KC-130H Hercules, the last-mentioned flown for air-refuelling the F-5s; No 1 Sqn, II Group with six BAe (Hawker Siddeley) HS 748s and some EMB-110 Bandeirante light transports; No 2 Sqn, II Group, with six HS 748 Srs 2Cs delivered in 1976; and No 2 Sqn of a Parachute Transport Group, equipped with some of the 21 surviving DHC Buffalos purchased by the FAB. Most of the 86 EMBRAER Bandeirantes have been delivered to the FAB and comprise 56 C-95 transports, 20 C-95A freighters, six R-95 photo-survey aircraft and four EC-95 navaid calibration versions. An order for a Buffalo replacement could go to an EMBRAER design known as CX-2A and powered by two GE T64 turboprops, but this at present remains in the project stage. Based at Brasilia are the *Grupo de Transporte Especial* (GTE) or Special Transport Group, made up of two squadrons, operating two Boeing 737-200s, one BAC Viscount, eight HS 125s, six Bell 206 JetRangers and some Bandeirantes on VIP and government flights. Five EMB-121 Xingu light twins have been delivered to the GTE, while another recent purchase involves 12 licence-built EMB-810C Senecas for service with the GTE and other units in a liaison capacity. Four further squadrons fly EMB-110s, which have replaced Douglas C-47s, and two more squadrons operate the remaining Buffalos not flown by the Parachute Group. At Belem, six Consolidated PBY-5A Catalinas are employed on SAR and transport duties, although these veterans are long overdue for replacement.

Helicopters equip a counter-insurgency unit at Santos and total six UH-1Ds, four Bell 206s and four Hughes OH-6As. For navaid checking and survey duties two BAe (Hawker Siddeley) HS 125s and the four EMB-110As (EC-95s) have replaced three EC-47s. Training equipment is mainly home-produced — 100 T-23 Uirapurus for primary work, 132 T-25 Universals for basic training, plus eight more

Designated AT-26 Xavante, the Aermacchi MB.326GC is a more powerful and strengthened version of the Italian trainer, licence-built in Brazil for training and tactical Coin missions. The 167 delivered equip squadrons in the 14th and 4th Fighter Groups.

Though the Brazilian FAB (air force) manages all fixed-wing power, the Forca Aeronaval deploys a sizeable helicopter force, largest of which are the Sikorsky SH-3D Sea Kings of No 1 ASW Squadron.

on order to balance attrition, and some AT-26s for jet training. Helicopter training is carried out on 30 Bell H-13Js at Santos, Sao Paulo. For liaison duties there are some 40 Neiva L-42 Regentes, while in the observation role some 70 U-42 Regentes are operated.

Forca Aeronaval: The Brazilian naval air arm has been a helicopter operator since 1965, when the President decreed that all fixed-wing aircraft were to be operated under FAB con-

trol. Consequently, the navy supplies the Sikorsky SH-3 Sea Kings for operation aboard the *Minas Gerais*, while the air force contributes the S-2s, although the fixed-wing type comes under naval control once aboard. Six SH-3Ds are in service with No 1 ASQ Sqn and when ashore are absed at the main airfield of San Pedro de Aldeia. A total of nine Westland Lynx helicopters have been ordered for operation from six *Niteroi*-class frigates built or under construction in the UK and Brazil, and the first two aircraft were accepted by the navy in 1978. A liaison and general-duties squadron operates three Westland Whirlwind 3s, 18 Bell 206Bs and two Westland Wasps; six more Wasp HAS.1s were delivered in 1977 – 78 to take the inventory to eight aircraft. A training squadron has 10 Hughes 269/300s, though these are gradually being withdrawn from use.

Peru

Fuerza Aerea del Peru: The Peruvian air force continues to be one of the more modern air arms in South America. Having failed to procure an up-to-date Western strike aircraft in 1976, it ordered Sukhoi Su-22 'Fitter-C' fighter-bombers. A total of 32 single-seat and four two-seat combat trainer Su-22Us are now in service, and they are believed to have replaced the North American F-86Fs in Grupo 12, comprising two squadrons. To assist in training Peruvian pilots, 12 ex-Cuban air force Mikoyan-Gurevich MiG-21s were delivered to the FAP, together with Cuban instructors. Currently flying in the strike role are two squadrons of a three-squadron Bomber Wing (Grupo 21), with 32 BAC B.2/B.56/B(I).8 Canberras plus two T.4 trainers and 11 B(I).68s. delivered in 1976 from ex-RAF stocks via Marshall of Cambridge in the UK. A third unit in the wing operates 12 Cessna A-37B Dragonfly light attack aircraft ordered in 1974 and delivered in 1976. Peru's Dassault Mirage force began arriving in 1968, and the initial 20 5Ps and two two-seat 5DPs have been increased to a total of 36 aircraft by later re-orders. These fly with two squadrons of Grupo 13 in the strike/interceptor role, and the third squadron of the wing is believed to be flying the second batch of 12 A-37Bs. The total Peruvian A-37B order was for 36 aircraft, delivery of the final 12 having been completed towards the end of 1977. A further fighter wing (Grupo 12) flies the survivors of 16 Hawker Hunter F.62s and the Su-22s. A maritime-reconnaissance and SAR unit (Grupo 31) has four Grumman HU-16B Albatross amphibians.

The transport element of the FAP comprises Grupo 41, based at Jorge Chavez air base and flying six Lockheed L-100-20s, mainly for pipeline work. A second squadron in the wing has 16 DHC Buffaloes, while a third unit operates six Douglas C-47s, a few Curtiss C-46s, five Douglas DC-6s and four Douglas C-54s. A light transport unit has seven DHC Twin Otters, some equipped as floatplanes. Twenty Antonov An-26 tactical freighters are

being supplied by the Soviet Union, the first four aircraft having arrived late in 1977, and these are expected to replace the older types currently in FPA service. AeroPeru, the result of a reorganisation of Satco, the airline element of the air force, has three Fokker F28s and two F27-600s for services within the country. Grupo 8 operates 18 Beech Queen Airs on liaison duties, while 12 Pilatus Turbo-Porters are used for light transport tasks. A Presidential Flight operates a Fokker F28. Helicopters include 17 Bell 212s, 20 Bell 47Gs. 12 Aérospatiale (Sud) Alouette IIIs and six Soviet-supplied Mil Mi-8s, the last mentioned being used mainly for oil-exploration work. Also in service are five Mi-6 heavy-lift helicopters delivered last year. Training duties

are performed by 19 Cessna T-41As, six Pitts S-2As, 26 Cessna T-37Bs, six Beech T-34s, 15 North American T-6s and eight Lockheed T-33As in the armed trainer role. The National Air Photographic Service uses two Gates Learjet 25Bs for survey work.

The Peruvian army operates in the liaison and communication role and has five Helio Couriers and five Cessna 185s. Eight Bell 47Gs and four Alouette IIIs fly on AOP duties.

Servicio Aeronaval: Delivered to Peru in October 1977 was the first of two Fokker F27M maritime-patrol aircraft ordered in 1976. An unconfirmed report states that a further two are on option. Nine Grumman S-2E Trackers operate from Jorge Chavez air base

on ASW duties with the Peruvian naval air arm. Fleet requirements, support work and training are performed from Callao by six Douglas C-47s and a Piper Aztec; training duties are flown by two Beech T-34s. To replace the last mentioned type, six Beech T-34C-1 Turbo-Mentors were ordered in 1977 and deliveries are complete. A further order has been fulfilled for six anti-submarine Agusta AB 212 ASW helicopters for use aboard frigates being built in Italy for the Peruvian navy. Other helicopters include 10 Bell JetRangers, two Alouette IIIs, five Bell 47Gs and six Bell UH-1D/Hs; four Agusta-built SH-3Ds have been ordered. A total of 42 Mi-8s are in the naval inventory, of which 36 are currently in store.

Chile

Fuerza Aerea de Chile: Opposition to the present right-wing Chilean government by Britain continues, thus precluding any arms dealing between the two countries, particularly Hawker Siddeley Hunter spares and overhauls. Chile has therefore turned to the USA for modern combat aircraft, acquiring batches of Cessna A-37s and some Northrop F-5Es, while from Brazil she has purchased transport, maritime patrol and training aircraft. The FAC is organised into Grupos Aereos (Air Groups), each made up of one Escuadrilla or squadron. The prime front-line unit is Grupo 7 at Antofagasta in the north of the country, operating the 15 Northrop F-5Es and three two-seat F-5Fs ordered in 1974 and delivered two years later. Two fighter-bomber units, Grupos 8 and 9 at the same base are equipped with 33 HS Hunter FGA.71s and five Hunter T.72 two-seaters, delivered in batches since 1967. It was revealed officially in June 1978 that as a result of lack of spares only 20 Hunters were still flying. A further two light strike Grupos, No 1 at Iquique and No 12 at Punta Arenas, have the Cessna A-37Bs, with a total of 34 aircraft between them from two batches delivered in 1975 and 1977.

For heavy transport work, Grupo 10 at Los Cerrillos is equipped with two Lockheed C-130H Hercules as well as five Douglas DC-6As, one Aérospatiale SA.330 Puma and about 10 Douglas C-47s. Light utility duties and communications work is flown by Grupo 5 at Puerto Montt, with nearly 20 DHC Twin Otters, and Grupo 6 at Punta Arenas, equipped with five Beech Twin Bonanzas. Helicopters are encompassed within Grupo 3 at Temuco and number six Sikorsky S-55Ts, six Hiller SL-4s and six UH-12Es, 10 Bell UH-1Hs, and six Aérospatiale Lamas for SAR flights. At Quintero, Grupo 11 operates nine Beech 99s for navigation training, while for jet tuition there are 30 Cessna T-37Bs. Some 50 Beech T-34s and a number of Cessna T-41s are flown on piston-engined training duties. Also at Quintero is Grupo 2, which operates Grumman HU-16B Albatross amphibians in the SAR and ASW roles. For survey duties the Servicio de Aerofotogrametrico at Los Cerrillos

air base operates two Gates Learjet 35s and a Beech King Air 100.

Armada de Chile: The Chilean Navy air component operates five HU-16B Albatross on SAR and coastal patrol duties, while a land-based element with four ex-USN Lockheed SP-2E Neptunes flies long-range ASW and MR missions. Helicopter SAR duties are performed by some Aérospatiale Alouette IIIs, four Bell JetRangers and 14 Bell 47Gs. For transport and fleet requirement

duties there are two CASA C-212s, three EMBRAER EMB-110C Bandeirantes and a Piper Navajo, with about six Beech T-34As flown on training work. A further six aircraft, this time of the EMB-111A (M) maritime patrol version, were ordered in 1977 and deliveries have been made.

Ejército de Chile: The air element of the Chilean Army is equipped with nine Aérospatiale SA.330 Pumas, two Bell JetRangers, three Bell UH-1Hs and six

Aérospatiale Lama rescue helicopters. A fixed-wing portion used for liaison and utility work operates two CASA C-212 light transports, four Cessna O-1 Bird Dogs, two Piper Cherokee Sixes and at least four Piper Navajos. Ten Neiva T-25 Universals were acquired in 1975 for the dual strike/trainer role, and 18 Cessna Hawk XPs are in service at Santiago for basic training. In addition a number of civilian light aircraft are at the disposal of the force.

The Cessna A-37B Dragonfly equips two light strike units of the Fuerza Aerea de Chile.

Uruguay

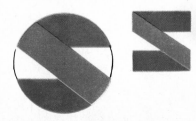

Fuerza Aérea Uruguaya: Few modern aircraft have been acquired by the FAU over the past year and even the reported transfer of 20

North American F-86F Sabres from Argentina has failed to materialise, the deal being vetoed by the US Government. The air force is currently made up of three commands: Tactical Air Command with two Air Brigades, Training Air Command and Material Air Command. Aircraft have in the main been supplied by the USA, although some equipment has been bought from Brazil. Air Brigade 1 controls Aviation Group 1 (Fighter), equipped with six armed Lockheed AT-33As; Aviation Groups 3 and 4 (Transport), flying 12 Douglas C-47s, three Fairchild FH.227s, two Fokker F27 Mk 100s and two Beech Queen Air liaison

aircraft; Aviation Group 5 (Seek and Attack), equipped with eight Cessna A-37Bs delivered in 1976; and Aviation Group 6, flying four EMBRAER EMB-110 Bandeirante light transports for both civil and military use. A further Bandeirante — designated EMB-110B1 — is used by AG 6 for dual photo/transport work.

Air Brigade 2 controls only one Group, No 1 (Tactical Reconnaissance), operating 10 North American T-6Gs, 10 Beech AT-11s and six Cessna U-17 Skywagons. Helicopters include two Hiller UH-12s for SAR work, two Bell UH-1Hs and four UH-1Bs for troop-

carrying duties. Training Command has a Command and Air Staff School equipped with about six Cessna T-41s and a couple of Beech C-45s.

Aviación Naval Uruguaya: Flying from the shore bases of Punta del Este and Laguna del Sauce are three Grumman S-2A Trackers used for ASW patrols. These are supported by three Beech SNB-5s flown for training, a Beech T-34B for primary tuition, four T-6s and some North American SNJ-4s. Two Bell 47Gs and some Sikorsky SH-34s are flown.

Bolivia

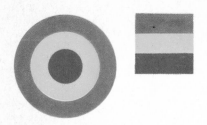

Fuerza Aerea Boliviana: Established as a separate military force in September 1957, the Bolivian Air Force (FAB) has divested itself of much of its outdated equipment acquired over the years since World War II. It recently traded six of its seven remaining air-worthy Cavalier F-51D Mustangs for five more Lockheed/Canadair T-33A/Ns — the seventh Mustang being retained for a museum. The T-33s have been acquired from ex-Canadian stocks and join 10 survivors of 13 aircraft of a similar type delivered some years ago; they equip the Air Pursuit Group (*Grupo Aereo de Caza*) at El Alto air base. For interception duties an Air Pursuit Group at Santa Cruz operates five ex-Venezuelan North American F-86F Sabres, but the service is known to be keen to procure a more modern combat aircraft; types under consideration include the Northrop F-5E and the EMBRAER AT-26 Xavante. Twelve Hughes 500M helicopter gunships, delivered in 1968, equip the Special Air Operations Group (*Grupo de Operacoes Aereas Especiais*) at Reboré. Based at Tarija is Air Cover Group No 1 (*Grupo Aereo de Cobertura*) flying 12 North-American AT-6 strike aircraft, while a Combined Air Group (*Grupo Aereo Misto*) at Cochabamba operates a number of Bell UH-1Hs delivered in 1975, a number of Aérospatiale Lama rescue helicopters and some North American T-6s.

A military airline, *Transportes Aereos Militares,* forms the transport wing of the air force, providing passenger and cargo services to remote areas. Main base is at El Alto, La Paz, and the largest type in use at present is the Lockheed C-130H, of which three are in use. Other aircraft flown by the unit total one Lockheed Electra, two Douglas DC-6s, three of six Convair CV-440s purchased in 1972, four Convair CV-580s, two DC-4s, six of seven IAI Arava light transports and seven Douglas C-47s. For Presidential use the FAB has a Rockwell Sabreliner 60. Liaison and utility work are performed by 15 Cessna 185s, two Cessna Turbo Centurions and two Cessna 402s. In addition there is a single Fairchild Turbo-Porter, two Beech Super King Air 200s and a Cessna 421B. The Military Aviation College at Santa Cruz conducts primary and advanced tuition on Brazilian and American aircraft types. As a result of congestion at the joint civil and military airfield, the college is to move to Santa Rosa by 1982. Present equipment is divided into two Flight Sqns, the first operating about 12 Aerotec T-23 Uirapuru of 18 originally delivered for primary cadet training, and the second unit having ten T-6s and two North American T-28 Trojans for basic work; six Italian SIAI-Marchetti SF.260Ms have been received to modernise this part of the training syllabus. Replacing the older piston-engined trainers are a batch of Pilatus PC-7 Turbo-Trainers, understood to total 14. Six Cessna T-41Ds and some Cessna 310s are also in use. The National Photogrammetry Service operates a single Gates Learjet 25B received in late 1975 and fitted with a Wild RC-10 camera; more recently a Cessna 402 joined the service, similarly adapted for aerial photography.

Paraguay

Fuerza Aerea del Paraguaya: A single counter-insurgency squadron with 12 armed North American T-6s constituted the sole combat element of this air force until late in 1978 when the USA supplied the FAP with six Cessna A-37Bs. For transport and supply work there is an assortment of types including five ex-Varig Douglas DC-6Bs donated by Brazil in 1976, 10 Douglas C-47s, two Douglas C-54s, on Convair C-131, one DHC Twin Otter and a single DHC Otter. Helicopters number 14 Bell H-13s and three Hiller 12Es. Training is conducted on eight ex-Brazilian Fokker S-11 primary trainers, eight Aerotec T-23 Uirapurus, 10 North American T-6s and an armed Morane-Saulnier MS.760 Paris. Five Cessna 185s fly liaison duties and the navy has two Bell 47Gs for river patrol and communications work plus two Cessna 150M trainers.

Argentina

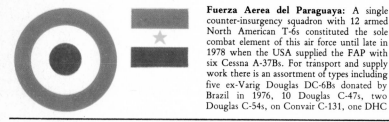

Fuerza Aerea Argentina: The FAA's flying elements are operated within the responsibility of Air Operations Command, within which are five Air Brigades. Each brigade, which roughly equates to an RAF wing, has up to three squadrons, each with a nominal establishment of three four-aircraft elements. The Second Air Brigade (II *Brigada Aerea*), with headquarters at General Urquiza air base, Entre Rios, controls I *Escuadron de Bombardeo* (nine BAC Canberra B.62s and two T.64s) and II *Escuadron de Exploración y Ataque* (25 FMA IA 35 Huanqueros and about 12 of the 30 FMA IA 58 Pucará COIN aircraft ordered). Delivery of Pucarás to Reconquista air base — home of II *Escuadron,* one of two squadrons scheduled to get the type — has been well behind schedule; the FAA's requirement still stands at about 100 aircraft. The remaining II Brigade squadron is I *Escuadron Fotografico,* equipped with about 20 IA 35s.

Under the control of IV *Brigada Aerea* is I *Escuadron* at El Plumerillo air base, Mendoza, with 25 McDonnell Douglas A-4P Skyhawk fighter-bombers replacing 20 North American F-86F Sabres which have been placed in storage, and II and III *Escuadron* equipped with locally-built Morane-Saulnier MS.760 Paris armed trainers. McDonnell Douglas A-4P Skyhawks also form the main equipment of the IV and V *Escuadron de Caza-Bombardeo* of the V *Brigada Aerea* at General Pringles air base, San Luis. The Skyhawks are refurbished US Navy A-4B/Cs delivered in 1966 and 1970; some 45 are in use with V *Brigada,* making a total inventory of some 70 aircraft. To update these machines, Ferranti D126R Isis weapons-aiming sights are being fitted following an initial order placed in 1976; further orders are likely.

The VII *Brigada Aerea* at Moron air base, Buenos Aires, operates the FAA's sole interceptor unit — I *Escuadron de Caza,* equipped with Dassault Mirages. A total of 12 IIIEAs and two IIIDAs are in service, and plans for the purchase of a further 80 Mirages have been shelved for economic reasons. Instead seven more IIIEAs have been ordered to make up for attrition, and 26 Israeli-built versions of the Dassault Mirage, known as Daggers and powered by SNECMA Átar engines, have been delivered. In addition, the Brigade has a helicopter attack squadron, I *Escuadron de Exploración y Ataque,* equipped with 14 Hughes 300Ms and six Bell UH-1H gunships.

For transport duties I *Brigada Aerea* at El Palomar air base, Buenos Aires, comprises I *Escuadron* with three Lockheed C-130E and four C-130H Hercules (a fifth C-130H was destroyed in 1975); a VIP unit for presidential and government use flying one BAe (Hawker-Siddeley Aviation) HS 748 Srs 2, one Fokker-VFW F.28 Mk 1000C, one Rockwell Sabreliner and a Boeing 707-320B; and a unit with 22 FMA IA 50 Guarani IIs (including 14 transports, two survey and one VIP version). El Palomar, base for a number of C-47s, is also HQ of the state military airline LADE (*Lineas Aereas del Estado*), which operates passenger and cargo services to remote areas of the country. The airline's fleet comprises five F.28 Mk 100Cs, five Fokker-VFW F.27 Mk 400s, five F.27 Mk 600s, three Douglas DC-6s and seven DHC Twin Otters.

For short-range liaison work there are 14 Rockwell Shrike Commanders and an SAR unit — *Escuadron de Busqueda y Salvamento* — equipped with three Grumman HU-16B Albatross for coastal duties and six Aérospatiale Lamas for high-altitude rescue. Delivery of two Swearingen Merlin IVAs for air force aeromedical work has been made. For logistic support of Argentina's Antarctic bases, I *Escuadron Antartico* operates from Rio Gallegos, Santa Cruz, equipped with a number of types including one Sikorsky S-61R, three DHC Beavers, three DHC Otters and one Douglas LC-47. Helicopters in FAA include two S-61NRs, four Bell UH-1Ds, six Sikorsky UH-19s and four Bell 47Gs. For general-purpose duties, eight Bell 212s were ordered in February 1978, with deliveries made in the summer, and five Boeing-Vertol CH-47C Chinooks have been ordered for joint air force and army use.

Training duties come under the command of the *Grupo Aerea Escuela,* and flying training is conducted on some 35 Beech T-34As and 12 MS.760 Paris trainers at Cordoba. A replacement for the long-serving T-34s is actively

The Fuerza Aerea Argentina's II Escuadron flies the locally built IA.58 Pucará.

being sought, one proposal being the FMA IA 62 project announced in 1977. For operational conversion, pilots move to the squadrons at brigade level.

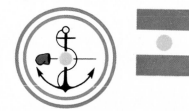

Comando de Aviación Naval Argentina: The navy operates a single aircraft-carrier, the 16,000-ton ex-Royal Netherlands Navy *Karel Doorman,* since renamed *25 de Mayo,* aboard which are deployed detachments of McDonnell Douglas A-4Q Skyhawks and Grumman S-2A Trackers, from a total of 15 and six respectively. The service in 1978 received four ex-USN S-2Es to replace the older As, and these are shore-based at Comandante Espora NAB. The *Armada Argentina* also operates eight Aermacchi M.B. 326GB jet trainers for continuation training in connection with the A-4Q squadron. At the Naval Training School at Punta de Indio air base some 28 North American T-28 Fennecs provide pilot training for both shore and carrier operations; a number of Beech AT-11s are used for twin conversion. To modernise the naval training programme, 15 Beech T-34Cs have been delivered, to replace the ageing T-28s. Maritime reconnaissance is performed by 10 Lockheed SP-2H Neptunes, four having been acquired from US stocks in 1977, and a few remaining Consolidated PBY-5A Catalinas. Fleet support and transport duties are flown by eight Douglas C-47s, three Lockheed L.188 Electras, three Douglas C-54s, two Douglas DC-4s, one Guarani II, and one BAe (Hawker Siddeley) HS 125-400 for calibration work. Three DHC Beavers, a DHC Twin Otter, two Beech Super King Air 200s and about four Queen Airs are flown on communication duties. The helicopter force is grouped into No 4 Naval Air Wing at Comandante Espora, and has nine Aérospatiale Alouette IIIs, four Sikorsky S-61D Sea Kings, five Sikorsky S-55s and a few Bell 47Gs. Two Westland Lynx HAS.23 ASW helicopters have been received to equip Argentinian frigates.

A small coastguard force known as *Prefectura Naval Argentina* is equipped with five Short Skyvan 3M transports and six Hughes 500M helicopters.

Comando de Aviación del Ejército: The Argentine Army has a fixed-wing fleet of four Piper Navajos, two DHC Twin Otters, one Beech Queen Air, one Beech King Air and a Rockwell Sabreliner for VIP use. Five Rockwell Turbo Commander 690As are being procured from a batch being assembled in the country. By far the largest type in use is the Aeritalia G222 STOL transport, three of which have been procured. The army is also receiving four Swearingen Merlin IIIAs for liaison and VIP work. Helicopters total six Aérospatiale Lamas delivered in 1975, seven Fairchild-Hiller FH-1100s, seven Bell JetRangers, 20 Bell UH-1Hs, two Bell 212s and two Bell 47Gs. Five Cessna 207 Turbo Skywagons carry out tactical and AOP duties, and five Cessna T-41Ds are flown on training work. For survey and mapping work, the Army uses a specially modified Cessna Citation fitted with Wild RC-10 cameras, while for use in the Andes, three Pilatus Turbo-Porters have been purchased.

North America

If Britain is vulnerable to air attack, having only some 70 home-based interceptors, the United States is positively naked, having just over 300 air-defence fighters — a mixture of F-4D Phantoms, F-106 Delta Darts and even older F-101 Voodoos flown by the USAF and Air National Guard. Most of the Nike-Hercules SAM batteries have also been phased out.

It is hardly surprising that the appearance of the Soviet Tu-26 Backfire bomber has created alarm in US political and defence circles. The age of the intercontinental ballistic missile has so diverted attention from the threat posed by manned aircraft that the US homeland would be wide open to attack by a new generation of strategic bombers.

Growing accuracy of Soviet ballistic missiles may soon make the USAF ICBM force vulnerable — in theory at least — to a first strike intended to blunt any US counterattack. With this leg of the strategic "Triad" apparently open to attack, President Carter's decision to reduce the B-1 bomber to a research and development project seems rash. In the 1980s, Strategic Air Command will be operating B-52 bombers so old as to be by USAF rules vintage aircraft.

Like most wars, the Vietnam conflict focused attention on short-term improvements to existing aircraft, especially since nearly all types then in use by the US armed forces were totally unsuited to limited warfare. The giant jolt which that conflict gave to the US defence establishment, and especially to the procurement machine, has since 1970 been compounded by accelerating inflation which, taken in conjunction with public disenchantment with defence, has made it much more difficult to match the Soviet Union even in quality of weapons, let alone in quantity. Almost total absence of any modern ICBM, especially one that cannot be caught at a fixed location, and run-down in manned bombers, has not been balanced by any increase in tactical strength, though the F-15 and A-10 are providing important new capabilities that by the mid-1980s will be numerically powerful. The Navy and Marines are likewise being modernised by the F-14 and F-18 and may eventually surmount political hurdles and achieve a dispersed-base V/STOL capability with the potentially vital AV-8BS.

Lack of money, however, has resulted in replacement of the C-130 being shelved, the KC-10A Extender being bought two at a time, and a complete absence of a modern first-pass attack platform in the class of the European Tornado. Canada has been even more hit by shortage of funds, and at the time of writing appears to have to settle for one of the relatively limited US tactical aircraft — the F-16 or F-18 — to replace the CF-101 and CF-104.

Canada **56**   United States of America **53**

United States of America

United States Air Force: The Strategic Air Command maintains the USAF deterrent and all nine ICBM wings, and the manned bomber force comes under its control within the 8th and 15th Air Forces. The bomber element has 19 wings of Boeing B-52s, comprising 269 B-52G/Hs (some equipped with SRAMs and fitted with an electro-optical viewing system) and 80 structurally modified B-52Ds. Only one B-52 unit is now permanently based overseas, the 43rd Wing on Guam; approximately 20 home-based B-52Fs equip one training unit. SAC B-52s began sea-surveillance flights in 1976 in co-operation with the US Navy, in addition to their regular long-range strategic missions. Each of the bomber wings has attached to it an associated Boeing KC-135 Stratotanker element. Formed into 35 squadrons with 615 aircraft, these also support other commands on air-refuelling duties and include 80 aircraft assigned to the Air Reserve Force. Four squadrons in two wings, the 380th and 509th, operate 70 SRAM-equipped FB-111As, while SAC's reconnaissance force comprises the 9th Strategic Reconnaissance Wing with nine Lockheed SR-71s and its supporting KC-135Q tankers at Beale AFB. Two further wings with 20 Lockheed U-2s, nine DC-130s (for drone launching), and about 50 Boeing RC-135s and EC-135s fly a variety of tasks, including electronic reconnaissance, atomic sampling, etc. In addition, 12 Air Guard units fly KC-135s assigned to SAC duties, and eventually 14 ANG units will have KC-135s.

Aerospace Defense Command, while regarded more as a missile warning force, still maintains its important air-defence commitment over the continental US with the co-operation of the Canadians under the North American Air Defence Command (NORAD). The interceptor force comprises six active and six Air National Guard General Dynamics (Convair) F-106 squadrons totalling some 150 aircraft (reducing to five units as one squadron converted to F-4s in 1978), three McDonnell

Douglas F-101B Voodoo ANG units with 60 aircraft and two McDonnell Douglas F-4 Phantom units, one based in Iceland (57th FIS) and the other in Hawaii (154th FIG). There are two groups of Martin EB-57s with the ANG and a further squadron in the active inventory. The ADC's Lockheed EC-121 Warning Star element has been centralised at Homestead AFB, Fla, under the command of the Air Force Reserve. All 10 remaining EC-121Ts are now assigned to AFRES, seven flying from Florida and three from Iceland. Plans call for the replacement of the F-106s by a new interceptor and the replacement of the Voodoo force with F-4s.

The Tactical Air Command is the USAF's quick-reaction force, incorporating fighter, reconnaissance, transport and special operations units. Approximately 1,700 aircraft operate within TAC and its two air forces, the 9th with headquarters at Shaw AFB, SC, and 12th headquartered at Bergstrom AFB, Tex.

TAC is currently phasing a number of new types into service. Following a year with the 355th TF Training Wing at Davis-Monthan AFB, Fairchild A-10As are now fully operational with the 354th TFW at Myrtle Beach. Funding has so far been allocated for 339 aircraft. Plans call for a total of five wings of A-10s, each with four 18-aircraft squadrons.

The eventual total USAF buy remains at 733 machines. McDonnell Douglas F-15s are now fully operational with the 1st TFW at Langley AFB, the 49th TFW at Hollman and the 33rd TFW at Eglin, the last-mentioned brought to operational status by October 1979. More than 400 F-15s have been delivered out of a total of 729 plus 20 development aircraft scheduled for USAF service with a total of 19 squadrons.

In March 1977 the 552nd Airborne Warning and Control Wing at Tinker AFB received its first Boeing E-3A AWACS aircraft, rising to 16 by early 1979. The first F-16 wing is the 388th TFW at Hill AFB, which received its

By late 1979 the USAF had received 60 per cent of its planned force of 729 F-15 Eagle fighters. This F-15A, with AIM-7E2 and AIM-9J missiles, was one of the first to be delivered to the first operator, the 1st Tac Ftr Wing at Langley AFB.

continued

53

first aircraft early in 1979. Present types in use include two active AF squadrons with 44 Republic F-105G 'Wild Weasel' Thunderchiefs, eight squadrons with 210 Vought A-7Ds, eight General Dynamics F-111E/F squadrons with 180 aircraft, seven RF-4C squadrons with 121 aircraft, and 30 squadrons with 664 F-4C/D/E Phantoms. Seven special-operations squadrons fly 42 Rockwell OV-10As, 68 Cessna O-2A/Bs, 27 C/AC-130s and five EC-135s. Most of TAC's 82 Northrop T-38s and 66 F-5Es are used for 'Red Flag' combat training at Nellis AFB, Nev. Total TAC helicopter inventory is 19 Bell UH-1s, 15 Sikorsky CH-3s and four Sikorsky CH-53s. A total of 20 Lockheed TR-1 high-altitude reconnaissance aircraft are on order for the possible use of TAC. Air National Guard units attached to TAC include three wings and five groups of Vought A-7D Corsair IIs, four wings and eight groups of North American F-100D Super Sabres, two wings and two groups of F-105B/Ds, two Cessna A-37B groups, two wings and six groups of F/RF-4Cs, one RF-101 group, and two wings and four groups of O-2As.

US Air Forces Europe is a part of NATO, with some 28 squadrons based with the 3rd AF in the UK, 16th in Spain and 17th in Germany. Planned for USAFE are three wings of Fairchild A-10As to be based in Europe, one (81st TFW at Bentwaters with six squadrons) based in England and two in Germany at Sembach and Leipheim; first deliveries were made in January 1979. The second unit to get F-15 Eagles was the 32nd TFS at Soesterburg. The first F-15 wing is the 36th TFW at Bitburg, which has 72 aircraft. Another new type is the Northrop F-5E Tiger, 20 of which equip the 527th TF Training Aggressor Sqn at Alconbury. At RAF Lakenheath the 48th TFW has exchanged its F-4Ds for F-111Fs. About 400 F-4 Phantoms equip five wings of 14 squadrons (81st TFW, Bentwaters, UK; 401st TFW Torrejón, Spain; 50th TFW, Hahn, Germany; 52nd TFW, Spangdahlem, Germany; 86th TFW, Ramstein, Germany). Other major USAFE units include one wing (20th TFW, Upper Heyford, UK) of three squadrons of 80 F-111Es, two reconnaissance wings with 60 RF-4Cs (one squadron with the 10th TRW at Alconbury, UK, and two squadrons with the 26th TRW at Zweibrucken, Germany), and a rotational squadron of some 15 C-130E/Hs detached to Mildenhall in the UK. At the same base are a number of SAC rotational KC-135s. For aeromedical duties four McDonnell Douglas C-9A Nightingale transports are based at Rhein-Main, Germany. At the same base there is another C-130E/H squadron rotated from the USA. At Sembach 30 OV-10As are deployed with the 601st Tactical Control Wing, which also has seven CH-53Cs. Located at Woodbridge, UK, the 67th ARRS is controlled by Military Airlift Command (MAC) but provides rescue helicopters and aircraft for all Europe in the shape of four Sikorsky HH-53Cs and seven HC-130H/Ns. A number of support units are based in Europe, flying Rockwell T-39s, Beech C-12As, Lockheed VC-140Bs, Bell UH-1Ns and HH-1Hs.

The Pacific Air Forces, with is headquarters in Hawaii, comprises the 5th AF based in Japan and 13th AF in the Philippines. Main units are as follows: under 5th AF command, 8th TFW at Kunsan AB, Korea, with F-4s; 18th TFW at Kadena AB, Okinawa, with 90 F-4/RF-4Cs; and the 51st Composite Wing at Osan AB, Korea, with F-4s and OV-10s. The 3rd TFW is based at Clark AFB, Philippines, and flies F-4s and a squadron (26th TF Training Sqn) of F-5Es, while at Hickham itself a support wing has a number of EC-135s, Lockheed T-33As and O-2s.

The Alaskan Air Command operates from Elmendorf AFB and has a C-130E squadron (17th ARRS), an F-4E squadron with 26 aircraft assigned to ADC (43rd TFS), an HH-3E/HC-130 squadron for SAR duties (71st ARRS), and a tactical operations unit with T-33s, EB-57s and a T-39 (5041st TOS). Also operated is the 25th Tac Support Sqn with O-2s at Eielson and an Air Guard unit with eight C-130s (176th TAG).

Military Airlift Command includes the Air Weather Service, the Aerospace Rescue and Recovery Service and the Aeromedical Airlift Wing. Two Air Forces, the 21st and 22nd, incorporate 13 squadrons with 271 Lockheed C-141s (to be stretched to C-141B standard) and four squadrons with 76 Lockheed C-5As. Six other squadrons have 23 C-9As. Six other squadrons have 23 C-9As (including three VC-9Cs with the 89th MAW), 11 VC-140s, two Boeing VC-137s, three VC-137Bs, four Convair C-131s, 11 C-135s and 14 WC-130s. The large tactical force of C-130E/H Hercules has some 276 aircraft flying with 14 active AF units, while the supporting Air National Guard inventory has 13 groups and five wings of C-130s. Also MAC-assigned is an ANG group of 19 DHC C-7 Caribous and two groups flying HH-3/HC-130 rescue aircraft. Three T-39 training/liaison units are attached to the 89th MAW with 105 aircraft, and being delivered are 34 C-12s for the use of air at-

Northrop delivered 1,187 T-38 Talons, which apart from the Japanese T-1 are the only supersonic trainers (other than dual versions of combat aircraft). USAF Air Training Command still operates more than 725 of these unusual but popular machines.

tachés around the world. Helicopters include more than 120 Bell UH-1Fs for missile site support, 30 UH-1Hs for base rescue duties, 51 HH-1Ns, 46 HH-3Es and 33 of 72 HH-53B/Cs in USAF service.

The Air Training Command with headquarters at Randolph AFB, Texas, operates a total of 1,629 aircraft, comprising 692 Cessna T-37s, 822 Northrop T-38s, 96 Cessna T-41s and 19 Boeing T-43s. The Navigator Training Wing at Mather AFB, Calif, operates as a joint USAF/USN/USMC/Coast Guard unit with the T-43s. At the USAF Academy, Colorado Springs, two DHC UV-18B Twin Otters, delivered in 1977 provide platforms for cadet parachute training. The Air Force Reserve is a large unmobilised training and support element with headquarters at Dobbins AFB, Ga, and flies many of the roles of the active AF. Reserve elements are divided into three air forces (4th, 10th and 14th AF) within the US, flying 11 C-130 squadrons, two DH C-7 squadrons, four Fairchild C-123K squadrons, two KC-135 squadrons, one EC-121T unit, three F-105 squadrons, five A-37B squadrons, one AC-130 unit, four ARRS squadrons with HH-1H, HH-3E and HC-130 aircraft, one CH-3E unit and a weather squadron with WC-130s.

The USAF's re-equipment programme is now well under way, with new types steadily replacing older combat aircraft. McDonnell Douglas F-15 Eagles and Fairchild A-10A Thunderbolt IIs are giving the Tactical Air Command new muscle in the air-superiority and ground-attack fields. In 1980, the air force plans to introduce the General Dynamics F-16 air combat fighter into service; 1,388 are required (including 98 two-seat F-16Bs), of which 200 are to be based in Europe. A large part of the USA's deterring ability in the future was to have been based on the Rockwell B-1A variable-geometry strategic bomber, but this was cancelled in June 1977. However, the USAF continues to finance the programme and four prototype aircraft are flying. The reinstatement of this project is apparently dependent on the SALT negotiations with the Soviet Union, and if continued a total of 241 B-1As would be procured. Another cancelled programme is the AMST Lockheed C-130 replacement. The two aircraft involved, the Boeing YC-14 and McDonnell Douglas YC-15, are being proposed as possible cruise-missile carriers. A total of 34 Boeing E-3A AWACS aircraft is still seen as the USAF requirement for an efficient force. So far three R&D and 16 production aircraft have been funded, with six E-3As in service by early this year. Boeing's other major military programme, the E-4 Command Post, continues with three aircraft delivered, a fourth ordered as an E-4B and two more planned. To meet the USAF's Advanced Tanker/Cargo Aircraft (ATCA) requirement, 20 McDonnell Douglas KC-10As have been ordered in a first contract worth $28 million, which will cover initial engineering and the purchase of long-lead items.

United States Navy: The USN operates a fleet of 13 attack carriers, with the *Dwight D. Eisenhower* commissioned in 1978 and the *Carl Vinson* under construction for service in 1981. The important McDonnell Douglas F-18 Hornet Naval Strike Fighter programme is now underway following the first flight of the prototype in November 1978 which is due to be followed by 11 development aircraft. The first of a planned 800 aircraft are expected to join the US Navy and USMC in 1982, initially replacing Phantoms. Six active and four reserve Navy squadrons (185 aircraft) are due to receive F-18s, and 345 of the type will replace Vaght A-7s later in the 1980s. Also on order are 278 Beech T-34C Turbo-Mentors for the training units, and from the same company T-44As are being delivered for multi-engine training, replacing T-2B/Cs. Grumman F-14A Tomcats continue to join USN squadrons, with 12 units fully equipped and deployed. More than 350 had been delivered up to the beginning of 1980 and full procurement stands at 521 aircraft. Some of the F-14As are being converted to the reconnaissance role. All 187 Lockheed S-3A Vikings have been delivered to the 12 ASW squadrons assigned the type. The US Navy's LAMPS competition was won by the Sikorsky SH-60, and the first of four prototypes made its initial flight in 1979; the total requirement stands at 204 Sh-60s. From the same company, the USN is buying 18 CH-53E heavy-lift helicopters.

Each of the attack carriers has approximately 85-95 aircraft organised into a Carrier Air

So-called 'snake' or 'lizard' camouflage covers the A-10A Thunderbolt II close air support aircraft of the six squadrons of the 81st Tac Ftr Wing of USAF Europe, which operate from RAF Bentwaters in the UK and four forward bases in W. Germany.

Wing with the following units: two interceptor squadrons with F-4B/Js or F-14As, two to four attack squadrons with A-7s or Grumman A-6s, a detachment from one of five reconnaissance squadrons with Rockwell RA-5C Vigilantes, a detachment from an electronic warfare squadron with Grumman EA-6B Prowlers or EA-6As transferred from the USMC, a detachment from an AEW squadron with Grumman E-2B/C Hawkeyes, and a detachment from a helicopter support squadron with Kaman H-2 seasprites. A variation on the CAW used by some attack carriers has been occasioned by the run-down in ASW carriers. These attack carriers, such as the USSS *Saratoga* and *Kennedy*, now operate two F-14 units, two A-7 units with a reduced complement, one A-6E unit, one ASW unit with Sikorsky SH-3s or Lockheed S-3As and one EA-6B electronic warfare unit. A total of 65 E-2A/B Hawkeyes have been delivered, and there are 77 E-2Cs delivered or on order.

Currently the US Navy has nearly 1,900 combat aircraft in 28 interceptor squadrons (F-4/F-14), 41 attack squadrons (27 with A-7s, 12 with A-6s and two with A-4s) and six reconnaissance squadrons with RA-5s and one with Vought RF-8Gs. Land-based long-range maritime patrol duties are performed by 24 squadrons in five patrol wings with about 280 Lockheed P-3A/B/C/ Orions of some 428 delivered to the service. Twelve EP-3Es are flying in the recce role, together with some Convair EC-131s and Lockheed EC-130s. There are seven helicopter support squadrons with Kaman UH-2s, Boeing UH-46s and HH-2Ds, and a mine counter-measures unit with 30 RH-53Ds. Ten Sikorsky SH-3 ASW squadrons have some 80 aircraft, while six transport squadrons provide worldwide fleet support equipped with 30 Douglas C-118s, seven C-130Fs, 12 C-9Bs, 12 Rockwell CT-39s, 20 Grumman C-1s and 12 Grumman C-2s. Late in 1977, the USN ordered 22 Beech C-12As for liaison duties, with an anticipated total procurement of 66 aircraft. Twenty training squadrons in seven wings operate Lockheed T-1As. Convair T-2B/Cs, LTV T-28s North American TA-4Fs, McDonnell Douglas TS-2As and Grumman T-29Bs. Sixty TA-7Cs have been ordered for conversion from existing A-7B/C Corsairs for advanced training. A Fighter Training Aggressor Sqn is equipped with 10 F-Es and three two-seat F-5Fs. Helicopter training is conducted on Bell TH-1s, Bell UH-1Ds and Bell TH-57As.

In addition to the active units, the US Navy and Marine Corps have a number of Reserve units; four of F-4s, three of A-7s, three of A-4s, two of RF-8Gs, two of Douglas KA-3s, and two Grumman E-1 squadrons. There are also two S-2 units, three SH-3 units, eight with P-3As, four with Lockheed SP-2Hs and three with C-118s.

United State Marine Corps: This compact air force supports US Marine ground troops wherever they operate and is divided into three Marine Air Wings (1st MAW at Okinawa, 2nd MAW at Cherry Point, 3rd MAW at El Toro) with the 4th MAW at Glenview controlling reserve forces. Most numerous type in the USMC inventory is the F-4 Phantom, and 12 fighter-bomber squadrons are equipped with 144 F-4B/Js which have been converted to F-4N/S standard. Some 270 McDonnell Douglas F-18 Hornets are planned to replace the F-4s in the mid-1980s following the transfer of the F-14 order to the US Navy. In the light attack role there are five squadrons with about 70 A-4F/M Skyhawks, and three squadrons and a training unit flying 110 BAe AV-8A Harriers, including eight two-seat TAV-8As. A total of 336 AV-8Bs is required by the USMC to replace the -8As and A-4s at present in use, but development work on the project has been temporarily halted in the FY79 budget. Five all-weather attack squadrons have some 60 A-6A/E Intruders, while three reconnaissance squadrons operate a total of 42 EA-6As and RF-4B Phantoms. The USMC has 15 EA-6B Prowlers on order to replace the EA-6As, and the first aircraft were delivered to VMAQ-2 late in 1977, followed by the remaining machines in 1979; the redundant EA-6As are being passed to the USN.

The USMC transport force has three

squadrons equipped with 46 KC-130F Hercules tanker/transports; up to 14 updated KC-130Rs are planned for procurement. Three C-9Bs are operated for high-speed transport duties. For observation duties there are three OV-10A squadrons, a helicopter assault force of nine squadrons flies 170 CH-46F Sea Knights, and a further six squadrons have about 100 CH-53D Sea Stallions. A batch of 33 updated CH-53E Super Stallions is on order for heavy-lift duties. Six utility squadrons operate 116 UH-1E/Ns and three attack helicopter squadrons have 74 AH-1J Sea Cobras, plus TOW-armed Bell AH-1Ts on order for the USMC, with delivery completed in 1979.

The USMC reserve force controlled by the 4th MAW has six A-4E/F attack squadrons, three F-4N fighter squadrons, one KC-130F refuelling squadron, one OV-10A unit, one AH-1G unit, two UH-1E squadrons, eight CH-46 squadrons and three CH-53A squadrons.

United States Army: The worlds largest helicopter operator, with some 9,000 machines, the US Army also has more than

1,000 fixed-wing aircraft in service. To replace the large force of some 4,000 Bell UH-1s, the Sikorsky UH-60A Black Hawk has been ordered into production, with initial procurement totalling 200 machines. Similarly, the Hughes AH-64A has been selected to replace the AH-1 HueyCobra in army service. AH-64 procurement is expected to total some 536 machines, including the three prototypes.

For liaison duties the Army has 2,200 Bell OH-58A Kiowas, and there are 1,400 Hughes OH-6A Cayuse LOHs. Fifty-four UH-1Hs are being delivered and most of the early UH-1B/C/Ds have been updated to H standard. Attack helicopter support is provided by almost 1,000 Bell AH-1Gs of which 290 have been converted to Q standard with TOW missiles. Bell AH-1S HueyCobra orders total 148. By 1984, the US Army will have a fleet of 986 fully updated AH-1S helicopters equipped with TOW antitank missiles which will include the 290 Q versions at present in service and due for modernisation in 1982-83. Older types in service include Sikorsky H-34s, Bell H-13s and Sikorsky UH-19s. Medium and heavy-lift support is performed by Boeing CH-47A/B/C Chinooksand 80 Sikorsky CH-54

Tarhe Skycranes. A large training force includes some 300 Hughes TH-55A primary helicopter trainers. Fixed-wing types include about 200 Grumman OV-1 Mohawks, and numbers of Beech U-21 Utes and Beech U-8 Seminoles. Fifty-six Beech C-12A Super King Airs, named Hurons, are being delivered for utility work, and two DHC OV-18A Twin Otters have been delivered to the Alsaka National Guard. Fixed-wing training is done on 250 Cessna T-41s and 60 Beech T-42s.

Seven Grumman F-14A Tomcats, all in tight formation with wings at 68°, present an impressive and unusual sight because this sweep angle is seldom chosen in subsonic regimes. This part-squadron comes from CVA-65 *Enterprise,* the first nuclear carrier.

For 15 years the Lockheed SR-71 series of 'Blackbird' strategic reconnaissance aircraft have been the fastest military aircraft in the world. Supported by special-fuel KC-135Q tankers, they equip SAC's 9th Strategic Recon Wing at Beale AFB.

Canada

Canadian Armed Forces — Air: Canada has one of the few unified armed forces in the world, having four commands, a Canadian Forces Europe HQ, a Northern Region HQ and a Forces Training System. The formation of Air Command on 2 September 1975 does not signify a return to the three-services system but means rather that the Canadian Armed Forces will now have three distinct commands for sea, land and air operations.

Air Command with headquarters at Winnipeg consists of four operational groups (Maritime Air Group, Air Defence Group, 10 Tactical Air Group and Air Transport Group) and exercises command and control over the Air Training Schools and the Air Reserve. It is responsible also for providing trained air and ground crews to operate the three Lockheed/Canadair CF-104 Starfighter squadrons of No 1 Canadian Air Group, which is under command and control of the Commander, Canadian Forces Europe.

Maritime Air Group operates four long-range patrol squadrons (Nos 404 and 405 Sqn at Greenwod, No 407 at Comox, BC and No 415 at Summerside) and a Maritime Patrol Evaluation Unit flying 26 Canadair CP-107 Argus aircraft. A replacement for these long-serving machines has been ordered in the form of 18 Lockheed Orion patrol aircraft, designated CP-140 Aurora in CAF service. The first Aurora is scheduled to be delivered in May 1980 and the last in March 1981. Provisional plans call for No 407 Sqn to receive the first four aircraft. A total of 16 Grumman CP-121 Trackers are shore-based and employed in short-range coastal patrols with No 880 MR Squadron at Shearwater and No 406 Operational Training Squadron on the east coast at Halifax, and VU-33 at Comox on the west coast. In addition to the fixed-wing aircraft, Maritime Air Group operates a fleet of 32 Sikorsky CH-124 Sea King helicopters. Two squadrons, HS-423 and HS-443 at Halifax, provide helicopters and crews to operate from destroyers and replenishment ships of Maritime Command.

Air Defence Group is integrated with the USAF through the NORAD joint air defence agreement and has an aircraft complement of four squadrons including an operational training squadron flying 56 McDonnell Douglas CF-101B Voodoos (Nos 409 Sqn at Comox, 416 Sqn at Chatham, 425 Sqn at Bagotville and 410 Sqn also at Bagotville). No 414 Sqn has an electronic warfare role and for this task operates a few remaining Canadair CF-100 Mk 5 Canucks and some Canadair CT-133 Silver Stars from North Bay. Also flown by this squadron are three Dassault CC-117 Falcons converted into ECM trainers.

10 Tactical Air Group operates all air resources engaged in close support of the army. It has two squadrons, Nos 433 at Bagotville and 434 at Cold Lake, Alta, of Canadair CF-5As totalling 24 aircraft with air-to-air refuelling capability. Approximately 25 CF-5As are in storage. The helicopter fleet of 56 Bell CH-118 Iroquois, 74 Boeing CH-136 Kiowas and seven Boeing-Vertol CH-147 Chinooks supports six squadrons (Nos 408, 427, 430, 422 and 403, with No 450 Transport Helicopter Sqn flying the Chinooks) in Canada; one (444) at Lahr, Germany, operates Kiowas in the liaison role.

Air Transport Group has two squadrons, No 435 at Edmonton, Alta and No 436 Sqn at Trenton, Ont, with 19 Lockheed CC-130E Hercules and five CC-130Hs; No 437 Sqn also at Trenton with five Boeing CC-137s, of which two have been converted to the tanker role to support the CF-5s; and No 412 Sqn at Upland, Ottawa, with seven Canadair Cosmopolitans and four Dassault Fan Jet Falcons flown for VIP and government use. SAR duties are performed by four units, Nos

Fighter pilot training on the Canadair/Netherlands CF-5B is conducted for the Canadian Armed Forces by 419 Tactical Fighter Training Squadron at Cold Lake, Alberta. One of the two 12-aircraft CF-5A squadrons is also based there.

413 Sqn at Summerside, 424 Sqn at Trenton, 440 Sqn at Edmonton (still equipped with three CC-129 Dakotas), 442 Sqn at Comox, equipped with some Bell CH-118 Iroquois and CH-135 Twin Hueys, 10 Boeing-Vertol CH-113/113A Labrador/Voyageur helicopters, 14 DHC CC-115 Buffaloes and eight DHC CC-138 Twin Otters.

An Air Reserve Group has been formed, operating four reserve wings and seven squadrons across the country on light transport and SAR duties. These units comprise four squadrons with DHC CSR-123 Otters, one squadron with Douglas CC-129 Dakotas, and one squadron each of DHC CC-138 Twin Otters and Grumman CP-121 Trackers.

Air training is the direct responsibility of Air Command and the four training bases are situated at Winnipeg; Portage la Prairie, Man; Moose Jaw, Sask; and Cold Lake, Alta. The Air Navigation School at Winnipeg trains navigators to wings standard using four Hercules aircraft. At Portage la Prairie, No 3 Flying School provides initial selection and flying training for pilot candidates, using 25 Beech CT-134 Musketeers. Trainees are then posted to No 2 Flying School at Moose Jaw, Sask, where training to wings standard is carried out, using the Canadair CT-114 Tutor jet trainer, of which some 85 are in service. From Moose Jaw, new pilots train further on CH-136 Kiowa helicopters, jet fighters, or multi-engined aircraft before entering squadron service. Beginning in January 1976, fighter training was conducted by the newly formed 419 Tactical Fighter Training Squadron at Cold Lake, Alta. The tactical fighter pilot course lasts five months and includes 92 hours of flying on the CF-5 fighter. This course prepares pilots for operational employment on the CF-5s and for further operational training on CF-101s and CF-104s.

Canada's contribution to NATO's 4th ATAF comprises 1 Canadian Air Group of three CF-104 Starfighter squadrons (Nos 421, 439 and 441) at Baden Soellingen in Germany employed in the conventional attack role. A fourth squadron, No 417 Sqn, based in Canada acts as an OTU and provides augmentation crews to bring the three European-based units up to wartime strength. Some 85 CF-104Gs and 22 CF-104D two-seaters are on inventory. The 1st CAG was the recipient of two CC-132 DHC-7s ordered to replace the Cosmopolitans used for transport and VIP flights.

The outcome of Canada's New Fighter Aircraft programme is still awaited as the CAF considers proposals for a replacement for the CF-101 and CF-104. A multi-role aircraft is being sought by the service, and the types under consideration have been reduced to two, the General Dynamics F-16 and the McDonnell Douglas F-18A/L Hornet. To improve its Tutor jet trainers, the CAF has initiated a modification programme involving some 113 aircraft to begin with, followed by a further 45 at a later date if resources permit.

The Canadian Armed Forces operates nearly 100 of a formerly larger force of single- and two-seat CF-104 Starfighters, chiefly in order to maintain a combat ready 1 Canadian Air Group based at European airfields and assigned to 4th ATAF for conventional attack.

The World's Military Aircraft

At the start of the 1980s the McDonnell Douglas F-4 Phantom was the leading fighter with several of the most important non-Communist air forces.

Aermacchi AM.3C

The AM.3 was a joint venture by Aerfer Industrie Aerospaziali Meridionali SpA of Turin and Aermacchi of Varese. The first of two prototypes was built by Macchi and flew on 12 May 1967, to be followed by the Aerfer-built second prototype on 22 August 1968. Both aircraft were powered by a 340-hp (254-kW) Continental GTSIO-520-C engine. The AM.3C is a high-wing observation/liaison aircraft intended to replace the Cessna L-19s then serving with the Italian army.

The high wing is braced on each side by a single strut. The wing is of similar concept to that of the Aermacchi AL.60, with an all-metal D-spar torsion-box structure with piano-type ailerons and Fowler-type flaps. The AM.3 has a welded chrome-molybdenum steel-tube fuselage, covered forward with light-alloy skinning, the cabin area having glass-fibre reinforced plastic panels. The rear fuselage is a light alloy semi-monocoque. The wing is attached to the fuselage at three easily accessible points for swift removal. The cantilever all-metal tail unit has a variable camber tailplane and the rudder is fitted with a spring-tab.

Each leg of the fixed landing gear has a tubular strut with an oleo-pneumatic shock absorber. The fixed tailwheel is steerable. The fully-glazed, raised cabin has two seats in tandem with dual controls. A third seat at the rear can be removed to accommodate a stretcher or freight, with access via three doors in the sides of the cabin.

The roles of the AM.3C production version include forward air control, observation, liaison, cargo or passenger transport, casualty evacuation and tactical ground support. An anticipated Italian army order did not materialise, the SIAI-Marchetti SM.1019 being preferred, but 40 AM.3Cs were delivered to South Africa, the first aircraft of the order being delivered in May 1972. Three were purchased by Ruanda.

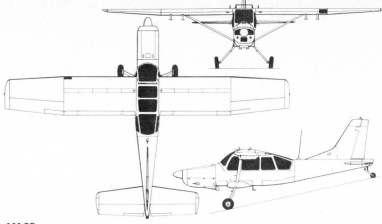

AM-3C

Type: three-seat light tactical support/observation aircraft.
Powerplant: one 340-hp (254-kW) Piaggio-Lycoming GSO-480-B1B6 six-cylinder horizontally-opposed air-cooled piston engine
Performance: maximum speed at 8,005 ft (2440 m) 173 mph (278 km/h); maximum cruising speed at 75% power at 8,005 ft (2440 m) 153 mph (246 km/h); maximum range at cruising speed 615 miles (990 km); service ceiling 27,559 ft (8400 m); take-off run 279 ft (85 m); landing run 217 ft (66 m)
Weights: empty 2,381 lb (1080 kg); maximum take-off (with underwing weaponry) 3,748 lb (1700 kg)

Dimensions: span 41 ft 5.6 in (12.64 m); length 28 ft 7.7 in (8.73 m); height 8 ft 11 in (2.72 m); wing area 219.2 sq ft (20.36 m²)
Armament: carried on two underwing hardpoints; each can carry up to 375 lb (170 kg) of external stores. Alternative loads for each hardpoint are: a pod with two 7.62-mm

(0.3-in) machine-guns; or a General Electric-Minigun with 1,500 rounds; a pod with six 70-mm (2.75-in) rockets; or a single AS.11 or AS.12 wire-guided missile; or a single 250-lb (113.4-kg) bomb
Operators: South Africa, Ruanda

Aeritalia G91R

The Fiat G91 design was the winner of a NATO requirement for a light fighter/tactical support aircraft formulated in December 1953 and issued to European aircraft manufacturers early in 1954. Although the proposal that the G91 should become standard equipment in NATO air forces was not realised, the aircraft was subsequently built in substantial numbers in Italy and, under licence, in Germany, and equipped the air forces of three countries.

Externally resembling a scaled-down North American F-86K Sabre, the Fiat G91 was first flown on 9 August 1956 and during technical evaluation trials in France in 1957 the aircraft met all the requirements of the official specification, particularly regarding the ability to operate with or without external loads from semi-prepared grass airstrips.

The initial Fiat G91 production version was a ground-attack fighter. Deliveries commenced early in 1958, and the G91 became operational with the Italian air force in February 1959. After extensive trials the Fiat G91 was also adopted by the new Federal German air force in 1958 and a licence-production agreement between Fiat and Flugzeug Union Süd (Messerschmitt-Dornier-Heinkel) was signed on 11 March 1959.

The Fiat G91 is simple, light and easy to fly, and has generally proved itself in service. The basic aircraft was progressively made more versatile by various combinations of underwing stores and the evolution of new combat tactics. The importance of high-speed armed reconnaissance led to the development of a specialised photographic reconnaissance version of the basic G91 already by 1957. The initial variant, the Fiat G91/1, first flown in 1959, was essentially a standard G91 ground-attack fighter equipped with three 70-mm focal length cameras in a shortened nose section for front and oblique photography; it was also possible to take vertical photographs from high altitudes. Adopted by the Italian air force, this modification also aroused interest in the USA and 10 G91R/1 aircraft were evaluated by the USAF during 1961 – 62.

The G91R/1a is similar, but features improved navigational aids as fitted to the G91R/3 variant to make it independent of ground installations; the maximum underwing ordnance has also been increased. A variant with reinforced structure, wheel brakes of increased capacity, tubeless tyres and some equipment changes was designated G91R/1B and also became operational with the Italian air force. This was followed by the G91R/3, which was similar to the G91R/1B, but built to West German specifications: it carries an armament of two 30-mm cannon instead of machine-guns. It also features certain equipment changes, including the installation of doppler radar and Position and Homing In-

dicator. The first Federal German air force unit equipped with the G91R/3 was commissioned on 5 May 1962. This version was also subject to the first licence-production agreement between Fiat and FUS in Germany; of the total of 344 aircraft 74 were built by Fiat (with 12 assembled by Dornier) and the remaining 270 in Germany, the first jet combat aircraft built in Germany since 1945.

The first Dornier-built G91R/3 was flown on 20 July 1965, the last in May 1966. Two Fiat G91R/3s were also evaluated by the US Army in the USA early in 1961.

The next variant, the G91R/4, was basically a G91R/3 with R/1 armament and some equipment changes. A total of 50 were procured by US authorities under the MAP scheme for Greece and Turkey but diverted in-

stead to the Federal German air force; later, the remaining 40 aircraft were transferred to the Portuguese air force.

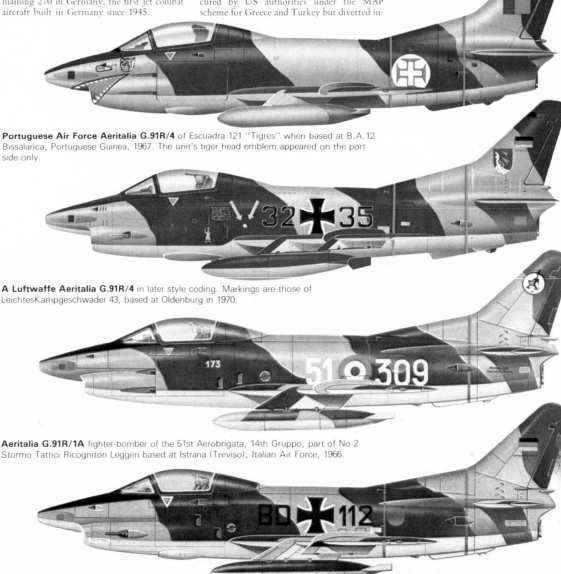

Portuguese Air Force Aeritalia G.91R/4 of Escuadra 121 "Tigres" when based at B.A.12 Bissalanca, Portuguese Guinea, 1967. The unit's tiger head emblem appeared on the port side only.

A Luftwaffe Aeritalia G.91R/4 in later style coding. Markings are those of LeichtesKampfgeschwader 43, based at Oldenburg in 1970.

Aeritalia G.91R/1A fighter-bomber of the 51st Aerobrigata, 14th Gruppo, part of No 2 Stormo Tattici Ricognitori Leggeri based at Istrana (Treviso), Italian Air Force, 1966.

Luftwaffe Aeritalia G.91R/3 ground-attack aircraft used for weapon training by Waffenschule 50 at Erding, mid-sixties.

At present, the remaining G91R/3s are being phased out of Federal German air force service.

Type: single-seat tactical strike/reconnaissance fighter
Powerplant: one 5,000-lb (2268-kg) Fiat-built Bristol Siddeley Orpheus 803 turbojet
Performance: (at basic take-off weight) maximum speed at sea level 668 mph (1075 km/h); maximum level speed at 5,000 ft (1520 m) 675 mph (1086 km/h or Mach 0.87); economical cruising speed

403 mph (650 km/h); initial rate of climb 6,003 ft (1830 m) per minute; service ceiling 42,978 ft (13100 m); combat radius (standard fuel) 200 miles (320 km); ferry range 1,150 miles (1850 km)
Weights: empty 6,835 lb (3100 kg); basic operational take-off 11,995 lb (5440 kg); maximum take-off 12,125 lb (5500 kg)
Dimensions: wing span 28 ft 1 in (8.56 m); length overall 33 ft 9¼ in (10.30 m); height overall 13 ft 1¼ in (4.00 m); wing area 176.74 sq ft (16.42 m²)
Armament: G91R/1: four 0.50-in

(12.7 mm) Colt-Browning machine-guns (300 rpg) plus four underwing pylons (two inner for two 500-lb/227-kg bombs, tactical nuclear weapons, Nord 5103 air-to-air guided missiles, clusters of six 3-in (76-mm) air-to-air rockets, honeycomb packs of 31 air-to-ground folding-fin rockets, pods containing one 0.50-in (12.7-mm) machine-gun with 250 rds; two outer for Nord 5103 missiles, 205-lb/113-kg bombs, honeycomb packs of 19 folding-fin rockets, or gun pods as above) Photographic equipment: three 70-mm Vinten cameras
G91R/1A: as above, except for improved

navigational equipment
G91R/1B: as above, but with detailed improvements
G91R/3: two 30-mm DEFA cannon (125 rpg) instead of machine-guns; three 70-mm Vinten cameras; pylon loads similar
G91R/4: as G91R/3 but with four 0.50-in (12.7-mm) machine-guns; camera and pylon equipment same
G91R/6: an experimental variant with two 30-mm DEFA cannon and two AS.20 or AS.30 missiles on underwing pylons
Operators: Italy, Portugal, West Germany

Aeritalia G91T

The Fiat G91T two-seat version of the G91 ground-attack fighter was evolved during 1958 for advanced training at transonic speeds. Intentionally, the G91T was designed with minimum modifications to produce an aircraft that would be suitable for both training and combat tasks at short notice. The airframe is similar to the basic G91 except for a slightly longer fuselage with a new cockpit for two in tandem, the rear seat being slightly raised, under an electrically-actuated canopy.

The first G91T was flown on 31 May 1960 powered by a Bristol Orpheus BOr.803-02 turbojet engine. A total of 76 were produced for the Italian air force under the designation G91T/1. The Fiat G91T/3 differs only in equipment changes. Some 66 were produced for the Federal German air force (44 built by Fiat and 22 under licence in Germany). The last Dornier-built G91T/3 was delivered to the Federal German air force on 19 October

1972. Both the G91T/1 and T/3 have provision for cameras in the fuselage nose.

The G91T/4 was a proposed G91T/1 variant with Lockheed F-104G Starfighter electronics, but it remained in the project stage.

Type: two seat transonic trainer
Powerplant: one 5,000-lb (2268-kg) Fiat-built Bristol Siddeley Orpheus 803 turbojet
Performance: (at basic take-off weight) max-

imum level speed at 5,000 ft (1524 m) 640 mph (1030 km/h); economical cruising speed 403 mph (650 km/h); service ceiling 40,000 ft (12200 m); take-off to clear 50 ft (15 m) 4,750 ft (1450 m)
Weights: basic operating 8,520 lb (3865 kg); basic take-off 12,125 lb (5500 kg); maximum take-off 13,340 lb (6050 kg)
Dimensions: span 28 ft 1 in (8.56 m); length 38 ft 3½ in (11.67 m); height 14 ft 7¼ in (4.45 m); wing area 176.74 sq ft (16.42 m²)

Armament: two 0.50-in (12.7-mm) Colt-Browning machine-guns; two underwing pylons for light bombs, missiles, or extra fuel tanks
Operators: Italy, Portugal, West Germany

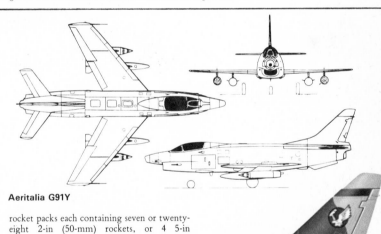

Two-seat G.91T/3 advanced trainer on the strength of the Luftwaffe's Waffenschule 50 at Erding, 1966.

Aeritalia G91Y

The Aeritalia (Fiat) G91Y is essentially a twin-engined development of the G91. Project work in response to a specific Italian air force requirement for a light ground-attack/fighter-reconnaissance aircraft began in 1965. The G91Y was based on the G91T airframe, the major change being the introduction of two General Electric J85-GE-13A turbojets in place of the single Bristol Siddeley Orpheus 803, giving a significant boost in power (over 60%) at a minimum increase in powerplant weight. This improved power/weight ratio enables the new aircraft to carry considerably heavier military loads and/or more fuel, apart from the improved safety factor in combat and the ability to cruise with one engine stopped to extend the flight endurance.

The complete airframe structure has been extensively redesigned, incorporating the latest aerodynamic innovations and avionics, including an integrated nav/attack system.

Two prototypes of the G91Y were built, the first flying on 27 December 1966. The flight tests were generally successful and the new aircraft was accepted by the Italian air force. The pre-production batch comprises 20 aircraft, , the first of which was flown in July 1968. At that time, plans were in hand for several variants of the basic G91Y, such as the G91Y/T basic/advanced trainer and the G91Y/S project to meet Swiss specifications for a ground-attack aircraft, but none of these were built.

In the event, the pre-production series was followed by the initial 35 production G91Ys for the Italian air force, with deliveries commencing in September 1971. Total production for the Italian air force amounted to 75 aircraft, including the first series.

The G91Y production version differs from the prototypes in having a slightly slimmer rear fuselage without the two ventral fins initially fitted. The pilot is equipped with a zero-zero ejector seat and accommodated in an armoured, pressurized and air-conditioned cockpit.

Type: single-seat tactical strike/reconnaissance fighter
Powerplant: two 2,725 lb (1236 kg) dry or 4,080 lb (1850 kg) with afterburning General Electric J85-GE-13A turbojets
Performance: (at maximum take-off weight) maximum speed at sea level Mach 0.93; maximum speed at 30,000 ft (9145 m) Mach 0.95;

economical cruising speed at 35,000 ft (10670 m) Mach 0.75; maximum rate of climb at sea level (with afterburning) 17,000 ft (5180 m) per minute; service ceiling 41,000 ft (12500 m); take-off to 50 ft (15 m) 3,610 ft (1100 m); typical combat radius at sea level 372 miles (600 km); lo-lo-lo mission with 2,910 lb (1320 kg) load 240 miles (385 km); ferry range with maximum fuel 2,175 miles (3500 km)
Weights: basic empty 8,117 lb (3682 kg); normal take-off 17,196 lb (7800 kg); maximum overload 19,180 lb (8700 kg)
Dimensions: span 29 ft 6½ in (9.01 m); length 38 ft 3½ in (11.67 m); height 14 ft 6½ in (4.43 m); wing area 195.15 sq ft (18.13 m²)
Armament: two 30-mm DEFA cannon; four underwing pylons for 1,000-lb (454-kg) bombs, 750-lb (340-kg) napalm containers,

Aeritalia G91Y

rocket packs each containing seven or twenty-eight 2-in (50-mm) rockets, or 4 5-in (127-mm) rocket containers
Operators: Italy

Aeronautica Militare Italiano G.91T/1 of the Scuola Volo Basico Avanzato Aviogetti at Amendola (Foggia), Italy, 1966.

The Aeronautica Militare Italiano's No 8 Wing at Cervia San Giorgio is equipped with the twin-engined G91Y.

Aeritalia G222

The initial Aeritalia G222 originated with NBMR-4 (NATO Basic Military Requirement Four) formulated in 1962, resulting in several V/STOL tactical transport projects (using combined cruise turboprops and lift jets), none of which were realised. However, the research project contract for the G222 V/STOL transport awarded to Fiat by the Italian air force in 1963 was extended to cover the type's subsequent development in more conventional form. An official contract for two military transport prototypes, originally designated G222TCM, and a static test airframe, was finally signed in 1968, the aircraft being considered a successor to the ageing Fairchild C-119 transports then in Italian service. Delays caused by changes in official policy, take-over of the parent company, and funding problems held up the completion of the first prototype, and it was not flown until 18 July 1970. The second prototype joined the flight-test programme on 21 July 1971. These aircraft have 3,060/2,870-shp (2283/2141-kW) CT64-820 turboshaft engines and are unpressurized; the production model is pressurized, and fully air-conditioned and able to operate from semi-prepared airstrips in all weathers.

The highly successful trials resulted in a firm Italian order for 44 production G222s in August 1972; by that time arrangements had been made to involve most of the Italian aircraft industry in the G222 programme.

The G222 airframe was redesigned once more to take the more powerful General Electric T64-P4D turboprop engines and incorporate other detail improvements. The production prototype was flown on 23 December 1975, by which time Aeritalia had also obtained its first export order from Argentina.

The fuselage of the basic G222 transport version is an all-metal fail-safe structure, the underside of which forms a loading ramp. In standard troop-transport configuration the G222 carries 44 fully equipped troops (32 sidewall seats and 12 folding seats), as a paratroop transport 32 (in sidewall seats). As an ambulance, the G222 has space for 36 stretcher cases and two seated casualties, plus four medical attendants, while converted for cargo transport the aircraft has provision for a 3,305-lb (1500-kg) capacity cargo hoist and 135 tie-down points.

The basic G222 airframe is most suitable for adaptation to other military and civil roles, such as maritime patrol/anti-submarine warfare, surveillance and navaid/radar inspection. A prototype of the ECM version, designated G222VS (*Versione Speciale*) was flown on 9 March 1978 and is now undergoing protracted operational suitability trials. It is equipped with extensive electronic installations, and carries a flight crew of two, plus 10 systems operators.

A navaid/radar investigation/calibration version has also been completed and the prototype, designated G222RM (*Radiumissura*) is at the flight-test stage. Externally similar to the standard transport version this modification has facilities to check VOR, ILS, TACAN and DME; it also has optional secondary survey capabilities for multiple control of approach and ground-control radars.

Another new version intended mainly for export to the Middle East and now under development is the G222 tactical transport powered by 3,400-shp (3536-kW) Rolls-Royce Tyne turboprop engines. The first flight of the Tyne-powered prototype, designated G222L, is projected for July 1979.

In the civil field, successful trials have been carried out with a G222 SAMA fire-fighting modification (rebuilt second G222 prototype with 1,836-Imperial gallon/6300-litre water tank), and projects exist for crop-spraying and aerial photogrammetry variants.

By late autumn 1978 some 20 G222s had been delivered, including two prototypes, 14 production aircraft for the Italian air force, three for Argentina and one for the United Arab Emirates (Dubai). The Libyan Arab Republic has issued a letter of intent to purchase 20 G222L tactical transports, scheduled for delivery in 1980 – 81, and negotiations are in progress with Malagasy, Thailand and Tunisia.

Type: twin-turboprop general-purpose transport
Powerplant: two 3,400-shp (2536-kW) Fiat-built General Electric T64-GE-P4D turboprops driving Hamilton Standard 63E60 three-blade variable-pitch propellers; provision in fuselage for eight Aerojet General jet-assisted take-off rockets, delivering a total additional thrust of 7,937 lb (3600 kg) for take-off in overload condition
Performance: (standard transport at maximum take-off weight) maximum speed at 15,000 ft (4575 m) 336 mph (540 km/h); cruising speed at 14,750 ft (4500 m) 224 mph (360 km/h); maximum rate of climb at sea-level 1,705 ft (520 m) per minute; time to 14,750 ft (4500 m) 8 minutes 35 seconds; service ceiling 25,000 ft (7620 m); take-off run

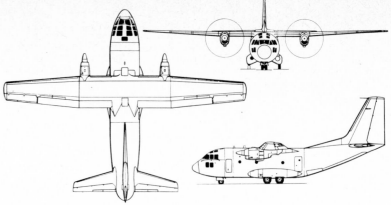

Aeritalia G222 (T64 engines)

2756 ft (840 m); range with maximum payload at optimum cruising speed at 19,685 ft (6000 m) 435 miles (700 km); range with 44 fully-equipped troops 1,380 miles (2220 km); ferry range with maximum fuel 3,075 miles (4950 km)
Weights: (standard transport) empty 32,165 lb (14590 kg); maximum payload 18,740 lb (8500 kg); normal take-off 54,013 lb (24500 kg); maximum take-off and landing 58,422 lb (26500 kg)
Dimensions: span 94 ft 2 in (28.70 m); length 74 ft 5½ in (22.70 m); height 32 ft 1¾ in (9.80 m); wing area 882.6 sq ft

(82.00 m²)
Operators: (operational or on order) Argentina, Italy, Libya, United Arab Emirates (Dubai)

Based at Dubai and shown in the markings of the Dubai Air Force is this Aeritalia G.222 tactical transport, delivered November '76.

This Aeritalia G.222 is serving with the Aeronautica Militare Italiano's No 46 Transport Brigade based at Pisa, which is receiving 44 of these all-Italian machines operated by Nos 2 and 98 Squadrons. They are replacing C-119s.

Aeritalia/Macchi AM-X

During 1976-77 the Italian air force (AMI) formulated its ideas on a next-generation multi-role tactical aircraft. It is a most interesting specification, rather like a smaller Vought A-7, and the missions are: close interdiction, reconnaissance, certain categories of close air support, offensive operation against airfields, and defence against low-flying aircraft. Later there is likely to be a specialized anti-ship version as well as a two-seater for EW and training (and possibly other roles). Wisely, the whole concept has been launched on a design-to-cost basis, the price per aircraft

being set at the equivalent of only £2.1 million in January 1978 values. The specification has been passed to NATO and discussions have been held at government level with Sweden, which has a similar need (not now to be met by the cancelled Saab B3LA or other Swedish design). Project definition is to be completed by late 1979, the first of six prototypes is to fly in late 1982, first delivery should follow in 1985, and the AMI requirement of 180 is to be complete by 1991. The AM-X will replace the Aeritalia G91 and Lockheed F-104G, serving alongside the costly all-weather Panavia Tor-

nado. The AM-X will almost certainly be subsonic but will have good sensors, navigation and weapon-aiming systems, and capability far in advance of current trainer and light attack aircraft. It will make maximum use of Tornado technology, and might well have a swing wing.

Type: single-seat tactical combat aircraft
Powerplant: one 11,030-lb (5000-kg) Rolls-Royce Spey 807 turbofan, without afterburner (made largely under licence in Italy by companies to be decided)

Performance: maximum speed at all heights about Mach 0.8; mission radius see under Armament
Armament
Weights: maximum loaded about 19,840 lb (9000 kg)
Dimensions: not disclosed but about the size of the G91
Armament: total weapon load 3,000 lb (1360 kg) plus two air-to-air missiles and internal gun for low-altitude mission radius of 207 miles (335 km); maximum load over shorter radius 6,000 lb (2725 kg)
Operators: under development for Italy

Aermacchi AL.60 Trojan

European exclusive manufacturing rights for the manufacture of the Lockheed 60 light utility transport were obtained by Aermacchi in 1960 and the first AL.60 appeared in April 1961. It is a high-wing cabin monoplane of an all-metal construction. The wing has piano-hinged ailerons and hand-operated Fowler flaps. The fixed tricycle landing gear has cantilever steel-tube main legs connected to an oleo-pneumatic shock absorber mounted horizontally under the cabin floor. The nose gear is steerable.

The pilot and co-pilot sit side-by-side, and behind them is provision for two benches, each seating three. As a casevac aircraft the AL.60 can take two stretchers plus one sitting patient and a medical attendant. The main cargo/casualty loading door is on the right, and a sliding door to the rear on the left can be used for dropping parachutists or supplies. There are normal doors forward on either side.

Lockheed-Azacarte SAI in Mexico have sold

a considerable number of civil variants, including specialized aircraft for agricultural use. The Mexican designation is LASA.60 'Santa Maria', and 18 built in Mexico were sold to that country's air arm for use primarily as search and rescue aircraft. The Aermacchi military variant, designated AL.60C5, has been purchased by the Central African Empire (10) and Canada. A similar variant has been supplied to Rhodesia as the Trojan.

Type: (AL.60 C.5 Conestoga/Trojan) utility aircraft
Powerplant: one 400-hp (298-kW) Lycoming IO-720-A1A horiztonally-opposed air-cooled piston engine
Performance: maximum speed 156 mph (251 km/h) at sea level; economic cruising speed 108 mph (174 km/h) at 5,000 ft (1524 m); range with maximum fuel load 644 miles (1037 km); service ceiling 13,615 ft (4150 m); rate of climb at sea level 1,083 ft (330 m) per

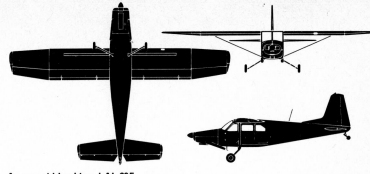

Aermacchi-Lockheed AL.60F

minute; take-off run 644 ft (196 m); landing run 846 ft (258 m)
Weights: empty equipped 2,395 lb (1086 kg); maximum take-off 4,500 lb (2041 kg)
Dimensions: span 39 ft 4 in (11.99 m); length 28 ft 10½ in (8.80 m); height 10 ft

10 in (3.3 m); wing area 210.4 sq ft (19.55 m²)
Armament: none
Operators: Canada, Central African Empire (Conestoga), Rhodesia (Trojan), Mauritania, Mexico, South Africa

---

Aermacchi M.B. 326

In an unbroken history dating back to before World War I, Aeronautica Macchi has produced more than 7,000 examples of aircraft of its own design; something like 10 per cent of that total are members of the M.B.326 family of jet trainers and light attack aircraft. In company with the BAC Jet Provost and Air Fouga Magister, it is one of the classic types of its genre, having been in constant production for two decades.

Design began in 1954, and the first prototype made its initial flight on 10 December 1957, powered by a 1,750-lb (794-kg) static thrust Viper 8 turbojet. The second prototype, and 15 pre-production examples ordered by Italy's *Aeronautica Militare*, standardized on the 2,500-lb (1134-kg) Viper 11. The basic airframe, designed by Dr-Ing Ermanno Bazzocchi of Aermacchi, is simple, robust, stressed to g limits of +8 and −4, has well-equipped, pressurized tandem cockpits with twin ejection seats, and is intended for use in all stages of flying training from *ab initio* upwards. The first M.B.326s entered Italian service in February 1962, the AMI eventually receiving 85 of the initial model in addition to the 15 pre-production aircraft.

Ground-attack potential was first offered by Aermacchi on a proposed model known as the M.B.326A, to be equipped with six underwing attachments for alternative gun or rocket pods, bombs or other weapons. Such a version was not then required by the Italian air force, but similar armed models were ordered by Tunisia (eight M.B.326Bs) and Ghana (nine M.B.326Fs). Four examples of an unarmed M.B.326D were produced as airline pilot trainers for Alitalia. The M.B.326H, for the Royal Australian Air Force (87) and Navy (10), had full armament provisions; they were assembled or licence-built in that country by CAC (Commonwealth Aircraft Corporation). M.B.326Ms were produced, in two models, for the South African Air Force: 40 unarmed Italian-built aircraft for use in the training role, and about 125 assembled or licence-built in Transvaal by the Atlas Aircraft Corporation. The latter, known as the Impala Mk 1, have provision for externally-mounted armament.

All of the foregoing aircraft had the Viper 11 as powerplant. Increased power was intro-

duced in the spring of 1967, with the flight of the first Viper 540-powered M.B.326G prototype. Combined with some local reinforcement of the airframe, this can carry almost twice as heavy a weapons load as the Viper 11-engined models, and in production form is known as the M.B.326GB. This has been, or is being, built in Italy for the Argentine navy (eight) and the air forces of Zaïre (17) and Zambia (20); a version with some features of the GB, but the Viper 11 engine, is the Italian air force's M.B.326E, six of which are newly-built and six converted from earlier M.B.326s. The largest overseas order to date has come from South America, where EMBRAER of Sao José dos Campos has virtually completed the manufacture of 170 armed GCs (similar to the GB) under the designation AT-26 Xavante for the air forces of Brazil (167) and Togo (three).

Aermacchi's most recent two-seat version, the M.B.326L, is based upon the single-seat M.B.326K (see separate description) and likewise features a further increase in engine power by the use of a Viper 600 series engine. Two of the customers for the K model have also ordered the L type: Dubai (one) and Tunisia (four). Although fully equipped with dual controls for training, the M.B.326L retains the full attack/close-support potential of the K variant.

Said to be practically viceless, the M.B.326 undoubtedly owes much of its success to the basic simplicity and robustness of its design, excellent stability and control at low speeds, plus considerable manoeuvrability, versatility, and (on the latest models) load-carrying capacity.

Type: two-seat basic/advanced trainer and light attack aircraft
Powerplant: one Rolls-Royce Viper turbojet: 2,500-lb (1134-kg) static thrust Viper 11

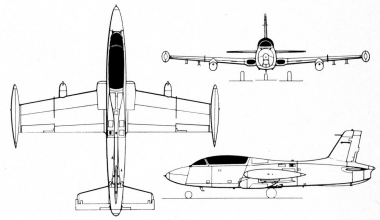

Aermacchi M.B.326E

in early models; 3,410-lb (1547-kg) static thrust Viper 20 Mk 540 in GB, H and M; 4,000-lb (1814-kg) static thrust Viper 632-43 in L
Performance: maximum speed (326) 501 mph (806 km/h), (GB, clean) 539 mph (867 km/h); range on internal fuel (326) 1,035 miles (1665 km), (GB, clean) 1,150 miles (1850 km); combat radius (B, with armament) 290 miles (460 km), (GB, with armament) 403 miles (648 km); maximum rate of climb at sea level (B, with armament) 2,300 ft (700 m) per minute, (GB, with armament) 3,100 ft (945 m) per minute; service ceiling (326, clean) 41,000 ft (12500 m), (GB, clean) 47,000 ft (14325 m), (GB, with armament) 39,000 ft (11900 m)
Weights: empty (326) 4,930 lb (2237 kg), (E) 5,772 lb (2618 kg), (GB, trainer) 5,920 lb (2685 kg); maximum take-off (326) 8,300 lb (3765 kg), (B) 10,000 lb (4535 kg), (GB, trainer) 10,090 lb (4577 kg), (GB, with armament) 11,500 lb (5216 kg)

Dimensions: span over tip-tanks (early models) 34 ft 8 in (10.56 m), (GB) 35 ft 7¼ in (10.85 m); length (early models) 34 ft 11¼ in (10.65 m), (GB) 35 ft 0¼ in (10.67 m); height 12 ft 2 in (3.72 m); wing area (early models) 204.5 sq ft (19.00 m²), (GB) 208.3 sq ft (19.35 m²)
Armament: two optional 7.7-mm (0.303-in) machine-guns in fuselage in early models, with six underwing points for machine-gun pods, rockets and/or bombs, or camera pod(s); maximum external load 2,000 lb (907 kg) on early models, 4,000 lb (1814 kg) on GB and L
Operators: Argentina, Australia, Bolivia, Brazil (Xavante), Dubai, Ghana, Italy, South Africa (Impala 1), Togo (Xavante), Tunisia, Zaïre, Zambia

One of the eight Aermacchi **M.B.326B** advanced trainers purchased in 1965 by the Tunisian Republican Air Force.

Aermacchi M.B. 326K/Atlas Impala Mk 2

Perhaps the most surprising aspect of this single-seat version of the Aermacchi M.B.326 family is the length of time that was allowed to elapse before it made its appearance, given the propensity for almost every new jet trainer to be offered as an 'ideal' vehicle for the close-support role. Aermacchi had proved at an early stage in its evolution that the basic two-seat M.B.326 was an extremely manoeuvrable yet stable weapon-launching platform, and the early armed versions, the M.B.326B and F, would normally be flown anyway with the second seat vacant in a ground-attack role. Nevertheless, the development of a genuine single-seat model offered attractive

possibilities, especially with the introduction of more powerful variants of the Rolls-Royce Viper engine.

Substitution of the Viper 540 for the original Viper 11 had allowed the weapon load to be effectively doubled from that of the early models, and with the still more powerful Series 600 engine available, the opportunity was taken to augment the offensive capability of the single-seat M.B.326K by installing a pair of electrically-operated cannon in the lower forward fuselage. Into the space normally occupied by the second cockpit have gone the ammunition drums for these guns, the avionics formerly housed in the nose, and an

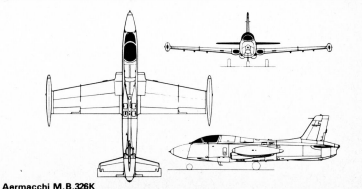

Aermacchi M.B.326K

continued

additional fuel tank. For the more demanding needs of low-level manoeuvring and weapon carriage/delivery, the airframe has been strengthened in selected areas, and servo assistance is provided for the ailerons. At first, Aermacchi felt that these changes were sufficient to justify the new designation M.B.336, but decided later to retain the already-established basic one and call the new version the M.B.326K.

Two prototypes of the M.B.326K were completed, the first of these making its maiden flight on 22 August 1970, more than 12½ years after the debut of the original M.B.326, with a 3,360-kg (1524-kg) static thrust Viper 540. The intended powerplant, the higher-rated Viper 632-43, was installed in the second aircraft, which joined the flight test programme in 1971. Despite the widespread popularity of the earlier two-seat models, a first customer for the K did not emerge until 1974, when three examples were ordered for the Dubai Police Air Wing (together with one example of the K's two-seat counterpart, the M.B.326L). Later that year Aermacchi delivered seven M.B.326Ks to South Africa, where Atlas Aircraft Corporation was soon due to end its licence production of the two-seat M.B.326M (Impala 1). In 1975 these were followed by Italian-built KDCs (knock-down components) for 15 more single-seaters, and since assembling these locally Atlas has manu-

factured a version of the K under licence in South Africa as the Impala 2. Except for the installation of different avionics, the Impala 2 is similar to the standard M.B.326K, but uses the lower-powered Viper 540 engine. In 1976 Italian-built Ks were ordered by the air forces of Ghana (six) and Tunisia (eight), two of the original customers for the early armed versions of the M.B.326.

The presence of built-in guns, and the variety of underwing weapons available (see specification below), mean that the M.B.326K is not necessarily confined to low-level ground-attack or close air support missions. It can carry a camera pod, for low- and medium-altitude tactical reconnaissance, without detriment to the attack weapon-carrying capacity of the remaining wing stations. Or, with twin cannon and heat-seeking dogfight missiles under the wings, it can perform in a visual interception role. Provision exists for a laser rangefinder and a bomb delivery computer to be installed if required by a customer.

Type: single-seat close air support or tactical reconnaissance aircraft, and limited air-to-air interceptor
Powerplant: one 4,000-lb (1814-kg) static thrust Rolls-Royce Viper 632-43 turbojet (M.B.326K); 3,360-lb (1524-kg) static thrust Viper 540 (Impala Mk 2)
Performance: (M.B.326K) maximum speed, clean, at 5,000 ft (1525 m) 553 mph (890 km/h); maximum speed, with armament, at 30,000 ft (9150 m) 426 mph (686 km/h); typical combat radius, according to altitude and external load 167-644 miles (268-1036 km); ferry range with two drop-tanks more than 1,323 miles (2130 km); maximum rate of climb at sea level, clean, 6,500 ft (1980 m) per minute; maximum rate of climb at sea level, with armament 3,750 ft (1143 m) per minute
Weights: empty equipped 6,885 lb (3123 kg); take-off, clean, 10,240 lb (4645 kg); maximum take-off, with armament 13,000 lb (5897 kg)
Dimensions: span over tip-tanks 35 ft 7 in (10.85 m); length 35 ft 0¼ in (10.67 m);

height 12 ft 2 in (3.72 m); wing area 208.3 sq ft (19.35 m²)
Armament: two 30-mm DEFA 553 cannon in lower fuselage, each with 125 rounds; and up to 4,000 lb (1814 kg) of external stores on six underwing stations, typical loads including four 1,000-lb (454-kg) bombs, or two 750-lb (340-kg) and four 500-lb (227-kg) bombs, or six 7.62-mm (0.3-in) Minigun pods, or two AS.11 or AS.12 air-to-surface missiles, or two Matra 550 Magic air-to-air missiles, or various launchers for 37-mm, 68-mm, 100-mm, 2.75-in or 5-in rockets, or (on innermost port station) a four-camera reconnaissance pod
Operators: Dubai, Ghana, South Africa (Impala 2), Tunisia

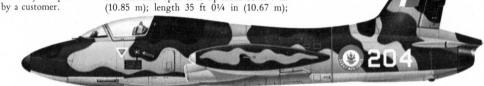

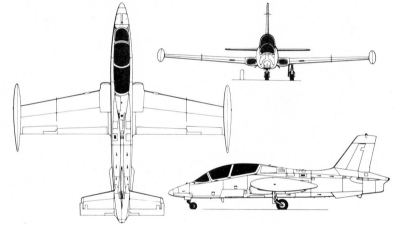

Aermacchi M.B. 326K D single-seat light strike aircraft of the Union Air Force, Dubai; three form a counter-insurgency flight.

Aermacchi M.B. 339

Following the receipt of a study contract from the Italian air force in 1972, Aeronautica Macchi undertook no fewer than nine separate design studies in its efforts to evolve a second-generation jet trainer to succeed the M.B.326 and Aeritalia (Fiat) .G91T during the 1980s. Seven of these were variants of a design known as the M.B.338, with numerous permutations of single or twin Viper, Larzac, Adour, RB.401 and TFE 731 turbojets or turbofans. Not surprisingly, the single-Viper versions would have offered little advance in performance over the later models of the M.B.326; neither, as it turned out, did the intermediately-powered models, which also would have been more expensive to produce than the M.B.326; while the two most powerful versions, with a single Adour and twin Larzacs respectively, offered a marked increase in performance only at a considerably higher cost.

The most encouraging studies were the two proposed models of the M.B.339, powered by either a single Larzac turbofan (M.B.339L) or a single Viper 600 series turbojet (M.B.339V). Moreover, a major part of the M.B.339 airframe was common with that of the M.B.326K, only the forward fuselage, with its modified cockpit and much superior all-round view, plus the enlarged vertical tail, being essentially different. In February 1975 the Italian air force decided to adopt the Viper-powered version to meet its requirements, and the first of two prototypes made its initial flight at Venegono airfield on 12 August of the following year. Only comparatively minor modifications, to provide an anti-skid braking system for the main landing gear and a steerable nosewheel, plus improved air-conditioning in the cockpit, were introduced on the second prototype, which flew for the first time on 20 May 1977. (An amusing subliminal touch is Aermacchi's use of the word 'nine' in various languages in the registration of the development aircraft: I-NOVE for the first prototype, I-NINE for the second, and I-NEUF for the first production machine.)

Redesign of the forward fuselage permits the rear (instructor's) seat to be elevated above that of his pupil in the now-fashionable manner, the elongated tandem canopy providing an all-round view much improved over that from the M.B.326. Both occupants have Martin-Baker zero-zero ejection seats, fitted only in the E, K, and L models of the earlier M.B.326. The avionics are suitably increased and updated to include Tacan, navigation computer, blind landing instrumentation, IFF (identification friend or foe), and both VHF and UHF radio. Fuselage and permanent wingtip tanks give a total 311 Imperial gallons

(1413 litres) of usable fuel as standard, with a 75-Imperial gallon (340-litre) drop-tank able to be carried on the middle pylon under each wing.

Following the two prototypes (the second of which represents the production standard), the Italian air ministry ordered an initial batch of 15 M.B.339s, of an expected total of about 100. Although developed initially as an Italian air force trainer, the 339 retains the six wing hardpoints of its predecessor. Thus, Aermacchi has achieved a successor to the M.B.326 with a compromise design. It may lack some sophistication and the performance 'edge' of the British Aerospace Hawk or Dassault-Breguet/Dornier Alpha Jet. However, these factors may be more than offset by the lower unit cost, plus the commonality with an already well-proven airframe.

Type: tandem two-seat basic/advanced jet trainer and close-support aircraft
Powerplant: one 4,000-lb (1814-kg) Piaggio-built Rolls-Royce Viper 632-43 turbojet
Performance: maximum limiting Mach number 0.86 (603 mph/971 km/h equivalent airspeed); maximum speed at sea level 558 mph (898 km/h); maximum speed at 30,000 ft (9150 m) 508 mph (817 km/h) or Mach 0.77; maximum range on internal fuel 1,093 miles (1760 km); maximum range with two underwing drop-tanks 1,310 miles (2110 km); maximum rate of climb at sea level 6,600 ft

Aermacchi M.B.339

(2012 m) per minute; service ceiling 48,000 ft (14630 m)
Weights: empty equipped 6,889 lb (3125 kg); take-off, clean 9,700 lb (4400 kg); maximum take-off, with underwing stores 13,000 lb (5895 kg)
Dimensions: span over tip-tanks 35 ft 7½ in (10.86 m); length 36 ft 0 in (10.97 m); height 13 ft 1¼ in (3.99 m); wing area 207.74 sq ft (19.30 m²)
Armament: six underwing hardpoints, the outer pair each able to carry a 750-lb (340-kg)

store and the others 1,000 lb (454 kg) each, subject to a maximum load of 4,000 lb (1814 kg). The two inboard points can carry 30-mm or multi-barrel 7.62-mm guns in a Macchi pod, and the two centre points are 'wet' for the carriage of drop-tanks. Wide variety of weapon loads including bombs, napalm, AS.11/AS.12 or Magic missiles, launchers for 50-mm, 68-mm or 2.75-in rockets, or a single four-camera reconnaissance pod
Operators: Italy

First (on the right) and second prototypes of the Aermacchi M.B.339, the improved and updated successor to the M.B.326. The first of an initial batch of 15 production aircraft for the Aeronautica Militare flew in 1978, and 100 in all are on order.

Aero 3

First flown in 1956, the Aero 3 entered production in 1957. It was designed to a Yugoslav air force specification for use in the primary training and army co-operation roles.

Approximately equivalent to the DHC Chipmunk, the Aero 3 is entirely of wooden construction, unlike the Canadian all-metal aircraft. It succeeded the earlier Aero 2 in service from 1958, and has full dual controls and blind-flying equipment. The single-piece canopy may be jettisoned if necessary.

A few Aero 3s remain in service but by the late 1970s were being replaced by the UTVA-75.

Type: two-seat primary trainer
Powerplant: one 190-hp (142-kW) Lycoming O-435A piston engine
Performance: maximum speed 143 mph (230 km/h); cruising speed 112 mph (180 km/h); range at cruising speed 422 miles (680 km); ceiling 14,000 ft (4300 m)

Weights: loaded 2,646 lb (1198 kg)
Dimensions: span 34 ft 5 in (10.5 m); length 28 ft 1 in (8.58 m); height 8 ft 10 in (2.7 m)
Operators: Yugoslavia

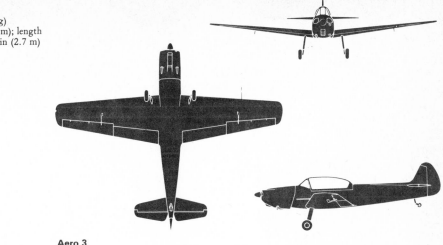

Aero 3

Aero L-29 Delfin

Even among the air forces of the Warsaw Pact nations, where large production contracts are common, manufacturing figures of over 3,000 of a single type of jet trainer indicate a successful design. The first studies leading to the Aero L-29 were made in 1955 by a team under K. Tomas and Z. Rublic. Known as the XL-29, the prototype flew for the first time on 5 April 1959, powered by a Bristol Siddeley Viper turbojet. The second prototype, which made its initial flight in July 1960, and a small pre-production batch of L-29s for service evaluation, had the nationally-designed M 701 turbojet.

A year later the Delfin (dolphin) was subjected to competitive evaluation against the Yakovlev Yak-30 and PZL-Mielec TS-11 Iskra. As a result, all Warsaw Pact countries (except Poland, which decided to continue supporting its own TS-11) decided to adopt the Delfin as their standard basic and advanced jet trainer. The first production Delfin was completed in April 1963, and approximately 3,500 had been built before the run ended some 12 years later. More than 2,000 of these were supplied to the Soviet air force, whose L-29s were assigned the reporting name 'Maya' by the NATO Air Standards Co-ordinating Committee, and about 400 to the Czech air force. Others were supplied to the air forces of Bulgaria, the German Democratic Republic, Hungary and Romania. From its introduction the Delfin enabled these services to inaugurate 'all-through' training on jet aircraft, by replacing earlier piston-engined types. It was designed not only for basic pilot training but also for advanced and combat weapon training.

The L-29's concept is based upon a straightforward, easy-to-build design, simple to fly and uncomplicated to operate. Flight controls are manual, with generous wing flaps and a perforated airbrake on each side of the rear fuselage. The Delfin does not readily stall or spin, and its safety and reliability are said to be high. There is a manual backup for the landing gear, and both occupants are provided with ejection seats though, unlike modern trainers, the instructor's (rear) seat is no higher than the pupil's. Runway requirements are modest, and it can operate from grass, sand or water-logged airstrips.

Aero also built a small batch of the single-seat L-29A Delfin Akrobat, for aerobatic displays, but this did not go into large-scale production. Neither did an attack version, the L-29R, but the standard L-29 was supplied to a number of countries (including Egypt) equipped for this role, with a modest weapon load on two underwing pylons. The L-29 was superseded in production at the Aero factory in the mid-1970s by the L-39.

Type: tandem two-seat basic and advanced jet trainer
Powerplant: one 1,960-lb (890-kg) Motorlet M 701 VC-150 or S-50 turbojet
Performance: maximum speed at 16,400 ft (5000 m) 407 mph (655 km/h); maximum speed at sea level 379 mph (610 km/h); maximum range on internal fuel 397 miles (640 km); maximum range with two underwing drop-tanks 555 miles (895 km); maximum rate of climb at sea level 2,755 ft (840 m) per minute; service ceiling 36,100 ft (11000 m)

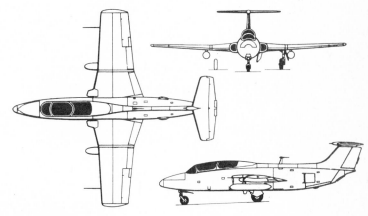

Aero L-29 Delfin

Weights: empty 5,027 lb (2280 kg); maximum take-off 7,231 lb (3280 kg)
Dimensions: span 33 ft 9 in (10.29 m); length 35 ft 5½ in (10.81 m); height 10 ft 3 in (3.13 m); wing area 213.1 sq ft (19.80 m²)
Armament: provision for two 7.62-mm gun pods, two 220-lb (100-kg) bombs, eight air-to-surface rockets or two drop-tanks, on pylon under each wing

Operators: Bulgaria, China, Czechoslovakia, Egypt, East Germany, Guinea, Hungary, Indonesia, Iraq, Nigeria, Romania, Syria, Uganda, USSR, Vietnam

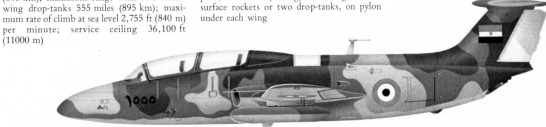

Serving in the basic and advanced training roles with the Egyptian Arab Air Force is the Czechoslovak L-29 Delfin.

Aero L-39 Albatros

Designed before the Soviet armed intervention in Czechoslovakia in 1968, the L-39 is now well on the road to emulating its predecessor, the L-29 Delfin, as the standard jet trainer for Warsaw Pact (except Poland) and other air forces. Aero began with three prototypes, the middle one of which flew for the first time on 4 November 1968; the other two were subjected to structural and fatigue tests. Pilot for the first flight was Rudolf Duchon, who had also been responsible for the early test programme of the L-29 nine years before. The powerplant selected for the L-39 is the Soviet-designed Ivchenko AI-25 turbofan, and most of the early delays in the aircraft's development are thought to be the result of problems encountered in relating this to the L-39's airframe, so rendering it acceptable for licence production in Czechoslovakia. One of the chief problems seems to have been the supply of air to the engine: by late 1970, at which time five flying prototypes had been completed, modified intakes of greater length and increased area were noticed on these develop-

ment aircraft. During the following year, a pre-production batch of 10 L-39s was built to the modified configuration, and series production began in late 1972. By 1979, more than 1,000 had been ordered, of which more than half had been completed.

These are of three main versions. The basic L-39, for elementary and advanced jet training, has been supplied in quantity to the Czech and Soviet air forces, plus those of other Warsaw Pact nations, as a successor to the L-29; it began to enter service in 1974. When equipped for weapons training, the two-seater is known as the L-39Z. A single-seat armed variant, for use in the light close-support and ground-attack roles, is designated L-39D; Iraq is known to be among the operators of this version.

Dipl-Ing Jan Vlcek, who led the Aero design team responsible for the L-39, has produced a physically attractive little aeroplane with a significant improvement in performance over its predecessor (Mach 0.83 top speed, compared with the L-29's Mach 0.75).

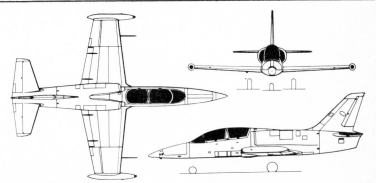

Aero L-39 Albatros

Tandem seating (on zero-height ejection seats in the L-39) is retained, but naturally with the rear (instructor's) seat elevated to improve his view forward. Simultaneously, this enables the lower-placed front cockpit to slope downward towards a finely-pointed nose that reduces drag and contributes to enhanced performance. Construction is modular, the airframe

being broken down into only three major sub-assemblies (wing, fuselage, and rear fuselage/tail unit) to facilitate major maintenance and overhaul. The entire wing, except for the moving surfaces, is in one piece, including the permanent tip-tanks, and the swept fin is integral with the rear fuselage; the latter is removable to provide easy access to the

continued

engine for servicing. Including detachables such as nose-cone, control surfaces, landing gear and canopies, the entire L-39 airframe consists of little more than a couple of dozen basic components. This enables any one to be replaced quickly and easily; plenty of access panels are provided for reaching individual systems or installations. A first-class all-round view is available from both pressurized cockpits, and dual controls are, of course, standard. The rear seat is removed in the L-39D, presumably providing space, if required, for avionics or an additional fuel tank. A small auxiliary power unit (APU), in the form of a compressed-air turbine and generator, makes the aircraft independent of ground power sources for engine starting, fuel flow or other services.

Type: tandem two-seat basic and advanced jet trainer (L-39), weapons trainer (L-39Z) and single-seat light ground-attack aircraft (L-39D)
Powerplant: one 3,792-lb (1720-kg) Walter Titan turbofan (Ivchenko AI-25-TL built under Czech licence by Motorlet)
Performance: maximum speed at sea level 435 mph (700 km/h); maximum speed (trainer, clean) at 19,685 ft (6000 m) 485 mph (780 km/h), (L-39D) at same altitude with four rocket pods 391 mph (630 km/h); range on internal fuel (trainer) 528 miles (850 km), (L-39D with rocket pods) 485 miles (780 km); maximum range with two drop-tanks and no weapons 994 miles (1600 km); maximum rate of climb at sea level (trainer) 4,330 ft (1320 m) per minute, (L-39D) 3,150 ft (960 m) per minute; service ceiling (trainer) 37,730 ft (11500 m), (L-39D) 29,525 ft (9000 m)
Weights: empty 7,341 lb (3330 kg); take-off (trainer, clean and with tip-tanks empty) 10,075 lb (4570 kg); maximum take-off (L-39D with four rocket pods) 11,618 lb (5270 kg)
Dimensions: span 31 ft 0½ in (9.46 m); length 40 ft 5 in (12.32 m); height 15 ft 5½ in (4.72 m); wing area 202.4 sq ft (18.80 m²)
Armament: (L-39D) up to 2,425 lb (1100

Assured at launch of sales throughout the Warsaw Pact nations, other than Poland, the Czech Aero L-39 Albatros has found a growing list of export customers and should by the late 1980s rival the 3,000-plus production runs of its predecessor, the L-29 Delfin.

kg) of weapons on four underwing points, including bombs of up to 1,102-lb (500-kg) size, pods of 57-mm or 130-mm rockets, gun pods, a single five-camera reconnaissance pack, or two drop-tanks; centreline point under fuselage for podded gun, believed to be a

Soviet GSh-23 of 23-mm calibre with about 180 rounds
Operators: Afghanistan, Bulgaria, Czechoslovakia, East Germany, Hungary, Iraq, Romania, USSR

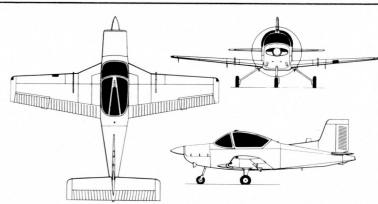

A desert-camouflaged Aero L-39 Albatros flown by the Iraqi Air Force College at Rashid.

Aerospace Airtrainer CT/4

The origins of this light primary trainer can be traced to Australian Henry Millicer's design, which won a Royal Aero Club competition in 1953 and which was subsequently built in Australia by Victa as a civil tourer/trainer. In 1971 the New Zealand company Aero Engine Services Ltd (AESL), later amalgamated with Air Parts, bought the rights to a four-seat development known as the Aircruiser and decided to convert the design to the military training role. One of the first priorities was to strengthen the airframe, which was initially cleared only from +3.8 to −1.5g. The prototype, stressed from +6 to −3g and featuring a hinged, clear-Perspex canopy, side-by-side seating for two with an optional third seat aft and stick-type control columns, first flew on 23 February 1972.

More than 80 Airtrainers now equip six air arms. They are used primarily for training, although modified versions with underwing hardpoints have been evaluated. Australia operates 31 aircraft with No 1 Flight Training School (FTS) at Point Cook, and a further six at the Central Flying School, East Sale, have taken over the tasks previously performed by Commonwealth Aircraft Winjeels. Six Airtrainers equipped with underwing hardpoints are used to train forward air controllers. The Royal New Zealand Air Force, happy to operate a home-grown trainer, bought 13 aircraft and a further six airframes for spares. Based at Wigram FTS, they are used for basic training and replace the North American Harvard, with which New Zealand has had a long association. From the Airtrainer, pilots move on to British Aerospace Strikemaster Mk 88s for operational strike and jet conversion training. The Royal Thai Air Force, with the ever present threat of clashes along the Thai-Cambodia border, trains its recruit pilots on 24 Airtrainers (along with 12 SIAI-Marchetti SF.260MTs, four Cessna T-41Ds and 10 Continental-powered de Havilland

Chipmunks) at Korat Air Base.

Type: two/three-seat aerobatic light trainer
Powerplant: one 210-hp (157-kW) Teledyne Continental IO-360-H flat-six air-cooled piston engine
Performance: maximum design speed 265 mph (426 km/h); maximum level speed at sea level 178 mph (286 km/h), at 10,000 ft (3050 m) 163 mph (262 km/h); range on internal fuel, 10% reserve, 75% power at 5,000 ft (1525 m) 790 miles (1271 km); maximum rate of climb at sea level 1,350ft (411 m) per minute
Weights: empty equipped 1,490 lb (675 kg); maximum take-off 2,400 lb (1088 kg)
Dimensions: span 26 ft 0 in (7.92 m); length 23 ft 2 in (7.06 m); height 8 ft 6 in (2.59 m); wing area 129 sq ft (11.98 m²)
Armament: a variety of stores on underwing hardpoints
Operators: Australia, Hong Kong, Indonesia, New Zealand, Singapore, Thailand

Aerospace Airtrainer CT/4

The Aerospace Airtrainer CT-4 originated in a design contest held by the Royal Aero Club in 1953. The winner was an Australian, who eventually had it built as the Victa Airtourer. New Zealand built the military trainer version, here seen in RNZAF service.

Aérospatiale SA.313B/SA.318C Alouette II

Of conventional configuration but sturdy design, the Aérospatiale Alouette II was one of the first true light multi-purpose helicopters and excelled in a variety of roles. This adaptability was facilitated by its reliable turboshaft engine, easy maintenance, and landing gear, which could be either of wheel or skid type, or floats, with provision for emergency flotation gear.

The Alouette II originated as Sud-Est SE.3120 Alouette (Lark), a three-seat light helicopter designed mainly for agricultural purposes. The first SE.3120 prototype was flown on 31 July 1952, powered by a 200-hp (149-kW) Salmson 9NH radial engine, and a year later established a new international helicopter closed-circuit duration record of 13 hours 56 minutes.

The basic airframe was then completely redesigned with the 360-shp (269-kW) Turboméca Artouste I turboshaft, and the first of two prototypes, designated SE.3130, was flown on 12 March 1955, followed by three pre-production aircraft in 1956. The Alouette II was granted a French certificate of airworthiness on 2 May 1956, and was soon in demand on the international market. In 1957 Sud-Est merged with Sud-Aviation, at which time the designation of the Alouette II was altered to SA.313B, remaining unchanged after Sud's take-over by Aérospatiale.

From the beginning, the Alouette II proved a most successful design and was found particularly suitable for operations in higher altitudes. Thus, during the period 9 – 13 June 1958, an Artouste-powered Alouette II set up an international helicopter altitude record of 36,027 ft (10984 m) for all classes, and a height record of 31,440 ft (9583 m) in the 1000/1750-kg category. By September 1960 no less than 598 Alouette IIs had been ordered by customers in 22 different countries, and it was being assembled by Republic in the USA and Saab in Sweden. It also became the first French aircraft of any kind, and the first helicopter in the world, to be granted an American certification.

A development of the Alouette II with a 400-shp (298-kW) Turboméca Turmo II engine, with the designation SE.3140, was announced in May 1957 but did not reach the production stage. Another derivative, powered by the more economical Astazou IIA

turboshaft engine and featuring a new centrifugal clutch, was far more successful. The first prototype, designated SA 3180, was flown on 31 January 1960 and after thorough trials an extension of the Alouette II French certificate of airworthiness was granted on 18 February 1964. Production, as the SA.318C, commenced in the same year, with first deliveries taking place in 1965. Of generally similar appearance and versatility, the SA.318C has a slightly higher level speed, longer range, and was capable of lifting heavier loads, but is less suitable for operations in higher altitudes. The success of the basic Alouette II design is reflected in the growing number of civil and military customers: by 1 June 1967 a total of 988 Alouette IIs (including those with Astazou engines) had been ordered (and 969 delivered); by 21 May 1970 this total had increased to 1,200 (923 with Artouste and 277 with Astazou engines); this total included 450 Alouette IIs delivered to the French air force, army and navy as well as private customers. By the spring of 1975, when the production of this helicopter was terminated, the number of Alouette IIs sold had reached 1,300, and it was used by 126 civil and military operators in 46 countries.

In the military field, the Alouette II (particularly with the Artouste engine) has found widespread use in a variety of roles: anti-submarine warfare, close ground-support, battlefield reconnaissance, light transport, flying crane (payload 1,100 – 1,322 lb (500 – 600 kg), casualty evacuation (two stretchers, one/two sitting cases, one attendant), aerial photography, and training. A wide range of suitable optional equipment was available and fitted to customer's requirements.

A substantial number of Alouette IIs are still in active service in many parts of the world.

Type: (SA 313B Alouette II) light general-purpose helicopter
Powerplant: one 530-shp (derated to 360-shp) (395-/269-kW) Turboméca Artouste IIC-6 turboshaft
Performance: (at maximum take-off weight) maximum speed at sea level 115 mph (185 km/h); maximum cruising speed at sea level 102 mph (165 km/h); rate of climb at sea level 825 ft (252 m) per minute; service ceiling

7,050 ft (2150 m); hovering ceiling in ground effect 5,400 ft (1650 m); hovering ceiling out of ground effect 3,000 ft (920 m); range with maximum fuel at sea level 350 miles (565 km); range with 1,200-lb (545-kg) payload at sea level 62 miles (100 km); range with 860-lb (390-kg) payload at sea level 186 miles (300 km); flight endurance with maximum fuel at sea level 4 hours 6 minutes
Weights: empty 1,973 lb (895 kg); maximum take-off 3,527 lb (1600 kg)
Dimensions: diameter of main rotor 33 ft 5⅝ in (10.20 m) diameter of tail rotor 5 ft 11 in (1.81 m); length (rotor blades folded) 31 ft 10 in (9.70 m); width (rotor blades folded) 6 ft 10 in (2.08 m); height 9 ft 0 in (2.75 m); main rotor disc area 880 sq ft (81.7 m²)
Armament: optional: can be fitted with two AS.11 missiles; ASW variants carry homing torpedoes
Operators: Algeria, Bangladesh, Belgium, Cameroun, Chad, Dominican Republic, Finland, France, India, Indonesia, Israel, Ivory Coast, Kampuchea, Laos, Lebanon, Libya, Mexico, Morocco, Nigeria, Pakistan, Peru, Portugal, South Africa, Sweden, Switzerland, Tunisia, West Germany, others (list includes past and present users; many Alouette IIs have changed hands since their original sales and are almost impossible to track down)

Type: (SA.318C Alouette II Astazou) light general-purpose helicopter
Powerplant: one 530-shp (derated to 360-shp) (395-/269-kW) Turboméca Astazou IIA turboshaft
Performance: (at maximum military take-off weight) maximum speed at sea level 127 mph (205 km/h); maximum cruising speed at sea level 105 mph (170 km/h); rate of climb at sea level 1,312 ft (400 m) per minute; service ceiling 10,800 ft (3300 m); hovering ceiling in ground effect 4,985 ft (1520 m); hovering ceiling out of ground effect 2,950 ft (900 m); range with maximum fuel at sea level 447 miles (720 km); range with 1,322-lb (600-kg) payload 62 miles (100 km); range with 1,058-lb (480-kg) payload 186 miles (300 km); maximum flight endurance at sea level 5 hours 18 minutes
Weights: empty 1,961 lb (890 kg); maximum take-off (civil version) 3,527 lb (1600 kg); maximum take-off (military version) 3,630 lb (1650 kg)
Dimensions: diameter of main rotor 33 ft 5⅝ in (10.20 m); diameter of tail rotor 6 ft 3 in (1.91 m); length of fuselage (tail rotor turning) 31 ft 11¾ in (9.75 m); width (rotor blades folded) 7 ft 6½ in (2.30 m); height 9 ft 0 in (2.75 m); main rotor disc area 880 sq ft (81.7 m²)
Operators: see under SE.313B

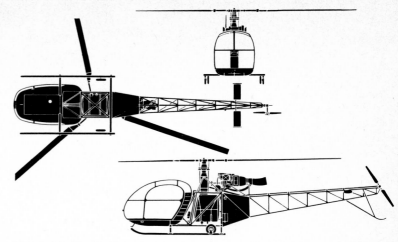

Aérospatiale Alouette II

Aérospatiale SA.316B/SA.319B Alouette III

The Aérospatiale Alouette III is an enlarged and most successful development of the Alouette II, with increased cabin capacity, improved equipment, more powerful turbine engine and generally enhanced performance. The prototype, designated SE.3160, was first flown on 28 February 1959, followed by the first production series known as SA.316A. In June 1960 an Alouette III with seven people aboard demonstrated its extraordinary performance by making landings and take-offs at an altitude of 15,780 ft (4810 m) on Mont Blanc in the French Alps. Five months later the same Alouette III with two crew and a 550-lb (250-kg) payload made landings and take-offs at an altitude of 19,698 ft (6004 m) in the Himalayas — both hitherto unprecedented achievements for a helicopter. The SA.316A was built for domestic and export market and, in June 1962, became subject to a licence-production agreement with HAL in India. The first Indian-assembled Alouette III was flown on 11 June 1965.

Various experimental developments followed, including an all-weather variant which made its initial flight on 27 April 1964. The subsequent SA.316B, first flown on 27 June 1968, featured strengthened main and tail rotor transmissions and was generally slightly heavier, but could carry more payload. It became the principal production version, with first deliveries made in 1970, and was an immediate export success. The Alouette III prototypes and the first two production series were powered by Turboméca Artouste IIIB turboshaft engines, replaced by the Artouste IIID on the SA.316C, built in limited numbers only.

The Alouette III cabin is more enclosed than that of the Alouette II, and can accom-

France's ALAT (Army light aviation) is almost wholly helicopter-equipped. Here seen against rugged mountains, the Alouette III is numerically the leading machine. This one comes from the Gendarmerie, without missiles.

continued

modate up to seven persons (or pilot and six fully equipped troops). All passenger seats are easily removable to provide an unobstructed cargo space. There is provision for an external sling for hauling loads up to 1,650 lb (750 kg) or, for the air/sea rescue role, a hoist of 380-lb (175-kg) capacity. Like most other light general-purpose helicopters, the Alouette III can also be used for casualty evacuation, carrying two stretcher cases and two seated persons behind the pilot. But the most popular military modifications became the two-seat light attack version armed with a selection of anti-personnel and anti-armour weapons, and the naval version, used principally in anti-submarine role.

Experiments with the thermally more efficient and more economical Astazou turboshaft engine led to the SA.319B, which is a direct development of the SA.316B. The first experimental SA.319B prototype was completed and flown in 1967, but full production did not start until 1973.

The Alouette III variants were even more successful on the international market than those of its predecessor, and by 1 April 1978 no less than 1,382 machines had been sold (with 1,370 delivered) to 190 civil and military operators in 72 countries. In addition to licence-production by HAL at Bangalore in India (200), similar agreements were signed with ICA-Brassov in Romania (for 130) and Switzerland (for 60). In Indian service the Alouette III has proved so successful that a special armed version known as Chetak is now under development by HAL. Since 1972 the Rhodesian Air Force has acquired at least 60 SA.319s from South Africa.

Type: SA 316B Alouette III general-purpose helicopter
Powerplant: one 870-shp (649-kW) Turbo-méca Artouste IIIB turboshaft, derated to 570 shp (425 kW)
Performance: (standard version, at maximum take-off weight) maximum speed at sea level 130 mph (210 km/h); maximum cruising speed at sea level 115 mph (185 km/h); maximum rate of climb at sea level 850 ft (260 m) per minute; service ceiling 10,500 ft (3200 m); hovering ceiling in ground effect 9,450 ft (2880 m); hovering ceiling out of ground effect 5,000 ft (1520 m); range with maximum fuel at sea level 298 miles (480 km); range at optimum altitude 335 miles (540 km)
Weights: empty 2,520 lb (1143 kg); maximum take-off 4,850 lb (2200 kg)
Dimensions: diameter of main rotor 36 ft 1¾ in (11.02 m); diameter of tail rotor 6 ft 3¼ in (1.91 m); length (rotor blades folded) 32 ft 10¾ in (10.03 m); width (rotor blades folded) 8 ft 6¼ in (2.60 m); height 9 ft 10 in (3.00 m); main rotor disc area 1,026 sq ft (95.38 m²)
Operational equipment: (assault role with reduced crew) choice of one 7.62-mm (0.3-in) AA52 machine-gun on tripod behind the pilot's seat, firing to starboard through door space, or one 20-mm MG 151/20 cannon in open turret-type mounting port side of cabin, or four AS.11 or two AS.12 wire-guided anti-tank missiles on external launching rails, or 68-mm rocket pods.
Users: *see* under SA.319B Alouette III (Astazou)

Type: SA 319B Alouette III (Astazou) light general-purpose helicopter
Powerplant: one 870-shp (649-kW) Turbo-méca Astazou XIV turboshaft, derated to 600 shp (448 kW)
Performance: (at max take-off weight) maximum speed at sea level 136 mph (220 km/h); maximum cruising speed at sea level 122 mph (197 km/h); maximum rate of climb at sea level 885 ft (270 m) per minute; hovering ceiling in ground effect 10,170 ft (3100 m); hovering ceiling out of ground effect 5,575 ft (1700 m); range with six passengers (take-off at sea level) 375 miles (605 km)
Weights: empty 2,527 lb (1146 kg); maximum take-off 4,960 lb (2250 kg)
Dimensions: diameter of main rotor 36 ft 1¾ in (11.02 m); diameter of tail rotor 6 ft 3¼ in (1.91 m); length (rotor blades folded) 32 ft 10¾ in (10.03 m); height 9 ft 10 in (3.00 m); main rotor disc area 1,026.5 sq ft (95.38

m²)
Operational equipment/armament: optional, fitted according to role. As light assault helicopter can be armed with one internally-mounted 7.62-mm (0.3-in) AA52 machine gun, or (with two crew) one 20-mm MG 151/20 cannon, or four AS.11 or two AS.12 wire-guided missiles of external mounts, or 68-mm rocket pods; successful trials have been flown with HOT missiles; in ASW role, two Mk 44 homing torpedoes, or one Mk 44 torpedo and MAD gear; in ASV role, two AS.12 wire-guided missiles
Operators: (military) Abu Dhabi, Argentina, Austria, Bangladesh, Belgium, Burma, Denmark, Dominican Republic, Ecuador, Ethiopia, France, Ghana, Hong Kong, India, Indonesia, Iraq, Ireland, Israel, Ivory Coast, Jordan, Laos, Lebanon, Libya, Malagasy, Malaysia, Mexico, Morocco, Nepal, Netherlands, Pakistan, Peru, Portugal, Rhodesia, Romania, Saudi Arabia, Singapore, South Africa, Switzerland, Tunisia, Venezuela, Yugoslavia, Zaire, Zambia

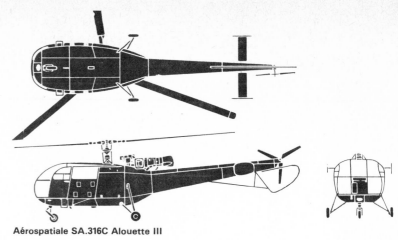

Aérospatiale SA.316C Alouette III

Aérospatiale Alouette III of 3 Sqn, Royal Malaysian Air Force, based at Kuala Lumpur and used for liaison and forward air control duties.

Aérospatiale Alouette III of the Força Aerea Portuguesa, operated in Portuguese Guinea in 1971 and based at Bissau Airport.

Shown in the markings of the Royal Jordanian Air Force, this Aérospatiale Alouette III is one of 15 in service based at Amman.

Aérospatiale Alouette III in the markings of the Tunisian Republican Air Force which currently has six of the type in use.

Aérospatiale Caravelle 3/6R

The prototype Aérospatiale (Sud-Aviation) Caravelle made its first flight on 27 May, 1955, with the second following just under a year later. This first French jet airliner attracted considerable attention with its novel placing of the engines on the rear-fuselage sides, a position which was subsequently adopted by other major transport aircraft manufacturers.

The first Caravelles to enter service, Srs 1s, appeared on Air France and SAS routes in mid-1959. These were followed by a number of passenger variants offering the same basic passenger accommodation but with increasingly powerful engines, and the Srs 6R managed to break into the US market when 20 were ordered by United Air Lines, deliveries being made between June 1961 and February 1962.

Later variants offered still more powerful engines, increased wing area and a stretched fuselage which, in the Srs 12, could accommodate up to 140 passengers, compared with earlier types' 64-70 passengers.

A total of 282 Caravelles had been built when the last aircraft, a Srs 12, was completed in 1972, but only a handful found their way into military service.

Only the earlier Caravelles were used by the military and a few are still in service. The Central African Empire's *Force Aérienne Centrafricaine* used an ex-Sterling Airways Caravelle as a personal transport for Emperor Bokassa, while the President of Chad has a similar personal Srs 6R which is operated by the *Escadrille Tchadienne*. President Tito has a Caravelle 6N and a Boeing 727 for his personal use, operated by the Yugoslav air force.

The Swedish air force, the *Flygvapen*, operates two former SAS Caravelle Srs 3s on transport and VIP services from Malmslatt.

In its home country, the Caravelle is in small-scale service with the French air force. Three Srs 3s are in use, with one operated for presidential business by the *Groupe des Liaisons Aériennes Ministérielles* at Villacoublay, near Paris, while other Caravelles have replaced a number of Douglas DC-6As and Bs at Evreux, where they are used for services to French bases in the Pacific.

Type: twin-jet airliner
Powerplant: (Srs 3) two 11,400 lb (5170 kg) Rolls-Royce Avon 522 turbojets; (Srs 6R) two 12,600 lb (5725 kg) Rolls-Royce Avon 533R turbojets
Performance: (Srs 3) maximum cruising speed at 25,000 ft (7620 m) at 90,000 lb (40820 kg) 500 mph (805 km/h); (Srs 6R) maximum cruising speed at 25,000 ft (7620 m) at 94,800 lb (43000 kg) 525 mph (845 km/h); take-off distance at maximum weight (Srs 3) 6,000 ft (1830 m); (Srs 6R) 6,800 ft (2073 m); landing distance at maximum weight (Srs 3) 5,900 ft (1800 m), (Srs 6R) 5,650 ft (1720 m); range with maximum payload, 300-mile (480-km) diversions and reserves (Srs 3) 1,056 miles (1700 km), (Srs 6R) 1,430 miles (2300 km)
Weights: (Srs 3) empty 53,320 lb (24185 kg); maximum take-off 101,413 lb (46000 kg); (Srs 6R) empty 57,935 lb (26280 kg); maximum take-off 110,230 lb (50000 kg)
Dimensions: (Srs 3 and 6R) span 112 ft 6 in (34.30 m); length 105 ft 0 in (32.01 m); height 28 ft 7 in (8.72 m); wing area 1,579 sq ft (146.7 m²)
Operators: Central African Republic, Chad, France, Mauritania, Sweden, Yugoslavia

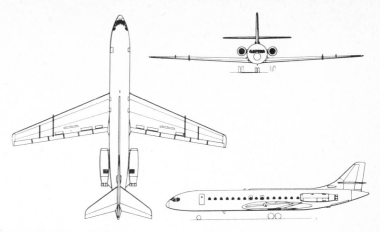

Aérospatiale Caravelle 6R

Aérospatiale Caravelles are used by the French *Armée de l'Air* for global services between France and the Pacific nuclear test bases, despite their extremely limited range. Another, illustrated, is a VIP aircraft based at Villacoublay near Paris.

Aérospatiale SA.365 Dauphin 2

The Aérospatiale Dauphin is being developed in several versions, with single and twin engines, as a replacement for the Aérospatiale Alouette III. The first version to fly was the SA.360, with a single Astazou XVI turboshaft, on 2 June, 1972. It was later re-engined with the Astazou XVIIIA and modifications were incorporated; in May 1973 this helicopter set up three speed records in its class. A second SA.360 prototype flew on 29 January, 1973 and French airworthiness certification was awarded in December 1975. The first twin-engine Dauphin to fly was the SA.365 prototype, on 24 January, 1975, and development of both versions is proceeding, with orders for more than 70 achieved to date. The only military order announced is for two SA.365s for the Sri Lanka air force. This formed part of a financial agreement signed between France and Sri Lanka in November 1977. The two Dauphins will operate from bases at Katunayake and China Bay on government and VIP duties.

A development of the SA.360, the SA.361H, has flown with a 1,400-shp (1044-kW) Turboméca Astazou XXB turboshaft and the Aérospatiale Starflex rotor head originally developed for the AS.350 helicopter. The SA.361H is a military version capable of anti-tank operations with eight HOT missiles (firing trials were completed in May 1978) or for ground attack using combinations of 20-mm cannon, 7.62-mm machine guns or rockets. As a transport the SA.361H can carry up to 10 assault troops.

Type: twin-turbine general-purpose helicopter
Powerplant: two 650-shp (485-kW) Turboméca Arriel turboshafts
Performance: (at a weight of 6,614 lb (3000 kg)) maximum speed 196 mph (315 km/h); cruising speed 158 mph (255 km/h); maximum rate of climb at sea level 2,460 ft (750 m) per minute; service ceiling 19,680 ft (6000 m); hovering ceiling in ground effect 11,000 ft (3350 m); hovering ceiling out of ground effect 8,530 ft (2600 m); maximum range (no reserves) 289 miles (465 km)
Weights: empty 3,946 lb (1790 kg); maximum take-off 7,495 lb (3400 kg)
Dimensions: main rotor diameter 38 ft 4 in (11.68 m); length 43 ft 7 in (13.29 m); height to top of rotor head 11 ft 6 in (3.50 m); main rotor disc area 1,154 sq ft (107.15 m²)
Operators: Sri Lanka

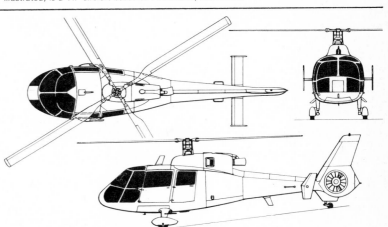

Aérospatiale SA.360 Dauphin

Though no Aérospatiale Dauphin helicopters had been ordered for tactical military roles in mid-1979 this illustration shows how the type could perform as a multi-role assault airlifter. Single- and twin-engined models exist.

Aérospatiale Fouga 90

Though in June 1979 no order for it had been placed, this new basic trainer is hoped by Aérospatiale to find wide markets because of its low cost of acquisition and upkeep. It was designed as a modernized descendent of the Magister (whose original manufacturer, Air Fouga, was absorbed by Potez, which in turn vanished into Aérospatiale). The main differences introduced by the Fouga 90 are simple turbofan engines of very low fuel consumption, a much deeper mid-fuselage to seat the instructor in a high rear cockpit with good all-round view, and completely updated systems and avionics. Most of the rest of the airframe is similar or even identical to the Magister, and it is possible that Aérospatiale would consider re-building customers' Magisters to Fouga 90 standard. The main difficulty facing the nationalized concern is that the armed forces of France are not supporting the programme and have announced their intention of continuing with their existing Magisters at least until 1985. Accordingly the Fouga 90 is a company project, and a prototype was flown on 20 August 1978 in order to confirm estimated figures and demonstrate to potential buyers. Limiting load factors are +7 and −3 g, and Martin-Baker F10KX zero/zero seats are fitted, to suit the aircraft to weapons training and use as a light attack platform. There is no internal armament.

Type: basic and transition trainer, and light attack aircraft
Powerplant: two 1,520-lb (690-kg) Turboméca Astafan IIG turbofans
Performance: maximum speed at height 398 mph (640 km/h); service ceiling 40,000 ft (12195 m); range with maximum fuel 1,150 miles (1850 km)
Weights: empty 5,732 lb (2600 kg); maximum loaded, clean 7,716 lb (3500 kg); maximum loaded, with weapons 9,259 lb (4200 kg)
Dimensions: span (without tip tanks) 39 ft 3 in (11.96 m); length 34 ft 0½ in (10.38 m); height 10 ft 1¼ in (3.08 m)
Armament: four underwing hardpoints, inner pair each rated at 551 lb (250 kg) and outer pair each rated at 331 lb (150 kg); options include 30-mm cannon pods, AS.11 or AS.12 wire-guided missiles, or various bombs, rocket pods and other stores
Operators: none yet (summer 1979)

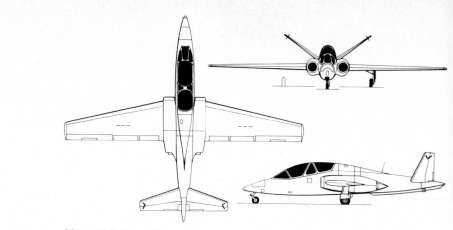

Aérospatiale Fouga 90

Though no order had been placed by late 1979, the Fouga 90 is claimed by Aérospatiale to be the cheapest available military jet trainer. It was derived from the first jet trainer in the Armée de l'Air, the Magister of 1953. Although 929 Magisters were delivered, the Armée de l'Air has denied intention to buy the Model 90.

Aérospatiale (Nord) 262 Frégate

The Aérospatiale N 262 is a pressurized development of the Nord M.H.260 Super Broussard (first flown on 29 July 1960) and features the same distinctive high wing/underslung engine nacelles/main undercarriage into fuselage fairings scheme, permitting a low loading level. Design work on the Nord 262 began early in 1961 and incorporated experience gained with the six M.H.260s built. The Nord 262 prototype, first flown on 24 December 1962, was followed by three pre-production aircraft and after extensive tests the Series A was officially approved for passenger service in the spring of 1965, although production deliveries of Series B aircraft had already started in 1964. At the time of its appearance the Nord 262 was acclaimed as one of the more economical contenders for 'Douglas DC-3 replacement' class, and had a considerable sales appeal to both civil and military customers. A project to revise the basic design as a STOL transport with lift jets remained on paper, but the conventional N 262 was constantly improved. In the autumn of 1967 trials began with an N 262 equipped with automatic landing equipment which enabled the aircraft to land in poor weather conditions. In 1969 two new versions were announced, designated Series C and Series D; later both these series were renamed Frégate, and were the final production version.

The standard early production version was the N 262 Series A with two 1,080-shp (806-kW) Turboméca Bastan VIC turboprop engines. The type received FAA Type Approval on 15 March 1965, and the first production deliveries were made on 17 August 1965, preceded by Series B aircraft (see below). Users included the French air force (6) and the French navy (15); another 46 Series A

machines were delivered to various commercial customers.

N 262 Series B is the designation allocated to the first four production aircraft. The first Series B aircraft was flown on 8 June 1964, received official certification on 16 July 1964 and entered service eight days later.

The Frégate Series C is the commercial version with more powerful Bastan VII turboprop engines, which also dispense with the water-methanol injection system of Series A and B aircraft. The new powerplants improve take-off performance from 'hot and high' airfields, and give higher single-engine ceiling and better cruising speed. After prolonged flight tests with the new engines and various aerodynamic improvements the Series C was introduced into production in 1970 alongside Series A aircraft. Official certification was granted on 24 December 1970. The standard version has a crew of two and carries 26 passengers, with provision for quick change to a cargo configuration.

The Frégate Series D is the military counterpart to the Series C, intended to fulfil various transport tasks and aerial survey missions. As an army transport, the Frégate Series D can carry either 22 or 29 troops, or 18 paratroops, or (after quick conversion), an equivalent amount of cargo. Fitted out as an ambulance the Frégate can accommodate 12 stretcher cases and two medical attendants. For aerial survey the Frégate can carry a whole range of cameras and survey equipment, plus a fully equipped darkroom. As in the civil versions, all accommodation is pressurized, sound-proofed and air-conditioned.

Deliveries of the Nord 262s and Frégates on order were completed in 1976, and in an attempt to restart production Aérospatiale pro-

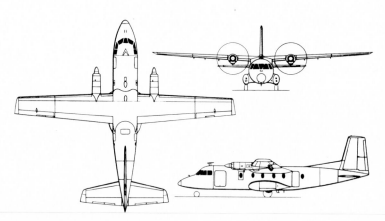

Aérospatiale (Nord) 262 Frégate

posed an improved version designated Nord 262A-II in commuter/third-level transport/military training/coastal patrol variants. The prospective market was estimated at 150 aircraft, and the plan was linked with the development of the Mohawk 298 (N262 with PT6A turboprops) in the USA. However, in May 1978 the French government declined to support the resumption of Frégate production.

Type: (Series D) light transport/multi purpose utility
Powerplant: two 1,145-shp (854-kW) Turboméca Bastan VII turboprops
Performance: (at maximum take-off weight) maximum speed 260 mph (418 km/h); maximum and economical cruising speed 254 mph (408 km/h); rate of climb at sea level 1,380 ft (420 m) per minute; service ceiling 28,500 ft (8690 m); service ceiling on one engine at 21,000 lb (9525-kg) 15,000 ft (4920 m); range with 26 passengers and baggage (no reserves) 900 miles (1450 km)
Weights: basic empty 13,668 lb (6200 kg); basic operational 15,928 lb (7225 kg); maximum payload 6,779 lb (3075 kg); maximum take-off 23,810 lb (10800 kg)
Dimensions: span 74 ft 1¾ in (22.60 m); length 63 ft 3 in (19.60 m); height 20 ft 4½ in (6.21 m); wing area 601 sq ft (55.79 m²)
Operators:: Congo Republic, France, Gabon, Upper Volta.

Aérospatiale SA.315B Lama

Initially evolved to meet an Indian armed forces requirement of 1968 and intended primarily for operations in 'hot and high' conditions, the basic design of the SA.315B Lama combines a reinforced Alouette II airframe with SA.316B Alouette III dynamic components, including its Artouste powerplant and rotor system. The SA.315 prototype was first flown on 17 March 1969, received the French certificate of airworthiness on 30 September 1970, and the name Lama bestowed by its manufacturer in July 1971.

From the outset the SA.315B excelled in load-to-altitude performance. During a series of demonstration flights in the Indian Himalayas in 1969 an SA.315B, carrying a crew of two and 308 lb (120 kg) of fuel, landed and took off at the highest altitude ever recorded, 24,600 ft (7500 m). On 21 June 1972, a Lama with only a pilot aboard, established a helicopter absolute height record of 40,820 ft (12552 m). These achievements, and the high reputation for reliability established by its close relations, the Alouette II and III, ensured a good reception on the market. Already in 1971 arrangements were completed for licence production of the SA.315B by HAL at Bangalore in India. The first Indian-assembled Lama flew on 6 October 1972, with deliveries commencing in December 1973. The HAL-produced Lama is renamed Cheetah.

Similar to the Alouette series, the SA.315B

Lama can be fitted out for various commercial roles, such as a light passenger transport or for agricultural tasks, while the military variants include conversions for liaision, observation, photography, air/sea rescue (hoist capacity 352 lb/160 kg), transport (maximum external load 2,500 lb/1135 kg), ambulance (two stretchers and one medical attendant), and other tasks. Its altitude performance makes it particularly suited for mountainous districts: the production Lama can transport underslung external loads of up to 2,204 lb (1000 kg) at an altitude of 8,200 ft (2500 m). Another important factor is its universal landing gear consisting of skids with removable wheels for ground handling, provision for floats for normal operations from water and emergency flotation gear, inflatable in the air.

In 1978 agreement was reached between Aérospatiale and Helibras in Brazil for the assembly of SA.315B Lama helicopters, leading to full licence production at a later stage.

Type: general-purpose helicopter
Powerplant: one 870-shp (649-kW) Turboméca Artouste IIIB turboshaft, derated to 550 shp (410-kW)
Performance: (at 5,070 lb/2300 kg) maximum cruising speed 75 mph (120 km/h); maximum rate of climb at sea level 768 ft (234 m) per minute; service ceiling 9,840 ft (3000 m); hovering ceiling in ground effect

Though superficially similar to the 1953-designed Alouette II, the Aérospatiale SA 315B Lama has markedly superior performance, gained from the Artouste engine and transmission, to the Alouette II.

9,675 ft (2950 m); hovering ceiling out of ground effect 5,085 ft (1550 m)
Weights: empty 2,251 lb (1021 kg); normal take-off 4,300 lb (1950 kg); maximum take-off with externally-slung cargo 5,070 lb (2300 kg)
Dimensions: diameter of main rotor 36 ft 1¾ in (11.02 m); diameter of tail rotor 6 ft 3¼ in (1.91 m); length of fuselage 33 ft 8 in (10.26 m); height 10 ft 1¾ in (3.09 m); main rotor disc area 1,026.5 sq ft (95,38 m²)
Operators: by 1 April 1978 total of 250 Lamas had been ordered (of which 215 delivered) by 84 operators in 26 countries; licence-built by HAL for the Indian army as the Cheetah

Aérospatiale (Fouga) CM.170 Magister/CM.175 Zéphyr

Apart from a BAe 125-700 executive transport the only jets in the Irish Army Air Corps are six Aérospatiale Fouga Magisters, which replaced the Vampires. Though they have two FN machine guns and rocket launchers they are used as pilot trainers.

One of the most-widely used trainer/light attack aircraft, the Air Fouga (later Potez and now Aérospatiale) CM.170 Magister was produced to meet an *Armée de l'Air* requirement for a jet trainer (the first in the world). The prototype made its first flight on 23 July 1952, and a pre-production batch of 10 was ordered the following year. An initial order of 95 for the *Armée de l'Air* was placed in 1954 and the first production aircraft made its maiden flight on 13 January 1954. Since then over 400 Magisters have been produced for the *Armée de l'Air* alone.

A specially-equipped naval version was produced for the *Aéronavale*, designated CM.175 Zéphyr. Two prototypes and 30 production aircraft were built to this standard, and the Zéphyr provides naval pilots with their initial experience of operating from an aircraft-carrier.

In addition to French-manufactured Magisters offered for export, the trainer was manufactured under licence in West Germany by Flugzeug-Union-Sud for *Luftwaffe* training school. However, with the transfer of most German flying training to the United States by the end of the 1960s, the Magister was phased out of service. Valmet OY in Finland built 62 Magisters under licence (in addition to 18 purchased from France) and Israel Aircraft Industries also acquired manufacturing rights for the type, building many for light tactical use as well as training. Total production was 916 aircraft.

Aérospatiale (Fouga) CM.170 Magister

IAI-built CM 170 Magister (No 242) used in the basic flying training role by Heyl Ha'Avir of Israel Defence Force/Air Force at Hatzerim air base.

IAI-built CM 170 (No 207) of the Heyl Ha'Avir aerobatic team. These aircraft were often used in the ground-attack role during the Arab-Israeli wars of 1967 and 1973.

CM 170 Magister of the French national aerobatic team "Patrouille de France" in pre-1972 colour scheme and with the emblem of Groupement d'Instruction 312.

continued

The Magister is all-metal. The mid-mounted wings have single-slotted flaps and airbrakes. The butterfly-type tail has surfaces separated by 110°.

Fuel is housed in two fuselage tanks of 56-Imperial gallon (255-litre) and 104-Imperial gallon (475-litre) capacity, with wingtip tanks each holding 27.5 Imperial gallons (125 litres).

The tandem cockpits are pressurized and air-conditioned, with individually-regulated oxygen supplies. Ejection seats are not fitted. VHF, blind flying equipment and radio compass are standard in the trainer, while UHF, Tacan and IFF may be fitted to armed Magisters.

Armament combinations include two 7.5-mm (0.295-in) or 7.62-mm (0.3-in) machine-guns mounted in the nose, with 200 rounds of ammunition per gun. A gyro gun-sight is fitted in both cockpits, the rear one having periscopic sighting. Underwing ordnance loads include two Matra Type 181 pods each with eighteen 37-mm rockets, two launchers each mounting seven 68-mm rockets, four 55-lb (25-kg) air-to-ground rockets, eight 88-mm rockets, two 110-lb (50-kg) bombs, or two Nord AS.11 air-to-ground guided missiles.

About 300 Magisters of the 437 originally procured remain in service with the *Armée de l'Air* and will continue until the mid-1980s. A 150-hour basic flying training course is provided for commissioned pupils at the *Ecole de l'Air* at Salon-de-Provence and similar instruction is provided for other ranks at *Groupement Ecole* 315, Cognac. Magisters also serve with *Groupement Ecole* 313 to provide instructor training for the *Armée de l'Air* and basic flying training for overseas students. The *Force Aérienne Belge*'s Magisters at the *Ecole de Pilotage Avancé*, Brustem, began to be replaced by Dassault-Breguet/Dornier Alpha Jets in 1979, although the Magister will continue to serve in various second-line units. Finland's Magisters at the Central Flying School, Kauhava, are to be replaced by the BAe Hawk.

Israel is the foremost operator of the Magister as a light attack aircraft, some 80 remaining in service as both trainers and operational aircraft. The Magister was particularly successful during the Six-Day War of June 1967, flying ground attack sorties on both the Egyptian and Jordanian fronts. The Irish Army Air Corps also operates the Magister in the dual light attack/training role, six Super Magisters being based at Baldonnel near Dublin.

Type: Jet trainer and light attack aircraft.
Powerplant: (Magister) two 880-lb (400-kg) Turboméca Marboré IIA turbojets; (Super Magister) two 1,058-lb (480-kg) Turboméca Marboré VI.
Performance: (Magister) maximum speed at 30,000 ft (9144 m) 444 mph (715 km/h), (Super Magister) 463 mph (745 km/h); (Magister) service ceiling 36,090 ft (11000 m), (Super Magister) 44,300 ft (13500 m); (Magister) range 575 miles (925 km), (Super Magister) 585 miles (940 km)
Weights: empty equipped 4,740 lb (2150 kg); take-off with external tanks 6,835 lb (3100 kg); maximum take-off 7,055 lb (3200 kg)
Dimensions: span over tip tanks 39 ft 10 in (12.15 m); length 33 ft (10.06 m); height 9 ft 2 in (2.80 m); wing area 186.1 sq ft (17.30 m²)
Armament: two 7.5-mm (0.295-in) or 7.62-mm (0.3-in) machine-guns in the nose, and underwing rockets, bombs or Nord AS.11 missiles
Operators: Algeria, Bangladesh, Belgium, Cameroon, Finland, France, Ireland, Israel, Lebanon, Libya, Morocco, Rwanda, Salvador, Senegal, Togo, Uganda

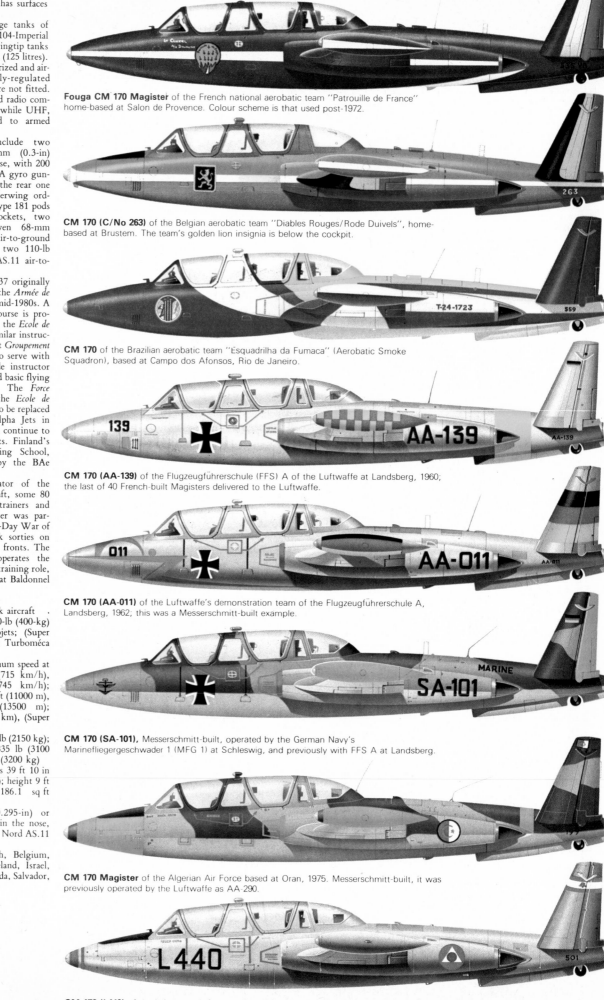

Fouga CM 170 Magister of the French national aerobatic team "Patrouille de France" home-based at Salon de Provence. Colour scheme is that used post-1972.

CM 170 (C/No 263) of the Belgian aerobatic team "Diables Rouges/Rode Duivels", home-based at Brustem. The team's golden lion insignia is below the cockpit.

CM 170 of the Brazilian aerobatic team "Esquadrilha da Fumaca" (Aerobatic Smoke Squadron), based at Campo dos Afonsos, Rio de Janeiro.

CM 170 (AA-139) of the Flugzeugführerschule (FFS) A of the Luftwaffe at Landsberg, 1960; the last of 40 French-built Magisters delivered to the Luftwaffe.

CM 170 (AA-011) of the Luftwaffe's demonstration team of the Flugzeugführerschule A, Landsberg, 1962; this was a Messerschmitt-built example.

CM 170 (SA-101), Messerschmitt-built, operated by the German Navy's Marinefliegergeschwader 1 (MFG 1) at Schleswig, and previously with FFS A at Landsberg.

CM 170 Magister of the Algerian Air Force based at Oran, 1975. Messerschmitt-built, it was previously operated by the Luftwaffe as AA-290.

CM 170 (L440) of the Lebanese air force and used for advanced training at Rayak, Lebanon.

Aérospatiale Rallye 100S

Basic training of French naval aviators is a task recently entrusted to 10 Aérospatiale Rallyes delivered to the *Aéronavale* in April 1974. Previously, the MS.733 Alcyon had been used to assess flying aptitude and for recreational flying, but retirement of the Alcyon resulted in the Aéronavale seeking new equipment. Its selection was the MS.880B Rallye 100S which entered service with the *Section de Vol Sportif 'Ecole Navale* at Lanvéoc-Poulmic.

The Rallye 100S is a two-seat low-wing light aircraft of all-metal construction, originally designed by La Société Morane-Saulnier in a national competition for light training types. Initial models of the Rallye entered production in 1961. There were two versions: the MS.880B Rallye Club and the MS.885 Super Rallye, powered by 100-hp (74.5-kW) and 145-hp (108-kW) Continental engines respectively. Substantial orders were forthcoming from civilian flying clubs in France and in export markets from Liberia to Peru, and over 400 Rallyes had been built when Morane-Saulnier went bankrupt in 1963.

The company was acquired by the Sud-Aviation subsidiary, SOCATA, which proceeded to develop the basic airframe with a variety of engines. Variants included the 150/180-hp (112/134-kW) Rallye Commodore and the Rallye Minerva, powered by a 220-hp (164-kW) Franklin 6A-350-C1 engine and marketed in the United States as the Minerva by Waco Aircraft Company. The majority of Rallyes are four-seaters and the higher-powered models have larger vertical tail surfaces, strengthened airframes and improved canopies and undercarriage fairings.

The success of Aérospatiale/SOCATA with the Rallye in military use has been limited but, in 1977, they produced the Rallye 235G. Powered by a 235-hp (175-kW) Lycoming O-540 engine, it was fitted with a strengthened wing incorporating hardpoints to carry four rocket-launchers or two machine-gun pods and two rocket-launchers. No sales of this variant had been recorded by the end of 1978.

Type: MS.880B Rallye 100S two-seat elementary trainer
Powerplant: one 100-hp (74.5-kW) Rolls-Royce Continental O-200A four-cylinder horizontally-opposed piston engine
Performance: maximum speed 121 mph (195 km/h); cruising speed at 75% power 106 mph

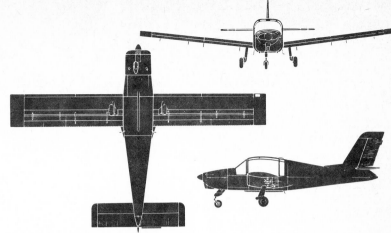

Aérospatiale Rallye 100

(170 km/h); stalling speed (flaps down) 47 mph (75 km/h); rate of climb 540 ft (165 m) per minute; maximum range 455 miles (720 km); STOL take-off distance 430 ft (130 m); service ceiling 10,500 ft (3200 m)
Weights: Empty 990 lb (450 kg); maximum

take-off 1,700 lb (770 kg)
Dimensions: span 31 ft 11 in (9.74 m); length 23 ft 1 in (7.04 m); height 9 ft 2 in (2.80 m); wing area 132.2 sq ft (12.28 m²)
Operators: Dominica, France, Libya (235GT)

The Rallye 235G is the world's most warlike single-engined lightplane, as this four-pylon specimen emphasizes. Built by Socata, a subsidiary of France's Aérospatiale, the manoeuvrable Rallye is normally a four-seater but can swap seats for stores.

Aérospatiale TB-30

In September 1978 first details were given of the Aérospatiale TB-30 piston-engined trainer, designed in collaboration with the *Armée de l'Air* to meet a new need for a light trainer able to weed out pupils before starting basic flying training on the jet Aérospatiale (Fouga) Magister. Like several other air forces this move is a response to rising costs, and the TB-30 is a simple and robust tandem two-seater whose design has been steadily refined by the Aérospatiale aircraft division over a period of several years. Features include a metal airframe with a life in the military training role of not less than 10,000 hours, a cockpit resembling that of a jet combat aircraft, and equipment for full basic flying training, including aerobatic, instrument, night, formation, navigation, combat manoeuvres and VFR/IFR navigation. Later it is probable that liaison (four-seat) and tactical attack versions will be marketed. The prototype was to fly in the last quarter of 1979, and production will be entrusted to the company's SOCATA subsidiary at Tarbes.

Type: primary trainer
Powerplant: one 300-hp (224-kW) Lycoming IO-540-K flat-six piston engine
Performance: (estimated) maximum speed in dive 287 mph (463 km/h); maximum cruising speed 218 mph (352 km/h); range with maximum fuel 750 miles (1200 km)
Weights: empty, not released; maximum loaded 2,645 lb (1200 kg)
Dimensions: span 24 ft 3¼ in (7.4 m); length 24 ft 3¼ in (7.4 m); height 8 ft 10¼ in (2.7 m)
Armament: under study for later versions
Operators: designed for *Armée de l'Air* and other French users

Aérospatiale SA.321 Super Frelon

Evolved from the smaller Sud-Aviation SA.3200 Frelon (Hornet) medium transport helicopter first flown on 10 June 1959, the Super Frelon was designed with technical assistance from Sikorsky Aircraft in the USA and built in cooperation with Fiat in Italy. As a result the SA.321 series embodies some typical Sikorsky characteristics such as watertight hull for amphibious operations, float-type sponsons housing the main landing gear, and a Sikorsky-designed rotor system. The first Super Frelon prototype, originally designated SA.3210-01, was flown on 7 December 1962, powered by three 1,320-shp (985-kW) Turboméca Turmo IIIC-2 engines, representing the troop transport version. In July 1963 this aircraft set up serveral international helicopter records, including a speed of 212 mph (341 km/h) over a 3-km course, and a speed of 217.77 mph (350.47 km/h) over a 15/25-km course. The second prototype, flown on 28 May 1963, was representative of the maritime version and featured stabilizing floats on the main landing gear supports. This was followed by four SA.321 pre-production aircraft, and an *Aéronavale* order for 17 aircraft designated SA.321G. This version was designed specifically for maritime patrol/anti-submarine role and became the first Super Frelon series to go into production. The SA.321G prototype was flown on 30 November 1965, and production deliveries started early in 1966. These helicopters carry comprehensive ASW/AS equipment and can also operate from helicopter-carriers; the tail section folds, and the shock-absorber legs of the tricycle undercarriage can be lowered to assist stowage.

The SA.321F commercial version, first flown on 7 April 1967, was approved for passenger service in June 1968. A faster and longer-ranged utility/public transport version, SA.321J, had joined the commercial field even before that date. Its prototype was first flown on 6 July 1967, and the SA.321J was granted a French certificate of airworthiness on 20 October 1967.

The Super Frelon had attracted foreign interest even before it had entered French service and the first export orders were soon in hand. The Super Frelons built for Israel were designated SA.321K and were fitted out as military transports, but after delivery in 1967 often proved their value in the airborne assault role. Similar military transports supplied to South Africa and Libya are designated SA.321L. These helicopters carry a crew of three and 27 – 30 troops; their rear loading ramps can be opened in flight.

The latest versions in production and service are the SA.321Ja passenger/cargo transport, a heavier version of the SA.321J and the SA.321H, a simplified universal military helicopter without stabilizing floats, external fairings or de-icing equipment. Like all military Super Frelon series, it can be fitted out as a troop transport (27 – 30 men), ambulance (crew, 15 stretchers and two medical attendants), ASR aircraft (provision for a hoist of 606-lb/275-kg capacity) and cargo transport (11,023 lb/5000 kg of internal or external cargo), but it is also suitable for ASV tasks and can be fitted out to customer's specifications.

Variants

SA.3200 FRELON. Troop transport: three Turmo IIIB turboshafts, two crew + 28 troops; swing-tail cargo loading. Prototype first flown 10 June 1959; two built; established basic Super Frelon configuration.
SA.3210.01 AND .02 SUPER FRELON. Prototype troop transport (first flown 7 December 1962) and maritime versions (first flown 28 May 1963): three 1,320-shp (985-kW) Turmo IIIC-2 engines
SA.321. Four pre-production aircraft
SA.321F SUPER FRELON. Civil passenger transport: three 1,320-shp (985-kW) Turmo IIIC-6 engines; designed to carry 34/37 passengers over 108 miles (175 km) stage lengths at a cruising speed of 143 mph (230 km/h), with 20 minutes reserve fuel. Prototype first flown 7 April 1967; French C of A granted on 27 June 1968, American C of A 29 August 1968.
SA.321G SUPER FRELON. Amphibious maritime/AS version: three Turmo IIIC-6 engines;

five crew; Sylphe panoramic radar in outrigger floats, maximum four homing torpedoes, dipping sonar. First production example flown 30 November 1965; deliveries from early 1966; total 24 built. (first SA.321 Super Frelon production series)
SA.321H SUPER FRELON. Simplified military service version: transport, attack and maritime tasks: three Turmo IIIE-6 engines. Current production SA.321
SA.321J SUPER FRELON. Utility/public transport: designed to carry maximum of 27 passengers with baggage over 435 miles (700 km) stage lengths at a cruising speed of 151 mph (243 km/h), with 20 minutes fuel reserves. Prototype flown 6 June 1967; French C of A granted 20 October 1967
SA.321Ja SUPER FRELON. Passenger/cargo transport: generally similar to SA.321J but maximum take-off weight increased to 28,660 lb (13000 kg); three Turmo IIIC engines; maximum 27 passengers. French C of A granted in December 1971
SA.321K SUPER FRELON. Non-amphibious military transport/assault version for Israel (military version of SA.321J): three Turmo IIIC engines
SA.321L SUPER FRELON. Non-amphibious military transport version for South Africa and Libya: three Turmo IIIC engines

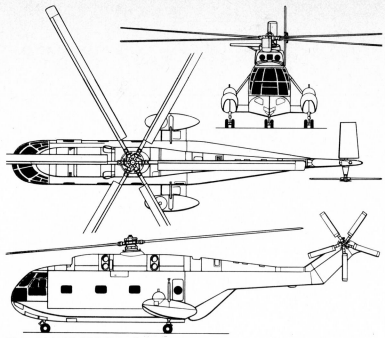

Aérospatiale SA.321G Super Frelon

Aérospatiale SA.321M Super Frelon, one of nine purchased by the Libyan Arab Republic Air Force.

One of eight Aérospatiale SA.321K Super Frelon assault helicopters used by the Heyl Ha'Avir, in service since 1966.

Type: (SA.321) heavy duty helicopter
Powerplant: (SA.321G) three 1,550-shp (1156-kW) Turboméca Turmo IIIC-6 turboshafts (Turmo IIIE-6 in SA.321H)
Performance: (at maximum take-off weight) maximum permissible speed at sea level 171 mph (275 km/h); cruising speed at sea level 155 mph (250 km/h); maximum rate of climb at sea level 1,312 ft (400 m) per minute; service ceiling 10,325 ft (3150 m); hovering ceiling in ground effect 7,120 ft (2170 m); normal range at sea level 509 miles (820 km); range at sea level with 7,716 lb (3500 kg) payload 633 miles (920 km); endurance in

ASW role 4 hours
Weights: empty (SA.321G) 15,130 lb (6863 kg); empty (SA.321H) 14,775 lb (6702 kg) maximum take-off (both versions) 28,660 lb (13000 kg)
Dimensions: diameter of main rotor 62 ft 0 in (18.90 m); diameter of tail rotor 13 ft 1½ in (4.00 m); length of fuselage 63 ft 7¾ in (19.40 m); width (SA.321G) 17 ft 0¾ in (5.20 m); height (SA.321G, rotor blades and tail folded) 16 ft 2½ in (4.94 m); height at tail rotor 21 ft 10¼ in (6.66 m); main rotor disc area 3,019 sq ft (280.55 m²)
Operational equipment: (SA.321G) self-

contained navigational system with doppler radar, Sylphe panoramic radar, dipping sonar; provision for maximum of four external homing torpedoes; Both SA.321G and SA.321H can be fitted with anti-surface vessel weapon system: two Exocet missiles with Omera-Segid Héraclès ORB-31D radar for target indication
Operators: By 1 May 1978 total of 97 Super Frelons sold (91 delivered) to 10 operators in eight countries. In military service in China, France, Iran, Israel, Libya and South Africa.

France's Aéronautique Navale uses the big Super Frelon in both the ASW and Commando assault-transport roles.

Aérospatiale/Westland SA.341/342 Gazelle

The SA.341 Gazelle all-purpose lightweight helicopter originated as Aérospatiale project X 300 to meet a French army requirement for a light observation helicopter. The designation was changed to SA.340 soon afterwards. The finished design showed close affinity to the SA.318C Alouette II, and eventually used the same Astazou II powerplant and transmission system. Unlike Alouette II, however, the new helicopter features a fully enclosed fuselage structure and has two pilots side-by-side, with full dual controls. It also introduced two innovations: the fenestron, or shrouded tail rotor, and a rigid modified Bölkow-type main rotor. And it shows every sign of sharing its predecessor's sales success and popularity.

While still in the final design stages the SA.340 attracted British interest leading to a joint development and production share-out agreement signed on 22 February 1967 and officially confirmed on 2 April 1968. The first prototype, designated SA.340.001 was flown on 7 April 1967, and the second on 12 April 1968. These were followed by four pre-production SA.341 Gazelles (first flown on 2 August 1968), of which the third was equipped to British army requirements, assembled in France, and then re-assembled by Westland in the UK as the prototype Gazelle AH.1. It was first flown on 28 April 1970.

On 14 May 1970 the first Aérospatiale-built SA.341 pre-production aircraft, in slightly modified form, established three new speed records for helicopters of its class, arousing even more foreign interest.

The first French production Gazelle, SA.341.1001, was cleared for its initial test flight on 6 August 1971; it had a longer cabin than its predecessors, an enlarged tail unit and an uprated Astazou IIIA engine. The initial Westland-assembled Gazelles followed early in 1972 (first flown on 31 January 1972). These comprised the first AH.1 for the British army, HT.2 for the Fleet Air Arm, and HT.3 for the RAF. The Gazelle entered service in the UK in May 1973, successfully passing the personnel familiarisation/training stage, and was then released for operational deployment, primarily to the Army Air Corps. The Gazelles procured by the Fleet Air Arm and RAF are used mainly for training purposes.

In the meantime, Gazelles in France had begun replacing Alouette IIs in service in increasing numbers, and the much faster light helicopter was acclaimed an unqualified success. No special modification is necessary to convert the Gazelle into an ambulance: two stretchers can be carried, one above the other, in the left side of the cabin, leaving space for the pilot and one seated medical attendant. There is also provision for a variety of operational equipment that can be fitted according to role, including a 1,540 lb (700 kg) cargo sling, a 300 lb (135 kg) rescue hoist, photographic or survey equipment, and armament. Military loads can comprise two rocket pods, wire-guided missiles or fixed forward-firing machine-guns, as well as reconnaissance flares and smoke markers.

The commercial success of this lightweight helicopter is evident from the official Aérospatiale and Westland sales figures: by 1 January 1973 a total of 289 Gazelles had been sold to, or ordered by, 19 operators in 10 countries; by 1 April 1978 these numbers had increased to 745 sold (670 delivered) to 115 civil and military operators in 29 countries.

The Aérospatiale-Westland co-production agreement was followed on 1 October 1971 by a licence-production agreement between Aérospatiale and SOKO in Yugoslavia for 112 Gazelles, and talks are in progress with other potential licence producers.

Variants

SA.341B GAZELLE AH.1. British Army version: Astazou IIIN engine; Nightsun searchlight, Decca Doppler 80 radar and automatic chart display. First Westland-assembled example flown on 31 January 1972; first entered operational service on 6 July 1974. Total 158.
SA.341C GAZELLE HT.2. Fleet Air Arm training version: Astazou IIIN engine; stability augmentation system and a hoist incorporated. First flown on 6 July 1972; first entered service on 10 December 1974. Total 30.
SA.341D GAZELLE HT.3. RAF training version: Astazou IIIN engine, stability augmentation system; Schermuly flares installation. First deliveries to service on 16 July 1973. Total 14.
SA.341E GAZELLE HCC.4. RAF communications version: Astazou IIIN engine. As a result of funding problems only one procured to date.
SA.341F GAZELLE. Basic French Army version: Astazou IIIC engine. Total of 166 to date.
SA.341G GAZELLE. Civil/commercial version: Astazou IIIA engine; officially certificated for passenger service on 7 June 1972; Subsequently became first helicopter to obtain US approval for operations under IFR Cat.1 conditions with a single pilot; Also developed into a so-called 'Stretched Gazelle', with rear section of the cabin modified to provide additional 8 in (20 cm) legroom for the rear passengers.
SA.341H GAZELLE. Military export version: Astazou IIIB engine; subject to licence-production agreement signed on 1 October 1971 with SOKO in Yugoslavia (112 aircraft)
SA.342F. 110 of the initial batch of 166 SA.342Fs now being modified to carry 4 Euromissile HOT missiles to supplement the 70-odd Alouette IIIs in ALAT (French army) service as an interim measure pending the first deliveries of the new SA.342M late this year.
SA.342J GAZELLE. Civil version of SA.342L. 870-shp (649-kW) Astazou XIV engine, improved 'Fenestron' tail rotor, increased take-off weight. Approved for service on 24 April 1976; deliveries commenced in 1977.
SA.342K GAZELLE. Military export version for 'hot and dry' areas: 870-shp (649-kW) Astazou XIVH engine with momentum-separation shrouds over air intakes. First flown on 11 May 1973. Initial sales to Kuwait.
SA.342L GAZELLE. Military counterpart of SA.342J: 870-shp (649-kW) Astazou XIV engine; adaptable for wide range of armaments and equipment.
SA.342M. Anti-armour helicopters 1 × Astazou XIV H turboshaft engine of 870 shp. Has revised avionics providing full night attack capability, incl. SFIM 85G autopilot and jetpipe deflectors to reduce infra-red detection. Armed with Euromissile HOT missiles; est AUW 5070 lb (2300 kg). Total of 160 ordered for the French army (ALAT); deliveries commencing late in 1979 will be in several batches. SA 342M will replace the 70-odd Alouette IIIs armed with SS.11 missiles now in service.

Type: (SA.341/342) five-seat utility helicopter
Powerplant: (SA.341): one 590-shp (440-kW) Turboméca Astazou IIIA turboshaft
Performance: (SA.341 at maximum take-off weight) maximum permissible speed at sea level 193 mph (310 km/h); maximum cruis-

ing speed at sea level 164 mph (264 km/h); economical cruising speed at sea level 144 mph (233 km/h); maximum rate of climb at sea level 1,770 ft (540 m) per minute; service ceiling 16,400 ft (5000 m); hovering ceiling in ground effect 9,350 ft (2850 m); hovering ceiling out of ground effect 6,560 ft (2000 m); range at sea level with maximum fuel 416 miles (670 km); range with pilot and 1,102 lb (500 kg) payload 223 miles (360 km)
Weights: (SA.341G) empty 2,002 lb (908 kg); maximum take-off 3,970 lb (1800 kg)
Dimensions: diameter of main rotor 34 ft 5½ in (10.50 m); diameter of tail rotor 2 ft 3⅜ in (0.695 m); length 39 ft 3⁵/₁₆ in (11.97 m); width (rotor blades folded) 6 ft 7⁵/₁₆ in (2.015 m); height 10 ft 2⅝ in

(3.15 m); main rotor disc area 931 sq ft (86.5 m²)
Armament: provision for two pods of Matra or Brandt 2.75-in (68-mm) rockets, four AS.11 or two AS.12 wire-guided anti-tank missiles, four or six HOT wire-guided missiles, two forward-firing 7.62-mm (0.3-in) machine-guns, reconnaissance flares or smoke markers
Operators: by 1 April 1978 total of 745 sold (670 delivered) to 115 civil and military operators in 29 countries. In military service in Egypt, France, India, Iraq, Kuwait, Libya, Syria, UK; single examples in Senegal and Trinidad-Tobago; licence-built by Westland Helicopters in the UK, and SOKO in Yugoslavia

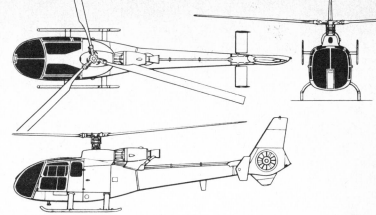

Aérospatiale/Westland SA.341 Gazelle

Aérospatiale SA.342 Gazelle with 'Fennestron' shrouded fan anti-torque tail rotor.

Armed with side-mounted machine gun pods, this Aérospatiale SA 342K Gazelle of the Kuwait Air Force is one of 24 in service with two squadrons.

Central Flying School, Shawbury, is where the RAF trains its future helicopter pilots. A Westland/Aérospatiale Gazelle HT.3 of the CFS is shown here.

Aérospatiale/Westland SA.330 Puma

The Puma was originally developed by Sud-Aviation to meet a French army requirement for an all-weather/all-climate medium tactical transport helicopter capable of day and night operations. The design was finalised as a twin-engined aircraft with a large four-blade main rotor, semi-retractable tricycle landing gear (with provision for emergency pop-out flotation units), two independent hydraulic systems and dual flight controls as standard.

The first of two SA.330 prototypes was flown on 15 April 1968, powered by Turmo IIIC-4 engines, the last of six pre-production aircraft on 30 July 1968, and the first SA.330B production aircraft in September 1968. Deliveries to the French army (ALAT) began in March 1969, and the helicopter became operational in June 1970.

In 1967, while still under construction, the SA.330 was selected for the RAF Tactical Transport Programme and became subject to a joint production agreement between Aérospatiale and Westland in the UK. The last pre-production SA.330 was modified to RAF specifications and extensively tested during 1969. The first Westland-built SA.330E Puma HC.1 was flown on 25 November 1970, and the first RAF Puma squadron formed in 1971. All RAF Pumas feature a rescue hoist of 606-lb (275-kg) capacity and an internally-mounted cargo sling of 5,511-lb (2500-kg) capacity as standard. In 1979 40 additional Pumas are to be received by the RAF, probably in order to replace the ageing Wessex assault helicopters.

The initial military export version of the Puma, designated SA.330C, was first flown in September 1968 and options were soon taken up by several foreign air arms. The parallel civil passenger and cargo development, the SA.330F, made its first flight on 26 September 1969 and received its French certificate of airworthiness in October 1970.

Operational experience with the first civil and military series led to the introduction of more powerful Turmo IVA engines. The re-engined civil version, the SA.330G, and its military counterpart, the SA.330H, were initially produced with the Turmo IVA, later replaced by the Turmo IVC with air intake de-icing. First deliveries took place in 1973.

A subsequently more detailed redesign resulted in the SA.330J civil version and its military counterpart, the SA.330L, introduced in 1976. Apart from increased take-off weight these current production versions are notable as the first helicopters outside the USSR to be certified for all-weather operations including flights in icing conditions.

The SA.330L (and earlier military versions) can be used as tactical transports (16–20 troops), cargo transports, air ambulances (six stretchers and six seated casualties), or assault/fire support helicopters, with a wide range of armament available for this role.

The success of this medium-size transport helicopter is reflected in its widespread sales to various civil and military operators. By the spring of 1975 a total of 400 Pumas (with 386 delivered) had been sold to 37 operators in 32 countries; by 1 April 1978 these figures had risen to 573 Pumas (510 delivered) sold to 45 operators in 38 different countries, and negotiations are in progress for a possible licence-production by P.T. Nurtanio in Indonesia.

Variants

SA.330. Two prototypes and six pre-production aircraft: first flown 15 April 1968; last 30 July 1968.
SA.330B Puma. Military version for the French Army (ALAT) and French AF: total 130 ordered and delivered. First flown January 1969; became operational in June 1970. 1,328/1,185-shp (991/884-kW) Turmo IIIC-4 engines. Production complete.
SA.330C Puma. Export version of SA.330B: First flown September 1968. No longer in production.
SA.330E Puma. RAF, as Puma HC.1: Turmo IIIC-4 engines. First of 40 Westland-built/assembled Pumas flown 25 November 1970; Became operational with RAF in 1971; Deliveries completed in 1974.
SA.330F Puma. Commerical passenger/cargo version: 1,435/1,385-shp (1071/1033-kW)

Turmo IVA engines; 15/17 passengers, or 5,511 lb (2500 kg). First flown 26 September 1969; French C of A 12 October 1970; certificated for increased take-off weight (14,770 lb/6700 kg) on 12 January 1972. Production complete.
SA.330G Puma. Commercial passenger/cargo version: as SA.330F, but with 1,575-shp (1175-kW) Turmo IVC engines. Production complete.
SA.330H Puma. Military version: as SA.330C but with uprated Turmo IVC engines. Production complete.
SA.330J Puma. Civil passenger/cargo version, introduced in 1976: increased take-off weight; internal cargo raised to 7,055 lb (3200 kg); Turmo IVC engines with de-iced air intakes. Certificated for flights in icing conditions. Current production.
SA.330L Puma. Military version of SA.330J; current production.

Type: (SA.330L) medium transport helicopter
Powerplant: two 1,575-shp (1175-kW) Turboméca Turmo IVC turboshafts
Performance: (SA.330L at 13,230 lb/6000 kg) maximum permissible speed 182 mph (294 km/h); maximum cruising speed 168 mph (271 km/h); maximum rate of climb at sea level 1,810 ft (552 m) per minute service ceiling 19,680 ft (6000 m); hovering ceiling in ground effect 14,435 ft (4400 m); hovering ceiling out of ground effect 13,940 ft (4250 m); maximum range at normal cruising speed (no reserves) 355 miles (572 km)
Weights: (SA.330L) empty 7,970 lb (3615 kg); maximum take-off and landing 16,315 lb (7400 kg)
Dimensions: diameter of main rotor 49 ft 2½ in (15.00 m); diameter of tail rotor 9 ft 11½ in (3.04 m); length 59 ft 6½ in (18.15 m); width (rotor blades folded), 11 ft 5¾ in (3.50 m); height 16 ft 10½ in (5.14 m); main rotor disc area 1,905 sq ft (176.7 m²)
Armament: (optional) provision for various combinations of weapons, including side-firing 20-mm cannon, axial-firing 7.62-mm (0.3-in) machine-guns and/or rockets and missiles
Operators: (in service or on order) Abu Dhabi, Algeria, Argentina, Cameroun, Chile, Ecuador, France, Indonesia, Ivory Coast, Kuwait, Mexico, Nigeria, Pakistan, Portugal, Romania, South Africa, Spain, UK, West Germany, Zaire, Zambia, others

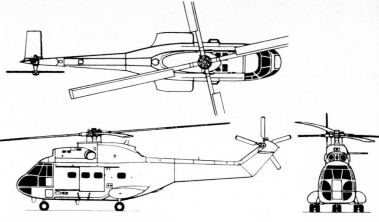

Aérospatiale/Westland SA.330 Puma

These Puma HC.1 transport helicopters are from 38 Group at Odiham, centre of the RAF's tactical aircraft capability, where the type equips 33 and 320 Sqns.

Westland/Aérospatiale SA.330 Puma HC.1 of 230 Sqn, Royal Air Force, operated from Odiham, Hants.

In the markings of the Abu Dhabi Air Force, part of the United Arab Emirates Air Force, this Aérospatiale SA.330 Puma is shown fitted with a sand filter in front of the engines for desert use.

Aérospatiale SA.332 Super Puma

The SA.332 Super Puma is a development of the Aérospatiale SA.330 Puma with more powerful Turboméca Makila turboshafts, multi-purpose air intakes, lightweight rotor head with uprated transmission and thermically de-iced main rotor blades, and wider-track landing gear. Most of these features have already been test-flown on modified SA.330 Pumas, and a fully representative SA.332 Super Puma prototype was first flown on 13 September 1978; since then it has flown at maximum weight of up to 17,180 lb (7800 kg) and speed of 180 mph (289.5 km/h). Certification tests began in March 1979. Production of this new version was commenced in August 1978, with the first completed aircraft scheduled for autumn 1980.

In its initial commercial form, the SA.332 Super Puma will have the same capacity as the SA.330 (two crew plus 19 passengers) but will have more improved performance. The design also has potential for development into a 'stretched' version with three/four added seats and more fuel.

Type: medium transport helicopter
Powerplant: two 1,775/1,323-shp (1324/987-kW) Turboméca Makila turboshaft
Performance: (estimated) maximum cruising speed 179 mph (289 km/h); economical cruising speed 167 mph (268 km/h); hovering ceiling out of ground effect (on one engine) 9,350 ft (2850 m); range with maximum fuel (no reserves) 420 miles (676 km)
Weights: empty 8,565 lb (3885 kg); maximum take-off 16,755 lb (7600 kg)
Operators: none at present.

Aerotec T-23 Uirapuru

Aerotec, a small Sao Paulo-based company formed in 1962, designed the Uirapuru in the early 1960s as a private venture, the prototype 108-hp Lycoming O-235 flying for the first time on 2 June 1965. A second prototype with a 150-hp Lycoming O-320-A was followed in January and April 1968 by two military pre-production aircraft (also 150 hp). A few months earlier, in October 1967, the *Forca Aérea Brasileira* had placed an initial order for 30 examples with 160-hp (119-kW) engines (which became the standard powerplant), side-by-side seating for instructor and pupil, and dual controls, under the designation T-23. Subsequent orders raised the FAB total to 100, and these are used for primary flying training by the Air Force Academy (*Academia de Forca Aérea*) at Pirassununga, Sao Paulo.

The airframe is built primarily of light alloy, and has a non-retractable landing gear with a steerable nosewheel. The cockpit canopy is jettisonable in flight. Aerotec also exported military Uirapurus to the air forces of Bolivia (18) and Paraguay (8), and has supplied about 20 A-122Bs (the military model has the company designation A-122A) to Brazilian state-supported civilian flying clubs. Production of the original Uirapuru came to an end in early 1977 after 155 of the two models had been built, but in 1978 – 79 Aerotec was developing under FAB contract the A-132 Uirapuru II, which will be fully aerobatic. This has the same powerplant as the T-23, which it is intended to replace, but will have 29 ft 6¼ in (9.00 m) span wings, a length of 22 ft 6¾ in (6.88 m), a flat-sided fuselage, enlarged vertical tail surfaces, no underfin, updated avionics, and an improved cockpit canopy and instrument layout. Up to 80 are expected to be ordered.

Type: two-seat primary trainer
Powerplant: one 160-hp Lycoming O-320-B2B flat-four piston engine
Performance: maximum speed at sea level 141 mph (227 km/h); maximum cruising

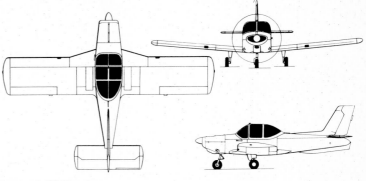

Aerotec A-122 Uirapuru

speed (75% power) at sea level 115 mph (185 km/h); range with maximum fuel 495 miles (800 km); maximum rate of climb at sea level 836 ft (255 m) per minute; service ceiling 14,760 ft (4500 m)
Weights: empty 1,191 lb (540 kg); maximum take-off 1,825 lb (840 kg)
Dimensions: span 27 ft 10¾ in (8.50 m); length 21 ft 8 in (6.60 m); height 8 ft 10 in (2.70 m); wing area 145.3 sq ft (13.50 m²)
Armament: none
Operators: Bolivia, Brazil, Paraguay

Agusta A 106

One of Italy's oldest aviation companies, Agusta was established in 1907, and entered the helicopter field in 1952 when a licence to build the Bell 47 was acquired. This was followed by a series of other licence agreements with both Bell and Sikorsky, but in more recent years Agusta has developed several of its own designs.

The smallest to come to fruition, even though only in a very modest way, the A 106 was flown in prototype form in November 1965. A small production batch followed in the early 1970s and about five of these are operated by the air arm of the Italian navy *(Marinavia)* from 'Impavido' class ships in the anti-submarine warfare role, supplementing larger naval ASW helicopters such as the SH-3D, AB 204AS and AB 212ASW.

The A 106 has a two-blade main rotor and conventional tail rotor, and auxiliary flotation gear can be fitted to the skid framework, which has removable wheels for ground manoeuvring.

Operations in poor visibility are assisted by comprehensive instrumentation and electronics, and the Ferranti company has developed an electronic three-axis stability augmentation system for the A 106, providing a stable firing platform and damping out external disturbances.

Type: ASW helicopter
Powerplant: one 300-shp (224-kW) Turboméca-Agusta TAA 230 turboshaft (derated) with maximum continuous rating of 260 shp (194 kW)
Performance: (at take-off weight including two torpedoes) maximum speed at sea level 109 mph (176 km/h); cruising speed 104 mph (167 km/h); maximum rate of climb 1,220 ft (372 m) per minute; hovering ceiling in ground effect 9,850 ft (3000 m); hovering ceiling out of ground effect 3,775 ft (1150 m); range 150 miles (240 km); range with maximum internal and external tanks 460 mile (740 km)
Weights: empty 1,300 lb (590 kg); normal take-off 2,954 lb (1340 kg); maximum take-off weight 3,086 lb (1400 kg)
Dimensions: main rotor diameter 31 ft 2 in (9.50 m); length (rotors turning) 36 ft 0 in (10.97 m); fuselage length 26 ft 3 in (8.00 m); length (main and tail rotors folded) 22 ft 8 in (6.90 m); height to top of rotor head 8 ft 2 in (2.50 m); width over skids 6 ft 2 in (1.88 m); main rotor disc area 763 sq ft (70.9 m²)

Armament: two Mk 44 homing torpedoes, two sonobuoys and 10 depth charges; for ground attack work two 7.62-mm (0.3-in) machine-guns and launching tubes for ten 80-mm (3.15-in) rockets can be fitted
Operators: Italy

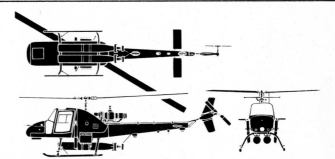

Agusta A 106

Though small and powered by a unique baby turbine engine of only 250 hp (the Turbomeca-Agusta TAA230), the Italian-designed Agusta A 106 carries two Mk 44 torpedoes and remains in limited use as an ASW platform based on the *Impavido* class ships.

Agusta A 109

The basic A 109A is notable as the first Agusta-designed helicopter to be built in large series, and is the end product of a special market analysis initiated in 1965. Initially envisaged for commercial use only, the A 109 was designed around a single 690-shp (515-kW) Turboméca Astazou XII engine, but mainly for additional safety considerations redesigned in 1967 to take two 370-shp (276-kW) Allison 250-C14 turboshafts. The projected A 109B military utility model was abandoned in 1969 in favour of the eight-seat A 109C Hirundo (Swallow) civil version, the first of three prototypes flying on 4 August 1971. Protracted trials, minor alterations and other factors caused unforeseen delays and the first A 109 pre-production aircraft was not completed until April 1975. Delivery of production machines, designated A 109A, commenced in 1976.

In addition to its designed role as a light passenger transport, the A 109A can be adapted for freight carrying, as an air ambulance, or for search-and-rescue tasks. It proved a great commercial success and by early 1978 the A 109A was subject to some 250 orders and options.

The obvious military potential of the A 109A was soon recognised and in 1975 Agusta SpA concluded a co-operation agreement with Hughes Aircraft, manufacturers of the TOW (Tube-launched Optically-tracked Wire-guided) missile. Subsequent trials carried out by the Italian army in 1976-77 with five A 109A helicopters armed with various TOW missiles were extraordinarily successful and resulted in two military derivatives, for light attack/anti-armour/close support tasks, and naval operations.

The first military version is available in several variants: as a light attack helicopter (two or three crew, two machine-guns, HOT or TOW missiles, or rocket-launchers), equipped for battlefield reconnaissance, artillery observation or electronic warfare, or as a radio relay post. It can also be converted into a light troop/personnel transport (pilot plus seven troops) or as an air ambulance (two stretchers and two medical attendants). Optional additional equipment includes armoured seats for the crew and emergency flotation gear. All variants can also be fitted with infra-red suppression systems.

The A 109A maritime derivative, currently under development, also retains the same general configuration, structure and powerplant but has been specially designed for shipboard service. Variants include ASW, anti-ship, electronic warfare, armed and coast guard patrol surveillance, air ambulance, search-and-rescue, and utility. In addition to the necessary specialised equipment, the A 109A maritime version features four-axis autostabilisation, radar altimeter, full dual flight controls, automatic navigation system, and anchorage points for deck mooring. It has universal supports for external loads, and a fixed landing gear. For armed patrol the maritime A 109A is equipped and armed to customer's requirements. The basic coast guard configuration carries a search radar, low-light level TV camera, and a special installation for external high efficiency loudspeakers. For search-and-rescue tasks the maritime A 109A is fitted with a 330-lb (150-kg) capacity electrically-operated hoist, emergency flotation gear and search radar. The maritime A 109A can also be modified for other duties, including fire fighting, crash rescue, military command post and liaison.

The maritime A 109A ECM variant is fitted with a radar display, direction finder, electromagnetic emission analyser and jamming equipment.

Type: light general-purpose helicopter
Powerplant: two Allison 250-C20B turboshaft engines, each developing 420 shp (313 kW) for take-off, 385 shp (287 kW) continuous power, derated to 346 shp (258 kW) for twin-engine operation
Performance: (at 5,400 lb/2450 kg) maximum permissible level speed 193 mph (311 km/h); maximum cruising speed at maximum continuous power 165 mph (266 km/h); optimum cruising speed at sea level 143 mph (231 km/h); maximum rate of climb at sea level 1,620 ft (493 m) per minute; service ceiling 16,300 ft (4968 m); hovering ceiling in ground effect 9,800 ft (2987 m); hovering ceiling out of ground effect 6700 ft (2042 m); maximum range at sea level 351 miles (565 km); maximum endurance at sea level 3 hours 18 minutes
Weights: empty 3,120 lb (1415 kg); maximum take-off 5,402 lb (2450 kg)
Dimensions: diameter of main rotor 36 ft 1 in (11.00 m); diameter of tail rotor 6 ft 8 in (2.03 m); length of fuselage 35 ft 1¾ in (10.71 m); height 10 ft 10 in (3.30 m); main rotor disc area 1,022.6 sq ft (95.0m²)
Armament: two 7.62-mm (0.3-in) flexibly-mounted machine-guns and two XM-157 rocket-launchers (each with seven 2.75-in/70-mm rockets) basic; alternative weapons include HOT or TOW missiles and an electrically-operated 7.62-mm (0.3-in) Minigun on a flexible mount; a fully

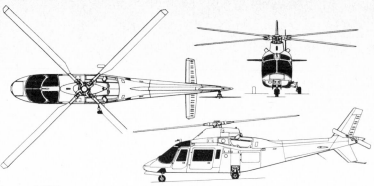

Agusta A-109C

automatic 7.62-mm (0.3-in) MG 3 machine-gun; an XM-159C launcher for nineteen 2.75-in (70-mm) rockets, an Agusta launcher for seven 81-mm (3.2-in) rockets, or a 200A-1 launcher for nineteen 2.75-in (70-mm) rockets.
Naval version (ASW role): two homing torpedoes, six marine markers; MAD gear optional
Naval version (ASV role): high-performance long-range radar plus AS.12 or other wire-guided missiles; other naval equipment fitted according to mission
Operators: (in service or ordered/on option) Argentina, Belgium, France, Mexico, the Philippines, Switzerland, UK, USA, Yugoslavia, other countries

This is the first of five Agusta A 109A helicopters being evaluated by the Italian Army (and now also ordered for inventory service by Argentina). Of the first five, three have a complete Hughes TOW missile and sight system, while the other two are furnished for liaison and rescue duties. By 1980 Agusta were tooling to build the military A 109A.

Agusta A 129 Mangusta

The Agusta A 129 is a light anti-armour helicopter developed from the A 109A and is now in the detail design stage. It uses most of the dynamic components, but features a completely new narrow fuselage with an upwards-staggered cabin (pilot in upper seat). Both positions are equipped with full flying controls, instruments and armoured seats. The partial armour in cockpit is designed to withstand 7.62-mm (0.3-in) bullets.

Initially proposed in 1973, the design was modified following firing trials with TOW missiles in 1977. Agusta now has an Italian army development contract for three prototypes, the first of which is scheduled to fly in December 1980.

The initial Italian army requirement is estimated at 60 A 129s, with deliveries expected to commence in 1982-83.

Type: A 129-19 light anti-armour helicopter
Powerplant: two 800-shp (597-kW) Avco Lycoming LTS101-850 turboshafts, derated to 525 shp (392 kW)
Performance: (estimated, at mission take-off weight) maximum permissible diving speed with 28 rockets 193 mph (311 km/h); maximum level speed at 3,280 ft (1000 m) with eight TOW missiles 177 mph (285 km/h); maximum rate of climb at sea level 1,970 ft (600 m) per minute; hovering ceiling in ground effect 11,155 ft (3400 m); hovering ceiling out of ground effect 8,860 ft (2700 m); endurance (anti-armour mission, with 20 minutes reserves) 2 hours 30 minutes; maximum ferry range with internal fuel at 155 mph (249 km/h) 391 miles (629 km)
Weights: empty equipped 4,976 lb (2257 kg); mission take-off weight 7,385 lb (3350 kg);

maximum take-off weight 7,716 lb (3500 kg)
Dimensions: diameter of main rotor 39 ft 0½ in (11.90 m); diameter of tail rotor 6 ft 6¾ in (2.00 m); stub wing span 10 ft 2 in (3.10 m); length overall (tail rotor turning) 41 ft 0 in (12.50 m); width of fuselage (max) 3 ft 1½ in (0.95 m); main rotor disc area 1,197 sq ft (111.2 m²)
Armament: eight HOT or TOW anti-tank missiles; air-to-surface rockets; 7.62-mm (0.3-in) Minitat machine-gun system
Operator: under development for Italian Army

Agusta-Bell AB 47 (see Bell Model 47)

Agusta-Bell AB 204 (see Bell Model 204)

Agusta-Bell AB 205 (see also Bell Model 205)

The Agusta-Bell AB 205 is a variant of the Bell Model 205 built under Bell Helicopter Textron licence granted in 1966 to Costruzioni Aeronautiche Giovanni Agusta SpA in Italy. It is generally similar to the earlier Bell Model 204 but introduced a longer fuselage with increased cabin space, more powerful engine and other improvements, resulting in better load-carrying characteristics. The Bell Model 205 military prototype, the YUH-1D, was first flown on 16 August 1961 and deliveries to the US armed forces commenced in autumn 1963. The initial production version UH-1D was superseded by the re-engined UH-1H in autumn 1967, and is the version licence-built by Agusta.

In its basic military form, the AB 205 corresponds to Bell UH-1D/UH-1H series in service with the US forces and elsewhere. Like its American counterpart, the AB 205 has proved a most useful multi-purpose utility helicopter

and is widely exported. It is equipped for night flying and can be employed for troop, passenger or equipment transport, casualty evacuation, rescue and other tasks, as well as tactical ground support. According to role, the basic airframe can be easily adapted to take floats, snow skids, rescue hoists and stretchers, or fitted with armament. Stripped of all internal fittings, the cabin has a clear volume of 220 cu ft (6.2 m³) for cargo carrying.

A civil modification designated AB 205A-1 represents the Bell Model 205A-1 built under licence by Agusta since 1969, with minor modifications. Apart from being slightly longer, the Italian-built variant is powered by the same type of engine as the AB 205 military series (T53-L-13B) while the Bell 205A-1 has a different sub-type (T53-L-13A) of similar power rating. The AB 205A-1 can carry a pilot and 14 passengers (or an equivalent commercial cargo), and is designed for rapid con-

version to other tasks: as an air freighter, flying crane (capacity 5,000 lb/2268 kg), ambulance (six stretchers and one/two medical attendants), rescue helicopter or VIP transport.

Type: multi-purpose military/utility helicopter
Powerplant: one 1,400-shp (1044-kW) Lycoming T53-L-13B turboshaft engine, derated to 1,250 shp (933-kW) for take-off
Performance: (at normal take-off weight) maximum level speed at sea level 138 mph (222 km/h); cruising speed 132 mph (212 km/h); maximum rate of climb at sea level 1,800 ft (548 m) per minute; hovering ceiling in ground effect 17,000 ft (5180 m); hovering ceiling out of ground effect 11,000 ft (3350 m); maximum range (standard tanks, no reserves) 360 miles (580 km); maximum endurance (standard tanks, no reserves) 3

hours 48 minutes
Weights: empty (standard) 4,800 lb (2177 kg); normal take-off 8,500 lb (3680 kg); maximum take-off 9,500 lb (4309 kg)
Dimensions: diameter of main rotor 48 ft 3½ in (14.72 m); diameter of tail rotor 8 ft 6 in (2.59 m); length of fuselage 41 ft 10¾ in (12.77 m); length overall (main rotor fore and aft) 57 ft 9⅜ in (17.62 m); width overall 9 ft 0½ in (2.76 m); height overall 14 ft 8 in (4.48 m)
Operators: Iran, Italy, Kuwait (withdrawn early 1978), Morocco, Saudi Arabia, Spain, Turkey, Uganda, United Arab Emirates, Zambia and others

Agusta-Bell AB 206 JetRanger (see also Bell Model 206)

The original Bell Model 206 was designed to meet a US Army requirement and flown in prototype form (as the OH-4A) on 8 December 1962. The subsequent Model 206A was built in both commercial and military versions, as the OH-58A Kiowa for the US Army and the TH-57A SeaRanger training helicopter for the US Navy. The civil and military variants were generally similar, except for larger-diameter main rotors, internal and equipment changes, and proved most reliable in service. US production terminated in 1972.

A long established partnership was continued by granting licence-production rights to Agusta SpA in 1966, and the first Italian-built AB 206A JetRanger five-seat commercial helicopters became available in 1967. Apart from very minor local modifications these machines were similar to their American counterparts and were powered by Allison 250-C18 turboshaft engines. Production of the improved Bell Model 206B JetRanger II began in 1971 and was followed by the Agusta AB 206B in 1972, powered by Allison 250-C20 engines. This new version was a successful combination of basically the same airframe with a more powerful engine resulting in improved performance, particularly in 'high and hot' conditions, for only a small weight penalty. The parallel military variants, the AB 206A-1 and AB 206B-1 JetRanger II, correspond to the Bell OH-58A Kiowa series. They differ mainly in in having larger-diameter main rotors, locally strengthened airframe and different equipment. The military variants also feature additional cabin doors. Although provision is made for fitting one centrally-mounted flexible machine-gun, most Italian-built military JetRangers are used for other tasks, such as anti-submarine/anti-shipping duties (particularly in Sweden), liaison, freight carrying (maximum 3,350 lb/1520 kg carried externally), rescue and air ambulance work.

The AB 206A and AB 206B series have been widely exported for use by civil and military operators, often with modifications to suit local requirements. Thus, the AB 206As delivered to Sweden (Swedish military designation HKP 6) feature extended skid landing gear and underfuselage weapon racks. Production of the AB 206A has now terminated.

The Bell Model 206L LongRanger, a more extensively revised development, appeared in September 1974. Designed as a seven-seat general purpose light helicopter, it was evolved from the JetRanger II and powered by an uprated Allison 250-C20B engine. It has a longer fuselage allowing maximum space for bulky internal cargo (maximum 2,000 lb/ 907 kg) and a new rotor. Optional equipment includes emergency flotation gear. Its military uses are limited to light personnel transport, cargo carrying, rescue and ambulance tasks. The generally similar Agusta licence-built

variant is known as AB 206L LongRanger.

The latest development in this series, the Bell Model 206B JetRanger III, is also powered by the Allison 250-C20B turboshaft engine but has an enlarged and improved tail rotor mast and other detail modifications. With these improvements the JetRanger III has a higher hover ceiling and has a generally better performance at altitude. Production deliveries of the Agusta-built AB 206B JetRanger III started early in 1978.

Type: (JetRanger II) light general-purpose helicopter
Powerplant: one 400-shp (298-kW) Allison 250-C20 turboshaft engine, derated to 317 shp (236-kW)
Performance: (at 3,200 lb/1452 kg) maximum speed at sea level 138 mph (222 km/h); cruising speed 133 mph (214 km/h); maximum rate of climb at sea level 1,358 ft

(414 m) per minute; hovering ceiling in ground effect 12,000 ft (3660 m); hovering ceiling out of ground effect 8,000 ft (2440 m); maximum range (standard fuel, no reserves) 418 miles (673 km); maximum endurance (standard fuel, no reserves) 4 hours.
Weights: empty (standard) 1,504 lb (682 kg); maximum take-off (internal load) 3,200 lb (1452 kg); maximum take-off (external load) 3,350 lb (1519 kg)
Dimensions: diameter of main rotor 35 ft 4 in (10.77 m); length overall (rotors turning) 39 ft 2 in (11.94 m); length of fuselage 32 ft 4 in (9.85 m); main rotor disc area 980.5 sq ft (91.1 m²)
Operators: Iran, Italy, Saudi Arabia, Spain, Turkey, Uganda and others.

Type: (AB 206A-1) light utility helicopter
Powerplant: one 317-shp (236-kW) Allison 250-C18 turboshaft

Performance: (at 3,000 lb/1360 kg AUW) maximum speed at sea level 131 mph (211 km/h); cruising speed 127 mph (204 km/h); maximum rate of climb at sea level 1,560 ft (475 m) per minute; hovering ceiling in ground effect 10,000 ft (3325 m); hovering ceiling out of ground effect 6,000 ft (1825 m); maximum range (standard fuel, no reserves) 368 miles (592 km); maximum endurance (standard fuel, no reserves) 4 hours.
Weights: empty (standard) 1,504 lb (682 kg); maximum take-off (internal load) 3,000 lb (1360 kg); maximum take-off (external load) 3,350 lb (1519 kg)
Dimensions: diameter of main rotor 35 ft 4 in (19.77 m); length of fuselage 32 ft 4 in (9.85 m); main rotor disc area 980.5 sq ft (91.1 m²)
Operators: Iran, Italy, Kuwait (withdrawn in Feb 1978), Saudi Arabia, Spain, Sweden, Turkey, and others

The Agusta-Bell 206 JetRanger family are used in large numbers by many air forces in Europe and the Near East, where Bell's Italian licensee has sales rights. Italy's air force (AMI) uses 60, while the Italian light aviation (ALE) has no fewer than 142, used chiefly for light observation and other tactical duties. The ALE machines do not carry anti-tank weapons.

Agusta-Bell AB 212 (see also Bell Model 212)

The basic AB 212 twin-engined utility transport helicopter is essentially the Bell Model 212 Twin Two-Twelve produced under licence by Agusta SpA in Italy. Deliveries of the Italian-built version started in late autumn 1971.

The Bell Model 212 was derived from the Model 205, differing primarily in having two turboshaft engines coupled to a single reduction gearbox to drive both main and tail rotors. Other changes include generally improved dynamics, structure and systems. Initially evolved in 1968 – 69 to meet a Canadian requirement, the design was also adopted by the US armed forces as UH – 1N and later released for export. A parallel commerical version is the Bell Model 212 Twin Two-Twelve, differing only in internal layout, equipment and some performance details; this was the version subject to the intial Agusta licence production agreement.

The standard AB 212 carries a pilot and up to 14 passengers, but the cabin is easily adaptable to other configurations, including VIP transport. Like its US counterpart, the AB 212 is intended for conversion to alternative roles and optional kits are available to customer's requirements. These include a rescue hoist, external cargo hook, auxiliary fuel tanks, and float and snow landing gear. The cabin can also be converted into an ambulance and has space for six stretchers and two medical attendants. The production aircraft are being constantly improved and adapted to suit new requirements. By early 1978 more than 80 AB 212s had been delivered, with others on order for Italian and various foreign commercial and military customers.

Development of the AB 212ASW version began late in 1971 and the design incorporated experience gained from considerable naval operations with the single-engined AB 204AS. Basically an extensively modified AB 212, the AB 212ASW is intended for a wide range of maritime tasks, from anti-submarine and anti-shipping operations (search and strike) to coastal patrol, search and rescue, and vertical supply of ships at sea. By altering internal installations the AB 212ASW can be converted into a troop transport and fire support helicopter, or an aerial ambulance; it can also be used for liaison and in the ECM role. Like its lighter predecessor, the AB 212ASW is designed to operate from small shipboard plat-

Italian Navy (Marinavia) Agusta-Bell AB.212ASW anti-submarine helicopter.

forms. Apart from some local strengthening, a dorsal radome and the necessary deck mooring attachments, the AB 212ASW airframe is essentially the same as that of the commercial AB 212, but it has added protection against salt-water corrosion. The main changes are internal. Depending on the mission, the crew can be three or four (one or two pilots and radar/electronics operators). The AB 212ASW carries complete instrumentation for day and night maritime operations in all weathers, and the electronics include (in ASW role) a high-discrimination search radar, sonar and other equipment. A specially-designed cockpit display shows the pilot or pilots all flight parameters for each phase of the ASW operations, and the design incorporates provision for the installation of future radar equipment and advanced ECM systems. With special search radar and target data transmission system the AB 212ASW can also be used as a passive guidance post for ship-launched surface-to-surface stand-off missiles.

For other tasks, the AB 212ASW can be fitted with either a 5,000-lb (2270-kg) capacity external cargo hook, a 595-lb (270-kg) rescue hoist, inflatable emergency pontoons, and internal and external auxiliary fuel tanks.

Completed in 1972, the AB 212ASW prototype was evaluated by the Italian navy during 1973 and entered service in 1976. It is currently in production to meet orders from the Italian navy and several foreign customers.

Type: utility transport helicopter
Powerplant: one 1290-shp (962-kW) Pratt &

Whitney Aircraft of Canada PT6T-3 Turbo Twin Pac coupled turboshaft, rated at 1,130-shp (843-kW) for continuous running
Performance: (at 10,000 lb/4536 kg) cruising speed at sea level 127 mph (204 km/h); maximum rate of climb at sea level 1,860 ft (567 m) per minute; service ceiling 17,000 ft (5180 m); hovering ceiling in ground effect 13,000 ft (3960 m); hovering ceiling out of ground effect 9,900 ft (3020 m); maximum range at 5,000 ft (1525 m) with standard fuel (no reserves) 307 miles (494 km)
Weights: empty (standard) 5,800 lb (2630 kg); maximum take-off 11,200 lb (5081 kg)
Dimensions: diameter of main rotor 48 ft 0 in (14.63 m); diameter of tail rotor 8 ft 6 in (2.59 m); length of fuselage 46 ft 0 in (14.02 m); height overall 14 ft 5 in (4.40 m); width over skids 8 ft 8 in (2.64 m); main rotor disc area 1,810 sq ft (17.30 m^2)
Operators: (in service or on order) Argentina, Austria, Italy, West Germany and others

Type: (AB 212ASW) medium anti-submarine, anti-shipping and general maritime helicopter
Powerplant: one 1,875-shp (1399-kW) Pratt & Whitney Aircraft of Canada PT6T-6 Turbo Twin Pac coupled turboshaft, derated to 1,290-shp (962-kW)
Performance: (at maximum take-off weight) maximum permissible level speed 150 mph (240 km/h); maximum speed at sea level 122 mph (196 km/h); maximum cruising speed with armament 115 mph (185 km/h);

maximum rate of climb at sea level 1,300 ft (396 m) per minute; hovering ceiling in ground effect (with Mk 46 torpedoes) 10,500 ft (3200 m); hovering ceiling out of ground effect (at 10,000 lb/4763 kg) 1,300 ft (396 m); average search endurance with Mk 46 torpedoes at 103.5 mph/167 km/h and 10% reserve fuel 3 hours 12 minutes; search range on ASV mission (with AS.12 missiles and 10% reserve fuel) 382 miles (615 km); maximum endurance with auxiliary tanks (no reserves) 5 hours
Weights: empty equipped 7,540 lb (3420 kg); take-off (with two Mk 46 torpedoes) 11,176 lb (5070 kg); take-off (with AS.12 missiles) 10,961 lb (4973 kg); take-off (search and rescue mission) 10,883 lb (4937 kg)
Dimensions: diameter of main rotor 48 ft 0 in (14.63 m); diameter of tail rotor 8 ft 6 in (2.59 m); length of fuselage 46 ft 0 in (14.02 m); height overall (tail rotor turning) 14 ft 5 in (4.40 m); maximum width (with Mk 46 torpedoes) 12 ft 11½ in (3.95 m); width (with AS.12 missiles) 13 ft 8¼ in (4.17 m); main rotor disc area 1,810 sq ft (168.1m^2)
Armament: (ASW role) two Mk 44 or Mk 46 homing torpedoes, or depth charges (ASV role) maximum of four AS.12 or other air-to-surface wire-guided missiles
Operators: (in service or on order) Iran, Italy, Peru, Spain, Turkey, Venezuela and others

Based on the Bell 212 Twin Two Twelve twin-engined helicopter, the Agusta-Bell 212 ASW was developed at Agusta's works near Milan as an anti-submarine platform for the Italian Marinavia and export customers. This is the civil-registered demonstrator with dummy torpedo. Today the usual torpedo is the Mk 46 instead of the Mk 44 shown.

Agusta-Bell AB 214 (see Bell Model 214)

AIDC T-CH-1

The Chinese Nationalist air force has had an aircraft production facility in Taiwan since 1948, when the former Bureau of Aircraft Industry moved there from mainland China. The BAI's present-day successor is the AIDC (Aero Industry Development Center), which was set up in March 1969 and in the same year began building more than 100 American Bell UH-1H Iroquois helicopters for the Nationalist army. The AIDC is fully capable of building modern military aircraft, as it will need to be following the USA's recognition of mainland China, and is currently engaged in licence manufacture of Northrop F-5E/F Tiger IIs for the CNAF. Its production know-how is backed by a national aircraft design capability, which began work on the T-CH-1

(presumably Trainer-China-No 1) in November 1970.

The T-CH-1 was the first aircraft to be designed in Nationalist China although, except for a switch to a turboprop engine (also built in Taiwan under licence), it is clearly based very closely on the airframe of the piston-engined North American T-28 Trojan, which has been operated for many years by the CNAF in a training capacity and to fulfil a light ground-attack role. Two prototypes (XT-CH-1A and XT-CH-1B) were completed, making their respective maiden flights on 23 November 1973 and 27 November 1974. The second was modified to weapons training and light COIN (counter-insurgency) configuration, and this capability is retained in

the 50 T-CH-1s ordered for the CNAF. Production of these began at Taichung in May 1976, and about 40 of them had been delivered by the beginning of 1979, to replace T-28s in service. CNAF primary training is given on the PL-1B Chienshou, an AIDC licence-built variant of the American Pazmany PL-1, before progressing on to the T-28 or T-CH-1; more advanced training is provided by the Lockheed T-33A and Northrop T-38A Talon.

Type: tandem two-seat trainer and light ground-attack aircraft
Powerplant: one 1,450-ehp (1081-kW) Lycoming T53-L-701 turboprop
Performance: maximum level speed 368 mph (592 km/h) at 15,000 ft (4570 m);

maximum cruising speed 253 mph (407 km/h) at 15,000 ft (4570 m); range with maximum fuel 1,250 miles (2010 km); maximum rate of climb at sea level 3,400 ft (1036 m) per minute; service ceiling 32,000 ft (9755 m)
Weights: empty 5,750 lb (2608 kg); take-off (clean) 7,500 lb (3402 kg); maximum take-off 11,150 lb (5057 kg)
Dimensions: span 40 ft 0 in (12.19 m); length 33 ft 8 in (10.26 m); height 12 ft 0 in (3.66 m); wing area 271 sq ft (25.18 m²)
Armament: provision for underwing gun and rocket pods, light bombs, etc
Operators: Nationalist China (Taiwan)

AISA I-115

Iberavia SA and AISA (Aeronautica Industrial SA) of Madrid collaborated in the mid-1940s on construction of various types of aircraft, including the I-11 and I-115 trainers. Subsequently, AISA took over Iberavia's aircraft department and continued development of the two types. The prototype I-115 made its first flight on 16 July, 1952 and, following orders from the Spanish Air Force, a production line was laid down. The all-wooden I-115 was intended to replace the CASA I-131L (licence-built Bücker Jungmann) in the primary-training role and quantity production began in

1954. A total of 200 was built for the air force before production ceased. A few I-115s remain in air force service with the designation E-9, but the majority has either been scrapped or handed over for flying-club use. The last units to use the I-115 in the training role are *Escuadrones* 792 and 912, the former being part of the Central Air Academy (*Academia General del Aire*) at San Javier while the latter is a refresher training unit with General Staff Group 91 (*Grupo del Estado Mayor* 91) at Madrid-Getafe Airport. In the liaison role, some I-115s are serving alongside CASA 127s

(Do 27s) with *Escuadrillas de Enlace* 901 at Madrid-Getafe, 902 at Tablada, 903 at Zaragoza and 905 at Torrejon.

Type: two-seat primary or single-seat aerobatic trainer
Powerplant: one 150-hp (112-kW) ENMA Tigre G-IV-B piston engine
Performance: (all figures for two-seat trainer version) maximum speed 149 mph (240 km/h); cruising speed 127 mph (204 km/h); landing speed with flaps 51 mph (81 km/h); take off distance to 50 ft (15 m):

1,245 ft (380 m); landing distance from 50 ft (15 m) 1,146 ft (350 m); initial climb 686 ft (225 m) per minute; ceiling 14,430 ft (4400 m); endurance (at 70% power) 5 hours
Weights: empty 1,346 lb (612 kg); loaded 1,980 lb (900 kg)
Dimensions: span 31 ft 3 in (9.54 m); length 24 ft 1 in (7.35 m); height 6 ft 10 in (2.10 m); wing area 150.6 sq ft (14.00 m²)
Operators: Spain

Antonov An-2 Colt

Believed to have been built in larger numbers than any other aircraft designed since World War II, the Antonov An-2 'Colt' was reported to be continuing in production in 1978 in the absence of any complete replacement. The Antonov bureau was during the year reported to be working on a new general-purpose and agricultural aircraft, but until this appears there is likely to be a continuing market for this inelegant but supremely practical aircraft.

The An-2 has several claims to uniqueness. It was the only biplane to be put into production on any scale after World War II, and as well as being the first aircraft specifically designed for agricultural duties, it is the only aircraft of that type ever to succeed in many other roles. As well as excelling as a light transport, with its outstanding STOL performance, it is also widely used as a parachute trainer by organisations such as DOSAAF, the Soviet Union's paramilitary training organisation.

The Antonov design bureau was formed in May 1946 with the specific task of producing a utility aircraft for the Soviet Union's Ministry of Agriculture and Forestry. The new type was to replace the Polikarpov Po-2, which had itself been built in greater numbers than almost any other aircraft. To begin with, the aircraft was designated Skh-1 (Agricultural-1), but later the designation An-2 was adopted.

The first aircraft of the type flew in August 1947, and after flight-testing and some modification the aircraft went into production in late 1948. The biplane layout was chosen for its combination of good field performance

with viceless low-speed handling, both of paramount importance for the agricultural role. The layout was unique for an aircraft of its time in that the fuselage filled the entire gap between the wings, which were braced by a single I-strut on each side. The structure was all-metal apart from the fabric-skinned wings and tailplane. The wings carry slotted trailing-edge flaps, and the ailerons droop at low speeds.

More than 5,000 An-2s were built in the Soviet Union between 1948 and 1960, and production in that country ceased temporarily in 1962. In 1957, however, production of the An-2 had started in China, as the Fong Shou No 2, and several thousand of these are reported to have been built. The Soviet bloc's main source of aircraft has, however, been WSK-Mielec in Poland. Production of the An-2 by WSK started in 1960, and still continues. Soviet production was resumed in 1964, with several hundred of the An-2M type, with larger tail surface, a new variable-pitch propeller and a hermetically sealed cabin to exclude chemicals from the cockpit during spraying operations. Polish production switched to this improved version.

Special versions of the An-2 include the An-2TD parachute trainer and the An-2V floatplane (designated An-2W in Poland), which has a reversible-pitch propeller for deceleration on water. The An-2 can also be fitted with skis. A military observation version with an almost entirely glazed rear fuselage was tested in 1948, but did not go into production. Another special version was the WSK-Mielec Lala-1, converted from an An-2

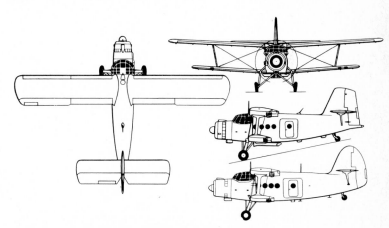
Antonov An-2M Colt (lower side view of An 2P)

as a testbed for the M-15 agricultural aircraft, designed as a replacement for the Antonov type. However, the An-2 continues in service in transport and paratrooping roles, and is likely to continue to do so for some time to come.

Type: 14-seat transport and general-purpose aircraft
Powerplant: one 1,000-hp (746-kW) Shvetsov ASh-62R nine-cylinder radial engine
Performance: maximum speed at 5,750 ft (1750 m) 160 mph (256 km/h); cruising speed 105 – 120 mph (170 – 190 km/h); ceiling 14,750 ft (4500 m); range 525 miles (845 km); take-off run 490 – 590 ft

(150 – 180 m); landing run 560 – 590 ft (170 – 180 m)
Weights: empty 7,500 lb (3400 kg); fuel load 2,000 lb (900 kg); payload 2,850 lb (1300 kg); maximum take-off 12,125 lb (5500 kg)
Dimensions: span (upper) 59 ft 8 in (18.18 m), (lower) 46 ft 9 in (14.24 m); length 40 ft 8 in (12.4 m); height (tail up) 20 ft 0 in (6.10 m); wing area 769.8 sq ft (71.52 m²)
Operators: military operators include Afghanistan, Albania, Bulgaria, China, Cuba, Egypt, Ethiopia, East Germany, Hungary, Iraq, Mali, Monglia, North Korea, Poland, Romania, Somalia, Sudan, Syria, Tanzania, Tunisia, USSR, Vietnam.

Antonov An-12 Cub

The Soviet equivalent of the Lockheed C-130 Hercules, the Antonov An-12 'Cub' was the result of a chain of development which started in the mid-1950s. By that time it was recognised that the turboprop engine, offering far higher power/weight ratios than the piston engines, as well as power outputs considerably greater than most piston engines, would revolutionize the design of military transport aircraft. Such aircraft generally operate over short distances; the fact that the fuel consumption of the turboprop was at the time higher than that of the piston engine was thus of secondary importance compared with the prospect of a military freighter with sufficient power to lift a large payload from a short and unprepared field.

The first Antonov aircraft designed around

this formula was the twin-engined An-8, which was designed in 1953 – 54 and made its first flight in the autumn of 1955. Like the contemporary C-130, it adopted what has become the classic layout for a military freighter, with high wing, landing gear in side fairings on a fuselage with a flat, low-level floor, and a rear loading door with integral ramp under the unswept rear fuselage.

The An-8 was tested with turboprops from the Kuznetsov and Ivchenko bureaux, both these Soviet design teams including many German engineers captured in 1945. Invchenko's AI-20 was chosen as the powerplant for the An-8, about 100 of which were built for the VTA (the Soviet military air transport force).

An Aeroflot requirement for an airliner designed for rough-field operations led to the

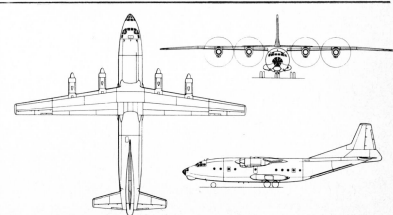
Antonov An-12 Cub

continued

development of the four-engined An-10 airliner from the An-8, and it was this type which formed the basis for the An-12. The wing and tail were initially largely unchanged, despite the 40% greater weight of the airliner, but the An-10 had a much larger, pressurized fuselage and four AI-20s. Lateral and longitudinal stability problems resulted in anhedral being applied to the outer wing panels, an Antonov trademark which was to persist until the appearance of the An-72 in 1977. The An-10 entered service in 1959, but following an accident at Kharkov in May 1972 the entire fleet was withdrawn, apparently because of structural problems.

The military An-12, differing from the airliner in having a more unswept rear fuselage and an integral rear loading ramp, flew in 1958 and from the early 1960s became the standard Soviet military transport. A peculiarly Soviet feature of the military versions is the rear gun turret, although this lacks radar guidance and can be only a token defence. (Indian An-12s were, however, used as bombers in the 1965 Indo-Pakistan war, escaping without loss.) Later in their service life, Russian air force An-12s were fitted with improved radar equipment.

Although the type does not seem to have been pressed into service in as many roles as the C-130, the An-12 has since 1970 been seen in the electronic counter measures (ECM) and electronic intelligence (Elint) role, joining the increasing number of Russian aircraft loitering in the vicinity of war zones and NATO exercises. The Elint version, known to Nato as 'Cub-B', features a number of ventral bulges covering variously-tuned receiver aerials, and the cabin is presumably equipped with operators' consoles. The fact that the 'Cub-B' has been seen in the vicinity of naval exercises may suggest that it forms part of the growing AV-MF (Soviet Naval Aviation) fleet of long-range land-based aircraft. The ECM Cub-C features prominent radomes, including a rear installation which replaces the tail turret. Like the Ilyushin Il-38, 'Cub-C' was seen in Egyptian markings before the rift between the two states widened, but this is probably no more than a cover for overseas basing of Soviet-manned aircraft, feeding their gleanings of monitored data back to the Soviet Union for interpretation.

Type: heavy tactical freighter, (Cub-B) ECM aircraft and (Cub-C) electronic intelligence

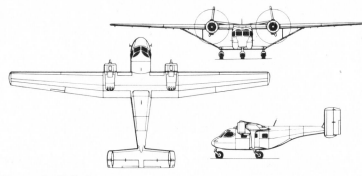

The civil transports of Aeroflot, such as this An-10, are always available for immediate use by the military VTA, the military transport force.

(Elint) platform
Powerplant: four 4,000-shp (2984-kW) Ivchenko AI-20K turboprops
Performance: maximum cruising speed 400 mph (640 km/h); economic crusing speed 360 mph (580 km/h); service ceiling 33,500 ft (10200 m); range with 22,000-lb (10000-kg) payload 2,100 miles (3400 km)
Weights: empty (estimated) 75,000 lb (35000 kg); maximum payload 44,000 lb

(20000 kg); maximum take-off 134,500 lb (61000 kg)
Dimension: span 124 ft 7 in (38.0 m); length 108 ft 6 in (33.1 m); height 32 ft 3 in (9.83 m); wing area 1,309 sq ft (121.73 m²)
Armament: two 23-mm NR-23 cannon in tail turret
Operators: Algeria, Bangladesh, Egypt, India, Indonesia, Iraq, Poland, Sudan, USSR, Yugoslavia

Antonov An-14 Clod/An-28

The Antonov An-14 'Clod' was designed in 1957 as a STOL (short take-off and landing) freighter and feederliner, with handling characteristics which would enable it to be flown by inexperienced pilots. With its high aspect-ratio braced wing and twin fins, it shows signs of inspiration from the French Hurel-Dubois transports of the early 1950s, the experimental designs which also led to the British Short Skyvan and 330.

The development of the An-14 was protracted, and it was not until 1965 that the type entered service. Production versions feature a very different tail design from the prototype, and the planform of the wing and the arrangement of the high-lift devices are also modified. The nose was slightly lengthened, and clamshell doors were fitted to the rear fuselage.

If the evolution of the An-14 had been slow, that of its turboprop development, the An-28, has been even less hurried. It was announced in 1967 that a turboprop version was under development, and the first prototype, designated An-14M, flew at Kiev in

September 1969. Powered by two 810-shp (604-kW) TVD-850 turboprops, the new version was stretched to accommodate up to 15 passengers, and weighed 12,500 lb (5600 kg) fully loaded. A production prototype of the aircraft was demonstrated in 1974, at which time the change in designation to An-28 was announced. The Soviet press continues to report the progress of the An-28, and Aeroflot is to introduce it as a feederliner in 1980. Production is planned by PZL in Poland.

All variants of the An-14 and An-28 share the same pod-and-boom fuselage layout, permitting easy loading of cargo in the freight role. The high wing carries full-span double-slotted flaps and slats, ailerons being built into the outer flap sections.

Type: light STOL transport (specification for An-14)
Powerplant: two 300-hp (224-kW) Ivchenko AI-14RF radial piston engines
Performance: cruising speed 105 – 120 mph (170 – 180 km/h) at 6,560 ft (2000 m); max-

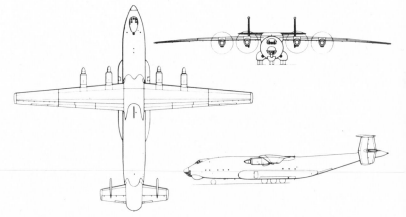

Antonov An-14 Clod

imum range with six passengers or 1,200 lb (570 kg) payload 400 miles (650 km); service ceiling 16,400 ft (5000 m); take-off run 330 – 360 ft (100 – 110 m); landing run 360 ft (110 m)
Weights: empty 5,700 lb (2600 kg); normal take-off 7,600 lb (3450 kg); maximum take-

off 8,000 lb (3630 kg)
Dimensions: span 72 ft 3 in (22.0 m); length 37 ft 3½ in (11.36 m); height 15 ft 2½ in (4.63 m); wing area 422.8 sq ft (39.72 m²)
Operators: Bulgaria, East Germany, Yugoslavia, USSR (air forces and Aeroflot)

Antonov An-22 Cock

One of the most technically impressive of Soviet aircraft designs, the mighty Antonov An-22 'Cock' strategic freighter took the world by surprise when it arrived at the Paris air show in June 1965. It has since become a symbol of Soviet imperialism, spearheading the shipment of arms to client states in Africa and elsewhere, using its vast range and payload to fly long diversions and so avoid hostile territory. Its combination of range with field performance is outstanding, and in many respects it outshines the later Ilyushin Il-76 'Candid' by a large margin.

Following the development of the twin-engined An-8 into the An-10 and An-12, and the design and testing of the An-24, the Antonov bureau turned its attention to a very large strategic freighter closely based on the successful An-12. The An-22 is very unusual, in fact, in being a successful example of a direct scaling-up process. The wing of the An-22 is an almost exact 1.7:1 linear scale of the An-12 wing, and is typically Antonov with its anhedralled outer panels. The major difference in shape between the two aircraft is in the rear fuselage and tail. Rear fuselage aerodynamics and structure are probably the most demanding area in the design of a large military transport, with the linked problems of drag around a rear ramp and aerodynamic tail loads on an open-ended fuselage. The An-22's twin-fin layout was probably chosen to reduce flex loads on the fuselage compared with those associated with the single fin of the An-12, and also possibly to fit into hangars.

The key to the An-22's efficiency is its high wing-loading, comparable with that of the

Boeing 747. This is an almost inevitable effect of the square cube law when the design of a smaller aircraft is scaled up so dramatically. Despite the high loading, however, the An-22 has an excellent field performance as a result of the fact that much of the wing is 'blown' by the slipstream of the four contra-rotating propeller units. Like those of the An-12, the flaps are double-slotted. Early An-22s had propellers with a diameter of 18 ft 6 in (5.6 m), similar to those of the Tu-20; production aircraft have propellers of 20 ft 4 in (6.4 m), presumably because the An-22 cruises at a lower speed than the swept-wing Tupolev, and propeller tip speeds are less critical.

Another operationally significant feature is the landing gear, designed to permit operations from unprepared strips. Each main gear is installed in a side blister, and comprises three twin-wheel units with large low-pressure tyres. An APU (auxiliary power unit) is fitted in the front of the right blister. The APU also seems to be used to pressurize the cabin (most large modern aircraft use engine bleed air for pressurization).

The An-22 carries a crew of five or six, and there is a cabin in the forward fuselage for about 28 passengers, possibly including a relief crew on long flights. The main hold can accommodate a twin SA-4 'Ganef' missile launcher on its tracked carrier, as well as any of the Soviet Union's armoured fighting vehicles, including main battle tanks. The hold is fitted with mechanical handling, including electric roof cranes and winches. The rear doors can be opened for air-dropping; like most Soviet freighters, the An-22 has a glazed nose and is

extensively fitted with radar; later aircraft have a forward-looking weather radar in the tip of the nose, a large navigation/mapping set aft of the nose glazing, and an unidentified avionic housing ahead of the second radar.

Design of the An-22 started in 1962 to meet civil and military requirements, following the Soviet government's decision to support the exploitation of natural resources in Siberia by air. The civil and military requirements were compatible, because the new aircraft was intended to carry heavy construction equipment and machinery as well as armoured vehicles. The first aircraft flew on 27 February, 1965, and was demonstrated at a day's notice at the

Paris air show in June of that year. It was the world's largest and heaviest aircraft until the first flight of the Lockheed C-5 in June 1968. The first production An-22 entered service with Aeroflot in 1967 — a short gestation period, particularly by Soviet standards, for so large an aircraft.

Only about 100 of these giant freighters have been built, and production is generally thought to have ended in 1974. Deliveries are believed to have been shared about equally between the Soviet VTA (air transport force) and Aeroflot, but the civil aircraft are equipped to the same standard as military variants and are always available for

Antonov An-22 Cock

military use. Aeroflot aircraft have been used for military airlifts where the presence of a red-starred VTA aircraft might have been provocative.

Despite its spectacular weight-lifting capability and field performance, the An-22 is probably of only limited use to the Soviet Union. Perhaps its most important role in the future will be to sustain an internal airlift capability linking the European and Chinese fronts. It is also useful in its role of supporting client states, but so large a freighter is probably out of place at a short frontal airstrip. As the US Air Force has found with the Lockheed C-5A, it is hard to justify a large force of super-heavy freighters when most items of military equipment can be carried in smaller aircraft such as the Il-76 or Lockheed C-141; the only item which really demands C-5 or An-22 capacity is the main battle tank, and tanks cannot be airlifted in significant numbers except by a force of freighters that even the Soviet Union could scarcely contemplate acquiring.

In 1977 the Antonov bureau was reported to be working on the design of a more advanced replacement of the An-22, an aircraft in the C-5A class and designated An-40.

Type: heavy strategic freighter
Powerplant: four 15,000-shp (11190-kW) Kuznetsov NK-12MV turboprops
Performance: maximum speed 460 mph (740 km/h); cruising speed 320 mph (520 km/h); service ceiling 25,000 ft (7500 m); range with 100,000-lb (45000-kg) payload 6,800 miles (11000 km); ground roll at maximum weight 5,000 ft (1500 m)
Weights: empty 250,250 lb (113500 kg); maximum payload about 175,000 lb (80000 kg); maximum take-off 550,000 lb (250000 kg); wing loading 148 lb/sq ft (725 kg/m²)
Dimensions: span 211 ft 4 in (64.42 m); length (prototype) 189 ft 7 in (57.8 m); height 41 ft 2 in (12.55 m); wing area 3,713 sq ft (345 m²)
Operator: USSR

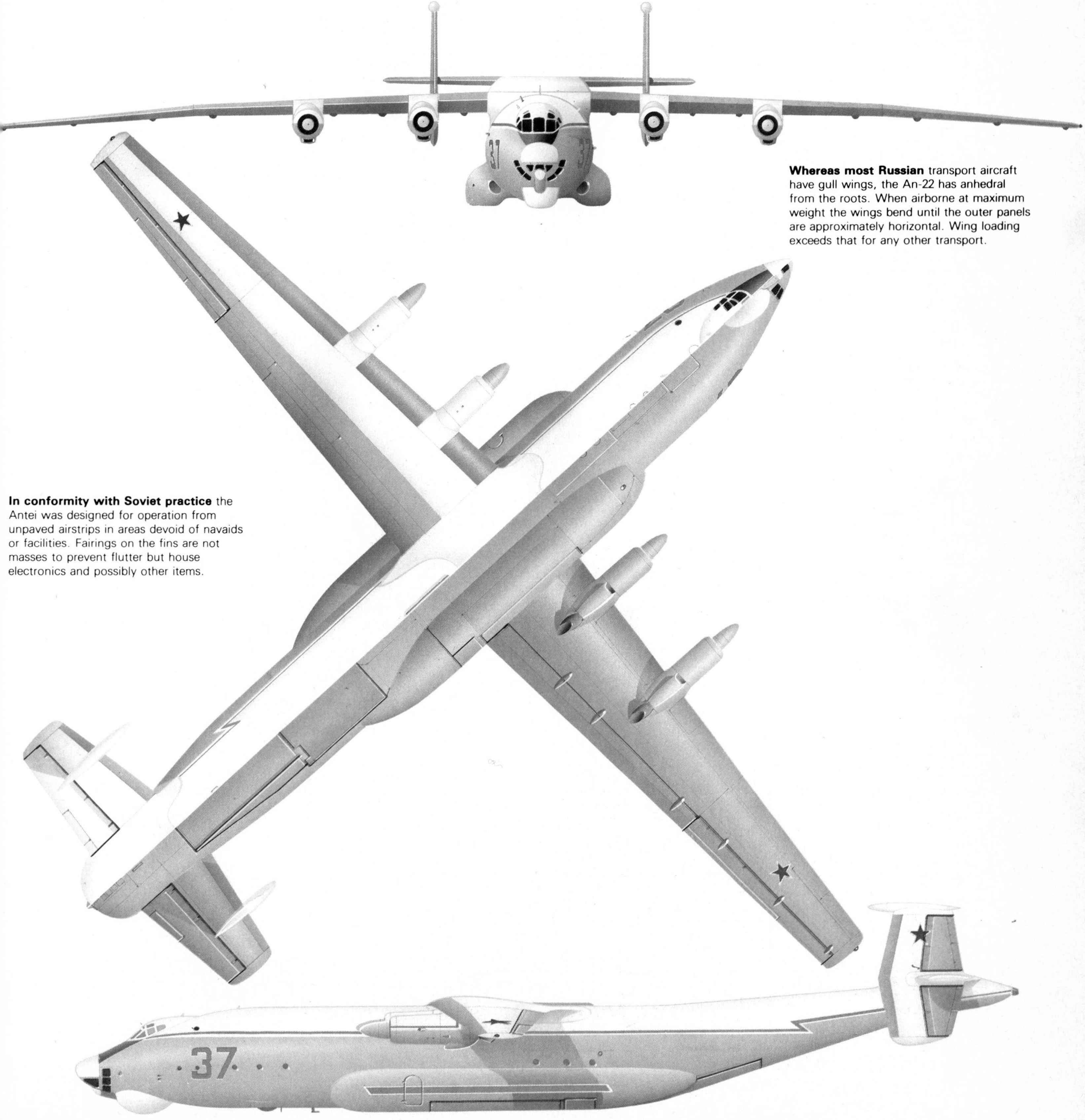

Whereas most Russian transport aircraft have gull wings, the An-22 has anhedral from the roots. When airborne at maximum weight the wings bend until the outer panels are approximately horizontal. Wing loading exceeds that for any other transport.

In conformity with Soviet practice the Antei was designed for operation from unpaved airstrips in areas devoid of navaids or facilities. Fairings on the fins are not masses to prevent flutter but house electronics and possibly other items.

The VTA (military air transport force) received about 50 An-22 Antei heavy logistic cargo transports between 1969 and 1974. Other examples were supplied to Aeroflot, the civil aviation organisation. Several have been lost on overseas flights and in difficult missions within the USSR.

Antonov An-24 Coke

Originally a civil airliner, the Antonov An-24 'Coke' VIP and government transport became the progenitor of the An-26 'Curl' military freighter. The design was undertaken in 1957 to meet a requirement for a turboprop replacement for the Lisunov Li-2 'Cab' and Ilyushin Il-14 'Crate'. Flown in December 1959, the An-24 resembles earlier Antonov designs in the wing planform and the anhedralled outer wing panels, but the mainwheels retract into the engine nacelles rather than fuselage fairings, and the structure makes extensive use of welding and bonding rather than riveting. The type went into service with Aeroflot in October 1962. Most of the production aircraft were An-24Vs, with 28-40 seats and, in some cases, a side freight door and convertible cabin. The An-24V Series II was introduced in 1967 with the more powerful AI-24T engine to improve hot-and-high performance, and this was delivered in 46-seat and 50-seat layouts.

All An-24Vs were delivered with a TG-16 gas-turbine auxiliary power unit in the right nacelle, an unusual piece of equipment for an aircraft in this class. In the An-24RV, also introduced in 1967, this was replaced by a small

Tumansky turbojet to boost take-off performance in hot-and-high conditions. The intake for the small auxiliary engine is located on the inboard side of the nacelle. Take-off weight of the An-24RV is increased to 48,060 lb (21800 kg) and this can be maintained up to ISA + 30° conditions. More than 1,000 An-24s are believed to have been built, and the type appears to be continuing in production alongside the later An-26 and An-32. Service experience is said to have proved the theoretical advantages of bonded structures in reducing maintenance costs and improving corrosion resistance.

Type: short-range transport or VIP aircraft
Powerplant: two 2,550-shp (2148-kW) Ivchencko AI-24 turboprops plus (An-24RV) one 1,980-lb (900-kg) Tumansky RU-19-300 turbojet
Performance: cruising speed 315 mph (500 km/h) at 20,000 ft (6100 m); maximum range with 30 passengers 1,490 miles (2400 km); range with 12,125-lb (5520-kg) payload 340 miles (550 km); take-off run to 35 ft (11 m) 2,900 ft (885 m); landing run from 50 ft (15

m) 3,700 ft (1130 m)
Weights: empty 29,320 lb (13600 kg); maximum take-off landing 46,300 lb (21000 kg)
Dimensions: span 95 ft 10 in (29.2 m);

length 77 ft 3 in (23.5 m); height 27 ft 4 in (8.3 m); wing area 780 sq ft (72.5 m²)
Operators: Czechoslovakia, East Germany, Hungary, Poland.

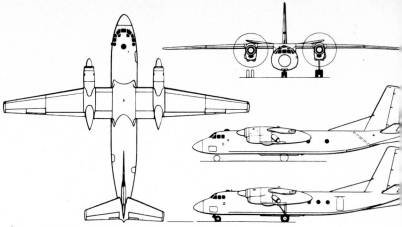

Antonov An-24 Coke (lower side view of An 24V)

Antonov An-26 Curl/An-30 Clank/An-32 Cline

Development of a military freighter from the Antonov An-24 'Coke' airliner was logical, especially in view of the increased performance available with the addition of an auxiliary engine in the An-24RV. (A similar development had been undertaken in the UK, where the Andover C.1 was modified from the Hawker Siddeley HS.748.)

The first rear-loading variant of the An-24 was the An-24TV, demonstrated in 1967. The aerodynamic shape of the rear fuselage was largely unchanged, but a loading hatch suitable for air-dropping was added beneath the rear fuselage, together with an internal winch and conveyor system. The original An-24TV had only two engines, but the first aircraft was modified in 1967-69 as the An-24RT with a booster engine as fitted to the An-24RV. The An-24RT could not accept large loads through the rear door, and does not appear to have gone into large-scale production. However, it forms the basis for the An-30 'Clank' photographic survey aircraft, first displayed in 1974. This aircraft features an extensively glazed nose and ventral ports for cameras or other survey equipment. As far as can be seen it has no directly military role (although it could form the basis of a maritime-patrol aircraft), but is more likely to be used in the search for mineral resources within the Soviet Union.

Before the development of the An-30, however, a new version of the basic aircraft appeared. Displayed in 1969, the An-26 'Curl' introduced a redesigned rear fuselage, in-

cluding a door large enough to admit any load which can be accommodated in the cabin and a rear-loading ramp. Small vehicles can be driven into the hold, while other cargoes can be handled by built-in powered conveyors and winches. A large bulged observation window is fitted to the left side of the fuselage, just aft of the flight-deck, presumably for increased accuracy in paradropping operations. The An-26 appears to be the standard light tactical transport of the Warsaw Pact air forces, and considerable efforts to export the type have been made. It is likely to replace the remaining examples of the Ilyushin Il-14 'Crate' and Lisunov Li-2 'Cab' still in transport service.

The latest development of the An-26 appears to be intended to overcome the hot-and-high performance problems which afflict the earlier aircraft, even with the auxiliary engine in operation. First revealed in 1977, the An-32 is powered by completely different engines from those fitted to the earlier aircraft: 5,180-shp (3864-kW) Ivchenko AI-20Ms, yielding almost twice as much power as the AI-24s of the An-26. The AI-20M is an uprated version of the An-12 powerplant. The

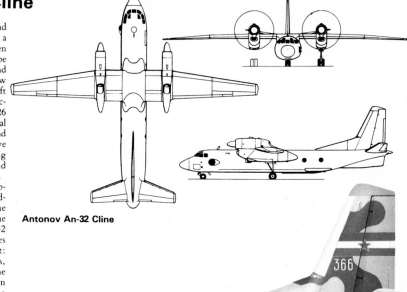

Antonov An-32 Cline

A Yugoslav Air Force Antonov An-26 Curl transport, one of a number in service with this air arm.

Though unimpressive in its range/payload capability, the Soviet-built Antonov An-26 is a tough and serviceable machine based on the An-24 but fitted with a rear ramp/door for large loads and for heavy dropping in flight. This example, making a slow fly-past with takeoff flap, is serving with the Yugoslav air force, where it replaced the wartime C-47.

greater power demands propellers of greater diameter than those fitted to the An-26; in order to avoid total redesign of the wing, the engines have had to be mounted well above the wing, so that the propeller axes are above the widest point of the fuselage. Another advantage of this arrangement is that the engine-out control problems are less severe than they would be if the engines were moved outboard. Even so, the An-32 has more ventral fin area than the An-26, to compensate for the greater installed power and the destabilizing effect of the bigger cowlings and propellers. The high thrust line has presumably caused some problems in pitch control; production versions of the An-32 feature extended chord on the outboard leading-edge of the wing, resulting in a dog-tooth, and fixed inverted slots on the tailplane leading edge. The wing may also be provided with spoilers. The An-32 dispenses with the booster engine and weighs 57,300 lb (24000 kg) for take-off, resulting in a great improvement in power/weight ratio. According to the Soviet exporters, the greater power of the An-26 permits operations at airfields as high as 15,000 ft (4600 m). The An-32 was reported to be in production in 1978.

Type: (An-26 and An-32) light tactical transport; (An-30) photographic survey aircraft (specifications for An-26)
Powerplant: two 2,820-shp (2104-kW)

Ivchenko AI-24T turboprops and one 1,980-lb (900 kg) Tumansky RU-19-300 turbojets
Performance: maximum cruising speed 270 mph (435 km/h) at 20,000 ft (6100 m); range with 12,130-lb (5500-kg) payload 560 miles (900 km); range with 6,800-lb (3100-kg) payload 1,370 miles (2200 km); take-off field length 4,200 ft (1240 m); landing field length 5,700 ft (1740 m)
Weights: empty 33,120 lb (15020 kg); maximum take-off and landing 53,000 lb (24000 kg)
Dimensions: span 95 ft 9 in (29.2 m); length 78 ft 1 in (23.8 m); height 28 ft 6 in (8.575 m); wing area 807 sq ft (75 m²)
Operators: Bangladesh, Cuba, Hungary, Peru, Poland, Romania, Somalia, USSR, Yugoslavia.

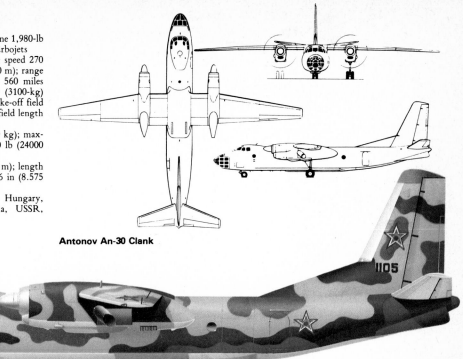

Antonov An-30 Clank

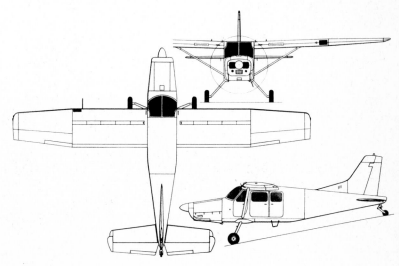

A further derivative of the widely-used An-24 is the An-30 Clank combined photographic and transport aircraft.

Antonov An-72 Coaler

The prototype of the Antonov An-72 twin-turbofan STOL military freighter, the first jet aircraft produced by the Antonov bureau, is reported to have flown in December 1977 and was revealed to the West shortly afterwards. Its service status is uncertain; the prototype was shown in Aeroflot markings, but the type has obvious military applications.

Photographs of the An-72 released by early 1979 do not allow the accurate estimation of dimensions, but the general characteristics of the aircraft can be gauged by the size of the engines and the type's close resemblance to the Boeing YC-14 military transport. The Antonov bureau has elected to adopt the Boeing-developed concept of 'upper-surface-blowing', in which the exhaust from high-bypass-ratio turbofans is directed across specially designed trailing-edge flaps, which divert the jet thrust downwards by the so-called Coanda effect. This principle demands the location of the engines above and ahead of the wing, close inboard to minimize the engine-out asymmetric problems. A T-tail is in consequence necessary, to lift the tailplane out of the wash from the engines.

The An-72 is considerably smaller than the US transport, being powered by two Lotarev

D-36 three-shaft turbofans of 14,500 lb (6500 kg) thrust each, the first high-bypass-ratio engines to be developed in the Soviet Union. Comparison with the YC-14 suggests that the maximum take-off weight would be in the region of 65,000 lb (30000 kg). Cruise speed is about Mach 0.7, but beyond this it is difficult to determine performance with any accuracy. The much larger Boeing YC-14 was designed to use 2,000-ft (600-m) strips.

The wing of the An-72 is fitted with full-span slats and double-slotted trailing edge flaps on its outer sections, with the special USB flaps inboard. The main landing gear comprises four independent single-wheel units, retracting into bulges on the fuselage side. The fuselage is pressurized and is fitted with a rear loading door and integral ramp for the accommodation of small vehicles. Two ventral fins are fitted to the rear fuselage on either side of the ramp; they may be designed to reduce turbulence around the tail for parachute dropping.

It has been suggested that the An-72 may be a flying scale model of a larger military freighter, intended to prove the upper-surface-blowing concept, and that the aircraft may have flown before its 'official' first flight in

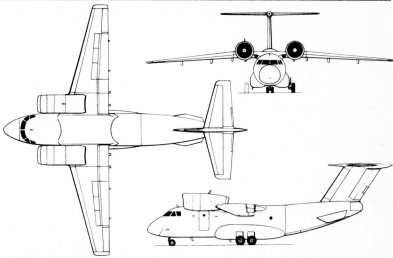

Antonov An-72 Coaler

1977. The main problem in the design of an upper-surface-blowing STOL aircraft is ensuring stability and control in the event of an engine failure in partially jet-borne flight, and this demands high-authority sophisticated

autopilots. Unless these problems can be solved, the An-72 is unlikely to enter service.

Specification unavailable

Atlas C4M Kudu

Atlas Aircraft Corporation is the only South African manufacturer of military aircraft for the South African air force, and is best known for its production of single- and two-seat versions of the Italian Aermacchi M.B.326 for the SAAF under the name Impala. It is also building sub-assemblies for the Dassault Mirage F1 strike fighters ordered and operated by the SAAF. Atlas insists that it developed the C4M/Kudu entirely in South Africa, but there is a clear design connection with an earlier Italian type, the Aeritalia/Aermacchi AM.3C, of which 40 were built for the SAAF for use on observation and light close-support duties, and the C4M's Lycoming engines are licence-built in Italy.

The Kudu, as the military C4M is known, is intended primarily as a general-purpose transport, having less cockpit glazing than the AM.3C, and accommodates a crew of two and four to six troops or passengers in the cabin. Freight (up to a maximum load of 1,235 lb/560 kg) can be carried instead of passengers, loading being via a double door on the left side, and there is a sliding door for parachute jumping on the right side. Other military applications include supply dropping and aerial survey, there being a 3.77 sq ft

(0.35 m²) trap-door in the fuselage floor which can be used as a camera opening or for air-dropping; and doubtless the Kudu is also capable of use as an aeromedical transport. The first (civil) prototype of the C4M made its initial flight on 16 February 1974, followed by a military Kudu prototype on 18 June 1975. South African reticence where military matters are concerned makes genuine information on production difficult to come by, but it seems probable that about 20-30 Kudus may have been built by the end of 1978.

Type: six/eight-seat STOL utility light transport
Powerplant: one 340-hp Lycoming GSO-480-B1B3 flat-six piston engine
Performance: maximum speed at 8,000 ft (2440 m) 161 mph (259 km/h); maximum cruising speed at 10,000 ft (3050 m) 145 mph (233 km/h); range with 882-lb (400-kg) payload (including reserves) 460 miles (740 km); range with maximum fuel (including reserves) 806 miles (1297 km); maximum rate of climb at sea level 800 ft (244 m) per minute; service ceiling 14,000 ft (4270 m)
Weights: empty 2,711 lb (1230 kg); maximum take-off and landing 4,497 lb (2040 kg)

Atlas C4M Kudu

Dimensions: span 42 ft 10¾ in (13.075 m); length 30 ft 6½ in (9.31 m); height 12 ft 0 in (3.66 m); wing area 225.7 sq ft (20.97 m²)

Armament: none
Operator: South Africa

Beech Model 18/C-45 Expeditor/Navigator

Beech Aircraft Company's Model 18, a modest but efficient and reliable twin-engined light transport, was ordered in small numbers by both the USAAF and US Navy in 1940. Versions of the 'Twin-Beech' were in production for a record 32 years, some 8,203 in all being built. Considerable numbers are still in service in 1979, and this speaks a great deal for the excellence of design and construction.

The original Army Air Force contract was for 11 six-seat C-45s, with two 450-hp (336-kW) Pratt & Whitney R-985-17 Wasp Junior radial piston engines. The C-45A had 420-hp (313-kW) R-985-AN-1 engines; the C-45B had revised interior arrangement; and the extensively built C-45F had seven seats and an extended nose. After January 1943 these became redesigned as UC-45A/B/F and acquired the name Expeditor (in the USA spelled Expediter). Versions served with more than 40 air forces during and after World War II. Other versions for the USAAF included the AT-7 Navigator navigation trainer with 450-hp (336-kW) R-985-25 engines, followed by floatplane AT-7As and winterised AT-7Bs. Last of this series was the AT-7C. The AT-11 Kansan, evolved from the AT-7, was a bombing and gunnery trainer of which more than 1,500 were built. Other air force variants included F-2/-2A/-2B photo-reconnaissance aircraft equipped with oxygen and various camera arrangements, and CQ-3 control aircraft for radio-controlled targets. Many surviving aircraft were remanufactured after 1951, being redesignated C-45G with autopilot and C-45H without, for use primarily as six-seat transports. Some -Gs were modified later as TC-45G navigation trainers.

US Navy designations proliferated to much the same extent. Initial contracts were for JRB-1 Voyager (later Expeditor) photo-reconnaissance aircraft, followed by JRB-2 transports, JRB-3 reconnaissance aircraft, and JRB-4s equivalent to the USAAF's C-45Bs. The SNB-1 Kansan was the same as the AT-11, the SNB-2 Navigator equivalent to the AT-7, the SNB-2H an air ambulance, and the SNB-2P a photo-reconnaissance trainer. Post-war remanufacture produced the SNB-3Q ECM trainer, JRB-6 transport, and SNB-5 and SNB-5P trainers, the latter two being redesignated subsequently as TC-45J and RC-45J respectively. It is these remanufactured aircraft, in the main, which continue in service in 1979.

Type: light transport/trainer/reconnaissance aircraft

Beech C-45 Expeditor

Powerplant: (SNB-1) two 450-hp (336-kW) Pratt & Whitney R-985-AN-3 radial piston engines
Performance: (SNB-1) maximum speed at sea level 209 mph (336 km/h); cruising speed 117 mph (188 km/h); range 898 miles (1445 km)
Weights: (SNB-1) empty 6,203 lb (2814 kg); maximum take-off 8,000 lb (3629 kg)

Dimensions: span 47 ft 8 in (14.53 m); length 34 ft 3 in (10.44 m); height 9 ft 4 in (2.84 m); wing area 349 ft (32.42 m²)
Armament: (SNB-1) one 0.30-in (7.62-mm) gun in dorsal turret, and 10 100-lb (45-kg) bombs
Operators: Canada, Japan, USAF, US Navy, many others

Beech Model 24 Musketeer

On 23 October 1961 Beech flew the prototype of a two/six-seat light aircraft which, at that time, was the smallest in its entire range. Known as the Model 23 Musketeer, this aircraft continues in production in 1979, although no longer named Musketeer, and since 1961 about 4,000 have been built.

An attractive cabin monoplane of low-wing configuration, its cantilever wing has fairly pronounced dihedral (6°30') to confer good inherent stability, plus single-slotted trailing-edge flaps which are manually (optionally electrically) actuated. The tail has a large swept fin, for good directional stability. Landing gear is a fixed tricycle unit. Three variants were originally marketed as Custom, Sport and Super, these having different engines and standards of installed equipment.

The Sport, in particular, was intended as an 'off the shelf' two-seat (optionally four-seat) primary trainer with limited aerobatic capability, powered by a 150-hp (112-kW) engine, whereas the 4/6-seat Custom and Super had 180-hp (134-kW) and 200-hp (149-kW) engines respectively. Most of the Musketeers have been supplied for private or club use, but they have also been manufactured for armed services.

During 1970 a total of 20 two-seat Sports were acquired by the *Fuerza Aérea Mexicana*, with blind-flying instrumentation and suitable screening to eliminate the pupil's external view, for instrument training. A further 25 were supplied to the Canadian Armed Forces in 1971 for use as primary trainers, with the designation CT-134.

Type: two/six-seat light aircraft
Powerplant: (Sport) one 150-hp (112-kW) Lycoming O-320-E3D flat-four piston engine
Performance: (Sport) maximum speed 140-mph (225-km/h) at sea level; maximum cruising speed 131 mph (211km/h) at 7,000 ft (2135 m); maximum range with maximum fuel (with allowances for warm-up, take-off and climb, and 45-minute reserves) 883 miles (1421-km)
Weights: (Sport) empty equipped 1,390 lb (630 kg); maximum take-off 2,250 lb (1021 kg)
Dimensions: span 32 ft 9 in (9.98 m); length 25 ft 1 in (7.65 m); height 8 ft 3 in (2.51 m); wing area 146 sq ft (13.56 m²)
Armament: none
Operators: Canada, Hong Kong, Mexico

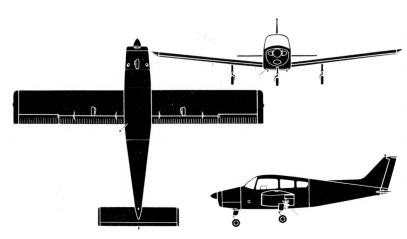

Beech Model 24 Musketeer (Sundowner C23)

The Beech Musketeer, a popular lightplane (since renamed by Beech the Sierra or Sundowner), serves the Canadian Armed Forces as *ab initio* trainer. Called the CT-134, it equips No 3 Flying School at Portage La Prairie to weed out inept pupils.

Beech Model A36 Bonanza/QU-22

Beech Bonanzas, of one kind or the other, have been winging their peaceful way across the world's skies since 1945. The original V-tailed Bonanza prototype first flew on 22 December 1945, a Christmas present *par excellence* for Beech, for they and their derivatives continue in production in 1979, something like 14,000 having been built.

One version, the Model A36 which was introduced in 1968, was intended for use as a passenger or utility aircraft, with emphasis on the latter role. It has a slightly larger cabin, with double cargo doors on the right side, but the most noticeable change is the replacement of the distinctive V-tail by a conventional unit with swept vertical surfaces. Electrically-retractable tricycle landing gear is standard, and powerplant consists of one 280-hp (209-kW) Continental IO-520 flat-six engine.

War in Vietnam was to lure many aircraft into military service for deployment in unexpected roles: one of these was the A36 Bonanza. A network of interconnected roads and trails, hidden by dense jungle, made the task of infiltration easy, and the detection and elimination of infiltrators extremely difficult. Under the American Igloo White programme, air-dispensed sensors were distributed in areas where it was believed there was enemy activity. These sensors could transmit data on troop or truck movements over short ranges

to orbiting aircraft, which relayed this information to a control centre able to initiate appropriate action. One of the aircraft used for this relay task was the A36 Bonanza.

Under the USAF's Pave Eagle programme, some 40 A36s were procured for conversion as relay aircraft. The intention was that they should be equipped with a microwave command guidance system, so that they could be flown to and operate in any particular area as RPV (drone) aircraft, and these entered service under the designation QU-22B. The normally sleek nose of the Bonanza was blunted by the installation of a Continental GTSIO-520 engine which, through the medium of a large reduction gear, drove a large-diameter, slow-turning quiet propeller. Special communications systems were installed. Despite their 'drone' capability, those used operationally in Vietnam were flown conventionally by a pilot.

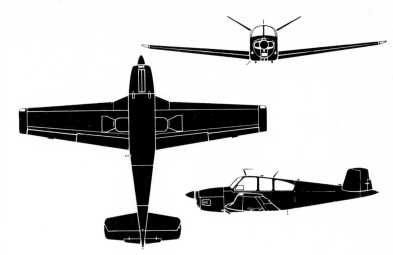

Type: six-seat lightweight utility aircraft
Powerplant: (QU-22B) one 340-hp (254-kW) or 375-hp (280-kW) Continental GTSIO-520 flat-six piston engine
Performance: (A36) maximum speed 204 mph (328 km/h) at sea level; maximum cruising speed 195 mph (314 km/h); maximum range (with maximum fuel, allowances for warm-up, take-off, climb, 45-minute reserves) 980 miles (1577 km)

Beech Model A36 Bonanza/QU-22

Weights: (A36) empty equipped 2,020 lb (916 kg); maximum take-off 3,600 lb (1633 kg)
Dimensions: (A36) span 33 ft 5½ in (10.20 m); length 26 ft 8 in (8.13 m); height

8 ft 5 in (2.57 m); wing area 181 sq ft (16.81 m²)
Armament: none
Operators: US Air Force

Beech Model 45/T-34 A/B Mentor

With an aircraft of which the basic design was so right from the outset that there has been little change since its first flight in 1945, it would have been strange if it had not been used fairly extensively in military service. The aircraft in question is the Beech Bonanza, some details of which appear in the A36 Bonanza entry.

The USAF's hesitation in resolving the problem of whether or not to introduce all-through jet training, has been mentioned under the Beech T-34C Mentor and Cessna T-37 headings. Following a decision after World War II to continue to use piston-engine aircraft for the *ab initio* phase of pilot training, three examples of the Beech Model 45 were evaluated for this role, as were examples of similar aircraft designed by other manufacturers. Beech had developed this aircraft from the V-tail Bonanza, realising astutely that there was good long-term market potential for a modern primary trainer.

The fundamental design was ideal for a trainer, for it included electrically-operated trailing-edge flaps and electrically-retractable tricycle landing gear with a steerable nosewheel. A new conventional tail unit replaced the distinctive V-tail, and design emphasis at this stage went into the creation of a good two-seat tandem cockpit layout. Provid-

ed with dual controls, seated on individual adjustable seats in a heated and ventilated environment, both instructor and pupil have plenty of room. A definite plus in the Model 45's design is the long continuous transparent canopy which encloses both cockpits, and which provides an excellent all-round view for both occupants.

Ordered into production as the USAF's new primary trainer on 4 March 1953, 450 were built for that service, 100 by the Canadian Car & Foundry Company of Montreal, Canada, and these duly entered service from 1954 as the T-34A Mentor with the Air Training Command's primary training schools.

The US Navy had a similar requirement, and following evaluation of the Model 45 in 1953-54, placed an initial order for 290 T-34Bs on 17 June 1954. Subsequent contracts brought total production for the US Navy to 423 examples.

Fuji in Japan also built the Model 45 under licence, producing 140 for the JASDF and 36 for the Philippine air force. The type was built also in Argentina, and was supplied under the US Military Assistance Program to friendly nations.

Type: two-seat primary trainer

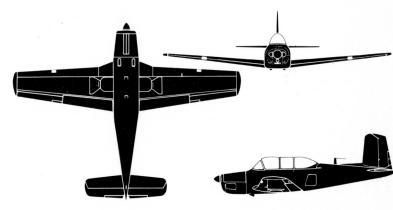

Beech T-34B Mentor

Powerplant: one 225-hp (168-kW) Continental O-470-13 flat-six piston engine
Performance: maximum speed 189 mph (304 km/h) at sea level, cruising speed 173 mph (278 km/h) at 10,000 ft (3050 m); range 975 miles (1569 km)
Weights: empty 2,055 lb (932 kg); max-

imum take-off 2,900 lb (1315 kg)
Dimensions: span 32 ft 10 in (10.01 m); length 25 ft 10 in (7.87 m); height 9 ft 7 in (2.92 m); wing area 177.6 sq ft (16.50 m²)
Armament: none
Operators: Argentina, Japan, Philippines, US Air Force, US Navy

Beech Model 45/T-34C

In 1948 Beech built as a private venture a two-seat trainer evolved from the V-tail civil Bonanza. The trainer differed primarily in having tandem seating for pupil and instructor, and by the substitution of a conventional tail unit. This aircraft was designated the Beech Model 45 Mentor, and flew for the first time on 2 December 1948.

At about this same period the USAF, in common with many other air forces, was trying to make up its mind about the trend of future primary training. The problem facing them all was whether or not, as a result of the introduction into service of turbine engines, all training should be on jet-powered aircraft. At the time it was a difficult question to answer. It meant not only that the most ham-fisted of student pilots would have to cope from the outset with aircraft of much higher performance, but that at the same time they would be faced with the problem of handling a power unit which had not then been developed to a point of great reliability. On the plus side they would work throughout their training with turbine engines and a constant handling technique: retention of piston-engine power for primary trainers would bring the need for a transition phase from piston to tur-

bine engines at some stage. USAF planners chose the latter as the most prudent course at that time.

Among the various types which were evaluated were three examples of the Beech Model 45, two powered by the 205-hp (153-kW) Continental E-185-8 engine, one by a 225-hp (168-kW) Continental E-225-8, and all three were designated YT-34 by the USAF. These three aircraft made their first flights in May, June and July 1950, and were tested extensively during the competition period, being flown not only by evaluation pilots, but also in the primary training role with pupils and instructors. Almost three years later, on 4 March 1953, the USAF selected the Model 45 as its new primary trainer, under the designation T-34A Mentor, and ultimately 450 were built for that service, 350 by Beech and 100 by the Canadian Car & Foundry Company in Montreal, Canada. US Navy evaluation of the Model 45 began soon after the USAF had placed its initial contract with Beech, and on 17 June 1954 the US Navy ordered 290 of these trainers, under the designation T-34B. A total of 423 were acquired eventually. In July 1951 one of the original prototypes was modified to mount two 0.30-in (7.62-mm)

Beech T-34C, two-seat turboprop-powered primary trainer, for service with the US Navy. Developed in 1948 from the civil Bonanza, it was used extensively as a piston-engined trainer until conversion to turboprop power in 1973 brought new orders.

continued

machine-guns in the wings and provided with underwing racks for six rockets or two 150-lb. (68-kg) bombs, and this was evaluated by the USAF as a potential light ground-support aircraft, but no orders materialised.

Not surprisingly, in the jet age, most piston-engine trainers were gradually phased out of service, being replaced by sleeker, purpose-built jets which formed the first component of an all-jet training scheme, from *ab initio* to the moment when the pupil was considered fit for posting to an operational squadron.

The US Navy decided in 1973 to investigate the possibility of retaining the tried and trusted Mentor in service, and gave Beech a contract to convert two T-34Bs to turboprop power. The first of these flew for the first time on 21 September 1973, and following a satisfactory evaluation programme Beech has received contracts for some 170 new production aircraft under the designation T-34C Mentor. In addition to the new turboprop engine, these aircraft have air-conditioned accommodation for pupil and instructor, and advanced avionics. A developed T-34C-1 is also available, equipped to operate for forward air control missions, as well as for tactical strike and armament systems training. T-34Cs first entered service with the Naval Air Training Command at Whiting Field, Milton, Florida, in November 1977, and the US Navy has anticipated a requirement of some 300 of these aircraft.

Type: two-seat turboprop-powered primary trainer
Powerplant: one 715-shp (533-kW), torque-limited output 400-shp (298-kW), Pratt & Whitney Aircraft of Canada PT6A-25 turboprop
Performance: (T-34C) maximum speed 257 mph (414 km/h); maximum cruising speed 247 mph (398 km/h); range at 20,000 ft (6100 m) 749 miles (1205 km)
Weights: empty 2,630 lb (1193 kg); maximum take-off (T-34C) 4,274 lb (1938 kg), (T-34C-1) 5,500 lb (2495 kg)
Dimensions: span 33 ft 3 7/8 in (10.16 m); length 28 ft 8½ in (8.75 m); height 9 ft 10 7/8 in (3.02 m); wing area 179.9 sq ft (16.71 m²)
Armament: (T-34C-1) four underwing hardpoints with a maximum total capacity of 1,200 lb (544 kg), which can include practice bombs or flares, BLU-10/B incendiary bombs, Mk-81 bombs, SUU-11 Minigun pods, LAU-32 or -59 rocket pods, AGM-22A anti-tank missiles, or towed target equipment
Operators: (T-34C) US Navy; (T-34C-1) Argentina, Ecuador, Indonesia, Morocco, Peru

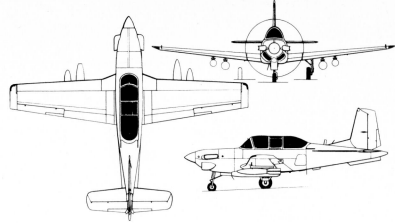

Beech T-34C-1

To modernise the Fuerza Aerea Ecuatoriana's training elements, 20 Beech T-34Cs have been delivered.

Beech Model 50 Twin Bonanza/65 Queen Air/U-8 Seminole

In late 1951 the US Army was evaluating a number of commercial aircraft capable of meeting its requirements for a communications and light transport aircraft for deployment with US Army units around the world. An 'off the shelf' design was considered essential to limit procurement costs to a minimum, and the final choice was the Beech Twin Bonanza. Four of these aircraft were acquired for evaluation under the designation YL-23, the first being delivered on 30 January 1952. A production order for 55 L-23As was placed subsequently, this representing the start of a long association between Beech and the US Army, which has continued to this day.

The L-23As were followed into US Army service by 40 generally similar L-23Bs, and the first of 85 new L-23Ds was delivered in November 1956. A total of 93 L-23A and -23B aircraft then remained in service, and these were all re-worked to L-23D standard in the period 1956-58. Additionally, during 1956 the US Army acquired six aircraft that were generally similar to the commercial D.50 Twin Bonanza, under the designation L-23E. To complete this early series, during the period 1958-60 the L-23 was developed for radar reconnaissance, equipped with Side-Looking Airborne Radar (SLAR), and some 20 of these aircraft entered US Army service under the designation RL-23D. With the change of designations brought about by the tri-service system adopted in 1962, L-23D, RL-23D and L-23E aircraft became redesignated U-8D, RU-8D and U-8E respectively, and acquired the name Seminole.

In January 1959 Beech made the initial flight of the first of three pre-production aircraft which the US Army had ordered for evaluation under the designation L-23F. These were derived from the Beech Model 65 Queen Air, the prototype of which was designed and constructed in early 1958, and made its first flight on 28 August 1958. The Model 65 represented Beech's first move towards a whole new range of business/utility aircraft; and its more spacious fuselage, offering accommodation for a crew of one or two and up to nine passengers, representing a payload increase of some 700 lb (318 kg) with very much the same cruising speed and range, appeared an attractive proposition to the US Army.

The evaluation of the L-23Fs was carried out by the Army Aviation Board at Fort Rucker, and after successful trials an initial order was placed with Beech in March 1959, leading to eventual procurement of 71 examples: with redesignation in 1962, these aircraft became known as U-8F Seminoles. They are of all-metal construction, of cantilever low-wing monoplane configuration, and with a conventional semi-monocoque fuselage structure of light alloy. Landing gear is of the electrically-retractable tricycle type, for most lightplane manufacturers have tended to stay clear of the complexities of hydraulic systems until the structural weight of the units to be moved has left no real alternative. Powerplant of the aircraft comprises two Lycoming flat-six horizontally-opposed supercharged engines with direct fuel injection, each driving a three-blade fully-feathering constant-speed propeller. This reliable powerplant not only confers good load-carrying ability and performance, but provides a single-engine rate of climb of 245 ft (75 m) per minute and a 12,100-ft (3690-m) service ceiling. Standard seating of the U-8F is for a crew of two on the flight deck and six passengers in the cabin, the entire accommodation being air-conditioned. Some U-8Fs were converted subsequently to U-8G standard, with improved cabin accommodation for four passengers, and unsupercharged engines. Queen Air 65s were also selected for service with Japan's JMSDF as transports and navigation trainers, and serve also with the air forces or Uruguay and Venezuela.

Type: six/eleven-seat light transport
Powerplant: two 340-hp (254-kW) Lycoming IGSO-480 flat-six piston engines
Performance: maximum speed at 12,000 ft (3660 m) 239 mph (385 km/h); maximum cruising speed at 15,200 ft (4630 m) 214 mph (344 km/h); range with 264 US gallons (1000 litres) of fuel and allowances, including 45 minutes reserve at maximum cruising speed 1,115 miles (1794 km)

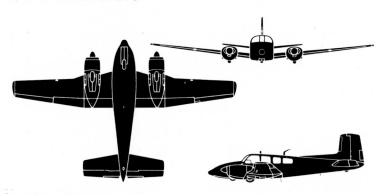

Beech Model 50 Twin Bonanza

Weights: empty 4,990 lb (2263 kg); take-off 7,700 lb (3493 kg)
Dimensions: span 45 ft 10½ in (13.98 m); length 35 ft 6 in (10.82 m); height 14 ft 2½ in (4.33 m); wing area 277.06 sq ft (25.73 m²)
Armament: none
Operators: Japan, Uruguay, Venezuela, US Army

Among the numerous military versions of twin-engined Beech aircraft are the L-23/U-8 Seminoles derived from the Twin Bonanza and (seen here) original Model 65 Queen Air. The US Army also uses many later U-21 Utes and big C-12 Huron turboprops.

Beech Model 65/90 King Air/U-21 Ute/T-44

In the early summer of 1963, Beech flew for the first time a new Model 65-90T. This was a Model 65 Queen Air, of the type which had fostered the L-23F/U-8F family, converted to enjoy the smooth power of turbine engines with the installation of 500-shp (373-kW) Pratt & Whitney PT6A-6 turboprops. On 17 March 1964, this prototype was handed over to the US Army for testing, under the designation NU-8F. In fact, this represented a stage in the development of the Model 65-90 King Air, the prototype of which first flew on 20 January 1964.

Testing of the NU-8F had shown the potential of this aircraft, and in October 1966 the US Army awarded Beech a contract for the supply of 48 aircraft under the designation U-21A. Amendment of the basic civil design was started immediately, and the prototype of the military U-21A, the Beech Model 65-A90-1C, flew for the first time in March 1967. Delivery of these aircraft started on 16 May 1967, and under subsequent contracts more than 120 have entered service with the US Army. Beech's original contract was a little unusual, for under its terms the company was responsible also for the training of 20 flying instructors and 20 mechanic instructors, to ensure that the service reaped the full benefit of this new aircraft.

The U-21A, which became named Ute, was an unpressurized version of the civil King Air, and was acquired to serve as a utility aircraft. Powerplant of the U-21A comprised two 550-shp (410-kW) Pratt & Whitney Aircraft of Canada PT6A-20 turboprops, these driving three-blade fully-feathering reversible and constant-speed propellers. Apart from the changes which resulted from the introduction of new engines, the airframe of the U-21A was generally similar to that of the U-8F. Internally, however, the cabin accommodation was made more versatile: there is still seating for a crew of two, but the cabin can be changed to accommodate 10 fully-equipped troops, or six passengers in a staff transport role, or three stretcher cases, and three walking injured, plus medical attendants. In addi-

tion, the seating can be removed rapidly to offer a clear space for up to 3,000 lb (1361 kg) of cargo. One noticeable external difference between the U-8F and U-21A is the latter's swept vertical tail.

Several specialized variants of the U-21 have been built for reconnaissance duties, most of them flown by the Army Security Agency in an electronic reconnaissance role. These include RU-21As and RU-21Ds, with the same powerplant as the U-21A, and RU-21Bs, -21Cs, and -21Es with 620-shp (462-kW) PT6A-29 engines which permit a maximum take-off weight of 10,900 lb (4944 kg). Because of their special duties, many of these reconnaissance variants have extensive arrays of aerials, plus unusual fairings and pods. They have, in addition, comprehensive avionics which include an all-weather navigation and communications system, weather radar and a transponder.

Another transport version is the U-21F, of which five examples were supplied to the US Army with deliveries beginning in October 1971. These derive from the Beech King Air 100, a pressurized model with increased capacity and 680-shp (507-kW) PT6A-28 turboprops.

A later variant has been evolved from the King Air C90, equipped with 750-shp (559-kW) PT6A-34B turboprops flat-rated to 550 shp (410 kW), under the designation T-44A. Selected by the US Navy to meet its VTAM (X) requirement for an advanced pilot trainer, it has been modified, especially in the avionics equipment, to satisfy special require-

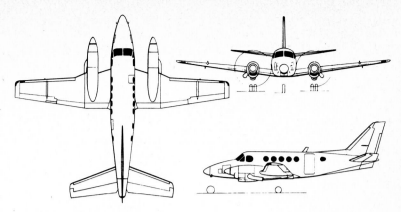

Beech Model 65/90 King Air/U-21 Ute

ments. Thus, in addition to a standard commercial installation, the T-44A has UHF, UHF/DF, and Tacan, plus a selector panel which enables the instructor to initiate any one of 10 avionics or instrument failures on the pupil's instrument panel.

The first of 61 aircraft ordered in 1976 was delivered on 5 April 1977 to the USN Training Command at NAS Corpus Christi, Texas, and all were scheduled for delivery by the end of 1979.

Type: military utility transport/special-purposes aircraft and advanced trainer
Powerplant: (U-21A) two 550-shp (410-kW) Pratt & Whitney Aircraft of Canada PT6A-20 turboprops
Performance: maximum speed at 11,000 ft

(3350 m) 249 mph (401 km/h); maximum cruising speed at 10,000 ft (3050 m) 245 mph (394 km/h); range with maximum payload, cruise at 25,000 ft (7620 m), plus allowances and 30 minutes reserve 1,167 miles (1878 km)
Weights: empty equipped 5,464 lb (2478 kg); take-off 9,650 lb (4377 kg)
Dimensions: span 45 ft 10½ in (13.98 m); length 35 ft 6 in (10.82 m); height 14 ft 2½ in (4.33 m); wing area 279.7 sq ft (25.98 m²).
Armament: none
Operators: US Army, US Navy

US Navy T-44A advanced trainer version of the Beech King Air.

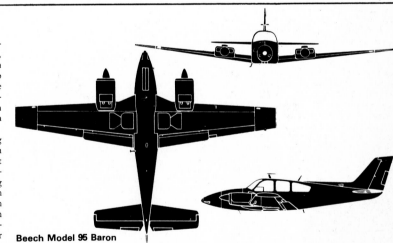

Beech Model 95 Baron/T-42A Cochise

Back in the mid-1950s, Beech began the construction of a new twin-engined aircraft which flew for the first time on 6 August 1956. Known as the Model 95 Travel Air, this was a four/five-seat cabin monoplane powered by two Lycoming piston engines. In the early 1960s this was further developed as the Model D95A Travel Air, powered by two 180-hp (134-kW) Lycoming IO-360-B1B flat-four fuel-injection engines, and featuring electrically-retractable tricycle type landing gear, cabin heating, full blind-flying instrumentation and communication and navigation avionics as standard equipment.

In November 1960 Beech introduced a new aircraft developed from the Travel Air. Known as the Beech Model 95-55, this had more powerful engines and improved all-weather capability, and the most conspicuous external change was the provision of swept vertical tail surfaces. Substitution of 260-hp (194-kW) Continental IO-470-L flat-six engines gave an immediate improvement in 12.5% in maximum speed, and increased the maximum take-off weight by almost 21.5%. Early versions of the Model 95-55 had accommodation for four, but the improved capability offered by the Continental engines made possible optional five- and six-seat layouts. Beech's current designation of this aircraft is the Baron Model 95-B55, the name Baron preceding the Model designation, as there were five other versions of the Baron available for civil use in 1979. The Model 95-B55 is still powered by Continental IO-470-L engines, each driving a two-blade constant-speed and fully-feathering propeller. The single-slotted trailing-edge flaps and the tricycle type landing gear are both electrically operated. The cabin is heated and ventilated, the heating system serving also for windscreen defrosting. An alcohol de-icing system is available optionally for the pilot's window, and pneumatically-operated de-icing boots for the wing and tail unit leading-edges are also optional.

The Baron 95-B55 has good baggage stowage, with 400 lb (181 kg) aft of the cabin, 300 lb (136 kg) in the fuselage nose, plus an optional extension of the aft compartment to accept an additional 120 lb (54 kg). A wide cargo door is available to order, and with unnecessary seats removed the 10 ft 1 in (3.07 m) long cabin can accommodate a significant load of cargo.

In the early 1960s the US Army was seeking a suitable twin-engine aircraft to serve as an instrument trainer. A primary requirement was that submission for the selective competition must be 'off the shelf' aircraft, requiring minimal additional expenditure to make them suitable for the army role. Thus the Baron 95-B55, which was equipped as standard with blind-flying instrumentation, turn coordinator, sensitive altimeter, and many other useful or desirable equipment features, was found to conform most nearly to the US Army's requirement, and in February 1965 this aircraft was selected as winner of the competition. A total of 65 was ordered under the designation T-42A, and given the name Cochise. Subsequently, in 1971, five more were ordered and supplied to the Turkish army under the Military Assistance Program.

Barons, as opposed to T-42A Cochise aircraft, have been supplied for service with the Spanish Air Ministry (19) and Japanese Civil Air Bureau (6) for use in an instrument training capacity.

Type: four/six-seat cabin monoplane/instrument trainer
Powerplant: two 260-hp (194-kW) Continental IO-470-L flat-six fuel-injection engines
Performance: maximum speed 231 mph (372 km/h); maximum cruising speed at 10,000 ft (3050 m) 216 mph (348 km/h); range with maximum fuel at maximum cruising speed, including allowances and 45 minutes reserve, 918 miles (1477 km)

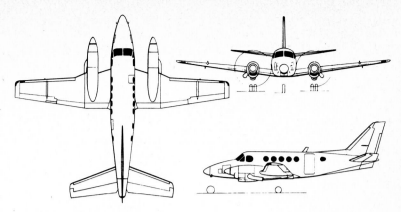

Beech Model 95 Baron

Weights: empty 3,226 lb (1463 kg); maximum take-off 5,100 lb (2313 kg)
Dimensions: span 37 ft 10 in (11.53 m); length 28 ft 0 in (8.53 m); height 9 ft 7 in

(2.92 m); wing area 199.1 sq ft (18.50 m²)
Armament: none
Operators: (T-42A) Turkey, US Army

Standard twin-engined fixed-wing trainer of the US Army, the T-42A Cochise is a close relative of the civil Beech Baron, bought off-the-shelf but fitted with Army communications and additional navaids and avionics. A total of 60 are in use.

Beech Model 100 King Air/200 Super King Air/C-12A Huron/RU-21J

The U-8 is a military variant of the Beech King Air 90; the U-21F evolved from the later King Air 100. Both have a wing of the same span, but the fuselage of the latter is of fail-safe construction, pressurized, and 4 ft 5 3/8 in (1.36 m) longer. In addition, the King Air 100 has more powerful engines and four-blade propellers. In October 1970, Beech began the design of an improved model known as the Super King Air 200, differing in a number of respects to provide improved performance and a higher gross weight. Structural changes include increased wing span, and consequently greater fuel capacity in the bladder type cells in each wing. A T-tail with fixed-incidence tailplane has been adopted, and cabin pressurization increased from 4.6 lb/sq in (0.32 kg/cm^2) to 6.0 lb/sq in (0.42 kg/cm^2) to permit a higher cruising altitude and service ceiling. Engine power has been increased by the installation of two 850-shp (634-kW) Pratt & Whitney Aircraft of Canada PT6A-41 turbo props.

Construction of the prototype began in late 1971, and this flew for the first time on 27 October 1972; construction of the first production aircraft was initiated in June 1973.

By the end of 1973, the US Army had already acquired considerable operating experience of King Airs, and with a requirement for additional light transport/cargo aircraft placed a contract with Beech in August 1974 for the supply initially of 34 slightly modified Super King Airs, of which 14 were intended for service with the USAF, and 20 with the US Army. These were allocated the designation C-12A Huron, the major difference between these aircraft and the civil Super King Air 200s being the use of reduced power engines, 750-shp (559-kW) Pratt & Whitney PT6A-38 turboprops, each driving a three-blade fully-feathering and reversible constant-speed propeller. As with the U-21 which preceded it, the contract which Beech was awarded by the US Army covered also inspection, maintenance and servicing on a worldwide basis, and the provision of certain strategic bases fully stocked with essential spares. Options in the contract allowed for the purchase of additional aircraft by either the USAF or US Army.

At the time of the acquisition of the initial examples of the C-12A, the US Army also took delivery of three aircraft equipped specially to fulfil an electronic reconnaissance role. These have the designation RU-21J, and serve with the Army Security Agency for special missions. Modified by Beech under the requirements of the US Army's Cefly Lancer programme, these easily recognisable aircraft have an extensive array of external antennae, and because of the comprehensive avionics equipment carried are approved for a take-off weight of 15,000 lb (6804 kg), 20% higher than the maximum take-off weight of the civil Super King Air 200.

Both the USAF and US Army exercised their options to purchase additional C-12As in 1975, 1976 and 1977. Under these options the US Army added 60 aircraft to its inventory. In 1977 the US Navy ordered 22 under a new contract, the first batch out of a total of 66 which this service hopes to acquire, and these later options and the new contract are expected to keep production of militarised Super King Airs under way into the 1980s.

The standard C-12A Huron has accommodation for a crew of two on a flight deck, with dual controls and flight instrumentation, and seating for eight passengers. The cabin accommodation and seating is so arranged that the type can be converted rapidly for all-cargo missions. There is a large baggage area in the aft fuselage, and this has provision for the storage of survival equipment.

Type: military utility transport and special purposes aircraft

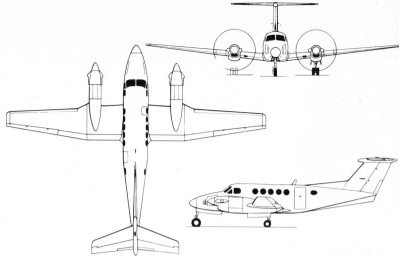

Beech C-12A Huron

Powerplant: two 750-shp (559-kW) Pratt & Whitney Aircraft of Canada PT6A-38 turboprops
Performance: maximum speed at 14,000 ft (4265 m) and weight of 10,000 lb (4536 kg) 299 mph (481 km/h); maximum cruising speed at 30,000 ft (9145 m) and weight of 10,000 lb (4536 kg) 272 mph (438 km/h); range at maximum cruising speed 1,824 miles (2935 km)
Weights: basic empty 7,800 lb (3538 kg); maximum take-off 12,500 lb (5670 kg)

Dimensions: span 54 ft 6 in (16.61 m); length 43 ft 9 in (13.34 m); height 15 ft 0 in (4.57 m); wing area 303 sq ft (28.15 m^2)
Armament: none
Operators: USAF, US Army, US Navy

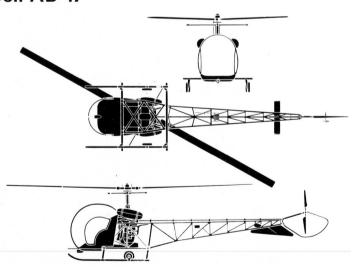

Beech C-12A, military version of the Super King Air 100.

Bell Model 47/H-13 Sioux/HTL/HUL/Agusta-Bell AB-47

On 8 December 1945, Bell flew the prototype of a classic helicopter design, the Model 47. On 8 March 1946 this was awarded the first Approved Type Certificate issued for a civil helicopter anywhere in the world. It remained in continuous production by Bell into 1973, and was also built under licence by Agusta in Italy from 1954 to 1976. The Model 47 has been used on a large scale by armed forces all over the world, its simplicity and low cost more than outweighing its limited capabilities.

In 1947 the USAF (then USAAF) procured 28 Model 47As, powered by 157-hp (117-kW) Franklin O-335-1 piston engines, for service evaluation: 15 were designated YR-13, three YR-13As were winterized for cold-weather trials in Alaska, and the balance of 10 went to the US Navy for evaluation as HTL-1 trainers. Little time was lost by either service in deciding that the Model 47 was an excellent machine, and the orders began to flow in.

The US Army's first order was issued in 1948, 65 being accepted as H-13Bs; all US Army versions were later named Sioux. Fifteen of these were converted in 1952 to carry external stretchers, with the designation H-13C. Two-seat H-13Ds with skid landing gear, stretcher carriers, and Franklin O-335-5 engines followed, and generally similar three-seat dual control H-13Es. H-13Gs differed by introducing a small movable elevator, and the H-13H introduced the 250-hp (186-kW) Lycoming VO-435 engine. Some of the H-13Hs were used also by the USAF, as were two H-13Js with 240-hp (179-kW) Lycoming VO-435s acquired for the use of the US President. Two H-13Hs converted for trial purposes, with an increased-diameter rotor and 225-hp (168-kW) Franklin 6VS-335 engine, were designated H-13K. In 1962 US Army H-13E, -G, -H and -K aircraft were redesignated with the prefix letter O, for observation. US Air Force H-13H and H-13Js were given the U prefix as utility helicopters.

Later acquisitions were the three-seat OH-13S to supersede the OH-13H, and the TH-13T two-seat instrument trainer.

US Navy procurement began with 12 HTL-2s and nine HTL-3s, but the first major version was the HTL-4, followed by HTL-5s with an O-335-5 engine. HTL-6 trainers incorporated the small movable elevator. HUL-1s were acquired for service on board icebreaking ships, and the final HTL-7 version for the US Navy was a two-seat dual-control instrument trainer with all-weather instrumentation. In 1962 the HTL-4, HTL-6, HTL-7 and HUL-1 were redesignated respectively TH-13L, TH-13M, TH-13N and UH-13P.

The Model 47 has been built under licence by Agusta in Italy, Kawasaki in Japan, and Westland in the UK (the 47G-2 for the British army, with the name Sioux), and in various roles Model 47s have served with more than 30 armed services.

Type: two/three-seat utility helicopter
Powerplant: (TH-13T) one 270-hp (201-kW) Lycoming TVO-435-25 six-cylinder vertical piston engine
Performance: (UH-13H) maximum speed 100 mph (161 km/h); cruising speed 85 mph (137 km/h); range 238 miles (383 km)
Weights: (UH-13H) empty 1,564 lb (709 kg); maximum take-off 2,450 lb (1111 kg)
Dimensions: main rotor diameter 37 ft 1½ in (11.32 m); tail rotor diameter 5 ft 10 in (1.78 m); length (rotors turning) 43 ft 2½ in (13.17 m); height 9 ft 3¾ in (2.84 m); main rotor disc area 1,085 sq ft (100.80 m^2)
Armament: none
Operators: have included Brazil, Burma, UK, Italy, Japan, Philippines, South Korea, Taiwan, Thailand, US Army, US Coast Guard and US Navy

Bell Model 47G/H-13 Sioux

This US Army H-13 trainer is one of a number still operational with that service, together with much larger numbers in other countries. No military user is known to have converted to turbine engines, though civil users have.

Bell Model 204/UH-1 Iroquois/Agusta-Bell AB 204

In 1955 the US Army initiated a design competition to speed the procurement of a new helicopter suitable for casualty evacuation, instrument training, and general utility duties. In June 1955 the US Army selected the Bell Helicopter Company's proposal, this having the company designation Model 204, and which became known to the US Army, initially, as the H-40, changed to HU-1 when it entered service, and given the name Iroquois. It was also the first of the 'Hueys', a nickname evolved from the HU-1 designation which, in 1962 became redesignated UH-1 under the tri-service rationalisation scheme.

The US Army's first order was for three prototypes, under the designation XH-40. The first made its first flight on 22 October 1956, and these were used by Bell for test and development. Just prior to that first flight, six pre-production YH-40s were ordered and all were delivered by August 1958. One remained with Bell, but the others were distributed one each to Eglin AFB and Edwards AFB, and three to Fort Rucker, for trials. Duly ordered into production, nine pre-production HU-1As were delivered on 30 June 1959, and were followed into service by 74 production examples, of which 14 went to the Army Aviation School at San Diego. The latter aircraft had dual controls and were used as instrument trainers. First major use overseas was with the 55th Aviation Company in Korea, and HU-1As were among the first US Army helicopters to operate in Vietnam.

The Model 204 displayed its Bell parentage for all to see by the stabilising bar above and at right angles to the two blades of the main rotor, and also by the small elevator surfaces attached to the rear fuselage. Its tubular skid-type landing gear was ideal for utility operations.

Accommodation was provided for a crew of two and six passengers or two stretchers. The powerplant consisted of a 700-shp (522-kW) Lycoming T53-L-1A turboshaft engine, and this made the Model 204 the first turbine-powered aircraft, rotary- or fixed-wing, to be ordered by the US Army.

The HU-1A was followed into service by an improved HU-1B, of which more than 700 were built, early production having 960-shp (716-kW) Lycoming T53-L-5 engines, and late production models 1,100-shp (820-kW) T53-L-11 engines. Other improvements in the HU-1Bs included redesigned main rotor blades, and an enlarged cabin to accommodate a crew of two, and seven passengers or three stretchers. In the autumn of 1965 the UH-1B was superseded in production by the UH-1C which had an improved 'door-hinge' rotor with wide-chord blades, this new main rotor conferring some increase in speed and improved manoeuvrability. A few UH-1As operating in Vietnam were equipped with rocket packs and two 0.30-in (7.62-mm) machine-guns for use in the close-support role, and the success of these resulted in many UH-1Bs serving in a similar capacity, armed mainly with four side-mounted 0.30-in (7.62-mm) machine-guns, or two similarly-mounted packs each containing 24 rockets. Other military versions of the Model 204 include the UH-1E for the US Marine Corps, generally similar to the UH-1B, but equipped with a personnel hoist, rotor brake and special avionics, the first delivery to Marine Air Group 26 being made on 21 February 1964, and from October 1965 Bell's new 'door-hinge' rotor being fitted to production aircraft; the UH-1F for the USAF, generally similar to the UH-1B but with a 1,290-shp (962-kW) General Electric T58-GE-3 turboshaft, increased diameter rotor, and able to accommodate a pilot and 10 passengers; a similar TH-1F training version of the above for the USAF; the HH-1K SAR version for the US Navy, similar to the UH-1E but with 1,400-shp (1044-kW) T53-L-13 engine; TH-1L and UH-1L training and utility versions respectively of the UH-1E with T53-L-13 engine; and three UH-1Ms with night sensor equipment for evaluation by the US Army.

The model 204B was built in small numbers by Bell for civil use and military export. Generally similar to the UH-1B, these were of 10-seat capacity, had the larger-diameter rotors of the UH-1F, and T53-L-11 engine.

Model 204Bs and UH-1s have been built by Fuji in Japan, under sub-licence from Mitsubishi, and continue in production in 1979. Agusta in Italy has also built the Model 204B in large numbers under licence for both armed services and commercial users, many powered by Rolls-Royce Gnome turboshafts. Agusta also developed a special ASW version with dipping sonar, advanced avionics, and armed suitably for anti-submarine attack, and these AB 204AS helicopters serve with the Italian and Spanish navies.

Type: general utility helicopter
Powerplant: (late production UH-1C) one 1,400-shp (1044-kW) Lycoming T53-L-13 turboshaft
Performance: (UH-1C) maximum speed at sea level 148 mph (238 km/h); cruising speed at 5,000 ft (1525 m) 143 mph (230 km/h); range with maximum fuel (no allowances) 382 miles (615 km)
Weights: (UH-1F) operating, empty 4,902 lbs (2224 kg); maximum gross 9,000 lbs (4082 kg)
Dimensions: (UH-1C) diameter of main rotor 44 ft 0 in (13.41 m); diameter of tail rotor 8 ft 6 in (2.59 m); length (rotor fore and aft) 42 ft 7 in (12.98 m); height 12 ft 8½ in (3.87 m); main rotor disc area 1,520 sq ft (141.21 m²)

Bell Model 204/UH-1 Iroquois

Armament: 0.30-in (7.62-mm) machine-guns, rocket packs, homing torpedoes, or air-to-surface missiles, according to version
Operators: Austria, Canada, Ethiopia, Greece, Iran, Italy, JGSDF (Japan), Kuwait, Lebanon, Morocco, Norway, Oman, RAAF, RAN, RNZAF, Spain, Sweden, Switzerland, Turkey, USAF, US Army, USMC, USN Zambia

Bell Model 204/UH-1B Iroquois. The military version of the Bell Model 204 was the first turbine-powered aircraft to enter service with the US Army. UH-1Bs armed with machine-guns or rockets were deployed in a close-support role in Vietnam.

Bell Model 204 (actually Agusta-built AB 204B) of the Austrian Luftstreitkräfte HG III based at Linz.

Bell Model 205/UH-1D/UH-1H Iroquois (see also Agusta-Bell AB 205)

The undoubted success of the Bell UH-1A/B Iroquois gave convincing proof that there was little wrong with the basic design of this utility helicopter. As detailed in the Model 204 entry, the UH-1A/B was developed continuously for differing roles and with progressively more powerful engines.

In early 1960 Bell proposed an improved version of the Model 204 design with a longer fuselage, plus additional cabin space resulting from relocation of the fuel cells, thus providing accommodation for a pilot and 14 troops, or space for six stretchers, or up to 4,000 lb (1814 kg) of freight. In July 1960, therefore, the US Army awarded Bell a contract for the supply of seven of these new helicopters for service test, these having the US Army designation YUH-1D and being identified by Bell as their Model 205. The first of these flew on 16 August 1961, and following successful flight trials was ordered into production for the US Army, the first of these UH-1Ds being delivered to the 11th Air Assault Division at Fort Benning, Georgia, on 9 August 1963. The powerplant of these aircraft was the 1,100-shp (820-kW) Lycoming T53-L-11 turboshaft, and the standard fuel storage of 220 US gallons (832 litres) could be supplemented by two internal auxiliary fuel tanks to give a maximum overload capacity of 520 US gallons (1968 litres) of fuel. Large scale production of the UH-1D followed for the US Army, as well as for the armed forces of other nations, and 352 were built under licence by Dornier in Germany for service with the German army and air force.

The UH-1D was followed into production by the more or less identical UH-1H which differed, however, in the use of the more powerful 1,400-shp (1044-kW) Lycoming T53-L-13 turboshaft engine. Delivery of this version to the US army began in September 1967, and the type was still in production in early 1979. Built extensively for the US Army, nine were supplied to the RNZAF, and under the terms of a licence agreement which was negotiated in 1969, the Republic of China (Taiwan) produced a total of 118 of these aircraft for service with the Nationalist Chinese Army. Variants of the UH-1H include the CH-118 (originally CUH-1H) built by Bell for the Canadian Armed Force's Mobile Command, with the first of 10 being delivered on 6 March 1968; and the HH-1H local base rescue helicopter of which 30 were ordered for the USAF on 4 November 1970, and of which deliveries were completed during 1973.

The UH-1D/H was employed extensively on a very wide range of duties in south-east Asia and was regarded by many as *the* workhorse helicopter in Vietnam. In particular, the type played a major role in special warfare operations in Laos, Cambodia, and in some of the remote areas of South Vietnam, and USAF historians have commented that in this latter theatre of operations nearly all battlefield casualties were evacuated by UH-1 helicopters.

As at March 1979 at least 11 205As were in the service of Rhodesia, having been acquired from Israel via bogus 'Singapore customer' documents in order to circumvent US embargo on sales of American equipment to Rhodesia. All 205As in Rhodesia Air Force service are now fitted with armament and armour protection.

Bell also produce a commercial version of the UH-1H under the designation Model 205A-1. It is powered by a 1,400-shp (1044-kW) Lycoming T5313B turboshaft, derated to 1,250-shp (932-kW). Normal fuel capacity of the Model 205A-1 is 215 US gallons (814 litres), optional fuel capacity 395 US gallons (1495 litres). Because it is intended for a wide range of users, special attention has been given to interior design to permit quick conversion for air freight, ambulance, executive, flying crane and search roles. Maximum accommodation is for a pilot and 14 passengers.

Agusta in Italy also build the Model 205 under licence with the designation AB 205A-1, this being virtually the same as the Bell production model. Customers have included the Italian armed forces, as well as those of several other countries.

Type: civil and military utility helicopter
Powerplant: (UH-1H) one 1,400-shp (1044-kW) Lycoming T53-L-13 turboshaft
Performance: (UH-1H) maximum and cruising speed 127 mph (204 km/h); range with maximum fuel (no allowances or reserves) 318 miles (512 km)
Weights: (UH-1H) empty 5,210 lb (2363 kg); basic operating (troop carrier) 5,557 lb (2521 kg); mission weight 9,039 lb (4100 kg); maximum take-off 9,500 lb (4309 kg)
Dimensions: (UH-1H) diameter of main rotor 48 ft 0 in (14.63 m); diameter of tail rotor 8 ft 6 in (2.59 m); length (rotor fore and aft) 57 ft 9⅝ in (17.62 m); height 14 ft 6 in (4.45 m); main rotor disc area 1,809 sq ft (168.06 m²)
Armament: none
Operators: Iran, Italy, Kuwait, Morocco, RAf, Rhodesia AF, RNZAF, Saudi Arabia, Spain, Taiwan, Turkey, United Arab Emirates, US Army, West Germany, Zambia

Bell UH-1H Iroquois

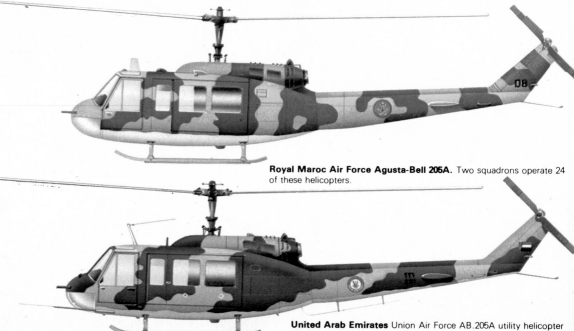

Bell Model 205/UH-1H Iroquois turbine-powered utility helicopter. Used extensively during US military operations in South Vietnam, these rotary-wing aircraft gained a remarkable reputation as a result of their widespread use for casualty evacuation from front-line areas.

Royal Maroc Air Force Agusta-Bell 205A. Two squadrons operate 24 of these helicopters.

United Arab Emirates Union Air Force AB.205A utility helicopter based at Dubai Airport.

Bell Model 206 JetRanger/OH-58 Kiowa/TH-57 SeaRanger (see also Agusta-Bell AB 206)

In 1960 the US Army launched a design competition for a new aircraft which it identified as a Light Observation Helicopter (LOH). Perhaps, more truthfully, it was seeking two or three helicopters in just one all-purpose design, for the LOH was required to fulfil casualty evacuation, close support, observation, photo-reconnaissance and light transport missions. Prior to that time no one aircraft had been able to embrace such a wide range of duties, and the specification called for four seats, a 400-lb (181-kg) payload, and cruising speed of around 120 mph (193 km/h). Twelve US helicopter manufacturers put forward design proposals, from which Bell, Hiller and Hughes were each contracted to build five prototypes for competitive evaluation. From the tests which followed, the Hughes HO-6 (later OH-6A) was selected for production as the US Army's LOH.

If the US Army had some doubts of the capabilities of Bell's HO-4 submission, the company did not share them, and after losing the competition built a new prototype which it designated as the Model 206A JetRanger. This flew for the first time on 10 January 1966, and on 20 October 1966 this aircraft received FAA certification, after which it entered production for commercial customers, and was built also by Agusta in Italy. The JetRanger was fundamentally the same as the OH-4A (formerly HO-4) prototypes, except for fuselage modifications to provide seating for five. It has been built in large numbers since 1966, and continues in production in 1979 under the designation Model 206B JetRanger III, having been the subject of progressive development and improvement programmes.

The US Army had expected to procure some 4,000 examples of the LOH, but became somewhat disenchanted with Hughes when

the unit cost began to climb rather steeply, and the production rate to fall off. As a result, the US Army's LOH competition was reopened in 1967 and, on 8 March 1968, Bell's Model 206A was announced as the winner. With production under the designation OH-58 Kiowa starting without delay, 2,200 of these aircraft were delivered by the end of 1973. The OH-58 differs from the commercial JetRanger by having a larger-diameter rotor, with detail changes in internal layout and the provision of military avionics. Initial deliveries to the US Army began on 23 May 1969, and within something less than four months the Kiowa was deployed operationally in Vietnam.

Of the original 2,200 ordered for the US Army, 74 were withdrawn from the production line for delivery to the Canadian Armed Forces from December 1971 under the designation COH-58A, and redesignated subsequently CH-136. An additional US Army contract for 74 aircraft was issued in January 1973 to replace these aircraft.

Australia acquired an equivalent to the US Army's LOH under the designation Model 206B-1 Kiowa, 12 being supplied by Bell and 44 produced under an offset agreement. The Commonwealth Aircraft Corporation in Australia was responsible for final assembly, and only the powerplant and avionics came from the United States.

Under a US Army development contract, a single OH-58A was equipped with a more powerful 420-shp (313-kW) Allison T63-A-720 turboshaft engine and an improved flat glass canopy. This modified aircraft has the designation OH-58C, but no decision to produce this version in quantity has been reached by early 1979. Other versions include 12 OH-58Bs, similar to the OH-58A, supplied to the Austrian air force in 1976, and the US Navy has 40 TH-57A SeaRangers. These lat-

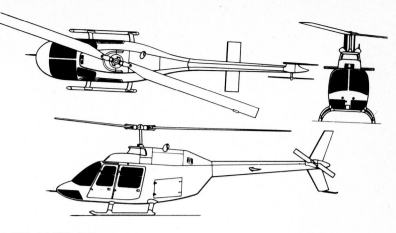

Bell Model 206B JetRanger

ter aircraft are dual-control trainers, which were ordered on 31 January 1968, to fulfil the requirement for a primary training helicopter for service with Naval Air Training Command at Pensacola, Florida. They are basically civil Model 206A JetRangers with US Navy avionics.

Agusta, in Italy, has manufactured the Model 206 under licence since 1967, and has built many hundreds for both civil and military service. Current production version is the AB 206B JetRanger III.

Type: light observation helicopter
Powerplant: (OH-58A) one 317-shp (236-kW) Allison T63-A-700 turboshaft
Performance: (OH-58A) maximum speed at sea level 138 mph (222 km/h); cruising speed 117 mph (188 km/h); maximum range at sea

level with 10% reserves 299 miles (481 km)
Weights: (OH-58A) empty 1,464 lb (664 kg); operating 2,313 lb (1049 kg); maximum take-off 3,000 lb (1361 kg)
Dimensions: (OH-58A) main rotor diameter 35 ft 4 in (10.77 m); length (rotor turning) 40 ft 11¾ in (12.49 m); height 9 ft 6½ in (2.91 m); main rotor disc area 978.8 sq ft (90.93 m²)
Armament: (Agusta-built HKP 6 for Swedish Navy) depth bombs, mines, and torpedoes can be carried on under-fuselage mountings; (OH-58) a variety of gun, rocket and other armament options.
Operators: Australia, Austria, Brazil, Canada, Iran, Italy, Saudi Arabia, Spain, Sweden, Turkey, US Army, US Navy

OH-58C development version of the Bell OH-58A Kiowa. This has an uprated 420-shp (313-kW) Allison T63-A-720 turboshaft engine, and a flat glass canopy to eliminate reflections. If this version enters production it is likely to introduce many improved avionics, maintenance and survivability features.

Bell Model 209/AH-1 HueyCobra

The Korean War, which started on 25 June 1950, showed very quickly how the helicopter had important contributions to offer in that style of land warfare.

With their unique capability of taking off from and landing on virtually any surface which could support their laden weight, they were able to infiltrate behind enemy lines to rescue aircrew, many of whom were injured, and to pick up wounded infantrymen from 'no man's land' situations. It was clear too that if helicopters could infiltrate enemy territory for rescue operations, they could carry out similar sorties to put men, weapons and supplies behind an enemy's lines. Soon transport helicopters were designed to perform this task, but it was necessary to evolve well armed aircraft to provide escort and fire support for them, a role which could be fulfilled most effectively only by other helicopters.

One of the first of the aircraft to be developed for deployment in this latter category was Bell's Model 209. This company had begun investigation of the armed-helicopter concept in 1963 with the OH-13X Sioux Scout, a tandem-seat derivative of the Model 47, and when aircraft within this category were required urgently for operational use in Vietnam, an interim step to meet the requirement was taken by arming examples of the Model 204 Iroquois, a single-rotor turbine-powered helicopter. The Model 204 had originally the US Army designation H-40, later changed to HU-1, and it was this designation which gave rise to the popular nickname of Huey for these aircraft, tending to make the official name Iroquois superfluous. HU-1As were among the first US Army helicopters to serve in Vietnam. Thirteen of these were modified to carry two machine-guns and 16 air-to-surface rockets, and were flown by the Army Utility Tactical Transport Helicopter Company. HU-1Bs were equipped more specifically for an armed escort role, with a pair of electrically-operated

machine-guns mounted on each side of the fuselage, or with up to 48 air-to-surface rockets, 24 on each side. In 1962, under a new US tri-service designation scheme, these two aircraft became redesignated UH-1A and UH-1B respectively, but despite this the 'Huey' nickname was to persist.

While these Model 204 types were exploring, and proving, the escort helicopter concept, Bell were busy pushing through a crash programme to meet the US Army's AAFSS (Advanced Aerial Fire Support System) requirement (to replace the costly Lockheed AH-56 Cheyenne) this taking the form of a redesign of the well-proven Model 204. Thus, the privately-funded prototype retained the wide-chord rotor of the UH-1C, as well as its transmission systems and Lycoming T53-L-13 turboshaft engine. The fuselage, however, was entirely new, its most notable features being the narrow frontal area (3 ft 2 in (0.97) m at its widest point), short stub wings and a machine-gun turret mounted beneath the fuselage nose. This flew for the first time on 7 September 1965, and was transferred to Edwards AFB in December 1965 for service trials to be carried out. Little time was needed for the US Army to satisfy itself that Bell's Model 209 was suitable for the AAFSS requirements, it being announced on 11 March 1966 that it was intended to order the aircraft into production. Designated originally AH-1G and named HueyCobra, the first two pre-production prototypes were ordered on 4 April 1966, and nine days later a first batch of 110 were contracted for the earliest possible delivery, this proving to be June 1977, with initial deployment to Vietnam starting in the autumn of that year. Of the total of 1,178 ordered by mid-1971, 38 were assigned to the US Marine Corps pending delivery of a twin-turbine version, designated AH-1J, treated in a separate entry.

The comparatively small size of the AH-1 made it ideal for use in forward areas, easily

concealed beneath small camouflage nets or under cover of trees. To make for ease of operation this aircraft had a fixed skid landing gear, and the 10 ft 4 in (3.15 m) span stub wings not only served for the carriage of weapons, but contributed also to total lift, and thus offloading the rotor in normal cruising flight. Performance of the AH-1G was such that in operational service it proved capable of reaching a target in about half the time taken by the UH-1 Iroquois, was able to operate in the combat zone for a longer period, and had more than twice the firepower. Because it was intended primarily for escort and support operations, the HueyCobra had seats, side panels, and protection for other vital areas of NOROC armour.

The most important feature, having regard to its specialised role, was the provision of adequate armament. Late production AH-1Gs had a tactical armament turret, beneath the nose, capable of housing two XM-28 Mini-guns, or two XM-129 40-mm grenade launchers, or one XM-28 and one XM-129; maximum rate of fire of the guns was 4,000 rounds per minute. Weapons carried beneath the stub-wings were up to 76 2.75 in (69.85 mm) air-to-surface rockets, or two XM-18E1 Minigun pods. A six-barrel cannon was made available for the AH-1G in late 1969, this XM-35 armament subsystem having a maximum rate of fire of 750 rounds per minute.

Later versions have included the anti-armour AH-1Q carrying eight TOW anti-tank missiles; the AH-1R, a variant of the AH-1G with uprated power plant, gearbox, and transmission; and the AH-1S, which is a variant of the AH-1Q with uprated power plant. A total of 690 AH-1Gs are to be modified to AH-1S standard, and 290 already converted are identified as the Modernised AH-1S. New contracts cover the Production AH-1S, which will have a flat-plate cockpit canopy and other changes, and the Upgunned AH-1S with a turreted cannon, more flexible

fire control system, and some electronics changes. The first production AH-1S entered US Army service on 16 March 1977.

Type: armed escort and close-support helicopter
Power Plant: (AH-1G) one Lycoming T53-L-13 turboshaft engine derated to 1,100 shp (820 kW); (AH-1R/S) one 1800-shp (1,342-kW) Lycoming T53-L-703 turboshaft engine.
Performance: (AH-1G) maximum speed at maximum take-off weight 172 mph (277 km/h); maximum range at S/L with maximum fuel and 8% reserves 357 miles (573 km); (AH-1S) maximum speed at maximum take-off weight with TOW missiles 141 mph (227 km/h); maximum range at S/L with maximum fuel and 8% reserves 315 miles (507 km)
Weights: (AH-1G) empty 6,073 lb (2754 kg); mission 9,407 lb (4266 kg); maximum take-off 9,500 lb (4309 kg); empty 6,479 lb (2939 kg); mission 9,975 lb (4525 kg); maximum take-off 10,000 lb (4535 kg)
Dimensions: diameter (main rotor) 44 ft 0 in (13.41 m); diameter (tail rotor) 8 ft 6 in (2.59 m); length (rotors fore and aft) 52 ft 11½ in (16.14 m); height 13 ft 6¼ in (4.12 m); main rotor disc area 1,520.4 sq ft (141.20 m²)
Armament: (AH-1G/R) XM-28 subsystem with two 7.62-mm Miniguns and 4,000 rounds of ammunition for each gun; or two SM-129 40-mm grenade launchers, each with 300 rounds; or one of each of the above; XM-35 subsystem with one 20-mm six-barrel cannon and 1,000 rounds of ammunition; four XM-159 packs each containing seven air-to-surface rockets; or two XM-18E† Minigun pods; (AH-1Q/S) eight BGM-71A TOW air-to-surface missiles; plus rockets on stub-wings; M-197 turret cannon with 750 rounds of ammunition.
Operators: Israel, Spain, US Army, US Marine Corps

Though produced as a company venture, thought to have no chance against the Army-sponsored AH-56A Cheyenne (a far more advanced and complex platform), the AH-1G HueyCobra became a smashing success, starting with orders for 1078 from the US Army alone. This photograph shows an AH-1G, many of which have been rebuilt to 1Q or 1S standard.

This is an AH-1G of which 690 surviving examples are being rebuilt as AH-1S TOW/Cobras. Later new-build TOW/Cobras are identifiable by their flat-plate angular-looking cockpit canopy.

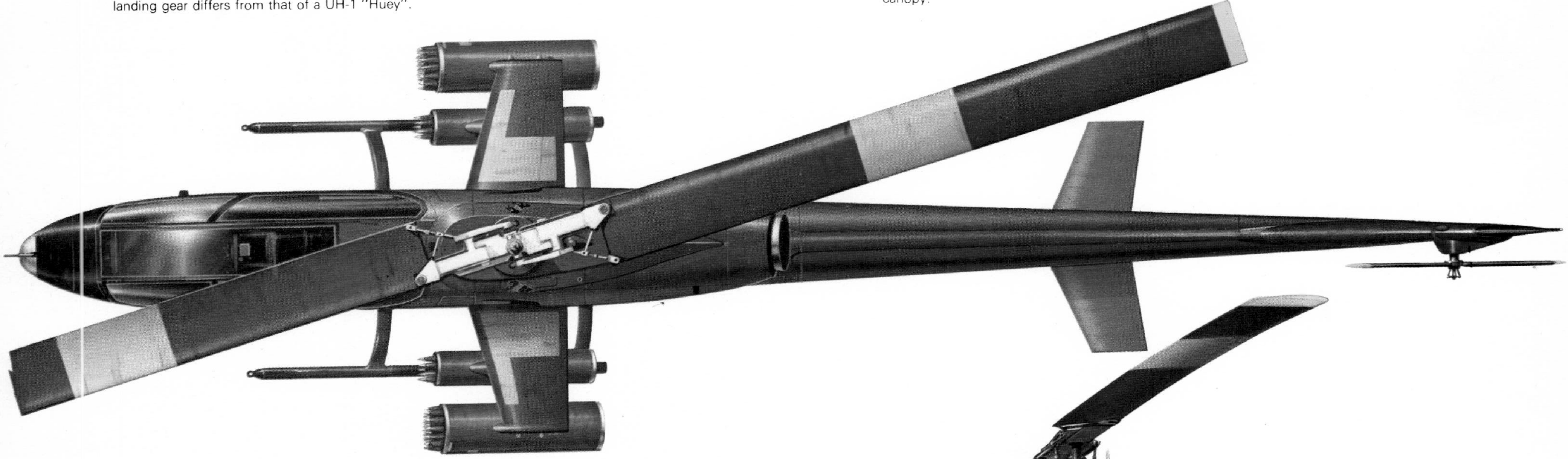

The various Cobra versions all seat the pilot behind the gunner, the latter having control of the XM28 armament system with under-nose turret, in this case mounting two 7.62mm Miniguns with 8,000 rounds.

16369

UNITED STATES ARMY

The slim fuselage, is emphasised in this plan view, which also shows the stub wings (in this case carrying 7- and 19-tube rocket launchers) and the small swept rear stabilizer. Skid landing gear differs from that of a UH-1 "Huey".

The slim frontal silhouette is remarkable. The "door hinge" main rotor, similar to that of the UH-1C, is shown in the sloping rest position; in the air it tilts slightly nose-down.

93

Bell Model 209/AH-1J SeaCobra/AH-1T TOWCobra

Somewhat confusingly, the Bell Model 209 appears in two basic families: the single-engine Model 209/AH-1, and the twin-engine version which is described here. This latter variation of the original Model 209, which was ordered into production to meet the US Army's AAFSS (Advanced Aerial Fire Support System) requirement, was produced originally for service with the US Marine Corps, who required that their version of this attack helicopter should have the extra reliability offered by a twin-engine powerplant. The USMC had shown early interest in the potential of a well armed close-support helicopter, for it seemed an ideal aircraft for deployment in support of the type of operations which are typically and traditionally those of the US Marines. Their evaluation of the US Army's AH-1G led to the initial order to Bell in May 1968 for 49 aircraft under the designation AH-1J SeaCobra. Pending delivery of these, the USMC acquired 38 single-engine AH-1G HueyCobras for training and initial deployment, and these entered service in 1969.

The AH-1J SeaCobra is dimensionally basically similar to the US Army's AH-1G. The major difference is in the powerplant, the SeaCobra having a 1,800-shp (1342-kW) Pratt & Whitney Aircraft of Canada T400-CP-400 turboshaft, the militarised version of the same company's PT6T-3 Turbo Twin Pac unit, with two PT6 power sections. In this particular installation the engine and transmission are flat-rated for a normal continuous power output of 1,100 shp (820 kW), but there is a take-off and five-minute emergency power rating of 1,250 shp (932-kW). Reference to the AH-1G will show that this take-off rating represents a power increase of 13.6%, and as a result the tail rotor pylon of the AH-1J has been strengthened and the blade chord of the tail rotor increased to cope with the additional loading and torque.

Armament differs from that of the HueyCobra, with the chin-mounted turret housing a three-barrel 20-mm XM197 cannon developed by the General Electric Company. A lightweight version of that company's M61 cannon, this weapon has a firing rate of 750 rounds per minute, but as the total ammunition carried in the magazine is 750 rounds, a 16-round burst limiter is included in the firing mechanism. As with the AH-1G/H, various stores can be carried on the four hardpoints beneath the small stub wings.

On 22 December 1972 Bell announced receipt of an order from the US Army for 202 AH-1Js and these, generally similar to those for the USMC, were acquired by Iran, via the US government, deliveries to that country beginning in 1974. The initial batch of 49 SeaCobras for the USMC was followed, in 1973, by an order for 20 more, for delivery during 1974–75, and on 5 June 1974 Bell received an order to modify the last two aircraft from this production run so that they could carry an increased payload and also have improved performance.

This version of the Model 209 was known initially as the Improved SeaCobra, but has since acquired the USMC designation AH-1T. It differs from the AH-1J in having a more powerful 1,970-shp (1469-kW) Pratt & Whitney Aircraft of Canada T400-WV-402 turboshaft. Resulting from the use of this engine, the AH-1T has an improved rotor and tail rotor related to the type developed for the Bell Model 214, an uprated transmission system, a slightly lengthened fuselage to accommodate more fuel, and a lengthened tail boom. The USMC has ordered 57 production aircraft, the first of these being delivered to the USMC on 15 October 1977. Since that time it has been decided to modify 23 of these to launch eight Hughes BGM-71A TOW air-to-surface wire-guided missiles. These are carried in double two-round pods mounted on the stub-wings, and are guided to the target via the crew's helmet sights and a stabilized TOW sight. This version of the Model 209 is known as the TOWCobra.

Type: close-support armed helicopter
Powerplant: (AH-1J) one 1,800-shp (1342-kW) Pratt & Whitney Aircraft of Canada T400-CP-400 turboshaft; (AH-1T) one 1,970-shp (1469-kW) Pratt & Whitney Aircraft of Canada T400-WV-402 turboshaft

Performance: (AH-1J) maximum speed 207 mph (333 km/h); maximum range (no reserves) 359 miles (578 km)
Weights: (AH-1J) operating 7,261 lb (3294 kg); basic combat 9,972 lb (4523 kg); maximum take-off 10,000 lb (4536 kg); (AH-1T) empty 8,014 lb (3635 kg); operating 8,608 lb (3905 kg); maximum take-off 14,000 lb (6350 kg)
Dimensions: (AH-1J) main rotor diameter 44 ft 0 in (13.41 m), tail rotor diameter 8 ft 6 in (2.59 m), length (rotor turning) 52 ft 11½ in (16.14 m), height 13 ft 6¼ in (4.12 m), main rotor disc area 1,520.4 sq ft (141.25 m²); (AH-1T) main rotor diameter 48 ft 0 in (14.63 m), tail rotor diameter 9 ft 8½ in (2.96 m), length (rotor turning) 58 ft 0 in (17.68 m), main rotor disc area 1,809.5 sq ft (168.11 m²)
Armament: (AH-1J) XM197 20-mm gun in chin turret, and two underwing hardpoints on each stub wing can accommodate weapons which include XM-18E1 0.3 in (7.62 mm) Minigun pods, and XM-157 (seven-tube) or XM-159 (19-tube) folding-fin rocket pods;

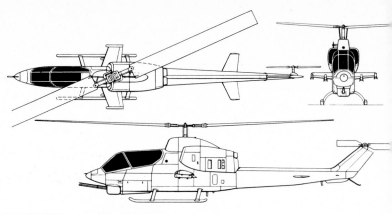

Bell AH-1T (improved SeaCobra)

(AH-1T) eight TOW missiles in four two-round launchers on outboard stub wing hardpoints, plus other weapons on vacant hard-points and XM197 gun in chin turret
Operators: (AH-1J) Iran, US Marine Corps; (AH-1T) US Marine Corps

Bell AH-1T SeaCobra, known also as the Model 209 improved SeaCobra, which has been developed from the twin-engine AH-1J SeaCobra. Ordered for the US Marine Corps, these helicopters have an uprated powerplant, a new dynamic system and advanced technology features.

Bell single-engine Model 209 HueyCobra/AH-1S, an advanced TOW-missile equipped version of the AH-1G/Q. A distinctive feature is the flat plate canopy, designed especially to eliminate unwanted reflections.

Bell Model 212/UH-1N Twin Two-Twelve (see also Agusta-Bell AB 212)

First intimation of a twin-engined version of the Bell Model 205 came on 1 May 1968, when Bell Helicopter Company announced that the Canadian government had approved development of a new general-purpose helicopter. This was to use the basic UH-1 airframe, combined with the PT6T Turbo Twin Pac powerplant produced by Pratt & Whitney Aircraft of Canada. The Canadian authorities later ordered 50, with options on 20 more. The Canadian helicopters were designated initially as CUH-1N, but the official Canadian military designation is CH-135. At the same time the United States armed services announced orders for this aircraft which Bell had designated the Model 212, and which was allocated the tri-service designation UH-1N.

These initial orders comprised 79 for the USAF, 40 for the US Navy and 22 for the US Marine Corps; later orders totalled 159 for the US Navy and Marine Corps.

Despite Canadian origins, the first production examples of the UH-1N were delivered to the USAF in 1970, but it was not until 3 May 1971 that the first CH-135 for the Canadian Armed Forces was handed over officially with the balance of the order being completed within a year. Other air forces which ordered military versions of this helicopter include those of Argentina and Bangladesh.

Simultaneously with the production of military helicopters, Bell began to manufacture a commercial version which is known as the Twin Two-Twelve and this first received FAA certification in October 1970. Generally similar to the military UH-1N, these commercial helicopters differ primarily by having changes in avionics and equipment, but also have the capability of carrying a load of 5,000 lb (2268 kg) externally, compared with the UH-1N's external load of 4,000 lb (1814 kg).

In January 1973 Bell announced development of an IFR version of the Twin Two-Twelve, this having a new avionics system, full blind-flying instrumentation, and an automatic stability augmentation system. This was an attractive proposition to many civil operators, and especially those offering support services to offshore oil rigs, and many of the initial orders were for utilisation in this role. Three of these aircraft were acquired by Peru and were considered so suitable that a follow up order for 14 more aircraft represented Bell's largest single order for non-military helicopters.

The PT6T (T400) powerplant of the Model 212 was developed initially for this aircraft, financed jointly by Bell, the Canadian government, and Pratt & Whitney Aircraft of Canada. It not only provides 1,800 shp (1342 kW) at its take-off rating, but offers true engine-out capability, plus improved performance in hot day/high altitude operations. This is due to its unique construction, comprising two Pratt & Whitney PT6 turboshaft engines mounted together and each driving into a combining gearbox with a single output shaft. In the event of an engine failure, the remaining engine can continue to drive the helicopter's rotors through the combining gearbox, and has adequate power to permit

safe operation to a suitable landing area.

The Bell Model 212 is built under licence by Agusta in Italy with the designation AB 212, and the first deliveries of these aircraft were made in late 1971. They are generally similar to the Bell production aircraft, but Agusta has developed an anti-submarine variant which has the designation AB 212ASW. These have the more powerful PT6T-6 Twin Pac turboshaft, which has a take-off rating of 1,875 shp (1398 kW), local airframe strengthening, and with deck mooring equipment. Initial deliveries were made to the Italian navy's 5° Gruppo Elicotteri during 1976.

Type: general-purpose/ASW/ASV helicopter
Powerplant: (UH-1N) 1,800-shp (1342-kW) Pratt & Whitney Aircraft of Canada PT6T-3 Turbo Twin-Pac turboshaft engine, flat rated to 1,290 shp (962 kW) for take-off
Performance: (UH-1N) maximum cruising speed at sea level 115 mph (185 km/h); maximum range with standard fuel at sea level (no reserves) 248 miles (399 km)
Weights: (UH-1N) maximum take-off and mission 10,500 lb (4763 kg); (Twin Two-Twelve) maximum take-off 11,200 lb (5080 kg)

Bell Model 212

Dimensions: diameter of main rotor 48 ft 2¼ in (14.69 m); diameter of tail rotor 8 ft 6 in (2.59 m); length (rotors fore and aft) 57 ft 3¼ in (17.46 m); height 14 ft 10¼ in (4.53 m); main rotor disc area 1,809 sq ft (168.06 m²)

Armament: (AB 212ASW) homing torpedoes, depth charges, and air-to-surface missiles
Operators: Argentina, Bangladesh, Canada, Italy, Japan, Norway, Peru, US Air Force, US Marine Corps, US Navy

Bell UH-1N general-purpose helicopter. Modern rotary-wing aircraft in this class offer completely new standards of performance as a result of using advanced main rotors and twin-turbine powerplants. Either turbine is able to maintain safe flight if one engine fails.

Bell Model 214/Huey Plus/Agusta-Bell AB 214

On 12 October 1970, Bell announced that it had developed as a company-funded project an improved version of the military Model 205/UH-1H, to which it had given the designation Model 214 Huey Plus. The prototype was powered by a 1,900-shp (1417-kW) Lycoming T53-L-702 turboshaft engine, driving a newly-developed main rotor of increased diameter to derive the maximum efficiency from the high-powered turboshaft engine. The airframe was basically that of the Model 205, but had been modified to increase the strength of areas and components which would be put under stress by the increased engine torque and new rotor. Minor internal rearrangement made possible the provision of accommodation for a crew of two and up to 12 passengers. Maximum speed at max take-off weight was 190 mph (306 km/h), but despite this 49.6% increase in speed by comparison with the Model 205, the Model 214

failed to attract the US Army.

However, on 22 December 1972 Bell announced that it had received an order from the US Army for the supply of 287 of these aircraft, to be acquired by Iran through the US government under the designation Model 214A, and six more were ordered in March 1977. These Model 214As were to be powered by the 2,930-shp (2185-kW) Lycoming LTC4B-8D turboshaft engine, enabling this aircraft, with a strengthened transmission, to carry an increased payload. In February 1976, the government of Iran ordered 39 more aircraft, designated Model 214Cs, which were to be equipped especially for search and rescue missions. These orders were increased by a total of 400 Model 214 aircraft when Bell and the Iranian government agreed in 1975 to establish a helicopter manufacturing industry in Iran. This plan was changed in March 1978 to cover the manufacture in Iran of 50 Model

Agusta-Bell AB 214

continued

214As, and 350 of a new version designated Model 214ST with 19-seat capacity and powered by two 1,625-shp (1212-kW) General Electric T700-GE-TIC turboshaft engines.

In early January 1979 it was reported that the post-Shah Iranian government had terminated this project, but it is believed that Bell will continue with development of the 214ST in the US as a company-funded project. Delivery of Model 214As for Iran began on 26 April 1975, and Bell have also developed a civil version known as the Model 214B BigLifter, which received FAA certification on 27 January 1976.

Type: single-engine utility helicopter
Powerplant: (214A) one 2,930-shp (2185-kW) Lycoming LTC4B-8D turboshaft

Performance: (214A) cruising speed 161 mph (259 km/h); maximum range at maximum take-off weight 283 miles (455 km)
Weights: (214A) maximum take-off

13,800 lb (6260 kg); maximum take-off with external load 15,000 lb (6804 kg)
Dimensions: (214A) main rotor diameter 50 ft 0 in (15.24 m); tail rotor diameter

9 ft 8 in (2.95 m); main rotor disc area 1,963.5 sq ft (182.4 m²)
Armament: none
Operators: Iran

Iranian Army Aviation Bell 214A transport helicopter.

Most capable of all versions of the prolific Bell 'Huey' helicopter, the Model 214 Big Lifter has a Lycoming T55 turboshaft engine and uprated dynamic parts, enabling it to carry a maximum of 16 persons for very short ranges. The 214 was ordered by Iran, but many of the large force of 287 delivered to that country may be grounded through lack of spares.

Beriev Be-6 Madge

Designed by G.M. Beriev, who had been responsible for a long line of seaplane and flying-boat designs since 1928, the Beriev Be-6 'Madge' flew in prototype form in 1947 under the project designation LL-143, powered by two 2,000-hp (1492-kW) Shvetsov ASh-72 engines. After successful trials the type was ordered into production as the Be-6 with the more powerful Shvetsov ASh-73 radials of 2,300 hp (1716-kW). It replaced several antiquated single- and twin-engined flying-boats built in small numbers after World War II. In the production aircraft, the single 23-mm cannon in the nose and twin 20-mm cannon in a tail turret were deleted, retaining only a dorsal barbette with twin 20-mm cannon. The tail gun position was replaced by magnetically detection (MAD) gear, and after the type entered service a retractable radome was fitted in the hull behind the second 'step'. Offensive weapons (mines, depth charges and torpedoes) are carried on underwing pylons outboard of the engine nacelles.

The Be-6 normally carried a crew of eight and was in a similar class to the US Martin Mariner. It served with the Soviet Navy (AV-

MF) in the long-range maritime reconnaissance role from about 1949 to 1967, when it was replaced by the turboprop-powered Be-12 'Mail' amphibian.

A few Be-6s are still in service, mainly on fishery patrol and protection duties.

Type: twin-engine maritime reconnaissance flying-boat
Powerplant: two 2,300-hp (1716-kW) Shvetsov ASh-73TK radial piston engines
Performance: maximum speed 258 mph (415 km/h) at 7,875 ft (2400 m); maximum range 3,045 miles (4900 km); maximum endurance 16 hours
Weight: loaded 51,588 lb (23400 kg)
Dimensions: span 108 ft 3 in (32.91 m); length 73 ft 10 in (22.50 m); height 24 ft 7 in (7.45 m)
Armament: twin 20-mm cannon in a remotely-controlled dorsal barbette; mines, torpedoes and depth charges carried beneath wings
Operators: USSR

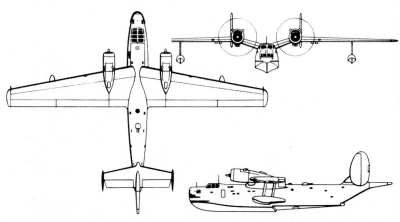

Beriev Be-6 Madge

Beriev Be-12 Tchaika (Mail)

Together with the Japanese Maritime Self-Defence Force, the AVMF (Soviet Naval Aviation) is the last major service to operate fleets of combat flying-boats and amphibians. Elsewhere, the role of the patrol flying-boat was taken over by long-range landplanes in the 1950s. This process may continue, as no amphibious replacement for the Beriev Be-12 Tchaika (seagull), codenamed 'Mail' by NATO, has been reported, and the AVMF has now introduced its first specialized landplane for the maritime reconnaissance role, the Ilyushin Il-38 'May'.

The Beriev design bureau, based at Taganrog on the Sea of Azov, has been the main supplier of marine aircraft to the Soviet navy since 1945, most of its aircraft going to the Northern and Black Sea Fleets. The origins of the Be-12 go back to the LL-143 prototype of 1945, which led in 1949 to the Be-6, 'Madge'. This latter twin-engined flying-boat served with success until 1967.

Following the Be-6, the Beriev team carried out a considerable amount of research into jet-powered flying boats, producing the straight-winged Be-R-1 of 1952 and the swept-wing Be-10 of 1960-61. The latter, powered by two Lyulka AL-7RVs (unreheated versions of the Su-7 powerplant), established a number of seaplane records in 1961, but only three or four are believed to have been built.

The lessons learned in the design of the Be-R-1 and Be-10, however, were incorporated in the design of a much improved flying-boat based loosely on the Be-6 and originally identified by NATO as a re-engined version of the older type. In fact, the Be-12 bears little more than a general resemblance to the Be-6, sharing only the gull-wing layout and twin tail of its predecessor. The greater power and lighter weight of the turboprop engines have permitted the forward extension of the hull, with a new planing bottom similar to that of the Be-10. The prominent spray suppressor around the bows of the Be-10 is also a feature of the turboprop aircraft. The most significant change, however, was the addition of a massive and sturdy retractable landing gear, making the Be-12 amphibious and thus considerably more versatile than the earlier Beriev designs. The turreted gun armament of the Be-6 has been deleted, being replaced by a MAD (magnetic anomaly detector) 'sting' in the tail, above the tailwheel well, while the search radar is carried in a long nose housing instead of the ventral retractable 'dustbin' radome of the Be-6. One of the drawbacks of the high-wing layout, the excessive height of the engines above the ground, has been mitigated by the design of the engine cowling panels, which drop down to form strong

working platforms.

The considerable weight-lifting capability of the Be-12 was demonstrated in a series of class records for amphibians set up in 1964, 1968 and 1970, suggesting a normal weapons load as high 11,000 lb (5000 kg). The Be-12 can load on the water through large side hatches in the rear fuselage, and stores can be dropped through a watertight hatch in the hull aft of the step. Unlike land-based ASW platforms, a marine aircraft can, in reasonably calm conditions, settle on the water and search with its own sonar equipment, rather than relying exclusively on sonobuoys. It is assumed that the Be-12 has this capability.

With the increasing use of the Mil Mi-14 'Haze' ASW helicopter and the Ilyushin Il-38 'May', there would seem to be a diminishing ASW role for the Be-12, although the type will certainly remain in service as a high-speed search-and-rescue (SAR) vehicle. It is also believed to have been used for mapping, geographical survey and utility transport. By Soviet standards the type was not built in large numbers, only 75 being reported in service in the late 1970s.

Type: maritime patrol amphibian
Powerplant: two 4,190-shp (3126-kW) Ivchenko AI-20D turboprops
Performance: maximum speed 380 mph (610 km/h); economical patrol speed 200 mph (320 km/h); maximum range 2,500 miles (4000 km)
Weights: estimated empty 48,000 lb (21700 kg); maximum take-off about 65,000 lb (30000 kg)
Dimensions: span 97 ft 6 in (29.7 m); length 99 ft (30.2); height on land 23 ft (7.0 m)
Armament: bombs, rockets or guided ASMs on underwing pylons; depth charges and sonobuoys in fuselage bays
Operator: USSR

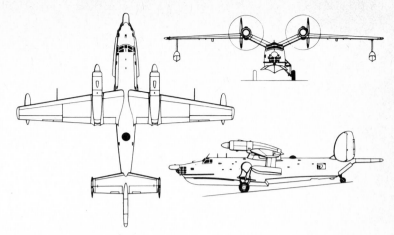

Beriev Be-12 (M-12) Mail

Called Tchaika (Seagull) by the Soviet AV-MF (naval air force), the Beriev M-12 (designated Be-12 by Beriev's design bureau) is a versatile turboprop amphibian.

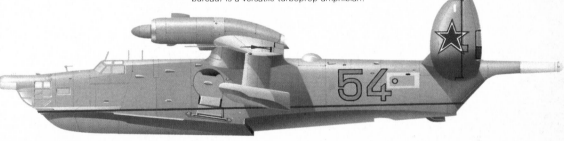

The Soviet Naval Air Force or AV-MF still operates a number of Beriev Be-12 Mail medium-range maritime patrol amphibians.

Boeing B-52 Stratofortress

By normal standards long since rendered obsolete as a result of its unacceptable vulnerability to anti-aircraft missiles, the mighty Boeing B-52 Stratofortress has seen two would-be successors fall by the wayside, and remains one of the three US strategic deterrents (the other two being the land and sea-launched missiles). More than a billion dollars has been spent on the 320 or so aircraft remaining in the front-line fleet to improve their safety, reliability, performance and weapon-delivery accuracy.

At Offutt Air Force Base, Nebraska, the headquarters of the US Air Force Strategic Air Command, an American journalist in 1976 was told that some of these B-52s would be operating into the next century. This claim was made at a time when the B-52's supersonic successor, the Rockwell B-1, was well into its flight-test programme and regarded as the linchpin of SAC's airborne might. With the cancellation of the swing-wing B-1 shortly after this, a huge responsibility has once more been thrown back on to the 25-year old heavyweight.

If the B-52 does reach the year 2000 it will probably have had the longest career of any front-line combat type. By that time the youngest of these subsonic bombers will have been on the flight-line for 40 years.

What was to become SAC's 'long rifle' began life in 1948 as a turboprop successor to

The B-52H Stratofortress was expected to be retired, with all other versions, in about 1975, but will almost certainly still be in use in 2000. Several times the original purchase price has been spent on structural and avionics improvements.

continued

the piston-engined Boeing B-50, itself a development of the B-29 Superfortress, whose nuclear missions against Japan brought World War II to a close in 1945. Designers were faced with a quandary: the B-50's successor was clearly going to have turbine engines, but how to use them? Ordinary jet engines of the period were so thirsty that a huge airframe would be needed to carry all the fuel. The answer was to harness them to large propellers, as the Soviet Union was to do later with its Tupolev Tu-95 'Bear'. Deciding on the right propulsion system was perhaps the biggest headache facing the early jet-bomber designers. Turboprops were the obvious answer, because they were more economical than pure jets, but on the other hand they were more complicated and less reliable.

Then, in 1949, Pratt & Whitney brought out the J57 engine. Far and away superior to any other US powerplant, it was to become over the next 30 years one of aviation's really great engines. Originally giving 7,500-lb (3402-kg) thrust, it helped to change the philosophy of both Boeing and the USAF.

Boeing and its rival in the big-bomber stakes, Convair, fought bitterly to get the contract for the new USAF bomber. Convair had already provided the mammoth B-36, and so had a wealth of experience with heavyweights. But its proposed YB-60, though cheaper than the competing B-52, could not equal its performance, and Boeing won the day.

The prototype B-52 took to the air for the first time on 15 April 1952. Its technology was based on the medium-range B-47 that had flown five years previously. Thus it had an extremely thin, shoulder-mounted wing, with engines clustered in podded pairs, and a tandem mainwheel arrangement with wing-mounted outrigger wheels to keep the wings level on the ground.

The first three production aircraft were designated B-52As, though they spent their lives at Boeing as test and development aircraft, beginning an improvement programme that has gone on to this day. The first version to join the USAF was the B-52B, virtually identical to the -A but with a navigation/bombing system. Of the 50 built, 27 were converted as RB-52B reconnaissance versions.

The B-52C was substantially improved in performance and equipment, and was the first model to have the white anti-radiation under-surface finish. It was succeeded by the B-52D, with an improved fire-control system for the tail armament of four 0.5-in (12.7-mm) machine-guns. As the B-52Ds were being turned out by Boeing's Wichita plant (the production line was progressively transferred there because of the huge build-up of KC-135 tanker construction at the Seattle factory), the USAF was thinking about the giant bomber's successor. This was to be the WS-110, later the North American B-70.

But the B-70 was years in the future, and B-52 improvement continued with the B-52E, having a more advanced navigation and weapons system, and with a new flight-deck layout to house the equipment displays. Continuing weight increases called for more power, especially at take-off, and the B-52F had a later version of the J57 engine, fitted like earlier versions with water injection to boost take-off power.

The B-52G, which was initially planned to be the final version pending arrival of the B-70, brought along a host of major improvements, and was the biggest single advance of any model. The airframe was substantially redesigned to save weight and to make it safer; integral wing-tanks greatly increased fuel capacity; the tail gunner was relocated in the crew compartment, this saving considerable weight; the fin was shortened; and provision was made for launching ECM decoys and stand-off missiles. The decoy was a small jet aeroplane known as the Quail, designed to have a radar signature similar to that of the bomber to confuse missile radars. One hundred and ninety-three B-52Gs were built, the last in 1960. The missile to go with it was the AGM-28 Hound Dog, which had a range of 750 miles (1207 km). The B-52G in fact was to be less a bomber than the first stage of a missile.

Packed with conventional bombs, a black-bellied BUFF (Big Ugly Fat Fella), alias the B-52D, thunders aloft from the switchback runway at Guam for the 9½-hour mission to Vietnam in 1967. A training wing of this conventional-warfare model is still at Guam.

Meanwhile, Boeing and the USAF were planning between them yet another version, the B-52H, to which the specification applies. This really was the final model. It was characterized by two major changes: the introduction of the new Pratt & Whitney TF33 turbofan engines, which at once gave a much greater thrust increase and a considerably lower specific fuel consumption, and structural changes which permitted the aircraft to fly at low altitudes without excessive fatigue problems. It also exchanged the four 0.5-in (12.7-mm) tail guns for a single fast-firing 'Gatling' type gun. It was built to carry Skybolt ballistic missiles under the wings and Quail decoys in the bomb-bay.

The final B-52H, the last of 744 B-52s, rolled out of Wichita in June 1962. The Skybolt missile, which had also been ordered by the RAF, was cancelled in December of that year, while the B-70 project had already been terminated. The B-52s were clearly going to have to soldier on for a long time while the USAF made up its mind what to do about a replacement.

In 1963 the B-52D was studied as a CBC (conventional bomb carrier) and the following year rebuilding of B-52Ds began at Wichita to permit the type to carry 105 'iron' bombs of 750-lb (340-kg) nominal weight, but actually weighing 825 lb (374 kg). In 1965 rebuilt CBC aircraft started to hammer suspected Communist hideouts in South Vietnam and the supply route from North Vietnam known as the Ho Chi Minh trail. The B-52s operated from Andersen AFB on Guam island, 2,600 miles (4185 km) away in the Pacific. Each mission lasted some 10 to 12 hours, with air-refuelling by means of Boeing KC-135 tankers. The B-52s were more feared than any other US weapon.

With little sign of progress around the negotiating table, the B-52s were authorized in April 1966 to bomb North Vietnam. To cut the cost of what was turning out to be a very expensive war, and to provide quicker reaction, the big bombers were deployed to U Tapao airfield in neighbouring Thailand, cutting the journey by three-quarters and dispensing with the need for air-refuelling.

Through the late 1960s and early 1970s the

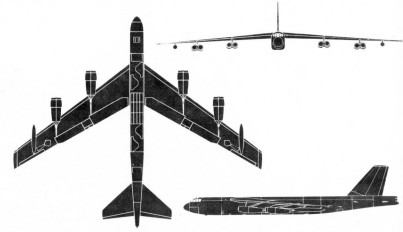

Boeing B-52H Stratofortress

B-52E Stratofortress

B-52G Stratofortress

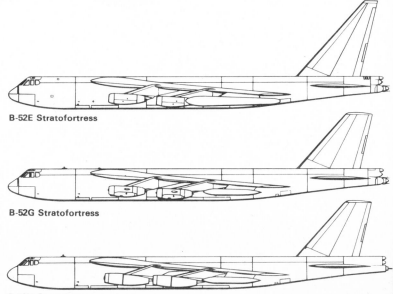

B-52H Stratofortress

bombers continued to rain high-explosive bombs on Vietnam, aided by improved navigation and weapon-delivery techniques and to some extent protected by ever-increasingly sophisticated ECM devices. For 11 days in late 1972, pausing only to celebrate Christmas, the huge bombers pounded North Vietnam's capital Hanoi and its harbour Haiphong into ruins during the most savage bombing campaign in the history of air warfare. But SAM defences were intense and 15 aircraft were lost. This caused concern at SAC, but the US forces were shortly afterwards withdrawn.

Since then the USAF launched a new B-52 successor, initially called AMSA (Advanced Manned Strategic Aircraft), later becoming the Rockwell B-1. This also has been cancelled, and there is nothing on the horizon to follow the B-52. Meanwhile a new generation of weapons has come along, such as the SRAM (Short-Range Attack Missile) and the ALCM (Air-Launched Cruise Missile). The SRAM entered service with the B-52G and H versions, and in 1977 the Hound Dog stand-off missile was withdrawn. Apart from a training wing of B-52Ds at Guam, SAC strength is made up of G and H versions. These have been structurally rebuilt and fitted with 14 to 18 new sensor and avionic systems.

Data for B52H only:
Type: long-range strategic bomber
Powerplants: eight 17,000-lb (7711-kg) Pratt & Whitney TF33-P-3 turbofans
Performance: maximum speed Mach 0.95 or 630 mph (1014 km/h) at 40,000 ft (12192 m); typical cruising speed 565 mph (909 km/h) at 36,000 ft (10973 m); service ceiling 55,000 ft (16764 m)
Weight: maximum take-off 505,000 lb (229066 kg)
Dimensions: span 185 ft (56.39 m); length 157 ft (47.85 m); height 40 ft 8 in (12.4 m)
Armament: one T-171 20-mm gun in General Electric rear gun position, 20 SRAM missiles (ALCM due to become operational in the 1980s) and Quail decoys
Operators: US Air Force

This **B-52D,** originally aircraft 56-581 but repainted 0-60581 in red on the new camouflage and black scheme for changed circumstances, was photographed during early 'Arc Light' bombing missions over Vietnam in 1966. It has the Big Belly structural rebuild.

USAF Strategic Air Command Boeing B-52G fitted with latest electro-optical viewing system blisters beneath the nose.

Boeing C-97/KC-97

In early 1942 Boeing initiated a design study to examine the feasibility of producing a transport version of the B-29 Superfortress. In due course the company's proposal was submitted to the USAAF for consideration and, because at that time a long-range transport was a much-needed type of aircraft, a contract for three prototypes was awarded on 23 January 1943. Identified by Boeing as the Model 367, and designated XC-97 by the US Air Force, the first made its maiden flight on 15 November 1944.

The XC-97 had much in common with the B-29, including the entire wing and engines. At first view the fuselage, a 'double-bubble' section, appeared to be entirely new, but in fact the lower 'bubble' was basically B-29 structure, and so was the tail unit attached to the new and larger upper 'bubble'. On 6 July 1945, following brief evaluation of the prototypes, 10 service-test aircraft were ordered. These comprised six YC-97 cargo transports, three YC-97A troop carriers, and a single YC-97B with 80 airline-type seats in its main cabin.

The first production contract, on 24 March 1947, for 27 C-97As with 3,250-hp (2424-kW) Pratt & Whitney R-4360-27 engines, specified accommodation for 134 troops, or the ability to carry a 53,000 lb (24040 kg) payload. Three transport versions followed, under the designation VC-97A, C-97C and VC-97D, and following trials with three C-97As equipped with additional tankage and a Boeing-developed flight refuelling boom, KC-97E flight-refuelling tankers went into production in 1951. This version was powered by 3,500-hp (2610-kW) R-4360-35C engines. The KC-97Fs which followed differed only in having R-4360-59B engines. Both the -97E and -97F were convertible tanker/transports, but for full transport capability the flight-refuelling equipment had to be removed. The most numerous variant, with 592 built, was the KC-97G which had

full tanker or full transport capability without any on-unit equipment change.

When production ended in 1956 a total of 888 C-97s had been built, and many were converted later for other duties. KC-97Ls had increased power by the installation of a 5,200-lb (2359-kg) thrust General Electric J47-GE-23 turbojet beneath each wing to improve rendezvous compatibility with Boeing B-47s. KC-97Gs converted to all-cargo configuration were redesignated C-97G, and in all-passenger configuration became C-97K. Search and rescue conversions were HC-97G, and three KC-97Ls went to the Spanish air force, being designated TK-1 in that service. Several have served in many roles with Israel's air force.

Type: long-range transport or flight-refuelling tanker
Powerplant: (KC-97G) four 3,500-hp (2610-kW) Pratt & Whitney R-4360-59 Wasp Major radial piston engines
Performance: (KC-97G) maximum speed 375 mph (604 km/h); cruising speed 300 mph (483 km/h); range 4,300 miles (6920 km)
Weights: empty 82,500 lb (37421 kg); maximum take-off 175,000 lb (79379 kg)
Dimensions: span 141 ft 3 in (43,05 m); length 110 ft 4 in (33.63 m); height 38 ft 3 in (11.66 m); wing area 1,720 sq ft (159.79 m²)
Armament: none
Operators: Israel, Spain, US Air Force, US Air National Guard

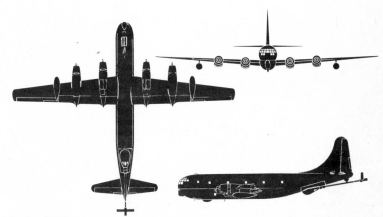

Boeing KC-97

One of the many home-produced success stories of the Israeli Heyl Ha'Avir is the rebuild of several Boeing 377 Stratocruisers as multi-role military freighter/tankers, since supplemented by ex-USAF KC-97s.

Boeing C-135 series

In August 1954 the USAF announced that it intended to procure a number of tanker/transports developed from the prototype Boeing 367-80 which had first flown a few weeks earlier. These were allocated the designation KC-135A and the first of these made its initial flight on 21 August 1956. Ten months later, on 28 June 1957, the first was delivered to Castle AFB, California. Since that time a family of variants have been built in large numbers for service with the USAF, primarily as tankers (Stratotankers) or cargo transports (Stratolifters), but many have been built or converted for special purposes.

Designated Model 717 by Boeing, these aircraft differ primarily from the later Model 707 by having a smaller-diameter fuselage, deletion tion of cabin windows, reduced size and weight, and the capability of carrying 80 passengers or an equivalent weight in cargo on the main deck. All equipment for the tanker role is accommodated on the lower deck, or normal cargo area, this including the pivoted 'flying boom' refuelling gear. Subsequently this was modified for probe-and-drogue refuelling of Tactical Air Command or US Navy Marine Corps aircraft. Two modified KC-135As are used by the US Federal Aviation Agency (FAA) to check navigation aids throughout the United States.

Other variants of the Model 717 tanker/-transport include the KC-135B, generally similar to KC-135As but powered by turbofan engines. Seventeen were built to serve as Airborne Command Posts for the Strategic Air Command. These aircraft, subsequently redesignated EC-135C, have TF33 turbofan engines, a flight-refuelling receptacle as well as a boom, suitable avionics to act as a control centre, and a crew of 16. EC-135A is the designation of turbojet-powered aircraft equipped to act as backups to the EC-135Cs. The EC-135G/H/K are turbojet-powered command posts with more advanced equipment, and the EC-135J is a turbofan-powered variant of the EC-135H. EC-135L aircraft are turbojet-powered KC-135As equipped for a dual role of command posts and airborne communications relay stations.

Special-purpose test aircraft for use by USAF Systems Command carry the designations C-135A, JKC-135A, KC-135A, and NKC-135A. RC-135Ds with turbojet engines and RC-135Cs and RC-135Es with turbofan engines all have the boom deleted and are equipped instead with sophisticated avionics and a crop of radar antennae for various reconnaissance, Elint and other missions. C-135F is the designation applied to 12 dual-purpose tanker/transports (with booms terminating in a drogue) supplied to the French air force. Last of the Stratotanker variants are three NC-135As equipped initially to monitor the blast of nuclear weapons during tests, and used also during 1965 with special equipment to study a total solar eclipse.

The Model 717 Stratolifter family differs from the foregoing by being equipped specifically to serve as long-range transports, with the refuelling boom deleted. There is a structural similarity between these two basic 'tanker/lifter' types, but interior changes in the latter provide accommodation for up to 126 troops, or 44 stretchers plus 54 sitting casualties. Galley and toilet facilities are provided at the rear of the cabin, and provision is made for an alternative all-freight role. The initial version is the C-135A with turbojet engines, first flown on 19 May 1961, and delivered to MATS on 8 June 1961 to become the service's first strategic jet transport.

Other versions include C-135Bs, similar to the above but with turbofan engines; four RC-135A (Boeing Model 739) reconnaissance aircraft for the 1,370th Photo Mapping Wing of the MAC; 10 similar RC-135Bs with turbofan engines; VC-135B is the designation of 11 C-135Bs modified to serve as VIP transports; and 10 WC-135Bs, similar to

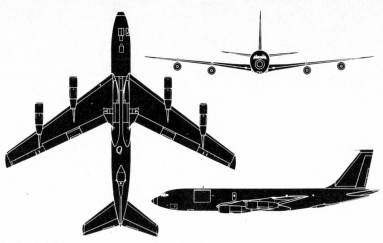

Boeing C-135

C-135Bs, are equipped for long-range weather reconnaissance duties.

Type: turbine-powered tanker/transport
Powerplant: (KC-135A derivatives) four 13,500-lb (6124-kg) Pratt & Whitney J57-P-59W turbojets; (C-135B) four 18,000-lb (8165-kg) thrust Pratt & Whitney TF33-P-5 turbofans
Performance: /C-135B) maximum speed 600 mph (966 km/h); average cruising at 35,000 ft (10670 m) 530 mph (853 km/h)
Weights: (C-135B) operating empty 102,300 lb (46403 kg); maximum take-off 275,500 lb (124965 kg)

Dimensions: (KC-135A) span 130 ft 10 in (39.88 m); length 136 ft 3 in (41.53 m); height 38 ft 4 in (11.68 m); wing area 2,433 sq ft (226.03 m²)
Armament: none
Operators: France, US Air Force

Boeing KC-135 Stratotanker of the United States Air Force.

The tenth of 732 Boeing KC-135 tanker/transports seen in its youth; today most of this vast force have been rebuilt for use in many different or additional roles, there being no fewer than 22 sub-types of this noisy and sometimes marginal, but always strategically useful, multi-role aircraft.

Boeing C-137/707

Although stemming from the same basic design which had produced for the US Air Force the important C-135/KC-135 in its many variants, the Boeing Model 707 differs in a number of important details. It was, of course, the first jet transport aircraft to be completed and flown in the United States, the initial flight of this company-funded prototype being made on 15 July 1954. Designated originally 367-80, this aircraft was known to two generations of Boeing workers as the 'Dash Eighty', and this venerable old lady flew for a variety of purposes from 1954 until honourable retirement and presentation to the Smithsonian Institution in 1972.

The British-built de Havilland Comet I had given the world a first glimpse of the potential of a turbojet transport, and Boeing's 367-80 was the first new design to benefit from the experience gained with swept wings and more efficient two-shaft engines. Boeing appreciated the glittering prize awaiting for the first really successful turbine-powered transport, and concentrated its effort, know-how, money, and more than a touch of genius, in finalizing the design of this new prototype. It was intended to demonstrate the possibilities of such an aircraft as a military flight-refuelling tanker, for which the USAF had an increasing demand, as well as for a civil transport. Boeing had developed also a rigid flight-refuelling boom which could be lowered and 'flown' for the steady transfer of fuel at a flow rate of 1,000 US gallons (3785 litres) a minute; during the early test programme, the 367-80 was fitted with such a boom and demonstrated extensively to show the capability of such an aircraft to refuel the majority of in use, or projected, USAF Strategic Air Command aircraft without them needing to effect a rendezvous

at speeds or altitudes significantly lower than those which were their normal cruising parameters. The result of the comprehensive tests showed that this Boeing tanker could be of vital importance to the future of the SAC and it was ordered in large numbers for service under the designation KC-135.

Having decided that it needed this special version of the 367-80 for its own military use, the USAF then authorized Boeing to proceed with the development of a commercial transport which would be basically similar. Two versions followed: the Model 707 medium-range transport, and the intermediate-range 720. It was, however, the first model was to be developed extensively for intercontinental services, and continues in production in 1979, all models being larger and much heavier than the KC-135. The first version was the 707-120, powered by four 13,500-lb (6123-kg) thrust Pratt & Whitney JT3C-6 turbojet engines, and three of these were ordered by the USAF in May 1958 to serve as VIP transports or for the carriage of high-priority cargo. Because these aircraft derived from the civil transport family of the 367-80, which was distinguished particularly by its larger-diameter fuselage with cabin windows and greater dimensions, they were given a C-137 designation rather than the C-135 of the tanker/transports. Thus, when they entered service in 1959 they had the designation VC-137A. They had, of course, a very different interior from the commercial 707, with VIP accommodation and special-purpose compartments. When re-engined later with Pratt & Whitney TF33 turbofans these aircraft were redesignated VC-137Bs. A single VC-137C was added to the fleet in 1962, similar to the commercial

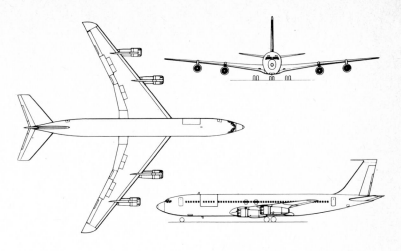

Boeing 707-320C

707-320B, and this became the Presidential transport, known as 'Air Force One'.

The German *Luftwaffe* has also acquired four 707-320Cs as VIP or special freight transports, the Portuguese air force four, the Iranian air force five, and the Canadian Armed Forces five, this last nation designating them CC-137. The Canadian and Iranian models have various boom and hose-reel fits for flight-refuelling.

Type: VIP or special freight transport
Powerplant: (VC-137C) four 18,000-lb (8165-kg) thrust Pratt & Whitney JT3D-3 turbofans

Peformance: (VC-137C) maximum speed 627 mph (1009 km/h); maximum cruising speed at 25,000 ft (7620 m) 600 mph (966 km/h); range with maximum fuel, allowances for climb and descent, no reserves 7,610 miles (12247 km)
Weight: (VC-137C) maximum take-off 327,000 lb (148325 kg)
Dimensions: (VC-137C) span 145 ft 9 in (44.42 m); length 152 ft 11 in (46.61 m); height 42 ft 5 in (12.93 m); wing area 3,010 sq ft (279.63 m²)
Armament: none
Operators: Canada, Germany, Iran, Portugal, and US Air Force

Air Force One is the aircraft (of whatever type) conveying the President of the United States. The title is usually borne by AF Serial 62-6000 or (illustrated) 72-7000, Boeing VC-137C (320B military version) of the MAC 89th Military Airlift Group.

Boeing E-3 Sentry

The requirement for an Airborne Warning And Control System (AWACS) aircraft was first proposed by the USAF in 1963, at which time it was planned for up to 64 specially-equipped aircraft to be provided. They were then considered essential to alert US air defence of approaching Soviet bomber attacks, and to act as mobile control centres in no fixed geographical position, able to control all national air activities in both nuclear or conventional combat operations. Since the origination of the concept, economic considerations have made it necessary to reduce considerably the number of aircraft to be acquired initially.

Though an AWACS is a development of the traditional Airborne Early-Warning (AEW) aircraft, the entire concept is far more all-embracing. It also fulfils the roles of the Airborne Command Post (ACP), typified by the EC-135 variants which have served with the USAF's Strategic Air Command. AWACS is a combination of both families, with advanced on-board avionics that make possible the simultaneous co-ordination of many differing air operations, so that these aircraft could command and control the entire air effort of a nation, embracing strike, interception, reconnaissance and interdiction, plus the backup roles of support and airlift.

Two main areas of use have been planned by the USAF, with the Tactical Air Command (TAC) using its AWACS aircraft for airborne surveillance, and as a command centre for the rapid development of TAC forces. A differing role is envisaged for the same aircraft by Aerospace Defense Command (ADC), who regard the AWACS aircraft as 'hard to find' command and control posts.

Boeing was the successful one of two contenders for the supply of an AWACS aircraft, being awarded a contract on 23 July 1970 to provide two prototypes under the designation EC-137D. The company's proposed AWACS was based on the airframe of the Boeing Model 707-320B commercial transport, and the prototypes were modified in the first place to carry out comparative trials between the prototype downward-looking surveillance radars designed by the Hughes Aircraft Company and Westinghouse Electric Corporation. These tests continued into the autumn of 1972, and on 5 October the USAF announced that Westinghouse had been selected as prime contractor for the advanced radar that was to be the essential core of the AWACS. This has the difficult task of seeking and identifying low-flying targets at ranges as great as 230 miles (370 km), and in the case of high altitude attack at even greater ranges.

The USAF has acquired an extensive knowledge of the operation and capabilities of the Boeing Model 707, especially in the form of the smaller EC-135 variants which have served well and long. It was clear that with far more advanced equipment the same aircraft could

provide the desired potential, thus ensuring that equipment acquired for and experience derived from the EC-135 would offer an important and reliable contribution to the AWACS concept.

Very little modification of the basic 707-320B airframe was required to make it suitable for the new role. Most important, and an external identification feature *par excellence*, is the large rotodome assembly carried on two wide-chord streamlined struts, which are secured to the rear upper fuselage. New engine pylon fairings are provided for the more powerful turbofan engines which power the pre-production EC-137Cs and production aircraft, the latter having the designation E-3A (the original choice of eight General Electric TF34 engines was abandoned to save money). The remainder of the essential avionics aerials (antennae) are housed within the wings, fuselage, fin and tailplane. Internal modifications include the provision of floor reinforcement, and new cooling and wiring installations. The normal crew consists of four flight crew and 13 AWACS specialists. The main operating area above the floor is equipped with nine MPCs (Multi-Purpose Consoles) for the specialist mission crew. Other crew manage systems and radar maintenance.

Not surprisingly, the mass of avionics equipment necessary for the E-3A to fulfil its appointed role needs considerable electrical power, and this is supplied by generators with a combined capacity of 600 kVA. Complex cooling and air-conditioning systems ensure dissipation of excessive heat and the creation of an ideal working environment for crew and equipment. Thus, a liquid cooling system protects the radar transmitter, which is housed in the aft cargo hold, while a conventional air-cycle and ram-air environmental control system is responsible for crew comfort and the safe operation of other avionics equipment.

The overfuselage rotodome is 30 ft 0 in (9.14 m) in diameter and has a maximum depth of 6 ft 0 in (1.83 m). It incorporates the AN/APY-1 surveillance radar and IFF/TADIL C antennae. During operational use the rotodome is driven hydraulically at 6 rpm, but in non-operational flight it is rotated at ¼ rpm to ensure that low temperatures do not cause the bearing lubricant to congeal and prevent emergency operation. The initial

Boeing E-3A Sentry AWACS of the United States Air Force. The first of 34 aircraft on order was delivered in March 1977.

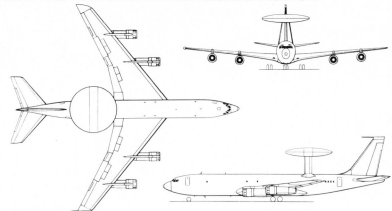

Boeing E-3A Sentry

Boeing E-3A cutaway drawing key

1 Weather radar scanner
2 Glide-slope aerial
3 Forward pressure bulkhead
4 Pilot's station
5 Central control console
6 Co-pilot's station
7 Flight engineer's station
8 Oberver/supernumary
9 Navigator's table
10 Navigator's overhead panel
11 Flight deck door
12 In-flight refuelling receptacle
13 Communication consoles (one unmanned TAC)
14 Forward entry door
15 Nosewheel hydraulic actuator
16 Nosewheel box
17 Twin nosewheels
18 Nosewheel doors
19 Forward cargo hold equipment bay
20 Flight essential avionics
21 Communications
22 Data processor functional group
23 Computer operator console
24 Bailout jettison mechanism
25 Bailout chute
26 DC power
27 Power distribution
28 Multi-purpose consoles (nine off)
29 VHF aerial
30 Engine intakes
31 Secondary inlet doors
32 Turbocompressor intakes
33 Turbocompressor outlets
34 Nacelle pylons
35 Leading-edge wing flap
36 Main tank No 3 (4,069 US gal/15 400 l each wing)
37 Fuel system dry bay
38 Main tank No 4 (2,323 US gal/8 791 l each wing)
39 Reserve tank (439 US gal/ 1 660 l each wing)
40 Vent surge tank
41 HF antenna
42 Starboard outboard aileron
43 Tab
44 Starboard outboard spoiler (extended)
45 Starboard outboard flap
46 Flap tracks
47 Aileron/spoiler linkage
48 Starboard inboard aileron
49 Control tab
50 Starboard inboard flap
51 Starboard inboard spoiler (extended)
52 Emergency overwing escape
53 Duty officer station (TAC)
54 Fuselage frame/production break
55 Front spar pick-up point
56 Landing lights
57 Front spar
58 Fuel tank end rib
59 Inboard wing stringers
60 Centre-section fuel tank (10,193 US gal/38 582 l)
61 Wing top skin
62 Floor support members
63 Rear spar pick-up point
64 Mainwheel bay
65 Keel beam
66 Radar receiver and signal processor
67 Radar maintenance station
68 Radar transmitter equipment
69 Rear cargo hold equipment bay

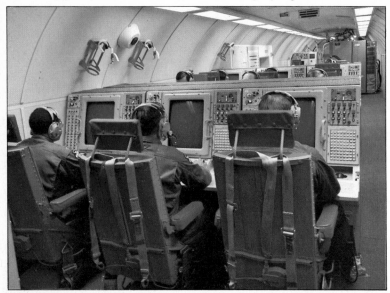

Operators seated at the MPCs (Multi-Purpose Consoles) of a Boeing E-3A Sentry AWACS (Airborne Warning and Control System), one of the most expensive production aircraft. The 552nd Wing at Tinker AFB has 20.

Westinghouse radar operates on pulse doppler technology, providing long-range, accuracy and downlook capability: it scans mechanically in azimuth and electronically from ground level up into the stratosphere. Westinghouse was awarded a contract in 1976 to develop maritime surveillance capability which could be an add-on feature to the existing radar and this, if adopted, would be retrofitted to in-service E-3As.

Heart of the AWACS is an IBM 4-Pi CC-1 high-speed computer, with a processing speed of some 740,000 operations per second, main memory capacity of 114,688 words, and mass memory size of 802,816 words. Navigation is provided by duplicated Carousel IV INS (Inertial Navigation System), AN/ARN-120 Omega and AN/APN-213 Doppler. Installed communications equipment provides HF, VHF and UHF for transmission/reception of information in clear/secure mode, in either vocal or digital form.

The first production E-3A was delivered to the USAF's 552nd Airborne Warning and Control Wing at Tinker AFB, Oklahoma, on 24 March 1977. A total of 10 were scheduled for delivery by the end of 1978, and production funding for a total of 22 aircraft had been approved by mid-1978. NATO plans to acquire 18 E-3As for basing in West Germany, and approval had been given for the sale of seven to Iran, now unlikely to be delivered.

Type: airborne early-warning and command post aircraft
Power Plant: four 21,000-lb (9525-kg) Pratt & Whitney TF33-PW-100/100A turbofans
Performance: no information
Weights: no information
Dimensions: span 145 ft 9 in (44.42 m); length 152 ft 11 in (46.61 m); height 42 ft 5 in (12.93 m); wing area 3,050 sq ft (283.35 m²)
Aramament: none
Operators: USAF (1978)

The easily identifiable Boeing E-3A Sentry Airborne Warning and Control System (AWACS) aircraft for service with the USAF. The 30-ft (9.14-m) diameter rotodome houses a 24-ft (7.32-m) diameter antenna.

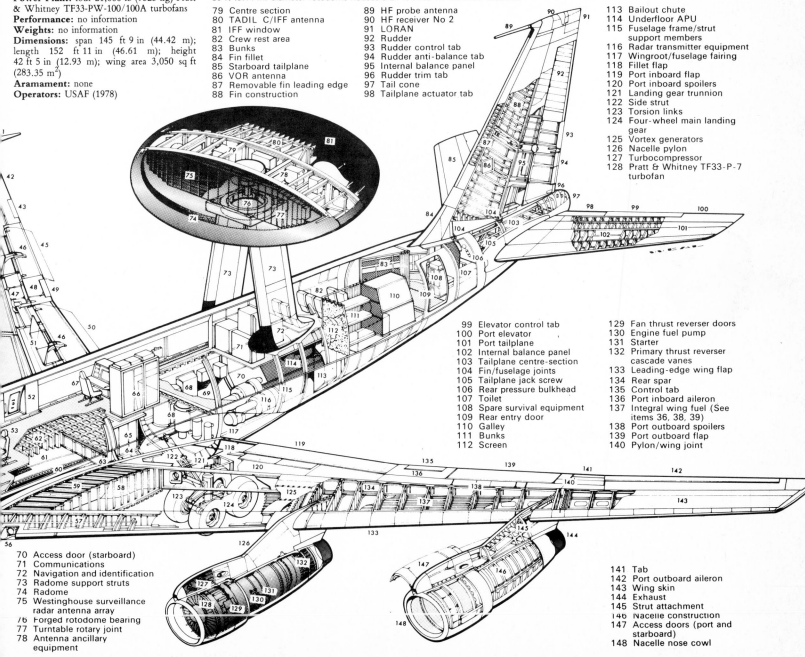

79 Centre section
80 TADIL C/IFF antenna
81 IFF window
82 Crew rest area
83 Bunks
84 Fin fillet
85 Starboard tailplane
86 VOR antenna
87 Removable fin leading edge
88 Fin construction
89 HF probe antenna
90 HF receiver No 2
91 LORAN
92 Rudder
93 Rudder control tab
94 Rudder anti-balance tab
95 Internal balance panel
96 Rudder trim tab
97 Tail cone
98 Tailplane actuator tab

113 Bailout chute
114 Underfloor APU
115 Fuselage frame/strut support members
116 Radar transmitter equipment
117 Wingroot/fuselage fairing
118 Fillet flap
119 Port inboard flap
120 Port inboard spoilers
121 Landing gear trunnion
122 Side strut
123 Torsion links
124 Four-wheel main landing gear
125 Vortex generators
126 Nacelle pylon
127 Turbocompressor
128 Pratt & Whitney TF33-P-7 turbofan

99 Elevator control tab
100 Port elevator
101 Port tailplane
102 Internal balance panel
103 Tailplane centre-section
104 Fin/fuselage joints
105 Tailplane jack screw
106 Rear pressure bulkhead
107 Toilet
108 Spare survival equipment
109 Rear entry door
110 Galley
111 Bunks
112 Screen

129 Fan thrust reverser doors
130 Engine fuel pump
131 Starter
132 Primary thrust reverser cascade vanes
133 Leading-edge wing flap
134 Rear spar
135 Control tab
136 Port inboard aileron
137 Integral wing fuel (See items 36, 38, 39)
138 Port outboard spoilers
139 Port outboard flap
140 Pylon/wing joint

70 Access door (starboard)
71 Communications
72 Navigation and identification
73 Radome support struts
74 Radome
75 Westinghouse surveillance radar antenna array
76 Forged rotodome bearing
77 Turntable rotary joint
78 Antenna ancillary equipment

141 Tab
142 Port outboard aileron
143 Wing skin
144 Exhaust
145 Strut attachment
146 Nacelle construction
147 Access doors (port and starboard)
148 Nacelle nose cowl

Boeing E-4/747

No matter how good they may be, a country's strategic forces are of little use in war unless it is possible to maintain reliable and coherent command and control of these forces. To ensure that it retains just such a capability, even in the aftermath of a nuclear attack, the United States Department of Defense has made plans to cope with all foreseen eventualities. It has created a National Military Command System, through which National Command Authorities are able to issue orders, and receive a feedback of information to show whether the orders were effective or not.

Currently there are three major command sources, the first two being the National Military Command Center, and the Alternate National Military Command Center. The latter is underground, for obvious reasons, but both of these have fixed geographical positions, and it has been appreciated for some number of years that an airborne command post would represent something approaching the ideal, its mobility in three dimensions making it a far more difficult target for an enemy to locate, especially in sufficient time to prevent retaliation to a surprise attack. This thinking led to procurement of the Boeing EC-135 Airborne Command Post (ABNCP), and these special versions of the Boeing C-135 family have been operational in this role since.

That the retention of a viable ABNCP is critical can be appreciated by considering that just one of these aircraft can control America's force of ICBMs, its manned bombers, and its nuclear-powered missile-carrying submarines. Confidence in the created National Military System depends upon a survivable ABNCP, and DoD planners are in the process of replacing the ageing EC-135 by a new Boeing

E-4 Advanced Airborne Command Post (AABNCP) which it is believed will have much increased survivability. This new and vital aircraft relies upon utilisation of the Boeing 747 airframe, and the announcement of an initial contract for two 747Bs to be converted to serve as AABNCP aircraft was first released on 28 February 1973. Follow-up contracts for two more aircraft were awarded in July and September 1973. It was announced subsequently that the total planned force is six aircraft, and it was anticipated that these would be fully operational in 1983.

Three aircraft of the initial four which were contracted became operational as E-4As in an ABNCP role. They were built with Pratt & Whitney F105 engines, and had avionics and equipment removed from EC-135 aircraft. The first of these E-4As, which represents an interim development stage, was handed over in December 1974. The second and third followed in May and September 1975, all three delivered initially to Andrews AFB, Maryland. Since that time they have shown that, as a result of their ability to accommodate a larger battle staff of up to 60, they are more flexible than the EC-135s which they have replaced.

The remaining three aircraft have more advanced avionics and equipment, and different engines, under the designation E-4B. The first was delivered to the USAF in August 1975, and the installation of its advanced command, control and communications equipment was scheduled for completion towards the end of 1979. These large aircraft can carry almost three times the payload of the EC-135s, providing work area for a much larger battle staff. Thus, the main deck comprises a work area for the battle staff, briefing room, conference room, communications control centre,

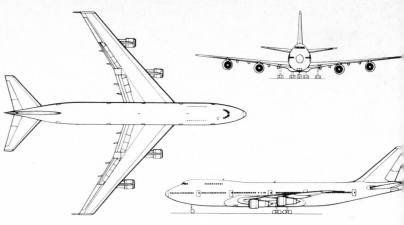

Boeing E-4B/747

National Command Authorities' area, and a rest area.

The three E-4As are being updated to E-4B standard, and in addition to advanced avionics will have a high-capacity air-conditioning system to maintain an equitable temperature for their operation, a large capacity electrical generating system, SHF and LF/VLF communications, and nuclear thermal shielding.

Boeing 747s are used in transport, air refuelling and electronics roles by Iran.

Type: special-purpose airborne command post
Powerplant: four 52,500-lb (23814-kg) thrust General Electric F103-GE-100 turbofans
Performance: not known
Weights: not known
Dimensions: span 195 ft 8 in (59.64 m); length 231 ft 4 in (70.51 m); height 63 ft 5 in (19.33 m); wing area 5,500 sq ft (510.95 m²)
Armament: none
Operators: Iran, US Air Force

United States Air Force Boeing E-4B airborne command post.

Heaviest, most powerful and most costly military aircraft in the world, the Boeing E-4B is the USAF Advanced Airborne Command Post which in time of emergency would carry the executive arm of the US government. Six are expected to be needed.

Boeing T-43/737

The success of Boeing's Model 707, the company's first commercial jet transport and also the first such aircraft to be built and flown in the United States, was to provide funds for the development of a family of smaller related aircraft. The last of these was the Model 737. On 19 February 1965, the company announced that it was to build this twin-turbofan short-range transport, the first order coming from a foreign customer, Lufthansa. The first of these aircraft made its first flight on 9 April 1967.

While retaining the family likeness, the 737 had its two engines in nacelles attached direct to the wings, with a conventional tail unit. It is, however, much reduced in wing span and length compared with the Model 707, but was designed to use many of the fuselage assemblies and components already in production for other models. The first deliveries were made in late 1967, and since that time there has been continuing improvement in this aircraft, which has proved to be an attractive investment for short-haul operators, to the extent that total orders are in excess of 700 in early 1979, when production was at a rate of three aircraft per month and increasing.

The first production version had the designation Model 737-100: this had maximum seating capacity for 115 passengers and was powered by Pratt & Whitney JT8D-7 or -9 engines. It was followed by the longer-fuselage Model 737-200, with maximum seating for 130 passengers, the Model 737-200C convertible passenger/cargo version, the Model 737-200QC convertible with quick conversion feature by use of palletised seating, and the Model 737-200 Business Jet, with luxurious business interiors. From the 135th production aircraft a number of improvements were introduced and from that time the model designations had the word Advanced added as a prefix. Thus, the current versions available in 1979 are the basic Advanced 737-200, Advanced 737-200C/QC, and Advanced 737-200 Executive Jet, with 14,500-lb (6577-kg) thrust JT8D-9A turbofans as standard powerplant, and 15,500-lb (7031-kg) JT8D-15 or 16,000-lb (7257-kg) JT8D-17 engines optional.

Experience in Vietnam had shown that the USAF had inadequate facilities for the training of navigators, and a decision was made to procure an 'off the shelf' aircraft with a desirable specification to replace the Convair T-29 (a militarised version of the Convair-Liner) then in service. In May 1971 the USAF announced that the Model 737 had been selected to fulfil this role, and Boeing was awarded a $82.4 million contract for the supply of 19 aircraft under the designation T-43A. First flight was made on 10 April 1973, and all of these aircraft were delivered to Mather AFB, California, by the end of July 1974.

Although the general configuration of these training aircraft was the same as that of the commercial 737-200, there were a number of detail and interior changes to make them suitable for their specific role. Doors and windows were reduced to one and nine respectively on each side of the fuselage, the cabin floor was strengthened to accommodate avionics consoles, and an 800-US gallon (3027-litre) auxiliary fuel tank was mounted in the aft cargo compartment.

Each of these aircraft accommodates, in addition to the normal flight crew, 12 trainees, four advanced trainees and three instructors. They are operated in conjunction with ground-based simulators, which simplifies student training over a wide range of missions, including high and low-level flight by day or night, high-speed flight, and the requirements of airways navigation. On-board equipment is updated from time to time to ensure that it is the same as that used in USAF operational aircraft.

The basic Model 737 is used by several other air forces and governments.

Type: two turbofan commercial transport/military navigation trainer
Powerplant: (T-43A) two 14,500-lb (6577-kg) thrust Pratt & Whitney JT8D-9 turbofans
Performance: (T-43A) cruising speed at 35,000 ft (10670 m) Mach 0.7 or 464 mph (747 km/h); operational range (MIL-C-5011A

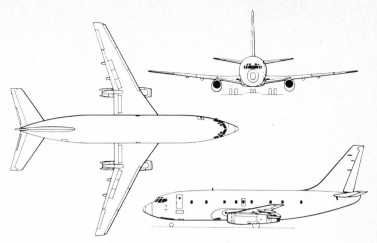

Boeing T-43A/737

reserves) 2,995 miles (4820 km); endurance 6 hours
Weights: (T-43A) maximum take-off 115,500 lb (52390 kg); maximum landing 103,000 lb (46,720 kg)

Dimensions: span 93 ft 0 in (28.35 m); length 100 ft 0 in (30.48 m); height 37 ft 0 in (11.28 m); wing area 980 sq ft (91.04 m²)
Armament: none
Operators: (T-43A) US Air Force

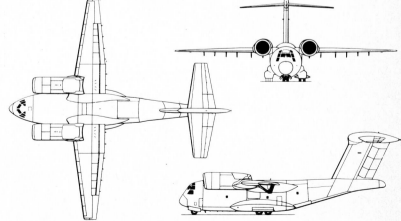

The Boeing T-43A is the chief navigation trainer of the US Air Force, a fleet of 19 operated by the 323rd Flying Training Wing at Mather AFB, California, having replaced 77 Convair T-29s. The T-43A is based on the Boeing 737-100, although with major changes.

Boeing YC-14

In 1971 the USAF issued the specification for a new AMST (Advanced Military STOL Transport) as a replacement for its fleet of Lockheed C-130 Hercules transports. The Hercules had originated from a specification 20 years earlier, and in putting together its requirement for this new transport the USAF planners had in mind the very important development in powerplants and aerodynamics which had taken place since 1951. In early 1972 Requests For Proposals were sent to nine US manufacturers, and those of the Boeing Aerospace Company and McDonnell Douglas Corporation were selected for competitive evaluation under the respective designations of YC-14 and YC-15.

STOL (short take-off and landing) capability was crucial. Boeing's design was based on the use of a supercritical wing, which provides highly efficient performance at high subsonic speeds. To this deep flat-topped wing Boeing added an advanced USB (upper surface blowing) concept, mounting the twin engines above the wing so that their efflux is exhausted over the wing. When the wing's leading-edge and Coanda-type trailing-edge flaps are extended, the high-speed flow from the engines clings to the upper surface and is directed downard by the flaps to provide powered lift.

The first of two YC-14s was flown on 9 August 1976, and at the completion of very successful testing, in the late summer of 1977, the two YC-14 (and two YC-15) prototypes were returned to the manufacturers. No further funding for development or procurement has been allocated from government funds, the C-130 remaining in production to save money. One of the roles for which the YC-14 was studied was the CMC (cruise-missile carrier), able to carry and launch 32 cruise missiles.

Type: advanced military STOL transport
Powerplant: two 51,000-lb (23133-kg) thrust General Electric F103 (CF6-50D) turbofans
Performance: maximum speed 504 mph (811 km/h) at optimum altitude; maximum speed at sea level 403 mph (649 km/h)
Weights: operating empty 117,500 lb

Boeing YC-14

(53297 kg); maximum STOL take-off 170,000 lb (77111 kg); maximum take-off 237,000 lb (107501 kg)
Dimensions: span 129 ft 0 in (39.32 in);

length 131 ft 8 in (40.13 m); height 48 ft 4 in (14.73 m); wing area 1,762 sq ft (163.69 m²)
Armament: none
Operators: none (in 1979 prototypes only)

Boeing 727

Following the successful introduction into service of the Boeing 707, the company announced its intention to make available a short/medium-range version which would be basically similar in fuselage design. The major change was in the powerplant, comprising three turbofan engines smaller than the four which powered the 707, all mounted at the rear.

The engine chosen was the 14,000-lb (6350-kg) thrust Pratt & Whitney JT8D-1, two mounted on the sides of the rear fuselage and the third mounted centrally in the tailcone, with its inlet above the fuselage. Apart from the T-tail, small triple-slotted wing, reduced fuel capacity and twin-wheel main gears the 727 is similar to the 707/720 series; the upper fuselage section is identical, and many other parts and systems are interchangeable.

The first 727-100, a production aircraft, made its first flight on 9 February 1963, and with the next three aircraft completed the 1,100-hour flight-test programme before FAA certification was awarded on 24 December 1963. The 727 has since been marketed in several versions, including the 727-100C with a convertible cargo/passenger interior, 727-100QC with quick-change convertible in-

terior, 727-100 Business Jet, 727-200 lengthened-fuselage version to accommodate a maximum of 189 passengers, advanced 727-200 with a restyled interior and increased fuel capacity, and proposed 727-200C convertible version. Only the -200 models remain in production in 1979, but Boeing's 727 has the distinction of being the most numerous jet airliner, with 1,700 ordered by early 1979.

Unlike the remainder of the Boeing family of commercial transports, no 727s have been procured by the US armed forces. Several have been obtained by other countries for military or government service, however.

Type: three turbofan short/medium-range transport
Powerplant: (727-200) three 14,500-lb (6577-kg) thrust Pratt & Whitney JT8D-9A turbofans (sometimes more powerful versions)
Performance: (727-200) maximum speed at maximum take-off weight 621 mph (999 km/h) at 20,500 ft (6250 m); maximum cruising speed 599 mph (964 km/h) at 24,700 ft (7530 m); maximum range with 27,500-lb (12474-kg) payload, ATA domestic reserves, with 9,730 US gallons (36831 litres) fuel 2,994 miles (4818 km)
Weights: (727-200) empty 97,600 lb

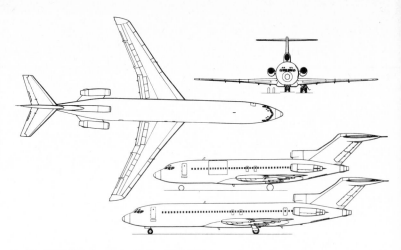

Boeing 727-200 (upper side view of 727-100C)

(44271 kg); maximum take-off 209,500 lb (95028 kg)
Dimensions: (727-200) span 108 ft 0 in (32.92 m); length 153 ft 2 in (46.69 m);

height 34 ft 0 in (10.36 m); wing area 1,700 sq ft (157.93 m²)
Armament: none
Operators: Belgium, Yugoslavia

Boeing Vertol 107/CH-46/UH-46 Sea Knight

Shortly after the formation of Vertol Aircraft Corporation in March 1956 the company initiated a design study for a twin-turbine commercial transport helicopter. In formulating the design, special attention was given to ensuring that it would be suitable also for military use if the armed forces showed an interest in its procurement. As a result, the tandem rotor layout which had been developed fully by Vertol, and the Piasecki Helicopter Corporation before it, was chosen because of its known performance and reliability. Twin turbines were chosen to power this new helicopter, for despite the fact that they had not then acquired a long history of reliability and economy, there was no doubt that these engines offered a superior power/weight ratio, and were improving progressively all the time. To limit noise and provide maximum cabin space these engines were mounted above the fuselage, at the aft end of the cabin. To speed the loading/unloading operation a large ramp formed the undersurface of the upswept rear fuselage, and was sufficiently robust to allow straight-on loading of vehicles and/or bulky freight. A sealed and compartmented fuselage made it possible for this new helicopter to be operated from water as well as land surfaces.

Construction of a prototype (company designation Model 107) began in May 1957, and the first flight was recorded on 22 April 1958. Company testing and development progressed well, and an extensive demonstration tour aroused considerable interest. First of the armed forces wishing to evaluate this new helicopter was the US Army which, in July 1958, ordered 10 slightly modified aircraft under the designation YHC-1A, and the first of these flew on 27 August 1959 for the first time. By that time the US Army had become more interested in a larger, more powerful helicopter which Vertol had developed from the Model 107 and, in consequence, reduced its order to only three YHC-1As. Subsequently, the company equipped the third of these with 1,050-shp (783-kW) General Electric T58-GE-6 turboshaft engines and rotors of increased diameter. The aircraft was also fitted out with a commercial interior as the Model 197-II prototype, which first flew on 25 October 1960. By that time Vertol had become a division of The Boeing Company.

When the US Marine Corps showed an interest in this aircraft one was modified as the Boeing Vertol Model 107M, with GE-8B engines (see data), and this was successful in winning the USMC's design competition in February 1961, and was ordered into production under the designation HRB-1 (changed to CH-46A in 1962), and given the name Sea Knight. Since that time Sea Knights have been used extensively by both the USMC and the US Navy. The former uses these helicopters

for troop transport, the latter mainly in the vertical replenishment (VERTREP) role, carrying stores, ammunition and personnel from logistic support ships to combat ships at sea.

The first CH-46A flew on 16 October 1962, and testing continued into late 1964, with the first US Marine squadrons taking these aircraft into service in early 1965. Since then a number of versions have been built, including the CH-46D for the USMC, generally similar to the CH-46A, but with 1,400-shp (1044-kW) T58-GE-10 turboshaft engines; the CH-46F for the USMC, generally similar to the CH-46D, but with additional avionics; the UH-46A Sea Knight, similar to CH-46A, procured by the US Navy with first deliveries to Utility Helicopter Squadron 1 in July 1964; and the UH-46D for the US Navy, virtually the same as the CH-46D. The US Marine Corps plans to update 273 of its Sea Knights to CH-46Es, with 1,870-shp (1394-kW) General Electric T58-GE-16 turboshafts and other improvements. Six utility models for the RCAF were delivered in 1963-4 under the designation CH-113 Labrador: these are almost identical to the CH-46A except for increased fuel capacity. Twelve aircraft similar to the CH-46A were delivered to the Canadian army during 1964-65 under the designation

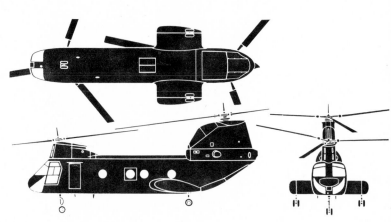

Boeing Vertol CH-46 Sea Knight

CH-113A Voyageur. In 1962-63 Vertol supplied Model 107-IIs to Sweden for service with the air force for search and rescue, and with the navy for ASW and minesweeping duties, both with the designation HKP-4.

Kawasaki in Japan acquired from Boeing Vertol worldwide sales rights for the Model

107-II, and continues to produce these helicopters in 1979 under the designation KV-107/II.

Type: tandem-rotor utility transport helicopter

A Boeing Vertol UH-46 ship-replenishment helicopter, basically the same as the CH-46 Sea Knight of the US Marines, nudges forward to the aft platform — which looks only a little larger than a pocket handkerchief — of DD703 *Wallace L. Lind*, an old destroyer.

Powerplant: (CH-46A) two 1,250-shp (932-kW) General Electric T58-GE-8B turboshafts
Performance: (CH-46D) maximum speed 166 mph (267 km/h); maximum cruising speed 165 mph (266 km/h); range at AUW of 20,800 lb (9435 kg) with 4,550-lb (2064-kg) payload and 10% reserves 238 miles (383 km)
Weights: (CH-46D) empty equipped 13,067 lb (5927 kg); maximum take-off 23,000 lb (10433 kg)
Dimensions: (CH-46D) rotor diameter (each) 51 ft 0 in (15.54 m); length (rotors turning) 84 ft 4 in (25.70 m); height 16 ft 8½ in (5.09 m); main rotor disc area (total) 4,086 sq ft (379.6m²)
Armament: none
Operators: Canada, Japan, Sweden, Thailand, US Marine Corps, US Navy

The Japanese Ground Self-Defence Force operates Kawasaki (Boeing) KV-107-11 assault helicopters.

Boeing Vertol 114/234/CH-47 Chinook

Following the evaluation of submissions by five US helicopter manufacturers, the US Army selected Boeing Vertol's Model 114 as most nearly meeting its requirements for a 'battlefield mobility' helicopter. This was expected to be suitably equipped for all-weather operations, to lift a load of 2 US tons (4,000 lb(1814 kg) internally or of 8 US tons (16,000 lb/7258 kg) suspended from an external sling, carry a maximum of 40 troops with full equipment, to have straight-in rear loading, be suitable for casualty evacuation roles, and be able to airlift any component of the Martin Marietta Pershing missile system. An initial contract for five YHC-1Bs was placed in June 1959, but soon after entering service these were redesignated YCH-47A and given the name Chinook.

Boeing Vertol's Model 114 was, in effect, a larger and more powerful version of the CH-46 Sea Knight. The non-retractable landing gear is of quadricycle configuration, and the fuselage has sealed and compartmented fairing pods on each side of the lower fuselage and extending for almost three-quarters of the fuselage length, to supplement the buoyancy of the sealed lower fuselage for water operations. The first YHC-1B made its first flight on 21 September 1961, by which time the first production contract for CH-47A aircraft had been placed. These were powered initially by 2,200-shp (1641-kW) Lycoming T55-L-5 turboshaft engines, subsequently by 2,650-shp (1976-kW) T55-L-7 turboshafts, and deliveries of CH-47As began in December 1972.

Since that time a number of versions have been built, including the CH-47B, a development with more powerful 2,850-shp (2125-kW) T55-L-7C turboshafts, redesigned rotor blades and other detail refinements, the first of two prototypes making its first flight during October 1966, with deliveries beginning on 10 May 1967. The current production version has the designation CH-47C/Model 234 and is powered by two 3,750-shp (2796-kW) T55-L-11C turboshafts, has a strengthened transmission system, and increased fuel capacity. The first of these aircraft made its initial flight on 14 October 1967, and deliveries of production aircraft began in early 1968. Nine aircraft similar to the CH-47C have been built for the Canadian Armed Forces, under the designation CH-147. Deliveries began in September 1974. The CH-147 has the latest safety features and an advanced flight-control system, and has a maximum land take-off weight of 50,000 lb (22,680 kg) and emergency water take-off weight of 46,000 lb (20865 kg). During the war in Vietnam, four ACH-47As were built, similar in configuration to the CH-47A, but equipped with armour and armament which included a 40-mm grenade launcher in the nose, a 20-mm forward firing cannon and a 7.62-mm (0.3-in) machine-gun or a 19-round rocket pack mounted on a pylon, one on each side of the fuselage, plus five gun positions for air gunners stationed in the cabin, each having a 0.50-in or 7.62-mm machine-gun on a flexible mounting. Three of these were evaluated in Vietnam, but no further examples were built.

Chinooks operated in South-east Asia proved most valuable, not only for the transport of troops and supplies, and for casualty evacuation, but also for the recovery of disabled aircraft and the airlift of refugees. Chinooks are still considered an important component of the US Army's helicopter air logistic forces, and all surviving CH-47A/B aircraft are being modernised, this being initially to CH-47C standard. However, under a US Army development programme one example of each version (A,B and C) is being equipped with new Lycoming T55-L-712 turboshafts, an auxiliary power unit (APU) and other advanced equipment, under the prototype designation YCH-47D.

Chinooks are built in Italy for European and Middle East customers, with manufacture beginning in 1970. Elicotteri Meridionali acquired from Boeing Vertol co-production and marketing rights in 1968, and construction of the airframe to CH-47C standard is carried out by SIAI-Marchetti. Boeing Vertol is also developing in America a Model 234LR Commercial Chinook for civil transport and offshore oilfield support.

Type: tandem-rotor medium transport helicopter
Powerplant: (CH-47C) two 3,750-shp (2796-kW) Lycoming T55-L-11C turboshafts
Performance: (CH-47C) average cruising speed 153 mph (246 km/h); ferry range with maximum intergral and internal auxiliary fuel (at optimum altitude, 10% reserves) 1,331 miles (2142 km)
Weights: empty 21,162 lb (9599 kg); maximum take-off 46,000 lb (20865 kg)
Dimensions: rotor diameter (each) 60 ft 0 in (18.29 m); length (rotors turning) 99 ft 0 in (30.18m); height 18 ft 7¾ in (5.68 m); main rotor disc area (total) 5,655 sq ft (525.35 m²)
Armament: none, except as detailed above for ACH-47A
Operators: Australia, Austria, Canada, Germany, Iran, Italy, Korea, Libya, Morocco, Spain, Thailand, Turkey, US Army, US National Guard, Vietnam

Boeing Vertol CH-47C Chinook

The US Army has over 620 Chinook heavy-lift helicopters, one of which is seen here with rear doors open and an old M56 Scorpion slung underneath as a test load. The US Army hopes to have most Chinooks rebuilt by Boeing Vertol to advanced CH-47D standard.

Italian-built Boeing CH-47C Chinook in the markings of the Libyan Arab Republic Air Force.

British Aerospace (Hawker Siddeley) Andover C.1

The Hawker Siddeley Andover C.1 was developed from the HS.748 Series 2 to meet a Royal Air Force requirement for a rear-loading STOL transport aircraft. Work on the design began in 1962, and the original HS.748 prototype (G-APZV) acted as guinea pig. Modifications to the aircraft include a new wide-span centre wing, shortened outer wings, raised tail of new design to make room for the rear ramp/door, and more powerful engines with larger propellers. A then-unique modification was a kneeling undercarriage, which allows exact alignment of the cabin floor with the decking surface of a loader/unloader vehicle.

The prototype was re-registered G-ARRV and flew on 21 December 1963. The first production machine (one of 31 ordered by the Royal Air Force) did not fly until 9 July 1965. Deliveries to No 46 Sqn RAF Transport Command, and to No 52 Sqn of the Far East Air Force, Singapore, began in 1966.

Typical Andover loads comprise 58 troops, 40 paratroops, 24 stretcher patients, or up to 15,350 lb (6963 kg) of freight. A Ferret scout car and a ¼-ton Land-Rover can be dragged out in flight by parachute. Paratroops use an inward-opening door on the left of the rear fuselage.

Only nine of these aircraft remain in service with the Royal Air Force. Six of the Royal Air Force's remaining Andover C.1s were converted in 1977 for flight checking and calibration duties, replacing Hawker Siddeley Argosy E.1s. The first, designated Andover E.3, were delivered to No 115 Sqn in 1978. The RAF also uses the Andover CC.2, with the HS.748 airframe and described under that designation. Ten were sold to the Royal New Zealand Air Force in 1976; six serve with No 1 Sqn at Whenuapai for trooping and freighting, while the remaining four equip No 42 Sqn and are tasked with VIP flying and twin continuation training.

Type: multi-role transport
Powerplant: two 3,245-ehp (2421-kW) Rolls-Royce Dart 201 turboprops
Performance: maximum cruising speed at 15,000 ft (4570 m) and 40,000 lb (18145 kg) weight 265 mph (426 km/h); range with payload of 8,530 lb (3870 kg) and reserves for 230-mile (370-km) diversion, 30-min hold and 5% block fuel 1,158 miles (1865 km); range with maximum payload and same reserves 311 miles (500 km); sea-level rate of climb at maximum gross weight 1,180 ft (360 m) per minute

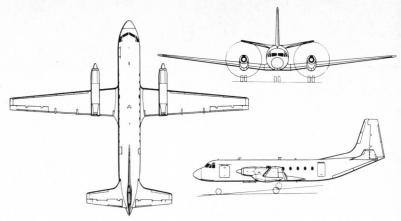

British Aerospace Andover C.1

Weights: empty equipped 25,516 lb (11574 kg); maximum take-off 50,000 lb (22680 kg); maximum overload limit 51,000 lb (23133 kg)
Dimensions: span 98 ft 3 in (29.94 m); length 78 ft 0 in (23.77 m); height 30 ft 1 in (9.17 m); wing area 831.4 sq ft (77.2 m²)

Armament: none
Operators: New Zealand, UK

British Aerospace (Hawker Siddeley) 748/Andover C.2/Coastguarder

Better known as an airliner, the BAe (HS) 748 has sold in large numbers as a military transport. Fifty per cent (including the Andover CC.1) of the 350 sold earn their keep by hauling cargo and personnel for armed services. The type's large-span wing and powerful turboprops give good field performance, and carriage of bulky and outsize loads is facilitated by an optional cargo door on the left behind the wing. Military specialization extends to a strengthened floor, fittings according to role, and overload take-off and landing weights, which produce a corresponding improvement in payload/range performance.

The 748 evolved from an Avro design for a short/medium-range twin-turboprop airliner embarked on in January 1959. The first prototype flew on 24 June 1960 and was produced as the Series 1 for seven years. Included in this batch were two Andover CC.2s for the Queen's Flight. The Series 2A, the current military variant, differs from the Series 2 (in production from 1967) in having more powerful Rolls-Royce Dart 534-2 or 535-2 engines. The latter powerplant is now standard.

The latest in this line is the Coastguarder, British Aerospace's bid to gain a foothold in the overcrowded maritime patrol and protection market. The prototype was converted from a Series 2A and flew on 18 February 1977. Changes have since been extended to fitting a wet wing. Although basically still a 748, the Coastguarder has undergone a number of modifications, revolving primarily around the electronics. A standard crew comprises two pilots, two beam observers and a tactical navigator. An important part of the Coastguarder's duties will be search and rescue, and to this end a 1-ft (0.3-m)-diameter chute is fitted in the rear fuselage, through which can be ejected five-man dinghies and marker flares. The tactical navigator, seated over the wing, has an MEL Marec radar display and plotting table, Decca 72 doppler and a Decca 9447 tactical air navigation system computer and display. The radar provides 360° coverage over 230 miles (370 km) for the tactical navigator, and 285 miles (460 km) for the pilot. A 'zoom' effect allows selective magnification of any part of the display. As with the other military variants, the Coastguarder can be converted to carry seats on full-length rails. For air-dropping of survival equipment to accident victims, the wide rear door is optional.

Both the Australian air force and navy operate 748s; the air force has two as VIP transports and eight for navigation training, while the navy's Nowra-based VC-851 Sqn operates two of the type for ASW training and transport work. Three, with wide doors, are used by the Belgian air force for transport work, and Brazil flies 12, six of which are Series 2Cs, with No 1 Sqn, I Group and II

Group. Delivered in 1971, a single 748 comprises the transport element of the Royal Brunei Malay Regiment Air Wing. Satena, the military airline of Colombia, has three of the type, and a further five are operated under a similar scheme by Tame, the military airline of Ecuador. India, whose Hindustan Aeronautics builds the type, has 81 BAe 748s on strength, and neighbouring Nepal has a single Series 2A delivered in 1975 for royal use. The royal flight of the Thai air force also uses two 748s, and a VIP flight of the Zambian air force operates a single example.

Type: transport
Powerplant: two 2,280-ehp (1687-kW) Rolls-Royce Dart 534-2 or 535-2 single-shaft turboprops
Performance: cruising speed 281 mph (452 km/h); maximum rate of climb at sea level 1,420 ft (433 m) per minute; range with maximum payload 1,066 miles (1714 km); range with maximum fuel 1,624 miles (2613 km)
Weights: empty equipped 25,453 lb (11545 kg); maximum take-off 46,500 lb (21092 kg); optional overload maximum take-off 51,000 lb (23133 kg)
Dimensions: span 98 ft 6 in (30.02 m); length 67 ft 0 in (20.42 m); height 24 ft 10 in (7.57 m); wing area 810.75 sq ft (75.35 m²)
Armament: none
Operators: Argentina, Australia, Belgium, Brazil, Brunei, Colombia, Ecuador, India, Nepal, New Zealand, Thailand, UK, Zambia

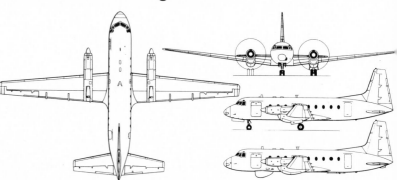

British Aerospace 748 Srs 2A/Andover C.2 (lower side view of Coastguarder)

British Aerospace Andovers were delivered to the RAF in several subtypes, including the completely redesigned C.1 STOL freighter. This example, XS794, is the last of six CC.2 passenger transports, pictured in August 1977 with No 32 Sqn at RAF Northolt.

Queen's Flight HS Andover CC.2 maintained by the Royal Air Force at Benson, Oxfordshire.

British Aerospace (Hawker Siddeley) Buccaneer

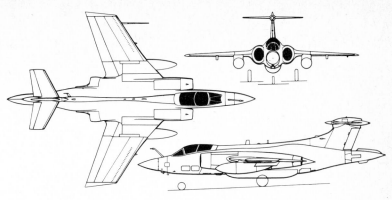

British Aerospace Buccaneer S.2B

Designed by a team under B.P. Laight of Blackburn Aircraft Ltd in the days before most pioneer British aircraft companies lost their separate identities in the mergers of the 1960s and 1970s, the Buccaneer was itself something of a pioneer. It has consistently proved to be a far better aeroplane than many have given it credit for, and is still giving valuable service more than 25 years after its conception. Developed to Royal Navy requirement NA.39 (issued in the early 1950s) as a two-seat carrier-based low-level strike aircraft, it was the first such type in the world actually to be built for this high-speed under-the-radar means of penetrating enemy airspace. The airframe design incorporated a number of then-novel features, such as a full wings-and-tail boundary layer control system for maximum lift; area-ruling of the bulky fuselage; and the fuselage tail-cone was split vertically and hinged so that the two halves could be deployed as airbrakes.

Blackburn's B.103 design was chosen in 1955 to meet the NA.39 requirement, an order being placed in July of that year for an evaluation batch of 20 aircraft; the first nine of these were allocated primarily for manufacturer's trials (initial flight being made on 30 April 1958), and the next five to the Ministry of Aviation for further development. Powerplant of the pre-production models was a pair of 7,000-lb (3175-kg) static thrust de Havilland Gyron Junior DGJ.1 turbojets; the full naval 'kit' of folding wings and nose, arrester hook, plus catapult points, was introduced on the fourth example, which carried out the first carrier compatibility trials. The fifth NA.39 was used for weapon testing, and numbers 15 to 20 were used to equip No 700Z Flight at RNAS Lossiemouth, an Intensive Flying Trials Unit formed in 1961 to prepare the aircraft for entry into Fleet Air Arm service.

An initial production order, for 40 aircraft, had been placed in October 1959, these being designated Buccaneer S.1. The first example made its maiden flight on 23 January 1962, and on 17 July of the same year No 801 Squadron of the Fleet Air Arm was commissioned as the first operational Buccaneer squadron. The squadron embarked in HMS *Ark Royal* in the following January. Two additional squadrons, Nos 800 and 809, were later formed with the S.1, replacing Supermarine Scimitars in the strike role. Production of this model ended in December 1963, powerplant being the Gyron Junior 101 of 7,100 lb (3220 kg) static thrust.

The S.1 was decidedly underpowered, and the Rolls-Royce Spey turbofan was therefore selected to power the major Buccaneer production variant, the S.2. Two of the pre-production NA.39s served as Mk 2 prototypes in 1963, the first of 84 production S.2s making its initial flight on 5 June 1964. With lower fuel consumption, plus some 30 per cent more power, the S.2 (identifiable by its larger, oval-shaped intakes) had a considerably better range than the S.1, a factor further enhanced by the provision in this variant for in-flight refuelling. This model began entering FAA service in October 1965, eventually equipping Nos 800, 801, 803 and 809 Squadrons, operating from the aircraft-carriers *Ark Royal*, *Eagle* and *Victorious*. Last to retire was No 809 from HMS *Ark Royal*, in 1979. A fully 'navalised' version of the Buccaneer, although scheduled for operation from shore bases, was the Mk 50 supplied in 1965 to the South African air force. These 16 aircraft, to aid their potential use from 'hot and high' airfields, were fitted with a Bristol Siddeley BS.605 twin-chamber rocket motor in the rear of the fuselage, enabling a 30-second boost of 8,000 lb (3628 kg) static thrust to be added to that of the basic powerplant to provide increased power for take-off.

The Royal Navy Buccaneer S.2s were not, however, retired when the progressive depletion of Britain's carrier force caused their withdrawal from Fleet Air Arm service. From 1969 onwards they were instead transferred to the Royal Air Force, whose first Buccaneer squadron (No 12) became operational with the type in July 1970, followed shortly afterwards by No 208 Squadron. With some changes to the internal systems and equipment to meet their new operator's requirements, they were then redesignated S.2A, about 70 aircraft being converted in this manner. Subsequently they underwent a further updating/modification programme, from which they emerged as Buccaneer S.2Bs, the primary difference being a capability to deliver the Martel anti-radar TV-guided missile. Other changes involved a new, bulged weapons bay door (accommodating an additional fuel tank) and detail improvements to the airframe. Apart from those converted to the new S.2B standard, 43 more were ordered as new-production aircraft, the first of these making its initial flight on 8 January 1970. The S.2B equips Nos 15 and 16 Squadrons, based at RAF Laarbruch in Germany. Two other RAF Buccaneers acted as systems trials aircraft for the Panavia Tornado multi-role combat aircraft. Before their retirement, the remaining Royal Navy Buccaneers also underwent comparable modifications, receiving the new designation S.2C (without Martel capability) and S.2D (with Martels).

It is the Buccaneer's high subsonic speed, plus an ability to accept continually updated systems and weapons throughout its career, that have kept it a viable front-line combat aircraft for nearly two decades. Aside from the usual capacity for underwing-mounted weapons, it has the novel feature of a rotary bomb door, on the inside of which conventional or nuclear weapons can be carried. By rotating to expose these for delivery, it avoids the drag penalty of the more orthodox type of door which opens into the surrounding airstream, so avoiding adverse effects upon its performance at the crucial moment of weapon release. The tough airframe is ideal for the high-g weaving flight paths demanded by the terrain-following nature of its primary low-level attack role. On-board systems provide night and all-weather attack capability; Doppler-type navigation, moving-map display linked to a computer, and radar acquisition of the target are standard.

Type: tandem two-seat low-level strike and reconnaissance aircraft
Powerplant: two 11,255-lb (5105-kg) Rolls-Royce Spey 101 turbofans
Performance: (except Mk 1) maximum speed at 200 ft (61 m) 645 mph (1038 km/h); typical hi-lo-hi range with weapons 2,300 miles (3700 km); endurance with two in-flight refuellings 9 hours; maximum rate of climb at sea level 7,000 ft (2134 m) per minute; service ceiling over 40,000 ft (12200 m)
Weights: (except Mk 1) empty about 30,000 lb (13610 kg); typical take-off 46,000 lb (20865 kg) to 56,000 lb (25400 kg); maximum take-off 62,000 lb (28123 kg); typical landing 35,000 lb (15876 kg)
Dimensions: (except Mk 1) span 44 ft 0 in (13.41 m); span folded 19 ft 11 in (6.07 m); length 63 ft 5 in (19.33 m); length folded 51 ft 10 in (15.79 m); height 16 ft 3 in (4.95 m); height folded 16 ft 8 in (5.08 m); wing area 514.7 sq ft (47.82 m²)
Armament: (S.2B) four 1,000-lb (454-kg) bombs, multi-sensor reconnaissance pack, or 440-Imperial gallon (2000-litre) fuel tank, on inside of rotary bomb door; up to 3,000 lb (1360 kg) of bombs and/or missiles on each of four underwing attachments; making total possible weapons load of 16,000 lb (7257 kg)
Operators: South Africa, UK

Used for low-level strike and reconnaissance duties, the HS Buccaneer S.2B equips three Royal Air Force squadrons in Germany.

Buccaneer S.2Bs of No 15 Sqn, RAF, with two more about half a mile away, streak across the North Sea on a simulated low-level attack mission from their German base at Laarbruch. The Buccaneer is unusual in being able to attack in the clean configuration.

British Aerospace (Scottish Aviation) Bulldog

The BAe Bulldog originated in 1968 as a military trainer development of the Beagle Pup, and flew for the first time on 19 May 1969. When Beagle Aircraft Ltd went into liquidation early in the following year the un-completed second prototype was taken over by Scottish Aviation Ltd (now the Scottish Division of British Aerospace), eventually making its first flight on 14 February 1971. Beagle had received an order from the Swedish government for 78 Bulldogs, and Scottish Aviation produced these also (58 for the Swedish air force and 20 for the Swedish army) as the Model 101 (Swedish designation Sk 61) from 1971 onwards. Other Series 100 Bulldogs were built for the air forces of Malaysia (15) and Kenya (5), as the Models 102 and 103. Model 104 was to have been the designation for the Royal Air Force's T.1 version, to equip the University Air Squadrons, but these Bulldogs (130 were built) were redesignated Model 121 as the first of a new and improved Series 120 line, subsequently produced also for the air forces of Ghana (13), Hong Kong (2), Jordan (13), Kenya (9), Lebanon (6) and Nigeria (32).

All versions have normal side-by-side seating for instructor and pupil, with dual controls, and are fully aerobatic (stressed to +6 and −3 g) as two-seaters; there is space for a third (rear) seat if required. The cockpit canopy is rearward-sliding and jettisonable. Construction is all-metal, and the tricycle landing gear is non-retractable, although Scottish Aviation has flown (in August 1976) a 'Series 200' prototype with retractable gear and other aerodynamic and performance improvements. Another company aircraft, known as the Model 124, has demonstrated the Bulldog's ability to carry a range of small ordnance for weapons training or a light ground-attack role.

Type: two/three-seat primary trainer
Powerplant: one 200-hp (149-kW) Lycoming IO-360-A1B6 flat-four piston engine
Performance: maximum speed at sea level 150 mph (241 km/h); maximum cruising speed at 4,000 ft (1220 m) 138 mph (222 km/h); range with maximum fuel (55% power, no reserves) 621 miles (1000 km); maximum rate of climb at sea level (Srs 100) 1,006 ft (306 m) per minute, (Srs 120) 1,034 ft (315 m) per minute; service ceiling (Srs 100)

17,000 ft (5180 m), (Srs 120) 16,000 ft (4875 m)
Weights: basic operating, empty (Srs 100) 1,420 lb (644 kg), (Srs 120) 1,475 lb (669 kg); maximum take-off (two-seat, fully aerobatic) (Srs 100) 2,150 lb (975 kg), (Srs 120) 2,238 lb (1015 kg); maximum take-off (three-seat or semi-aerobatic, Srs 100 and 120) 2,350 lb (1066 kg)
Dimensions: span 33 ft 0 in (10.06 m); length 23 ft 3 in (7.09 m); height 7 ft 5¾ in (2.28 m); wing area 129.4 sq ft (12.02 m²)
Armament: normally none, but has provision for up to 640 lb (290 kg) of gun or rocket pods, wire-guided air-to-surface weapons, 110-lb (50-kg) bombs or other stores, on four underwing hardpoints
Operators: (model numbers in brackets) Ghana (122, 122A), Hong Kong (128), Jordan (125), Kenya (103, 127), Lebanon (126), Malaysia (102), Nigeria (123), Sweden (101), UK (121)

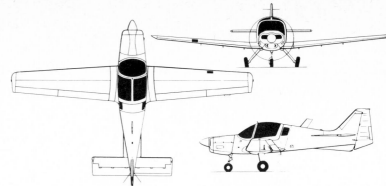

British Aerospace Bulldog T.1

Red and white RAF Training Command colours on a Scottish Aviation Bulldog T.1 primary trainer.

Scottish Aviation SK 61 Bulldog primary trainer of F5, Kungl Krigsflygskolan (Royal War Flying School), Royal Swedish Air Force.

British Aerospace (BAC) Canberra

A total of 27 marks of BAe (BAC) Canberra were built, including seven variants of the Martin B-57 for the US Air Force, during a production run of more than 10 years. Britain manufactured 901 aircraft, Australia made 48 for the Royal Australian Air Force, and the USAF flew 403 built under licence by Martin in Baltimore, Maryland, for a total of 1,352.

It is testimony to the Canberra's capability that 11 air arms throughout the world still operate the type 30 years after it first flew. The first prototype (VN799) took to the air for the first time on 13 May 1949. Designed by E.W. 'Teddy' Petter of the English Electric Company, the A.1, as it was originally known, was a remarkably agile aeroplane at low level. It had been designed in response to ministry specification B.3/45 but the customer soon realised that the radar bombing system was the weak spot, not the platform. In the light of lengthy development delays with the delivery system, a new specification was issued, transforming the Canberra into a simpler, visual bomber with a third crew member. Four prototypes had been built, one with Nene engines, before production switched to the new-specification B.2, of which 415 were manufactured in Great Britain. Four companies — English Electric, Shorts, Avro and Handley Page — were involved in British manufacture of the type, the three subcontractors building respectively 60, 75 and 75 aircraft.

Some of the more important British-built marks included the PR.3 reconnaissance version with stretched fuselage to house more fuel, the T.4 side-by-side trainer, the B.6 with wet wings and more power, the reconnaissance PR.7 and, later, Shorts' high-altitude

PR.9 with enlarged span, extended chord, off-set canopy and much more powerful Avon 206 engines. The PR.9's fighter-style offset cockpit was pioneered by the most versatile of all the marks, the B(I).8. This was a two-seat long-range night interdictor, high-altitude bomber and target marker, whose armament is listed below. The U.10 was an unmanned target modified from the B.2 by Shorts.

The *Fuerza Aérea Argentina*'s I *Escuadrón de Bombardeo*, based at Entre Rios, operates nine B.62s and two T.64s, the bombers being rebuilds. Amberley-based No 2 Sqn of the Royal Australian Air Force still flies eight Government Aircraft Factories-built B.20s for photo-reconnaissance and target towing, and four T.21s for training. Five of six B.6s originally delivered to Ecuador are still in service. The Ethiopian air force flew many sorties with its two surviving B.52s (four delivered) during the Ogaden war in 1977-78. Three Canberras in service with the West German *Luftwaffe* for communications and other special duties. Three bomber units (Nos 5, 16 & 35) of the Indian air force fly a total of 86 Canberra B(I).58s, B.74s, B(I).12s and T.13s, and No 106 Sqn, a photo-reconnaissance unit, is equipped with 12 PR.7s. Two squadrons of the *Fuerza Aérea del Peru*'s *Grupo* 21 bomber wing fly 32 Canberra B.2/B.56/B(I).8s, two T.4 trainers and 11 B(I).68s supplied in 1976 by the British com-

pany Marshalls of Cambridge; all are ex-RAF machines. The Rhodesian air force, heavily involved in anti-guerrilla operations, flies some eight Canberras out of a batch of 15 B.2s and three T.4s. Equipping Old Sarum-based No 5 Sqn, they are known to be suffering from spar fatigue and are being cannibalised to keep the

rest in the air. More than one is reported to have been lost in action. The South African air force, restricted by an arms ban just as tight as that imposed on Rhodesia, still has six

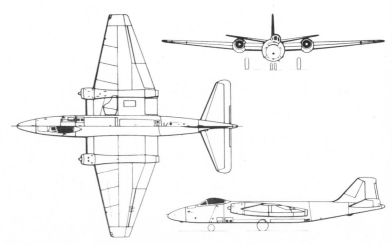

British Aerospace Canberra PR.9

BAC Canberra PR.9 of 39 Sqn, Royal Air Force, based at RAF Wyton, with the unit's bomb emblem on the fin.

Canberra B(I).12s and three T.4s, all serving with No 12 Sqn at Waterkloof. The Royal Air Force's No 39 Sqn, based at Wyton, flies PR.9s in the high-altitude photo-reconnaissance role, and No 51 Sqn, an electronic-surveillance unit, flies B.6s. Electronic-countermeasures T.17s equip the joint-service No 360 Sqn. Operational conversion is performed by Marham-based 231 OCU, which shares this airfield with No 100 Sqn, flying B.2s, E.15s, T.19s and T.4s. St Mawgan-based No 7 Sqn is equipped with B.2s, T.4s and TT.18s. The *Fuerzas Aéreas Venezolanas* has one squadron, No 39, of Canberras comprising 18 B.2s, seven B(I).8s, two T.4s and two PR.3s, based at Maracay.

Type: two/three-seat bomber, reconnaissance aircraft and trainer
Powerplant: two 7,500-lb (3357-kg) Rolls-Royce Avon 109 turbojets; (PR.9) two 11,000-lb (4990-kg) Avon 206
Performance: maximum speed at sea level 517 mph (827 km/h) or Mach 0.68; maximum speed at 40,000 ft (14630 m) 541 mph (871 km/h); range with maximum fuel (no reserves) 3,630 miles (5840 km); range with maximum load (no reserves) at 2,000 ft (600 m) and 10 minutes over target at full power 805 miles (1295 km); maximum rate of climb at sea level 3,400 ft (1035 m) per minute
Weights: empty equipped 27,950 lb (12678 kg); maximum take-off 54,950 lb (24925 kg); maximum zero-fuel 33,180 lb (15050 kg); maximum landing 40,000 lb (18145 kg)
Dimensions: span 64 ft 0 in (19.51 m), (PR.9) 67 ft 10 in (20.67 m); length 65 ft 6 in (19.96 m), (PR.9) 66 ft 8 in (20.32 m); height 15 ft 8 in (4.77 m); wing area 960 sq ft (89.19 m²), (PR.9) 1,045 sq ft (97.08 m²)
Armament: six 1,000-lb (454-kg) or one

4,000-lb (1814-kg) and two 1,000-lb (454-kg) or eight 500-lb (226-kg) bombs internally, plus up to 2,000 lb (907 kg) of stores on underwing pylons; four Hispano 20-mm cannon; sixteen 4.5-in flares internally; two AS.30 missiles; two packs of 37 rockets externally
Operators: Argentina, Australia, Ecuador, Ethiopia, India, Peru, Rhodesia, South Africa, UK, Venezuela, West Germany

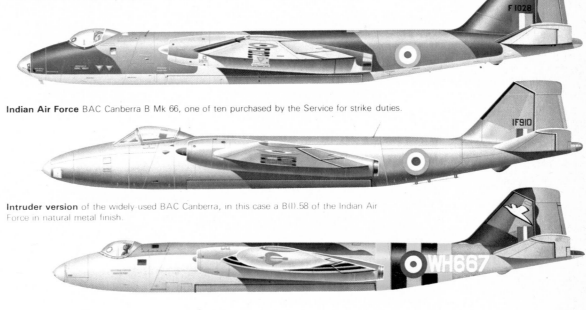

Indian Air Force BAC Canberra B Mk 66, one of ten purchased by the Service for strike duties.

Intruder version of the widely-used BAC Canberra, in this case a B(I).58 of the Indian Air Force in natural metal finish.

BAC Canberra B.2 of 10 Sqn, Royal Air Force, with the markings carried at the time of the Suez invasion in 1956.

British Aerospace (Hawker Siddeley) 125/Dominie

The BAe (HS) Dominie T.1 is a military version of de Havilland's first-generation business jet, the DH.125 (later HS.125). The first 125 flew on 13 August 1962 and was followed by the first production model on 12 February 1963. Impressed by the performance, roominess and low cost of the aircraft, the Royal Air Force ordered 20 in September 1962, and the first Dominie T.1 flew for the first time 30 December 1964. The service now uses two other variants: the CC.1 communications aircraft based on the civil Series 400; and the CC.2, also for communications but based on the stretched and improved-performance 125-600. The latest BAe 125, the -700 with Garrett AiResearch TFE731 turbofan engines, has not yet been bought by the military. In the case of the Royal Air Force, this could be a sign that the service is adequately equipped at present, and can wait for the possible Rolls-Royce RB.407-powered -800.

The Dominie T.1 navigation trainer normally carries a crew of five, comprising one pilot, a supernumerary crew member, two students and an instructor. The students sit in rearward-facing seats with an instructional panel and worktop in front of them. Comprehensive equipment is fitted for the use of both pilot and students, including Collins HF, Marconi VHF, Plessey UHF, Marconi

Royal Air Force British Aerospace HS.125 Series 600 designated CC.2, of 32 Sqn, at Northolt for VIP use.

VOR/ILS, ADF, intercom, Decca Navigator Mk 1 and Sperry gyro-magnetic compass. For the students there is a periscopic sextant station in the centre fuselage, Ekco weather radar, Decca doppler and two ground position indicators. External modifications include a belly fairing forward of the wing housing the Decca and doppler aerials, and a small ventral fin. Nineteen Dominies remain in service with the Royal Air Force (Support Command), and two communications squadrons, Nos 32 and 207, fly four -400s (CC.1s) and two -600s (CC.2s).

The Argentine navy operates a single BAe 125-400 for calibration work, and the Brazilian air force's *Grupo de Transporte Especial* operates eight. The Royal Malaysian

Air Force's No 2 Sqn continues to fly two on VIP/government missions. No 21 Sqn of the South African air force flies four 125s on VIP duties.

Type: navigation/pilot/radio-operator trainer, communications and liaison aircraft
Powerplant: two 3,000-lb (1360-kg) Rolls-Royce Viper 301 turbojets (Srs 3 and 400 Dominie); 3,750-lb (1701-kg) Viper 601-22 (Srs 600)
Performance: (Srs 600) maximum speed 570 mph (917 km/h); (Srs 600) cruising speed at 28,000 ft (8534 m) 522 mph (840 km/h); (Srs 600) initial rate of climb 4,900 ft (1493 m) per minute, (other marks) 4,000 ft (1219 m); (Srs 600) range with maximum payload of 2,000 lb

(907 kg) and maximum fuel (with reserves) 1,796 miles (2891 km)
Weights: (Srs 600) empty equipped 12,530 lb (5683 kg) (other marks) 10,100 lb (4581 kg); (Srs 600) maximum take-off 25,000 lb (11340 kg) (other marks) 21,200 lb (9615 kg)
Dimensions: span 47 ft 0 in (14.33 m); (Srs 600) length 50 ft 6 in (15.39 m), (other marks) 47 ft 5 in (14.45 m); (Srs 600) 17 ft 3 in (5.26 m), (other marks) 16 ft 6 in (5.03 m); wing area 353 sq ft (32.8 m²)
Armament: none
Operators: Argentina, Australia, Brazil, Malaysia, South Africa, UK

Distinguished by its bulged belly housing Decca doppler radar, and a bright red fuselage stripe, the Dominie T.1 equips 6 FTS at Finningley where the RAF's navigation training is centred. Some 19 are in use.

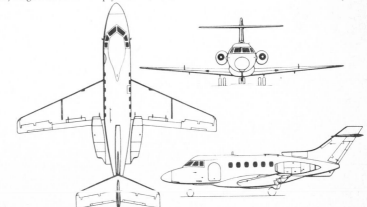

British Aerospace Dominie T.1

British Aerospace (Hawker Siddeley) Harrier

A decade after its entry into service the BAe (HS) Harrier is still, with the sole exception of the USSR's later but far less sophisticated Yakovlev Yak-36 'Forger', unique as the world's only operational V/STOL (vertical/short take-off and landing) combat aircraft. The origins of its design go back 12 years further still, to 1957, when Sir Sydney Camm of Hawker Aircraft and Dr Stanley Hooker of Bristol Siddeley Engines got together to design a tactical aircraft around Bristol's radical new turbofan engine, then known as the BS.53. Evolved specifically to give jet-lift to vertical take-off fixed-wing aircraft, the BS.53's exhaust airflow was discharged through four nozzles, in fore-and-aft pairs, each of which could be pivoted through more than 90° to vector (direct) the exhaust thrust rearward, vertically downward, or to any intermediate angle. Around the Pegasus, as the engine was eventually christened, Camm designed an essentially conventional all-metal shoulder-wing monoplane of compact dimensions, with anhedral on the wings and tailplane, a single-seat cockpit in the nose, and a large semi-circular fixed-geometry air intake on each side of the fuselage. The landing gear was less orthodox, comprising a single nosewheel and twin main wheels, mounted in tandem on the centreline, plus a small balancer wheel on a retractable outrigger leg at each wingtip.

Known in its original form as the Hawker P.1127, the first of six prototypes made its

A British Aerospace Harrier GR.1A of the recently-disbanded 20 Sqn of the Royal Air Force, in the ground-attack role.

initial hovering flight on 21 October 1960. Less than a year later, on 12 September 1961, the first complete transitions were made to and from vertical and horizontal flight. Vertical take-off was accomplished by vectoring the thrust from the engine downward; after a safe height was reached, the four nozzles were rotated slowly rearward to provide forward thrust for the transition to horizontal flight. As soon as forward speed increased sufficiently for wing lift to support the aircraft, the nozzles were rotated fully aft. This sequence was reversed for vertical landings. To stabilize the aircraft during hovering and low-speed manoeuvres, small reaction control jets mounted in the nose, tail and each wingtip were activated; operated by the control column and rudder pedals, these utilized compressed air bled from the engine.

In-flight transitions soon became commonplace, and Hawker Siddeley was awarded a contract for nine more advanced pre-

production aircraft to undergo evaluation in the fighter/ground-attack role. These were known as the Kestrel F(GA).1, the first example making its maiden flight on 7 March 1964. Subsequently, a special three-nation squadron was formed in the UK, with pilots from the Royal Air Force, the Federal German *Luftwaffe* and all three US services. Between April and November 1965 this unit tested the Kestrel under various simulated operational conditions.

Before this, however, the British government had already ordered, in February 1965, another six development aircraft. These were the first to be given the name Harrier, and the first made its initial flight on 31 August 1966. By that time the Mach 2 Hawker Siddeley P.1154 multi-role V/STOL aircraft intended for the RAF and Royal Navy had been replaced by production Harriers for the RAF only. The single-seat Harrier GR.1 was developed for ground-attack/reconnaissance, and the

tandem two-seat T.2 for combat readiness training. Total orders for the RAF subsequently rose to 132 single-seaters and 19 of the two-seat version, the first production examples of each model making their maiden flights on 28 December 1967 and 24 April 1969 respectively.

The Harrier officially entered service with the Royal Air Force on 1 April 1969 — the service's 51st birthday — the first aircraft being used to equip an Operational Conversion Unit at RAF Wittering, Northants. In the following year the first T.2s entered service, and both initial models were powered by Pegasus 101 turbofans of 19,000-lb (8618-kg) static thrust. They were later upgraded, being redesignated GR.1A and T.2A after refitting with 20,000-lb (9072-kg) Pegasus 102s; currently, they are designated GR.3 and T.4, powered by Pegasus 103s, and equip one RAF squadron in the UK and three in Germany. The RAF generally operates the Harrier GR.3

British Aerospace Harrier GR Mk 3 cutaway drawing key

1	Starboard navigation light
2	Detachable wingtip
3	Outrigger wheel fairing
4	Hydraulic retraction jack
5	Leg fairing (upper section)
6	Starboard outrigger wheel
7	Leg fairing (lower section)
8	Telescopic oleo strut
9	Roll reaction valve
10	Roll reaction outlet
11	Aileron hinge fairing
12	Bonded aluminium honeycomb structure
13	Fuel jettison pipe
14	Aileron hinge
15	Tandem aileron jack and autostabilizer
16	Pylon spigot
17	Starboard outer pylon
18	Leading-edge duct to roll-reaction valve
19	Leading-edge wing fences
20	Riveted rolled stringers
21	Fuel/air valves
22	Pylon spigot
23	Starboard inner pylon
24	Wing fuel tank
25	Wing leading-edge dog-tooth
26	Tank pressurizing air
27	Aileron control rod
28	Front spar web
29	Machined skin plank
30	Centre spar web
31	Rear spar web
32	Main wing attachment point
33	Rear spar/fuselage attachment point
34	Fuselage rear fuel tank
35	Rear nozzle heat shield
36	Vibration-isolating equipment rack
37	IFF-SSR transponder
38	TACAN trans-receiver
39	Ram-air turbine
40	HF tuner
41	HF notch aerial
42	Tailfin attachment bracket
43	Tailfin structure
44	Total temperature sensor
45	ECM pod
46	VHF aerial
47	Rudder
48	Tailplane front spar
49	Tailplane nose ribs
50	Tailplane extension ribs
51	Bonded aluminium honeycomb structure
52	Tail antenna
53	Tail navigation light
54	Pitch and yaw-reaction valve
55	Rudder/yaw-reaction nozzle linkage
56	Pitch and yaw-reaction valve ducting
57	IFF notch aerial
58	Compass flux valve

59	Plastic tail bumper
60	Port all-moving tailplane
61	Ventral fin structure
62	UHF stand-by aerial
63	Rear fuselage access hatch
64	Hydraulic filter No 2 (tailplane)
65	Tandem tailplane jack
66	Rudder cable tensioner
67	UHF stand-by
68	Batteries shelf
69	Airbrake jack
70	Lox container (1.1 Imp gal/ 5 l)
71	Extruded L-section longeron
72	Airbrake (extended)
73	Rigid live-axle mounted mainwheels
74	Multi-disc brakes
75	Torque links
76	Mainwheel leg
77	Pre-closing mainwheel door
78	Mainwheel leg fairing
79	Machined main gear beams
80	Rear bevel gearbox
81	Transverse drive shafts
82	Compensating engine rear support member
83	Rear exhaust nozzle
84	No 2 hydraulic reservoir nitrogen charging connection
85	Titanium heat shield (internal)
86	Reservoir No 2 system
87	Rear nozzle bearings
88	Starboard centre fuel tank
89	Longitudinal drive shaft to rear nozzles
90	Gearbox
91	Master shut-off (butterfly) valve (reaction control system)

92	Nozzle rotation air motors
93	Port 30-mm Aden cannon
94	Case ejection
95	Link ejection
96	Rigid feed chute
97	Ammunition box
98	Port aileron
99	Outrigger wheel fairing
100	Port outrigger wheel
101	Roll reaction outlet
102	Port navigation light
103	Port outer pylon
104	Port inner pylon
105	Ejector release unit
106	Port cannon fairing (starboard weapon deleted for clarity)
107	Blast suppressor
108	Frangible cap fairing
109	Front attachment point
110	Roll reaction valve ducting
111	Air filter
112	Front bevel gearbox
113	Transverse drive shafts
114	Fabricated engine front mounting frame
115	Intermediate chain
116	Chain and sprocket nozzle actuation
117	Fan air nozzle
118	Ground servicing points No 2 system: hydraulics, fuel and air supply external connections
119	GTS/APU
120	Venting air

as a STOVL (short take-off and vertical landing) aircraft, since with a short take-off run it can carry a greater load of weapons than when taking off vertically. Equipment includes an inertial system, flight-refuelling probe, head-up display and laser rangefinder. Both the two-seater and the single-seater have the same nominal weapon-carrying capability, though the two-seater has a greater empty weight.

At about the time the Harrier entered RAF service, an initial buy of 12 was made by the US Marine Corps. This service, one of the first in the world to exploit the helicopter for tactical warfare in Korea and Vietnam, well appreciated the operational flexibility offered by VTOL. The prospect of allying this to the performance of a fixed-wing jet combat aircraft was too strong to resist, and the initial order was soon raised to 110, including eight two-seaters. USMC Harriers, designated AV-8A and TAV-8A respectively, have Pegasus 103 engines, but lack several of the navigation/attack systems of the RAF's GR.3. Instead they carry AIM-9 Sidewinder missiles for air-to-air combat, in which role the US Marine Corps pilots have added a remarkable new trick to the Harrier's repertoire. Known as VIFF (Vectoring In Forward Flight), this makes use of the thrust-vectoring facility in dogfighting situations, where it gives the aircraft an unprecedented manoeuvrability that no other warplane can match. The USMC has

This Harrier GR.3 of RAF No 4 Sqn at Gutersloh would probably be one of the NATO machines to escape an attack.

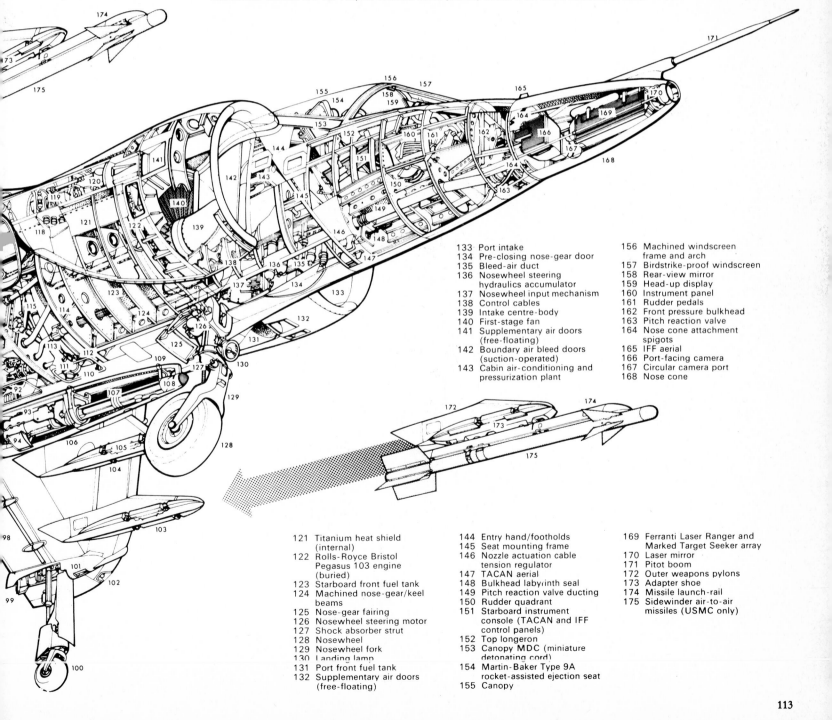

133 Port intake
134 Pre-closing nose-gear door
135 Bleed-air duct
136 Nosewheel steering hydraulics accumulator
137 Nosewheel input mechanism
138 Control cables
139 Intake centre-body
140 First-stage fan
141 Supplementary air doors (free-floating)
142 Boundary air bleed doors (suction-operated)
143 Cabin air-conditioning and pressurization plant

156 Machined windscreen frame and arch
157 Birdstrike-proof windscreen
158 Rear-view mirror
159 Head-up display
160 Instrument panel
161 Rudder pedals
162 Front pressure bulkhead
163 Pitch reaction valve
164 Nose cone attachment spigots
165 IFF aerial
166 Port-facing camera
167 Circular camera port
168 Nose cone

121 Titanium heat shield (internal)
122 Rolls-Royce Bristol Pegasus 103 engine (buried)
123 Starboard front fuel tank
124 Machined nose-gear/keel beams
125 Nose-gear fairing
126 Nosewheel steering motor
127 Shock absorber strut
128 Nosewheel
129 Nosewheel fork
130 Landing lamp
131 Port front fuel tank
132 Supplementary air doors (free-floating)

144 Entry hand/footholds
145 Seat mounting frame
146 Nozzle actuation cable tension regulator
147 TACAN aerial
148 Bulkhead labyrinth seal
149 Pitch reaction valve ducting
150 Rudder quadrant
151 Starboard instrument console (TACAN and IFF control panels)
152 Top longeron
153 Canopy MDC (miniature detonating cord)
154 Martin-Baker Type 9A rocket-assisted ejection seat
155 Canopy

169 Ferranti Laser Ranger and Marked Target Seeker array
170 Laser mirror
171 Pitot boom
172 Outer weapons pylons
173 Adapter shoe
174 Missile launch-rail
175 Sidewinder air-to-air missiles (USMC only)

one training and three operational squadrons equipped with the Harrier, and is campaigning strongly for the Advanced Harrier, the AV-8B developed by McDonnell Douglas. Another development is the Sea Harrier.

To date, the only other operator of the standard Harrier, equivalent to the USMC versions, is the Spanish navy, by whom the aircraft is known as the Matador. Eleven AV-8Ss and two TAV-8Ss equip one Spanish squadron. In early 1979, controversy, promoted by the USSR, surrounded the British government's decision, in principle, to supply Harriers to the People's Republic of China, which is reported to require a large number of these unique aircraft.

Type: V/STOL close-support/reconnaissance aircraft (single-seat models) and combat readiness trainer (two-seaters)
Powerplant: one 21,500-lb (9752-kg) Rolls-Royce Pegasus 103 vectored-thrust turbofan
Performance: maximum speed at low altitude more than 737 mph (1186 km/h); maximum Mach number in dive 1.3; combat radius with 3,000-lb (1360-kg) external load (AV-8A) after vertical take-off 57 miles (92 km), with short take-off 414 miles (667 km); range with one in-flight refuelling (GR.3) 3,455 miles (5560 km); time to climb to 40,000 ft (12200 m) from vertical take-off 2 minutes 22.7 seconds; service ceiling more than 55,000 ft (15240 m)
Weights: basic operating weight empty, including crew (GR.3) 12,300 lb (5580 kg); (AV-8A) 12,200 lb (5533 kg); (two-seaters) 13,750 lb (6237 kg); maximum take-off (single-seat, short take-off) over 25,000 lb (11340 kg)
Dimensions: span 25 ft 3 in (7.70 m); length (AV-8A) 45 ft 6 in (13.87 m); length (GR.3 with laser nose) 45 ft 7¾ in (13.91 m); length (two-seater) 55 ft 9½ in (17.00 m); height (single-seater) 11 ft 4 in (3.45 m); height (two-seater) 13 ft 8 in (4.17 m); wing area 201.1 sq ft (18.68 m²)

Armament: centreline and four wing attachments for external stores, maximum demonstrated load being 8,000 lb (3630 kg); RAF aircraft cleared for operations with more than 5,000 lb (2268 kg); ventral strakes can be replaced by two 30-mm Aden gun/ammunition pods in lieu of centreline store; wing points able to carry various combinations of bombs, gun pods, rockets and flares; provision in AV-8A for two 30-mm Aden guns and Sidewinder air-to-air missiles
Operators: Spain, UK, US Marine Corps

Each of the low-drag inlet cowls, with outward-cambered lips, is provided with a row of eight spring-loaded suction-relief doors which open to admit additional air to the engine at near-zero airspeeds. To provide even better "breathing" in the jet-lift mode, the McDonnell Douglas AV-8B development has a double row of these doors on each side, although the engine is essentially the same; it also has long rectangular front nozzles.

Perhaps the chief alteration to the appearance of RAF Harrier GR.3s and T.4s has been the addition, usually as a modification to aircraft already in service, of a Ferranti Type 106 laser ranger and market-target seeker in a modified nose. This improves the delivery accuracy of air/ground weapons and locks automatically on to laser-lit targets, including those marked or "designated" by a laser directed by friendly ground troops.

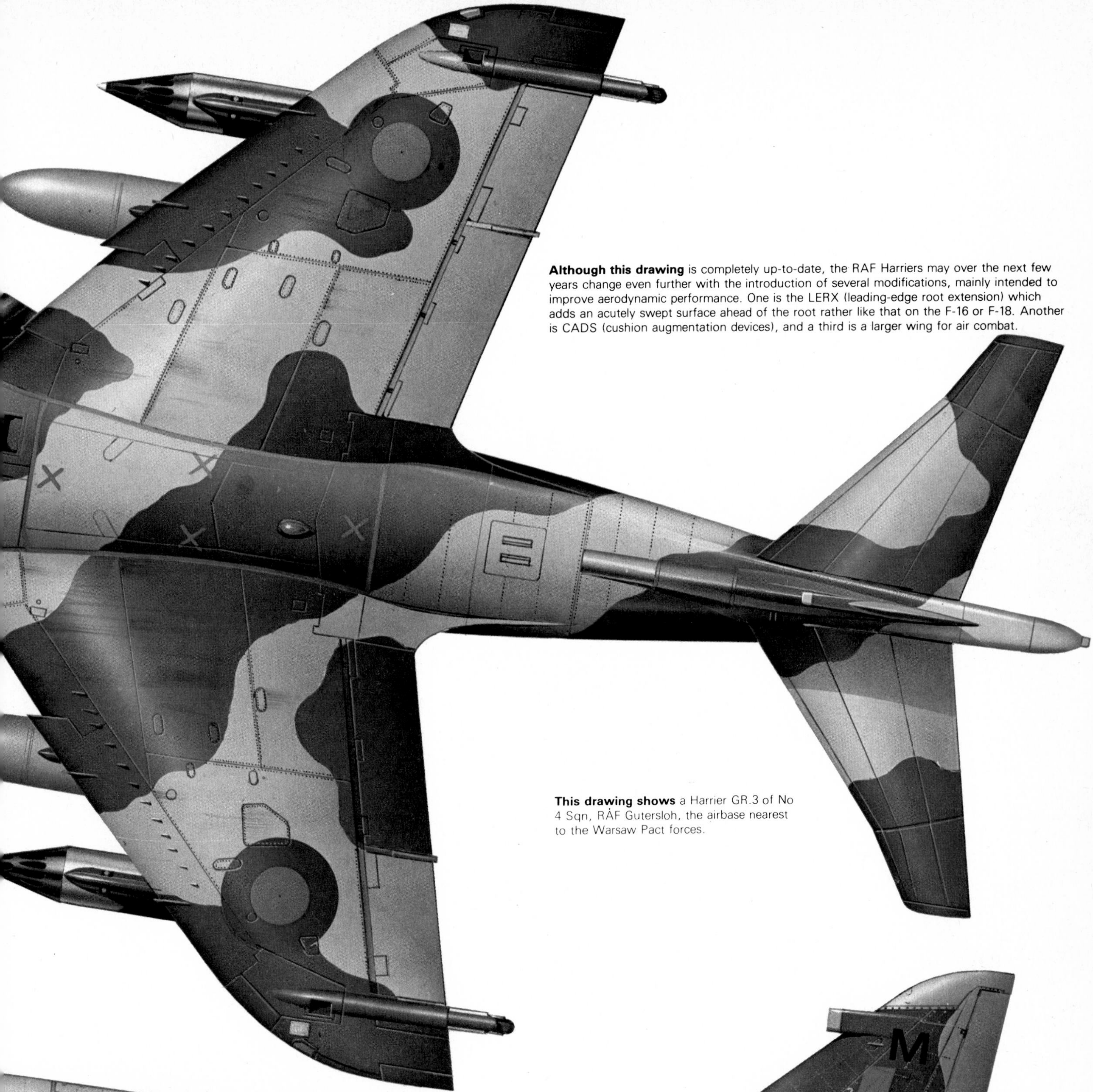

Although this drawing is completely up-to-date, the RAF Harriers may over the next few years change even further with the introduction of several modifications, mainly intended to improve aerodynamic performance. One is the LERX (leading-edge root extension) which adds an acutely swept surface ahead of the root rather like that on the F-16 or F-18. Another is CADS (cushion augmentation devices), and a third is a larger wing for air combat.

This drawing shows a Harrier GR.3 of No 4 Sqn, RAF Gutersloh, the airbase nearest to the Warsaw Pact forces.

This aircraft is fitted with ARI-18228 analog-controlled rear warning radar receivers, with front/rear aerials (yellow) on the fin and at the rear of the tail-nozzle fairing. Ajax and other ECM equipment is said to be carried, together with MB Associates MFCD (multiple flare and chaff dispenser). Not fitted to XZ 131 in this drawing are the bolt-on ferry wingtips, which add more than 4 ft to the span, or the clip-on FR probe.

British Aerospace (Hawker Siddeley) Hawk

The British Aerospace Hawk, originally known as the Hawker Siddeley HS.1182, is replacing the Royal Air Force's Gnat, Jet Provost and Hunter trainers. By early 1979 the aircraft had additionally been ordered by three export customers, and British Aerospace sees a market for up to 3,000 Hawk-type machines by the mid-1980s.

The HS.1182 was selected for the RAF in 1971 in preference to a BAC design; five months later the Adour turbofan was chosen in place of the Rolls-Royce Viper turbojet. In March 1972 an order was placed for 176 Hawks. There was no prototype and only one pre-production aircraft, the first 10 production Hawks being allocated to the test programme. This saved considerable time, and the first two operational aircraft were handed over to the RAF in November 1976.

The Hawk is a tandem-seat transonic ground-attack and training aircraft of conventional layout, with a low-mounted wing. Its primary structure is designed for a safe fatigue life of 6,000 hours in the exacting conditions demanded by the RAF. Simplicity of design and manufacture are emphasized to ensure that the aircraft has a high utilization rate and is inexpensive to operate. One man can prepare the aircraft for its next flight in less than 20 minutes between sorties, and in the weapon-training role it can be re-armed by four men in less than 15 minutes.

Low operating costs are contributed to by the efficient Adour turbofan, which is an unaugmented version of that employed in the SEPECAT Jaguar. The Adour is of modular construction, so the spares holding is reduced. Any module can be changed without the need to rebalance the rotating assemblies, and large doors beneath the engine bay permit easy access and removal. An integral gas-turbine starter running off the aircraft's fuel supply makes the Hawk independent of external aids.

The Hawk had a remarkably trouble-free development programme, entering service only 27 months after its maiden flight. All performance objectives were met, and the top speed proved to be higher than expected. The aircraft has reached Mach 1.15 in a dive and has a maximum level speed of Mach 0.88, allowing student pilots to experience transonic handling before they progress to true supersonic types. Even better figures could be achieved by fitting a more powerful engine, and possibilities which have been examined by the manufacturer include the uprated -56 version of the Adour and an unaugmented version of the Turbo-Union RB.199 turbofan. A single-seat Hawk, with additional fuel and/or avionics, has been studied by British Aerospace.

The RAF operates the aircraft for weapon instruction as well as flying training, with three pylons. The centreline pylon is normally occupied by an Aden cannon pod, with Matra rocket launchers or practice bombs beneath the wings. Potential export customers often demand heavier armament, however, and British Aerospace has tested the Hawk with about 40 combinations of air-to-surface and air-to-air weaponry. Two stations can be fitted beneath each wing, giving a total of five, and the use of multiple racks allows the aircraft to carry an exceptional 6,500 lb (2954 kg) of stores in the form of six 1,000-lb (454-kg) bombs plus the Aden gunpack. Wingtip air-to-air missiles can also be fitted.

By the end of 1978, deliveries to the RAF were running at six aircraft a month, with 100 delivered. British Aerospace has also been awarded a contract by the US Navy to study the modifications necessary to make the aircraft suitable for its VTX-TS requirement, aimed at replacing the fleet of Rockwell T-2 Buckeyes and McDonnell Douglas TA-4 Skyhawks. Changes would include altering the landing gear for operations from aircraft-carriers, and fitting an arrester hook.

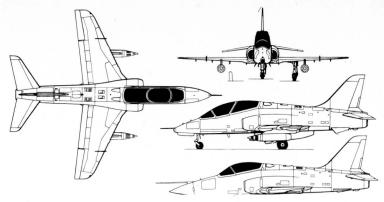

British Aerospace Hawk T.1
(lower side view of proposed single-seat attack variant)

A **British Aerospace** Hawk T Mk 1 in the markings of No 4 Flying Training School, Royal Air Force, based at RAF Valley.

Type: multi-role trainer and light attack aircraft
Powerplant: one 5,340-lb (2427-kg) Rolls-Royce/Turboméca Adour turbofan
Performance: maximum level speed at sea level 625 mph (1000 km/h); maximum speed 662 mph (1060 km/h); ceiling 50,000 ft (15240 m); time to 30,000 ft (9145 m) 6 minutes 20 seconds; ferry range (clean) 1,520 miles (2433 km); ferry range with two 100-Imperial gallon (455-litre) auxiliary fuel tanks 1,933 miles (3093 km)
Weights: take-off (trainer role) 11,100 lb (5030 kg); maximum take-off 17,097 lb (7755 kg); maximum landing at 13-ft (3.96-m) per second descent 10,250 lb (4650 kg)
Dimensions: span 30 ft 9½ in (9.39 m); length 38 ft 11 in (11.85 m); height 13 ft 1 in (4.0 m); wing area 179.64 sq ft (16.69 m²)
Armament: up to 6,500 lb (2954 kg) of stores, including Aden 30-mm cannon pod and six 1,000-lb (454-kg) bombs; also Matra 155 rocket launchers, practice bombs and a wide range of other stores
Operators: ordered by Finland (50), Indonesia (8), Kenya (12), and used by UK

A BAe Hawk T.1 from the Tactical Weapons Unit at RAF Brawdy does a slow roll to show off its centreline 30-mm Aden gun pod and two SNEB rocket pods on the wings.

British Aerospace (Hawker) Hunter

Another design by Sydney Camm, continuing the tradition of the Hurricane, Typhoon, Tempest, Fury and Sea Fury, the Hunter has been Britain's most successful post-war fighter. A total of 1,985 were built, including 445 built under licence in Belgium and Holland. Not only an extremely capable warplane, the Hunter will always be remembered by its pilots as a sheer delight to fly. It has served with 19 air arms around the world, and is still operational with 14 of them. All surviving variants are powered by the Rolls-Royce Avon turbojet, though the Armstrong Siddeley Sapphire powered the Mks 2 and 5. The prototype, P.1067, flew on 20 June 1951, and was followed exactly one month later by the first prototype Hunter F.1. The first production F.1 flew on 16 May 1953, and the first two-seater approximately two years later. Deliveries of brand-new aircraft continued until 1966, during which time the breed was continually improved. All versions of the aircraft were supersonic in a shallow dive, and power, armament and fuel capacity were progressively increased to reach a peak in the Mk 9. This variant, embodying all the lessons to come out of the earlier marks, is

powered by the 10,150-lb (4604-kg) Rolls-Royce Avon 207; it packs a greater punch, in the form of heavier underwing capacity, and is generally beefed up to capitalise on its improved potency in the ground-attack role. So great an improvement was this mark that the manufacturer has had a steady flow of refurbishing and remanufacturing work over the years, more than 700 aircraft having undergone the treatment.

The United Emirate air force has a ground-attack squadron formed in 1970, operating eight FGA.76s and two T.77 trainers from Sharjah. Chile, with 37 Hunters (33 FGA.71s and four T.77s), is faced with a grave problem as the British government, which opposes the government of this South American country, continues to prohibit any arms dealing. In mid-1978 only 20 of the Hunters were flying, the remainder being grounded for lack of spares and service support. Five ground-attack squadrons of the Indian air force fly some 130 F.56/T.66s. Iraq, with a variety of Russian and Western machines on strength, still operates 30 FGA.9/FR.10s (46 delivered) in three strike squadrons. Kenya's one fighter-bomber squadron flies five FGA.9s received in

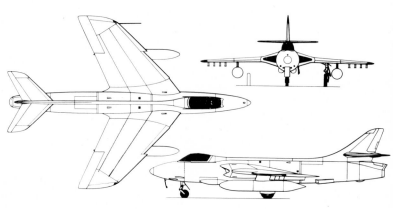

British Aerospace Hunter FGA.9

1974. A ground-attack squadron of the Kuwait air force has retired its four single-seat FGA.57s but five two-seat T.67s continue to operate alongside Mk 83 Strikemasters. Lebanon's *Force Aérienne Libanaise* is spearheaded by 17 F.70s (including six bought in 1975 to make up for attrition) and two T.66 two-seaters. The Sultan of Oman's air force, now equipped with SEPECAT Jaguars, continues to fly some 15 FGA.6s from Thumrayt. Oman bought 31 Hunters from Jordan in 1975, and those not operational are kept in storage. A fighter wing of the *Fuerza Aérea del Peru* flies F.52s (16 delivered). The Qatar air force has two FGA.78s (a third was destroyed in 1977) and one T.79, all based at Doha, mainly for use on coastal patrol duties. Rhodesia, heavily involved in anti-guerilla operations, flies nine FGA.9s with two squadrons (Nos 1 and 2) based at Thornhill. The Republic of Singapore air force flies about 30 single-seaters (Mk 74s) with Nos 140 and 141 Sqns, in addition to seven T.75s and four reconnaissance FR.74As. Fiercely neutral Switzerland operates nearly 150 Hunters, the fleet having been bolstered in 1974 by an order for 60 to tide the air force over until a new air-superiority fighter was chosen (the Northrop F-5E was eventually selected). The Swiss aircraft are particularly capable: they carry Sidewinder missiles and Saab bombing computers, and equip nine squadrons for ground-attack and two for surveillance. Two forces of the United Kingdom use the Hunter: an RAF tactical weapons unit based at Brawdy has 80-odd Mk 6As in Nos 63, 79 and 234 Sqns, and 30 aircraft equip a second unit at Lossiemouth. Hunters are also occasionally detached to Gibraltar on training missions. Some 20 are based at Valley for training. The Fleet Air Arm flies GA.11s.

Type: single-seat fighter, fighter-bomber and fighter-reconnaissance; or two-seat training aircraft
Powerplant: one 10,150-lb (4604-kg) Rolls-Royce Avon 207 single-shaft turbojet
Performance: Maximum speed 710 mph (1144 km/h) at sea level; 620 mph (978 km/h) or Mach 0.94 at height; range (internal fuel) 490 miles (689 km); range (with 230-Imperial gallon/1046-litre drop-tanks) 1,840 miles (2965 km); initial rate of climb 8,000 ft (2438 m) per minute
Weights: empty equipped 13,270 lb (6020 kg); clean 17,750 (8051 kg); maximum take-off 24,000 lb (10885 kg)
Dimensions: span 33 ft 8 in (10.26 m); length (single-seaters) 45 ft 10½ in (13.98 m); length (two-seaters) 48 ft 10½ in (14.9 m); height 13 ft 2 in (4.26 m); wing area 349 sq ft (32.4 m²)
Armament: four 30-mm Aden cannon in self-contained, removable package beneath cockpit floor; external stores include two 1,000-lb (454-kg) bombs, two clusters of six 3-in (76.2-m) rockets, two 100-Imperial gallon (456-litre) or 230-Imperial gallon (1046-litre) drop-tanks, two Sidewinder or (exceptionally) Firestreak air-to-air missiles
Operators: Abu Dhabi, Chile, India, Iraq, Kenya, Kuwait, Lebanon, Oman, Peru, Qatar, Rhodesia, Singapore, Switzerland, UK

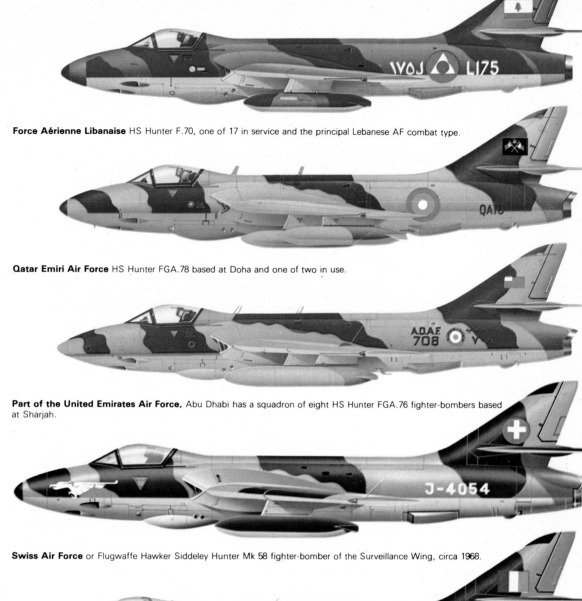

Force Aérienne Libanaise HS Hunter F.70, one of 17 in service and the principal Lebanese AF combat type.

Qatar Emiri Air Force HS Hunter FGA.78 based at Doha and one of two in use.

Part of the United Emirates Air Force, Abu Dhabi has a squadron of eight HS Hunter FGA.76 fighter-bombers based at Sharjah.

Swiss Air Force or Flugwaffe Hawker Siddeley Hunter Mk 58 fighter-bomber of the Surveillance Wing, circa 1968.

Indian Air Force HS Hunter Mk 56. In 1979 the type equipped four squadrons.

HS Hunter T Mk 7 two-seat advanced trainer of No 4 Flying Training School, RAF Valley.

British Aerospace (Hunting) Jet Provost

For 20 years the Royal Air Force's standard basic trainer, the BAe (formerly Hunting, then BAC) Jet Provost replaced the piston-engined Hunting Provost between 1959 and 1961. The concept of *ab initio* jet training had been tested using the Jet Provost T.1 in 1955.

The production Jet Provost T.3 flew on 22 June, 1958 and deliveries commenced a year later. In 1961 the more powerful T.4 entered service and enabled the RAF's basic flying syllabus to be extended, thus reducing usage of more expensive advanced trainers. Export versions, designated T.51 and T.52, were developed with armament, enabling them also to be employed in the light attack role.

The Jet Provost is all-metal. Side-by-side

Martin-Baker lightweight ejection seats are fitted.

Internal fuel totals 182 Imperial gallons (827 litres) in six wing tanks. Tip tanks each carry an additional 48 Imperial gallons (827 litres). The wings incorporate slotted flaps and airbrakes. RAF aircraft were delivered with Rebecca and UHF navigation and radio, with VHF and radio compass available on export models. Armed export versions carry two machine-guns in the intake walls, with 600 rounds of ammunition per gun. An underfuselage gunpack, housing two 0.5-in (12.7-mm) machine-guns with 100 rounds per gun, can also be fitted. Alternative underwing ordnance loads include: 24 Sura rockets,

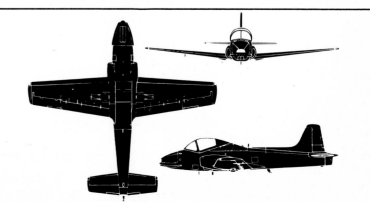

British Aerospace Jet Provost T.5

continued

twelve 25-lb (11.3-kg) or 8-cm (3.15-in) Oerlikon rockets, six 60-lb (27.2-kg) rockets, eight 25-lb (11.3-kg) bombs, or two 100-lb (45.4-kg) bombs.

In 1967 the T.5 (export version BAC.145) introduced a pressurized cabin with better view and a lengthened nose housing avionics. A new wing has greater fatigue life, and increased capacity for fuel and underwing weapons.

In mid-1967 BAC completed refurbishing 157 T.3 and 5, fitting DME and VOR to produce the T.3A and 5A.

RAF pilot training is divided between graduate entrants and direct entrants. The former receive some 85 hours' instruction on the Bulldog T.1 with a University Air Squadron. A further 75 hours' flying the Jet Provost T.3A at the RAF College, Cranwell, brings them to 'wings' standard, and a further 60 hours on Jet Provost T.5As completes the course at Cranwell.

Direct entrants are posted to No 1 Flying Training School at Linton-on-Ouse, Yorks, which also flies Jet Provost T.3As and T.5As. They require 100 hours on the Jet Provost to reach 'wings' standard (receiving no preliminary piston-engined training) and thereafter 60 hours on the T.5A. At No 3 FTS at Leeming, Yorkshire, Jet Provosts are used for refresher training for pilots who are returning to flying after a ground posting. Trainee navigators at No 6 FTS Leeming, Yorks, also fly in the Jet Provost. The Central Flying School at Cranwell, responsible for the training and standardization of flying instructors, is another important user of the type.

Foreign users of the Jet Provost include Iraq, which flies 16 T.52 in the light-attack role; Sri Lanka, which has eight T.51s with a training unit; the Sudan, with three BAC.145s used for light attack; and Venezuela, which is replacing its T.52 weapons trainers with Rockwell T-2D Buckeyes.

Type: basic jet trainer and light attack aircraft
Powerplant: one 1,750-lb (795-kg) Rolls-Royce Viper 102 (T.3); one 2,500-lb (1135-kg) Rolls-Royce Viper 202 (T.52 and T.5)
Performance: maximum speed at 20,000 ft (6100 m) 410 mph (660 km/h) (T.52); maximum speed at 25,000 ft (7600 m) 440 mph (708 km/h) (T.5); service ceiling 21,700 ft

This **British Aerospace Jet Provost T.3** is on a dual exercise making a circuit of the city of York. The JP equips the Central Flying School at Leeming and also No 3 Flying Training School at Dishforth, in both Mk 3 and 5 versions.

BAC Jet Provost T.5 basic trainer on the strength of the Royal Air Force College, Cranwell, Lincs.

(6600 m) (T.3); service ceiling 34,500 ft (10500 m) (T.5); range with maximum fuel 700 miles (1130 km) (T.52); range with maximum fuel (tip tanks fitted) 900 miles (1450 km) (T.5)
Weights: normal take-off 7,400 lb (3365 kg) (T.52); normal take-off 7,630 lb (3460 kg)

(T.5); maximum landing 7,250 lb (3288 kg) (T.52); maximum overload 9,200 lb (4173 kg) (T.5)
Dimensions: span (over tanks) 36 ft 11 in (11.25 m); length 32 ft 5 in (9.88 m) (T.3 and 52); length 33 ft 7½ in (10.25 m) (T.5); height 10 ft 2 in (3.10 m); wing area 213.7 sq

ft (19.80 m²)
Armament: two 0.303-in (7.7-mm) machine-guns and twin 0.5-in (12.7-mm) machine-gun pack, rockets, or 200-lb (91-kg) bomb load (T.52)
Operators: Iraq, Sri Lanka, Sudan, UK, Venezuela

British Aerospace (Scottish Aviation) Jetstream

The decision by British Aerospace in 1978 to relaunch the Jetstream has brought new life to a project which began with the Handley Page company in the mid-1960s. The new Jetstream 31 is powered by twin Garrett AiResearch TPE 331-10 turboprops flat rated to 840 shp (627 kW), and differs only in detail from the 26 military Series 200s used by the RAF and RN.

First flight of the Jetstream 31 was scheduled for late 1979 and British Aerospace expects to begin deliveries in 1981. The Jetstream 31 is offered in three versions, one designed for special customers such as the military.

The British Aerospace market surveys of 1977-1978 leading to the Jetstream relaunch paralleled those of a dozen years previously. These led Handley Page to draw up a specification for the medium-sized twin turboprop which became the Jetstream. The new aircraft was to replace the Beech 18 and DH Dove, offering greater cabin comfort than types like the turboprop Beech King Air but costing less than executive jets. The aircraft came out 1,000 lb (454 kg) too heavy, 30 mph (48 km/h) too slow and 70 per cent above the target price. Despite its problems, which have generally been resolved with development, the Jetstream is of straightforward layout with an unswept low wing, a pressurized fuselage, and a tailplane set half way up the fin. Its structure and systems are conventional, although it is a mini-airliner rather than king-sized business aircraft.

The standard Jetstream was to have had the 811-shp (605-kW) Turboméca Astazou XIV, and this was launched in 1966, 165 being on

order by mid-1967. The first flew in August 1967. The US government gave the project a boost in December 1967 when it ordered 11 military Jetstream 3Ms for the USAF as C-10As and took options on 300. The 3M prototype flew in March 1968, powered by 840-shp (627-kW) Garrett AiResearch TPE 331-310W turboprops. The 3M had a higher take-off weight than the Mk 1 and was equipped with a larger door, strengthened floor and removable jump seat. Two military prototypes had flown and the 11 initial 3Ms were on the line when, following receivership, the Radlett factory closed on 2 March 1970. Some 36 Jetstreams had been completed.

Production and design rights were eventually sold to Scottish Aviation, who had originally been subcontracted by Handley Page to build all Jetstream wings. In February 1972 the RAF ordered 26 Jetstreams from Scottish Aviation and the first flew in April 1973. These are similar to the civil Series 200 with Astazou XVIC2 engines, new 'eyebrow' windows and revised instrumentation. They were constructed substantially from parts built by Handley Page, and the Scottish company was reluctant to invest in a new production line, not least because of the possibility of nationa-

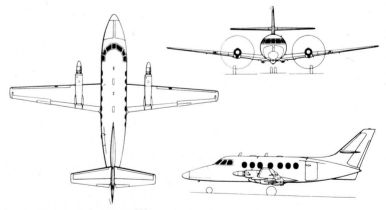

British Aerospace Jetstream 200

The Jetstream T.1 is flown by the RAF's Multi-Engined Training School at Leeming, Yorks.

ization. The RAF operates eight Jetstream T.1s as multi-engine pilot trainers, and the Royal Navy 14 T.2s for observer training. The naval aircraft replaced Sea Princes and have an MEL E190 weather and terrain-mapping nose radar.

British Aerospace was eventually formed in April 1977 and re-examined Jetstream prospects. About 30 Handley Page aircraft are still in service and a number of specialist US companies are already offering re-engined and updated second-hand examples.

Type: trainer, liaison or light transport aircraft
Powerplant: (Srs 200, T.Mk 1 or T.Mk 2) two 996-ehp (743-kW) Turboméca Astazou XVIC2 turboprops; (Jetstream 31) two

840-shp (627-kW) Garrett AiResearch TPE 331-10 turboprops
Performance: (Srs 200, T.Mk 1 or T. Mk 2 at maximum take-off weight) maximum level speed 282 mph (454 km/h); economical cruising speed 269 mph (433 km/h); range with maximum fuel (full reserves) 1,380 miles (2224 km)
Weights: (Srs 200, T.Mk 1 or T.Mk 2)

empty 7,683 lb (3485 kg); maximum take-off and landing 12,566 lb (5700 kg); maximum zero fuel 12,250 lb (5556 kg)
Dimensions: span 52 ft 0 in (15.85 m); length 47 ft 1½ in (14.37 m); height 17 ft 5½ in (5.32 m); wing area 270 sq ft (25.08 m²)
Armament: none
Operator: UK

British Aerospace (BAC) Lightning

When the BAC (now part of BAe) Lightning finally entered service in 1960 it heralded a new era for the Royal Air Force. Prime mover behind the project was 'Teddy' Petter, father of the BAC (English Electric) Canberra bomber. It was in 1947 that a study contract was awarded for a supersonic research aircraft. The resulting English Electric P.1A flew on 4 August 1954, and later exceeded Mach 1 on two unreheated and rather basic Armstrong Siddeley Sapphire turbojets. Three research prototypes were built, two for intensive flying trials and one for testing to destruction in a ground rig. These early aircraft had an elliptical nose air intake. In 1954 the design underwent extensive change to make it a practical service aircraft. Three operational prototypes, designated P.1B and featuring Avon turbojets, with a centre-body air intake, were built. The first P.1B (XA847) flew on 4 April 1957. Some 19 months later the Air Ministry adopted the name Lightning. On 25 November 1958, the P.1B, fitted with crudely afterburning Avons, exceeded Mach 2 for the first time. After a further 20 pre-production aircraft had been built and proven (this was a radically new aircraft to the Air Ministry), the Lightning was finally cleared to enter service in 1960.

The RAF now had a highly supersonic all-weather interceptor with excellent performance but it also had severe maintenance headaches.

The Lightning F.1 had a Ferranti Airpass Mk 1 interception and fire-control radar in the central nose cone, guided missiles (heat-seeking Firestreaks) and truly supersonic performance. The first production model of this operational version, designated F.1, flew on 29 October 1959, and deliveries to RAF No 74 Sqn began the following summer. F.1s were also supplied to Nos 56 and 111 Sqns. The final production aircraft of this mark, the F.1A, had provision for flight refuelling and UHF radio. Next development was the F.2, with better range, ceiling and speed, more advanced electronics, Hawker Siddeley Red Top air-to-air missiles in place of Firestreaks, liquid-oxygen breathing system and a steerable nosewheel. The first F.2 flew on 11 July 1961, and the type later equipped Nos 19 and 92 Sqns in Germany. A total of seven T.2 and T.4 trainers were delivered to Saudi Arabia in 1966–67. The F.3, a further development, was powered by 16,360-lb (7420-kg) Avon 300-series reheat turbojets. It had no guns, and for long-range ferrying two large over-wing jettisonable fuel tanks could be fitted, along with a flight-refuelling probe under the port wing. The first F.3, incorporating a larger, square-tip fin, flew on 16 June 1962, and the type entered service with No 74 Sqn in mid-1964, subsequently re-equipping also Nos 23, 29, 56 and 111 Sqns. The F.6 was the result of a long-overdue decision in 1965 to follow BAC's advice and nearly double the fuel capacity and fit the cambered, kinked wing leading-edge which had first been flown nine years earlier. This latter modification allowed operation at greater weights. Increased fuel capacity (in the form of a much enlarged ventral tank), coupled with the low subsonic drag of the new leading edge, gave the F.6 a tremendous improvement in effectiveness. Both Saudi Arabia and Kuwait bought a developed version of the F.6, designated F.53. Saudi Arabia still operates 31 F.53s (32 delivered), two F.54s, three F.52s and five two-seat T.55s. Twenty of the F.53s fly with No 2 Sqn at Tabuk in the north on interception duties, and the remaining aircraft operate from the OCU (Operational Conversion Unit) at Dharan. Kuwait's 10 F.53s and two T.67 two-seat trainers are no longer

operational, having been replaced by Mirage F.1s.

Type: (F.6) single-seat supersonic all-weather interceptor, strike and reconnaissance aircraft
Powerplant: two 15,680-lb (7112-kg) Rolls-Royce Avon 302 turbojets
Performance: maximum speed Mach 2.3 or 1,500 mph (2415 km/h) at 40,000 ft (12190 m); range (internal fuel only) 800 miles (1288 km); initial rate of climb 50,000 ft (15240 m) per minute; time to operational height (around 40,000 ft/12190 m) and speed of Mach 0.9 (clean) 2 minutes 30 seconds; acceleration from Mach 1 to Mach 2 + (clean) 3 minutes 30 seconds.
Weights: empty equipped about 28,000 lb (12700 kg); loaded 50,000 lb (22680 kg)
Dimensions: span 34 ft 10 in (10.61 m); length 55 ft 3 in (16.84 m); height 19 ft 7 in (5.97 m); wing area 380.1 sq ft (35.31 m²)
Armament: large, two-portion ventral pack contains fuel tank (rear) and (forward) either more fuel or a pack housing two 30-mm Aden guns (120 rounds each); operational packs mounted ahead of ventral bay include two Firestreak or Red Top air-to-air missiles, or 44 2-in (50.8-mm) spin-stabilized rockets, or five Vinten 360 70-mm cameras, or (night recon-

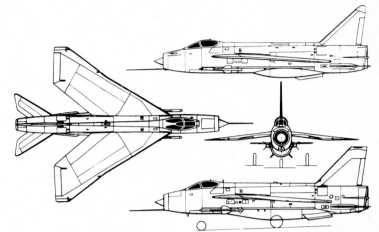

**British Aerospace Lightning F.6
(upper side view of F.1)**

naissance) cameras and linescan equipment and underwing flares; underwing/overwing hard-points can carry up to 144 rockets or six 1,000-lb (454-kg) HE, retarded or fire bombs.
Operators: Saudi Arabia, UK

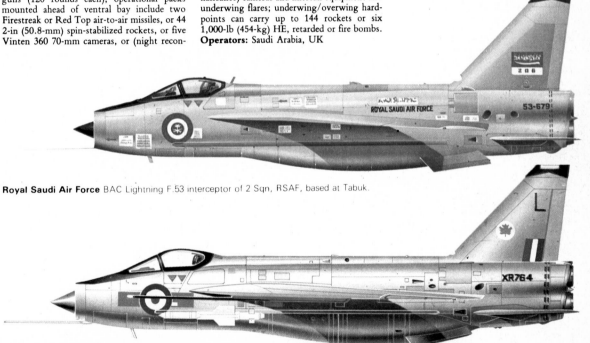

Royal Saudi Air Force BAC Lightning F.53 interceptor of 2 Sqn, RSAF, based at Tabuk.

BAC Lightning F.6 of 5 Sqn, Royal Air Force Strike Command, based at Binbrook for the air defence of Great Britain.

Still a mainstay of Britain's air defences, the popular but ageing Lightning will survive until the entry to service of the Tornado F.2; this is a Mk 6 aircraft from No 5 Sqn based at RAF Binbrook, pictured over an oil rig.

British Aerospace (Hawker Siddeley) Nimrod MR and R

The name Nimrod, after the 'mighty hunter' of the Book of Genesis, was a most suitable choice for this aircraft. Its own genesis lies in the world's first jet airliner, the de Havilland Comet, which was adopted as a military transport by the Royal Air Force in 1955. Some 10 years later, in early 1965, when the RAF was seeking a new maritime patrol aircraft, the British government decided not to authorize the development of an entirely new aeroplane, but to see what could be done by adapting the basic airframe of the Comet 4. The outcome of that programme is now acknowledged as one of the finest overwater patrol and anti-submarine aircraft in service in the world to-day.

Nimrod development began with the allocation of two ex-airline Comet 4Cs, which in 1965-66 were modified as Hawker Siddeley 801 prototypes for the new design. Principal modifications were the substitution of four Rolls-Royce Spey turbofan engines for the Avon turbojets of the Comet, and the addition of a new, unpressurized lower compartment beneath the basic pressure shell of the original airliner. The new lower fuselage was used to house a search radar, much of the specialized avionics, and the 48 ft 6 in (14.78 m) weapons bay. The first HS.801 was flown on 23 May 1967; the second, which retained its original Avon engines and was used primarily as a maritime avionics testbed, followed it into the air on 31 July 1967. Wings and horizontal tail surfaces remained essentially those of the Comet 4C, as did the landing gear, apart from being strengthened for the higher operating weights. Additional new structural features were a large dorsal fin, a fat ECM (electronic countermeasures) pod on top of the main fin, a magnetic anomaly detector (MAD) boom behind the rear fuselage, a searchlight in the right leading-edge fuel tank, and underwing pylons for air-to-surface missiles.

An initial contract was placed for 38 production aircraft, to be known as the Nimrod MR.1; the first of these flew on 28 June 1968, and deliveries began to No 201 Squadron of RAF Strike Command in October of the following year. A further batch of eight MR.1s was ordered in 1972, to permit the equipping of six RAF squadrons (Nos 42, 120, 201, 203, 206 and one other) with this version of the Nimrod. In the previous year, however, three examples of a different version, known as the R.1, were received by No 51 Squadron. These have a shorter, blunt tailcone and the wing leading-edge pods are of a modified size and shape. It is obvious that these three aircraft are employed for electronic reconnaissance and the monitoring of foreign emissions, although they are described officially as 'calibration' aircraft.

Primary Nimrod roles, for which it carries a standard crew of 12, are those of anti-submarine warfare, maritime surveillance of the United Kingdom defence area (including the North Sea and the eastern Atlantic) and anti-shipping strike. The large weapons bay can accommodate a wide variety of ordnance, in addition to which there is ample storage space in the rear of the pressurized fuselage compartment for sonobuoys, marine markers and other detection gear. Twelve hours is a typical patrol endurance, and an on-station patrol of more than six hours can be maintained at a distance of 1,150 miles (1850 km) from its shore base. This capability is made possible by cruising on only two engines, with the other pair shut down, and the Nimrod can, if necessary, cruise and climb on only one engine. Range can be extended still further by installing up to six auxiliary fuel tanks in the

weapons bay. Search radar in the nose is an ASV-21D by EMI, and a Marconi computer-based system provides integrated navigation/weapon selection and delivery with appropriate operator displays in the tactical compartment. If required, the Nimrod can be used in a secondary transport role, with seats for up to 45 troops.

Since 1975 the RAF's fleet of MR.1 Nimrods has been undergoing a modernization programme, being re-delivered from 1978 in updated form as MR.2s. In consequence, only five of the eight additional Nimrods ordered in 1972 were actually delivered as MR.1s: one of the others was utilized as a Mk 2 development aircraft, while the seventh and eighth have been allocated to a similar role in the evolution of the early-warning Nimrod AEW.3. Though the MR.2 is a major rebuild, the essence of the conversion is to modernize and improve the operational equipment. A new Marconi digital computer, able to store much more information than that in the MR.1, is integrated with a Ferranti inertial navigation system; the new EMI radar, appropriately known as Searchwater, has its own

British Aerospace Nimrod MR.2

Royal Air Force HS Nimrod MR.1 long-range maritime patrol aircraft of 203 Sqn, Kinloss, Scotland.

British Aerospace Nimrod MR Mk 1 cutaway drawing key

1 Dielectric radome
2 Taxi lamp
3 ASV-21D Search and weather radar
4 Radome hoist point
5 Front pressure bulkhead
6 Windscreen (area enlarged from original Comet)
7 Four windscreen wipers
8 Instrument panel coaming
9 Co-pilot's seat
10 Eyebrow window
11 Pilot's seat
12 Pitot head
13 Twin nosewheels
14 Sonics homing aerial
15 Doppler bay
16 Forward radio pack
17 Autolycus unit
18 Autolycus equipment rack
19 Port D.C. electrics crate
20 Engineer's station
21 Emergency escape hatch
22 Starboard DC electrics crate
23 Crew entry door
24 Periscopic sextant
25 Equipment systems crate
26 Toilet
27 Ground supply socket
28 Weapons-pannier door ground control
29 Weapons-pannier door
30 Door strut
31 Mixed ASW weapons load
32 Tank blow-off
33 "On-top" sight
34 Port beam lookout's seat

35 Domed observation window (hinged, pressure-bearing, with sight linked to computer)
36 Starboard beam lookout's seat
37 Domed observation window (fixed)
38 Analogue computer rack
39 Digital computer rack
40 Blackout curtain
41 Map projector station
42 Routine navigator
43 Plot cathode ray tube
44 Tactical navigator
45 Wireless operator
46 Tactical commander
47 Sonics stations (2)
48 Sonics operators (2)
49 ASV operator
50 Partition
51 Space provision for extra sensor operator's station
52 Radio trough
53 Sonics cupboard
54 Port AC electrics crate
55 Starboard AC electrics crate
56 Aft radio rack
57 ESM/MAD operator
58 Machined inner-wing skin
59 Undercarriage bay upper panel
60 Starboard weapons pylon
61 Flow spoiler

62 Searchlight, 70m candle power
63 External fuel tank
64 Wing bumper
65 Fixed slot
66 Integral fuel tanks
67 Skin butt-joint rib
68 Over-wing filler
69 Starboard navigation light
70 Wingtip fuel vent
71 Starboard aileron
72 Aileron tab

sub-system, based on a Ferranti digital computer, for data processing. The Searchwater system, designed to function in spite of hostile ECM, can detect submarines or surface vessels over long ranges, track several different targets simultaneously, and present a clutter-free display to the operators in the tactical compartment. The AQS-901 acoustics processing and display systems (also computer-based) are believed to be the most advanced in the world, and are compatible not only with all NATO sensors but also the new Australian Barra buoy. Communications include twin HF transceivers and teletype/encryption system. The crew complement remains unchanged, comprising two pilots, two navigators, flight engineer, radio operator, radar operator, two sonics systems operators, another for the ECM/MAD installations, plus two observers whose job also includes loading the sonobuoy and marker launchers. A galley, eating and rest areas are provided in the centre fuselage. Nimrods are expected to serve well into the 1990s, and in many respects the MR.2 is superior to all other similar platforms.

Type: anti-submarine patrol, anti-shipping strike and electronic reconnaissance aircraft
Powerplant: four 12,140-lb (5507-kg) Rolls-Royce Spey 250 turbofans
Performance: maximum speed 575 mph (926 km/h); maximum transit speed 547 mph (880 km/h); economical transit speed 490 mph (787 km/h); typical patrol speed at low level (on two engines) 230 mph (370 km/h); typical mission endurance 12 hours; typical ferry

range 5,755 miles (9265 km); normal operational ceiling 42,000 ft (12800 m)
Weights: typical empty 86,000 lb (39010 kg); normal maximum take-off 177,500 lb (80510 kg); maximum overload take-off 192,000 lb (87090 kg); typical landing 120,000 lb (54430 kg)
Dimensions: span 114 ft 10 in (35.00 m); length (except R.1) 126 ft 9 in (38.63 m); length (R.1) 118 ft 0 in (35.97 m); height 29 ft 8½ in (9.08 m); wing area 2,121 sq ft (197.05 m²)
Armament: wide variety of ASW weapons, in six lateral rows, in 48 ft 6 in (14.78 m) long ventral bay; these may include up to nine torpedoes plus depth charges, or combinations of mines, bombs, depth charges or nuclear weapons of various sizes; alternatively, weapons bay can be occupied by up to 15,100 lb (6849 kg) of auxiliary fuel in six supplementary tanks, or by a combination of weapons and fuel. Bay for sonobuoys and launchers in rear of pressurized fuselage. Hardpoint under each wing for mine, gun pod or rocket pod, or (if required, though currently deleted from RAF aircraft) an air-to-surface missile
Operator: UK

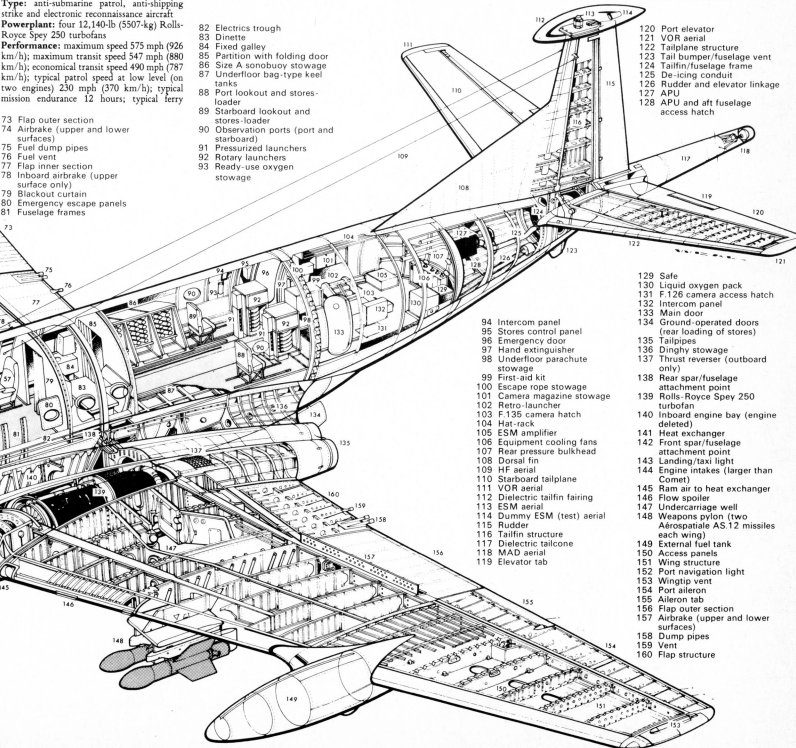

The watcher watched, as BAe Nimrod MR.1 XV246 is photographed (in colour) whilst itself photographing the Soviet ASW helicopter cruiser *Leningrad* (in black and white). The date was March 1972 when both Nimrod and ship were relatively new and immature.

73 Flap outer section
74 Airbrake (upper and lower surfaces)
75 Fuel dump pipes
76 Fuel vent
77 Flap inner section
78 Inboard airbrake (upper surface only)
79 Blackout curtain
80 Emergency escape panels
81 Fuselage frames

82 Electrics trough
83 Dinette
84 Fixed galley
85 Partition with folding door
86 Size A sonobuoy stowage
87 Underfloor bag-type keel tanks
88 Port lookout and stores-loader
89 Starboard lookout and stores-loader
90 Observation ports (port and starboard)
91 Pressurized launchers
92 Rotary launchers
93 Ready-use oxygen stowage

94 Intercom panel
95 Stores control panel
96 Emergency door
97 Hand extinguisher
98 Underfloor parachute stowage
99 First-aid kit
100 Escape rope stowage
101 Camera magazine stowage
102 Retro-launcher
103 F.135 camera hatch
104 Hat-rack
105 ESM amplifier
106 Equipment cooling fans
107 Rear pressure bulkhead
108 Dorsal fin
109 HF aerial
110 Starboard tailplane
111 VOR aerial
112 Dielectric tailfin fairing
113 ESM aerial
114 Dummy ESM (test) aerial
115 Rudder
116 Tailfin structure
117 Dielectric tailcone
118 MAD aerial
119 Elevator tab

120 Port elevator
121 VOR aerial
122 Tailplane structure
123 Tail bumper/fuselage vent
124 Tailfin/fuselage frame
125 De-icing conduit
126 Rudder and elevator linkage
127 APU
128 APU and aft fuselage access hatch

129 Safe
130 Liquid oxygen pack
131 F.126 camera access hatch
132 Intercom panel
133 Main door
134 Ground-operated doors (rear loading of stores)
135 Tailpipes
136 Dinghy stowage
137 Thrust reverser (outboard only)
138 Rear spar/fuselage attachment point
139 Rolls-Royce Spey 250 turbofan
140 Inboard engine bay (engine deleted)
141 Heat exchanger
142 Front spar/fuselage attachment point
143 Landing/taxi light
144 Engine intakes (larger than Comet)
145 Ram air to heat exchanger
146 Flow spoiler
147 Undercarriage well
148 Weapons pylon (two Aérospatiale AS.12 missiles each wing)
149 External fuel tank
150 Access panels
151 Wing structure
152 Port navigation light
153 Wingtip vent
154 Port aileron
155 Aileron tab
156 Flap outer section
157 Airbrake (upper and lower surfaces)
158 Dump pipes
159 Vent
160 Flap structure

British Aerospace (Hawker Siddeley) Nimrod AEW.3

Detailed studies for an AEW (airborne early warning) version of the Hawker Siddeley Nimrod began in 1973, to replace the RAF's Avro Shackletons in a role now recognised as vital to the defence of the United Kingdom. The capacious fuselage and ample reserve of power in the standard MR versions of this aircraft give it considerable potential for carrying alternative equipment and performing other duties. After much deliberation whether or not to participate in a controversial NATO plan to buy the Boeing E-3A, the British government decided in March 1977 to finance instead a developed version of the Hawker Siddeley (now British Aerospace) Nimrod. This has enabled the design to be tailored to British needs, instead of the overall European defence network centred on West Germany. In particular, the Nimrod AEW.3 is designed for superior performance over sea areas.

In terms of outward appearance, the AEW.3 violates even further the good looks of the original de Havilland Comet design, chiefly through the appearance, at each end of the fuselage, of a grotesquely swollen radome. These contain the front and rear 8 ft by 8 ft (2.44 m by 2.44 m) phased-array scanners for a new Marconi radar system, designed specifically for this platform to fulfil the basic over-water mission, but compatible also with the air defence requirements of central Europe. Because of their fore-and-aft location, the scanners' efficiency is not obscured by other parts of the airframe, as is the case with the dorsally-mounted radar of the American Grumman E-2C or E-3A. An on-board digital computer controls the flow of data from the

scanners (target range, speed, and other data), and also correlates this information with a control station on the ground. The scanners, which are interfaced with the Nimrod's IFF (identification, friend or foe) system, are also part of a pulse-Doppler radar installation capable of ship surveillance as well as aircraft detection, and highly resistant to electronic jamming. Thus, despite its AEW designation, the Nimrod's function could more accurately be defined by the AWACS (airborne warning and control system) description applied by the Americans to the Boeing E-3A. The Nimrod's systems can detect, track and classify aircraft, missiles or ships; control an interceptor fighter force; direct retaliatory strike aircraft; serve as an airborne air traffic control centre; or manage a search and rescue operation.

The other outward sign of change in the Nimrod AEW.3 is the presence at each wingtip of a pod containing electronic support measures (ESM) equipment. Internally, the sophisticated detection/tracking/classification gear goes hand in hand with dual inertial navigation systems; tactical situation displays (six consoles); UHF, HF, U/VHF and LF communications; a flight director; plus many other electronic aids.

As an aerodynamic prototype, a Comet 4C was converted at Woodford, and this made its first flight on 28 June 1977, sporting the forward (nose-mounted) radome only. Two other development aircraft, the first of which was due to fly in 1979, have been set aside from the supplementary batch of eight Nimrods originally ordered as MR.1s in 1972. Subject to satisfactory evaluation programmes

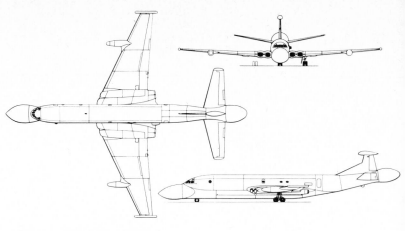

British Aerospace Nimrod AEW.3

for both the aircraft and the various on-board avionics packages, it is intended to procure an initial quantity of 11 production AEW.3s for the RAF, for entry into service during the early 1980s. These will be produced by the conversion of existing Nimrod airframes rather than as new-production machines, and will replace the ageing Shackleton AEW.2s, which currently equip No 8 Squadron, from about 1982 onwards.

Type: airborne early warning and control aircraft
Powerplant: four 12,140-lb (5507-kg) Rolls-Royce Spey 250 turbofans
Performance: endurance more than 10 hours; no other figures released officially, but likely to differ only marginally from MR versions
Weights: no details released
Dimensions: span over ESM pods 115 ft 1 in (35.08 m); length 137 ft 5½ in (41.76 m); height 33 ft 0 in (10.06 m); wing area 2,121 sq ft (197.05 m²)
Armament: none
Operator: under development for UK

British Aerospace (BAC) One Eleven

Announced in May 1961, the BAC (British Aircraft Corporation) One-Eleven twin-jet airliner was ordered straight from the drawing board by British United Airways and the first production models were designated Srs 200.

The prototype made its maiden flight on 20 August, 1963, followed by the first production aircraft, a Model 201, on 19 December, 1963. It should be explained that within the Series group individual Model numbers were allocated to each customer. By 1972, orders for 56 aircraft had been received and the type had broken into the US market with an order by Braniff for 14 Model 203s, followed by 18 Model 204s and three Model 215s for Mohawk Airlines, and 30 of the 400-series for American Airlines.

Two Model 217s were supplied to the Royal Australian Air Force as executive transports and are in service with No 34 (VIP) Squadron at Fairbairn, Canberra, for government transport and liaison. In Mexico, a One-Eleven serves alongside a Boeing 727, Lockheed JetStar, BAe (HS) 125 and Fokker F.27 plus several older aircraft, with the *Escuadron de Transport Presidencial* at Mexico City. Two Model 423s supplied to the Brazilian air force have since been sold to the Ford Motor Company in the UK for their private services within Europe.

On 27 August, 1970, BAC's Srs 400/500 One-Eleven development aircraft G-ASYD flew as the prototype for the Srs 475. This variant has the standard Srs 400 fuselage with

the wings and powerplant of the heavier Srs 500. The undercarriage has been modified to use low-pressure tyres for operation from runways with poor surfaces and low strength. First orders for the Srs 475 came from civil operators — Faucett of Peru took two Model 476s, Air Pacific two Model 479s and Air Malawi one Model 481.

The Srs 475 production received a boost when the Sultan of Oman's Air Force ordered three in June 1974. These replaced Viscounts and are in service with No 4 Squadron at Seeb Airport, Muscat. All three are fitted with a wide cargo door forward of the wing and have quick-change passenger/cargo interior configuration.

About 220 One-Elevens have been ordered to date and there is an agreement with Romania under which about 80 Srs 475s and 500s will be built under licence by Grupul Aeronautic Bucuresti (Bucharest Aircraft Group). Some of these may go to military customers. Standard seating is for 89 passengers.

Type: twin-jet commercial airliner
Powerplant: two 12,550-lb (5692-kg) Rolls-Royce Spey 512 DW turbofans
Performance: (Srs 475) maximum cruising speed at 21,000 ft (6400 m) 541 mph (871 km/h) at maximum take-off weight; take-off distance at sea level (maximum weight) 5,290 ft (1612 m); landing distance at sea level (maximum weight) 4,720 ft (1439 m); landing run at sea level (maximum

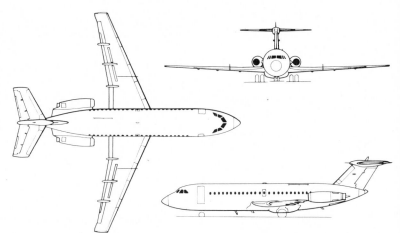

British Aerospace One Eleven 475

weight) 2,710 ft (826 m); range with maximum fuel and reserves for 230 miles (370 km), diversion and 45-minute hold 2,285 miles (3677 km)
Weights: (Srs 475) basic operating 51,731 lb (23464 kg); maximum take-off 98,500 lb (44678 kg); maximum landing 87,000 lb (39462 kg); maximum ramp 92,500 lb (41957 kg); maximum zero-fuel 73,000 lb (33112 kg)
Dimensions: (Srs 475) span 93 ft 6 in

(28.50 m); length 93 ft 6 in (28.50 m); height 24 ft 6 in (7.47 m); wing area 1,031 sq ft (95.78 m²)
Operators: Australia, Mexico, Oman

British Aerospace (Hunting) Pembroke/Sea Prince

First flown in 1948, the Percival Prince was a high-wing feederliner transport, but its suitability for military training and communications work was evident. The Pembroke, its military counterpart, made its maiden flight in November 1952. Major differences included an 8 ft 6 in (2.6 m) increase in span, reinforced floor and strengthened twin-wheel main gears.

The RAF received 44 Pembroke C.1 staff transports, for up to eight passengers, production ceasing in 1958. The generous ground clearance afforded the propellers by the high wing, together with the sturdy tricycle landing gear, permitted operation from unprepared airstrips inaccessible even to its predecessor, the Avro Anson.

Six Pembroke C-(PR).1, with fuselage-

mounted cameras, were supplied to the RAF for photo-reconnaissance in 1956. These saw extensive service in Malaya with No 81 Squadron. Twelve similar aircraft were supplied to the Belgian air force, the first of several foreign customers, which included the air arms of Sweden, Denmark and Finland. A small number of transport Pembrokes was also diverted by the RAF to the Royal Rhodesian Air Force. The major overseas operator was the *Luftwaffe*, which had 33 freighter, ambulance, survey and crew-training aircraft. The Royal Navy Sea Prince C.1 communications aircraft was similar to the civil Prince II. The four ordered in 1951 were followed by 42 larger T.1 'flying classrooms', with provision for three trainee radar operators apiece. The final naval variant was the Sea Prince C.2

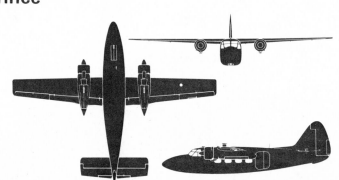

British Aerospace Pembroke/Sea Prince C.2

passenger transport.

By 1979 the only Pembrokes known to be in first-line squadron service were a small number on the strength of RAF Germany. Flying with No 60 Sqn from Wildenrath, they carry out regular communications flights to West Berlin and between RAF installations in West Germany. All have had to be re-sparred by British Aerospace to prolong safe airframe life. The Royal Navy's Sea Prince trainers have been superseded by BAe Jetstreams.

Type: staff transport, light freighter and utility aircraft
Powerplant: two 540-hp (403-kW) Alvis Leonides 127 radial engines
Performance: maximum speed at 2,000 ft (610 m) 220 mph (354 km/h); cruising speed at 8,000 ft (2440 m) 150 mph (241 km/h); range at 150 mph (241 km/h) at 8,000 ft (2440 m) 1,030 miles (1657 km); service ceiling 22,000 ft (6070 m); initial rate of climb 1,500 ft (457 m) per minute
Weights: empty equipped 8,970 lb (4068 km); loaded 13,000 lb (5900 kg)
Dimensions: span 64 ft 6 in (19.6 m); length 46 ft 0 in (14.0 m); height 16 ft 1 in (4.9 m); wing area 400 sq ft (37.16 m²)
Armament: none
Operator: UK

British Aerospace Sea Harrier

In 1969, watching a Harrier taking off vertically from the aft platform of the USS *Coronado,* a US admiral is reported to have said: 'You Brits gave us the angled deck, the mirror sight and the steam catapult — and now you've taken them all away!' The admiral had a point; conversely, it is just as well for the Royal Navy, which has seen its aircraft-carrier force eroded away to nothing by successive governments over the past two decades, that Britain developed the BAe (HS) Harrier. Not only has this unique warplane revolutionised land-based tactical combat techniques, but its ability to operate from aft-platform warships, as well as aircraft-carriers, has introduced a new factor into the tactics of naval warfare.

Harriers and their predecessors have carried out innumerable trials and demonstrations from a wide variety of warships over the past 17 years. With the Royal Navy and the US Marine Corps both keenly interested in an advanced version for their own use it was naturally hoped that such a variant could be evolved as a joint effort with McDonnell Douglas, Hawker Siddeley's American licensee. Unfortunately, the British government decided in 1975 that there was 'not enough common ground' between the two requirements, and declined to participate. Britain then decided to go it alone in developing a Harrier variant for the Royal Navy. Although this does not incorporate a new wing, as does the McDonnell Douglas AV-8B, it offers significant improvements in operational capability compared with the Harriers of the Royal Air Force.

Most significant change is a completely new forward fuselage with a higher cockpit giving more avionic and panel space, and all-round pilot view for combat. In the nose is the Ferranti Blue Fox multi-mode radar, which folds 180° to the left for shipboard stowage. The radar was air-tested in two Hawker Hunter T.8s, and gives the Sea Harrier both air-to-air interception and air-to-surface capability. Other upgraded avionics include Decca Doppler radar, digital navigation and weapon-aiming computers, comprehensive ECM (electronic countermeasures) including ARI.18223 in the fin, plus a pilot's head-up display. Designated FRS.1 (fighter/reconnaissance/strike), the Sea Harrier can carry the full range of weapons or surveillance equipment available for the land-based version, plus a pair of AIM-9L Sidewinders for air-to-air combat, and various precision air-to-surface weapons.

Thirty-four Sea Harriers have so far been ordered for the Royal Navy, destined for Nos 800, 801 and 802 Squadrons of the Fleet Air Arm, to serve principally in the new 'Invincible' class of command cruisers, with five Harriers to each ship. The former carrier HMS *Hermes,* now classified as an LPH (landing platform, helicopters), will also operate Sea Harriers. No aircraft, however, can carry its maximum payload from its minimum take-off run, and to increase payload capability and pilot safety in the event of engine failure, and also to provide additional lift to overcome wind-over-the-deck problems, the cruiser-based Sea Harriers will operate from a 'ski-jump', a curving 7° ramp located at the forward end of the take-off area.

No prototypes of the Sea Harrier were considered necessary, the initial flight being made on 20 August 1978 by the first production example. Entry into Fleet Air Arm service is scheduled for late 1979 or early 1980. During 1978 the Indian navy, whose Hawker Sea Hawk carrier fighters are long overdue for replacement, placed an order for 10 Sea Harriers; these will be operated from the carrier INS *Vikrant.* Several further possible orders were being negotiated in 1979.

Type: single-seat shipboard fighter/reconnaissance/strike aircraft
Powerplant: one 21,500-lb (9752-kg) Rolls-Royce Pegasus 104 vectored-thrust turbofan
Performance: no details released, but generally similar to Harrier GR.3
Weights: approximately the same as the Harrier GR.3
Dimensions: span 25 ft 3¼ in (7.70 m); length 47 ft 7 in (14.50 m); length (nose folded) 42 ft 3 in (12.88 m); height 12 ft 2 in (3.71 m)
Armament: same as for Harrier GR.3, plus

British Aerospace Sea Harrier FRS.1

provision for carrying two AIM-9L Sidewinder infra-red homing missiles and/or two air-to-surface missiles under wings
Operators: on order for India, UK

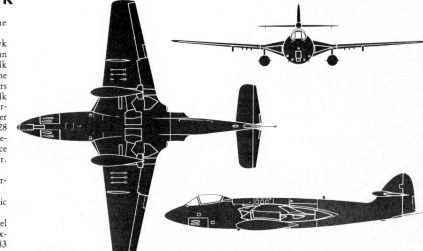

The Royal Navy Sea Harrier FRS.1 is certain to sustain an important manufacturing programme extending into the next century, despite the fact it is starting off with the same wing and other limitations of the original Harrier. The front end is wholly new.

British Aerospace (Hawker/AW) Sea Hawk

Aesthetically one of the most appealing of Sydney Camm's early jet fighters, the Hawker-built prototypes of the Sea Hawk were completed to Specification N.7/46, and the first of three was flown on 2 September 1947. Hawker subsequently built 35 Sea Hawk F.1s before transferring all future development and production to Armstrong Whitworth. A further 60 F.1s and 40 F.2s were produced by that company, which then introduced the FB.3 fighter-bomber, with a stronger wing to carry external stores. Production of 116 FB.3s was followed by 97 FGA.4s (fighter/ground-attack), all models up to this point having a 5,000-lb (2268-kg) Nene 101 engine with twin nozzles, allowing fuel to be carried in the rear fuselage. Conversion of some Mk 3s to the Nene 103 produced the FB.5, and production for the Royal Navy ended with 86 FGA.6s, with the Nene 103 but otherwise similar to the Mk 4. (The specification refers to the Mk 6.) The Sea Hawk served with the Royal Navy until the end of 1960, and 22 export Mk 50s with the Royal Netherlands Navy until the end of 1964. The other major export versions were the Mk 100 and all-weather Mk 101 ordered by the West German Marineflieger. They were similar to the FGA.6 but for a taller fin and rudder and, on the Mk 101, an Ekco Type 34 search radar in a pod under the starboard wing. Operated from shore bases, they were replaced by Lockheed F-104G Starfighters in the mid-1960s.

Sole remaining operator of the Sea Hawk today is the Indian navy, which in the autumn of 1959 ordered 24 aircraft similar to the Mk 6. Some of these were new-built (although the production line had closed some three years earlier), the rest being refurbished ex-RN Mk 6s. They equipped No 300 Squadron in the aircraft carrier INS *Vikrant* and were joined later by 12 more ex-RN Mk 4s and Mk 6s, plus 28 Mk 100/101s from Germany. A score or so remain in service, the intention being to replace them in the 1980s with the BAe Sea Harrier.

Type: single-seat shipboard fighter/attack aircraft
Powerplant: one 5,400-lb (2449-kg) static thrust Rolls-Royce Nene Mk 103 turbojet
Performance: maximum speed at sea level Mach 0.79 or 602 mph (969 km/h); maximum speed at 20,000 ft (6100 m) Mach 0.83 or 587 mph (945 km/h); combat radius (clean) 230 miles (370 km); combat radius with two 500-lb (227-kg) bombs and two 90-gallon (409-litre) drop-tanks 288 miles (463 km); maximum rate of climb at sea level 5,700 ft (1737 m) per minute; time to 35,000 ft (10670 m) 11 minutes 50 seconds; service ceiling 44,500 ft (13565 m)
Weights: empty 9,720 lb (4409 kg); take-off with two 90-gallon (409-litre) drop-tanks 15,198 lb (6894 kg); maximum take-off 16,200 lb (7348 kg)
Dimensions: span 39 ft 0 in (11.89 m); span folded 13 ft 4 in (4.06 m); length 39 ft 8 in (12.09 m); height 8 ft 8 in (2.64 m); wing area 278.0 sq ft (25.83 m²)
Armament: four 20-mm Hispano cannon in

British Aerospace Sea Hawk FGA.6

nose, with 200 rounds per gun; underwing points for four 500-lb (227-kg) bombs; or two 500-g (227-kg) bombs plus twenty 3-in (76-mm) or sixteen 5-in (127-mm) rockets; or two AIM-9 Sidewinder air-to-air missiles; or four 90-gallon (409-litre) drop-tanks
Operators: India

British Aerospace (Avro) Shackleton MR.3

Although anachronistic alongside modern jet equipment, the BAe (Avro) Shackleton continues to fill an important role in maritime protection and patrol. The ancestry of the aircraft stems back to the Avro Type 696, a variant of the Lincoln bomber designed for maritime reconnaissance. The MR.3 is, as its designation suggests, the third (and final) variation on the theme. It supersedes the MR.2, itself an improved version of the MR.1 with a longer, more streamlined nose, sharper tail and ventral radar mounted in a retractable 'dustbin' aft of the wings. Distinguishing features of the MR.3 include wingtip tanks, a tricycle undercarriage, deletion of the mid-upper turret and numerous other detail refinements.

The first MR.3 flew on 2 September 1955, on the eve of that year's SBAC display at Farnborough. It pioneered the battleship-grey paint scheme subsequently adopted for all the marks, and also introduced a few creature comforts for the crew, which in previous versions had had to suffer interminable hours of throbbing from the Rolls-Royce Griffon engines. A sound-proofed wardroom allowed some form of retreat on long patrols, the record duration for which was set by an aircraft of No 206 Sqn in February 1959: it stayed aloft for an impressive 24 hours 21 minutes patrolling the Canary Islands. Although endurance had always been a strong point of the Shackleton, the MR.3 introduced

yet more tankage, raising total capacity to 4,248 gallons (19285 litres). The increased gross weight called not only for a modified undercarriage — the MR.3 rolls on four main landing wheels and a twin nosewheel — but also for more power. The rating of the Griffon piston engines had remained unchanged throughout development of the airframe; at 2,455 hp (1831 kW) each, they were put under some strain in the MR.3, and in 1966 most of the RAF aircraft were updated to Series 3 standard. This modification entailed fitting a 2,500-lb (1134-kg) thrust Rolls-Royce Viper 203 turbojet in the outer nacelle of each wing, taking some load off the Griffons on take-off and climb.

Entry into service was delayed by a number of factors, including a cutback in the production contract in March 1956. The need for an improved version had been recognised soon after the MR.1 entered service in 1951. Landplanes were taking over from flying-boats, putting great demand on range and endurance, but the MR.3 did not fly with Coastal Command until the end of 1957, some eight years after the Shackleton prototype had flown. First squadron to be equipped with the MR.3 was No 220. A total of 34 MR.3s were subsequently delivered to the RAF, the final example being handed over in June 1959. British Aerospace Nimrod MR.1/2s have now replaced the Shackletons, however, the older type having been progressively phased out

British Aerospace Shackleton MR.3

during the 1970s. South Africa, forced by a near-universal arms ban to make the most of what it already has, still operates seven MR.3s. Respurred to extend their useful lives, they fly from D.F.Malan Airport, Cape Town, with No 35 Sqn on long-range maritime patrol duties guarding the vital tanker route round the Cape of Good Hope.

Type: maritime reconnaissance/anti-shipping aircraft
Powerplant: four 2,455-hp (1831-kW) Rolls-Royce Griffon 57A piston engines plus (Series 3) two 2,500-lb (1134-kg) Rolls-Royce Viper 203 turbojets

Performance: maximum speed 302 mph (486 km/h); typical range at 200 mph (320 km/h) at 1,500 ft (460 m) 3,660 miles (5890 km); sea-level rate of climb 850 ft (260 m) per minute; service ceiling 19,200 ft (5850 m)
Weights: empty equipped 57,800 lb (26218 kg); maximum loaded 98,000 lb (44450 kg)
Dimensions: span 119 ft 10 in (36.5 m); length 92 ft 6 in (28.2 m); height 23 ft 4 in (7.1 m); wing area 1,421 sq ft (132.4 m²)
Armament: at least 10,000 lb (4536 kg) of depth charges, torpedoes or other weapons in belly bay; two 20-mm cannon in nose (gunner positioned above, bomb aimer below)
Operators: South Africa, UK

British Aerospace (Avro) Shackleton AEW.2

The airborne early-warning version of the verteran Avro Shackleton was developed in 1971 to provide the Royal Air Force with warning of low-level intruders in the UK air-defence region. It replaced the Westland (Fairey) Gannet AEW.3 which, with the run-down of aircraft-carrier operations, was left no seaborne base. The AEW Shackleton's APS-20F radar in the forward fuselage, with scanner in the chin position, was even older than the airframe, having served first in Douglas AD-4W Skyraiders and then in Gannet AEW.3s. Other changes included Orange Harvest electronic countermeasures and increased fuel capacity.

The first Shackleton AEW.2 flew from Woodford on 30 September 1971, and the 12 aircraft converted to the role entered service with No 8 Sqn in 1972, this unit having been formed in January of that year at Kinloss. Its aircraft named after characters in *The Magic Roundabout* television series, are the last survivors of this ageing design still in service with the RAF. The aircraft are now based at Lossiemouth and will be replaced by 11 British Aerospace AEW.3 Nimrods from 1982.

The AEW.2 normally carries a crew of nine, comprising captain, co-pilot, radio navigator, navigating navigator, engineer and four radar operators. There are three radar displays, so having a fourth operator allows a little flexibility and rest-time, no small consideration on a 12-hour mission. The Gannet, which the Shackleton replaced, had a normal mission endurance of about three hours, some two of which would have been on task, so two operators for its two scopes were adequate. The senior radar operator is the Tactical Co-ordinator (Tacco), who is responsible for seeing that the other operators, the equipment and the aircraft are used to the best effect tactically. Unlike its pioneer predecessors (used by the Americans from 1946), the updated APS-20F radar is ground-stabilized from the aircraft's doppler. It also differs in being north-stabilized. Lack of height finding equipment makes interception direction a somewhat harder task than it need be: the McDonnell Douglas Phantom, with more powerful radar than its RAF partner, the BAe (BAC) Lightning, is for this reason easier to direct. Apart from the Orange Harvest electronic countermeasures, limited in range and more suited to the maritime patrol role, the AEW Shackleton carries an APX-7 IFF (identification friend or foe) interrogator and both active and passive SIF (selective identification facility) operating through a coded pulse within the IFF signal. With the SIF in the active mode the operator can place a 'window' over a par-

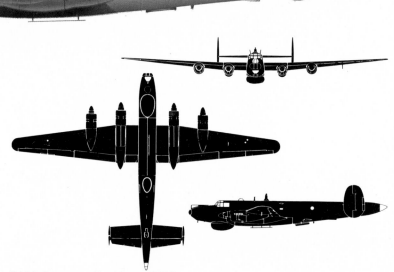

Avro Shackleton AEW Mk 2 of 8 Sqn, Royal Air Force, at RAF Lossiemouth.

ticular target; in the passive mode a particular interceptor liaising with a Shackleton would be the only aircraft tallying with all IFF returns. Radio includes two PTR 175 VHF/UHF, two R52 UHF and a pair of Collins 618T single-sideband HF sets. An airborne moving-target indicator fitted to the aircraft in 1974 cuts out returns from surface vessels when necessary.

Type: nine-seat airborne early-warning aircraft
Powerplant: four 2,455-hp (1816-kW) Rolls-Royce Griffon 57A liquid-cooled piston engines
Performance: maximum speed 272 mph (439 km/h); typical operating ceiling 20,000 ft (6100 m); rate of climb (initial) 850 ft (260 m) per minute; endurance 14 hours; range about 4,000 miles (6437 km)
Weights: empty 57,000 lb (25855 kg); gross 98,000 lb (44450 kg)
Dimensions: span 120 ft 0 in (36.58 m);

British Aerospace Shackleton AEW.2

length 87 ft 3 in (26.59 m); height 16 ft 9 in (5.1 m)

Armament: electronic countermeasures only
Operator: UK

An airborne early-warning Shackleton, WL 754 of No 8 Sqn, RAF, going out on patrol from Lossiemouth in August 1977. The Shackleton AEW.2 was a rebuild of an outdated MR patrol platform with a 'third-hand' radar previously used in the AD-4W and Gannet.

British Aerospace (BAC) Strikemaster

Although based on a 1950s design, the BAe (BAC) Strikemaster offers a number of air forces relatively cheap, effective firepower. It is derived from the Hunting (later BAC/British Aerospace) Jet Provost, which in turn was a radical development of the Percival Provost piston-engined basic trainer. The Jet Provost proved to be a highly successful trainer, selling in large numbers to the RAF and overseas air arms, and was progressively upgraded. The final versions are pressurized and more powerful. The next step was to give the aircraft teeth, and the BAC 145 was the first multi-role attack version. This was in turn refined to produce the relatively more sophisticated Strikemaster, a private-venture project which has side-by-side ejection seats and eight underwing hardpoints capable of carrying up to 3,000 lb (1360 kg) of stores. This ordnance capacity, coupled with the more powerful Viper Mk 535 turbojet engine, makes the Strikemaster particularly suitable for counter-insurgency combat operations, reconnaissance, and pilot and weapons training.

The first Strikemaster flew on 26 October 1967, and a total of 145 have since been sold. Ten more were built in 1978 against the possibility of new or repeat orders. The Strikemaster did, in fact, set a world record for repeat orders by export customers, so effective has it proved. Of the 16 Strikemaster Mk 89s bought by Ecuador, 14 survivors equip a strike/trainer unit. Ecuador is a good example of a re-order customer: its initial order covered eight aircraft but this was later increased to 12, delivery of which began in early 1973. Delivery of a further four was completed in July 1976. The Strikemaster is one of 29 types operated by the *Fuerza Aerea Ecuatoriana* and works alongside Cessna A-37s and Lockheed T-33As in the training and strike role. It is, probably more than any other factor, the Strikemaster's versatility and value for money which have made it so successful. It can operate from rough strips, lifting as much as a specialised bomber would have been carrying in the 1930s and delivering it at 400 + mph (640 + km/h). Until the announcement in 1977 of a $75 million order for Northrop F-5E/Fs, the Strikemaster, along with five BAe (HS) Hunter FGA.9s, was the Kenyan Air Force's most potent warplane. Five Mk 87s equip a strike/trainer unit, and these are soon to be supplemented by 12 BAe Hawks. Kuwait, with a firm commitment to protect its rich oil-fields, operates a modern and highly potent force and has a ready place for the Strikemaster. Of 12 aircraft originally bought in 1969 and 1971, nine Mk 83s equip a ground-attack squadron, operating alongside five Hunter T.67s. The Strikemaster is closely integrated into the Royal New Zealand Air Force, which operates 16 Mk 88s with No 14 Sqn at Ohakea. Delivery of the first 10 was completed in October 1972 and six more were ordered in the spring of 1974. They are used for operational strike training and advanced flying training as the next step up from the CT/4 Airtrainer. Oman, whose 10-year-old Dhofar conflict ended in 1976, has since its formation with British assistance in 1958 traditionally bought British, including 24 Strikemaster Mk 82/82As. Delivery of the first 12 Mk 82s was completed in December 1969, and 12 Mk 82As were handed over by July 1976. Twelve aircraft are still operating in the ground-attack and advanced training roles with No 1 Sqn at Salalah, with two held in reserve, and five were sold to Singapore early in 1977. Saudi Arabia bought 46 Strikemaster Mk 80/80As: No 9 Sqn is a purely basic jet

training unit, and No 11 Sqn operates in the weapon training role. A counter-insurgency squadron of the Sudanese Air Force flies three Mk 55s (BAC 145s).

Type: (BAC 167) two-seat light tactical support aircraft and trainer
Powerplant: one 3,410-lb (1547-kg) dry Rolls-Royce Viper 535 turbojet
Performance: maximum design speed 518 mph (834 km/h); maximum level speed at 18,000 ft (5485 m) (clean) 450 mph (724 km/h); combat radius with 3,000-lb (1360-kg) weapon load (lo-lo-lo, 5 minutes over target, 10% reserves) 145 miles (233 km); ferry range 1,615 miles (2600 km); initial climb (max fuel, clean) 5,250 ft (1600 m) per minute
Weights: empty equipped 6,195 lb (2810 kg); with two crew, full internal fuel and practice bombs and racks 10,600 lb (4808 kg); maximum allowed 11,500 lb (5215 kg)
Dimensions: span 36 ft 10 in (11.23 m); length 33 ft 8½ in (10.27 m); height 10 ft 11½ in (3.34 m); wing area 213.7 sq ft (19.85 m²)
Armament: Two 7.62-mm (0.3-in) FN machine-guns (fixed forward-firing, with 550

rounds each); underwing stores (maximum 3,000 lb/1361 kg) include two 75- and 50-Imperial gallon (341- and 227-litre) drop-tanks, four Matra launchers each containing 18 68-mm SNEB rockets, four LAU-68 seven-round rocket-launchers, four 540-lb (245-kg) ballistic or retarded bombs, four 551-lb (250-kg) or 1,102-lb (500-kg) bombs, 24 practice bombs, BAe/Vinten five-camera reconnaissance pod, or Sura 80-mm rockets.
Operators: Ecuador, Kenya, Kuwait, New Zealand, Oman, Saudi Arabia, Singapore, Sudan

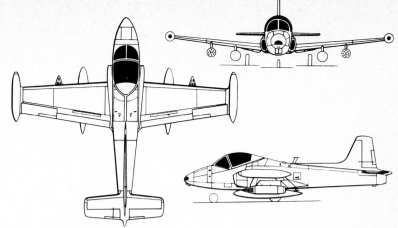

British Aerospace Strikemaster 167

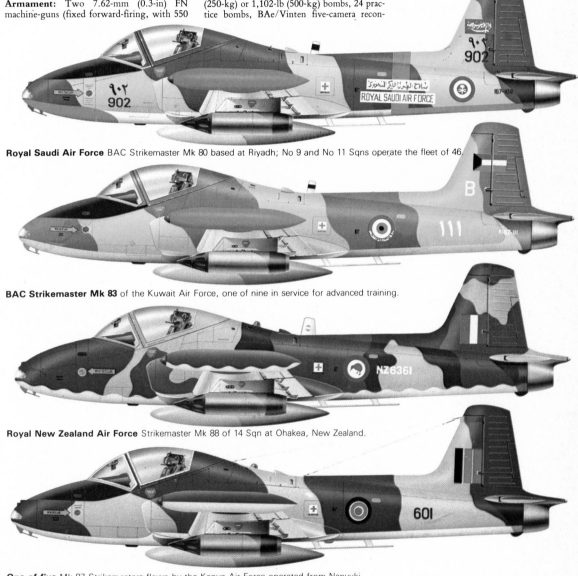

Royal Saudi Air Force BAC Strikemaster Mk 80 based at Riyadh; No 9 and No 11 Sqns operate the fleet of 46.

BAC Strikemaster Mk 83 of the Kuwait Air Force, one of nine in service for advanced training.

Royal New Zealand Air Force Strikemaster Mk 88 of 14 Sqn at Ohakea, New Zealand.

One of five Mk 87 Strikemasters flown by the Kenya Air Force operated from Nanyuki.

British Aerospace (Hawker Siddeley) Trident 2E

Design of the DH.121 Trident began in 1957, and construction started at the end of July 1959 to meet a British European Airways requirement for a short-range airliner. There was no prototype, and the first production Trident 1 for BEA flew on January 9, 1962.

A total of 117 Tridents of various marks were built, consisting of 24 Srs 1s, 15 Srs 1Es, 50 Srs 2Es, 26 Srs 3Bs and two Super 3Bs. The main foreign user is the People's Republic of China, which ordered 33 Trident 2Es and two

Super 3Bs; the last Trident built was a 2E for China, flown on 17 April 1978.

The 2E has accommodation for up to 115 passengers and, while no direct military deliveries were made, photographic evidence indicates that at least two 2Es have been transferred from CAAC, the Chinese airline, to the country's air force. This service also received four Trident 1Es from Pakistan International Airlines, one subsequently being lost in a crash. Another Chinese Trident was lost

in an accident in March 1979.

Type: medium-range passenger transport
Powerplant: three 11,900-lb (5425-kg) thrust Rolls-Royce Spey 512-5W turbofans
Performance: maximum design limit speed at maximum take-off weight M 0.95; cruising speed at 27,000 ft (8230 m) 605 mph (972 km/h), at 30,000 ft (9150 m) 596 mph (959 km/h); take-off with 21,378-lb (9697-kg) payload for 1,000-mile (1610-km) stage 6,400

ft (1950 m); range with maximum fuel and 16,520-lb (7493-kg) payload 2,500 miles (4025 km) with 250-mile (450-km) reserve and 45-minute hold at 15,000 ft (4570 m)
Weights: empty operating 73,200 lb (33203 kg); maximum take-off 144,000 lb (65315 kg)
Dimensions: span 98 ft 0 in (29.87 m); length 114 ft 9 in (34.97 m); height 27 ft 0 in (8.23 m); wing area 1,462 sq ft (15.82 m²)
Operators: China

British Aerospace (BAC) VC10 C.1

The Royal Air Force's BAe VC10 C.1 is a specially-modified variant of the VC10 civil transport. The first VC10 C.1 (Model 1106), 14 of which had been ordered for RAF Transport Command (now no 38 Group, RAF Strike Command), flew in November 1965. Deliveries to No 10 Sqn at RAF Brize Norton, Oxfordshire, began the following year.

The C.1 version is based on the standard (not Super) civil model, but incorporates a number of the improvements featured on the Super VC10. These include more powerful Conway engines, increased gross weight, and a 'wet' fin. Reversers are fitted on the outer engines, the leading edge is extended, the nose has a flight-refuelling probe, and an APU (Artouste 526) is fitted in the tailcone to provide ground power at remote locations.

The VC10 C.1 has a large cargo door on the left of the forward fuselage, and the strengthened floor has a 20-in (50-cm) grid of 10,000-lb (4500-kg) lashing points. In the trooping role, rearward-facing seats can accommodate up to 150, though a 125-seat layout is usual on scheduled flights. In the casevac role, up to 78 stretcher patients can be carried, but an alternative layout, more appropriate to peacetime needs, provides for nine stretcher cases and 61 seated patients. Cargo capacity is 54,000 lb (24495 kg).

The wing has a 32° 30' sweepback at quarter chord. Fowler flaps are fitted, and slats extend over the major part of the leading edge. Spoilers on the upper surface also serve as air-brakes.

When the VC10 began to operate with No 10 Sqn, British defence commitments were worldwide, with significant forces stationed in the Far East and Persian Gulf. However, in January 1968 a Defence White Paper announced drastic cuts in the resources of all three services and the withdrawal of most forces stationed outside Europe. Consequently the importance of the strategic transport role diminished. RAF Transport Command became Air Support Command in 1967, and five years later the formation was reduced to Group status within RAF Strike Command.

Nevertheless, a strategic airlift capability has been found vital. Relief operations and the evacuation of British citizens from trouble spots highlight the need for an intercontinental air transport force. Among recent such operations in which RAF VC10s have participated are the evacuation of over 13,000 civilians from war-torn Cyprus in July 1974, the evacuation of 5,700 people from Angola in October the following year, the reinforcement of the British garrison in Belize when that country was threatened by invasion from neighbouring Guatemala in 1977, and the evacuation of British citizens from Iran in early 1979.

Currently 11 VC10 C.1s are on the strength of No 10 Sqn, each named in honour of a British airman awarded the Victoria Cross.

Type: long-range strategic transport
Powerplant: four 21,800-lb (9890-kg) Rolls-Royce Conway Mk 250 turbofans
Performance: cruising speed at 38,000 ft (11600 m) 550 mph (886 km/h); rate of climb at sea level 3,050 ft (930 m) per minute; range with maximum fuel 7,128 miles (11470 km); range with maximum payload 4,720 miles (7600 km)
Weights: maximum take-off 323,000 lb (146500 kg); maximum landing 225,000 lb (102100 kg)
Dimensions: span 146 ft 2 in (44.55 m); length 158 ft 8 in (48.36 m); height 39 ft 6 in (12.04 m); wing area 2,932 sq ft (272.4 m²)
Operator: UK

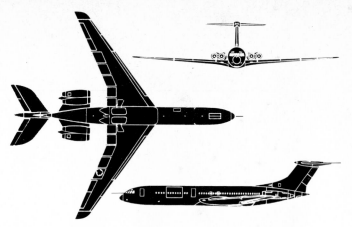

British Aerospace VC10 C.1

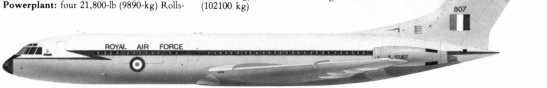

Royal Air Force BAC VC10 of 10 Sqn at Brize Norton, Oxon, used for long-range transport flight.

British Aerospace VC10 Tanker

The RAF followed the United States's lead in air-to-air refuelling by converting 45 Vickers Valiant jet bombers to perform this role from 1958, but the Handley Page Victor, again a former mainstay of Britain's nuclear V-force, took over the refuelling role in the mid-1960s. By the late 1970s, when the Victors were beginning to be worn out, the RAF was obliged to consider types to supplement and eventually replace them.

The aircraft chosen was the BAe (BAC) VC10. No stranger to RAF service, the type had entered service with Transport (later Air Support) Command in mid-1966 with No 10 Squadron. The VC10 is the heaviest aircraft to be flown by the RAF, and can carry a full payload of 150 troops for 3,650 miles (5870 km) without refuelling. Between 1959 and 1961 Vickers had undertaken design studies which had included tanker, maritime reconnaissance and bomber variants of the basic design, but only the transport was proceeded with. In addition to the RAF's 14 aircraft, some 40 VC10s saw service with civil operators.

Ten aircraft were earmarked for conversion to tanker configuration: six VC10s and four larger Super VC10s acquired from East African Airways. These former airliners are being converted at Filton by the BAe Aircraft Group and will enter service alongside the Victor K.2 aircraft of Nos 55 and 57 Squadrons at RAF Marham, Norfolk from 1980. Each will have three hose-reels, additional tanks for transfer fuel, cargo floor and doors, and extensive military avionics. One of the chief tasks of these aircraft will be refuelling support of the Panavia Tornado F.2.

An important additional factor behind the programme is the rumoured development by the Soviet Union of a new long-range missile to be carried by variable-geometry Tupolev 'Backfire' bombers. To counter this threat, the limited range of the RAF's air defence fighters must be increased: it is anticipated that the VC10s will play a crucial role in permitting earlier interceptions to be made.

Details of the VC10 Tanker were classified at the time of writing: the data below therefore refers to the original Super VC10.

Type: long-range transport
Powerplant: four 22,500-lb (10200-kg) Rolls-Royce Conway 550 turbofans
Performance: maximum cruising speed at 38,000 ft (11580 m) 568 mph (914 km/h); range with maximum payload at 550 mph (885 km/h) 4,630 miles (7450 km)
Weights: empty 149,000 lb (67130 kg); loaded 335,000 lb (151950 kg)
Dimensions: span 146 ft 2 in (44.55 m); length 171 ft 8 in (52.32 m); height 39 ft 6 in (12.04 m); wing area 2,932 sq ft (272.4 m²)
Armament: none
Operators: UK

British Aerospace (Handley Page) Victor K.2

One of two bombers designed around Specification B.35/46, the Handley Page HP.80 Victor was the last of the V-bombers to enter service with the Royal Air Force. The Avro Vulcan, to the same requirements, had become operational in mid-1956. Technically highly advanced for its time, the Victor was designed to operate fast and high, above virtually all known defences. As it turned out, when the aircraft did finally enter service in 1956 after a lengthy development phase, it had been overtaken by fighters and missiles capable of interception at its designed operating altitudes.

A crescent-shaped wing was chosen to allow the highest possible cruise Mach number. Four Armstrong Siddeley Sapphire 200-series turbojets, buried in the sharply swept root, powered the Victor B.1. Construction was primarily of light-alloy double-skin sandwich with either corrugated or honeycomb filling. It was the B.1 which was first offered to the RAF, but in the light of its reduced effectiveness the service later demanded better protection. Eventually 50 of the resulting version, redesignated B.1A, were operated; they were fitted with more sophisticated electronic countermeasures (ECM) housed in the rear fuselage and were generally better equipped.

In 1964 Handley Page was contracted to convert the remaining B.1/1As into probe-and-drogue flight-refuelling tankers for the RAF. Operational aircraft were fitted with a Flight Refuelling Mk 20b pod under each wing to replenish high-speed tactical aircraft and fighters. A Flight Refuelling Mk 17 hose drum in the rear of the bomb bay supplied bombers and transport aircraft. To raise capacity, two extra fuel tanks were fitted in the remainder of the bomb bay, which could be modified quickly to retain bombing capability as necessary. The first six tankers, designated K.1/1A, carried only the under-wing refuelling points, and these aircraft entered service with No 55 Sqn at Marham in August 1965. In 18 months of trials the six K.1s transferred 6,718,700 lb (3044914 kg) of fuel in 10,646 real and practice refuelling contacts and participated in nearly 40 overseas exercises. Two BAC Lightning fighters could be supplied simultaneously at the rate of 150 Imperial gallons (680 litres) per minute. Nos 57 and 214 Sqns were equipped with three-point K.1As, and No 55 Sqn received its first improved models in the spring of 1967.

British Aerospace Victor K.2

Royal Air Force Handley Page Victor K. Mk 2 tanker aircraft of 55 Sqn, RAF Marham, Norfolk.

By 1954 design was in hand on the Victor Mark 2, and the first B.2 flew on 20 February 1959. This larger version was much heavier and more powerful, the engines being 20,600-lb (9344-kg) Rolls-Royce Conway 201 turbofans. Changes compared with the Mk 1 included greater span, larger air intakes, a dorsal fillet forward of the fin and a retractable scoop on each fuselage side to supply two turbo-alternators for the totally new electrical system. A Turboméca Artouste turbine in the starboard wing root drove the APU (Auxiliary Power Unit) which also supplied ground power. Armament was the Hawker Siddeley Blue Steel stand-off bomb (air-to-surface missile), which became operational in February 1964 with No 139 Sqn at Wittering. Two years earlier this squadron had been also the first unit to receive the updated Victor. Although considerably improved, the Victor B.2 was no less vulnerable at height, and the aircraft's role was changed to include low-level attack, and only 34 were built, 22 being cancelled.

The Victor SR.2, a strategic reconnaissance version of the Victor B.2, had the primary role of high-altitude maritime reconnaissance. A single aircraft could radar-map the entire Mediterranean in one seven-hour sortie, and four could map the North Atlantic in six hours. Photoflash bombs allowed night operations. Despite its bulk, a production Victor B.1 exceeded Mach 1 in a shallow dive in 1957, and routine high-speed flights included England to Malta in two hours (655 mph/1050 km/h), and an Atlantic crossing in three hours eight minutes (644 mph/1030 km/h). A number of Victor B.2s were converted to the strategic reconnaissance role, but 24 K.2 tanker conversions of the B.2 are now serving with Nos 55 and 57 Sqns and 232 OCU at Marham. The K.2 is a complete rebuild, by British Aerospace at Woodford, with three hose-reels and reduced span.

Type: five-seat strategic bomber (B.1/1A, B.2); four-seat flight-refuelling tanker (K.1A, K.2).
Powerplant: four 11,000-lb (4990 kg) Armstrong Siddeley Sapphire 202 turbojets (Mk 1/1A); four 20,600-lb (9344-kg) Conway 201

The BAe (Handley Page) Victor K.2 is the RAF's standard air-refuelling tanker, seen here serving with No 55 Sqn from Marham and refuelling a Jaguar GR.1 of No 54 Sqn in March 1978. Ex-civil VC10 and Super VC10 transports are being rebuilt for the tanker role.

turbofans (B.2, SR.2, K.2)
Performance: maximum speed (both marks) 640 mph (1030 km/h) or Mach 0.92 at 40,000 ft (12192 m); maximum cruising height 45,000 ft (13700 m) (Mk 1), 55,000 ft (16750 m) (Mk 2); combat radius (Mk 2) 1,725 miles (2780 km) at high/low level, 2,300 miles (3700 km) at high level, 4,600 miles (7400 km) with flight-refuelling

Weights: empty 79,000 lb (35834 kg) (Mk 1), 91,000 lb (41,277 kg) (Mk 2); maximum take-off 180,000 lb (81650 kg) (Mk 1), 233,000 lb (101150 kg) (Mk 2)
Dimensions: span 110 ft 0 in (33.53 m) (B.1), 120 ft 0 in (36.58 m) (B.2), 117 ft 0 in (35.7 m) (K.2); length 114 ft 11 in (35.05 m); height 28 ft 1½ in (8.59 m) (Mk 1), 30 ft 1½ in (9.2 m) (Mk 2); wing area 2,406 sq ft

(223.5 m²) (Mk 1), 2,597 sq ft (241.3 m²) (Mk 2)
Armament: internal bay for various nuclear or conventional weapons, including up to 35 1,000-lb (454-kg) bombs; one Blue Steel Mk 1 air-to-surface missile semi-recessed beneath fuselage (B.2); electronic countermeasures; no armament on tankers
Operators: UK

British Aerospace (Hawker Siddeley/Avro) Vulcan

To carry out the strategic bombing of Germany during World War II, Britain developed a trio of four-engined bombers, of which the Handley Page Halifax and Avro Lancaster were the star performers. When, in 1946, the air staff issued its requirements for a post-war jet-driven generation of strategic bombers, it was to be the same two companies that were responsible for the aircraft that fulfilled the need: Handley Page with the crescent-winged Victor and Avro with the delta-winged Vulcan. In both cases the configuration was new and untried, yet each survived early teething troubles to become highly successful in their chosen role and adaptable to a number of others; they have also enjoyed a period of Royal Air Force service far in excess of that of their illustrious forebears.

Delta wings were to undergo a considerable vogue in the 1950s, but at the time the RAF issued its Specification B.35/46, a year after the end of World War II, no powered delta-wing aircraft had been flown, and A.V. Roe's brilliant technical director, Roy Chadwick, decided to air-test the configuration initially by building a series of smaller research aircraft with a generally similar shape. The first of these was the single-seat Avro 707, flown for the first time on 4 September 1949 and powered by a 3,500-lb (1588-kg) static thrust Rolls-Royce Derwent 5 turbojet. Twenty-six days later it crashed, killing test pilot S.E.Esler. This was hardly an auspicious beginning, but the modified 707B, flown by R.J. (Roly) Falk, took to the air on 6 September 1950 and quickly displayed extremely docile handling qualities. One major modification was made on the third aircraft, the 'high speed' Avro 707A, when the dorsal intakes for the engine were relocated in the wing roots; the 707A flew for the first time on 14 June 1951, and was followed by a second

The British Aerospace Vulcan B.2 is another long-serving type which has been continually updated, some of the electronics changes showing externally. The RAF also has four rebuilt as SR.2 strategic reconnaissance platforms, serving with No 27 Sqn at Scampton.

continued

707A on 20 February 1953. Last of the research prototypes, the Avro 707C, flew on 1 July the same year and was completed as a side-by-side two-seater, to provide training in the particular techniques necessary in flying a tailless delta.

Long before this, in January 1948, Avro had received the go-ahead for two prototypes of the full-size B.35/46 design, the Avro 698, some 20 times the weight of the little 707s. However, the British government remained wary of the unorthodox design; a production contract did not follow until June 1952, and in the meantime the more conventional Vickers Valiant was ordered as a back-up in the event of a possible failure of the Handley Page and Avro types. When the Avro 698 prototype first flew on 30 August 1952, it was powered by four 6,500-lb (2948-kg) static thrust Rolls-Royce Avon RA.3 turbojets, substituting for the planned installation of Bristol B.E.10 (Olympus) engines which were not then ready. In the following year it was refitted with 8,000-lb (3629-kg) static thrust Armstrong Siddeley Sapphires; Olympus Series 100 engines, of 9,750-lb (4423-kg) static thrust, were installed in the second prototype, which made its maiden flight on 3 September 1953.

A little less than 18 months later, on 4 February 1955, Falk flew the first production Vulcan B.1 (four 10,000-lb/4536-kg static thrust Olympus Mk 101s), and at the SBAC Display at Farnborough in the following September eclipsed even his own outstanding earlier performances by slow-rolling the second production example of this 99-ft (30.18-m) span bomber. Any remaining doubts — and there were not many — about the control and stability of such a large aeroplane, with no separate tailplane or elevators, were quickly dispelled. The only noteworthy problem was a slight buffeting when pulling g at high altitude, and this was remedied by decreasing the angle of sweepback on the centre panels of each wing, giving a kinked and cambered leading edge instead of the former straight line. This was applied to existing Vulcan 1s, successive batches of which introduced more powerful models of the Olympus engine; the eventual standard for all Vulcan 1s was the 13,500-lb (6123-kg) static thrust Olympus 104. Deliveries of 45 B.1s began in February 1957, to No 230 Operational Conversion Unit; first operational squadron, from July 1957, was No 83, followed by Nos 101 and 617. The internal bomb bay was large enough to carry twenty-one 1,000-lb (454-kg) bombs or mines, and pressurized accommodation was provided for a five-man crew: pilot and co-pilot (on ejection seats), navigator, radar operator and an air electronics officer. All B.1s still in service in 1961 were upgraded to B.1As with a new tailcone containing ECM (electronic countermeasures) equipment.

Major production version, however, was the B.2, with more powerful engines, much larger wings and capability for carrying the Hawker Siddeley Blue Steel thermonuclear stand-off missile. The new wings, of markedly thinner section and fitted with elevons, began flight testing on the second Vulcan prototype

on 31 August 1957, and the first production Vulcan 2 (17,000-lb/7711-kg static thrust Olympus 201s) flew on 30 August 1958. On receipt of the new version, Nos 83 and 617 Squadrons passed on their Mk 1As to Nos 44 and 50 Squadrons; No 617 was the first, in February 1963, to become operational with the Blue Steel. Additional Vulcan squadrons included Nos 9, 12 and 35, production of approximately 50 of this version ending in 1964.

As the B.1/1As were phased out, all of the squadrons listed came to fly the B.2, and after the Skybolt fiasco of 1961 – 62, followed by the adoption of the submarine-launched Polaris missile as Britain's primary nuclear deterrent, it became necessary to adapt the Vulcan for low-level operation, to maintain its capability to penetrate enemy airspace against improved-quality Soviet detection radars and

surface-to-air missiles. To this new requirement the Vulcan adapted very successfully, carrying conventional HE bombs and adopting a two-tone camouflage of green and grey for its new role instead of the all-white finish employed previously. Continuing improvement in power was maintained, Vulcans being re-engined in 1962 – 64 with 20,000-lb (9072-kg) static thrust Olympus 301 engines. The Vulan's third role, that of strategic reconnaissance, began in 1973 when a number of bombers were converted to SR.2s for this purpose; since 1974, these have been operated by No 27 Squadron.

The following data are for the B.2.
Type: low-level tactical bomber and strategic reconnaissance aircraft
Powerplant: four 20,000-lb (9072-kg) static

thrust Rolls-Royce Olympus 301 turbojets
Performance: maximum speed at high altitude 645 mph (1038 km/h); cruising speed at high altitude about 625 mph (1006 km/h); combat radius without refuelling 1,725 miles (2776 km); combat radius with one in-flight refuelling 2,875 miles (4627 km); range with normal bomb load about 4,600 miles (7403 km); service ceiling about 65,000 ft (19810 m)
Weights: maximum take-off about 250,000 lb (113400 kg)

Royal Air Force Hawker Siddeley Vulcan B.2 long-range strategic bomber, in low-visibility markings, from the Waddington Wing.

British Aerospace Vulcan B Mk 2 cutaway drawing key

1 Wing tip antennae
2 Starboard navigation light
3 Starboard wing tip construction
4 Outboard aileron
5 Inboard aileron
6 Rear spar
7 Outboard wing panel ribs
8 Front spar
9 Leading edge ribs
10 Cranked leading edge
11 Corrugated leading-edge inner skin
12 Retractable landing and taxying lamp
13 Fuel tank fire extinguisher bottles
14 Outer wing panel joint rib
15 Honeycomb skin panel
16 Outboard elevator
17 Inboard elevator
18 Elevator hydraulic jacks
19 No 7 starboard fuel tank
20 No 5 starboard fuel tank
21 Diagonal rib
22 Leading edge de-icing air duct
23 Wing stringer construction
24 Parallel chord wing skin panels
25 No 6 starboard fuel tank
26 No 4 starboard fuel tank
27 No 3 starboard fuel tank
28 Main undercarriage leg
29 Eight-wheel bogie
30 Mainwheel well door
31 Fuel tank fire extinguishers
32 Inboard leading edge construction
33 De-icing air supply pipe
34 Fuel collectors and pumps
35 Main undercarriage wheel bay
36 Retracting mechanism
37 Airborne auxiliary power plant (AAPP)

38 Electrical equipment bay
39 Starboard engine bays
40 Rolls-Royce (Bristol) Olympus 301 engines
41 Air system piping
42 Engine bay dividing rib
43 Engine fire extinguishers
44 Jet pipes
45 Fixed trailing edge construction
46 Jet pipe nozzles
47 Rear equipment bay
48 Oxygen bottles
49 Batteries
50 Rudder power control unit
51 Rear electronics bay
52 Electronic countermeasures system equipment
53 Cooling air intake
54 Tail warning radar scanner
55 Tail radome
56 Twin brake parachute housing
57 Brake parachute door
58 Rudder construction
59 Rudder balance weights and seals
60 Fin de-icing air outlet
61 Di-electric fin tip fairing
62 Passive electronic countermeasures (ECM) antennae
63 Fin construction
64 Fin leading edge
65 Corrugated inner skin
66 Communications aerial
67 Fin de-icing air supply
68 Bomb-bay rear bulkhead

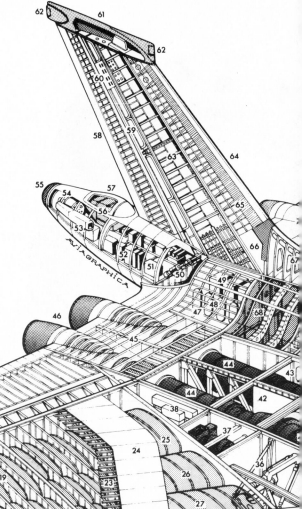

Dimensions: span 111 ft 0 in (33.38 m); length (including refuelling probe) 105 ft 6 in (32.16 m); length (without probe) 99 ft 11 in (30.45 m); height 27 ft 2 in (8.28 m); wing area 3,964 sq ft (368.27 m²)
Armament: no defensive armament; up to twenty-one 1,000-lb (454-kg) bombs in internal weapons bay
Operators: UK

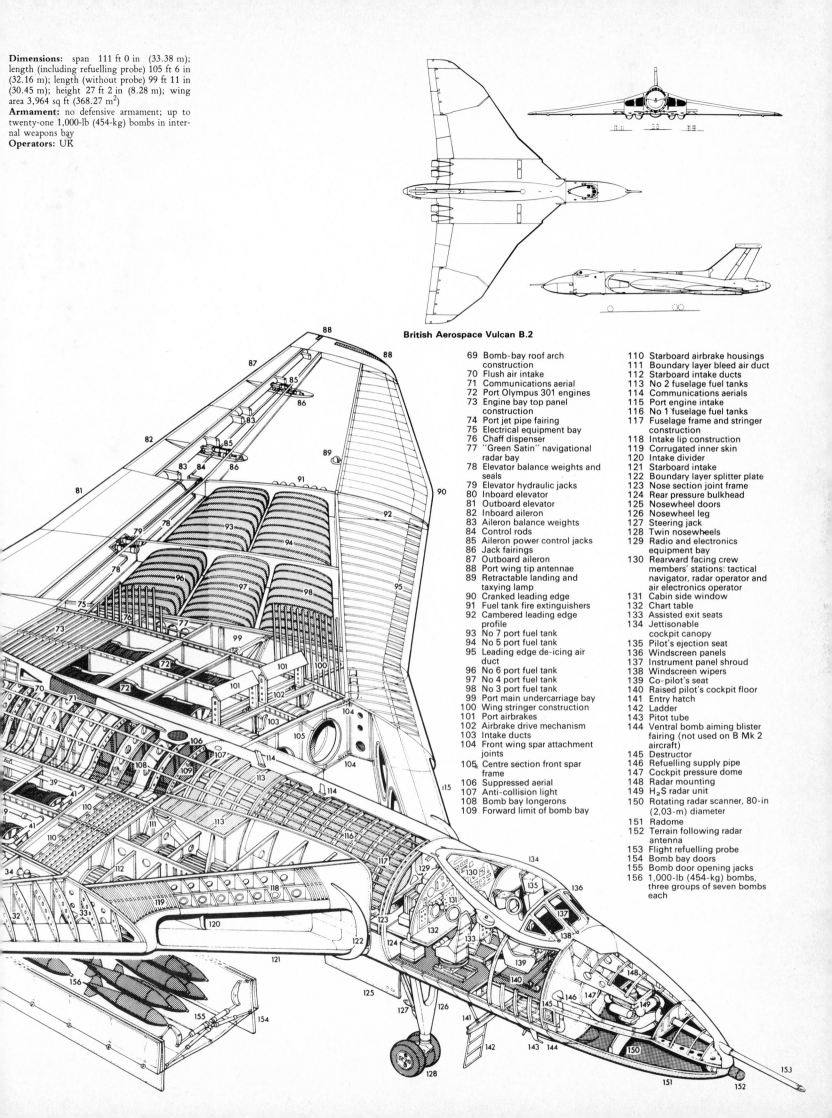

British Aerospace Vulcan B.2

69 Bomb-bay roof arch construction
70 Flush air intake
71 Communications aerial
72 Port Olympus 301 engines
73 Engine bay top panel construction
74 Port jet pipe fairing
75 Electrical equipment bay
76 Chaff dispenser
77 "Green Satin" navigational radar bay
78 Elevator balance weights and seals
79 Elevator hydraulic jacks
80 Inboard elevator
81 Outboard elevator
82 Inboard aileron
83 Aileron balance weights
84 Control rods
85 Aileron power control jacks
86 Jack fairings
87 Outboard aileron
88 Port wing tip antennae
89 Retractable landing and taxying lamp
90 Cranked leading edge
91 Fuel tank fire extinguishers
92 Cambered leading edge profile
93 No 7 port fuel tank
94 No 5 port fuel tank
95 Leading edge de-icing air duct
96 No 6 port fuel tank
97 No 4 port fuel tank
98 No 3 port fuel tank
99 Port main undercarriage bay
100 Wing stringer construction
101 Port airbrakes
102 Airbrake drive mechanism
103 Intake ducts
104 Front wing spar attachment joints
105 Centre section front spar frame
106 Suppressed aerial
107 Anti-collision light
108 Bomb bay longerons
109 Forward limit of bomb bay

110 Starboard airbrake housings
111 Boundary layer bleed air duct
112 Starboard intake ducts
113 No 2 fuselage fuel tanks
114 Communications aerials
115 Port engine intake
116 No 1 fuselage fuel tanks
117 Fuselage frame and stringer construction
118 Intake lip construction
119 Corrugated inner skin
120 Intake divider
121 Starboard intake
122 Boundary layer splitter plate
123 Nose section joint frame
124 Rear pressure bulkhead
125 Nosewheel doors
126 Nosewheel leg
127 Steering jack
128 Twin nosewheels
129 Radio and electronics equipment bay
130 Rearward facing crew members' stations: tactical navigator, radar operator and air electronics operator
131 Cabin side window
132 Chart table
133 Assisted exit seats
134 Jettisonable cockpit canopy
135 Pilot's ejection seat
136 Windscreen panels
137 Instrument panel shroud
138 Windscreen wipers
139 Co-pilot's seat
140 Raised pilot's cockpit floor
141 Entry hatch
142 Ladder
143 Pitot tube
144 Ventral bomb aiming blister fairing (not used on B Mk 2 aircraft)
145 Destructor
146 Refuelling supply pipe
147 Cockpit pressure dome
148 Radar mounting
149 H₂S radar unit
150 Rotating radar scanner, 80-in (2,03-m) diameter
151 Radome
152 Terrain following radar antenna
153 Flight refuelling probe
154 Bomb bay doors
155 Bomb door opening jacks
156 1,000-lb (454-kg) bombs, three groups of seven bombs each

Britten-Norman Islander/Defender

Since its first flight in June 1965, the Britten-Norman Islander has been built in several different versions, examples have rolled off five different production lines, and ownership of the design rights have been vested in four different companies.

The original BN-2 Islander was conceived by Desmond Norman and John Britten as a cheap, simple, twin-engined aircraft capable of carrying up to 10 people including the pilot. Detailed design work began in early 1964 and in just over a year the first prototype had taken to the air. Production aircraft has uprated 260-hp (194-kW) O-540-E4C5 engines in place of the original 210-hp (157-kW) Rolls-Royce Continental IO-360-Bs and a 4-ft (1.2-m) increase in wing span. The aircraft was an immediate success.

To boost supply the small Isle of Wight company signed an agreement in 1968 with IRMA (Intreprinderea de Reparat Material Aeronautic) of Romania for the quantity production of Islanders under licence. The first IRMA-built aircraft flew in August 1969. In addition, Britten-Norman placed a contract with the British Hovercraft Corporation for the manufacture, up to final assembly stage, of 236 Islanders, followed by a further 134.

The very success of the Islander strained the finances of Britten-Norman and by 1971 these problems became acute. Price Waterhouse was appointed receiver and a new company named Britten-Norman (Bembridge) was formed. The uncertainty lasted until August 1972 when Britten-Norman became part of the Fairey Group. The new holding company, Fairey Britten-Norman, brought together the B-N factory at Bembridge, Isle of Wight, and the Fairey works at Gosselies, Belgium. While Gosselies concentrated on production, Bembridge carried out final finishing, design, marketing and product support.

At the 1974 Farnborough Air Show, Fairey Britten-Norman announced another international venture. The National Aero Manufacturing Corporation (NAMC), a subsidiary of the Philippine Aerospace Development Corporation, had arranged to build Islanders under licence. Britten-Norman initially supplied six finished aircraft but these were followed by 14 unpainted, untrimmed aircraft for fitting out. NAMC is now assembling 20 aircraft from kits supplied by Britten-Norman. It was anticipated that a further 60 aircraft would be built in the Philippines using jigs and detailed parts supplied from Europe. Although Philippines Aero Transport will operate most of the aircraft covered by the agreement, some have been supplied to the Philippines Armed Forces for air/sea rescue duties and about 25 will be repurchased by Britten-Norman for sale in other parts of the world. The agreement with the Philippines also covered the development of an amphibious version.

The excessive cost of aircraft built at Gosselies was one of the primary reasons why the Fairey Group found itself in financial difficulties at the end of 1977. Part of the aircraft manufacturing side of the group, without Gosselies, was re-formed as Britten-Norman (Bembridge), and the design rights and production jigs and tools for the Islander and its development were again up for sale. The delivery of Romanian-produced aircraft continued, but the future looked uncertain. After negotiations which involved Grumman, Shorts and SAAB, it was announced in July 1978 that Pilatus Aircraft of Switzerland, part of the Oerlikon-Bührle Group, had acquired all the assets. The agreements with Romania and the Philippines were continued and Pilatus made it clear that further developments of the Islander family were likely.

The Islander, with its simple high wing, fixed undercarriage and modest cruising speed was easy to fly and maintain right from the start. The engines were well proven and the formula lent itself to a wide range of applications. The original BN-2 Series 1 was followed on the production line by the BN-2A Series 2 after June 1969. The option of 300-hp (224-kW) fuel-injection Lycoming IO-540-K1B5s or supercharged 260-hp (194-kW) O-540-E4C5s was made available, as were extended wingtips containing auxiliary fuel tanks. The latest production variant is the BN-2B Islander II and this is available with a choice of engines, with extended wing tips or with an extended nose incorporating additional baggage space.

Military applications seemed obvious and the aircraft displayed its outstanding qualities by landing and taking off unassisted from the deck of HMS *Hermes* in May 1968. At the 1971 Paris Show the company displayed its newly developed Defender. It was aimed at low-cost search and rescue, internal security, patrol, forward air control, troop transit, logistic support, and casualty evacuation.

The equipment fitted to production Defenders depends on customer requirements, but up to four underwing pylons for offensive stores can be provided. Typical loads include machine-gun packs, rockets, wire-guided missiles, bombs, flares, grenades or drop tanks. The Maritime Defender has a nose-

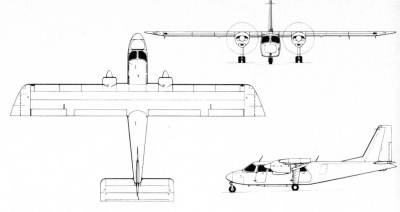

Britten-Norman 2B Islander

mounted search radar and can carry searchlights, loudspeakers, flares, dinghies or weapons.

Versions are also available for firefighting, crop spraying and aerial surveying. The turbo-prop powered Turbo Islander first flew in April 1977 but production deliveries have yet to begin. One Islander has been modified to accept twin Dowty Rotol ducted propulsors which offer a dramatic reduction in noise, and improved performances. There are no production plans for this variant at present.

Type: general-purpose light transport capable of carrying (Defender) light pod-mounted armaments or (Maritime Defender) optional nose search radar
Powerplant: (standard) two 260-hp (194-kW) Lycoming O-540-E4C5 flat-six piston engines; optional 300-hp (224-kW) Lycoming IO-540-K1B5s
Performance: (at maximum take-off weight) maximum level speed (clean) 176 mph (283 km/h), (loaded pylons) 168 mph (270 km/h); maximum range with full payload (clean) 418 miles (672 km), (loaded pylons) 375 miles (603 km)
Weights: empty 3,708 lb (1682 kg); maximum take-off 6,600 lb (2993 kg); maximum landing 6,300 lb (2855 kg); maximum zero

fuel 6,200 lb (2810 kg)
Dimensions: span 53 ft (16.15 m); length (Defender) 35 ft 8 in (10.86 m); length (Defender Maritime) 36 ft 4 in (11.07 m); height 13 ft 9 in (4.18 m); wing area (standard) 325 sq ft (30.19 m²)
Armament: Four NATO standard wing pylons capable of accepting twin 7.62-mm (0.3-in) machine-gun pods, 250-lb (113-kg) or 500-lb (227-kg) general-purpose bombs, Matra rocket packs, wire-guided missiles, SURA rocket packs, reconnaissance flares, grenades, smoke bombs, markers or drop tanks.
Operators: Abu Dhabi, Belgium, Botswana, Ghana, Guyana, Hong Kong, India, Israel, Jamaica, Malagasy, Mauritania, Oman, Mexico, Malawi, Panama, Philippines, Qatar, Rhodesia, Rwanda, Venezuela. Government operators include Brazil, Egypt, Lesotho, Liberia, Nigeria, Thailand, Turkey, Zaire and Zambia.

Britten-Norman Defender of 5 Sqn, Sultan of Oman's Air Force, at Seeb. Seven aircraft are in service for utility duties.

Britten-Norman BN-2A Mk III Trislander

It took just six weeks for the second Britten-Norman Islander prototype to be converted to a 17-seat trimotor, with stretched fuselage and a third engine on a new fin. The first flight on 11 September 1970 proved that there were no unusual handling characteristics and the BN-2A Mk III Trislander was born.

Modifications were kept to a minimum and Trislanders are 75 per cent built from Islander parts. They have a 90-in (2.29-m) fuselage plug forward of the wing, strengthening plates in the centre section, reinforced rear fuselage, new main landing gear and new fin and rudder. The extended nose, optional on the Islander, is standard. A stand-by rocket below the rear engine nacelle is available to assist take off and climb away in the event of engine failure.

Like the Islander, the three-engined development has a military potential and Britten-Norman offers the Trislander M for trooping, supply dropping, maritime patrol, and search and rescue. The aircraft could have a patrol endurance of nine hours and could carry radar or a variety of other avionics and mission equipment. Although nearly 100 civil Trislanders have been sold, no customers have yet been confirmed for the military counterpart.

Type: general-purpose light transport also suitable for maritime patrol, search and rescue duties
Powerplant: three 260-hp (194-kW) Lycoming O-540-E4C5 flat-six piston engines, plus stand-by rocket engine available as option
Performance: (at maximum take-off weight) maximum level speed 181 mph (291 km/h); cruising speed 155 mph (249 km/h); maximum range with full payload 259 miles (417 km)
Weights: empty 5,800 lb (2631 kg); maximum take-off and landing 10,000 lb (4536 kg); maximum zero fuel 9,700 lb (4400 kg)
Dimensions: span 53 ft 0 in (16.15 m); length 49 ft 3 in (15.01 m); height 14 ft 2 in (4.32 m); wing area 337 sq ft (31.31 m²)
Armament: four underwing pylons to carry fuel tanks, life raft and survival pack pods or offensive stores as on the Defender
Operator: none

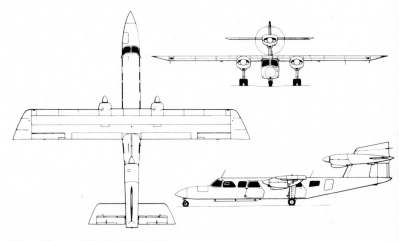

Britten-Norman BN-2A Mk III Trislander

Canadair CL-28 Argus

The Canadair CL-28 (military designation CP-107) Argus was designed to meet a 1952 requirement for a maritime patrol and anti-submarine warfare (ASW) aircraft to succeed the Avro Lancaster MR.10 and Lockheed P2V Neptune in service with the Royal Canadian Air Force's Maritime Air Command. The aircraft was based on the Bristol Britannia airliner, the wings, tail and undercarriage being virtually identical on both machines. The fuselage was redesigned to incorporate two weapons bays, and pressurization was eliminated as it was not necessary at the low altitudes customarily used by maritime reconnaissance aircraft.

The first Argus Mk 1 flew from Canadair's factory at Montreal on 28 March 1957. It was followed by 12 further aircraft built to Mark 1 standard, fitted with American APS-20 radar in a chin-mounted radome. The 20 Argus Mk 2s were fitted with British ASV-21 radar mounted in a smaller radome. Production ended in July 1960, with the completion of the RCAF's last Argus Mk 2.

The normal crew complement of the Argus is 15, comprising three pilots, two flight engineers, three navigators and seven ASW systems operators. This enables the crew to work in shifts during a patrol which can last up to 20 hours, a crew rest area with bunks and a galley being provided.

The crew stations comprise an observer/bomb aimer's position in the glazed nose; the flight deck with provision for pilot, co-pilot and flight engineer; and behind them the routine navigator and radio operator's positions. A rear compartment houses six or seven members of the ASW team under a tactical co-ordinator, with two beam lookout positions behind this compartment.

The ASW equipment carried by the Argus includes search radar, a magnetic anomaly detector (MAD) carried on an 18 ft (5.49 m) tail boom, electronic countermeasures equipment and a diesel exhaust detector. Sonobuoys are carried in an aft fuselage compartment, which also houses flares and marine markers. Offensive stores (acoustic homing, torpedoes and depth charges) are carried in the two internal weapons bays.

In addition to the long-range maritime patrol and anti-submarine warfare tasks, the Argus can undertake minelaying duties and act as an emergency transport. The aircraft's maritime patrol duties include Arctic patrols, fishery surveillance, search and rescue, and pollution monitoring.

In May 1958 No 405 Squadron based at Greenwood, Nova Scotia, began to convert to the Argus and was followed by No 404, which shared the same base, in April 1959. A third east coast Argus squadron (No 415) was formed at Summerside, Prince Edward Island, in June 1961. Ten years after the Argus entered Canadian Service, a fourth unit was equipped with the type (by which time the RCAF had been absorbed in the Canadian Armed Forces), when No 407 Squadron on Canada's west coast at Comox, British Columbia, began to replace its Lockheed Neptunes with Arguses. Unlike the east coast squadrons, this unit was not assigned to NATO, but it nevertheless worked closely with United States forces. Also in 1968 No 449 Squadron was formed at Greenwood to train maritime crews, a task previously performed by No 2 Operational Training Unit.

As it soldiered on into the 1970s, the Argus began to show increasing signs of old age. Early in 1972 the entire fleet was grounded because of a fault in the undercarriage. Later that year a requirement for an Argus replacement, the Long Range Patrol Aircraft (LRPA), was drawn up. Three years later it was announced that the Argus fleet would be reduced to 26 aircraft as an economy measure. The six redundant aircraft (one Argus Mk 2 had been lost in an air accident in 1965) were accordingly withdrawn between May and August 1975.

The LRPA selected, the CP-140 Aurora (a version of the Lockheed P-3 Orion), is scheduled to replace the Argus between May 1980 and March 1981.

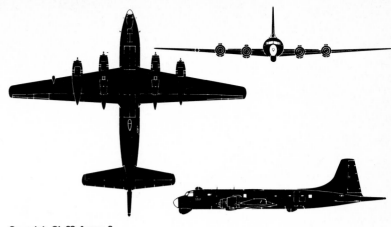

Canadair CL-28 Argus 2

Type: long-range maritime patrol aircraft
Powerplant: four 3,400-hp (2536-kW) Wright Cyclone R-3350-EA1 Turbo-Compound 18-cylinder engines
Performance: maximum speed 315 mph (507 km/h) at 10,000 ft (3050 m); service ceiling 25,000 ft (7620 m); normal range 4,000 miles (6438 km); maximum range 5,900 miles (9495 km); endurance 20 hours
Weights: empty equipped 81,000 lb (36740 kg); maximum take-off 157,000 lb (71215 kg)
Dimensions: span 142 ft 3½ in (43.35 m); length 128 ft 9½ in (39.54 m); height 38 ft 8 in (11.78 m)
Armament: a total of 8,000 lb (3630 kg) of depth charges, mines, bombs or homing torpedoes in two fuselage weapons bays; provision for two wing hardpoints for air-to-surface missiles or free-fall stores weighing up to 3,800 lb (1720 kg)
Operator: Canadian Armed Forces

Canadair based the CL-28 Argus ASW and ocean-patrol aircraft on the Britannia, although differences were so great the advantages were problematical. Called CP-107 by the CAF, these long-endurance platforms are soon to be replaced by the smaller CP-140 Aurora.

Canadair CL-41 Tutor

The Canadair CL-41's development programme was privately funded by the company, because of the Canadian government's early lack of interest in this basic jet trainer. Two prototypes were built, powered by a 2,400-lb (1088-kg) Pratt and Whitney JT12A-5 turbojet, the first flying on 13 January 1960. In September 1961 the Canadian government ordered 190 CL-41As for the Royal Canadian Air Force (now the Canadian Armed Forces) with the designation CT-114 Tutor. These were powered by the General Electric J85-CAN-40 turbojet of 2,850-lb (1290-kg) thrust. Delivery took place in 1963-6.

Further development resulted in the CL-41G armament trainer and light attack air-

Canadair CL-41G Tebuan armed jet trainer of the Royal Malaysian Air Force. Two squadrons, Nos 6 and 9, operate the 16 surviving Tebuans of 20 originally supplied; this machine was on the strength of 9 Sqn at Kuantan.

continued

craft. This has uprated engines and six under-wing hardpoints; the landing gear is modified for soft field operation, and 'zero level' automatic ejection seats are fitted. In March 1966 the Royal Malaysian Air Force ordered 20, named Tebuan (wasp) in Malaysian service.

Features include side-by-side seats, upward-opening canopy, lateral door-type airbrakes, 'T' tail, and steerable nosewheel. Internal fuel totals 258 Imperial gallons (1170 litres), in five cells in the fuselage.

Main user of the CT-114 Tutor in the Canadian Armed Forces is Training Command's No 2 Flying Training School at Moose Jaw, Saskatchewan. After primary training on the Beech CT-134 Musketeer, pupils do some 200 hours on the CT-114 to reach 'wings' standard, and proceed to specialized training for combat jets, multi-engined types or helicopters.

Ten Tutors were modified for the Golden Hawks (later Snowbirds) aerobatic team and the type also serves with the Flying Instructors' School. These units share the Moose Jaw base with No 2 FTS.

In 1976 the Canadian Armed Forces began a 113-aircraft modification programme which includes provision of external fuel tanks, upgrading of avionics, changes to the canopy electrical system and relocation of the engine ice-detector probe.

Deliveries to Malaysia began in 1967 and a new base was constructed to accommodate the Tebuans at Kuantan on the peninsula's east coast. Two squadrons fly the type: No 9 Sqn is an advanced training unit, while No 6 operates in the light strike role.

Type: two-seat training and tactical support aircraft
Powerplant: (CL-41G) one 2,950-lb (1340-kg) General Electric J85-J4 turbojet
Performance: maximum level speed at 28,500 ft (8700 m) 480 mph (774 km/h); service ceiling 42,200 ft (12800 m); maximum range 1,430 miles (2300 km)
Weights: empty 5,296 lb (2400 kg); maximum take-off 11,288 lb (5130 kg); maximum landing 8,900 lb (4040 kg)
Dimensions: span 36 ft 5.9 in (11.13 m); length 32 ft (9.75 m); height 9 ft ¾ in (2.84 in); wing area 220 sq ft (20.44 m²)
Armament: six wing hardpoints can carry up to 4,000 lb (1815 kg) of bombs, rockets, gun pods or air-to-air missiles
Operators: Canada, Malaysia

The **Canadair CL-41 Tutor,** called CT-114 by the Canadian Armed Forces, has equipped several CAF display teams as well as serving as standard pilot trainer to 'wings' standard at Moose Jaw. Over 100 are being updated in both structure and systems.

Canadair CL-66 Cosmopolitan

With the advent of turboprop engines, a number of airliner manufacturers examined the possibility of re-engining airframes which had been designed for piston engines. Very few of the projects became actual hardware, but the Cosmopolitan was an exception.

Production of the Convair 440 was completed in 1958, by which time nearly 1,000 of the 240/340/440 transports had been built, of which almost half were delivered to the US military services. Convair was concentrating on development of the 880/990 series, but Pacific Airmotive Corporation undertook conversion of a number of 340/440 airframes to take Allison 501 turboprops for several airlines, the resulting aircraft being designated CV-580. Convair themselves fitted the Rolls-Royce Dart to produce the CV-640.

Meanwhile, the Royal Canadian Air Force was in the market for a twin-turboprop transport and, under an agreement between Convair and Canadair, the CV-440 jigs and tools were transferred to the latter company's factory at Cartierville, Montreal. In collaboration with the British aero-engine manufacturer Napier, Canadair proposed to use the 3,500-hp (2611-kW) Napier Eland turboprop married to newly-manufactured CV-440 airframes under the company designation Canadair 540 (the CL-66 in Canadair's own terminology). Two pre-production aircraft, actually re-engined CV-440s, were used for demonstration purposes and Royal Canadian Air Force crew training; they were designated

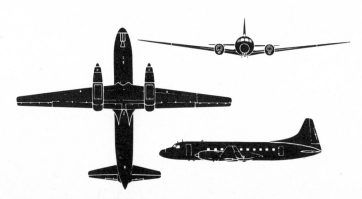

Canadair CL-66 (CC-109) prior to refitting with Allison 510 engines

Canadair 540C, and were later bought by Quebecair in a 52-passenger configuration. The first production 540 flew in January 1960 and 10 were built for the RCAF, by whom they were designated CC-109 Cosmopolitan. Following the collapse of Napier the CC-109 fleet were re-engined by Allison with the Model 501 turboprop and brought up to the same airframe standard as the Convair 580. As civil passenger transports the aircraft were offered with accommodation for 48 to 64, depending on configuration, while the RCAF

version was convertible with a reinforced floor and 10-ft (3.04-m) cargo loading door; the payload is 14,300 lb (6486 kg).

In addition to its 10 Cosmopolitans, the RCAF eventually acquired the two Quebecair aircraft plus Canadair's demonstrator. Most of the Cosmopolitans are still in service, the majority with No 412 Squadron at Trenton and at Uplands, Ottawa, for VIP and utility transport work. Others are detached to the Canadian Forces in Europe headquarters at Lahr and to the NORAD headquarters at Col-

orado Springs. The German-based aircraft will soon be replaced by two de Havilland Canada DHC-7 four-turboprop transports, an order for which was announced in 1978.

Type: twin-turboprop military transport
Powerplant: two turboprops (see text)
Performance: maximum speed 340 mph (547 km/h); cruising speed at 46,000 lb (20865 kg) at 20,000 ft (6100 m) 322 mph (518 km/h); climb to 10,000 ft (3050 m) 6 minutes 24 seconds; climb to 20,000 ft (6100 m) 15 minutes 36 seconds; range

(45-minute fuel reserve) with 48 passengers 1,244 miles (1996 km); range with extra tanks in same conditions 2,275 miles (3660 km); take-off distance 4,550 ft (1388 m); landing distance 4,020 ft (1226 m)
Weights: empty 32,333 lb (14666 kg); maximum take-off 53,200 lb (24130 kg) maximum landing weight 50,670 lb (22985 kg)
Dimensions: span 105 ft 4 in (32.12 m); length 81 ft 6 in (24.84 m); height 28 ft 2 in (8.49 m); wing area 963.82 sq ft (89.54 m²)
Operators: Canada

Canadair CL-215

The Canadair CL-215 was designed to meet a requirement for a firefighting amphibian which could replace the miscellany of types used in the 'water bomber' role in the 1960s. The basic parameters of the CL-215 design emerged from a symposium on forest-fire protection held in Ottawa in December 1963. Early in 1966 it was decided to put the type into production. The Canadian Province of Quebec and the French *Protection Civile* were the first customers, ordering 20 and 10 CL-215s respectively to undertake its primary role of forest fire detection and suppression. However, the robust and versatile amphibian was also available to military customers for the search and rescue and utility roles.

From the outset simplicity of design was a primary requirement, with ease of maintenance and reliability of equipment (achieved through the incorporation of already-proven systems wherever practicable) also receiving careful attention. Protection against salt-water corrosion was achieved through the use of corrosion-resistant materials and by carefully sealing components during assembly.

The CL-215 is an aircraft of substantial size. It has a single-step hull, and fixed stabilizing floats are mounted just inboard of the wing tips. The tricycle undercarriage comprises a twin nosewheel and single mainwheels, the former retracting into the hull and the latter being raised to lie flat against the hull during operations from water.

The high-mounted wing and tailplane are single-piece structures, with ailerons and flaps occupying the entire wing trailing edge. All fuel is carried in flexible wing cells, and the engine nacelles are integral with the wing structure.

For its firefighting role the CL-215 can lift 1,200 Imperial gallons (5450 litres) of water or retardent fluid in two fuselage tanks. The water is scooped from a convenient lake or river through two retractable inlets mounted under the hull while the CL-215 taxies across the surface. It then takes off and flies to the area of the fire where the load is jettisoned in under a second. The operation is repeated until the fire is under control. In most environments a load can be dropped at least every 10 minutes.

Configured for the search and rescue role, the CL-215 carries a crew of six. In addition to the pilot and co-pilot, a flight engineer is housed on the flight deck. The navigator's station is located farther back in the forward fuselage, and two observers are carried in the rear fuselage. The basic avionics (typically HF, VHF and VHF/HM transceivers, ADF, VOR/ILS/glide slope and marker beacon) are augmented by an AVQ-21 weather and search radar in the nose, a radio altimeter, an UHF/VHF homer and DME. Maximum endurance is 12 hours.

First flight of the CL-215 was on 23 October 1967, and deliveries to France began in May 1969. In March 1970 Quebec Province received the first of a reduced order of 15 CL-215s, the surplus machines going to France (2), Spain (2) and Greece (1). The Spanish Air Force was favourably impressed by an evaluation of the two CL-215s orderered by the Ministry of Agriculture and these machines, together with a new order for eight, formed the equipment of *Escuadron 404*. Based at Torrejon, this unit operates in the firefighting, search and rescue and casualty evacuation roles.

The second largest military operator of the CL-215 is Greece's Hellenic Air Force,

which purchased a total of eight. Primarily operating in the forest protection role, the Greek CL-215s have nevertheless successfully demonstrated the aircraft's capability as a troop transport.

The Royal Thai Navy operates two CL-215s as patrol and search and rescue amphibians. The aircraft were delivered during the summer of 1978, the 10,000-mile (16094-km) ferry flight taking the aircraft across the Atlantic and then on to India, by way of Egypt and the Persian Gulf.

Type: twin-engined utility and firefighting amphibian
Powerplant: two 2,100-hp (1566-kW) Pratt & Whitney R-2800-83 eighteen cylinder radial engines, each driving a Hamilton Standard three-bladed propeller
Performance: cruising speed at 10,000 ft (3050 m) 181 mph (290 km/h); rate of climb at sea level 1,000 ft (305 m) per minute; range at maximum cruise power 1,150 miles (1851 km)
Weights: empty equipped 26,600 lb (12000 kg); maximum take-off (land)

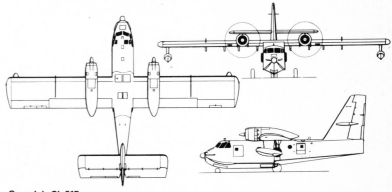

Canadair CL-215

43,500 lb (19730 kg); maximum take-off (water) 37,700 lb (17100 kg); maximum payload (utility version) 6,260 lb (2840 kg)
Dimensions: span 93 ft 10 in (28.6 m); length 65 ft ½ in (19.82 m); height (wheels extended) 29 ft 8 in (8.92 m)
Accommodation: two crew and 19 passengers; (search and rescue) six crew, four seats or six stretchers; (casevac) nine stret-

chers; (troop transport) 36 troops
Operators: Spanish Air Force, Hellenic Air Force (Greece), Royal Thai Navy

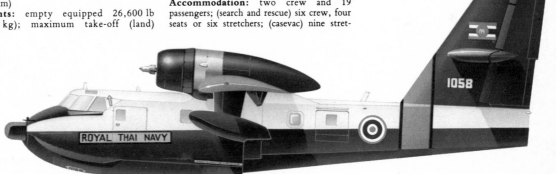

One of two Canadair CL-215-amphibians delivered to the Royal Thai Navy in 1978 and operated from Bangkok on search-and-rescue duties.

One of the Province of Quebec's Canadair CL-215 amphibians pictured on the St Lawrence river at Quebec City. Designated initially as a firefighting aeroplane, the CL-215 also serves in the search and rescue and patrol roles.

CASA C-101 Aviojet

Spain's aircraft industry is quite small, but a number of indigenous designs have emerged in recent years following licence production of designs from Germany and other countries. CASA (Construcciones Aeronauticas SA) is one of the oldest European aircraft companies and was founded in 1923. Since then it has been busily engaged in aircraft production and is also a large sub-contractor, being involved in such programmes as the Airbus A300 and the HFB 320 Hansa, together with licence production of the Northrop F-5 for the Spanish air force, and considerable overhaul work for both the Spanish and US air forces.

In 1972 Hispano Aviación SA merged with CASA and by mid-1978 the two companies had built some 3,500 aircraft, including the HA-200 jet trainer. Work on this aircraft, the F-5 and the Hansa stood CASA in good stead when it was asked to design a replacement for the HA-200, and in September 1975 the company was awarded a development contract for a basic and advanced jet trainer. Six prototypes were covered, four for flight test and two for fatigue testing. The first prototype, by then wearing the company designation C-101, flew on June 27, 1977, followed in September by the second. The third and fourth followed on 26 January and 17 April 1978 respectively and, following manufacturer's trials, were handed over to the Spanish air force for service testing in late 1978, by which time the name Aviojet had been chosen. The military designation will be E.25.

Assistance in the design stage came from MBB in West Germany, while the US Northrop company helped with the jet inlet and wing design. Imported components include Dowty landing gear, tandem Martin-Baker ejection seats, US-built air-conditioning and pressurization system, Garrett-AiResearch engine and Sperry STARS integrated flight control system.

Production of the initial batch of 10 Aviojets began in early 1978 to meet orders for 60 for the Spanish air force as a replacement for the Hispano HA-200 and HA-220s, of which 80 or more are still in service. All these will eventually need to be replaced and further orders for Aviojets up to a total of around 120 are expected. Deliveries were due to begin in October 1979 and the Aviojet was to enter service with the training units in 1980.

Construction is on a modular basis for ease of maintenance and low cost, with ample internal space available for training equipment; there is a large bay behind the rear cockpit for quick-change equipment packages and a variety of underwing and underfuselage stores can be carried on hardpoints (see specification).

The Martin-Baker Mk 10E seats are of the zero-zero type, while the cockpit canopy is in two sections which open sideways; there is a separate internal windscreen for the raised rear cockpit.

As in the case of the HA-200/220 it seems likely that a strike variant will be developed to replace the 20 or so HA-220s still in service.

Type: basic and advanced jet trainer and light strike aircraft
Powerplant: one 3,500-lb (1587-kg) thrust Garrett-AiResearch TFE731-2-25 turbofan
Performance: maximum speed at sea level 420 mph (676 km/h); maximum speed at 25,000 ft (7620 m) Mach 0.69; cruising speed at 35,000 ft (10675 m) Mach 0.61; rate of climb at sea level 3,350 ft (1021 m) per minute; service ceiling 41,000 ft (12495 m); take-off run to 50 ft (15 m) 2,950 ft (900 m); landing run from 50 ft (15 m) 2,165 ft (660 m); ferry range 2,485 miles (4000 km)
Weights: basic operating 6,519 lb (2957 kg); maximum take-off (trainer) 10,361 lb (4700 kg); maximum take-off (ground-attack) 12,345 lb (5600 kg)
Dimensions: span 34 ft 9 in (10.60 m); length 40 ft 2 in (12.25 m); height 13 ft 11 in (4.25 m); wing area 215.3 sq ft (20.00 m²)
Armament: underfuselage attachment for a 30-mm cannon, a 12.7 mm (0.5-in) gun, reconnaissance camera or laser designator; three hardpoints under each wing can carry up to 4,410 lb (2000 kg) of stores consisting of rocket pods, missiles, bombs or napalm canisters; a tow target can also be carried beneath each wing
Operators: Spain

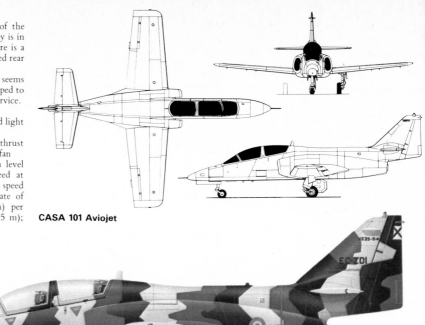
CASA 101 Aviojet

Striking splinter camouflage on the fourth prototype of the new Spanish CASA C.101 Aviojet.

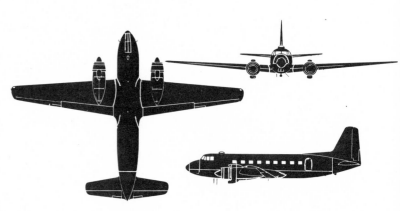
First prototype of the CASA C-101 Aviojet, flown in June 1977. Production by CASA and MBB of West Germany is geared to 1980 service in the EdA (Spanish air force), and France is sales agent for Africa and South America (no foreign sales by April 1979).

CASA 207 Azor

The Spanish aircraft industry has produced four different types of twin-engined transport since the end of World War II, the first of these being the CASA 201 Alcotan, a dual military/civil type of modest size, and the second the somewhat similar CASA 202 Halcon; both were produced in small numbers only. Third, and to date the largest, the Azor is essentially a scaled-up development of the Halcon. It flew for the first time on 28 September 1955 and was intended originally for the domestic civil market. Here it found no takers, but the aircraft was rescued from obscurity by the Spanish government, which placed an initial order for 10 for the *Ejército del Aire*.

Carrying a crew of four and having cabin accommodation for up to 40 passengers, this first model received the Spanish air force designation T.7A and began to enter service in 1960; two of the 10 were fitted experimentally with Pratt & Whitney Double Wasp engines. The original batch was followed by a further 10 aircraft, configured for either paratroop transport or freight-carrying duties. Designated CASA 207C (military designation T.7B), they are distinguishable by large cargo-loading double doors at the rear of the fuselage, and can transport up to 37 paratroops or 7,385 lb (3350 kg) of freight. The two CASA 207 prototypes, as well as the 20 production Azors, were utilised by the Spanish air force, which still had about a dozen in service

in 1978, with the 35th Wing of its Transport Command at Madrid-Getafe. In 1973 CASA proposed a four-turboprop STOL design, known as the CASA 401, to replace the Azor; but this was eventually abandoned in favour of the smaller twin-turboprop CASA 212 Aviocar.

Type: short/medium-range troop and cargo transport
Powerplant: two 2,040-hp (1520-kW) Bristol Hercules 730 fourteen-cylinder radial piston engines
Performance: maximum level speed at 4,920 ft (1500 m) 261 mph (420 km/h); maximum cruising speed at 12,340 ft (3760 m) 249 mph (400 km/h); range with 6,614-lb (3000-kg) payload 1,460 miles (2350 km); maximum rate of climb at sea level 1,080 ft (330 m) per minute; service ceiling 26,250 ft (8000 m)
Weights: empty equipped (207A) 23,370 lb (10600 kg); maximum payload (207A) 6,806 lb (3087 kg); maximum payload (207C) 8,818 lb (4000 kg); maximum take-off (207A) 35,275 lb (16000 kg); maximum take-off (207C) 36,376 lb (16500 kg)
Dimensions: span 91 ft 2½ in (27.80 m); length 68 ft 5 in (20.85 m); height 25 ft 5 in (7.75 m); wing area 923.5 sq ft (85.80 m²)
Armament: none
Operator: Spain

CASA 207 Azor

CASA C-212 Aviocar

The Spanish air force's requirement to replace several of its elderly transport aircraft such as the Douglas DC-3, the licence-built Junkers Ju 52/3m and the CASA Azor led to CASA drawing up a specification for a twin-turboprop transport which would be a general-purpose aircraft capable of adaptation for a number of roles. The possibility also of civil orders was not overlooked.

The result is the C-212 Aviocar, designed for a crew of two and up to 18 troops or, in a civil configuration, 19 passengers. The first prototype flew on 26 March, 1971 and was demonstrated with verve at the Paris air show only 10 weeks later; its STOL performance was well demonstrated although the main spar suffered some damage apparently as a result of reverse pitch being applied while the aircraft was still several feet above the runway.

The second prototype flew in October 1971 and the test programme continued, being rewarded by an order from the Spanish air ministry for an initial batch of eight pre-production aircraft, which made their maiden flights between November 1972 and February 1974. The type was given the Spanish air force designation T.12. The C-212A (T.12B) is a utility transport, and the first of 45 was delivered on 20 May, 1974; the first squadron to be equipped with the new type was No 461 at Gando in the Canary Islands.

Five examples of the C-212AV were ordered as VIP transports and the first arrived in May 1976. Of the eight pre-production Aviocars, six were completed as C-212B (TR.12A) photographic and survey versions with two Wild RC-10 cameras and a darkroom, and the other two became C-212E navigation trainers. Following the delivery of these two aircraft, the Spanish air force ordered three more of the same type to bring its total Aviocar orders to 61.

Other military export customers have included Indonesia (13), Jordan (3) and Portugal (20) for the C-212A, Jordan (1) C-212AV and Portugal (4) C-212B. The most recent military customer has been Chile, which has ordered eight Aviocars, four each for the army and navy. For civil use the government of Nicaragua bought five C-212As, but the basic commercial version is the C-212C of which three were ordered by Pertamina in Indonesia for operation by Pelita Air Service and Merpati Nusantara Air Lines, and the Turkish operator Bursa Hava Yollari has two.

As a result of considerable sales interest in the Far East, CASA concluded a licence agreement with Nurtanio Aircraft Industries in Indonesia; production began in mid-1976 and 18 had been completed by 1979. Production rate was established at one per month increasing to two a month by 1982. At present it is envisaged that around 80 aircraft will come from the Nurtanio line.

CASA has received orders for about 150 Aviocars and more than 120 had been delivered by 1979; the production rate is about 30 aircraft a year.

In April 1978 CASA flew the prototype of a higher-powered and heavier Aviocar, the C-212-10. This was a conversion of the 138th production aircraft, featuring a strengthened airframe and two 865-shp (645-kW) Garrett-AiResearch TPE331-10 turboprops. The more powerful engines enable the maximum take-off weight to be increased by 2,205 lb (1000 kg) to 16,534 lb (7500 kg) and the maximum payload from 4,410 lb (2000 kg) to 7,054 lb (3200 kg).

In its troop-transport configuration the standard Aviocar can carry light vehicles or up to 18 fully-equipped troops; the rear loading ramp can be used for paratroop and cargo drops. In the ambulance role 12 stretcher (litter) patients and two attendants can be carried. As a navigation trainer desks for five pupils and an instructor can be fitted.

The VIP versions supplied to the Spanish and Jordanian air forces have 12 passenger seats and folding tables.

Type: utility transport
Powerplant: two 750-shp (560-kW) Garrett-AiResearch TPE331-5-251C turboprops
Performance: maximum speed at 12,000 ft (3660 m) 223 mph (359 km/h); cruising speed

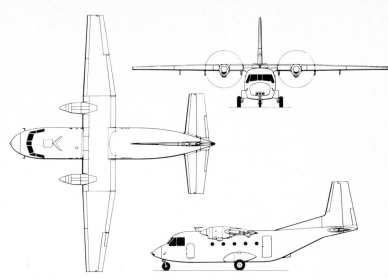

CASA 212 Aviocar

at 12,000 ft (3660 m) 171 mph (275 km/h); rate of climb at sea level 1,800 ft (548 m) per minute; service ceiling 26,700 ft (8140 m); take-off run to 50 ft (15 m) 1,588 ft (484 m); landing run from 50 ft (15 m) 1,263 ft (385 m); range with maximum fuel and 2,303-lb (1045-kg) payload 1,093 miles (1760 km)
Weights: empty 8,609 lb (3905 kg); maximum take-off (14,330 lb (6500 kg)
Dimensions: span 62 ft 4 in (19.00 m); length 49 ft 10 in (15.20 m); height 20 ft 8 in (6.30 m); wing area 430.56 sq ft (40.0 m²)
Operators: Chile, Indonesia, Jordan, Portugal, Spain

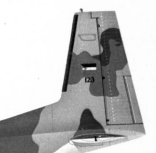

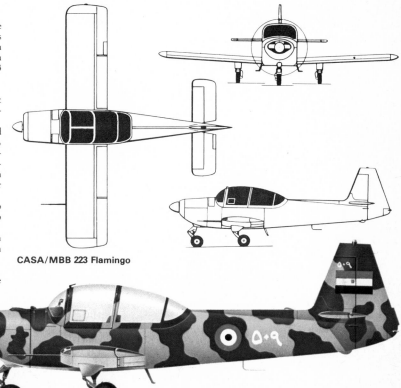

One of four CASA C-212 Aviocars operated by the Royal Jordanian Air Force from Amman.

CASA/MBB 223 Flamingo

The Flamingo spent so much of its development and production life undergoing changes of management that its relative obscurity is perhaps not surprising. Its origins go back to the German company SIAT (Siebel-werke-ATG) which was itself a successor to the famous pre-war Klemm lightplane company. When aircraft design and production was again permitted in Germany in 1955, SIAT was one of the first to enter this field, with a four-seat sporting and touring monoplane known as the SIAT 222. SIAT's second design, the Model 223 Flamingo, won a government-sponsored design competition in the early 1960s for a fully-aerobatic club and training aircraft, and the first of two prototypes was flown on 1 March 1967. It was originally proposed in two versions, the basic aerobatic 223K two-seater and the four-seat, extended-span 223N, but after changes in requirements the two production versions emerged as the 223A1, a 'two plus two' utility model, and the 223K1 single-seat aerobatic variant. In 1970, SIAT became a member of the MBB (Messerschmitt-Bölkow-Blohm) industrial group, production continuing as the MBB 223 until early 1972, when MBB transferred the whole Flamingo programme to Hispano Aviación of Spain. At that time German production had totalled 50, including 15 for the Turkish air force.

The first Spanish-built Flamingo was flown on 14 February 1972, but later in the same year Hispano was taken over by the Madrid-based Construcciones Aeronáuticas SA (CASA). A second series of 50 was built by Hispano/CASA, of which 30 were reportedly for the Syrian air force and three others for the

Spanish air force. Whether any of these three military operators still employ Flamingoes seems open to doubt — especially the Syrian air force, which was heavily re-equipped with aircraft from the Soviet Union after the 1973 war with Israel.

Type: one/four-seat trainer and utility aircraft
Powerplant: one 200-hp (149-kW) Lycoming IO-360-C1B flat-four piston engine
Performance: (two-seat) maximum speed 151 mph (243 km/h); cruising speed (75% power) 134 mph (216 km/h); range (including reserves) 547 miles (880 km); maximum range 715 miles (1150 km); maximum rate of climb at sea level 846 ft (258 m) per minute; service ceiling 12,300 ft (3750 m)
Weights: (two-seat) empty equipped 1,510 lb (685 kg); maximum take-off 2,315 lb (1050 kg)
Dimensions: span 27 ft 2 in (8.28 m); length 24 ft 4½ in (7.43 m); height 8 ft 10¼ in (2.70 m); wing area 123.8 sq ft (11.50 m²)
Armament: none
Operators: Spain, Syria, Turkey (but see text)

CASA/MBB 223 Flamingo

The Syrian Arab Air Force operates 48 CASA/MBB 223 Flamingo primary trainers, procured during 1977

Cerva CE.43 Guépard

The Cerva CE.43 Guépard (cheetah) is an all-metal version of the Wassmer WA4/21, itself a development of the WA.40 and WA.41 Baladou. Wassmer Aviation's origins go back to 1905, but it was only in 1955 that the company began to build Jodels and later went on to design its own range of light aircraft.

The WA4/21 prototype flew in March 1967; it was certificated in November of that year, and 25 had been built by 1970. Construction is of steel tube with a fabric-covered fuselage and a plywood-covered wing, but in order to provide an alternative metal version Wassmer Aviation and Siren SA in 1971 formed a joint company, known as *Consortium Européen de Réalisation et de Ventes d'Avions* (CERVA).

The dimensions of the CE.43 and WA.4/21 are identical but the former is slightly heavier. A prototype was flown in May 1971 and presented at the Paris Air Show later in the month. The second prototype was delivered to *Service de la Formation Aéronautique* (SFA) while a third airframe went to the *Centre d'Essais Aéronautique de* Toulouse (CEAT) for static testing.

Following certification on 1 June 1972, a government contract was awarded covering five CE.43s for SFA and 18 for the *Centre d'Essais en Vol* (CEV). By early 1974 there were 12 CE.43s on the production line and first deliveries to private customer in France, Germany, Finland and Africa began in 1975. A total of 43 had been delivered by January 1977.

Components for the CE.43 were built by Siren at Argenton-sur-Creuse while final assembly, equipment, installation and flight testing was carried out by Wassmer at Issoire.

Prototypes of two new versions have flown under French government contract — the CE.44 Couguar (cougar) on 24 October 1974 powered by a 285-hp (213-kW) Continental Tiara and the CE.45 Léopard with a 310-hp (231-kW) Lycoming TIO-540, but Wassmer went into liquidation in 1977.

Type: four-seat light aircraft
Powerplant: one 250-hp (187-kW) Lycoming IO-540 piston engine
Performance: maximum speed at sea level 199 mph (320 km/h); maximum cruising

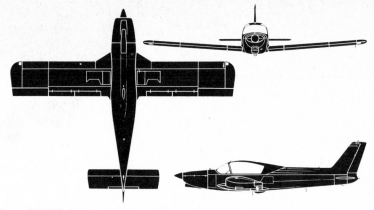

Cerva CE.43 Guépard

speed at 75% power at 6,560 ft (2000 m) 193 mph (310 km/h); service ceiling 16,400 ft (5000 m); range 1,740 miles (2800 km)
Weights: empty 1,863 lb (845 kg); loaded 3,130 lb (1420 kg)

Dimensions: span 32 ft 9 in (10.0 m); length 25 ft 7 in (7.80 m); height 9 ft 5 in (2.86 m); wing area 172 sq ft (16.0 m²)
Operators: France

Cessna Model 150

A two-seat cabin monoplane, the Cessna Model 150 is one of the world's most popular light aircraft, well over 20,000 having been built in the US and about 2,000 in France by Reims Aviation.

The prototype of the Model 150 first flew in September 1957, and was the aircraft with which Cessna re-entered the two-seat light aircraft market when production started in August 1958. In 1977 the Model 150 was being produced in Standard, Commuter, Commuter II and Aerobat versions. This last version embodies structural changes permitting a licence in the Aerobatic category for load factors of +6g and −3g at full gross weight. The Aerobat combines the economy and versatility of the Standard model with an aerobatic capability permitting the execution of manoeuvres such as barrel and aileron rolls, snap rolls, loops, vertical reverses and chandelles.

Of all-metal construction, the high-set wing is braced by a single strut. The landing gear is of the non-retractable tricycle type, with toe-operated single-disc hydraulic brakes on the main wheels. Nosewheel steering assists ground manoeuvring.

The enclosed cabin has side-by-side seating, and full dual controls can be fitted if required. Comprehensive standard equipment is fitted,

including a stall-warning indicator. Extensive optional communications and navigational equipment is available, including systems such as the Cessna 300 Series nav/com (navigation and communication radio) with 360-channel com and 160-channel nav with remote VOR indicator; 300 Series transceiver with 360 com channels; 300 Series nav/com with 360-channel com, 200 channel nav with remote VOR/LOC or VOR/ILS indicator; Series 300 ADF; marker beacon with three lights and aural signal; and transponder with 4096 code capability and slimline microphone. Other optional equipment includes blind-flying instrumentation; a rate of climb indicator; turn co-ordinator indicator; and outside air temperature gauge.

In addition to its widespread use as a private-owner and club aircraft, the Cessna 150 is also used for liaison duties by several of the world's smaller air forces.

Type: two-seat cabin monoplane
Powerplant: one 100-hp (74.5-kW) Continental O-200-A flat-four piston engine
Performance: maximum design speed 162 mph (261 km/h); maximum cruising speed (75% power) at 7,000 ft (2135m) 122mph (196 km/h); economical cruising speed at 10,000 ft (3050 m) 95 mph (153 km/h); stall-

Cessna C150 Aerobat

ing speed (flaps down, power off) 48 mph (78 km/h)
Weights: empty equipped 1,000 lb (454 kg); maximum take-off 1,600 lb (726 kg)
Dimensions: span 32ft 8½in (9.97 m);

length 23 ft 11 in (7.29 m); height 8 ft 6 in (2.59 m); wing area 157 sq ft (14.59 m²)
Operators: Ecuador, Haiti, Ivory Coast, Netherlands, Paraguay, Somalia, Sri Lanka

---

Cessna Model 170/172/T-41 Mescalero

The evolution of Cessna's Model 170 is mentioned under the entry for the O-1 Bird Dog. The Model 172, which was to follow, is of the same basic design, but introduced a tricycle landing gear and a swept fin and rudder.

The USAF's decision to provide all-through jet training for its pupil pilots proved to be too costly, as mentioned under the Cessna T-37 entry, with the result that the US Air Force had an urgent requirement for a piston-engined trainer. This was needed to re-introduce a 30-hour period of basic training on an aircraft type which long experience had shown to be far more economical in operation. This served to weed out pupils lacking pilot

aptitude.

Having reached this conclusion, in July 1964 the US Air Force lost little time in seeking a suitable 'off the shelf' trainer which had a sufficiently long background in use to ensure that it would give little trouble. Cessna's Model 172 was chosen, 170 were ordered on 31 July 1964 as the T-41A Mescalero, and the first were in use six weeks later; by July 1965 all had been delivered. They serve at civilian flying schools with government contracts for USAF *ab initio* training, and carry both USAF serial numbers and FAA civil registrations. In 1967 an additional 34 were procured.

The US Army bought 255 T-41Bs with the

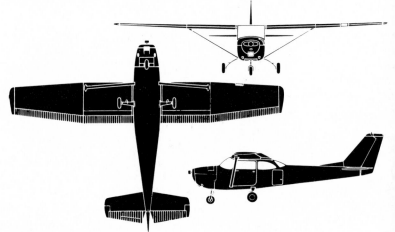

Cessna T-41A Mescalero

210-hp (157-kW) Continental IO-360-D flat-six engine. T-41C is the designation of 45 at the USAF Academy, virtually identical to the T-41B. Production ended with 226 similar T-41Ds for supply to nations eligible under the Military Assistance Program.

Type: two-seat basic trainer/utility aircraft
Powerplant: (T-41A) one 145-hp (108-kW) Continental O-300-C flat-six piston engine
Performance: (T-41B) maximum speed 153 mph (246 km/h) at sea level; maximum

cruising speed 145 mph (233 km/h) at sea level; maximum cruising range at 10,000 ft (3050 m) 800 miles (1287 km)
Weights: (T-41B) empty 1,230 lb (558 kg); maximum take-off 2,300 lb (1043 kg)
Dimensions: span 36 ft 2 in (11.02 m); length 26 ft 11 in (8.20 m); height 8 ft 9½ in (2.68 m); wing area 174 sq ft (16.16 m²)
Armament: none
Operators: Colombia, Ecuador, Peru, Saudi Arabia, Singapore, Turkey, US Air Force, US Army

Cessna have supplied Type 170/172 trainers (often with US military designation T-41A) to many air forces; this T-41A is operated by the Ecuadorean Army aviation.

Cessna Model 180/185/U-17 Skywagon

Cessna's Model 170, from which the O-1 Bird Dog was evolved, was a classic design of which traces could be seen in many subsequent aircraft that originated from this company. In modernised form, with tricycle landing gear, this design remains the basis of several of the company's lightplanes in production in 1979.

The Cessna 180, announced in January 1953, was generally similar to the 170. It differed by having a more powerful Continental engine, constant-speed propeller, and larger tail. After 4,000 had been built, 15 were supplied to the Australian army, serving with No 16 Army Light Aircraft Squadron in a light observation and reconnaissance role.

In July 1960 Cessna flew the prototype Model 185, with more powerful engine, still further increase in fin/rudder area, and changes in tyres and tyre pressure for operation at increased gross weight. Delivery of production aircraft began in March 1961 and when, about a year later, the USAF was seeking to purchase a light utility aircraft for supply to countries eligible for aid under the Military Assistance Program, Cessna's 185 was selected as meeting the requirement and ordered under the designation U-17. More

than 300 were supplied eventually, the initial version being the U-17A of which 169 had been delivered by July 1965, powered by the 260-hp (194-kW) Continental IO-470-F flat-six piston engine. They were followed by 136 U-17Bs with the 300-hp (224-kW) Continental IO-520D flat-six engine. Both Peru and South Africa bought aircraft equivalent to the U-17B direct from Cessna for their armed services. Final production version was the U-17C with Continental O-470-L engine, this having a carburettor instead of direct fuel injection.

Type: one/six-seat utility aircraft
Powerplant: (U-17B) one 300-hp (224-kW) Continental IO-520-D flat-six piston engine
Performance: (U-17B) maximum speed 178 mph (286 km/h); maximum cruising speed 169 mph (272 km/h) at 7,500 ft (2285 m); range with maximum standard fuel and no reserves 600 miles (966 km); maximum range with maximum optional fuel 1,075 miles (1730 km)
Weights: (U-17B) empty equipped 1,580 lb (717 kg); maximum take-off 3,300 lb (1497 kg)
Dimensions: span 36 ft 2 in (11.02 m);

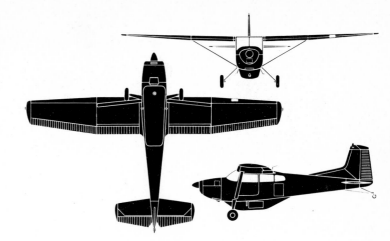

Cessna C185

length 25 ft 6 in (7.77 m); height 7 ft 6 in (2.29 m); wing area 174 sq ft (16.16 m²)
Armament: none

Operators: Bolivia, Costa Rica, Laos, Peru, South Africa, Vietnam

---

Cessna Model 206 Super Skywagon/207 Skywagon

Cessna's Model 185 had the civil name Skywagon and when an improved version was evolved this was designated Cessna 206 Super Skywagon. Changes included replacement of the tailwheel landing gear with one of tricycle type; introduction of conical-camber wingtips to reduce induced drag; enlargement of the tailplane and flaps; addition of double cargo doors on the right side to permit the loading of freight measuring 4 × 3 × 3 ft (1.22 × 0.91 × 0.91 m); and a more powerful 285-hp (213-kW) Continental IO-520-A flat-six engine. Production of the Model 206 ended in 1964, but examples remain in service with several armed forces.

On 3 January 1969 Cessna flew the first production example of the lengthened seven-seat Model 207, which reverted to the name Skywagon. This introduced a second access door on the right; a 120-lb (54-kg) capacity baggage compartment, forward of the cabin; and the more powerful IO-520-J engine. Both 206 and 207 can be flown with cargo doors removed for the air-dropping of supplies,

parachuting and photography. Both can carry a 300-lb (136-kg) glassfibre cargo pack beneath the fuselage, and ambulance kits comprising a stretcher, oxygen supply and attendant seat are available. The Model 207 also serves with several armed services.

Type: (206) one/six-seat; (207) one/seven-seat utility aircraft
Powerplant: (206) one 285-hp (213-kW), (207) one 300-hp (224-kW) Continental IO-520 flat-six piston engine
Performance: maximum speed at sea level (206) 174 mph (280 km/h), (207) 168 mph (270 km/h); maximum cruising speed (206) 163 mph (262 km/h) at 6,000 ft (1830 m), (207) 159 mph (256 km/h) at 6,500 ft (1980 m); maximum range with maximum fuel and no reserves (206) 1,020 miles (1642 km), (207) 925 miles (1489 km)
Weights: empty (206) 1,690 lb (767 kg), (207) 1,900 lb (862 kg); maximum take-off and landing (206) 3,600 lb (1633 kg) (207) 3,800 lb (1724 kg)

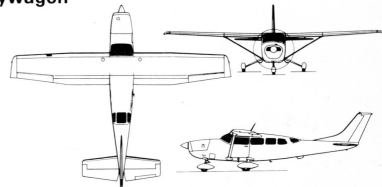

Cessna Model 206 Super Skywagon/207 Skywagon

Dimensions: span (206) 36 ft 7 in (11.15 m), (207) 35 ft 10 in (10.92 m); length (206) 27 ft 9 in (8.46 m), (207) 31 ft 9 in (9.68 m); height (206) 9 ft 9 in (2.97 m), (207) 9 ft 6½ in (2.91 m); wing area (206) 175.5 sq ft (16.30 m²), (207) 174 sq ft (16.16 m²)
Armament: none
Operators: Bolivia, Guatemala, Guyana, Indonesia, Israel, Liberia, Mexico, Paraguay

---

Cessna Model 305A/O-1 Bird Dog

The dust of World War II had hardly settled before the US Army began the inevitably slow task of procuring new aircraft which, based upon immediate past experience, would hopefully be free of the shortcomings of their predecessors. In the late 1940s the specification for a two-seat liaison and observation monoplane was circulated to US manufacturers of light aircraft, and the Cessna Aircraft Company's submission was declared the winner. In June 1950 an initial contract was awarded for 418 examples of the aircraft which Cessna identified as their Model 305A.

Cessna's design was based upon their successful Model 170, a lightweight strut-braced high-wing monoplane, powered by a 145-hp (108-kW) Continental flat-six engine, which provided accommodation for a pilot and three passengers. The Model 305A differed by having the aft fuselage redesigned, the turtleback of the 170 disappearing so that a window could give a clear view to the rear, and by the provision of transparent panels in the wing centre-section, which formed the cabin roof. A wider access door was provided so that there was room to load a standard stretcher, for which support brackets were installed.

Deliveries of production aircraft began in December 1950, under the designation L-19A and with the name Bird Dog, and 2,486 had been delivered by October 1954, of which 60 were diverted to the US Marine Corps which designated them OE-1. An L-19A-1T instrument-trainer version was developed in 1953, TL-19D trainers with constant-speed propellers in 1956, and an improved L-19E with higher gross weight, was the final production version to bring the grand total of

Bird Dogs to 3,431. With redesignation in 1962, the US Army's L-19A, TL-19D and L-19E aircraft became O-1A, TO-1D and O-1E respectively. The US Marines' OE-1 became O-1B, and this service also acquired 25 higher powered O-1Cs. US Army trainers, derived from standard production aircraft, also had the designations TO-1A, and TO-1E.

Bird Dogs were operated in small numbers during the Korean War, but the USAF acquired many of the Army's O-1s for use by Forward Air Controllers in Vietnam, former TO-1Ds and O-1As becoming re-designated O-1F and O-1G respectively when equipped for this role. O-1s were supplied to many nations and built under licence by Fuji in Japan.

continued

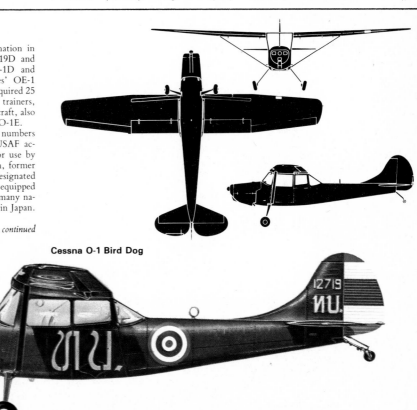

Cessna O-1 Bird Dog

Cessna O-1A Bird Dog (51-12719) operated by a Royal Thai Army air observation and liaison flight in 1957.

Type: liaison and observation aircraft
Powerplant: (O-1E) one 213-hp (159-kW)
Continental O-470-11 flat-six piston engine
Performance: (O-1E) maximum speed 130
mph (209 km/h); range 530 miles (853 km)
Weights: (O-1E) empty 1,614 lb (732 kg);
maximum take-off 2,400 lb (1089 kg)
Dimensions: span 36 ft 0 in (10.97 m);
length 25 ft 9 in (7.85 m); height 7 ft 3½ in
(2.22 m); wing area 174 sq ft (16.16 m²)
Armament: none
Operators: Austria, Brazil, Canada, Chile,
France, Italy, Japan, Kampuchea, South
Korea, Laos, Lebanon, Norway, Pakistan,
Thailand, US Air Force, US Army, US
Marine Corps, Vietnam

Large numbers of Cessna O-1 Bird Dogs remain in use in many countries, often (as in the case of this example supplied to what was then the VNAF of South Vietnam) simply left freely by US forces. Such aircraft can be maintained by local resources.

Cessna Model 310/320/U-3

In 1952 Cessna initiated the design of a new 5/6-seat light twin, the prototype of which flew for the first time on 3 January 1953. Designated Model 310, this was to prove a popular design, and continues in production in 1979, over a quarter of a century after the type's first flight. During this period more than 4,500 examples have been built. Of low-wing monoplane configuration, and provided with tricycle landing gear, the prototype was powered by two 225-hp (168-kW) Continental O-470 flat-six engines, each driving a two-blade metal constant-speed and fully-feathering propeller. This engine had been developed originally for military use under the company designation E225, and its use to power the Cessna 310 was one of its first civil applications.

Early production aircraft were powered by the 260-hp (194-kW) Continental IO-470, and an outstanding feature of the design at that time were the two wingtip fuel tanks which then represented the entire fuel tankage. Production deliveries began in 1954, and steady product improvement has continued since that time. Current production Model 310s are powered by two 285-hp (213-kW) Continental IO-520-M piston engines. A *de luxe* version with 285-hp (213-kW) Continental TSIO-520 turbo-

charged engines, individual seats, air-conditioning and an oxygen system as standard was introduced in 1966. This was known as the Turbo-System Executive Skynight and for a short period was identified also as the Cessna 320. It continues in production in 1979, but is known now as the Turbo-System T31- and has 285-hp (213-kW) TSIO-520-B turbocharged engines.

In the mid-1950s the USAF initiated a competition to select a suitable 'off the shelf' design to serve in an administrative liaison and cargo aircraft category. Twin-engine power was an essential requirement, and a slightly modified version of the Model 310 was ordered for service with the USAF under the designation L-27A, subsequently redesignated U-3A. A total of 160 U-3As were acquired, and were followed into service by 36 U-3Bs with limited 'all-weather' capability. A small number of Cessna 310s also serve with the French air force.

Type: 5/6-seat cabin monoplane/administrative liaison and cargo aircraft
Powerplant: (U-3B) two 260-hp (194-kW) Continental IO-470-V flat-six piston engines
Performance: (U-3B) maximum speed 236 mph (380 km/h); maximum cruising speed at 6,500 ft (1980 m) 221 mph (356 km/h); range

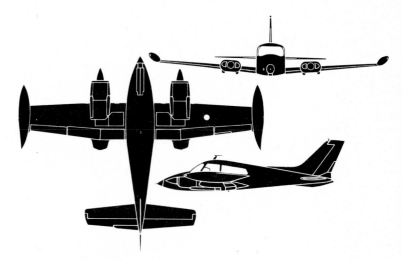

Cessna Model 310/320/U-3

at maximum cruising speed (standard fuel, no reserves) 774 miles (1246 km)
Weights: empty 3,214 lb (1458 kg); maximum take-off 5,300 lb (2404 kg)
Dimensions: span 36 ft 11 in (11.25 m);

length 29 ft 3 in (8.92 m); height 10 ft 6 in (3.20 m); wing area 179 sq ft (16.63 m²)
Armament: none
Operators: France, US Air Force

The Cessna U-3B is an administrative liaison and utility cargo transport for the US Air Force (36 delivered). Apart from having a swept fin, it is generally similar to the original U-3A (previously L-27A) model, of which 160 were bought in the late 1950s.

Cessna Model 318/T-37

It has been mentioned in the Beech T-34 entry how, in 1950, the USAF was uncertain whether to introduce a turbine-engine aircraft as a trainer: in putting the T-34 into production they opted for the available and cheaper piston engine. This decision was, of course, merely putting off the evil hour: just two years later the problem arose again, and after extensive discussion, and with considerable trepidation, a design competition was initiated to find a suitable aircraft for development as a jet trainer for primary flying instruction.

However hesitant the USAF decision-makers in 1950, the basic idea was really good sense. The very different handling techniques for piston and turbine engines meant that, after learning to fly on a piston-engined aircraft, there was a new big step to be taken in converting to turbine-powered aircraft. If pupils started from scratch with turbine power, it would offer at least one area of continuity in flying training. Those opposed to the plan feared that the accident rate might soar because of the higher-performance aircraft, or that there might be an excessive number of engine failures as a result of incorrect handling of what was, after all, a very new type of power unit. However, the decision was made to go ahead: The problem, when it arrived, was of a very different nature.

The winner of the competition, announced in early 1953, was the Cessna Aircraft Company's proposal which they identified as the Model 318, a perfectly straightforward monoplane of all-metal construction, with pupil and instructor seated in what had long been considered to be an ideal side-by-side arrangement (contrary to the normal US tandem practice). Powerplant consisted of two Continental turbojets (Americanized versions of the French Turboméca *Marboré*) mounted within the wing roots on each side of the fuselage. The tailplane was mounted above the fuselage about one-third of the way up the fin to ensure that the airstream flowing past it was unaffected by the jet efflux.

Following selection of the Model 318 as the programme winner, two prototypes were ordered under the designation XT-37, the first of which made its initial flight on 12 October 1954. It was powered by the prototype engines built by Continental, designated YJ69-T-9, each of which developed 920-lb (417-kg) thrust. The first production batch of 11 aircraft, which were designated T-37As, were ordered during 1954, and the first of these flew on 27 September 1955. The T-37As, of which 534 were built under successive contracts, were slow in entering service due to the fact that a number of changes and modifications were carried out before they

were considered acceptable for training purposes.

When introduced into service, in 1957, the T-37s were used initially as basic trainers, the pupils transferring to these aircraft only after completing their primary training on Beech T-34 Mentors. In April 1961 the original plan for all-through jet training was initiated: instead of a quiet amble in the traditional kind of primary trainer with a speed range of perhaps 60 – 140 mph (97 – 225 km/h), the pupil flew from the very beginning of his training in an aircraft which had a speed range of 85 – 425 mph (138 – 684 km/h). No catastrophic accident rate resulted, as had been feared by many, but one point which had not been fully considered was the much higher training cost using these turbine aircraft. There is inevitably a varying pupil rejection rate at the end of primary training, and it was decided in 1964 to revert to light piston-engine trainers, which are much cheaper to operate, for this primary phase, so that T-37 pupils were those left after the first weeding-out.

T-37Bs with more powerful engines and improved nav/com systems were introduced into service in November 1959, and all surviving T-37As were converted retrospectively to this standard. Final version was the T-37C with provision for armament and wingtip fuel tanks. When production ended in 1977 a combined total of 1,268 T-37s had been built for the USAF and for export.

Type: two-seat jet primary trainer
Powerplant: (T-37B/C) two 1,025-lb (465-kg) thrust Continental J69-T-25 turbojets
Performance: (T-37B) maximum speed at 20,000 ft (6100 m) 425 mph (684 km/h); cruising speed at 35,000 ft (10670 m); range with standard fuel at cruising speed 870 miles (1400 km)
Weight: (T-37B) maximum take-off 6,574 lb (2982 kg)
Dimensions: span 33 ft 9.3 in (10.29 m); length 29 ft 3 in (8.92 m); height 9 ft 2 in (2.79 m); wing area 183.9 sq ft (17.08 m²)
Armament: (T-37C) two 250-lb (113-kg) bombs, or four Sidewinder missiles, or jettisonable pods which can contain a 0.50-in (12.7-mm) machine-gun with 200 rounds, two 2.75-in (69.8-mm) folding fin rockets, and four 3-lb (1.4-kg) practice bombs
Operators: Brazil, Chile, Colombia, Greece, Kampuchea, Pakistan, Thailand, Turkey, US Air Force, West Germany

These **Cessna T-37s** are among 685 serving as the Phase II undergraduate pilot trainer of the US Air Force. This flight-line is at Randolph AFB, now home of instructor training; undergrads fly at Columbus, Laughlin, Vance, Reese, Williams and Sheppard.

Cessna Model 318E/A-37 Dragonfly

During 1962 two Cessna T-37 trainers were evaluated by the USAF's Special Air Warfare Center to consider their suitability for deployment in the counter-insurgency (COIN) role. The aircraft chosen for this evaluation were two T-37Bs, and these were first tested with their original powerplant of two 1,025-lb (465-kg) thrust Continental J69-T-25 turbojets, at a take-off weight of 8,700 lb (3946 kg), which was almost 33% above the normal maximum take-off weight. After a first test period, the airframes were modified to accept two 2,400-lb (1089-kg) thrust General Electric J85-GE-5 turbojets. This vast increase in power made it possible for the aircraft, then designated YAT-37D, to be flown at steadily increasing maximum take-off weights until a safe upper limit of 14,000 lb (6350 kg) was reached. There was, clearly, plenty of scope for the carriage of a worthwhile load of weapons.

This exercise had been more academic than essential, until the need of the war in Vietnam made the USAF take a closer look at this armed version of what had proved to be an excellent trainer. Accordingly, Cessna were requested to convert 39 T-37B trainers to a light-strike configuration, a contract being awarded in 1966: this related to the conversion of new T-37B aircraft taken from the production line. The new model based on the earlier experiments with the two YAT-37Ds, and

equipped with eight underwing hardpoints, provided with wingtip tanks to increase fuel capacity, and was powered by derated General Electric J85-GE-5 turbojets.

Delivery of these aircraft to the USAF began on 2 May 1967, and during the latter half of that year a squadron numbering 25 of these aircraft, designated A-37A and named Dragonfly, underwent a four-month operational evaluation in South Vietnam. Following this period of investigation, they were transferred for operational duty with the 604th Air Commando Squadron at Bien Hoa; in 1970 they were assigned to the South Vietnamese air force.

During this period, Cessna had been busy building the prototype of a purpose-designed light-strike aircraft based on the T-37 airframe, and this flew for the first time in September 1967. Little time was lost in evaluating this, and the first of the initial pro-

continued

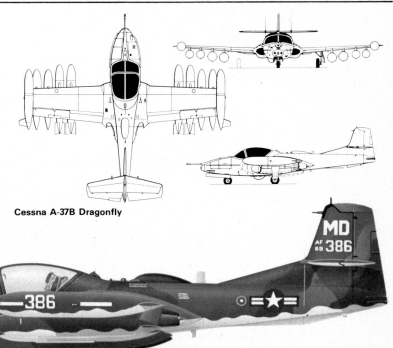

Cessna A-37B Dragonfly

Cessna A-37B Dragonfly flown by the 104th Tactical Fighter Squadron, Maryland Air National Guard, US Air Force.

duction batch of A-37Bs was started quickly enough for the first production deliveries to begin in May 1968.

The A-37B differed in its construction from the prototype YAT-37D which had been evaluated in 1963–64. The airframe had been stressed for 6-g loading, maximum internal fuel capacity was increased to 507 US gallons (1920 litres), with the ability to carry four auxiliary tanks with a combined capacity of 400 US gallons (1516 litres), and there was also provision for flight-refuelling. Powerplant was changed to two General Electric J85-GE-17A turbojets. A GAU-2B/A 7.62-mm Minigun was installed, and the eight underwing hardpoints were able to carry in excess of 5,000 lb (2268 kg) of mixed stores. For the assessment of results both gun and strike cameras were carried, and while the provision of armour would have added a significant weight penalty which could not be afforded, some measure of protection for the crew of two was provided by the inclusion of layered nylon flak-curtains installed around the cockpit.

By the time that production ended in 1977, a total of 577 A-37Bs had been built, and in addition to serving with the USAF had been supplied in small numbers to friendly nations. Many were transferred to the US Air National Guard, and to the South Vietnam air force.

Type: two-seat light strike aircraft
Powerplant: two 2,850-lb (1293-kg) thrust General Electric J85-GE-17A turbojets
Performance: maximum speed at 16,000 ft (4875 m) 524 mph (843 km/h); maximum cruising speed at 25,000 ft (7620 m) 489 mph (787 km/h); range with maximum fuel at 25,000 ft (7620 m) with reserves 1,012 miles (1629 km); range with maximum payload, including 4,100 lb (1860 kg) external weapons 460 miles (740 km)
Weights: empty equipped 6,211 lb (2817 kg); maximum take-off 14,000 lb (6350 kg)
Dimensions: span 35 ft 10½ in (10.93 m); length 28 ft 3¼ in (8.62 m); height 8 ft 10½ in (2.71 m); wing area 183.9 sq ft (17.08 m²)
Armament: can include bombs, incendiary bombs, cluster bombs, rocket pods and gun pods
Operators: Chile, Ecuador, Guatemala, Thailand, US Air Force, US Air National Guard, South Vietnam

This Cessna A-37B Dragonfly was photographed in VNAF markings in August 1971, near Da Nang AB where much Vietnamese pilot training was carried out. Several Dragonflies are among the types still operating with today's Vietnamese People's AF.

Cessna Model 337 Skymaster/O-2 Milirole

After several years of study and evaluation, Cessna completed the design of a somewhat unorthodox 4/6-seat light aircraft. Their company's aim had been to produce a low-cost and easy-to-fly aeroplane, which would be comfortable, and offered the safety and advantages of a twin-engine powerplant. It is in the layout of the powerplant that the unorthodox features appear: one engine and tractor propeller is mounted conventionally in the nose; the second, high in the aft fuselage, turns a pusher propeller. Contra-rotation of the propellers ensures that there are no torque effects at take-off maximum power, and with both engines mounted on the centreline of the fuselage, single-engine operation (of either engine) has proved undemanding even for comparatively inexperienced pilots. Two slim metal booms are integrated with the structure of the high-mounted strut-braced wing, and these have twin fins and rudders at their aft end, with a tailplane and elevator between the booms, the tailplane serving also to consolidate this 'frame' structure. The twin booms have ample clearance between them for the 76-in (1.93-m) diameter rear propeller.

Cessna's prototype of this aircraft, which the company designated Model 336 Skymaster, flew for the first time at Wichita, Kansas, on 28 February 1961, and FAA certification was awarded on 22 May 1962. The Model 336 prototype had fixed landing gear, as did the 195 production aircraft, the first of which was delivered in May 1963. In February 1965 the Model 336 was followed into production by a generally similar but much improved version which has the designation Model 337 Skymaster, this introducing hydraulically-retractable tricycle-type landing gear. The latter aircraft continues in production in 1979 as the Skymaster II, and since May 1972 has been available also with turbocharged engines, a pressurized cabin and air-conditioning. Well over 2,000 Model 336/337 Skymasters had been built by early 1979.

Reims Aviation in France, which manufactures Cessna aircraft under licence for sale in Europe, Africa and Asia, has also built a small number of unpressurized and pressurized 337s, these all being powered by Rolls-Royce Continental engines. The name *Milirole* was applied to the basic unpressurized F 337 for a short time. Since 1974 Reims have developed a special unpressurized STOL version, designated FTB 337, which can be provided with a wide range of equipment to make it suitable for such duties as maritime or overland patrol and rescue.

War in Vietnam brought a new task for air units known as Forward Air Control (FAC), a pilot in a lightplane carrying out tasks not very different from those of artillery observers in earlier years of aviation history. In the modern application, however, they spot not for artillery units on the ground, but seek guerrillas operating in jungle terrain and mark their position for the airborne 'artillery' which they call in to the attack. Experience in Vietnam suggested that the mission could be made more effective with FAC aircraft operated by a pilot and Forward Air Navigator (FAN), the latter being able to concentrate on the FAC mission without having to fly the aircraft.

Cessna's Model 337 was selected 'off the shelf' in late 1966 as being ideal for this role, and equipped with four underwing pylons to carry flares, rockets and such light ordnance as a 7.62-mm (0.3-in) Minigun pack. These were designated O-2A, and 501 were supplied to the USAF. In addition, a version equipped for psychological warfare missions entered USAF service under the designation O-2B. This carried a powerful air-to-ground broadcasting system using three 600-Watt amplifiers and a battery of highly directional speakers. Total procurement of O-2B aircraft amounted to 31. Both versions carried advance nav/com systems. Twelve O-2As were supplied to the Imperial Iranian Air Force in early 1970. A twin-turboprop O-2T/O-2TT did not proceed beyond USAF evaluation.

Type: tandem-engine cabin monoplane
Powerplant: two 210-hp (157-kW) Continental IO-360 flat-six piston engines

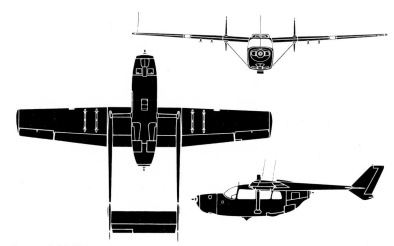

Cessna O-2A Milirole

Performance: maximum speed at sea level 206 mph (332 km/h); maximum cruising speed at 5,500 ft (1675 m); 196 mph (315 km/h); range at maximum cruising speed (standard fuel, no reserve) 780 miles (1255 km)
Weights: empty 2,705 lb (1227 kg); maximum take-off 4,630 lb (2100 kg)

Dimensions: span 38 ft 2 in (11.63 m); length 29 ft 9 in (9.07 m); height 9 ft 2 in (2.79 m); wing area 202.5 sq ft (18.81 m²)
Armament: (O-2A) flares, rockets, Minigun pack
Operators: Ecuador, Iran, Venezuela, US Air Force

The unusual Cessna O-2 series, with push/pull engines derived from the Skymaster, was the chief lightplane FAC (forward air control) platform in Vietnam. By 1969 the USAF had 346 of the multi-role O-2A, illustrated, plus 164 'psy-war' O-2B aircraft.

Cessna Model 402/411/421

When it flew for the first time on 18 July 1962, Cessna's Model 411 then represented the largest business aircraft in the company's extensive range of light aircraft. In overall configuration it had a close relationship to the company's Model 310, which had served the USAF as a light twin-engine administrative liaison and cargo aircraft from December 1960 under the designations L-27A or U-3. It differed, however, by having slightly increased wing span and area, a longer fuselage, and the introduction of more powerful 340-hp (254-kW) Continental GTSIO-520-C turbocharged engines. There had, of course, been some detail refinements, and the permanently fixed wingtip fuel tanks had undergone some alteration in their shape to improve their aerodynamic characteristics and reduce drag. These aircraft have accommodation for a crew of two, and can seat from four to six passengers according to the interior layout, and each seat in the main cabin has a reading light, ventilator and oxygen outlet.

On 26 August 1965 Cessna flew the prototype of a generally similar aircraft which served for two new models, Models 401 and 402, and when FAA certification of the Model 401 prototype was awarded on 20 September 1966 it covered also the Model 402. These two aircraft represented lower-cost versions of the Model 411, differing primarily by having two

300-hp (224-kW) Continental TSIO-520-E flat-six engines and some reduction in basic installed equipment. The Model 401 accommodates a crew of two and four to six passengers, but the Model 402 has a cabin layout which permitted a quick change from nine-seat commuter use to an all-cargo configuration.

Cessna's six-seat Model 421, first announced on 28 October 1965, is generally similar to these two latter aircraft, except for the provision of a new fuselage of fail-safe structure to permit cabin pressurization, installation of 375 hp (280 kW) Continental GTSIO-520-D turbocharged engines, and the introduction of an AiResearch air-conditioning and pressurization system.

All three of these aircraft, namely the Models 402, 411 and 421, have proved useful to air forces for 'off the shelf' buys of communications aircraft: for example, 402s serve with the Royal Malaysian air force and 411s with the French air force.

Type: six/nine-seat light transport aircraft
Powerplant: (421) two 375-hp (280-kW) Continental GTSIO-520-L flat-six geared and turbocharged piston engines
Performance: (421) maximum speed 297 mph (478 km/h) at 20,000 ft (6095 m); maximum cruising speed 279 mph

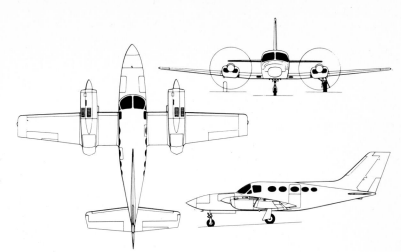

Cessna Model 402/411/421

(449 km/h) at 25,000 ft (7620 m); range (with allowances for start, taxi, take-off, climb, descent and 45-minutes reserves at 45% power, at maximum cruising speed with maximum fuel at 25,000 ft (7620 m) 1,440 miles (2317 km)
Weights: (421) empty 4,572 lb (2074 kg); maximum take-off 7,450 lb (3379 kg)

Dimensions: (421) span 41 ft 1½ in (12.53 m); length 36 ft 4½ in (11.09 m); height 11 ft 5½ in (3.49 m); wing area 215 sq ft (19.97 m²)
Armament: none
Operators: Bolivia, Finland, France, Indonesia, Malaysia, Mexico, Saudi Arabia, Turkey

Cessna Model 500 Citation

The Cessna Citation was the first of the new generation of quiet and economical turbofan business jets, and its development represented an enormous financial commitment for Cessna Aircraft Company. It was the answer to growing environmentalist pressure, and when it first flew on 15 September 1969 it posed a serious commercial threat to the BAC HS 125, Dassault Falcon 20, North American Sabreliner and Learjet types which had hitherto dominated the market.

The Citation is an all-metal, pressurized, low-wing monoplane. It has seating for up to eight people including two crew — although the Citation I S/P version of the aircraft is certificated for single-pilot operation. Initial aircraft, delivered in 1971, were competitively priced at $695,000 including a full Category II avionics package, a computerized maintenance programme and training for the customer's pilots and mechanics. In a subsequent development Cessna produced the Citation II, with uprated JT-15D engines and a stretched 12-seat cabin. The prototype Citation II first flew on 31 January 1977, with first deliveries in April 1978. The Citation III is an entirely new and larger aircraft with a supercritical wing, scheduled to enter service in 1981.

The first military user of the Citation was the Venezuelan air force which took delivery of the 92nd production aircraft in 1973; this is operated by the *Comando Aereo Logistico* on general transport duties. The *Ejercito Argentino* also purchased a Citation, which entered service with the *Instituto Geografico Militar*. It had a Wild RC-10 dual camera installation fitted in a large fairing under the centre fuselage, and is employed on mapping and photographic surveillance missions.

The US forces have not, as yet, used the Citation but an extensive evaluation was carried out by the US Coast Guard prior to their decision to purchase the Dassault Falcon Guardian.

Type: seven/eight-seat light communications aircraft
Powerplant: two 2,200-lb (998-kg) Pratt & Whitney Aircraft of Canada JT15D-1 turbofans
Performance: maximum speed 403 mph (648 km/h); maximum cruising speed 400 mph (644 km/h); long-range cruising speed at 35,000 ft (10670 m) 321 mph (514 km/h); maximum rate of climb 3,100 ft (945 m) per minute; service ceiling 35,000 ft (10670 m); balanced field length 3,575 ft (1090 m); maximum range with full fuel and 45 minutes reserves at long-range cruising speed 1,404 miles (1664 m)
Weights: empty equipped 6,520 lb (2960 kg); maximum take-off 11,500 lb (5217 kg)

Dimensions: span 43 ft 9 in (13.34 m); length 43 ft 6 in (13.26 m); height 14 ft 4 in (4.40 m); wing area 260 sq ft (24.15 m²)
Operators: Argentina, Venezuela

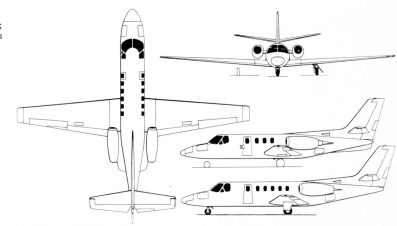

Cessna Model 500 Citation

Cessna's Citation is among the cheapest executive jets, making it popular with a number of air forces, including the FAV of Venezuela. This Citation I is used for VIP transport and other urgent missions. Some air forces use Citations for training.

Consolidated Aeronautics PBY-5 Catalina

Requiring a new monoplane patrol flying-boat to replace the liberally-strutted Consolidated P2Y and Martin P3M flying-boats in service in 1933, the US Navy ordered competitive prototypes from Consolidated Aircraft and Douglas Aircraft, and it was the former company's XP3Y-1 which was ordered into production. In due course, as the Catalina, the type became used extensively by the US forces and their allies and has been built in larger quantity (approximately 4,000 examples) than any other flying-boat in history.

Experience in the construction of the P2Y helped in the design of an efficient two-step hull, above which was mounted an internally-braced parasol wing that was sufficiently near to a true cantilever structure to require only two streamlined bracing struts on each side. This clean design was enhanced by a then-unique feature: stabilizing floats which retracted in flight to form the wingtips. The powerplant comprised two 825-hp (615-kW) Pratt & Whitney R-1830-58 Twin Wasp radial engines. Armament comprised four 0.5-in (12.7-mm) machine-guns and up to 2,000 lb (907 kg) of externally-hung ordnance.

The first production PBY-1s equipped Navy Patrol Squadron VP-11F in late 1936. They were followed by the PBY-2/-3 and -4, which differed primarily in their powerplant. The first PBY-5s entered service on 18 September 1940, with 1,200-hp (895-kW) R-1830-92

engines, waist blisters for beam gunners, and a revised tail. In late 1939 Consolidated had flown an XPBY-5A prototype which introduced retractable tricycle landing gear to confer amphibious capability, and following evaluation the US Navy ordered the remaining PBY-5s on the production line to be completed as amphibians. Thereafter, construction continued into 1945 with PBY-5A/-5B and -6A aircraft, which differed mainly in powerplant and armament. PBYs supplied to the RAF in 1940 were named Catalina by that service, this name being adopted also by the US Navy on 1 October 1941.

PBYs were also built in the Soviet-Union, which designated them GST, and it is uncertainty regarding the large number constructed by that nation which makes it necessary to use the 'approximately 4,000' figure for total production. A total of 230 Canadian-built aircraft were designated PBV-1A by the US Navy, but these all served with the USAAF as OA-10A amphibians. Many more examples were built in Canadian factories, those PBYs which served with the RCAF having the name Canso. In addition a slightly revised version was built by the Naval Aircraft Factory at Philadelphia, Pennsylvania, these being designated PBN-1 and named Nomad.

Catalina flying-boats were retired from US Navy service soon after the end of World War II, but many amphibians remained in use for several years, primarily in the air-sea rescue

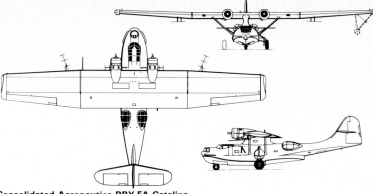

Consolidated Aeronautics PBY-5A Catalina

role. Some of these fine flying-boats still serve in 1979 with the armed forces of seven nations.

Type: flying-boat and amphibious patrol-bomber
Powerplant: (PBY-5A) two 1,200-hp (895-kW) Pratt & Whitney R-1830-92 Twin Wasp radial piston engines
Performance: (PBY-5A) maximum speed 175 mph (282 km/h) at 7,000 ft (2135 m); cruising speed 113 mph (182 km/h); range 2,350 miles (3782 km)
Weights: (PBY-5A) empty 20,910 lb (9485 kg); maximum take-off 35,420 lb

(16066 kg)
Dimensions: (PBY-5A) span 104 ft 0 in (31.70 m); length 63 ft 10 in (19.46 m); height 20 ft 2 in (6.15 m); wing area 1,400 sq ft (130.06 m²)
Armament: (PBY-5A) three 0.3-in (7.62-mm) machine-guns, two 0.5-in (12.7-mm) machine-guns and up to 4,000 lb (1814 kg) of other weapons.
Operators: Argentina, Brazil, Chile, Dominica, Ecuador, Mexico, Taiwan

Convair (General Dynamics) C-131 Samaritan/T-29

With the requirement in the second half of the 1940s for a large 'flying classroom' type of trainer, for the instruction of navigators and radar operators, the USAF ordered two prototype XAT-29s from Consolidated-Vultee Aircraft Corporation (Convair), soon to be the Convair Division of the General Dynamics Corporation. The XAT-29 was based on the pressurized civil transport known as the Convair-Liner which, in its initial 240 version, had accommodation for 40 passengers.

The first XAT-29 made its initial flight on 22 September 1949, and following evaluation by the USAF a production contract was placed for T-29As, of which 46 were built. These differed from the Convair 240 by being unpressurized, and fitted with a totally different interior. The T-29A had 14 positions for student navigators and four astrodomes. The T-29B was pressurized and provided for the simultaneous training of 10 navigators and four radar operators, and the generally similar T-29C had more powerful engines. The T-29D was an advanced navigation/bombing trainer, with the K-system bombsight and camera scoring equipment.

The first USAF transport variant was the C-131A Samaritan for casualty evacuation, based on the Convair 240. This had large loading doors for stretchers or cargo, and was equipped to accommodate 27 stretchers or 37 sitting casualties. These were followed by 36 C-131B transport/electronic test-bed aircraft; by 33 C-131D/VC-131D transports of which 27 and six were to Convair 340 and 440 standard respectively; and finally by 15 C-131E ECM trainers delivered during 1956 – 57. RC-131Fs were photo-survey conversions of C-131Es, and a single similarly-derived RC-131G was equipped to check airways navigational aids. Two aircraft re-engined with turboprops to provide handling experience with this type of powerplant, and four similarly-modified C-131Ds, were used as VIP transports under the designation VC-131H.

The US Navy received 36 R4Y-1 (C-131F) cargo, personnel and evacuation transports; a single R4Y-1Z (VC-131F) VIP transport; and two R4Y-2 (C-131G) transport versions of the Convair 440. They also operated a small number of T-29Bs transferred from the USAF. The Canadian Armed Forces received eight aircraft similar to the VC-131H but designated CC-109 Metropolitan, and a number of ex-civil Convair 440s are used by the Bolivian, German, Italian and Spanish air forces.

Type: short/medium-range transport
Powerplant: (C-131B) two 2,500-hp (1864-kW) Pratt & Whitney R-2800-99W

Double Wasp radial piston engines
Performance: (C-131B) maximum speed 293 mph (472 km/h); cruising speed 254 mph (409 km/h); range 450 miles (724 km)
Weights: (C-131B) empty 29,248 lb (13267 kg); maximum take-off 47,000 lb (21319 kg)
Dimensions: span (T-29B) 91 ft 9 in (27.97 m), (C-131B) 105 ft 4 in (32.11 m); length (T-29B) 74 ft 8 in (22.76 m), (C-131B) 79 ft 2 in (24.13 m); height (T-29B) 26 ft 11 in (8.20 m), (C-131B) 28 ft 2 in (8.59 m); wing area (T-29B) 817 sq ft (75.90 m²), (C-131B) 920 sq ft (85.47 m²)
Armament: none
Operators: Bolivia, Canada, Germany, Italy, Spain, US Air Force, US Navy

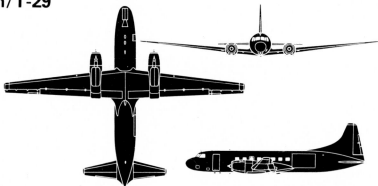

Convair C-131 Samaritan

Very few military versions of the CV-240, 340 or 440 Convair-Liner remain in use; this is a C-131 Samaritan, but the only examples still in American service are EC-131 electronic platforms of the Navy.

Convair (General Dynamics) F-102 Delta Dagger

Convair's F-102, mentioned also under the Convair (General Dynamics) F-106 entry, evolved from the company's XF-92A delta-wing research aircraft which had been built under post-war USAF contract. The German aerodynamicist and designer Dr Alexander Lippisch gave assistance in the design of this latter aircraft, which made its first flight on 18 September 1948. Only a single example was built, although the initial contract was for three aircraft, and in 1952 the USAF handed the XF-92A over to NACA (NASA's predecessor) after it had demonstrated a speed of 630 mph (1014 km/h) during tests and when powered by an Allison J33-A-29 turbojet engine.

Even before the contract for the XF-92A was awarded, the USAF had formulated an Advanced Development Objective (ADO) for an interceptor which would have performance considerably superior to that of Soviet intercontinental jet bombers. However this ADO was probably one of the most revolutionary in US Air Force history because, for the first time, it regarded this projected interceptor as a weapon system. It was realised that for far too long it had been customary to procure an airframe and its weapons as separate items in the hope that, when united in production form, these units would integrate as a satisfactory weapon. The time had come to investigate a Weapon System Concept, in which all the differing units were planned from the outset as a compatible system.

With these ideas in mind, Requests For Proposals were sent out on 18 June 1950 for a new interceptor, then identified as Project MX-1554. Four months later, the Hughes Aircraft Company was awarded a contract for development of Project MX-1179, this being the Electronic Control System (ECS) with which the MX-1554 system would be compatable. In spite of the extended development period of the design chosen to satisfy the MX-1179 concept, the MX-1179 failed to materialise within an acceptable time-scale for this aircraft and was abandoned. Instead the Huges E-9 fire-control system, later redesignated MG-3, was adopted, and finally replaced by the MG-10.

Six airframe manufacturers submitted proposals in January 1951, Convair, Lockheed and Republic being chosen to develop their designs to a mockup stage. However, it did not take the US Air Force long to realise that it could not afford these three projects and on 11 September 1951 gave Convair a Letter Contract which authorised use of the Westinghouse J40 turbojet, pending availability of the more powerful Wright J67, a version of the Bristol Olympus. A decision to proceed with production of Convair's proposal was made on 24 November 1951: as explained in the F-106 entry, the F-102, as it became designated, was thus an interim project until the 'Ultimate Interceptor' should reach fruition. The J40 and J67 subsequently failed to

mature, and the chosen engine bcame the Pratt & Whitney J57. The first YF-102A prototype made its initial flight on 24 October 1953, but was lost in an accident only nine days later. By that time, however, it had demonstrated that performance of this tailless delta was below the required figures: this dismal forecast was to be confirmed by the second YF-102A when it flew on 11 January 1954.

The year 1954 must be one etched permanently in the memories of Convair's design staff, for realisation of anything approaching the desired supersonic speed and ceiling seemed unattainable. In fact, it was not until a major redesign incorporated the area-ruled fuselage concept, which had emerged as a result of research carried out by Richard Whitcomb at NACA, that a better looking prototype flew on 19 December 1954. Its fuselage was lengthened and increased in volume at the ends, while being slightly slimmer alongside the wing. Powered by an advanced Pratt & Whitney J-57-P-23 turbojet that was to power production aircraft, this prototype achieved a speed of Mach 1.22 and altitude of 53,000 ft (16150 m) during its first flight.

It was not until April 1956 that F-102As entered service with Air Defense Command's 327th Fighter-Interceptor Squadron at George AFB, California, and procurement finally totalled 889. In addition, 111 TF-102A two-seat side-by-side trainers were built for the USAF, these retaining full operational armament and capability. An improved F-102B was planned, but this materialised eventually as the F-106 Delta Dart (q.v.).

F-102As were deployed to Thule, Greenland, in June 1958, but the installation of Tacan equipment delayed the introduction of these aircraft into Europe and Alaska until early 1960. At about the same time, F-102As joined the Pacific Air Forces, and the type remained in service in both the European and Pacific theatres of operation for almost a

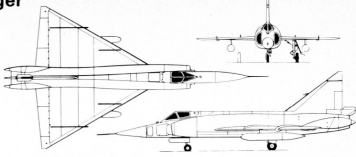

Convair F-102A Delta Dagger

decade. They were first introduced into the conflict in Vietnam in March 1962, and by 1967-68 a minimum of 14 F-102s were held on 5-minute standby at all times, with the remainder of the force on 1-hour call. Over the period March 1962 to December 1969, when these aircraft were withdrawn from south-east Asia, they had a remarkable safety record for, despite their operation in an air defence role, plus some combat patrols in support of SAC's B-52 operations, only 15 aircraft were lost.

Modernisation of the F-102A was almost continuous throughout its service life, and progressive programmes introduced data-link equipment, the improved MG-10 fire control system, in-flight refuelling, the substitution of more advanced missiles, and the addition of an infra-red search and tracking system. In 1974 six F-102As were converted to QF-102A (2) manned drone aircraft and PQM-102A (4) RPVs under the Pave Deuce programme, their role to represent MiG-21s in connection with the flight test and development programme of the McDonnell Douglas F-15A Eagle.

From 1961 F-102s began a slow process of transfer from deployment with active USAF squadrons into those of the Air National Guard (ANG), remaining operational with the ANG until 1977: all had been withdrawn from service by the end of 1978. During 1971 a number of F-102s were transferred to the

Greek and Turkish air forces, but by early 1979 these also had been withdrawn from service.

Type: supersonic all-weather fighter-interceptor
Powerplant: one 17,200-lb (7802-kg) Pratt & Whitney J57-P-23 or -25 afterburning turbojet
Performance: maximum speed Mach 1.25 or 825 mph (1328 km/h) at 36,000 ft (10970 m); range approximately 1,100 miles (1770 km)
Weights: maximum take-off as point interceptor 28,150 lb (12769 kg); maximum take-off as area interceptor, with two 215-US-gallon (814-litre) drop tanks 31,276 lb (14187 kg)
Dimensions: span 38 ft 1½ in (11.62 m); length 68 ft 4½ in (20.84 m); height 21 ft 2½ in (6.46 m); wing area 661.5 sq ft (61.45m²)
Armament: includes two AIM-26/26A Falcon missiles, or one AIM-26/26A plus two AIM-4A Falcons or one AIM-26/26A plus two AIM-4C/D, or six AIM-4A, or six AIM-4C/D; aircraft not modified for interchangeable use of AIM-26 or AIM-4 missiles in the weapons bay, could also carry twelve 2.75-in (69.8-mm) folding-fin rockets inside the bay doors
Operators: Grece, Turkey, US Air Force, US Air National Guard

This GD (Convair) F-102 Delta Dagger is not parked on the duty runway; it has just opened up for takeoff, despite the empty cockpit. It is a Sperry/Fairchild PQM-102A used in threat evaluation and other hazardous missions, flown by a remote pilot.

Curtiss-Wright C-46 Commando

On 26 March 1940 Curtiss-Wright flew the prototype of a 36-seat commercial airliner which had the company designation CW-20. Its large-capacity fuselage aroused US Army interest for cargo/transport/casualty evacuation, and a militarized version with 2,000-hp (1491-kW) Pratt & Whitney R-2800-43 engines was ordered into production under the designation C-46 and named Commando. When these first entered service in July 1942 they were the largest and heaviest twin-engine aircraft to serve with the USAAF, and proved such a valuable transport in the Pacific theatre of operations that well over 3,000 were to be built before production ended.

Apart from differing engines and fewer cabin windows, the original C-46s were generally similar to the CW-20 prototype. The C-46As which followed had a large cargo door on the left side, a strengthened floor, and folding seats for 40 troops. Pratt & Whitney R-2800-51 engines provided better performance at altitude. This was to prove of great importance, for C-46As transporting vital supplies 'over the hump' of the eastern Himalayas to China from India were found to have better

performance than the Douglas C-47 at the altitudes involved. They were to make a vital contribution to the success of this airlift.

In the Pacific the C-46 played a significant role in the island-hopping operations which culminated in Japanese surrender, and 160 R5C-1s of the US Marine Corps made an important contribution. Later versions for the USAAF included C-46D/E/F and a single C-46G, and Commandos were to remain in service with both the USAAF/USAF and USMC after World War II had ended. The USAF employed C-46s operationally during the Korean War, as well as in the early stages of hostilities in Vietnam. Since 1945 the C-46 has been the leading aerial workhorse of Latin America, and some also remain in service with air forces in 1979.

Type: troop and cargo transport
Powerplant: (C-46A) two 2,000-hp (1491-kW) Pratt & Whitney R-2800-51 Double Wasp radial piston engines
Performance: (C-46A) maximum speed 269 mph (433 km/h) at 15,000 ft (4570 m); cruising speed 183 mph (295 km/h); range

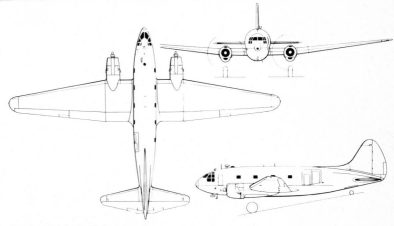

Curtiss-Wright C-46 Commando

1,200 miles (1931 km)
Weights: (C-46A) empty 32,400 lb (14696 kg); maximum take-off 56,000 lb (25401 kg)
Dimensions: wing span 108 ft 1 in (32.94 m); length 76 ft 4 in (23.27 m); height

21 ft 9 in (6.63 m); wing area 1,360 sq ft (126.34 m²)
Armament: none
Operators: Brazil, Dominica, Honduras, Japan, Peru, South Korea, Taiwan, Uruguay, Zaire

Dassault Etendard

Although it is a carrier-based attack aircraft, the Dassault Etendard (flag or standard) was conceived as a land-based ground-support aircraft for the French air force. It was developed in response to a NATO requirement for a light, high-subsonic strike fighter capable of operating from unpaved forward strips. Included in the NATO specification was a requirement that the aircraft should be powered by the Bristol Orpheus turbojet, which had a modest (for this class of aircraft) thrust of around 4,800 lb (2177 kg). The designation of this aircraft was Etendard VI. Another variant, the Etendard II with two 2,420-lb (1097-kg) Turboméca Gabizo turbojets, was the first to fly, on 23 July 1956. But Marcel Dassault, highly sceptical of such low-powered designs, privately financed a version powered by the much more powerful SNECMA Atar 08 and designated Etendard IV. This version flew on 24 July 1956, and was turned down by the French air force, which decided against the concept of such a light interceptor. Italy's Fiat G91 subsequently won the NATO competition. But far from going under, the Etendard IV was put through a protracted modification programme to meet the needs of the Aéronavale, which required carrier-based attack and reconnaissance aircraft. The Etendard IV was put into production in two forms to fulfil these roles. The first was designated Etendard IVM and deployed aboard the carriers *Foch* and *Clemenceau* (*Flottilles* 11F and 17F). The prototype of this variant flew for the first time on 21 May 1958, and was followed by six pre-production aircraft. The first of 69 production Etendard IVMs for the French navy was delivered on 18 January 1962, and production was completed in 1964. The seventh Etendard was the prototype of the IVP, a reconnaissance/tanker version, of which 21 were ordered. First flight was made on 19 November 1960. The primary design changes include nose and ventral stations for three and two reconnaissance cameras, an independent navigation system, a fixed nose-probe for flight-refuelling, and a 'buddy-pack' hose-reel

unit designed by Douglas to allow Etendard-to-Etendard refuelling. Compared with the original land-based aircraft, both maritime versions are equipped with such standard naval features as long-stroke undercarriage, arrester hook, catapult attachments and associated strengthening, folding wing-tips and a high-lift system which combines leading-edge and trailing-edge flaps, as well as two perforated belly air-brakes. The Etendard IVM also carries Aïda all-weather fire-control radar. Both marks of Etendard are being replaced by the Super Etendard, but for the present *Flottilles* 11F and 17F (home bases Landivisiau and Hyères respectively when not deployed aboard the 27,300-ton carriers *Clemenceau* and *Foch*) fly 36 Etendard IVM aircraft. A reconnaissance squadron (*Flottille* 16F) based at Landivisiau operates 14 Etendard IVPs. The Super Etendard will also replace 32 LTV F-8E (FN) Crusaders.

Type: single-seat transonic carrier-based strike aircraft
Powerplant: one 9,700-lb (4400-kg) SNECMA Atar 8B single-shaft turbojet
Performance: maximum speed 683 mph (1099 km/h) at sea level; maximum speed 673 mph (1083 km/h) or Mach 1.02 at 36,090 ft (11000 m); maximum design speed Mach 1.3; combat range (low-level attack role) 370 miles (600 km); combat range (medium-altitude mission) 1,000 miles (1600 km); (ferry) range 1,860 miles (3000 km); rate of climb (sea level) 19,685 ft (6000 m) per minute
Weights: empty equipped 13,500 lb (6123 kg); normal take-off 18,010 lb (8170 kg); maximum take-off 22,650 lb (10,275 kg)
Dimensions: span 31 ft 6 in (9.6 m); span (folded) 25 ft 7 in (7.8 m); length 47 ft 3 in (14.4 m); height 14 ft 2 in (4.3 m); wing area 312 sq ft (29 m²)
Armament: two 30-mm DEFA cannon; four underwing hardpoints for a maximum of 3,000 lb (1360 kg) of rockets, bombs, Nord 5103 (AA.20) air-to-surface or Sidewinder air-to-air missiles, or external fuel tanks
Operators: France (*Aéronavale*)

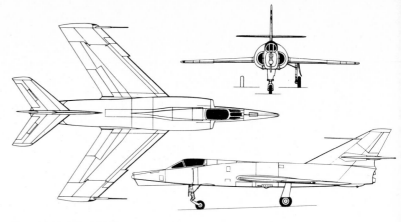

Dassault Etendard IV M

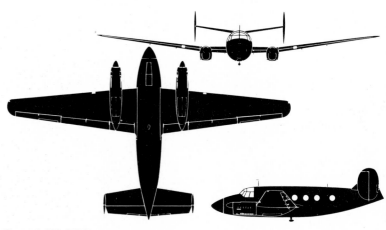

The Dassault Breguet Etendard IVP is an unarmed photo-reconnaissance aircraft which operates with the French *Aéronavale* from a shore base, Landivisiau, with *Flottille* 16F. Despite the Super Etendard the old IVP is likely to remain until at least 1985.

Dassault MD.315 Flamant

Now more than 30 years of age, the portly Dassault Flamant has had a long career as a utility transport and aircrew trainer since the prototype made its maiden flight on 10 February 1947. This had the designation MD 303, and was evaluated successfully at the *Centre d'Essais en Vol* at Brétigny later that year. Production Flamants, the first of which was flown in January 1949, were intended mainly for service with the *Armée de l'Air* in France's overseas territories, and deliveries to AOF (*Afrique Occidentale Française*) squadrons began in October 1950. There were three main versions. First of these, the MD 311, was a bombing, navigation and photography trainer; 39 were built. More numerous, and longer-serving, were the six-seat MD 312 military liaison/communications aircraft and the 10-seat MD 315 light utility transport. These models (production totals were 142 and 137 respectively) were used over a long period by the *Armée de l'Air* and, in the case of the MD 312, by the *Aéronavale*. Over 200 were still in service in the mid-1960s, though none are now operated by the French armed forces. Convertible from passenger to cargo or aeromedical transport, several were passed on to other air forces such as those of Cambodia

(now Kampuchea), Madagascar, Tunisia and South Vietnam as they were withdrawn from French service. Only about half a dozen remain, these being operated by the former French colonies of Cameroun, Malagasy, the Republic of Niger, and Tunisia.

One MD 315 was converted as the MD 316, with 820-hp (612-kW) SNECMA 14X Super Mars radial engines; this flew on 17 July 1952. A single-finned second prototype, the MD 316T, had 800-hp (597-kW) Wright R-1300-C7BA1 Cyclone radials. These new models were intended for crew training and commercial transport operation, but neither reached production status. The following specification applies to the MD 315.

Type: multi-purpose transport
Powerplant: two 580-hp (433-kW) SNECMA-Renault 12S 02-201 12-cylinder inverted-Vee piston engines
Performance: maximum speed at 3,280 ft (1000 m) 236 mph (380 km/h); typical cruising speed 186 mph (300 km/h); maximum range at 172 mph (277 km/h) 755 miles (1215 km); maximum rate of climb at sea level 984 ft (300 m) per minute; service ceiling 26,245 ft (8000 m)

Dassault MD.315 Flamant

Weights: empty 9,370 lb (4250 kg); maximum take-off 12,787 lb (5800 kg)
Dimensions: span 67 ft 11 in (20.70 m); length 41 ft 0¼ in (12.50 m); height 14 ft 9¼ in (4.50 m); wing area 508.06 sq ft (47.20 m²)
Armament: none
Operators: Cameroun, Malagasy, Niger, Tunisia

Dassault MD.450 Ouragan

France has probably produced more jet fighters that have fired their guns in anger than any other country outside the USA or USSR. The Dassault Ouragan (hurricane), her first postwar jet fighter, is now almost extinct, the sole survivors being a dozen or so ex-Israeli air force aircraft refurbished and sold to Salvador in the mid-1970s. The private venture prototype was first flown on 28 February 1949, lacking armament, a pressurized cockpit, or the wingtip fuel tanks standard on production aircraft. Three prototype and 12 pre-production Ouragans were followed by an in-

Dassault MD.450 Ouragan, one of 104 supplied to the Indian Air Force with which it was known as the Toofani.

itial contract for 150 production aircraft, subsequently increased to 350. The first production Ouragan flew on 5 December 1951, and the last was completed in mid-1954. Replacement of *Armée de l'Air* de Havilland Vampires began in 1952; three *escadres* (groups) were equipped, but began phasing the fighter out in favour of its improved descendant, the Mystère IVA, in May 1955, though the last Ouragan did not disappear from a French operational unit until six years later, and 50 or so still served as advanced trainers in the mid-1960s. Four aircraft, known as 'Barougans', were fitted with twin-wheel 'diabolo' main-wheel units and a brake parachute, and between 1954–57 evaluated this arrangement for possible use from Algerian desert strips, but the idea was not adopted.

Seventy-five Ouragans were acquired by the Israeli air force from 1955 (24 new and 51 ex-*Armée de l'Air*), and in the Suez and later Middle East campaigns the type proved an agile and stable weapon platform, particularly for ground attack. An earlier customer was the Indian air force, to whom 104 Toofanis (the Hindi word for hurricane) were delivered from

1953. These were later replaced by Mystère IVAs and Folland Gnats but, so far as is known, were not used operationally during the Indo-Pakistan conflicts of the 1950s and 1960s.

Type: single-seat fighter/ground-attack aircraft
Powerplant: one 5,004-lb (2270-kg) static thrust Hispano-Suiza-built Rolls-Royce Nene Mk 104B turbojet (5,180-lb/2350-kg thrust Mk 105A in Indian aircraft)
Performance: (with Nene 104B) maximum speed at sea level 584 mph (940 km/h); maximum speed at 39,370 ft (12000 m) 516 mph (830 km/h); combat radius (interceptor, clean) 280 miles (450 km); ferry range 572 miles (920 km); maximum rate of climb at sea level 7,480 ft (2280 m) per minute; service ceiling 42,650 ft (13000 m)
Weights: basic empty 9,132 lb (4142 kg); normal loaded (ground attack, with tip-tanks and 16 RPs) 16,323 lb (7404 kg); maximum take-off (ground-attack, with tip-tanks and maximum external load) 17,416 lb (7900 kg)
Dimensions: span (over tip-tanks) 43 ft 2 in (13.16 m); length 35 ft 2¾ in (10.74 m);

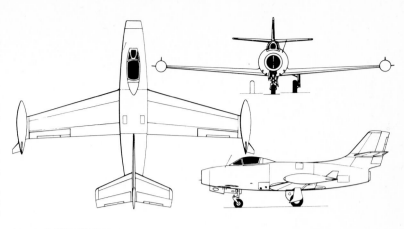

Dassault MD.450 Ouragan

height 13 ft 7 in (4.14 m); wing area 256.18 sq ft (23.80 m²)
Armament: four 20-mm Hispano 404 Model 50 cannon in underside of forward fuselage, with 125 rounds per gun; underwing hard-

points for two 1,000-lb (454-kg) bombs, sixteen 105-mm (4.13-in) rockets, or eight rockets and two 100-gallon (458-litre) napalm tanks
Operators: Salvador

Dassault MD.452 Mystère IV

Two years after his release from Buchenwald concentration camp, Marcel Dassault began designing jet fighters, and he has kept the French air force (and many others) well supplied ever since. His first type, the straight-winged Ouragan, was developed first into the Mystère IIC with slightly-swept wings (150 of these were built) and then into the Mystère IVA which, although bearing the same name, was virtually a completely new design. A thinner wing, with more sweep, and a longer, oval-section fuselage were combined with a French-built version of the Rolls-Royce Tay turbojet in the prototype (first flown on 28 September 1952), nine pre-series aircraft and the first 50 production IVAs. These were part of an 'offshore' procurement of 225 Mystère IVAs, ordered in April 1953 and paid for by US government funds to assist in strengthening the NATO alliance, to which France then belonged. The more powerful Hispano-Suiza Verdon 350 engine, a French development of the Tay, went into the remaining 175 US-funded IVAs and further quantities ordered by the French government, which had brought the total built to 421 by the time that production ended in late 1958. The type's *Armée de l'Air* service began in 1955 with the 12e *Escadre de Chasse* at Cambrai-Epinoy.

Some still remain in French service in an operational training role, and for several years the Mystère IVA (like the Ouragan) was used by the *Patrouille de France* aerobatic team. Exports included 110 to India and 60 to Israel, and the latter country still retains a dozen or so for combat training. French Mystères fought in the 1956 Suez campaign, and those supplied to Israel shortly afterwards have been involved in every major Arab-Israeli clash since then. Derived prototypes included the Mystère IVB, which led to the supersonic Super Mystère B-2.

Type: single-seat fighter-bomber
Powerplant: one 7,716-lb (3500-kg) static thrust Hispano-Suiza Verdon 350 turbojet
Performance: maximum speed at sea level 696 mph (1120 km/h); maximum speed at

39,370 ft (12000 m) 615 mph (990 km/h); range (clean) 572 miles (920 km); maximum rate of climb at sea level 8,858 ft (2700 m) per minute; service ceiling 49,215 ft (15000 m)
Weights: empty equipped 12,941 lb (5870 kg); normal take-off 16,535 lb (7500 kg); maximum take-off 20,944 lb (9500 kg)
Dimensions: span 36 ft 5¾ in (11.12 m); length 42 ft 2 in (12.85 m); height 15 ft 1 in (4.60 m); wing area 344.44 sq ft (32.00 m²)
Armament: two 30-mm DEFA cannon in underside of forward fuselage; provision for retractable underfuselage Matra 101*bis* pack of 55 Brandt unguided air-to-air rockets; up to 1,984 lb (900 kg) of bombs, two 19-tube Matra rocket pods, or twelve T-10 air-to-ground rockets, on four underwing hard-points
Operators: France, Israel

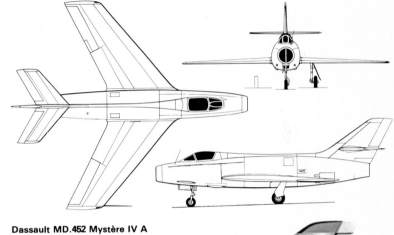

Dassault MD.452 Mystère IV A

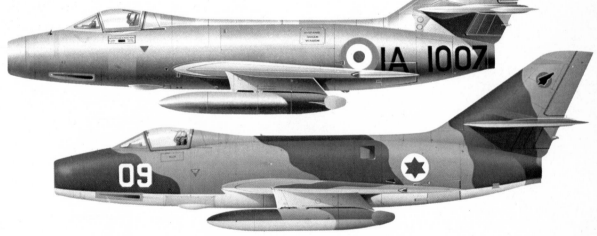

Indian Air Force Dassault Mystère IVA. Almost obsolete at the time of the Indo-Pakistan conflict, the type flew close support missions during the war.

Israeli Defence Force/Air Force Dassault Mystère IVA depicted in the camouflage carried at the time of the 1967 Arab-Israeli war.

Dassault-Breguet Mirage F1

The Dassault Mirage F1 is effectively a successor to the extremely successful Dassault Mirage III/5 series, although it differs substantially from the design which was originally planned to replace this family. In 1964 Dassault was awarded a French government contract to build a prototype of the F2 two-seat fighter, with a conventional wing and tailplane, and powered by a SNECMA/Pratt & Whitney TF306 turbofan. This aircraft made its maiden flight in June 1966, and in December of that year it was followed into the air by the first F1, a smaller single-seat fighter which Dassault had designed as a private ven-

ture and sized to the smaller Atar turbojet.

The F1 crashed, but still proved a more attractive proposition than its larger brother, and in September 1967 the French government ordered three pre-production F1s together with a structural test airframe. The first of these new aircraft made its maiden flight in March 1969 and completed its initial series of

flight trials some three months later. Despite being powered by a SNECMA Atar 9K31, which produced less thrust than the 9K50 adopted later, the first pre-production F1 notched up a series of impressive performances during this early period. These included a

continued

continued

Kuwait Air Force Mirage F1 CK interceptor operational with one squadron; 18 are in use with the unit plus two two-seat trainers.

speed of Mach 2.12 or 1,405 mph (2260 km/h) at 36,090 ft (11000 m), and 808 mph (1300 km/h) at low level.

The F1 has proved to be more than an adequate successor to the Mirage III as a multi-role aircraft, with emphasis on a large payload, easy handling at low altitude and a high rate of climb. Compared with its predecessor, the F1 has a higher maximum speed (Mach 2.2 rather than Mach 2), three times the endurance at high Mach numbers, three times the patrol time before and after an interception, twice the tactical range at sea level, a 30% shorter take-off run at greater maximum weight, 25% lower approach speed, and improved manoeuvrability at both subsonic and supersonic speeds.

The short take-off and landing performance results from the high-lift system, comprising leading-edge droops and large flaps, fitted to the sharply swept wing. At its average mission weight the F1 can take off and land within 1,700 ft to 2,600 ft (500 to 800 m). Although the Mirage III and F1 have practically identical external dimensions — and in particular the same wetted area — the internal fuel capacity of the later aircraft is 40% more than that of its forebear. This has been achieved by eliminating bladder-type tanks and replacing them with integral fuel space.

The F1 was designed for the best operational efficiency and the greatest possible flexibility. The ability to operate from short, rough strips is enhanced by the use of twin wheels on the main landing gear and by the adoption of medium-pressure tyres, combined with a landing speed of 167 mph (267 km/h), which is high, but still less than that of the delta-winged Mirages. The main landing gear

legs are mounted on the fuselage, leaving the wings free for the carriage of stores.

A fast reaction time is a necessity for an interceptor, and almost equally so for an attack aircraft, and the F1 is acceptable on this score. The ground handling equipment is kept to a minimum, and that which is used is fully air-transportable. A self-starter is used, and the high-pressure refuelling system allows all internal tanks to be filled in about six minutes; this contributes to a turn-round time of 15 minutes between two missions where identification of intruders rather than interception is required.

The F1's Thomson-CSF Cyrano IV mono-pulse radar has 80 per cent greater range than the Cyrano II fitted in Mirage IIIs and allows intruders to be intercepted at all altitudes, even if they are flying low in ground clutter, though the radar cannot rival a pulse-doppler type in this capacity. Targets to be tracked are selected manually by the pilot, who then transfers his attention to the Thomson-CSF electromechanical head-up display while the radar continues to track its designated target automatically. The weapons can be fired automatically by the fire-control computer, or manually with the computer supplying the pilot with clearance to engage the target.

A Mirage F1 can be scrambled within two minutes of the order being given, thanks to the use of the GAMO self-propelled preparation truck. This supplies electrical power to preheat the navigation and weapon-system equipment, circulates a fluid to cool the radar and controls the cockpit air-conditioning, as well as carrying a sunshade on a telescopic arm so that the pilot can sit at readiness for extended periods in the heat of the day. When the

pilot is ordered to scramble he starts the engine in the normal way. The sunshade is automatically withdrawn, the air-conditioning and radar-cooling systems are switched off and, as soon as the F1's engine is running fast enough for the alternators to supply sufficient electrical power, the connector to GAMO is automatically ejected and the pilot can begin to taxi.

The variant in service with the French air force is the F1 C interceptor, the first production example of which made its maiden flight in February 1973. The initial batch comprised 105 aircraft, and a further 109 are expected to be acquired eventually. The F1 A is a ground-attack and VFR (visual flight rules) fighter version, with only a ranging radar instead of the Cyrano IV, and simpler avionics. The deletion of some of this equipment allows extra fuel to be carried. The F1 A is built under licence by Atlas Aircraft in South Africa as well as being supplied directly by Dassault. The F1 E was planned in two versions: one with the Atar 9K50 and the other with the SNECMA M53. The latter version made its maiden flight in December 1974 and was offered to Belgium, Holland, Denmark and Norway in competition with the Saab Viggen and General Dynamics F-16. This contest was won by the US aircraft and the M53-powered aircraft was discontinued. The F1 E has more advanced avionics suiting the aircraft to the all-weather role.

The F1 B, which took to the air for the first time in May 1976, is a dual trainer. Changes from the single-seat variants are minimal, although no internal guns are carried. This can be remedied by fitting external pods containing the weapons. The radar screen and head-

up display are repeated in the rear cockpit, allowing the F1 B to act as a fully operational trainer.

Type: single-seat interceptor and ground-attack fighter

Powerplant: one 15,870-lb (7214-kg) SNECMA Atar 9K50 afterburning turbojet

Performance: maximum speed Mach 2.2 or 1,450 mph (2320 km/h) at 39,990 ft (12190 m); maximum speed at sea level Mach 1.2 or 920 mph (1472 km/h); maximum combat radius 400 miles (640 km) with 3,520-lb (1600-kg) load at low level; endurance 3 hours 45 minutes; time to climb to Mach 2 at 39,990 ft (12190 m) 7 minutes 30 seconds; stabilized supersonic ceiling 60,695 ft (18500 m).

Weights: empty 16,315 lb (7400 kg); operational (pilot, guns, internal fuel) 24,030 lb (10900 kg); operational (with air-to-air missiles) 25,350 lb (11500 kg)

Dimensions: span 27 ft 8 in (8.44 m); length 50 ft (15.25 m); height 13 ft 9 in (4.50 m); wing area 269 sq ft (25 m²)

Armament: two 30-mm DEFA 553 cannon with 125 rounds per gun and (intercept mission) two R.550 Magic air-to-air missiles, or two AIM-9 Sidewinder air-to-air missiles, or two R.530 or Super 530 air to air missiles with option of two Magic; or (attack mission) up to 8,818 lb (4000 kg) on seven hardpoints, with combinations such as eight 1,000-lb (454-kg) bombs, or four 36-round rocket launchers, or gun pods, or one AS.30 or AS.37 Martel air-to-surface missile, or other payloads such as napalm

Operators: Ecuador, Egypt, France, Greece, Iraq, Kuwait, Libya, Morocco, South Africa, Spain, Syria (?)

The Dassault-Breguet Mirage F1-C is the standard interceptor of the French *Armée de l'Air*. This, the 21st off the line, is serving with *12ème Escadre de Chasse* at Cambrai; it is toting a Matra R.530 air-to-air missile and two much better Magics.

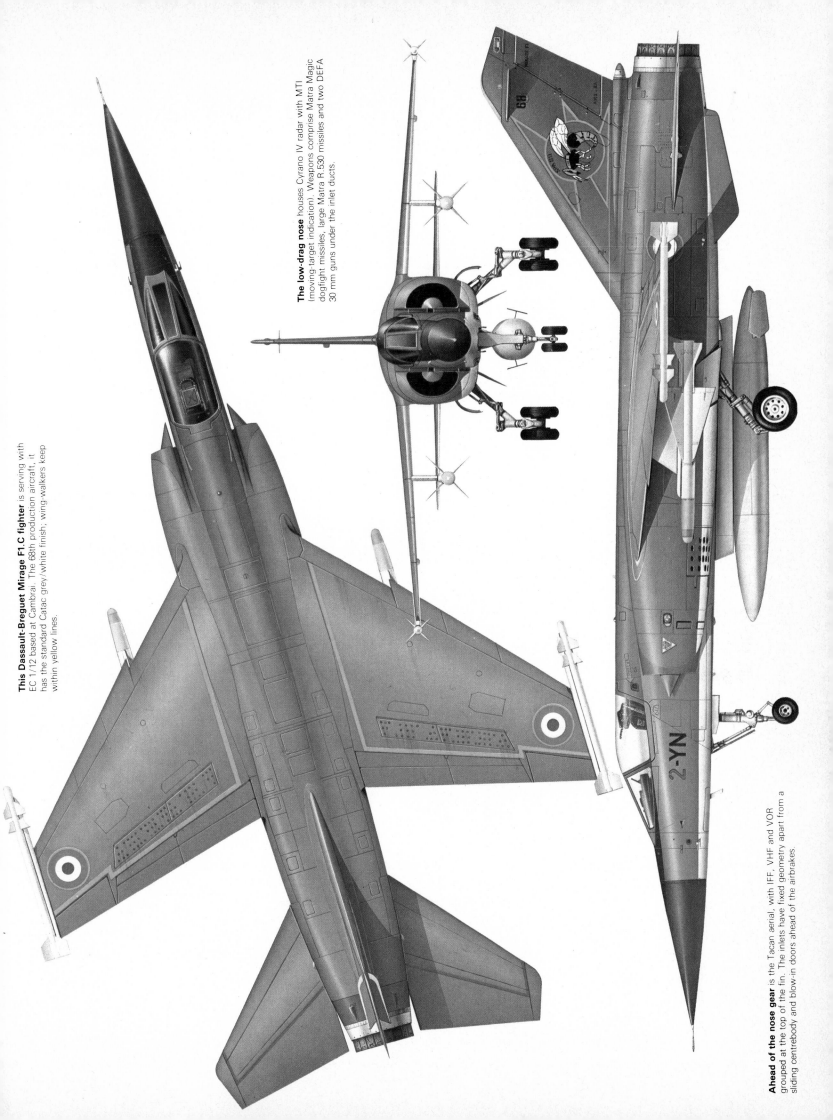

This Dassault-Breguet Mirage F1.C fighter is serving with EC 1/12 based at Cambrai. The 68th production aircraft, it has the standard Catac grey/white finish; wing-walkers keep within yellow lines.

The low-drag nose houses Cyrano IV radar with MTI (moving-target indication). Weapons comprise Matra Magic dogfight missiles, large Matra R.530 missiles and two DEFA 30 mm guns under the inlet ducts.

Ahead of the nose gear is the Tacan aerial, with IFF, VHF and VOR grouped at the top of the fin. The inlets have fixed geometry apart from a sliding centrebody and blow-in doors ahead of the airbrakes.

Dassault Mirage III/5

The Dassault Mirage III holds the distinction of being the first European aircraft to fly at twice the speed of sound, which it achieved in October 1958, and it has since gone on to become one of the world's most successful military aircraft. Dassault was one of three companies which built prototypes to meet a requirement formulated by the French air staff in the early 1950s. The specification called for a small supersonic interceptor with good armament and a fast rate of climb, and capable of acting independently of ground control. French aircraft engines at that time were not very powerful, and the new type was needed quickly, so the air staff decided that the best solution was a combination of jet and rocket propulsion to allow intruders to be intercepted at high altitudes.

Sud-Ouest's answer was the Trident, which was powered by a large rocket motor and two small turbojets. Sud-Est adopted the opposite combination, its Durandal having a large turbojet and a small rocket. Dassault's MD.550 had two small Viper turbojets plus a rocket. The type was named Mirage, because Dassault intended it to be 'like a desert vision, so that enemy pilots should see it but never catch up with it'.

The misconception of the official requirement soon became evident to Dassault, for the dependence on rocket propulsion severely limited the aircraft's endurance, and Dassault believed it would be preferable to use a single large turbojet. As a private venture he therefore decided at the end of 1955 to build a single prototype of a new design retaining the tailless delta planform but with a larger fuselage to house a single SNECMA Atar 101G turbojet.

The Mirage III-001 took to the air in November 1956 and quickly provided valuable information about the aerodynamics, flight controls and variable supersonic intakes which would be required of a production fighter. By this time the French air force was showing marked interest in the project, and a pre-production batch of 10 Mirage IIIs was ordered only six months after the type's maiden flight. The first of these flew in May 1958, and the initial production contract was awarded in October of that year. Two years later the first Mirage IIIC made its maiden flight, and the next month it was handed over to the French air force. The Mirage III was therefore delivered to a customer only three and a half years after the first contract had been placed.

Despite its thin flapless wing, inefficient at low speeds, the Mirage III can take off from and land on a 2,600 ft (800 m) runway while carrying its standard air-to-air armament. The Mirage IIIC is a single-seat interceptor powered by a SNECMA Atar 9B of 13,228-lb (6000-kg) static thrust. Its rate of climb and ceiling can be increased by fitting an SEP 844 rocket motor rated at 3,307 lb (1500 kg) thrust, which can be jettisoned after use if desired. Alternatively, an extra fuel tank can be fitted in the same space if the rocket is not installed. So far as is known, no export customers use the rocket installation. The Mirage IIIC carries a Thomson-CSF Cyrano Ibis fire-control radar; its normal armament comprises Matra R.530 and AIM-9 Sidewinder air-to-air missiles in addition to the two built-in cannon carried as an alternative to rocket fuel.

The next major version was the Mirage IIIE, a long-range fighter-bomber. Its fuselage is slightly longer, and an Atar 9C is installed. The use of Cyrano II radar, together with a doppler radar and navigation computer, allows the IIIE to fly at low level in all weathers and to carry out blind attacks, though it cannot hug the ground or strike point targets as can the General Dynamics F-III and Panavia Tornado. Other major variants in the series include the Mirage IIIB and IIID two-seat trainers; the IIIO built under licence in Australia; and the IIIR reconnaissance version with five OMERA Type 31 cameras or the SAT Cyclope infra-red package. The Mirage IIIS was built under licence in Switzerland and carries a Hughes Taran fire-control system, with the same company's Falcon missiles replacing French types. Some of the last Mirage IIIs supplied to South Africa are

Three Mirage IIICJ interceptors in Heyl Ha'Avir markings. The natural metal finish aircraft were operational at the time of the 1967 war, while the camouflaged example is from the later '73 conflict. No 758 carries the Israeli-designed Shafrir air-to-air missile and has a score of five Arab aircraft to its credit.

Dassault Mirage IIIR reconnaissance aircaft of 33 Escadre de Reconnaissance 1 Catac, l'Armee de l'Air, at Strasbourg.

Pakistan Air Force Dassault Mirage IIIEP of 5 Sqn, PAF.

This Dassault Breguet Mirage IIIE, the 512th off the assembly line, is seen in the stand-off attack role armed with an AS.37 anti-radar Martel. France has not bought the more useful British-developed TV-guided version of this collaborative missile.

powered by the more powerful SNECMA Atar 9K50.

Israel asked for a simplified ground-attack version, the Mirage 5. This retains the basic airframe of its predecessor, but has miniaturized electronics tailored to its new role. The smaller electronics volume has allowed the fuel capacity to be increased by 110 gallons (500 litres), and the weapon load has also been improved by the use of up to seven attachment points. The Mirage 5, which made its maiden flight in May 1969, does not carry the Cyrano fire-control radar but can be fitted with an Aida II ranging radar in its place. Two-seat and reconnaissance versions have been built and the Mirage 5, like the III, is designed for a service life of 5,000 hours flying over a period of 25 years. The Israeli batch of 50 was paid for, but were then embargoed by General de Gaulle and finally used by France. Belgium also adopted this 'primitive' derivative, which is intended for visual missions in good weather, and built 110 under licence.

A further development is the Mirage 50, which is basically a Mirage 5 fitted with an Atar 9K50 engine. The Mirage Milan (kite), with retractable foreplanes, was abandoned. Fixed canard foreplanes are used, however, on the IAI Kfir C2 (itself an adaptation of the Mirage 5). Such surfaces greatly alleviate the problems associated with the tailless delta configuration.

Type: single-seat interceptor (IIIC), all-weather fighter-bomber (IIIE), reconnaissance aircraft (IIIR), two-seat trainer (IIIB and IIID), or ground-attack aircraft and day fighter (5 and 50)
Powerplant: (IIIE and 5) Mach 2.2 or 1,460 mph (2336 km/h) at 40,000 ft (12190 m); cruising speed Mach 0.9 at 36,090 ft (11000 m); maximum level speed at sea level 863 mph (1390 km/h); ground-attack combat radius (5) 760 miles (1220 km); time to Mach 1.8 at 60,040 ft (18300 m) with SEP rocket and one AAM (IIIE) 7 minutes 40 seconds; time to Mach 1.8 at 49,870 ft (15200 m) (5) 6 minutes 48 seconds
Weights: empty (IIIE) 15,875 lb (7200 kg); empty (5) 15,210 lb (6900 kg); mission take-off, clean (IIIE), 21,605 lb (9800 kg); mission take-off, clean (5) 20,500 lb (9300 kg); maximum take-off (IIIE and 5) 29,760 lb (13500 kg)
Dimensions: span (IIIE and 5) 27 ft (8.22 m); length (IIIE) 49 ft 3 in (15.03 m); length (5) 50 ft 10 in (15.50 m); height (IIIE) 13 ft 11 in (4.25 m); height (5) 14 ft 9 in (4.50 m); wing area (IIIE and 5) 375 sq ft (35 m²)
Armament: (IIIE) two 30-mm DEFA cannon and (ground-attack mission) one AS.30 air-to-surface missile or two 1,000-lb (454-kg) bombs under the fuselage and two 1,000-lb (454-kg) bombs beneath the wings; (intercept mission) one or two R.530 air-to-air missiles and guns or Sidewinder air-to-air missile; (5) two 30-mm DEFA cannon and up to 8,818 lb

(4000 kg) of stores including 1,000-lb (454-kg) bombs, JL-100 rocket pods with eighteen 68-mm projectiles each, napalm, AS.30 air-to-surface missile, etc
Operators: (III) Argentina, Australia, Brazil, Egypt, France, Israel, Lebanon, Libya, Pakistan, South Africa, Spain, Switzerland, Venezuela; (5) Abu Dhabi, Belgium, Colombia, Egypt, France, Gabon, Libya, Pakistan, Peru, Venezuela, Zaire; (50) Sudan

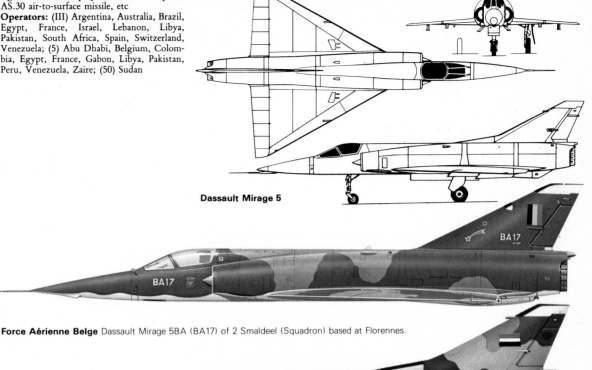

Dassault Mirage 5

Force Aérienne Belge Dassault Mirage 5BA (BA17) of 2 Smaldeel (Squadron) based at Florennes.

Libyan Arab Republic Air Force Mirage 5D fighter-bomber, one of 60 equipping two squadrons and a training unit.

Union Air Force (Abu Dhabi) Mirage 5AD (513) fighter-bomber based at Abu Dhabi International Airport.

Egyptian Arab Air Force Mirage IIIEE (alias 5SDE) equips one regiment. These aircraft were, passed on by Saudi Arabia.

Dassault Mystère-Falcon 20 Series G/HU-25A Guardian

The Dassault Falcon 20 (originally known as the Mystère 20) was designed as a transport for the executive market. It has since found favour with military customers as a VIP transport and in more specialized roles. Developed in conjunction with Sud-Aviation (Aérospatiale), who produced the wings and tailplane, the prototype flew on 4 May 1963. The first production aircraft, flown on 1 January 1965, differed in being fitted with CF700 turbofans; Aérospatiale built the fuselage and tail, while Dassault was responsible for the wings.

The fuselage of the Falcon 20 is an all-metal, fail-safe structure of circular cross-section. The low-mounted wing has a sweepback of 30° at quarter chord and incorporates leading-edge slats inboard and outboard with a fence. Hydraulic airbrakes are mounted forward of double-slotted flaps.

A total of 1,374 Imperial gallons (5200 litres) of fuel is carried in two fuselage and two wing tanks. Twin wheels are fitted on all three units of the tricycle undercarriage, and a braking parachute is standard. Controls are

powered.

The French armed forces still use the designation Mystère 20. The 65e Escadre handles short-range liaison from Villacoublay, while five with VIP furnishing operate from the same airfield with the Groupe des Liaisons Aériennes Ministerielles. A trainer, also operated by Libya, is fitted with Mirage IIIE radar and navigation equipment. The Aéronavale's Falcon 10s provide proficiency, radar and continuation training.

The Canadian Armed Forces has four CC-117 VIP transports with No 412 Sqn. Three are ECM trainers with No 414 Sqn at North Bay, Ontario. The Royal Norwegian Air Force's No 333 Sqn operates two in the dual role of ECM and navaid calibration.

In January 1977 the US Coast Guard ordered 41 Falcon 20Gs, to be designated HU-25A Guardian for maritime surveillance. Japan has expressed interest in the Falcon 20G for similar duties.

The primary difference between the 20G and earlier Falcons is the fitting of the more-powerful ATF 3 turbofan, sufficient for

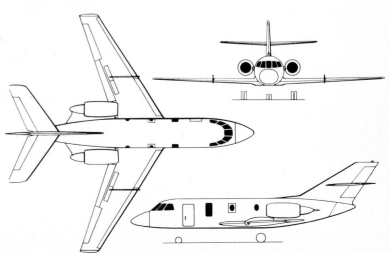

Dassault Mystère-Falcon 20G

continued

greater weights with avionics for overwater search and rescue, maritime law and treaty enforcement and environmental protection. Communications equipment includes dual HF, VHF-AM, IFF, single VHF-FM and UHF. Navaids include an inertial platform, Omega, dual VOR/ILS/MB, DME, ADF, radio altimeters, R-nav system and Tacan. Search and weather radar is standard, while optional sensors include SLAR, infra-red and ultra-violet scanners, reconnaissance camera and television. The 20G's fuselage is modified to in-

corporate two observation windows and a drop hatch, and provision is made for external pods to be carried. The US Coast Guard's HU-25As are being delivered one per month from mid-1979 and replace the Grumman HU-16E Albatross amphibian at six Coast Guard stations.

Type: twin-turbofan transport
Powerplant: two 4,500-lb (2040-kg) General Electric CF-700-2D-2 turbofans; (20G) two 5,300-lb (2400-kg) Garrett AiResearch ATF

3-6 turbofans
Performance: maximum cruising speed at 25,000 ft (7620 m) 536 mph (862 km/h); (20G) maximum cruising speed at 40,000 ft (12200 m) Mach 0.8; absolute ceiling 42,000 ft (12800 m); range with maximum fuel (45-minute reserves) 2,080 miles (3350 km); (20G) range with crew of 5, 2,600 miles (4185 km)
Weights: empty equipped 16,600 lb (7530 kg); maximum take-off 28,660 lb (13000 kg); (20G) maximum take-off 32,000 lb (14500 kg)

Dimensions: span 53 ft 6 in (16.3 m); length 56 ft 3 in (17.15 m); height 17 ft 5 in (5.32 m); wing area 440 sq ft (41 m²); (20G) wing area 450 sq ft (41.8 m²)
Armament: none
Operators: Australia, Belgium, Canada, Central African Empire, Egypt, France, Gabon, Iran, Libya, Norway, Pakistan, US Coast Guard

Dassault-Breguet Br.1050/Alizé

The Breguet Alizé (tradewind) is descended from an early post-1945 design, the Vultur, which was test-flown with a mixed powerplant comprising an Armstrong Siddeley Mamba turboprop as the prime mover, boosted for high-speed over-the-target dashes by a Rolls-Royce Nene turbojet in the tail. When the role was changed from attack to anti-submarine search and strike, the luxury of the extra engine was no longer justified, and a more straightforward design resulted.

First flown on 6 October 1956, the Alizé represented no mean feat of packaging, managing to contain in a modest-sized airframe an internal weapons bay, a CSF radar in a retractable ventral 'dustbin', and a three-man crew (pilot and two sensor operators), in addition to a retractable landing gear and other necessary electronic and naval equipment. The first prototype was followed by a second, and then by three pre-production examples, before Breguet flew the first of 75 production Alizés for the French *Aéronavale* on 26 March 1959. These entered service later that year and equipped the operational *Flottilles* 4F and 9F (based on the carriers *Foch* and *Clémenceau*) as well as a shore-based training unit, *Flottille* 6F. Those with 9F were replaced by Super Frelon ASW helicopters in the early 1970s, and the two currently-operational units are 4F (covering the Atlantic) and 6F (Mediterranean). In 1979

Dassault-Breguet announced a major structural rebuild and electronic updating programme to suit the Alizés of the *Aéronavale* for service until 1990.

The Indian navy received 12 Alizés in 1961 (and additional ex-*Aéronavale* aircraft later). These are in service with No 310 Squadron at Garuda, with a detachment maintained in the carrier INS *Vikrant* (the former HMS *Hercules*). The *Vikrant* made extensive use of its Alizés during the Indo-Pakistan conflict of 1971, but attrition then and since has reduced the effective number still in Indian service to little more than a handful.

Type: three-seat shipboard anti-submarine aircraft
Powerplant: one 2,100-ehp (1566-kW) Rolls-Royce Dart RDa.21 turboprop
Performance: maximum speed at 10,000 ft (3050 m) 292 mph (470 km/h); maximum speed at sea level 286 mph (460 km/h); normal patrol speed at 1,475 ft (450 m) 146 mph (235 km/h); normal endurance (standard fuel) about 5 hours 5 minutes; normal range 1,533 miles (2500 km); maximum endurance (with auxiliary fuel) 7 hours 40 minutes; ferry range 1,783 miles (2870 km); maximum rate of climb at sea level 1,380 ft (420 m) per minute; service ceiling over 20,500 ft (6250 m)
Weights: empty equipped 12,566 lb (5700

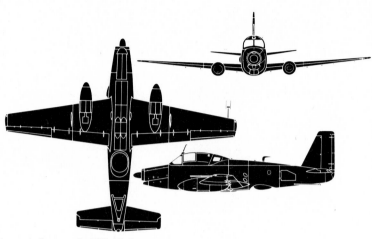

Dassault-Breguet Br.1050 Alizé

kg); maximum take-off 18,078 lb (8200 kg)
Dimensions: span 51 ft 2¼ in (15.60 m); span folded 22 ft 11½ in (7.00 m); length 45 ft 5¾ in (13.86 m); height 15 ft 7 in (4.75 m); wing area 387.5 sq ft (36.00 m²)
Armament: one 500-kg (1,102-lb) homing torpedo or three 160-kg (353-lb) depth charges in internal fuselage weapons bay; eight under-

wing attachment points for two 160-kg (353-lb) or 175-kg (386-lb) depth charges (on in board pair) and six 127-mm (5-in) rockets or two AS.12 air-to-surface missiles (outboard); and sonobuoys in front portion of each mainwheel fairing
Operators: France, India

Dassault-Breguet Atlantic

The Breguet Atlantic has the distinction of being the first combat aircraft to be designed and built as a completely multi-national project. In January 1958, NATO issued an NBMR (NATO Basic Military Requirement) for a long-range maritime-patrol aircraft. Breguet submitted its Br.1150 project, which was studied along with 24 other designs from a total of nine countries, and in November of that year the alliance's group of experts selected the French company's submission. The choice was unanimously approved by the 15 NATO members at the end of 1958, and responsibility for the construction of prototypes and production Atlantics was entrusted to SECBAT (*Société d'Etudes et de Construction du Breguet Atlantique*). The original SECBAT members, led by Breguet (now Avions Marcel Dassault-Breguet Aviation), comprised Sud-Aviation (later part of Aérospatiale) in France, the Belgian ABAP grouping (Fairey, FN and SABCA), Dornier in Germany and Fokker (now part of Fokker-VFW) in the Netherlands. A similar multi-national organisation was set up to build the Tyne turboprop engines, which had been designed by Rolls-Royce: other members were SNECMA in France, FN in Belgium and MAN in Germany. The Hawker Siddeley Dynamics propellers were constructed by Ratier in France.

The United States at no time planned to buy Atlantics itself but contributed to the cost of the programme, along with Belgium, France, Germany and the Netherlands. Italy joined the programme in 1968, and some of the work was allocated to Aeritalia in exchange. Britain and Canada contributed representatives to the NATO panel of experts which laid down the requirements of the Atlantic programme but these countries, like the US, did not participate in the programme. Canada had developed the Canadair Argus, and the United Kingdom the Hawker Siddeley Nimrod. Belgium benefited from work on the Atlantic programme but has bought none.

The first prototype Atlantic made its maiden flight at Toulouse in October 1961 and was followed by two other aircraft before the initial production machine took to the air in September 1964. The French navy began to receive the type in July 1965, eventually accepting two-thirds of the 60 aircraft in the first batch; the other 20 were put into service by the German navy. The first Atlantic in the second production batch made its initial flight in January 1971 and was later supplied, along with eight others to the Netherlands navy. The Italian air force received the remaining 18 aircraft in this batch, deliveries ending in July 1974. Production thus totalled 87, of which three have since been transferred from the French navy to Pakistan.

The Atlantic's main mission is to hunt and attack submarines, but the aircraft can fulfil a wide variety of secondary roles including anti-ship missions, minelaying, coastal reconnaissance, fleet escort and the direction of air-sea rescue missions. The aircraft is a land-based twin-engined type with a double-bubble fuselage and a wing of high aspect-ratio. The twin-lobe cross-section of the fuselage allows most of the upper section to be pressurized, offering an unobstructed cabin of constant width over a length of more than 49 ft (15 m). The unpressurized lower lobe comprises a central section, with a weapons bay 27 ft 6 in (9 m) long, closed by circular doors which slide along the fuselage sides. This arrangement avoids obstructing the panoramic field of view for the search radar, which is mounted in

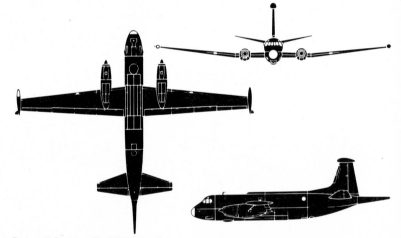

Dassault-Breguet Br. 1150 Atlantic

a retractable dustbin under the chin, and minimizes drag when the doors are open. It also ensures easy access from the side when the aircraft is on the ground, allowing complex items of ordnance to be loaded simply.

The slender wing of high aspect ratio ensures good fuel economy in cruising flight and a tight turning radius at low altitude — an essential feature for finding and attacking fast submarines. Extensive use is made of light-alloy honeycomb sandwich material in the Atlantic's construction, the honeycomb being bonded between twin metal sheets to form

wing and fuselage structural panels. This material provides a very stiff but light skin structure with exceptional fatigue life.

The Atlantic's Thomson-CSF search radar can detect a submarine's schnorkel at ranges of

Aeronautique Naval Breguet Atlantic anti-submarine patrol aircraft. Four units are equipped with 35 aircraft.

up to 46 miles (75 km) even in rough seas. Sonobuoys are jettisoned through chutes in the rear fuselage, and the 'sting' for a magnetic-anomaly detector (MAD) is mounted behind the tail section. Information from the sensors is fed to individual displays in the Plotac display and control system.

Various improved versions of the Atlantic have been studied under a number of designations, including Mk II and M4, and in March 1977 the French government finally decided to launch preliminary design work on this project, now known as ANG (Atlantic *Nouvelle Génération*). This was followed in February 1978 by a go-ahead for the programme, with the French navy to receive 42 ANGs. The schedule laid down in 1978 calls for the first ANG prototype, converted from a Mk 1 Atlantic, to make its maiden flight in the second half of 1980, with the second following in the first half of 1981. Production ANGs

would be delivered from mid-1984.

The ANG will be of similar construction to the Mk 1, with some structural improvements, but the avionics are completely new. The heart of the ANG is a digital tactical system designed by Thomson-CSF and including that company's *Iguane* (iguana) long-range search radar. *Iguane* uses pulse-compression and frequency-agility techniques, allowing it to detect targets in heavy seas and to counter jamming. Other equipment includes the SADANG system to process signals from several sonobuoys simultaneously, an Apar 13 radar countermeasures set which analyses signals transmitted by enemy ships and identifies them by comparing them with a stored library, and a CIMSA 15M 125F computer to handle communication between various parts of the system. The ANG will also be fitted with a forward-looking infra-red (FLIR) sensor, allowing the crew to see their

target at night and through haze.

At one time the uprated Atlantic was planned to have two Rolls-Royce M45 turbofans in addition to its Tyne turboprops, but this proposal has since been dropped. France is proceeding alone with development of the ANG but hopes to sell the aircraft to existing Atlantic operators such as Germany and Italy. These plans received a setback at the end of 1978, however, when the Netherlands rejected the offer of ANGs and selected the Lockheed P-3C Orion.

Type: anti-submarine and maritime-patrol aircraft
Powerplant: four 6,100-ehp (4551-kW) Rolls-Royce Tyne 21 turboprops, built by a multi-national consortium
Performance: maximum design speed 408 mph (658 km/h); maximum sea-level speed 368 mph (593 km/h); cruising speed 345 mph

(556 km/h) or Mach 0.5 at 24,935 ft (7600 m); typical patrol speed 196 mph (315 km/h); ceiling 30,020 ft (9150 m); maximum endurance 18 hours; maximum range 5,180 miles (8340 km); sea-level take-off run at maximum gross weight 5,750 ft (1750 m)
Weights: empty equipped 55,115 lb (25000 kg); maximum take-off 98,105 lb (44500 kg); maximum fuel weight 40,740 lb (18500 kg); maximum ordnance load 6,614 lb (3000 kg)
Dimensions: span 119 ft 1 in (36.30 m); length 104 ft 2½ in (31.75 m); height 37 ft 4 in (11.33 m); wing area 1,293 sq ft (120.0 m²)
Armament: bombs, 385-lb (175-kg) depth charges, air-to-surface rockets, Mk 44 or LX.4 homing torpedoes, AM.39 Exocet anti-ship missiles, AS.37 Martel anti-radiation missiles, AS.12 air-to-surface missiles
Operators: France, Italy, Netherlands, Pakistan, West Germany

Dassault-Breguet Mirage 2000

Although called Mirage, and having a plan form similar to that of the well-known Mirage III, the Dassault-Breguet Mirage 2000 is a completely new aircraft. Dassault was building the French air force *Avion de Combat Futur* (ACF) when the project was cancelled in 1975, only six months before the prototype was due to fly. The French air force had decided that the ACF, a twin-engined aircraft based on SNECMA M53-5 bleed-turbojets was too big. It wanted a smaller aircraft, with approximately the performance of the General Dynamics F-16 lightweight fighter.

On 18 December 1975 the French government gave a go-ahead on this new programme, which was styled the Mirage 2000. Four prototypes were ordered and Dassault decided to build a fifth example to aid the development of export versions. At the same time Dassault took the unprecedented decision to fund as a private venture the continued development of an ACF-size aircraft, now accorded the designation Mirage 4000. It is the largest private-venture military aircraft programme ever undertaken.

The Mirage 2000 is the sixth aircraft in the Mirage family. Dassault produced a simple single-engined supersonic aircraft in the Mirage III and scaled-up to a twin-engined layout it became the Mirage IV supersonic bomber. Prototypes were also built of the large IIIT and tailed F2 types. The company flirted in vertical take-off and landing research using the Balzac and Mirage IIIV, and put into production the Mirage F1. A prototype variable-geometry aircraft, the Mirage G, was also built, but eventually Dassault decided to stay with the devil it knew, and both new Mirage designs are conventional deltas, though of much improved types.

In the Mirage 2000, for which the 19,840 lb (9000 kg) SNECMA M53-5 bleed-turbojet engine had to provide a thrust:weight ratio of 1:1 at combat weights, the aircraft has been made as small and as light as possible. To enhance manoeuvrability, the aircraft has an electronic fly-by-wire flight control system which allows the aircraft centre of gravity range to be extended further aft than on a conventional aircraft. This produces less basic stability, and is a concept previously applied on the American F-16. Quadruplex pitch and roll controls are installed, and triplex rudder controls.

The delta wing is large compared with Dassault's previous designs, reduced wing-loading providing better low-speed performance, and permitting higher turn-rates at high altitude. The wing has almost no camber, but leading-edge flaps (very rare on deltas) and large trailing-edge elevons, which droop as flaps during manoeuvres, can produce more lift per unit area than the inefficient conventional delta wing. The aerodynamic and control innovations are more radical than is apparent at first sight. A slight blending on the wing root into the fuselage helps to provide about 955 gallons (4340 litres) of internal fuel volume, and two 374-gallon (1700-litre) drop tanks can be added.

Nine hardpoints, five under the fuselage and four under the wings, can carry up to

11,025 lb (5000 kg) of ordnance. Normal air-interception duties will be carried out with two Matra Super 530 and two Matra 550 Magic air-to-air missiles. Two 30-mm DEFA cannon are mounted in the fuselage. Sidewinder missiles can be carried instead of Magic on export versions.

The lightweight airframe has been achieved by using the simplest possible structure with a large proportion of titanium and boron/carbon-fibre panels. It is estimated that 220 lb (100 kg) of weight was saved by using fibre components alone. Movable half-cone centre bodies, which Dassault has always preferred to variable-ramp intakes, are used to control engine airflow over the wide speed range. Arrester gear and a brake chute are fitted to reduce landing field length.

An X-band pulse-doppler radar with a range of about 62 miles (100 km) has been developed for the air-interceptor version. It uses a flat-plate aerial and has integral IFF equipment. A

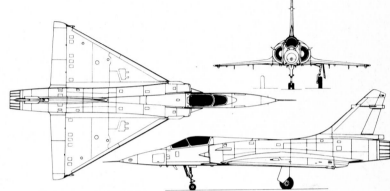

Dassault-Breguet Mirage 2000

modified set is proposed for the multi-role version, and this will use an inverted-cassegrain aerial. The air-interceptor radar has a continuous-wave illumination mode for

doppler-homing missiles.

Dassault test pilot Jean Coureau made the first flight of the Mirage 2000 on 10 March 1978, reaching Mach 1.3. The aircraft was

The Dassault-Breguet Mirage 2000 01 pictured south of its test base at Istres, heading out over the Mediterranean. A totally different animal from the primitive Mirage III and 5, it is — amazingly — being backed up by the un-ordered Super Mirage 4000.

flown from Istre, although it had been built at St Cloud. The second Mirage 2000 flew on 18 September 1978 and three more are due to fly before 1980, including a two-seater. The French air force is reported to want up to 400 examples, but only 130 are expected to be ordered for the air-interceptor role. The remainder are probably be strike and reconnaissance aircraft. Mirage 2000 deliveries will begin in 1982, and production should reach four aircraft per month by 1984.

Type: single-seat multi-role fighter
Powerplant: one 19,840-lb (9000-kg) SNECMA M53-5 continuous-bleed after burning turbojet
Performance: estimated maximum speed Mach 2.3 or 1,520 mph (2445 km/h) above 36,090 ft (11000 m); estimated tactical radius with two Matra Super 530 and two Matra 550 Magic air-to-air missiles and two 374-gallon

France's newest air superiority interceptor, the delta-winged Dassault Mirage 2000, seen in initial prototype form.

(1700-litre) drop tanks 435 miles (700 km); time to Mach 2 at 49,210 ft (15000 m) from brake release with four air-to-air missiles 4 minutes; range (with drop tanks) 932 miles (1500 km); service ceiling 65,600 ft (20,000 m)
Weights: estimated empty 14,080 lb (6400 kg); normal take-off (with internal fuel

and four air-to-air missiles) 21,825 lb (9900 kg); maximum take-off weight (maximum external ordnance) 33,070 lb (15000 kg)
Dimensions: (estimated) span 29 ft 6 in (9.00 m); length 50 ft 3½ in (15.33 m); height 17 ft 6 in (5.30 m); wing area 430.5 sq ft (40.00 m²)

Armament: two 30-mm DEFA cannon and (air-superiority) two Matra 550 Magic plus two Matra Super 530 air-to-air missiles or (strike) up to 11,025 lb (5000 kg) of ordnance on nine external points (five under fuselage, four under wing)
Operator: France (on order)

Dassault-Breguet Super Mirage 4000

Technically this twin-engined multi-role aircraft may be sensible, but as a programme it passes all belief. In a world in which partnerships of several major nations are hard-pressed to create new aircraft in this class, Dassault has announced it is developing the Super Mirage 4000 (sometimes simply called 'Mirage 4000') as a company venture, without even a customer. The company stated that the Chief-of-Staff who in December 1975 selected the small Mirage 2000 as the next-generation combat aircraft for the *Armée de l'Air* would not be in office when delivery became due in the 1980s, and that it would be desirable to offer his successor the choice of a much larger twin-

engined machine. To some degree the 4000 makes use of information gained in building the *Avion de Combat Futur*, a similar-sized twin-engined machine with a fixed-angle swept wing and tailplane, cancelled when the Mirage 2000 was selected instead. In configuration, however, it resembles a scaled-up 2000, with variable-camber delta wing, but with the important addition of substantial canard surfaces projecting from the front of the engine inlet ducts. Another difference is that the airbrakes are not above and below the wing but above the fuselage, immediately behind the canards.

Engines are two M53, initially at the

available 18,740-lb (8500-kg) rating but later at the M53-5 rating of 19,840 lb (9000 kg). The 4000 prototype, which was built in 1978 and was scheduled to fly in October of that year (but did not do so until 9 March 1979), is a single-seater with the minimum of equipment in order to reduce cost in early flight development. It is intended that the 4000 should carry an advanced radar, two 30-mm DEFA cannon, Matra 550 Magic close-range air-to-air missiles on rails under the outer wings, and various other weapons depending on mission. Features include active fly-by-wire controls, large internal fuel capacity in wings, fuselage and fin, composite structure, and ad-

vanced avionics and cockpit displays. A twin-cockpit version is being studied. Dassault has hinted that no such aircraft would exist without a customer, though there has been no indication of who this might be; the *Armée de l'Air* has stated it has no requirement for this costly aircraft, and Saudi Arabia has informally denied involvement. Missions are described as 'interception and low-altitude penetration attacks', despite the fact that the two missions are incompatible with a fixed-geometry wing.

Dassault-Breguet Super Etendard

As its name implies, the Dassault-Breguet Super Etendard is an updated version of Dassault's Etendard IVM carrier-based attack aircraft. The need for a replacement for the original aircraft had been recognised in the mid-1960s, and the maritime variant of the SEPECAT Jaguar, designated model M, was intended to fill this role. This version differed from the land-based Jaguar in having single main wheels, extended undercarriage stroke, all the modifications required for carrier operations and equipment tailored to the naval strike role. Despite its completion of flight and carrier trials, the Jaguar M was cancelled, primarily on grounds of cost and politics. Having evaluated the McDonnell Douglas A-4 Skyhawk and LTV A-7 Corsair II (France already operates the same company's F-8 Crusader), the *Aéronavale* decided to adopt an improved Etendard. Dassault converted two standard Etendard IVM airframes, and the first of three Super Etendard prototypes flew on 28 October 1974. Power comes from a single SNECMA Atar 8K-50 turbojet, a non-afterburning version of the Atar 9K-50 which powers the Dassault Mirage F-1 multi-mission fighter and attack aircraft.

The Super Etendard contains many improvements over the earlier aircraft, not the least of which are 10% more thrust (at a lower specific fuel consumption) and new high-lift devices on the wing, which together permit a heavier gross weight on the catapult strop and, consequently, greater fuel capacity and armament. Air-to-air refuelling capability is retained, including the 'buddy-pack' system. Range is therefore considerably improved. Although the Super Etendard is classified as a 'strike fighter' with a ceiling of 52,000 + ft (15850 + m), it will spend much time at low level in the tactical attack role.

Among the new equipment is a highly sophisticated and accurate nav/attack integrated electronic system. At the heart of the new fit is a Thomson-CSF/Eléctronique Marcel Dassault Agave X-band monopulse radar with an air-to-air detection range of 25.3 miles (40.7 km). The radar's other modes permit air-to-air search and target designation for transmission either to a gunsight or to the active homing head of an antiship missile; ground mapping; fully automatic air-to-air and air-to-sea tracking; and air-to-

air, air-to-sea and air-to-ground ranging. A Thomson-CSF head-up display operates in conjunction with a Singer-Kearfott inertial navigation and weapon-aiming system built under licence by the French company Sagem.

The first prototype was used to prove the engine installation, testing the external load-carrying capabilities and performing firing trials of the AM.39 Exocet air-to-surface anti-ship missile, of which the Super Etendard carries one under the starboard wing. The second prototype flew on 25 March 1975, and was involved in navigation-system and bombing trials. By November 1977 it had logged more than 400 hours in slightly less than 400 flights, which also found it being subjected to shipboard trials away from the waters of the Mediterranean, where the early trials had been conducted.

The third prototype was the first example with the new wing to fly. The first production aircraft flew on 27 November 1977, and deliveries began on 28 June 1978, when the third production aircraft was handed over to the *Aéronavale*. A total of 71 Super Etendards are required by the French Navy, and the schedule will see 13 aircraft delivered in 1978, another 22 in 1979 and the remainder by the summer of 1981. The first flottille to be re-equipped will be 11F, based at Landivisiau/*Clémenceau*. Flottille 14F's F-8 Crusaders, at the same base, will be replaced in 1979, followed finally by Hyères-/*Foch*-based Flottille 17F's Etendard IVMs. The Super Etendard is expected to remain operational until 1992.

Type: single-seat transonic carrier-based attack aircraft
Powerplant: one 11,265-lb (5110-kg) SNECMA Atar 8K-50 single-shaft turbojet
Performance: maximum speed 745 mph

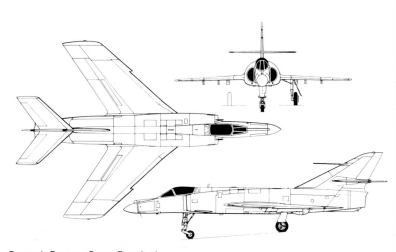

Dassault-Breguet Super Etendard

(1200 km/h) at sea level, Mach 1 at altitude; range at altitude (clean) more than 1,243 miles (2000 km); initial rate of climb 24,600 ft (7500 m) per minute; service ceiling 45,000 ft (13700 m)
Weights: empty equipped 14,220 lb (6450 kg); maximum take-off 26,455 lb (12000 kg)
Dimensions: span 31 ft 6 in (9.6 m); span folded 25 ft 7 in (7.8 m); length overall 46 ft 11½ in (14.31 m); height overall 12 ft 8 in (3.86 m); wing area 305.7 sq ft (28.4 m²)
Armament: two 30-mm DEFA cannon (125 rounds each) in bottom of engine air-intake trunks; underfuselage hardpoints for 551-lb (250-kg) bombs; four underwing hardpoints for 882-lb (400-kg) bombs; Magic air-to-air

missiles or rocket pods; optional, one AM.39 Exocet air-to-surface missile under starboard wing and one external fuel tank under port wing
Operators: France (Aéronavale)

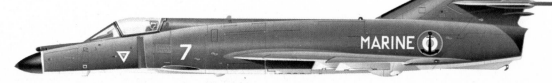

Seventh production Super Etendard carrier-based attack aircraft of the Aéronautique Naval. A total of 71 are on order.

Dassault-Breguet Falcon 10

The baby of the Dassault-Breguet Mystère/Falcon family of business jets, the Falcon 10 was known at first as the 'Minifalcon' when announced at the end of the 1960s. Like the rest of the family, it has rear-mounted turbofan engines and is basically a scaled-down version of the Falcon 20. A prototype, originally with turbojet engines, flew for the first time on 1 December 1970 and six months later set a 1000-km (621-mile) closed-circuit speed record in its class of 578.13 mph (930.4 km/h). A similar record over 2000 km (1,243 miles) was set by the third prototype in May 1973, a month after the first production aircraft had flown, and sales have since topped the 150 mark.

The only specific military model is the Falcon 10MER, three of which are used by the *Aéronavale* (French Naval Aviation, which has an option for two more) for general liaison and communications duties and to give training to pilots of the Dassault Super Etendard carrier fighter. Two are in service with the SRL (*Section Réacteur de Landivisiau*) near Brest, and one is based at Hyères, near Toulon. The SRL, which also operates eight Morane-Saulnier Paris light aircraft, has a threefold function: to provide instrument and night fly-ing training for pilots of carrier aircraft (Etendard, Super Etendard and Vought F-8 Crusader); liaison flights for French naval headquarters, the Commander of Naval Aviation, and the C-in-C of the French Atlantic Fleet; and support missions for the ships of the Atlantic Fleet. The Falcon 10MER has also been found to make a good mock intruder, to provide training for ground control radar crews and interceptor pilots. Its other *Aéronavale* duties include medical evacuation readiness training, simulated anti-shipping strikes to test the readiness of ships' crews, and calibration of shipborne radars.

Type: four/seven-passenger aircrew trainer and light transport/liaison aircraft
Powerplant: two 3,230-lb (1465-kg) Garrett AiResearch TFE 731-2 turbofans
Performance: maximum cruising speed at 30,000 ft (9145 m) 568 mph (915 km/h); range with four passengers, with reserves 2,209 miles (3555 km)
Weights: empty equipped 10,760 lb (4880 kg); maximum payload 2,337 lb (1060 kg); maximum take-off 18,740 lb (8500 kg)
Dimensions: span 42 ft 11 in (13.08 m);

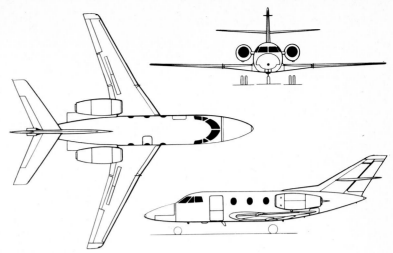

Dassault-Breguet Falcon 10

length 45 ft 5 in (13.85 m); height 15 ft 1½ in (4.61 m); wing area 259.4 sq ft (24.10 m²)

Armament: none
Operator: France

Dassault-Breguet Mirage IV

The French, renowned for their highly nationalistic policies, decided in 1954 to create their own nuclear deterrent force. One of the first priorities was to develop a launch platform for the weapons. The project was headed by Dassault in association with a number of other companies, including Sud-Aviation (responsible for the wing and rear fuselage) and Breguet (tail surfaces). In the face of a requirement calling for a long, high-speed mission (likely to the Soviet Union), Dassault looked initially at developments of the Vautour but later directed its attention at a 1956 design for a twin-engined night fighter. Basically a scaled-up Mirage III, the project underwent many changes in size and proposed powerplant as speed, load and range requirements were formulated. It was decided finally to make large-scale use of in-flight refuelling. (Twenty-three Boeing KC-135Fs are now on strength to support the bombers: this tanker force is split into three squadrons, each with four aircraft, and the remaining 11 are based at Istres.)

The original prototype Mirage IV flew on 17 June 1959, and was powered by two 13,225-lb (6000-kg) SNECMA Atar 09 augmented turbojets. Take-off weight was approximately 55,100 lb (25000 kg). On its 14th test flight (in July 1959) it reached Mach 1.9, and it attained Mach 2 on its 33rd flight. Three pre-production prototypes, the first of which flew on 12 October 1961, followed the prototype. Powered by a pair of 14,110-lb (6400-kg) Atar 09Cs, this aircraft was larger and more representative of the production Mirage IVA, incorporating a large circular radome under the centre fuselage forward of the semi-recessed nuclear free-fall bomb. The first pre-production aircraft underwent bombing trials and development at Colomb-Béchar; the second aircraft, a similar machine, was used to develop the navigation and flight-refuelling systems; and the third aircraft, a completely operational model with Atar 09Ks, full equipment including nose-probe for refuelling, and armament, flew on 23 January 1963. Satisfied with the trials, the French air force ordered 50 production Mirage IVAs for delivery in 1964 – 65. A repeat order for a further 12 was placed later. Fifty of the 62 delivered are expected to remain in service in the nuclear strike role until 1985, when silo-based S-3 strategic missiles (first operational in 1976) will maintain the country's deterrent until the year 2000. A total of 33 aircraft on call for service equip six squadrons in two wings (91 and 94 *Escadres*) dispersed among six bases. Twelve have been converted for long-range, high/low-level reconnaissance, which will be the type's main role from 1985. Although a heavy machine and fairly 'hot' to operate, the Mirage IVAs of the French air force are on extremely quick alert. They can take off straight out of the hardened shelters in which they are housed, with their engines running at full power, and have even operated off short, unpaved strips with the aid of auxiliary take-off rockets and fast-drying chemicals sprayed onto the surface to harden the ground run.

In the 1950s the manned fighter was seen in Britain as soon becoming obsolescent, a theory which, with hindsight, led to a chain of highly dubious decisions. It now transpires that the heavy manned bomber may become extinct as technology allows the development of guidance systems which will make cruise missiles a more effective method of deterring hostilities. The USA has cancelled the Rockwell B-1 manned supersonic bomber in favour of proposed air-launched cruise missiles. In 1977 it was announced that a strategic cruise missile is under development in France — the Mirage IVA might be a launch platform.

Type: two-seat supersonic strategic bomber
Powerplant: two 15,432-lb (7000-kg) reheat SNECMA Atar 9K turbojets.
Performance: maximum dash speed at 40,060 ft (13125 m) 1,454 mph (2340 km/h or Mach 2.2); maximum sustained speed 1,222 mph (1966 km/h or Mach 1.7) at 60,000 ft (19685 m); tactical radius (dash to target, high-subsonic return) 770 miles (1240 km); ferry range 2,485 miles

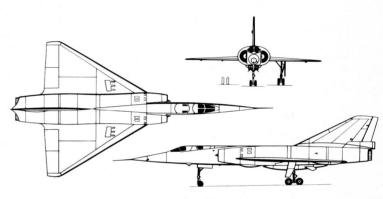

Dassault-Breguet Mirage IV A

(4000 km); time to 36,090 ft (11000 m) 4 minutes 15 seconds
Weights: empty equipped 31,967 lb (14500 kg); maximum loaded 73,800 lb (33475 kg)
Dimensions: span 38 ft 10½ in (11.85 m); length 77 ft 1 in (23.5 m); height 17 ft 8½ in (5.4 m); wing area 840 sq ft (78 m²)
Armament: electronic countermeasures; one 60-kiloton freefall bomb recessed in belly; or, alternatively, up to 16,000 lb (7257 kg) of ordnance on wing and fuselage hardpoints

Operator: France (Armée de l'Air Commandement des forces Aériennes Stratégique)

Dassault Mirage IVA of L'Armée de l'Air's "Force de Frappe", with a crew of two. It carried a nuclear weapon.

The USA may have cancelled its supersonic bomber, the Rockwell B-1, but France will continue to operate a manned, supersonic nuclear deterrent until at least 1985 in the form of 50 Dassault-Breguet Mirage IV strategic bombers.

Dassault Super Mystère B2

First flown on 2 March 1955, the Super Mystère shortly afterwards exceeded the speed of sound in level flight, subsequently becoming the first European aircraft with a Mach 1-plus performance to enter full-scale service. Developed from Dassault's earlier Mystère IVA via an interim Rolls-Royce Avon-engined variant known as the Mystère IVB, the Super Mystère differed chiefly in having a new thinner-section wing with more marked sweepback, a flat oval air intake (similar to that of the North American F-100 Super Sabre), and a larger and more swept fin and rudder.

Production began in 1956, the first series-built aircraft flying for the first time on 26 February 1957; deliveries to the *Armée de l'Air* began later that year. One hundred and eighty were produced (plus five pre-production examples) over the next two years, including 24 for the Israeli Self-Defence Forces/Air Force. Those in French service had, in addition to the armament listed, a capability to carry an AIM-9 Sidewinder air-to-air missile beneath each wing. In February 1958 Dassault flew a prototype Super Mystère B-4, powered by a 13,228-lb (6000-kg) thrust Atar 9 afterburning turbojet, but this programme was overshadowed by the greater promise of the Mirage III, and the B-4 did not go into production.

By the late 1970s only a few B-2s remained in French service, most having been replaced by Mirage F1s, but the type still served with the Israeli air force, and Israel has supplied Honduras with 12 examples of a version modified locally to take a 9,300-lb (4218-kg) thrust non-afterburning Pratt & Whitney J52-P-8A turbojet. Despite the absence of an afterburner, this version is said to have a considerably longer rear fuselage than the standard Super Mystère, and can carry a wider variety of external stores. This version appeared in the early 1970s, and was used with some success in the Yom Kippur War of October 1973.

Type: single-seat fighter and fighter-bomber
Powerplant: one 9,833-lb (4460-kg) SNECMA Atar 101G-2 or G-3 afterburning turbojet
Performance: maximum speed at sea level 646 mph (1040 km/h); maximum speed at 39,370 ft (12000 m) 743 mph (1195 km/h); normal range 600 miles (965 km); maximum rate of climb at sea level at normal loaded weight 17,500 ft (5340 m) per minute; service ceiling 55,775 ft (17000 m)
Weights: empty equipped 15,282 lb (6932 kg); normal loaded 19,842 lb (9000 kg); maximum take-off 22,046 lb (10000 kg)
Dimensions: span 34 ft 5¾ in (10.51 m); length 46 ft 1 in (14.04 m); height 14 ft 11 in (4.55 m); wing area 376.74 sq ft (35.00 m²)
Armament: two 30-mm DEFA 552 cannon in underside of forward fuselage; retractable internal pack of thirty-five 68-mm SNEB rockets in lower fuselage; and up to 2,205 lb (1000 kg) of bombs, rocket pods, drop-tanks or other stores on two underwing hardpoints
Operators: France, Honduras and Israel

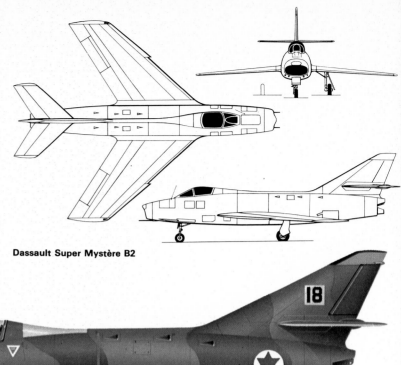

Dassault Super Mystère B2

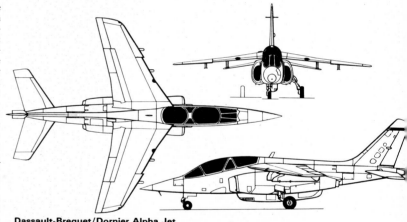

The Super Mystères of the Israeli Heyl Ha'Avir saw considerable action which included numerous air combats.

Dassault-Breguet/Dornier Alpha Jet

An international project between France and West Germany, the Dassault-Breguet/Dornier Alpha Jet will serve with *l'Armée de l'Air* in the advanced training role, and with the *Luftwaffe* with the additional tasks of light strike and reconnaissance. On 22 July 1969 the governments of France and West Germany announced that they had a requirement for a new subsonic basic and advanced training aircraft. A total of around 200 each was envisaged, to replace the Lockheed T-33s and Fouga Magisters then in service and beginning to show their age. France had originally hoped to fill this role with the two-seat SEPECAT Jaguar, but it was eventually realised that so powerful a supersonic trainer was foolish, so an alternative had to be found. On 24 July 1970 it was announced that the Alpha Jet had been selected to equip the two forces not only in the training role but also for battlefield-reconnaissance duties and light strike, following a change in *Luftwaffe* requirements. Despite these differing specifications, the basic structure, engines and landing gear are virtually identical in all versions. As well as France and Germany, the air forces of Belgium (33 aircraft), Morocco (24), Ivory Coast (12), and Togo (5) have placed orders for the Alpha Jet. Under a licence-production agreement Egypt will build 160 aircraft, a deal with which Dassault-Breguet/Dornier can feel well satisfied as the order followed a protracted evaluation of other aircraft including the British Aerospace Hawk, which is cheaper, has higher performance and a longer fatigue life. In response to the US Navy's requirement for a new advanced trainer, Dassault-Breguet/Dornier have teamed up with Lockheed-California to enter the Alpha Jet in the VTX competition. If chosen, the Franco-German aircraft would be built under licence by Lockheed and would represent a welcome (for Europe) change of direction in the predominanly eastward flow of aircraft sales across the Atlantic. Licence production could also come out of the manufacturing agreement signed in the spring of 1978 between the French government and the Arab Organisation for Industrialisation.

The whole programme has suffered a slippage of more than two years, causing a corresponding delay to production deliveries. The go-ahead decision was taken on 26 March 1975, nearly 18 months after the first prototype flew on 26 October 1973. The first *Luftwaffe* aircraft flew on 12 April 1978, nearly six months after the first series aircraft. The first of 33 aircraft for Belgium took to the air on 20 June 1978. Production is centred in France, along with flight testing, as Dassault Breguet is prime contractor and Dornier industrial collaborator. The assembly line in Belgium will be closed down in 1980, by which time all the country's aircraft are due to have been delivered. In 1978 the Alpha Jet cost in the region of $4.5 million, making it the most expensive of the new generation of trainers. It is also, however, one of the most capable at the cost of seven maintenance man-hours per flying hour, and a limited fatigue life of 10,000 hours. Aspect ratio may be increased to improve single-engine performance.

Dassault-Breguet/Dornier Alpha Jet

After prolonged delays, production series of the Dassault-Breguet/Dornier Alpha Jet at last began in late 1978. This photograph shows the first Belgian example, now in service at Brustem, replacing the T-33A.

France's Alpha Jets will replace T-33s and Mystère IVs, which have been used for advanced and weapons training for some reason France does not fit zero-zero ejection seats, though the West Germans do. Students will spend some 70 hours on a new basic trainer and then a similar period on Magisters before moving up to the more complex Alpha Jet. Belgian students will move straight from SIAI-Marchetti SF.260 primary trainers to the new jet. Weapon-training and light strike variants for the *Luftwaffe* will be able to carry nearly 5,000 lb (2268 kg) of stores on one centre-fuselage and four underwing hardpoints. The German aircraft will be equipped with a simple nav/attack system. Hi-lo-hi radius of action with a representative warload is about 345 miles (556 km), and about 607 miles (370 km) on a lo-lo-lo mission.

Type: two-seat advanced trainer and light strike/reconnaissance aircraft
Powerplant: two 2,976-lb (1350-kg) SNEC-MA/Turboméca Larzac 04 two-shaft turbofans

Performance: maximum speed at sea level 622 mph (1000 km/h); maximum speed at 30,000 ft (9144 m) or Mach 0.85; combat radius (including 5 minutes combat) with maximum external load 254 miles (410 km); combat radius (ground-attack, lo-lo-lo), 391 miles (630 km); ferry range (internal fuel and two 68.2-Imperial Gallon (310-litre) drop-tanks) 1,725 miles (2780 km); time to 30,000 ft (9145 m) under 7 minutes
Weights: empty equipped (trainer) 7,374 lb (3345 kg); empty equipped (strike) 7,716 lb

(3500 kg); normal take-off (trainer, clean) 11,023 lb (5000 kg); normal take-off (strike) 13,448 lb (6100 kg); maximum take-off (strike, external stores) 15,983 lb (7250 kg)
Dimensions: span 29 ft 10¾ in (9.11 m); length 40 ft 3¾ in (12.29 m); height 13 ft 9 in (4.19 m); wing area 188.4 sq ft (17.5 m²)
Armament: underfuselage pod containing a 30-mm DEFA or 27-mm Mauser cannon (150 rounds each) or 7.62-mm (0.3-in) machine-gun (250 rounds); four underwing hardpoints each carrying up to thirty-six 68-mm (2.68-in) rockets or high-explosive/retarded bombs up

to 882 lb (400 kg) in weight, or cluster dispensers, or drop tanks etc; provision also for air-to-air (Magic) or air-to-surface (Maverick) missiles
Operators: Belgium, France, Ivory Coast, Morocco, Togo, West Germany

Dassault-Breguet/Dornier Alpha Jet shown in the operational camouflage planned for the 200 aircraft on order for the Luftwaffe.

De Havilland DH.104 Dove/Devon

Design of the DH.104 Dove began towards the end of World War II, and the prototype flew at Hatfield on 25 September 1945. It was intended as a replacement for the DH.89A Dragon Rapide biplane, was of all-metal construction and scored two firsts — the first British transport with a tricycle undercarriage and the first with braking propellers. It rapidly went into production and soon attracted the attention of the military authorities. The 48th production aircraft was modified to Air Ministry specification C.13/47 as a military communications version, and this variant went into production as the Devon C.1; a total of 41 were handed over to the RAF, with deliveries beginning in late 1947. The Devon incorporated several minor changes to meet RAF requirements, such as removal of the right-hand front passenger seat for installation of a dinghy, and addition of a jettisonable cabin door. RAF Devons were re-engined later in their life with 400-hp (298-kW) Gipsy Queen 70-3 engines to bring them up to Dove 8 standard.

The Royal Navy acquired 13 Doves from 1955 under the designation Sea Devon C.20. A number of Devons and Sea Devons are still in service. India and New Zealand were the only other countries to use the designation Devon: the first of 22 for the Indian air force was delivered in March 1948, and the RNZAF received 30, deliveries beginning in mid-1948. The biggest overseas military customer for the Dove was Argentina which received 54, but these are now out of service.

A total of 544 Doves, including two pro-

totypes, had been built when manufacture ceased in 1967, and of these about 240 were at one time in military use.

Type: twin-engine light transport
Powerplant: (Devon C.1) two 330-hp (246-kW) DH Gipsy Queen 71 or 400-hp (298-kW) Gipsy Queen 70-3 inline piston engines
Performance: maximum speed at 8,000 ft (2440 m) 210 mph (337 km/h); cruising speed at 8,000 ft (2440 m) 179 mph (288 km/h); initial rate of climb 850 ft (259 m) per minute; service ceiling 20,000 ft (6100 m); range 1,000 miles (1600 km) with 1,700 lb (771 kg) payload
Weights: empty 5,780 lb (2621 kg); maximum 8,500 lb (3855 kg)
Dimensions: span 57 ft 0 in (17.37 m); length 39 ft 4 in (11.98 m); height 13 ft 4 in (4.06 m); wing area 335 sq ft (31.12 m²)
Operators: Eire, Ethiopia, India, Jordan, Lebanon, Malaysia, New Zealand, Paraguay, Sri Lanka, Sweden, UK, Zaire

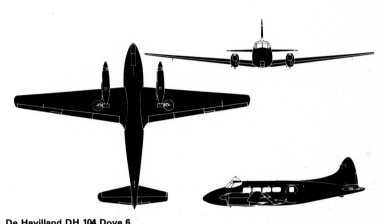
De Havilland DH.104 Dove 6

This HS Devon C.2 carries the badge of RAF 207 Sqn stationed at Northolt.

De Havilland DH.114 Heron 2

Following the success of the de Havilland Dove, the manufacturers decided to scale up the design, but when this was first considered at the time of the Dove's first flight in 1945, the market for a larger version had not appeared. The prototype de Havilland Heron featured a large number of Dove components, with the fuselage about 10 ft (3.04 m) longer, providing accommodation for 17 passengers, and first flew at Hatfield on 10 May, 1950. The first production aircraft was delivered to New Zealand National Airways in April 1952.

Of the early production Herons, 48 were Srs 1B aircraft with a fixed tricycle undercarriage, but the seventh production aircraft became the prototype Srs 2 with retractable landing gear, and all military Herons were variants of the Srs 2. The prototype was temporarily transferred to the RAF for a short period in mid-1956 for Princess Margaret's East African tour, but the first production Srs 2 was the 50th production Heron.

A total of 29 Herons have seen military service; an early customer was the South African air force which received two Srs 2Bs in October 1955. A Heron which was forcibly militarized was the aircraft belonging to the governor general of the Congo: it was cap-

tured by Katangan rebels and transferred to the Katanga air force in 1960.

Two Srs 2Ds were delivered to the Jordan Arab Air Force in January 1959 and two to the West German *Luftwaffe* in 1957–58. The Kuwait air force received an ex-civil Heron 2D in May 1962 and the Iraqi air force took delivery of a new Srs 2C in September 1956 plus a Srs 2D for the Royal Flight; the latter was subsequently tranferred to normal air force duties and was written off in a crash.

The Ghana air force bought a new Srs 2D in June 1961 and in December the following year took over two Srs 2Ds from Ghana Airways; two served for a time with 112 *Escadrille de Transport Moyen* in Zaire. None of the above mentioned Herons remain in military service. In September 1959 two Heron 2Ds were delivered to the Royal Ceylon Air Force (now Sri Lanka Air Force), followed a year later by two more. Two of these remain in service, converted by the Riley Aeronautics Corporation to 290-hp (216-kW) Lycoming IO-540-G1A5 engines. These aircraft are now in full-time use for tourist flying, but using service pilots.

Two late production Heron 2Ds delivered in August and September 1963 to the Royal

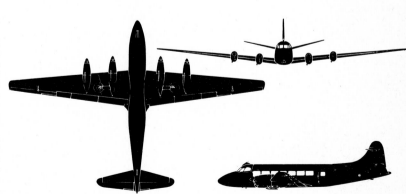
De Havilland DH.114 Heron 2

Malaysian Air Force are still in service with No 2 Squadron, a VIP unit which also operates Doves, Fokker Fellowships and BAe (HS) 125s. Few Herons saw military service in Britain but four of those which did received the supreme accolade in being chosen for the Royal Flight. The first, a Srs 2B, was delivered to the RAF in May 1955. Nos 2 and

3 were delivered in April 1958 and designated Heron C(VVIP).3, while No 4 was a Srs 4 which was handed over in June 1961. The royal Herons were eventually replaced by BAe (HS) 748s; three were sold to Saunders Aircraft in Canada and the other was transferred to the Royal Navy where it is still in service with the Yeovilton station flight. One other

continued

155

Heron was used by the RAF, a Srs 2B delivered in September 1954 for use by the Joint Services Mission in Washington. It was subsequently used by several other air attachés before being sold to a Danish civil operator. The Royal Navy acquired five ex-civil Herons in 1961. Two Srs 2Bs came from Airlines

(Jersey) Ltd in March and April, and three Srs 2s from Overseas Aviation in March. All were delivered to No 781 Squadron at Lee-on-Solent with the designation Sea Heron C.20 and four are still in use with this unit.

Type: four-engine light transport

Powerplant: four 250-hp (187-kW) DH Gipsy Queen 30-2 engines
Performance: (Srs 2D) cruising speed 183 mph (295 km/h) at 8,000 ft (2348 m); rate of climb at sea level 1,075 ft (327 m) per minute; take off distance to 50 ft (15.2 m) 2,425 ft (740 m); landing distance from 50 ft

(15.2 m) 2,065 ft (630 m)
Weights: (Srs 2D) empty 8,150 lb (3697 kg); maximum 13,500 lb (6123 kg)
Dimensions: span 71 ft 6 in (21.80 m); length 48 ft 6 in (14.78 m); height 15 ft 7 in (4.72 m); wing area 499 sq ft (46.36 m²)
Operators: Malaysia, Sri Lanka, UK

De Havilland DH.100/113/115 Vampire

The de Havilland Vampire was Britain's first single-jet fighter, the prototype flying at Hatfield on 20 September, 1943, piloted by Geoffrey de Havilland, only 16 months after the beginning of detail design. The type entered service with the RAF in 1946 as the Vampire F.1 and a number of this early variant were used for experimental work.

Development led to the Vampire F.3 which eventually replaced the F.1s in RAF service, and the F.3 was the basis for a series of export Vampires, four going to Norway and 85 to Canada. Arrangements were made for production of the Vampire in Australia and 80 were built by de Havilland Aircraft Pty Ltd, powered by Australian-built Rolls-Royce Nene engines and designated Vampire FB.30.

A ground-attack version of the Vampire F.3, with strengthened wing and reduced span, entered production as the FB.5 and this attracted a number of export orders. Examples were supplied to France, Sweden, Egypt, Finland, Iraq, Lebanon, Norway, New Zealand and Venezuela. Some standard FB.5s were supplied to the Indian and South African air forces, and production licences were negotiated successfully with a number of countries. In Italy, Macchi built 80 FB.52As, Switzerland 178 F.6s and France 67 FB.5s. The last were assembled by SNCASE from British-made components, but subsequently SNCASE built 183 Goblin-powered FB.5s and 250 FB.53s with French-built Rolls-Royce Nene engines, in which form they were designated SE.535 Mistral.

The last single-seat Vampire variant to see service with the RAF was the FB.9, a version of the FB.5 with cockpit air-conditioning; FB.9s were also delivered to Rhodesia, Jordan and Ceylon. Total UK production of single-seat Vampires amounted to 1,157 aircraft

when the line closed in December 1953. The only single-seaters believed to be still in military service are a handful of FB.1/FB.50s in Dominica, a few FB.9s in Rhodesia and about 30 FB.6s in Switzerland.

Brief mention must be made of the DH.113 Vampire NF.10, a two-seat night-fighter development of which 95 were built, mainly for the RAF. A few were delivered to Italy as NF.54s and 29 ex-RAF aircraft were sold to the Indian air force between 1954 and 1958. No Vampire night fighters remain in service.

Experience with the wide side-by-side (Mosquito-type) seating of the Vampire NF.10 proved invaluable in the development of the DH.115 Vampire trainer, flown on 15 November, 1950 as a private venture with Martin-Baker ejection seats. The foresight of de Havilland was rewarded by production orders from the RAF and Royal Navy. First RAF deliveries were made in 1952 while those of the RN version, which was basically similar, began in 1954; the respective designations were Vampire T.11 and Sea Vampire T.22. More than 530 went to the RAF and 73 to the RN from a total UK production of 804, completed in 1958. Export deliveries, as Vampire T.55s, were made to Austria (5), Burma (8), Ceylon (5), Chile (5), Egypt (12), Eire (6), Finland (5), India (5), Indonesia (8), Iraq (6), Lebanon (3), New Zealand (12), Norway (4), Portugal (2), South Africa (21), Sweden (57), Switzerland (39), Syria (2), and Venezuela (6). Ex RAF T.11s were supplied to Jordan (2) and Rhodesia (4). Additionally, 109 were built in Australia under the designation T.33, 34 and 35, and 50 were assembled in India.

Chile and Rhodesia have a few T.55s still in service, but the biggest user is Switzerland with more than 30 in use alongside Vampire FB.6s, training students to wings standard.

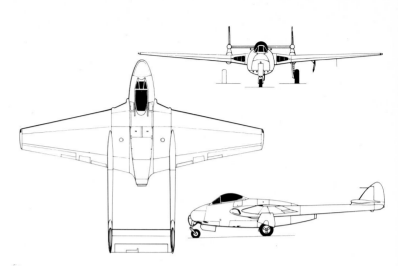

De Havilland DH.100 Vampire FB.5

Type: jet fighter and trainer
Powerplant: (FB.6) one 3,350-lb (1518-kg) DH Goblin 3 turbojet; (T.11) one 3,500-lb (1587-kg) DH Goblin 35 turbojet
Performance: (FB.6) maximum speed 548 mph (882 km/h) at 30,000 ft (9144 m); initial rate of climb 4,800 ft (1463 m) per minute; range 1,220 miles (1963 km) at 30,000 ft (9144 m); service ceiling 42,800 ft (13044 m). (T.11) maximum speed 549 mph (883 km/h) at 20,000 ft (6096 m); initial rate of climb 4,500 ft (1341 m) per minute; range 787 miles (1266 km); service ceiling 40,000 ft (12192 m)
Weights: (FB.6) empty 7,283 lb (3303 kg);

(FB.6) all-up 12,390 lb (5620 kg); (T.11) empty 7,380 lb (3347 kg); (T.11) all-up 11,150 lb (5058 kg)
Dimensions: (FB.6) span 38 ft 0 in (11.58 m); length 30 ft 9 in (9.36 m); height 6 ft 2 in (1.87 m); wing area 262 sq ft (24.33 m²) (T.11) span 38 ft 0 in (11.58 m); length 34 ft 6 in (10.50 m); height 6 ft 2 in (1.87 m); wing area 262 sq ft (24.33 m²)
Armament: (FB.6) four 20-mm cannon in nose and provision for underwing stores; (T.11) two 20-mm cannon in nose plus 8 rockets and two 500-lb (227-kg) bombs
Operators: Dominica, Rhodesia, Switzerland

De Havilland FB.50 Venom

Some 30 years after the prototype's first flight, the de Havilland Venom remains in front-line service with the Swiss air force. This is a remarkable record, especially for a jet fighter.

An improved version of the Vampire, the Venom prototype flew from Hatfield on 2 September 1949. The type reached the RAF in August 1952, serving in Germany, the Near East and Far East with 18 squadrons, as well as No 14 Sqn, Royal New Zealand Air Force. The two-seat night-fighter Venom NF.2 and NF.3 served with the RAF between 1953 and 1957, and the Royal Swedish Air Force flew the type until 1960. Foreign users of Venom fighter-bombers included Venezuela and Iraq.

The Venom FB.1 was fitted with a Rotax cartridge starter. Martin-Baker ejection seats were fitted to later FB.1s, and the FB.4 introduced powered ailerons and rudders to improve control at high subsonic speeds. The fins were modified, and provision was made for underwing drop tanks in addition to tip tanks.

In 1951 Switzerland decided to build the Venom under licence as a follow-on to the Vampire FB.6. Work on 150 Venom Mk.50s, completed to FB.1 standard, began in 1953. Manufacture was undertaken by a consortium which comprised the Federal Aircraft Factory (EFW) at Emmen, Pilatus at Stans and the Flug und Fahrzeugwerke at Altenrhein. A further batch of 100, to FB.4 standard, was completed in 1957.

Flying from airfields in mountain valleys up to 4,500 ft (1400 m) above sea level, the Venom's manoeuvrability is a great asset. Today, maintenance of the aged aircraft presents problems, though monthly flying hours are not high as the Venom units are manned by part-time militia. Some 100 remain in service, equipping *Fliegerstaffeln* 2, 3, 6, 9, 13, 15 and 20 assigned to the close-support role. Among

the modifications introduced by the Swiss are a redesigned nose housing UHF communications, strengthening of the inner wing sections for rocket launchers, and fitting of link collectors beneath the cannon. Eight Venoms with underwing camera pods fly alongside the Dassault Mirage IIIRS tactical-reconnaissance aircraft of *Fliegerstaffel* 10.

Replacement was first considered in 1966, but it was not until 1975 that it was decided to order 72 Northrop F-5Es. These will enable the Venom to be retired in the early 1980s.

Type: ground-attack fighter
Powerplant: one 5,150-lb (2338-kg) de Havilland Ghost 105 turbojet
Performance: maximum speed at 30,000 ft (9150 m) 557 mph (896 km/h); range 1,075 miles (1730 km); service ceiling 48,000 ft (14600 m); rate of climb from sea level 7,230 ft (2200 m) per minute
Weights: loaded 15,310 lb (6950 kg)
Dimensions: span 41 ft 8 in (12.7 m); length 33 ft 0 in (10.06 m); height 6 ft 8 in (2.03 m); wing area 279.75 sq ft (25.99 m²)
Armament: four 20-mm Hispano cannon with 150 rounds per gun, plus up to 2,000 lb (910 kg) of bombs or rockets
Operators: Switzerland

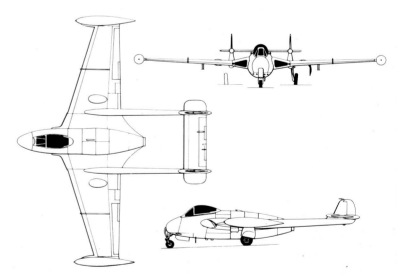

De Havilland Venom FB.4

Swiss Air Force de Havilland Venom FB.50 in tactical camouflage. The type was licence-built by the Federal Aircraft Factory.

De Havilland Canada DHC-1 Chipmunk

The DHC-1 Chipmunk was designed to succeed de Havilland's classic Tiger Moth biplane trainer. Flying for the first time at Downsview, Toronto, on 22 May 1946, the tandem-seat stressed-skin monoplane was the first indigenous design of the Canadian de Havilland company. The prototype, put through its paces by Pat Fillingham from the parent company at Hatfield, was powered by a 145-hp (108-kW) de Havilland Gipsy Major 1C.

Chipmunks built to the prototype's specification were designated DHC-1B-1, while those with a Gipsy Major 10-3 were DHC-1B-2s. An order for 60 1B-2s from the Royal Canadian Air Force were designated Chipmunk T.30, and distinguished by a bubble canopy.

Downsview built 218 Chipmunks, the last in 1951. Two were evaluated by the Aeroplane and Armament Experimental Establishment at Boscombe Down. As a result, the fully-aerobatic Chipmunk was ordered from Hatfield and Chester to Specification 8/48 as an *ab initio* trainer for the RAF.

The RAF received 735 Chipmunks out of 1,000 manufactured in Britain. The first to wear RAF roundels were flown by the Oxford University Air Squadron from February 1950; thereafter, the type replaced the Tiger Moth with all 17 university air squadrons, as well as equipping many RAF Volunteer Reserve flying schools in the early 1950s. National service pilots underwent their initial training on the 'Chip', which was served intermittently at the RAF College, Cranwell. Perhaps the most famous Chipmunk pilot was the Duke of Edinburgh, who gained his wings in an all-red machine at White Waltham in late 1952.

A few Chipmunks of 114 Squadron were pressed into service in Cyprus on internal security flights during the troubles of 1958.

Under an agreement concluded between de Havilland and the General Aeronautical Material Workshops (OGMA) of Portugal, 60 Chipmunks were licence-manufactured from 1955 for the Portuguese air force. Other users included Burma, Ceylon, Colombia, Denmark, Iraq, Ireland, Jordan, Lebanon, Malaya, Saudi Arabia, Syria, Thailand and Uruguay.

Type: tandem two-seat primary trainer
Powerplant: one 145-hp (108-kW) de Havilland Gipsy Major 8 air-cooled inline engine
Performance: maximum speed at sea level 138 mph (222 km/h); cruising speed at sea level 119 mph (191 km/h); cruising range at 116 mph (187 km/h), at 5,000 ft (1525 m) 280 miles (445 km); service ceiling 15,800 ft (4820 m); rate of climb at sea level 840 ft (256 m) per minute
Weights: empty 1,425 lb (646 kg); loaded 2,014 lb (914 kg)
Dimensions: span 34 ft 4 in (10.45 m); length 25 ft 5 in (7.75 m); height 7 ft 0 in (2.13 m); wing area 172 sq ft (15.97 m²)
Armament: none
Operators: Portugal

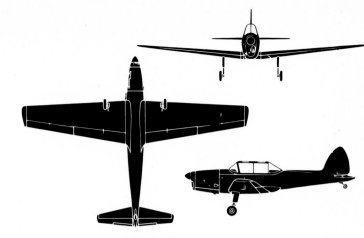

De Havilland Canada DHC-1 Chipmunk

De Havilland Canada Chipmunk T Mk 10 WB550. This famous RAF trainer remains in use primarily in Air Experience Flights.

De Havilland Canada DHC-2 Beaver

Design of the Beaver light utility transport was started in Toronto in late 1946, influenced by the Ontario Department of Lands and Forests. The prototype took to the air on 16 August 1947 with Russ Bannock at the controls. Type certification in Canada followed in March 1948. A ready market had been foreseen in the numerous 'bush' operators in the Canadian prairies, but it was as a military transport that the type was to make its mark.

The Beaver was entered in a design competition jointly sponsored by the US Air Force and US Army in 1951 for a new liaison aircraft. These services purchased six Beavers for evaluation purposes under the designation YL-20; the type's subsequent success made it only the second non-American type to be purchased in quantity since World War II. Once Congressional approval had been obtained, large-scale acquisition commenced. It is a tribute to the sturdy construction of the Beaver that very few changes were specified by the US authorities; these were mainly concerned with instrumentation and equipment, and were easily complied with.

Most Beavers were for the export market. Some 970 were delivered to the American armed forces, designated L-20 and, since 1962, U-6A. The Beaver's wide track and ease of maintenance, features intended for operation in the snowy wastes of the Canadian north, proved equally attractive in Korea in the 1950s

and, later, Vietnam. A pilot and up to seven passengers can be accommodated; alternatively, the tough floor with cargo attachments can carry 1,500 lb (680 kg). Wheels, skis, floats, or an amphibious float assembly can be fitted.

Over 20 countries ordered the Beaver for military use in addition to the United States and Canada. Some, such as the 24 supplied to the Royal Netherlands Air Force, were covered by America's postwar Mutual Assistance Defense Program. The British Army Air Corps took delivery of 46 Beavers. DH at Hatfield produced a Beaver 2, with Alvis Leonides engine and enlarged tail surfaces; no production resulted. Greater success was achieved by Toronto's Beaver 3 or Turbo-Beaver with a 578-ehp (431-kW) Pratt and Whitney PT6A-6 turboprop; 60 were built, the majority for civil use.

The US Army operated more Beavers than any other single type of fixed-wing aircraft. Several were operated on skis in Alaska during the early 1950s in a high-visibility red and white. USAF Strategic Air Command used 58 to support ICBM sites. The few dual-control Beavers of the US Navy were designated TU-6A.

Nearly 1,700 Beavers had been manufactured when de Havilland Canada made the decision to curtail production in the mid-1960s, in favour of larger and more powerful STOL aircraft.

De Havilland Canada DHC-2 Beaver

Type: light utility transport
Powerplant: one 450-hp (336-kW) Pratt & Whitney R-985 Wasp Junior air-cooled radial engine
Performance: maximum speed at 5,000 ft (1520 m) 163 mph (262 km/h); cruising speed at 5,000 ft (1520 m) 143 mph (230 km/h); cruising range on internal fuel 455 miles (732 km); maximum range 733 miles (1180 km); service ceiling 18,000 ft (5485 m); initial climb rate 1,020 ft (311 m) per minute
Weights: empty 2,850 lb (1290 kg); loaded 5,100 lb (2310 kg)
Dimensions: span 48 ft 0 in (14.63 m); length 30 ft 3 in (9.22 m); height 9 ft 0 in (2.74 m); wing area 250 sq ft (23.22 m²)
Armament: none
Operators: Canada, UK

De Havilland Canada DHC-3 Otter

The all-metal de Havilland Canada DHC-3 Otter was designed to carry 2,240 lb (1016 kg) of freight or 14 passengers and was built in quantity in the early 1950s for the US Army, US Navy and Royal Canadian Air Force. The majority of the 466 examples built went to military customers although about 100 were delivered to civil operators.

Powered by a single 600-hp (448-kW) Pratt & Whitney R-1340 Twin Wasp radial, the Otter followed closely the layout and design philosophy of the earlier DHC-2 Beaver. It was, in fact, originally known as the King Beaver. Despite Canada's harsh climate and large areas with sparse populations, single-engined aircraft had been used successfully to

open up the country. The choice of a single engine for a new 14-seater was not therefore unusual. The parallel-chord wing is fitted with double-slotted flaps. The prototype made its maiden flight in December 1951 and the first of 66 Otters for the RCAF were employed on search and rescue operations in the Arctic, paratrooping, and aerial photography.

Quantity deliveries to the US Army began in 1955 under the designation U-1A, US Navy aircraft being designated UC-1 (changed to U-1B in 1962). The US armed forces expected to use the Otter for supplying troops in forward areas but in peacetime the aircraft found a number of roles reflecting its Canadian origins. The first six US aircraft were assigned

De Havilland Canada DHC-3 Otter

continued

to Alaska. Others were used on expeditions to the Antarctic and in 1957 – 58 an Otter provided the sole transport and reconnaissance support for the British component of the Commonwealth Trans-Antarctic Expedition. At one time or another 10 nations used the Otter for Arctic surveys. An RAF crew flew the Trans-Antarctic Expedition Otter on an 11-hour sortie across the South Pole.

Like the Beaver and Twin Otter, the Otter is capable of operating from wheels, floats or skis, and an amphibian version was also offered. Production ceased in 1968.

Type: STOL light utility aircraft
Powerplant: one 600-hp (448-kW) Pratt & Whitney R-1340-S1H1-G air-cooled radial piston engine

Performance: (at maximum take-off weight, landplane at sea level) maximum speed 153 mph (246 km/h); maximum cruising speed 132 mph (212 km/h); economical cruising speed 121 mph (195 km/h); range with 2,100-lb (953-kg) payload and reserves 875 miles (1410 km)
Weights: (landplane) empty 4,431 lb (2010 kg); maximum take-off and landing 8,000 lb

(3629 kg)
Dimensions: (landplane) span 58 ft 0 in (17.69 m); length 41 ft 10 in (12.80 m); height 12 ft 7 in (3.83 m); wing area 375 sq ft (34.83 m²)
Armament: none
Operators: Australia, Burma, Canada, Chile, Colombia, Ghana, India, Indonesia, Norway, US Army, US Navy

De Havilland Canada DHC-4 Caribou

DHC took the decision to build the DHC-4 in 1956 and the aim was to develop an aircraft with the load carrying capability of the DC-3 and the STOL performance of the Beaver and Otter. The Canadian army placed an order for two and the US Army followed with five. The US Secretary of Defense waived a restriction which limited the US Army to fixed-wing aircraft with empty weight less than 5,000 lb (2268 kg).

The prototype flew in July 1958. The high wing had a characteristic centre section with marked anhedral. The rear door was designed as a ramp for items weighing up to 6,720 lb (3048 kg). In the trooping role up to 32 soldiers could be carried. The Caribou served with the RCAF as the CC-108 and with the US Army as the AC-1 (1962 designation, CV-2A). As a result of its evaluation of the first five aircraft the US Army adopted the Caribou as standard equipment and placed orders for 159.

The second batch were uprated and designated CU-2B. Following tension on the border between China and India, the US Army handed over two Caribous to the Indian air force in early 1963. In January 1967 the 134 Caribous still in service with the US Army were transferred to US Air Force charge as C-7As or C-7Bs. The aircraft was a general sales success and examples flew with air forces throughout the world. In Canadian service the Caribou was replaced by the DHC-5 Buffalo and surplus examples were sold to a number of nations including Columbia, Oman and Tanzania. Many of the Canadian aircraft had been loaned to the United Nations and seen extensive international service. Production ceased in 1973.

Type: STOL tactical transport
Powerplant: two 1,450-hp (1080-kW) Pratt & Whitney R-2000-7M2 air-cooled radial piston engines
Performance: (at maximum take-off weight) maximum speed at 6,500 ft (1980 m) 216 mph (347 km/h); maximum cruising speed at 7,500 ft (2285 m) 182 mph (293 km/h); range with maximum payload and full reserves 242 miles (390 km)
Weights: empty 18,260 lb (8283 kg); maximum take-off and landing 28,500 lb (12930 kg); maximum zero fuel 27,000 lb (12250 kg)
Dimensions: span 95 ft 7½ in (29.15 m); length 72 ft 7 in (22.13 m); height 31 ft 9 in (9.70 m); wing area 912 sq ft (84.73 m²)
Armament: none
Operators: Abu Dhabi, Australia, Cameroon, Canada, Ghana, India, Kenya, Kuwait, Malaysia, Oman, Spain, Taiwan, Tanzania, Thailand, Uganda, US Air Force, Zambia

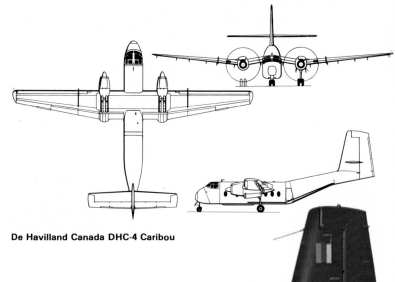

De Havilland Canada DHC-4 Caribou

Royal Malaysian Air Force de Havilland Canada DHC-4 Caribou shown in 1970 when flown by 5 Sqn, RMAF.

De Havilland Canada DHC-5 Buffalo

De Havilland Canada began work on the Caribou II in May 1962 in response to a US Army request for proposals for a new 41-seat STOL tactical transport. DHC was selected from 25 candidates to build four evaluation aircraft and the first made its maiden flight in April 1964. It was designed to be compatible with the Boeing-Vertol Chinook helicopter and to carry loads such as the Pershing missile, 105-mm howitzer or a ¾-ton truck. These four aircraft were delivered to the Army as YAC-2s, since redesignated C-8A. Although no further US orders followed, the Canadian Armed Forces took delivery of 15 DHC-5As designated CC-115s; six have since been converted to the maritime patrol role. Following delivery of 24 to the Brazilian air force and 16 aircraft to the Peruvian air force in 1972 the production line closed.

In 1974 DHC proposed two developed versions to the Indian air force. Designated DHC-5B and DHC-5C respectively, they were powered by General Electric CT64-P4C and Rolls-Royce Dart RDa.12 engines. Although no Indian order was forthcoming, the company judged that there was a continuing demand and invested $4 million in Buffalo improvements. The line was re-opened in 1974 to produce initially 19 of the improved D-model. A further 24 followed.

Because of the interest of the Canadian Department of Industry, Trade and Commerce, DHC and NASA in STOL capability and the suitability of the C-8A Buffalo as a test bed, an agreement was signed in 1970 between the Canadian and American governments covering the development of a jet research aircraft. Based on the Buffalo, it was designated NASA/DITC XC-8A. This much-modified aircraft, with clipped wings, fixed undercarriage and powered by two Rolls-Royce Spey

engines, made its first flight in May 1972. Apart from its unique augmentor wing, the engines make use of vectored nozzles.

The Buffalo has also spawned two other interesting research aircraft. The first to fly was the XC-8A ACLS fitted with an air-cushion landing system. This derivative can take off and land on an air cushion which, when inflated, looks like an elongated tyre inner tube. The first ACLS take-off by the Buffalo was on 31 March, 1975 and the first ACLS landing 11 days later. Aircraft fitted with the ACLS would be able to operate from rough fields, soft soil, swamps, water, ice or snow. The NASA/Boeing QSRA quiet short-haul research aircraft is the third Buffalo development, with four turbofans blowing over a new wing.

Type: STOL tactical transport
Powerplant: (DHC-5A) two 2,650-shp (1976-kW) General Electric T64/P2 turboprops; (DHC-5D) two 3,133-shp (2336-kW) General Electric T64-415 turboprops
Performance: (DHC-5A at maximum take-off weight) maximum cruising speed 271 mph (435 km/h); economical cruising speed 208 mph (335 km/h); range with maximum payload and full reserves 507 miles (815 km); (DHC-5D at maximum take-off weight) max-

imum cruising speed 288 mph (463 km/h); range with maximum payload and full reserves 691 miles (1112 km)
Weights: (DHC-5A) empty 23,157 lb (10505 kg); maximum take-off 41,000 lb (18598 kg); maximum landing 39,000 lb (17690 kg); maximum zero fuel 37,000 lb (16783 kg); (DHC-5D) empty 25,160 lb (11412 kg); maximum take-off 49,2000 lb (22316 kg); maximum landing 46,900 lb (21273 kg); maximum zero fuel 43,500 lb (19730 kg)
Dimensions: span 96 ft 0 in (29.26 m); length 79 ft 0 in (24.08 m); height 28 ft 8 in

(8.73 m); wing area 945 sq ft (87.8 m²)
Armament: none
Operators: Brazil, Canada, Ecuador, Kenya, Mauritania, Peru, Sudan, Togo, United Arab Emirates, Zaïre, Zambia

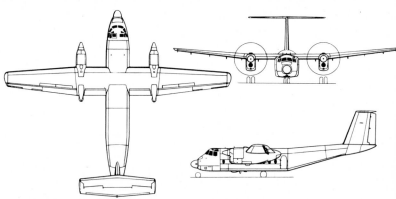

De Havilland Canada DHC-5D Buffalo

The Force Aérienne Togolaise is one user of the de Havilland Canada DHC-5D Buffalo, with its short take-off and landing properties.

De Havilland Canada DHC-6 Twin Otter

DHC had in the early 1960s fitted two PT6 turboprops to a basic DHC-3 Otter airframe. But the new 20-seat DHC-6 Twin Otter, while retaining the same fuselage cross-section, involved an almost complete redesign. The span was extended, struts moved inboard, nosewheel landing gear fitted, doors enlarged, cockpit revised and fin area increased. The first development aircraft flew on 20 May 1965. Orders built up slowly for the production Series 100, and there was a steady flow of military and paramilitary orders.

Among the current military users are the Canadian Armed Forces, with eight examples designated CC-138s. These are used for search and rescue, and utility duties. The US Army also has two examples, designated UV-18As, for service with the Alaska National Guard.

After 110 Series 100 aircraft had been delivered, DHC introduced the long-nosed Series 200. This aircraft has a much-improved baggage volume and 115 were built. The short-nose remained a standard production fit on float-equipped aircraft.

The Series 300 introduced more power and more payload/range.

Twin Otters are available with a fire-bombing tank attached to the belly. A 10-ft (3.05-m) ventral pod is an optional extra for carrying up to 600 lb (272 kg) of cargo or baggage. Like other DHC designs, the Twin Otter can operate from wheels, skis or floats. When floats are fitted small fins are added to the horizontal tailplane to maintain directional stability. DHC expects that the Twin Otter will remain in production for some years and in 1979 began negotiations with the Chinese government about possible licence production.

Type: light STOL utility transport
Powerplant: (Srs 100) two 578-ehp (430-kW) Pratt & Whitney Aircraft of Canada PT6A-20 turboprops; (Srs 300) two 652-ehp (486-kW) Pratt & Whitney Aircraft of Canada PT6A-27 turboprops.
Performance: (Srs 100 at maximum take-off weight) maximum cruising speed 184 mph (297 km/h); range with 2,150-lb (977-kg) payload 835 miles (1344 km); (Srs 300 at maximum take-off weight) maximum cruising speed 210 mph (338 km/h); range with 2,550-lb (1160-kg) payload 892 miles (1435 km)
Weights: (landplane Srs 100) empty 5,850 lb (2653 kg); maximum take-off and landing 10,500 lb (4763 kg); maximum zero fuel 10,150 lb (4603 kg); (landplane Srs 300) empty 7,415 lb (3363 kg); maximum take-off 12,500 lb (5700 kg); maximum landing 12,300 lb (5579 kg); maximum zero fuel 11,695 lb (5304 kg)
Dimensions: (landplane) span 65 ft 0 in

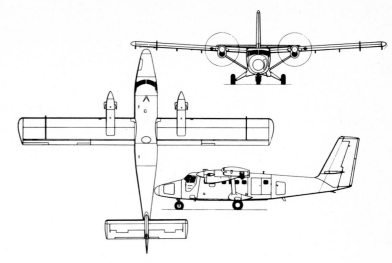

De Havilland Canada DHC-6 Twin Otter 3N

(19.81 m); (Srs 100) length 49 ft 6 in (15.09 m); height 18 ft 7 in (5.66 m); wing area 420 sq ft (39.02 m²); (Srs 300) length 51 ft 9 in (15.77 m); height 19 ft 6 in (5.94 m); wing area 420 sq ft (39.02 m²)

Armament: none
Operators: Argentina, Canada, Chile, Ecuador, Ethiopia, Jamaica, Norway, Panama, Paraguay, Peru, US Army

---

De Havilland Canada DHC-7R Ranger Dash-7

De Havilland Canada began project studies of a 40-50 seat STOL airliner in the late 1960s when enthusiasm in inter-city STOL operations was at its height. The airlines remained sceptical, however, and worries about noise and pollution were compounded by the 1973 oil crisis. While other aircraft manufacturers rapidly lost interest, DHC pressed ahead and the 50-seat pressurized Dash-7 made its first flight on 27 March 1975. Development costs, paid for largely by the Canadian government, DHC and major equipment suppliers, were $120 million.

Airline orders for such a costly and specialized vehicle have been slow to materialize, but DHC remains confident that sales will build up in a similar manner to other DHC designs. In order to broaden the market, DHC has examined a number of developments including the DHC-7R Ranger maritime patrol aircraft. The Canadian Armed Forces currently operate six DHC Buffaloes in the coastal patrol role and there is a strong possibility that these will be replaced by Rangers in due course. The Dash-7R has an increased fuel tankage to push endurance to 10-12 hours. A belly-mounted search radar provides 360° scan, and the package of electronics and reconnaissance equipment would be chosen to match the requirements of the customer. The Ranger could double as a transport with 26 seats in the rear of the cabin without any of the reconnaissance equipment having to be removed. Like the civil aircraft, the Ranger can be fitted with a freight door measuring 5 ft 10 in (1.778 m) by 7 ft 7 in (2.31 m).

The Dash-7 is unique amongst airliners in being able to operate with a full payload from grass runways as short as 2,300 ft (701 m). The Dash-7 Ranger would be able to use short, semi-prepared airstrips close to an area of military interest, and this is claimed to give it a distinct advantage over the more traditional maritime reconnaissance aircraft. Good take-off performance also means it can operated from hot-and-high airfields in remote areas.

Type: (Dash-7) STOL tactical transport; (Ranger) STOL maritime reconnaissance aircraft
Powerplant: four 1,120-shp (835-kW) Pratt & Whitney Aircraft of Canada PT6A-50 turboprops
Performance: (Dash-7) maximum cruising speed at 8,000 ft (2440 m) and with 41,000 lb (18600 kg) of payload 271 mph (436 km/h); maximum range with 50 passengers and full reserves 810 miles (1303 km); (Ranger) maximum cruising speed at sea level and at maximum take-off weight 268 mph (432 km/h); patrol endurance 9 hours 30 minutes
Weights: (Dash-7) empty 26,850 lb (12178 kg); maximum take-off 43,500 lb (19731 kg); maximum landing 41,500 lb (18824 kg); maximum zero fuel 39,000 lb (17690 kg); (Ranger) empty 28,500 lb (12927 kg); maximum take-off (45,000 lb (20411 kg); maximum landing 41,000 lb (18597 kg); maximum zero fuel 39,000 lb (17690 kg)
Dimensions: span 93 ft 0 in (28.35 m); length 80 ft 8 in (24.58 m); height 26 ft 2 in (7.98 m); wing area 860 sq ft (79.9 m²)
Armament: unarmed, but Ranger is equipped for flare and life-raft dropping
Operators: (Dash-7) Canadian Armed Forces; (Ranger) Canadian Coastguard

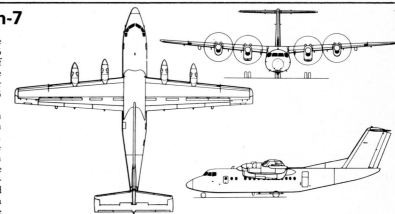

De Havilland Canada DHC-7 Ranger Dash-7

Dornier Do 27

The Dornier Do 27 was the first aircraft to enter production in Germany after World War II. Claudius Dornier recommenced activities in Spain in 1949, his Oficinas Tecnicas Dornier working closely with the Spanish CASA. The initial fruits of this collaboration were evident with the first flight of the Do 25 in June 1954. Prepared to meet a Spanish air ministry specification, the STOL transport was powered by a single 150-hp (112-kW) ENMA Tigre engine; 50 similar aircraft subsequently appeared under the designation CASA C-127.

Developed from this, the prototype Do 27 was flown on 8 April 1955. Production took place in Germany at Dorniër-Werke, the first example flying in October 1956. With a large 'wraparound' windscreen and generous five-seat layout, the Do 27A proved popular. Deliveries began at 20 aircraft per month.

The main military Do 27A and dual-control Do 27B differed little. The strutless, high wing provided ease of access for loading passengers or freight. Large flaps gave an amazing STOL capability. By far the largest user was the Federal German Republic, with well over 400. Another early customer was the Swiss *Flugwaffe*, whose initial seven aircraft sported a wheel-and-ski undercarriage. A prototype floatplane, the Do 27S, was built and flown; another was re-engined with the Turboméca Astazou turboprop. Production of the standard Do 27 exceeded 600 units in all its sub-versions before the line closed in 1965.

Type: STOL liaison and utility transport
Powerplant: one 275-hp (205-kW) Lycoming GO-480 air-cooled piston engine
Performance: maximum speed at 3,280 ft (1000 m) 155 mph (250 km/h); cruising speed at 3,280 ft (1000 m) 127 mph (205 km/h); cruising range 540 miles (870 km); service ceiling 18,400 ft (5500 m); climb to 3,280 ft (1000 m) 2 minutes 36 seconds; take-off to clear 50-ft (15-m) obstacle (maximum fuel, no wind) 558 ft (160 m); landing from 50 ft (15 m) 525 ft (170 m)
Weights: empty 2,167 lb (983 kg); loaded 3,460 lb (1570 kg)
Dimensions: span 39 ft 4½ in (12.0 m); length 31 ft 4 in (9.54 m); height 8 ft 10¾ in (3.28 m); wing area 208.8 sq ft (19.4 m²)
Armament: none
Operators: 14 countries including Israel, Spain, Switzerland, West Germany

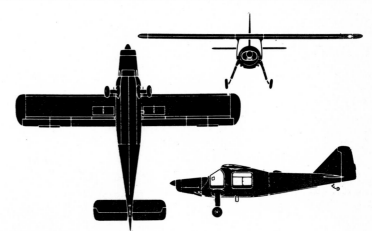

Dornier Do 27

Dornier Do 28D Skyservant

In the early 1950s Dipl-Ing Claudius Dornier established design offices in Madrid. Under the auspices of the Spanish aircraft manufacturer CASA, prototypes of the Do 25 and Do 27 STOL transports were flown in 1954 and 1955 respectively.

When the postwar embargo on aircraft manufacture in Germany was lifted, production of the Do 27 was transferred there, deliveries commencing in late 1956. Some 30 months later came the first flight of the twin-engined Do 28. To retain the STOL qualities of an aerodynamically clean high wing, the 225-hp (190-kW) Lycoming engines were mounted on stub-wings, flanking the six-seat cabin. Some 120 examples of the Do 28A and B were built.

The prototype Do 28D Skyservant flew on 23 February 1966. Its box-like fuselage seated 12 passengers, and 380-hp (283-kW) engines were installed.

The production Do 28D-1 was later fitted with wheel spats, wing fences and a large dorsal spine. These first four were the first to be delivered to the *Luftwaffe,* as VIP transports, in 1970.

By this time 101 had been allocated to the *Luftwaffe* as communications transports, a further 20 going to the *Marineflieger.* Skyservant roles include photographic survey, ambulance and para-dropping duties. Its robust construction and a take-off run of the order of 920 ft (280 m) has made it suitable for operation in Africa and other harsh environments. Most Skyservants exported are Do 28D-2s, lengthened by 6 in (15 cm), with larger fuel tanks in the engine nacelles and aerodynamic improvements to wing and tailplane. Dual controls became standard, and new landing lights were installed in the detachable fibreglass wingtips, which have anhedral. Freight doors may be replaced by a sliding door for supply-dropping. Additional stores or 55-gallon (250-litre) fuel tanks may be attached to underwing hardpoints.

A Skyservant with turboprops flew in April 1978. Dubbed the TurboSky, the Do 28D-5 has two 400-shp (298-kW) Avco Lycoming LTP 101-600s. Turboprop power and reliability, combined with a near aerobatic manoeuvrability and STOL capability, may attract orders from several air arms.

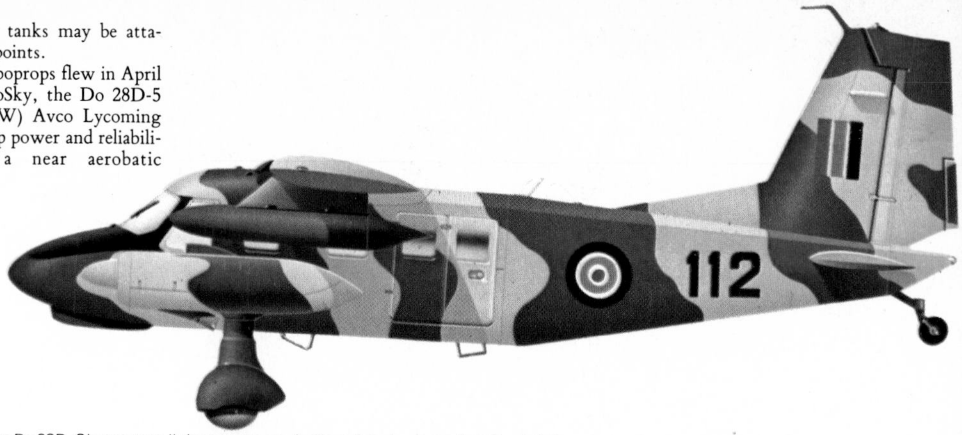

Kenya Air Force Dornier Do28D Skyservant light transport, believed to be based at Eastleigh.

Type: light passenger, freight and liaison transport
Powerplant: two 380-hp (283-kW) Lycoming IGSO-540 piston engines
Performance: maximum speed at 10,000 ft (3050 m) 201 mph (323 km/h); cruising speed 143 mph (230 km/h); range with 12 passengers 497 miles (800 km); range with 3,000-lb (1360-kg) payload 125 miles (200 km); service ceiling 24,000 ft (7300 m)
Weights: empty 4,615 lb (2095 kg); maximum loaded 8,040 lb (3647 kg)
Dimensions: span 49 ft 2½ in (15.0 m); length 37 ft 4¾ in (11.4 m); height 12 ft 9½ in (3.9 m); wing area 302 sq ft (28.06 m^2)
Armament: none
Operators: Cameroon, Ethiopia, Israel, Kenya, Malawi, Nigeria, Somalia, Thailand, West Germany, Zambia.

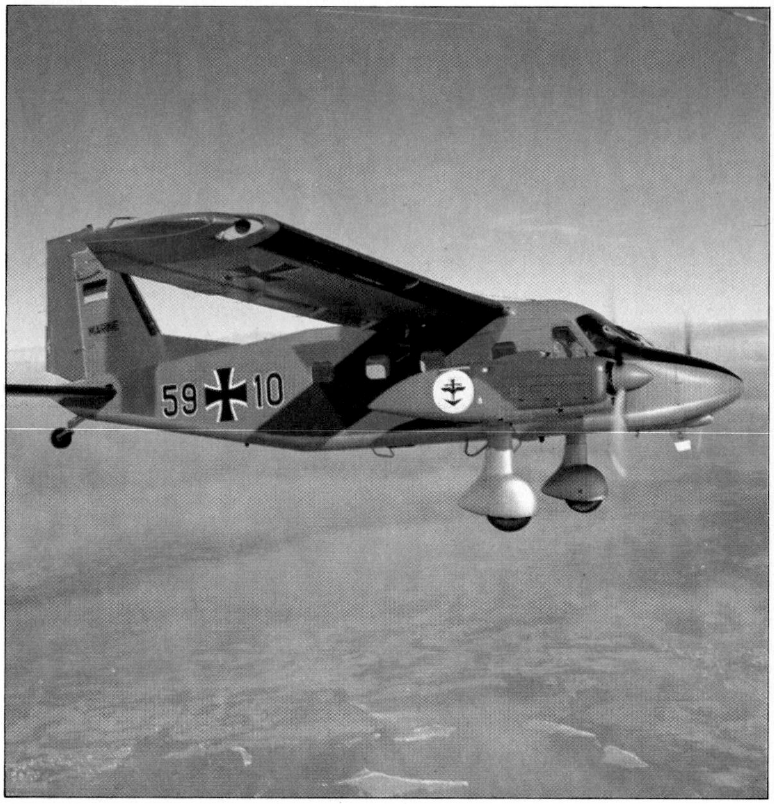

The Dornier Do 28D-2 Skyservant, here seen in service with the Federal German *Marineflieger,* is a STOL communications aircraft able to carry 13 passengers or a wide range of other loads. Dornier is trying to define advanced turboprop successors.

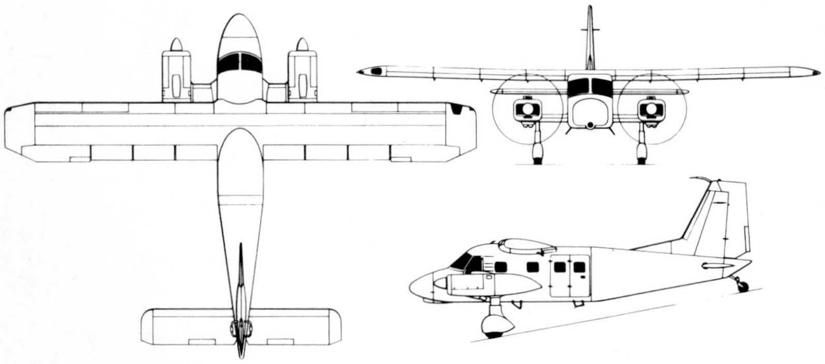

Dornier Do 28D Skyservant

Douglas A-1 Skyraider

Ed Heinemann, chief engineer at Douglas El Segundo (who also created the Boston/Havoc, Invader, Skynight, Skyray, Skywarrior, Skyrocket and Skyhawk) was so unimpressed by the XBTD-1 series built to US Navy specification for a carrier-based dive-bomber/torpedo-carrier that he took it upon himself to design a simpler machine which he judged more useful. At first designated XBT2D-1 and flown on 18 March 1945, it became the Douglas AD-1 Skyraider, and was to enjoy an amazingly long and varied career.

Flown by a pilot only, the AD-1 was at the time the largest production single-seater. Of low-wing monoplane configuration, the design was based on the Wright R-3350 radial engine, smaller than the R-4360 of other prototypes. Although there was plenty of internal space this was not used for weapons; instead the folding wings were given no fewer than seven hardpoints on each side, and a robust structure gave the Skyraider great integrity. Wartime experience had shown that the most important characteristic for an aircraft in this category was the ability to deliver a wide range of weapons. Douglas ensured that the

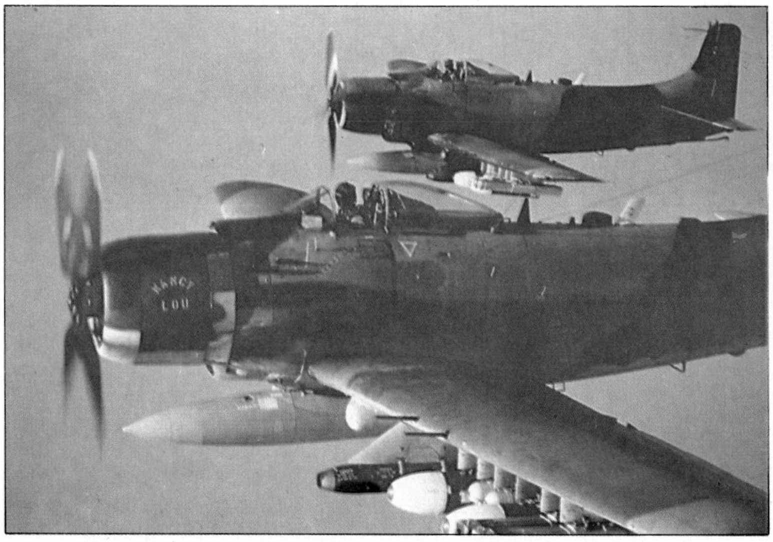

It has proved difficult to ascertain if any Skyraiders remain in genuine military service in 1980, though large numbers are still flying in several countries out of the 3,180 produced. These single-seat A-1H multi-role platforms of the USAF were escorting a 'Jolly Green' rescue helicopter in Vietnam, their pylons laden with weapons and equipment. One or two remain in US trials and research units.

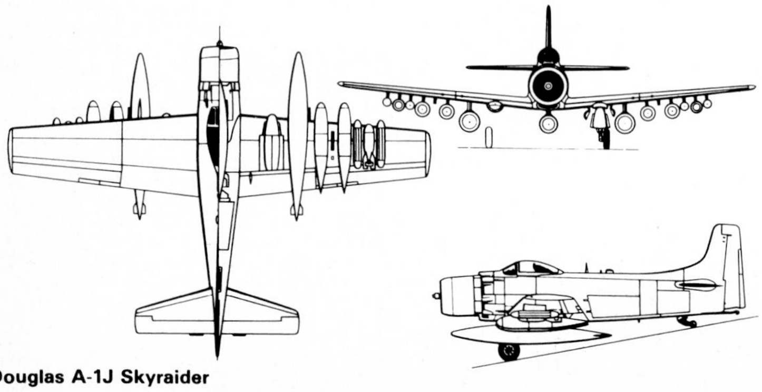

Douglas A-1J Skyraider

AD was capable of this, and its basic versatility was such that 3,180 had been built when production ended in 1957.

Just too late for World War II, the AD-1 proved a valuable weapon in the Korean War, when its heavy weapon load and up to 10-hour endurance contrasted sharply with the jets. The AD-1 to AD-4 versions differed in detail, but the AD-5 had a wider cockpit seating two (side-by-side) and several early versions had APS-20 radar and a rear cabin for two/three operators for AEW missions. The AD-5 introduced conversion kits for ambulance,

freight, transport or target towing. The AD-6 and -7 were chiefly advanced single-seaters. Large numbers of single-seat versions were used by the French *Armée de l'Air* in Algeria.

In 1962 Skyraiders were redesignated A-1A to A-1J, and in South Vietnam the USAF's 1st Air Commando Group of the Tactical Air Command used A-1E/-1H and -1J versions with great success, continuing to use them after the US Navy Skyraiders had been withdrawn from that theatre. Called 'Sandy' or 'The Spad', A-1 versions were among the most hardworked and versatile aircraft in that

theatre. A few Skyraiders continue to serve with several armed forces.

Type: one/two-seat attack-bomber
Powerplant: (AD-7/A-1J) one 2,800-hp (2088-kW) Wright R-3350-26WB radial piston engine
Performance: (A-1J) maximum speed at 18,500 ft (5640 m) 320 mph (515 km/h); cruising speed at 6,000 ft (1830 m) 190 mph (306 km/h); range 900 miles (1448 km)
Weights: (A-1J) empty 10,550 lb (4785 kg); maximum take-off 25,000 lb (11340 kg)

Dimensions: span (most) 50 ft 0 in (15.24 m), (A-1J) 50 ft 9 in (15.47 m); length (most) 38 ft 2 in (11.63 m), (A-1J) 38 ft 10 in (11.84 m); height (most) 15 ft 5 in (4.70 m), (A-1J) 15 ft 8¼ in (4.78 m); wing area 400 sq ft (37.16 m²)
Armament: two or four 20-mm cannon, plus up to 8,000 lb (3629 kg) of weapons on 15 hardpoints, including bombs, depth-charges, mines, napalm, rockets and torpedoes
Operators: Central African Empire, Chad, Gabon, Kampuchea, Vietnam

Douglas A-3 Skywarrior

The largest and heaviest aircraft designed for operation from an aircraft carrier when the Douglas El Segundo division's project design was completed in 1949, the A3D Skywarrior originated from a US Navy requirement of 1947. An attack-bomber with strategic strike capability was envisaged, tailored to the giant new aircraft-carriers that were ultimately (after prolonged opposition from the USAF) to materialize as the 'Forrestal' class of four ships, as it was believed that the moment had come to exploit the potential of the rapidly-developing gas turbine engine.

The Douglas design was that of a high-wing monoplane, with retractable tricycle lan-

ding gear, two podded turbojets beneath the wing, and a large internal weapons bay to accommodate up to 12,000 lb (5443 kg) of varied weapons. The wings were swept back 36° and had high aspect ratio for long range, all tail surfaces were swept, and the outer wing panels and vertical tail folded.

The first of two prototypes made its maiden flight on 28 October 1952, powered by 7,000-lb (3175-kg) Westinghouse XJ40-WE-3 engines, but the failure of this engine programme meant that the 9,700-lb (4400-kg) thrust Pratt & Whitney J57-P-6 powered the production A3D-1. The first of these A3D-1s flew on 16 September 1953, and deliveries to

Douglas TA-3B Skywarrior

Designed to an exacting specification of 1948 for nuclear long-range attack from carriers, the Skywarrior is still in use in unarmed KA-3 and EKA-3 form with Reserve units operating from a number of shore stations.

the US Navy's VAH-1 attack squadron began on 31 March 1956.

In 1962 the designation was changed to A-3, the initial three-seat production version becoming A-3A. Five of these were modified subsequently for ECM missions under the designation EA-3A. A-3Bs which entered service in 1957 had more powerful J57-P-10 engines and a flight-refuelling probe. A reconnaissance variant with cameras in the weapons bay was designated RA-3B, and EA-3B identified ECM aircraft with a four-man crew in the weapons bay. Other designations include 12 TA-3B trainers for radar operators, one VA-3B executive transport, and the final variants in US Navy service were KA-3B flight-refuelling tankers and 30 EKA-3B tanker/countermeasures/strike aircraft. The EKA-3B remains a standard USN Reserve aircraft in 1979.

Type: carrier-based attack bomber
Powerplant: (A-3B) two 10,500-lb (4763-kg) thrust Pratt & Whitney J57-P-10 turbojets
Performance: (A-3B) maximum speed 610 mph (982 km/h) at 10,000 ft (3050 m); range 1,050 miles (1690 km)
Weights: (A-3B) empty 39,409 lb (17876 kg); maximum take-off 82,000 lb (37195 kg)
Dimensions: span 72 ft 6 in (22.10 m); length 76 ft 4 in (23.27 m); height 22 ft 9½ in (6.95 m); wing area 812 sq ft (75.43 m²)
Armament: two 20-mm guns in radar-controlled rear turret, and up to 12,000 lb (5443 kg) of assorted weapons in internal weapons bay; (EKA-3B) none
Operators: US Navy

Douglas B-26 Invader

The USAAF issued a requirement for an attack aircraft in 1940, before it had information on World War II combat operations in Europe. Consequently, three prototypes were ordered in differing configurations: the Douglas XA-26 bomber with a bomb-aimer's position; XA-26A heavily-armed night-fighter; and XA-26B attack aircraft with a 75-mm cannon. After flight testing and careful examination of reports from Europe and the Pacific, the A-26B Invader was ordered into production, and initial deliveries were made in April 1944.

The A-26B had six 0.5-in (12.7-mm) machine-guns in the nose, remotely controlled dorsal and ventral turrets each with two 0.5-in (12.7-mm) guns, and up to 10 more 0.5-in (12.7-mm) guns in underwing and under-fuselage packs. Heavily armoured, and able to carry up to 4,000 lb (1814 kg) of bombs, the A-26B was potentially a formidable weapon. Moreover, its two 2,000-hp (1491-kW) Pratt and Whitney engines conferred a maximum speed of 355 mph (571 km/h), making the A-26 the fastest US bomber of World War II, F-8 Mosquitoes being photographic aircraft. Invaders remained in USAF service until well into the 1970s.

Missions with the 9th Air Force in Europe began in November 1944, at the same time as the type became operational in the Pacific. A-26Cs with a bomb-aimer's position entered service in 1945, but saw only limited use before World War II ended. With little employment ahead of them, so far as anyone could see, one A-26B and subsequently 140 A-26Cs were converted as target tugs for the US Navy with the designation JD-1. Some of

these were converted later to launch and control missile test vehicles and drones, becoming JD-1Ds. These designations became UB-26J and DB-26J in 1962.

USAF A-26B and A-26C aircraft became B-26B and B-26C in 1948, and retained this designation in 1962. Both versions saw extensive service in the Korean war, and were again used in a counter-insurgency role in Vietnam. A special COIN version with very heavy armament and extra power was developed by On-Mark Engineering in 1963, a prototype being designated YB-26K. Subsequently about 70 B-26s were converted to B-26K standard, later redesignated A-26A. Some were redeployed in Vietnam and others supplied to friendly nations under the Military Assistance Program. B-26s were used also for training (TB-26B and TB-26C) and transport (CB-26B and VB-26B), and as DB-26C RPV launch and control aircraft.

Type: light bomber
Powerplant: two 2,000-hp (1491-kW) Pratt & Whitney R-2800-27 or -79 Double Wasp radial piston engines
Performance: (B-26B) maximum speed 373 mph (600 km/h) at 10,000 ft (3050 m); cruising speed 284 mph (457 km/h); range 1,400 miles (2253 km)

Douglas A-26B

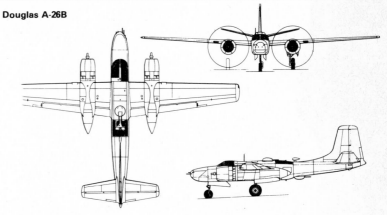

Weights: (B-26B) empty 22,850 lb (10365 kg); maximum take-off 35,000 lb (15876 kg)
Dimensions: span 70 ft 0 in (21.34 m); length (B-26B) 50 ft 0 in (15.24 m), (B-26C) 51 ft 2 in (15.60 m); height (B-26B) 18 ft 6 in (5.64 m), (B-26C) 18 ft 3 in (5.56 m); wing area 540 sq ft (50.17 m²)
Armament: (B-26B) 10 0.5-in (12.7-mm) machine-guns, (B-26C) six 0.5-in (12.7-mm) machine-guns; both able to carry up to 4,000 lb (1814 kg) of bombs

Operators: Colombia, Dominica, Nicaragua; previously 16 countries plus US Army Air Force, US Air Force, US Air National Guard, US Navy

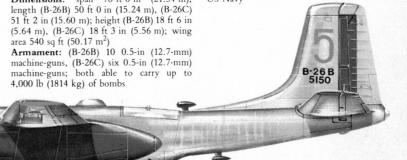

Forca Aerea Brasileira Douglas B-26 Invader in the markings of 5° Grupo de Aviacao de Bombardeo.

Douglas DC-3/C-47 Skytrain/Skytrooper

Probably the most famous civil transport in aviation history, the Douglas DC-3 has achieved a reputation in military usage which is if anything even greater. During World War II these aircraft were to be found wherever there were Allied military services, and General 'Ike' Eisenhower was to comment that, in his opinion, the C-47 was one of the four major tools of war which had contributed to Allied victory.

In 1935 Douglas had flown the prototype of a Douglas Sleeper Transport which led to a 21-seat 'day-plane' designated DC-3. The latter was soon in wide use with US and world airlines. It was the most advanced airliner then in service, offering new standards of comfort, safety and reliability. The last factor is significant, but the DC-3 was not just reliable: partly by chance it has proved also to be enduring and fatigue-free, and in 1979, 44 years after that first flight, many remain in both civil and military use.

The US Army's interest in the new generation of civil transports evolved by the Douglas Aircraft Company began with the purchase of a single DC-2 from FY 1936 funds. This was designated C-32 when it entered service, and was followed by C-33s with a cargo-loading door; C-34s with a passenger door and different interior; a single C-38 with DC-3 type tail unit; C-39s with more powerful engines; and single examples of the C-41 and C-42 with more powerful engines, C-41A with a *de luxe* interior for 23 passengers, and two extra C-42s converted from C-39s.

The potential of these aircraft had convinced the US Army of their excellence of design and construction, and a study of the DC-3 enabled the US Army to outline to Douglas the modifications required for its use as a military transport. These included more powerful engines, strengthening of the rear fuselage and cabin floor, and the provision of large loading doors. The airline-type interior disappeared, replaced by utility seats lining the cabin walls. Powerplant of the initial production version, and of most subsequent production, comprised two 1,200-hp (895-kW) Pratt & Whitney R-1830-92 Twin Wasp radial engines. Ordered in large numbers in 1940, these aircraft became designated C-47 and acquired the name Skytrain.

Versions to serve with the US Army include the basically similar C-47/-47A, most of which had a shorter tailcone with a glider-tow cleat; C-47Bs with increased fuel and supercharged engines: TC-47B navigation trainers; C-53 Skytrooper troop-carriers; and C-117 staff transports. The designations C-48, -49, -50, -51, -52, -68 and -84 applied to civil transports impressed from US domestic airlines for service with the USAAF. C-47D and TC-47D were the designations applied to former C-47B/TC-47B aircraft from which the two-speed superchargers had been deleted. VC-47A, -47B and -47D identified staff transport versions, and the later designation C-117 applied also to surviving VC-47s, redesignated as C-117C. SC-47B and SC-47D were designations for aircraft supplied to MATS for air/sea rescue, with provision for carrying a releasable lifeboat beneath the fuselage.

C-47s were notable glider tugs, involved in actions in Sicily, Italy, Burma, Normandy, Arnhem and the Rhine crossing. Those supplied to Britain under Lend-Lease were named Dakota, and took part in all the above operations. C-47s took part in the Berlin Airlift, were involved in the Korean War and, under the designation AC-47D, were deployed as well-armed gunships in Vietnam.

The US Navy and Marine Corps used similar aircraft under a number of designations, although the original and basic identification was R4D. In 1962 those which continued in service acquired the tri-service C-47 designations. Like the US Army, the USN and USMC used the R4D initially for the primary personnel or cargo transport roles. Later duties included radar countermeasures, air/sea warfare training, research and trials and, equipped with skis, transport in the Antarctic.

Type: basically troop, personnel and cargo transport
Powerplant: (C-47) two 1,200-hp (895-kW) Pratt & Whitney R-1830-92 Twin Wasp 14-cylinder two-row radial piston engines
Performance: (C-47) maximum speed 230 mph (370 km/h); time to 10,000 ft (3050 m) 9 minutes 36 seconds; range 1,500 miles (2414 km)
Weights: (C-47) empty 18,200 lb (8255 kg); maximum take-off 26,000 lb (11793 kg)
Dimensions: span 95 ft 6 in (29.11 m); length 63 ft 9 in (19.43 m); height 17 ft 0 in (5.18 m); wing area 987 sq ft (91.69 m²)
Armament: AC-47D gunships were equipped with General Electric 7.62-mm (0.3-in) Miniguns, firing through the fuselage door aperture and right-hand windows
Operators: more than 50 air forces have been or are still equipped with military transports of the C-47 type, including the RAF, USAAF/USAF, US Navy and US Marine Corps

Douglas C-47 of the Israel airline Arkia at the time of the 1956 war in Egypt.

Douglas DC-4/C-54 Skymaster

Douglas Aircraft Company flew the prototype of a new four-engine civil transport on 21 June 1938. This had the company designation DC-4E and was intended for transcontinental services. The prototype was unsuccessful, and was sold to Japan. Chastened, the company produced a slightly smaller and much more efficient aircraft with the designation DC-4A. Features of this aircraft included the first monocoque constant-section fuselage suitable for eventual pressurization (though for the present this was not included) and a retractable tricycle landing gear, with twin main wheels on each unit and a single-wheel steerable nose unit. Powerplant comprised four Pratt & Whitney R-2000-3 radial piston engines.

When America became involved in World War II the DC-4As on the Santa Monica production lines were commandeered by the USAAF, and the aircraft of the initial batch of 24 were designated C-54 Skymasters. These were virtually drab-painted civil airliners, the first flying in February 1942, but contracts were soon drawn up for militarized versions capable of deployment for the transport of troops, cargo and casualties. First of these for the USAAF was the C-54A with strengthened floor, cargo door and handling equipment, followed by the C-54B/D/E and G, with development following the line of maximum seating capacity (50) for short/medium-range operations and restricted seating (20) for long-range flights. As the R5D Skymaster, the DC-4 was also built for the US Navy in many variants, total combined construction for these two services exceeding 1,000 aircraft.

Like the DC-3, this new Douglas design was to prove long-lived. With World War II ended, they were to serve with distinction in the Berlin Airlift and the Korean War, and small numbers remain in use with military services in 1979.

Type: four-engine transport aircraft
Powerplant: (C-54A) four 1,350-hp (1007-kW) Pratt & Whitney R-2000-7 Twin Wasp radial piston engines
Performance: (C-54A) maximum speed 265 mph (426 km/h); time to 10,000 ft (3050 m); 14 minutes 11 seconds; range

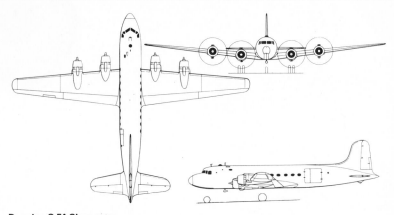

Douglas C-54 Skymaster

3,900 miles (6276 km)
Weights: (C-54A) empty 37,000 lb (16783 kg); maximum take-off 62,000 lb (28123 kg), (C-54B) 73,000 lb (33112 kg)
Dimensions: span 117 ft 6 in (35.81 m); length 93 ft 10 in (28.60 m); height 27 ft 6 in (8.38 m); wing area 1,460 sq ft (135.63 m²)
Armament: none
Operators: have included the US Air Force, US Army Air Force and US Navy, among a wide range of military services

Douglas DC-6/C-118 Liftmaster

The success of the DC-4, in both civil and military use, ensured that Douglas would continue development of the design, and the DC-6 was little more than a larger pressurized version with more powerful engines.

Development of this larger version originated in the closing year of the war when, because of the widespread commitment of US services in the Pacific theatre of operations, one of the primary requirements was for effective transport aircraft which were capable of being deployed as personnel transports, cargo carriers, or for medical evacuation. As a result, Douglas designed the XC-112A, which flew for the first time on 15 February 1946.

Civil DC-6s were built alongside 166 aircraft for the USAF and US Navy, partially to support the operations of the Military Air Transport Service (MATS). Those which served with the Air Force had the designation C-118A, and could accommodate 74 passengers, or 27,000 lb (12247 kg) of cargo, or 60 stretcher cases. The 29th DC-6 was fitted out with a VIP interior for President Truman; the VC-118 'Independence' had a cabin for 24 passengers, or night accommodation for 12, and an executive stateroom.

DC-6s in US Navy service included 61 R6D-1s and four R6D-1Zs with VIP interiors; these became C-118B and VC-118B in 1962. Other military services have also acquired DC-6s, the majority of them ex-civil, and many continue in service in 1979.

Type: four-engine transport aircraft
Powerplant: (C-118A) four 2,500-hp (1864-kW) Pratt & Whitney R-2800-52W Double Wasp radial piston engines
Performance: (C-118A) maximum speed 356 mph (573 km/h) at 19,600 ft (5975 m); cruising speed 313 mph (504 km/h) at 20,400 ft (6220 m); normal range 3,820 miles (6148 km); ferry range 4,610 miles (7419 km)
Weights: (C-118A) empty 51,495 lb (23358 kg); maximum take-off 97,200 lb (44089 kg)

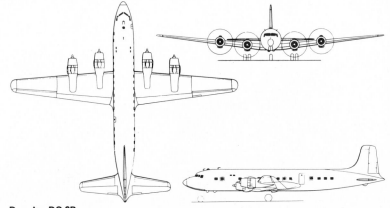

Douglas DC-6B

Dimensions: span 117 ft 6 in (35.81 m); length 100 ft 7 in (30.66 m); height 28 ft 5 in (8.66 m); wing area 1,457 sq ft (135.36 m²)
Armament: none

Operators: have included the US Air Force and Navy among a wide range of military services

EMBRAER EMB-110 Bandeirante

The EMBRAER EMB-110 Bandeirante turboprop light transport was created in the mid-1960s, initially as a replacement for the fleet of Beech Super 18s and C-45s used by the *Forca Aérea Brasileira*. It was developed by a team led by the French designer Max Holste under the aegis of the Brazilian Air Ministry's *Centro Técnico Aerospacial* (CTA). The initial study received the designation PAR6504 with the FAB type number YC-95. It was a low-wing monoplane of conventional layout powered by two Pratt & Whitney Aircraft of Canada PT6A-20 turboprops of 550 shp (410 kW) each.

The first prototype was constructed by the *Institute de Pesquisas e Desenvolvimento* (IPD), a part of the CTA, at Sao José dos Campos near Sao Paulo. The first flight took place on 26 October 1968, and this prototype is now preserved in the Brazilian Air Force Museum.

In some respects the three prototypes fell short of the FAB specification. This led to installation of 680-shp (507-kW) PT6A-27 engines for the production C-95 (EMB-110), and the nacelles were redesigned to permit full retraction of the main landing gear legs. Other changes included increased fuel capacity, the use of five square windows instead of three round portholes, a lengthened rear fuselage, and an enlarged tail.

There was no manufacturing facility capable of handling the project, however, and this led to the establishment of the Empresa Brasiliera de Aeronautica SA (EMBRAER) with a 51% government stake. A factory was set up at Sao José dos Campos to manufacture 80 C-95s. The engines, landing gear, instrumentation and avionics are imported.

The EMB-110 became the basis for a range of aircraft, and the initial FAB order was soon modified to include 20 of the EMB-110K1 model. This embodies a 33-in (0.84-m)

fuselage stretch ahead of the wing, and a ventral fin. This variant uses PT6A-34 engines, and has been fitted with a forward entry door on the left and a large freight door behind the wing. It is primarily employed as a cargo aircraft by the FAB, with the designation C-95A. In addition to the cargo role this version can carry 19 paratroops, dropped from an exit in the freight door.

Also operating with the FAB are three EMB-110As (EC-95s) for ground-aid calibration. In addition, EMBRAER has developed the EMB-110B1 with a large fairing beneath the rear fuselage for vertical survey cameras, increased fuel capacity and PT6A-34 engines. Six have been supplied to the FAB under the designation R-95.

The Bandeirante has been exported successfully. The *Fuerza Aérea Uruguaya* has taken six aircraft, of which five are EMB-110C transports for TAMU and one is an EMB-110B1. The other military order has come from the *Servicio de Aviación de la Armada de Chile* which has three EMB-110C(N) aircraft which differ from standard in having a full de-icing system.

Type: 16-passenger transport and utility aircraft
Powerplant: two 680-shp (507-kW) Pratt & Whitney Aircraft of Canada PT6A-27 turboprops

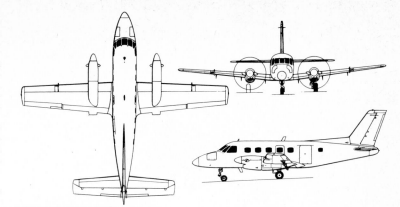

EMBRAER EMB-110P Bandeirante (Brazilian Air Force C-95)

Performance: maximum cruising speed at 7,500 ft (2285 m) 280 mph (452 km/h); economical cruising speed at 10,000 ft (3050 m) 212 mph (341 km/h); stalling speed 82 mph (132 km/h); maximum rate of climb at sea level 1,450 ft (442 m) per minute; service ceiling 25,300 ft (7700 m); take-off run 1,480 ft (452 m); range at 10,000 ft (3050 m) with 45-minute reserve 1,266 miles (2038 km)
Weights: empty equipped 7,054 lb (3200 kg); maximum take-off 11,684 lb (5300 kg)

Dimensions: span 50 ft 2 in (15.30 m); length 46 ft 8 in (14.22 m); height 15 ft 6 in (4.73 m); wing area 312.13 sq ft (29.00 m²)
Operators: Brazil, Chile, Uruguay

This EMBRAER EMB-110 Bandeirante is a Forca Aerea Brasileira C-95A freighter version, one of 20 in service.

EMBRAER EMB-111/P-95

A significant newcomer to the ranks of maritime patrol aircraft, the EMBRAER EMB-111 is a development of the EMB-110 Bandeirante to meet the needs of the Brazilian air force (FAB). As the P-95, at least 16 were ordered for the Coastal Command of the FAB and initial deliveries were made in 1978. The Chilean navy also ordered six of the similar EMB-111(N).

The EMB-111 is similar in most respects to the short fuselage C-95 Bandeirante (EMB-110) but it has PT6A-34 engines and a ventral fin. Wingtip fuel tanks bring fuel capacity up to 560 Imperial gallons (2545 litres). Maximum endurance exceeds 8 hours, which allows the type to be used on search and rescue, inspection of civilian and military surface craft, protection of oil rigs, pollution control and other tasks. Five crew are normally carried, comprising a pilot, co-pilot, two observers and a radar operator. Equipment includes a galley, toilet, eight-man liferaft, Motorola locator beacon, and survival stores which are dropped via the rear door.

A prominent nose radome houses the aerial

for a Cutler-Hammer APS-128 SPAR-1 search radar. This can identify low-profile targets at 60 miles (96 km) in disturbed sea conditions. The display is repeated on a cockpit monitor.

Brazil's air arm, Forca Aerea Brasileira, operates 12 EMBRAER EMB-111 maritime patrol aircraft from Salvador.

A Litton LN-33 inertial navigation system is interfaced with the radar. Three underwing pylons can carry depth charges, bombs or three rocket pairs, and a 50-million candlepower searchlight is carried on the right wing.

Type: maritime patrol aircraft
Powerplant: two 750-shp (560-kW) Pratt & Whitney Aircraft of Canada PT6A-34 turboprops
Performance: maximum speed at 10,000 ft (3050 m) 251 mph (404 km/h); long-range cruising speed at 10,000 ft (3050 m) 216 mph (347 km/h); stalling speed (flaps down) 82 mph (132 km/h); rate of climb at sea level 1,320 ft (403 m) per minute; service ceiling at

12,000 lb (5443 kg) 23,720 ft (7230 m); maximum range with 45-minute reserves 1,695 miles (2725 km)
Weights: empty equipped 7,502 lb (3403 kg); maximum take-off 15,432 lb (7000 kg)
Dimensions: span 52 ft 4½ in (15.96 m); length 48 ft 8 in (14.83 m); height 15 ft 6½ in (4.74 m); wing area 312 sq ft (29.00 m²)
Armament: assorted underwing stores
Operators: Brazil, Chile

Brazil's FAB 7º Grupo uses the P-95, FAB designation of the EMBRAER EMB-111 offshore patrol aircraft. This twin-turboprop product of the world's sixth-largest aircraft company has APS-128 nose radar, Litton inertial navigation system and searchlight.

EMBRAER EMB-111 (Brazilian Air Force P-95)

Embraer EMB-121 Xingu

EMBRAER's EMB-121 owes much to the EMB-110 but is, in fact, the first of the Brazilian company's -12 series of light pressurized twins: the EMB-120 Araguaia and EMB-123 Tapajos are pressurized commuter airliners and the EMB-121 Xingu has a shorter fuselage for nine passengers and an airstair door.

The prototype EMB-121 made its first flight on 10 October 1976. The aircraft was intended primarily to compete with the Beech King Air 90 and Mitsubishi MU-2, but initial demand came from the Brazilian air force, which ordered five as VIP transports. Designated VU-9, these aircraft were delivered to the *Grupo de Transporte Especial* in Brasilia during 1978.

The VU-9 seats five; the two-crew cockpit is screened-off, and resembles that of the C-95. Standard avionics fit for the VU-9 includes dual RCA vhf, Collins ADF, and Sunair hf, Sperry SPZ-200 autopilot and Bendix Weathervision radar.

The wings of the EMB-121 are similar to those of the Bandeirante but are reduced in span; the large fin is swept and has the tailplane mounted on top. Full de-icing is fitted.

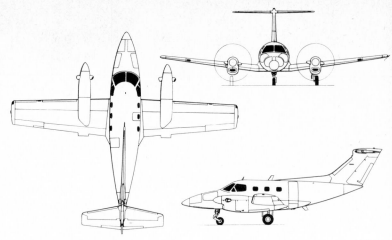

Type: five/nine-seat transport
Powerplant: two 680-shp (507-kW) Pratt & Whitney Aircraft of Canada PT6A-28 turboprops
Performance: maximum speed at 15,000 ft (4575 m) 294 mph (473 km/h); long-range cruising speed at 20,000 ft (6100 m) 247 mph (398 km/h); stalling speed (flaps down) 81 mph (131 km/h); maximum rate of climb at sea level 1,900 ft (580 m) per minute; take-off run 1,706 ft (520 m); service ceiling 27,300 ft (8,320 m); maximum range with 45-minute reserve 1,646 miles (2650 km)
Weights: empty equipped 7,663 lb (3476 kg); maximum take-off 12,346 lb (5600 kg)
Dimensions: span 46 ft 4¾ in (14.14 m); length 40 ft 5 in (12.32 m); height 16 ft 2½ in (4.94 m); wing area 296.0 sq ft (27.50 m²)
Operator: Brazil

Embraer EMB-121 Xingu

Embraer EMB-810 see Piper PA34/Emb 810

Fairchild A-10 Thunderbolt II

Considering that the close support role figures prominently among the normal commitments of most air forces, it is at first sight surprising that so few aircraft have actually been designed for the job. The answer is, of course, that the task has traditionally been done by superannuated air combat aircraft, whose performance is no longer up to the mark. Close support is an obligation to ground forces, and air forces are much keener to spend their budgets on air combat or strategic aircraft.

A few aeroplanes have been specially adapted for ground attack, and especially for anti-tank work, by the addition of special weapons, mainly large-calibre guns. The Hawker Hurricane IID, for example, had twin Vickers 40-mm cannon under the wings and was notably effective against Axis tanks in the Western Desert during 1942. At the same time Germany was producing the Henschel Hs 129, the very first really specialised close support aeroplane. With its 75-mm gun firing a 15.2-lb (6.9-kg) projectile, it could stop a Josef Stalin tank dead in its tracks with one round. After the war, France built the Potez 75, also with a 75-mm gun, but the type failed to reach production.

But now a unique aeroplane has appeared, which may well tip the balance of power between NATO forces and the massed might of the Warsaw Pact armoured forces in Central Europe — and the ability of this force to move fast and far under cover of darkness was shown by the overnight invasion of Czechoslovakia in 1968. The Fairchild A-10 Thunderbolt II was born of the recognition that the adaptation of air combat aircraft would no longer suffice to produce adequate ground attack/anti-tank capability. They were actually too fast, lacked the manoeuvrability needed for battlefield warfare, and their weapons were unsuitable against the growing resistance to damage of tanks.

The request for a specialised aeroplane to replace the hodge-podge of Martin B-57s, Cessna T-37s and Douglas A-1 Skyraiders, to mention just three, was made by the United States Air Force as long ago as 1966. Basically what it wanted was something better than the piston-engined Skyraider but cheaper than the Vought A-7 Corsair II. It had to be reliable, tough, easy both to fly and to maintain in the field, capable of loitering over or 'hanging around' the battlefield for long periods with heavy loads of ordnance (after the manner of the 1944 Typhoon cab-rank patrols), but capable of turning on a sixpence.

In 1967 the USAF solicited proposals from no fewer than 21 companies. Most of the entries came up with turboprop propulsion, and the USAF, dissatisfied, went back to its studies; it was not clear that any of the designs put up for consideration would be a significant advance on the already existing types.

But by 1970 the USAF felt it could issue a realistic specification, and two companies,

Northrop and Fairchild, were chosen to build competitive aeroplanes under the new 'Fly before Buy' policy adopted by the US Defense Department. The USAF planners defined four principal aims: combat effectiveness, survivability, simplicity, and responsiveness. Broadly translated, these equated in order to (a) a warload of 16,000 lb (7258 kg) with partial fuel, or 12,000 lb (5443 kg) with full tanks, (b) sufficient armour or, failing that, enough redundancy of equipment to withstand considerable punishment and still get home, (c) a modest financial outlay, consistent with another newly announced policy called 'Design to Cost', and (d) the ability to operate from primitive or unprepared areas (meadows, for example) sufficiently close to the front line that little time be lost getting there in response to calls from the local ground force commander.

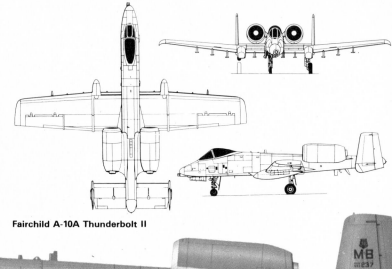

Fairchild A-10A Thunderbolt II

This Fairchild A-10A Thunderbolt II is from the 354th Tactical Fighter Wing, USAF Tactical Air Command.

This A-10A was photographed while firing its extremely powerful tank-killing gun. One of the 11 pylons is carrying a laser-guided 'smart bomb'.

The competitive A-X (Attack, Experimental) programme ran for two years, with the Fairchild A-10 in January 1973 being judged the winner over its Northrop A-9 rival. Development went ahead smoothly, production beginning in 1975, the first squadrons forming in 1976 and 1977. The first units were in 1978 deployed to Europe, the arena for which the A-10 was designed.

From the beginning, the primary armament was to be a special anti-tank gun with seven barrels rotating round a common axis, after the manner of the Gatling-type guns used in the Lockheed F-104G Starfighter and the McDonnell Douglas F-4E Phantom, but firing 30-mm rather than 20-mm rounds. These shells, weighing 1.6 lb (0.73 kg) travelling at two-thirds of a mile a second, and containing lethal warheads, were to have sufficient energy to penetrate the heaviest armour existing or projected.

Two companies, Philco-Ford and General Electric, competed to build the gun, and their relative merits and performance were decided in a shoot-off. GE emerged the winner. Its GAU-8/A Avenger gun is the most potent airborne weapon of its type ever built. Weighing 4,091 lb (1856 kg) with its huge drum containing 1,350 armour-piercing shells, the gun is 22 ft (6.7 m) long, and so bulky that the aeroplane had to be built around it. It takes up virtually all the forward part of the fuselage, so mounted that it fires along the centreline. This is essential, because otherwise the tremendous recoil — 18,000 lb (8165 kg), or the combined thrust of the two engines acting rearwards — would seriously disturb the aim, and perhaps cause the aeroplane to go out of control.

For all its conventional, even clumsy, appearance, the A-10 is as cleverly thought out as, say, the Grumman F-14 or McDonnell Douglas F-15 fighters. Its large wing provides the lift to keep it turning tightly over the bat-

This so-called lizard camouflage is now standard in Tactical Air Command A-10 units, in place of the overall grey previously used. This aircraft, which does not have unit insignia, has the pilot ladder extended.

continued

Taken during the type's flight development, this impressive photograph shows an AGM-65A Maverick precision air-to-ground missile being fired from a Fairchild Republic A-10A Thunderbolt II over a US range. Note the split ailerons opened above and below the wing for use as airbrakes.

tlefield at 300 kt (345 mph/556 km/h), carrying more than seven tons (7.11 tonnes) of bombs or rockets; it also supplies the space needed for these stores, which take up a considerable amount of room. The maximum speed is startlingly low: only 450 kt (518 mph/834 km/h). A fully retracting undercarriage is not therefore essential. The two General Electric TF34 turbofan engines are mounted over the rear fuselage, where they do not get in the way of the pilot's field of view and where their relatively cool exhaust tends to be hidden by the wing during an attack, further reducing the A-10's vulnerability to heat-seeking missiles.

The pilot sits in a thick titanium 'bath', resistant to all but the heaviest-calibre shells. The most important areas of the aeroplane are also armoured, or are designed so that, if they are hit, the aeroplane can still fly back to base.

Type: single-seat close support/anti-tank bomber

Powerplant: two General Electric TF34-GE-100 high-bypass turbofans, each of 9,065 lb (4112 kg) thrust
Performance: nominal cruise speed (no external stores) 345 kt (397mph/640km/h); design maximum speed, 450 kt (518 mph/722 km/h); take-off roll (maximum weight) 3,800 ft (1158 m); loiter endurance (250 nautical miles from base, 18 Mk82 bombs and 750 rounds of GAU-8 ammunition), 2 hours
Weights: operating weight (aircraft ready to fly, less fuel, ammunition and pilot) 24,000 lb (10886 kg); maximum external payload (full internal fuel) 11,980 lb (5434 kg); maximum payload (with partial fuel) 16,000 lb (7258 kg); empty weight 20,700 lb (9389 kg)
Dimensions: span 57 ft 6 in (17.53 m); length 54 ft 4 in (16.26 m); height 14 ft 8 in (4.47 m); wing area 506 sq ft (47.01 m²)
Armament: one 30-mm rotating-barrel gun plus various combinations of external stores
Operators: US Air Force

Fairchild A-10A Thunderbolt II Cutaway Drawing Key

1 Cannon muzzles
2 Nose cap
3 ILS aerial
4 Air-to-air refuelling receptacle (open)
5 Nosewheel bay (offset to starboard)
6 Cannon barrels
7 Rotary cannon barrel bearing
8 Gun compartment ventilating intake
9 L-band radar warning aerial
10 Electrical system relay switches
11 Windscreen rain dispersal air duct
12 Pave Penny laser search and tracking pod
13 Windscreen panel
14 Head-up display symbol generator
15 Pilot's head-up display screen
16 Instrument panel shroud
17 Air-to-air refuelling pipe
18 Titanium armour cockpit enclosure
19 Rudder pedals
20 Battery
21 General Electric GAU-8/A 30-mm seven-barrelled rotary cannon
22 Ammunition feed ducts
23 Steering cylinder
24 Nose undercarriage leg strut
25 Nosewheel
26 Nosewheel scissor links
27 Retractable boarding ladder
28 Ventilating air outlets
29 Ladder stowage box
30 Pilot's side console panel
31 Engine throttles
32 Control column
33 McDonnell Douglas ACES 2 ejection seat
34 Headrest canopy breakers
35 Cockpit canopy cover
36 Canopy hinge mechanism
37 Space provision for additional avionics
38 Angle-of-attack probe
39 Emergency canopy release handle
40 Ventral access panels to gun compartment
41 Ammunition drum (1,350-rounds)
42 Ammunition drum armour plating
43 Electrical system servicing panel
44 Ventral fin
45 Spent cartridge-case return chute
46 Control cable runs
47 Avionics compartments
48 Forward/centre fuselage joint bulkhead
49 Aerial selector switches
50 IFF aerial
51 Anti-collision light
52 UHF/TACAN aerial
53 Starboard wing integral fuel tank
54 Wing skin plating
55 Outer wing panel attachment joint strap
56 Starboard fixed wing pylons
57 ALE-37A chaff dispenser pod

58 ALE/ALQ-119 electronic countermeasures pod
59 Pitot tube
60 Starboard drooped wing tip fairing
61 Split aileron/deceleron mass balance
62 Deceleron open position
63 Starboard aileron/deceleron
64 Deceleron hydraulic jack
65 Aileron hydraulic jack
66 Control linkages
67 Aileron tab
68 Tab balance weight
69 Slotted trailing edge flaps
70 Outboard flap jack
71 Flap synchronising shafts
72 Fuselage self-sealing fuel cells (maximum internal fuel capacity 10,700 lb/4 853 kg)
73 Fuselage main longeron
74 Longitudinal control and services duct
75 Air conditioning supply duct
76 Wing attaching fuselage main frames
77 Gravity fuel filler caps
78 Engine pylon fairing
79 Pylon attachment joint
80 Starboard intake
81 Intake centre cone
82 Engine fan blades
83 Night/adverse weather two-seater variant
84 Radar pod (forward looking infra-red in starboard pod)
85 Engine mounting struts
86 Nacelle construction

87 Oil tank
88 General Electric TF34-GE-100 turbofan
89 Rear engine mounting
90 Pylon trailing edge fillet
91 Engine exhaust duct
92 Fan air duct
93 Rudder hydraulic jack
94 Starboard tail fin
95 X-band aerial
96 Rudder mass balance weight
97 Starboard rudder
98 Elevator tab
99 Tab control rod
100 Starboard elevator
101 Starboard tailplane
102 Tailplane attachment frames
103 Elevator hydraulic jacks
104 Tailcone
105 Tail navigation light
106 Rear radar warning receiver aerial
107 Honeycomb elevator construction

108 Port vertical tailfin construction
109 Honeycomb rudder panel
110 Rudder hydraulic jack
111 Formation light
112 Vertical fin ventral fairing
113 Tailplane construction
114 Tailplane control links
115 Port engine exhaust duct
116 Tailboom frame construction
117 VHF/AM aerial
118 Fuel jettison
119 VHF/FM aerial
120 Fuel jettison duct
121 Hydraulic reservoir
122 Port engine nacelle attachment joint
123 Cooling system intake and exhaust duct
124 Engine bleed air ducting
125 Auxiliary power unit
126 APU exhaust
127 Engine nacelle access door
128 Air conditioning plant

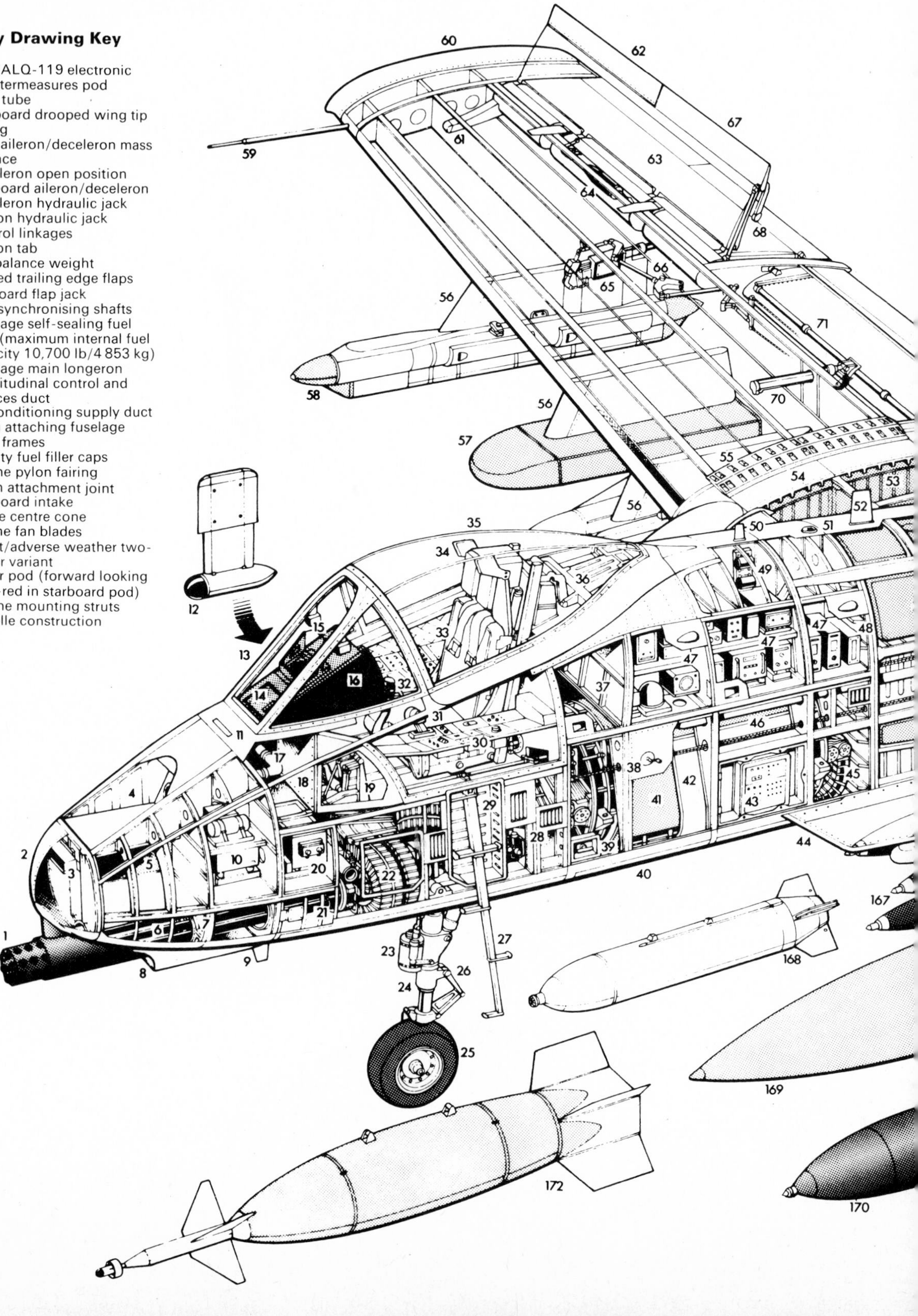

129 Port engine intake
130 Trailing edge wing root fillet
131 Fuselage bomb rack
132 Inboard slotted flap
133 Flap guide rails
134 Rear spar
135 Flap shroud structure
136 Honeycomb trailing edge panel
137 Outboard slotted flap
138 Port deceleron open position
139 Aileron tab
140 Aileron hinges
141 Port split aileron/deceleron
142 Drooped wing tip fairing construction
143 Port navigation light
144 Honeycomb leading edge panels
145 Wing rib construction
146 Centre spar
147 Leading edge spar
148 Two outer fixed pylons (1,000-lb/453,6-kg capacity)
149 ALE/ALQ-119 electronic countermeasures pod
150 ALE-37A chaff dispenser
151 Port mainwheel
152 2,500-lb (1 134-kg) capacity stores pylon

153 Main undercarriage leg strut
154 Undercarriage leg doors
155 Main undercarriage leg pivot fixing
156 Port mainwheel semi-recessed housing
157 Pressure refuelling point
158 Undercarriage pod fairing
159 Outer wing panel attachment joint
160 Port wing integral fuel tank
161 Inboard leading edge slat
162 Slat hydraulic jacks
163 Slat endplate
164 2,500-lb (1 134-kg) stores pylon
165 3,500-lb (1 588-kg) capacity fuselage pylon
166 Bomb ejector rack
167 Mk 82 500-lb (226,8-kg) bombs
168 Rockeye anti-armour cluster bomb
169 600-US Gal (2 271-l) long range ferry tank
170 Mk 84 2,000-lb (907-kg) bomb
171 Maverick air-to-ground missile
172 Paveway 3,000-lb (1 360-kg) laser guided bomb

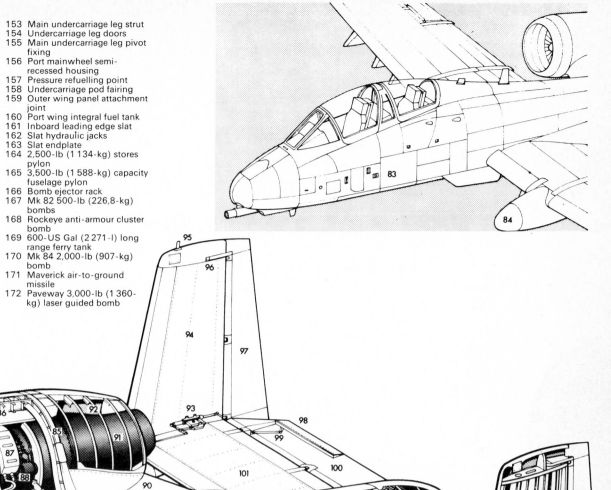

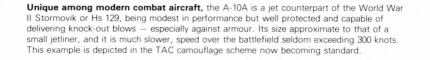

Unique among modern combat aircraft, the A-10A is a jet counterpart of the World War II Stormovik or Hs 129, being modest in performance but well protected and capable of delivering knock-out blows — especially against armour. Its size approximate to that of a small jetliner, and it is much slower, speed over the battlefield seldom exceeding 300 knots. This example is depicted in the TAC camouflage scheme now becoming standard.

The large TF34 turbofan engines are in an unusual location, partly for convenience and partly to reduce the infra-red (IR) signature and thus make the A-10A less vulnerable to heat-seeking missiles. In many typical attitudes the engines are blanketed by the wing or vertical tails from IR seekers, and in any case these engines are externally cool and smokeless. They are identical left/right, and the A-10 can get home on one.

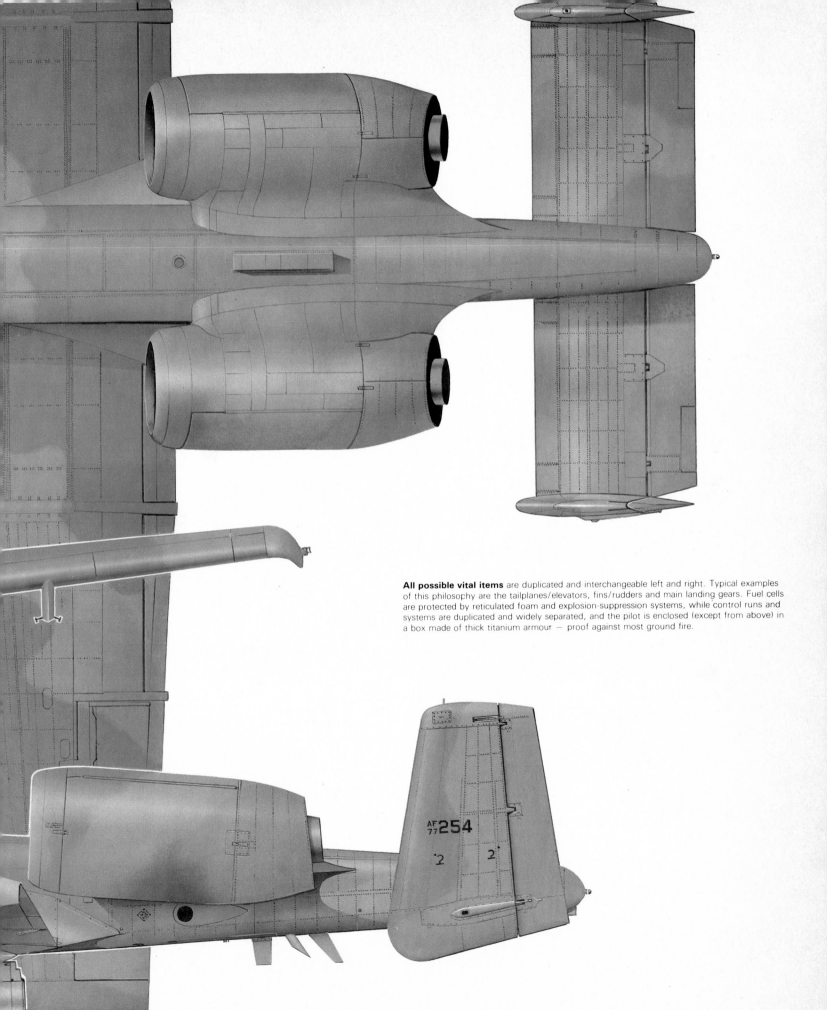

All possible vital items are duplicated and interchangeable left and right. Typical examples of this philosophy are the tailplanes/elevators, fins/rudders and main landing gears. Fuel cells are protected by reticulated foam and explosion-suppression systems, while control runs and systems are duplicated and widely separated, and the pilot is enclosed (except from above) in a box made of thick titanium armour — proof against most ground fire.

Among the great variety of tactical weapons carried by this strange platform are the AGM-65A Maverick IR-homing missile (triplets on Nos 3 and 9 pylons), Hobos electro-optically guided heavy bomb (No 4 station) and various Paveway laser-guided "smart bombs" (No 8 station). Few sensors or avionic weapon subsystems are carried internally, but like most A-10As this example has a Pave Penny laser pod under the right front fuselage.

Fairchild AU-23A Peacemaker (see Pilatus PC-6 Turbo Porter/Fairchild AU-23A)

Fairchild C-119 Flying Boxcar

In 1941 Fairchild began the design of a specialised military freight aircraft for the US Army. At that time it represented the largest aircraft in which Fairchild had been involved and, not surprisingly, was regarded by them as an important project. Hence, a considerable amount of time and effort was devoted to the evolution of a design which would secure for the company the US Army's intended production contract. Under the company identification Model F-78, Fairchild arrived at a design which featured a pod-type fuselage with a high-mounted wing, thus ensuring that the cargo hold was free from obstruction. The tail unit was carried on twin booms, with central tailplane and elevator, and twin fins and rudders. The two R-2800 engines were mounted conventionally, but their nacelles were extended rearwards as tail booms. Access to the cargo compartment was via rear clamshell-type doors, permitting straight-in loading of military vehicles up suitable ramps. Ordered into production as the C-82A Packet in 1944, after the prototype had flown, more than 200 were built for the USAAF after World War II.

In 1947 Fairchild developed an improved version of this transport, with a new flight deck positioned lower and further forward, a recontoured nose, changes in the tail design, and provision of more powerful 3,000-hp (2238-kW) Pratt & Whitney R-4360 Wasp Major engines. One example, modified from a C-82, flew for the first time in November 1947. Following USAF evaluation, this version was ordered into production as the C-119 Flying Boxcar and the production C-119B began to enter service in December 1949. This differed from the converted C-82, which had become designated C-119A, by having a new, wider fuselage, which could accommodate 62 troops when used for troop ferry missions, and some structural changes to the wings to permit operation at the higher gross weight of 74,000 lb (33566 kg), powerplant comprised two R-4360-20 engines.

Following 54 C-119Bs into service came the first of 303 C-119Cs with changes to the tail unit and 3,250-hp (2425-kW) R-4360-20WA engines with water injection. Other production Boxcars included 210 C-119Fs with different engines, small changes to the tail unit, and gross weight increased to 85,000 lb (38555 kg). Last major production model was the C-119G, powered like the -Fs with Wright R-3350 engines, and of which 484 were built.

In addition to production for the USAF, the US Navy acquired 41 aircraft equivalent to the C-119C, which had the designation R4Q-1

and the name Packet. Most of these served with the US Marine Corps. These were followed into service by 58 R4Q-2s, similar to the USAF's C-119F, which were operated by both the US Navy and the US Marine Corps.

Variants of the C-119 have included 68 C-119Js with 'beaver tail' rear doors and an air-openable ramp, converted from C-119Fs; a YC-119K prototype with two General Electric J85 turbojets as auxiliary engines, pod-mounted on pylons beneath each wing; a YC-119H prototype with a wing of increased span and area, and larger tail unit; and nine JC-119s used by the USAF's 6593rd Test Squadron for air retrieval of space capsules in connection with the Discoverer satellite programme in 1960.

In late 1967 Fairchild began development of a gunship version of the C-119, and 52 were converted from C-119Gs. These consisted of 26 AC-119Gs, each with four side-firing 7.62-mm (0.3-in) Miniguns and an AN/RVQ-8 target-illuminator, followed by 26 AC-119Ks with a similar Minigun installation plus two M61 20-mm cannon. These latter aircraft also had the J85 auxiliary booster jets which had been evaluated with the YC-119K prototype.

Of the total of 1,051 Flying Boxcars that were built originally for the USAF, or for supply to countries benefitting from the Military Assistance Program, about 100 remained in service in early 1979.

Type: tactical transport and gunship
Powerplant: (C-119K) two 3,700-hp (2759-kW) Wright R-3350-89B Cyclone 18-cylinder twin-row radial piston engines, plus two 2,850-lb (1293-kg) General Electric J85-GE-17 turbojets
Performance: (C-119C) maximum speed 281 mph (452 km/h) at 18,000 ft (5485 m); range with maximum fuel 1,770 miles (2849 km)
Weights: (C-119C) empty 39,800 lb (18053 kg); maximum take-off 74,000 lb (33566 kg); (C-119K): empty 44,747 lb (20297 kg); maximum take-off 77,000 lb (34927 kg)
Dimensions: (C-119C) span 109 ft 3 in (33.30 m); length 86 ft 6 in (26.36 m); height 26 ft 4 in (8.03 m); wing area 1,400 sq ft (130.06 m²)
Armament: (AC-119G and AC-119K) includes SUU-11 pods each containing one 7.62-mm (0.3-in) Minigun, and SUU-16 pods each containing one 20-mm M61 cannon, with comprehensive night sensors
Operators: Belgium, Brazil, Ethiopia, India, Italy, Taiwan, US Air Force, US Marine Corps, US Navy, Vietnam

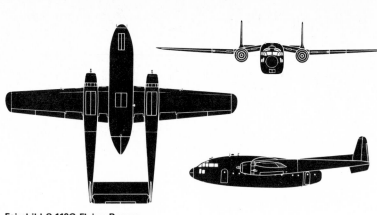

Fairchild C-119G Flying Boxcar

The Fairchild C-119 Flying Boxcar remains a widely used tactical airlifter, but this dramatic view was taken during flight testing of the AC-119K Shadow night gunship at the company plant at St Augustine, Florida.

Fairchild C-123 Provider

In 1943 the Chase Aircraft Company was founded to undertake the design, development and production of a heavy assault cargo glider for the US Army. Following the successful demonstration of the XCG-18A cargo glider, five YG-18A pre-production examples followed, and one of these was converted to a light assault transport aircraft by the addition of two wing-mounted radial engines, under the designation YC-122. YC-122A/B/C aircraft followed for service trials, leading to the construction of two prototypes of an even larger troop/cargo transport. These were designated XCG-20 in glider form and XC-123 in powered configuration, the latter being known to Chase as the MS-8 Avitruc. It was powered by two Pratt & Whitney R-2800 Double Wasp engines and flew for the first time on 14 October 1949. Chase received a contract in 1952 for five pre-production aircraft under the designation C-123B, and these were built and flown in 1953. In that same year the Kaiser-Frazer Corporation acquired a majority holding in the Chase Aircraft Company, and was awarded a production contract by the USAF for 300 C-123Bs. Subsequently, the USAF had reason to cancel this contract in mid-1953, renewing it with the Fairchild Company which assumed responsibility for continued development and production of the C-123B.

Fairchild's interest in the development of the C-123 resulted in the provision of a large dorsal fin to improve directional stability, and the first of the Fairchild-built C-123Bs flew for the first time on 1 September 1954. Production of 302 for the USAF followed, this total including one airframe for static testing, and 24 for delivery to Saudi Arabia (6) and Venezuela (18) under the Military Assistance Program. At a later date four were supplied to Thailand.

In 1962 Fairchild produced a prototype YC-123H, which had a wide-track landing gear to overcome problems which had been experienced with C-123Bs being taxied in strong crosswinds. In addition, a General Electric CJ610 (similar to the J85) turbojet was pod-mounted beneath each wing to evaluate the performance improvement offered by this auxiliary power. This flew for the first time on 30 July 1962, and was subsequently tested in South Vietnam in a counter-insurgency role, which resulted in a modification programme to convert 183 aircraft to this configuration. These were powered by the military version of the General Electric J85, and the first modified aircraft, designated C-123K, made its initial flight on 27 May 1966. Most of the C-123Ks were deployed in Vietnam, where they were the chief tactical support transports. Some were converted later for operation as multi-

Fairchild C-123K Provider

sensor night gunships under the designation AC-123K. Other variants have included 10 C-123Js, these having two Fairchild J44-R-3 turbojets (mounted in wingtip pods) for auxiliary power, and modified for operation by

the USAF in Alaska, where they were used in support of DEW-Line installations. The C-123J also has provision for wheel/ski landing gear, some being transferred at a later date to the Alaskan Air National Guard.

UC-123Bs were deployed in Vietnam to spray defoliating liquid over forest areas where the Viet Cong were believed to be operating, and the designation NC-123K applied to AC-123Ks when their deployment as gunships ended and they were converted back to serve in a transport role. Eight C-123B Providers were acquired by the US Coast Guard in 1962, on loan from the USAF, and these were used as cargo transports, operating under their original designation. Some C-123s in south-east Asia were transferred for service with the Cambodian air force, and all but one squadron of C-123s operating in Vietnam were transferred to the South Vietnam air force. Nothing is known of the fate of these aircraft after the fall of South Vietnam.

Type: tactical transport aircraft
Powerplant: (C-123K) two 2,500-hp (1865-kW) Pratt & Whitney R-2800-99W Double Wasp radial piston engines, and two 2,850-lb (1293-kg) thrust General Electric J85-GE-17 turbojets
Performance: (C-123B) maximum speed 245 mph (394 km/h); cruising speed 205 mph (330 km/h); range 1,470 miles (2366 km)
Weights: (C-123B) empty 29,900 lb (13562 kg); maximum take-off 60,000 lb (27216 kg)
Dimensions: span 110 ft 0 in (33.53 m); length 76 ft 3 in (23.92 m); height 34 ft 1 in (10.39 m); wing area 1,223 sq ft (113.62 m²)
Armament: (AC-123K) 7.62-mm (0.3-in) Minigun installations

Operators: Kampuchea, Saudi Arabia, South Korea, Thailand, US Air Force, US Coast Guard, Venezuela, Vietnam

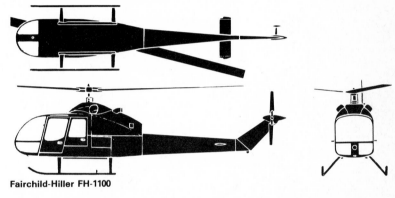

This Fairchild C-123K Provider was photographed in March 1976 during spray training at Fort Stuart, Georgia. The Provider was the type used to defoliate vegetation in Vietnam to try to deny cover to the Viet Cong. Training was carried out with water.

Fairchild-Hiller FH-1100

The US Army's Light Observation Helicopter (LOH) competition resulted in competitive prototypes being built by Bell, Hiller and Hughes. The Bell Model 206 and the Hughes OH-6 Cayuse are described separately. Hiller's HO-5 prototypes were powered by 250-shp (186-kW) Allison T63-A-5 turboshafts, and the first flew on 21 January 1963. Following evaluation of the competing prototypes, the Hughes design was ordered into production.

Hiller subsequently became a subsidiary of Fairchild, the company becoming the Fairchild Hiller Corporation. In 1965 it was announced that the four/five-seat utility helicopter would enter production under the designation FH-1100, and the first example was completed in June 1966.

Powerplant of the FH-1100 is a 317-shp (236-kW) Allison 250-C18, derated to 274 shp (204 kW) for take-off, with a maximum continuous rating of 233 shp

(174 kW). Standard accommodation is for a pilot and passenger on side-by-side front seats, with three passengers on rear seats which can be folded to provide space for cargo or two stretchers and an attendant.

The FH-1100 can carry a variety of weapons (see below). Following the initiation of production, several armed forces acquired these helicopters for a wide range of roles.

Type: four/five seat utility helicopter
Powerplant: one 317-shp (236-kW) Allison 250-C18 turboshaft
Performance: maximum cruising speed 127 mph (204 km/h); range (with maximum payload, standard fuel at sea level, no reserves) 348 miles (560 km)
Weights: empty 1,396 lb (633 kg); maximum take-off 2,750 lb (1247 kg)
Dimensions: main rotor diameter 35 ft 4¾ in (10.79 m); tail rotor diameter

Fairchild-Hiller FH-1100

6 ft 0 in (1.83 m); length (rotors turning) 39 ft 9½ in (12.13 m); height 9 ft 3½ in (2.83 m); main rotor disc area 984 sq ft (91.41 m²)
Armament: two 7.62-mm (0.3-in) machine-

guns, or two grenade launchers in armament packs, or anti-submarine weapons
Operators: Argentina, Brazil, Chile, Costa Rica, Cyprus, Ecuador, Nigeria, Panama, Philippines, Salvador, Thailand

Fairchild Republic F-105 Thunderchief

Republic Aviation Corporation's F-84 Thunderjet, the last turbine-powered subsonic straight-wing fighter-bomber to serve operationally with the USAF, was followed into service by the generally similar F-84F and RF-84F, these differing primarily by the adoption of swept wings and tail surfaces. This course had been adopted to produce quickly and cheaply a higher performance fighter-bomber, and the success of the project can be determined by the fact that Republic's combined production figures for the F-84F/RF-84F series totalled more than 3,000 aircraft.

When the F-84F Thunderstreak entered service in 1954, Republic had already spent some years in studying the design of a higher performance fighter-bomber which the company hoped would prove an acceptable successor to the Thunderstreak. At much the same time, North American proposed an improved version of the F-100, under the designation F-100B, but this differed so much from the basic F-100 design that it was allocated the designation YF-107A when three prototypes were ordered for evaluation. However, when Republic had submitted its AP-63 proposal to the USAF, the design appeared to have great potential, and two YF-105A prototypes were ordered. The first of these made its initial flight on 22 October 1955, exceeding Mach 1 on this flight; the first YF-107A flew initially

on 10 September 1956, but this latter aircraft was cancelled in favour of the F-105.

Inspection of an F-105 mockup was carried out in October 1953 and only minor changes in the configuration were required. The major area of concern at that time was whether the Allison J71 turbojet engine, which has been selected provisionally to power the F-105, would meet its thrust requirements, and a decision was made to use the Pratt & Whitney J57 turbojet as an interim powerplant. The question of a suitable engine was important, for Republic had planned a massive aircraft that could carry up to 12,000 lb (5443 kg) of mixed weapons. The company recognised the changing role of the 'fighter', and provided an internal bomb bay which at that time was tailored mainly to nuclear weapons.

No production F-105As were built, for with installation of the more powerful Pratt & Whitney J75 afterburning turbojet the

continued

Fairchild Republic F-105D Thunderchief

Republic F-105D Thunderchief of the 192nd Tactical Fighter Group, Virginia National Air Guard, based at Byrd Field, Sandston, Va.

designation was changed to F-105B. The prototype YF-105B flew for the first time on 26 May 1956, but development problems were to delay acceptance of the first production F-105B until 27 May 1958, and in August 1958 — three years later than planned originally — the first deliveries of operational aircraft were made to the USAF's 335th Tactical Fighter Squadron at Eglin AFB, Florida. Even then, it was not until mid-1959 that the USAF had acquired its first complete squadron of F-105Bs.

Design of the F-105 included a highly swept wing, swept tail surfaces and a petal-type speed brake comprising four segments of the rear nozzle fairing. Conventional ailerons were used for low-speed roll control, plus spoilers for control at high speeds.

The most unusual feature of the F-105B and subsequent Thunderchiefs were the sweptforward oblique-shockwave air intakes, coupled with an area-ruled fuselage. Major production version was the F-105D, with all-weather capability, much improved avionics, and detail improvements. This was followed by the twoseat F-105F with a lengthened fuselage and larger fin which, although intended originally for combat proficiency evaluation and transition training to the F-105, was used operationally because of the shortage of F-105 air-

craft generally. The designation F-105G was applied to F-105Fs modified to Wild Weasel configuration, with advanced ECM avionics which included an internally mounted jamming system, and able to deploy Shrike and ARM anti-radar missiles. After return from operations in Vietnam about 30 F-105Ds were modified with the T-Stick II bombing system, its avionics housed in a saddleback fairing along the top of the fuselage. This equipment conferred more precise navigation and improved blind bombing capability. Various subtypes were extremely important in south-east Asia in 1967-73. The F-105 was generally known as the 'Thud' or 'Lead Sled'.

Type: long-range tactical fighter-bomber
Powerplant: (F-105D) one 26,500-lb (12020-kg) afterburning thrust Pratt & Whitney J75-P-19W turbojet
Performance: (F-105D) maximum speed (clean) Mach 2.1 or 1,387 mph (2232 km/h) at 36,000 ft (10970 m); maximum cruising speed 836 mph (1345 km/h) at optimum altitude; combat radius 900 miles (1448 km); ferry range 2,200 miles (3541 km)
Weights: (F-105D) empty 27,500 lb (12474 kg); maximum take-off 52,838 lb (23967 kg)
Dimensions: span 34 ft 11¼ in (10.65 m); length 64 ft 0 in (19.51 m); length (F-105F) 67

ft 0⅛ in (20.43 m); height 19 ft 8 in (5.99 m); wing area 385 sq ft (35.77 m²)
Armament: one General Electric M61 20-mm Vulcan multi-barrel gun; more than

14,000 lb (6350 kg) of stores carried internally and externally
Operators: US Air Force, US Air National Guard

With nose receptacle open, this ANG F-105D is seen from a KC-135 tanker.

F & W C-3605

Development of the Farner-Werke C-3605 two-seat target-tug can be traced back to the Fabrique Fédérale C-3602, two prototypes of which were built in 1939-40 for long-range reconnaissance and ground-attack works. Following flight tests, modifications were made and an initial batch entered production as the C-3603. Ten were built and after service evaluation a further 142 followed, serving with the Swiss air force between 1942 and 1952 in the combat role. Two others, designated C-3603-1 TR, were produced for training and parachute tests. In 1945 a C-3603-1 was converted for target-towing; after considerable flight testing a successful installation was evolved and fitted to 20 other aircraft within a year.

Further improvements followed, and in 1946 Farner-Werke at Grenchen converted a C-3603-1 into a more advanced target-tug. A long tube was fitted from the rear cockpit to eject the target sleeve above the tail-plane and between the twin fins, with a cable-cutting device available to the pilot. Twenty C-3603s were converted to this standard.

Development of the basic airframe meanwhile continued with the C-3604, a version using the 1,250-hp (933-kW) Saurer YS-2 engine in place of the 1,000-hp (746-kW) Hispano-Suiza used in earlier models. A prototype and 12 production C-3604s were built, entering service in 1947-48. Spares produced for the C-3603 and not used enabled a further six C-3603-1s to be assembled in 1948.

During the early 1950s a requirement for an aircraft to tow illuminated targets at night

was met with the conversion of a C-3603-1, and this machine remained in service until replaced by the C-3605 in 1972. Further conversions of 40 C-3603-1s to target-tugs began in 1953, while another aircraft was fitted beneath one wing with a winch built by ML Aviation in the UK for high-speed towing, with a water ballast tank beneath the other wing. In the same year, 20 more C-3603-1s were converted by the military at Dübendorf for catastrophe relief using underwing supply containers.

The ultimate development of the C-3603 airframe came when the Hispano-Suiza engines of the 40 C-3603-1 conversions began to wear out. Various types of foreign aircraft, including the Westland (Fairey) Gannet, Rockwell (North American) Bronco, Dornier Skyservant, Shorts Skyvan, Mitsubishi MU-2, Sud Marquis and North American Trojan, plus the Pilatus Turbo-Porter, were considered but all were rejected for various reasons and a proposal to re-engine the C-3603-1 with a Lycoming T53-L-7A turboprop was accepted. A prototype was converted and flown on 19 August 1968; it was handed over to the Swiss air force in December 1968 for acceptance trials which proved satisfactory and, with a few modifications, a series of 23 aircraft were re-engined and given the new designation C-3605. A third, central, fin was added and the lower weight of the turboprop necessitated a major 6 ft (1.82 m) increase in the length of the nose.

The first C-3605s entered service in 1971; special equipment includes the target-towing

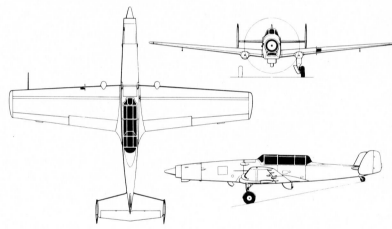

F & W C-3605

winch in the rear cockpit with 6,560 ft (2000 m) of cable.

Type: two-seat target-tug
Powerplant: one 1,100-shp (820-kW) Lycoming T53-L-7 turboprop
Performance: maximum speed at 10,000 ft (3050 m) 268 mph (432 km/h); cruising speed at 10,000 ft (3050 m) 261 mph (420 km/h); rate of climb at sea level 2,470 ft (753 m) per minute; service ceiling 32,800 ft (10000 m); take-off run to 50 ft (15 m) 1,005 ft (307 m);

landing run from 50 ft (15 m) 1,695 ft (516 m); range with 10% reserves 605 miles (980 km)
Weights: empty 5,806 lb (2634 kg); maximum take-off (with drop tanks) 8,192 lb (3716 kg)
Dimensions: span 45 ft 1 in (13.74 m); length 39 ft 6 in (12.03 m); height 13 ft 3 in (5.05 m); wing area 308.9 sq ft (28.70 m²)
Operators: Switzerland

FFA AS.202 Bravo

Originally conceived as a joint Swiss/Italian production, the Flug- und Fahrzeugwerke AG Altenrhein (FFA) Bravo was to be built in both countries — as the AS.202 in Switzerland and as the SA.202 in Italy — but in the event SIAI-Marchetti constructed the second prototype only and it was decided, because of shortage of production space, to produce the type exclusively in Switzerland. The first prototype was Swiss-built and flew on 7 March, 1969. A production line was established by FFA at Altenrhein, on Lake Constance, the former Swiss branch of the Dornier company.

A third prototype was built, and the first production Bravo flew on 22 December, 1971. Two versions were initially available, the AS.202/15 and AS.202/18A, powered respectively by 150- and 180-hp (112- and 134-kW) Lycoming engines. The latter had an inverted-flight oil system.

The /15 achieved Swiss certification on 15 August, 1972, and FAA certification on 16

November, 1973. By early 1978, 28 of the 32 ordered had been delivered.

The first /18 flew on 22 August, 1974 and was certificated in Switzerland on 17 December, 1976. Orders received for the /18 by mid-1978 totalled 72, including 48 Srs. 18A-1s for the Iraqi air force, 14 for the Moroccan air force, and eight for the Uganda air force. Two were also supplied for the Oman Royal Flight.

Flown in 1978 and making its overseas public debut at the SBAC display at Farnborough in September that year, the AS.202/26A is powered by a 260-hp (194-kW) Lycoming O-540 engine giving a greatly improved performance, including a maximum speed of 240 mph (385 km/h), maximum rate of climb at sea level 1,240 ft (348 m) per minute and ceiling of 22,000 ft (6700 m). The increased performance has however resulted in a range penalty, reducing this to 560 miles (900 km).

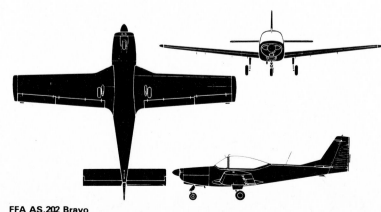

FFA AS.202 Bravo

Type: two/three-seat light touring or training aircraft
Powerplant: (AS.202/15) one 150-hp

(112-kW) Lycoming O-320-E2A flat-four piston engine;
(AS.202/18A) one 180-hp (134-kW) Lycom-

ing AEIO-360-B1F flat-four piston engine
Performance: (AS.202/15) maximum speed at sea level 131 mph (211 km/h); cruising speed at 8,000 ft (2440 m) 131 mph (211 km/h); maximum rate of climb at sea level 633 ft (193 m) per minute; service ceiling 14,000 ft (4265 m); take-off run to 50 ft (15 m) 1,558 ft (475 m); landing run from

50 ft (15 m) 1,362 ft (415 m); range (no reserves) 553 miles (890 km)
(AS.202/18) maximum speed at sea level 150 mph (241 km/h); cruising speed at 8,000 ft (2440 m) 141 mph (227 km/h); maximum rate of climb at sea level 922 ft (281 m) per minute; service ceiling 18,000 ft (5490 m); take-off run to 50 ft (15 m) 1,312 ft (400 m);

landing run from 50 ft (15 m) 1,362 ft (415 m); range (no reserves) 704 miles (1134 km)
Weights: (AS.202/15) empty 1,388 lb (630 kg); maximum take-off 2,202 lb (999 kg); (AS.202/18) empty 1,466 lb (665 kg); maximum take-off 2,315 lb (1050 kg)

Dimensions: (both versions) span 32 ft 0 in (9.75 m); length 24 ft 7 in (7.50 m); height 9 ft 3 in (2.81 m); wing area 149 sq ft (13.86 m²)
Operators: Iraq, Morocco, Oman, Uganda

FMA IA-35 Huanquero

The DINFIA company was founded in 1927 as the FMA (Fábrica Militar de Aviones) and after name-changes in 1943 and 1952 became the Dirección Nacional de Investigaciones y Fabricaciones Aeronáuticas (DINFIA), a state enterprise, in 1957. In 1968 the company reverted to its original FMA title.

The company currently consists of two large divisions, one designing, manufacturing and testing rockets and instrumentation (IIAE), while the FMA division proper controls the Córdoba aircraft-manufacturing facility.

FMA has built a number of original designs including, in 1959, the IA-38 four-engine tailless cargo transport designed by Dr Reimar Horten, who had produced a number of such projects in Germany.

The IA-35 prototype flew on 21 September 1953 and went into production for the Argentine air force in five versions, the first production aircraft flying on 29 March 1957. The versions are the IA advanced trainer, IU bombing and gunnery trainer, II light transport, III ambulance and IV photographic. All have 620-hp (463-kW) El Indio engines except the IU, which is fitted with two 720-hp (537-kW) engines of the same basic type.

As a navigational trainer, the IA carries pilot and co-pilot, radio operator, instructor and four pupils; it has instrument flying equipment, a camera, and oxygen. Armament

details of the IU are shown in the specification above. The type II is a light transport with a crew of three and seats for seven passengers. Wingtip fuel tanks can increase the standard 4 hours 40 minutes endurance by three hours, and underwing pylons can carry supply containers; only one type II was built. The type III ambulance can accept four stretcher cases plus a medical attendant, and crew of three, while the photographic version, the type IV, carries an operator for its Fairchild 225 camera in addition to the normal crew.

The original intention was to produce a batch of 100 IA-35s but in the event this was cut back considerably; 34 had been built by mid-October 1962 and its seems unlikely that total production exceeded 50. Of these, some 45 are thought to be still in service, their numbers about equally divided between II *Escuadrón de Exploración y Ataque* at Reconquista and I *Escuadrón Fotográfico*. The II *Escuadrón* is in process of converting to the FMA IA-58 Pucará.

A prototype of a civil version of the IA-35 flew on 28 May 1960. Powered by two 750-hp (560-kW) IA-19SR-1 El Indio engines, the same as those fitted to the IA-35-IU, it could accommodate 10 passengers and was named Pandora. This variant attracted little interest, however, and there was no further development, probably because the company was concentrating on the more advanced IA-50

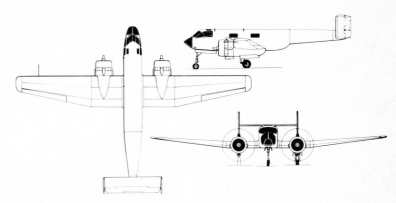

FMA IA-35 Huanquero

Guaraní twin-turboprop transport, flown in February 1962.

Type: general-purpose utility transport
Powerplant: two 620-hp (463-kW) IA-19R El Indio piston engines
Performance: maximum speed at 9,840 ft (3000 m) 225 mph (362 km/h); maximum cruising speed at 9,840 ft (3000 m); 217 mph (350 km/h); economical cruising speed at sea level 200 mph (320 km/h); rate of climb at sea level 984 ft (300 m) per minute; service ceiling

21,000 ft (6400 m); range 975 miles (1570 km)
Weights: empty 9,480 lb (4300 kg); loaded 13,670 lb (6200 kg)
Dimensions: span 64 ft 3½ in (19.6 m); length 45 ft 10 in (13.98 m); height 12 ft 2 in (3.70 m); wing area 452 sq ft (42 m²)
Armament: (as bombing and gunnery trainer) two 0.5-in (12.7-mm) Browning machine-guns, up to 440 lb (200 kg) of bombs and up to four 2.25-in (57-mm) rockets under each wing
Operators: Argentina

FMA IA-50 Guarani

The decision to produce a twin-turboprop light transport for the Argentine air force was quite an advanced concept for the late 1950s, and at the time of the first flight of the FMA IA-50 Guarani I on 6 February 1962, none of the North American companies had flown a light transport with turboprops except for Grumman with its Gulfstream I (although, of course, the British Vickers Viscount had been flying since 1948).

The prototype Guarani used some structural components of its predecessors, the FMA IA-35 Huanquero and the civil Pandora, and to enable flight testing to begin with the new engines the Guarani I retained the twin tail assembly of the earlier aircraft. Its two Turboméca Bastan IIIA turboprops were each rated at 858 shp (640-kW). The first of the definitive Guarani IIs featuring the production version's single highly swept fin and rudder and the 930-shp (694-kW) Bastan VIA flew on 23 April, 1963 and featured de-icing equipment and a shorter rear fuselage to save weight.

A second prototype and one pre-production model were produced, the latter being fitted with a Bendix autopilot for evaluation purposes, before full-scale production commenced on an initial batch of 23 Guarani IIs, the first two of which were in service by March 1967 at El Palomar, Buenos Aires. This batch of aircraft also included a VIP executive transport

for use by the President of Argentina, four photographic models and a staff transport for the Argentine navy. A further 15 Guaranis were ordered in October 1969 and these were made lighter by redesign of the interiors and replacement of certain steel components by aluminium. The first of this new batch was fitted with a combined wheel/ski undercarriage for use in support of Argentine bases in the Antarctic. The unit responsible for this work, I *Escuadrón Antarctico* based at Rio Gallegos, Santa Cruz, operates a miscellaneous collection of aircraft including DHC Beavers, DHC Otters, a Douglas C-47 and a Sikorsky S-61L helicopter. Other Guaranis in the second production batch included two for ground radio aids calibration, with seating for five equipment operators using an extensive array of electronic equipment. These aircraft have wing-tip fuel tanks.

As a light transport, the Guarani's standard seating is for 10 to 15 passengers, and an airstair/door is fitted. The executive version has 10 seats, while as a paratroop carrier there are 15 bench seats. In the ambulance role, three pairs of stretchers and two seats for medical attendants are provided. All variants are fitted with a toilet at the rear, a forward baggage hold and a galley.

Type: light transport
Powerplant: two 930-shp (694-kW) Tur-

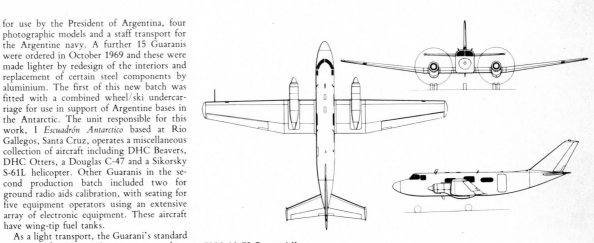

FMA IA-50 Guarani II

boméca Bastan VIA turboprops
Performance: maximum speed 310 mph (500 km/h); cruising speed 280 mph (450 km/h); rate of climb at sea level 2,640 ft (805 m) per minute; service ceiling 41,000 ft (12500 m); take-off run to 50 ft (15 m) 2,200 ft (640 m); landing run from 50 ft (15 m) 1,970 ft (600 m); range with maximum fuel 1,600 miles (2575 km); range with maximum payload

1,240 miles (1995 km)
Weights: empty 8,650 lb (3924 kg); maximum take-off 16,204 lb (7350 kg)
Dimensions: span 64 ft 3 in (19.59 m); length 50 ft 2 in (15.30 m); height 18 ft 5 in (5.61 m); wing area 450 sq ft (41.81 m²)
Operators: Argentina

FMA IA-58 Pucará

The IA-58 Pucará, originally known as Delfin, is a twin-turboprop counter-insurgency aircraft developed by FMA (*Fábrica Militar de Aviones*), part of the Argentine air force's *Aérea de Material Córdoba* division, to meet an air force requirement. Following testing of an unpowered aerodynamic prototype, the first powered Pucará made its maiden flight in August 1969. The second prototype, which took to the air in September 1970, was fitted with Turboméca Astazou XVIG turboprops in place of the AiResearch TPE 331s used in the initial aircraft, and the French powerplant

Argentinian FMA IA-58 Pucará attack aircraft of II Escuadron de Exploration y Ataque based at Reconquista AFB, Argentina.

continued

has been the standard for all subsequent Pucarás. The first production machine made its initial flight in November 1974, and 20 had been delivered by the autumn of 1978. A further 18 were due to follow in 1979, and the Argentine air force's order for 40 is expected to be expanded to 70. Other South American countries have expressed an interest in acquiring Pucarás.

The Pucará is named after the stone strongholds built on mountain tops by the Incas and Aimaras to protect themselves from attack, and the aircraft is likewise designed to withstand a determined onslaught. Its main mission is armed reconnaissance over land and sea, together with fire support; counter-insurgency roles can also be carried out. The two-man crew sit in tandem, with the co-pilot's seat 10 in (25 cm) higher than that of the pilot so that both have the best all-round view. The windscreen and cabin floor are designed to stop machine-gun bullets.

The IA-58 is an all-metal aircraft with a T-tail and rough-field landing gear. It can dive at maximum speed from cruising height to bring its armament to bear on targets of opportunity, and its tight turning radius allows the crew to keep their target in sight even in difficult mountain terrain. The IA-58 can operate from small grass fields 'no larger than a football pitch', and the take-off run can be reduced to only 262 ft (80 m) by fitting three rockets to the centreline pylon. This STO performance would allow the Pucará to be operated from aircraft carriers, and the large

clearance between the propeller tips and ground ensures that no damage will result from landings on uneven surfaces.

The Pucará packs a powerful punch in the form of two Hispano-Suiza HS-804 20-mm cannon each with 270 rounds and four Browning 7.62-mm machine-guns each with 900 rounds. Studies have been made of an alternative installation comprising a pair of 30-mm cannon and only two Brownings. The Matra 83-A 3 illuminated reflex sight with adjustable depression angle gives great flexibility in weapon delivery. Both the guns and the external stores, carried on four wing pylons and one on the centreline, are operated by buttons on the control column. A programmer allows stores to be released in any quantity from two to 40, with two firing modes available: step (single, pairs or salvo) and ripple (single, pairs or salvo). The interval between weapons can be varied from 0.02 to 2 seconds.

Features designed to allow operations from front-line bases with the minimum of support include direct access to main components on the ground, self-starting engines, duplicated systems, and a high ratio of operating to maintenance time.

Type: reconnaissance, close-support and counter-insurgency aircraft
Powerplant: two 988-hp (735-kW) Turboméca Astazou XVIG turboprops
Performance: maximum level speed at 9,840 ft (3000 m) 312.5 mph (500 km/h); maximum diving speed 469 mph (750 km/h); service ceil-

ing 32,810 ft (10000 m); stalling speed (gear and flaps up) 78 mph (125 km/h); take-off run over a 50-ft (15-m) obstacle 984 ft (300 m); initial sea-level rate of climb 3,547 ft (1080 m) per minute; radius of action — outward flight at 19,680 ft (6000 m), penetration and 5 minutes over target at height of 492 ft (150 m), return at 26,240 ft (8000 m), with 10% reserves — 250 miles (400 km) with 3,306-lb (1500-kg) payload, and aircraft weighing 14,300 lb (6500 kg)
Weights: empty 8,810 lb (4000 kg); maximum take-off 14,960 lb (6800 kg); maximum

payload 5,984 lb (2720 kg)
Dimensions: span 47 ft 6¾ in (14.50 m); length 46 ft 9 in (14.25 m); height 17 ft 10½ in (5.36 m); wing area 326.1 sq ft (30.30 m²)
Armament: two Hispano-Suiza HS-804 20-mm cannon and four Browning 7.62-mm (0.3-in) machine guns plus up to 3,564 lb (1620 kg) of external ordnance on five stations: typical weapons include general-purpose, fragmentation and incendiary bombs; mines; one or two torpedoes; and up to three AGM-12B Bullpup air-to-surface missiles
Operator: Argentina

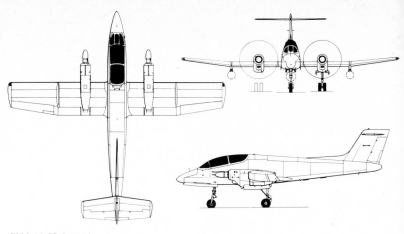

FMA IA 58 Pucará

Fokker S.11 Instructor

Although the Fokker factory at Amsterdam was practically destroyed in World War II, the technical staff was maintained virtually intact. The factory was rebuilt in the space of a year after the cessation of hostilities and a simple low-wing trainer, the S.11 Instructor, selected as the company's first postwar product. Nothing controversial was considered for the new aircraft, which flew in 1947. It had an all-metal wing with fabric-covered ailerons, and the steel-tube fuselage was fabric-covered. The fixed main legs bent, grasshopper-like, under the wing; the tailwheel was steerable for taxiing.

The Royal Netherlands Air Force bought 40, followed by 41 for Israel. Italy's Macchi company built 150 under licence, designated M.416 in Italian air force service. Meanwhile, Fokker Industria Aeronautica SA was established at Rio de Janeiro's Galeao Airport in 1954. The first Brazilian-produced S.11 was accepted by the Brazilian air force on 29 December 1955 and 100 were subsequently delivered.

The S.12, with a nosewheel, was also

manufactured in Brazil, 50 being delivered. Little modification was needed to accommodate the new undercarriage, as the wing had been stressed to support the gear in either position.

The 40 Instructors of the Royal Netherland Air Force provided elementary flying training with No 5 Instruction Squadron at Gilze-Rijen. With the introduction of more modern primary trainers in the 1970s, many S.11s were released to the civil market.

Type: two/three-seat primary trainer
Powerplant: one 190-hp (142-kW) Lycoming O-435-A air-cooled piston engine
Performance: maximum speed at sea level 134 mph (215 km/h); cruising speed at sea level 106 mph (170 km/h); normal range 430 miles (695 km); service ceiling 12,120 ft (4000 m); take-off run in 6-mph (10-km/h) wind 640 ft (195 m)
Weights: empty equipped 1,710 lb (775 kg); normal take-off 2,370 lb (1075 kg)
Dimensions: span 36 ft 1 in (11.0 m); length

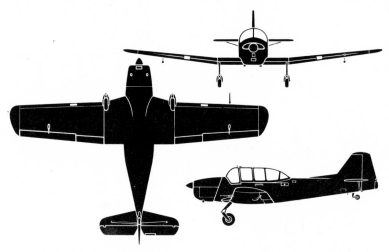

Fokker S.11 Instructor

25 ft 7 in (7.8 m); height 7 ft 0½ in (2.15 m); wing area 199 sq ft (18.49 m²)

Armament: none
Operator: Netherlands

Fokker-VFW F27 Friendship/Maritime

In March 1976, some 21 years after the maiden flight of the F27 Friendship prototype, Fokker-VFW flew the first F27 Maritime. In the 1950s and 1960s the Friendship was sold mainly to civil operators, but most recent orders have been from government agencies or the military.

The F27 Maritime is a major new development, equipped with a Litton search radar in a belly radome, inertial navigation system, radar altimeter, new autopilot and uprated communications. Although the Maritime does not carry offensive stores, two racks each holding 16 flares can be installed in the engine nacelles. Fuel capacity is increased to give an endurance of 10 to 12 hours. Designed as a medium-range patrol aircraft, its roles include fishery patrol, surveillance of offshore oil platforms and coastal shipping lanes, search and rescue, and environmental control. The rear fuselage has bulged observation windows.

The original 32-seat F27 Mk 100 sold well and 83 were built before it was supplemented by the more powerful Mk 200 (first flight 1959), the freight-door equipped Mk 400 Combiplane (first flight 1961), the Mk 500 with a 5-ft (1.5-m) fuselage stretch (first flight 1967) and the current Mk 600 (first flight 1968). The 500 and 600 both have freight

doors, the 600 retaining the shorter fuselage of the 200. The 300 was a freight version of the 100, only 13 being built. Britain supplies engines, undercarriages and propellers, but major sections of structure are constructed in France and West Germany.

Fairchild built and sold 205 F-27s and FH-227s between 1958 and 1973, these differing only in details. Although the F-27 is the same length as the F27, the stretched FH-227 is about 12 in (30.5 cm) longer than the F27 500. Total sales of Dutch-built examples have now passed 500, making it the top-selling European airliner.

The basic military versions are the 400M, capable of carrying 45 parachute troops or 13,550 lb (6145 kg) of freight or 24 stretchers and nine attendants, and the 500 M with accommodation for 50 paratroopers, 14,590 lb (6620 kg) of freight or 30 stretchers and attendants.

The F27 Maritime is aimed at customers who cannot afford expensive patrol aircraft such as the Lockheed Orion. Three examples have been ordered by Spain and two are in service with the Peruvian navy. Although Fokker-VFW remains confident of orders, competition is fierce. Every manufacturer with an aircraft even remotely suitable has proposed

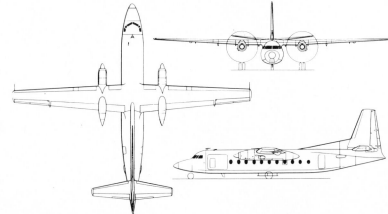

Fokker-VFW F27 Friendship 500

a maritime derivative.

Type: (Mk 400M/500M) medium-range military transport; (Maritime) medium-range maritime patrol and fishery protection aircraft
Powerplant: two 2,140-shp (1596-kW) plus 525-lb (238-kg) thrust Rolls-Royce Dart Mk 532-7R turboprops
Performance: (Mk 400M/500M at max-

imum take-off weight) normal cruising speed 298 mph (480 km/h); range with full payload and reserves 1,375 miles (2213 km); (Maritime at maximum take-off weight with pylon tanks) normal cruising speed 265 mph (427 km/h); search speed 168 mph (270 km/h); endurance 10 to 12 hours
Weights: (400m) empty 23,360 lb (10596 kg); maximum take-off 45,000 lb (20410 kg);

maximum landing 41,000 lb (18600 kg); maximum zero fuel 37,500 lb (17010 kg); (500M) empty 24,325 lb (11034 kg); maximum take-off 45,000 lb (20410 kg); maximum landing 42,000 lb (19050 kg); maximum zero fuel 39,500 lb (17900 kg); (Maritime with typical equipment fit) empty 27,400 lb (12430 kg); maximum take-off 45,000 lb (20410 kg); maximum landing 43,500 lb (19730 kg); maximum zero fuel 39,500 lb (17920 kg)
Dimensions: span 95 ft 2 in (29.00 m); length (Mk 400M/Maritime) 77 ft 3½ in (35.56 m); height (Mk 400M/Maritime) 27 ft 11 in (8.50 m); length (Mk 500M) 82 ft 2½ in (25.06 m); height (Mk 500M) 28 ft 7¼ in

(8.71 m); wing area 753.5 sq ft (70.0 m²)
Armament: normally unarmed apart from racks for flares installed in the rear of the engine nacelles

Operators: Algeria, Argentina, Burma, Ghana, Indonesia, Iran, Italy, Ivory Coast, Netherlands, Nigeria, Pakistan, Peru, Philippines, Senegal, Spain, Uruguay

Peru's naval air arm, Servicio Aeronavale, operates two Fokker F.27M Maritimes, the first being illustrated.

Fokker-VFW F28 Fellowship

The Fokker F28 jet retains many of the qualities of the F27 — good field performance, the ability to operate from unsophisticated airports, simple maintenance — and like the earlier design, was sold initially to airlines. However, in the mid-1970s a number were sold to governmental agencies, and some are operated by air forces.

Like the F27, the F28 is collaborative venture. Fokker-VFW builds the cockpit section, centre section and wing root fairing, and carries out assembly at Schiphol. Messerschmitt-Bölkow-Blohm in West Germany supplies most of the fuselage aft of the wing, including nacelles and support subs. VFW in West Germany is responsible for the rear fuselage and tail, and Shorts of Belfast builds the outer wings and landing-gear doors. Equipment includes Dowty-Rotol landing gear and Smiths autopilot.

Fokker announced plans for a 65-seat jet successor to the F27 in 1962. The initial schemes showed an aircraft much like the F28 of today with a high tail, rear engines and a wing of modest sweep. A unique airbrake forming the rear of the fuselage is employed in place of thrust reversers.

The initial production version is designated Mk 1000. In 1971 the Mk 2000 featured an

85-in (2.15-m) fuselage stretch to accommodate up to 79 passengers. A new wing, with extended tips and leading-edge slats, was applied to the Mk 1000 to produce the Mk 5000, and to the Mk 2000 to give the Mk 6000. Fokker then deleted the slats and is selling the short body and new wing as the Mk 3000 and the long body and new wing as the Mk 4000. A large cargo door is an optional extra.

Type: medium-range transport
Powerplant: (Mk 3000/4000/6000) two 9,900-lb (4491-kg) Rolls-Royce RB.183-2 Spey Mk 555-15H turbofans
Performance: (at 63,934 lb/29000 kg) maximum level speed Mach 0.75; maximum cruising speed at 30,000 ft (9150 m) 523 mph (843 km/h); economical cruising speed at 30,000 ft (9150 m) 421 mph (678 km/h); range at long-range cruise speed with full reserves (Mk 3000 with 65 passengers) 1,611 miles (2593 km), (Mk 4000 with 85 passengers) 1,151 miles (1852 km), (Mk 6000 with 79 passengers) 1,185 miles (1908 km)
Weights: (Mk 3000) empty 36,000 lb (16324 kg); maximum take-off 70,988 lb (32200 kg); maximum landing 64,000 lb (29030 kg); maximum zero fuel 56,000 lb (25400 kg); (Mk

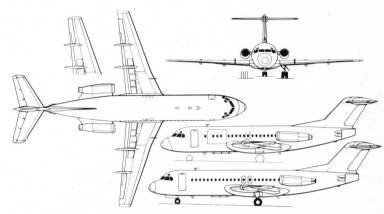

Fokker-VFW F28-4000 Fellowship. (upper side view of 1000C)

4000) empty 37,394 lb (16962 kg); maximum take-off 70,988 lb (32200 kg); maximum landing 64,000 lb (29030 kg); maximum zero fuel 57,500 kb (26080 kg); (Mk 6000) empty 38,318 lb (17381 kg); maximum take-off 72,995 lb (33110 kg); maximum landing 64,000 lb (29030 kg); maximum zero fuel 56,000 lb (25400 kg)
Dimensions: span 82 ft 3 in (25.07 m);

length (Mk 3000) 80 ft 6½ in (24.55 m); (Mk 4000/Mk 6000) 87 ft 9½ in (26.76 m); height 27 ft 9½ in (8.47 m); wing area (Mk 6000) 850 sq ft (78.97 m²)
Armament: none
Operators: Australia, Congo, Ghana, Ivory Coast, Malaysia, Netherlands, Nigeria, Peru, Tanzania, Togo

Fournier RF-4

In 1960 René Fournier designed and built an ultra-light single-seat aircraft designated RF.01. The intention was to combine the characteristics of a light sporting aircraft with those of a sailplane, and the RF.01 was an extremely clean design powered by a 25-hp (18.65-kW) converted Volkswagen engine with dual ignition and carburettors.

The success of the prototype resulted in support from the French government in laying down a production line, and a second prototype was built. Two pre-production aircraft designated RF-2 were flown, the first in June 1962, and production models became the RF-3, the first of which flew in March 1963, receiving its certificate of airworthiness three months later; production deliveries began in November the same year.

René Fournier had entered into a partnership in 1962 with Alpavia SA for production of the RF-3, and 95 were built before an improved model, the RF-4D, appeared.

In 1966 a further change of company took place when Sportavia-Putzer was formed in Germany to take over manufacture of the RF

designs. A total of 160 RF-4Ds were built and several achieved notable flights. In May 1969, Miro Slovak flew one across the Atlantic in 175 hours 42 minutes to win the *Evening News* £1,000 prize for the best performance in the *Daily Mail's* transatlantic race by a light aircraft under 5,000 lb (2268 kg).

Further developments of the basic RF-4 design include the 'stretched' RF-5 two-seater and the Sportavia SFS-31 Milan which combines the RF-4 fuselage and tail unit married to the 49 ft (15 m) span wing of the Scheibe SF-27M sailplane.

The only known military user of the RF-4 is Egypt which received six. They are believed to be used for AOP and electronic-intelligence work where their wooden construction and small engine give low radar and infra-red signatures.

Type: single-seat light aircraft
Powerplant: one 40-hp (30-kW) converted Volkswagen 1,200-cc four-cylinder car engine
Performance: maximum cruising speed 112 mph (180 km/h); economical cruising

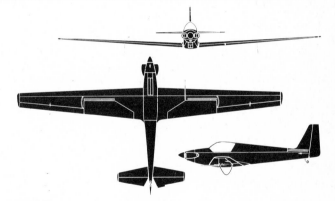

Fournier RF-4D

speed 100 mph (160 km/h); stalling speed 43.5 mph (70 km/h); rate of climb at sea level 690 ft (210 m) per minute; service ceiling 19,700 ft (6000 m); take-off run 427 ft (130 m); landing run 328 ft (100 m); range with maximum fuel 415 miles (670 km)
Weights: empty 584 lb (265 kg); maximum

take-off in utility role 859 lb (390 kg)
Dimensions: span 36 ft 11 in (11.26 m); length 19 ft 10 in (6.05 m); height (tail down) 5 ft 2 in (1.57 m); wing area 120.6 sq ft (11.20 m²)
Operators: Egypt

Fuji KM-2/KM-2B/T-3

The Fuji KM-2 primary trainer is a development of the civil KM prototype and first flew on 16 July, 1962. A contract for 25 aircraft was placed by the Japanese Maritime Self-Defence Force and deliveries took place between September 1962 and May 1965. Three more were subsequently ordered in 1968 and these had been delivered by February 1970. Around 25 are still in service.

The Japan Air Self-Defence Force which is currently using around 80 Beech T-34A Mentors in the primary training role, has selected the Fuji KM-2B as its replacement under the designation T-3. The KM-2B is a further modification of the KM-2 design, incorporating the airframe and powerplant of the

Japanese aircraft with the two-seat cockpit layout of the T-34A.

The first KM-2B, a civil aircraft, flew on 26 September, 1974 and received its Japanese certification on 26 November, 1974. First of six pre-production aircraft flew on 17 January, 1978, while the first of 32 ordered for the JASDF was delivered in March 1978. The force plans to order a further batch of 22 later, and a liaison/search and rescue version is being considered.

Type: (KM-2B) primary trainer
Powerplant: one 340-hp (254-kW) Lycoming IGSO-480-A1A6 piston engine
Performance: maximum speed at 16,000 ft

(4875 m) 234 mph (377 km/h); cruising speed at 8,000 ft (2440 m) 204 mph (328 km/h); rate of climb at sea level 1,520 ft (463 m) per minute; take-off run to 50 ft (15 m) 1,650 ft (503 m); landing run from 50 ft (15 m) 1,430 ft (436 m); range 600 miles (965 km)
Weights: empty 2,469 lb (1120 kg); maximum loaded 3,329 lb (1510 kg)
Dimensions: span 32 ft 10 in (10.00 m); length 26 ft 4 in (8.03 m); height 9 ft 11 in (3.02 m); wing area 177.6 sq ft (16.50 m²)
Operators: Japan

Fuji LM-1/LM-2

The Fuji LM-1 Nikko is an adaptation of the Beech B-45 Mentor airframe with the military training equipment removed. Interior modifications included conversion to take four or five passengers, and 27 Nikkos were supplied to the Japanese Ground Self-Defense Force under US offshore procurement in the mid-1950s. Two civilian versions were built and one was later modified to form the prototype of the KM-2 (sic). Two other LM-1s were converted to LM-2s by the substitution of the much more powerful 340-hp (254-kW) Lycoming IGSO-480 engine for liaison work with the JGSDF. Around half of the LM-1/LM-2s delivered are still in service, but the type is gradually being retired and replaced by helicopters.

Type: four five-seat general-purpose

monoplane
Powerplant: (LM-1) one 225-hp (168-kW) Continental O-470-13 air-cooled piston converted
Performance: (LM-1) maximum speed at sea level 185 mph (298 km/h); cruising speed at 3,000 ft (910 m) 148 mph (238 km/h); rate of climb at sea level 990 ft (302 m) per minute; service ceiling 15,000 ft (4575 m); take-off run to 50 ft (15 m) 1,642 ft (501 m); landing run from 50 ft (15 m) 1,110 ft (339 m); range 895 miles (1440 km) at 3,000 ft (910 m)
Weights: (LM-1) empty 2,080 lb (945 kg); maximum loaded 3,527 lb (1600 kg)
Dimensions: (LM-1) span 32 ft 10 in (10.00 m); length 25 ft 11 in (7.9 m); height 9 ft 7 in (2.92 m); wing area 177.6 sq ft (16.49 m²)
Operators: Japan

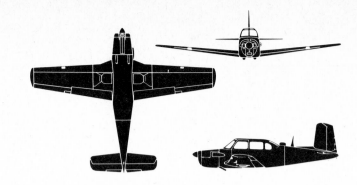

Fuji LM-1/LM-2

Fuji T-1

The honour of building Japan's first post-World War II domestically produced jet aircraft went to the Fuji company with its T1F2 trainer. By the end of the war in the Pacific, the Japanese aircraft industry had produced more than 100,000 aircraft and the country's aviation technology was well advanced. However, from 1945 aircraft development and manufacture was prohibited under the terms of the armistice agreement and while other countries forged ahead in the immediate post-war years, Japan's industry lay dormant.

The situation was changed from April 1952 when government approval was given for the industry to be revived, first with overhaul and maintenance of US military aircraft and, from several years later, production of new aircraft, which were initially foreign types built under licence. As successor to the well-known Nakajima company, Fuji Heavy Industries was established in July 1953 and its aviation division built a number of Beech Mentors. Later developments of this basic design, the LM and KM series are described elsewhere, while other types built under licence included the Bell 204 helicopter.

When it became necessary to consider replacing the North American T-6 (Harvard) trainer, the Japanese Defense Agency issued a design requirement and Fuji's entry was the T1, competing against designs from Shin Meiwa and Kawasaki. Fuji won, and three T1s were ordered on 11 July, 1956.

The first prototype flew on 8 January, 1958, with a Bristol Orpheus turbojet, and the second flew the following month. It had been intended to use the Japanese Ishikawajima-Harima J3 turbojet in the T1F1, but delays in engine development led to the use of the British engine in the first two batches of T1s, each comprising 20 aircraft; these were designated T1F2, and deliveries of the first 20 were completed in June 1961 with the second 20 following by July 1962. They received the Japanese Air Self-Defense Force designation T1A. A prototype of the T1F1 was converted from a T1F2 and flown on May 17, 1960 with the J3-IHI-3 engine developing 2,645-lb (1200-kg) thrust. As a result of successful flight trials, despite the reduced power, the JASDF ordered 20 T1F1s under the designation T1B, and delivery took place between September 1962 and June 1963.

Further development followed with the T1F3, which flew in April 1965 powered with a development of the Ishikawajima-Harima engine, the J3-IHI-7, giving 3,085-lb (1400-kg) thrust, and the JASDF planned to re-engine all T1Bs with this engine, redesignating them T1C. Most of the 50 or more Fuji jet trainers in JASDF service are with the 13th Wing at Ashiya. Because of this airfield's proximity to the sea, the T1s are painted in anti-corrosion white instead of the natural metal finish used on other JASDF trainers.

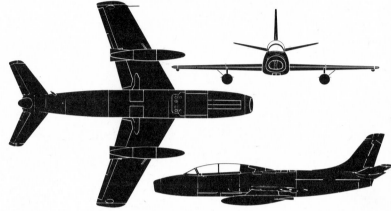

Fuji T1A

Type: (T1F2/T1A): intermediate jet trainer
Powerplant: one 4,000-lb (1814-kg) Rolls-Royce Orpheus 805 turbojet
Performance: maximum speed at 20,000 ft (6100 m) 575 mph (925 km/h); cruising speed at 30,000 ft (9150 m) 385 mph (620 km/h); cruising speed at 10,000 ft (3050 m) 357 mph (575 km/h); rate of climb at sea level 6,500 ft (1980 m) per minute; service ceiling 52,000 ft (15850 m); take-off run to 50 ft (15 m) 2,000 ft (610 m); landing run 1,920 ft (585 m); range on internal fuel 805 miles (1300 km); range with underwing tanks 1,210 miles (1950 km)

Weights: empty 5,335 lb (2420 kg); normal take-off 9,150 lb (4150 kg); take-off with underwing tanks 11,020 lb (5000 kg)
Dimensions: span 34 ft 5 in (10.50 m); length 39 ft 9 in (12.12 m); height 13 ft 4 in (4.08 m); wing area 239.2 sq ft (22.22 m²)
Armament: one Colt-Browning 0.50-in (12.7-mm) machine-gun in nose; if underwing tanks are not carried, each rack can be used for a gun pod, Sidewinder air-to-air missile, 750-lb (340-kg) bomb, napalm bomb or cluster of 2.75-in (70-mm) air-to-air rockets
Operators: Japan

GAF (Government Aircraft Factories) Nomad/Mission Master/Search Master

The GAF Nomad is a twin-turboprop STOL utility transport developed for a variety of roles, including maritime patrol. The first of two Model N2 prototypes made its maiden flight in July 1971, and the standard N22B short-fuselage production version is known as the Mission Master in military service. A fishery-production and anti-smuggling variant, the Search Master, has since been developed.

The basic Nomad is a high-wing aircraft with full-span double-slotted flaps for STOL operations, allowing it to take off in 600 ft (183 m). The aircraft is designed for single-pilot operation and can accommodate 12 passengers or a typical disposable load of 4,250 lb (1931 kg). Double doors on the left give access to the cabin and a dropping hatch, the doors of which can be operated from the cockpit, has a capacity of 500 lb (227 kg). The Mission Master can also carry up to 2,000 lb (909 kg) of stores on four underwing pylons, which can be fitted with gun or rocket pods. Surveillance and night-vision aids may be fitted in a nose bay, and removable seat armour and self-sealing fuel tanks can be incorporated.

The aircraft's powerplant, a pair of Allison 250-B17B turboprops, is the first application of this engine in a fixed-wing type. Its more normal use is as a turboshaft in helicopters such as the Bell JetRanger and Hughes 500, but the Model 250 has proved to be very suitable for driving a propeller instead of a rotor, with excellent power and reliability combined with low noise.

The maritime-patrol Search Master is based on the standard N22B Mission Master and is

The GAF Mission Master is the military version of the N22B short-body model of the Australian twin-turboprop Nomad STOL transport. This 'MM' for the Australian Army has four wing pylons, transparent cockpit roof and comprehensive communications.

available in two versions: the Search Master B, with a nose-mounted Bendix RDR-1400 search radar; and Search Master L, incorporating the Litton LASR-2 radar in a radome beneath the belly. The RDR-1400 can detect a wooden boat 40 ft (12 m) long at a range of 22.5 miles (36 km) and can pick up a 150 ft (46 m) object at twice this distance. The radar can also detect weather out to ranges of 270 miles (432 km) and can interrogate transponders within 185 miles (296 km). The LASR-2, a derivative of the APS-503 which equips the Canadian Armed Forces' Sikorsky Sea King helicopters, is similar to the radar installed in the Fokker-VFW F27M maritime-patrol aircraft and is mounted under the Search Master's fuselage, giving it a 360° scan.

The L version has a slightly slower cruising speed than the B, but the superior radar performance more than compensates for this reduction. Against a target with a cross-section of 10,750 sq ft (1000 m²) in sea state three and with the aircraft cruising at 5,000 ft (1524 m), the Search Master L has a radar range of 115 miles (184 km) — twice that of the B version — and on an eight-hour patrol it surveys more than 3.2 times the ocean area.

Even greater improvements are achieved against small targets.

The Search Master is also equipped with a Litton LTN-72 inertial navigator which supplies all the information needed to carry out a search over large tracts of sea and which can feed directly into the autopilot to fly an efficient pattern. Larger fuel tanks are fitted to increase the aircraft's range, and bubble windows are fitted in the fuselage sides to aid visual observation. The Search Master's crew comprises pilot, co-pilot, radar operator and navigator. Stores such as reconnaissance pods can be attached to underwing pylons, and an RC-9 camera may be fitted in a hatch in the cabin floor, which is also suitable for delivering flares or other droppable items.

Type: utility transport and maritime-patrol aircraft
Powerplant: two 400-shp (298-kW) Allison 250-B17B turboprops
Performance: maximum speed at sea level 193 mph (309 km/h); economical cruising speed 161 mph (258 km/h); sea-level rate of climb 1,410 ft (429 m) per minute; ceiling 23,500 ft (7164 m); maximum range at 161

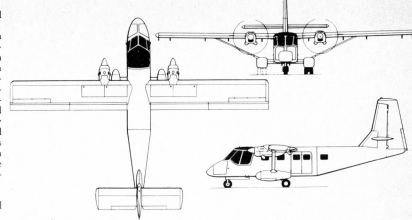

GAF Nomad 22

mph (258 km/h) with reserves and auxiliary fuel 1,300 miles (2080 km)
Weights: typical operating 4,750 lb (2159 kg); maximum take-off 9,000 lb (4090 kg)
Dimensions: span 54 ft (16.46 m); length 41

ft 2½ in (12.56 m); height 18 ft 1½ in (5.53 m); wing area 145.3 sq ft (13.50 m²)
Operators: (Mission Master) Australia, Indonesia, Papua New Guinea, Philippines; (Search Master) Indonesia

---

Gates Learjet 25B

One of the world's most successful business jets, the Learjet not only has the appearance of a fighter but was the direct outcome of a jet fighter design. In 1955 the Flug und Fahrzeugwerke AG (FFA) built and tested the P-1604 fighter, aiming at a Swiss air force order which did not in fact materialise. The aircraft came to the attention of William P. Lear, a talented engineer who headed the successful electronics and aircraft company, Lear Incorporated. He decided to recruit the FFA design team and he formed the Swiss American Aviation Corporation (later Lear Jet Corporation) to develop a light transport based on the P-1604.

In 1962, Lear Jet Corporation moved to Wichita, Kansas, and the prototype of the new Learjet first flew on 7 October 1963. It had a streamlined fuselage mounting two General Electric CJ610-1 turbojets in rear fuselage pods, and employed wing and tip tanks which recalled its P-1604 ancestry. The Model 23 could accommodate two crew and five passengers, and the performance of the prototype justified every hope of its creator. The Lear Jet development team pushed the aircraft through the civil certification procedure in the short space of nine months, and the first commercial delivery of a production Model 23 was made in October 1964.

Orders came initially from business concerns, with no US military orders despite company presentations to the Pentagon. The USAF and US Navy preferred the Rockwell (North American) T-39 Sabreliner, largely because of its greater cabin volume and higher payload. The only Learjet for governmental use was one machine delivered to NASA's Ames Research Center in September 1965. In 1966 Lear Jet announced the Model 24 featuring increased gross weight and improvements to the pressurization system, and this was further developed into the Model 24B which employed more powerful CJ610-6 powerplants. It was this model which found the first true military application, in the unusual role of target towing. Two aircraft were sold to Swedair Ltd to undertake contracts for the armed forces of Sweden, Denmark and Austria, and they were fitted with a PM-7C dart target housed externally under the rear fuselage together with an under-fuselage chaff dispenser pod for ECM training missions. The high performance of the Learjet made it highly suitable for sorties involving SAAB-35s and -37s and Swedish anti-aircraft batteries.

Shortly after introduction of the Model 24 the company brought out the stretched Learjet 25 with capacity for two extra passengers and with the large oval windows of earlier aircraft replaced by smaller rectangular units. This window arrangement was introduced in the smaller Model 24D of 1970 and the company (now named Gates Learjet) also announced the short range Model 24C. The new series started to find favour with overseas users, the

500th Learjet (a -24D) being delivered to the Mexican navy in 1975. A Model 25D went to the *Fuerza Aerea Boliviana* for high-speed communications, and the Yugoslav government received two -25Bs in military markings for their Belgrade-based VIP flight. The most popular task for military Learjets has been high-altitude photography and remote sensing. For this application, the aircraft is fitted with a large single or dual integral camera pod just forward of the wing. In many South American countries aerial mapping is a military task and the air arms of Ecuador, Peru, Bolivia and Argentina all received Learjets in this configuration. Operating at 41,000 feet (12497 m), the versatile Learjet can also be used for standard military photo-reconnaissance but is rapidly convertible for normal transport if required.

Type: 10-seat light communications, target-towing, photographic and special-duties aircraft
Powerplant: two 2,950-lb (1338-kg) General Electric CJ610-6
Performance: maximum cruising speed

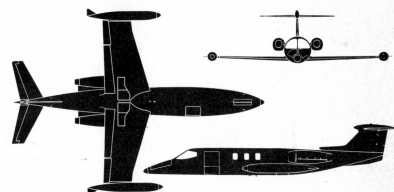

Gates Learjet 25

Mach 0.81 or 534 mph (860 km/h); maximum rate of climb 6,050 ft (1844 m) per minute; time to 41,000 ft (12497 m) 19 minutes; balanced field length 5,186 ft (1581 m); take-off distance over 35-ft (10.67-m) obstacle 3,400 ft (1036 m); maximum range with full fuel 1,900 miles (3080 km); service ceiling 41,000 ft (12497 m)

Weights: Empty 7,355 lb (3336 kg); maximum take-off 15,000 lb (6804 kg)
Dimensions: span 35 ft 7 in (10.85 m); length 47 ft 7 in (14.50 m); height 12 ft 3 in (3.73 m); wing area 231.8 sq ft (21.53 m²)
Operators: Bolivia, Peru, Yugoslavia; operators of the Learjet 24 include Ecuador and Mexico; and of the Model 35A Argentina

Best-selling executive jet, the Learjet has been sold in various models to a number of air forces, usually for VIP liaison. This is a specially equipped Model 24 used by the civil operator Swedair as a target tug for hire to Sweden, Denmark and Austria.

General Dynamics F-16

Small, lightweight, agile, hard to see and hard to hit, the General Dynamics F-16 is one of the most promising fighter designs to emerge in recent years. Its origins go back to February 1972, when General Dynamics, Boeing, LTV, Lockheed and Northrop all submitted proposals to the US Air Force for a new lightweight fighter (LWF) with exceptional manoeuvrability. Two months later General Dynamics and Northrop were each given contracts for two prototypes, to be flown against one another (and other contemporary USAF fighters) in a competitive fly-off to decide the winner. The choice was not an easy one, for both General Dynamics' YF-16 and Northrop's twin-engined YF-17 gave equally excellent performances, neither really deserving to lose. As subsequent events have shown, neither did actually lose, for although the YF-17 was unsuccessful in the US Air Force competition, its direct derivative, the F-18 Hornet, now seems assured of large orders from the US Navy and possibly other customers.

Originally there was no intention of building an LWF in quantity, but this was overturned by the emergence of a large export market, initially in Europe. Selection of the F-16 for the USAF was announced in January 1975, and five months later came the news that four European air forces (those of Belgium, the Netherlands, Norway and Denmark) had chosen the F-16 to replace Lockheed Starfighters and other types in their respective modernization programmes. Another substantial contract followed in October 1976, when the Imperial Iranian air force ordered 160, to carry total orders beyond the 1,000 mark. The USAF now plans to have nearly 1,400 eventually, and the four NATO countries have ordered 348. The latter will be divided 116 to Belgium, 102 to the Netherlands, 72 to Norway and 58 to Denmark; there are assembly lines in Belgium and the Netherlands in addition to that in the USA. In all cases the totals include a proportion of tandem two-seat F-16B fighter/trainers.

The first YF-16 prototype made its maiden flight on 20 January 1974. An exhaustive fly-off against the YF-17 occupied almost the whole of that year, and after the F-16's acceptance a further eight modified development aircraft were built: six single-seat F-16As and two two-seat F-16Bs. The first of these flew on 8 December 1976 and the last in June 1978. The production go-ahead was announced in the spring of 1978, when General Dynamics was authorized to start building the first 105 aircraft for the USAF, the first 192 for Europe, and the first 55 for Iran. August 1978 saw the initial flight of a series-built F-16A, and in the winter of 1978-79 the 388th Tactical Fighter Wing at Hill AFB, Utah, became the first USAF unit to receive the new fighter; European deliveries began shortly afterwards.

The engine is almost identical with that used in the twin-engined McDonnell Douglas F-15, and although the USAF is deeply concerned about the engine's continuing troubles, the type's maturity must be an advantage. The inlet is a simple fixed-geometry hole on the underside of the fuselage, though this reduces the maximum speed.

Some of the latest technology can be seen in the aerodynamic structure, and in the avionics and fire-control systems of the F-16. For example, the way that the wings are blended into the body, instead of being 'stuck on', not only helps to save weight but increases the overall lift at high angles of attack and reduces drag in the transonic speed range. Moveable flaps on the wing leading- and trailing-edges, controlled automatically by the aircraft's speed and altitude, enable the wing to assume an optimum configuration for lift under all conditions of flight. The highly-swept strakes that lead forward alongside the nose provide further lift; they also prevent wing-root stall, reduce buffeting, and improve directional stability and roll control. A lot of thought has gone into cockpit design to get the canopy shape, seat angle and instrument layout just right, so that the pilot has the maximum field of view and maximum efficiency with a minimum of fatigue: a most important factor in an aircraft liable to pull up to 9 g in an air-

The **General Dynamics F-16,** likely to be named eventually, was a mere demonstrator of advanced light-fighter technology that suddenly found itself in international production as a multi-role combat aircraft.

General Dynamics F-16 cutaway drawing key

1 Pitot tube
2 Radome
3 Planar radar scanner
4 Scanner drive motors
5 ADF antenna
6 Front electronics equipment bay
7 Westinghouse radar electronics
8 Forward radar warning antenna
9 Cockpit front bulkhead
10 Instrument panel shroud
11 Missile control electronics
12 Fuselage forbody strake fairing
13 Marconi-Elliot head-up display
14 Side stick controller (fly-by-wire control system)
15 Cockpit floor
16 Frameless bubble canopy
17 Canopy fairing
18 Ejection seat (30-deg tilt back)
19 Pilot's safety harness
20 Throttle
21 Side control panel
22 Cockpit frame construction
23 Ejection seat headrest
24 Cockpit canopy seal
25 Canopy hinge
26 Rear avionics bay (growth area)
27 Cockpit rear bulkhead
28 Boundary-layer splitter-plate
29 Fixed geometry air intake
30 Antenna
31 Aft retracting nosewheel
32 Shock absorber scissor link
33 Retraction strut
34 Nosewheel door
35 Intake trunking
36 Cooling louvres
37 Gun gas suppression nozzle
38 Air conditioning system pipes
39 Forward fuselage fuel tanks
40 Canopy aft glazing
41 Drop tank, capacity 370 US gal (1 400 l)

49 Ammunition drum (500 × 20-mm rounds)
50 Ammunition drum flexible drive shaft
51 Hydraulic gun drive motor
52 Leading edge control shaft
53 Hydraulic service bay
54 Hydraulic reservoir
55 Leading edge manoeuvre flap drive motor
56 Antenna
57 No 2 hydraulic system reservoir
58 Leading edge control shaft
59 Inboard pylon
60 Wing centre pylon
61 Mk 82 500-lb (227-kg) bombs
62 Outboard wing pylon
63 Missile launcher shoe
64 AIM-9L Sidewinder missile
65 Starboard navigation light
66 Aluminium honeycomb leading edge construction
67 Static dischargers
68 Fixed trailing edge section
69 Multi-spar wing construction
70 Integral wing fuel tank
71 Starboard flaperon
72 Fuel system piping
73 Access panels
74 Centre fuel tank panels
75 Centre fuselage fuel tank
76 Intake duct
77 Wing mounting bulkheads
78 Flight refuelling receptacle
79 Pratt & Whitney F100-PW-100(3) turbofan
80 Engine gearbox, airframe mounted
81 Gearbox drive shaft
82 Ground pressure refuelling receptacle

90 Anti-collision light power supply
91 Starboard tailplane
92 Graphite-epoxy fin skins
93 Fin construction
94 Aluminium honeycomb leading edge construction
95 Steel leading edge strip
96 Antenna
97 Anti-collision light
98 Tail radar warning antenna
99 Aluminium honeycomb rudder construction
100 Rudder servo-actuator
101 Radar warning power supply
102 Tail navigation light
103 Fully variable exhaust nozzle
104 Split trailing edge airbrakes (upper and lower surfaces)
105 Airbrake jack
106 Port tailplane
107 Static dischargers
108 Graphite-epoxy tailplane skins
109 Aluminium honeycomb construction
110 Titanium tailplane spar
111 Tailplane pivot mounting
112 Tailplane servo-actuator
113 Nozzle sealing fairing
114 Fueldraulic nozzle actuators

42 Forbody blended wing root
43 TACAN aerial
44 Fuel tank access panel
45 Cannon barrels
46 Forbody frame construction
47 M-61 rotary cannon
48 Ammunition feed and link return chutes

83 Flaperon servo-actuator
84 Rear fuselage frame construction
85 Integral fuel tank
86 Front engine mounting
87 Antenna
88 Fin root fairing
89 Flight control system hydraulic accumulators

115 Afterburner tailpipe
116 Rear fuselage bulkheads
117 Rear engine mountings
118 Formation light
119 Chaff and flare dispenser
120 Fuselage sidebody fairing
121 Runway arresting hook
122 Ventral fin, port and starboard

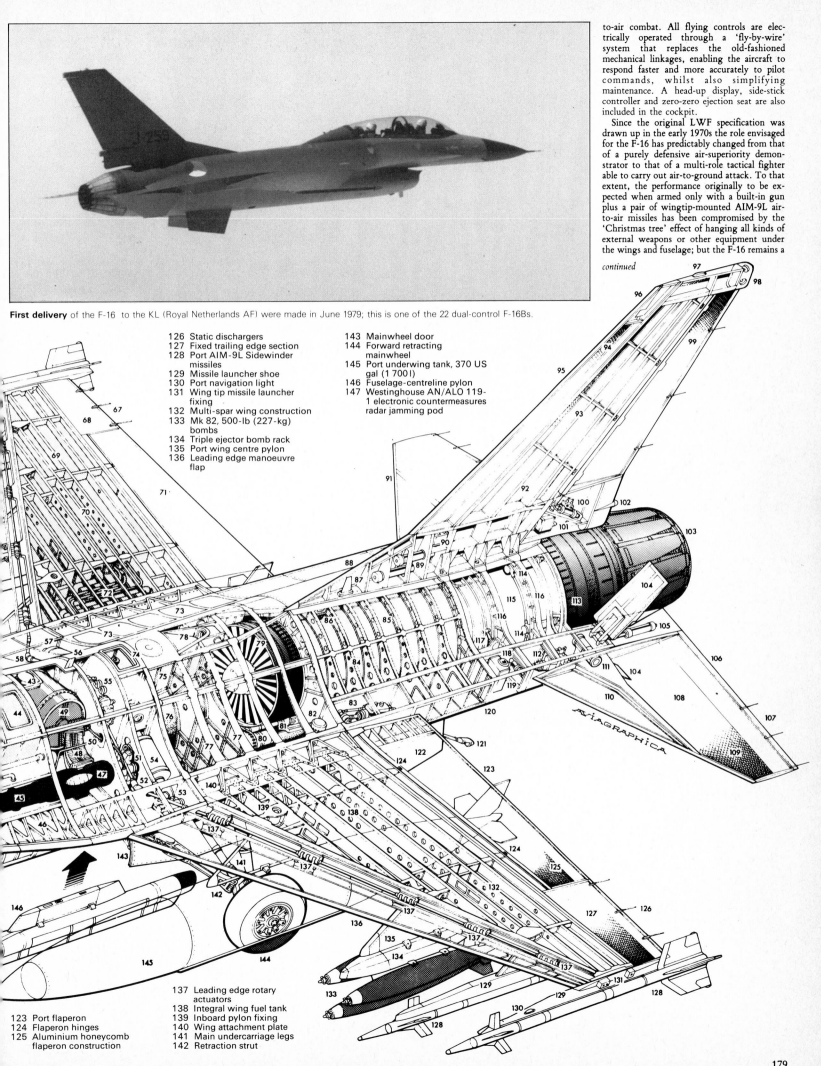

to-air combat. All flying controls are electrically operated through a 'fly-by-wire' system that replaces the old-fashioned mechanical linkages, enabling the aircraft to respond faster and more accurately to pilot commands, whilst also simplifying maintenance. A head-up display, side-stick controller and zero-zero ejection seat are also included in the cockpit.

Since the original LWF specification was drawn up in the early 1970s the role envisaged for the F-16 has predictably changed from that of a purely defensive air-superiority demonstrator to that of a multi-role tactical fighter able to carry out air-to-ground attack. To that extent, the performance originally to be expected when armed only with a built-in gun plus a pair of wingtip-mounted AIM-9L air-to-air missiles has been compromised by the 'Christmas tree' effect of hanging all kinds of external weapons or other equipment under the wings and fuselage; but the F-16 remains a

continued

First delivery of the F-16 to the KL (Royal Netherlands AF) were made in June 1979; this is one of the 22 dual-control F-16Bs.

126 Static dischargers
127 Fixed trailing edge section
128 Port AIM-9L Sidewinder missiles
129 Missile launcher shoe
130 Port navigation light
131 Wing tip missile launcher fixing
132 Multi-spar wing construction
133 Mk 82, 500-lb (227-kg) bombs
134 Triple ejector bomb rack
135 Port wing centre pylon
136 Leading edge manoeuvre flap

143 Mainwheel door
144 Forward retracting mainwheel
145 Port underwing tank, 370 US gal (1 700 l)
146 Fuselage-centreline pylon
147 Westinghouse AN/ALQ 119-1 electronic countermeasures radar jamming pod

123 Port flaperon
124 Flaperon hinges
125 Aluminium honeycomb flaperon construction

137 Leading edge rotary actuators
138 Integral wing fuel tank
139 Inboard pylon fixing
140 Wing attachment plate
141 Main undercarriage legs
142 Retraction strut

179

most impressive performer even under full-load conditions, naturally regaining its full measure of agility once the weapons have been delivered. Though limited in all-weather attack capability, the F-16A carries a good range of modern avionics. Based on a digital computer, the Westinghouse multi-mode pulse-Doppler radar has a look-down range, eliminating ground 'clutter', of 23-35 miles (37-56 km), and a look-up range of 29-46 miles (46-74 km). In air-to-air fighting, the pilot has a choice of one missile-firing mode plus two gunnery modes ('snap-shoot' and optical lead-computing) available on the cockpit stores control panel. Air-to-ground attacks can be made under visual, blind or electro-optical delivery conditions, by day or night and to some degree in adverse weather. Combined with a long-life structure, low radar signature, active and passive countermeasures, plus first-class manoeuvrability, the F-16 is clearly destined to make an outstanding contribution to the tactical defence of the United States and Western Europe for many years to come. By 1980 the USAF anticipates a mission reliability factor of 80 per cent based on a rate of 1½ sorties per aircraft per day.

Countries attempting to buy the F-16 early in 1979 included Israel and Turkey, while the type was also being evaluated by Australia and Canada; Iran's change of government has led to the cancellation of that country's order.

Type: single-seat tactical fighter (F-16A) and two-seat combat trainer (F-16B)
Powerplant: one 23,810-lb (10800-kg) Pratt & Whitney F100-PW-100(3) afterburning turbofan
Performance: maximum speed (YF-16) at 36,000 ft (10970 m) with two Sidewinders Mach 1.95 or 1,289 mph (2074 km/h); combat radius (YF-16) with two Mk 82 bombs 340 miles (547 km), (F-16A) about 575 miles (925 km); ferry range (F-16A) with drop-tanks 2,303 miles (3705 km); service ceiling (F-16A) about 60,000 ft (18290 m); maximum rate of climb (YF-16) with two Mk 82 bombs 42,000 ft (12802 m) per minute
Weights: (F-16A) operational empty 14,567 lb (6607 kg); internal fuel 6,972 lb (3162 kg); maximum external load 15,200 lb (6894 kg); design take-off gross, clean 22,500 lb (10205 kg); maximum take-off without external tanks 22,785 lb (10335 kg), with external load 33,000 lb (14968 kg)
Dimensions: span (over missiles) 32 ft 10 in (10.01 m); length 47 ft 7¾ in (14.52 m); height 16 ft 5¼ in (5.01 m); wing area 300 sq ft (27.87 m²)
Armament: one 20-mm General Electric M61A-1 multi-barrel cannon in left wing/body fairing, with 500 rounds; one AIM-9J/L Sidewinder infra-red homing missile at each wingtip (radar-homing Sparrow or AMRAAM later) for air-to-air interception; six underwing hardpoints and one under fuselage for up to 15,200 lb (6894 kg) of attack weapons or drop-tanks (10,500 lb/4763 kg if full internal fuel is carried). Stores under wings/fuselage can include four more Sidewinders or Sparrows, Pave Penny laser tracking pod, single or cluster bombs, flare pods, air-to-surface missiles, laser-guided and electro-optical weapons
Operators: Belgium, Denmark, the Netherlands, Norway, USAF

The weapons illustrated comprise triplets of free-fall bombs (typically Mk 82) and four Sidewinders (AIM-9J depicted but operational standard will be the 9L).

The unswept wing has an automatic variable camber with flaps and hinged leading edges. In subsonic cruise the wing is flat. At supersonic speeds it is curved slightly up, while for subsonic manoeuvre the leading edge goes down fully.

Low-visibility two-tone grey is the standard USAF colour scheme for TAC-F16s, and following successful trials will probably in future include the radome, the 30 sq ft of which will be coated with an anti-static non-eroding grey layer,

Relaxed static stability and a high-reliability stability augmentation system are reflected in the unusual shape and especially the large-area strakes and blended wing/fuselage which also offers valuable space for avionics and gun.

USAF
50747

Airbrakes are above and below the trailing edge of each wing/body strake, just inboard of the horizontal tails. The latter augment the roll performance which stems also from the wing trailing-edge surfaces, known as flaperons.

General Dynamics (Convair) F-106 Delta Dart

In the early 1950s it became clear that the 'Ultimate Interceptor' being developed by Convair would not be operational by its 1954 deadline. Faced with this problem, the US Air Force decided to procure from Convair a less sophisticated, interim interceptor. This became designated the F-102A Delta Dagger: the original MX-1554 Ultimate Interceptor was then designated the F-102B, and it is this aircraft which became eventually the F-106 Delta Dart.

It was fortunate that the USAF adopted such a policy, for the F-102A ran into serious development problems, and it was not until April 1956 that the first production examples of this 'interim' aircraft entered service. In the same period the F-102B was virtually at a standstill, starved of funds and still awaiting its Wright J67 powerplant, though the Hughes MX-1179 electronic control system (ECS) was ready before the airframe. When the F-102A tests were seen to be successful the US Air Force contracted for 749 examples; at the same time, November 1955, an order was placed for 17 F-102Bs. The Hughes MA-1 (ex-MX-1179) fire control system, and a mock up of the proposed cockpit with radically new equipment and cockpit displays was available for inspection in December 1955.

On 17 June 1956 the F-102B was redesignated officially as the F-106, reflecting the fact that the original requirement had now changed considerably. When the initial details became known, on 28 September 1956, it was clear that the USAF had raised its sight somewhat. Convair were now required to produce an aircraft capable of intercepting enemy vehicles in all weathers at altitudes up to 70,000 ft (21335 m) and within a radius of 430 miles (692 km). Armed with guided missiles, and/or rockets with atomic warheads, the F-106 was expected also to carry out interceptions at speeds of up to Mach 2.0 at heights of up to 35,000 ft (10670 m), under automatic guidance from SAGE installations integrating with the MA-1 fire control system.

Two YF-106A prototypes made their first flights on 26 December 1956 and 26 February 1957, but flight tests were disappointing, and it was painfully obvious that there were still many shortcomings. Maximum speed was some 15% below the required figure, but causing greater concern was the slow rate of acceleration, and neither of these factors were helped by delays in the Pratt & Whitney J75-P-9 turbojet which had been substituted for the Wright J67 chosen originally. To aggravate the situation still further, the MA-1 ECS was not performing well, and a shortage of funds almost caused the USAF to scrap the entire F-106 programme.

To salvage something from this difficult situation, the USAF decided to reduce its planned procurement of 1,000 F-106s by some 65%. So much had already been spent on the programme that it seemed sensible to continue development so that the US Air Force would acquire eventually a smaller but high quality force of interceptors. Engine intake modifications, and eradication of some of the bugs from engine and avionics, made it possible for the first deliveries of aircraft with an initial operational capability to be made to the 498th Fighter Interceptor Squadron at Geiger AFB, Washington, in October 1959. Production of 277 F-106As and 63 F-106B two-seat combat trainers (which retained full combat capability), ended in December 1960. Improved F-106C, F-106D and F-106X variants were also projected, but none were built.

Late production F-106As differed in equipment from those which entered service in 1959, which meant that modification programmes to bring all aircraft to a common standard were running concurrently with the production of new aircraft. This was but the tip of the iceberg, for the need to retain the F-106s in front-line service with Aerospace Defense Command (ADC) has meant the updating programmes have been almost continuous since that time. These have included the installation of ejection seats operable in supersonic flight, the provision of flight refuelling capability and of drop tanks suitable for supersonic operations; improved radar, automatic flight control and DC power

system under the MEISR (Minimum Essential Improvement in System Reliability) programme; introduction of an M-61 20-mm multi-barrel gun, lead-computing gunsight, clear cockpit canopy, and radar homing and warning (RHAW) system under ADC's Six-shooter programme; and the installation of a Hughes solid-state digital computer.

In early 1979, ADC still retained six squadrons of F-106 aircraft to defend the United States from conventional attack, these being supported by five F-106, three F-101 and two F-4 squadrons flown by the Air National Guard. During 1978, one of the ANG's F-106 squadrons was replaced by the second F-4 squadron.

Current events show that the USAF did well to persevere in its efforts to get the F-106 into service in 1959, believing in its capability sufficiently to accept and make the best possible use of some 35% of the number planned originally. It is now twenty years since that decision, and the F-106s are still in the front-line of the nation's defence: they are likely to remain there until the early 1980s when sufficient advanced fighter/interceptors will become available to take over this role.

Type: supersonic all-weather interceptor

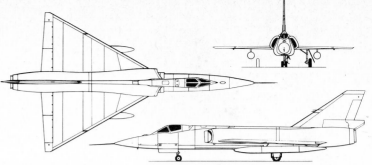

Convair F-106A Delta Dart

Powerplant: one 24,500-lb (11113-kg) reheat Pratt & Whitney J75-P-17 turbojet
Performance: maximum speed Mach 2.3 or 1,519 mph (2445 km/h) at 36,000 ft (10970 m); combat radius with external fuel tanks 729 miles (1173 km)
Weights: empty 23,646 lb (10726 kg); maximum take-off (F-106A, area interceptor mission) 38,700 lb (17554 kg)
Dimensions: span 38 ft 3½ in (11.67 m); length 70 ft 8¾ in (21.56 m); height 20 ft 3¼ in (6.18 m); wing area 631.3 sq ft 58.65 m²)

Armament: one Douglas AIR-2A Genie or AIR-2B Super Genie rocket, and four Hughes AIM-4F or AIM-4G Super Falcon air-to-air missiles carried in internal weapons bay; many aircraft have also one 20-mm gun
Operators: US Air Force

General Dynamics (Convair) F-106A Delta Dart of the 159th Fighter Interceptor Squadron, Florida National Air Guard.

The General Dynamics F-106A Delta Dart is another willing old bird soldiering on through lack of a replacement; this one is operating from the Air Defense Weapons Center at Tyndall AFB. By 1979 it was intended that the F-15 should help in this role.

General Dynamics F-111/FB-111

It needs no more than a glance at the current inventory of the Soviet air force to see how one country, at least, has moved heavily in favour of variable-geometry or 'swing-wing' aircraft in the past 10 to 15 years. For the nation that first put this principle into practice in a production aircraft, however, the progress from prototype to successful service warplane made a far from happy story. The major advantages offered by a variable-geometry aircraft are a high supersonic performance with the wings swept back; economical subsonic cruising speed with them fully spread; a long operational or ferry range; and relatively short take-off and landing runs at very high weights. So, when the US Air Force's Tactical Air Command was seeking a strike aircraft to replace the Republic F-105 Thunderchief, as outlined in its SOR (Specific Operational Requirement) 183 of 14 June 1960, it was very interested in the results of experiments with variable-geometry wing configurations that had recently been conducted by NASA's Langley Research Center at Hampton, Virginia. The US Navy, at the same time, was looking for a new fleet air defence fighter to succeed the McDonnell Douglas F-4 Phantom, and eventually the Department of Defense decreed that the two requirements should be combined in a single programme known as TFX, or Tactical Fighter, Experimental.

The Defense Secretary, Robert McNamara, stuck to this decision despite strong objections from both services, and his department rejected all six designs originally submitted in late 1961. However, a design from Defense, and a joint offering by General Dynamics and Grumman, were considered worthy of study

contracts. At three subsequent 'paper' evaluation conferences, after successive refinements of the two designs, the Boeing contender appeared to be a clear favourite and was almost universally recommended for adoption. To McNamara, however, it was technologically too advanced and lacked the commonality between the air force and navy versions that he believed was essential. He therefore overruled his advisers, and on 24 November 1962 a development contract for 23 aircraft was awarded to General Dynamics. Of these, 18 were to be basic tactical F-111As for the USAF and five were F-111Bs, developed primarily by Grumman for the US Navy.

The F-111B began to run into trouble almost immediately; despite a long and intensive flight development programme the type was eventually cancelled in July 1968. The aircraft had consistently proved overweight, quite unable to meet the performance required of it, and only seven examples were completed: the five development machines, plus two of the 231 production F-111Bs which the US Navy had planned to order.

The F-111A, on which all subsequent models were based, had an almost equally unhappy early history after its first flight on 21 December 1964, but eventually it was cleared for service and deliveries of 141 production examples began in October 1967, to the 474th Tactical Fighter Wing at Nellis AFB, Nevada. In spring 1968 the 428th Tactical Fighter Squadron took six F-111As to Thailand for operational trials over Vietnam — and lost three of them in four weeks. Groundings and modifications followed, and when 48 more F-111As were sent to Vietnam in 1972-73,

they flew over 4,000 combat sorties in seven months for the loss of only six aircraft. One of the modifications was to the engine air inlet geometry; the next 94 aircraft were built with an enlarged inlet (to suit more powerful engines which were not fitted) and designated F-111E.

Meanwhile, the designation F-111C had been applied to 24 aircraft ordered by the Royal Australian Air Force in 1963, but as a result of extensive modifications and escalating costs the delivery of these did not begin until 1973. They have the increased-span wings of the FB-111A and a strengthened landing gear. Another export order was placed in 1966 when the Royal Air Force ordered 50 F-111Ks, but these were cancelled two years later and the two that were almost complete became YF-111As for the USAF, the rest becoming FB-111As.

The third production tactical version for the USAF (96 were built) was the F-111D, which combined a slightly more powerful engine with the modified inlets of the E model. It also introduced 'Mk II' avionics, which included an AN/APQ-30 attack radar, a digital (instead of analogue) computer, AN/APN-189 Doppler navigation equipment, and head-up displays for both crew members; several other installations were improved versions of the 'Mk I' systems in the F-111A and E. These avionics had great potential, but proved extremely costly and troublesome.

The fourth and last tactical production version, the F-111F, has been described as 'the aircraft that the F-111 should have been from the beginning'. It has a much more powerful TF30 engine, with which it first flew in May

1973, and 'Mk IIB' avionics which, while more advanced than those in the A and E, are less complex than those in the F-111D. In this form the F-111 finally emerged as the superb combat aeroplane that it was planned to be, with excellent range, efficiency and reliability in the worst possible weather. Unfortunately, by the time that it was ready for production, costs had risen so much that the USAF could only buy 94 aircraft. The F-111E wing is based at RAF Upper Heyford, and the F-111F wing at RAF Lakenheath, both in England.

However, the combined force of Ds and Fs make the total look rather more respectable, and the Tactical Air Command will improve its overall effectiveness still further if, as seems likely, it is allowed the 40 examples it wants of the electronic countermeasures EF-111A. These would be converted from existing F-111As, and would replace the present EB-66 versions of the Douglas Destroyer for the task of suppressing hostile radars. Two prototypes have been converted by Grumman (first flight 10 March 1977), and have already demonstrated their capabilities. They have ALQ-99E noise jammer equipment inside a canoe-shaped radome under the weapons bay, with the receiver and antennae for the system in a large fin-tip pod. The installation is the same as that of the Grumman EA-6B Prowler, but without the extra two crew.

The other major basic version, serving with the Strategic Air Command, is the FB-111A. This has, in effect, the F-111D fuselage and intakes, the larger wings of the F-111B/C, strengthened landing gear, and yet another variant of the TF30 engine. For the strategic role, the avionics are related to the Mk IIB fit.

One of the first General Dynamics F-111A swing-wing attack aircraft, flying in the loiter mode with wings at 16° sweep. Violent Congressional arguments centred around the decision to procure this slightly disappointing initial version in quantity; the final F-111F is a vast improvement but only 106 could be afforded.

Potentially important, the EF-111A electronic-warfare platform packages the ALQ-99 tac-jammer system of the Navy EA-6B Prowler into an F-111 airframe without the two extra crew members. There have been funding problems, but batches for inventory service are expected to become operational in 1980.

As an alternative to bombs the FB-111A can be equipped with six Boeing AGM-69A SRAMs (short-range attack missiles), two carried internally. Seventy-six FB-111As were built (instead of the 210 planned), and these equip two 30-aircraft wings.

Type: two-seat all-weather attack aircraft (F-111), electronic warfare aircraft (EF-111) and strategic bomber (FB-111)

Powerplant: two Pratt & Whitney TF30 afterburning turbofans: TF30-P-3s of 18,500-lb (8390-kg) static thrust in A and C; TF30-P-9s of 19,600-lb (8890-kg) static thrust in D and E; TF30-P-100s of 25,100-lb (11385-kg) static thrust in F; TF30-P-7s of 20,350-lb (9230-kg) static thrust in FB-111

Performance: maximum speed (clean) at 35,000 ft (10670 m) and above, Mach 2.2 (1,450 mph/2335 km/h); maximum speed (clean) at low level Mach 1.2 (800 mph/1287 km/h); range with internal and external fuel (A and C) 3,165 miles (5093 km), (F) more than 2,925 miles (4707 km), (EF) 2,416 miles (3889 km); service ceiling (clean) (A) 51,000 ft (15550 m), (F) 60,000 ft (18300 m), (EF) 50,000 ft (15250 m)

Weights: empty (A) 46,172 lb (20943 kg), (C) 47,300 lb (21455 kg), (D and E) about 49,000 lb (22226 kg), (F) 47,175 lb (21398 kg), (FB) about 50,000 lb (22680 kg), (EF) 53,600 lb (24313 kg); maximum take-off (A) 91,500 lb (41504 kg), (C) 114,300 lb (51846 kg), (D and E) 99,000 lb (44906 kg), (F) 100,000 lb (45359 kg), (FB) 119,000 lb (53977 kg), (EF) 87,800 lb (39825 kg)

Dimensions: span fully spread (A, D, E and F) 63 ft 0 in (19.20 m), (C and FB) 70 ft 0 in (21.34 m); span fully swept (A, D, E and F) 31 ft 11½ in (9.74 m), (C and FB) 33 ft 11 in (10.34 m); length 73 ft 6 in (22.40 m), (EF) 77 ft 0 in (23.47 m); height 17 ft 1½ in (5.22 m), (EF) 20 ft 0 in (6.10 m); wing area fully spread (A, D, E and F) 525 sq ft (48.77 m²), (C and FB) 550 sq ft (51.10 m²); wing area fully swept (A, D, E and F) 657.3 sq ft (61.07 m²)

Armament: (F) two 750-lb (341-kg) B-43 bombs, or one 20-mm M61 multi-barrel cannon and one B-43 bomb, in internal weapons bay; three underwing hardpoints on each outer wing panel, the inner four pivoting to keep stores aligned as wings sweep, the outer two non-pivoting and jettisonable. All six wing points 'wet', for carriage of drop-tanks instead of weapons; maximum ordnance load (E) 29,000 lb (13154 kg), (FB) 37,500 lb (17010 kg) as fifty 750-lb (341-kg) bombs, two in internal bay and 48 on wing pylons

Operators: Australia, USAF

In front view the F-111 looks odd, with giant tyres on levered landing gear able to cushion the loads of "no flare" landings, and the rotating gloves on the fixed inner-wing leading edges turned to an acute negative angle of attack. Side-by-side seating is unusual in a supersonic combat aircraft (the rightseater's canopy is open in this view). Prominent are four tandem triplets of 500 lb retarded bombs, each actually 527 lb.

The monster radome covers three radar antennas, the main scanner for the General Electric APQ-113 multi-mode radar and the two small aerials for the terrain-following radar (TFR), usually Texas Instruments APQ-110. To the rear is the cockpit capsule, capable of being bodily severed from the fuselage and shot out with crew, thereafter serving as a survival shelter or lifeboat, the control column taking on a new task as the water-baling handle.

The wings of all F-111 versions can swing from 16° to the exceptionally high angle of 72°30' (most swing-wing aircraft are limited to about 68°). This drawing shows both limits, and the unique and questionable closeness of wing and stabilizer (tailplane) at the maximum-sweep position. The wings of two production versions, the FB-111A and F-111C, are longer; the tips are aligned with those of the stabilizer.

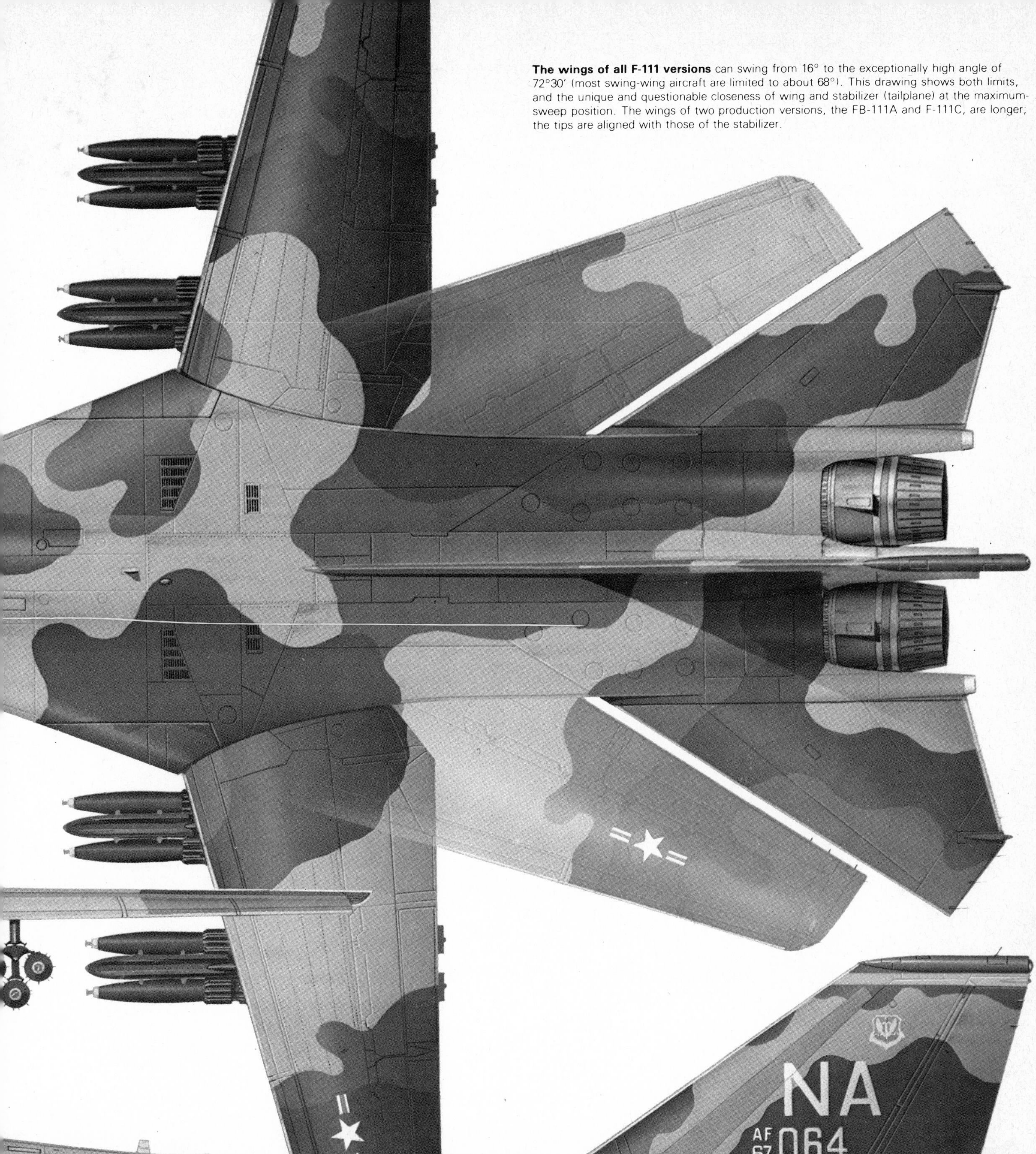

NA

AF
67 064

These drawings show an aircraft from the final production block of F-111As, the original model with low-thrust engines and small-area inlets. It is shown with weapon-bay doors open, though the bay usually carries items other than weapons and in a few aircraft houses the M61 gun. Countermeasure pods, such as the ALQ-119, are carried immediately to the rear of the main gears on ventral pylons which are unavailable for other loads.

Grumman A-6 Intruder

During the Korean War the US services flew more attack missions than any other type, in the case of the US Navy and US Marine Corps mostly with elderly piston-engined aircraft. What they learned during this conflict convinced them of the need for a specially-designed jet attack aircraft that could operate effectively in the worst weather. In 1957 eight companies submitted 11 designs in a US Navy competition for a new long-range, low-level tactical strike aircraft. Grumman's G-128, selected on the last day of the year, was to fulfil that requirement admirably, becoming a major combat type in the later war in South-East Asia, and leading to a family of later versions.

Eight development A-6As (originally designated A2F-1) were ordered in March 1959, a full-scale mockup was completed and accepted some six months later, and the first flight was made on 19 April 1960. The jet-pipes of its two 8,500-lb (3856-kg) static thrust Pratt & Whitney J52-P-6 engines were designed to swivel downwards, to provide an additional component of lift during take-off, but this feature was omitted from production aircraft, which instead have jet-pipes with a permanent slight downward deflection. The first production A-6As were delivered to US Navy Attack Squadron VA-42 in February 1963, and by the end of the following year deliveries had reached 83, to VA-65, VA-75 and VA-85 of the US Navy and VMA(AW)-242 of the US Marine Corps. First unit to fly on combat duties in Vietnam was VA-75, whose A-6As began operating from the USS *Independence* in March 1965, and from then onwards Intruders of various models became heavily involved in the fighting in South-East Asia. Their DIANE (Digital Integrated Attack Navigation Equipment) gave them a first-class operating ability and efficiency in the worst of the humid, stormy weather offered by the local climate, and with a maximum ordnance load of more than 17,000 lb (7711 kg) they were a potent addition to the US arsenal in South-East Asia.

Production of the basic A-6A ran until December 1969 and totalled 482 aircraft, plus another 21 built as EA-6As, retaining a partial strike capability but developed primarily to provide ECM (electronic countermeasures) support for the A-6As in Vietnam and to act as elint (electronic intelligence) gatherers. The first EA-6A was flown in 1963, and six A-6As were also converted to EA-6A configuration. A more sophisticated electronic warfare version, the EA-6B, is described separately.

The next three variants of the Intruder were also produced by the conversion of existing A-6As. First of these (19 converted) was the A-6B, issued to one USN squadron and differing from the initial model primarily in its ability to carry the US Navy's AGM-78 Standard ARM (anti-radiation missile) instead of the AGM-12B Bullpup. For identifying and acquiring targets not discernible by the aircraft's standard radar, Grumman then modified 12 other A-6As into A-6Cs, giving them an improved capability for night attack by installing FLIR (forward-looking infra-red) and low light level TV equipment in a turret under the fuselage. A prototype conversion of an A-6A to KA-6D in-flight refuelling tanker was flown on 23 May 1966, and production contracts for the tanker version were placed. These were subsequently cancelled, but 62 A-6As were instead converted to KA-6D configuration, equipped with Tacan (tactical air navigation) instrumentation and mounting a hose-reel unit in the rear fuselage to refuel other A-6s under the 'buddy' system. The KA-6D is also able to operate as a day bomber, or as an air/sea rescue control aircraft, and since the withdrawal of the EKA-3B from seagoing duty has been the standard carrier-based tanker.

On 27 February 1970, Grumman flew the first example of the A-6E, an advanced, upgraded development of the A-6A, which the A-6E succeeded in production. Procurement of nearly 350 of this version is planned for USN and USMC squadrons, of which some 120 are newly-built and about 230 are converted from A-6As. The basis of the A-6E, which retains upgraded forms of the airframe and powerplant of the earlier models, is a new avionics fit, founded on the addition of a Norden AN/APQ-148 multi-mode navigation/attack radar, an IBM/Fairchild AN/ASQ-133 computerized navigation/attack system, Conrac armament control unit, and an RCA video-tape recorder for assessing the damage caused during a strike mission. The Norden radar provides ground mapping, terrain avoidance/clearance, and target identification/tracking/rangefinding modes, with cockpit displays for both the pilot and navigator/bombardier, who sit side by side in the well-forward cockpit. It replaces the two older radars of the A-6A.

Following the first flight of a test aircraft on 22 March 1974, all US Navy and US Marine Corps Intruders are to be progressively updated still further under a programme known as TRAM (Target Recognition Attack Multisensor). To the A-6E-standard Intruder, this adds a Hughes turreted electro-optical package of FLIR and laser detection equipment, integrated with the Norden radar; adds CAINS (Carrier Airborne Inertial Navigation System) to the existing navigation equipment; provides the capability for automatic landings on carrier decks; and incorporates provisions for the carriage and delivery of automatic-homing and laser-guided air-to-surface weapons. The first US Navy squadron to be equipped with the A-6E/TRAM version was VA-165, which was deployed aboard the USS *Constellation* in 1977.

Including training squadrons, the Intruder equipped some 20 US Navy and US Marine Corps squadrons in the late 1970s, and it is expected that eventually all aircraft will be brought up to the A-6E standard. The title of 'miniature B-52' (bestowed by the North Vietnamese and Viet Cong) is well earned, for the Intruder's maximum weapon load, all carried externally, represents about 30 per cent of its maximum land take-off weight, and can be made up of a greater variety of weapons, nuclear or conventional, than any previous US naval attack aircraft. With its truly all-weather operating ability, plus a highly sophisticated set of avionics for navigation and pin-point precision bombing by day or night, it is certain to maintain a highly important contribution to US naval air power on land or at sea for many years to come.

Type: two-seat carrier or shore-based attack aircraft

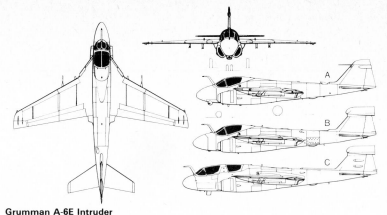

Grumman A-6E Intruder
(side views of A: A-6E; B: EA-6A; C: EA-6B Prowler)

Powerplant: two 9,300-lb (4218-kg) static thrust Pratt & Whitney J52-P-8A or -8B turbojets
Performance: maximum speed at sea level (A-6A, clean) 685 mph (1102 km/h), (A-6E, clean) 648 mph (1043 km/h); maximum speed at high altitude (A-6A, clean) 625 mph (1006 km/h); range with full weapon load (A-6E) 1,924 miles (3096 km); ferry range with maximum internal and external fuel (A-6E) 2,723 miles (4382 km); maximum rate of climb at sea level (A-6E, clean) 9,200 ft (2804 m) per minute; service ceiling (A-6A) 41,660 ft (12700 m), (A-6E, clean) 47,500 ft (14480 m)
Weights: empty (A-6A) 25,684 lb (11650 kg), (EA-6A) 27,769 lb (12596 kg), (A-6E) 25,740 lb (11675 kg); maximum take-off (A-6E, catapult) 58,600 lb (26580 kg), (A-6E, field) 60,400 lb (27397 kg)
Dimensions: span 53 ft 0 in (16.15 m); span folded 25 ft 4 in (7.72 m); length 54 ft 9 in (16.69 m); height 16 ft 2 in (4.93 m); wing area 528.9 sq ft (49.1 m²)
Armament: one underfuselage and four underwing attachments for maximum external load of 15,000 lb (6804 kg) in A-6A, or 18,000 lb (8165 kg) in A-6E; wide variety of nuclear or conventional weapons, typical loads ranging from thirty 500-lb (227-kg) bombs, in clusters of six, to three 2,000-lb (907-kg) bombs plus two 250-gallon (1135-litre) drop-tanks; air-launched missiles can include Bullpup (A-6A), Standard ARM (A-6B) and Harpoon (A-6E)
Operators: US Marine Corps, US Navy

Grumman's KA-6D Intruder is the standard seagoing tanker of the 13 US Navy Carrier Air Wings. Distinguished chiefly by its hose-reel under the rear fuselage, it can transfer over 21,000 lb (9526 kg) of fuel; alternatively it can fly day attack or control missions.

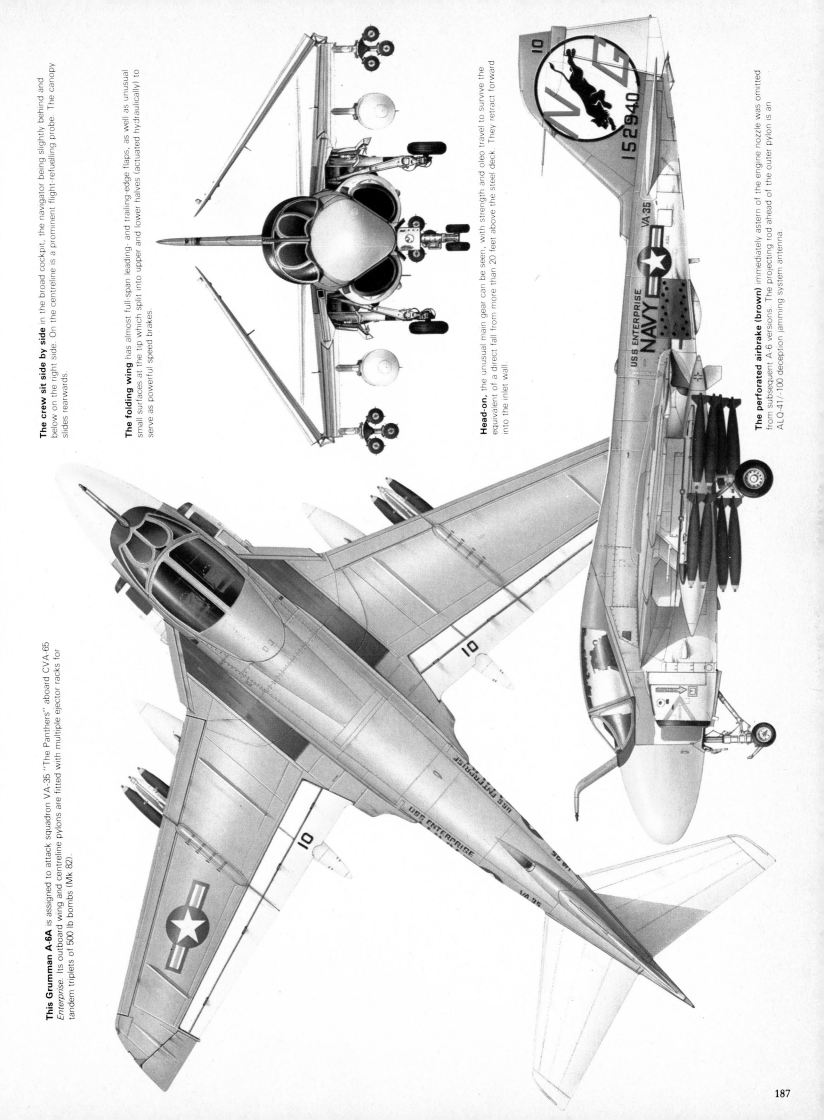

The crew sit side by side in the broad cockpit, the navigator being slightly behind and below on the right side. On the centreline is a prominent flight-refuelling probe. The canopy slides rearwards.

The folding wing has almost full-span leading- and trailing-edge flaps, as well as unusual small surfaces at the tip which split into upper and lower halves (actuated hydraulically) to serve as powerful speed brakes.

Head-on, the unusual main gear can be seen, with strength and oleo travel to survive the equivalent of a direct fall from more than 20 feet above the steel deck. They retract forward into the inlet wall.

This Grumman A-6A is assigned to attack squadron VA-35 ''The Panthers'' aboard CVA-65 *Enterprise*. Its outboard wing and centreline pylons are fitted with multiple ejector racks for tandem triplets of 500 lb bombs (Mk 82).

The perforated airbrake (brown) immediately astern of the engine nozzle was omitted from subsequent A-6 versions. The projecting rod ahead of the outer pylon is an ALQ-41/-100 deception jamming system antenna.

Grumman EA-6B Prowler

A US Navy requirement for a carrier-based strike aircraft resulted, in 1956, in a number of submissions to satisfy the specification. The submissions were no easy task to finalise, for whilst the US Navy was seeking a subsonic aircraft with long range and/or endurance, it was not really the aeroplane but what it contained that mattered. Experience gained in Korea had shown that the real need was for a strike aircraft that could fly at tree-top height to slip beneath the curtain of enemy radar, and then have the capability to find and attack any target by day or night in all weather conditions.

Grumman's G-128 submission was chosen for development from 11 proposals, and this materialised as the A-6A, which first flew in prototype form on 19 April 1960. When it entered service on 1 February 1963, it was the world's first all-weather day/night attack aircraft with the capability of detecting and identifying tactical and strategic targets under zero-visibility conditions, and against which it could launch conventional or nuclear weapons.

This very advanced aircraft did not come cheaply, for the ability to get to a target in any weather is not provided by the airframe, but rather by the very sophisticated electronics which it carries, and the avionics to make such performance possible can cost perhaps two or three times as much as the aircraft. Neither is it an ultimate weapon, for from the moment that an aircraft like this is deployed, the enemy is working to overcome the temporary operational lead the new system provides. Defensively speaking, this can mean more advanced and powerful radar systems, and quick-reaction surface-to-air missiles with homing capability.

To offset such defence, there has been extensive development of electronics countermeasures (ECM) aircraft able to mislead or suppress enemy radars, and as an interim ECM escort aircraft for A-6 Intruders a special EA-6A version was developed and first flown as a prototype in 1963. Retaining some strike capability, this is primarily equipped for the ECM role, with more than 30 different aerials to detect, locate, classify and jam the radiations from enemy radar systems. A total of 27 EA-6As were procured for the US Marine Corps pending development of an even more specialized variant for this role.

Thus, Grumman's EA-6B Prowler has been evolved to satisfy this requirement, an advanced version of the EA-6A which has been completely redesigned to carry the extra avionics necessary for it to fulfil this demanding role. Externally it looks little different from the basic A-6A, but it has a nose section which has been extended by 4 ft 6 in (1.37 m), and a distinctive fin pod housing highly sensitive surveillance receivers. The major changes are internal and these include accommodation for two additional crew members, reinforced wings and strengthened landing gear to match higher gross weight and extended fatigue life, reinforced underfuselage structure, greater fuel capacity, and more powerful J52-P-408 engines.

The Prowler's advanced ECM is based upon the ALQ-99 tactical noise jamming system, and up to 10 jamming transmitters can be carried. Jammers are packaged into up to five external pods, each with electrical power provided by a turbogenerator on the nose. A central computer processes sensor and receiver information, enabling detection, identification, direction finding and jamming to be initiated automatically, or with manual assistance from two back-seat crew.

It is expected that a total of 77 or 90 of the aircraft will be acquired to equip at least 12 squadrons. The first production aircraft was delivered in January 1971, and production was continuing in 1979. Improved jamming capability for in-service and future-production aircraft will result from the introduction of ICAP (Increased Capability) modifications, and aircraft so modified have been returned to service since 1978.

Type: four-seat carrier or land-based advanced ECM aircraft
Powerplant: two 11,200-lb (5080-kg) Pratt & Whitney J52-P-408 turbojets
Performance: (no external jammers) maximum speed at sea level 651 mph (1048 km), cruising speed at optimum altitude 481 mph (774 km/h), combat range with maximum external fuel 2,399 miles (3861 km), range (with maximum payload, 5% reserves plus 20 minutes at sea level) 1,099 miles (1769 km); (with five tactical jamming pods) maximum speed 623 mph (1003 km/h), cruising speed at optimum altitude 481 mph (774 km/h), ferry range 2,022 miles (3254 km)
Weights: empty 32,162 lb (14588 kg); stand-off jamming configuration take-off 54,461 lb (24703 kg); ferry range configuration take-off 60,610 lb (27492 kg); maximum take-off 65,000 lb (29484 kg)
Dimensions: span 53 ft 0 in (16.15 m); span (wings folded) 25 ft 4 in (7.72 m); length 59 ft 5 in (18.11 m); height 16 ft 2 in (4.93 m); wing area 528.9 sq ft (49.13 m²)
Armament: none
Operators: US Marine Corps

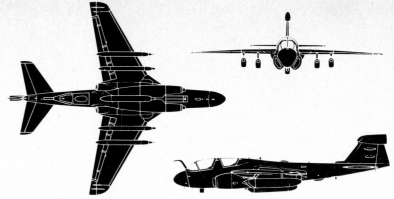

Grumman EA-6B Prowler

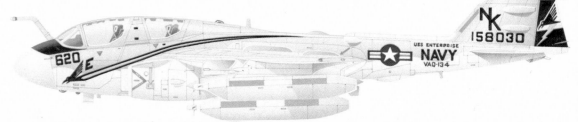

Electronic warfare is the role of the Grumman EA-6B Prowler. This example is from VAQ-134, US Navy, operating from the USS Enterprise.

Grumman EA-6B Prowlers of US Navy carrier squadron VAQ-129 represent a high point in seagoing air technology. Their ALQ-99 ECM system costs more than the rest of the aircraft and is managed by two backseat operators. Five jammer pods can be added.

Grumman C-2A Greyhound

The rapid delivery of high-priority personnel, urgently needed stores and mail to the US carrier fleet at sea was obviously one which could be carried out effectively by aircraft. Thus, carrier on-board delivery (COD) aircraft have for many years been considered an essential component of US naval aviation, and special derivatives of several types have been evolved to meet this requirement.

One of the first aircraft to be re-configured for this purpose was the Grumman C-1 Trader, evolved from the S-2 Tracker ASW aircraft. Provided with a new fuselage, these have accommodation for nine passengers, and first entered service with the US Navy in 1955. They were designated originally TF-1 and more than 80 were built.

The increasing usage of these COD aircraft made it desirable in the early 1960s to investigate the procurement of an aircraft with much greater capacity. Grumman had won a design competition in 1957 to build for the US Navy an airborne early-warning (AEW) aircraft, one which would be able to operate from carriers at sea to extend their 'eyes' beyond the limits imposed by a sea level vantage point. The resulting Grumman E-2 Hawkeye had long-range radar 'eyes' among its equipment, requiring a fairly large airframe to contain advanced avionics and crew so that it could effectively carry out this task.

With the Hawkeye operating successfully from and to aircraft carriers at sea, it was logical that the US Navy should look favourably on a COD version of this aircraft when it was proposed by Grumman in 1962. Three C-2A prototypes were ordered (one for static testing), and the first of these made its initial flight on 18 November 1964, being accepted by the US Navy in the following month.

A total of 25 of these aircraft were built for COD service, being generally similar to the E-2 except for deletion of the large over-fuselage radome and the provision of a new, higher-capacity fuselage. This, in addition to being wider and deeper, has an aft-loading cargo door which forms the undersurface of the upswept rear fuselage, and includes an integral loading ramp.

In addition to these changes, the tail looks very different. The large radome of the Hawkeye creates complex airflow patterns, resulting in a large tail unit with a tailplane which has 11° of dihedral and inward-canted fins and rudders. That of the Greyhound has no dihedral, with the result that the fins and rudders are vertical. The hydraulically-

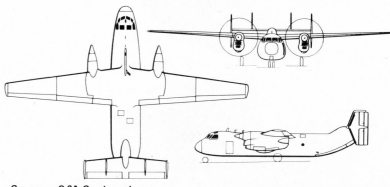

Grumman C-2A Greyhound

retractable tricycle landing gear is generally similar, except that the nose unit has been strengthened for operations at higher gross weight. Total fuel capacity has been increased considerably, the two main wing tanks with their combined total of 1,824 US gallons (6905 litres) capable of being supplemented by two external tanks on the fuselage sides to add 900 US gallons (3407 litres) and two 1,000 US gallon (3786 litre) long-range tanks in the cabin to give a combined total of 4,724 US gallons (17883 litres). Beech or Douglas buddy refuelling packs can be carried instead of the fuselage side tanks, and there is provision for a flight-refuelling probe.

Accommodation of the Greyhound also differs considerably, the cargo compartment floor being strengthened to cater for heavier loads, and provided with flush tracks for the attachment of cargo tie-down fittings. In addition to the carriage of alternative palletized loads, 39 troops, or 20 stretchers and four nursing staff,

can be accommodated.

In 1979, the C-2A remains the standard US Navy COD transport. A COD version of the Lockheed S-3A Viking has failed to win US Navy acceptance, and studies for a C-2A replacement are proceeding.

Type: naval COD transport aircraft
Powerplant: two 4,050-shp (3020-kW) Allison T56-A-8/-8A turboprops
Performance: maximum speed at optimum altitude 352 mph (566 km/h); range at average cruising speed of 297 mph (478 km/h) at 27,300 ft (8320 m) 1,650 miles (2655 km)
Weights: empty 31,154 lb (14131 kg); maximum take-off 54,830 lb (24870 kg)
Dimensions: span 80 ft 7 in (24.56 m); length 56 ft 8 in (17.27 m); height 15 ft 11 in (4.85 m); wing area 700.0 sq ft (65.03 m²)
Armament: none
Operators: US Navy

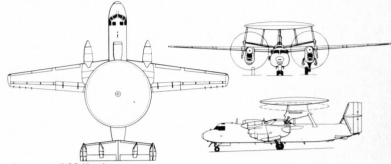

The Grumman C-2A Greyhound is a vital but lesser-known type in the US Navy's inventory. These COD (carrier on-board delivery) transports are the lifeline between the Fleet and shore, and can make cat-takeoffs and arrested landings with 39 passengers.

Grumman E-2 Hawkeye

The original concept of AEW (airborne early warning) was developed during World War II, when it was realised that an airborne surveillance radar could overcome the range limitations imposed by the curvature of the Earth on such detectors on land or on board ship. Early attempts to provide such an 'eye in the sky' were not particularly successful, but over the next three decades both the equipment and the AEW concept have developed to a considerable extent.

One company associated with AEW since its earliest days is Grumman, which claims with some justification that its E-2 Hawkeye was the first, as well as remaining the only, aircraft in service today that was designed from the outset as an AEW/tactical airborne command and control aircraft. Following a lineage that began with the TBF-3W Avenger, and continued with the AF-2W Guardian and the E-1B Tracer, the Hawkeye was the winner of a US Navy competition for a radar-carrying aircraft that would form part of an overall Naval Tactical Data System, the requirement for which was issued in 1956. The radar operator in the TBF-3W was quickly overwhelmed by the number of targets which he had to track on the face of the radar scope with a waxed pencil; the AF-2W and E-1B added video relays, so that the radar picture was on several scopes at a ground site or on board a parent aircraft carrier, but a high density of targets could still overshadow any number of assigned manual operators. In any case, manual operation restricted the number of tracks and interceptions the operators could handle.

What was needed was an aircraft of sufficient size to carry not only the radar but also digital computers which could detect targets automatically, select the best available means of interception, and generally keep a task force commander fully informed at all times of the disposition of friendly or hostile ships and aircraft in his area. Automation was the key: the operators had to be free of all routine activities in order to give their full attention to the tactical situation.

Grumman won the competition on 5 March 1957 with a design for a twin-turboprop aircraft carrying a crew of five (two pilots, radar operator, air control officer and combat information centre officer) and mounting a General Electric AN/APS-96 surveillance radar in a 24-ft (7.32 m) discus-shaped revolving radome on a pylon above the fuselage. To even out the airflow disturbed by this enormous excrescence, a wide-span dihedral tailplane was fitted, bearing four fins and twin rudders. Known originally as the W2F-1, the first prototype made its initial flight on 21 October 1960, powered by two Allison T56-A-8 turboprops. This was an aerodynamic prototype only: the full electronics systems were installed in the second Hawkeye, which made its maiden flight on 19 April 1961. In 1962 the designation was changed to E-2A, and the first of 62 examples of this version (including prototypes) was delivered to Squadron VAW-11 on 19 January 1964. Detachments of VAW-11 were assigned to various carriers in the Pacific

Fleet, the Atlantic Fleet receiving detachments of Hawkeyes from the second squadron, VAW-12, in 1965. Deliveries were completed in the spring of 1967.

Beginning in 1969 (a prototype conversion was flown on 20 February), all operational E-2As were modified to E-2B standard, differing mainly in having an improved computer, the microelectric Litton L-304, and provision for flight-refuelling. Over the next five years these were re-delivered to equip Squadrons VAW-113, -116, -125 and -126. They normally operate in teams of two or more aircraft, flying at altitudes of 30,000 ft (9150 m) to provide long-range early warning of potential threats from hostile surface vessels and fast-flying aircraft. The dorsal radome rotates once every 10 seconds while the Hawkeye is in flight; to facilitate stowage when on board its parent carrier, the telescopic pylon can be lowered 2 ft (0.61 m).

In the summer of 1971, following the first flight of a prototype on 20 January, Grumman began production of a new Hawkeye model, the E-2C. This heralded a significant improvement in operational capability, with a major upgrading of the principal avionics, and entered service in November 1973 with VAW-123. The initial order by the US Navy was for 11 E-2Cs, since increased to 47, including some TE-2C trainers. The E-2C has also been ordered by Israel (four) and Japan; the US Navy plans to acquire a further 36 by the end of 1984.

Major ingredients of the E-2C are the APS-125 radar, APA-171 radar and IFF (identification, friend or foe) antennae in the dorsal radome; an air-data computer in addition to

Grumman E-2C Hawkeye

the L-304; plus a carrier aircraft inertial navigation system (CAINS). The APS-125, developed jointly by General Electric and Grumman, is capable of detecting airborne targets in a 'land clutter' environment, at ranges up to 230 miles (370 km). It provides automatic detection and tracking over land or water, with simultaneous surveillance (though displayed separately if required) of air as well as surface traffic. The on-board data processing gear can track, automatically and simultaneously, more than 250 targets; it can also control over 30 airborne interceptions. As an addition to its radar system, the E-2C carries a passive detection system (PDS) which automatically detects the presence, direction and identity of any traffic in a 'high signal density' environment. The PDS can alert its operators to the presence of electronic emitters at distances up to almost 500 miles (805 km), establish the location of the emission, and identify the threat. At the same time, the E-2C's own radar system incorporates ECCM (electronic countermeasures) to help ensure its

own continued effectiveness in the face of hostile jamming. Despite the additional avionics, the E-2C still carries only a five-man crew.

The C-2 Greyhound is a transport derivative of the E-2.

Type: airborne early-warning and control aircraft
Powerplant: two 4,910-shp (3661-kW) Allison T56-A-425 turboprops
Performance: maximum speed 374 mph (602 km/h); cruising speed for maximum range 310 mph (499 km/h); patrol endurance 6 hours; maximum ferry range 1,605 miles (2583 km); service ceiling 30,800 ft (9390 m)
Weights: empty 37,678 lb (17090 kg); internal fuel load 12,400 lb (5624 kg); maximum take-off 51,569 lb (23391 kg)
Dimensions: span 80 ft 7 in (24.56 m); length 57 ft 7 in (17.55 m); height 18 ft 4 in (5.59 m); wing area 700.0 sq ft (65.03 m²)
Armament: none
Operators: Israel, Japan (on order), US Navy

Portrait of a Hawkeye, claimed by Grumman to be more cost/effective in most scenarios than the Boeing E-3A Sentry. All versions — E-2A, E-2B, E-2C (illustrated) and TE-2C — are closely similar externally but differ greatly in electronics and systems.

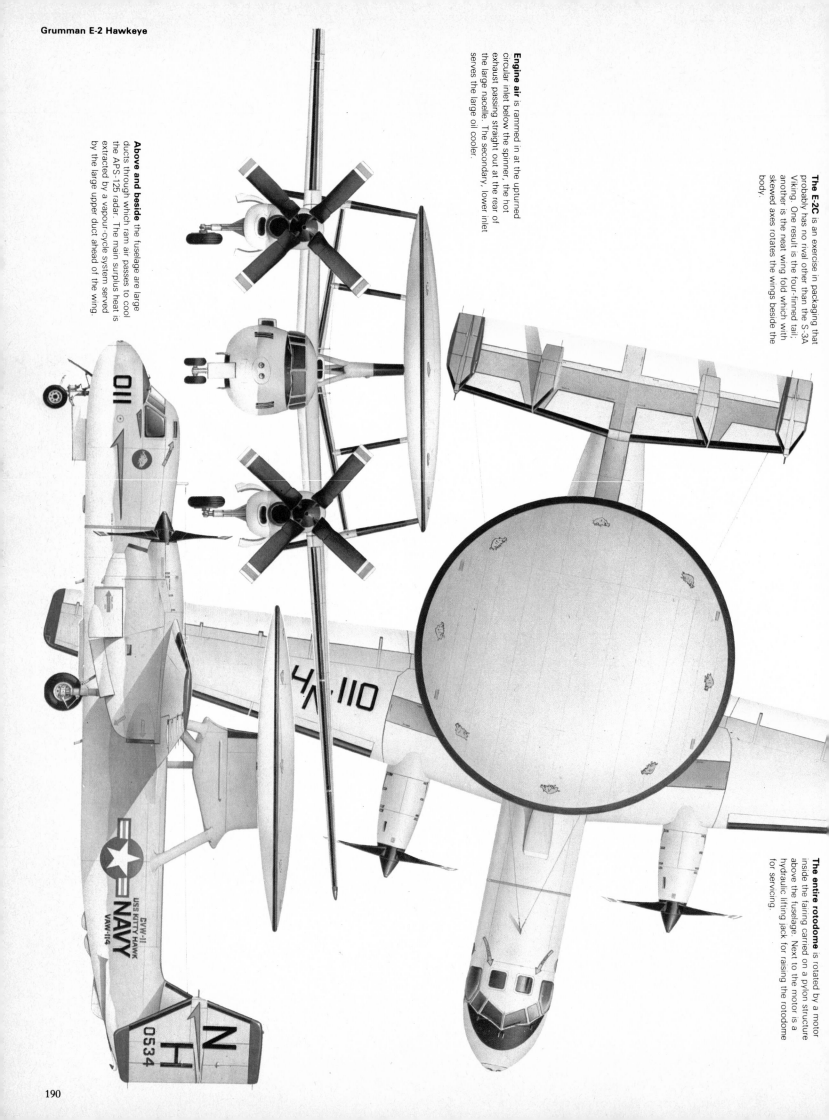

The E-2C is an exercise in packaging that probably has no rival other than the S-3A Viking. One result is the four-finned tail; another is the neat wing fold which with skewed axes rotates the wings beside the body.

Engine air is rammed in at the upturned circular inlet below the spinner, the hot exhaust passing straight out at the rear of the large nacelle. The secondary, lower inlet serves the large oil cooler.

Above and beside the fuselage are large ducts through which ram air passes to cool the APS-125 radar. The main surplus heat is extracted by a vapour-cycle system served by the large upper duct ahead of the wing.

The entire rotodome is rotated by a motor inside the fairing carried on a pylon structure above the fuselage. Next to the motor is a hydraulic lifting jack for raising the rotodome for servicing.

011

4—110

NAVY
CVW-11
USS KITTY HAWK
VAW-114

N
H
0534

Grumman F-14 Tomcat

Unquestionably one of the finest warplanes in the world today, the Grumman F-14 Tomcat is fulfilling the role that, in the mid-1960s, it was hoped would be undertaken by the naval version of the General Dynamics F-111 variable-geometry strike aircraft. By the time that the F-111B programme was eventually cancelled in the summer of 1968, Grumman (also responsible for developing the F-111B version) had already reached an advanced stage in designing a new swing-wing carrier fighter, following a US Navy competition in which four other designs were in contention. From these, the US Navy selected Grumman's G-303 proposal in January 1969 to fill this major gap in its front-line inventory. In the following May a detailed mock-up was completed for US Navy evaluation, and in the same year an initial contract was placed for six development aircraft (later increased to 12). The first of these made its maiden flight on 21 December 1970, but nine days later, on only its second flight, this prototype was coming in to land when the complete hydraulic system failed, resulting in the loss of the aircraft, although both crew members were able to eject to safety. Despite this setback, however, the development programme proceeded without further serious mishap, the second aircraft making its first flight on 24 May 1971.

Designed to later technology than the pioneering F-111, the F-14 was designed from the outset for operation from USN fleet carriers, and is unique among variable-geometry aircraft so far designed in having, in

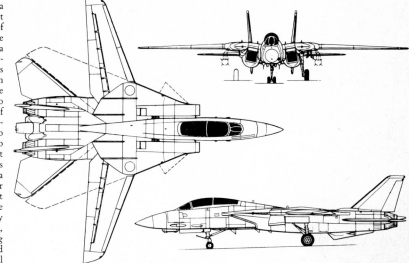

The Grumman F-14A Tomcat, one of the US Navy's most powerful warplanes.

addition to variable-sweep outer wings, a smaller moveable foreplane (Grumman calls it a glove vane) inside the leading-edge root of the fixed inboard portion of each wing (the glove box). The outer wings pivot to give a leading-edge sweep of 68° when in the fully-aft position, reducing to 20° when the wings are in the fully-forward position. As the main wings pivot backwards, the glove vanes can be extended forward into the airstream to regulate any alterations in the centre of pressure and prevent the aircraft from pitching. By deploying its variable-sweep wings to the best advantage, the Tomcat is thus able to vary its flying configuration to the different aerodynamic and performance requirements needed when taking off from, or landing on, a carrier, taking part in an air-to-air dogfight, or carrying out a low-level attack mission against a surface target. In air-to-air fighting, the variation of wing sweep can be undertaken by the in-built automatic flight control system, relieving the pilot of this task and enabling him to concentrate on out-manoeuvring and shooting down his opponent. With additional control surfaces which include full-span

continued

Grumman F-14A Tomcat

This Grumman F-14A Tomcat is probably operating out of NAS Miramar in southern California, but appears to have tail insignia of USS *Constellation*. It is fully armed with four long-range Phoenix, two medium-range Sparrows and two close-range AIM-9s.

A menacing F-14A Tomcat armed with all three clases of air-to-air missile — Phoenix, Sparrow and Sidewinder — may be that illustrated in another photograph in a tight turn. The unit is almost certainly VF-211, a famed US Navy fighter outfit.

trailing-edge flaps, spoilers, leading-edge slats and all-moving horizontal tail surfaces, the Tomcat is a superbly manoeuvrable warplane; longitudinal stability is assured by the use of twin outward-canted fins and rudders. It is also very strong structurally, many of the airframe components being manufactured of boron-epoxy or other composites, or titanium.

The primary role of the Tomcat is to provide long-range air defence of the US fleet, and the two-man crew (pilot and naval flight officer) are seated in tandem on zero-zero ejection seats under a single long, upward-opening canopy, which affords a fine all-round view. An excellent weapons platform, the Tomcat's armament for the air defence role includes air-to-air missiles such as the medium-range AIM-7 Sparrow and close-range AIM-9 Sidewinder (the latter being mounted on launchers attached beneath the glove box on each side), and for unexpected dogfights a Gatling-type multi-barrel cannon. Primary interception armament, however, consists of six Hughes Phoenix air-to-air missiles, four of which are mounted on pallets which fit into the semi-recessed Sparrow positions under the aircraft's belly, with an additional Phoenix underneath each wing glove box alongside the underwing Sidewinders. The Phoenix is

currently the longest-range air-to-air missile in use anywhere in the world (more than 124 miles/200 km), and the Tomcat is the only combat aircraft equipped to carry it. In conjunction with the extremely powerful Hughes AWG-9 radar mounted in the nose, it provides the Tomcat with the unique ability to detect and attack an airborne target while it is still 100 miles (160 km) away. The F-14A also has a secondary capability in the low-level attack role, in which event the air-to-air missiles can be replaced by up to 14,500 lb (6577 kg) of externally-mounted bombs or other weapons.

The initial F-14A model of the Tomcat has been in service with the US Navy since October 1972, when the first deliveries were made to squadrons VF-1 and VF-2. It was an aircraft of the latter unit which, in March 1974, flew the first operational Tomcat sortie from the carrier USS *Enterprise*. Subsequent acceptance of the fighter into regular USN service was both enthusiastic and without major incident until 1975, when a series of powerplant, structural and systems problems were encountered. However, these have been largely resolved, one resultant modification being an increase in available thrust with the afterburners on. (Shortage of power and other pro-

Grumman F-14A Tomcat cutaway drawing key

1 Anti-collision beacons
2 DECM/RCVR antenna
3 Honeycomb rudders
4 Honeycomb-sandwich fin skin
5 Rear navigation light
6 Fuel dump line
7 Exhaust nozzles
8 Engine rear mount/ stabilizer mounting spectacle beam
9 Tailplane actuator
10 Tailplane pivot mounting
11 Boron-epoxy stabilizer
12 Honeycomb trailing edge
13 APR-25 receiving antenna
14 Wing position (fully swept)
15 Ventral fin
16 Engine oil-cooler air intake
17 UHF-band blade antenna
18 Aft fuselage structure
19 Multi-bolt fin attachments
20 Arresting hook damper
21 Tailplane control linkage
22 Airbrake (upper surface)
23 Revised (reduced) aft fuselage planform (aircraft No 87 onwards)
24 Fin spigot mounting
25 Vent tank
26 Aft fuselage integral tanks
27 Finroot fairing
28 Port tailplane

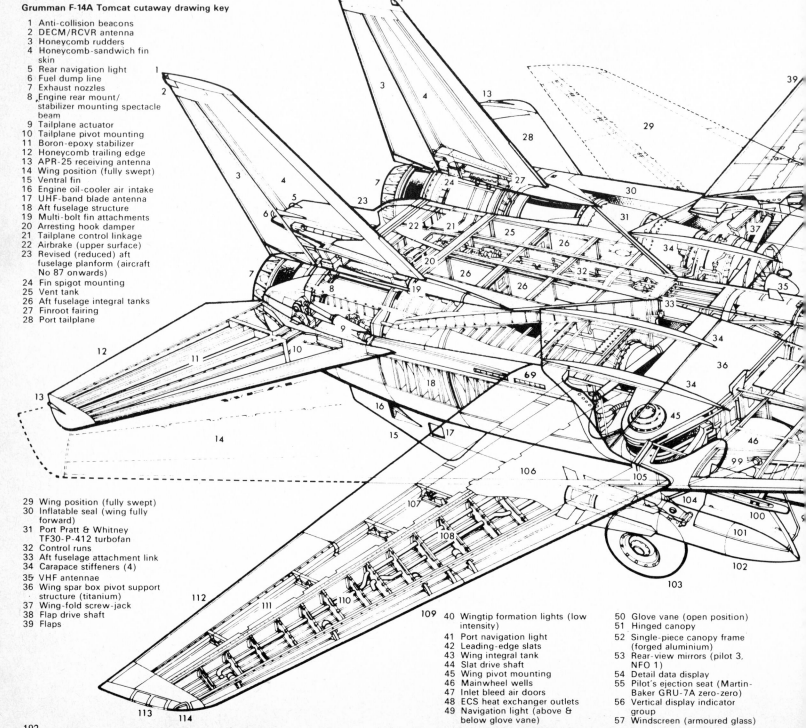

29 Wing position (fully swept)
30 Inflatable seal (wing fully forward)
31 Port Pratt & Whitney TF30-P-412 turbofan
32 Control runs
33 Aft fuselage attachment link
34 Carapace stiffeners (4)
35 VHF antennae
36 Wing spar box pivot support structure (titanium)
37 Wing-fold screw-jack
38 Flap drive shaft
39 Flaps

40 Wingtip formation lights (low intensity)
41 Port navigation light
42 Leading-edge slats
43 Wing integral tank
44 Slat drive shaft
45 Wing pivot mounting
46 Mainwheel wells
47 Inlet bleed air doors
48 ECS heat exchanger outlets
49 Navigation light (above & below glove vane)

50 Glove vane (open position)
51 Hinged canopy
52 Single-piece canopy frame (forged aluminium)
53 Rear-view mirrors (pilot 3, NFO 1)
54 Detail data display
55 Pilot's ejection seat (Martin-Baker GRU-7A zero-zero)
56 Vertical display indicator group
57 Windscreen (armoured glass)

pulsion problems have threatened replacement with different engines, however.) The US Navy plans to acquire some 390 Tomcats, about 80 per cent of which had been delivered by the beginning of 1979 to equip more than a dozen US Navy and US Marine Corps squadrons. At that time the Naval Air Training Center at Patuxent River, Maryland, was developing a tactical air reconnaissance pod system (TARPS) to extend further the versatility of the F-14A, seen as the interim replacement for the Rockwell RA-5C Vigilante.

Eight F-14As were exported to the Imperial Iranian Air Force in the mid-1970s, but cost escalation curtailed the development of the proposed F-14B and F-14C models for the US Navy. Two prototypes of the former were produced by refitting F-14As with 28,090-lb (12741-kg) static thrust Pratt & Whitney F401-P-400 turbofans, the first of these making its initial flight on 12 September 1973. Development of the F-14C, with the same engines plus new avionics and weapons, was also halted.

continued

This Grumman F-14A Tomcat, probably recovering aboard the first nuclear carrier, CVA-65 *Enterprise,* is painted in an unusual scheme which embraces the radome, which most units do not paint. The ship's fore/aft axis is shown by the direction of the wake.

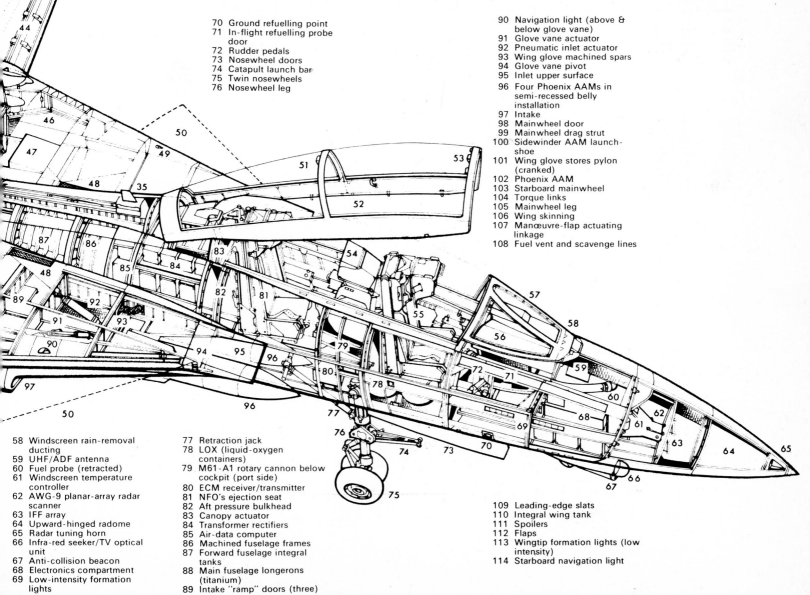

70 Ground refuelling point
71 In-flight refuelling probe door
72 Rudder pedals
73 Nosewheel doors
74 Catapult launch bar
75 Twin nosewheels
76 Nosewheel leg

90 Navigation light (above & below glove vane)
91 Glove vane actuator
92 Pneumatic inlet actuator
93 Wing glove machined spars
94 Glove vane pivot
95 Inlet upper surface
96 Four Phoenix AAMs in semi-recessed belly installation
97 Intake
98 Mainwheel door
99 Mainwheel drag strut
100 Sidewinder AAM launch-shoe
101 Wing glove stores pylon (cranked)
102 Phoenix AAM
103 Starboard mainwheel
104 Torque links
105 Mainwheel leg
106 Wing skinning
107 Manœuvre-flap actuating linkage
108 Fuel vent and scavenge lines

58 Windscreen rain-removal ducting
59 UHF/ADF antenna
60 Fuel probe (retracted)
61 Windscreen temperature controller
62 AWG-9 planar-array radar scanner
63 IFF array
64 Upward-hinged radome
65 Radar tuning horn
66 Infra-red seeker/TV optical unit
67 Anti-collision beacon
68 Electronics compartment
69 Low-intensity formation lights

77 Retraction jack
78 LOX (liquid-oxygen containers)
79 M61-A1 rotary cannon below cockpit (port side)
80 ECM receiver/transmitter
81 NFO's ejection seat
82 Aft pressure bulkhead
83 Canopy actuator
84 Transformer rectifiers
85 Air-data computer
86 Machined fuselage frames
87 Forward fuselage integral tanks
88 Main fuselage longerons (titanium)
89 Intake "ramp" doors (three)

109 Leading-edge slats
110 Integral wing tank
111 Spoilers
112 Flaps
113 Wingtip formation lights (low intensity)
114 Starboard navigation light

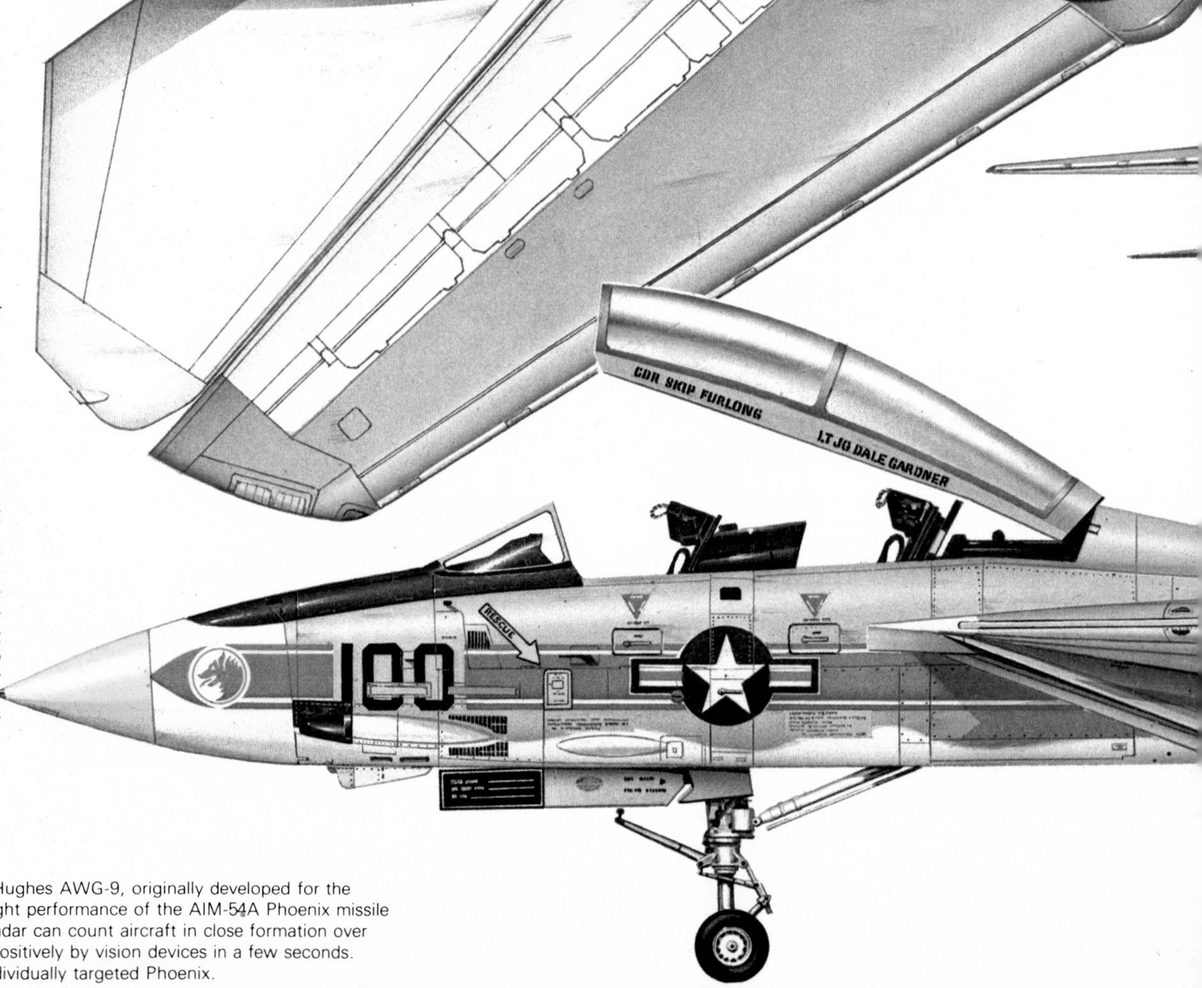

Type: tandem two-seat carrier-borne multi-role fighter

Powerplant: two 20,900-lb (9480-kg) static thrust Pratt & Whitney TF30-P-412A after-burning turbofans

Performance: maximum speed at altitude Mach 2.34 or 1,564 mph (2517 km/h); maximum speed at sea level Mach 1.2 or 910 mph (1470 km/h); range (interceptor, with external fuel) about 2,000 miles (3200 km); service ceiling over 56,000 ft (17070 m); maximum rate of climb at sea level (normal gross weight) over 30,000 ft (9145 m) per minute

Weights: empty 39,310 lb (17830 kg); normal take-off 58,539 lb (26553 kg); take-off with four Sparrows 58,904 lb (26718 kg); take-off with six Phoenix 69,790 lb (31656 kg); maximum take-off 74,348 lb (33724 kg)

Dimensions: span unswept 64 ft 1½ in (19.45 m); span swept 38 ft 2½ in (11.65 m); length 61 ft 2 in (18.89 m); height 16 ft 0 in (4.88 m); wing area 565.0 sq ft (52.49 m²)

Armament: one General Electric M61A-1 20-mm multi-barrel Vulcan cannon in forward fuselage with 675 rounds; four AIM-7 Sparrow or AIM-54 Phoenix air-to-air missiles under fuselage; two AIM-9 Sidewinder air-to-air missiles, or one Sidewinder plus one Phoenix or Sparrow, under each wing glove box; tactical reconnaissance pod containing cameras and electro-optical sensors; or up to 14,500 lb (6577 kg) of Mk 82/83/84 bombs or other weapons

Operators: Iran, US Marine Corps, US Navy

The radar in the nose of the F-14A is the Hughes AWG-9, originally developed for the defunct F-111B to match the tremendous flight performance of the AIM-54A Phoenix missile and transferred to the F-14 in 1968-9. This radar can count aircraft in close formation over 100 miles away, and they can be identified positively by vision devices in a few seconds. They can then be hit automatically by six individually targeted Phoenix.

The plan view shows the great distance between the pivots of the swing wings, unlike most early variable-sweep projects. The pivots are joined by the structural heart of the aircraft, a wing box made of electron-beam welded titanium (in the earlier F-111, this was riveted and bolted from D6AC steel, causing problems). The large fixed "glove" inboard of each pivot houses a swinging vane extended by an actuator at high angles of attack.

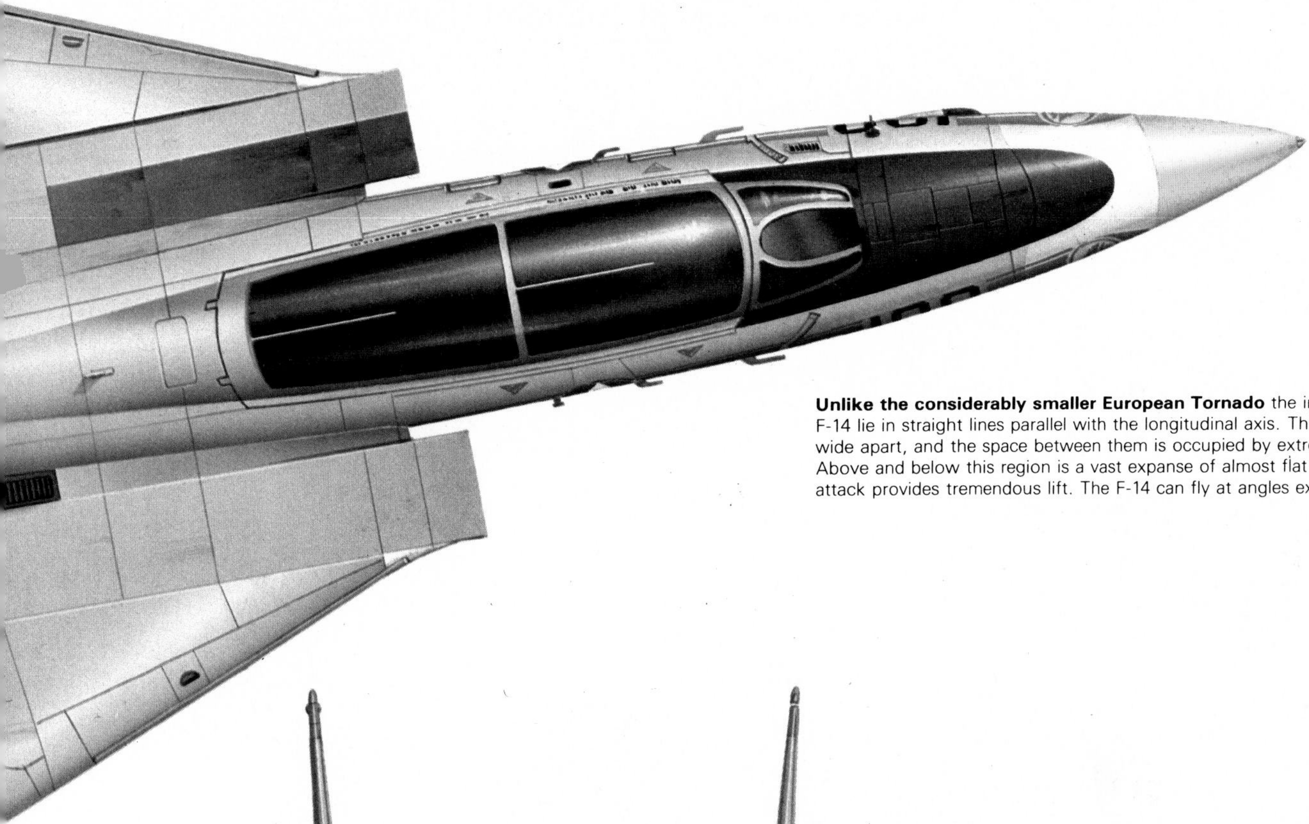

Unlike the considerably smaller European Tornado the inlet ducts and engines of the F-14 lie in straight lines parallel with the longitudinal axis. This means that the engines are wide apart, and the space between them is occupied by extremely large integral fuel tanks. Above and below this region is a vast expanse of almost flat skin which at high angles of attack provides tremendous lift. The F-14 can fly at angles exceeding 60°!

The F-14's swing wing, here seen in the maximum 68° position, is believed to be unique in being governed not only by the pilot but also by an automatic sweep programmer for peak flight performance and manoeuvrability in all flight regimes. In a close dogfight, the wings automatically pivot in and out continually, giving exceptional manoeuvrability. The F-14 was also one of the first aircraft with twin outward-canted vertical tails.

Grumman HU-16 Albatross

In the spring of 1931, a new entrant to the US aircraft industry was awarded a US Navy contract to build the prototype of a two-seat biplane fighter for operation from aircraft-carriers. The company was the Grumman Aircraft Engineering Corporation; the aircraft, when it entered service, was designated either FF-1 or SF-1, according to usage, the former denoting fighter, the latter scout. From that time until the present day, Grumman has been an important builder of naval aircraft of many types, and succeeding generations of naval pilots around the world have come to know the superb engineering and reliability of these Grumman aircraft.

Some two years after the award of that first contract, on 4 May 1933, Grumman flew the prototype of a general utility amphibian, the XJF-1, which became initially the JF-1 Duck when the first production aircraft were delivered in late 1934. This amphibian, the first of the US Navy's Grumman 'birds', was followed by the twin-engine monoplane JRF Goose in 1937, which, with the smaller Widgeon, served in World War II. A decade later, Grumman flew the prototype of the much larger Model G-64 amphibian.

Work started on the design of this aircraft in 1944, and apart from being almost twice as big as the Goose, it is a distinguished-looking boat-type amphibian with a conventional two-step hull. The cantilever monoplane wing is set high on the hull, and stabilizing floats are mounted about one-third span inboard from each wingtip. Underwing hardpoints just outboard of each engine can be used to carry drop tanks of different capacities, up to a maximum of 300 US gallons (1136 litres), as well as bombs or depth charges, and each of the floats can be used to contain 200 US gallons (757 litres). Standard fuel, comprising 675 US gallons (2555 litres) is contained in two wing centre-section tanks.

An interesting feature of the design includes the retractable tricycle landing gear, giving amphibious capability, and in some versions, a sprung ski beneath the hull and small skis beneath each of the stabilizing floats making it possible for the Albatross, as Grumman named the G-64, to operate onto and from ice surfaces. This enabled the company to advertise this aircraft as 'a unique triphibian'. Versions which were intended specifically for sea rescue operations have a 'barn' or 'Dutch'-type door on the left side of the fuselage, so that only the upper half need be opened in rough weather for the loading or unloading of stretchers. These rescue aircraft also carry three life-rafts: two in the cabin and one, inflatable automatically, housed in an upper hull compartment aft of the wing.

The prototype ordered by the US Navy for service as a utility aircraft had the designation XJR2F-1, and this flew for the first time on 24 October 1947. In service these became designated UF-1, and a modified version introduced in 1955 was UF-2. This latter aircraft had increased wing span, a cambered wing leading-edge, ailerons and tail surfaces of increased area, and more effective de-icing boots for all aerofoil leading edges. In the tri-service rationalisation of designations in 1962, these aircraft became UH-16C and HU-16D respectively. Winterized aircraft for antarctic service were UF-1Ls, later LU-16Cs, and five UF-1T dual-control trainers became TU-16Cs.

The USAF found the G-64 attractive for rescue operations, the majority of the 305 ordered serving with the MATS Air Rescue Service under the designation SA-16A. An improved version, equivalent to the US Navy's UF-2, entered service in 1957 as the SA-16B: in 1962 these became HU-16A and HU-16B respectively. HU-16E was the designation of Albatross aircraft operated by the US Coast Guard, and 10 supplied to Canada were CSR-110s. An anti-submarine version with nose radome, retractable MAD gear, ECM radome and searchlight was introduced in 1961, and this could carry a small number of depth charges. The versatile Albatross continues in service with several air forces and navies.

Type: utility and rescue amphibian
Powerplant: two 1,425-hp (1063-kW) Wright R-1820-76A/76-B Cyclone radial piston engines
Performance: maximum speed 236 mph (380 km/h) at sea level; cruising speed 150 mph (241 km/h); range with 1,275 US gallons (4826 litres) of fuel 2,700 miles (4345 km); maximum endurance 22 hours 54 minutes

Dimensions: (HU-16D) span 96 ft 8 in (29.46 m); length 61 ft 3 in (18.67 m); height 25 ft 10 in (7.87 m); wing area 1,035 sq ft (96.15 m²)
Armament: (ASW) depth charges
Operators: Argentina, Brazil, Canada, Chile, Indonesia, Italy, Japan, Philippines, Portugal, Spain, Taiwan, US Air National Guard, US Air Force, US Navy, US Coast Guard

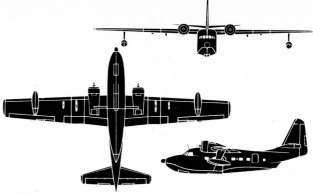

Grumman HU-16 Albatross

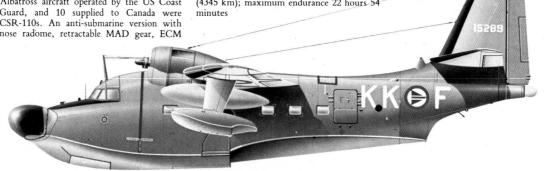

Royal Norwegian Air Force Grumman HU-16B Albatross. Skv 333 at Sola operated the type in 1968 before changing to Orions.

Grumman OV-1 Mohawk

In the mid-1950s, both the US Army and US Marine Corps drew up specifications for a battlefield surveillance aircraft. Their requirements were generally similar: to carry a variety of reconnaissance equipment, to have rough-field capability, and be able to operate on a STOL basis. It proved possible for both services to agree on a common design. Thus, in 1957 the US Navy, acting as programme manager for both the US Army and the US Marine Corps, ordered nine examples of Grumman's G-134 design for test and evaluation. These were designated initially YAO-1A, subsequently YOV-1A, and the first of these aircraft made its maiden flight on 14 April 1959.

Early evaluation left little doubt of the excellence of the design, but even before the prototype had made its first flight the US Marine Corps had withdrawn from the initial contract, and no examples of that service's OF-1s were built. Instead, the flight-test programme was speeded up, and before the end of 1959 the US Army had placed production contracts for OV-1A and OV-1B aircraft, the basic OV-1 acquiring the name Mohawk.

First turboprop-powered aircraft to enter service with the US Army, the OV-1 is comparatively slow but highly manoeuvrable, and to help offset its vulnerability as a result of its speed and role, has a well-armoured cockpit with a 0.25-in (0.64-cm) thick aluminium-alloy floor, flak curtains on both fore and aft bulkheads, and bullet-resistant windscreens. Although conventional in its basic configuration, detail design has produced an easily identified and unusual-looking aircraft. The midset monoplane wing is quite normal, but the two turboprop engines mounted high on each wing have their centrelines canted outward and upward. The tail unit, with three sets of fins and rudders, has considerable dihedral so that, while the centre fin is vertical, the end-plate fins are canted in. Moreover, because it is desirable to provide the two-man crew with the best possible downward view, the sides of the cockpit are deeply bulged. As a final dash of the eccentric, in the OV-1B version the side-looking airborne radar (SLAR) is housed in an 18-ft (5.49-m) glass-fibre container carried on pylons below the fuselage and offset to the right.

However, beautiful or not, the Mohawk was designed to carry out a tactical observation and battlefield surveillance role in direct support of army operations, a role which it soon demonstrated it could perform successfully. Normal deployment of Mohawk aircraft was four to each army division, and although these aircraft were capable of being armed, it was DoD policy from 1965 that US Army fixed-wing aircraft should not carry weapons, to avoid conflict and confusion with USAF close-support aircraft. However, like many other US aircraft, a number were deployed in Vietnam with underwing arms, a JOV-1A with four 500-lb (227-kg) capacity pylons having demonstrated suitability for the armed reconnaissance role.

The basic version is the OV-1A, equipped for day and night visual or photo reconnaissance, and provided with dual controls. The OV-1B which followed has increased wing span, SLAR and an internal camera with in-flight processor; the dual controls have been deleted. Next production version was the OV-1C, similar to late production version OV-1As but with the AN/AAS-24 infra-red (IR) surveillance system. Final version was the OV-1D with side loading doors to accept a pallet with SLAR, IR, or other sensors; in addition to production aircraft, more than 80 OV-1B/-1Cs were converted to OV-1D standard. The designations RV-1C and RV-1D apply respectively to OV-1C and OV-1D aircraft modified permanently for electronic-reconnaissance missions.

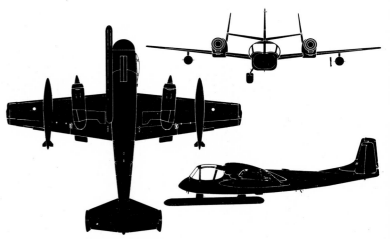

Grumman OV-1B Mohawk (with SLAR)

US Army Grumman OV-1B Mohawk of the 23rd Special Warfare Aviation Detachment.

Type: two-seat multi-sensor observation aircraft

Powerplant: (OV-1D) two 1,400-shp (1044-kW) Lycoming T53-L-701 turboprops

Performance: (OV-1D) maximum speed at maximum rated power (SLAR mission) 289 mph (465 km/h) at 10,000 ft (3050 m), (IR mission) 305 mph (491 km/h); maximum range with auxiliary fuel (SLAR mission) 944 miles (1519 km), (IR mission) 1,011 miles (1627 km); maximum endurance at 161 mph (259 km/h) at 15,000 ft (4570 m) on a SLAR mission 4 hours 20 minutes, on an IR mission 4 hours 32 minutes

Weights: (OV-1D) empty equipped 12,054 lb (5468 kg); normal take-off (SLAR mission) 15,741 lb (7140 kg), (IR mission) 15,544 lb (7051 kg); maximum take-off (SLAR mission) 18,109 lb (8214 kg), (IR mission) 17,912 lb (8125 kg)

Dimensions: span (OV-1A/-1C) 42 ft 0 in (12.80 m), (OV-1B/-1D) 48 ft 0 in (14.63 m); length 41 ft 0 in (12.50 m); height 12 ft 8 in (3.86 m); wing area (OV-1A/-1C) 330 sq ft (30.66 m²), (OV-1B/-1D) 360 sq ft (33.44 m²)

Armament: normally none, but bombs, rockets and Minigun pods have been carried on underwing pylons

Operators: Israel and US Army

The Grumman OV-1 Mohawk is a unique STOL platform for carrying sensors over land battlefields. This US Army OV-1D is burdened with APS-94 SLAR (side-looking airborne radar), tanks and bombs. Many have been converted to serve as EW/Elint aircraft.

Grumman S-2 Tracker/ E-1 Tracer/C-1 Trader

In the years immediately after World War II, the US Navy's carrier-based ASW effort was based upon the use of twin-aircraft hunter/ killer teams. Typical was the twinning of the Grumman Avenger, with TBM-3W or TBM-3W-2 radar-equipped search aircraft locating enemy submarines for the TBM-3S or TMB-3S-2 aircraft which made the attack with suitable anti-submarine weapons. There were clearly some snags to such a twin-aircraft attack: for example, malfunction of one meant that the second was virtually useless. Furthermore, the location problem was aggravated by the introduction into service of deeper-diving nuclear-powered submarines. A larger amount of more sophisticated avionics was needed for their detection, as well as for the launch and guidance of air-to-underwater weapons.

In the late 1940s the US Navy finalised its ideas on the kind of single hunter/killer aircraft which it needed to fulfil this role, and Grumman designed a fairly large twin-engine high-wing monoplane, designated G-89, to meet this requirement. The high-wing configuration maximized the cabin space to provide room for on-board equipment, and additional stowage space for expendable sonobuoys was provided in the rear of the engine nacelles. Other features included a large weapons bay, retractable search radar in the rear fuselage, MAD boom in a retractable fairing, searchlight beneath the starboard wing, plus folding wings and arrester hook for carrier operations.

On 30 June 1950 Grumman was awarded a contract to build for evaluation a single prototype of the G-89, the US Navy designation for this aircraft being XS2F-1, and this aircraft

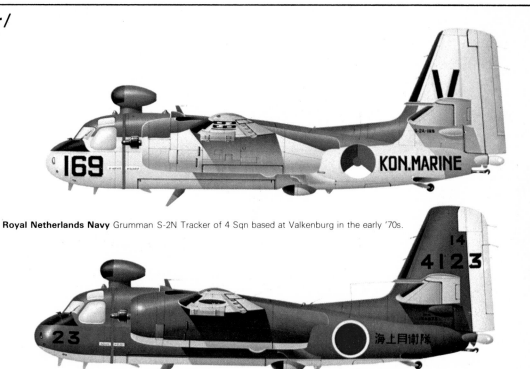

Royal Netherlands Navy Grumman S-2N Tracker of 4 Sqn based at Valkenburg in the early '70s.

Japanese Maritime Self-Defence Force S-2A Tracker.

flew for the first time on 4 December 1952. S2F Tracker, WF Tracer and TF Trader versions were to appear in due course, and under

continued

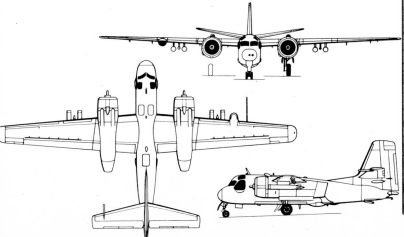

Grumman S-2 Tracker

The Grumman S-2 Tracker has for more than 25 years been an extremely useful shore-based ASW platform, although designed for carrier use by the US Navy, a duty taken over by the S-3A. A few S-2Es, much updated, remain with the US Naval Reserve.

the 1962 tri-service rationalisation of designations these became respectively S-2, E-1, and C-1 series aircraft. The S-2A, the first production version of the Tracker, began to enter service with the US Navy's Anti-Submarine Squadron VS-26 in February 1954. In addition to the 500-plus examples built for the US Navy, more than 100 S-2As were exported to friendly nations. A number of these aircraft were used in a training role under the designation TS-2A.

The designation S-2B applied to S-2A aircraft which had been modified to carry AQA-3 Jezebel passive long-range acoustic search equipment, working in conjunction with Julie active acoustic echo-ranging by explosive charge. S-2C was the designation of the next production version, which had an enlarged weapons bay with an offset extension on the left side, and these also had a larger tail to compensate for a higher gross weight. Many S-2B/B/C aircraft were converted subsequently for utility use, such as target towing and light transports, under the designations US-2A/B/C respectively. A small number of S-2Cs were also modified to serve in a photo-reconnaissance role under the designation RS-2C.

The second major production version was the S-2D, of which the initial example flew for the first time on 21 May 1959. This had a wing of increased span, still larger tail surfaces, plus greater fuel capacity and stowage for double the number of sonobuoys in each engine nacelle, for a combined total of 32. In addition, the forward fuselage was lengthened and widened to improve accommodation for the four-man crew. S-2Ds began to enter service in May 1961, and eventually equipped at least 15 US Navy squadrons. Those modified later to carry more advanced search equipment had the designation S-2E, and production of these ended in 1968 with a batch of 14 for the Royal Australian Navy. S-2F was the designation of S-2Bs retrofitted with the same advanced search equipment as that installed in the S-2Es. The de Havilland Aircraft of Canada company built 100 Trackers for the Royal Canadian Navy, the first 43 as CS2F-1s and the remainder with improved equipment as CS2F-2s.

Type: naval anti-submarine aircraft
Powerplant: two 1,525-hp (1137-kW) Wright R-1820-82WA Cyclone radial piston engines
Performance: (S-2E) maximum speed at sea level 265 mph (426 km/h); patrol speed 150 mph (241 km/h) at 1,500 ft (455 m); ferry range 1,300 miles (2092 km); endurance with maximum fuel (10% reserves) 9 hours.
Weights: (S-2E) empty 18,750 lb (8505 kg); maximum take-off 29,150 lb (13222 kg)
Dimensions: (S-2E) span 72 ft 7 in (22.12 m); length 43 ft 6 in (13.26 m); height 16 ft 7 in (5.05 m); wing area 496 sq ft (46.08 m²)
Armament: one Mk 47 or Mk 101 nuclear depth bomb or similar store in weapons bay, 60 echo-sounding depth charges in fuselage, 32 sonobuoys in engine nacelles, plus a variety of bombs, rockets or torpedoes on six underwing hardpoints
Operators: Argentina, Australia, Brazil, Canada, Italy, Japan, Netherlands, Taiwan, Thailand US Navy, Uruguay

JMSDF TS-2A Tracker.

US Navy S2F-1 Tracker of VS-21 in original midnight blue finish.

A trainer version of the Tracker, designated TS-2A, of US Navy Training Sqn VT-28.

Grumman S-2E Tracker of VS-21, operating from the USS Kearsage, CVSG-53.

Royal Thai Navy S-2A Tracker, one of about ten in service, and based at Bangkok.

Grumman TC-4 Gulfstream I

In the mid-1950s Grumman began the design of a twin-turboprop executive transport which was intended for a crew of two and 10–14 passengers in typical corporate versions. An alternative high-density layout could accommodate a maximum of 24 passengers. Because of its proven reliability in operation, the Rolls-Royce Dart turboprop was selected by Grumman, and two of these engines, driving Rotol four-blade constant-speed propellers, comprise the powerplant of this G-159 Gulfstream I aircraft. The overall layout is that of a conventional low-wing monoplane transport, with a retractable tricycle landing gear with twin wheels on each unit. The entire accommodation is pressurized by a system able to maintain a 5,500 ft (1675 m) cabin altitude up to

25,000 ft (7620 m), the baggage compartment also being pressurized. An auxiliary power unit (APU) is installed to provide electrical power and air-conditioning prior to main-engine starting. The prototype of the Gulfstream I flew for the first time on 14 August 1958, and FAA certification was awarded on 21 May 1959.

As early as 1962 the US Navy decided to acquire a small number of these aircraft for use as navigation trainers and transports, under the designation T-41A, and, later, TC-4B. Nothing came of these early attempts to procure the G-159, however, and it was not until there was an urgent requirement to expand the training capacity for bombardier/navigators to serve with Grumman A-6A In-

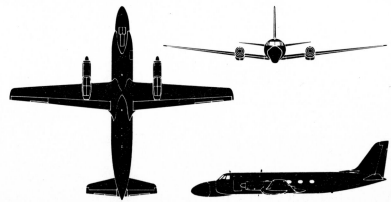

Grumman TC-4C Gulfstream I

truder Squadrons that a go-ahead was given to acquire nine aircraft under the designation TC-4C. These were readily distinguishable from other Gulfstreams by the addition of a bulbous nose radome to house the radar (at first the two sets of the A-6A, but later the new radar of the A-6E). Internally, the cabin was laid out with a replica of an A-6A cockpit to accommodate a student pilot and student

bombardier/navigator, an instructor's position, and four consoles to provide four more students with radar/computer readouts. The first of these TC-4Cs flew for the first time on 14 June 1967.

Prior to that, in the summer of 1963, the US Coast Guard had acquired two Gulfstream Is to serve as VIP transports, being allocated the service designation VC-4A.

Type: twin-engine bombardier/navigator trainer and VIP transport
Powerplant: (TC-4C) two 1,987-shp (1482-kW) Rolls-Royce Dart 529-8X turboprops
Performance: maximum cruising speed 348 mph (560 km/h) at 25,000 ft (7620 m); range with maximum fuel and 10% reserves 2,300 miles (3700 km)

Weight: (TC-4C) maximum take-off 36,000 lb (16329 kg)
Dimensions: span 78 ft 6 in (23.93 m); length 67 ft 11 in (20.70 m); height 22 ft 9 in (6.93 m); wing area 610.3 sq ft (56.70 m²)
Armament: none
Operators: US Coast Guard, US Navy

Grumman VC-11A Gulfstream II

In 1965 Grumman announced the intention to build a turbofan-powered executive transport with the name Gulfstream II, but although the name might suggest that this latter aircraft is simply a turbofan-powered version of the Gulfstream I, the two aircraft in fact have little in common. No prototype was built, and on 2 October 1966 the first production Gulfstream II aircraft made its initial flight. FAA certification was gained a year later, and the first production delivery was made in December 1967, since when well over 200 have been sold.

Grumman's satisfaction with the Rolls-Royce engines which powered the first Gulfstream led to the selection of two Spey turbofans pod-mounted on the rear fuselage. The cantilever low-set monoplane wings have a moderate sweepback of 25°, and all flight controls, including those of the T-tail, are hydraulically powered. The twin-wheel landing gears have modulating anti-skid units.

Typically, there is seating for 19 passengers

in the main cabin. The US Coast Guard acquired a single example as a VIP transport, this being operated under the designation VC-11A. Several armed forces have procured these aircraft for similar duties.

Type: executive transport
Powerplant: two 11,400-lb (5171-kg) thrust Rolls-Royce Spey 511-8 turbofans
Performance: maximum cruising speed 581 mph (935 km/h) at 25,000 ft (7620 m); NBAA VFR range with crew of three, passenger payload of 2,000 lb (907 kg), fuel amounting to 28,600 lb (12973 kg) and 30-minute reserves 4,123 miles (6635 km)
Weights: typical operating empty (no tip-tanks) 36,544 lb (16576 kg), (with tip-tanks) 37,186 lb (16867 kg); maximum take-off 65,500 lb (29710 kg)
Dimensions: span 68 ft 10 in (20.98 m); span (over tip-tanks) 71 ft 9 in (21.87 m); length 79 ft 11 in (24.36 m); height 24 ft 6 in (7.47 m); wing area 809.6 sq ft (75.21 m²)

Grumman VC-11A Gulfstream II

Armament: none
Operators: Cameroun, Gabon, Ivory Coast, Nigeria, US Coast Guard

Grumman TF-9T Cougar

In 1946 Grumman began the design of a carrier-based fighter for the US Navy, the initial XF9F-2 prototype making its first flight on 24 November 1947, and by May 1949 the first F9F-2 Panthers were entering service with Navy Squadron VF-51. The Panther was not only the first jet fighter to be designed and built by Grumman, but was also the US Navy's first jet fighter to be used in combat, being deployed in Korea in 1950.

Soon after the Panther entered service, Grumman began development of a swept-wing variant under a US Navy contract dated 2 March 1951, and the prototype XF9F-6 flew for the first time on 20 September 1951. Although the F9F portion of the designation was the same as that of the Panther, confirming that it was a variant of the original design, the new name of Cougar also confirmed that it was a rather different aeroplane.

The main difference, of course, lay in the wing and the changes necessitated by it. That of the Panther was a conventional straight wing with ailerons and trailing-edge flaps interconnected with hinged leading-edges; that

of the Cougar had sweep-back of 35°, spoilers replacing ailerons, larger flaps, leading-edge slats, and fences. A more powerful engine was also installed. In this form, F9F-6 Cougars entered service with VF-32 in November 1952.

They were followed by generally similar F9F-7s, F9F-8s with a longer fuselage and wing modifications, and the F9F-8T trainer with a still longer fuselage to accommodate pupil and instructor in tandem. In 1962 these last were redesignated TF-9J, many being flown operationally in Vietnam for various missions.

Type: carrier-based fighter
Powerplant: (TF-9J) one 7,200-lb (3266-kg) thrust Pratt & Whitney J48-P-8A turbojet
Performance: (TF-9J) maximum speed 705 mph (1135 km/h) at sea level; time to 40,000 ft (12190 m) 8 minutes 30 seconds; range 600 miles (966 km)
Weight: (TF-9J) maximum take-off 20,600 lb (9344 kg)
Dimensions: (TF-9J) span 34 ft 6 in

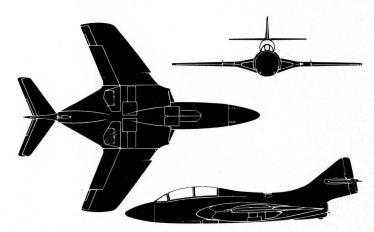

Grumman TF-9J Cougar

(10.52 m); length 44 ft 5 in (13.54 m); height 12 ft 3 in (3.73 m)
Armament: (TF-9J) two 20-mm cannon and up to 2,000 lb (907 kg) of weapons on under-

wing hardpoints
Operators: Argentina; formerly US Navy, US Marine Corps

Helio AU-24A Stallion

The unique STOL abilities of the Helio U-10 Courier came to be well accepted by military and civil users throughout the world during the early 1960s. However, it became clear that a somewhat larger version of the Super Courier, powered by a turboprop engine, would be attractive for a broader utility role.

The result was the HST-550 Stallion, and, when the prototype first flew on 5 June 1964, it was clearly a completely redesigned aircraft with only superficial resemblance to the Courier. Of all-metal construction, the HST-550 is powered by a Pratt & Whitney Aircraft of Canada PT6A-27 turboprop, and the cabin accommodates a pilot and up to 10 passengers. The rear cabin bulkhead is constructed to allow long loads to be extended into the rear fuselage when the aircraft is used in the freight configuration.

In August 1965 the aircraft was certificated, but few civil buyers were willing to pay the price of over $100,000. However, the USAF had formulated its 'Credible Chase' programme, calling for a multi-role STOL aircraft, and the Stallion was selected for a fly-off with the Fairchild-Hiller Peacemaker, 15 of each type being ordered in early 1970. The AU-24A, as it was designated, featured an in-

creased gross weight, hardpoints under wings and fuselage, and a cabin gun mounting. Its role was armed reconnaissance, close air support, forward air control (FAC) and general transport.

In the event, the Vietnam war had changed course before Credible Chase reached fruition. No further orders were placed, and the USAF transferred all but one of the AU-24As to the Khmer Air Force. How many survived is unknown, but three AU-24As did manage to escape to Thailand with refugees when the Khmer Rouge overthrew the American-backed Cambodian government.

Type: 11-seat STOL utility and COIN aircraft
Powerplant: one 680-shp (507-kW) Pratt & Whitney Aircraft of Canada PT6A-27 turboprop
Performance: maximum speed at 10,000 ft (3050 m) 216 mph (348 km/h); maximum cruising speed 206 mph (332 km/h); minimum-control speed (power on) 42 mph (68 km/h); maximum rate of climb 2,200 ft (671 m) per minute; service ceiling 25,000 ft (7620 m)
Weights: Empty 2,860 lb (1297 kg); maxi-

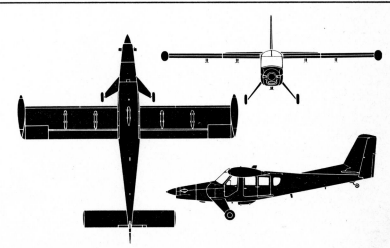

Helio AU-24A Stallion

mum take-off 5,100 lb (2313 kg)
Dimensions: span 41 ft 0 in (12.50 m); length 39 ft 7 in (12.07 m); height 9 ft 3 in (2.81 m); wing area 242 sq ft (22.5 m²)
Armament: one demountable M-197 20-mm cannon on fuselage doorframe fixture; two

hardpoints under each wing for stores including CBU-14A/A bomb dispensers, and one fuselage hardpoint for one 500-lb (227-kg) HE bomb
Operators: USAF, possibly Kampuchea

Helio U-10 Courier

The Helio U-10 Courier has its origins in the remarkable Koppen-Bollinger Helioplane of 1949. With full-span automatic leading-edge slats and dual-purpose ailerons, the Helioplane's slow flight performance soon attracted the US Army's interest, resulting in an evaluation order for one YL-24. The YL-24 was delivered in 1952 and was of mixed construction with a fabric-covered rear fuselage and powered by a 145-hp (108-kW) Continental C-145-4 engine. Despite the type's versatility, however, the US Army did not order L-24s, and Helio Aircraft tackled the commercial market with the all-metal H-391 Courier.

In 1961, the USAF ordered three H-395 Super Couriers for assessment and this led to an initial production order for L-28As for Strategic Air Command, followed by procurement on behalf of the Air National Guard and the US Army. The L-28A was later designated U-10A, and was joined by two further variants. The U-10B was a long-range version capable of missions in excess of nine hours duration, and the U-10D was an increased-weight aircraft with accommodation for a pilot and five passengers.

The Vietnam war saw the U-10 employed in a wide range of roles. It was ideal for clandestine operations, dropping agents into small jungle strips, and it was able to mount light weapons in its main door for support missions. U-10s used sky shouting equipment on propaganda sorties, and did forward air control and communications (FAC) work with the USAF and the 2nd Wing of the Royal Thai Air Force.

Exports of the Courier included two float-equipped machines for the *Fuerza Aerea del Peru* and two were used by the Guyana Defence Force for some time. After the end of the Vietnam war, the USAF U-10s were largely repatriated and many were sold on the US civil market, although a few still serve with Air National Guard units.

Type: six-seat STOL communications and utility aircraft
Powerplant: one 295-hp (220-kW) Lycoming GO-480-G1D6 six-cylinder horizontally-opposed piston engine
Performance: maximum speed at sea level 167 mph (269 km/h); maximum cruising speed at 75% power at 8,500 ft (2600 m) 165 mph (265 km/h); minimum power-on speed 30 mph (48 km/h); landing run 270 ft (82 m); rate of climb at sea level 1,150 ft (350 m) per minute; standard range (U-10A) 660 miles (1062 km)
Weights: empty 2,080 lbs (943 kg); maximum take-off 3,400 lb (1542 kg)
Dimensions: span 39 ft 0 in (11.89 m); length 31 ft 0 in (9.45 m); height 8 ft 10 in (2.69 m); wing area 231 sq ft (21.46 m2)
Armament: light arms mounted in main door opening as required
Operators: Guyana, Peru, Thailand, USAF, US Army

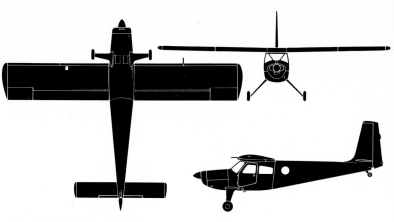

Helio U-10 (H-250) Super Courier

Heliopolis Gomhouria 2

The Heliopolis Gomhouria is an Egyptian-built version of the pre-war German Bücker Bü 181 Bestmann and was the first military aircraft to be produced in quantity in Egypt.

The Heliopolis aircraft factory was founded in 1950 as part of the Egyptian Military Factories Directorate; its initial production consisted of a batch of 60 Gomhourias for the Egyptian air force. This Mk 1 version was powered by a 105-hp (78-kW) Walter Minor engine, and was followed by the Continental-powered Mk 2.

Around 300 Gomhourias are reported to have been built, and export customers have included Jordan, Sudan and Saudi Arabia. About six Mk 2s remain in use in Algeria, while Egypt still has more than 100. The Egyptian air force's training academy at Bilbeis uses Gomhourias for initial student training; they then pass on to Yakovlev Yak-18s before moving to Aero L-29s for jet conversion.

Type: primary trainer
Powerplant: one 145-hp (108-kW) Continental C-145 piston engine
Performance: maximum speed at sea level 136 mph (220 km/h); cruising speed at sea level 124 mph (200 km/h); cruising speed at 6,500 ft (2000 m) 127 mph (205 km/h); rate of climb at sea level 810 ft (246 m) per minute; service ceiling 15,740 ft (4800 m); take-off to 50 ft (15 m) 1,149 ft (350 m); range 490 miles (788 km)
Weights: empty 1,333 lb (515 kg); loaded 1,826 lb (800 kg)
Dimensions: span 34 ft 9 in (10.6 m); length 25 ft 11 in (7.9 m); height 6 ft 9 in (2.05 m); wing area 145 sq ft (13.46 m2)
Operators: Algeria, Egypt, Jordan, Sudan

HFB 320 Hansa

West Germany entered the business-jet field when the first prototype HFB 320 Hansa flew on 21 April, 1964. Design had begun three years before at Hamburger Flugzeugbau's factory at Hamburg/Finkenwerder Airport. HFB was part of the North European group of aircraft manufacturers who were at that time licence-producing the Lockheed F-104G Starfighter and other projects; the Hansa was the company's first design.

The first prototype was lost in a crash during May 1965, but a second prototype had been flying since the previous October and the type was in production. The first production Hansa flew on 2 February, 1966, and an initial batch of 10 was laid down, with a similar number to follow. The first 15 Hansas had General Electric CJ610-1 engines, the following 20 the more powerful CJ610-5, and subsequent production the CJ610-9.

In addition to its executive role, the Hansa was offered for a wide variety of military duties including VIP transport, liaison, casualty evacuation, navigation training, radio and radar reconnaissance and light freighting.

Competition was extremely strong, and although the Hansa with the unusual swept-forward wing attracted some attention it did not attract many orders. A few went to civil operators in the USA and Italy; three were supplied to the RLS (*Rijksluchtvaartschool*) in the Netherlands for training and calibration work, but the biggest user, and the only military one, was the West German *Luftwaffe*, which accepted about 16 of approximately 40 Hansas built. The FBS (*Flugbereitschaftsstaffel*) operates six Hansas from Köln/Bonn Airport on VIP and support flights alongside Boeing 707s and Lockheed JetStars, while at Lechfeld the FVSt (*Flugvormeesungsstaffel*) uses two Hansas on calibration work and four others for electronic countermeasures and similar missions.

Type: twin-jet executive transport
Powerplant: two 3,100-lb (1406-kg) General Electric CJ610-9 turbojets
Performance: maximum cruising speed at 25,000 ft (7620 m) 513 mph (825 km/h); rate of climb at sea level 4,250 ft (1295 m) per minute; time to 25,000 ft (7600 m) 12 minutes; take-off run to 50 ft (15 m) 2,740 ft (835 m) at 17,640 lb (8000 kg); range 1,472 miles (2370 km) with 1,200 lb (545 kg) load and 45 minutes reserves; service ceiling 40,000 ft (12200 m)
Weights: empty (passenger version) 11,960 lb (5425 kg); empty (freighter version) 11,874 lb (5386 kg); maximum take-off 20,280 lb (9200 kg)
Dimensions: span 47 ft 6 in (14.49 m); length 54 ft 6 in (16.61 m); height 16 ft 2 in (4.94 m); wing area 324.4 sq ft)30.14 m2)
Operators: West Germany

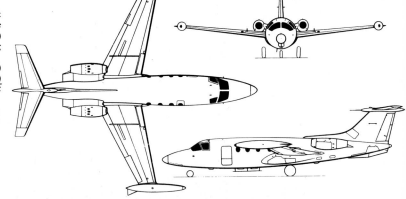

HFB 320 Hansa

The HFB 320 Hansa became a product of the giant MBB combine. Noted for its swept-forward wings (which thus pass behind the cabin) this neat business jet serves here in radar-equipped form as a *Luftwaffe* liaison/trainer; four more are due 1980–81.

Hiller OH-23 Raven

First flown as the Hiller UH-12A in 1950, this helicopter became the standard light observation machine for the US Army as the OH-23 Raven. It was the first helicopter approved by the US military for 1,000 hours of operation between major overhauls.

The commercial models UH-12A to 12D became, in military service, the OH-23A to 23D respectively, and the US Army received a total of 998 of these versions. The UH-12E was basically a three-seat dual-control version of the OH-23D intended for the civil market, but attracted military interest as the OH-23G. The OH-23F was the military version of the Model E4, a four-seat version featuring a 25-inch (63-cm) extension to the fuselage and various minor changes. This model had high-compression pistons which gave an equivalent of 340 hp (254 kW) from the 305-hp (228-kW) Lycoming VO-540 engine. Twenty-two OH-23Fs were used by the US Army in central and south America in 1962, transporting personnel engaged in the Inter-American Geodetic Survey. A US Army OH-23G set up six international helicopter speed records in October 1963; the service used several hundred OH-23Gs which eventually replaced the OH-23Ds.

Overseas customers for the various versions of the OH-23 included Argentina, Bolivia, Colombia, Chile, Cuba, Dominica, Guatemala, Guyana, Mexico, Morocco, the Netherlands, Paraguay, Switzerland, Thailand and Uruguay. The OH-23G was supplied to the Canadian army, with whom it served under the designation CH-112 Nomad, and the Royal Navy which used ex-US Navy HTE-2 trainers for pilot training at Culdrose, Cornwall, as the Hiller HT.2.

Although a number of these helicopters are still in use with civil operators throughout the world, few remain in military service. It is believed that several are used for liaison work by the air forces of Chile and Uruguay, while the Thai army, which received six OH-23Fs in 1976, may still have some in use. Guatemala had a single OH-23G in 1974, and the Dominican air force a pair of UH-12Es.

Type: three-seat military helicopter
Powerplant: one 323-hp (241-kW) Lycoming VO-540-A1B piston engine
Performance: (H-23D) maximum speed 95 mph (153 km/h); cruising speed 82 mph (132 km/h); maximum rate of climb at sea level 1,050 ft (320 m) per minute; vertical rate of climb at sea level 650 ft (198 m) per minute; service ceiling 13,200 ft (4020 m); hovering ceiling in ground effect 5,200 ft (1585 m); hovering ceiling out of ground effect 1,250 ft (380 m); range 205 miles (330 m)
Weights: (H-23D) empty 1,816 lb (824 kg); loaded 2,700 lb (1225 kg)

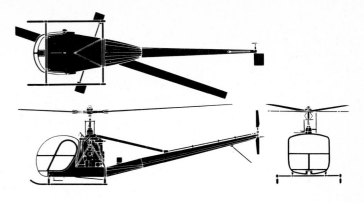

Hiller OH-23 Raven

Dimensions: main rotor diameter 35 ft 6 in (10.67 m); length 28 ft (8.53 m); height (to top of rotor head) 9 ft 9 in (2.98 m); main rotor disc area 989.8 sq ft (89.4 m²)
Operators: Chile, Dominica, Guatemala, Paraguay, Thailand, Uruguay

---

Hindustan Aeronautics Gnat/Ajeet

While the Folland (later Hawker Siddeley, now British Aerospace) Gnat was rejected by the RAF, though later accepted as a trainer, it was built in some numbers in India, where it achieved considerable success in aerial combat in its original design role of lightweight fighter.

First flight of the prototype, developed from the less powerful Folland Midge, took place on 18 July 1955. The design was simple, yet brilliant. The designer, W.E.W. Petter, had produced an advanced aircraft capable of being built in completely unsophisticated factories at a cost only one third that of fighters with comparable performance, and having operating costs to match. Typical of the approach to lighten and simplify the airframe was the use of the mainwheel doors as airbrakes.

After evaluation at Folland's Chilbolton airfield by an Indian air force test pilot, the Indian government signed an agreement with Folland for licence production to be undertaken by Hindustan Aircraft (now Aeronautics) Ltd at Bangalore, following the supply of 23 complete Gnats and components for a further 20 to be assembled by HAL.

A Gnat was shipped by the Ministry of Supply in late 1957 for trials in India, and became the first such aircraft in the Indian air force's inventory. The first Indian squadron to be equipped with Gnats was No 23 at Poona, which began to convert from de Havilland Vampires when six Folland-built Gnats were delivered to Ambala in March 1960.

Following assembly of UK-built Gnat components in 1959, the first Gnat built entirely in India from indigenous raw materials flew on 21 May, 1962, and full production began the following year at an average rate of two per month. A fourth Gnat squadron was being formed when the war with Pakistan broke out in September 1965 and the Gnat was soon 'blooded' in combat, scoring several successes over Pakistani North American Sabres. As a result of the Gnat's excellent combat performance, the Indian government reaffirmed its faith in the design by awarding further contracts. Production continued until January 1974, by which time 213 had been built. This was not, however, the end of the line. HAL had for some time been seeking a way of improving the basic Gnat design, and in 1974 had completed studies of a Mark 2, to be known as the Ajeet (invincible).

The last two production Gnats, which would have been nos 214 and 215, were completed as prototypes for the Ajeet, flying on 6 March and 5 November 1975, while the first production aircraft flew on 30 September 1976. The most important change is the wet wing, accomodating as much fuel as the Gnat's drop tanks and thus freeing the pylons for weapons for the same mission radius. A later Martin-Baker ejection seat, the Mk GF4, permits ejection at zero feet and speeds down to 104 mph (167 km/h) compared with the 300 ft (91 m) and 149 mph (241 km/h) of the Gnat's Folland Type 2G seat. Improved flight control communications and navigation systems are fitted and from Ajeet No 21 the Ferranti F.195 Iris sight is fitted. Initial production of the Ajeet fighter is planned as 100 aircraft but this may eventually be doubled over a four year period. HAL is rebuilding Gnats to Ajeet standard and has developed a two-seat trainer Ajeet, the first being completed in 1979. It retains the fighter's attack capability, though despite a length increase of 2 ft 3½ in (0.7 m), the second cockpit (with its own windscreen and canopy) is fitted at the cost of deleting two fuselage fuel tanks. If necessary, another 60-gallon (273-litre) tank can be fitted in place of the cannon.

Type: fighter and ground attack aircraft
Powerplant: one 4,520-lb (2050-kg) Rolls-Royce Orpheus 701 turbojet
Performance: (Gnat) maximum level speed M 0.98; climb to 45,000 ft (13720 m) 5 minutes 15 seconds; service ceiling over 50,000 ft (15240 m); take-off run to 50 ft (15 m) 2,620 ft (800 m); landing run from 50 ft (15 m) 3,500 ft (1065 m); radius of action 500 miles (805 km); endurance 1 hour 15 minutes, doubled with underwing tanks
(Ajeet) maximum level speed at sea level 716 mph (1152 km/h); service ceiling 45,000 ft (13720 m); climb to 39,375 ft (12000 m) at take-off weight 7,803 lb (3359 kg) from brakes off 9 minutes 33 seconds; take-off run at sea level, weight 9,118 lb (4136 kg) with two rocket pods and two 33-gallon (150-litre) drop tanks 4,515 ft (1376 m); landing run at normal landing weight 3,435 ft (1047 m); combat radius in low level ground attack role with two 500-lb (227-kg) bombs 127 miles (204 km), with two rocket pods and two 33-gallon (150-litre) drop tanks 161 miles (259 km), with four rocket pods 120 miles (193 km) (all Ajeet performance figures at ISA + 30°C)
Weights: (Gnat) interceptor take-off 6,650 lb (3010 kg); tactical with wing tanks and armament 8,885 lb (4020 kg)
(Ajeet) empty 5,086 lb (2307 kg); maximum take-off 9,195 lb (4170 kg)
Dimensions: (Gnat) span 22 ft 2 in (6.75 m); length 29 ft 9 in (9.06 m); height 8 ft 10 in (2.69 m); wing area 136.6 sq ft (12.69 m²)
(Ajeet) span 22 ft 1 in (6.73 m); length 29 ft 8 in (9.04 m); height 8 ft 1 in (2.46 m)
Armament: (Gnat) two 30-mm Aden cannon in fuselage air intake fairings; two underwing pylons for two 500-lb (227-kg) bombs or twelve 3-inch (7.6-cm) rockets
(Ajeet) cannon as Gnat; four underwing pylons, two inner each capable of carrying one 500-lb (227-kg) bomb, and others for four Arrow pods each containing eighteen 68-mm rockets or two 33-gallon (150-litre) drop tanks
Operator: India

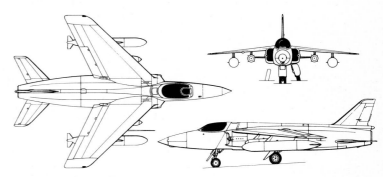

Hindustan Aeronautics Ajeet

Hindustan Aeronautics HPT-32

The Bangalore design office of Hindustan Aeronautics Ltd has given many diversified examples of its talents in the years since World War II, ranging from small Auster-type air observation posts to basic trainers (piston- and jet-engined), crop-sprayers, helicopters, and transonic jet-powered ground-attack fighters. Its 32nd design, as the designation reveals, is for a primary training aircraft, the HPT-32, which is intended for service in the early 1980s to replace the ageing HT-2, now long overdue for replacement.

First flown on 6 January 1977, the HPT-32 is an all-metal low-wing monoplane whose design contains no surprises. It conforms to the airworthiness requirements of FAR Part 23, being stressed to g limits of +6 and −3 for a full range of aerobatic manoeuvres, but is intended for a wide variety of instructional roles including *ab initio*, instrument, navigation, night flying, formation flying and weapon training; and also for glider or target towing. With four underwing pylons available for weapons or other stores, it will also be able to perform light ground-attack or supply-dropping missions. With a third (and possibly fourth) seat behind the side-by-side front seats of the standard trainer, other potential roles include search and rescue, liaison, reconnaissance, or civil touring. A second prototype was being built in 1979; meanwhile the first HPT-32 has undergone a few changes since its debut, resulting in a somewhat lighter aircraft with improved ceiling and climb rates. The production version is expected to have an Indian engine, of approximately the same power as the prototype's Lycoming, and may feature a retractable landing gear instead of the fixed tricycle type fitted to the prototype.

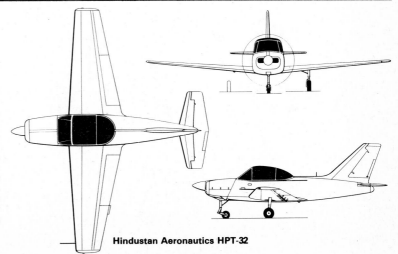

Hindustan Aeronautics HPT-32

continued

Type: two/three-seat basic trainer or four-seat liaison aircraft
Powerplant: (prototype) one 260-hp (194-kW) Lycoming AEIO-540-D4B5 flat-six piston engine
Performance: (at normal take-off weight of 2,756 lb (1250 kg)) maximum speed at sea level 135 mph (217 km/h); range with standard fuel at 5,000 ft (1525 m) 435 miles (700 km); maximum rate of climb at sea level 1,100 ft (335 m) per minute; service ceiling 15,580 ft (4750 m)

Weights: empty 2,041 lb (926 kg); normal take-off 2,756 lb (1250 kg); maximum take-off 3,031 lb (1375 kg)
Dimensions: span 31 ft 2 in (9.50 m); length 25 ft 3¾ in (7.715 m); height 10 ft 8¾ in (3.27 m); wing area 161.57 sq ft (15.01 m²)

Armament: up to 562 lb (255 kg) of weapons or other stores on four underwing hardpoints
Operators: India (under development)

Hindustan Aeronautics HT-2

As its designation indicates, the HT-2 was the second original design to be evolved by the Bangalore factory of Hindustan Aircraft Ltd, the first having been a wartime design for a troop transport glider. The HT-2 was thus India's first domestically-designed powered aeroplane, and was one of three types commissioned by the Indian government in September 1948 to cover the primary, basic and advanced training roles. In the event the HT-2 was the only one to proceed, the first of two prototypes flying on 13 August 1951 and the second on 19 February 1952. The former proving to be somewhat underpowered by its 145-hp (108-kW) de Havilland Gipsy Major 10 engine, the second aircraft was flown with a slightly more powerful Cirrus Major III, which became the standard production powerplant. Broadly similar to the contemporary de Havilland Chipmunk in general appearance, the HT-2 is an all-metal low-wing monoplane having a fixed, tailwheel-type landing gear. Tandem seating and dual controls are provided for instructor and pupil, under a long framed canopy. Production, which totalled 169, continued until 1958 to fulfil orders

from the Indian air force, Indian navy and civilian flying clubs.

In the hope of securing export sales India presented the Indonesian and Singapore governments each with an HT-2, but no orders were forthcoming. However, 12 were sold later to the Ghana air force, with whom they remained in service until replaced by Scottish Aviation Bulldogs in 1973. In India, only 50 or so remain in service and are long overdue for replacement. A new HAL primary trainer, the HPT-32, is now under development as such a replacement.

Type: two-seat primary trainer
Powerplant: one 155-hp (116-kW) Blackburn Cirrus Major III four-cylinder in-line piston engine
Performance: maximum speed 130 mph (209 km/h); maximum cruising speed 115 mph (185 km/h); maximum range 350 miles (563 km); maximum endurance 3 hours 30 minutes; maximum rate of climb at sea level 800 ft (244 m) per minute; service ceiling 14,500 ft (4420 m)
Weights: empty 1,540 lb (699 kg); max-

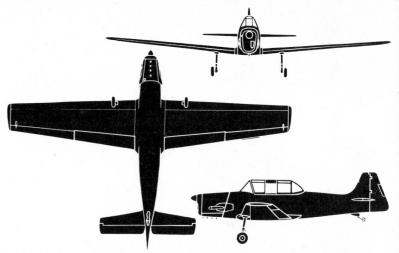

Hindustan Aeronautics HT-2

imum take-off 2,240 lb (1016 kg)
Dimensions: span 35 ft 2 in (10.72 m); length 24 ft 8½ in (7.53 m); height 8 ft 11 in (2.72 m); wing area 173.4 sq ft (16.11 m²)
Armament: none
Operators: India

Hindustan Aeronautics HJT-16 Kiran

HAL (Hindustan Aeronautics Ltd) followed the BAC (Hunting) Jet Provost in adopting side-by-side seating for the HJT-16 Kiran (ray of light), design of which began in 1959.

The first prototype did not fly until September 1964; the second followed 11 months later. A pre-production batch of 24 followed for the Indian air force, first delivery of six taking place in March 1968. The 50th aircraft was completed in late 1973 and the 125th by the beginning of 1978. The total requirement for Kirans by the Indian air force and navy is said to be 190.

The Kiran's cockpit is pressurized and the canopy is of the clamshell type. Two Martin-Baker Mk H4HA zero-altitude fully-automatic ejector seats are fitted.

An Indian-designed engine, the HJE-2500, was developed for the Kiran and tests began at the end of 1966. It seems unlikely that it will ever be installed in production aircraft, but many lessons have been learned.

In order to make full use of the Kiran's capabilities in the light attack and armament training roles, later production models are fitted with a hardpoint beneath each wing for weapons or a drop tank. In this form it becomes the Mark 1A.

A more powerful development of the basic

aircraft, known as the Mark 2, has a derated HAL Orpheus 701 turbojet giving 3,400-lb (1542-kg) thrust, improving speed, climb and manoeuvrability. The prototype flew on 30 July 1976 and a second followed some months late, in 1979.

The Kiran Mark 2 has two hardpoints beneath each wing giving a weapons capability of up to four 500-lb (227-kg) bombs, or four 68-mm rocket pods or 25-lb (11.34-kg) bomb carriers or combinations of these loads. Alternatively, four 50-Imperial gallon (227-litre) drop tanks can be carried.

Type: basic trainer
Powerplant: one 2,500-lb (1134-kg) Rolls-Royce Viper 11 turbojet
Performance: maximum speed at sea level 432 mph (695 km/h); maximum speed at 30,000 ft (9150 m) 427 mph (688 km/h); cruising speed 201 mph (324 km/h); time to reach 30,000 ft (9150 m) 20 minutes; take-off run 1,450 ft (442 m); endurance without external tanks 1 hour 45 minutes at 265 mph (426 km/h) at 30,000 ft (9150 m)
Weights: empty 5,644 lb (2560 kg); maximum take-off with underwing tanks 9,039 lb (4100 kg)
Dimensions: span 35 ft 1 in (10.70 m);

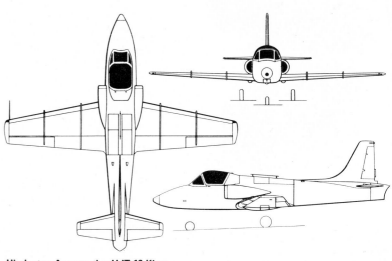

Hindustan Aeronautics HJT-16 Kiran

length 34 ft 9 in (10.60 m); height 11 ft 11 in (3.63 m); wing area 204.5 sq ft (19.00 m²)
Armament: current production aircraft have a hardpoint beneath each wing capable of carrying a variety of stores: each hardpoint can

carry one 500-lb (227-kg) bomb, or a 50-Imperial gallon (227-litre) drop tank or a pod with two 7.62-mm (0.3-in) machine-guns, or seven 68-mm SNEB rockets in a pod
Operator: India

Hindustan Aeronautics HAOP-27 Krishak Mk II

On 28 September 1958, Hindustan Aeronautics Ltd flew a prototype of the HUL-26 Pushpak, a two-seat ultra-light cabin monoplane which was subsequently produced in series and became a popular lightplane for use by Indian civil flying clubs. The next HAL design was evolved originally as a slightly larger, four-seat multi-purpose version of the Pushpak, and two Krishak Mk I prototypes (190-hp/142-kW Continental engine) made their initial flights in November 1959 and November 1960. No production of this version was undertaken, but when, a few years later, the Indian army issued a requirement for a three-seat air observation post and liaison aircraft, HAL evolved the three-seat Krishak Mk II to meet it. The prototype of this made its first flight in 1965, and over the next four years 68 production Krishak IIs, first ordered in 1964 and bearing the designation HAOP-27, were delivered to the Indian air force.

The steel-tube fuselage and metal wings, both fabric-covered, are essentially similar to

those of the Pushpak, fuel being carried in two standard tanks in the wings and, optionally, in an underfuselage auxiliary tank. Pilot and co-pilot sit side by side, with an excellent all-round view from the extensively glazed cabin; to their rear can be installed an optional third seat or, for an air ambulance role, a single stretcher. The Krishaks replaced most of the British Auster AOP.9s in Indian service, but up to the mid-1960s the two types still equipped four squadrons (Nos 659, 660, 661 and 662) of the Indian air force, which flew them in a support role in conjunction with the army's Regiment of Artillery. These fixed-wing AOP aircraft began to be replaced from 1974 onwards by Cheetah helicopters, a HAL licence-built version of the Aérospatiale SA.315B Lama.

Type: two/three-seat air observation post and light utility aircraft
Powerplant: one 225-hp (168-kW) Continental O-470-J flat-six piston engine
Performance: maximum speed at sea level

Hindustan's HAOP-27 Krishak was a satisfactory three-seat observation aircraft, over 50 being built, but nearly all have now been replaced in Indian army service by the SA.315B Cheetah, a version of the Aérospatiale Alouette helicopter made by Hindustan.

130 mph (209 km/h); maximum speed at 5,000 ft (1525 m) 116 mph (187 km/h); range with auxiliary fuel 500 miles (805 km); maximum rate of climb at sea level 900 ft (274 m) per minute; service ceiling 19,500 ft (5945 m)
Weights: empty 1,970 lb (894 kg); max-

imum take-off 2,800 lb (1270 kg)
Dimensions: span 37 ft 6 in (11.43 m); length 27 ft 7 in (8.41 m); height 7 ft 9 in (2.36 m); wing area 200.0 sq ft (18.58 m²)
Armament: none
Operators: India

Hindustan Aeronautics HF-24 Marut

India's first, and so far only, indigenous jet fighter, the HAL HF-24 Marut (wind spirit) has not been an unqualified success. Development was protracted, performance disappointing, and the search for an engine capable of carrying it to its intended Mach 2 maximum speed unfruitful. Nevertheless, all national aerospace industries have to start somewhere, and HAL deserves credit for a brave try, considering that before the Marut its design and manufacturing effort had been confined largely to piston-engined light aircraft.

The lack of home-produced experience in designing jet aircraft was offset by acquiring the services of a team of German engineers, headed by Dipl-Ing Kurt Tank, the brilliant wartime technical director of Focke-Wulf. This team began work on the HF-24 in June 1956 and stayed until 1967, after which development was continued by an all-Indian team. After preliminary trials with a full-size two-seat glider built to the same basic configuration, two prototype HF-24s were built, making their initial flights on 17 June 1961 and 4 October 1962 respectively.

The two prototypes were followed in 1963-64 by 18 pre-production aircraft, before series manufacture began of the Marut Mk I as a ground-attack fighter. A token delivery of two of these aircraft was made to the Indian air force on 10 May 1964; 12 others were delivered later, the remaining four being retained for various test purposes. Of all-metal low-wing configuration, the Marut has 45° swept wings, twin Orpheus 703 non-afterburning turbojets side by side in the fuselage, and a Martin-Baker Mk 84C zero-height ejection seat for the pilot. The first production Mk I was flown on 15 November 1967, and by the time of the December 1971 war with Pakistan Maruts equipped three IAF squadrons (Nos 10, 31 and 220), acquitting themselves well in operations, without loss. Mk I production, including development aircraft, totalled 129, but no additional squadrons were equipped with the type. Later examples feature extended-chord.

In addition to the single-seater, HAL also developed a two-seat combat proficiency trainer version of the Marut, known as the Mk IT. The first of two Mk IT prototypes was flown on 30 April 1970, and 18 were eventually built, with the two seats in tandem under a long, one-piece canopy, and dual controls for the occupants. The Mk IT is used for all-weather ground-attack, instrument flying and weapons training.

Production of the Marut ended in 1977. Over the years a number of attempts have been made to push the performance up to Mach 2, one of which involved the conversion of a pre-production Marut to Mk IA standard by fitting afterburners to the existing Orpheus 703 engines. Entirely new powerplants studied have varied from the German-designed, Egyptian-built Brandner E300 turbojet in the latter half of the 1960s to the more recent study of the Turbo-Union RB.199 turbofan which powers the Panavia Tornado. None of these has yielded satisfactory results, and the idea of a Mach 2 Marut now seems to have been abandoned. In 1978-79 the aircraft was still under consideration as the basis for development of a new tactical fighter, but the recent Indian purchase of the SEPECAT Jaguar makes this possibility seem equally unlikely.

Type: single-seat ground-attack fighter (Mk I); two-seat operational trainer (Mk IT)
Powerplant: two 4,850-lb (2200-kg) static thrust HAL-built Rolls-Royce Orpheus 703 turbojets
Performance: maximum speed at 39,375 ft (12000 m) (Mk I) Mach 1.02 or 675 mph (1086 km/h), (Mk IT) Mach 1.00 or 661 mph (1064 km/h); maximum indicated airspeed at sea level (Mk I) 691 mph (1112 km/h); combat radius (Mk IT) at low level 148 miles (238 km), at 39,375 ft (12000 m) 246 miles (396 km); ferry range (Mk IT) at 30,000 ft (9150 m) 898 miles (1445 km); time to 40,000 ft (12200 m), aircraft clean 9 minutes 20 seconds
Weights: empty (Mk I with ventral drop-tank) 13,658 lb (6195 kg), (Mk IT) 13,778 lb (6250 kg); maximum take-off (Mk I) 24,048 lb (10908 kg), (Mk IT) 23,836 lb (10812 kg)
Dimensions: span 29 ft 6¼ in (9.00 m); length 52 ft 0¾ in (15.87 m); height 11 ft 9¾ in (3.60 m); wing area 301.4 sq ft (28.00 m²)
Armament: four 30-mm Aden Mk 2 cannon with 120 rounds per gun, two on each side of forward fuselage; retractable Matra Type 103 pack of fifty 68-mm SNEB air-to-air rockets in belly (not in Mk IT); four underwing points for 1,000-lb (454-kg) bombs, Type 116 SNEB rocket pods, T10 air-to-surface rocket clusters, napalm, or drop-tanks
Operators: India

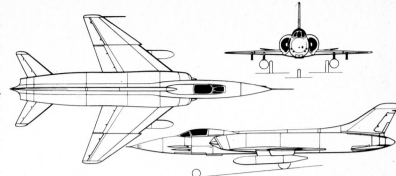

Hindustan Aeronautics HF-24 Marut

Called Marut (Wind Spirit), the Hindustan HF-24 is roughly in the class of the Hunter, and was designed by a team led by Dr Kurt Tank, creator of the Focke-Wulf 190. This is one of the dual trainer Mk 1T versions, most of which have only two 30-mm cannon.

Hindustan Aeronautics HF-24 Marut Mk 1 fighter of the Indian Air Force; three squadrons operate the type in the IAF.

Hispano HA-200/HA-220 Saeta

In 1954 Hispano Aviación produced the HA-100 Triana advanced trainer, designed under the supervision of Professor Willy Messerschmitt. Four prototypes were followed by 40 production aircraft, which entered service with the Spanish air force from 1958 as armament trainers, under the designation E-12.

Hispano used major HA-100 components in the first Spanish jet aircraft, the HA-200, the prototype of which first flew on 12 August, 1955. It was followed by a second prototype and 30 production aircraft designated HA-200A Saeta (arrow) by the manufacturer and E-14 by the Spanish air force. The first production HA-200A flew on 11 October 1962.

Egypt showed interest in the HA-200, and a licence agreement was reached whereby a production line was established at the Helwan air works near Cairo. The variant chosen was the HA-200B, named Al-Kahira, and Egypt obtained a batch of 10 pre-production HA-200B aircraft built by Hispano, the first flying on 21 July, 1960. It was planned that 90 aircraft would be built in Egypt, and these were used until supplanted by the Aero L-29 Delfin.

The next development in Spain was the HA-200D with improved systems, wheels, brakes and armament. Production of 55 HA-200Ds for the Spanish air force was completed in early 1968, and 40 of these were subsequently upgraded in respect of armament to HA-200E standard.

This variant, also known as the Super Saeta, had more powerful Marboré engines, provision for rocket pods and updated Bendix electronics. A single-seat model went into production as the HA-220 attack aircraft with the military designation C-10, after a launching order for 25 by the Spanish air force in December 1967; ten had been delivered by mid-February 1972. The HA-220 retains the long canopy of the HA-200, but the rear cockpit holds a tank. A bullet-proof windscreen is fitted, and the seat has armour at front and rear. A wide range of underwing armament can be carried.

In all, Hispano supplied 110 production HA-200/220s to the Spanish air force, although by the time production deliveries had been completed, the company had been merged with CASA. About 80 HA-200/220s are still in service in Spain. *Escuadrón* 214 has about 20 HA-220s based at Morón as part of the 21st Wing, Tactical Air Command, while in the training role some 60 HA-200s remain with *Escuadrón* 793 at San Javier. The HA-200s will be replaced by the CASA C-101 Aviojet, and presumably a strike version of the latter will be developed as an HA-220 replacement.

Type: advanced trainer
Powerplant: (HA-200B and D) two 880-lb (400-kg) Turboméca Marboré IIA turbojets; (HA-200E) two 1,058-lb (480-kg) Turboméca

Marboré VI turbojets
Performance: (HA-200D) maximum speed at maximum take-off weight 404 mph (650 km/h); cruising speed 330 mph (530 km/h); rate of climb at sea level 2,755 ft (840 m) per minute; service ceiling 39,360 ft (12000 m); take-off run to 50 ft (15 m) 1,740 ft (530 m); landing run from 50 ft (15 m) 2,300 ft (700 m); range at 29,500 ft (9000 m) 930 miles (1500 km).
(HA-200E) maximum speed at maximum take-off weight at sea level 413 mph (665 km/h); maximum speed at 23,000 ft (7000 m) 429 mph (690 km/h); cruising speed at 19,700 ft (6000 m) 360 mph (579 km/h); rate of climb at sea level 3,050 ft (930 m) per minute; service ceiling 42,650 ft (13000 m); take-off run to 50 ft (15 m) 2,625 ft (800 m); other figures

as for HA-200D
Weights: (HA-200D) empty equipped 4,035 lb (1830 kg); maximum take-off 7,385 lb (3350 kg)
(HA-220E) basic operating 4,453 lb (2020 kg); maximum take-off 7,937 lb (3600 kg)
Dimensions: (all versions) span 34 ft 2 in (10.42 m); length 29 ft 5 in (8.97 m); height 9 ft 4 in (2.85 m); wing area 187.2 sq ft (17.40 m²)
Armament: underwing hardpoints for rocket launchers, bomb racks and photo-reconnaissance equipment; provision for one 20-mm Hispano-Suiza cannon in the fuselage; HA-200E has Matra 38 underwing attachments for range of weapons
Operators: Egypt, Spain

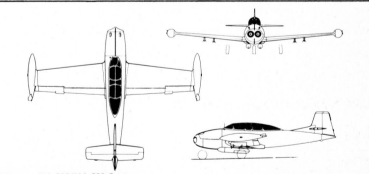

Hispano HA-200/HA-220 Saeta

Hughes Model 269/300/300C/TH-55A Osage

The diminutive but versatile Hughes TH-55A Osage is a military version of Hughes' original Model 269A, a re-engineered and simplified follow-on from the two-seat Model 269. Five 269As bought by the US Army under the designation YHO-2HU in 1958 completed a highly successful evaluation programme in the command and observation roles. In 1964 the type was chosen as the force's standard two-seat training helicopter, and by 1969 a total of 792 had been delivered. The conflict in Vietnam demanded the use of helicopters on a scale never seen before, and TH-55As are still operated to train pilots to fly the 9,000 rotary-wing aircraft in the US Army inventory.

The basic design has undergone many changes over the years. The first three-seat variant, the Model 300, appeared in 1963. Five years later, in July 1968, construction began of the Model 300C. Powered by a 190-hp (142-kW) Lycoming piston engine, this three-seat aircraft first flew in August 1969 and offered a 45% increase in payload. The 300CQ is 75% quieter than earlier models. Adoption of a larger engine called for a number of structural changes, including enlarging the tail rotor and fin, and lengthening the tailboom and rotor mast to accommodate the longer and heavier main rotor blades. Hughes has also experimented with alternative powerplants. A TH-55A has flown with a 185-hp (138-kW) Wankel RC2-60 rotary engine, and another has been fitted with a 317-shp (236-kW) Allison 250-C18 turboshaft. Kawasaki built 48 Osages for the Japan Ground Self-Defence Force (JGSDF), and the Model 300C is also built under licence in Italy by Breda Nardi.

Algeria uses six 269s for training; the Brazilian navy's 10 269/300s are now being phased out of the training role; Guyana has

the type primarily for police work; Italy has trained many pilots on the type; Japan's GSDF is replacing much of its fixed-wing fleet with helicopters, including 38 TH-55Js; Nicaragua has one for training; the Sierra Leone Defence Force, formed in 1973 and with an inventory of six aircraft, operates one; and the largest user, the US Army, still operates some 300.

Type: two/three-seat light training helicopter
Powerplant: one 180-hp (134-kW) Avco Lycoming HIO-360-A1A four-cylinder, horizontally opposed, air-cooled piston engine (300C: 190-hp/142-kW HIO-360-D1A)
Performance: maximum design speed (300) 87 mph (140 km/h), (TH-55A) 86 mph (138 km/h), (300) 105 mph (169 km/h); maximum cruising speed (300) 80 mph (129 km/h), (TH-55A) 75 mph (121 km/h), (300C) 100 mph (161 km/h); range (maximum fuel, no reserve), (300) 300 miles (480 km), (TH-55A) 204 miles (328 km), (300C) 232 miles (373 km); maximum rate of climb at sea level 1,140 ft (347 m) per minute
Weights: empty equipped (300) 958 lb (434 kg), (TH-55A) 1,008 lb (457 kg), (300C) 1,039 lb (471 kg); maximum take-off and landing (300, TH-55A) 1,670 lb (757 kg), (300C) 1,900 lb (861 kg)
Dimensions: rotor diameter (300, TH-55A) 25 ft 3½ in (7.71 m), (300C) 26 ft 10 in (8.18 m); length overall (rotors turning) (300, TH-55A) 28 ft 10¾ in (8.8 m), (300C) 30 ft 11 in (9.42 m); height (tail rotor turning) 8 ft 2¾ in (2.5 m); main rotor disc area (300, TH-55A) 503 sq ft (46.73 m²), (300C) 565.5 sq ft (52.5 m²)
Armament: none
Operators: Algeria, Brazil, Guyana, Italy, Japan, Nicaragua, Sierra Leone, US Army

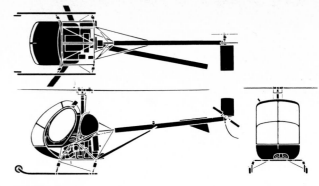

Hughes TH-55A Osage

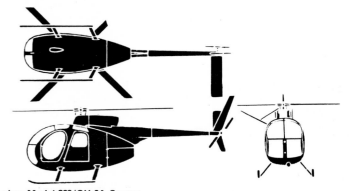

The US Army bought 792 Hughes TH-55A Osage light helicopters as standard rotary-wing trainers, and some 300 are still in use in this role. Virtually every Army helicopter pilot learns to fly on the Osage.

Hughes Model 369/OH-6 Cayuse

The Hughes Model 369 was designed to meet the requirements of the US Army's Light Observation Helicopter (LOH) specification, which was issued to US aircraft manufacturers in 1960. There was a likelihood of large-scale production for the winning design, which explains why no fewer than 12 companies made submissions. The US Army selected those of Bell, Hiller and Hughes as the most suitable proposals, and in the spring of 1961 ordered five prototypes from each for evaluation.

When ordered by the US Army the Hughes Model 369 was given the designation HO-6, but it was under the revised tri-service designation of OH-6 that it flew for the first time on 27 February 1963. The US Army's trials of the competing prototypes began at Fort Rucker, Alabama, in November of that year, and on 26 May 1965 it was announced that the Hughes submission had won the competition and was being ordered into production.

The US Army's initial order was for 714 of these helicopters, and it was expected that Hughes would manufacture the total requirement, which was predicted to be 4,000 examples. In fact, although Hughes received further contracts to bring the total requirement for the OH-6 to 1,434, this was to prove the end of the line for Hughes, for it was Bell that built the balance of the 4,000 after the US Army became dissatisfied with the rising costs of the OH-6. This was the result of a political storm which raged over the award of the contract to Hughes, which was said to have bid below costs.

That this should be the case was most unfortunate, for although the OH-6 Cayuse, as it became known, was falling behind its production schedule, as well as costing more to produce than had been anticipated, in its OH-6A production form as delivered to the US Army in the summer of 1966 it really was a superb light helicopter with sparkling performance. As proof of this statement, OH-6A helicopters were used by both service and civilian pilots to set up a whole series of international helicopter records, including all class helicopter records for a straight-line distance of 2,213 miles (3561 km), a sustained altitude of 26,448 ft (8061 m), and a speed of 141.51 mph (227.74 km/h) over a 1,243-miles (2000-km) closed circuit. Many other records

were broken in this helicopter's own class, including a maximum speed of 172.41 mph (227.47 km/h).

Undoubtedly, the key to the success of this light helicopter was the combination of the well developed fully-articulated four-blade main rotor, which had evolved from that designed for the Hughes Model 200, and the small, lightweight Allison T63-A-5A turboshaft engine which powered it. The term 'lightweight' is, of course, somewhat arbitary: in fact, the T63-A-5A weighs only 136 lb (61.7 kg) dry, and any engine with a take-off rating of 317 shp (236 kW) cannot come much lighter than that, its weight being only 5% of the overload take-off weight of the Cayuse. In practice, however, the engine is derated to 252.5 shp (188 kW) for take-off and has a maximum continuous rating of 214.5 shp (160 kW), which explains its high-altitude record, and which also gives the OH-6 excellent 'hot and high' performance.

Accommodation is for a crew of two, with two folding seats in the rear cabin which, when folded out of the way, provide sufficient room for four fully equipped troops seated on the floor, or space for a worthwhile load of cargo.

OH-6As began to enter service with the US Army in September 1966, and delivery of the

total 1,434 on order had been completed by August 1970. The Cayuse is employed for a wide range of duties, even including offensive operations by the provision of armament kits for mounting on the left side of the fuselage, these comprising the XM-27 7.62-mm (0.3-in) machine-gun or XM-75 grenade-launcher.

Type: light observation helicopter
Powerplant: one 317-shp (236-kW) derated Allison T63-A-5A turboshaft
Performance: maximum cruising speed at sea level 143 mph (230 km/h); normal range

413 miles (665 km/h) at 5,000 ft (1525 m); ferry range 1,560 miles (2511 km)
Weights: empty equipped 1,156 lb (524 kg); design take-off 2,400 lb (1089 kg); overload take-off 2,700 lb (1225 kg)
Dimensions: main rotor diameter 26 ft 4 in (8.03 m); tail rotor diameter 4 ft 3 in (1.30 m); length rotors turning 30 ft 3¾ in (9.24 m); height 8 ft 1½ in (2.48 m); main rotor disc area 544.63 sq ft (50.60 m²)
Armament: XM-27 7.62-mm (0.3-in) machine-gun or XM-75 grenade launcher
Operators: US Army

Hughes Model 369/OH-6A Cayuse

Popularly called the Loach, from its LOH (light observation helicopter) role, the Hughes OH-6A Cayuse is one of the world's smallest, fastest and most nimble rotary wing machines. Similar machines are built in Italy, Japan, Argentina and S. Korea.

Hughes Model 500M/Defender

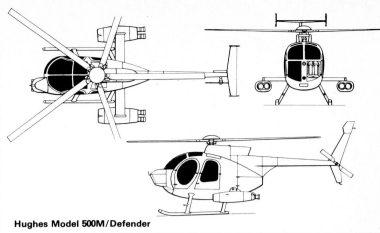

Hughes announced on 21 April 1965 that it was the company's intention to market a commercial equivalent of the military OH-6A. Three versions were to be available: the basic Model 500, a five-seat executive; the utility Model 500U (later 500C), which would carry seven persons or up to 1,710 lb (776 kg) of freight; and a military Model 500M, basically the same as the US Army's OH-6A, but configured for sale to foreign military customers. These variants differed from the military OH-6A mainly in their powerplant. The Models 500 and 500M retained the same basic Allison T63-A-5A, but in these applications rerated to 278 shp (207 kW) for take-off, and with a maximum continuous rating of 243 shp (181 kW). The 500C has the commercial 400-shp (298-kW) Allison Model 250-C20 turboshaft, derated to the same levels as the T63-A-5A, but giving improved 'hot and high' performance. Deliveries of these helicopter models began in 1968, and the 500M proved an attractive buy for many foreign air forces, including those of Colombia, Denmark, Mexico, the Philippines, and Spain. In addition, licence manufacture of the Model 500 has been undertaken by BredaNardi in Italy, Kawasaki in Japan and RACA in Argentina.

The development of a more advanced version began in 1974, introducing a number of changes to enhance performance. The more powerful Allison 250-C20B was introduced: this develops a maximum of 420 shp (313 kW), but is derated in this application to 375 shp (280 kW) for take-off, and has a maximum continuous rating of 350 shp (261 kW). There are two readily noticeable external changes, the first being the provision of a T-tail, with a small-span horizontal stabilizer, with diminutive end-plate fins, mounted at the tip of the dorsal fin. This replaces the earlier unit which had a similar ventral/dorsal fin arrangement, but had also a fixed stabilizer with considerable dihedral mounted on the starboard side of the fin. The other major external change is the introduction of a five-blade main rotor similar to that installed on the experimental OH-6C. In fact, as early as April 1976 Hughes had been working on a modified OH-6A which was known as 'The Quiet One', and it was for this aircraft that the slower-rotating five-blade main rotor had originally been developed. This latter aircraft also had a four-blade tail rotor, but to avoid excessive weight that of the 500D, as this new helicopter is known, has only two blades of slightly increased diameter, plus a longer and strengthened tail boom to cater for the increased torque. Other changes include strengthening of the lower fuselage and landing gear, and the introduction of a small fairing over the rotor hub to eliminate a slight problem of buffeting with the prototype. This flew for the first time in August 1974, followed by the first flight of a production aircraft on 9 October 1975, initial deliveries being made in December 1976.

During 1976 Hughes made extensive studies of armed helicopters, from which the conclusion was reached that the Model 500D could, with minimal modification, be marketed as a low-cost multi-mission combat helicopter. The resulting Model 500M-D Defender created a favourable impression and is currently being manufactured extensively by Hughes and its licensees. Changes include the installation of self-sealing fuel cells and armour, provision for the carriage and deployment of a variety of weapons, and inclusion of the Hughes Black Hole Ocarina IR suppressor, which reduces the Defender's vulnerability to infra-red (heat) seeking missiles by a considerable factor. Amongst the weapons carried is the TOW missile, the installation including two weapon pods on each side of the fuselage, plus a telescopic nose sight for the gunner and a steering indicator for the pilot. The simple Hughes Chain Gun, of 30-mm calibre and with firing rates of up to 750 rpm, can also be fitted.

Defenders have been delivered to Colombia, Mauritania and South Korea, and this latter country is to assemble 60 – 70 from American components.

Type: lightweight commercial/military helicopter
Powerplant: (500M-D) one 420-shp (313-kW) Allison 250-C20B turboshaft, derated to 375 shp (280 kW), and with a maximum continuous rating of 350 shp (261 kW)
Performance: maximum cruising speed at sea level 160 mph (257 km/h); range at sea level (with allowance for 2-minute warm-up, standard fuel and no reserves) 300 miles (483 km)
Weights: empty 1,320 lb (599 kg); maximum take-off 3,000 lb (1361 kg)
Dimensions: main rotor diameter 26 ft 5 in (8.05 m); length (rotors turning) 30 ft 6 in (9.30 m); height 8 ft 3½ in (2.53 m); main rotor disc area 547.81 sq ft (50.89 m²)
Armament: (500M-D) includes 2.75-in (69.9-mm) rockets, 7.62-mm (0.3-in) Minigun, 30-mm Chain Gun; Mk 44 or Mk 46 homing torpedoes; or four TOW air-to-surface missiles
Operators: Argentina, Colombia, Denmark, Italy, Israel, Japan, Mauritania, Mexico, South Korea, Spain

Hughes Model 500M/Defender

The **Hughes 500M-D Defender** angered Britten-Norman by confusingly using the latter's established name, but that does not alter the fact that this is the most useful tactical helicopter of its size. This example was equipped with a TOW missile system, seen firing.

Hughes YAH-64

'Soviet ground forces outnumber US ground forces by virtually every criterion (sic): total ground force personnel; number of divisions; and ground force systems, especially tanks (5:1), personnel carriers (2.5:1), artillery pieces (4:1), and heavy mortars (2.5:1).' The words are those of Gen George Brown (USAF), Chairman of the Joint Chiefs of Staff, who used them during 1978 in an analysis for the US Congress, referring in particular to the threat with which NATO forces are confronted in Europe.

It was the knowledge of this growing threat that brought authorization in June 1973 for the US Army to initiate a two-phase development for an Advanced Attack Helicopter (AAH). Phase I represented the competitive stage, for selection of the most suitable helicopter to advance to the Phase II stage of full-scale development of the helicopter and its integrated avionics and weapons systems. Both Bell Helicopter Company and Hughes were awarded a contract, in July 1973, for static test and ground test vehicles, plus two flying prototypes to be flown in competitive evaluation. Bell's submission carried the designation YAH-63 and that designed by Hughes YAH-64. It was the latter which was announced to be the winner on 10 December 1976.

Hughes was awarded a $317.7 million contract covering engineering development over

This prototype **Hughes YAH-64** advanced attack helicopter is firing unguided rockets, but the primary anti-tank weapon of the production AH-64A is expected to be the precision-guided Hellfire. A total of 536 is expected to be ordered.

continued

four years, and no production decision is likely before the termination of this phase of the programme in late 1980. Simultaneously, since 1977 Martin Marietta and Northrop have been developing the competing TADS (Target Acquisition and Designation System) and PNVS (Pilot's Night Vision System) for competitive evaluation in late 1979. Pending construction of three development aircraft (AV-01, 2 and 3), the original prototypes were flown extensively to evaluate planned design modifications. Those introduced under the Mod 1 programme included swept tips on the main rotor blades, an increased-diameter tail rotor, and the addition of the Hughes-developed 'Black Hole' infra-red suppressor. Mod 2 brought these prototypes very close to the final configuration for production aircraft, and introduced changes in cockpit windows and electronics-bay fairings.

In mid-1979 the AH-64 was regarded as one of the US Army's top priority programmes, with the US Army planning to procure a total of 536 AAH aircraft. These have been allocated provisionally to the Airborne Division (39), Air Mobile Division (75), Heavy Division, selected (36), Armored Cavalry Regiment (18), and Air Cavalry Combat Brigade (129). At this same time, initial tests had been carried out with the firing of Hellfire anti-tank missiles (at first without a definitive guidance system), and two of the first three development aircraft were being transferred to Martin Marietta and Northrop for installation of the competing TADS and PNVS equipment. These systems will provide the crew with the capability to detect, recognise, and engage enemy targets at stand-off range by day or night, or under adverse weather conditions. TADS includes direct-view optics, forward-looking infra-red (FLIR), TV, laser designator/rangefinder, and laser tracker. PNVS is a sophisticated FLIR system.

Extensive thought and design work has gone to enhance survivability of the AAH which, when flown in anger, will operate in an environment that is especially hostile to a helicopter. Thus the 'Black Hole' infra-red suppressor system breaks up the hot gas plume from the engine exhaust to reduce its temperature below the lock-on threshold of any known infra-red detection systems. The main rotor blades and fuel tank are unlikely to be damaged critically by strikes from projectiles up to 23-mm calibre, and the aircraft's basic structure is designed to be crashworthy, with a 95% probability of crew survival at a crash impact rate of 42 ft (12.8 m) per second.

For attack, its main purpose in life, the AH-64 will carry up to 16 Hellfire missiles, or 76 FFAR rockets, or a mix of both, plus the lightweight Hughes-developed XM230El 30-mm Chain Gun, which has a normal firing rate of 800 rounds per minute. With a range of 920 miles (1480 km), the AH-64 will be able to self-deploy across the North Atlantic in four stages: for longer ranges it is air transportable; a Lockheed C-5A Galaxy can accommodate six of these helicopters.

Three additional development aircraft (AV 04, 5 and 6) were under construction in mid-1979, and will be utilized in continuing US Army development testing into the Summer of 1981.

Type: advanced attack helicopter
Powerplant: two 1,536-shp (1145-kW) General Electric T700-GE-700 turboshafts
Performance: maximum speed 192 mph (309 km/h); maximum range with internal fuel 380 miles (612 km); ferry range with internal and external fuel 920 miles (1480 km)
Weights: empty 10,268 lb (4657 kg); maximum take-off 17,650 lb (8006 kg)
Dimensions: main rotor diameter 48 ft 0 in (14.63 m); tail rotor diameter 8 ft 4 in (2.54 m); length overall (rotors turning) 57 ft 9 in (17.60 m); height to top of rotor hub 12 ft 6¾ ft (3.83 m); main rotor disc area 1,809 sq ft (168.06 m²)
Armament: Hellfire missiles, FFAR rockets, and one XM230El 30-mm Chain Gun
Operators: (from December 1982 if procured) US Army

Ilyushin Il-14 Crate

Although obsolescent in its original roles as airliner and military freighter, the Ilyushin Il-14 'Crate' remains in service for secondary duties, and in 1976 it was reported that the type was entering service with Russian Frontal Aviation electronic intelligence (Elint) units in East Germany. The type is also used as a navigation trainer by a number of air forces.

The Il-14 was developed as an improved version of the Il-12, which had been designed in 1944 and flown in 1946 as a replacement for the Lisunov Li-2 (Soviet-built Douglas C-47). Compared with its predecessor, the Il-14 featured more powerful engines and a redesigned wing of slightly thicker section, intended to improve handling characteristics. The fin and rudder were enlarged to improve engine-out behaviour. The type made its maiden flight in 1950 and entered service with Aeroflot in 1954.

About 1,200 Il-14s are believed to have been built in the Soviet Union in 1950-58, when the type was superseded on Soviet production lines by turbine-powered transports. However, about 80 of the type were built by VEB in the German Democratic Republic, and some 120 produced in Czechoslovakia as the

Avia-14. The Avia-14 corresponded to the Il-14M, a stretched version of the original aircraft, while the Avia-14T was a freighter version with optional wing-tip tanks. Some Czech-built aircraft were supplied to the Soviet Union.

The Russian air force Elint version of the Il-14 preceded the Il-18 'Coot-C' into service, and has probably been replaced in this role by the more advanced aircraft. The older type may, however, be retained as an Elint trainer.

Type: medium transport, electronic intelligence (Elint) aircraft, and navigation trainer
Powerplant: two 1,900-hp (1417-kW) Shvetsov ASh-82T radial piston engines
Performance: maximum speed 268 mph (430 km/h) at 7,800 ft (2400 m); cruising speed 200-215 mph (320-350 km/h) at 8,200-9,800 ft (2500-3000 m); range with 7,300-lb (3300-kg) payload 250 miles (400 km); range with 3,500-lb (1600-kg) payload 1,000 miles (1750 km)
Weights: (Il-14M) empty 28,000 lb (12700 kg); maximum payload 7,300 lb (3300 kg); maximum fuel with tip-tanks·7,000 lb (3175

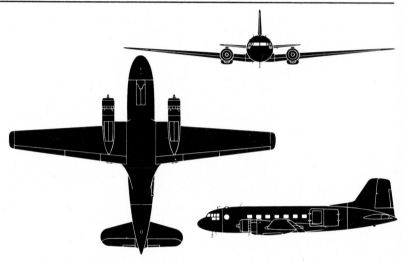

Ilyushin Il-14 (military)

kg); maximum take-off 38,500 lb (17500 kg)
Dimensions: span 104 ft (31.7 m); length 69 ft 11 in (21.31 m); wing area 1,080 sq ft (100 m²)

Operators: Czechoslovakia, Poland, India, Egypt, USSR, Yugoslavia

Ilyushin Il-18 Coot

The first Soviet airliner designed from the outset as a turbine-powered commercial transport, the Ilyushin Il-18 'Coot' made its initial flight in July 1957. Although a close contemporary of the US Lockheed Electra, it was rather larger, being closer in size to the Vickers Vanguard and Bristol Britannia. Despite this, it relies on manual controls, commonly found on Soviet commercial aircraft.

Early Il-18s were flown with both Kuznetsov NK-4 and Ivchenko AI-20 turboprops. The latter was standardized, but severe problems with this engine caused accidents in the early years of operations from 1958. The capacity of the Il-18 was increased from 80 passengers in early versions to 120 in later aircraft. The Il-18D featured increased power, weight and fuel capacity and became the main production version in airliner form. Its economics, although not outstanding, were

better than those of contemporary Soviet jet transports and the type was extensively used by Aeroflot and other airlines in Warsaw Pact countries. Other examples have been used as government and VIP transports, but no convertible passenger/freight version has been produced, and its value as a military transport is therefore limited.

About 600 Il-18s are reported to have been built by the late 1960s, but by 1975 the type

was being phased out of service with Aeroflot in favour of the Tupolev Tu-154 'Careless' trijet. About this time, with the closely related Il-38 'May' maritime reconnaissance aircraft in production, it was decided to use the basic Il-18 for the electronic intelligence (Elint) role, backing up Antonov An-12 'Cub-Bs'. It seems likely that both the 'Cub-B' and the Elint Il-18, codenamed 'Coot-A', are based on old airframes retired from the VTA (Military

The Ilyushin Il-18, called 'Coot' by NATO, is used in small numbers by most Warsaw Pact air forces as passenger transports.

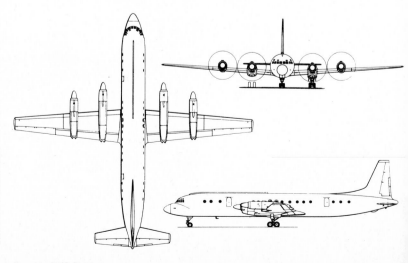

Ilyushin Il-18 Coot

Transport Aviation) or Aeroflot, and remanufactured for their new roles.

The 'Coot-A' was observed in early 1978, and has been seen in overland and over-water service. Given the wide-ranging nature of Elint activities, it is probable that both the 'Coot-A' and 'Cub-B' are operated by the AVMF (Soviet Naval Aviation). Their missions involve monitoring transmissions on the periphery of NATO-controlled areas, and patrolling in the vicinity of NATO exercises, suggesting that they may be involved in communications between widely-spaced Soviet units: (the US forces use the similar Lockheed Hercules for the same role.) Another activity is the so-called 'provocative' mission, collo-

quially known to the Royal Air Force as 'ringing the fire alarm': a 'Coot-A' was intercepted and photographed by an RAF fighter in 1978, suggesting that it was involved in an investigation of the UK Air Defence Region. The value of such missions is that they provoke a flurry of communications among the defending forces and provide a mass of data for later analysis.

The 'Coot-A' is fitted with a very large canoe fairing below the fuselage, possibly containing a highly sensitive directional receiver antenna. Other aerials are mounted in pods on the fuselage side, and in dorsal and ventral radomes. The prominent dorsal radomes may indicate the use of satellite communication for

real-time transmission of intercepted signals to a processing station. (The radar installations are strongly reminiscent of those on the US Navy's Lockheed EP-3E Orion, which also has a ventral cause.) The crew presumably includes a complement of systems operators, and working conditions are presumably far superior to those aboard the converted bombers which previously bore the brunt of Russian Elint work.

Type: medium transport and ('Coot-A') electronic intelligence/communications aircraft
Powerplant: four 4,250-ehp (3170-kW) Ivchenko AI-20M turboprops
Performance: cruising speed 380-390 mph

(610-625 km/h) at 26,250 ft (8000 m); range with 30,000-lb (13500-kg) payload 2,500 miles (4000 km); range with maximum fuel 4,000 miles (6500 km)
Weights: empty 77,000 lb (35000 kg); maximum fuel load 51,920 lb (23550 kg); maximum take-off 141,000 lb (64000 kg)
Dimensions: span 122 ft 8½ in (37.4 m); length 117 ft 9½ in (35.9 m); wing area 1,507 sq ft (140 m²)
Operators: Afghanistan, Algeria, Bulgaria, Czechoslovakia, East Germany, North Korea, Poland, Romania, USSR, Vietnam, Yugoslavia

Ilyushin Il-28 Beagle

China is by far the most important user of the Ilyushin Il-28 'Beagle', a now elderly tactical bomber. Some hundreds of the type were manufactured in China under a licence taken out before the Sino-Soviet rift. Production of the bomber, designated B-5, and of a trainer version continues despite the age of the design. Other air forces continue to use the Il-28 for various second-line duties: the Finnish air force operated several as target-tug into the late 1970s. The last Soviet force to use the type for combat duties was the AVMF (Soviet Naval Aviation) which adopted the Il-28T torpedo-bomber fairly late in the type's career. The AVMF Il-28Ts were almost certainly adapted from surplus Frontal Aviation Il-28s when the AVMF Tupolev Tu-14 'Bosuns' were retired in the mid-1960s.

The Il-28 was, like many first-generation Soviet jets, powered by derivatives of the Rolls-Royce Nene turbojets which had been supplied to the Soviet Union by the British government immediately after World War II. These offered greater power and better reliability than the engines then being developed by Russian and German engineers in the country's own establishments. The first prototype flew in August 1948 on the power of two British-built Nenes: the later aircraft were fitted with Soviet-built RD-45s or VK-1s. The Il-28 was of rather unusual appearance; the leading-edge of the wing was completely unswept and the trailing-edge was swept forwards, giving the aircraft a long-nosed appearance. The tail was abbreviated, possibly because of the weight of a bulky tail gun turret similar to that on the Tupolev Tu-4 'Bull', a copy of the Boeing B-29. Unlike contemporary US bombers, the Il-28 had a manned tail turret rather than a radar-controlled installation. In contrast with the wings, the tail surfaces were sharply swept back. Swept tail surfaces were standard on all straight-wing Soviet bombers of the day, for reasons which are not altogether clear; the intention may have been to avert compressibility problems around the rear turret.

Pre-production aircraft with RD-45s began to appear in late 1949, and deliveries of production aircraft, powered by the VK-1, started in 1951. Deliveries to Frontal Aviation greatly increased the striking power of the force, which hitherto had relied on the piston-engined Tu-2 'Bat'. The Il-28 retained the visual bombardier nose of the older piston-engined bombers, but at a fairly early stage in production the type was also fitted with all-weather bombing radar in a ventral fairing. Later aircraft were fitted with a tail-warning radar beneath the rear turret, but the guns remained manually aimed.

The Il-28 formed the main striking strength of the initial Warsaw Pact air forces, particularly those of Poland, Czechoslovakia and, later, East Germany. Other versions included the Il-28U 'Mascot' conversion trainer, with a second pilot's station and canopy in place of the bombardier nose. Like many Soviet conversion trainers, the Il-28U has no combat capability. Some Il-28R photographic and electronic reconnaissance aircraft were also put into service.

At least 1,000 Il-28s were built in the Soviet Union. The type was replaced in Soviet air force service by the Yakovlev Yak-28 'Brewer'. In general, however, non-Soviet Warsaw Pact forces have not been re-equipped

with comparable offensive aircraft. The Ilyushin bomber also possesses the distinction of being the first jet aircraft operated by Aeroflot; a few examples of the type, designated Il-20, were put into service by the airline in 1955 carrying high-priority freight and mail, as a means to gain jet experience before the arrival of the Tu-104 'Camel'.

Type: three-seat light bomber
Powerplant: two 6,040-lb (2740-kg) Klimov VK-1 centrifugal-flow turbojets
Performance: maximum speed at 14,765 ft (4500 m) 560 mph (900 km/h); maximum speed at sea level 500 mph (800 km/h); cruising speed 480 mph (770 km/h) at 33,000 ft (10000 m); range with a 2,200-lb (1000-kg) bombload 1,350 miles (2180 km) at 33,000 (10000 m)
Weights: empty 26,455 lb (13000 kg); maximum 46,300 lb (21000 kg)
Dimensions: span 70 ft 4½ in (21.45 m); length 57 ft 11 in (17.65 m); wing area 654.4 sq ft (60.8 m²)
Armament: internal bay for up to 6,500 lb (3000 kg) of bombs or two air-launched torpedoes; two fixed NR-23 23-mm cannon in nose and two NR-23 in tail turret
Operators: Afghanistan, Algeria, Bulgaria, China, Czechoslovakia, Iraq, North Korea, Nigeria, Poland, Romania, Somalia, South Yemen, Syria, USSR, Vietnam.

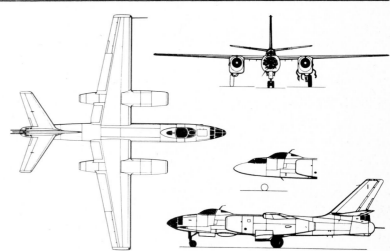

Ilyushin Il-28 Beagle (inset nose of Il-28U Mascot)

Chinese Air Force B-5 light bomber (Soviet Il-28 built under licence) of which more than 400 are in use.

The Il-28 has had a very long active life, indicating an excellent all-round design. This is a clean-looking example recently in Soviet service, which has escaped being rebuilt as a dual trainer, multi-sensor reconnaissance aircraft or EW/Elint platform.

Ilyushin Il-38 May

Compared with the Il-18 airliner the Il-38 has the wing further forward, balancing heavy equipment loads in the forward fuselage. The main weapon bay is ahead of the wing, where it can extend up to floor level. The ECM/Elint version called 'Coot-A' carries its equipment here.

Head-on the shallow space available for internal weapons is obvious, as is the basically clean form of this converted civil aircraft. Operating crew of most versions is reported to be 12, probably made up of four flight crew and eight sensor operators.

So far all Il-38 'May' aircraft seen by Western aircraft have been painted a medium grey overall, with no insignia except for national markings and a low-figure number on the tail. The former practice of displaying an airframe number has been discontinued, and on naval Tu-16 'Badger' aircraft it has been painted out.

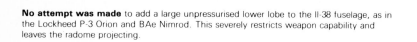

No attempt was made to add a large unpressurised lower lobe to the Il-38 fuselage, as in the Lockheed P-3 Orion and BAe Nimrod. This severely restricts weapon capability and leaves the radome projecting.

The Soviet Union was a latecomer in the field of specialized maritime reconnaissance and anti-submarine-warfare (ASW) aircraft, as it came late to the manufacture of airborne early warning systems. For this reason it is usually assumed that Soviet systems such as the Ilyushin Il-38 'May' and the Tu-126 'Moss' are not up to the same standards as Western counterparts; but their operational effectiveness depends on hard-to-assess details of their sensors and internal equipment.

The closest Western equivalent of the Il-38 is the Lockheed P-3 Orion. Both were developed from medium-range airliners of about the same vintage, although the Il-18 which forms the basis of the Il-38 is a rather larger aircraft than the Lockheed Electra. However, the histories of the two types are different. The first Orion entered service some 10 years before the Il-38 appeared, and by the time the Soviet aircraft had entered service the P-3's systems had been modernized twice to keep abreast with the growing threat from Russian ballistic-missile-firing submarines (SSBNs). More recently, the P-3C has undergone various Update programmes, acquiring new types of sensor and improved versions of systems already fitted. None of this development effort has been paralleled visibly on the Il-38, no changes in equipment having been observed since the type entered service.

Neither has the Soviet Union the benefit of the West's long experience of ASW, dating back to the Battle of the Atlantic in World War II. The Lockheed Neptune, for example, had no known equivalent in the Soviet Union. Jet aircraft such as the Tu-16 were too inefficient at low speeds and altitudes to be used effectively in the ASW role, which was mainly

the province of flying-boats such as the Beriev Be-6 and M-12, with relatively short range.
. In the early 1960s, when the United States Navy's force of Polaris-armed SSBNs was being built up, there was no aircraft in the Soviet naval air force (AVMF) which could counter the increasing threat. With the development of the Poseidon missile, the area from which US SSBNs could threaten large sectors of the Soviet Union increased well beyond the area which could be covered, even partially, by Be-6s and M-12s. The need for a specialized ASW aircraft grew with the deployment of the longer-ranged missile to replace the Polaris, and Il-38 development appears to have coincided with the introduction of Poseidon. The aircraft was first observed in 1974, but by that time it appears to have been in service for some years, and so design probably began in about 1965. About 100 Il-38s have been delivered to the AVMF, and some have been supplied to India; it is possible that the latter aircraft have a reduced standard of equipment, like the Lockheed P-3F supplied to Iran.

The airframe of the Il-38 is certainly stronger than that of the Il-18 airliner, in order to withstand the stresses of manoeuvring at low altitude in gusty weather. It is also likely that the ASW aircraft can take off at a higher gross weight than the airliner (the P-3C for instance, is very much heavier than the Electra) and it would be logical to expect the engines to be similar to the uprated AI-20s fitted to the Antonov An-32 STOL freighter.

A highly significant feature of the Il-38 design is the fact that the wing is set much farther forward than on the airliner. This indicates that the forward fuselage contains a concentration of heavy equipment. On either

side of the fuselage, ahead of the wing, there is fitted what appears to be an air intake and outlet. One explanation for this feature, and for the short front fuselage, is that a large processor is installed forward, with the main tactical control compartment above the wing and extending towards the rear. The aft fuselage presumably includes sleeping accommodation for relief crews and galley facilities, which are light.

Unlike that of the Orion, the main radar of the Il-38 is mounted under the forward fuselage immediately aft of the nosewheel bay. Radar is a major search aid for an ASW aircraft, but in these days of nuclear-powered submarines it has to be of high performance if it is to be effective. It is not known whether the Il-38 radar can match Western sets in its ability to distinguish small solid echoes such as periscopes from 'glint' off the water surface.

The weapon bay of the Il-38 is installed well forward; this feature does not in itself account for the forward shift of the wing, as it is shared by the P-3, where the wing is in the same relative position as on the original Electra. The weapon bay houses sonobuoys as well as offensive weapons, whereas the P-3 has separate sonobuoy stowage in the rear fuselage. Underfloor capacity immediately ahead of the wing is probably used for fuel tankage. The Il-38 carries the symbol of the ASW aircraft's trade: a magnetic anomaly detector (MAD) installed in a long tailboom.

Radar, MAD and acoustic sensors appear to be the main sources of raw data for the Il-38, but its effectiveness will also depend on the processing equipment fitted and its ability to select and pass information to the crew. Electronic surveillance measures (ESM) are not

conspicuous, although there is a fin-top antenna. Also apparently absent are infra-red and low-light level visual sensors, both standard on the latest Western types. Going purely on external signs, the Il-38 is so far observed appears to be a first-generation type in terms of its operational equipment; however, it can be expected that more effective versions are under development and will appear in AVMF service in due course.

Development of a large, long-range subsonic military aircraft was reported in 1979, with both the strategic missile-launching and ASW roles apparently in mind. However, the new type may be intended more for the high-altitude surveillance role formerly undertaken by the Tu-20 than for ASW of the sort carried out by the Il-38 and its Western equivalents.

Type: maritime reconnaissance and ASW aircraft
Powerplant: four 5,200-shp (3879-kW) Ivchenko AI-20M turboprops
Performance: maximum speed 400 mph (640 km/h); patrol speed 290 mph (460 km/h); endurance 16 hours; range 5,200 miles (8300 km)
Weights: empty 90,000 lb (40000 kg); maximum take-off 150,000 lb (68000 kg)
Dimensions: span 122 ft 9 in (37.4 m); length (including MAD boom) 129 ft 10 in (39.6 m); height 33 ft 4 in (10.3 m); wing area 1,500 sq ft (140 m²)
Armament: internal weapons bay for homing torpedoes, nuclear and conventional depth charges and sonobuoys
Operators: India, USSR

Ilyushin Il-76 Candid

Superficially similar to the Lockheed C-141 StarLifter, the Ilyushin Il-76 'Candid' is in fact a heavier and more powerful aircraft, more capable of operations from short, unpaved runways. It is replacing the Antonov An-12 'Cub' as the main tactical transport of the Soviet VTA (air transport force); it is also in service with Aeroflot, and Il-76s of both operators have been used to supply arms to Soviet client states.

The design of the Il-76 started in the late 1960s, to meet a joint civil/military requirement. Aeroflot needed an aircraft smaller and more flexible than the An-22 'Cock', while the VTA could presumably see a requirement for a faster aircraft than the big Antonov turboprop for use in forward areas. The requirement which emerged was for an aircraft which could carry twice the maximum payload of the An-12 over sectors longer than the older aircraft's maximum range. The new transport had to be able to use the same short and semi-prepared strips as the An-12, setting problems in undercarriage and wing design.

There is little room for flexibility in the design of a heavy military freighter. Loading and unloading requires a rear ramp and a floor at truck-bed height, so that a low wing is ruled out; wing wake then makes a low-set tailplane risky, so that aircraft of this type tend to have T-tails. The Ilyushin design bureau, headed from the mid-1960s by General Designer Novozhilov, adopted this generally conventional layout for the Il-76. It was the first Soviet transport to have podded engines,

hung on low-drag pylons reminiscent of those of the Douglas DC-8-62. The engines are set well inboard compared with those of Western airliners, and are probably set too low to have any blowing effect on the flaps. The wing is fitted with extensive high-lift devices, including slats, triple-slotted trailing-edge flaps, and spoilers for low-speed roll control.

A unique feature of the Il-76 is its rough-field landing gear, more complex than that of the C-141. The main gear comprises four units, each a single axle with four wheels abreast, while the nose gear also has four wheels abreast. The original Il-76 was designed to have a 'footprint pressure' no higher than that of the An-12.

Internally, the Il-76 is equipped with a cargo roller floor, two 6,500-lb (3000-kg) winches and two roof cranes with a total capacity of 22,000 lb (10000 kg).

In addition to the normal crew of two pilots, a flight engineer and a navigator, there is accommodation for a loadmaster and a radio operator. The navigator occupies a cabin below the flight deck, with a glazed nose. Production Il-76s have two radomes similar to those of late-production An-22s, one housing a weather radar and the other containing mapping equipment. The final member of the crew, on military Il-76s, is the tail gunner: the apparently archaic armament of twin 23-mm cannon fitted to the An-12 is retained on its jet replacement.

The first Il-76 was flown in March 1971, and was demonstrated at the Paris air show

two months later. Prototype and early production aircraft were designed closely to the original specification, which demanded 3,100-mile (5000-km) range with 88,000-lb (40000-kg) payload, and had a maximum take-off weight of 346,000 lb (157000 kg). This is believed to have been matched by limited fuel capacity. From 1977 production appears to have concentrated on the Il-76T, with some 20 per cent more fuel. It is likely that more of the Il-76T wing is wet, allowing payload to be traded for extra range.

Take-off and landing runs for the lighter early Il-76 are quoted at 2,800 ft (850 m) for the 1,500 ft (450 m) respectively; these are almost certainly ground rolls, but still suggest that the Il-76 could comfortably use a 5,000 ft (1500 m) strip. This performance is impressive, if not in the class of the US Advanced Medium STOL Transport (AMST) prototypes, and makes the Il-76 a tactical transport to be reckoned with. It has also been used extensively in the airlift role, and air-dropping trials have been carried out.

More than 100 Il-76s are now in service, and the VTA is probably replacing all its 600 An-12s with the new type. Reports of a tanker version under development may have been premature: the Il-86 wide-body airliner would seem to be a more suitable basis for such a development and would now be available in the same timescale. In 1978 the first examples of the Il-76 were reported to be in service outside the Soviet Union, but in the case of Iraq they are unarmed versions, at least

ostensibly civil in intent. The type does not yet appear to have been released as a military aircraft for supply outside the Soviet Union. Deliveries to Aeroflot appeared to be gaining momentum in 1978, suggesting that the VTA was relaxing some of its demands for priority in deliveries.

The Il-76T is probably the definitive version of the type for the time being, in the absence of any more advanced Soviet powerplant. An Il-76 was used as the flying test-bed for the Kuznetsov NK-86 engine, and the type was mentioned as a possible application for the engine, but there seems to be no sign that such a version is being built.

Type: strategic or tactical freighter
Powerplant: four 26,500 lb (12000 kg) Soloviev D-30KP turbofans
Performance: maximum speed 530 mph (850 km/h) or Mach 0.8; economical cruising speed 500 mph (800 km/h) or Mach 0.75; range with 77,000-lb (35000-kg) payload 4,000 miles (6500 km); ceiling 42,000 ft (13000 m)
Weights: empty 135,000 lb (62000 kg); maximum payload about 88,000 lb (40000 kg); maximum take-off 375,000 lb (170000 kg)
Dimensions: span 165 ft 8 in (50.5 m); length 152 ft 10½ in (46.59 m); height 48 ft 5 in (14.76 m); wing area 3,230 sq ft (300 m²)
Armament: (when fitted) two 23-mm cannon in radar-directed manned tail turret
Operators: Iraq, USSR

Like the American C-141, which appears to have been a model for this Russian transport, the wing is only slightly swept and was designed not for speed but for field performance. Compared with the USAF aircraft the power is much greater and the ability to operate from austere unpaved bases considerably better.

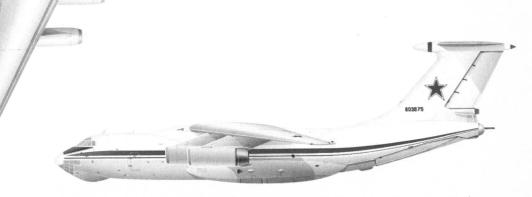

Though early Il-76 transports had anhedral from the roots (the wings bending level in flight) the latest example, seen at Paris in 1979, had gull wings with dihedral inboard of the outer engines.

The Soviet VTA military air transport force has been receiving Il-76 'Candid' transports since 1975, and numbers continued to increase in 1979. Most appear identical with the civil Aeroflot examples.

Israel Aircraft Industries 201 Arava

The civil prototype IAI-101 twin-turboprop STOL passenger/freight transport made its initial flight on 27 November 1969. It was named Arava 02 after the desert valley of Arava near the Dead Sea, and testing proceeded satisfactorily until 19 November 1970 when the aircraft disintegrated during wing-flutter tests, as a result of the failure of one of the wing struts. A second civil prototype was built, but the military version Arava 201 was already under construction and prototype 04 first flew on 7 March 1972. Registered 4X-IAB, it was demonstrated in gunship configuration with a 0.5-in (12.7-m) Browning machine-gun mounted in a blister on each side of the forward fuselage and another carried on a flexible tailcone mounting. Two hardpoints on the sides of the fuselage below the gun blisters accommodate up to 1,200 lb (544 kg) of offensive stores.

IAI offer the IAI-201 as an all-purpose military aircraft, easily adaptable to many configurations other than that of gunship. As an assault transport it carries 24 troops or a jeep-mounted 106-mm recoilless rifle and four-man crew; it can transport 17 paratroops plus dispatcher; the rear swing-fuselage section when replaced by a fairing allows the carriage of two one-ton cargo pallets; and as an ambulance 12 stretchers plus two medical attendants can be accommodated. Other missions which can be fulfilled by the Arava include those of tanker, anti-submarine aircraft,

navigational trainer and target tug.

The Israeli air arm has 14 Arava 201s to date, and export sales have been largely directed at Latin America, where to date some 50 machines have been sold to seven countries.

Structurally, the Arava 201 is a high-wing monoplane with a single bracing strut on each side. The wing has slight dihedral and is a light-alloy two-spar torsion-box structure, with two-spar ailerons, electrically operated double-slotted flaps and scoop-type spoilers for lateral control, all of light alloy. The spoilers are forward of the flaps and are linked to the ailerons. They act automatically when the ailerons are deflected more than 5° upwards.

The fuselage, with its two-man cockpit well forward, is a circular 'capsule' semi-monocoque light-alloy structure, with single-skin panels. The rear is cone-shaped and swings to the right for access, which is rendered easy by the short fixed tricycle undercarriage. Twin fins and rudders are carried on booms extending rearward from the nacelles of the twin 783-shp (584-kW) Pratt & Whitney PT6A-34 turboprops. The engines drive Hartzell HC-BT3TN-3D three-blade fully-feathering and reversing propellers.

Type: twin-turboprop STOL transport
Powerplant: two 783-ehp (584-kW) Pratt & Whitney PT6A-34 turboprops
Performance: maximum speed at 10,000 ft (3050 m) at full take-off weight 203 mph

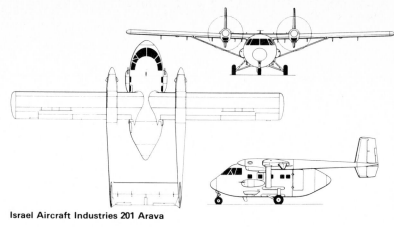

Israel Aircraft Industries 201 Arava

(326 km/h); economical cruising speed at 10,000 ft (3050 m) 193 mph (311 km/h); range with maximum fuel 806 miles (1297-m); service ceiling 26,575 ft (8100 m); rate of climb at sea level 1,565 ft (477 m) per minute; STOL take-off run 732 ft (223 m); STOL landing run 390 ft (119 m)
Weights: empty equipped (paratroop layout) 7,786 lb (3532 kg); maximum take-off 14,500 lb (6577 kg)
Dimensions: span 68 ft 6 in (20.88 m); length 42 ft 7.4 in (12.99 m); height

5 ft 6.9 in (1.70 m); wing area 470.2 sq ft (43.68 m²)
Armament: (gunship configuration) three 0.5-in (12.7-mm) Browning machine-guns, one in a blister either side of forward fuselage, with third weapon on a pintle mounting in the tail cone; (anti-submarine configuration) 12 sonobuoys and four Mk 44 torpedoes
Operators: Bolivia, Ecuador, Guatemala, Honduras, Israel, Mexico, Nicaragua, Salvador.

Though it soon proved its versatility and usefulness in warfare, the IAI 201 Arava was not originally ordered by the Israeli air force, which had to lease three (built for export) during the Yom Kippur war in October 1973. This example is from a batch of five delivered to the Fuerza Aerea Salvadorena in 1975-76.

Israel Aircraft Industries Barak

The first objective of the Israelis' Black Curtain programme of the late 1960s was to put a J79 engine into a French-built Mirage IIICJ, and this was successfully achieved in 1969-71. Conversion entailed complete remanufacture of much of the fuselage, with larger inlet ducts to handle the increased airflow, a shorter but fatter engine bay, with totally different engine

mounting locations, and a ram-air cooling inlet in an added dorsal fin to reduce temperature of the structure around the afterburner. The first batch of re-engined IIICJ aircraft were called Salvos, but later the J79-powered Mirage was named Barak (lightning). When the 'Yom Kippur' War broke out on 6 October 1973, five Baraks had been

completed and all were intensively and successfully used in that conflict. One of their features was racks for two Rafael Shafrir close-range air-to-air missiles, as were also being added to the surviving Mirage IIICJ force at that time. Total production of this type was small; as soon as possible it gave way to the completely redesigned Kfir, and the original

Black Curtain plan to re-engine all the IIICJ force was not carried out.

Data: as for Mirage IIICJ but with Kfir performance
Operator: Israel

Israel Aircraft Industries Kfir

Kfir (Lion Cub) has been developed by IAI to succeed the Dassault Mirage III in the interceptor and ground-attack roles. The Israeli Air Force received 72 single-seat Mirage IIICJs from April 1972, mainly for use as air-superiority fighters and for interception. In late 1966 Israel ordered 50 Mirage 5Js to complement the Mirage IIIs by concentrating on ground-attack, but following the Six-Day War in June 1967 the French government placed an embargo on the delivery of the Mirage 5Js, which were eventually put into service with France's *Armée de l'Air*. The Israeli Air Force therefore had to look elsewhere for equipment and, although the United States began to supply McDonnell Douglas F-4 Phantoms and McDonnell Douglas A-4 Skyhawks, the Israeli authorities decided to set up an indigenous production line to build combat aircraft.

The basic Mirage III/5 airframe was adopted as a starting point, with a General Electric J79 turbojet — the engine used in the Phantom — replacing the SNECMA Atar employed in the Mirage series. Mating the US powerplant with the Dassault-designed airframe proved difficult, however, and IAI produced the Nesher (Eagle) as an interim fighter to fill the gap until the new type was available. The Nesher was a locally built copy of the Mirage III/5, with some modifications but retaining the Atar 9C engine. The prototype Nesher is thought to have made its maiden flight in September 1969 and deliveries of production aircraft, equipped with Israeli avionics, began in 1972. About 40 Neshers are reported to have fought with the Israeli Air Force during the Yom Kippur War in October 1973.

The Kfir was revealed in April 1975, when two examples were put on display. The aircraft closely resembles the Mirage 5 but has a number of differences apart from the use of a

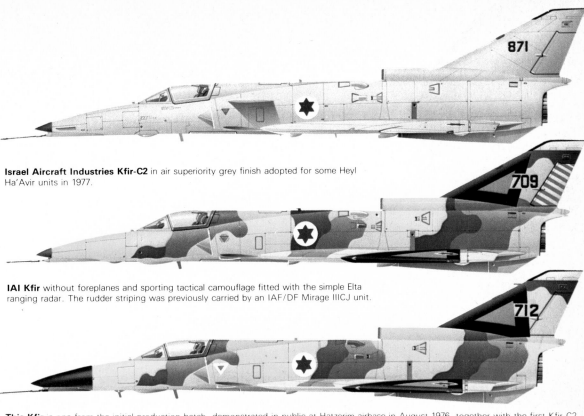

Israel Aircraft Industries Kfir-C2 in air superiority grey finish adopted for some Heyl Ha'Avir units in 1977.

IAI Kfir without foreplanes and sporting tactical camouflage fitted with the simple Elta ranging radar. The rudder striping was previously carried by an IAF/DF Mirage IIICJ unit.

This Kfir is one from the initial production batch, demonstrated in public at Hatzerim airbase in August 1976, together with the first Kfir-C2 with canard foreplanes. Fitted with the definitive radar, it was subsequently brought up to C2 standard.

continued

One of the first IAI Kfir-C2 multi-role fighters which entered production for the Heyl Ha'Avir (Israeli air force) in 1974. Several possible export sales for this cost-effective aircraft have failed to mature, or been blocked by the USA (because it has an American engine), but a sale of 50 to Taiwan was being fulfilled in 1980.

Israel Aircraft Industries Kfir

IAI Kfir-C2 cutaway drawing key

1 Fin-tip UHF antenna
2 Rear navigation light
3 ECM antenna
4 Fin construction
5 Rudder construction
6 Rudder bellcrank
7 Rudder control rods
8 Fin spar
9 Rudder jack

10 Anti-collision beacon
11 Brake parachute fairing
12 Parachute
13 Release mechanism
14 Tailcone fairing
15 Airflow guide vanes
16 Variable exhaust nozzle
17 Tailcone attachment frame
18 Cooling air outlet
19 Jetpipe inner ducting
20 Tail bumper
21 Tail avionics boxes
22 Fin attachment
23 Fin attachment frame
24 Rear fuselage
   construction

42 Leading edge fuel tank
43 Fuel supply piping
44 Fuselage fuel tanks
45 Turbojet intake
46 Engine starter
47 Port constant speed drive
   unit
48 Intake ducting
49 Fuselage frame construction
50 Pressure sensor
51 Inverted flight accumulator
52 Dorsal fairing
53 Oxygen bottles
54 Forward fuselage fuel tank

25 Compensator jack
26 Belly fuel tank
27 Engine mounting attachment
28 Cooling air outlet
29 Fin root intake fairing
30 Cooling air intakes
31 Main fuselage frame
32 Oil tank
33 General Electric J79-GE-17
   engine
34 Cooling air ducts
35 Engine front mounting cover
36 Port inboard elevon
37 Port outboard elevon
38 Port navigation light
39 Wing main fuel tank
40 Missile launcher
41 Shafrir air-to-air missile

55 Fuel filler
56 Canard foreplane
   construction
57 Canopy hinge attachment
58 Canopy external release
   handle
59 Ejection seat mounting
60 Avionics units
61 Martin Baker JM6 ejection
   seat
62 Jettisonable canopy cover
63 Ejection seat firing handles
64 Pilot's control console

65 Instrument panel
66 Reflector sight
67 Windscreen
68 Instrument pitot
69 Nose construction
70 Radar ranging unit
71 Radome
72 Pitot boom
73 Nose strake
74 Yaw sensing vane
75 Autopilot controller
76 Radio and electronics
   equipment
77 Inertial platform
78 Static inverter
79 UHF aerial
80 Rudder pedal
81 Radar console
82 Control column
83 Ejection seat adjusting
   handle
84 Control rod linkage
85 Nosewheel leg doors
86 Nosewheel leg

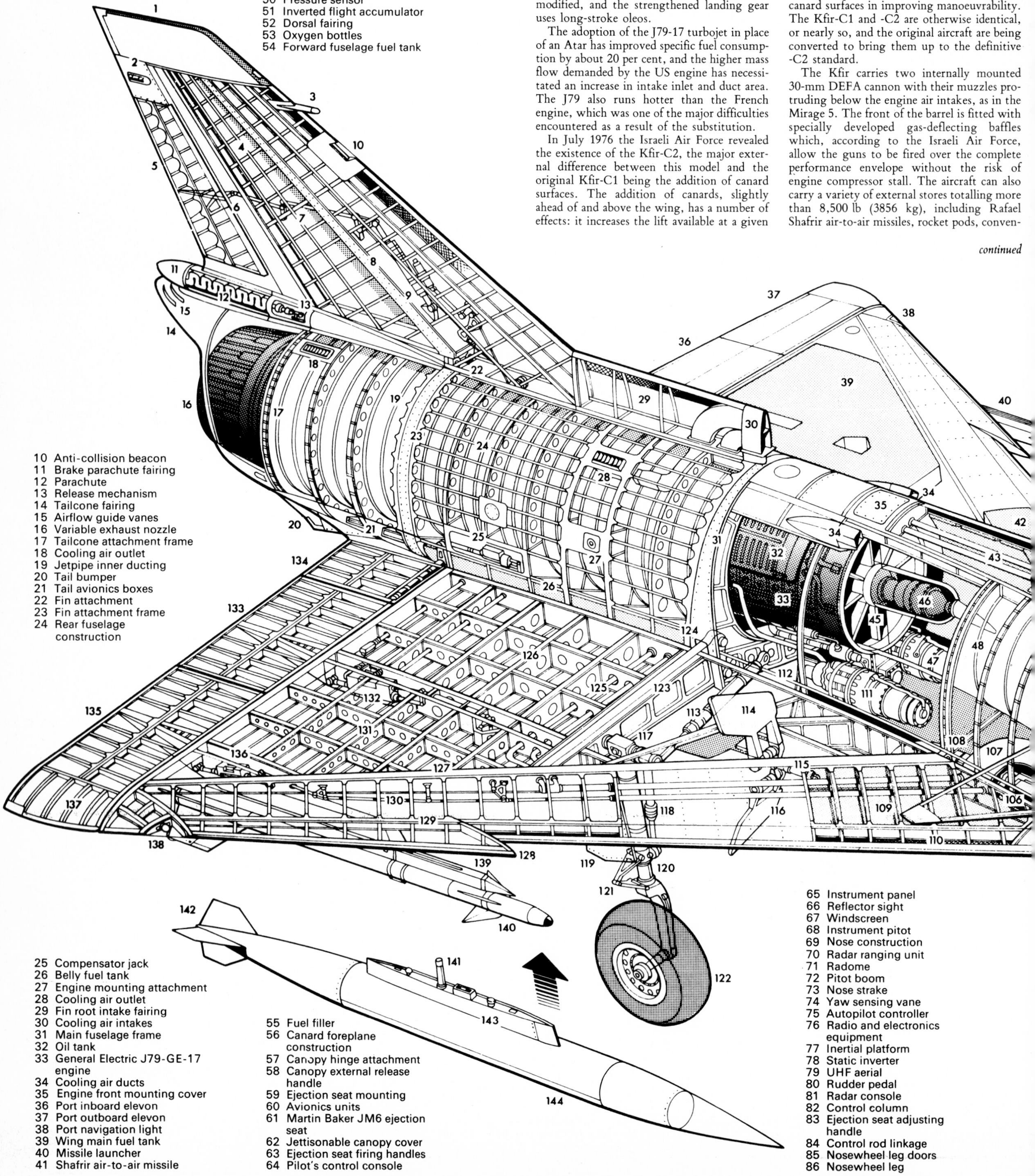

US engine and Israeli equipment. The rear fuselage is fatter and shorter than in the French-designed aircraft, with the variable exhaust nozzle protruding from the afterbody. The afterburner is cooled by air drawn from a scoop in the root of the fin. The forward section of Kfir's fuselage is larger than that of the Mirage, and the undersurface is flatter, while the nose itself has been lengthened. The leading edges of the 60° delta wing are also modified, and the strengthened landing gear uses long-stroke oleos.

The adoption of the J79-17 turbojet in place of an Atar has improved specific fuel consumption by about 20 per cent, and the higher mass flow demanded by the US engine has necessitated an increase in intake inlet and duct area. The J79 also runs hotter than the French engine, which was one of the major difficulties encountered as a result of the substitution.

In July 1976 the Israeli Air Force revealed the existence of the Kfir-C2, the major external difference between this model and the original Kfir-C1 being the addition of canard surfaces. The addition of canards, slightly ahead of and above the wing, has a number of effects: it increases the lift available at a given angle of attack, allows the aircraft to operate over a greater range of angles of attack, and reduces stability because the centre of lift and centre of gravity are moved closer together. The canards have been fitted mainly to improve manoeuvrability in combat, but they also allow the aircraft to operate from shorter runways. The Kfir-C2 has saw-teeth in the wing leading edges and small strakes along the nose, both these features complementing the canard surfaces in improving manoeuvrability. The Kfir-C1 and -C2 are otherwise identical, or nearly so, and the original aircraft are being converted to bring them up to the definitive -C2 standard.

The Kfir carries two internally mounted 30-mm DEFA cannon with their muzzles protruding below the engine air intakes, as in the Mirage 5. The front of the barrel is fitted with specially developed gas-deflecting baffles which, according to the Israeli Air Force, allow the guns to be fired over the complete performance envelope without the risk of engine compressor stall. The aircraft can also carry a variety of external stores totalling more than 8,500 lb (3856 kg), including Rafael Shafrir air-to-air missiles, rocket pods, conven-

continued

This Kfir-C2 lacks the M-2021 multimode radar and has instead the M-2001B ranging set which is limited to air/air or air/ground ranging of targets acquired visually. The large stores are finned drop tanks, though various ECM pods, bombs and air/air (Shafrir) and air/ground missiles can be carried.

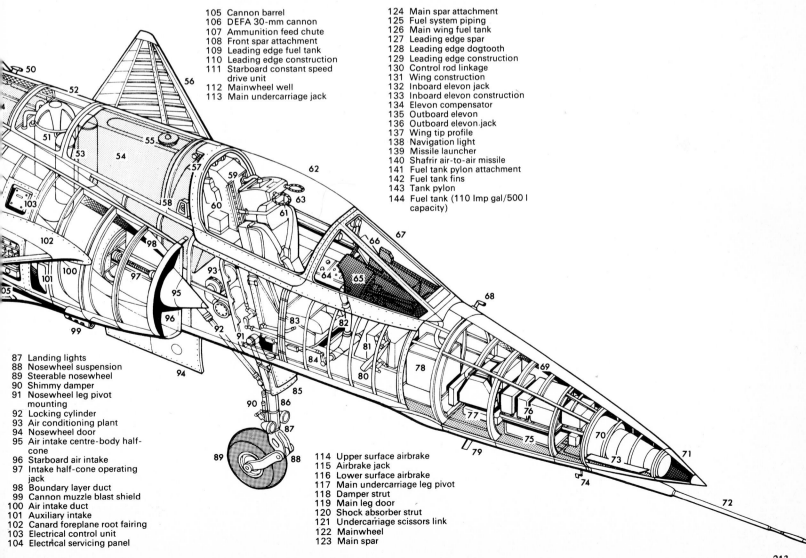

105 Cannon barrel
106 DEFA 30-mm cannon
107 Ammunition feed chute
108 Front spar attachment
109 Leading edge fuel tank
110 Leading edge construction
111 Starboard constant speed drive unit
112 Mainwheel well
113 Main undercarriage jack

124 Main spar attachment
125 Fuel system piping
126 Main wing fuel tank
127 Leading edge spar
128 Leading edge dogtooth
129 Leading edge construction
130 Control rod linkage
131 Wing construction
132 Inboard elevon jack
133 Inboard elevon construction
134 Elevon compensator
135 Outboard elevon
136 Outboard elevon jack
137 Wing tip profile
138 Navigation light
139 Missile launcher
140 Shafrir air-to-air missile
141 Fuel tank pylon attachment
142 Fuel tank fins
143 Tank pylon
144 Fuel tank (110 Imp gal/500 l capacity)

87 Landing lights
88 Nosewheel suspension
89 Steerable nosewheel
90 Shimmy damper
91 Nosewheel leg pivot mounting
92 Locking cylinder
93 Air conditioning plant
94 Nosewheel door
95 Air intake centre-body half-cone
96 Starboard air intake
97 Intake half-cone operating jack
98 Boundary layer duct
99 Cannon muzzle blast shield
100 Air intake duct
101 Auxiliary intake
102 Canard foreplane root fairing
103 Electrical control unit
104 Electrical servicing panel

114 Upper surface airbrake
115 Airbrake jack
116 Lower surface airbrake
117 Main undercarriage leg pivot
118 Damper strut
119 Main leg door
120 Shock absorber strut
121 Undercarriage scissors link
122 Mainwheel
123 Main spar

tional or anti-runway bombs, and guided air-to-surface weapons such as Maverick, Hobos and Shrike.

The majority of Kfir's avionics is supplied by Israeli companies, although some items are built under licence from overseas firms. In many cases the original equipment has been improved on by the licensee. The Thomson-CSF Cyrano radar fitted in Mirage IIIs proved to be inadequate for the Israeli Air Force's needs, so Elta has developed its EL/M-2001B ranging radar for the Kfir. This set can track low-flying aircraft even against a background of clutter and is claimed by the manufacturer to have no equivalent in the West. The EL/M-2001B feeds range data for air or ground targets into the central navigation and weapon-aiming system, which is based on an Elbit System-80 digital computer. Further information is supplied by the licence-built Singer Kearfott KT-70 inertial platform, allowing the nav-attack system to drive a head-up display supplied by Israel Electro-Optical Industries. The company based its HUD development on equipment built by Marconi Avionics for the Israeli Air Force's A-4 Skyhawks, although the unit fitted in the Kfir is of indigenous design. The HUD has two modes for delivery of air-to-ground weapons, another for air combat and a fourth for navigation.

The Israeli Air Force is expected to receive a total of about 160 Kfirs, and the type is also being offered for export. At least one proposed sale, to Ecuador, has however been embargoed by the United States, which refused to supply engines in support of such a deal. Some of the Israeli Air Force's Kfirs will be two-seat trainers, the first of which is due to fly during 1979.

Type: single-seat fighter and ground-attack aircraft
Power Plant: one General Electric J79-GE-17 (modified) turbojet rated at 17,900 lb (8119 kg) thrust with afterburning
Performance: maximum design speed (clean) at least Mach 2.2 or 1,450 mph (2335 km/h) at high altitude; tactical radius (as interceptor with two drop tanks) up to 330 miles (535 km); time to 36,000 ft (11000 m) 1.5 minutes
Weights: maximum combat for ground attack 32,120 lb (14600 kg); typical combat as interceptor with two Shafrir missiles 20,470 lb (9305 kg)
Dimensions: span 27 ft (8.23 m); length 50 ft 4 in (15.34 m); height 17 ft 1 in (5.22 m); wing area 392 sq ft (36.43 m²)
Armament: two 30-mm DEFA cannon and two Shafrir AAMs or air-to-ground weapons including bombs, rockets or missiles (such as Maverick, Hobos and Shrike)
Operator: Israel

Obviously slimmer than that of the Mirage III, and superficially similar to the Mirage 5, the Kfir's nose actually contains a better kit of avionics than any version of the French aircraft, all of it of Israeli manufacture. The Elta multi-mode radar is a modern pulse-doppler set, and other equipment includes a twin-computer flight control and stability-augmentation system, HUD (head-up display) and Elbit weapon delivery.

The most prominent external difference between the Kfir-C2 and the original Kfir and Mirage is the fixed canard, a pair of sweptback foreplanes above the engine inlet ducts which greatly improves field length, combat manoeuvrability, control about all axes and landing behaviour. Airflow at high angles of attack is also improved by a pair of narrow strakes along each side of the extreme nose, rather like those on Concorde.

In the front view the strakes and canards can be related to the height of the wing and engine inlets, the upper surfaces of the latter contributing with the top of the wide fuselage to the total aerodynamic lift at high angles of attack. At the rear can be seen the array of cooling-air ram inlets above the engine bay and in the leading edge of the dorsal fin. With good design these could give thrust rather than drag overall.

To accommodate the modified J79-GE-17 engine the rear fuselage is of larger diameter than that of the Mirage III, although it is markedly shorter. The ventral fairing and twin diagonal underfins are also quite unlike the French design. Less obvious are the many internal systems and structural changes, one of the latter being a strengthened main landing gear with increased shock-strut travel for rough-field operations at high weight.

Israel Aircraft Industries Nesher

As an intermediate stage in the development of an Israeli fighter derived from the Dassault-Breguet Mirage III, Israel Aircraft Industries first produced drawings and tooling for a direct copy of the French aircraft, with only detail changes. While the secret Black Curtain project was under way to re-engine the Mirage with the J79 turbojet, plans of the original aircraft and its Atar 09C engine arrived covertly in Israel from French and Swiss sources. In view of the time needed to develop a satisfactory J79-Mirage it was decided as an immediate measure to manufacture the Atar-powered aircraft under the name Nesher (Eagle). The decision to do so was taken in the winter 1969-70, and the first Nesher flew as

early as 1971. The aircraft was in most respects similar to the Mirage IIICJ but incorporated simplified avionics more akin to those of the Mirage 5. When the 'Yom Kippur' War broke out in 1973 the Nesher was fully operational with the Heyl Ha'Avir. Total production exceeded 50, the latter being the reported current operational strength.

Data: essentially as for Mirage IIIC
Operators: Israel, and possibly Argentina, which has announced an order for 26 aircraft called Dagger (one report states that these are probably refurbished ex-Israeli air force aircraft)

Israel Aircraft Industries Westwind

The Westwind is a twin-engined executive jet in current production by Israel Aircraft Industries. It has been the product of IAI since 1967, but the Westwind has a history which goes back a great deal further than that. The design originated with Aero Commander Inc of Bethany, Oklahoma, which conceived the Model 1121 Jet Commander as a contender for the lucrative business jet market of the early-1960s. The type was based on the design philosophy of the long line of Aero Commander piston twins and the turboprop Commander 680T. The prototype Jet Commander made its first flight on 27 January 1963 powered by a pair of General Electric CJ610 turbojets. With the wings positioned behind the cabin, the forward fuselage provided very quiet passenger accommodation and extremely good vision for all occupants. The engines were set on each side of the rear fuselage in accordance with accepted practice, and the horizontal tail unit was positioned on the fin and had substantial sweep-back. On the other hand, the wings were unswept, with equal-taper and fixed at the fuselage midposition.

The essential Federal Aviation Administration type certificate was granted to the Jet Commander on 4 November 1964, with the aircraft being approved under FAR.25 regulations, and the first delivery was made in January of the following year. Most aircraft went to commercial business users in the United States and 32 examples were delivered in the first year. A further 71 Jet Commanders were sold by 1967 when the design faced a major change of fortune.

In 1967 Rockwell Standard Corporation

(the owners of Aero Commander) merged with North American Aviation Inc and the American anti-trust laws came into play. It was decided that the new organization could not market both the Jet Commander and the Sabreliner. The Jet Commander was accordingly sold to Israel Aircraft Industries for a price of $25.0 million. In the hands of IAI the aircraft received a 2 ft 6 in (0.762 m) fuselage stretch, new CJ610-5 engines, an increase in gross weight to 18,500 lb (8392 kg) and the new name Commodore Jet Model 1123. Under this name, and later as the Westwind 1123, it returned to the world market and sales built up rapidly with a few aircraft reaching military users — largely through the US distributor, Atlantic Aviation. One example was delivered to the *Fuerza Aerea Panamena* for transport duties, and the *Fuerza Aerea Hondurena* also received a Westwind which was assigned to the VIP flight at Tegucigalpa. The Uganda air force bought a Jet Commander from IAI for use by President Amin, but this was later returned to Israel and sold to a US corporate customer.

The next development was the Model 1124 Westwind — essentially a Model 1123 with two Garrett AiResearch TFE-731-3 turbofan engines. It was this model which provided a basis for the main military derivative of the Westwind. In 1977 IAI supplied three Model 1123s to the Israeli navy and reworked these into Model 1124N maritime patrol aircraft. They were fitted with TFE-731-3-1G engines and equipped with a large nose radome accommodating a Litton LASR-2 search radar, together with the Global Navigation low-

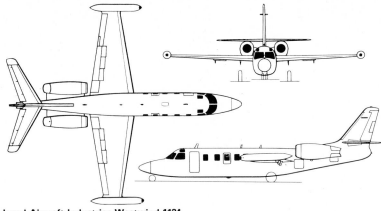

Israel Aircraft Industries Westwind 1124

frequency NS-500A navigation system. In an alternative configuration, the 1124N can be fitted with a retractable radome beneath the rear fuselage to house the search radar. The 1124N also has provision for a rear-fuselage MAD boom, and can be equipped with low-light level television. External stores, including sea-rescue drop modules, can be carried on fuselage pylons, and the aircraft can be fitted with ECM chaff dispensers and sonobuoy chutes. The Israeli navy is well satisfied with the 1124N, which is used for surveillance of merchant ships involved in possible clandestine operations and general maritime reconnaissance.

Type: 12-seat light transport and maritime surveillance aircraft

Powerplant: two 3,700-lb (1678-kg) static thrust Garrett AirResearch TFE-731-3-1G turbofans
Performance: maximum speed 542 mph (868 km/h) at 19,450 ft (5928 m); long-range cruising speed at 41,000 ft (12497 m) 462 mph (739 km/h); maximum range at long-range cruising speed with 45 minutes reserve 2,869 miles (4591 km); rate of climb 4,000 ft (1219 m) per minute; balanced field length 4,950 ft (1509 m); service ceiling 45,000 ft (13716 m)
Weights: empty 10,300 lb (4672 kg); maximum take off 22,850 lbs (10365 kg)
Dimensions: span 44 ft 9½ in (13.65 m); length 55 ft 0 in (16.8 m); height 15 ft 9½ in (4.81 m); wing area 308.3 sq ft (28.63 m²)
Armament: none
Operators: Honduras, Israel, Panama

Jodel D.140

Based on the smaller two-seat Jodels, the D.140 was developed by the *Société Aéronautique Normande* (SAN) as a four-seat tourer, but alternative configurations available included an ambulance version with capacity for a stretcher loaded through a baggage door behind the cabin. The prototype D.140, subsequently named Mousquetaire (musketeer), flew on 4 July 1958, and was followed by the first production aircraft four months later. By mid-1961 the production rate at SAN's Bernay factory had reached five per month, and some 65 had been delivered.

The design was developed, later versions incorporating various modifications. The D.140B had a revised instrument panel and foot-operated brakes; the D.140C Mousquetaire III featured swept vertical tail surfaces and the D.140E Mousquetaire IV had a larger wing, flaps and vertical tail, all-moving tailplane and improved ailerons. The D.140A had a modified airspeed indicator and when fitted with the D.140C tail became the D.140

AC.

The French air force bought 18 D.140Es for the *Ecole de l'Air* at Salon where they are used for recreational purposes. Later, 15 D.140R Abeilles were also obtained; this version, which first flew in mid-1965, was intended for glider- and banner-towing. It features an extensively glazed cabin to improve rearward vision, and can be fitted with skis for snow operation.

The Abeille (bee) is basically similar to the D.140E in specification but has an empty weight of 1,408 lb (639 kg), a maximum speed of 155 mph (250 km/h), a cruising speed of 140 mph (225 km/h) and a service ceiling of 16,725 ft (5100 m).

Type: four-seat light touring aircraft
Powerplant: one 180-hp (134-kW) Lycoming O-360-A2A piston engine
Performance: maximum speed 158 mph (254 km/h) at sea level; cruising speed at 75% power 149 mph (240 km/h) at 5,900 ft (1798

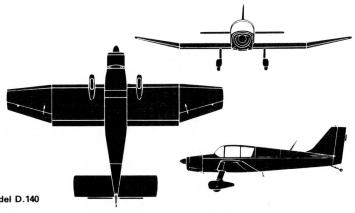

Jodel D.140

m); rate of climb at sea level 750 ft (230 m) per minute; take-off to 50 ft (15 m) 1,000 ft (305 m); service ceiling 16,400 ft (5000 m); range 870 miles (1400 km) at 140 mph (225 km/h)
Weights: empty 1,367 lb (620 kg); loaded

2,645 lb (1200 kg)
Dimensions: span 33 ft 8 in (10.27 m); length 25 ft 8 in (7.82 m); height 6 ft 9 in (2.05 m); wing area 199.13 sq ft (18.50 m²)
Operators: France

Junkers Ju 52/3m

The Junkers Ju 52/3m must surely qualify as the longest-serving military aircraft ever built; 47 years after the flight of the prototype in May 1932 three examples are still in service with the Swiss air force, and licence-built examples have only comparatively recently been retired from the Portuguese and Spanish air forces.

Based on the single-engined Ju 52, the /3m was an instant success and earned an enviable reputation for strength and reliability in many parts of the world.

Lufthansa was an early customer, and within 3½ years had more than 50; the Luftwaffe received a large number to form the backbone of its bomber strength in the mid-1930s, some of these latter aircraft serving with the Legion

Koudor in the Spanish Civil War. In World War II the Ju 52/3m was seen in all European and North African theatres of war in transport, troop-carrying, glider-towing and supply-dropping roles. Around 4,300 Ju 52/3ms were built in Germany, while more than 400 were built in France as the AAC.1 shortly after the end of the war. CASA in Spain produced 170 under licence.

The dearth of new civil transports in the early post-war years saw a number of French-built Ju 52/3ms and a few ex-Luftwaffe aircraft serving as interim civil airliners, even with British European Airways. Post-war military users included Bolivia, Czechoslovakia, France, the Netherlands, Portugal, South Africa, Spain and others.

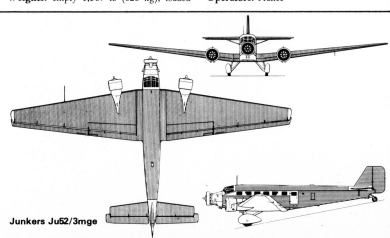

Junkers Ju52/3mge

The only military examples still in service are the three bought new by the Swiss air force and delivered from Germany on 4 October 1939. They were used for training observers and had interchangeable equipment to enable use as transports, including a gun position in the top of the fuselage and in a retractable 'dustbin' underneath.

During the licence-manufacture of the DH Vampire in Switzerland the three Ju 52/3ms were used to collect DH Goblin jet engines from Hatfield, while prior to this they had transported personnel and material between Germany and Switzerland when the Swiss air force was obtaining surplus North American Mustang fighters from US bases in Germany. All three aircraft are still used for transport and paratroop training, and fatigue tests have indicated that they are good for a number of years yet.

Forca Aerea Portuguesa Junkers Ju52/3m fitted with early spatted undercarriage.

Type: three-engine utility transport
Powerplant: (Swiss Ju52/3m, 4e) three 660-hp (492-kW) BMW 132A/3 radial piston engines
Performance: maximum speed 161 mph (260 km/h); cruising speed 124 mph (200 km/h); maximum rate of climb 790 ft (240 m) per minute; service ceiling 16,730 ft (5100 m); range 745 miles (1200 km); endurance 6½ hours.
Weights: empty 14,354 lb (6510 kg); loaded 23,157 lb (10500 kg)
Dimensions: span 95 ft 11 in (29.25 m); length 62 ft 0 in (18.9 m); height 18 ft 2 in (5.5 m); wing area 1,189.4 sq ft (110.5 m²)
Operators: Switzerland

Kaman H-2 Seasprite

In 1956 the US Navy initiated a design competition to procure a high-speed all-weather utility helicopter. Kaman's design proved sufficiently attractive to be selected as the winner later in 1956, and on 29 November 1957, the company received a contract for four prototypes plus an initial batch of 12 production aircraft. The service designation was HU2K-1 (changed in 1962 to UH-2A) and the name Seasprite. The prototype flew for the first time on 2 July 1959, but it was rather more than three years later that the first UH-2A production aircraft entered service with the US Navy's Helicopter Utility Squadron 2 (HU-2) at Lakehurst NAS, on 18 December 1962.

This new Kaman helicopter with a single main rotor and tail-mounted anti-torque rotor was something of an innovation for the company. In fact, it was their first design to dispense with side-by-side intermeshing rotors which they had once considered superior to the main-rotor/anti-torque rotor combination. Other unusual features of the design were the inclusion of retractable landing gear and a flotation hull, which meant that this helicopter could be operated direct from water. This was of considerable advantage, as the primary requirement for this new aircraft was in the carrier plane-guard, and search and rescue roles. From the general utility aspect the Seasprite was expected to cater also for casualty evacuation; courier service; emergency supply and resupply; reconnaissance; vertical replenishment, especially for small ships at sea; and tactical air control. To make possible its utilisation over such a wide range of duties, standard avionics included equipment for all-weather navigation, automatic flight stabilization and automatic navigation, and the Seasprite was also provided with an external cargo hook of 4,000-lb (1814-kg) capacity. Internal accommodation was for a crew of two and up to 11 passengers or four stretchers.

Initial production version was the UH-2A, powered by a single 1,250-shp (932-kW) General Electric T58-GE-8B turboshaft, and these aircraft first went to sea aboard USS Independence on 4 June 1963. They were followed into service by the UH-2B with reduced navigation avionics, and the first detachment of these went to sea with USS Albany on 8 August 1963. Service deployment under active conditions highlighted the desirability of providing increased engine power, and in March 1965 Kaman completed the first of two twin-engine conversions for evaluation. These had two T58-GE-8B turboshafts mounted in pods on each side of the rotor pylon, providing improved performance, plus the added reliability of a twin-engine installation. The success of this conversion meant that all surviving UH-2A and UH-2B aircraft were converted from 1967 onwards, and at the same time tail surface areas were increased slightly, and minor modifications made to the rotor pylon and cockpit. The resulting aircraft was designated UH-2C.

Next version to enter service was the HH-2C, an armed and armoured variant of the UH-2C, having a chin-mounted 7.62-mm (0.3-in) Minigun turret, waist-mounted machine-guns, extensive armour, and changes such as uprated transmission and dual wheels on the main landing gear to cater for the higher gross weight. They were followed by HH-2Ds with armament and armour deleted.

Increasing concern with the problem of nuclear submarines caused the US Navy to think hard and long about ways and means of coping with this menace, and in 1971 two HH-2Ds were modified to carry an experimental under-nose radar system. Two more were modified subsequently, and the results of their testing were incorporated into the US Navy's important Light Airborne Multi-Purpose System (LAMPS) programme. This is concerned with ASW and missile defence, and a number of HH-2Ds have been converted to SH-2D Interim-LAMPS configuration with the installation of ASW search radar, MAD, sonobuoys, the necessary associated avionics and controls, plus smoke markers and flares. To strike home at the identified target, Mk 46 homing torpedoes are carried.

While these HH-2Ds were being modified, Kaman was testing two other Seasprites with even more advanced avionics, and deliveries of this SH-2F version began in May 1973, with initial deployment on board USS Bagley. SH-2Ds and HH-2Ds have since been uprated to this SH-2F configuration. In addition to the advanced avionics, modifications include the provision of Kaman's new '101' rotor, strengthened landing gear, and the installation of more powerful engines (see data).

Type: naval ASW, anti-ship missile defence, search and rescue and utility helicopter
Powerplant: (SH-2F) two 1,350-shp (1007-kW) General Electric T58-GE-8F turboshafts
Performance: (SH-2F) maximum speed at sea level 165 mph (266 km/h); cruising speed 150 mph (241 km/h); range with maximum fuel 422 miles (679 km)
Weights: (SH-2F) empty 7,040 lb (3193 kg); take-off 12,800 lb (5806 kg)
Dimensions: (SH-2F) main rotor diameter 44 ft 0 in (13.41 m); tail rotor diameter 8 ft 2 in (2.49 m); length (rotors turning) 52 ft 7 in (16.03 m); height (rotors turning) 15 ft 6 in (4.72 m); main rotor disc area 1,520.5 sq ft (141.25 m²)
Armament: can include air-to-surface missiles, homing torpedoes, guns and rockets
Operators: US Navy

Kaman SH-2F Seasprite

Kaman's SH-2F Seasprite is a vastly more capable helicopter than the original single-engined Seasprites, and has for a decade been the "Interim LAMPS" platform for US Navy frigates and other ships, with radar, sonics, MAD bird and torpedoes.

Kaman H-43F Huskie

Winner of a US Navy competition for a liaison helicopter, the Kaman 600 entered production in 1950 as the HOK-1. A developed model, the OH-43D with a 600-hp (447-kW) Pratt & Whitney R-1340-81 radial engine, served with the US Marine Corps, 81 being built for use in cargo, medevac, search and rescue and liaison work.

The next variant was the UH-43C, of which 24 were delivered before the decision was taken to use turbine power for further development. The prototype H-43B, converted from a modified HOK-1, flew on 27 September 1956. Its development formed part of a USAF contract covering testing of the Lycoming XT53 engine. Production models of the H-43B began to come off the line in December 1958 powered by an 860-shp (642-kW) Lycoming T53-L-1B turboshaft derated to 825 shp (615 kW). The new model offered double the usable cabin space and payload of the H-43, made possible by mounting the engine above the cabin.

An original contract covered 116 H-43Bs for the USAF, and a further contract for 59 followed. The type was subsequently redesignated HH-43B, and export deliveries included 12 to the Burmese air force, some of which are still in service, and six to the Colombian air force.

Final model of the Huskie was the HH-43F

with a 1,150-shp (858-kW) Lycoming T53-L-11A turboshaft derated to 825-shp (615-kW). It was designed to replace the H-43B where altitude performance was required under hot weather conditions, and by use of internal tankage fuel capacity was increased by 291 gallons (1323 litres). The first HH-43F flew in August 1964 and production deliveries were made to Iran where the air force received 10 and the army 14; a few of the air force machines were still in service at the time of the 1979 revolution.

Type: crash rescue helicopter
Powerplant: one 1,150-shp (858-kW) Lycoming T53-L-11A turboshaft
Performance: maximum speed at sea level 120 mph (193 km/h); cruising speed 110 mph (177 km/h); initial rate of climb 2,000 ft (610 m) per minute; service ceiling 23,000 ft (7010 m); hovering ceiling in ground effect 20,000 ft (6096 m); hovering ceiling out of ground effect 16,000 ft (4876 m); range 504 miles (810 km)
Weights: empty 4,469 lb (2027 kg); loaded 8,800 lb (3991 kg) with underslung load
Dimensions: main rotor diameter 47 ft 0 in (14.32 m); length 25 ft 0 in (7.62 m); height 15 ft 6 in (4.72 m); main rotor disc area (both rotors) 3,470 sq ft (322.1 m²)
Operators: Burma, Colombia, Iran

Kaman H-43F Huskie

Last of the 'egg-beaters' with Kaman-style intermeshing rotors, the HH-43 Huskie is still used by several air forces. This example was pictured on jungle rescue duties in South Vietnam in 1967 with Detachment 12, 39th USAF Aerospace Rescue & Recovery Sqn.

Kamov Ka-25 Hormone

The Soviet naval air arm (AVMF) has for many years been a loyal customer of the design bureau named after Nikolai Kamov. Like the similarly named Kaman concern in the United States, the Kamov bureau has been associated with compact helicopters of close-coupled twin-rotor layout, but whereas Kaman developed the Flettner intermeshing rotor concept, the Soviet team chose the co-axial layout, originally applied to the experimental pre-World War II Breguet-Dorand. With no need for a long tail boom to counter torque, the fuselage of the co-axial helicopter can be made small and compact. This renders it particularly suitable for shipboard use, and all the helicopters operated by the AVMF from ships have been Kamov co-axial types.

The Ka-8 and Ka-10 'flying motorcycle' designs of 1945-55 aroused naval interest in the potential of shipboard helicopters for over-the-horizon target spotting; this 'airborne crow's nest' concept had been explored by the German navy in World War II. The Ka-15 cabin helicopter and the improved Ka-18 were ordered for AVMF service, but appear to have been used only on a small scale for experimental shipboard operations.

The Soviet Union's definitive shipboard helicopter, however, made its public debut in 1961, at the Tushino air display. More than four times as heavy as the Ka-15, the new helicopter was powered by twin turbines, six times as powerful as the piston engine of the older type, with scarcely any increase in weight and volume. As with land-based helicopters, the availability of the turboshaft engine vastly increased what could be achieved. Together with the natural compactness of the co-axial layout, the powerplant makes the Ka-25 look deceptively small; in fact it is

almost as heavy as the Mil Mi-4, and rather bigger than the Westland Wessex. At the time of writing it is probably the largest and most capable helicopter intended for operation from normal warships, and in effectiveness it comes into the same class as the much later Kaman SH-2F and Westland Lynx. The prototype Ka-25 was demonstrated with air-to-surface missiles on outriggers, but these appear to have been dummies.

Details of the Ka-25 design probably reflect lessons learned in trials with smaller helicopters. The twin-engine layout presumably confers a degree of security in the event of an engine failure, although the type does not seem over-endowed with power unless the engines can be run at a contingency rating higher than the figure quoted for the Ka-25K civil derivative. Both engines, however, have their own independent fuel supplies, a feature not always found on Soviet land-based helicopters; the type is fitted with autostabilization, powered controls, comprehensive communications and full all-weather navigation equipment. Most Ka-25s are fitted with emergency flotation 'boots' on each of the four landing gear legs, which inflate automatically in the event of a ditching.

The 'missile-armed' prototype seen in 1961 was codenamed 'Harp' by NATO, but for some reason best known to NATO the very similar production version was christened 'Hormone'. The first version of the Ka-25 to see service appears to have been the 'Hormone-B' fitted with a large chin radome broader than that of the 'Harp' prototype. The 'Hormone-B' is deployed on 'Kresta I' class cruisers and 'Kiev' class aircraft-carriers, and appears to be associated with long-range surface-to-surface cruise missiles such as the

SS-N-3 'Shaddock' (on the cruisers) and the SS-N-12 fitted to the 'Kiev' class. (The lead ship of the latter class, *Kiev*, made her maiden voyage in 1976, followed by *Minsk* in 1979.) The 'Hormone-B' seems to be a modern extension of the 'flying crow's nest' principle, using its radar to provide guidance and targeting information for the long-range missiles. The 'Kresta I' class appeared in 1967, marking the first shipboard deployment of the Ka-25. It would be logical for the 'Hormone-B' to lack some of the ASW equipment of the 'Hormone-A', in order to increase its range and ceiling and hence the area over which it can offer missile guidance.

The 'Hormone-A', the basic ASW variant, appeared shortly after the 'Hormone-B' on the helicopter-carriers *Moskva* and *Leningrad*, and on the new 'Kresta II' and 'Kara' cruiser classes. It also equips the 'Kanin' class destroyers. It forms the bulk of the helicopter complement of the 'Kuril' class carriers, which also carry a number of 'Hormone-B' radar pickets.

Little is known about the operational equipment of the 'Hormone-A', and equipment standards appear to vary; some aircraft are fitted with a box-like container on the fuselage side, while others have been seen with nose aerials possibly connected with ESM (electronic surveillance measures). As well as radar, the 'Hormone-A' almost certainly carries dunking sonar equipment in the cabin, and is likely to be fitted with a magnetic anomaly detector (MAD) in a towed 'bird'. The radome is smaller than that of the 'Hormone-B' and the radar is presumably less powerful. There may be an internal weapons bay, but usually the 'Hormone-A' crew would leave the 'kill' to the SS-N-14 ASW missiles of the

mother ship.

A new naval helicopter is expected to appear shortly, but there would seem to be no need in the immediate future for a Ka-25 replacement. The type appears well suited to the shipboard role, in which its compactness — without the complication of tail folding — counts for a great deal and the need for high performance or low silhouette is not urgent. The Ka-25 may fill other roles in addition to ASW and radar-picket duties, but as yet no details of these have been revealed.

Type: multi-role shipboard helicopter
Powerplant: two 900-shp (671-kW) Glushenkov GTD-3 turboshafts
Performance: maximum speed 135 mph (220 km/h); cruising speed 120 mph (200 km/h); hovering ceiling 2,000 ft (600 m); service ceiling 16,500 ft (5000 m); maximum endurance 4 to 5 hours; range with external fuel 400 miles (650 km)
Weights: empty about 10,500 lb (4750 kg); normal maximum 15,500 lb (7100 kg); overload 16,500 lb (7500 kg)
Dimensions: rotor diameter 51 ft 8 in (15.75 m); fuselage length about 34 ft (10.35 m); height 17 ft 8 in (5.4 m); rotor disc area 4,193 sq ft (389.7 m²)
Armament: two homing torpedoes or depth charges in internal weapons bay
Operator: USSR

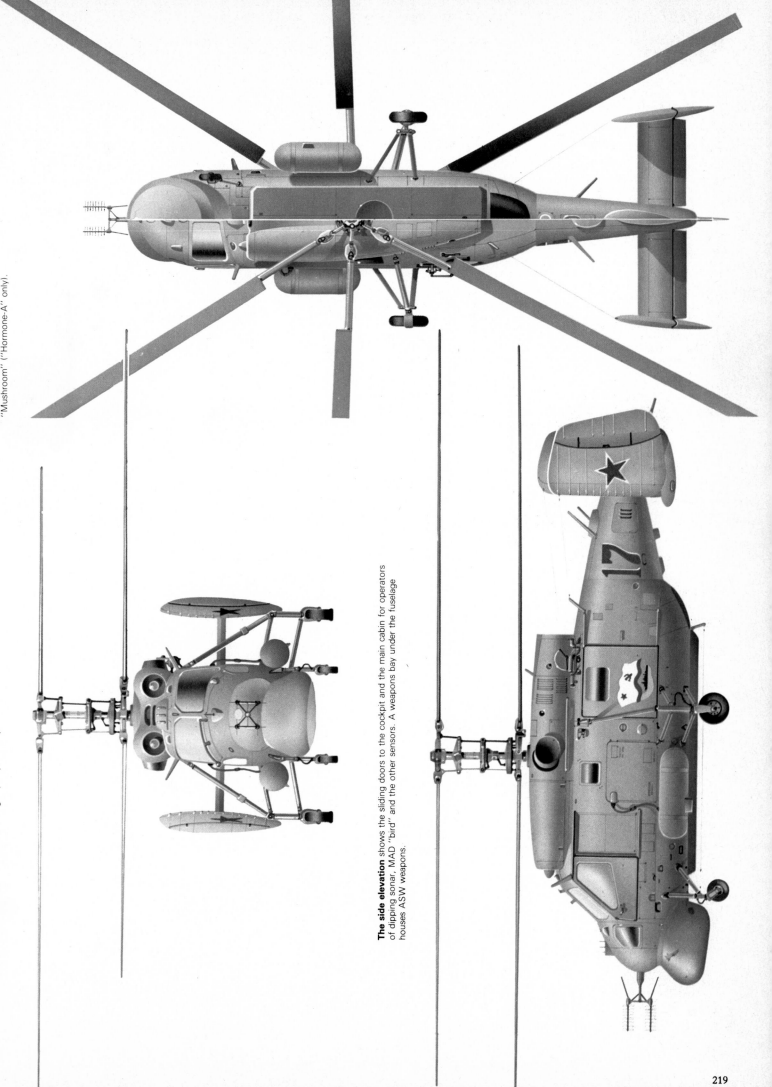

This Kamov Ka-25 "Hormone-A" anti-submarine helicopter is serving aboard a cruiser of the Kresta series. Co-axial rotors reduce overall dimensions for gusty shipboard operations.

Some confusion exists over NATO codenames for Ka-25 radars; the main undernose set is probably "Big Bulge" while the quad Yagi array in front of the nose may be the widely used "Mushroom" ("Hormone-A" only).

The side elevation shows the sliding doors to the cockpit and the main cabin for operators of dipping sonar, MAD "bird" and the other sensors. A weapons bay under the fuselage houses ASW weapons.

219

Kawasaki C-1

The Kawasaki C-1 was produced to replace Curtiss C-46 transports with the Japanese Air Self-Defence Force. Design was begun by NAMC in 1966. The first prototype was assembled at Kawasaki's Gifu factory and flew on 12 November 1970, the second following on 16 January 1971. Both aircraft were handed over to the Japanese Defence Agency for evaluation, which was completed in March 1973. Two pre-production C-1A aircraft were delivered in 1974.

The Air Self-Defence Force's Air Proving Group carried out a successful long-range flight with the XC-1 on 12 October 1973. The aircraft covered the 1,460-mile (2350-km) flight from Naha on Okinawa to Chitose in just over 4 hours, carrying a payload of 8,818 lb (4000 kg). Crew training began in 1974 at the Air Transport Wing at Iruma, and the first production C-1A was delivered in December 1974.

The initial production batch totalled 11, completed by March 1976. A second batch for 13 was delivered by February 1978. Two of this order were modified for long-range flying with an additional 1,040 Imperial gallons (4732 litres) of centre-section fuel. The Air Self-Defence Force requires a further 12 C-1s by the mid-1980s, so that Nos 1, 2 and 3 Squadrons can each have 12 aircraft instead of eight. Kawasaki is prime contractor, responsible for final assembly as well as building the wing centre-section and front fuselage. Mitsubishi builds the centre and rear fuselage sections and T-tail, Fuji the anhedralled outer wings and Nihon Hikoki the wing control surfaces.

Standard crew consists of pilot, co-pilot, navigator, flight engineer and loadmaster. The pressurized main cabin can seat up to 60

troops. In the paratroop role 45 can exit through doors on each side aft of the wing. In the casevac role 36 stretchers and medical attendants are carried. The cabin measures 35 ft 5¼ in (10.80 m) by 11 ft 9½ in (3.60 m) and is 8 ft 4¼ in (2.55 m) high, enabling such loads as a 2½-ton truck or 105-mm howitzer to be carried.

One C-1 has been earmarked for test work on air-to-air and air-to-surface missiles, including the XASM-1 for the Mitsubishi F-1. Other specialized variants have been studied for flight-refuelling, electronic-warfare, weather reconnaissance, and a stretched-fuselage transport.

The Air Self-Defence Force, Air Transport Wing currently operates the C-1A with Nos 1, 2 and 3 Squadrons, each with a unit establishment of eight aircraft.

Type: medium-range transport
Powerplant: two 14,500-lb (6580-kg) Mitsubishi-built Pratt & Whitney JT8D-M-9 turbofans
Performance: economical cruising speed at 35,000 ft (10700 m) 408 mph (657 km/h); service ceiling 38,000 ft (11580 m); maximum rate of climb at sea level 3,500 ft (1065 m) per minute; range with maximum fuel and 4,850-lb (2200-kg) payload 2,084 miles (3353 km)
Weights: empty 51,410 lb (23320 kg); normal take-off 85,320 lb (38700 kg); maximum take-off 99,210 lb (45000 kg); maximum payload 26,235 lb (11900 kg)
Dimensions: span 100 ft 4¾ in (30.6 m); length 95 ft 1¾ in (29 m); height 32 ft 9¼ in (9.99 m); wing area 1,297 sq ft (120.5 m²)
Armament: none
Operator: Japan

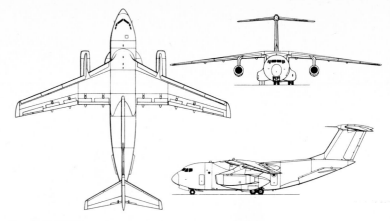

Kawasaki C-1A

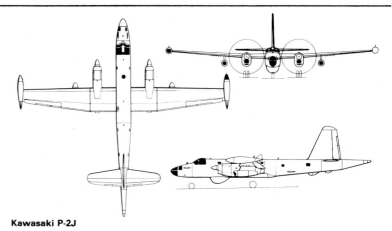

A production Kawasaki C-1 of the Japanese Air Self-Defence Force. Although very limited in payload and range, this twin-JT8D aircraft is being updated gradually, and the final batch have a centre-section tank added. Total deliveries by 1980 are to be 28.

Kawasaki P-2J

The Kawasaki P-2J was the outcome of a requirement for a new maritime patrol and anti-submarine aircraft for the Japanese Maritime Self-Defence Force (JMSDF). This was issued by the Defence Agency as part of the second Defence Build-up Programme to provide a successor for the JMSDF's fleet of 76 Lockheed P-2H Neptunes in the 1970s.

As 60 of the Neptunes had been built in Japan under licence by Kawasaki, a new maritime reconnaissance aircraft based on this design was decided upon, instead of the more costly alternative of buying the Lockheed P-3 Orion from the United States, as was later decided. Design of an updated Neptune was begun by Kawasaki in October 1961. Work commenced on the prototype, a modified P-2H, in 1965 and this aircraft made its first flight on 21 July the following year. The designation P-2J was decided on to conform with the US Department of Defense system, the last Lockheed-built production version of the Neptune being the P-2H. The JMSDF received the first production P-2J on 7 October 1969, and planned procurement of the type covers 83 aircraft.

The P-2J's unpressurized fuselage is basically that of the P-2H, being an all-metal semimonocoque structure. However, it has been extended by the insertion of a new 4 ft 2 in (1.27 m) section forward of the wing. The additional space houses a largely new set of avionics, which is one of the major improvements introduced by the P-2J.

The second important innovation is the substitution of turboprops for the P-2H's piston engines. The new engines are Japanese-built General Electric T64 turboprops. As on the P-2H, auxiliary turbojets are fitted to provide increased take-off power and to increase speed during an attack. These are of Japanese design and manufacture. Fuel capacity is 2,515 gallons (11433 litres), with a further 1,514 gallons (6882 litres) in the left wingtip tank. For ferrying, a 583 gallon (2650 litre) tank can be carried in the weapons bay.

The total crew complement is 12. Two pilots occupy the flight deck, the ASW tactical compartment houses seven and three are carried in the aft fuselage. An ordnance room and galley are located behind the tactical compartment.

Communications equipment includes UHF,

VHF and HF transceivers, and the navigation aids carried are doppler radar, Loran, Tacan, ADF, UHF/DF, radar altimeter and navigation plotter. Specialized ASW equipment embraces the elderly AN/APS-80 search radar, MAD, ESM, sonobuoy data display system, digital data processor and an integrated data display. A searchlight is housed in the right wingtip pod.

The current JMSDF shore-based anti-submarine force comprises five groups, of which three include the P-2J in their operational inventories. They are the 1st *Koku-gun* at Kanoya, the 2nd *Koku-gun* at Hachinoe and the 4th *Koku-gun* at Atsugi. In addition, the independent Okinawa *Koku-tai* operates the P-2J from Naha air base. The 203rd *Kyohiku Koku-tai* at Kanoya is the P-2J operational con-

Kawasaki P-2J

A Kawasaki P-2J of the Japanese Maritime Self-Defence Force's 2nd *Koko-gun*, based at Hachinoe, is pictured on patrol. This derivative of the Lockheed P-2 Neptune is the principal Japanese long-range maritime patrol aircraft, serving with four front-line units in this role.

version unit. The FY 1978 budget provided for the conversion of one P-2J to target-tug configuration, with the designation UP-2J. A further three such conversions are planned to fulfil the role currently undertaken by Grumman Trackers with the 61st *Koku-tai*.

Ironically the replacement for the P-2J (and the JMSDF's surviving P-2Hs) is to be the Lockheed P-3 Orion, which was ruled out as a Neptune replacement on the grounds of cost. Current plans envisage the production under licence of 45 P-3Cs by Kawasaki between 1981 and 1988.

Type: long-range maritime patrol aircraft.
Powerplant: two 3,060-ehp (2282-kW) General Electric T64-IHI-10E turboprops, each driving a three-blade metal variable-pitch propellor, and two 3,417-lb (7517-kg) Ishikawajima-Harima J3-IHI-7D turbojets in under-

wing pods.
Performance: maximum cruising speed 250 mph (402 km/h); maximum rate of climb at sea level 1,800 ft (500 m) per minute; service ceiling 30,000 ft (9150 m); range with maximum fuel 2,765 miles (4450 km)
Weights: empty 42,500 lb (19280 kg); maximum take-off 75,000 lb (34000 kg)

Dimensions: wing span (over tip tanks) 101 ft 3½ in (30.87 m); length 95 ft 10¾ in (29.23 m); height 29 ft 3½ in (8.93 m); wing area 1,000 sq ft (92.90 m^2)
Armament: anti-submarine homing torpedoes, depth charges or mines
Operators: Japanese Maritime Self-Defence Force

Kawasaki P-2J version of the Lockheed Neptune fitted with advanced ASW systems and powered by T64 turboprops.

Lockheed C-5 Galaxy

In 1963 the USAF's Military Air Transport Service (MATS), since redesignated Military Airlift Command (MAC), began to investigate the procurement of a very large strategic transport which would not only supplement the Lockheed C-141s in service, but would also have the capability of operating from the same airfields. This requirement was identified initially under the designation CX-4, which envisaged an aircraft with a maximum take-off weight of about 600,000 lb (272155 kg). Further study resulted in a new specification, designated CX-HLS, which called for an aircraft able to carry a payload of 125,000 lb (56699 kg) over a range of 8,000 miles (12875 km), or approximately double that payload over a shorter distance.

Requests for Proposals were issued in May 1964, and Boeing, Douglas and Lockheed were subsequently awarded contracts for development of their designs. At about the same time, General Electric and Pratt & Whitney were given contracts for the design and construction of prototype powerplants suitable for use by this large aircraft, which by then was expected to have a maximum take-off weight of around 700,000 lb (317515 kg). In August 1965, General Electric's GE1/6 turbofan engine prototype was selected for development: in its final form, this engine was designated TF39-GE-1. Two months later, Lockheed was named prime contractor for the airframe, and construction of the prototype began in August 1966, by which time the aircraft had been designated C-5A and named Galaxy. Major structural design, including the wing, was handled by a special company formed by 'brain drain' designers in Britain. This aircraft flew for the first time on 30 June 1968, and it and seven other examples were assigned to a test programme which extended into mid-1971. The ninth aircraft off the line, the first production/operational example, was delivered to MAC on 17 December 1969. Successful testing resulted in contracts for a total of 81 C-5As to equip four squadrons, and the last of these were delivered in May 1973. The original intention had been to acquire 115 of these aircraft to equip six squadrons, but cost escalation resulted in procurement of the reduced number.

Operational deployment of the Galaxy started in 1970, when the first of these aircraft began to supplement the airlift capability then provided by Lockheed C-141A StarLifter transports. It was discovered very quickly that they were a valuable addition to MAC's air fleet, operating reliably on supply missions from the United States to Europe and southeast Asia. In this latter area C-5As made their first deliveries to South Vietnam in August 1971, and in the months which followed, and particularly in the spring of 1972, made a major contribution to MAC's capability in south-east Asia. By comparison with the C-141A StarLifter which was then, and still is, an important component of the strategic airlift fleet, the Galaxy can lift a payload which is more than twice as heavy. More importantly, its lower deck has an unobstructed length of 121 ft 1 in (36.91 m) and width of 19 ft 0 in (5.79 m), which gives this aircraft the ability to carry practically any piece of the US Army's

equipment, including self-propelled howitzers, personnel carriers, and tanks, none of which can enter the constricted hold of the C-141. Typical of outsize loads which have been carried over transoceanic ranges are two M48 tanks, with a combined weight of 198,000 lb (89811 kg), and three Boeing Vertol CH-47 Chinook transport helicopters.

Payloads of this weight and size meant that the design team had to give close attention to the provision of landing gear able to cope with a take-off weight approaching 350 tons (355.6 tonnes); special facilities to make possible the quick loading and off-loading of outsize cargoes; and provisions for the carriage of large numbers of troops with their equipment when necessary. A basic requirement was the capability of operating from unpaved surfaces. So while the Galaxy has retractable tricycle-type landing gear, it differs very considerably from that of most civil transports. The nose unit has four wheels, and there are four main wheel units each consisting of a six-wheel bogie. All five units are mounted on oleo-pneumatic shock-absorbers which have a nor-

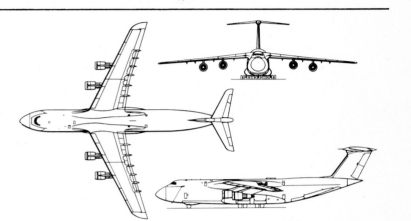

Lockheed C-5A Galaxy

mal extended position for take-off and landing, but which can be shortened for the loading or off-loading of heavy cargo, and especially to provide drive-on/drive-off facilities for tracked and wheeled vehicles. Other features of this landing gear include in-

continued

One of the 76 Lockheed C-5A Galaxy long-range transports in service with Military Airlift Command, USAF.

This illustration of the Lockheed C-5A Galaxy gives some scale to the size of this very large transport aircraft. With the visor type nose door raised, a Bell UH-1 Iroquois helicopter, itself almost 42 ft (12.80 m) long, can be loaded without difficulty.

flight deflation capability for all 28 wheels, for soft airstrips, provision of a fully-modulating anti-skid system, the ability to set all wheel units 20° to left or right to simplify operation in crosswinds, and the inclusion of castoring capability for the forward main units to ease ground handling. Forward loading is accomplished by raising the visor type upward-hinged fuselage nose and lowering a ramp. Simultaneous rear loading is carried out via a ramp which, when raised, forms the under-surface of the rear fuselage. With the landing gear 'kneeled', the floor-to-ground height is 4 ft 4¾ in (1.34 m) forward and 4 ft 9 in (1.45 m) aft.

Accommodation in the Galaxy is provided on two levels. The forward end of the upper cabin comprises a flight deck for a crew of five, with a rest area immediately aft for up to 15 relief crew. The rear area of this upper cabin, aft of the wing box, is equipped normally to provide seating for 75 troops. Although the Galaxy is intended primarily as a cargo carrier, there are provisions for accommodating up to 270 fully-equipped troops on the lower deck.

Despite the fact that, at the time of their introduction into service, the USAF had to cope with what were dimensionally the largest in-use aircraft in the world, they encountered few problems in handling the C-5A on a worldwide basis. In-flight refuelling capability makes possible their deployment with the heaviest of loads over whatever range is

necessary. One major setback in the service life of these aircraft has been the discovery that the wing structure has accrued fatigue damage at a higher rate than anticipated, threatening a reduced service life. Because of their importance to the USAF's airlift capability, Lockheed was awarded a contract in 1978 to manufacture new-design wings for the C-5A. If testing of two initial sets proves satisfactory, it is planned to equip the entire fleet of Galaxies with new wings, beginning in 1982, to ensure that these vital aircraft retain the 30,000-hour service life for which they were intended.

Type: heavy logistics transport aircraft
Powerplant: four 41,000-lb (18597-kg) thrust General Electric TF39-GE-1 turbofans
Performance: maximum speed at 25,000 ft (7620 m) 571 mph (919 km/h); average cruising speed 518 mph (834 km/h); range with design payload 3,749 miles (6033 km); range with 112,600-lb (51075-kg) payload 6,529 miles (10507 km)

Weights: basic operating 337,937 lb (153286 kg); design payload 220,967 lb (100229 kg); maximum take-off 769,000 lb (348813 kg)
Dimensions: span 222 ft 8½ in (67.88 m); length 247 ft 10 in (75.54 m); height 65 ft 1½ in (19.85 m); wing area 6,200 sq ft (576.00 m²)
Armament: none
Operators: US Air Force

By far the largest military transport in service with the West (unless an airlift version of the 747F were to be developed), the C-5A is a crucial item in NATO planning despite prolonged structural problems that have come to a head in the decision to build new wings for all aircraft in service. The basic USAF Military Airlift Command force numbers 76, in four squadrons.

Lockheed C-121 Constellation

The USAAF gained experience of operating the Lockheed L-49 Constellation during World War II, having requisitioned its initial examples from Lockheed's production line of civil aircraft soon after Pearl Harbor. The first flew on 9 January 1943, and when they entered service these 64-passenger pressurized transports were the largest and fastest in the USAAF's inventory. A total of 22 were used by the Air Transport Command under the designation C-69, and were sold to civil airlines at the end of the war.

Ten L-749s were procured by the USAF in 1948 as C-121s, becoming C-121As or VC-121As according to interior layout, except for one VC-121B with additional tankage. All were redesignated later as PC-121A. The US Navy adopted the L-49 Constellation in 1945 as the R7O-1, and acquired 50 L-749s under the designation R7V-1. Of these, 32 were transferred to the USAF, as C-121Gs, the rest becoming C-121Js in 1962.

Most important usage of the Constellation was in the airborne early-warning role, and following prototype evaluation of two PO-1Ws with large radomes above and below the fuselage, 142 WV-2 Warning Stars were procured by the Navy. Some with ECM equipment were WV-2Qs, and weather-reconnaissance versions were WV-3s. In 1962 these became EC-121K, EC-121M and WC-121N respectively. Some EC-121Ks were given new avionics in 1963, becoming EC-121Ps, and serving into the the 1970s.

The USAF rebuilt 120 C-121Cs into RC-121C AEW platforms, these later being redesignated EC-121Cs.

The RC-121D of 1955 had longer endurance, receiving advanced avionics in 1962 as the EC-121H. Subsequent updating programmes to provide increased capability for many electronic missions has resulted in the designations EC-121Q/R/S/T. The Indian air force acquired nine L-1049s from Air India, using them mainly in a maritime patrol role.

Type: long-range transport and AEW aircraft
Powerplant: (C-121G) four 3,250-hp (2424-kW) Wright R-3350-91 Turbo-Compound radial piston engines
Performance: (C-121G) maximum speed 368 mph (592 km/h) at 20,000 ft (6095 m); cruising speed 259 mph (417 km/h) at 10,000 ft (3050 m); range 2,100 miles (3380 km)
Weights: (C-121G) empty 72,815 lb (33028 kg); maximum take-off 145,000 lb (65771 kg)
Dimensions: span (C-121G) 123 ft 0 in

(37.49 m), (RC-121D) 126 ft 2 in (38.46 m); length 116 ft 2 in (35.41 m); height (C-121G) 24 ft 8 in (7.52 m), (RC-121D) 27 ft 0in (8.23 m); wing area (C-121G) 1,650 sq ft (153.29 m²), (RC-121D) 1,653.6 sq ft (153.62 m²)
Armament: none
Operators: India, Indonesia; formerly US Air Force, US Navy

The Lockheed EC-121 Warning Star has always been out of the limelight, although it is a great old aircraft continually updated over a 25-year period to fly new missions. This US Navy example is one of five 1972–73 vintage sub-types still flying.

Lockheed C-130 Hercules

Surely one of the most ubiquitous of all post-World War II aircraft, Lockheed's Model 382 was certainly well named, for it has proved itself able to perform far more and diverse labours than the 12 attributed to the Greek hero Heracles, known to the Romans as Hercules. Furthermore, it is another of the small number of types which, in 1979, will have been in production for one-third of the entire period of powered flight.

Its origin came in 1951 when the USAF made the decision to acquire a fleet of turbo-prop transports for use by the Military Air Transport Service (MATS), later the Military Aircraft Command (MAC), and by Tactical Air Command (TAC). This policy set in motion the design of three aircraft, designated C-130, C-132 and C-133. The second was a heavy logistic transport to be built by Douglas, but this was cancelled. This company did, however, build the C-133 Cargomaster, a heavy strategic freighter which served with MATS/MAC.

The tactical transport was originally known to USAF planners as the Logistic Carrier Supporting System SS-400L. The initial contract for two prototypes, placed on 11 July 1951, used the designation YC-130. Just over three years later, on 23 August 1954, the first of these made its first flight, and these two aircraft, like early series C-130As, were powered by four 3,750-shp (2796-kW) Allison T56-A-1A turboprop engines. The C-130, popularly called the 'Herky-Bird', was designed by Lockheed-California, but all production has been handled by Lockheed-Georgia. The first production contract was awarded in September 1952, and the first production C-130A flew for the first time at Marietta, Georgia, on 7 April 1955. Initial production deliveries went to TAC units in December 1956, these including the 463rd Troop Carrier Wing, and the 322nd Division USAFE.

The Hercules, as it became named, set a wholly new standard in tactical airlift. New features were pressurization, very good flight performance, and a full-section rear ramp-door. A high setting of the monoplane wing ensured that the cabin had minimal loss of capacity from the wing carry-through structure, and for the same reason, the main landing gear when retracted was enclosed in fairings built onto each side of the fuselage. Provision of weather radar altered the nose profile after only a few production aircraft had been constructed, and two other early modifications were carried out to increase fuel capacity and strengthen the floor and fuselage to cater for heavier loads. Access to the main cargo hold, 41 ft 5 in (12.62 m) in length, and with a maximum width of 10 ft 3 in (3.12 m), is via a hydraulically-operated loading ramp which, when closed, forms the undersurface of the rear fuselage. This represents the basic configuration of the C-130A, and a listing of the wide range of variants will trace the usage and purpose of a transport aircraft of which more than 1,500 examples have been built, and which was still in production in 1979.

Variants of the C-130A have included a single AC-130A gunship which was tested in Vietnam: armament included four 20-mm guns and four 7.62-mm (0.3-in) Miniguns. Two GC-130A (later DC-130A) aircraft were converted to carry up to four RPVs, and provided with electronics equipment to launch, control and monitor their flight. Eleven JC-130As were converted for the tracking of missiles and spacecraft, and additional fuel and oil capacity conferred an endurance of 12 to 13 hours; seven of these were reconverted as AC-130A gunships and deployed operationally in Vietnam in 1968–69. Seventeen RC-130As were equipped with TV viewfinder, cameras, mapping equipment, galley and five additional crew positions and delivered by the end of 1959 to MAC's 1,370th Photo Mapping Wing.

Next major version was the C-130B, the first of which entered service with the TAC on 12 June 1959. These had extra fuel capacity, strengthened landing gear, and 4,050-shp (3020-kW) Allison T56-A-7 turboprops driving four-blade propellers (standard on later versions). A total of 230 were built and, as well as being delivered to the USAF, were supplied also to the Indonesian, Pakistani,

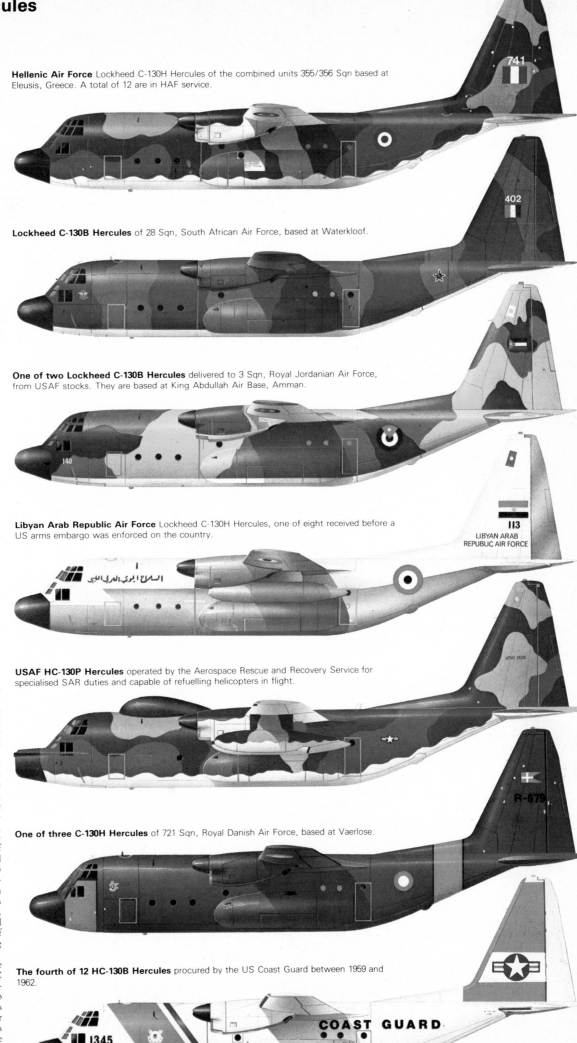

Hellenic Air Force Lockheed C-130H Hercules of the combined units 355/356 Sqn based at Eleusis, Greece. A total of 12 are in HAF service.

Lockheed C-130B Hercules of 28 Sqn, South African Air Force, based at Waterkloof.

One of two Lockheed C-130B Hercules delivered to 3 Sqn, Royal Jordanian Air Force, from USAF stocks. They are based at King Abdullah Air Base, Amman.

Libyan Arab Republic Air Force Lockheed C-130H Hercules, one of eight received before a US arms embargo was enforced on the country.

USAF HC-130P Hercules operated by the Aerospace Rescue and Recovery Service for specialised SAR duties and capable of refuelling helicopters in flight.

One of three C-130H Hercules of 721 Sqn, Royal Danish Air Force, based at Vaerlose.

The fourth of 12 HC-130B Hercules procured by the US Coast Guard between 1959 and 1962.

continued

Lockheed C-130 Hercules

Canadian and South African air forces. Variants of the C-130B have included 12 HC-130B search and rescue aircraft for the US Coast Guard, these having extra accommodation for a radio operator, two search observers and 22–44 passengers. Six C-130Bs were equipped with air-snatch satellite recovery equipment for use in connection with the Discoverer programme, and supplied to the USAF's 6,593rd Test Squadron based at Hickam AFB, Hawaii, in mid-1961. NC-130B was the designation applied to a single aircraft converted for STOL research, this having two turbojet engines pod-mounted beneath the outer wing to provide large volumes of bleed air for BLC blowing. RC-130B was the designation for survey and reconnaissance versions, similar to the earlier RC-130A. Under the designation WC-130B, 17 aircraft were converted for weather reconnaissance and research, and were distributed between the USAF's 53rd Squadron in Puerto Rico, the 54th Squadron on Guam, and the 55th Squadron in California. The designation C-130D applied to 12 wheel/ski-equipped version of the C-130A for operation in the An-

tarctic, or other ice/snowbound areas.

The C-130E was another major version, with increased fuel tankage to increase range, of which 503 examples were built. Derivatives included eight AC-130Es, an improved close-support gunship with extensive weapons and night sensors for service in Vietnam; DC-130E RPV launch and control aircraft, converted by Lockheed Aircraft Service Company (LASC); one special duty EC-130E for the US Coast Guard; three HC-130E SAR aircraft for the USAF. Two 'oddities', so far as alphabetical designation is concerned, are the C-130F, similar to the KC-130F assault transport with flight refuelling equipment to serve as a tanker, but without the refuelling equipment and underwing pylons: both versions were re-engined subsequently with 4,508-shp (3362-kW) Allison T56-A-15 turboprops.

Current production version is the C-130H, powered by T56-A-15 turboprops, of which well over 500 had been ordered and a lesser quantity delivered by early 1979. Variants include HC-130H long-range SAR aircraft with pick-up gear to lift persons or objects from the ground; JC-130H, four modified from

HC-130H, for retrieval of space capsules on re-entry; DC-130H, one modified by LASC for RPV launch and recovery; KC-130H flight refuelling tankers; C-130K, designation of 66 aircraft for service with the RAF; HC-130N SAR aircraft for retrieval of space capsules; HC-130P helicopter refuelling tankers; EC-130Q command communication aircraft for the US Navy; KC-130R tankers for the US Marine Corps; and LC-130R wheel/ski landing gear transport for service with the US Navy in the Antarctic.

In addition to the military versions of the Hercules, lengthened-fuselage but otherwise generally similar civil transports are manufactured under the designation L 100 series.

Type: military/civil medium/long-range transport
Powerplant: (C-130H) four 4,508-shp (3362-kW) Allison T56-A-15 turboprops
Performance: (C-130H) maximum cruising speed 386 mph (621 km/h); range with maximum payload, 5% reserve and allowances for 30 minutes at sea level 2,487 miles (4002 km); range with maximum fuel, reserve and

allowances as above 5,135 miles (8264 km)
Weights: (C-130H) operating (empty) 75,331 lb (34170 kg); maximum normal take-off 155,000 lb (70307 kg); maximum overload take-off 175,000 lb (79379 kg)
Dimensions: span 132 ft 7 in (40.41 m); length (except HC-130H) 97 ft 9 in (29.79 m); height 38 ft 3 in (11.66 m); wing area 1,745 sq ft (162.11 m²)
Armament: (gunship versions) has included 20-mm and 40-mm guns, a 105-mm howitzer, and 7.62-mm (0.3-in) Miniguns
Operators: Brazil, Canada, Egypt, Gabon, Indonesia, Israel, Jordan, South Korea, Kuwait, Pakistan, Peru, Philippines, Portugal, Saudi Arabia, South Africa, Spain, Sudan, UK, US Air Force, US Air National Guard, US Coast Guard, US Marines, US Navy, others

Lockheed C-130H Hercules cutaway drawing key

1 Radome
2 Sperry AN/APN-59 radar
3 External interphone connection
4 Nose-gear forward door
5 Twin nosewheels
6 Accumulators (port and starboard)
7 Nose landing gear shock strut
8 External electrical power receptacles
9 Battery compartment
10 Pilot's side console
11 Portable oxygen cylinder
12 Pilot's seat
13 Control column
14 Main instrument console
15 Windshields
16 Co-pilot's seat
17 Systems engineer's seat
18 Navigator's seat
19 Navigator's desk
20 Crew bunks (upper and lower)
21 Forward emergency escape hatch
22 Control runs in bulkhead
23 Fire-extinguisher
24 Crew closet
25 Galley
26 Access steps to flight deck
27 Crew entry well
28 Crew entry door
29 Lower longeron
30 Window ports
31 Cargo floor panels
32 Cargo floor support frames
33 Troop seats (stowed)
34 Overhead emergency equipment stowage
35 Fuselage frames
36 Booster hydraulic system reservoir and accumulator
37 Control runs
38 Starboard main landing gear access (sealed)
39 Wingroot frame strengthener
40 Fuselage/centre section join
41 Inboard leading-edge structure
42 Fuel valve inspection access
43 Nacelle panels
44 Starboard auxiliary tanks
45 Tank pylon
46 Fuel filler points
47 Fuel tanks
48 Dry bay
49 Allison T56-A-15 turbo-prop
50 Reduction gear
51 Four-blade reversible pitch Hamilton Standard propeller
52 Engine starter
53 Engine oil tank
54 Limit of wing walkway
55 Starboard navigation lights
56 Starboard aileron
57 Aileron tab
58 Outer wing flap
59 Centre-section flap
60 Centre-section wing box beam structure

61 Flap drive control
62 Internal corrugation
63 Aileron control linkage
64 Port main landing gear bay
65 Hydraulic actuator motor
66 Fire-extinguisher bottles
67 Main landing gear shock struts
68 Retraction mechanism
69 Air turbine motor (driven by GTC, item 71, to supply electric and hydraulic power)
70 Utility hydraulic system reservoir and accumulator

71 Gas turbine compressor (air supply for engine starting, ground conditioning and to drive ATM, item 69)
72 Main gear fairing
73 Landing light in outer door forward section
74 Twin tandem mainwheels
75 Main landing gear outer door
76 Inner door section
77 Air deflector door
78 Tank pylon
79 Port auxiliary tank
80 Spinner
81 Chin intake
82 Nacelle structure
83 Engine bearer

84 Exhaust outlet
85 Outboard leading-edge structure
86 Port navigation lights
87 Aileron control bell crank
88 Aileron structure
89 Aileron tab
90 Outer wing box beam structure
91 Flap structure
92 Idler bell crank
93 Auxiliary ground-loading ramp
94 Ramp actuating cylinder
95 Cargo ramp (lowered)
96 Port paratroop door
97 Cargo ramp floor panels
98 Ramp hinge line
99 Ramp actuating mechanism
100 Miscellaneous stores bin
101 Starboard paratroop door
102 Centre emergency escape hatch

Lockheed HC-130H Hercules air search, rescue and recovery aircraft; seven examples are in service with the US Coast Guard. These have a nose-mounted recovery system able to pick up from the ground persons, or objects weighing up to 500 lb (227 kg).

103 Wingroot fairing
104 Fuselage frames
105 Toilet
106 Urinal
107 Ramp and auxiliary hydraulic reservoir
108 Troop water bottles
109 Ramp actuator housing
110 Auxiliary hydraulic system reservoir
111 Static line stowage
112 Cargo door (upward hinged)

113 Dorsal fin fairing
114 Rear emergency escape hatch
115 Rudder boost assembly
116 Starboard tailplane
117 Starboard elevator
118 Fin auxiliary beam
119 Fin main beam
120 Fin rear beam
121 Fin leading-edge
122 Antenna
123 Anti-collision beacon
124 Rudder
125 Rudder structure
126 Rudder tab
127 Rudder front beam
128 Tail cone
129 Elevator control linkage
130 Elevator tab
131 Elevator structure
132 Tailplane box structure
133 Tailplane leading-edge
134 Cargo door rear hinge-line

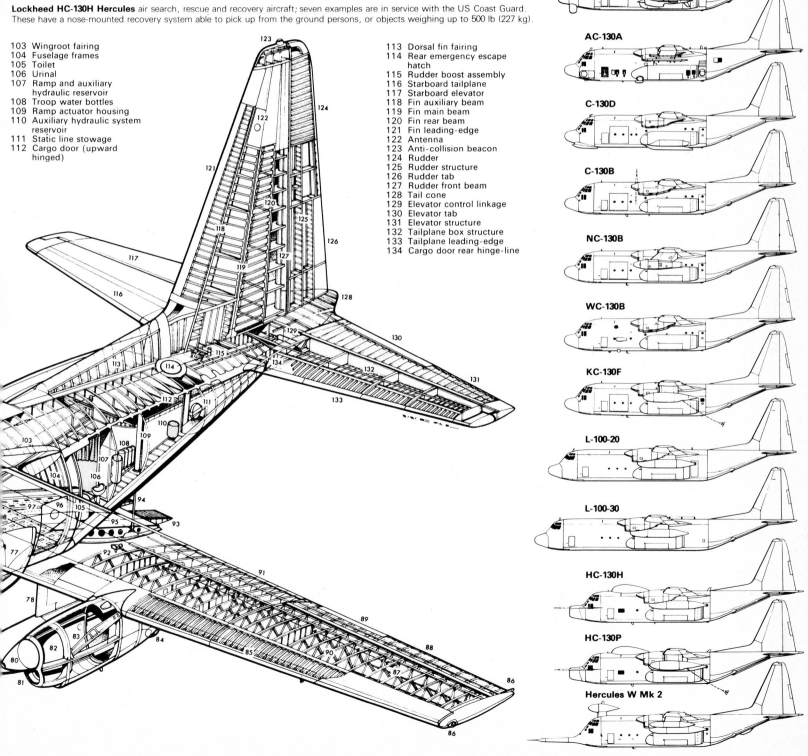

YC-130A
C-130A
JC-130A
DC-130A
AC-130A
C-130D
C-130B
NC-130B
WC-130B
KC-130F
L-100-20
L-100-30
HC-130H
HC-130P
Hercules W Mk 2

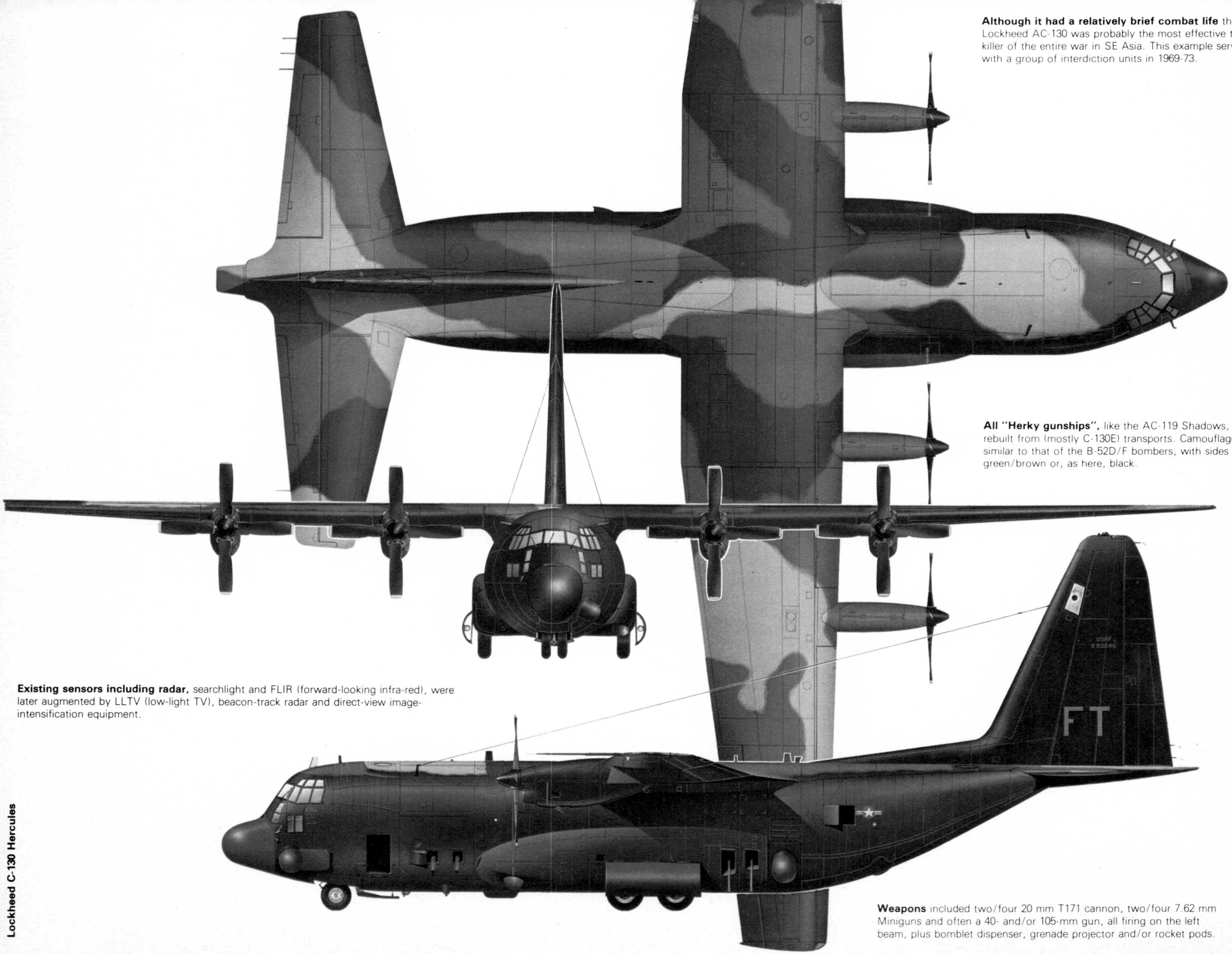

Existing sensors including radar, searchlight and FLIR (forward-looking infra-red), were later augmented by LLTV (low-light TV), beacon-track radar and direct-view image-intensification equipment.

Weapons included two/four 20 mm T171 cannon, two/four 7.62 mm Miniguns and often a 40- and/or 105-mm gun, all firing on the left beam, plus bomblet dispenser, grenade projector and/or rocket pods.

All "Herky gunships", like the AC-119 Shadows, were rebuilt from (mostly C-130E) transports. Camouflage was similar to that of the B-52D/F bombers, with sides green/brown or, as here, black.

Although it had a relatively brief combat life, the Lockheed AC-130 was probably the most effective truck killer of the entire war in SE Asia. This example served with a group of interdiction units in 1969-73.

Lockheed C-140 JetStar

The JetStar was produced as a private venture to meet US Air Force UCX requirements for a jet-powered utility aircraft for airways and air communications, transport, crew-readiness training and other duties.

The prototype flew for the first time on 4 September 1957, only 241 days after the basic design was finalised. Of conventional low-wing configuration, it was powered by engines mounted on the sides of the rear fuselage, following the contemporary fashion introduced by the French Caravelle airliner. The two prototype JetStars were each originally powered by two Bristol Orpheus turbojets, but one of these was re-engined in December 1959 with four Pratt & Whitney JT12 (J60) turbojets in the position representative of current production aircraft. Other improvements embodied on the prototype at the same time included a high-lift wing leading edge, twin-wheel landing gear and thrust reversers. The large distinctive external fuel tanks mounted at mid-span were intended to be an optional fitment, but became standard on the production aircraft.

In October 1959 the USAF announced that it had selected the JetStar, and subsequently a number were ordered by MATS. Five of these were used by the Special Air Missions wing, and others by the Airways and Air (now Air Force) Communications Service, which has the responsibility for inspecting military navigation aids. These aircraft carry the USAF designation C-140A. US Air Force support versions are designated T-40.

In addition to the service models, a civil version is available for commercial use. In this capacity the JetStar is unique among the world's business jet aircraft in being powered by four engines.

In the summer of 1973, Lockheed announced the development of an improved model, designated JetStar II. This has an airframe generally similar to that of earlier aircraft, but with detail changes in configuration and equipment. The major change was the replacement of the Pratt & Whitney engines by four AiResearch TFE731 turbofans. The new powerplant offers a significant increase in range and lower noise levels, as well as allowing an increase in maximum take-off weight. The new engines can be retrofitted into early airframes.

Normal accommodation is for a crew of two and 10 passengers, with a wardrobe/galley and toilet, and space for the storage of baggage. However, the layout and furnishing can be varied to suit customer requirements, and by reducing the number of seats very luxurious interiors can be provided. A jump-seat is available as an option for a third crew member. The passenger entry door is located at the forward end of the fuselage, on the left side, and opens by moving inward and sliding aft. The fourth window on each side is an emergency exit and is removed inwardly. The cabin is pressurized, air-conditioned, heated and ventilated. A high-pressure oxygen system for the crew and passengers is fitted as standard equipment. An altitude control valve activates the passenger system when the cabin altitude exceeds 14,000 ft (4267 m), the masks being presented automatically.

The JetStar can be fitted with special equipment for electronic countermeasures training, fighter interceptor training, target towing, air photography and mapping and other duties. Jet Star II production ceased at the end of 1979 after a total of 40 aircraft had been built.

Type: (JetStar II) executive and light utility jet transport
Powerplant: four 3,700-lb (1678-kg) AiResearch TFE731-3 turbofans
Performance: maximum level and cruising speed at 30,000 ft (9145 m) 547 mph (880 km/h); stalling speed 144 mph (232 km/h); range with maximum fuel and 30 minutes reserves 3,189 miles (5132 km); range with maximum payload and 30 minutes reserves 2,994 miles (4818 km)
Weights: basic operating weight 24,900 lb (11294 kg); maximum take-off weight 44,500 lb (20185 kg); maximum payload 2,600 lb (1179 kg)
Dimensions: span 54 ft 5 in (16.60 m); length 60 ft 5 in (18.42 m); height 20 ft 5 in (6.23 m); wing area 542.5 sq ft (50.40 m²)
Operators: USAF, Canadian Department of Transport

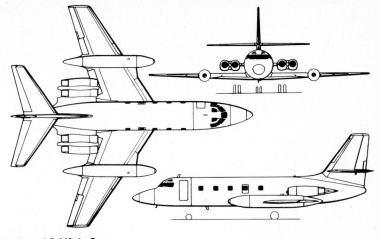

Lockheed C-140 JetStar

Lockheed CP-140 Aurora

To meet its requirement for a Long-Range Patrol Aircraft (LRPA) to replace Canadair CP-107 Argus aircraft which are currently in service, the Canadian government prepared Air Specification 15-14 in 1972. The LRPA was required for use by the Canadian Armed Forces for: ASW; arctic surveillance; ice reconnaissance; coastal, fisheries and shipping patrols; pollution control; resources location; search and rescue; and aerial survey. The government made a detailed evaluation of several 'off the shelf' aircraft before announcing, on 21 July 1976, its intention to purchase 18 special variants of the Lockheed P-3 Orion to fulfil this role.

The designation CP-140 Aurora has been allocated to this aircraft, which combines the basic airframe/powerplant/systems of the Orion with the avionics and data-processing systems of the Lockheed S-3A Viking, and the first of these was scheduled to make its first flight in the spring of 1979. Delivery of all 18 aircraft on order was scheduled for completion in March 1981.

Primary changes, by comparison with the P-3C Orion, are confined to the interior, and there are extensive modifications to the cabin. These include the provision of three observer's stations, a crew rest area, galley and dining area, toilet facilities, and an airborne maintenance station. The largest area is allocated to a tactical compartment, which has accommodation for a six-man team comprising a tactical navigator, a navigator/communicator, two acoustic-sensor operators and two non-acoustic sensor operators. Immediately aft of this tactical compartment is a camera bay and a search stores, with stowage for sonobuoys, Signals Underwater Sound (SUS) sensors, marine markers and flares. Three launch tubes permit in-flight delivery of mail and supplies to remote stations or ships, and are used to launch flares, marine markers and SUS with the cabin unpressurized. Cartridge-discharged sonobuoys can be launched with the cabin pressurized. A KA-107A day/night reconnaissance camera completes the equipment of this bay.

For ASW missions the weapons bay and 10 underwing hardpoints provide for a wide range of weapons to be carried, and the weapons bay can also accommodate the Canadian-developed SKAD/BR search and rescue kit during SAR operations.

Type: long-range ASW and maritime patrol aircraft

Powerplant: four 4,910-shp (3661-kW) Allison T56-A-14 turboprops
Performance: (estimated) maximum speed at optimum altitude 455 mph (732 km/h); endurance on station at 1,150 miles (1850 km) radius 8.2 hours; ferry range 5,180 (8336 km)
Weights: maximum permissible 142,000 lb (64410 kg)
Dimensions: span 99 ft 8 in (30.38 m); length 116 ft 10 in (35.61 m); height 33 ft 8½ in (10.27 m); wing area 1,300 sq ft (120.77 m²)
Armament: weapons bay and 10 underwing hardpoints for stores as yet unspecified
Operators: (from May 1980) Canadian Armed Forces

Lockheed C-141 StarLifter

Victory in battle often goes to the contestant who gets there 'firstest with the mostest', and the Lockheed C-141 StarLifter transport was developed to enable the United States to deploy large quantities of troops and heavy equipment very quickly indeed.

The aircraft was designed to specification SOR-182 (Specific Operational Requirement 182) issued for a turbofan-powered freighter and troop carrier for operation by the US Military Airlift Command, and was selected in a competition in which Boeing, Douglas and General Dynamics were contenders. The transport is the flying element of the US Logistics Support System 476L, the purpose of which is to provide global-range airlift for the MAC, and strategic deployment capabilities at jet speeds for the US Strike Command, which includes the Strategic Army Corps and the Composite Air Strike Forces of Tactical Air Command.

Of conventional construction, the StarLifter is of swept-wing configuration, the wing being mounted high on top of the fuselage to minimise cabin obstruction. The four engines are mounted on pylons carrying them well below and forward of the wing leading edge. A distinctive feature is the tall T-tail.

The 70 ft 0 in (21.34 m) long cabin has a maximum width of 10 ft 3 in (3.12 m) and a maximum height of 9 ft 1 in (2.77 m), and can accommodate 154 troops or 123 fully-equipped paratroops, or 80 stretchers with seats for up to 16 walking wounded or attendants. Two bunks and two seats are provided within the cabin for relief flight crew members. If required, a special pallet comprising a galley and toilet can be installed in the front of the cabin, this reducing the capacity to 120 passenger-type seats.

Two paratroop doors are provided at the aft end of the cabin. Clamshell doors and a rear ramp permit straight-in cargo loading. The ramp can be opened in flight for air-drops. Up to 5,283 cu ft (149.6 m³) of freight can be loaded on 10 pallets. The rollers and retaining rails for the pallets can be retracted into recesses to provide a flat floor when not in use.

The StarLifter demonstrated its load-carrying potential when it established a world record for heavy cargo drops by delivering 70,195 lb (31840 kg). Several aircraft were modified to carry the Minuteman ICBM in its special transport container, a total weight of 86,207 lb (39103 kg).

continued

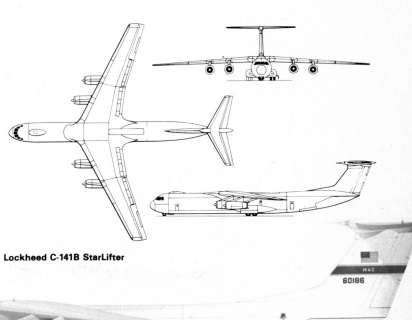

Lockheed C-141B StarLifter

Lockheed C-141B StarLifter, prototype long-fuselage conversion of the standard C-141A, of Military Airlift Command, USAF.

The StarLifter began squadron operations with MAC in April 1965 and soon demonstrated its usefulness in war when it was used extensively to carry troops and supplies across the Pacific to Vietnam and carry wounded back to the USA. This and other operational experience indicated the need to provide the StarLifter with a flight-refuelling capability. It was frequently found, moreover, that when loaded with a bulky rather than weighty load, the aircraft had not reached its maximum weight; that is to say, it could have carried still more. Though nothing could be done to enlarge the cross-section of the StarLifter's fuselage, the latter could be lengthened.

Accordingly, in mid-1976 Lockheed was awarded a contract to develop an extended C-141 with in-flight refuelling equipment. Designated YC-141B, a converted aircraft first flew on 24 March 1977. The fuselage extension consists of a 13 ft 4 in (4.06 m) plug inserted in front of the wing and a similar 10 ft 0 in (3.05 m) plug immediately aft of the wing. At the same time refined wing-root fairings were fitted. These not only reduce drag, thus permitting high speed and reducing fuel consumption, but also change the lift distribution, permitting the carriage of increased loads without affecting the fatigue life of the wing.

The enlarged cabin can accommodate 13 standard pallets, instead of the previous 10. The US Air Force plans to convert all of its 277 operational StarLifters (out of 284 built) to the new configuration by 1982, in effect adding the equivalent of an extra 90 aircraft.

Type: (C-141B) long-range logistics jet transport
Powerplant: four 21,000-lb (9525-kg) Pratt & Whitney TF33-P-7 turbofans
Performance: maximum level speed at 25,000 ft (7620 m) over 570 mph (920 km/h); maximum cruising speed over 560 mph (900 km/h); range with maximum fuel about 5,000 miles (8500 km); range with maximum payload about 4,000 miles (6450 km)
Weights: operating weight 149,848 lb (67970 kg); maximum payload (2.25 g) 89,152 lb (40439 kg); or (2.5 g) 68,877 lb (31242 kg); maximum ramp weight 344,900 lb (156444 kg)
Dimensions: span 159 ft 11 in (48.74 m); length 168 ft 4 in (51.3 m); height 39 ft 3½ in (11.98 m); wing area 3,228 sq ft (299.9 m²)
Operators: USAF

All Lockheed C-141A StarLifter strategic airlifters were delivered in natural metal finish, but in December 1977 this example tested a low-visibility paint scheme. It may become standard, as will the long-body and other improvements of the C-141B.

Lockheed Electra

The design of the Lockheed L-188 short/medium range turboprop airliner began in 1954. In 1955 Lockheed received an initial order for the L-188 'off the drawing board' from American Airlines, with the result that the prototype made its first flight on 6 December 1957, entering service with American and Eastern in January 1959. Of conventional layout, the L-188 Electra had large Fowler flaps, and a tricycle-type landing gear with twin wheels on each unit. The powerplant comprised four Allison 501 turboprop engines, the commercial version of the T56. The initial version accommodated 74 passengers, but later arrangements provided for a maximum of 98 passengers.

A total of 170 were built. As these aircraft were gradually replaced by jets, some were acquired by the military services of smaller nations for use in a cargo/transport role.

Type: short/medium-range transport
Powerplant: four 3,750-shp (2796-kW) Allison 501-D13 or 4,050-shp (3020-kW) Allison 501-D15 turboprops
Performance: maximum speed at 12,000 ft (3660 m) 448 mph (721 km/h); cruising speed at 22,000 ft (6705 m) 405 mph (652 km/h); range with maximum payload and 7,100-lb (3221-kg) fuel reserves 2,770 miles (4458 km); range with maximum fuel plus 1,000 US gallons (3785 litres) of auxiliary fuel with 2 hours reserves 3,460 miles (5568 km)
Weights: empty 57,300 lb (25991 kg); empty (extra fuel) 58,750 lb (26649 kg); maximum take-off 116,000 lb (52617 kg)
Dimensions: span 99 ft 0 in (30.18 m); length 104 ft 6½ in (31.86 m); height 32 ft 1 in (9.78 m); wing area 1,300 sq ft (120.77 m²)
Armament: none
Operators: Argentina, Bolivia, Panama

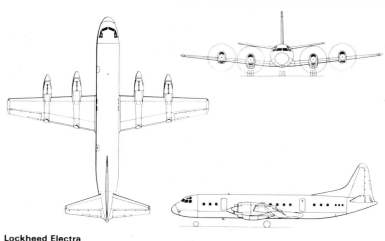

Lockheed Electra

Lockheed F-104 Starfighter

Although by the early 1950s, just over a decade after the first jet aircraft had flown, NACA (the National Advisory Committee for Aeronautics, now known as NASA) had flown a series of experimental Mach1 + aeroplanes to push back the speed and altitude frontiers, the fastest US service fighter was the Mach 0.8 North American F-86 Sabre, and the first true transonic fighter, the North American F-100 Super Sabre, had not yet flown.

This was the situation facing C.L. 'Kelly' Johnson, chief engineer of Lockheed, when in 1952 he set out to produce a fighter superior to anything being flown by the Communists over Korea. It was to be as small as possible, reversing the trend towards ever heavier aircraft exemplified by the Republic XF-91, McDonnell XF-88 Voodoo, and Lockheed's own XF-90. Small size, he reasoned, would permit a maximum speed about twice the speed of sound and great manoeuvrability on the power of only one engine, so cutting down on size, cost and complexity.

At that time designers were limited by the relatively low power available from the early jet engines. The best at the time was the Wright J65, a licence-built version of Britain's Armstrong Siddeley Sapphire. But General Electric was just about to launch the J79, the engine that was to become one of the most widely used of all Western turbine powerplants.

With the promise of this engine to come, Johnson went ahead with his design. He chose Mach 2.2 as the flat-out level speed, and investigated some 300 different shapes to find one that would provide the best compromise between speed, range, manoeuvrability, and landing and take-off performance. Throughout 1953, as the bitter air war finally ended in the Korean skies, Johnson continued to interview pilots just back from combat, to find out what they wanted; meanwhile model after model went through the Lockheed wind tunnels.

Since the discovery in Germany that swept wings produced less drag than straight ones at speeds around Mach 1, virtually all designers had gone over to them. But later work by

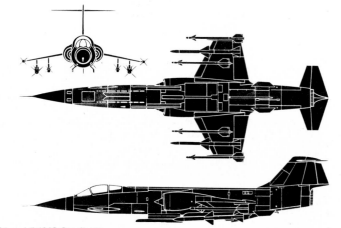

Lockheed F-104S Starfighter

NACA showed that swept wings were actually 'draggier' at speeds around Mach 2, and so Johnson chose a tiny straight wing only 4 inches (10.16m) thick at the deepest part, and with so sharp a leading edge that it had to be covered with a protective sheet on the ground to prevent injury. The wing was heavily anhedralled to overcome the 'aileron' effect of the large rudder. To increase the lift producd by the tiny wing, high-pressure air from the engine was blown over the flaps when they were depressed for landing. The tailplane was set high on the fin in an effort to avoid pitchup, a serious aerodynamic characteristic that was known to affect jet fighters when pulling very tight turns. There was very little room for equipment, and no attempt was made to incorporate AI (Airborne Interception) radar. Most controversially, the pilot was given a downward-firing ejector seat on the grounds that a conventional upward-firing one might hit the tailplane.

On 4 March 1954 the XF-104 prototype made its first flight with simple inlets feeding a J65 engine. There were many problems to overcome, and some 50 production F104As with advanced inlets feeding a J79 engine were assigned to the test programme in addition to the prototypes and pre-production aeroplanes. Development in fact took four years to accomplish, twice the anticipated duration, and far longer than any other US fighter up to that time. Clearance for use by the squadrons was granted in January 1958, but accidents and continued difficulties were so prolific that the F-104A was grounded three months later. In July 1958 the type was again cleared to fly.

During 1958 F-104As of the USAF Air Defense Command (responsible for the defence of the continental United States) set up international speed and altitude records. But the US Air Force was losing interest in the lightweight fighter formula, despite the efforts of Lockheed to turn the F-104 into a workable combat aircraft, and in 1959 they were transferred to the Air National Guard, the part-time reserve organisation.

The F-104 progamme by now had assumed considerable momentum, however, and the USAF was obliged to accept the next model, the greatly improved F-104C (the F-104B had been a two-seat version of the F-104A). This time, however, they went to the Tactical Air Command, where they stayed till 1965.

The F-104 story might have ended there had it not been for the decision of a group of NATO countries led by West Germany to build under licence a totally redesigned version. While the European aircraft industry was slowly regaining strength, there was certainly not enough experience to build a fighter guaranteed to match anything the Russians could put up. In the largest international programme up to then Germany, Italy, Holland, Denmark, Norway, Canada and Japan in-

Spain's Ejercito del Aire operated 21 Lockheed F-104G Starfighters in the '60s, based at Torrejon.

Force Aérienne Belge F-104G Starfighter of the 350 Sqn, No 1 Wing, based at Beauvechain, operating in the all-weather flight-interceptor role.

Royal Danish Air Force F-104G Starfighter in overall blue-grey finish, in 1965.

Royal Netherlands Air Force F-104G Starfighter of 4306 Sqn, based at Volkel. This unit currently performs reconnaissance duties with camouflaged Starfighters.

RNethAF F-104G of 322 Sqn at Leeuwarden assigned interceptor duties.

vestigated a dozen or so aircraft, and in February 1959 chose what had already become the most controversial of them, the F-104, for its new multimission attack fighter, to replace a variety of earlier types such as Gloster Meteors, Lockheed Shooting Stars, North American Sabres, and Republic Thunderstreaks. Lockheed's sales tactics in the matter were to be widely criticised over the next 20 years.

So the F-104G (G for Germany, with more than 700 aircraft) was launched, to keep production lines in many countries busy for the next seven years. The Super Starfighter was the most advanced fighter anywhere at the time of its introduction; apart from being the first Mach 2 + fighter outside the USA, Britain, Soviet Union and Sweden, it had a proper fire-control radar and the world's first miniature, high-accuracy inertial navigation system for squadron service.

But in the hands of its chief customer the

F-104G was destined to become as controversial as the F-104A before it. The number of accidents, which might have been expected to decrease with increasing familiarity, began to rise alarmingly, to the extent that in 1965 one Super Starfighter was being lost every 10 days. Eventually, however, the *Luftwaffe* pilots grew in experience and the ground crews learned how to maintain its aircraft more efficiently, and loss rates have been reduced.

continued

This Aeritalia F-104S Starfighter was one of the test fleet selected to complete development and service indoctrination trials with the Aspide, a medium-range AAM derived from the American Sparrow but claimed by the Italians to have numerous improved features. By 1980 the Aspide 1A should be entering combat service replacing the AIM-7E Sparrow.

Lockheed F-104 Starfighter

The most recent version of the F-104 family is the F-104S, an advanced interceptor for the Italian and Turkish air forces. This is basically the same as the -G model, but incorporates refinements developed over years of experience with the earlier models. But the main change was the substitution of a weapon system for air fighting rather than for ground attack. The main external differences were the addition of two wingtip-mounted Sparrow missiles (hence the 'S' in the designation), and the appearance of a pair of additional strakes under the rear fuselage. It first flew in 1968, and the 205 aeroplanes built in Italy were the last Starfighters to be built.

Of the many countries that took to F-104, only Pakistan has used the Starfighter in combat. In 1965 its Starfighters clashed with Indian fighters over the frontier between the two countries.

Lockheed's last big effort to sell the F-104 took place in 1970, when it proposed a version for the IFA (International Fighter Aircraft) competition, subsequently won by Northrop with its F-5E, and again a few years later in the LWF (Light-Weight Fighter) programme. The latter produced the General Dynamics F-16, which is to become the F-104's successor.

Type: single-seat multimission fighter
Powerplant: one General Electric J79-GE-11A of 10,000-lb (4536-kg) thrust, increasing to 15,800 lb (7167 kg) with afterburning
Performance: maximum speed 1,300 mph (2092 km/h) at 40,000 ft (12192 m); radius of action 690 miles (1110 km); service ceiling 55,000 ft (16764 m)
Weights: empty 14,0821-lb (6388 kg); maximum 28,779 lb (13054 kg)
Dimensions: span 21 ft 11 in (6.68 m); length 54 ft 9 in (16.69 m) height 13 ft 6 in (4.15 m); wing area 196.1 sq ft (18.22 m²)
Armament: one 20-mm General Electric M61 six-barrel cannon, wingtip-mounted Sidewinder air-to-air missiles; various external stores to total weight of 4,000 lb (1814 kg)
Operators: (all F-104 versions) Belgium, Canada, Denmark, Italy, Japan, Jordan, Netherlands, Norway, Pakistan, Spain, Turkey, USAF and West Germany

Luftwaffe F-104G of Jagdbombergeschwader 34 in 1965 with Nato green-grey uppersurface camouflage and blue-grey undersurface. On the intake is the JaboG 34 badge.

Marineflieger F-104G of MFG1 at Schleswig in the mid-sixties. The German Navy has two Starfighter units in service.

Luftwaffe F-104G of Jagdgeschwader 71 "Richthofen".

Royal Canadian Air Force Canadair-built F-104G Starfighter of 441 Sqn, No 1 Fighter Wing based at Marville, France, 1965. The aircraft has a Vicom camera pod.

Aeronautica Militare Italiano F-104G of 9° Gruppo of the 4 Aerobrigata with the unit's prancing horse insignia on the fin.

Lockheed P-2 Neptune

Originating from design studies made in the early years of World War II, Lockheed's land-based Neptune patrol aircraft was destined, from 1947 to 1962, to represent the foundation of the US Navy's land-based patrol squadrons. Strangely enough, the original design studies were made at a time when the US Navy had not envisaged that a land-based patrol aircraft would be included in its inventory of operational types.

The initial studies were made by Lockheed's Vega subsidiary in 1941, but at that time the impact of America's involvement in World War II concentrated most activities of the nation's aviation industry into the production of aircraft essential for the prosecution of the war in the Pacific, and support of the Allies in Europe and the Middle East. By 1944, however, there was an increasingly important requirement for a new land-based patrol bomber, and Lockheed dusted the cobwebs off its earlier designs and took a new look at the US Navy's requirement.

These, in fact, were basically similar to Lockheed's Model 26 design which had been formulated in 1941, and with but comparatively slight changes two prototypes and 15 production aircraft were ordered by the US Navy on 4 April 1944 under the designation P2V, the PV family having been the Ventura and Harpoon. The letter 'V' suffix denoted the Vega origin, despite the fact that Vega had lost its identity when absorbed into the Lockheed parent company in 1943. The first prototype XP2V-1 flew for the first time on 17 May 1945. It was seen to be fairly large aircraft, able to accommodate a crew of seven, and possessing a weapons bay which could carry two torpedoes or 12 depth charges, and armed with three pairs of 0.5-in (12.7-mm)

machine-guns in nose, dorsal and tail positions. The powerplant comprised two 2,300-hp (1715-kW) Wright R-3350-8 Duplex Cyclone radial piston engines. The initial 15 production aircraft ordered were designated P2V-1, and though almost identical to the prototypes, had underwing mountings for up to 16 rockets. In September 1946 one of these aircraft, stripped of all unessential equipment and provided with tankage for 50,400 lb (22861 kg) of fuel, set a world distance record. this was the Truculent Turtle, which between 29 September and 1 October 1946 completed a non-stop flight of 11,235 miles (18081 km) from Perth, Western Australia, to Colombus, Ohio.

Second production version was the P2V-2 with more powerful R-3350-24W engines, six nose-mounted 20-mm cannon and, in later ex-

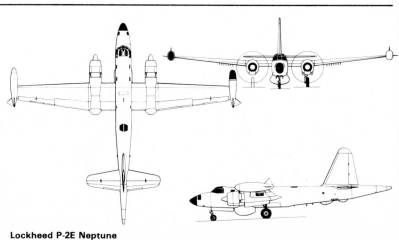

Lockheed P-2E Neptune

Lockheed's P-2 Neptune is still an important ocean-patrol and ASW platform, although this SP-2H (seen with VP-31 of the US Navy) is no longer in service. Many nations have found the P-2 difficult to replace, as modern equivalents cost over 10 times more.

amples, 20-mm guns in dorsal and tail positions. The following P2V-3, which had only the dorsal and tail guns plus advanced ASW avionics, proliferated into the P2V-3C for carrier-launched nuclear-weapon delivery, P2V-3Z armoured transports, and P2V-3Ws with APS-20 search radar. The P-2D (formerly P2V-4) had improved electronics and APS-20 search radar. Extensively built as a result of war in Korea was the P-2E (formerly P2V-5) with many changes. The powerplant comprised two 3,250-hp (2424-kW) Wright R-3350-30W Turbo-Compound engines, and variants included: the P2V-5F with two 3,400-lb (1542-kW) thrust Westinghouse J34-WE-34 turbojets mounted beneath the wing to improve performance for take-off and maximum speed; the P2V-5FE with advanced avionics; the P2V-5FS with Jezebel passive

underwater detection equipment; the P2V-5FD for drone (RPV) control; and the AP-2E for tactical land reconnaissance over Vietnam. The type was supplied also to the RAAF and RAF, and of those supplied to the latter most were transferred subsequently to Argentina (6), Brazil (14), and Portugal (12). P-2F (formerly P2V-6) designated a version of the P-2E with advanced avionics and minelaying capability, and when equipped with J34-WE-36 auxiliary turbojets this became the P-2G. MP-2Fs carried mines or Petrel AUM-N-2 air-to-surface missiles, and TP-2Fs were utilised in a training role. Final Lockheed production version was the P-2H (formerly P2V-7), first flown on 26 April 1954, of which many remain in service. This was the only Neptune to have underwing auxiliary turbojets as standard on all production aircraft, plus

many of the refinements introduced on P-2E and P-2F aircraft. SP-2H aircraft had Julie explosive echo-sounding and Jezebel acoustic search equipment, and LP-2Js were equipped for Arctic photo-reconnaissance. The USAF operated seven P2V-7Us in Vietnam as RB-69A ECM test and training aircraft, on loan from the US Navy, and also acquired a small number of AP-2H aircraft for special duties. Kawasaki in Japan built 48 P-2H ASW aircraft, and has since developed a new ASW for the JMSDF under the designation P-2J, plus one UP-2J for target towing.

Type: naval patrol bomber and ASW aircraft
Powerplant: (P-2H) two 3,500-hp (2610-kW) Wright R-3350-32W radial piston engines, plus two 3,400-lb (1542-kg) Westinghouse J34-WE-34 turbojets

Performance: (P-2H) maximum speed 403 mph (649 km/h) at 10,000 ft (3050 m); cruising speed 207 mph (333 km/h) at 8,500 ft (2950 m); ferry range 3,685 miles (5930 km)
Weights: (P-2H) empty 49,935 lb (22650 kg); maximum take-off 79,895 lb (36240 kg)
Dimensions: (P-2H) span 103 ft 10 in (31.65 m); length 91 ft 4 in (27.84 m); height 29 ft 4 in (8.94 m); wing area 1,000 sq ft (92.90 m²)
Armament: variations of 20-mm cannon, 0.5-in (12.7-mm) machine-guns, mines, torpedoes, depth charges, and air-to-surface missiles
Operators: Argentina, Australia, Brazil, France, Netherlands, Portugal, UK, US Air Force, US Navy, US Naval Reserve

---

Lockheed P-3 Orion

In early December 1957 the prototype of a new four-turboprop civil transport was flown by Lockheed. This had the company designation L.188, and the first deliveries of L.188A production aircraft to US airlines began in the autumn of 1958. Named Electra, about 170 were built in L.188A and L.188C versions, and these were supplied mainly to US and South American airlines.

In August 1957 the US Navy called for design proposals to meet Type Specification 146. This concerned the supply of a new advanced aircraft for maritime patrol and ASW (Anti-Submarine Warfare), and in order to save cost and, more importantly, to permit service introduction as quickly as possible, the US Navy suggested that a variant of an aircraft that was already in production would receive favourable consideration if generally suitable. Thus, Lockheed proposed a developed version of the civil Electra as its submission for the USN competition, and in April 1958 the US Navy announced that this had been selected. The initial research and development contract was awarded on 8 May 1958, and Lockheed proceeded immediately to modify the third civil Electra airframe as an aerodynamic prototype for US Navy evaluation of flight characteristics. This had a mock-up of the MAD (Magnetic Anomaly Detection) boom as an extension of the rear fuselage and a simulated weapons-bay, and made its first flight on 19 August 1958. An operational prototype with full avionics flew for the first time on 25 November 1959, this having the designation YP3V-1, and the name of Orion was adopted for these aircraft in late 1960. The first production P3V-1 made its initial flight on 15 April 1961, and six aircraft were involved in flight testing, operational evaluation and acceptance trials before the first deliveries of production aircraft to USN Patrol Squadrons VP-8 and VP-44 began on 13 August 1962. By that time the P3V-1 had been redesignated as the P-3 Orion.

Lockheed's Model 185 retains the wings, tail unit, basic fuselage structure, powerplant and many assemblies and systems of the Electra. It differs primarily by having a fuselage which has been reduced in length by 7ft 4in (2.24 m) and modified to incorporate a large weapons-bay. The change from a civil to military role involved also the provision of new avionics and other systems, including a pneumatic system for the launch of ASW stores and extra electrical power generation to cope with the demand of the much-increased avionics equipment. The basic fuselage is both pressurised and air-conditioned, but the weapons-bay is excluded, and the hydraulic system includes operation of the weapons-bay doors. Mines, depth-bombs, torpedoes or nuclear weapons can be carried in the weapons-bay, and 10 underwing pylons accommodate a variety of stores.

During more than 17 years of service there has been very considerable revision of the avionics equipment, as a result of changing threats and the inevitable progressive evolution of ASW equipment over this period. In other respects there have been few changes, except that the original 4,500-hp (3356 kW) Allison T56-A-10W turboprop was replaced by a more powerful version.

The original P-3A had what was then an advanced avionics system to equip it for an effective ASW role, for however sophisticated the weapons that such an aircraft can deploy, these are virtually useless unless the target can be identified and located. So, in addition to HF, VHF and UHF communications, the early Orions had inertial, doppler, Loran, and Tacan navigation systems, autopilot, sonobuoy signal receivers and indicators, MAD, and a modified ECM device which served as a direction finder, by detecting and locating electronic emissions from submarines.

Orions are operated normally by a crew of 10, five of these being regarded as tactical specialists who work in a compartment within the main cabin which contains electronic, magnetic and sonic detection equipment. And because these aircraft have a patrol endurance of up to 10 hours, a large crew rest area with galley is provided in the main cabin.

The initial P-3A production aircraft are being replaced in USN squadron service progressively by new production P-3Cs. It is plan-

continued

Lockheed P-3C Orion

US Navy Lockheed RP-3D version of the Orion employed for Project Magnet, the investigation of the Earth's magnetic field.

Iranian Air Force Lockheed P-3F Orion, one of six based at Bandar Abbas for maritime reconnaissance.

Lockheed P-3 Orion maritime patrol and anti-submarine warfare aircraft. Frequently updated and advanced avionics makes it possible to locate modern, deep-diving and quiet submarines against which the Orion can deploy a range of weapons.

ned that P-3A/B aircraft released from active service will, as they become available, be used to modernise the US Navy's reserve forces, gradually replacing the Lockheed P-2 Neptunes which at present are used by the reserve.

For an aircraft which has given good service over a period of more than 17 years, it is inevitable that a number of versions and variants have evolved. The major production versions are the P-3A, -3B and -3C.

A total of 157 examples of the P-3A were built, and from the 110th aircraft these were provided with more sensitive (so-called Deltic) ASW detection equipment and improved electronic displays. Three of this latter version were supplied to the Spanish Air Force. P-3Bs replaced P-3As on the production line during 1965, the new model having more powerful Allison turboprops (see data). Those which entered service with the USN were modified subsequently to allow for the carriage and deployment of AGM-12 Bullpup air-to-surface guided missiles on wing pylons. Five of this version were delivered to the RNZAF in 1966, 10 to the RAAF in 1968, and five to Norway in 1969.

Current production version is the P-3C. This has the same power plant as the -3B, but has an advanced system of sensors and control equipment identified as A-NEW. Heart of the system is a digital computer which processes all ASW information, and this then becomes available for retrieval or display at any time. Under the Update and Update II programmes, P-3Cs have been given even more advanced systems. Update III is under development in 1978 and 1979 to provide new ASW avionics for installation in 1980. Variants include two RP-3A special project reconnaissance aircraft, four WP-3As for weather reconnaissance, EP-3Bs for electronic reconnaissance, one RP-3D for a worldwide magnetic survey, two WP-3Ds to serve as airborne research centres, 10 EP-3E electronic reconnaissance aircraft for service with VQ-1 and VQ-2 squadrons, and six P-3Fs as long-range surveillance aircraft for the Royal Iranian Air Force. During the period 1979-90, Japan is to assemble four and build under licence 38 P-3Cs for the Japanese Maritime Self-Defence Force.

Lockheed P-3A Orion of US Navy patrol squadron VP-19 in original white and midnight blue finish.

Lockheed P-3C Orion of USN patrol squadron VP-50 in the current white and grey scheme.

Royal Norwegian Air Force P-3B Orion, named "Fridtjof Nansen", operated by 333 Sqn at Andoya; five are in service.

Type: ASW patrol/attack aircraft
Power Plant: (P-3B/C) four 4,910-ehp (3661-kW) Allison T56-A-14 turboprop engines
Performance: (P-3B/C) maximum speed at 15,000 ft (4750 m) at AUW of 105,000 lb (47627 kg) 473 mph (761 km/h); patrol speed at 1,500 ft (457 m) at above AUW 237 mph (381 km/h); mission radius 3 hr on station at 1,500 ft (457 m) at 1,550 miles (2494 km); maximum mission radius, no time on station,

at maximum normal take-off weight, 2,384 miles (3836 km)
Weights: (P-3B/C) empty 61,491 lb (27892 kg); maximum normal take-off 135,000 lb (61235 kg); maximum permissible weight 142,000 lb (64410 kg)
Dimensions: span 99 ft 8 in (30.38 m); length 116 ft 10 in (35.61 m); height 33 ft 8½ in (10.27 m); wing area 1,300 sq ft (120.77 m²)
Armament: (weapons bay) one Mk-25/39/

55/56 mine, or three Mk-36/52 mines, or three Mk-57 depth-bombs, or eight Mk-54 depth-bombs, or eight Mk-43/44/46 torpedoes; (underwing pylons) mines and rockets, torpedoes for ferrying, and a searchlight under the starboard wing. Maximum weapons load (P-3C) is 20,000 lb (9070 kg)
Operators: Australia, Iran, New Zealand, Norway, Spain, and the US Navy

Lockheed S-3 Viking

The evolution of nuclear-powered submarines, able to remain submerged for long periods and to range across the world's oceans, posed an entirely new threat to defence planners of all nations. When it became possible to launch ballistic missiles, with nuclear warheads, from a submerged submarine, it seemed that the ultimate weapon had been created. Clearly, the submarine had become a major weapon, and the US Navy considered it essential that no effort should be spared to develop a new generation of carrier-based hunter-killer aircraft to replace their Grumman S-2 Trackers which were no longer able to detect the more sophisticated, quieter and deeper-diving submarines being put into service by the Soviet Union.

Consequently, in 1967 the US Navy initiated a design competition to which submissions were received in April 1968 from Convair, Grumman, McDonnell Douglas, North American Rockwell, and Lockheed-California collaborating with LTV Aerospace. Following evaluation by Naval Air Systems Command, General Dynamics and Lockheed were requested in August 1968 to provide further contract definition and to make additional refinement. When these final proposals were evaluated in early 1969, Naval Air Systems Command selected that submitted by Lockheed.

When the initial $461 million contract was awarded by the US Navy in August 1969, Lockheed announced that the new anti-submarine aircraft, already designated S-3A, would be developed in partnership with Vought Aeronautics Division of LTV Aerospace and Univac Federal Systems Division of Sperry Rand. Vought was to design and build the wings, tail unit, landing gear and engine pods; Univac was responsible for an advanced digital computer to provide the high-speed data processing which would be

the key to the effectiveness of this new aircraft; and Lockheed was to build the fuselage, integrate the avionics system, and carry out final assembly and system integration.

The first prototype made its initial flight on 21 January 1972, and because of the urgency to put these aircraft into service additional funding was added to the initial contract to provide for eight research and development aircraft. Within little more than a year all eight were involved in the development programme, working to such effect that initial deliveries to the US Navy were made on 20 February 1974, the first aircraft going to Squadron VS-41. By that time the S-3A had acquired the name Viking, and when the US Navy ordered 13 production aircraft, on 4 May 1972, it had already been planned to equip 13 squadrons, each with 10 aircraft. Additional contracts placed since that date have covered the production of 187 aircraft in total, comprising the original eight R & D S-3As, plus 179 production aircraft, of which the last were delivered during 1978.

The S-3A is a fairly conventional aircraft for carrier operation: a shoulder-wing monoplane with wings that fold hydraulically on skew hinges to overlap for carrier stowage; the vertical tail also folds. Aerodynamic features include single-slotted Fowler flaps, leading-edge flaps which depress automatically at flap angles in excess of 15°, and conventional ailerons augmented by under- and over-wing spoilers. The powerplant comprises two high by-pass ratio turbofan engines on underwing pylons. The whole aircraft is stressed for catapult launching and arrested landings, yet is relatively more packed with equipment than any other aircraft, and incorporates a large weapons-bay. The short fuselage accommodates part of the fuel, a retractable FR probe, weapons bay and the landing gear whose main units are similar to those of the Vought F-8 Crusader, and nose unit similar to that of the Vought A-7 Corsair II. Accommodation is provided for a crew of four, comprising pilot, co-pilot, tactical operator and acoustic sensor operator, each in a McDonnell Douglas zero-zero ejection seat. The entire cabin is pressurised and air-conditioned, and each crew member's anti-exposure suit is ventilated with air from the same system.

To carry out its ASW role, the Viking has a comprehensive range of the most advanced

sonobuoys, and a MAD boom extendable from the rear fuselage. Non-acoustic sensors include the outstanding Texas Instruments APS-116 high-resolution radar, a forward-looking infra-red scanner in a retractable turret, and passive ECM in wingtip pods. Accurate navigation is ensured by an advanced inertial navigation system, augmented by doppler, Tacan and UHF/DF. HF and UHF communication systems are provided, and an ACLS (Automatic Carrier Landing System) is installed to facilitate all-weather operations. Heart of the ASW data processing is the Univac 1832A digital computer which receives inputs from all sensors, stores information for instant recall, and carries out weapon-trajectory calculations based on information

continued

United States Navy Lockheed S-3A Viking of anti-submarine squadron VS-24. A total of 187 Vikings were delivered.

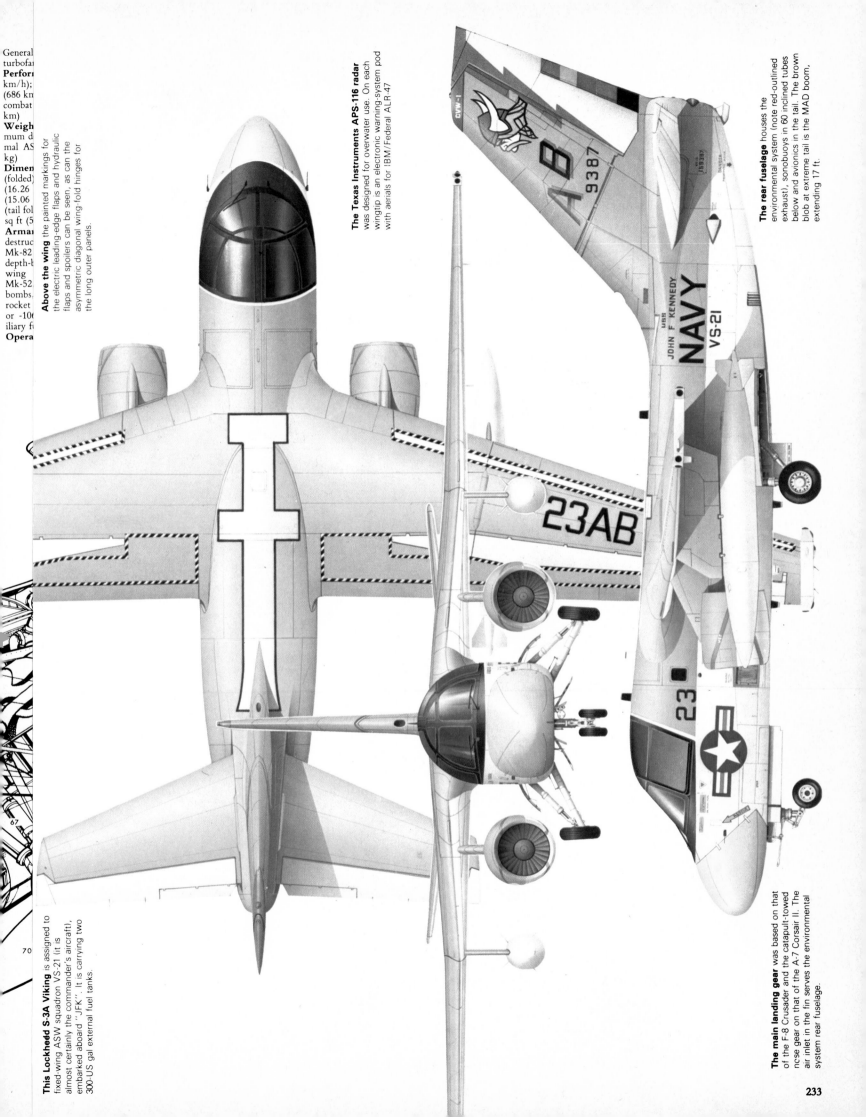

General
turbofar
Perfor
km/h);
(686 km
combat
km)
Weigh
mum d
mal AS
kg)
Dimen
(folded)
(16.26
(15.06
(tail fol
sq ft (5
Arman
destruc
Mk-82
depth-b
wing
Mk-52.
bombs.
rocket
or -10(
iliary f
Opera

This Lockheed S-3A Viking is assigned to fixed-wing ASW squadron VS-21 (it is almost certainly the commander's aircraft), embarked aboard "JFK". It is carrying two 300-US gal external fuel tanks.

Above the wing the painted markings for the electric leading-edge flaps and hydraulic flaps and spoilers can be seen, as can the asymmetric diagonal wing-fold hinges for the long outer panels.

The Texas Instruments APS-116 radar was designed for overwater use. On each wingtip is an electronic warning-system pod with aerials for IBM/Federal ALR-47

The rear fuselage houses the environmental system (note red-outlined exhaust), sonobuoys in 60 inclined tubes below and avionics in the tail. The brown blob at extreme tail is the MAD boom, extending 17 ft.

The main landing gear was based on that of the F-8 Crusader and the catapult-towed ncse gear on that of the A-7 Corsair II. The air inlet in the fin serves the environmental system rear fuselage.

233

Lockheed SR-71

Perhaps the most enigmatic aircraft in service, the delta-winged Lockheed SR-71 'Blackbirds' go about their clandestine business of keeping watch on the world's more serious trouble spots for the US Department of Defense and Central Intelligence Agency. Flying at altitudes of more than 80,000 ft (24384 m) they remain out of sight throughout their missions, showing up only as fast-moving traces on the radar screens of countries below, and perhaps occasionally revealing their presence as a sonic bang.

It is a reflection on their phenomenal performance that the many and continuing optical and electronic intelligence and surveillance tasks across the globe can be accomplished with so few aircraft flying so infrequently. The final and largest members of the 'Blackbird' family, so named for their midnight-blue thermally emissive finish, the SR-71As were built for the United States Air Force Strategic Air Command and are incorporated as a single squadron into the 9th Strategic Reconnaissance Wing based at Beale Air Force Base in California. The total number of aircraft has never been publicly disclosed, but is certainly more than 30 and has been augmented at least once. Unlike combat aircraft, which usually move about the world in strength of at least a squadron, the SR-71As are deployed in ones and twos as needed. A single SR-7A can always cover whatever operation is required, but usually it is desirable to ensure that a second aircraft is also on station to back up the first in the event of loss or unserviceability. As it is, each Blackbird clocks up a mere 200 hours a year, and most of this is simply to keep its crew proficient. The SR-71 has by far the highest performance of any Western aircraft, and considerable skill is needed from their two-man crews. The 9th SRW at Beale operates not only the SR-71s, but also about half Strategic Air Command's fleet of Lockheed U-2 reconnaissance aircraft.

Though originally regarded as a replacement for the U-2, the SR-71 and its stablemate are now seen as complementary to one another, and the U-2 will be kept in service indefinitely; indeed, a new version, the Tr-1 is planned for tactical use. The reason is that there are many high-altitude jobs for which the SR-71 is 'too good' and too expensive. Upper-atmosphere research is a case in point. The two aircraft operate alongside one another and there is never any doubt about which does what job.

The SR-71 is the surviving sister to an earlier and very advanced interceptor, the YF-12A. In the late 1950s and early 60s the leading Western nations were emphasising the importance of long-range interception to destroy enemy bombs outside the release range of their stand-off missiles. At the same time US planners were increasingly concerned about the vulnerability of high-altitude reconnaissance aircraft to surface-to-air missiles, worries that were to be justified by the shooting down in May 1960 over Russia of the U-2 flown by Francis Gary Powers. The two roles (long-range interception and strategic reconnaissance) called for much the same performance. Both needed high speed at high altitude, though the latter role was more demanding in terms of range.

The SR-71 design team was led by C.L. 'Kelly' Johnson, one of the most famous US designers. In the early 1950s he built the world's first aircraft capable of sustained flight at Mach 2 (the Lockheed F-104) and a few years later set out to build the Mach 3 + reconnaissance/interceptor aircraft. He faced three principal challenges: kinetic heating, fuel consumption and aerodynamic drag.

The surface temperature of any aeroplane rises as it goes faster, increasing rapidly over Mach 2, as a result of friction generated between its skin and the air molecules travelling over it. Traditional aluminium alloys cannot be used above Mach 2.2 because the equilibrium temperature of 120°C causes them to weaken dangerously. At over Mach 3 some structural components can reach 300°C, and so the Lockheed team was obliged to use titanium. Though strong, titanium is light, but in the 1960s it was difficult to fabricate and expensive.

To sustain such high speeds for long periods the SR-71A has perforce to consist largely of fuel tanks. It was always envisaged that air-refuelling would be employed to 'top up' after take-off, but even so great quantities of fuel are needed to feed the engines which have to use afterburning throughout the mission.

Like kinetic heating, aerodynamic drag increases rapidly with speed. To keep it as low as possible the team went for the slimmest fuselage and the thinnest wing, blending the two in a new drag-reduction method known as wing-body integration. The wing had to be a delta, so that it could be made thin and yet be sufficiently strong, and also to keep it within the shock-waves thrown off by the forward fuselage. But the delta has the disadvantage that the lift axis moves rearwards over the wing as the speed goes up, and so a force has to be applied to keep the nose up. Usually on deltas this is done by progressively feeding in 'up-elevon', but this would have added too much drag in the case of the SR-71, and so the sides of the forward fuselage were broadened out to form lifting 'chines'.

Two Pratt & Whitney J58 continuous bleed turbojet engines are at the heart of the highly complex propulsion system. It is rightly so-called; at low speed the efflux from the engines provides the force that drives the Blackbird through the sky, but as the speed increases the situation changes and at Mach 3 the engine produces only 18% of the thrust, the rest being generated at suction in the intakes (54%) and from the special ejector nozzles at the rear of the multiple-flow nacelles, (28%). The J58 burns special JP-7 fuel, supplied in flight by the purpose-equipped Boeing KC-135Q tankers at Beale.

The SR-71 went into service in 1966. Two other versions, the SR-71B and SR-71C, are dual-control trainers with reduced performance because of the extra drag produced by the projecting second cockpit. While SR-71s have made headlines with their record-breaking performances, their professional careers have always been shrouded in secrecy. It is likely that they observed the Arab/Israeli wars of 1967 and 1973, the Greek/Turkish flare-up, various parts of the war in Vietnam, deliveries of arms to Cuba, and many other crisis spots. Their information is supplemented by data from reconnaissance satellites because even the SR-71A is vulnerable to the most recent missiles.

Type: two-seat reconnaissance aircraft
Powerplant: two 32,500-lb (14700-kg) Pratt & Whitney J58 afterburning bleed turbojets
Performance: maximum speed Mach 3 to 3.5 at 80,000 ft (24384 m); maximum sustained cruising speed Mach 3; range 2,590 miles (4168 km)
Weight: (estimated) maximum operational 140,000 – 170,000 lb (64000 – 77000 kg)
Dimensions: span 55 ft 7 in (16.94 m); length 107 ft 5 in (32.74 m); height 18 ft 6 in (5.64 m)
Armament: none
Operators: US Air Force

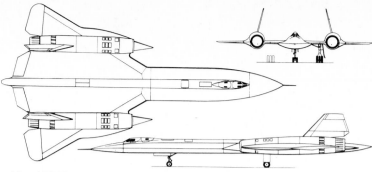

Lockheed SR-71A

A product of the famous Lockheed 'Skunk' works, this SR-71 is on the strength of the 9th Strategic Reconnaissance Wing at Beale AFB, California.

Despite being black — officially dark blue, but the popular name is Blackbird — the monster Lockheed SR-71A is a photogenic aircraft, especially after landing when it pops its drag 'chute. Sensors and EW subsystems are continually being updated.

Lockheed T-33/F-80 Shooting Star

The Lockheed F-80 Shooting Star was the first jet to enter service with the US Army Air Force. Work on the aircraft began in May 1943, when Lockheed was asked to design a fighter around the de Havilland Goblin engine.

The contract gave Lockheed 180 days to design, build and fly the fighter, then designated the XP-80. Working in a specially erected building, known as the 'Skunk Works', the company beat the construction deadline handsomely, the airframe being ready in only 143 days. Unfortunately, the engine sucked in the flimsy thin-wall inlet duct. Unselfishly, de Havilland took the engine from their second Vampire, shipped it to Burbank, and on 8 January 1944 the new fighter flew for the first time.

It was a sleek, low-wing monoplane, with a thin laminar-flow wing section and power-boosted ailerons. Official flight tests showed a top speed of 502 mph (808 km/h) at 20,850 ft (6360 m), although the engine developed only 2,460-lb (1117-kg) thrust instead of the rated 3,000 lb (1360 kg).

Meanwhile, General Electric had achieved 4,000 lb (1814 kg) thrust with their new I-40 engine. This, together with difficulties in the plans to build the Goblin in the US, resulted in the decision that production aircraft would be powered by the American engine. Soon there emerged from the 'Skunk Works' a second prototype, designated XP-80A. Slightly bigger and heavier, this flew for the first time on 10 June 1944. By the time the war ended, 45 had been delivered to USAAF squadrons, but they were too late to see combat. Two aircraft were flown to Italy for tests at operational bases, but they were deliberately kept away from any combat situation. These early production aircraft had a top speed of 558 mph (898 km/h).

When World War II ended, plans to produce 5,000 P-80s were drastically curtailed. However, the aircraft was chosen to re-equip front-line pursuit groups of the USAAF, and an order was placed for 677 P-80As in December 1945. These were powered by Allison J33 engines, had wing-tip tanks, and provision for wing bomb racks, rocket launchers or fuel tanks.

During the production of these aircraft, a thinner wing was developed, together with provision for JATO, improved armament and more powerful engines with water-alcohol injection. These improvements were embodied on the last 240 aircraft, which were designated P-80B. Further evolution resulted in the F-80C (the designation 'P' was changed to 'F' in 1948) with the J33-A-23 engine (the production version of the I-40) and provision for additional under-wing loads.

Serving with the US Far East Air Force in June 1950 were five F-80C jet wings and RF-80A tactical reconnaissance squadron, and these went into action when the Korean War

started. It was during this conflict that the F-80 made aviation history by engaging in what was probably the first combat between opposing jet fighters. On 8 November 1950, four F-80Cs of the 51st Fighter Interceptor Wing engaged four Mikoyan-Gurevich MiG-15s and shot one of them down. It was, however, somewhat of a lucky outcome, because the F-80 was generally inferior to the swept-wing Russian fighter.

A major development was the T-33A two-seat conversion trainer. Basically an F-80 with a lengthened fuselage to accommodate a second seat in tandem, the T-33A served with more than 30 air forces. Over 5,690 were built by Lockheed, a further 210 were assembled by Kawasaki in Japan and Canadair built 656 which, mostly powered by Rolls-Royce Nenes, were known as CL-30 Silver Stars. The RT-33A, a single-seat variant fitted with cameras for reconnaissance, was supplied to many countries, including Thailand and Turkey. The version used by the US Navy, designated TV-2, was the first operational jet trainer designed to perform pilot training operations from both sea-going carriers and land bases.

Tribute to the reliability and handling qualities of the T-33A is the fact that it was still being used by several air forces in 1979, more than 30 years after its first flight. Japan

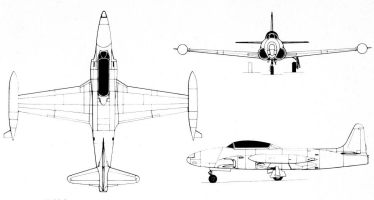

Lockheed T-33A

intends to continue using the aircraft at least until the mid-1980s.

Type: (F-80C) single-seat jet fighter
Powerplant: one 5,200-lb (2360-kg), with water injection, Allison J33-A-35 turbojet
Performance: maximum speed at sea level 600 mph (960 km/h); maximum speed at 25,000 ft 543 mph (874 km/h); stalling speed 105 mph (169 km/h); climb to 25,000 ft (7620 m) 7 minutes; combat ceiling 44,100 ft (13440 m); combat mission endurance 3 hours

12 minutes
Weights: empty 8,240 lb (3741 kg); loaded 15,336 lb (6963 kg)
Dimensions: span 38 ft 10½ in (11.85 m); length 34 ft 6 in (10.51 m); height 11 ft 4 in (3.45 m); wing area 237 sq ft (16.66 m²)
Armament: six 0.50-in (12.7-mm) machine-guns, plus two 1,000-lb (454-kg) bombs and eight rockets
Operators: (T-33 in 1979) Bolivia, Greece, Japan, Nicaragua, Portugal

Two T-birds over Alaska make a fine picture, and one that will soon be hard to repeat as the well-liked Lockheed T-33A becomes rarer in air forces around the world. These two were assigned to the USAF 317th FIS, and are seen over the Chugash mountain range.

Lockheed U-2/TR-1

When it became vital for the West to know the extent of military developments in the Soviet Union, and the deployment of that country's armed forces, the USA initiated a major programme of aerial reconnaissance. Initially, specially adapted versions of aircraft such as the Convair B-36 and Boeing B-47 bombers were used. In time, however, the Mikoyan-Gurevich MiG-15 began to intercept these aircraft, and in December 1954 the US decided to produce a specialized reconnaissance aircraft.

The result was the Lockheed U-2, built virtually by hand in the Lockheed company's secret 'Skunk Works' in Burbank. The U stood for 'Utility', one of the many steps taken to disguise the real purpose of the aircraft at that time.

The U-2 had a remarkable high-flying and long-range performance as a result of powerplant and configuration. The former was a Pratt & Whitney engine with wide-chord compressor blades for flight at high altitudes, and specially adapted to run on low-volatility fuel. The configuration, employing a high aspect ratio, glider-like wing, enabled the range to be extended by shutting down the

engine to flight-idle and gliding.

At a summit conference in July 1955, President Eisenhower proposed an 'Open Skies' policy as a means of reducing international tensions and increasing mutual trust. Under this plan, the US and the Soviet Union would have allowed the other to carry out unrestricted reconnaissance flights over their territory. Marshal Bulganin rejected the proposal. With this rejection, the wisdom of the U-2 project was underwritten and the first aircraft made its maiden flight in August 1955.

Despite payload restrictions, the aircraft bristled with data-gathering devices, including a long-focus camera, which scanned through seven apertures and could record on 4000 pairs of photographs an area some 125 miles (200 km) wide by 2,200 miles (3540 km) long, and an Elint receiver which monitored radio and radar transmissions from the ground. U-2 aircraft flew many missions which provided data important to US intelligence, not only over the Soviet Union, but also over China, North Vietnam and Cuba.

In April 1960 a set of U-2 prints taken over the Soviet Union revealed what appeared to be the first Russian ICBM installation. Plans

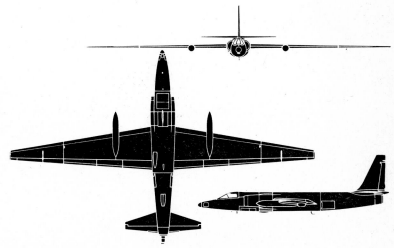

Lockheed U-2D

were made for another mission to be made and accordingly a U-2 was ferried to a base in Pakistan, ready for a long over-land flight of

2,900 miles (4700 km) over the Soviet Union, which was to have ended in Norway. During the flight, however, the U-2, piloted by Gary

continued

Powers, was knocked into a spin by the explosion of a ground-to-air missile and crashed.

The aircraft continued its work, however, and it was a U-2 flight over Cuba in 1962 which first revealed the Soviet Union's surreptitious attempts to install ballistic missiles in that country — and provided the foundation for the pressures which eventually resulted in their removal.

Some U-2s have been used for high-altitude weather reconnaissance and research. Designated U-2D and having two seats, these are instrumented with equipment supplied by NASA and the Wright Air Development Center. This equipment gathers data on phenomena such as clear-air turbulence, convective clouds, wind shear, jet streams and cosmic radiation.

In the 1960s one of 19 new versions was the U-2CT dual conversion with a separate cockpit for the instructor. Another new version was designated U-2R. This had a lengthened fuselage and redesigned wing of increased span, able to hold more fuel. From the U-2R has been developed the TR-1. This is being produced openly as a high-altitude tactical surveillance and reconnaissance aircraft for the USAF Tactical Air Command, with funds allocated for the production of an initial batch of 25 aircraft. Intended primarily for use in Europe, the TR-1 is equipped with an ASARS (Advanced Synthetic Aperture Radar System), all-weather SLAR (Side-Looking Airborne Radar) and extensive ECM (Electronic CounterMeasures) equipment. The SLAR is reported to have a stand-off range of about 35 miles (56 km).

Type: (TR-1) high-altitude reconnaissance aircraft
Powerplant: one 17,000-lb (7711-kg) Pratt & Whitney J75-P-13 turbojet

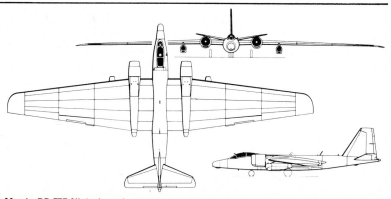

This dark stranger is a Lockheed U-2R, much larger than other versions of the clandestine U-2 mystery ship and in this case operating in black out of Davis-Monthan AFB with no marking save tail-number 10333 in red. This airframe is the basis of the TR-1.

Performance: maximum speed at 40,000 ft (12200 m) 430 mph (692 km/h); cruising speed 460 mph (740 km/h); service ceiling over 70,000 ft (21335 m); range 3,000 miles (4830 km)
Weights: unknown

Dimensions: span 103 ft 0 in (31.39 m); length 63 ft 0 in (19.20 m)
Operators: NASA, US Air Force

Martin B-57 Night Intruder

On 21 February, 1951, the third production English Electric Canberra B.2 flew to Baltimore, setting a transatlantic record and also becoming the first jet aircraft to complete an unrefuelled Atlantic crossing. The flight was historic in another way because The Martin Company was to undertake licence-production of the type for the USAF — the first foreign design built for US combat deployment since the end of World War I.

As the Martin Model 272, the initial US-built aircraft comprised a pre-production batch of eight to establish the line. They incorporated numerous engineering changes. The designation B-57A was given to this batch, fitted with Wright J65-W-1 (licence-built Armstrong Siddeley Sapphire) engines, and the first flew on 20 July 1953. These were followed by 67 externally similar RB-57As with cameras behind the bomb bay; the first of these went to Shaw AFB in early 1954. For the next three years the RB-57A served with the 363rd Tactical Reconnaissance Wing.

The first major change came with the next model, the B-57B night intruder, of which 202 were built — half of Martin's total of 403. The cockpit was changed to a tandem configuration. A rotary bomb bay was fitted (see specification) and the first B-57B flew on 28 June, 1954.

First deliveries of B-57Bs, beginning on 5 January 1955, were to the 461st Bombardment Wing of the USAF's Tactical Air Command, while the 345th Wing converted to the B-57B in 1956, followed by the 3rd Wing Pacific Air Forces.

The B-57B was in TAC service for a comparatively short time, being withdrawn by 1959. Some aircraft were issued to Air National Guard units from 1961, and 26 were supplied to the Pakistan air force, two of whose squadrons were equipped with the type.

A transition trainer version, the B-57C, served alongside the B-57B in TAC service, and 38 were built following the first flight on 30 December, 1954.

One other variant with a similar airframe was the B-57E, flown in April 1956. This was a multi-role version, capable of use as a bomber, reconnaissance aircraft, trainer or

target tug, for which purpose a detachable container was carried beneath the fuselage; 68 were produced, the last being coupled in 1959.

The two final versions were so far removed from the original Canberra design that the ancestry was almost unrecognisable. First was the RB-57D, of which 20 were built for high-altitude work, six as two-seat reconnaissance aircraft (RB-57D2) and the remainder as single seaters, of which several were used for electronic reconnaissance missions under the designation RB-57D(C), having enlarged bulbous nose and tail radomes increasing the length by 2 ft 4 in (71.12 cm) and wingtip fairings which, together with a completely new wing, raised the span to 107 ft 6 in (32.76

Martin RB-57F Night Intruder

The Martin B-57 in SE Asia did a tremendous job, often in close partnership with such diverse platforms as the O-2 slow-FAC Cessna and AC-130K night gunship. This example is being readied for a mission at Da Nang AB in May 1966. Attrition was low.

m). The RB-57Ds served for several years with the TAC. Pacific Air Forces, MATS (MAC) for air sampling, and the Aerospace Defense Command calibrating the NORAD radar network.

If the long-span RB-57D looked odd, the RB-57F was grotesque. General Dynamics was given a USAF contract to convert 12 B-57Bs into reconnaissance platforms capable of operating at up to 100,000 ft (30480 m). A completely new wing of 122 ft 5 in (37.32 m) span and 2,000 sq ft (185.8 m²) was designed. A new vertical tail increased the height to 19 ft (5.79 m), and length became 69 ft (21.03 m). The RB-57F had two 18,000-lb (8165-kg) Pratt & Whitney TF33-P-11 turbofans supplemented by two underwing 3,300-lb (1500-kg) Pratt & Whitney J60-P-9 turbojets. The first RB-57F was delivered on 18 June 1964.

The war in South-East Asia gradually brought the B-57 out of retirement and into the forefront of the battle as a FAC, ground attack, night reconnaissance, multi-sensor reconnaissance and early warning platform. Unfortunately, the multi-sensor B-57G never got into production (as conversions), but surviving B-57Bs were rebuilt as EB-57s of three subtypes used chiefly by the Aerospace Defense Command as standard EW platforms for tasks such as threat-evaluation and simulation, fighter affiliation, and jamming tests on NORAD.S.

Several of the B-57Bs supplied to Pakistan are believed still to be operational in the night attack role.

Type: originally reconnaissance bomber
Powerplant: (B-57B) two 7,200-lb (3265-kg) Wright J65-W-5 turbojets
Performance: (B-57B) maximum speed at 40,000 ft (12192 m) 582 mph (937 km/h); maximum speed at sea level 520 mph (837 km/h); rate of climb at sea level 3,500 ft (1066 m) per second; service ceiling 48,000 ft (14630 m); range 2,300 miles (3700 km)
(RB-57D) maximum speed at 40,000 ft (12192 m) 632 mph (1017 km/h); service ceiling 60,000 ft (18288 m)
Weights: (B-57B) empty 26,000 lb (11793 kg); maximum loaded 55,000 lb (24948 kg)
Dimensions: (B-57B) span 64 ft (19.5 m); length 65 ft 6 in (19.9 m); height 15 ft 7 in (4.75 m); wing area 960 sq ft (89.18 m²)
(RB-57D) span 106 ft (32.30 m); length 65 ft 6 in (19.9 m); height 14 ft 10 in (4.51 m)
Armament: (B-57B) eight 0.50-in (12.7-mm) Colt-Browning machine-guns or four 20-mm

This grotesque WB-57F was developed from the British Canberra by Martin and General Dynamics for extreme-altitude reconnaissance. This one was assigned by the USAF to NASA for Project Airstream, sampling nuclear radiation; Howard AFB, Canal Zone, 1977

Pakistan Air Force Martin B-57B of 7 Sqn, based at Masroor and camouflaged for the night attack role.

cannon in wings; underwing racks can accommodate mixed loads such as two 500-lb (227-kg) bombs and eight 5-in (12.7-cm) rockets, or napalm tanks; A rotary weapons bay in the fuselage has a capacity of up to 5,000 lb (2268 kg) of bombs or rockets, and these can be mounted on the bomb bay door as an internal load and rotated to provide an external load when approaching a target
Operators: Pakistan, US Air Force

Max Holste MH.1521 Broussard

Produced by one of the smaller French aircraft companies, Avions Max Holste (later merged into Aérospatiale), the Broussard was an enlarged version of the MH.152 flown in June 1951 with a 220-hp (164-kW) Salmson 8AS engine. An unusual feature is the twin-finned tail. Interest was shown by the French army and an initial batch of 24 was laid down, of which 18 went to the army. The prototype flew in November 1952 and the first production aircraft on 16 June, 1954.

A total of 335 Broussards were built and deliveries were made to a number of countries under the French military aid programmes. The Cameroun air force received three in 1961 and several more later; Chad, the Central African Republic, Dahomey and Haute Volta had three each; Congo six; Ivory Coast, Mauritania and Senegal two each; and Malagasy Republic, Niger and Gabon four each. A few are still in service.

The biggest user is still France, where examples are in service with the air force and army. The former still operated around 70 in 1976; six of these were based at Villacoublay, near Paris, with others at Metz, Bordeaux and Aix. Overseas detachments served in Djibouti and Pointe-à-Pitre. The French army had 37 Broussards on strength in 1976, operating throughout the country alongside helicopter units, but only eight are expected to be still in service by 1982.

The basic military variant is the MH.1521M. A version was produced with crop-spraying gear as the MH.1521A, and the experimental MH.1522, flown in February 1968, had double-slotted flaps and leading edge slats to give even better STOL performance.

A number of Broussards have been used by civil operators.

Type: six-seat light utility transport
Powerplant: one 450-hp (336-kW) Pratt & Whitney R-985-AN Wasp piston engine
Performance: maximum speed at sea level 168 mph (270 km/h); cruising speed at 50% power at 4,920 ft (1500 m) 143 mph (230 km/h); minimum flying speed with flaps 46.5 mph (75 km/h); minimum flying speed without flaps 55.8 mph (90 km/h); rate of climb at sea level 1,180 ft (360 m) per minute; range 500 miles (800 km) with 1,320 lb (600 kg) load; take-off run 510 ft (155 m); landing run 393 ft (120 m)
Dimensions: span 45 ft 1 in (13.74 m); length 28 ft 2 in (8.60 m); height 9 ft 2 in (2.80 m); wing area 273.3 sq ft (25.4 m²)
Operators: Cameroun, Central African Republic, Chad, Congo (Brazzaville), Dahomey, France, Gabon, Haute-Volta, Ivory Coast, Malagasy Republic, Mauritania, Niger, Senegal

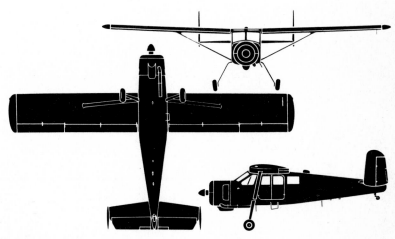

Max Holste MH.1521 Broussard

McDonnell Douglas A-4 Skyhawk

In 1950 the US Navy was busy preparing its specification for an advanced attack aircraft. Early experience in the Korean War, which started in mid-1950, had shown that such an aircraft was needed for deployment from aircraft-carriers, the mobile airfield/maintenance base that service planners then considered vital for global policing. The US Navy decided it needed a turboprop-powered aircraft, with a maximum weight of 30,000 lb (13607 kg), and capable of carrying a 2,000 lb (907 kg) bomb load.

When the Douglas Aircraft Company at El Segundo received a request for proposals the divisions's chief engineer, Ed Heinemann, had for some time been investigating the possibility of producing an advanced aeroplane which would be far less complex and much lighter in weight than the attack/fighter aircraft then in service. The US Navy's requirement provided a first opportunity to put these ideas into practice and it is unlikely that, in even his wildest dreams, he could have imagined in 1951 that his brain child would still be in production 28 years later.

Instead of producing a machine merely to satisfy the US Navy's requirement, Heinemann and his team set out to evolve the design of an attack aircraft which was far superior to anything which the US Navy had considered possible at that time. It developed as an aeroplane with a gross weight which was half that of the US Navy's specification, and which also had a maximum speed some 100 mph (160 km/h) faster than that specified. When the Douglas proposal was evaluated by the US Navy an increase in bomb load and range was requested, probably tongue-in-cheek, for it seems fairly certain that many of the US Navy's evaluation officers must have considered it most unlikely that Douglas would be able to develop a production aircraft that was anywhere near as good as the proposal. Just in case the El Segundo team really knew what it was about, they lost little time in awarding a contract for prototypes and pre-production aircraft under the designation A4D-1, later redesignated A-4 and named Skyhawk.

In its original form the Skyhawk was a small single-seat aircraft of delta-wing configuration, although a number of two-seat variants have been produced subsequently. Like many classic designs it happened to be right first time, and the XA4D-1 prototype which first flew on 22 June 1954 is superficially almost identical to single-seat production aircraft which are still in service. The wing is a three-spar structure forming an integral fuel tank, so small it need not fold, and with additional fuel carried within the fuselage aft of the lightweight ejection seat. There is a variable-incidence tailplane and hydraulically-powered elevator and rudder, the latter of unique construction with a central 'skin' and external stiffeners. The rear fuselage is detachable to provide easy access to the turbojet for servicing or replacement. The landing gear is of the hydraulically-retractable tricycle type, the main legs folding rearwards under the wing. Initial armament comprised two 20-mm two-barrel guns mounted in the wing roots, plus one underfuselage and two underwing hardpoints capable of carrying a variety of weapons up to a total weight of 5,000 lb (2268 kg). It is in the areas of powerplant, avionics and armament that the major changes have been made since the first pre-production aircraft flew on 14 August 1954.

The engine selected to power the prototype was a 7,200 lb (3266 kg) thrust Wright J65-W-2 (a licence-built Armstrong Siddeley Sapphire), but the first production A4D-1s, subsequently A-4As, of which deliveries to Navy Squadron VA-62 began on 26 October 1956, were powered by the 7,700 lb (3493 kg) thrust Wright J65-W-4 or -4B.

Not surprisingly, for an aircraft with such a long production history, there have been

Lt Beck's A-4 Skyhawk was pictured on the deck of the *JFK* in the early 1970s, possibly in SE Asian waters. His mount is not one of the later 'saddleback' or 'camel' versions, which remained in production for 25 consecutive years until February 1979.

McDonnell Douglas A-4M Skyhawk II single-seat attack bomber, in production until 1979 for the US Marine Corps. It is equipped as standard with a braking parachute which makes it possible to deploy this aircraft operationally from fields only 4,000 ft (1220 m) in length.

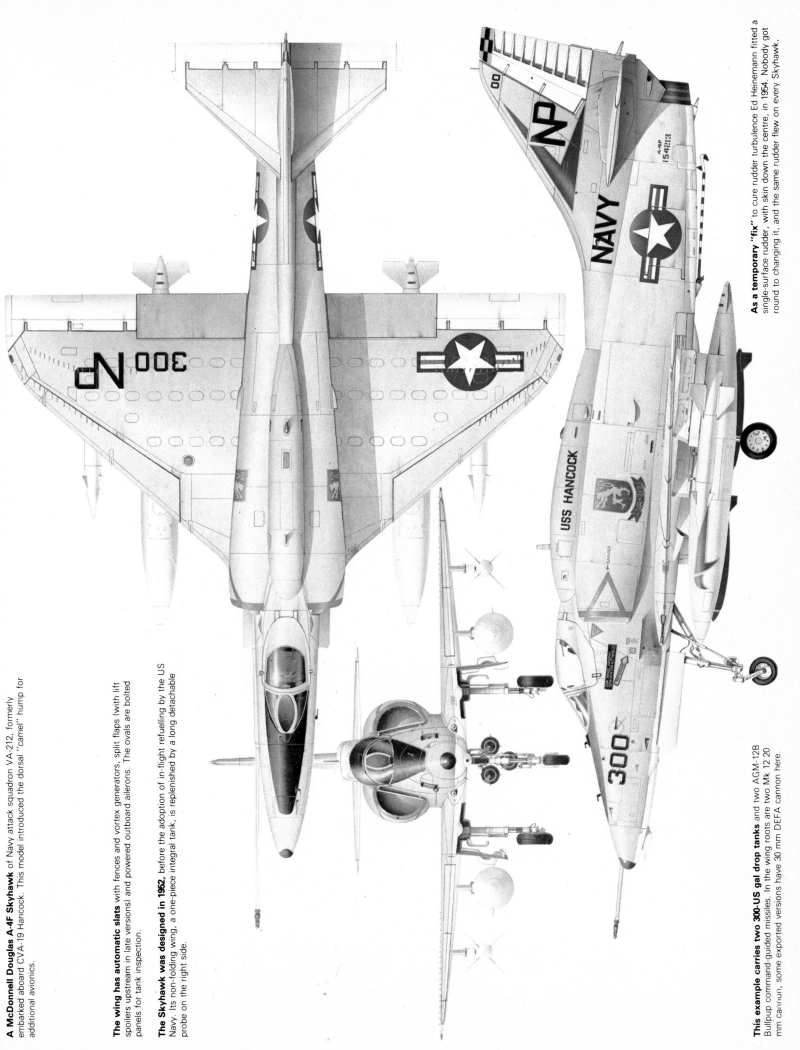

A McDonnell Douglas A-4F Skyhawk of Navy attack squadron VA-212, formerly embarked aboard CVA-19 Hancock. This model introduced the dorsal "camel" hump for additional avionics.

The wing has automatic slats with fences and vortex generators, split flaps (with lift spoilers upstream in late versions) and powered outboard ailerons. The ovals are bolted panels for tank inspection.

The Skyhawk was designed in 1952, before the adoption of in-flight refuelling by the US Navy. Its non-folding wing, a one-piece integral tank, is replenished by a long detachable probe on the right side.

As a temporary "fix" to cure rudder turbulence Ed Heinemann fitted a single-surface rudder, with skin down the centre, in 1954. Nobody got round to changing it, and the same rudder flew on every Skyhawk.

This example carries two 300-US gal drop tanks and two AGM-12B Bullpup command-guided missiles. In the wing roots are two Mk 12 20 mm cannon, some exported versions have 30 mm DEFA cannon here.

McDonnell Douglas A-4 Skyhawk

many versions and variants. A brief mention of each of these will show the steady development of the type from the first production series to the A4-M/N Skyhawk IIs being built in early 1979.

The A-4A was followed by the A-4B (A4D-2) which had an engine of the same power, a Wright J65-W-16A or -20. Major changes included provision for carrying Bullpup missiles; introduction of a navigation computer, flight refuelling capability, and dual hydraulic system. Examples of this version used for training purposes, in the absence of a special-purpose trainer, were given the designation TA-4B.

The A-4C (A4D-2N) had the fuselage nose extended to accommodate new equipment necessary to improve all-weather capability, including an advanced autopilot, terrain clearance radar, and a low-altitude bombing system. Deliveries of 638 aircraft for USN and USMC began in December 1959.

The next production version was the A-4E (A4D-5) with an 8,500 lb (3855 kg) thrust Pratt & Whitney J52-P-6A turbojet, and this engine was fitted retrospectively to A-4A, -4B and -4C aircraft in operational service. The A-4E introduced a zero-height/90 knot (104 mph/167 km/h) ejection seat, and new under-fuselage/underwing pylons enabling this version to carry 8,200 lb (3719 kg) of weapons.

The A-4F attack bomber with the 9,300 lb (4218 kg) thrust Pratt & Whitney J52-P-8A turbojet, introduced lift spoilers to reduce landing run, nosewheel steering, a zero-zero ejection seat, improved protection against ground fire, and new avionics installed in a 'hump' fairing aft of the cockpit. Because of the hump, this and other recent versions are called 'Camels'; in S.E. Asia the A-4 served widely with the USN, USMC and USAF, and was popularly called the 'Scooter'.

It was followed by a TA-4F two-seat trainer (all two-seaters have one large canopy except for the TA-4S), TA-4J two-seat trainer, and the A-4M Skyhawk II in production in 1979. This latter version has a braking parachute as standard, and a number of detail improvements. Also in production is the A-4N, similar to the -4M, which is being built for Israel. A-4Gs and TA-4Gs for the Royal Australian Navy, and A-4Ks and TA-4Ks for the RNZAF, are both similar to the A-4F and TA-4F respectively. The A-4H and TA-4H have been supplied to Israel, A-4KU and TA-4KU to Kuwait, A-4P and A-4Q to the Argentine Air Force & Navy respectively. A-4S and TA-4S (two separate canopies) are designations for updated A-4Bs for the Singapore Air Defence Command, modified by Lockheed Aircraft Service Company. Remaining versions are the A-4L, a modified A-4C with uprated engine for the US Navy Reserve, and A-4Y, an updated A-4M, to which specification all -4Ms are to be modified. This has a new Head Up Display, redesigned landing gear, and Hughes Angle Rate Bombing system.

Type: single-seat attack bomber
Power Plant: (A-4M) one 11,200-lb (5080-kg) Pratt & Whitney J52-P-408 turbojet
Performance: (A-4M) maximum speed with 4,000-lb (1814-kg) bombload, 646 mph (1040 km/h); maximum ferry range 2,000 miles (3219 km)
Weights: (A-4M) empty 10,800 lb (4899 kg), take off 24,500 lb (11113 kg)
Dimensions: (A-4M) span 27 ft 6 in (8.38 m); length 40 ft 4 in (12.29 m); height 15 ft 0 in (4.57 m); wing area 260 sq ft (24.15 m²)
Armament: (A-4M) underfuselage hardpoint with a capacity of 3,500 lb (1588 kg); two inboard underwing hardpoints each with a capacity of 2,250 lb (1021 kg); two outboard underwing hardpoints each with a capacity of 1,000 lb (454 kg) Extensive range of weapons can be carried, including conventional or nuclear bombs, air-to-air and air-to-ground rockets, missiles and gunpods. Two 20-mm guns in wing roots are standard (Israeli have 30-mm)
Operators: Argentina, Australia, Israel, Kuwait, New Zealand, Singapore, US Marine Corps and US Navy

Israel Defence Force/Air Force A-4E Skyhawk, a version that seems likely for imminent retirement from service, later variants taking over the light strike role.

A-4P (C-241) converted from an ex-US Navy A-4B Skyhawk, of IV Grupo Caza-Bombardeo, Fuerza Aerea Argentina, based at Villa Reynolds in 1970.

US Navy two-seat TA-4J Skyhawk of Training Squadron VT-21, based at Naval Air Station Kingsville.

Royal Australian Navy A-4G Skyhawk of VF-805 Sqn, part of an Air Group flying from HMAS Melbourne, Australia's sole aircraft carrier.

Royal New Zealand Air Force A-4K Skyhawk strike aircraft of 75 Sqn based at Ohakea, North Island.

US Marine Corps A-4M Skyhawk of VMA-324, MCAS Beaufort, MD, 1971.

Kuwait Air Force A-4KU Skyhawk, one of 30 single-seaters equipping two strike squadrons stationed near Kuwait.

McDonnell Douglas AV-8B Advanced Harrier

Strong interest in the British Aerospace Harrier by the US Marine Corps resulted in an initial order for 12 examples in 1969, under the designation AV-8A, and these were equipped to carry AIM-9 Sidewinder missiles. Subsequent orders brought the total for USMC use to 102, of which eight were two-seat trainers designated TAV-8A, and all had been delivered by 1977. They were used to equip three USMC squadrons (VMA 231, VMA 513 and VMA 542) at Cherry Point, North Carolina.

Deployment by the US Marine Corps of the AV-8A Harrier jet V/STOL concept was operationally attractive. They needed, however, an aircraft with this capability that had virtually double the weapons payload/-combat radius of the AV-8A, and the Corps was encouraged in this belief by McDonnell Douglas, the type's US foster-parent. In late 1973 the British and US governments started to consider joint development of an AV-16A 'Advanced Harrier', but by early 1975 the British government had decided that there was 'not enough common ground' to take part in a joint programme. Instead, the USMC and McDonnell Douglas initiated a programme to convert two AV-8As as prototype YAV-8Bs, AV-8B being the designation allocated to the new US development.

These prototypes differ from the British-built AV-8A by the introduction of a supercritical wing of graphite/epoxy construction, a lift-improvement device to contain the engine exhaust air as it rebounds from the ground, increased-area trailing-edge flaps, drooped ailerons, redesigned engine air intakes, strengthened landing gear, and completely different subsystems and equipment. The first of these prototypes made its first flight at the McDonnell plant at St Louis, Missouri on 9 November 1978, and the second was due to fly in early 1979.

At that time it was anticipated that, subject to satisfactory flight testing, the USMC would initiate production of the first batch of a stated requirement for 350 aircraft, and a similar quantity was a possible requirement of the US Navy. Despite the operational need, the AV-8B has been politically handicapped by being 'foreign' and the Carter administration hoped to terminate the programme by eliminating it from the FY80 Defense Budget. The US Marines hoped in early 1979 to get this decision reversed.

Type: V/STOL strike aircraft

Powerplant: one 21,500-lb (9752-kg) thrust Rolls-Royce Pegasus Mk 803 (F402-RR-402) vectored-thrust turbofan
Performance: (estimated) operational radius (VTO) with 3,000-lb (1361-kg) external load 57 miles (92 km); operational radius (STO) with same external load 414 miles (666 km); ferry range over 2,000 miles (3220 km)
Weights: basic operating empty 12,550 lb (5693 kg); maximum take-off (VTO) 18,850 lb (8550 kg); maximum take-off (STO) 29,550 lb (13403 kg)
Dimensions: span 30 ft 4 in (9.25 m); length 46 ft 4 in (14.12 m); height 11 ft 7¾ in (3.55 m); wing area about 230 sq ft (21.37 m²)
Armament: twin underfuselage gun/ammunition packs each mounting a US 20-mm cannon or 30-mm Aden gun; one underfuselage and six underwing hardpoints with combined capacity of 9,200 lb (4173 kg); weapons carried can include MK-82 Snakeye

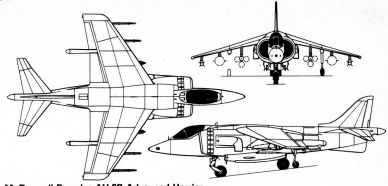

McDonnell Douglas AV-8B Advanced Harrier

bombs and laser or electro-optical guided weapons, and AIM-9L Sidewinders for air-to-air use

Operators: (1979) US Marine Corps prototypes only

After very successful flight evaluation in 1979 an order was placed for further development aircraft of the AV-8B, the first two prototypes of which were remanufactured British-built AV-8As.

McDonnell Douglas C-9 Nightingale/Skytrain II

When in 1966 the USAF required a new aeromedical transport for operation over medium range, a careful evaluation of existing civil transport aircraft was made to select the most suitable 'off the shelf' production model. This is today an essential exercise when only a comparatively small number of aircraft are required; for the days when a manufacturer could scratch out a design on the 'back of an envelope', and then build half-a-dozen at moderate cost, has long since gone.

Following their investigation, the US Air Force decided that the McDonnell Douglas DC-9 Series 30 most nearly met its requirements, and ordered eight of these aircraft in 1967. Whilst being generally similar to the standard DC-9, these had two 14,500-lb (6577-kg) thrust Pratt & Whitney JT8D-9 turbofan engines instead of the JT8D-7s then installed as standard in Series 30 plus a number of detail changes and a very different interior. Three entrances were provided to ease the problems of embarking and disembarking patients: two had hydraulically operated stairways, the third (forward) door, measuring 6 ft 9 in (2.06 m) high and 11 ft 4 in (3.45 m) wide, had a hydraulically-operated ramp to simplify the loading of stretchers and wheelchairs.

Internal changes provided for the accommodation of up to 40 patients on stretchers, or more than 40 ambulatory patients in standard seats, and a medical team of five. Within the interior is an intensive-care compartment in which ventilation and atmospheric pressure can be regulated independently of the main

cabin, and galley and toilets are provided both fore and aft.

Designated C-9A by the US Air Force, and appropriately named Nightingale, the first of these was delivered to Scott AFB on 10 August 1968, for operation by the MAC's 375th Aeromedical Wing. Thirteen more of these C-9As were ordered subsequently, and all 21 had been delivered to the USAF by February 1973.

Just before the completion of this order the US Navy, which had taken a close look at the civil transport and the USAF's C-9A, decided to procure a slightly modified version for service as a fleet logistic passenger/cargo transport. On 24 April 1972 five aircraft were ordered under the designation C-9B and named Skytrain II. The name was chosen to honour the venerable Douglas R4D Skytrain (DC-3 variant), which has served the US Navy so long and so well.

The C-9B has the JT8D-9 turbofan, plus the optional large cargo door forward which, in the C-9A is intended for the loading of stretchers. Normal access for passengers is via forward port and aft ventral doors, both of which have hydraulically-operated airstairs so that the aircraft can be independent of airport facilities. Normal seating capacity of the C-9B is for 90 passengers in a five-abreast seating arrangement, but a maximum of 107 can be accommodated in a high-density layout. A galley and toilet are provided at each end of the cabin. These aircraft can be operated also in all-cargo or passenger/cargo configuration, this enabling the US Navy to utilise its fleet of

C-9Bs to the maximum. Augmented fuel capacity confers a longer range than any other DC-9 variant.

The US Navy's original contract for five C-9Bs was increased later to eight aircraft, but a subsequent order placed in 1974 brought the total on order to 14. The first made its initial flight on 7 February 1973, and all had been delivered by mid-1976. Several are used by the US Marine Corps. The VC-9B is a VIP version. In addition to the above, two generally similar aircraft were sold to the Kuwait air force.

Type: military aeromedical or naval passenger/cargo transport
Powerplant: (C-9B) two 14,500-lb (6577-kg)

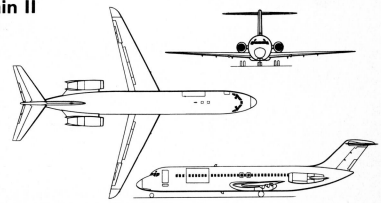

McDonnell Douglas C-9B Skytrain II

thrust Pratt & Whitney JT8D-9 turbofans
Performance: (C-9B) maximum cruising speed 576 mph (927 km/h); long-range cruising speed 504 mph (811 km/h); range at long-range cruising speed with 10,000-lb (4536-kg) payload at 30,000 ft (9145 m) 2,923 miles (4704 km)
Weights: (C-9B) operating empty (passenger) 65,283 lb (29612 kg); operating empty (cargo) 59,706 lb (27082 kg); maximum take-off 110,000 lb (49895 kg)
Dimensions: span 93 ft 5 in (28.47 m); length 119 ft 3½ in (36.36 m); height 27 ft 6 in (8.38 m); wing area 1,000.7 sq ft (92.97 m²)
Armament: none
Operators: Kuwait, US Air Force, US Marine Corps, US Navy

McDonnell Douglas F-4 Phantom II/R-4

Even before the 5,000th McDonnell Douglas F-4 Phantom II was delivered in mid-1978, the aircraft had a production history which far outstripped that of any other recent combat jet aircraft in the Western world. Only the Mikoyan-Gurevich MiG-21 can challenge its astonishingly large production total. The Phantom's success, originally attributable to its excellent fighter and strike aircraft qualities, was boosted by the demand for the type during the Vietnam war. During 1967 the production rate at McDonnell Douglas's St Louis factory peaked at 72 aircraft per month. The Phantom has been used as a front-line aircraft by 11 nations — and remains in service with 10 countries.

In 1953 McDonnell failed to win the contract for the first US Navy supersonic ship-borne fighter. A new design was started in-house in the same year, tailored to a specification which the company evolved from its contacts with leading naval personnel. After seeing a mock-up the US Bureau of Aeronautics (BuAer) ordered McDonnell to build two prototype F3H-Gs. After four months' work, in April 1954, the design was drastically revised to provide more internal fuel capacity, a two-seat cockpit and more comprehensive fire-control equipment. The strike/fighter which emerged from this revision was called the F-4 Phantom II (the Roman numeral initially distinguishing it from McDonnell's first jet fighter with the same name). The first flight took place on 27 May 1958 and the F-4 soon proved that it could live up to its claims. It could operate over a 290-mile (467-km) radius of action, loiter for up to two hours, and was the first aircraft which could detect, intercept and destroy any target which came within radar range. Other types in the same era still needed assistance from surface-based radar units.

The US Navy ordered only 375 aircraft initially, but it was evident from its earliest days that the Phantom was a good basic airframe for a wide variety of roles. The first 24 produc-

RAF Phantom FGR.2 (XT901) in the markings of 17 Sqn before it converted to Jaguars.

F-4D Phantom of the 306th Fighter Squadron, Imperial Iranian Air Force.

US Navy F-4B Phantom in the markings of VF-84 based on the aircraft carrier USS Independence.

This Phantom FGR Mk2 (XV500) carries the distinctive black and yellow lightning marking of 111 Sqn, RAF.

An F-4J Phantom of VF-21 shows a typical dive angle used in surface attack with 'iron bombs' (in this case retarded 500-pounders). The photograph was taken during the involvement in SE Asia, when traditional free-fall weapons began to be inadequate.

tion aircraft eventually entered service as F-4A Phantoms, and were followed into US Navy and Marine Corps service by the F-4B. This version had raised cockpits, higher-thrust J79 engines, a larger radar and several structural modifications. F-4B production eventually totalled 649 aircraft, plus 46 RF-4B reconnaissance versions for the US Marine Corps.

The US Air Force, which traditionally did not order US Navy aircraft, ordered the first of 583 minimum-change F-4Cs in July 1963, and later added 505 examples of the RF-4C tactical reconnaissance version. With a more powerful radar the aircraft became the F-4D, and no fewer than 825 examples of this type were built. Most of these were delivered to the US Air Force between 1965 – 68, although 32 examples went to Iran and 36 to Korea. Of the original F-4Cs, 36 were later sold to Spain.

Even more were to come. It was the F-4E Phantom which eventually became the most numerous version. This has more powerful engines, extra rear-fuselage fuel, APQ-120 solid-state radar and, in all but the first production blocks, a 20-mm M61 cannon under the nose. The first F-4E flew on 7 August 1965 and production deliveries began in 1967. About 1,477 examples were built, 949 for the US Air Force, and the rest for export. A large leading-edge slat on all late-model F-4Es improves manoeuvrability, and safety in ground-attack missions, and has been retrofitted to many of the earlier F-4Es. Australia operated 24 F-4Es while waiting delivery of its General Dynamics F-111s, and is the only former Phantom operator. Export orders for the F-4E, with the approximate order sizes, came from: West Germany (10), Greece (56), Iran (177), Israel (86), Japan (154), South Korea (19) and Turkey (40). The Japanese order includes 138 F-4EJs which are being licence-built by Mitsubishi. Other versions of this Phantom variant include the RF-4E (130 built for export) and F-4F (175 for West Germany), the latter being a simplified F-4E.

Some 116 US Air Force F-4Es are being

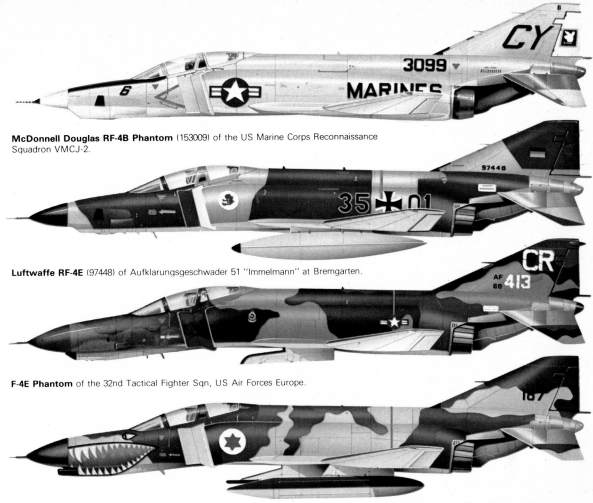

McDonnell Douglas RF-4B Phantom (153009) of the US Marine Corps Reconnaissance Squadron VMCJ-2.

Luftwaffe RF-4E (97448) of Aufklarungsgeschwader 51 "Immelmann" at Bremgarten.

F-4E Phantom of the 32nd Tactical Fighter Sqn, US Air Forces Europe.

F-4E at the time of the Israeli Holy Day war in 1973 when the type undertook long-range strike missions as well as air superiority tasks.

McDonnell Douglas F-4D Phantoms of the US Air Force lined up at Cam Ranh Bay AB, in what was then South Vietnam, in November 1966. They are configured for air-to-air missions, with Sidewinders, tanks and, in some cases, centreline gun pods.

converted to F-4G Wild Weasel aircraft, packed with electronic countermeasure (ECM) equipment to locate and either disrupt or attack enemy electronic stations. The first aircraft flew in 1975, and conversions will continue until 1981.

The F-4J is a further version for the US Navy and Marine Corps. Although similar to the F-4B it has improved AWG-10 radar and fire-control electronics, more powerful engines, and more internal fuel, and was the first version to have a leading-edge slot on the tailplane. Deliveries of 522 aircraft were spread over 1966 – 72. The type is being improved in service, stronger wing-root components and leading-edge wing slats being added to 302 aircraft, which are redesignated F-4S. A similar improvement programme for the F-4B did not incorporate the wing slats, but has brought 228 of the original aircraft up to F-4N standard.

Britain took delivery of 52 F-4K and 118 F-4M Phantoms to equip Fleet Air Arm and Royal Air Force squadrons. Both types have Rolls-Royce Spey 202/203 turbofan engines and several equipment modifications.

Total Phantom production, to early 1979, was 5,177 aircraft, comprising 1,264 for the original customer (US Navy and Marine Corps), 2,650 for the US Air Force, 1,135 for export and 138 built under licence in Japan. The type is still in production in Japan, where the last delivery should be made in 1981.

Several world records have been held by the F-4, including a world absolute speed record of 1,606.3 mph (2585 km/h) or Mach 2.6, set on 22 November 1961, and the world absolute altitude record of 98,537 ft (30034 m), set on 6 December 1958. These have since been beaten, but with 11 other distinctions at various times, including almost every time-to-height record, and a world low-altitude absolute speed record (902 mph/1452 km/h) which stood for 16 years, they distinguish the Phantom as one of the world's finest all-round military combat aircraft.

Type: (F-4E) two-seat shipboard/land-based multi-role fighter/strike aircraft
Powerplant: two 17,900-lb (8127-kg) General Electric J79-GE-17 afterburning turbojets
Performance: maximum design speed (clean) Mach 2.17 or 1,430 mph (2304 km/h) at 36,000 ft (10973 m); cruising speed with full internal fuel, four AIM-7E missiles and two 308-gallon (1400-litre) drop tanks 572 mph (924 km/h) at 33,000 ft (10050 m); typical combat radius on hi-lo-hi mission with two 308-gallon (1400-litre) drop tanks and four AIM-7E missiles 520 miles (840 km); ferry range 1,610 miles (2593 km); service ceiling (clean) 58,750 ft (17907 m); maximum rate of climb (clean) 49,800 ft (15179 m) per minute
Weights: empty equipped 31,853 lb (14461 kg); normal take-off (internal fuel, four AIM-7E missiles and two 308-gallon/ 1400-litre drop tanks) 53,814 lb (24430 kg); maximum take-off 61,795 lb (28055 kg)
Dimensions: span 38 ft 4 in (11.68 m); length 63 ft 0 in (19.20 m); height 16 ft 5 in (5.00 m); wing area 530 sq ft (49.24 m²)
Armament: one 20-mm M61A1 rotary cannon with 640 rounds, four AIM-7E Sparrow missiles semi-recessed under fuselage, or up to 3,020 lb (1371 kg) on centreline pylon, plus various combinations of missiles and stores on four wing pylons up to a weight of 12,980 lb (5888 kg)
Operators: Greece, Iran, Israel, Japan, South Korea, Spain, Turkey, UK, US Air Force, US Marine Corps, US Navy, West Germany

McDonnell Douglas F-4E Phantom II cutaway drawing key

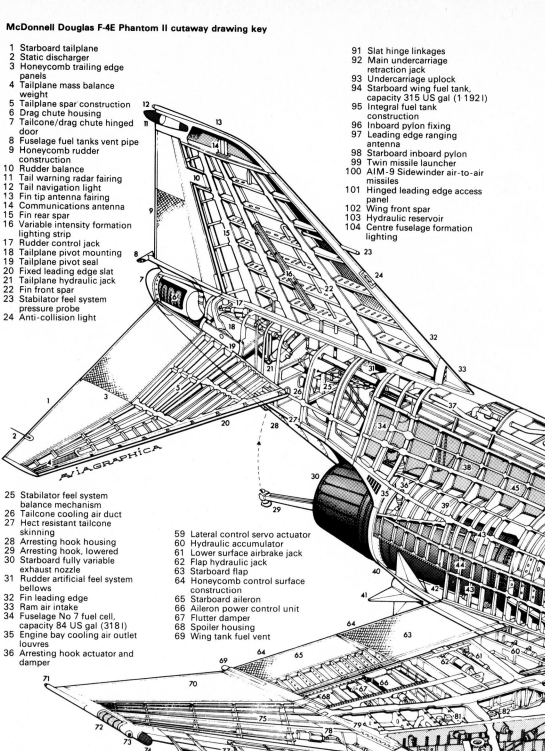

1 Starboard tailplane
2 Static discharger
3 Honeycomb trailing edge panels
4 Tailplane mass balance weight
5 Tailplane spar construction
6 Drag chute housing
7 Tailcone/drag chute hinged door
8 Fuselage fuel tanks vent pipe
9 Honeycomb rudder construction
10 Rudder balance
11 Tail warning radar fairing
12 Tail navigation light
13 Fin tip antenna fairing
14 Communications antenna
15 Fin rear spar
16 Variable intensity formation lighting strip
17 Rudder control jack
18 Tailplane pivot mounting
19 Tailplane pivot seal
20 Fixed leading edge slat
21 Tailplane hydraulic jack
22 Fin front spar
23 Stabilator feel system pressure probe
24 Anti-collision light
25 Stabilator feel system balance mechanism
26 Tailcone cooling air duct
27 Hect resistant tailcone skinning
28 Arresting hook housing
29 Arresting hook, lowered
30 Starboard fully variable exhaust nozzle
31 Rudder artificial feel system bellows
32 Fin leading edge
33 Ram air intake
34 Fuselage No 7 fuel cell, capacity 84 US gal (318 l)
35 Engine bay cooling air outlet louvres
36 Arresting hook actuator and damper
37 Fuel vent piping
38 Fuselage No 6 fuel cell, capacity 213 US gal (806 l)
39 Jet pipe shroud construction
40 Engine bay hinged access doors
41 Rear AIM-7E-2 Sparrow air-to-air missile
42 Semi-recessed missile housing
43 Jet pipe nozzle actuators
44 Afterburner jet pipe
45 Fuselage No 5 fuel cell, capacity 180 US gal (681 l)
46 Fuel tank access panels
47 Fuel system piping
48 Tailplane control cable duct
49 Fuselage No 4 fuel cell, capacity 201 US gal (761 l)
50 Starboard engine bay construction
51 TACAN aerial
52 Fuselage No 3 fuel cell, capacity 147 US gal (556 l)
53 Engine oil tank
54 General Electric J79-GE-17A turbojet engine
55 Engine accessories
56 Wing rear spar attachment
57 Mainwheel door
58 Main undercarriage wheel well

59 Lateral control servo actuator
60 Hydraulic accumulator
61 Lower surface airbrake jack
62 Flap hydraulic jack
63 Starboard flap
64 Honeycomb control surface construction
65 Starboard aileron
66 Aileron power control unit
67 Flutter damper
68 Spoiler housing
69 Wing tank fuel vent
70 Dihedral outer wing panel
71 Rear identification light
72 Wing tip formation lighting
73 Starboard navigation light
74 Radar warning antenna
75 Outer wing panel construction
76 Outboard leading edge slat
77 Slat control linkage
78 Slat hydraulic jack
79 Outer wing panel attachment
80 Starboard wing fence
81 Fuel vent system shut-off valves
82 Top of main undercarriage leg
83 Outboard pylon attachment housing
84 Inboard slat hydraulic jack
85 Starboard outer pylon
86 Mainwheel leg door
87 Mainwheel brake discs
88 Starboard mainwheel
89 Starboard external fuel tank, capacity 370 US gal (1 400 l)
90 Inboard leading edge slat, open

91 Slat hinge linkages
92 Main undercarriage retraction jack
93 Undercarriage uplock
94 Starboard wing fuel tank, capacity 315 US gal (1 192 l)
95 Integral fuel tank construction
96 Inboard pylon fixing
97 Leading edge ranging antenna
98 Starboard inboard pylon
99 Twin missile launcher
100 AIM-9 Sidewinder air-to-air missiles
101 Hinged leading edge access panel
102 Wing front spar
103 Hydraulic reservoir
104 Centre fuselage formation lighting
105 Fuselage main frame
106 Engine intake compressor face
107 Intake duct construction
108 Fuselage No 2 fuel cell, capacity 185 US gal (700 l)
109 Air-to-air refuelling receptacle, open
110 Port main undercarriage leg
111 Aileron power control unit
112 Port aileron
113 Aileron flutter damper
114 Port spoiler
115 Spoiler hydraulic jack
116 Wing fuel tank vent pipe
117 Port outer wing panel
118 Rearward identification light
119 Wing tip formation lighting
120 Port navigation light
121 Radar warning antenna
122 Port outboard leading edge slat

123 Slat hydraulic jack
124 Wing fence
125 Leading edge dog tooth
126 Inboard leading edge slat, open
127 Port external fuel tank, capacity 370 US gal (1 400 l)
128 Inboard slat hydraulic jack
129 Port wing fuel tank, capacity 315 US gal (1 192 l)
130 Upper fuselage light
131 IFF antenna
132 Avionics equipment bay
133 Gyro stabiliser platform
134 Fuselage No 1 fuel cell, capacity 215 US gal (814 l)
135 Intake duct
136 Hydraulic connections
137 Starter cartridge container
138 Pneumatic system air bottle
139 Engine bleed air supply pipe
140 Forward AIM-7 missile housing
141 Ventral fuel tank, capacity 600 US gal (2 271 l)
142 Bleed air louvre assembly, lower

151 Inter-canopy bridge section glazing
152 Radar operator's instrument console
153 Canopy jack
154 Port intake
155 Pilot's Martin-Baker ejection seat
156 Intake front ramp
157 Starboard intake
158 Bleed air holes
159 Boundary layer splitter plate
160 ALQ-72 electronic countermeasures pod (replaces forward Sparrow missile)
161 HOBOS 2000-lb (908-kg) guided bomb
162 Nosewheel door
163 AIM-7E-2 Sparrow missile semi-recessed housing
164 Forward formation lighting
165 Air conditioning plant
166 Battery
167 Pilot's starboard side console
168 Ejection seat safety harness
169 Engine throttles
170 Port intake front ramp
171 Forward cockpit canopy cover

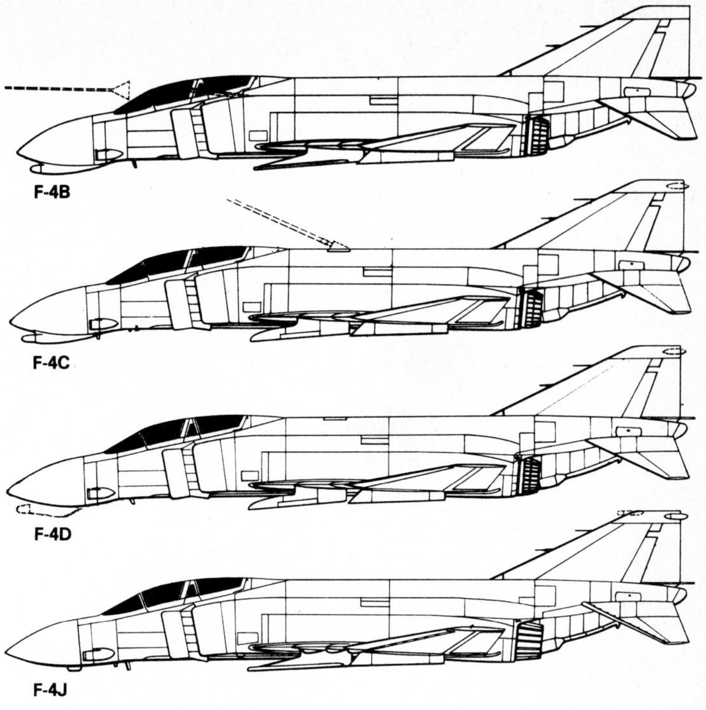

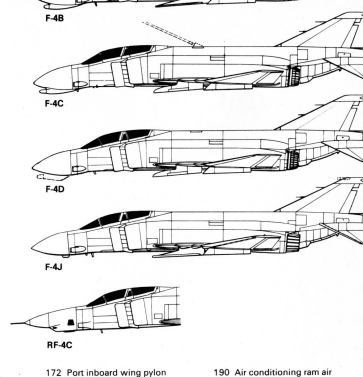

F-4B

F-4C

F-4D

F-4J

RF-4C

172 Port inboard wing pylon
173 Pylon attachments
174 Triple ejector release unit
175 Mk 84 low profile 500-lb (227-kg) bombs
176 Extended bomb fuses
177 Windscreen panels
178 Pilot's lead computing sight and head-up display
179 Instrument panel shroud
180 Control column
181 Rudder pedals
182 Cockpit front pressure bulkhead
183 Refrigeration plant
184 Communications antenna
185 Nosewheel jack

190 Air conditioning ram air intake
191 Angle of attack probe
192 Ammunition drum, 639 rounds
193 Rain dispersal duct nozzle
194 ADF antenna
195 Gun bay frame construction
196 M61A-1 20-mm rotary barrel cannon
197 Cannon fairing
198 AN/APQ-120 fire control radar
199 Radar antenna mounting
200 Gun muzzle fairing
201 Radar scanner
202 Radome
203 Pitot tube

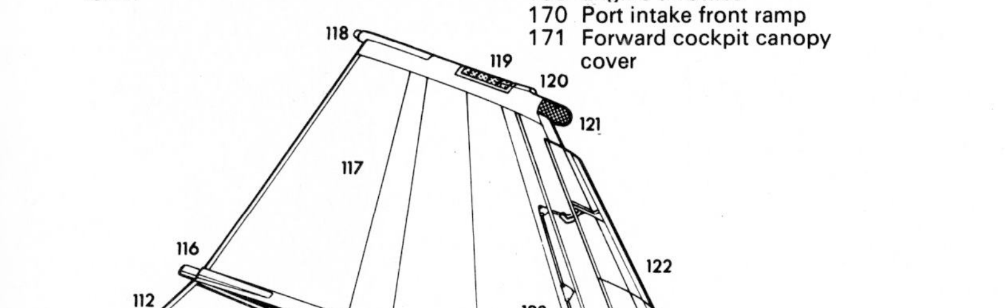

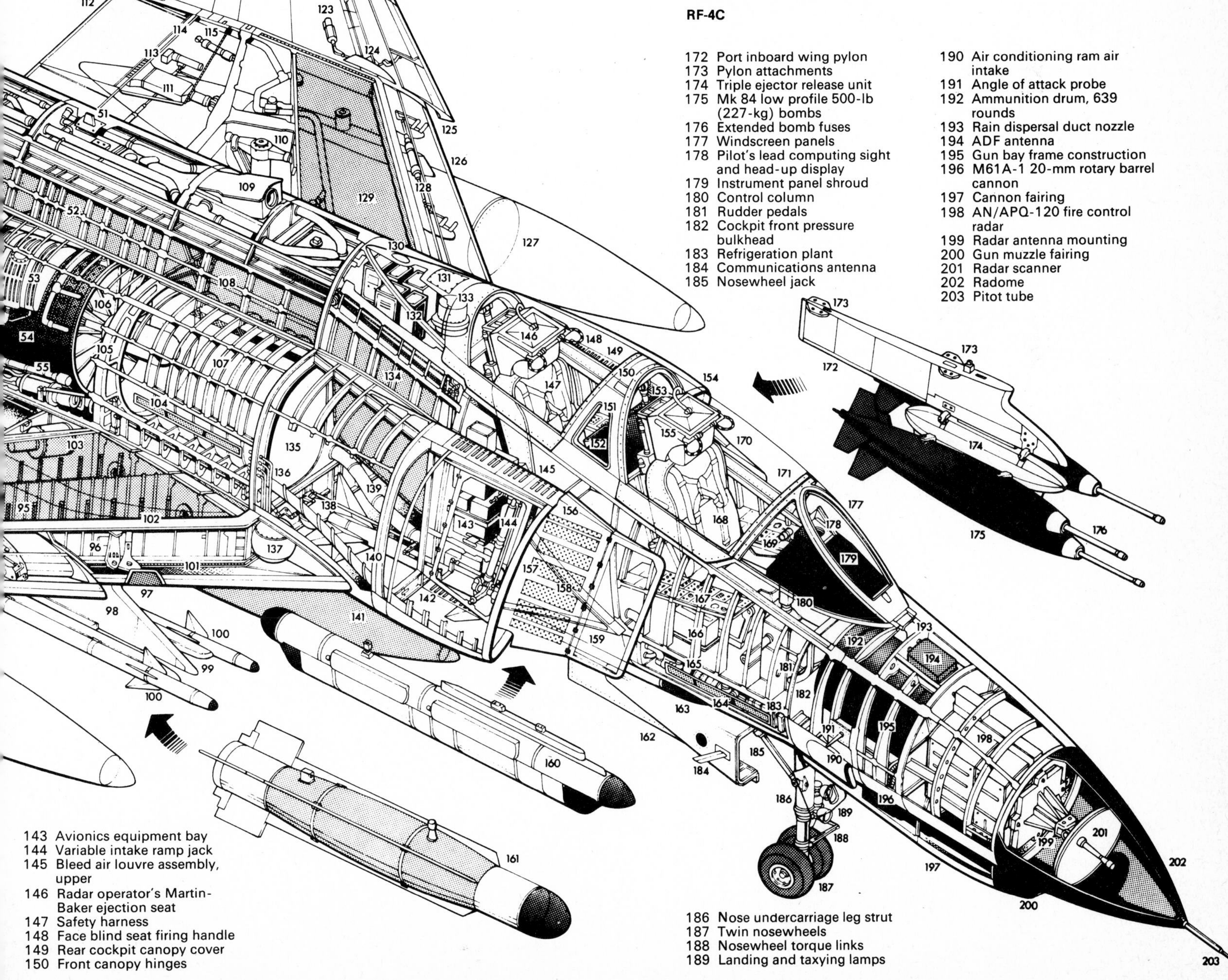

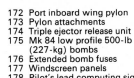

143 Avionics equipment bay
144 Variable intake ramp jack
145 Bleed air louvre assembly, upper
146 Radar operator's Martin-Baker ejection seat
147 Safety harness
148 Face blind seat firing handle
149 Rear cockpit canopy cover
150 Front canopy hinges

186 Nose undercarriage leg strut
187 Twin nosewheels
188 Nosewheel torque links
189 Landing and taxying lamps

247

The nose of the F-4E is longer and slimmer than that of earlier versions. One reason is the APQ-120 radar, a solid-state set much more modern than that of earlier sub-types. Lighter and with a smaller antenna than previous radars, it was moved forward so that, with the gun and ammunition, the weight would balance a new No 7 fuel cell in the rear fuselage. J79-GE-17 engines of increased thrust handle the greater weight.

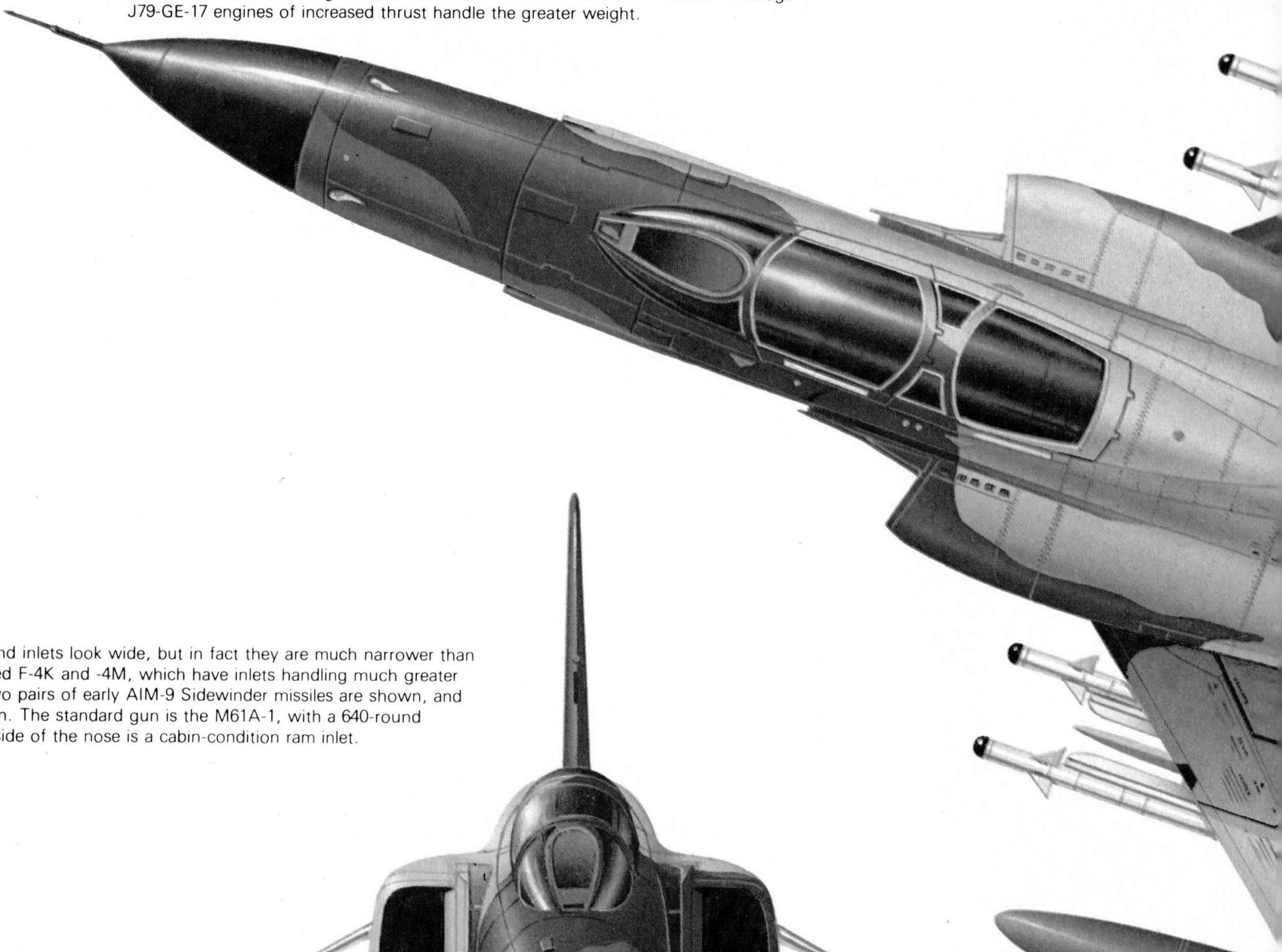

In head-on view the fuselage and inlets look wide, but in fact they are much narrower than those of the British Spey-powered F-4K and -4M, which have inlets handling much greater airflow. Supersonic tanks and two pairs of early AIM-9 Sidewinder missiles are shown, and the main gun access door is open. The standard gun is the M61A-1, with a 640-round ammunition tank. Low on each side of the nose is a cabin-condition ram inlet.

Another feature visible in the head-on view is the thickened inner wing introduced with the first land-based version, the F-4C. Whereas the Navy used hard high-pressure tyres, the Air Force needed wide tyres for forward-airbase operation, and also demanded greater-capacity brakes. (Many combat aircraft, including several Soviet tactical machines, have bulges resulting from the need to house larger low-pressure tyres for off-airstrip use.)

The axes of radar and gun slope downwards in side elevation, but the black boxes ensure that air-to-air firing is accurate! No F-4 in regular service has a HUD (head-up display), but the sight system has been progressively upgraded and made more versatile for lead-computing interception and air/ground delivery. The slope of the tandem cockpits was ahead of its time in the 1950s, and this assisted the original USAF philosophy of having a rated pilot in the back seat with controls.

All normal F-4 variants have broad-chord short-span blown flaps, outboard of which is the equally low-aspect-ratio inboard aileron. The wingtip, completely new on the slatted wing, has no movable surfaces. The unusual stabiliser (tailplane) is a single slab on each side, with no less than 23° of anhedral (downward-slope) and made of tough, heat-resistant titanium and steel. In some models the leading edge has an inverted slot.

JV
AF 70 308

USAF Phantoms display fewer prominent warning and countermeasure systems than those of the Navy, Marines and RAF, but 48 different defensive or offensive avionic items can be installed in tactical F-4 versions. Standard on the F-4E are three warners, two jammers, two chaff/flare dispensers and various subsidiary devices, as well as laser target designator, slatted wing, airfield arrester hook and often a TISEO zoom-lens video system.

McDonnell Douglas F-15 Eagle

Now spearheading the defence of the Western world, and likely to stay there well into the next century, the McDonnell Douglas F-15 Eagle has a flight performance unsurpassed by any other fighter. It is probably the only US fighter capable of catching the Soviet Union's very fast and high-flying Mikoyan-Gurevich MiG-25, and indeed very early in its career was being openly talked about as the 'Foxbat killer'. Israel and Iran are two countries that have raged impotently as this formidable Soviet spy-plane and long-range interceptor has streaked high along their borders (and, even over their territory), photographing military installations. With typical early-warning times quite long, as they have been in the mid-1970s, it has been immune from the efforts of the McDonnell Douglas F-4 Phantoms to bring them down. In at least one case Sparrow missiles from Israeli F-4s launched against 'Foxbats' operating from Libya have fallen impotently into the sea.

But all this has now changed. F-15s are now operational in Europe, Israel and Saudi Arabia, and the Mach 3/80,000-ft (24385-m) cruise performance of the MiG-25 will no longer be adequate to protect it over these areas. Although armed with the same Sparrow and Sidewinder combat missiles as its predecessor, the Phantom, the F-15 behaves as a much more powerful 'first stage', giving them considerably greater speed and height at launch.

In the early 1960s, while the fabulous F-4 was still fresh to the US Navy (its sponsor and first customer), American defence experts were beiginning to plan a fighter to follow it. Both the US Navy and US Air Force wanted an air-superiority aircraft, and many people saw the possibility of a common design. But as time went by the two services evolved substantially different requirements and with

Trio of Eagles over the Arctic demonstrate that US airpower has not yet entirely vanished. These three F-15As of the 36th TFW, based at Bitburg in West Germany, were photographed on detachment to Bodo Air Station, Norway, for 'Arctic Express 78'

McDonnell Douglas F-15A Eagle cutaway drawing key

1 Nose radome
2 Hughes attack radar scanner
3 Avionics racks
4 Forward bulkhead
5 Instrument panel shroud
6 Gunsight/weapon-sight
7 Curved windscreen (poly-carbonate with cast acrylic surfaces)
8 Polycarbonate one-piece canopy
9 Pilot's headrest
10 Ejection capsule (by McDonnell Douglas Corp)
11 Port control console
12 Nosewheel door
13 Retraction strut
14 Landing/taxi lights
15 Forward-retracting nose-wheel
16 Nosewheel fairing door
17 Port intake
18 Variable inlet
19 Inlet pivot line
20 Port missile station (Side-winder, Sparrow or advanced missile)
21 Avionics stowage
22 Wing-intake fairing
23 Flight refuelling receptacle
24 Auxiliary intake (and grille)
25 Canopy hinges
26 Provision for second crew member (TF-15)
27 Starboard inlet
28 GAU-7 20-mm gun barrels
29 Ammunition drum
30 Ammunition feed
31 Dorsal speed-brake (shaded, shown retracted)
32 Centre-section fuel tanks (4)
33 Starboard wing tank
34 Vent tank
35 Aluminium wing skinning
36 Honeycomb outboard leading-edge
37 Starboard wingtip antennae
38 Fuel vent pipe
39 Starboard aileron
40 Aileron actuator
41 Flap actuator
42 Starboard flap
43 Starboard Pratt & Whitney F100-PW-100 turbofan
44 Aluminium vertical tail surface leading and trailing edges (honeycomb)
45 Advanced composites construction
46 Starboard stabilator
47 ECM antennae
48 Tail navigation and formation keeping lights
49 Starboard rudder section (advanced composites construction)
50 Exhaust nozzle actuators
51 Exhaust pipe
52 Airfield arrester hook fairing
53 Titanium vertical tail surface spars
54 Stabilator spindle (titanium)
55 Aluminium stabilator leading and trailing edges (honeycomb)
56 Stabilator torque box (boron epoxy skin)
57 Leading-edge dog-tooth
58 Titanium centre-fuselage bulkheads
59 Intermediate frames
60 Wing/fuselage attachment points (seven lugs)
61 Port mainwheel
62 Aluminium front spar
63 Titanium wing spars (3)
64 Port flap
65 Port aileron
66 Wingtip
67 Wingtip antennae
68 Port navigation light

the example of the disastrous General Dynamics F-111A/F-111B fresh in their minds the planners let the two services have their own ways.

For several years the USAF and the companies studied a number of projects without any conviction that any of them were worth pursuing. The trouble was that not enough was known about the new generation of combat aircraft known to be under development in the Soviet Union. Then, in July 1967, the Soviet air force unveiled at Domodedovo airport near Moscow a whole fleet of new military aircraft. Two of them, the MiG-23 variable-geometry fighter, soon to be codenamed 'Flogger', and the clearly formidable MiG-25 'Foxbat', crystallised the suspicions long held by US defence experts.

In September 1968, after running its rule over the new Soviet designs, the USAF commissioned three companies to produce another set of competitive designs. They were McDonnell Douglas, Fairchild and North American, and in December 1968 the first-named was declared the winner. Undoubtedly its F-4 background helped, but all three companies put up extraordinarily detailed schemes. The winner, for example, had conducted no fewer than 13,000 hours of wind-tunnel testing, compared with 900 hours on which the F-4 had been chosen, and had submitted 37,500 pages of technical, industrial, commercial and administrative documentation. The new fighter was designated the F-15 Eagle, and the first of 20 test aeroplanes made its initial flight in July 1972. The type entered ser-

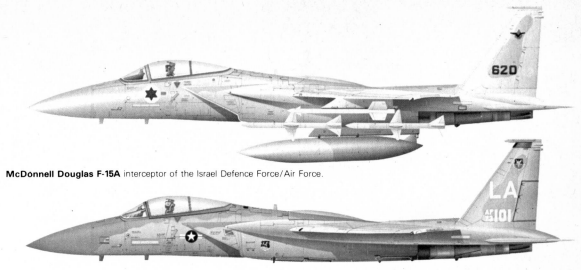

continued

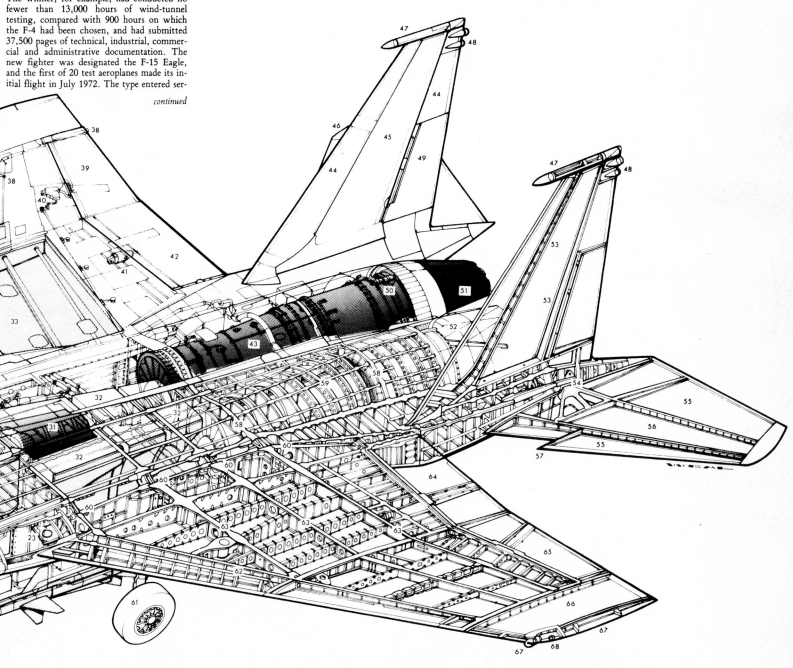

McDonnell Douglas F-15A interceptor of the Israel Defence Force/Air Force.

Shown in the early 'blue' camouflage finish is this F-15A Eagle of the 58th Tactical Training Wing, US Air Force, at Luke AFB, Arizona.

251

The F-15 Eagle has a clean exterior partly because all its EW/ECM systems were designed in from the start instead of hung on as afterthoughts. The chief system is Loral's immense ALR-56, which could hardly be fitted as a modification to any fighter.

vice in November 1974 and the first squadron was declared operational in January 1976.

Such is the importance of the F-15 in Europe that less than two years later three squadrons had been deployed to Germany to face the growing fleet of Soviet and eastern bloc warplanes ranged along the East German border. Export F-15s are now also finding their way to Israel, Saudi Arabia and Japan. So potent was the Eagle considered that the decision to permit export to Israel was long held up because of political implications in the Arab world.

In July 1979 the F-15 saw its first combat application in the skies over the Lebanon. The aircraft of the Israeli *Heyl Ha'Avir* flying in support of ground attacks by Kfirs and F-4s engaged Syrian MiG-21s. These successfully destroyed several Syrian aircraft and themselves suffered no losses.

When laying out the F-15, the St Louis team, as directed by the USAF, had four principal adversaries in mind: the MiG-23 and -25, most potent of the new Domodedovo types, the new Sukhoi Su-15 'Flagon' (also revealed at Domodedovo) and the MiG-21. The last has been around now for many years, and improved versions are likely to be developed for the Soviet satellite countries.

A thrust/weight ratio far greater than used in any previous fighter was specified. This was necessary for two reasons: to permit a rate of climb sufficient to catch any intruding MiG-25 with its Sparrow and Sidewinder anti-aircraft missiles, and to out-turn any likely foe in combat in order to bring its gun to bear.

The missiles were already standard armament on a number of US aircraft, but a new gun was to be specially designed for the F-15 to make it more lethal. The 25-mm GAU-7 rotating-barrel gun was to have a considerably greater killing power than the 20-mm calibre M61 weapon used in the F-4E Phantoms and Lockheed F-104 Starfighters. A competition to build the gun was held between General Electric and Philco-Ford, and won by the latter company, but both firms ran into such trouble with the new caseless ammunition that the programme was abandoned and the USAF had to fall back on the well tried M61.

To exploit fully the new fighter designs being studied by the US Air Force and US Navy, the Defense Department decided the time was right for new propulsion systems, and accordingly a third competition was held, between Pratt & Whitney and General Electric, the two top US engine companies. The former's F100 engine, after some initial problems, is shaping up to be a worthy successor to the General Electric J79, probably the most widely used military powerplant in the western world. As with most combat aircraft designed since the late 1960s, twin engines rather than one were chosen for better chances of survival.

The decision to carry only one crew member (its naval contemporary, the F-14, has a crew of two) meant that the F-15 had to be easy to fly and automated as far as possible. In particular it meant that the Hughes APG-63 pulsed-Doppler radar had to be easy to operate and read; pilots in combat or scanning the

skies cannot afford to be looking down into the cockpit all the time.

In a word, the F-15 is designed for 'seatpants' operation: the pilot flies the machine instinctively, his eyes constantly scanning the sky and seeing only one instrument, the head-up display. This instrument is a cathode-ray tube fed with information from the radar, showing the actual position of the target in the sky, its range, closing speed, missile safe firing distance and all the other information the pilot needs to attack the target.

In addition to picking up echoes from targets flying at the same altitude or higher (where echoes can only be produced by other aircraft), the radar can 'see' targets 'silhouetted' against the ground. This is immensely more difficult owing to the far greater strength of the ground returns compared with even the largest targets. It calls for highly sophisticated signal-processing techniques, using complex 'software' (computer programming) methods to get the most information out of the faint target returns. Improvements in

The wing commander's aircraft of the 49th TAC Fighter Wing at Holloman AFB, Albuquerque, New Mexico is painted in low-visibility grey (one of at least five colour schemes experimented with on Tactical Air Command Eagles). In 1979 it appeared likely that, while the RAF may switch to grey for interceptors, the F-15s are more likely to end up with two-tone blue. The objective is low visibility "eyeball" combat.

software in fact permit great improvements in radar performance without physical modifications to the equipment itself.

Meanwhile, taking a lesson from the Vietnam war, the designers have added a tail-warning radar to indicate the presence of a threat from behind — the traditional blind spot and worry of the air-combat pilot.

Type: single-seat air-superiority fighter
Powerplant: two Pratt & Whitney F100-PW-100 turbofan engines, each of 23,800-lb (10976-kg) thrust with afterburning
Performance: maximum speed 921 mph (1482 km/h) at low altitude, Mach 2.5 at altitude; maximum radius of action, 2,878 miles (4631 km) with three 600 US gallon tanks; maximum rate of climb 40,000 ft/min (12192 m/min); service ceiling 63,000 ft (19203 m)
Weights: empty 28,000 lb (12700 kg); maximum take-off 56,000 lb (25401 kg)

Dimensions: span 42 ft 10 in (13.05 m); length 63 ft 9 in (19.43 m); height 18 ft 8 in (5.63 m); wing area 608 sq ft (56.5 m²)
Armament: one 20-mm M61A1 rotating-barrel gun and up to eight air-air missiles (normally four AIM-7F Sparrow III and four AIM-9L Sidewinder) under guidance of APG-63 pulsed-Dopple radar with search range of 150 miles (241 km)
Operators: United States, Israel, Saudi Arabia, Japan

The F-15 carries more defensive/offensive electronics than any previous combat aircraft, including the ALR-56 radar warning system, a digital network with sensors all over the aircraft. The ALQ-128 is a launch warning/IFF system, ALQ-135 the internal countermeasures, ALQ-154 or 155 the tail-warning radar, and AAR-38 the infra-red (IR) tail warning system. Additional equipment can be accommodated in the "empty rear cockpit".

This F-15A has the production wingtip (prototypes were squared-off) but is not shown carrying the unique FAST (fuel and sensor, tactical) packs which fit against the sides of the fuselage and double fuel capacity. Above the wing on each side is a large body bulge housing the flight-refuelling boom receptacle on the left side and the M61 gun on the right. The engine inlets hinge downwards to work better at low speeds.

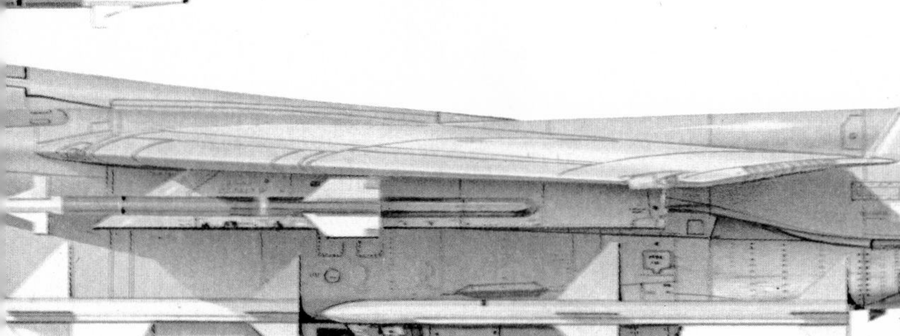

All F-15 weapons except the gun are hung externally. Unlike the F-4, whose Sparrows are semi-recessed to reduce drag, the F-15 carries these medium-range missiles neatly snuggled up against the right-angled lower edge of the box-like fuselage. Close-range missiles on this aircraft comprise two pairs of AIM-9J1 Sidewinders. Eventually all previous Sidewinder versions will be replaced by the AIM-9L.

253

McDonnell Douglas F-18

In the years between World Wars I and II the US Army Air Corps usually contracted for the manufacture of competitive prototypes of designs which were considered to be the most suitable submissions to meet a specific requirement. There were many advantages from such a policy, especially when manufacturers were seeking anxiously for military contracts, not the least of which was the fact that the prototypes could be test flown and evaluated, and even flown competitively, one against the other. World War II brought an end to this procedure, and many years were to elapse before this competitive prototype procurement method was reinstated.

One requirement for which this policy was used arose in the early 1970s, when the USAF was seeking what it chose to identify as a Lightweight Fighter (LWF). Early excursions into the design and development of supersonic combat aircraft had resulted in hardware which was big, heavy, complex and costly. The USAF's LWF project sought to investigate whether it was possible to evolve a lightweight, low-cost, high-performance air-superiority fighter. Competitive prototypes were considered essential to assist in evaluating the operational potential of such an aircraft, as well as making it possible to establish the role which an LWF would best be able to satisfy. Thus, Requests For Proposals were sent out in 1971, and by 28 February 1972 submissions had been received from five companies. From these, General Dynamics and Northrop were awarded contracts on 13 April 1972 to build two prototypes each, under the respective designations YF-16 and YF-17. First to fly, on 2 February 1974, was the General Dynamics YF-16, Northrop's first YF-17 flying on 9 June 1974. During the evaluation which followed, terminating at the end of December 1974, the YF-16s had flown in excess of 400 hours, the YF-17s more than 200. In September 1974 the USAF announced that the winner of the competition would be declared in January 1975, and at that time identified the aircraft as the Air Combat Fighter (ACF). On 13 January 1975 it was duly announced that the YF-16 had been selected for production by General Dynamics.

Northrop's YF-17 prototype was a markedly different aeroplane from the single-engine YF-16, being identified by its combination of a mid-wing monoplane configuration, outward-canted twin vertical tails, and with underwing air intakes for its two 14,000-lb (6350-kg) thrust General Electric YJ101-GE-100 afterburning by-pass turbojet engines. The rejection of this prototype was a disappointment to Northrop, for the company had devoted considerable time and funding since 1963 in the evaluation of an advanced tactical fighter derived from their P-530 Cobra project. There was, however, a silver lining to this particular cloud.

In early 1974 the US Navy initiated the study of a low-cost lightweight multi-mission fighter, then identified as VFAX, but in August 1974 the VFAX concept was terminated by the US Congress, which directed instead that the US Navy should investigate the YF-16/17 prototypes which had been built for the USAF. McDonnell Douglas had taken a close look at both of the competing prototypes, coming to the conclusion that Northrop's design most nearly met the US Navy's original requirement, and teamed up with Northrop to arrive at a new aircraft derived from the YF-17, with much greater fuel capacity and gross weight, which could be submitted to the US Navy for consideration.

This proposal, for what was identified initially as the Navy Air Combat Fighter (NACF), was received enthusiastically by the US Navy, and on 2 May 1975 it was announced that McDonnell Douglas (as prime contractor), Northrop and General Electric had all been awarded short-term contracts to refine their proposals. Less than 12 months later, on 22 January 1976, the US Navy announced that full-scale development was being initiated of this new naval combat/strike fighter, under the designation F-18 Hornet, and that 11 aircraft were to be produced initially for the flight test programme.

McDonnell Douglas and Northrop have planned carefully their joint participation, and in respect of the F-18 Northrop will develop and build the centre and aft fuselage, this representing about 40% of the total task. McDonnell Douglas will develop and build the remainder, and be responsible for final assembly and marketing of these naval aircraft. An international land-based version designated F-18L, with reduced fuel capacity and weight, is also planned, and Northrop will be responsible for sales and 60% of the construction of these aircraft.

The F-18 differs from the YF-17 prototype in a number of ways, primarily because of its different usage, but also to meet the requirements of the US Navy's specification. This means that its dimensions have been increased somewhat to cater for considerable additional internal fuel to confer the requisite range for the US Navy's intended missions; the fuselage nose is enlarged to accommodate a radar which can provide the specified 35-mile (56-km) search range; and the fuselage and landing gear have been strengthened to cater for the additional stresses of catapult launch and arrested landing.

Powerplant for the F-18 consists of two

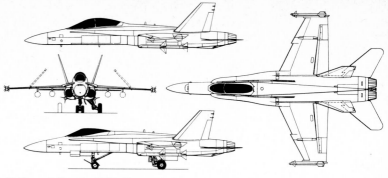

McDonnell Douglas F-18A Hornet

16,000-lb (7257-kg) General Electric F404-GE-400 augmented turbofan engines. This is a developed version of the XJ101 which powered the YF-17 prototypes, and it is interesting to note the change from turbojet to turbofan, indicated by the change from J to F in the engine designation, as a result of a slight increase in by-pass ratio.

This advanced naval aircraft is not only capable of high performance, but has avionics and equipment to enhance its combat/strike capabilities. It has part-graphite structure and fly-by-wire control system. Without moving his hands from the throttle or control stick the pilot has within the compass of his fingers

Artist's impression of what the F-18A Hornet will look like in operational markings, here VF-114 US Navy.

McDonnell Douglas F-18 Hornet cutaway drawing key

1 Radome
2 Radar scanner (see item 9)
3 Scanner drive mechanism
4 Gun muzzle
5 Gun gas vents
6 Cannon barrels
7 Radar package sliding rails
8 Low voltage formation lighting
9 Hughes AN/APG-65 multi-mode radar package
10 Infra-red sensor housing
11 Ammunition drum, 540 rounds
12 Angle of attack probe
13 Gun mounting
14 Flight refuelling probe, extended
15 Refuelling probe hydraulic jack
16 M61, 20-mm rotary cannon
17 Ammunition feed track
18 Communications antenna
19 Cockpit front bulkhead
20 Pressurization valve
21 Frameless windshield panel
22 Instrument panel shroud
23 Pilot's sight and Kaiser head-up display
24 Control column
25 Rudder pedals
26 Wing leading edge extension (LEX)
27 Nosewheel bay
28 Nosewheel doors
29 Retractable step
30 Catapult strop link, landing position
31 Strop link, launch position
32 Twin nosewheels
33 Catapult launch signal lights
34 Landing lamp
35 Cleveland nose undercarriage leg
36 Avionics bay
37 Control runs
38 Engine throttle controls
39 Pilot's port side console
40 Cockpit rear bulkhead
41 Martin-Baker SJU-5/A ejection seat
42 Starboard side console
43 Ejection seat firing handle
44 Cockpit canopy
45 Canopy open position
46 Canopy jack
47 2nd seat structural space provision (TF-18)
48 Forward fuselage fuel tank, deleted for TF-18
49 Honeycomb panel construction
50 Liquid oxygen container
51 Nose undercarriage retraction strut
52 Centreline drop tank, capacity 300 US gal (1 136 l)
53 Avionics bays
54 LEX frame construction
55 Port navigation light
56 Air conditioning ducting
57 Intake splitter plate
58 Air conditioning intake
59 Bleed air holes
60 Boundary layer control slot
61 Main fuel tanks, 10,860-lb (4 930-kg) internal fuel load
62 Communications aerial
63 Bleed air outlet louvres
64 Starboard leading edge extension
65 External fuel tank, capacity 610 US gal (2 309 l)
66 Laser spot tracker pod (LST), starboard fuselage station
67 Starboard inboard wing pylon
68 Pylon mounting
69 Mk 83 low drag general purpose (LDGP) bombs (A-18)
70 Bomb ejector rack
71 Starboard outer wing pylon
72 Pylon fixing
73 Leading edge dog-tooth
74 Wing fold hinge line
75 Outboard leading edge actuator
76 Drooping leading edge
77 Starboard wing tip missile launcher rail
78 AIM-9L Sidewinder air-to-air missile
79 Outer wing panel folded position
80 Starboard drooping aileron
81 Starboard double slotted flap
82 Flap guides
83 Wing integral fuel tank
84 Hydraulic flap jacks
85 Graphite/epoxy dorsal fairing panels
86 Fuel delivery piping
87 Fuselage longeron
88 Boundary layer bleed air duct
89 Air conditioning plant
90 Port intake
91 Intake ducting
92 Leading edge flap hydraulic jack
93 Flap sequencing control unit
94 Control cable runs
95 Wing attachment pin joints
96 Rear fuselage fuel tank
97 APU exhaust duct
98 Starboard engine bay
99 Fin attachment fixing
100 Fin construction
101 Fuel jettison pipe
102 Graphite/epoxy skin
103 Anti-collision light
104 Steel leading edge strip
105 Honeycomb panel
106 Aerial tuners
107 Electronic countermeasures aerials (ECM)
108 Fin tip antenna housing
109 Communications aerial
110 Radar warning receiver
111 Tail navigation light
112 Fuel jettison
113 Low voltage formation lighting
114 Honeycomb rudder construction
115 Rudder hydraulic jacks
116 Airbrake open position
117 Starboard tailplane
118 Port fin tip antenna housing

every switch necessary to engage in air-to-air combat or ground-attack. The array of instruments once commonplace in high-performance aircraft is replaced by cathode-ray tube displays, and all vital information is available on the head-up display (HUD) which enables the pilot to be aware of the state of his aircraft without taking his eyes from the target. The Hughes AN/APG-65 tracking radar is able to track accurately multiple targets, so that the Hornet will be able to 'sting' to great effect.

The first F-18 was rolled out on 13 September 1978 and made its first flight on 18 November 1978. The US Navy plans to acquire at least 800 of these aircraft, the first becoming operational in 1982. It is planned also to develop an attack version under the designation A-18, chiefly for the US Marine Corps, with sensors and instruments configured for surface attack, as well as the dual-control TF-18 trainer with reduced internal fuel. These are all included in the 800 total.

With the McDonnell Douglas Corporate HQ building in the background, the first prototype F-18 Hornet made its first flight at St Louis on 18 November 1978. The Navy and Marine Corps intend to buy 1,366 Hornets in 1982-90.

Type: single-seat carrier-based combat/strike aircraft
Powerplant: two 16,000-lb (7257-kg) General Electric F404-GE-400 afterburning turbofans
Performance: (estimated) maximum speed (clean) Mach 1.8; maximum speed at intermediate power Mach 1.0; ferry range (unrefuelled) more than 2,300 miles (3700 km)
Weights: take-off (fighter) 33,585 lb (15234 kg); take-off (fighter escort) 35,000 lb (15875 kg); maximum take-off more than 44,000 lb (19958 kg)

Dimensions: span 37 ft 6 in (11.43 m); length 56 ft 0 in (17.07 m); height 15 ft 3½ in (4.66 m); wing area 400 sq ft (37.16 m²)
Armament: carried on nine external weapon stations, with a maximum capacity of 13,700

lb (6214 kg) for high-g missions: weapons can include AIM-9 Sidewinder air-to-air missiles, AIM-7 Sparrow air-to-air missiles (F-18 only), bombs and rockets; sensor pods and fuel tanks can also be carried on these weapons stations;

M61 20-mm six-barrel gun mounted in nose
Operators: (from 1982) US Marine Corps, US Navy

119 Low voltage formation lighting
120 Airbrake housing
121 Airbrake hydraulic jack
122 Starboard engine tailpipe
123 Exhaust nozzle shroud
124 Variable area exhaust nozzle
125 Nozzle actuators
126 Afterburner duct
127 Port tailplane

128 Graphite/epoxy skin panels
129 Honeycomb construction
130 Steel leading edge strip
131 Deck arresting hook
132 Tailplane pivot
133 Tailplane hinge lever
134 Hydraulic servo actuator
135 Port engine bay
136 Engine access doors
137 Engine accessories

138 Main engine mounting
139 General Electric F404-GE-400 low bypass turbojet
140 Engine compressor face
141 Airborne auxiliary power plant (APU)
142 Airframe mounted auxiliary drive gearbox
143 Port flap actuators
144 Flap sequencing control
145 Flap guides
146 Port double slotted flap
147 Graphite/epoxy flap skins
148 Honeycomb panel construction
149 Wing fold actuator
150 Aileron hydraulic jacks
151 Port drooping aileron
152 Fixed portion of trailing edge
153 Port wing tip AIM-9 Sidewinder
154 Missile launcher rail
155 Honeycomb leading edge construction

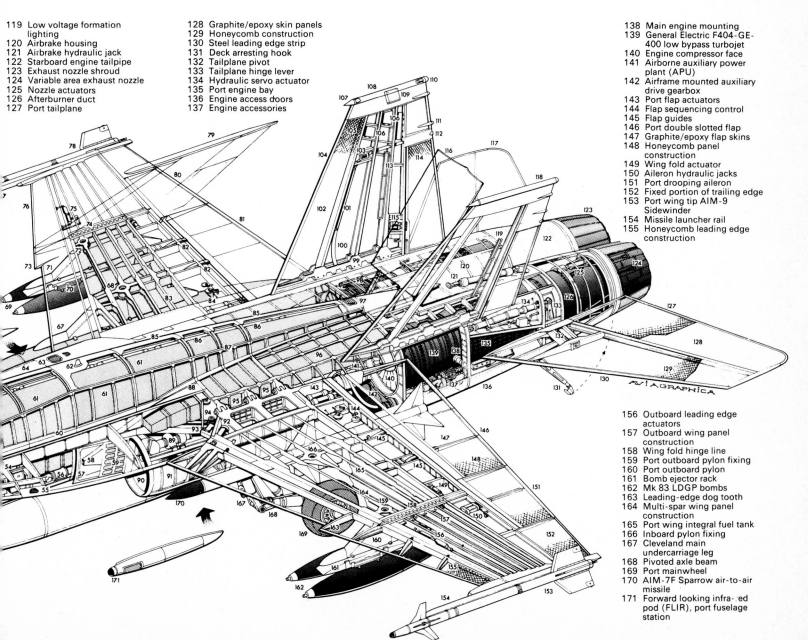

156 Outboard leading edge actuators
157 Outboard wing panel construction
158 Wing fold hinge line
159 Port outboard pylon fixing
160 Port outboard pylon
161 Bomb ejector rack
162 Mk 83 LDGP bombs
163 Leading-edge dog tooth
164 Multi-spar wing panel construction
165 Port wing integral fuel tank
166 Inboard pylon fixing
167 Cleveland main undercarriage leg
168 Pivoted axle beam
169 Port mainwheel
170 AIM-7F Sparrow air-to-air missile
171 Forward looking infra-red pod (FLIR), port fuselage station

McDonnell Douglas F-101 Voodoo

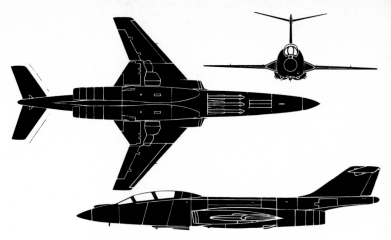

Detail design of a new penetration fighter to escort bombers of the USAF's newly formed Strategic Air Command was entrusted to the McDonnell Aircraft Company in 1946. Two prototypes were ordered under the designations XF-88 and XF-88A, both swept-wing aircraft with two turbojet engines, but the latter was to have afterburners to boost the thrust of its Westinghouse J34-WE-22 engines. Both prototypes flew, but the XF-88 contract was cancelled in 1948. Primary reasons for this was a shortage of funds, for with US defence plans which hinged on greater use of the nuclear deterrent, all available funding had to be concentrated on the continued procurement of the Convair B-37 pending the availability of a new generation of strategic bombers.

Nevertheless, the requirement for a long-range fighter to escort the B-36 was equally vital, and on 6 February 1951 the USAF issued a general operational requirement for such an aircraft. From the ensuing submissions McDonnell's was chosen as most suitable. The submission was for an improved version of the XF-88. However, no decision for production was made, and it was not until the shortcomings of in-service fighters as escorts for Boeing B-29 bombers involved in the Korean War became painfully clear that the USAF decided that it wanted McDonnell's new fighter urgently.

Consequently, the McDonnell aircraft was ordered in 1951 to provide Strategic Air Command (SAC) with the long-range fighter escort which it required for its B-36s, except that, as it could fly only one-fifth as far as the B-36, it was seen then as an interim interceptor which by some strange metamorphosis would develop at some stage into the anticipated long-range escort. On 30 November 1951 the aircraft was designated F-101 and christened Voodoo. But even before the first F-101 flew, on 29 September 1954, SAC had cancelled its requirement for this aircraft. It was decided, however, that subject to satisfactory evaluation, production of the Voodoo would continue for the Tactical Air Command.

Thus, on 2 May 1957, the first production F-101As were delivered to the SAC's 27th Fighter-Bomber Wing at Bergstrom AFB, Texas. Both the unit and its aircraft were due for transfer to Tactical Air Command (TAC) on 1 July 1957, and ultimately all the operational F-101As produced went to form the equipment of three squadrons of the TAC's 81st Tactical Fighter Wing. Of the total of 77

F-101As built, 27 were allocated for experimental and test purposes.

The operational F-101As were about twice as powerful as other current fighters, being powered by two 14,880-lb (6749-kg) thrust Pratt & Whitney J57-P-13 afterburning turbojets, and its large internal fuel capacity could be supplemented by three external tanks to provide a range in excess of 1,500 miles (2414 km). Its standard armament of four M-39 20-mm revolver cannon could be supplemented by three Falcon air-to-air missiles in the internal weapon bay. So far as speed was concerned, the F-101A could attain Mach 1.5 or 1,002 mph (1613 km/h) at 35,000 ft (10670 m). It gained the world absolute speed record of 1,208 mph (1944 km/h).

The F-101A was succeeded by the F-101C (only 47 built) which had structural strengthening for low-altitude operation and was provided with flight-refuelling capability. Most of the foregoing versions were modified subsequently for use by the US Air National Guard as the RF-101G and RF-101H respectively, equipped with nose-mounted cameras. Special-purpose reconnaissance versions were also built; RF-101As with six cameras in place of armament, and an improved RF-101C, combined production of these models totalling 200 aircraft.

For use by the Air Defense Command (ADC) a two-seat long-range interceptor was developed under the designation F-101B. The first of 480 entered service with the 60th Fighter Interceptor Squadron at Otis AFB, Massachussetts, on 5 February 1959, and some of these were equipped with dual controls as TF-101Bs. Following service with ADC (later ADCOM) 66 of these aircraft were transferred to the Royal Canadian Air Force, which shares with ADC defence responsibility within the NORAD command. When modified for Canadian use they were designated F-101F and TF-101F respectively, but were redesignated in RCAF service as CF-101B and CF-101F. They were exchanged subsequently for 66 similar aircraft with more advanced electronics.

Type: long-range all-weather interceptor
Powerplant: (F-101B) two 14,880-lb (6749-kg) afterburning Pratt & Whitney J57-P-55 turbojets

Performance: (F-101B) maximum speed Mach 1.85 or 1,221 mph (1965 km/h) at 40,000 ft (12190 m); range 1,550 miles (2494 km)
Weight: (F-101B) maximum take-off 46,500 lb (21092 kg)
Dimensions: span 39 ft 8 in (12.09 m); length 67 ft 4¾ in (20.54 m); height 18 ft 0 in (5.49 m); wing area 368 sq ft (34.19 m²)
Armament: (F-101B) three AIM-4D Falcon air-to-air missiles in internal weapon bay, plus two AIR-2A Genie air-to-air missiles under fuselage
Operators: Canada, Taiwan, US Air Force, US Air National Guard

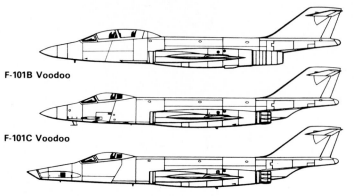

McDonnell Douglas F-101B Voodoo

F-101B Voodoo

F-101C Voodoo

RF-101C Voodoo

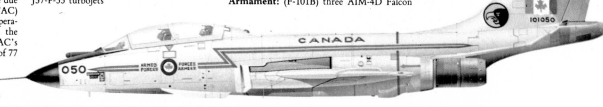

Two-seat McDonnell Douglas CF-101B Voodoo of 409 Sqn, Canadian Armed Forces, based at Comox on the Canadian west coast and part of Air Defence Group.

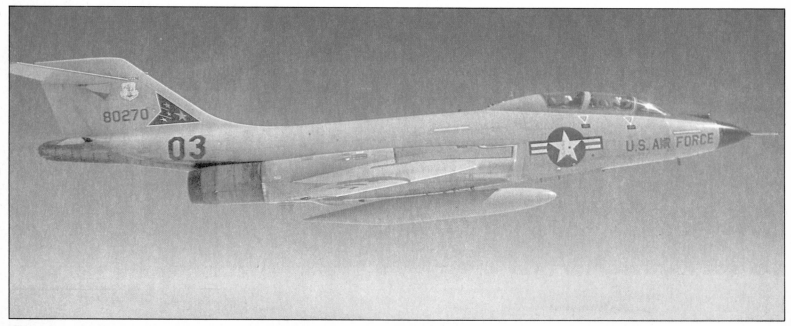

This well-preserved Voodoo is an F-101B still serving as an all-weather interceptor, the unit being the 123rd FIS, Oregon Air National Guard. It was photographed in late July 1977 during Exercise 'Overview', testing the efficiency of the USAF's new E-3A Sentry.

McDonnell Douglas KC-10A Extender

One of the problems which the USAF found to be highlighted during the Arab-Israeli conflict in 1973 was the refusal of many nations to allow American cargo/tanker aircraft to land in their territory. With aircraft of short/medium-range capability, such a procedure was necessary for the USAF's support aircraft to fulfil their role.

In the post-conflict analysis, the Military Airlift Command (MAC) was able to demonstrate that because of such action their capabilities had been limited considerably. It was essential for the future that MAC should have a cargo/tanker aircraft with greater range, for direct point-to-point flight without the need for an intermediate stop, or have adequate range in the tanker role to be able to offer a meaningful service to the aircraft which it had to support. During the submission of this requirment for consideration by the US Congress it was pointed out that just 17 of the Advanced Tanker/Cargo Aircraft (ATCA) which the USAF wished to procure, would be able to mount more efficiently and economically a support operation which requires currently a fleet of 40 KC-135 tankers plus additional cargo aircraft.

As a result of such discussions and consideration, the USAF was authorized to investigate the potential of existing commercial transports for modification to fulfil an ATCA role. Boeing's Model 747 and the McDonnell Douglas DC-10 were selected for evaluation, and on 19 December 1977 the USAF announced that the latter aircraft had been chosen for development as the ATCA for service with the MAC. The USAF plans initially to acquire two of these aircraft, subsequently designated KC-10A, and on 20 November 1978 McDonnell Douglas received authorization to begin production of these aircraft. Available funding will determine the future rate of procurement, but McDonnell Douglas believe that as many as 20 KC-10As may be acquired eventually. This compares with 732 of the KC-135 type.

The basic commercial airframe for conversion to the ATCA configuration is that of the DC-10 series 30CF convertible freighter. Extensive modification is needed, the primary task being that of providing adequate additional fuel capacity. This takes the form of seven bladder-type fuel cells installed in compartments below the main deck which serve normally for cargo. Three of these cells are installed forward of the wing, the remaining four aft, and these have a combined capacity of 117,829 lb (53446 kg) of fuel. These cells are interconnected into the aircraft's basic fuel system, which contains 238,236 lb (108062 kg) of fuel, and the combined total can be used for either extended range in a cargo role, or for flight refuelling. The KC-10A can thus carry in excess of 51,000 US gallons (193050 litres) of fuel, which means that in the tanker role a first-class system is needed to dispense such large quantities. McDonnell Douglas have developed an advanced refuelling boom, able to transfer fuel at a rate of 1,500 US gallons (5678 litres) a minute, and this is sited in the lower aft fuselage, where it is controlled by one operator. In addition, facilities will be available for probe-and-drogue refuelling, so that the KC-10A will be able to serve all types of US and NATO aircraft.

Seating is to be provided in the forward area of the main cabin so that a KC-10A could carry a fighter squadron's essential support personnel of 55 or 60, together with its immediately needed equipment. Additionally, KC-10As will be equipped to serve as cargo transports, with a cargo handling system which includes omni-directional rollers, powered rollers and a mobile winch for the easy movement of heavy cargo. Other modifications cover the provision of military avionics and minor equipment changes. It was anticipated that the first KC-10A would enter service with the MAC in 1980.

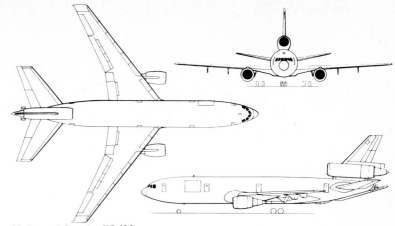

McDonnell Douglas KC-10A

Type: military flight-refuelling/cargo aircraft
Powerplant: three 52,500-lb (23814-kg) thrust General Electric F103 (CF6-50C1) turbofans
Performance: (estimated) maximum range with maximum cargo 3,800 miles (6115 km)
Weights: (estimated) operating empty (tanker) 239,747 lb (108747 kg); operating empty (cargo) 243,973 lb (110664 kg); design maximum take-off 590,000 lb (267620 kg)
Dimensions: span 165 ft 4.4 in (50.40 m); length 181 ft 7 in (55.35 m); height 58 ft 1 in (17.70 m); wing area 3,958 sq ft (367.70 m²)
Armament: none
Operators: (1980) US Air Force

McDonnell Douglas YC-15

The YC-15 was the McDonnell Douglas contender for the USAF's competition for an Advanced Medium Short take-off and landing Transport (AMST) to replace its fleet of Lockheed C-130 Hercules.

Powered by four turbofan engines, the YC-15 obtains its STOL performance by an advanced flap system. The engines, mounted on pylons extending forward from the wing leading edge, are positioned so that the exhaust nozzles are close to the undersurface of the wing. This provides a high-velocity flow which can be used to blow externally the large, two-segment, slotted flaps. The engines are fitted with multi-lobe nozzles that mix cool air with the hot exhaust, reducing the temperature to a level that does not require the use of special materials for the wing structure, though the flaps have to be made of titanium.

Lateral control is provided by a combination of aileron and triple inboard spoilers on each wing. For STOL landings the spoilers are used also as direct-lift controls, speed brakes and ground lift-dumpers. The control system is fully powered.

The wide fuselage has cabin space for about 150 fully equipped troops, or a wide range of the towed artillery and light armoured vehicles currently in the NATO inventory. One planned version was a totally self-contained mobile surgical hospital, complete with a casevac helicopter.

The YC-15 completed landing tests on soft fields, inflight drops of military loads and paratroop dummies, night trials, airborne tactical manoeuvres, formation flights and evaluation of its general performance, stability and control. Cargo drops included the parachuting of pallet loads weighing up to 20,000 lb (9072 kg) from an altitude of 2,000 ft (610 m).

Through lack of government funding the USAF did not proceed beyond the prototype stage of the AMST programme. However, McDonnell Douglas believe there will be a commercial requirement for an aircraft in this category. It is claimed that the YC-15 can be adapted for civil operations without extensive changes.

Type: advanced military STOL transport
Powerplant: four 16,000-lb (7257-kg) Pratt & Whitney JT8D-17 turbofans
Performance: maximum speed 500 mph (805 km/h); approach speed 98 mph (157.5 km/h); take-off field length with payload of 27,000 lb (12247 kg) 2,000 ft (610 m); operational radius with 27,000-lb (12247-kg) payload (short take-off) or 62,000-lb (28122-kg) payload (conventional take-off) 461 miles (742 km)
Weights: maximum take-off 216,680 lb (98284 kg)
Dimensions: wing span (second, larger wing) 132 ft 7 in (40.41 m); length 124 ft 3 in (37.87 m); height 43 ft 4 in (13.21 m); wing area (second wing) 2,107 sq ft (195.74 m²)
Operators: None

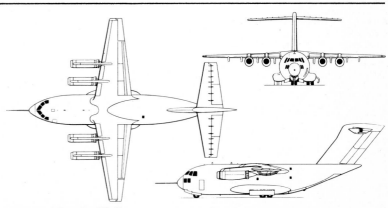

McDonnell Douglas YC-15

Seen here in its original configuration, with small wing and JT8D engines, the McDonnell Douglas YC-15 was one of the technically impressive Advanced Medium STOL Transport (AMST) contenders; no production money has been voted.

Messerschmitt-Bölkow-Blohm BO105

Rigid non-articulated rotor, two engines, compact size — all these combine to make the Messerschmitt-Bölkow-Blohm BO105 a particularly impressive helicopter. It is fully aerobatic and highly manoeuvrable, but also comparatively expensive. Its safety and versatility have made the BO105 a successful civil helicopter, and a few military forces find the type equally suitable. It is assigned multiple roles and can operate in all weathers. Nap-of-the-earth flying is a speciality to which the BO105 is well suited, the rigid rotor allowing it to hug contours like a leech. A conventional helicopter can tolerate no negative-g, restricted as it is by a much more mobile rotor assembly, but the BO105 can be pushed down the other side of such obstacles as trees, having been pulled up over them conventionally. Armed with up to six HOT or TOW missiles, the BO105 is a formidable opponent to any tank. West Germany's army air corps, the *Heeresflieger*, is receiving 212 BO105Ps each armed with six HOT anti-tank missiles, and a further 227 BO105Ms have been procured to replace Aérospatiale Alouette IIs in the liaison and communications role. Deliveries of the armed helicopter were due to begin in September 1979, and the type will enter service fully in 1980, when a regiment of 56 PAH-1s (service designation) will join each corps. They will be split into flights of seven aircraft, which will then be assigned to brigades or divisions. The Royal Netherlands Air Force (*Koninklijke Luchtmacht*) operates 30 BO105Cs with No 300 Sqn based at Deelen. Nigeria's air force has a requirement for 20 BO105Cs, four of which have so far been delivered for short-range search-and-rescue missions. Six more have been ordered, to supplement the force's helicopter strength, which also includes 10 Aérospatiale/Westland Pumas

and three Westland Whirlwinds, and 10 Alouette IIs in storage. The Philippine air force's No 505 Air Rescue Squadron flies BO105s assembled locally by the Philippine Aerospace Development Corporation, which has also supplied at least three to the navy for liaison work and general duties. Sudan has 20 BO105s on order. Boeing Vertol is responsible for sales in the Americas, and has developed a stretched version, called the Executaire, for the civil market.

The BO105 started life in 1962, the radical rotor system having been tested earlier on a ground rig. Government contracts covered this initial testing and also the construction of prototypes in 1964. Dipl Ing E. Weiland conceived the rotor, which in its developed, production form uses rigid, glass-fibre, folding blades. Sud Aviation (now part of Aérospatiale) was involved, and it was one of this company's helicopters, a Turboméca Astazou-powered Alouette II, which was used as a test bed for the initial trials. The first prototype BO105 was fitted with a conventional rotor assembly (from the Westland Scout) and a pair of Allison 250-C18 turboshafts but was

destroyed following resonance during ground trials; the second aircraft, similarly powered, pioneered the rigid rotor on the BO105. MTU-München Turbo 6022 engines were tried on the third development aircraft, but production machines are now all powered by the Allison turboshaft. Customers previously had the option of two versions of this engine: the 317-shp (236-kW) C18, now out of production, or the 400-shp (298-kW) C20, now standard. The *Heeresflieger's* PAH-1s are powered by a pair of 405-shp (302-kW) T63-A-720 turboshafts. German land forces will have had some two years experience with the Euromissile (Aérospatiale/MBB) HOT when the PAH-1s enter service, as the German army's RJpz-2 tank destroyers have been converted to carry the new missile in place of Aérospatiale SS.11s.

Operators: Netherlands, Nigeria, Philippines, Sudan, West Germany
Powerplant: two 400-shp (298-kW) Allison 250-C20 turboshafts; (PAH-1) two 405-shp (302-kW) Allison T63-A-720 turboshafts
Performance: maximum speed at sea level

167 mph (270 km/h); maximum cruising speed at sea level 144 mph (232 km/h); range with standard fuel and no reserves 363 miles (585 km) at sea level, 388 miles (625 km) at 5,000 ft (1525 m); maximum range with auxiliary tanks at sea level 621 miles (1000 km), at 5,000 ft (1525 m) 658 miles (1060 km); maximum rate of climb at sea level 1,870 ft (570 m) per minute; maximum rate of climb at sea level, on one engine 197 ft (60 m) per minute
Weights: empty equipped 2,645 lb (1200 kg); maximum take-off 5,070 lb (2300 kg)
Dimensions: rotor diameter 32 ft 2¾ in (9.82 m); length (rotors turning) 38 ft 10¾ in (11.84 m); height 9 ft 9½ in (2.98 m); main rotor disc area 811.2 sq ft (75.4 m²)
Armament: up to six Euromissile HOT or Hughes TOW anti-tank missiles with stabilized sight, plus various other options
Users: Netherlands, Nigeria, Philippines, Sudan, West Germany

The Netherlands Army Light Aircraft Group (Gp LV) operates a total of 30 MBB BO105C light observation helicopters in 300 Sqn.

Designated PAH-1 (for anti-armour helicopter Type 1) by the Federal German Heer (army), the MBB BO105P can carry six of the Euromissile Hot anti-tank weapons and the complex associated sight and tracking system. A total of 212 are being delivered at six per month. Meanwhile bids for a successor PAH-2 were being studied in late 1979.

Mikoyan-Gurevich MiG-15 Fagot/15UTI Midget

Although obsolete in its basic fighter version, the Mikoyan-Gurevich MiG-15 'Fagot' survives in considerable numbers in its two-seat trainer version and will remain in use, in some countries, until it is replaced by the Aero L-39 Albatros.

German and Russian research gave rise to the design of the MiG-15 in 1945-46, and the first prototype was not unlike the Focke-Wulf Ta 183 study of the late war years. Early difficulties occasioned by the lack of a suitable powerplant for the proposed fighter were solved when the British government decided to supply the Soviet Union with a batch of Rolls-Royce Nene turbojets. A copy was produced by the Klimov bureau under the designation RD-45; later uprated versions were designated in the VK-1 series.

The first prototype was lost soon after its first flight in July 1947, but a second and extensively revised prototype flew towards the end of the same year, and the aircraft was ordered into production in March 1948. Deliveries started in 1949, by which time the improved MiG-15SD, better known as the MiG-15bis, was flying in prototype form. The MiG-15UTI conversion trainer flew shortly afterwards.

The combat debut of the MiG-15 in Korea in November 1950 proved an unpleasant shock to the West. There was only one Allied fighter in the same class, the North American F-86 Sabre. Its better equipment, and the better training of the US pilots, allowed the US Air Force to achieve superiority over the MiG-15, but the Soviet fighter had a better climb rate, ceiling and acceleration even than this outstanding US type.

China, Poland and Czechoslovakia built MiG-15s, and the latter two countries converted many single-seaters into two-seaters after the MiG-15 was phased out of first line service. In the absence of any production trainer version of the MiG-17 or MiG-19, the MiG-15UTI moved out of its original role as conversion trainer and became the Eastern bloc's standard advanced trainer. Even today it is found in service all over the world.

Type: single-seat fighter and (MiG-15UTI) two-seat advanced trainer
Powerplant: one 5,950-lb (2700-kg) Klimov VK-1 centrifugal-flow turbojet
Performance: maximum speed 668 mph (1076 km/h) at 39,500 ft (12000 m); ferry range 1,250 miles (2000 m); initial climb rate 9,050 ft (2760 m) per minute; ceiling 51,000 ft (15500 m)
Weights: empty 7,500 lb (3400 kg); normal loaded 11,000 lb (4960 kg); maximum take-off 12,750 lb (5786 kg)
Dimensions: span 33 ft 1 in (10.08 m); length 35 ft 7½ in (10.86 m); height 11 ft 1¾ in (3.4 m); wing area 221.7 sq ft (20.6 ^{2})
Armament: one 37-mm N-37 and two 23-mm NS-23 cannon (later aircraft had the NS-23s replaced by NR-23 revolver cannon); underwing hardpoints for slipper tanks or up to 1,100 lb (500 kg) of stores
Operators: Albania, Algeria, Angola, Bulgaria, China, Cuba, Czechoslovakia, East Germany, Egypt, Finland, Guinea, Hungary, Iraq, Mali, Mongolia, Nigeria, North Korea, Poland, Romania, Somalia, South Yemen, Sri Lanka, Syria, Tanzania, Uganda, USSR, Vietnam

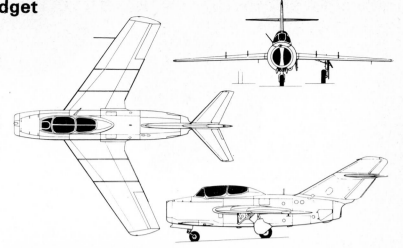

Mikoyan-Gurevich MiG-15UTI Midget

This MiG-15UTI was recently retired from service with the Finnish Ilmavoimat, but large numbers remain in use as trainers with other air forces, and spares are probably in production in Poland and China and possibly other countries.

Mikoyan-Gurevich MiG-17 Fresco

The Mikoyan-Gurevich MiG-17 'Fresco' was a completely redesigned development of the MiG-15, intended to remove the maximum speed restriction of Mach 0.92 which affected the earlier type. During flight trials the MiG-17 is claimed to have exceeded Mach 1 in level flight, but this performance was not attained in service.

Early production MiG-17s were fitted with the same VK-1 engine as the MiG-15, but the main production model, the MiG-17F, introduced the VK-1F with a simple afterburner. The wing of the MiG-17 was thinner and more sharply swept than that of its forebear, and the rear fuselage was slightly extended to reduce drag. First seen in 1955 was the MiG-17PF, a limited all-weather interceptor with radar in a central inlet bullet and the inlet lip. A further development was the MiG-17PFU, armed with four AA-1 'Alkali' guided air-to-air missiles, the Soviet Union's first missile-armed interceptor.

Although the MiG-17 was in theory obsolete by the mid-1960s, the type gave a good account of itself over Vietnam, being flown by most of the leading North Vietnamese pilots. Its US adversaries were hampered by rules under which they had to close to within visual range before firing, and unlike the MiG-17 they were not designed for close-range dogfighting.

The MiG-17 has been built in Poland (as the LIM-5 and -5P), Czechoslovakia (as the S-104) and China (as the Shenyang F-4). A special close-support version was developed in Poland as the LIM-6, with a deeper, longer-chord inner wing section, and dual mainwheels, rocket-assisted take-off gear and a braking parachute for operation from unprepared fields.

Type: single-seat fighter
Powerplant: one 7,500-lb (3400-kg) Klimov VK-1 afterburning turbojet
Performance: maximum speed 710 mph (1145 km/h) at 10,000 ft (3000 m); range 1,400 miles (2250 m); rate of climb 12,795 (3900 m) per minute; ceiling 54,500 ft (16600 m)
Weights: empty 9,000 lb (4100 kg); maximum take-off 14,750 lb (6700 kg)
Dimensions: span 31 ft 7 in (9.63 m); length 36 ft 4½ in (11.09 m); height 11 ft (3.35 m); wing area 243.3 sq ft (22.6 m²)
Armament: (MiG-17P, PF) three 23-mm NR-23 cannon and/or four AA-1 'Alkali' AAMs; two underwing hardpoints for drop tanks or stores up to 1,100 lb (500 kg)
Operators: Afghanistan, Albania, Algeria, Angola, Bulgaria, China, Cuba, Czechoslovakia, East Germany, Egypt, Guinea, Hungary, Iraq, Mali, Nigeria, North Korea, Poland, Romania, Somalia, South Yemen, Sri Lanka, Sudan, Syria, Tanzania, Uganda, USSR, Vietnam, Yemen

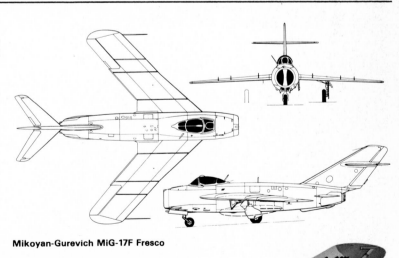

Mikoyan-Gurevich MiG-17F Fresco

MiG-17F of the Syrian Arab Air Force. This jet has all but been replaced in service with more modern aircraft.

Mikoyan-Gurevich MiG-19 Farmer

The Mikoyan-Gurevich MiG-19 'Farmer', the world's first production supersonic fighter remained in production in late 1978, and currently forms the backbone of the Chinese tactical air force in its Shenyang F-6 version. In the hands of Pakistan air force pilots it has proved its worth against considerably more modern and more costly opponents, with agility in combat which would do credit to a contemporary air-superiority fighter. Another good feature is the hard-hitting gun armament, with much greater projectile weight and muzzle velocity than most western 30-mm weapons.

Development of the MiG-19 started in the late 1940s, with a requirement for a new fighter designed around the newly developed Lyulka AL-5, the Soviet Union's first large axial-flow jet engine. Disappointing progess with this powerplant, however, led to the decision to redesign the Mikoyan prototype around two small-diameter Mikulin AM-5s. The first aircraft, the I-360, was distinguised by a T-tail, but was destroyed in flight-testing as a result of tailplane flutter. The I-350(M) was completed with a low-set tailplane, and was flown in late 1952. It was soon followed by the production MiG-19F with afterburning AM-5Fs, the first version to go supersonic in level flight in early 1953.

The initial MiG-19F and limited-all-weather MiG-19PF were less than successful, and were eventually withdrawn from service as a result of high accident rates. They were replaced by the MiG-19S, with an all-moving tailplane, refinements to flying controls and systems, and RD-9 engines. The latter was a largely redesigned development of the AM-5 produced by the Tumansky bureau, and was the first of many Tumansky engines believed to power all MiG fighters up to the MiG-27 'Flogger-D'. Deliveries of the definitive MiG-19S started in mid-1955 and the basic airframe thereafter continued almost completely unchanged to the end of the type's Russian production life. A measure of the basic good handling characteristics is the fact that the two-seat MiG-19UTI, although completed and flown, was never put into production; pilots found little difficulty in converting from the MiG-15UTI to the supersonic fighter.

The MiG-19S was rapidly followed by the MiG-19P, with Izumrud radar in an intake bullet fairing and the inlet lip, and from this version was developed the Soviet Union's first missile-armed fighter. The MiG-19PM suffered from engine problems resulting from rocket-plume ingestion, it formed the spearhead of the PVO air defence force for some years. However, more advanced versions of the MiG-19 were overtaken by the MiG-21 'Fishbed' and its developments.

Production of the MiG-19 was transferred from the Soviet Union to Czechoslovakia in 1958, the Aero works producing some 850 aircraft between 1958 and 1961. In that year, the Chinese Shenyang works produced the first examples of an unlicensed copy of the MiG-19S, designated F-6. By the mid-1970s at least 1,800 F-6s had been built in China, including a few F-7s based on the MiG-19P. A substantial number of F-6s was supplied to Pakistan in 1965-66 and 1972; Vietnam, Albania and Tanzania have also taken delivery of similar aircraft. The Pakistani aircraft have been modified with launch pylons for AIM-9 Sidewinder missiles, but it is not known whether Chinese aircraft carry a version of the equivalent K-13 'Atoll'. Points in favour of the MiG-19 include its excellent manoeuvrability and initial climb rate, products of its modest size, high power/weight ratio and (by modern standards) low wing-loading.

Type: single-seat fighter and limited all-weather interceptor
Powerplant: two 7,165-lb (3250-kg) afterburning Tumansky RD-9B turbojets
Performance: maximum speed (clean) 900 mph (1450 km/h) at 33,000 ft (10000 m) or Mach 1.4; maximum speed with external fuel tanks 715 mph (1150 km/h) at 33,000 ft (10000 m); initial climb rate 22,640 ft (6900 m) per minute; ceiling 57,400 ft (17500 m); ferry range with external fuel 1,350 miles (2200 km)
Weights: empty 11,400 lb (5172 kg); loaded

(clean) 16,300 lb (7400 kg); maximum take-off 19,600 lb (8900 kg)
Dimensions: span 29 ft 6½ in (9.0 m); length (excluding pitot tube) 41 ft 4 in (12.6 m); height 12 ft 9½ in (3.9 m); wing area 269 sq ft (25 m²)
Armament: three 30-mm NR-30 cannon plus rocket pods on underwing pylons; Pakistani aircraft have AIM-9 Sidewinders; MiG-19PM has no cannon but four K-5M 'Alkali' AAMs
Operators: Afghanistan, Albania, Bulgaria, China, Cuba, Iraq, North Korea, Pakistan, Tanzania, Uganda, USSR, Vietnam

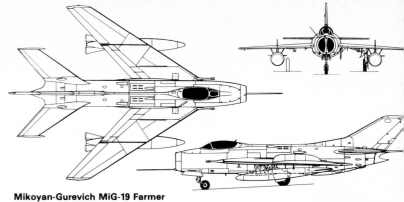

Mikoyan-Gurevich MiG-19 Farmer

MiG-**19SF** supplied by the Soviet Union to the Syrian Arab Air Force.

MiG-**19PM** limited all-weather interceptor of the Polish Air Force.

MiG-**19SF** (Shenyang F-6) of the Air Force of the People's Liberation Army. This type equips more than 40 regiments.

These MiG-19SF fighters are believed to have equipped a Soviet aerobatic display team organised by the Moscow Military District in 1958-66. The team then re-equipped with the MiG-21, and today flies the Su-15 'Flagon-F'. The true colour is carmine-red.

Mikoyan-Gurevich MiG-21 Fishbed/MiG-21U Mongol

The Mikoyan-Gurevich MiG-21 'Fishbed', still in production and apparently under development more than 25 years after it first flew must be judged a classic combat aircraft. Although its combat record has been mixed, it has had a profound influence on Western fighter design. At the time of writing, it remains the principal low-level air combat fighter of the Eastern bloc, working in conjunction with top-cover MiG-23s, and is unlikely to be fully replaced before the second half of the 1980s, even in Soviet service.

The origins of the MiG-21 lie in Korean War experience as do those of the Lockheed F-104. Both types stemmed from demands from pilots for an 'air-superiority' fighter from which all unneccessary equipment would be eliminated, and in which all aspects of the design would be subordinated to combat performance. Armament would be the minimum needed to knock down an enemy fighter.

The Mikoyan design bureau went even further in the direction of miniaturization than Lockheed, producing in 1955 the first of a series of prototypes designed around an engine not much larger than the Tumansky RD-9; two of the latter powered the MiG-19, itself not a large aircraft. The new engine, also of Tumansky design, was not available by 1955, so the swept-wing E-50 of that year was powered by an uprated RD-9E and a booster rocket.

In the following year the design bureau flew the swept-wing E-2A and the tailed-delta E-5, both powered by the newly developed RD-11 and armed with three 30-mm cannon. The tailed-delta layout of the E-5 resembled that of the Douglas Skyhawk in plan view, but featured a mid-set wing in line with the tailplane. The advantages of the layout included low drag and, as it turned out, excellent handling; on the debit side, its low-speed performance was not good and it was structurally complicated. However, the E-5 offered generally better performance than the E-2, and the tailed-delta was selected for production.

The first series aircraft were developed from the E-6 production prototype and were themselves designated E-66 by the Mikoyan bureau. They carried a simple radar-ranging sight and two K-13 'Atoll' air-to-air missiles in addition to two 30-mm cannon, but with only 11,250-lb (5100-kg) maximum thrust they were underpowered. A few aircraft of the type entered service with a trials unit in late 1957, with the designation MiG-21. The first large-scale production variant was the MiG-21F, powered by an uprated Tumansky R-11F-300 of 12,600-lb (5750-kg) thrust, which entered service in late 1959. Most of these had the left gun removed to save weight, and had a fin of longer chord than that of the early MiG-21.

After the appearance of the MiG-21F, the process of improving the MiG-21 began in earnest. The early MiG-21 was a clear-weather interceptor with little payload, range and armament. However, there were strict limits to what could be done to rectify the situation, because any extra equipment could have disastrous effects on the perfomance of what was basically a small aircraft.

The MiG-21F was delivered to India and Finland as well as to Warsaw Pact states, and was put into production in China and Czechoslovakia. By the time it was established in service, development of a limited-all-weather version was under way, an aerodynamic prototype being demonstrated at Tushino in 1961. This was the MiG-21PF, with an R1L radar in the centrebody of a redesigned inlet. Guns were removed, and the cockpit was faired into the fuselage, sacrificing rear vision for low drag.

Between 1964 and 1970 the MiG-21PF formed the basis for numerous modified sub-variants. In the course of production, a new brake-chute installation was added at the base of the fin. On the MiG-21SPS, plain flaps blown by engine-bleed air replaced the chord-extending Fowler flaps. Later the fin was again extended forwards, and some aircraft had provision for a GP-9 gun-pack containing the newly developed GSh-23 cannon. Also covered by the MiG-21PF designation was the introduction of the 13,700-lb (6200-kg) R-11F2S-300 engine and improved R2L radar.

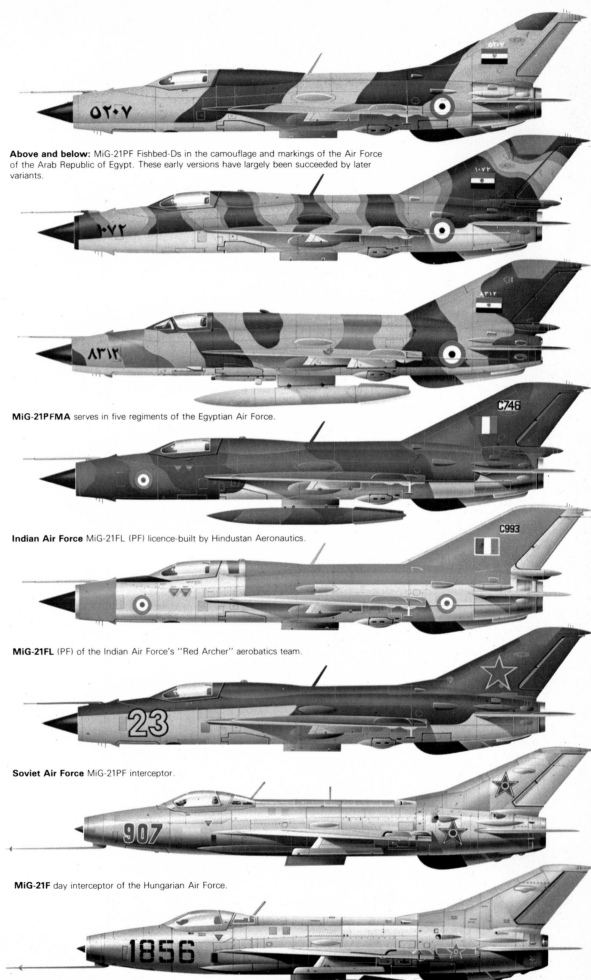

Above and below: MiG-21PF Fishbed-Ds in the camouflage and markings of the Air Force of the Arab Republic of Egypt. These early versions have largely been succeeded by later variants.

MiG-21PFMA serves in five regiments of the Egyptian Air Force.

Indian Air Force MiG-21FL (PF) licence-built by Hindustan Aeronautics.

MiG-21FL (PF) of the Indian Air Force's "Red Archer" aerobatics team.

Soviet Air Force MiG-21PF interceptor.

MiG-21F day interceptor of the Hungarian Air Force.

MiG-21F of the Air Force of the People's Liberation Army of China.

continued

Mikoyan-Gurevich MiG-21 Fishbed/MiG-21U Mongol

The next recognisable modification produced the MiG-21PFM, with a conventional sideways-hinged canopy and separate windscreen replacing the forward-hinged one-piece hood of the MiG-21F. It was followed by the MiG-21PFMA, with a deeper dorsal spine and four wing pylons, which formed the basis for the MiG-21R reconnaissance version with optical and electronic sensors in ventral and wing-tip pods. The next major modification came in 1970, with the service introduction of the MiG-21MF. This has an internal GSh-23 and the new Tumansky R-13 rated at 14,500 lb (6600 kg). The equivalent reconnaissance version is designated MiG-21RF.

In 1973 there appeared the first examples of a new MiG-21 development, the MiG-21SMT, with internal fuel and avionic equipment in a bulged dorsal spine. It has been followed by the structurally redesigned MiG-21bis, with the Tumansky R-25 and further improved avionics. The MiG-21bis is regarded by NATO as a true multi-role type, and some of the extra avionic installations are probably connected with newer Soviet weapons such as the AS-7 guided air-to-surface missile.

However, the MiG-21 is limited in range and payload by comparison with the MiG-27, while its dogfighting performance is not in the class of the latest Western fighters. it is thus likely that the MiG-21bis represents an interim development, pending production of a new aircraft to fill the air-to-air slot in the Soviet air arm. Meanwhile, the Mig-21bis has become the standard export version.

Other versions of the MiG-21 have included the MiG-21M, generally similar to the MiG-21MF but powered by the older R-11, which is built under licence in India. All trainer versions of the MiG-21 have similar forward fuselages and lack search radar: the MiG-21U is basically equivalent to an early MiG-21PF, the MiG-21US is equivalent to the MiG-21PFS and the MiG-21UM is derived from the MiG-21MF. It is likely that a MiG-21bis-derived trainer will emerge in due course.

continued

MiG-21MF cutaway drawing key

1 Pitot-static boom
2 Pitch vanes
3 Yaw vanes
4 Conical three-position intake centrebody
5 "Spin Scan" search-and-track radar antenna
6 Boundary layer slot
7 Engine air intake
8 Radar ("Spin Scan")
9 Lower boundary layer exit
10 Antennæ
11 Nosewheel doors
12 Nosewheel leg and shock absorbers
13 Castoring nosewheel
14 Anti-shimmy damper
15 Avionics bay access
16 Attitude sensor
17 Nosewheel well
18 Spill door
19 Nosewheel retraction pivot
20 Bifurcated intake trunking
21 Avionics bay
22 Electronics equipment
23 Intake trunking
24 Upper boundary layer exit
25 Dynamic pressure probe for q-feel
26 Semi-elliptical armour-glass windscreen
27 Gunsight mounting
28 Fixed quarterlight
29 Radar scope
30 Control column (with tailplane trim switch and two firing buttons)
31 Rudder pedals
32 Underfloor control runs
33 KM-1 two-position zero-level ejection seat
34 Port instrument console
35 Undercarriage handle
36 Seat harness
37 Canopy release/lock
38 Starboard wall switch panel
39 Rear-view mirror fairing
40 Starboard-hinged canopy
41 Ejection seat headrest
42 Avionics bay
43 Control rods
44 Air conditioning plant
45 Suction relief door

46 Intake trunking
47 Wingroot attachment fairing
48 Wing/fuselage spar-lug attachment points (four)
49 Fuselage ring frames
50 Intermediary frames
51 Main fuselage fuel tank
52 RSIU radio bay
53 Auxiliary intake
54 Leading-edge integral fuel tank
55 Starboard outer weapons pylon
56 Outboard wing construction
57 Starboard navigation light
58 Leading-edge suppressed aerial
59 Wing fence
60 Aileron control jack
61 Starboard aileron
62 Flap actuator fairing
63 Starboard blown flap — SPS (*sduva pogranichnovo sloya*)
64 Multi-spar wing structure
65 Main integral wing fuel tank
66 Undercarriage mounting/pivot point
67 Starboard mainwheel leg
68 Auxiliaries compartment
69 Fuselage fuel tanks Nos 2 and 3
70 Mainwheel well external fairing
71 Mainwheel (retracted)

72 Trunking contours
73 Control rods in dorsal spine
74 Compressor face
75 Oil tank
76 Avionics pack
77 Engine accessories
78 Tumansky R-13 turbojet (rated at 14,550 lb/6 600 kg with full reheat)
79 Fuselage break/transport joint
80 Intake
81 Tail surface control linkage
82 Artificial feel unit
83 Tailplane jack
84 Hydraulic accumulator
85 Tailplane trim motor
86 Tailfin spar attachment plate
87 Rudder jack
88 Rudder control linkage
89 Tailfin structure
90 Leading-edge panel
91 Radio cable access

92 Magnetic detector
93 Tailfin mainspar
94 RSIU (*radio-stantsiya istrebitelnaya ultrakorot-kykh vol'n* — very-short-wave fighter radio) antenna plate
95 VHF/UHF aerials
96 IFF antennæ
97 Formation light
98 Tail warning radar
99 Rear navigation light
100 Fuel vent
101 Rudder construction

MiG-21F of a Rumanian Air Force interceptor Regiment, 1967.

Sand camouflaged MiG-21RF of the Arab Republic of Egypt Air Force.

MiG-21MF of the Luftstreitkrafte und Luftverteidigung of the GDR.

MiG-21MF of the Czeskoslovenske Letectvo (Czech Air Force).

Indian Air Force Hindustan-built MiG-21PFM hastily camouflaged for service in the 1971 India-Pakistan war.

The CL (Czech air force) is one of the few in the Warsaw Pact to use at least some aircraft of its own design, and even the Soviet-designed MiG-21 was built in early versions. Today the CL uses about 170 MiG-21s of several tactical versions, as well as about 80 of the MiG-21R ("Fishbed-H") type which are dedicated to reconnaissance.

102 Rudder hinge
103 Braking parachute hinged bullet fairing
104 Braking parachute stowage
105 Tailpipe (variable convergent nozzle)
106 Afterburner installation
107 Afterburner bay cooling intake
108 Tailplane linkage fairing
109 Nozzle actuating cylinders
110 Tailplane torque tube
111 All-moving tailplane
112 Anti-flutter weight
113 Intake
114 Afterburner mounting
115 Fixed tailplane root fairing
116 Longitudinal lap joint

117 External duct (nozzle hydraulics)
118 Ventral fin
119 Engine guide rail
120 JATO assembly canted nozzle
121 JATO assembly thrust plate forks (rear mounting)
122 JATO assembly pack
123 Ventral airbrake (retracted)
124 Trestle point
125 JATO assembly release solenoid (front mounting)
126 Underwing landing light
127 Ventral stores pylon
128 Mainwheel inboard door
129 Splayed link chute
130 Twin 23-mm GSh-23 cannon installation

131 Cannon muzzle fairing
132 Debris deflector plate
133 Auxiliary ventral drop tank
134 Port forward air brake (extended)
135 Leading-edge integral fuel tank
136 Undercarriage retraction strut
137 Aileron control rods in leading-edge
138 Port inboard weapons pylon
139 UV-16-57 rocket pod
140 Port mainwheel
141 Mainwheel outboard door section

142 Mainwheel leg
143 Aileron control linkage
144 Mainwheel leg pivot point
145 Main integral wing fuel tank
146 Flap actuator fairing
147 Port aileron
148 Aileron control jack
149 Outboard wing construction
150 Port navigation light
151 Port outboard weapons pylon
152 "Advanced Atoll" infrared-guided AAM
153 Wing fence
154 Radio altimeter antenna

Mikoyan-Gurevich MiG-21 Fishbed/MiG-21U Mongol

Type: fighter/light strike and (MiG-21M variants) conversion trainer
Powerplant: (MiG-21bis, to which subsequent details refer) one 16,500 lb (7500 kg) Tumansky R-25 afterburning turbojet
Performance: maximum speed clean 1,320 mph (2125 km/h) or Mach 2 at 36,000 ft (11000 m); maximum speed with external stores at medium altitude 1,000 mph (1600 km/h) or Mach 1.5; maximum speed at sea level just over Mach 1; service ceiling about 50,000 ft (15000 m); hi-lo-hi combat radius about 300 miles (500 km)
Weights: empty 13,500 lb (6200 kg); maximum loaded 22,000 lb (10000 kg)
Dimensions: span 23 ft 6 in (7.16 m); length 51 ft 9 in (15.75 m); height 14 ft 9 in (4.49 m); wing area 247 sq ft (22.9 m²)
Armament: one twin-barrel 23-mm GSh-23 cannon, plus four wing hardpoints for 3,300 lb (1500 kg) of ordnance, including up to four K-13 (AA-2 'Atoll') or AA-8 'Aphid' air-to-air missiles, AS-7 'Kerry' air-to-surface missiles or unguided rockets; outer wing pylons or centreline pylon can be used for drop tanks
Operators: Afghanistan, Albania, Algeria, Angola, Bangladesh, Bulgaria, China, Cuba, Czechoslovakia, East Germany, Ethiopia, Egypt, Finland, Hungary, India, Iraq, Laos, Mozambique, Nigeria, North Korea, Poland, Romania, Somalia, Sudan, Syria, Tanzania, Uganda, USSR, Vietnam, Yemen, Yugoslavia.

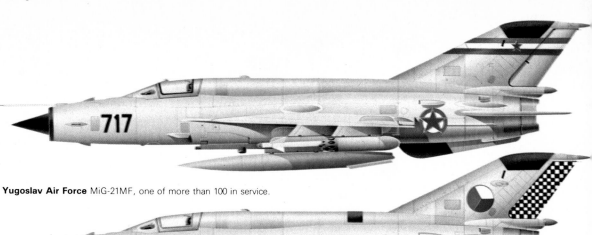

Yugoslav Air Force MiG-21MF, one of more than 100 in service.

One of the few MiG-21Rs in the Czech Air Force carrying unit insignia.

Soviet Air Force MiG-21MF of a fighter regiment assigned to the Kiev Military District.

Late-model MiG-21s, apparently of the SMT sub-type called 'Fishbed-K' by NATO, seen on a rare visit outside the Soviet Union. This version has augmented avionics, with rear-warning radar, and fuel tankage restored to the large fuselage spine fairing.

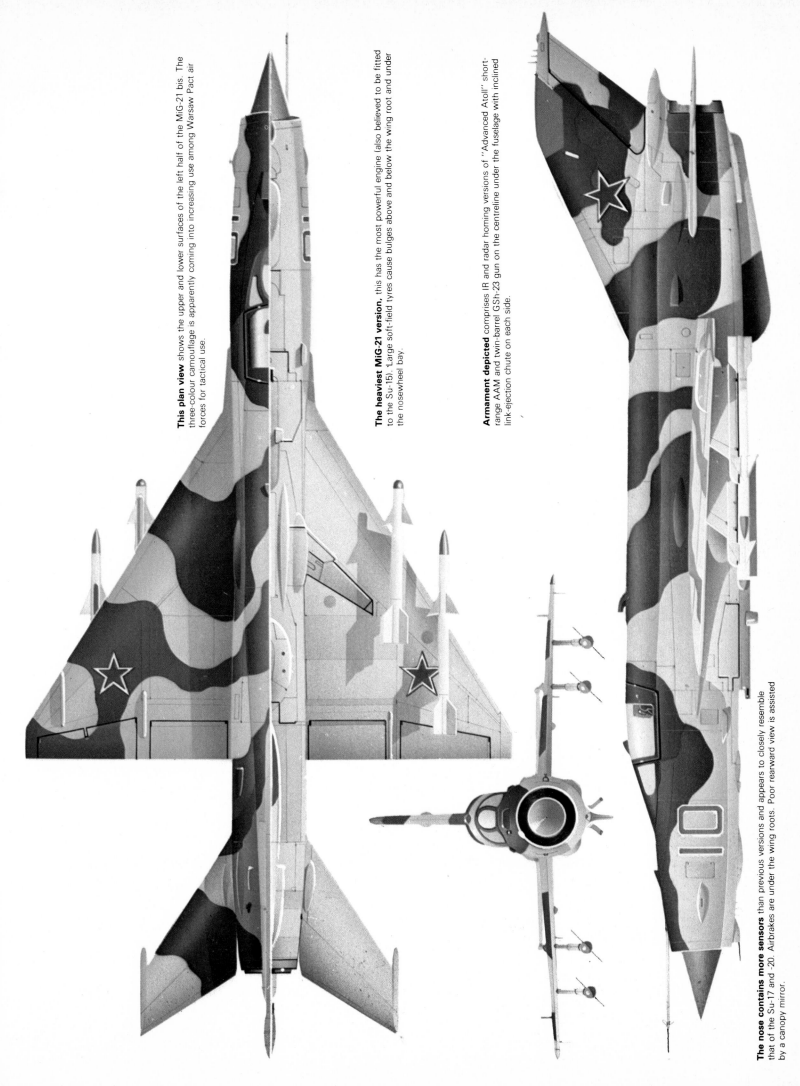

This plan view shows the upper and lower surfaces of the left half of the MiG-21 bis. The three-colour camouflage is apparently coming into increasing use among Warsaw Pact air forces for tactical use.

The heaviest MiG-21 version, this has the most powerful engine (also believed to be fitted to the Su-15). Large soft-field tyres cause bulges above and below the wing root and under the nosewheel bay.

Armament depicted comprises IR and radar homing versions of "Advanced Atoll" short-range AAM and twin-barrel GSh-23 gun on the centreline under the fuselage with inclined link-ejection chute on each side.

The nose contains more sensors than previous versions and appears to closely resemble that of the Su-17 and -20. Airbrakes are under the wing roots. Poor rearward view is assisted by a canopy mirror.

Mikoyan-Gurevich MiG-23 Flogger-A,B,C,E,F

The Mikoyan-Gurevich MiG-23 'Flogger' is almost certainly the most important of Soviet tactical warplanes, and production of this aircraft, and of its derivative the MiG-27 was reported to have attained a rate of 300 aircraft a year by 1976-77. The type has replaced many MiG-21s and Sukhoi Su-7s, and in 1978 was first deployed by the PVO air defence force. It has no direct Western equivalent, the near-contemporary Dassault-Breguet Mirage G being almost identical in concept but never put into production. The most closely comparable type in service is perhaps the Saab 37 Viggen, but the MiG-23 can probably best be likened to a 'miniaturised Phantom', later in timescale and more advanced, but intended for the same spectrum of roles. Modification fairly late in its development produced a type with better air-superiority characteristics than at first intended, but the MiG-23 cannot be compared with later specialized Western fighters.

Develoment of the MiG-23 was almost certainly initiated in 1963-64, before the Vietnam war and most Middle East experience of air combat. The aim was to produce for Frontal Aviation (FA) a tactical fighter which could match the payload/range of types such as the Lockheed F-104G, Republic F-105 and McDonnell Douglas F-4 Phantom without demanding massive runways. The last concern was also a feature of Western thinking at the time, leading to development of the Viggen and a short-lived NATO enthusiasm for V/STOL strike aircraft.

The Mikoyan evaluated at least two approaches to the FA requirements: the swing-wing MiG-23 and a tailed-delta type with a battery of Kolesov lift jets amidships (the latter codenamed 'Faithless' by NATO). It is also possible that a canard type was test-flown. The swing-wing prototype was the first such aircraft to fly in the Soviet Union, as distinct from the mid-span pivot principle used on the Su-17 and Tupolev Tu-26. Both the aircraft evaluated were designed to accept the Tumansky R-27, the first Soviet afterburning turbofan for military use.

The Mikoyan prototypes were evaluated in 1966-67, and the decision to go ahead with the swing-wing type was probably taken in 1968.

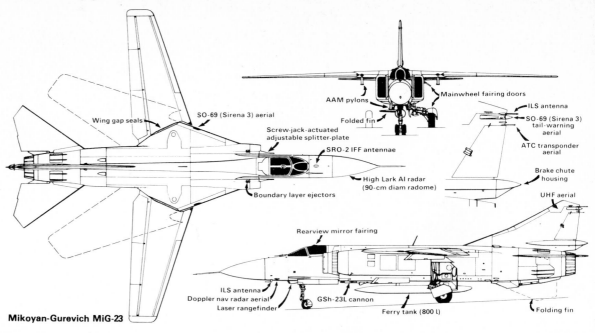

Mikoyan-Gurevich MiG-23

By that time, however, the importance of the air combat regime was being recognised; the MiG-23 may also have demonstrated generally unacceptable handling characteristics, as well as needing improvement in the air-to-air regime. In any event, although a few aircraft basically similar to the prototype (designated 'Flogger-A' by NATO) were put into service with trials units, several years elapsed before the highly modified MiG-23S 'Flogger-B' was introduced.

Compared with the prototype, the MiG-23S features an extremely large saw-toothed leading-edge extension which increases wing area and taper, reducing the shift of aerodynamic centre with wing sweep. The planform was also altered, the tail surfaces being moved aft. Together, most of the modifications would tend to make the aircraft more stable, while the additional wing area might restore some of the manoeuvrability thus sacrificed.

Libyan Air Force MiG-23 Flogger-E flown by an interceptor squadron originally based at Benghazi.

Still code-named 'Flogger-B' by NATO, this model of MiG-23S has a barely perceptible. kink in the fin leading edge, extended-chord tabs on the tailerons, pylons for swing-wing drop tanks (usable at 16° sweep only) and, for foreign visits, no laser or AAMs.

The notched wing planform distinguishes the MiG-23 series from other variable-sweep aircraft. Other unusual features include a folding ventral fin and a complex but space-saving main landing gear. Moveable surfaces include simple leading-edge droops on the outer sections of the moving wing panels, plain trailing-edge flaps and spoilers. The outermost of the three flap sections operate in conjunction with the spoiler and tailerons for roll control. Western testing shows strongly that variable-geometry wings should be matched with sophisticated high-lift systems.

Whereas design of the MiG-23 was biased towards the strike role, development was aimed at improving handling and manoeuvrability in the air-combat regime. No effort was made, however, to improve visibility, beyond the installation of rear-view mirrors.

Development of the MiG-23S equipment and armament went hand in hand with airframe and powerplant work. The aircraft is fitted with a radar considerably larger and more powerful than that fitted to the MiG-21, and is armed with specially developed medium-range and dogfighting missiles. All examples in FA service also carry a laser (or possibly infra-red) sighting aid beneath the nose.

The MiG-23S entered service in 1971-72. Early aircraft were powered by the 23,150-lb (10500-kg) Tumansky R-27, but by the time the aircraft was established in service work was under way on a more powerful engine: this was probably another example of development aimed at improving air-to-air combat capability. The R-27 is, however, still used in the MiG-23U 'Flogger-C' conversion trainer and the export 'Flogger-E'; the latter has a much-reduced standard of equipment, including AA-2-2 'Advanced Atoll' missiles and like the trainer, a radar apparently derived from the R2L of the MiG-21.

The AA-2 'Atoll' formed the interim armament of the MiG-23S until the newly developed AA-7 and AA-8 entered service in the mid-1970s. It is not clear at what point the R-29B replaced the R-27 as the standard engine, because the installation appears externally identical. It is also possible that later MiG-23S fighters have a better radar than the initial fit, which the US Department of Defense (DoD) compared to that of the McDonnell Douglas F-4J Phantom in 1971; in early 1979 the DoD credit the MiG-23/AA-7 combination with look-down/shoot-down capability, suggesting that the radar had been upgraded. In 1978, examples of the MiG-23S visiting France and Finland were seen to have smaller dorsal fin extensions than earlier aircraft, probably indicating a further effort to improve manoeuvrability. These aircraft also featured attachments for ferry tanks under the outer wing panels, standard on the MiG-27 but not previously seen on the MiG-23S. However, up to early 1979 these aircraft were still regarded as MiG-23S 'Flogger-Bs' rather than any major new type.

Type: air superiority fighter with secondary strike role of (MiG-23U) conversion trainer
Powerplant: (current production) one 25,350-lb (11500-kg) Tumansky R-29B afterburning turbofan
Performance: maximum speed 1,450 mph (2350 km/h) or Mach 2.2 at 36,000 ft (11000 m); maximum speed at sea level 840 mph (1350 km/h) or Mach 1.1; service ceiling 55,000 ft (17000 m); ferry range 1,750 miles (2800 km); combat radius 575 miles (930 km)
Weights: empty 25,000 lb (11300 kg); internal fuel 10,140 lb (4600 kg); normal take-off 38,000 lb (17250 kg); maximum 41,000 lb (18500 kg)
Dimensions: span (unswept) 46 ft 9 in (14.25 m); span (swept) 27 ft 2 in (8.3 m); length 59 ft 10 in (18.25 m); height 14 ft 4 in (4.35 m); wing area 400 sq ft (37.2 m²)
Armament: one internal 23-mm GSh-23 twin-barrel cannon, two glove hardpoints for AA-7 'Apex' medium-range air-to-air missiles, two belly hardpoints for AA-8 'Aphid' dogfight air-to-air missiles. The export 'Flogger-E' carries four AA-2-2 'Advanced Atoll' air-to-air missiles
Operators: Algeria, Bulgaria, Czechoslovakia, Egypt, Ethiopia, Libya, USSR

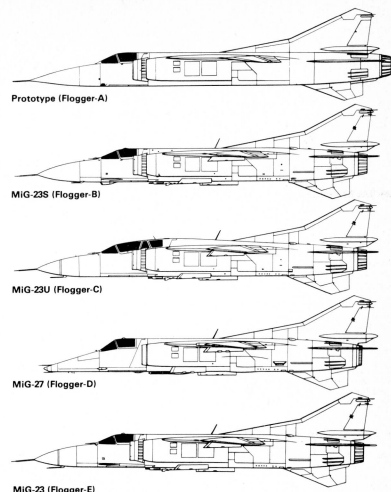

Prototype (Flogger-A)

MiG-23S (Flogger-B)

MiG-23U (Flogger-C)

MiG-27 (Flogger-D)

MiG-23 (Flogger-E)

The MiG-23S of Soviet Frontal Aviation use a braking parachute of cruciform pattern - made from overlapping red and white rectangles. This one, landing at a Finnish airbase, is steering to the left with its mudguarded nosewheels, with lower fin folded.

Mikoyan-Gurevich MiG-25 Foxbat

In early 1979 the US Department of Defense commented that the Mikoyan-Gurevich MiG-25 'Foxbat' was being produced 'mainly for export'. At that time the only known foreign recipients were Libya and Algeria, and it is uncertain whether their MiG-25s are interceptors or reconnaissance aircraft. In either case they give these nations the ability to defy all but the most sophisticated defence systems by virtue of sheer height and speed of penetration. Long ago the appearance of MiG-25s stimulated purchases of advanced weapon systems by the United States, Israel and the former Iranian regime, making the 'Foxbat' the best sales aid for McDonnell Douglas and Grumman yet devised. The type is also reported to form the basis of the Soviet Union's new air-defence system for the 1980s, but it is likely that the airframe is so highly modified for this role that a new designation will be applied.

The basic design goes back to 1957-59, when it seemed possible that the US Air Force would introduce a Mach 3, 70,000-ft (21350-m) bomber (the North American B-70) by 1964. Later the Lockheed A-11, intended as a strategic reconnaissance aircraft, clearly had a strike capability. Development of a Russian Mach 3 interceptor proceeeded as a matter of urgency, the first prototype flying around 1964. By this time, however, the B-70 had been cancelled and the pace of the Russian programme slowed.

The design of the E-266, as the Mikoyan bureau designated the new type, was influenced by that of the North American A-5 Vigilante. The two types both have large, thin-section shoulder wings of moderate sweep, vertical ramp inlets and identical fuselage and propulsion layouts. The main landing gear units are similar, and the twin fins of the E-266 are similar to those of the original Vigilante mock-up.

However, the Mach 3 requirement demanded a unique approach to structure and propulsion. The E-266 is constructed largely of fabricated steel sections, and the fuel tanks are of continuously welded steel sheet so that they can expand and contract with temperature without leaking. (Fuel-tank sealing proved to be a major problem with Mach 3 aircraft.) Power is provided by two extremely simple turbojets optimized for high-Mach performance; static pressure ratio is low, but at high speeds is multiplied by compression in the inlet ducts. The powerplant thus has some of the characteristics of a turbo-ramjet. At low speeds its efficiency is extremely poor, a factor exacerbated by the fact that only at high speeds is a substantial part of the lift generated by the intakes. The MiG-25 thus requires considerable nose-up trim at subsonic speeds, worsening its aerodynamic efficiency. It follows that the MiG-25 is a relatively inflexible machine, with poor loiter and mixed-profile performance, and poor manoeuvrability. It is commonly called a 'straight-line aircraft'.

The propulsion system, possibly including an early version of the electronic inlet control system, was tested on a modified Mikoyan-Gurevich I-75 interceptor, designated E-166, which is claimed to have exceeded Mach 2.8. However, it was not until 1967 that similar record speeds were set by E-266 development aircraft. By that time the airframe and engine appeared to be fully developed, with methanol-water injection for high-speed flight. However, it was another three years before production MiG-25s appeared in service, indicating protracted development of the offensive systems. The type received the NATO name 'Foxbat'.

There are two main versions, both deployed around 1970. The PVO air defence force operates the interceptor, possibly designated MiG-25P and known to NATO as 'Foxbat-A'. The radar and missile system is designed mainly for interceptions controlled from the ground or the Tupolev Tu-126 'Moss' AWACS aircraft. Although the 'Fox Fire' radar appears to be based on the 'Big Nose' radar of the two-seat Tu-28P, which operates with greater autonomy, the MiG-25 relies to a great extent on communication links and ground-guided trajectories rather than inertial or Doppler radar systems. Early MiG-25s carried the AA-5 'Ash' missile which arms the Tu-28P, and some may have carried the AA-3 'Anab'. The production-standard armament however, appears to be the massive AA-6 'Acrid', by far the largest air-to-air missile and even longer than the Western Hawk surface-to-air missile. The 'Fox Fire'/AA-6 system is not thought to have any look-down/shoot-down capability or multiple-target processing.

By the time the interceptor entered service, however, the MiG-25 had found a new role as a reconnaissance aircraft, using electronic and optical sensors. Although the range and sensor capacity of the MiG-25R are markedly inferior to those of the Lockheed SR-71, the aircraft can penetrate many defence systems in safety provided that there is a safe base close at hand. MiG-25Rs have been based in Egypt for uninterceptable overflights of Israel, and have flown from Poland in missions along the East German border for Elint probing of NATO defences. Two versions of the MiG-25R appear to exist: one, designated 'Foxbat-B' by NATO, has cameras as well as Elint dielectric panels, while the 'Foxbat-D' has more extensive Elint equipment but no cameras. Both types appear to be fitted with Doppler radar, and lack the compound leading-edge sweep of the interceptor.

The third confirmed variant is the MiG-25U 'Foxbat-C' conversion trainer, with a separate second cockpit in an extended nose. It has no operational systems. The West had an unusual chance to evaluate the MiG-25 in September 1976, when a Russian pilot landed an example of the interceptor version at a Japanese air base.

The US Department of Defense expects a 'modified MiG-25' carrying a look-down/-shoot-down system based on the new AA-X-9 missile to become operational in the early 1980s, with the ability to intercept low-flying strike aircraft. However, the limitations of the MiG-25, particularly in range and subsonic loiter capability, suggest that major modifications will be needed to turn the MiG-25 into a modern air defence fighter. It is possible that the two-seat interceptor which was undergoing weapons trials in 1978 shares little more than a fixed-wing, twin-fin configuration with the MiG-25; the DoD use of the designation 'Super MiG-25' for this aircraft suggests that this possibility is appreciated, and the type is not yet identified by a NATO reporting name in the 'Foxbat' series.

Type: interceptor and reconnaissance aircraft
Powerplant: two 27,000-lb (12250-kg) Tumansky R-31 afterburning turbojets
Performance: maximum speed (clean) Mach 3.0, equivalent to just under 2,000 mph (3200 km/h) at medium and high altitudes; maximum speed with external stores Mach 2.8; maximum sustained altitude 75,460 ft (23000 m); typical intercept radius 460 miles (740 km); range at Mach 3 900 miles (1500 km); initial climb rate 30,000 ft (9000 m) per minute
Weights: empty 44,000 lb (20000 kg); maximum take-off 82,500 lb (37500 kg)
Dimensions: (interceptor) span 46 ft (14 m); length 73 ft 2 in (22.3 m); height 18 ft 6 in (5.64 m); wing area 605 sq ft (56.2 m²)
Armament: up to four AA-6 'Acrid' air-to-air missiles (two radar and two infra-red) plus optional ventral gunpack probably containing GSh-23 cannon
Operators: Algeria, Libya, USSR

Possibly taken during a low-altitude fly-past, this unusual view of a MiG-25 shows the camera and SLAR-equipped reconnaissance version called "Foxbat-B" by NATO. For four years, from September 1971, aircraft of this type made reconnaissance missions across Israel, out of reach of F-4E Phantoms sent against them.

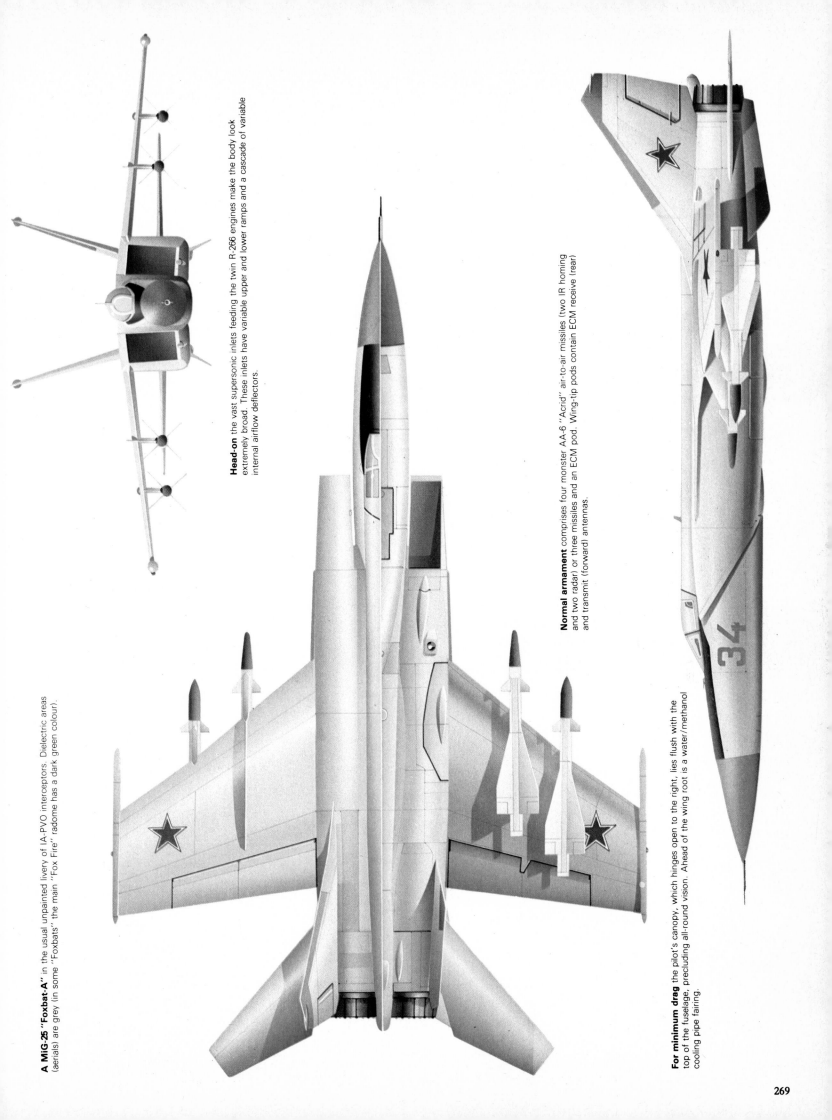

A MiG-25 "Foxbat-A" in the usual unpainted livery of IA-PVO interceptors. Dielectric areas (aerials) are grey (in some "Foxbats" the main "Fox Fire" radome has a dark green colour).

Head-on the vast supersonic inlets feeding the twin R-266 engines make the body look extremely broad. These inlets have variable upper and lower ramps and a cascade of variable internal airflow deflectors.

Normal armament comprises four monster AA-6 "Acrid" air-to-air missiles (two IR homing and two radar) or three missiles and an ECM pod. Wing-tip pods contain ECM receive (rear) and transmit (forward) antennas.

For minimum drag the pilot's canopy, which hinges open to the right, lies flush with the top of the fuselage, precluding all-round vision. Ahead of the wing root is a water/methanol cooling pipe fairing.

Mikoyan-Gurevich MiG-27 Flogger-D,-F

With the increasing optimization of the Mikoyan-Gurevich MiG-23 for the air-to-air role, it became increasingly attractive to develop a specialized version of the type for strike duties rather than employing the type as a multi-role aircraft as had been intended. This was the rationale behind the MiG-27, known to NATO as the 'Flogger-D', which presumably flew in 1972-73 (development having been initiated once the MiG-23 was reasonably well settled in service) and entered service with the Soviet Union's 16th Air Army in East Germany in 1975.

The main difference between the MiG-23 and the MiG-27 lies in the forward fuselage. The MiG-27 dispenses with the nose radar and has a slimmer nose giving a much better downward view. The nose cap houses a simple ranging radar; aft of this is a small window for a laser ranger, a radome which may cover a terrain-avoidance radar, and a Doppler aerial. Several other aerials appear on the leading edge of the wing gloves and on either side of the forward fuselage.

In order to save weight the variable inlets of the MiG-23 are dropped in favour of simple fixed structures; the medium-altitude high-speed performance thus sacrificed is not needed by the MiG-27 in any case. The secondary power nozzle of the engine is also simplified, probably to balance the weight saved in the forward fuselage. Weapon pylons are installed beneath the inlet ducts, rather than on the fuselage underside as on the MiG-23. The quoted weapon load is small by comparison with smaller Western aircraft, but represents an operating standard rather than the all-out ''Christmas-tree'' figure used in Western brochures. The twin-barrel GSh-23 gives way to a much harder-hitting six-barrel weapon, probably of 23-mm calibre although some reports claim that it is a 30-mm gun. The mainwheel tyres are fatter, to cope with greater weights.

Of uncertain status is an aircraft which represents a hybrid of the MiG-23 and MiG-27, with the powerplant and gun of the former and the latter's nose and pylon arrangement. It is probable that this aircraft, codenamed 'Flogger-F' by NATO, is an interim type, even though it has been supplied to Egypt. It is probably powered by the lower-thrust Tumansky R-27.

Pilots of the Soviet FA (Frontal Aviation) wear different flying clothing from some of the high-flying interceptor pilots of the PVO, who use partial-pressure suits. These FA pilots belong to a regiment equipped with the variable-sweep MiG-27 close-support and attack aircraft, of which about 1,000 are now estimated to be in service with the FA.

There is no direct trainer equivalent to the MiG-27, conversion being carried out on MiG-23Us despite the different propulsion systems. Some MiG-23Us have similar aerials to those of the MiG-27, suggesting that they are used for MiG-27 weapons training.

The closest Western equivalent to the MiG-27 is the smaller Jaguar, and like the Western aircraft it is probably intended for the medium-depth strike role rather than close-support duties or interdiction. However, with the aid of jetisonable drop tanks and rocket-assisted take-off, the MiG-27 can threaten a considerable area of Europe from dispersed forward bases in East Germany, being vastly more effective in payload range terms than its predecessors.

Weapons developed for the MiG-27 include cluster and fuel-air munitions as well as laser-guided and electro-optical 'smart' glide bombs. It is the first Soviet type to be seen with multiple stores racks: tandem racks can be fitted to both centreline and wing stations. The number of aerials on the airframe bear witness to an extensive internal ECM suite, augmented by external pods.

Type: tactical attack fighter
Powerplant: one 25,350-lb (11500-kg) Tumansky R-29B afterburning turbofan
Performance: maximum speed 1,050 mph (1700 km/h) or Mach 1.6 at 36,000 ft (11000 m); maximum speed (clean) at sea level 840 mph (1350 km/h) or Mach 1.1; service ceiling

55,000 ft (17000 m); ferrry range 1,750 miles (2800 km); combat radius 575 miles (930 km)
Weights: empty 24,000 lb (11000 kg); internal fuel 10,100 lb (4600 kg); normal take-off 39,500 lb (18000 kg); overload take-off 44,300 lb (20100 kg)
Dimensions: span (spread) 46 ft 9 in (14.25 m); span (swept) 27 ft 2 in (8.3 m); length 58 ft (17.7 m); height 14 ft 4 in (4.35 m); wing area 400 sq ft (37.2 m²)
Armament: one six-barrel rotary cannon, two multiple weapon points under each inlet duct and two multiple racks under gloves for maximum external weapon load estimated at 6,600 lb (3000 kg), including air-to-surface missiles.
Operators: Cuba, Egypt, Iraq, Syria, USSR

Landing after a sortie, this Soviet FA MiG-27 'Flogger-D' has its flaps fully down on the wings in minimum-sweep position, and the ventral fin folded to the right. Unlike most NATO air forces the FA regiments often operate for prolonged periods from rough unpaved temporary bases, thus giving an outstanding dispersion capability.

Head-on, with wings in the long-span loiter mode at only 16° sweep, the MiG-27 looks extremely clean with empty pylons and is a most efficient platform. Engine inlets are plain fixed-geometry rectangles.

The plan view shows the upper and lower sides of the left half of the aircraft. Range of sweep is considerable, from 16° to 72°, but the wing never comes close to the taileron-type horizontal tails.

Ahead of the centreline multiple ejector rack (which is aligned with those on the fixed inner-wing racks) is a six-barrel (23mm?) gun of unknown type. The ventral fin folds to the right when the landing gear is extended.

A MiG-27 of the type widely used by the Group of Soviet Forces in Germany. They bristle with sensors, ECM and other devices, including nose laser, CW radars, doppler and ASM guidance.

271

Mil Mi-1 Hare

By 1947 it had become clear to the Soviet leadership that helicopters would be necessary for many military and civil tasks, and a specification for a three-seat general-purpose helicopter was issued. One of three design bureaux asked to produce helicopter designs was that of Mikhail I. Mil, whose last previous design had been the A-15 autogiro of 1938. The first prototype, designated GM-1, flew in autumn 1948 and was the first Soviet production helicopter of the classic single-rotor layout. It was selected for production rather than the twin-rotor Bratukhin competitor and single-rotor Yakovlev Yak-100, and the Russian air force demonstrated the type for the first time in 1951 as the Mi-1 'Hare'.

Float-equipped (Mi-1P) and trainer (Mi-1U) versions of the basic versions were produced in quantity, in addition to Russian air force and navy co-operation and liaison aircraft. The overhaul life of critical components such as the transmission and rotor head was substantially improved during the production run, from 100 hours in 1951, to 500-600 hours in 1956, and to 1,000 hours in 1960.

The Mi-1 also started the record-breaking tradition which has typified Soviet helicopter development, setting up a variety of class records in the late 1950s. Long-distance records of up to 760 miles (1224 km) were set,

as well as a speed of 87 mph (141.2 km/h) on a 621-mile (1000 km) closed circuit.

Production of the Mi-1 in the Soviet Union tailed off in 1956-58, being gradually transferred to the Polish state aircraft factory, WSK-Swidnik. Both the airframe and engine were licence-built in Poland, WSK-manufactured aircraft being designated SM-1. About 150 SM-1s were delivered to the Soviet Union, and manufacture of the type paved the way for Polish production of the later Mi-2.

Type: utility and training helicopter
Powerplant: one 575-hp (429-kW) Ivchenko AI-26V seven-cylinder radial piston engine
Performance: maximum speed 125 mph (205 km/h); cruising speed 85 mph (140 km/h); range 370 miles (590 km); hovering ceiling 6,500 ft (2000 m)
Weights: empty 3,900 lb (1760 kg); normal loaded 5,300 lb (2400 kg); maximum loaded 5,650 lb (2550 kg)
Dimensions: main rotor diameter 47 ft 1 in (14.346 m); fuselage length 39 ft 4½ in (12.0 m); height 10 ft 10 in (3.3 m); main rotor disc area 1,739 sq ft (161.56 m²)
Operators: Albania, Bulgaria, China, Cuba, Czechoslovakia, East Germany, Finland, Iraq, Romania, Syria, USSR

This **Mil Mi-1** has been discarded by the *Ilmavoimat* (Finnish air force), but large numbers of similar helicopters are still nominally operational elsewhere, including Warsaw Pact forces. The last batches were built in Poland as the improved WSK SM-1.

Mil (PZL) Mi-2 Hoplite

The Mi-2 'Hoplite' was developed in the early 1960s by the Mil bureau as a straightforward turbine-powered version of the Mi-1, the availability of the shaft-turbine engine having revolutionised the design of the helicopter. The twin turbines develop 40% more power than the Mi-1's piston engine for barely half the dry weight, more than doubling the payload. The fuselage of the Mi-2 is completely different from that of its progenitor, carrying the engines above the cabin. Although some of the points of commonality between the Mi-1 and the Mi-2 were eliminated during development, the overall dimensions of the two types remain closely similar.

The Mi-2 was flown in 1962, but never put into production in the Soviet Union. Instead responsibility for the type was assigned to WSK-Swidnik now (PZL) in Poland as part of a Comecon rationalization programme, becoming the only Soviet-designed helicopter to be built solely outside the Soviet Union. Production in Poland started in 1965, and continues.

The Mi-2 is now the standard training helicopter of the Soviet Union, and has also been seen armed with anti-tank guided weapons. Its role, however, may be as a weapons trainer rather than an attack helicopter, as its slow speed and relatively old-technology rotor system (which limits its manoeuvrability for low-level 'nap-of-the-earth' flying) would render it vulnerable to defences. It is therefore more likely that pilots and weapon operators learn their skills on the Mi-2 before proceeding to the Mi-24 'Hind'.

PZL has developed a slightly enlarged version of the Mi-2, designated Mi-2M, but this 10-seat aircraft appears to be aimed mainly at the civil market. A reported version with a lighter skid landing gear (the only use of such a feature on a recent Warsaw Pact helicopter) has not been proceeded with, but efforts have been made to sell a US-engined version of the Mi-2 in the United States.

Type: eight-passenger transport attack and training helicopter

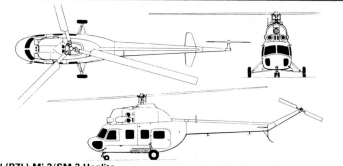

Mil (PZL) Mi-2/SM-2 Hoplite

Powerplant: two 400-shp (298-kW) Isotov GTD-350 turboshafts
Performance: maximum speed at sea level 130 mph (210 km/h); cruising speed 125 mph (205 km/h); maximum range 370 miles (590 km); range with eight passengers 150 miles (240 km); service ceiling 13,100 ft (4000 m)
Weights: empty 5,255 lb (2384 kg); maximum slung load 1,750 lb (800 kg); maximum take-off 8,160 lb (3700 kg)

Dimensions: main rotor diameter 47 ft 7 in (14.5 m); fuselage length 39 ft 2 in (11.94 m); height 12 ft 3½ in (3.75 m); main rotor disc area 1,727.6 sq ft (160.5 m²)
Armament: up to four AT-3 'Sagger' (possibly AT-5) anti-tank guided weapons or a combination of rocket pods and gun pods
Operators: Bulgaria, Czechoslovakia, Hungary, Poland, Romania, USSR

Mil Mi-4 Hound

Developed to flight-test status in only seven months following a personal edict from Stalin, the Mil Mi-4 'Hound' was at first considered to be a Soviet copy of the Sikorsky S-55 until it was realised that it was considerably larger than the later S-58. It was thus the first of a long line of large Mil helicopters.

The first prototype Mi-4 was completed in April 1952. It shared the basic layout of the S-55, with the powerful radial engine in the nose and quadricycle landing gear, but added a pair of clamshell loading doors capable of admitting a small military vehicle or most light infantry weapons such as anti-tank guns. It was thus a far more capable military transport than its Western contemporaries, and several thousand of the type were built.

The Mi-4 entered service in 1953. Early production aircraft had wooden-skinned rotor blades of very short life, but later aircraft had all-metal blades. Special versions include an amphibious development, tested in 1959, and the Mi-4V for high-altitude operations with a two-stage supercharger fitted to the ASh-82FN engine. The Mi-4 was also put into production at the Shenyang plant in China, as the Whirlwind-25 or H-5.

The Mi-4 has been one of the most important helicopters in service with the Soviet armed forces. At the 1956 Tushino air display, a formation of 36 Mi-4s demonstrated their ability to land a sizeable and well-equipped infantry force; later, the type became the Soviet Union's first armed helicopter, with a machine-gun in the nose of the navigator's

gondola and rocket pods on outriggers from the fuselage. This version was introduced as an interim armed helicopter with the expansion of the Soviet tactical air forces in the late 1960s. More recently, Mi-4s have been equipped with prominent aerials for communications jamming equipment.

With the rise of the Soviet navy, the Mi-4 found another new role: a number of the type were fitted with search radar beneath the nose and used as anti-submarine warfare aircraft in the Black Sea and Baltic areas. Other ASW equipment includes a magnetic anomaly detector (MAD) installed in a 'bird' towed behind the helicopter, and the type presumably also carries dunking sonar. The Mi-4 ASW variant paved the way for the later introduction of the Mi-14 'Haze'.

Type: 12-seat transport and anti-submarine warfare helicopter
Powerplant: one 1,700-hp (1268-kW) Shvetsou ASh-82V two-row radial piston engine
Performance: maximum speed 130 mph (210 km/h) at 5,000 ft (1500 m); cruising speed 100 mph (160 km/h); normal range 370 miles (590 km); ceiling 19,700 ft (6000 m); hovering ceiling 6,500 ft (2000 m)
Weights: empty 11,800 lb (5356 kg); maximum internal payload 3,840 lb (1740 kg); maximum take-off 17,200 lb (7800 kg)
Dimensions: main rotor diameter 68 ft 11 in (21.0 m); fuselage length 55 ft 1 in (16.79 m); height 14 ft 5¼ in (4.4 m); main rotor disc area 3,724 sq ft (346 m²)

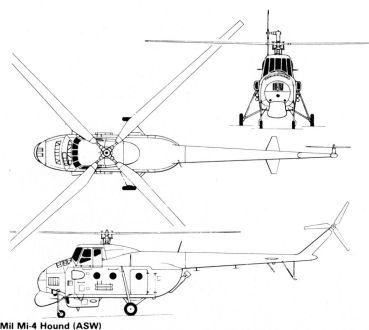

Mil Mi-4 Hound (ASW)

Armament: 7.62-mm machine-gun in ventral gondola, and rocket or gun pods; (ASW) depth charges or torpedoes
Operators: Afghanistan, Albania, Algeria, Bulgaria, China, Cuba, Czechoslovakia, East Germany, Egypt, Finland, Hungary, India, Iraq, Mali, Mongolia, North Korea, Poland, Romania, Somalia, Syria, USSR (AF and Navy), Vietnam, Yemen

Mil Mi-6 Hook/Mi-10 Harke

When the first of five prototypes of the Mil Mi-6 'Hook' was flown in September 1957, it was by far the largest helicopter in the world; what is more surprising is that with one exception (the same design bureau's apparently abortive Mi-12) it has retained that distinction and seems likely to do so into the foreseeable future.

The Mi-6 was the result of a joint military and civil requirement for a massive helicopter that would not only bring a new dimension to mobile warfare, with the ability to transport light armoured vehicles, but would also help in the exploitation of previously uncharted areas of the Soviet Union. Thus the requirement was not only demanding in terms of payload, calling for a disposable load half as great again as the fully loaded weight of the Mi-4, but also in terms of range.

The requirement was met by the first use of turbine power in a Soviet helicopter, and also by the provision of variable-incidence wings, first fitted in 1960 to the 30 pre-series aircraft, which carry 20% of the weight of the aircraft in cruising flight. Unusually the Mi-6 can make a rolling take-off at a weight greater than that at which it can take-off vertically. The engineering problems were formidable — the R-7 gearbox and rotor head alone weigh 7,055 lb (3200 kg), more than both the engines.

Like the Mi-4, the Mi-6 has clamshell doors at the rear of the cabin and can accommodate small armoured vehicles. Even larger loads can be lifted by the specialized flying-crane derivative of the Mi-6, the Mi-10 'Harke'; this features a much shallower fuselage than the Mi-6, and in its initial version is fitted with a vast quadricycle landing gear which allows it to straddle and lift loads as large as a motor-coach or a prefabricated building. The later Mi-10K has a shorter, lighter landing gear and rear-facing gondola beneath the nose for a crewman to direct lifting operations.

The Mi-6 and Mi-10 are not as widely used as the Mi-8 by the Soviet armed forces, possibly because such large helicopters are vulnerable in combat. A new heavy assault helicopter is, however, believed to be under development.

Type: heavy transport helicopter and (Mi-10) crane helicopter (specification Mi-6)
Powerplant: two 5,500-shp (4103-kW) Soloviev D-25V turboshafts
Performance: maximum speed 186 mph (300 km/h); crusing speed 155 mph (250 km/h); range with 26,500-lb (12000-kg) payload 125 miles (200 km); range with 8,800-lb (4000-kg) payload 620 miles (1000 km); service ceiling at maximum gross weight 14,500 ft (4400 m); hovering ceiling 8,200 ft (2500 m)
Weights: empty 60,050 lb (27240 kg); maximum internal payload 26,500 lb (12000 kg); normal take-off 89,300 lb (40500 kg); maximum vertical take-off 93,700 lb (42500 kg)
Dimensions: main rotor diameter 114 ft 10 in (350 m); fuselage length 108 ft 10¼ in (33.18 m); wing span 50 ft 2½ in (15.3 m) height on ground 30 ft 1 in (9.16 m); main rotor disc area 10,356.8 sq ft (962 m²)
Armament: in tactical role, one machine-gun in nose compartment
Operators: Algeria, Bulgaria, Egypt, Ethiopia, Iraq, Libya, Peru, Syria, USSR, Vietnam

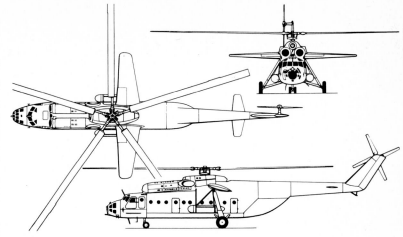

Mil Mi-6 Hook

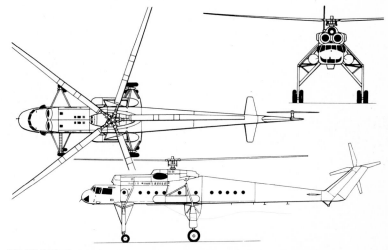

Mil Mi-10 Harke

Largest helicopters in the Americas are the five Mil Mi-6 supplied newly built by the Soviet Union in 1978 to the Fuerza Aerea del Peru. This powerful air force had in the past relied on Western manufacturers, but since 1975 has bought Russian.

Mil Mi-8 Hip

The Mil Mi-8 'Hip' relates to the earlier, piston-engined Mi-4 'Hound' as the Mi-2 'Hoplite' relates to the Mi-1 'Hare'. As in the case of the smaller helicopter, development started as a turbine-powered adaptation of the original design and proceeded to a point where there was little if any commonality between the new helicopter and its predecessor.

The first prototype of the Mi-8 was flown in 1961, with the four-blade rotor of the Mi-4 and a single Soloviev turboshaft of 2,700-shp (2014-kW). In 1962, however, the second prototype flew with the production standard twin-engine installation, and in 1964 a five-blade rotor was added. It was this version which went into production as the standard Warsaw Pact medium transport helicopter in about 1967.

The Mi-8 is widely used by the Soviet air force and other Warsaw Pact forces, apparently by the tactical units rather than by the VTA military transport force. It is broadly comparable with the land-based transport versions of the Sikorsky S-61 family, although there is so far no evidence that the type is used in the long-range rescue role as are the US Air Force's HH-3s. Its usefulness in military service is increased by its rear-loading doors, which allow the full width of the cabin to be used for bulky or awkward loads. The Mi-8 can, for instance, accommodate small military vehicles or infantry weapons such as anti-tank guns.

The data apply to the basic Mi-8T utility version, which has been offered for export for civil operators in the West. Defects of the civil design, which must add to the type's vulnerability in combat, include a fuel system which could be rendered inoperative by a single leak. However, it was reported in 1978 that an improved version of the Mi-8 was under development. About 1,000 of the basic version had been built by 1974.

Most military Mi-8s in Warsaw Pact service appear to be armed, usually carrying two weapon pylons on outriggers on each side of the fuselage. These are generally used for carrying rocket pods. Machine-guns do not seem to be permanently installed on the Mi-8, but it is reported that Soviet airborne troops are trained to fire their own small-arms from pivoted mountings in the windows. One report refers to an Mi-8 version with attachments for up to six rocket pods, each surmounted by a launcher for an anti-tank guided weapon. Some Mi-8s also feature an oblong housing under the tailboom; it is possible that this is the electrical battery, moved aft for centre-of-gravity considerations, rather than a doppler radar as reported elsewhere.

The Mi-8's armament is presumably intended for self-defence in the form of fire suppression during landings in hostile territory. The type is too large for aggressive use in combat, its size and conventional rotor system making it less manoeuvrable than a specialized attack helicopter. The ATGW-armed version does not appear to be standard. However, a salvo of unguided rockets may prove effective in keeping the defenders' heads down while the helicopters land and unload their cargoes, by far the most dangerous point of a mission.

A specialized role in which the Mi-8 has been seen is minesweeping, a number of aircraft of this type having been ferried to Egypt

in 1974 to assist in the clearing of the Suez Canal. It is not known whether this was an entirely *ad hoc* operation, or whether the Mi-8, rather than its amphibious relative the Mi-14 'Haze', is the Soviet navy's standard minesweeping helicopter. The Mi-8, however, does not appear to be operable at sea, the aircraft used in the Egyptian operation being carried shrouded on the deck of a helicopter carrier.

Type: twin-engined medium transport helicopter
Powerplant: two 1,500-shp (1119-kW) Isotov TV-2-1117A turboshafts
Performance: maximum speed 145 mph (230 km/h); cruising speed 125 mph (200 km/h); range with 6,500-lb (3000-kg) payload 265 mph (425 km); hovering ceiling 14,765 ft (4500 m)
Weights: empty 15,780 lb (7420 kg); maximum payload 8,800 lb (4000 kg); maximum take-off (VTO) 26,500 lb (12000 kg)
Dimensions: main rotor diameter 69 ft 10¼ in (21.29 m); fuselage length 60 ft 1 in (18.31 m); height 18 ft 4½ in (5.6 m); main rotor disc area 3,828 sq ft (355 m²)

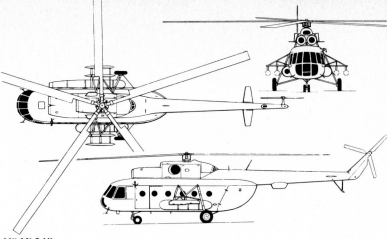

Mil Mi-8 Hip

Armament: normally, up to four 16 × 57-mm rocket pods on fuselage pylons
Operators: Afghanistan, Bangladesh, Czechoslovakia, East Germany, Egypt, Ethiopia, Finland, Hungary, Iraq, North Korea, Libya, Pakistan, Peru, Poland, Romania, Somalia, South Yemen, Syria, USSR, Vietnam, Yugoslavia

The Mil Mi-8 Hip remains the most numerous of helicopters in the Egyptian inventory with nearly 70 currently on strength.

Six Mil Mi-8P passenger helicopters, with the large windows of the civil version, form the chief rotary-wing transport element of Finland's Ilmavoimat. Since delivery they have been equipped with weather radar under the nose.

Mil Mi-14 Haze

It is not surprising that the Soviet navy's land-based anti-submarine warfare (ASW) helicopter, the Mil Mi-14 'Haze' should be derived from the Mi-8 'Hip'; what is surprising, however, is that its development should have taken so long to come about. Once the requirement was formulated, the evolution of the type was fairly rapid; the prototype, designated V-14, was reported to be flying in 1973, and the operational version was seen in service in 1977. It is steadily replacing such aircraft as the ASW version of the Mi-4 'Hound' (possibly designated Mi-4MA) while the Kamov Ka-25 'Hormone' will probably continue to be the Soviet navy's standard shipboard helicopter.

The powerplant, rotor system and much of the airframe of the Mi-14 appear similar to

those of the Mi-8, the structural difference between the two types being confined mainly to the lower part of the fuselage. The Mi-14 has a flying-boat bow, a watertight hull and rear sponsons carrying stabilizing floats. Unlike that of its land-based progenitor, the landing gear of the Mi-14 is retractable. The Mi-14 is clearly capable of water landings, although like the closely comparable Sikorsky SH-3 series it may be designed for water landings only in an emergency. This is also suggested by the location of the search radar under the nose; repeated immersion in salt water is hardly calculated to extend the life of electronic equipment, while the radome would not improve stability on the water. The tail bumper of the Mi-8 is retained, and carries a small pontoon to prevent the tail rotor from

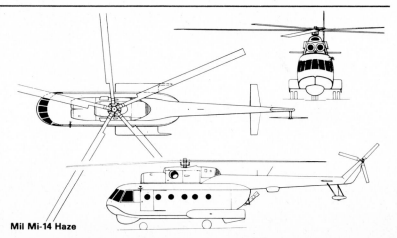

Mil Mi-14 Haze

striking the water. The sponsons presumably contain fuel, supplanting the side-mounted tanks of the land-based aircraft.

Externally visible operational equipment includes the search radar beneath the nose and magnetic anomaly detector 'bird' attached to the rear of the fuselage proper, under the tail boom, and towed on a long cable when in use, well away from the magnetic disturbance produced by the helicopter. It is likely that, like the SH-3, the Mi-14 carries a 'dunking' sonar in the fuselage, and that the helicopter can lower this into the water while hovering. Weapons are presumably carried on the lower fuselage sides forward of the sponsons, close to the centre of gravity.

The effectiveness of the Mi-14 is difficult to assess, depending as it does on the quantity of its sensors and the data processing equipment installed. It is likely that the systems installed are better than those of the Ka-25, and that like the other helicopter the Mi-14 will be updated and improved in service. Its main advantage over the Ka-25 is its greater range.

Becoming the standard shore-based Soviet Naval Aviation ASW helicopter, the Mil Mi-14 Haze-A has been developed from the Mi-8 Hip.

Type: amphibious (?) anti-submarine warfare (ASW) helicopter
Powerplant, Performance, Weights and

Dimensions are not known, but assumed to be generally similar to those of the Mi-8
Armament: offensive stores almost certainly

include mines, depth charges and homing torpedoes
Operators: USSR

Mil Mi-24 Hind

The Mil Mi-24 'Hind' is a large and intimidating armed helicopter, and has been a cause for controversy and a source of puzzlement in the West since it was first observed in 1973. At first it was thought to be a straightforward armed version of the Mi-8, but it soon became clear that the new helicopter was rather smaller than its predecessor, although apparently using the same engines. The early 'Hind-A' appeared to be a conventional squad-carrying helicopter, with the addition of rocket pods and missile rails. This sort of combination had been experimentally used by the US Army in Vietnam, but had led to the development of specialized armed helicopters with automatic turreted armament and small silhouette, designed to escort the troop carriers, while other helicopters armed with guided weapons

took on the enemy armour. The 'Hind-A', however, appeared to combine all three elements into one unwieldy package: a troop carrier with guns for self-defence, but equipped with rockets for defence suppression and anti-tank missiles for attacking enemy armour.

The conundrum of how the Mi-24 was to be used became even more perplexing with the arrival in 1975 of the 'Hind-D', adding to the earlier versions' armament a highly complex nose gun installation. The 'Hind-D' also features a more heavily protected cockpit, considerably less spacious than that of its predecessor. One fear was that the gun armament is intended for use against NATO's own anti-tank helicopters in Western Europe. By early 1979 it had been estimated that more than 800 'Hinds' were in service, both 'Hind-A to -C' and 'Hind-D' being in volume pro-

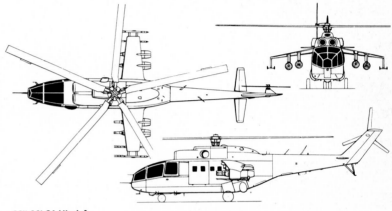

Mil Mi-24 Hind-A

One of the latest and best photographs of the Mil Mi-24 version known as 'Hind-A' to NATO, this appears to show a six-bladed main rotor, though this may be an illusion caused by the upward flexure of the blades. Since 1974 possibly 1,000 of several versions of these versatile machines have entered Soviet service.

duction. The 'Hind-C' lacks provision for anti-tank guided weapons, while the 'Hind-B' was an early variant which does not appear to have entered service.

The Mi-24 seems to combine the power-plant and transmission of the Mi-8 with a smaller rotor and airframe, retaining the fan-cooled transmission characteristic of large Mil turbine helicopters. The cabin is considerably smaller than that of the 28-seater Mi-8, but should be able to accommodate a 12-man infantry section without difficulty, off-loading them via a large side door forward of the anhedralled stub wings. The latter carry missiles on downward tip extensions, presumably to allow easy reloading from ground level while carrying the wing spar above the cabin. The rough-field landing gear is retractable.

The forward fuselage of the 'Hind-A' comprises a spacious 'greenhouse' canopy for the crew of three. Access to the flight-deck is via two large sliding windows, which can be opened in flight and may be used for defensive machine-guns. Visible avionic equipment includes a small blister under the forward fuselage (possibly a missile sight) and an electro-optical head on the left inner pylon.

The 'Hind-D' forward fuselage features two tandem blown canopies on separate cockpits, reducing the chance of both crewmen being disabled with one hit. The windscreens are made of flat armour glass. In the extreme nose is a turret mounting a four-barrel gun, possibly of 12.7-mm calibre, although most sources report that it is larger. Aft of the turret are two installations: a blister very similar to that under the nose of the 'Hind-A' and a larger installation which appears to contain a sensor slaved in elevation to the gun. This may be an assisted gunsight (either infra-red or TV). A large low-airspeed probe juts from the forward (gunner's) wind-

screen.

Now entering service on the 'Hind-D' is a new heavy anti-tank missile designated AT-6 'Spiral' by NATO, possibly weighing as much as 200 lb (90 kg) per round and with a 6-mile (10-km) range. It it likely to be laser-guided, with semi-active seeking, rather than wire-guided like the AT-2 'Swatter' previously carried by 'Hind-D'. It is also believed to be tube-launched, and it is possible that more than four could be carried on one helicopter.

Performance figures for the Mi-24 are difficult to assess, but records established by Soviet women pilots in a helicopter known as the 'A-10' may give a clue. Given that the Mi-24 has as much power as the larger Mi-8, the performance of the 'A-10' is roughly what might be expected. However, its power/weight ratio is considerably less than that of the latest US armed helicopters, and with its relatively old-technology rotor system (similar to that of the Mi-8) the Mi-24 is not likely to be agile. Its large size compared with the Western ideal of a combat helicopter will also make it vulnerable to hostile fire. A surprising feature of the design, which will adversely affect its survivability, is its complete lack of infra-red signature suppression; the exhausts are open from all aspects.

The Mi-24 has been described as a 'helicopter battle-cruiser' and this may not be too bad a summing-up of what the machine does. Its main advantage is its ability to fight in several different ways: by dropping an anti-tank platoon, complete with missiles, while defending itself against ground fire with the nose gun (or in the case of the 'Hind-A', with side guns); by acting as its own escort on troop-carrying flights; or by acting as a tank-killer pure and simple, with a vast capacity for even the heaviest reload rounds. An inevitable corollary of this 'combination of all arms' in a single aircraft, however, is that the vehicle's

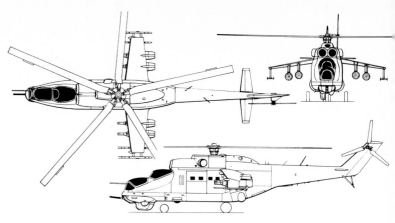

Mil Mi-24 Hind

size and weight rule out evasive flying, and render it difficult to escape alert and well-equipped defences.

Type: ('Hind-A to-C') assault helicopter and ('Hind-D') gunship
Powerplant: two 1,500-shp (1119-kW) Isotov TV-2 turboshafts
Performance: maximum speed 200 mph (320 km/h); cruising speed 160 mph (260 km/h); service ceiling 18,000 ft (5500 m)
Weights: empty 14,000 lb (6500 kg); loaded 22,000 lb (10000 kg)
Dimensions: main rotor diameter 56 ft (17 m); length of fuselage 56 ft (17 m); height 14 ft (4.25 m); main rotor area 2,463 sq ft (227 m²)
Armament: ('Hind-D') four-barrel cannon of 14.5- or 20-mm calibre in nose turret; (all versions) up to four pods each containing

thirty-two 57-mm rockets, plus up to four anti-tank missiles on stub wings; the 'Hind-A' has nose- and side-mounted guns
Operators: USSR

Serving in large numbers with the Soviet 16th Air Army, part of the GSFG (Group of Soviet Forces in Germany) the "Hind-D" is a multi-role attack helicopter of formidable capabilities. Now believed to be designated Mi-27, it has eight weapon pylons, a "Gatling" cannon and a comprehensive array of avionics and sensors. The long pole in the nose is a low-airspeed sensor.

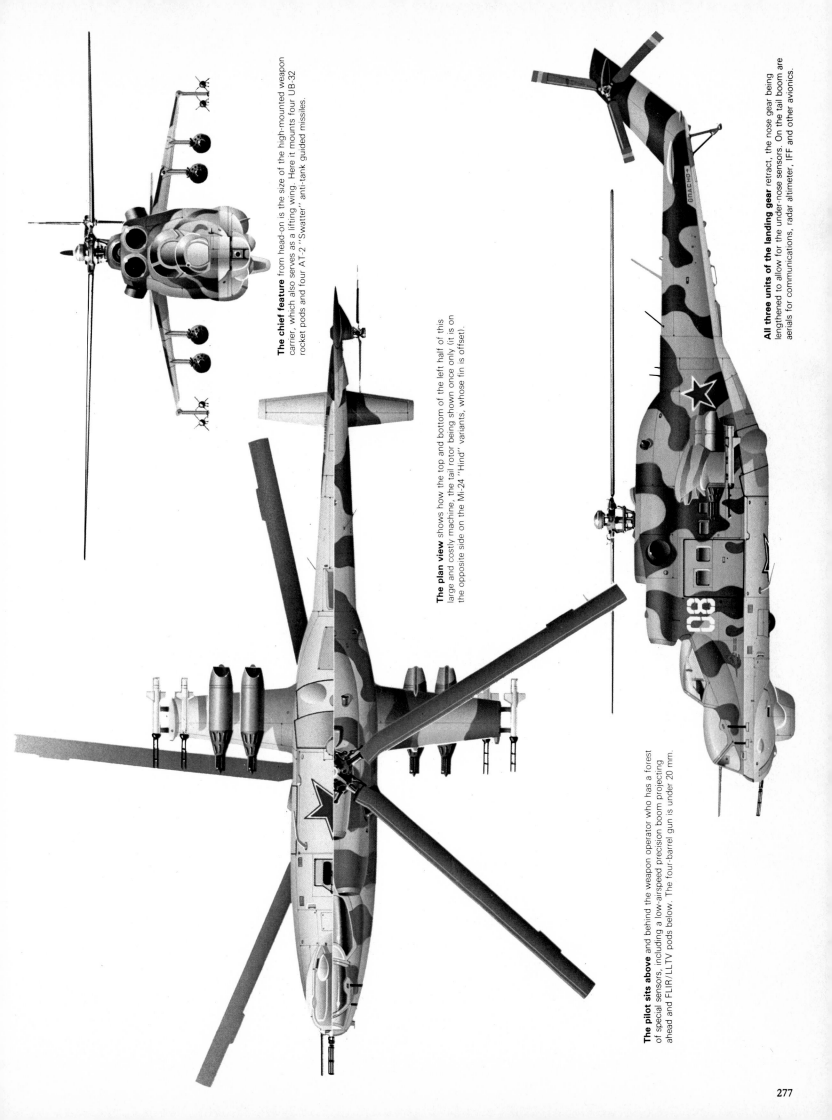

The chief feature from head-on is the size of the high-mounted weapon carrier, which also serves as a lifting wing. Here it mounts four UB-32 rocket pods and four AT-2 "Swatter" anti-tank guided missiles.

The plan view shows how the top and bottom of the left half of this large and costly machine, the tail rotor being shown once only (it is on the opposite side on the Mi-24 "Hind" variants, whose fin is offset).

All three units of the landing gear retract, the nose gear being lengthened to allow for the under-nose sensors. On the tail boom are aerials for communications, radar altimeter, IFF and other avionics.

The pilot sits above and behind the weapon operator who has a forest of special sensors, including a low-airspeed precision boom projecting ahead and FLIR/LLTV pods below. The four-barrel gun is under 20 mm.

Mitsubishi F-1

Mitsubishi's F-1 close-support fighter is an adaptation of the same company's T-2 supersonic trainer for the Japanese Air Self-Defence Force. Design work on the fighter, which was originally designated FS-T2-Kai, began in 1972 and the second and third production T-2 trainers (59-5106 and 59-5107) were converted to prototype F-1s. The first flight of 59-5107 in modified form was made on 3 June 1975, with the second machine following it into the air four days later.

The prototype retained the rear cockpit and canopy of the T-2, with a fire-control system and test equipment in place of the instructor. In the summer of 1975 the fighter prototypes were delivered to the JASDF Air Proving Wing at Gifu for service testing, which was satisfactorily concluded in November 1976.

The first production aircraft (70-8201) made its maiden flight on 16 June 1977, and was handed over to the JASDF at Mitsubishi's Komaki factory in September that year. In early 1979 production orders for 64 aircraft had been placed, against an anticipated requirement of 70.

Behind the cockpit is an avionics compartment (housing a bombing computer) and an inertial navigation system, and on the fin are radar warning aerials. The fuselage structure is basically that of the T-2. The wing has leading-edge flaps, the outer segments of which are extended to create a 'dog tooth', and single-slotted flaps ahead of which are slotted spoilers for roll control. Twin airbrakes and ventral fins are carried under the rear fuselage, aft of the mainwheel bays. The single-piece 'all flying' tailplane and rudder are hydraulically actuated. The landing gear has single wheels, and braking parachute and arrester hook are standard.

Power is provided by two Iskikawajima-Harima TF40-IHI-801A turbofans (licence-built Rolls-Royce/Turboméca Adours). Internal fuel is housed in seven fuselage tanks with a total capacity of 841 Imperial gallons (3823 litres). In addition, 180-Imperial gallon (821-litre) auxiliary fuel tanks can be carried on two underwing pylons, with a third beneath the fuselage.

The F-1's avionics fit includes dual UHF, IFF/SIF, head-up display, radio altimeter, attitude and heading reference system, air-data computer, Tacan, Ferranti inertial navigation system, and a radar warning and homing system. Mitsubishi Electric supplies the multi-mode radar and a fire control system and bombing computer. Built-in armament comprises a 20-mm JM-61 (General Electric) multi-barrel cannon, while four underwing hardpoints, fitted with multiple-ejector racks, allow up to twelve 500-lb (227-kg) bombs to be carried. Alternative loads include rocket pods, drop tanks or two Mitsubishi ASM-1 anti-ship

missiles. For self-defence, the F-1 can carry two or four Sidewinder or Mitsubishi AAM-1 air-to-air missiles on wingtip mountings.

The first JASDF unit to equip with the F-1 was the 3rd *Hiko-tai*, formerly a North American F-86F unit, which reformed with the Mitsubishi fighter at Misawa air base in the spring of 1978; the 8th *Hiko-tai* will follow. The JASDF's original plans called for three 18-aircraft squadrons, but more recent thinking favours a squadron strength of 25. This means that current procurement plans will provide aircraft for only two squadrons.

Type: ground attack fighter
Powerplant: two 7,070-lb (3206-kg) Ishikawajima-Harima TF40-IHI-801A afterburning turbofans

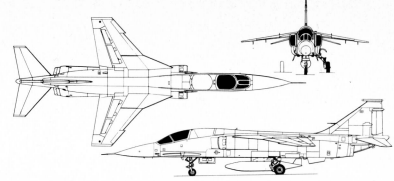

Mitsubishi F-1

Flight development prototype of the F-1, this aircraft was a rebuilt PC-7 T-2 with the rear cockpit occupied by instrumentation. Very few problems were encountered with basic aerodynamics or aircraft systems.

Performance: maximum speed at 36,090 ft (11000 m) Mach 1.6; maximum rate of climb at sea level 35,000 ft (10670 m) per minute; service ceiling 50,000 ft (15240 m); combat radius with 4,000-lb (1814-kg) warload and external tanks 218 miles (351 km)
Weights: empty equipped 14,017 lb 66358 kg); maximum take-off 30,146 lb (13674 kg)
Dimensions: span 25 ft 10¼ in (7.88 m); length 56 ft 9½ in (17.31 m); height 14 ft 4¼ in (4.38 m); wing area 228 sq ft (21.18 m²)
Armament: one 20-mm JM-61 cannon and 6,000 lb (2720 kg) of external stores, including bombs, rockets, drop tanks or Mit-

subishi ASM-1 air-to-surface missiles; wingtip attachments for up to four Sidewinder or Mitsubishi AAM-1 air-to-air missiles
Operator: Japan

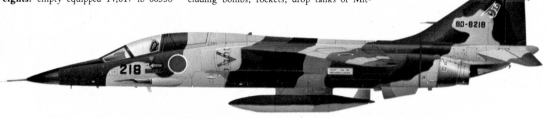

Mitsubishi F-1 fighter of 3 Sqn, 3rd Air Wing, Japanese Air Self-Defence Force, based at Misawa and formed in March 1978.

Mitsubishi MU-2

After the end of World War II the Mitsubishi Jukogyo Kabushiki Kaisha ceased aircraft production, but the 1952 peace treaty restored the opportunity for aviation development. The company undertook overhaul and licence assembly, and in 1959 started the design of a twin-turboprop light transport. The MU-2 was the world's first small twin-turboprop transport, the 562-shp (419-kW) Turboméca Astazou IIK being selected for the prototype MU-2A. Unusual features included full-span Fowler flaps and spoilers rather than ailerons. The aircraft was designed to have STOL characteristics. Its fuselage was pressurized and some 180 gallons (820 litres) of standard fuel capacity was contained in fixed wingtip tanks.

The first MU-2A flew on 14 September 1963, followed by a further two prototypes. These had a gross weight of 7,937 lb (3600 kg) and were able to attain a top speed of 328 mph (525 km/h). It was, however, obvious that the MU-2 could survive commercially only by entering the US market, and this meant a change of engine. As a result, the standard production version became the MU-2B, powered by two Garrett AiResearch TPE331-25A engines, and the first of this model flew at Nagoya on 11 March 1965.

The MU-2 has gone through a number of variants all based on the standard MU-2B or the stretched MU-2G. The short models include the MU-2B, C, D, E, F, K, M and P; stretched aircraft have been the MU-2G, J, L and N. Some variants have a more powerful TPE331. The MU-2C and -2E are pure military variants of the design.

From an early stage the MU-2 was assembled at San Angelo, Texas, from components built in Nagoya, and the MU-2 embodies a large American content in systems, engines and avionics. Some 420 MU-2s were in service in North America at the end of 1978. The Japanese market is small, but the military did adopt the MU-2 in a variety of applications. The first military model was the MU-2C, designated LR-1 for service with the JGSDF (Japanese Ground Self Defence Force). The initial LR-1 was based on the MU-2B, but was not pressurized and the wingtip tanks were replaced by additional rear-fuselage tankage. Later LR-1s were based on the MU-2K and MU-2M, and are used for reconnaissance and general transport. Provision is made for vertical cameras installed in forward-fuselage fairings, nose-mounted 13-mm guns, and SLAR.

The Air Rescue Wing of the JASDF has taken delivery of the MU-2S, based on the -2E which is readily identified by the thimble radome and bulged side windows. These

search and rescue aircraft have a large sliding door on the left to allow dinghy drops, and are fitted with supplementary tankage. MU-2JF calibration aircraft are based on the commercial model MU-2J.

Mitsubishi has not been permitted to export the MU-2 in its military form as a result of

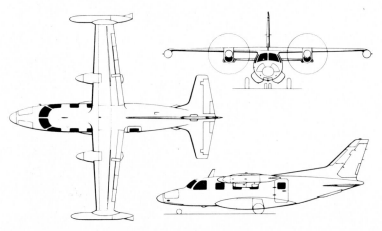

Mitsubishi MU-2L

Self-Defence law restrictions. However, like the Learjet, the type has been adopted by Swedair as a target-tug.

Type: (MU-2S) light search and rescue aircraft
Powerplant: two 715-shp (533-kW) Garrett

AiResearch TPE331-25A turboprops
Performance: maximum cruising speed at 10,000 ft (3050 m) 296 mph (474 km/h); economical cruising speed at 20,000 ft (6100 m) 280 mph (450 km/h); stalling speed (flaps down) 77 mph (124 km/h); rate of climb at sea level 2,200 ft (678 m) per minute; service ceiling 26,000 ft (7900 m); maximum range with 30-minute reserve 1,300 miles (2100 km)
Weights: empty equipped 5,650 lb (2560 kg); maximum take-off 10,053 lb (4560 kg)
Dimensions: span 39 ft 2 in (11.93 m); length 35 ft 1 in (10.70 m); height 12 ft 11 in (3.94 m); wing area 178 sq ft (16.55 m²)
Operator: Japan

Mitsubishi's MU-2 is fast and nimble, despite having propellers, and versions exist for many purposes.

Mitsubishi T-2

The Mitsubishi T-2, the first supersonic aircraft to be designed and built in Japan, is a two-seat trainer which bears more than a passing resemblance to the SEPECAT Jaguar attack aircraft and is powered by the same engine: the Rolls-Royce/Turboméca Adour turbofan, built under licence by Ishikawajima-Harima Heavy Industries as the TF40. Mitsubishi was selected as prime contractor in September 1967 and was awarded a contract to build prototypes in March 1970. The first of these XT-2s made its maiden flight in July 1971, the second following in December of that year. A month earlier the first aircraft had exceeded the speed of sound on its 30th flight. The prototypes were handed over to the Japanese Air Self-Defence Force in December 1971 and March 1972 respectively for further trials. Two additional development aircraft ordered in 1970 made their maiden flights in April and July 1972, and the flight-test programme was completed in March 1974.

The T-2 entered JASF service in 1975, and two squadrons had been equipped by the end of 1978. The total was expected to rise to 66 aircraft, with production continuing until March 1981. Some of the aircraft are fitted

with a single JM-61 six-barrel 20-mm cannon in the left side of the lower forward fuselage, allowing the aircraft to be used for weapon training, and two were built to FST-2 *Kai* standard as prototypes of the F-1 attack fighter.

The T-2 can carry up to three 183-Imperial gallon (833-litre) drop tanks beneath the wings and fuselage, and wingtip attachments for air-to-air missiles are provided. Other stores can be carried on the three standard pylons if desired.

Type: two-seat advanced and weapons trainer
Powerplant: two 7,140-lb (3245-kg) Ishikawajima-Harima Heavy Industries TF40-IHI-801A afterburning turbofans (licence-built Rolls-Royce/Turboméca Adours)
Performance: maximum level speed at 36,000 ft (10975 m) Mach 1.6; maximum sea-level rate of climb 35,000 ft (10670 m) per minute; ceiling 50,000 ft (15240 m); maximum ferry range with external tanks 1,785 miles (2870 km)
Weights: operational empty 13,662 lb (6197 kg); maximum take-off (clean) 21,330 lb (9675 kg)
Dimensions: span 25 ft 10¼ in (7.88 m);

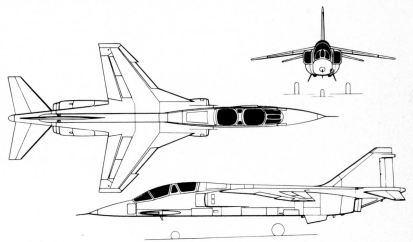

Mitsubishi T-2

length 58 ft 6¾ in (17.85 m); height 14 ft 4¾ in (4.39 m); wing area 228 sq ft (21.18 m²)
Armament: one JM-61 20-mm cannon in weapon-trainer version; wingtip attachments

for air-to-air missiles, and three pylons beneath wings and fuselage for a variety of stores
Operator: Japan

This neat machine, closely modelled upon the similarly powered Jaguar, was the original prototype Mitsubishi XT-2 trainer, flown in July 1971. From this have been developed not only the production T-2, standard supersonic trainer of the JASDF, but also the single-seat F-1 multi-role fighter.

Morane-Saulnier MS.760 Paris

In January 1953 Morane-Saulnier flew the prototype MS.755 Fleuret, a two-seat jet trainer which competed with the Fouga Magister for an air force order. The Fleuret, with its side-by-side seating, lost the competition but its design formed the basis for the MS.760 Paris. Although designed primarily as a high-speed liaison aircraft, the Paris can really be considered as the forerunner of the executive jet. The first prototype flew on 29 July, 1954. Interest was shown by the French military authorities and orders were placed on behalf of the air force and navy. The first production model was flown on 27 February, 1958, and by spring 1961 orders for 137 had been received from a number of countries for both civil and military use.

A batch of 48 sets of components was supplied to Argentina for assembly at the government factory in Cordoba, while another big customer was Brazil, which received 12 for training, 10 for liaison and eight for photographic work. Final delivery of the Brazilian batch, on 31 March, 1961, was a Paris II, with two 1,058-lb (480-kg) Marboré VI turbojets. This model superseded the Paris I and by the time production was completed in 1964 a total of 165 aircraft of the two series had been built, in addition to those assembled in Argentina.

France has the largest surviving Paris fleet in military use; about 25 are with the air force, based at Villacoublay, with others at Metz, Bordeaux and Aix. The navy still uses around 10, some of which are at Lann-Bihoué with *Escadrille* 25, while several others serve alongside Dassault Falcon 10s at Landivisiau on communications, radar and continuation training.

About 10 are still used by the Argentine air force for training at Cordoba, and the single Paris supplied to the Paraguayan air force by the Argentine government in 1962 is thought to be still in service for training at Campo Grande, Asunción.

Type: twin-jet liaison aircraft
Powerplant: two 882-lb (400-kg) Turboméca Marboré II turbojets
Performance: maximum speed 405 mph (650 km/h) at sea level; 345 mph (555 km/h) at 23,000 ft (7000 m); cruising speed 350 mph (570 km/h) at 16,400 ft (5000 m); initial rate of climb at sea level 2,264 ft (690 m) per minute; rate of climb at 23,000 ft (7000 m) 780 ft (240 m) per minute; service ceiling 32,800 ft (10000 m); range at 23,000 ft (7000 m) 930 miles (1500 km)
Weights: empty 4,280 lb (1945 kg); loaded 7,650 lb (3470 kg)
Dimensions: span (over tip tanks) 33 ft 3 in (10.15 m); length 33 ft 0 in (10.05 m); height 8 ft 6 in (2.60 m); wing area 193.68 sq ft (18.0 m^2)
Armament: (Paris I as a weapons trainer)

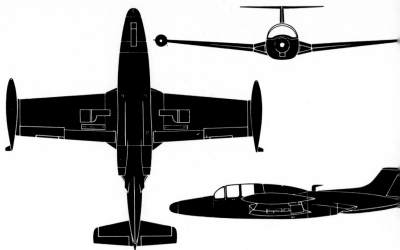

Morane-Saulnier MS.760 Paris

two 7.5-mm (0.295-in) nose-mounted machine-guns; racks for two 110-lb (50-kg) bombs or four 89-mm (3.5-in) rockets beneath wings
Operators: Argentina, France, Paraguay

Mudry CAP 10

In 1955 Auguste Mudry took the first steps towards the design of a fully-aerobatic monoplane, his objective being to produce a modern replacement for the pre-war Stampe SV-4 biplane. The popular Piel Super Emeraude (emerald) was taken as a basis for the design, resulting in a prototype known as the C.P.100. When this was lost in a fatal accident in January 1967, further modifications were made to the design to produce a new and improved version known as the CAP 10. More powerful than the Super Emeraude, the CAP 10 prototype was built by CAARP (Co-opérative des Ateliers Aéronautiques de la Région Parisienne), which since 1965 had been responsible for production of the Super Emeraude. The first CAP 10 made its initial flight in August 1968 and was, like the C.P.100, a side-by-side two-seater with dual controls. After manufacturer's trials, service evaluation, and the award of a French type certificate on 4 September 1970, an initial production batch of 50 was begun, CAARP building the fuselages, with Avions Mudry at Bernay building the rest and doing the final assembly and flight testing.

Construction is mainly of wood, with the rear fuselage fabric-covered and plastics used for the engine cowling and some other components. The airframe is stressed to g limits of +6 and -4.5. The French air force ordered 26 (later increased to 30), and deliveries of these began in the spring of 1970 to the *École de Formation Initiale du PN,* a flying school at Clermont-Ferrand-Aulnat where pilot selection and basic training are carried out. The CAP 10 is also used by the *Armée de l'Air's Équipe de Voltige Aérienne* (EVA), an aerobatic training, competition and display unit based at Salon-de-Provence. Current production models are designated CAP 10B.

Type: two-seat basic and aerobatic trainer
Powerplant: one 180-hp (134-kW) Lycoming IO-360-B2F flat-four piston engine
Performance: maximum diving and never-exceed speed 211 mph (340 km/h); maximum speed at sea level 168 mph (270 km/h); maximum cruising speed (75% power) 155 mph (250 km/h); range with maximum fuel 745 miles (1200 km); maximum rate of climb at sea level over 1,180 ft (360 m) per minute; service ceiling 16,400 ft (5000 m)
Weights: empty equipped 1,190 lb (540 kg);

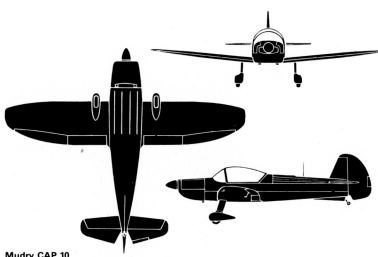

Mudry CAP 10

maximum take-off (aerobatic) 1,675 lb (760 kg); maximum take-off (utility) 1,830 lb (830 kg)
Dimensions: span 26 ft 5¼ in (8.06 m); length 23 ft 6 in (7.16 m); height 8 ft 4½ in (2.55 m); wing area 116.79 sq ft (10.85 m^2)
Armament: none
Operators: France

Mudry CAP 20

The Mudry CAP 20, although to outward appearances a direct development of the CAP 10, has in fact undergone quite a lot of redesign. Being intended solely for aerobatics, it is a single-seater, has a more powerful engine, and the airframe is stressed for g limits of +8 and -6. Other less obvious differences are that the dimensions are slightly smaller overall, and the wings have no dihedral (those of the CAP 10 have 5°) and no flaps. The canopy opens sideways to the right and, as in the CAP 10, the fuel system is adapted to permit short periods of inverted flight. The CAP 20 prototype (F-WPXU) made its first flight on 29 July 1969, its construction having been sponsored by the SGAC, the French civil aircraft licensing body, for national and international competitions. The French air force's *Équipe de Voltige Aérienne* received six examples of the CAP 20A initial production version, with lighter-weight landing gear, and modified wings with larger ailerons were introduced on the CAP 20B of 1974.

A new prototype (F-WVKY) was flown on 15 January 1976, with the designation CAP 20L-180. The suffix letter (for *léger*) indicates that this is a lighter model, and that the prototype had a 180-hp (134-kW) engine. The next batch of 25 production aircraft in 1978-79

have a more powerful engine and are designated CAP 20LS-200. Prior to the CAARP/Mudry merger in 1977, CAP 20 production took place at the former company's factory at Beynes, but both CAP types are now manufactured entirely by Mudry at Bernay; combined CAP 10/20 production (including civil sales) passed the 100 mark in 1978. A CAP 21, using a CAP 20L fuselage and a new wing, was then being developed.

Type: single-seat aerobatic aircraft
Powerplant: (CAP 20LS-200) one 200-hp (149-kW) Lycoming AIO-360-B1B flat-four piston engine
Performance: (CAP 20LS-200) maximum diving and never-exceed speed 230 mph (370 km/h); maximum cruising speed (75% power) 165 mph (265 km/h); maximum endurance 2 hours; rate of climb at sea level 2,755 ft (840 m) per minute
Weights: (CAP 20LS-200) empty 1,058 lb (480 kg); maximum take-off (aerobatic) 1,433 lb (650 kg)
Dimensions: span 24 ft 10 in (7.57 m); length 21 ft 2½ in (6.46 m); height 5 ft 0 in (1.52 m); wing area 112.7 sq ft (10.47 m^2)
Armament: none
Operators: France

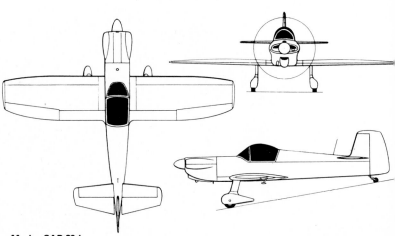

Mudry CAP 20 L

Myasishchev M-4/201 Bison

One of the Soviet Union's most underestimated aircraft, the Myasishchev bomber usually known as the M-4 'Bison' has probably been at least as important to the development of Long-Range Aviation (DA) and the AVMF (Soviet Naval Aviation) as the better known Tupolev Tu-20 'Bear'. The type is often dismissed as a near-failure, partly because it was not appreciated for many years that what had been identified as a special record-breaking version was in fact the difinitive production model of the aircraft.

The availability of the massive Mijulin AM-3 turbojet made it a logical step to incorporate four of these engines in a heavy bomber, as well as using them in the twin-engined Tu-16 'Badger'.

The Myasishchev bureau was formed in 1951 to build such an aircraft, and the first prototype flew in early 1953, shortly after its US contemporary, the Boeing B-52 Stratofortress. However, by that time it was clear that the original version would have inadequate range, and it appears that only a few of the AM-3-powered aircraft (designated 'Bison-A' by NATO) went into service. The heavier and considerably more powerful Myasishchev 201M 'Bison-B' flew in early 1955. Among other changes, two of the five gun turrets fitted to the original aircraft were removed to save weight.

The 'Bison-B' was one of the first Soviet types to carry a flight-probe, and many of the old 'Bison-As' were converted to tankers with a hose-reel in the bomb bay. With the rise of the Soviet navy, many of the 'Bison-Bs' were transferred to the AVMF as long-range reconnaissance aircraft, and later development, the 'Bison-C', carried a large search radar in an extended nose. All 'Bisons' have ventral radar installations and observation blisters, and appear to be equipped for electronic intelligence (Elint) operations.

The 201M established a series of impressive world records in 1959, although at that time the designation was thought to apply to the M-52 supersonic bomber; only in 1967 was it realised that the 201M was a 'Bison' variant. One aircraft attained 638 mph (1028 km/h) on a 1000-km (621-mile) closed circuit with a 59,525-lb (27000-kg) payload, simultaneously setting a record for zero payload over the same course. The 201M lifted a · 121,275-lb (55000-kg) payload to 43,036 ft (13121 m), a record unmatched by any aircraft until the appearance of the Lockheed C-5A.

The 201M has not been seen with air-to-surface missiles, possibly because its twin-bogie undercarriage design results in a lower ground clearance than that of the Tu-95. As a free-fall bomber, it was probably obsolete almost as soon as it entered service, the increasing performance of interceptors and missile systems rendering it a relatively easy target. As far as is known, the 'Bison' has never been converted for low-level attack as have the B-52 and BAe Vulcan. It is most unlikely that any of the 201Ms are still equipped as bombers, serving instead as tankers and reconnaissance aircraft. The old AM-3-powered 'Bison-As' have probably all been retired.

The powerplants of the 201M were identified as D-15s on the occasion of the record attempts; although D stands simply for 'engine', this system of designation was associated with the Soloviev bureau in the late 1950s and early 1960s, and the designation D-15 fits in with the numerical series of Soloviev engines. The D-20 flew in the Tu-124 'Cookpot' in 1960, and as the D-20 was an early low-bypass-ratio turbofan, it is possible that it is a scaled-down version of the 201M.

Type: strategic bomber, tanker and maritime reconnaissance aircraft (specification for Myasishchev 201 'Bison-C')
Powerplant: four 28,500 lb (13000 kg) Soloviev D-15 (almost certainly bypass) turbojets
Performance: maximum speed 680 mph (1100 km/h) or Mach 0.95 at 10,000 ft (3000 m); cruising speed 560 mph (900 km/h); service ceiling 56,000 ft (17000 m); range with 11,000-lb (5000-kg) weapon load 11,200 miles (18000 km)
Weights: empty 198,500 lb (90000 kg); normal take-off 365,000 lb (165000 kg); overload take-off 463,000 lb (210000 kg)
Dimensions: span 172 ft 2 in (52.5 m); length 175 ft 2 in (53.4 m); wing area 3,440 sq ft (320 m²)
Armament: Six 23-mm NR-23 cannon in dorsal, ventral and tail barbettes, and up to 33,000 lb (15000 kg) of internal stores
Operators: USSR

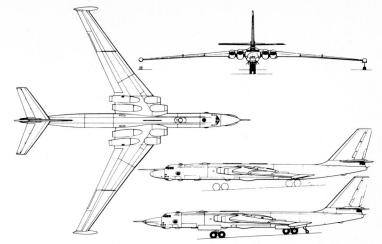

Myasishchev M-4 Bison C

Though built in the 1950s the large four-jet Myasishchev M-4 'Bison' continues as a strategic surveillance platform and tanker. This example is of the 'Bison-C' variety, believed to operate only with the AV-MF Naval Aviation.

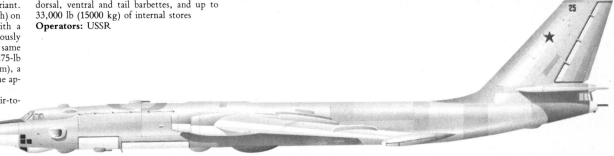

Myasishchev M-4 strategic bomber, code-named Bison-C, operated by the Aviatsiya Del'nevo Deistviya (Long Range Aviation) of the Soviet Air Force.

NAMC YS-11

The Nikon Aeroplane Manufacturing Corporation (NAMC) YS-11 twin-turboprop airliner was sponsored by the Japanese government and a group of private companies to provide a short/medium range transport for Japanese airlines and for export. The major industrial participants in the NAMC consortium are Mitsubishi Heavy Industries, Kawasaki Aircraft, Fuji Heavy Industries, Shin Meiwa Industry, Japan Aircraft Manufacturing Company and Showa Aircraft Industry. The prototype flew on 30 August 1962.

The YS-11 was built in four basic versions: the YS-11-100 is a passenger version seating 60, the YS-11A-200 offers an increase in payload of 2,970 lb (1350 kg), the YS-11A-300 is a mixed passenger/freight variant, while the YS-11A-400 is an all-cargo version capable of carrying 2,860 cu ft (81.0 m³) of freight or 42 troops. The wings carry Fowler flaps and house 1,600 Imperial gallons (7270 litres) of fuel in tanks inboard of the engines and integral tanks outboard. Standard avionics include VHF, VOR/LOC, ADF, marker beacon and ILS. Optional aids include weather radar, autopilot and DME. The YS-11 is designed for two-crew operation.

The Japanese Air Self-Defence Force took delivery of four YS-11-100s (FY 1964 and 1965 allocations), one YS-11A-218 (FY 1970),

one YS-11A-305 (FY 1968) and seven YS-11A-402s (FY 1969, 1970 and 1971). These operate with the Air Transport Wing (Yusoh Koku-dan), flying alongside the Kawasaki C-1A in No 1, 2 and 3 Sqns. The YS-11 is also used by the Air Self-Defence Force's Air Traffic Control and Weather Wing to check navaids.

In 1974 the Air Self-Defence Force decided to convert one of its YS-11 transports to replace a Curtiss C-46 in the ECM training role: ALQ-3 was installed and the aircraft (designated YS-11E) was delivered to the Electronic Warfare Training Unit (Koku Sohtai Denshi Kunren-tai), operating alongside modified Lockheed T-33As.

The second major user is Japan's Maritime Self-Defence Force, which operates 10. The roles undertaken by the naval YS-11s are transport and ASW training: the last of the 182 YS-11s produced was an ASW trainer, delivered on 1 February 1974. The 61st Koku-tai, based at Atsugi, flies four YS-11 transports and one Grumman S-2A. As with the Air Self-Defence Force's fleet, the naval YS-11s perform both personnel and cargo transport duties, two of the machines being YS-11-112s and two being YS-11A-404s. The six ASW trainers are YS-11A-206 series, designated YS-11T. They operate within the Maritime Self-

Defence Force's Air Training Command (Kyohiku-Koku-Shuhdan) and are assigned to the 205th Kyohiku Koku-tai (training squadron), based at Atsugi. ASV radar, ESM and other ASW sensors are fitted.

The Philippine air force operates four YS-11 in the VIP transport role with the 700th Special Mission Wing, based at Nichols Air Base, Pasay City.

Type: short/medium-range transport
Powerplant: two 3,060-ehp (2283-kW) Rolls-Royce Dart Mk 542-10 turboprops
Performance: maximum cruising speed at 15,000 ft (4575 m) 294 mph (472 km/h); economical cruising speed at 20,000 ft (6100 m) 292 mph (470 km/h); rate of climb at sea level 1,220 ft (372 m) per minute; range with maximum fuel 860 miles (1390 km); range with maximum payload 690 miles (1110 km)
Weights: empty equipped 32,170 lb (14590 kg); take-off 54,010 lb (24500 kg); payload 16,330 lb (7410 kg)
Dimensions: span 104 ft 11¾ in (32.0 m); length 86 ft 3½ in (26.30 m); height 29 ft 5 ¾ in (8.99 m); wing area 1,020.4 sq ft (94.8 m²)
Operators: Japan, Philippines

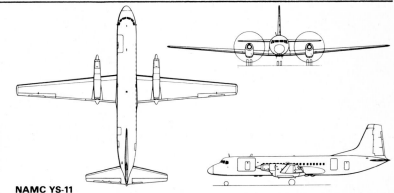

NAMC YS-11

Neiva C-42/L-42 Regente

Broadly resembling the Cessna 150/180 series of lightplanes, the Neiva Regente was built for the FAB (*Forca Aérea Brasileira*) in two basic versions, the C-42 and L-42. These were preceded by a civil-registered prototype, the Neiva Model 360C, which flew for the first time on 7 September 1961 at Sao José dos Campos and was powered by a 145-hp (108-kW) Continental O-300 engine. The C-42 (originally U-42) initial production version was generally similar, and 80 were built as utility transports for the FAB by the Sociedade Construtora Aeronáutica Neiva Ltda. The first of these made its maiden flight in February 1965, and the last was delivered during 1968.

Meanwhile, as a potential replacement for the Brazilian air force's L-6 Paulistinha (another Neiva design) and Cessna O-1 Bird Dog lightplanes in the air observation post and liaison roles, Neiva had in January 1967 flown a modified YL-42 prototype of the Regente. This differed from the C-42 in having a two/three-seat cabin, the fuselage to the rear being cut down to permit all-round glazing so as to improve the field of view; and a higher-powered flat-six engine with fuel injection replaced the flat-four of the C-42. Known in production form as the Neiva Model 420L,

and by the FAB designation L-42, this version of the Regente entered production in 1968, the first series-built example flying in June 1969. Deliveries of 40 production L-42s were completed in March 1971. Although the C-42 is unarmed, the L-42 can carry light weapons under the wings, and most of those in FAB service are operated by two *Esquadroes de Ligacao e Observacao* (liaison and observation squadrons) which, despite their title, also perform an additional COIN (counter-insurgency) role.

Type: four-seat light utility transport (C-42) and two/three-seat liaison and observation aircraft (L-42)
Powerplant: (C-42) one 180-hp (134-kW) Lycoming O-360-A1D flat-four piston engine; (L-42) one 210-hp (157-kW) Continental IO-360-D flat-six piston engine
Performance: (C-42) maximum speed at sea level 137 mph (220 km/h); cruising speed at 5,085 ft (1550 m) 132 mph (212 km/h); range with maximum payload 562 miles (904 km); range with maximum fuel 577 miles (928 km); maximum rate of climb at sea level 689 ft (210 m) per minute; service ceiling 11,810 ft (3600 m)
(L-42 has marginally better speed and range,

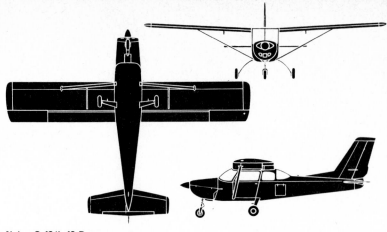

Neiva C-42/L-42 Regente

and approximately 33% better ceiling and climb)
Weights: (C-42) empty equipped 1,411 lb (640 kg); (L-42) empty equipped 1,623 lb (736 kg); (both) maximum take-off 2,293 lb (1040 kg)
Dimensions: span 29 ft 11½ in (9.13 m);

length 23 ft 7¾ in (7.21 m); height 9 ft 7¼ in (2.93 m): wing area 144.77 sq ft (13.45 m²)
Armament: L-42 has provision for light bombs, rockets or other stores on four underwing pylons
Operators: Brazil

Neiva T-25 Universal

The Neiva Model N621 Universal was designed in the early 1960s to meet a requirement, and first flew in prototype form on 29 April 1966. It is an all-metal low-wing monoplane, with a fully-retractable tricycle landing gear, and seats the instructor and pupil side by side (with full dual controls) under a rearward-sliding framed canopy. Fully aerobatic in two-seat configuration, it can also carry a third occupant on an optional third seat at the rear. Ordered by the Brazilian government in 1968 as a replacement for the North American T-6 Texan, the first production Universal was flown on 7 April 1971, and 150 were built initially for the Brazilian air force, with deliveries beginning in the following autumn and ending in early 1975. A further 28 were ordered in 1978. These all have the air force designation T-25, and serve both as basic, advanced and weapons trainers at the Brazilian Air Force Academy and as light ground-attack aircraft with reconnaissance/attack squadrons. The Chilean army received 10 similar aircraft in 1975.

A more powerful version, with greater attack capability, is the N622 Universal II, a YT-25B prototype of which was undergoing

development in 1978–79 as a potential successor to the original model. This differs from the earlier version principally in having a 400-hp (298-kW) Lycoming IO-720 flat-eight engine in a redesigned nose, and strengthened wings with six hardpoints, enabling it to carry a mixture of machine-gun or rocket pods, or small bombs. Other changes intended for the T-25B production version (about 80 of which are likely to be needed by the Brazilian air force) include a redesigned cockpit canopy, a taller fin and rudder, and a small dorsal fin.

Type: two/three-seat basic trainer
Powerplant: one 300-hp (224-kW) Lycoming IO-540-K1D5 flat-six piston engine
Performance: (two-seat) maximum speed at sea level 186 mph (300 km/h); maximum cruising speed (75% power) at sea level 177 mph (285 km/h); range at maximum (75% power) cruising speed (including reserves) 621 miles (1000 km); maximum rate of climb at sea level 1,312 ft (400 m) per minute; service ceiling 20,000 ft (6100 m)
Weights: empty equipped 2,535 lb (1150 kg); maximum take-off (two-seat) 3,306 lb (1500 kg); maximum take-off (three-seat)

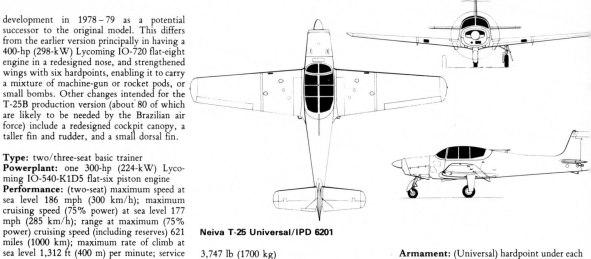

Neiva T-25 Universal/IPD 6201

3,747 lb (1700 kg)
Dimensions: span 36 ft 1 in (11.00 m); length 28 ft 2½ in (8.60 m); height 9 ft 9¾ in (3.00 m); wing area 185.14 sq ft (17.20 m²)

Armament: (Universal) hardpoint under each wing for a 7.62-mm gun pod; (Universal II) three hardpoints under each wing for gun pods, rocket pods and/or light bombs
Operators: Brazil, Chile

Nord 3202/3212

The early 1950s spawned a rash of new trainers as countries realised that their antiquated biplanes should have been phased out a decade before. In France an official competition was held for a new monoplane to equip the government-sponsored flying training schools.

Nord provided two prototypes, the N.3200 with a 260-hp (194-kW) Salmson-Argus 8AS-04 engine and the N.3201 with the smaller 170-hp (127-kW) SNECMA-Regnier. The lower-powered N.3201 flew first, on 22 June 1954, followed on 10 September by the N.3200.

The basic design won the competition, but the engine chosen for the production N.3202 was the 240-hp (179-kW) Potez 4-D32, and the prototype of this version flew on 17 April 1957.

The first of an initial batch of 100 reached the French army in July 1959; a year later 29

had been delivered. The N.3202 was used for basic flying, aerobatic and blind-flying training, and another version, the N.3212, was equipped with a radio compass for instrument training at Sidi-bel-Abbes.

Following completion of the first 50 aircraft, the second batch was fitted with the 260-hp (194-kW) Potez 4-D34. Production was completed in 1961, but around 50 are still in service at Dax where they provide a two-month selection course for trained pilots who then pass on to a six-month helicopter course.

Type: two-seat primary trainer
Powerplant: one 240-hp (179-kW) Potez 4-D32 piston engine
Performance: maximum speed at sea level 161 mph (260 km/h); maximum cruising speed 155 mph (249 km/h) at 4,265 ft (1300 m) or 146 mph (234 km/h) at 7,545 ft (2300 m); initial rate of climb 1,180 ft (360 m) per

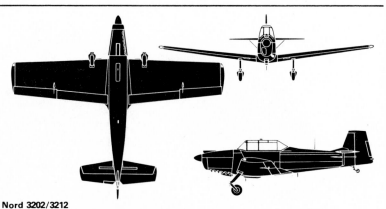

Nord 3202/3212

minute; minimum speed 51.5 mph (83 km/h); range 620 miles (1000 m)
Weights: empty 1,813 lb (824 kg); loaded 2,960 lb (1220 kg)

Dimensions: span 31 ft 2 in (9.50 m); length 26 ft 8 in (8.12 m); height 9 ft 3 in (2.82 m); wing area 175 sq ft (16.26 m²)
Operators: France

Nord Noratlas

The Nord 2501 Noratlas transport derives from the Nord 2500 of 1949. Following the twin-boom layout of the Fairchild C-82 and C-119, the prototype Noratlas flew on 27 November 1950. Over 200 were produced for the *Armée de l'Air*, deliveries commencing in 1953, and this service remains the major operator.

In 1956 the Federal German Republic signed a licence agreement with France to enable the Noratlas to be produced by Flugzeugbau Nord. The *Luftwaffe* took delivery of 186, 50 of them supplied from France. The type equipped three tactical transport wings (*Lufttransportgeschwader* 61, LTG 62 and LTG 63) each with two

18-aircraft squadrons. However, with deliveries of the Transall C.160D starting in April 1968, the Noratlas was gradually withdrawn, and by 1979 only a handful remain in second-line service.

In addition to the Nord 2501 transport version, the Nord 2504 was produced for the *Aéronavale*. This was equipped as an ASW

trainer, and extra power for take-off and manoeuvres was available from two Turboméca Marboré turbojets mounted in wingtip pods. Only one Nord 2504 was built and it first flew on 17 November 1958.

Power is provided by two French-built Bristol Hercules sleeve-valve radials, driving four-blade propellers. If the optional Hercules

758/759 power units are installed, reverse-pitch propellers are available. Fuel is carried in a centre-section tank of 1,120 Imperial gallons (5,090 litres). The flight deck in the extreme nose of the cargo pod houses five crew members. The pilot and co-pilot are side-by-side, with the navigator (to the right) and radio operator behind them. The flight engineer occupies a folding seat on the rear bulkhead.

The cargo hold has a reinforced floor and measures 32 ft 5 in (9.90 m) in length, with a maximum width of 7 ft 10 in (2.40 m) and a maximum height of 9 ft (2.75 m). Rear loading cargo doors open to the full cross-section of the hold (but have to be removed for air-dropping) and there is a door to the rear on the left. Loads can include vehicles, up to 1,800 cu ft (51.0 m³) of cargo, or 36 paratroops, or 45 troops, or stretchers in the casevac role.

The Noratlas remains the most important type in the inventory of the *Commandement du Transport Aérien Militaire*, in spite of the introduction of the Transall C.160. It is envisaged that modified and refurbished Noratlases will remain in French service until the mid-1980s, some 120 being in service in 1979.

Two *escadres* operate the Noratlas in the transport role, each having two 18-aircraft *escadrons*. They are the 62ᵉ *Escadre de Transport* at Reims and the 64ᵉ *Escadre* at Evreux. In the training role, the Noratlas serves with the *Centre d'Instruction des Equipages de Transport* at Toulouse (Francazals) and for navigator training with *Groupement Ecole* 316. Overseas units of the *Armée de l'Air* in Africa, the West Indies and the Pacific also fly the Noratlas.

The Greek air force's Air Matériel Command is a major operator, having acquired some 40 ex-*Luftwaffe* machines and the Israeli air force's 20. They operate in the cargo and troop transport role from Eleusis. About 10 Noratlases of the Portuguese air force remain in service, though they are being phased out as Lockheed C-130s and CASA Aviocars are received. A number were passed to the former Portuguese colonies of Angola and Mozambique, but their operational status is doubtful.

Type: medium-range transport
Powerplant: two 2,040-hp (1522-kW) SNECMA-built Bristol Hercules 738 or 758 radial air-cooled engines
Performance: maximum speed 273 mph (440

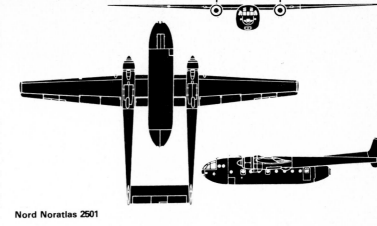

Nord Noratlas 2501

km/h); cruising speed at 9,850 ft (3000 m) 208 mph (335 km/h); rate of climb at sea level 1,230 ft (375 m) per minute; service ceiling 24,600 ft (7500 m); range 1,865 miles (3000 km)
Weights: empty equipped 28,765 lb (13075

kg); loaded 50,700 lb(23000 kg)
Dimensions: span 106 ft 7 in (32.50 m); length 72 ft (21.96 m); height 19 ft 8 in (6 m); wing area 1,089 sq ft (101.2 m²)
Operators: France, Greece, Niger, Portugal, West Germany

North American B-25 Mitchell

Named after General 'Billy' Mitchell, pioneer of US military aviation, the North American B-25 was one of the most outstanding medium bombers of World War II. Developed from the NA-40 attack-bomber of 1938, the original B-25 for the US Army made its maiden flight on 19 August 1940. Its two big engines, mounted under the shoulder-wing, and twin fins, gave the aircraft a distinctive appearance. Armament comprised four machine-guns in the fuselage, with provision for three more in the wing; the bomb load was 3,000 lb (1360 kg). On later production aircraft the dihedral on the outer wing panels was eliminated, giving the aircraft a gullwing appearance.

Special 'armament' modifications included the installation of 10 0.50-in (12.7-mm) machine-guns, and that of a standard army 75-mm gun in the nose. Aimed by two 0.50-in (12.7-mm) guns alongside it, this cannon was an especially effective weapon for use against shipping. Another version was armed with the same 75-mm gun plus 14 0.50-in (12.7-mm) machine-guns, for exclusive use in the Pacific area of operation.

Mitchells served with the US Army Air Force in the Pacific. In April 1942, 16 B-25Bs made an epic raid on Tokyo after taking off from the USS *Hornet* and flying 800 miles (1290 km), the attack being of great psychological but little military value.

Many Mitchells served with the Royal Air Force in Europe, where they were used principally as light day-bombers with Bomber Command and later with the 2nd Tactical Air Force, operating as close-support bombers with the Allied armies as they advanced through France and Holland. Before the invasion, Mitchells were used in attacks on northern France and on flying-bomb sites in the Pas de Calais.

After World War II Mitchells were replaced in the Allied air forces by newer, more advanced types, such as the Bristol Brigand and English Electric Canberra in the Royal Air Force. Many of the superceded bombers served for many years in secondary air forces, including those of several South American countries. Venzuela is reported to be the last user, B-25s remaining in service in that country until the late 1970s.

Type: (B-25D) medium-range light bomber
Powerplant: two 1,350-hp (1007-kW) Wright Double-Row Cyclone GR-2600 radial engines
Performance: maximum speed 292 mph (470 km/h) at 15,000 ft (4570 m); range 1,635 miles (2630 km) with 4,000 lb (1814 kg) of bombs, or 950 miles (1530 km) with maximum bomb load.
Weights: empty 16,000 lb (7257 kg); loaded 24,000 lb (10886 kg); maximum take-off 35,000 lb (15876 kg)
Dimensions: span 67 ft 7 in (20.61 m); length 52 ft 11 in (16.14 m); height 16 ft 4 in (4.98 m); wing area 610 sq ft (56.67 m²)
Armament: five 0.50-in machine guns in

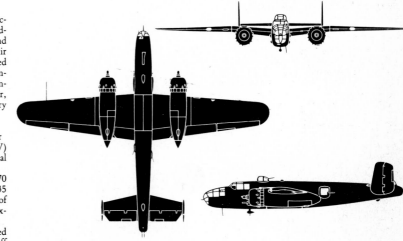

North American B-25J Mitchell

nose, dorsal and ventral positions. Maximum bomb load 6,000 lb (2722 kg)
Operators: none

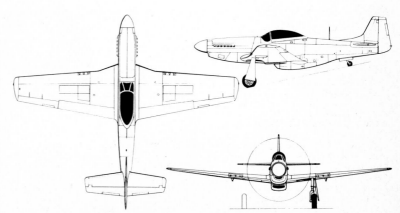

Fuerza Aerea Uruguaya North American B-25J Mitchell medium bomber, supplied by the United States in 1950.

North American F-51 Mustang

The North American Mustang evolved from a British requirement in 1940 for a fighter of more advanced design and with a better performance than any of the then current US fighters.

Early production models, fitted with 1,100-hp (821-kW) Allison V-1710 engines, arrived in Britain in November 1941 and were faster than any fighter then in service with the Royal Air Force. However, their 'low-altitude' engines limited the operational effectiveness of the Mustang, which was relegated to fighter-reconnaissance duties. A number were used for armament and powerplant experiments during which four were fitted with 'high-altitude' Rolls-Royce Merlin engines. This led to a major re-design to take advantage of the performance gain offered by the British engine, from which

evolved one of World War IIs great fighters.

The Mustang with Packard-built Merlins went into service with the US 8th Air Force in December 1943, escorting bomber formations, and its combination of speed, manoeuvrability and long range made it not only the most popular but also the most effective fighter operational over Europe in the last two years of World War II.

After World War II Mustangs served with many other air forces. The Australian contribution to the occupation of Japan consisted of three squadrons of P-51Ds, and these fought with the US 5th Air Force when the Korean conflict broke out in 1950, until they were replaced by Gloster Meteors.

The South African Air Force also used Mustangs to help stem the North Korean advance when the latter invaded South Korea,

North American P-51D Mustang

continued

until they were superseded by North American F-86 Sabres.

In 1967 the F-51 was put back into production for counter-insurgency duties. These new aircraft had two seats in tandem and updated systems and electronics, and improved armament. The most important family of rebuilds and new construction was produced by Cavalier Aircraft.

Mustangs continued to serve with many of the smaller air forces for another decade although during the last few years the operational serviceability of a number of these has been open to question. Two air forces at least had sizeable numbers of Mustangs in their inventories early in 1979.

Type: single-seat land-based fighter

Powerplant: one 1,680-hp (1253-kW) Packard Merlin V-1650-7 piston engine
Performance: maximum speed 442 mph (712 km/h) at 24,500 ft (7470 m); climb 10 minutes to 20,000 ft (6096 m); range (normal) 950 miles (1530 km)
Weights: empty 7,000 lb (3175 kg); loaded 9,200 lb (4173 kg)
Dimensions: span 37 ft 0 in (11.28 m); length 32 ft 3 in (9.84 m); height 8 ft 8 in (2.64 m); wing area 235 sq ft (21.83 m²)
Armament: four 0.50-in (12.7-mm) machine-guns and provision for 1,000 lb (453 kg) of bombs
Operators: Australia, Canada, China, Dominica, Haiti, Indonesia, Israel, New Zealand, South Africa, Sweden

North American F-86 Sabre

Designed to meet US Air Force requirements for a day-fighter which could also be used for escort duties, the North American F-86 Sabre as originally conceived had straight wings. However, an analysis of German research experiments in World War II indicated that a swept wing would significantly improve performance.

The first production models, designated F-86A, went into service in 1949. These aircraft had a top speed of 679 mph (1093 km/h) at sea level, a performance greatly superior to that of contemporary fighters such as the Lockheed P-80C and Gloster Meteor, the top speeds of which were below 600 mph (965 km/h).

This version saw service in the Korean War in the 1950s where its performance, together with skilful flying by experienced pilots, proved superior to that of the opposing vaunted MiG-15.

During its career, several versions of the F-86 were developed by North American, including the heavy radar-equipped F-86D interceptor, the F-86K (the F-86D with guns instead of rockets) and the powerful F-86H fighter-bomber. Mitsubishi-built reconnaissance fighters still serve in Japan. In Canada, Canadair produced 1,815 for the Royal Canadian Air Force and other customers under the designation CL-13, many of these being powered by Orenda engines. The most advanced version was the one developed by the Commonwealth Aircraft Corporation for the Royal Australian Air Force. These Australian Sabres were powered by Rolls-Royce Avon engines of 7,500-lb (3400-kg) static thrust and were armed with two 30-mm Aden cannon and Sidewinder air-to-air missiles.

In addition to its widespread use among NATO and British Commonwealth countries (those in Pakistan seeing action when that country found itself at war with India), Sabres were supplied to many other countries throughout the world. In fact, the demand became so great that in 1954 the F-86F was put back into production.

Biggest of the overseas users was Japan, where Mitsubishi assembled and built 300 Sabres. These continued to serve in the Japanese Air Self-Defence Force until the late 1970s. When withdrawn from front-line service Sabres continued to be used for training; the final stages of pilot tuition including no less than 290 hours on an F-86F, of which 220 hours were combat instruction.

Type: (F-86D) single-seat fighter
Powerplant: one 7,650-lb (2330-kg) General Electric J47-GE-17 after burning turbojet
Performance: maximum design speed 692 mph (1114 km/h) at sea level; maximum speed at 40,000 ft (12190 m) 612 mph (985 km/h); combat radius with full internal fuel 277 miles (446 km); maximum rate of climb 12,150 ft (3705 m) per minute at sea level
Weights: empty 13,518 lb (4123 kg); normal take-off 18,183 lb (5546 kg); maximum take-off (area interceptor) 19,975 lb (6092 kg)
Dimensions: span 37 ft 1½ in (11.32 m); length 40 ft 3 in (12.28 m); height 15 ft (4.57 m); wing area 287.9 sq ft (26.75 m²)
Armament: twenty-four 2.75-in (70-mm) Mighty Mouse rockets
Operators: (1979) Argentina, Bolivia, Ethiopia, Indonesia (in storage), Japan, Malaysia (in storage), Peru, Philippines, Portugal, South Korea, Tunisia, Uruguay, US Navy, Yugoslavia

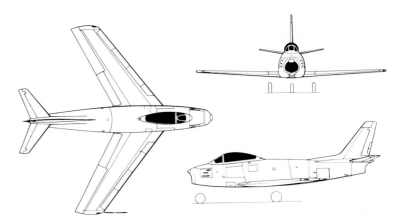

North American F-86F Sabre

One of the six Canadair Sabre Mk 6s acquired by the Fuerza Aerea Columbiana in the mid-fifties and equipping the Escuadron de Caza.

North American F-100 Super Sabre

The first of the USAF's so-called 'Century-series' fighters, because their designations were 100 or over, the North American F-100 is also regarded as being the world's first operational fighter capable of sustaining a speed in excess of Mach 1 in level flight. Its design originated as a private venture by North American Aviation for an improved successor to the North American F-86 Sabre, and was identified originally by the company as the Sabre 45 because of the aircraft's 45° of wing sweepback. This design proposal was submitted to the USAF for consideration, as it was understood that although the US Air force had submitted no requests for proposals, there was general interest in a supersonic air superiority fighter to become operational in 1955.

In October 1951 the USAF requested North American to proceed with development of the Sabre 45 design, resulting in a rapidly produced mockup which, when inspected in November, brought a demand for more than 100 detail changes. The company's involvement in accelerated production of the F-86 for deployment in Korea meant that reduced priority was given to the Sabre 45 project, and it was not until 21 March 1952 that inspection of the revised mockup could take place. This was then designated F-100A, as the result of an order for two YF-100A prototypes placed by letter contract on 3 January 1952, followed

Takeoff of F-100D Super Sabres of the 120th TFS from Phan Rang AB during the American involvement in Vietnam. Today a handful of 'Huns' are still airworthy with the Air National Guard and in Taiwan, and the last combat units are in Denmark and Turkey.

by an order for 23 production F-100As in 11 February 1952. The review of the F-100A by the Mockup Board showed that almost all of the desired changes had been incorporated in the design and, since it was regarded as being generally satisfactory, a follow-up contract for a further 250 aircraft was placed in August 1952.

In its original form there was a distinct family likeness to the F-86, except for the larger-area, increased-sweep wing, but by the time the building of the prototypes began there were other notable differences. These were concerned primarily with the configuration of the nose and tail unit. The former had acquired a flat oval intake for the single afterburning turbojet installed in the aft fuselage; the latter had become somewhat unconventional, with a slab tailplane mounted as low as possible, completely separated from fin and rudder. There were no flaps because the ailerons were mounted inboard to avoid the problem of control reversal, feared with so thin a wing, but full-span leading-edge slats were fitted.

The initial flight of the first prototype was made on 25 May 1953, and in a subsequent flight this aircraft demonstrated a speed of Mach 1.05 although powered by a derated prototype engine. The second prototype flew on 14 October 1953, and the first production F-100A on 29 October 1953: all three aircraft confirmed shortcomings in respect of flight control, stability, and pilot visibility. In addition, the Pratt & Whitney J57 engine was suffering problems with compressor stall.

Interim modifications were made to correct these deficiencies and on 27 September 1954 F-100As entered operational service with the Tactical Air Command's 479th Fighter Day Wing at George AFB, California. By early November all F-100s were grounded following serious accidents. The major problem was that at high speed and under high-g the aircraft had a tendency to yaw: if this instability was not recognised immediately and corrected the result was loss of control and break-up. Electronic and aerodynamic 'fixes' including extended wings and a taller vertical tail, were a temporary paliative; but it was not until introduction of a hydraulically-actuated electrically-controlled yaw damper on the subsequent F-100C, plus a pitch damper, that the problem was regarded as solved.

By the time that production ended in 1959, the USAF had accepted 2,249 Super Sabres for its own use, fewer than had been expected. The F-100A had been followed by the F-100C fighter-bomber with a strengthened wing for external loads, the F-100D fighter-bomber with an autopilot and other improved equipment and detail changes, and the longer-fuselage two-seat F-100F combat trainer with full operational capability. F-100s saw extensive service in Vietnam, and seven F-100Fs were equipped with anti-SAM (surface-to-air missile) avionics, under the designation Wild Weasel I, to counter North Vietnamese weapons, and in April 1966 were deployed to attack 'Fan-Song' fire-control radar systems. Like the McDonnell Douglas F-4 Phantom, the 'Hun' could operate effectively in both low attack and high combat roles.

Type: supersonic tactical fighter/fighter-bomber/combat trainer
Powerplant: (F-100D) one 17,000-lb (7711-kg) afterburning thrust Pratt & Whitney J57-P-21A turbojet
Performance: (F-100D): maximum speed Mach 1.3 or 864 mph (1390 km/h) at 36,000 ft (10970 m); cruising speed 565 mph (909 km/h) at 25,000 ft (7620 m); combat radius 530 miles (853 km)
Weights: (F-100D) empty 21,000 lb (9525 kg); maximum take-off 34,832 lb (15800 kg)
Dimensions: span 38 ft 9 in (11.81 m); length (F-100D) 47 ft 0 in (14.33 m); span (F-100F) 52 ft 6 in (16.00 m); wing area 385 sq ft (35.77 m²)
Armament: (F-100D) four M39 20-mm cannon, with six underwing hardpoints for rockets, bombs, air-to-air and air-to-surface missiles, or drop tanks
Operators: Denmark, France, Taiwan, Turkey, US Air National Guard (1979 Taiwan and Turkey only)

North American F-100D Super Sabre

Carrying low-visibility national markings and unit badge below the cockpit, this Royal Danish Air Force North American F-100D Super Sabre shares Denmark's defence with Saab Drakens and Lockheed Starfighters. This example comes from Escadrille 730 Skrydstrup.

F-100D-15-NA (54-2244) of Escadrille 730 Kongelige Danske Flyvevaben, based at Skyrydstrup, 1975. This unit is due to exchange its F-100s for F-16s in 1980.

F-100C-5-NA (54-1798) Super Sabre of 111th Sqn, Turk Hava Kuvvetleri, 1st Jet Air Base, Eskisehir, 1973.

All but a few of l'Armée de l'Air's Super Sabres have now been withdrawn from service. This example, an F-100D-10-NA (54-2160) is in the markings of Escuadron de Chasse 1/11 "Roussillon".

Shark-mouthed F-100C-20-NA (54-1939) Super Sabre of the 127th Tactical Fighter Sqn, Kansas Air National Guard, 1969.

USAF F-100D-61-NA (56-2910) of the 308th Tactical Fighter Sqn, 31st TFW, based at Tuy Hoa, Vietnam, 1970.

North American T-6 Texan

The North American T-6 is a two-seat advanced trainer, officially named Texan but better remember by Commonwealth pilots as the Harvard.

The aircraft was introduced in 1938 and was similar to and eventually replaced the USAAF's North American BC-1A basic combat trainer. The pilot and instructor sat in tandem enclosed cockpits, the low sill of which gave an excellent view. Complete dual flight and engine controls were fitted in each cockpit. The powerful and reliable Pratt & Whitney Wasp air-cooled radial engine gave a sprightly performance, and the forgiving but responsive flying controls combined to make the T-6 an ideal training aircraft. Its distinctive rasping noise, not heard by the occupants, was caused by the high tip-speed of the direct-drive propeller.

Early aircraft had a conventional aluminium-alloy monocoque fuselage, but in 1941, because of possible shortages of strategic materials, the structure was extensively redesigned to eliminate the use of aluminium-alloy and high-alloy steels. The wings, centre-section, fin, and the flying control surfaces

were made of spot-welded low-alloy steel, while the side panels of the forward fuselage and the entire rear fuselage were made of plywood. However, when the anticipated shortages did not materialise, the original method of construction was reintroduced.

Harvards were first delivered to the Royal Air Force in 1938, and remained a standard trainer at flying training schools for over 16 years. After their withdrawal in 1955 they continued in service with university air squadrons of Home Command as communications aircraft. Many Harvards also saw service in an operational armed role against the Mau Mau in Kenya and terrorists in Malaya.

The primary role of the T-6 as an armed trainer makes it suitable also for light ground attack duties. Because of this, and its strong construction, reliability and ease of flying, the T-6 continues to be used by numerous countries throughout the world.

Type: two-seat advanced trainer
Powerplant: one 550-hp (409-kW) Pratt & Whitney Wasp R-1340-AN-1 air-cooled radial
Performance: maximum speed 212 mph (341

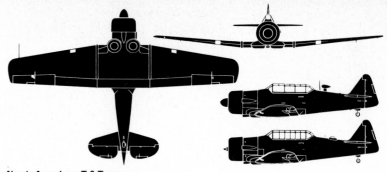

North American T-6 Texan

km/h); cruising speed 170 mph (272 km/h); service ceiling 21,500 ft (6560 m); range 870 miles (1400 km)
Weights: empty 4,158 lb (1888 kg); gross 5,617 lb (2550 kg)
Dimensions: span 42 ft 0 in (12.9 m); length 29 ft 6 in (9.0 m); height 11 ft 8½ in (3.5 m); wing area 253.7 sq ft (23.6 m²)
Armament: two forward-firing 0.30-in (7.62-mm) machine-guns and one 0.30-in (7.62-mm) machine-gun on flexible mounting

in rear cockpit; in addition, underwing rockets and light bombs can be carried for weapon training and close-support duties
Operators: Argentina, Bolivia, Brazil, Canada, Chile, Dominican Republic, France, Greece, Guatemala, Haiti, Honduras, India, Indonesia, Italy, Japan, Laos, Mexico, Morocco, New Zealand, Nicaragua, Pakistan, Paraguay, Portugal, Salvador, South Africa, Spain, Taiwan, Thailand, Tunisia, United Kingdom, Uruguay, Venezuela, Zaïre

North American T-28 Trojan

Requiring a primary and basic two-seat trainer to supersede the well-known T-6 Texan (Harvard), the USAF initiated a design competition in 1948 to procure a replacement. North American Aviation, which had designed and built the T-6 Texan, thus had very considerable experience of building training aircraft, and the company's NA-159 design was selected as the winning entry, an initial contract for two prototypes, designated XT-28, being awarded. The first of these made its initial flight on 26 September 1949, and following satisfactory evaluation was ordered into production for the USAF in 1950, with the designation T-28A and the name Trojan.

Deliveries to Air Training Command began in late 1950, and when production ended a total of 1,194 had been built. Of low-wing monoplane configuration, with pupil and instructor seated in tandem, the Trojan was the first trainer in US military service with a retractable tricycle-type landing gear. Powerplant consisted of an 800-hp (597-kW) Wright R-1300-1 radial piston engine. Although used mainly as a primary trainer, the Trojan could operate also in an armament training role, for there was provision for the carriage of light bombs or rockets beneath the wings, and for the installation of two 0.5-in (12.7-mm) machine-guns.

Following a decision made in 1952 to standardise on training aircraft for the US forces, the US Navy ordered the type into production under the designation T-28B. These differed from the USAF version by having a more

powerful 1,425-hp (1063-kW) Wright R-1820 Cyclone radial piston engine, an improved cockpit canopy and an airbrake on the undersurface of the fuselage. The T-28B, of which 489 were built, was followed by 299 T-28Cs which differed only by having an arrester hook for deck landing training.

Subsequently, many surplus T-28s were converted to serve as ground attack aircraft. Under the designation T-28D, North American modified 147 T-28As for the above role, this work including the installation of a 1,425-hp (1063-kW) Wright R-1820-56S engine, and the provision of six underwing hardpoints to carry a combat load of various weapons, including 0.50-in machine-gun packs, napalm, bombs and rockets, or external fuel tanks to give a ferry range of 1,200 miles (1930 km). A number were also converted to attack trainers under the designation AT-28D. Many T-28Ds were deployed in South Vietnam and the Congo, and were supplied also to the armed forces of several nations. Following evaluation of a T-28D by the French Air Force in North Africa, Sud-Aviation in France modified a considerable number of ex-USAF T-28As, under an arrangement with PacAero Engineering Corporation of Santa Monica, California. Under the name Fennec, these aircraft were given 1,425-hp (1063-kW) Wright R-1820-56S engines and armament comprising two 12.5-mm machine-guns in a pod beneath each wing, and mountings for four 300-lb (136-kg) bombs. The French Air Force Fennecs were used for a variety of reconnaissance,

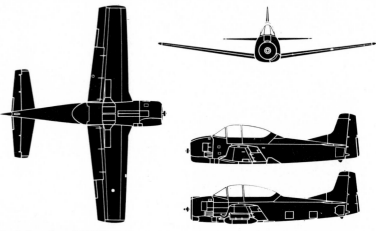

North American T-28A Trojan

patrol and close support duties in Algeria, replacing North American T-6 aircraft which had been similarly deployed for a number of years. Several Fennecs were supplied for service with the Argentine Navy.

Type: two-seat primary and basic trainer
Powerplant: (T-28B) one 1,425-hp (1063-kW) Wright R-1820 radial aircooled piston engine
Performance: (T-28B) maximum speed 343 mph (552 km/h); cruising speed at 30,000 ft (9145 m) 310 mph (499 km/h); maximum range at 10,000 ft (3050 m) 1,060 miles

(1706 km)
Weights: (T-28B) empty 6,424 lb (2914 kg); maximum take-off 8,486 lb (3849 kg)
Dimensions: span 40 ft 1 in (12.22 m); length 33 ft 0 in (10.06 m); height 12 ft 8 in (3.86 m); wing area 268 sq ft (24.90 m²)
Armament: (T-28D) six underwing hardpoints for the carriage of bombs, machine-gun packs, napalm and rockets
Operators: (trainers) US Air Force, US Navy; (armed variants) Argentina, Bolivia, France, Kampuchea, Laos, Thailand, US Air Force, Zaire

Northrop F-5A/F-5B Freedom Fighter

In 1954 the US government initiated a study to determine Asian and European requirements for a lightweight and comparatively inexpensive high-performance fighter, to be supplied to friendly nations via the Military Assistance Programme. As a result of this interest, Northrop began investigation of the requirement, identifying their initial work as the N-156 concept. Two years of private development followed before the USAF and Navy showed interest in a supersonic trainer derived from this work and this, designated T-38, was developed in parallel with the private venture N-156C. First flight of the prototype N-156C was made on 30 July 1959, and during which a speed in excess of Mach 1 was attained.

However, it was not until 23 April 1962 that the US Secretary of Defense approved USAF selection of the N-156C, this being designated subsequently F-5, the first single-seat F-5A prototype flying initially in May 1963. A two-seat version for fighter/trainer duties was developed and built simultaneously under the designation F-5B, and this entered operational service four months before the F-5A, with the 4441st Combat Crew Training Squadron at Williams AFB, Chandler, Arizona, on 30 April 1964. The first of the

F-5As were delivered to the same squadron in August of that same year.

The required performance was attained by installing two small turbojets with afterburners, and provision of a lightweight airframe which used new structural techniques and advanced aerodynamic features. These included wing leading-edge and trailing-edge flaps, area-ruled fuselage and two hydraulically-operated airbrakes on the undersurface of the fuselage. A rocket-powered ejection seat is provided for the pilot of an F-5A, and for both instructor and pupil of the F-5B version. The primary interception weapons comprised two nose-mounted Colt-Browning 20-mm guns and two AIM-9B Sidewinder missiles on wingtip launchers. One underfuselage and four underwing pylons permit the carriage of nearly three tons of weapons, including AGM-12B Bullpups and a wide variety of bombs and rockets.

To evaluate the combat potential of the F-5A, a 12-aircraft unit of the Tactical Air Command's 4503rd Tactical Fighter Wing was deployed to South-East Asia in October 1965, under the codename Project Skoshi Tiger. It was from this project that the F-5 acquired the nickname 'Tiger'. The aircraft

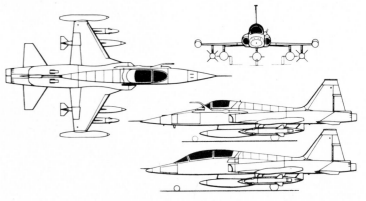

Northrop F-5A Freedom Fighter

deployed to Da Nang were diverted from the Military Assistance Programme, and provided with in-flight refuelling capability, armour protection, jettisonable pylons, additional avionics, and finished in camouflage paint. In a period of four months these aircraft flew more than 2,500 hours, in roles which included close support, interdiction and reconnaissance. In early 1966 the unit was moved to Bien Hoa AB, from where interdiction, armed recon-

naissance and combat air patrols against enemy MiG fighters were flown over North Vietnam. The unit was increased subsequently to 18 aircraft, becoming the 10th Fighter Command Squadron and assigned to the 3rd Tactical Fighter Wing based at Bien Hoa AB. These aircraft were transferred to the South Vietnamese Air Force in 1967.

Versions of the F-5 include the basic F-5A, the two-seat F-5B and the reconnaissance version RF-5A, which carries four KS-92A cameras mounted in the fuselage nose. The Royal Norwegian Airforce flies modified F-5As under the designation F-5G and reconnaissance versions under the designation RF-5G. Versions of the F5A/B built jointly by Canada and The Netherlands for their armed forces, are known as CF5A/D and NF-5AB respectively. Spanish versions of the F5 built under licence by AISA (CASA) are known as the C-9 and the CE-9.

Type: tactical fighter, fighter/trainer, and reconnaissance aircraft
Powerplant: two 4,080 lb (1850 kg) afterburning General Electric J85-GE-13 turbojets
Performance: maximum speed (F-5A) Mach 1.4 or 924 mph (1488 km/h) at 36,000 ft (10970 m); (F-5B) Mach 1.35 or 891 mph (1435 km/h) at 36,000 ft (10970 m); maximum cruising speed without afterburning (both versions) Mach 0.97 or 640 mph (1031 km/h) at 36,000 ft (10970 m); combat radius with maximum payload, plus allowances for 5 minutes combat at S/L (F-5A) 195 miles (314 km), (F-5B) 201 miles (323 km); combat radius with maximum fuel, plus allowances for 5 minutes combat at S/L (F-5A) 558 miles (898 km),(F-5B) 570 miles (917 km)
Weights: empty equipped (F-5A) 8,085 lb (3667 kg), (F-5B) 8,361 lb (3792 kg); maximum military load 6,200 lb (2812 kg); maximum take-off (F-5A) 20,677 lb (9379 kg), (F-5B) 20,500 lb (9298 kg)
Dimensions: span 25 ft 3 in (7.70 m); length (F-5A) 47 ft 2 in (14.38 m), (F-5B) 46 ft 4 in (14.12 m); height (F-5A) 13 ft 2 in (4.01 m), (F-5B) 13 ft 1 in (3.99 m); wing area 170 sq ft

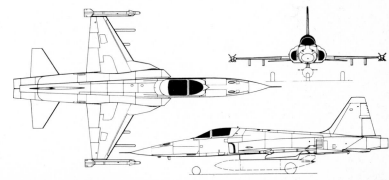

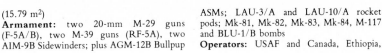

Pictured in its blastproof dispersal in 1967, this Northrop F-5A Freedom Fighter was one of the standard types supplied to the VNAF (air force of South Vietnam). Today few if any US types (certainly not the F-5) are operated by the VPAF.

(15.79 m²)
Armament: two 20-mm M-29 guns (F-5A/B), two M-39 guns (RF-5A), two AIM-9B Sidewinders; plus AGM-12B Bullpup

ASMs; LAU-3/A and LAU-10/A rocket pods; Mk-81, Mk-82, Mk-83, Mk-84, M-117 and BLU-1/B bombs
Operators: USAF and Canada, Ethiopia,

Greece, Iran, Libya, Morocco, Netherlands, Norway, Philippines, Republic of China (Taiwan), Republic of Korea, Spain, Thailand, Turkey and Vietnam

---

Northrop F-5E/F Tiger II

While production of the Northrop F-5A/B was in progress, the company developed as a private venture an improved version of the F-5, using as a prototype an F-5A airframe. First flown in March 1969, it was powered by two 5,000-lb (2267-kg) afterburning General Electric J85-GE-21 turbojets, providing almost 23% more power than the engines of the F-5. This higher-performance aircraft was offered to the USAF who were acting as the US government's instrument in the IFA competition for foreign customers as a follow-on to the F-5, but this force was unprepared to accept this as a replacement for the satisfactory and effective F-5 without extended flight testing to establish whether the new engines offered any really significant advantages. There were other factors which at that time caused some concern to the Secretary of Defense and the USAF. If Northrop's new fighter introduced new engines and some degree of advanced ideas, would it retain the proven capability of the F-5A/B to be operated and maintained successfully by nations which did not aspire to the technological experience of the USAF. Conversely, the USAF wanted a fighter with expanded performance, for the primary requirement was for a fighter able to fly air superiority missions against aircraft such as the Soviet-built MiG-21. The tentative name of Advanced International Fighter was attached to the new design but, effective or not, the USAF could not expect to receive funding for its development and production without the normal Congressional procedure of selecting a contractor. Thus, requests for proposals were sent to eight US manufacturers on 26 February 1970, and in the following month four companies replied, each offering a version of a fighter aircraft already in production. Ling-Temco-Vought proposed a variant of the F-8 Crusader, Lockheed of the F-104 Starfighter, McDonnell Douglas of the F-4 Phantom II and, of course, Northrop the advanced F-5. It was the last which was chosen for production to meet the requirements for what had by then become known as the International Fighter Aircraft (IFA), and on 20 November 1970 the USAF announced selection of Northrop as the prime contractor for this programme.

Northrop's finalised design for the aircraft which became designated F-5E and acquired the name Tiger II, differed in several respects from the F-5A, for experience gained by

deployment of that aircraft in South-East Asia had shown that good manoeuvrability was of more significance than high speed. Thus the IFA acquired a version of the full-span leading-edge manoeuvring flaps which had been evolved first for the NF-5A/Bs supplied to the Royal Netherlands Air Force. These, electrically-operated, could be used in conjunction with the electrically-operated single-slotted trailing-edge flaps. Other improvements included an increase of wing area of about 10%; modification of the tapered wing leading-edge extension, between wing and fuselage, to improve airflow over the wing, especially at high angles of attack; provision of two-position nosewheel gear, which

Northrop F-5E Tiger II

This 'foreign camouflaged' Northrop F-5E Tiger II is one of a fleet of over 60 operated by USAF Tactical Air Command for Red Flag exercises at Nellis AFB. Similar aircraft are used for Dissimilar Air Combat Training and Aggressor work by USAFE and the USN.

continued

increased the wing's angle of attack by 3° 22'
to reduce take-off distance, and also of arrester
gear which would make it possible for the IFA
to be operated from and to short runways; increased internal fuel capacity; introduction of
an integrated fire-control system; and, of
course, installation of the General Electric
J85-GE-21 engines which had initiated the
project.

The initial contract called for the production
of 325 F-5Es on a fixed-price-incentive basis,
and it is interesting to note that Northrop's
costs were higher than the target figure. One
of the primary reasons for this was the
cancellation of the Boeing SST (SuperSonic
Transport) programme, for the company had
used anticipated sub-contract earnings on this
latter progamme to arrive at the lowest possible initial cost for its new fighter. Costs also
rose because the added complexities of providing shorter take-off and manoeuvrability
created problems that had to be resolved,
despite utilisation of a well developed airframe.
For example, the need to limit weight increases dictated the use of costly titanium in
the aft fuselage section in the engine/tailpipe
shroud areas. Furthermore, the higher
powered J85-GE-21 engine was suffering from
a degree of unreliability, and the US Air Force
suspended flight testing for three months,
from 21 September 1972, to give General
Electric time to resolve the major problems.
Inevitably, such setbacks added to costs, but in
the final analysis it has been proved that
although unit costs were higher than
estimated by Northrop, they were below the
figure that the USAF had expected it might
have to pay. The first production aircraft made
its first flight on 11 August 1972, but the
F-5E was not accepted for sevice by the USAF
until 4 April 1973. At that date, the aircraft
which were being used by Tactical Air Command's 425th Tactical Fighter Training
Squadron at Williams AFB, Chandler,
Arizona, for operational testing were adopted
for service use. A lengthened-fuselage tandem
two-seat trainer has since been developed,
under the designation F-5F. This version retains the integrated fire-control system of the
F-5E, so that it may be used both for training
and combat, but has only a single M-39 gun.
The first flight of an F-5F was made on 25
September 1974, with deliveries of production
aircraft beginning in the summer of 1976.
The effectiveness of the F-5E in service use can
perhaps be judged best by the fact that the top
air combat training schools in the US, the
Navy's Fighter Weapon School and the Air
Force's Aggressor Squadron, both use F-5Es
as 'enemy' aircraft in combat training against
US squadrons of first-line operational tactical
fighters.

By early 1978 orders for the F-5E/F totalled
just over 1,000, in ratio of approximately 9:1,
of which about 75% had then been delivered.
An RF-5E reconnaissance version was approved for development on 31 March 1978, with a
prototype scheduled to make its first flight in
the spring of 1979. This will have a modified
forward fuselage that will be able to accommodate a wide variety of equipment for the
reconnaissance role. It is intended that during
the flight test programme of the RF-5E both
day and night photo-reconnaissance missions
will be flown.

Type: tactical fighter, fighter/trainer, and
reconnaissance aircraft
Powerplant: two 5,000-lb (2267-kg) afterburning General Electric J85-GE-21 turbojets
Performance: maximum speed (F-5E) Mach
1.64 or 1,083 mph (1743 km/h) at 36,000 ft
(10970 m); (F-5F) Mach 1.56, or 1,030 mph
(1657 km/h) at 36,090 ft (11000 m); maximum cruising speed (F-5E) Mach 0.98 or 647
mph (1040 km/h) at 36,000 ft (10970 m);
combat radius with maximum fuel, two AIM-
9E Sidewinders, plus allowances for 5 minutes
combat with maximum afterburning power at
15,000 ft (4570 m) 656 miles (1056 km); combat radius with 5,200-lb (2358-kg) weapons
load, two AIM-9E Sidewinders, maximum
fuel, plus allowances for 5 minutes combat at
military power at S/L 138 miles (222 km)
Weights: empty (F-5E) 9,683 lb (4392 kg),
(F-5F) 10,567 lb (4793 kg); maximum take-off
(F-5E) 24,664 lb (11187 kg), (F-5F) 25,147 lb

Northrop F-5E (159881) of the US Naval Fighter Weapons "Top Gun" School at Miramar NAS, Calif. Soviet style
numbers adorn the nose and the school emblem is on the fin.

Iranian Air Force F-5E (00933), one of 141 received by the Service replacing older F-5As.

Northrop F-5E (01568) of the 64th Fighter Interceptor Training Sqn, 57th Fighter Weapons Wing, at Nellis AFB, in the
so-called "snake" camouflage scheme.

Northrop F-5E (01545) of the 527th TFTAS at Alconbury, Hunts, in the "ghost" scheme emulating the
camouflage carried by some Soviet Air Force fighters.

"Lizard" camouflage applied to an F-5E (01528) of the 64th FITS, 57th FWW at Nellis AFB.

Fuerza Aerea de Chile F-5E of Grupo 7 at Antofagasta AFB. Delivered in 1976, the 15 F-5Es in Chilean service have a
dorsal fin extension housing the ADF antenna.

US Air Force F-5E (1508) of the 57th Fighter Weapons Wing, Nellis AFB, in one of several experimental camouflage
schemes employed by the "Aggressor" units.

Forca Aerea Brasileira F-5E (4820) of the 1° Escuadrao, 1° Grupo de Aviacao de Caca, at Santa Cruz AFB, Rio de Janeiro.

(11406 kg)

Dimensions: span 26 ft 8 in (8.13 m); span over missiles 27 ft 11¾ in (8.53 m); length (F-5E) 48 ft 2 in (14.68 m), (F-5F) 51 ft 7 in (15.72 m); height (F-5E) 13 ft 4 in (4.06 m), (F-5F) 13 ft 1¾ in (4.01 m); wing area 186 sq ft (17.3 m²)

Armament: two Colt-Browning M-39 20-mm guns (F-5E), one M-39 (F-5F); two AIM-9E Sidewinders; LAU-3/A and LAU-59/A rockets; Mk-82, Mk-84, Mk-117A1, BLU-27/B, BLU-32/B, and CBU-24/49 bombs

Operators: Brazil, Chile, Egypt, Iran, Jordan, Kenya, South Korea, Malaysia, Saudi Arabia, Singapore, Sudan, Switzerland, Taiwan, Thailand, and the USAF and USN (as trainers)

Chinese Nationalist Air Force F-5E (74-00959) "Chung Cheng" of 2nd Fighter Wing, Taiwan. Example illustrated is one of initial batch supplied direct from Northrop.

The Royal Saudi Air Force operates 70 Northrop F-5E Tiger IIs in four squadrons based at Taif and Khamis Mushayt.

Northrop T-38 Talon

As mentioned briefly in the description of the Northrop F-5A/B, the evolution of that tactical fighter had begun with Northrop's N-156 concept which, after two years of development as a private venture, had resulted in a supersonic trainer which in 1956 was identified as the N-156T and submitted as a proposal to the USAF. Three prototypes were ordered in December 1956 for development as a two-seat supersonic basic trainer (the first and, except for the Mitsubishi T18, only such aircraft in the world). The first of these made its initial flight on 10 April 1959 at Edwards AFB, California. By that time there had been a contract revision, concluded in June 1958, for the supply of six aircraft under the designation YT-38, plus one airframe for static testing.

Powerplant of the first two prototypes comprised two 2,100-lb (953-kg) thrust non-afterburning General Electric YJ85-GE-1 turbojets, but the remainder of the YT-38 trials aircraft had 3,600-lb (1633-kg) afterburning thrust YJ85-GE-5 engines. Whilst testing of the first two prototypes was satisfactory, early evaluation of the YT-38s with the more powerful engines left little doubt that the US Air Force was about to acquire an exceptional trainer, and the first contract was for 13 T-38As, which were given the name Talon. The first was delivered for service with the USAF's 3510th Flying Training Wing, at Randolph AFB, on 17 March 1961.

When it entered service, no aircraft could have looked less like a trainer than the Talon. Its slender area-ruled fuselage, narrow-span sharp-edged wings, and tailplane with anhedral, identified it at a glance as an advanced combat aircraft: many pupils wondered just what they were taking on. But despite its high-performance capability, with a Mach 1.3 speed at altitude, its stalling speed was as low as 146 mph (235 km/h) and very considerable design effort had been directed to make it an aeroplane which would not be too demanding on the pupil in the front seat. Both pupil and instructor are accommodated on rocket-powered ejection seats, the latter raised 10 in (0.25 m) higher than the pupil to improve the instructor's forward view. All flying controls are hydraulically powered by a duplicated system; directional and longitudinal stability augmenters are installed in series with the con-

trol system; and aileron design and area are such that the Talon can be flown and landed safely with one aileron inoperative.

The cumulative effect of such attention to the safety aspect, plus the inherent reliability of the entire aircraft and its systems, enabled the US Air Force to report in 1972 that the T-38 had maintained consistently the highest safety record of any supersonic aircraft in USAF service. During 1971 the T-38A accident rate was 1.2 per 100,000 flying hours, which was below half the average for the Air Force.

When production ended in early 1972, a total of 1,187 T-38s had been delivered to the USAF. Other users included the US Navy, which acquired five from the US Air Force, and NASA, which obtained a total of 24 from Northrop to serve as flight-readiness trainers for astronauts. In addition, 46 were supplied through the USAF for use by the German *Luftwaffe* in the training of German student pilots in the United States: these aircraft retain USAF military insignia.

Type: two-seat supersonic basic trainer
Powerplant: two 3,850-lb (1746-kg) afterburning thrust General Electric J85-GE-5A turbojets
Performance: maximum speed Mach 1.3 or 858 mph (1381 km/h) at 36,000 ft (10970 m); maximum cruising speed 627 mph (1009 km/h) at 36,000 ft (10970 m); range with maximum fuel, with 20 minutes reserve at 10,000 ft (3050 m) 1,140 miles (1835 km)
Weights: empty 7,164 lb (3250 kg); maximum take-off and landing 11,820 lb (5361 kg)
Dimensions: span 25 ft 3 in (7.70 m); length 46 ft 4½ in (14.14 m); height 12 ft 10½ in (3.92 m); wing area 170 sq ft (15.79 m²)
Armament: none
Operators: NASA, US Air Force, US Navy, West Germany

Just on 800 Northrop T-38A Talons serve with USAF Air Training Command, and 41 in US markings belong to the Federal German *Luftwaffe* which found American desert weather made for faster pilot graduation. This supersonic trainer has a good service record.

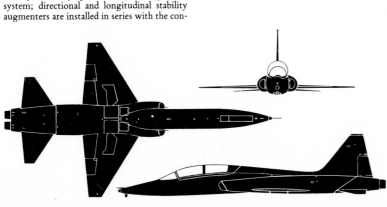

Northrop T-38 Talon

This gaggle of Northrop T-38A Talons are among the oldest of the breed in the whole US Air Force. although only Japan followed suit in buying a costly supersonic trainer (the Jaguar was sensibly reserved as a warplane) the T-38 proved safe and reliable.

Northrop YF-17/F-18L

The Northrop F-18L is the land-based version of the McDonnell Douglas F-18 Hornet carrier-based fighter, which in turn was derived from the Northrop YF-17 twin-engined fighter prototype entered for the US Air Force competition for a Lightweight Fighter. The USAF competition was won by the General Dynamics F-16.

McDonnell Douglas made a detailed study of the two aircraft and concluded that the Northrop YF-17 not only met most of the US Navy's requirements for a new combat fighter, but was also the easier to convert for operation from aircraft carriers. Following this company evaluation, McDonnell Douglas teamed with Northrop to propose a very much heavier, longer ranged development of the YF-17 to meet the US Navy requirements. The resulting aircraft, designated F-18 Hornet, is now in production for the US Navy.

Northrop, although losing the USAF Lightweight Fighter competition, believed that the YF-17 had certain inherent advantages for many overseas air forces, the main one being those afforded by twin engines against the single engine in the F-16. To meet this potential demand, Northrop have evolved a land-based version of the F-18, designated F-18L.

The chief distinguishing features of the F-18L are the absence of carrier gear (such as wing fold, catapult arm and arrester hook), and a considerable reduction in internal capacity which reduces gross weight by 40 per cent.

Externally, the two aircraft are very similar. Of advanced aerodynamic configuration, a distinctive feature is the highly-swept strakes extending along the fuselage from the wing leading edge, which provide vortex lift and control, and significantly reduce wing area. Other features of the fixed unswept wings are the large leading-edge manoeuvring flaps, and the ailerons which can be drooped along with the wing flaps to provide the advantages of full-span flaps for low approach speeds. The primary flying controls are operated by a fly-by-wire flight-control system, with a mechanical back-up.

Ease of maintenance has been given careful consideration in the design. Servicing points and panels are spaced apart, permitting simultaneous maintenance work. An engine can be changed in less than 30 minutes.

Type: single seat, lightweight fighter
Powerplant: two 16,000-lb (7257-kg) General Electric F404-GE-400 turbofans
Performance: maximum level speed at high altitude Mach 2.0; approach speed 127 mph (204 km/h); stalling speed 102 mph (163 km/h); maximum rate of climb with 50% fuel and two Sidewinders over 60,000 ft (18000 m)/min; combat radius 921 miles (1482 km)
Weights: maximum take-off (estimated) 33,000 lb (14970 kg)
Dimensions: span 37 ft 6 in (11.43 m); length 56 ft 0 in (17.07 m); height 15 ft 3 in (4.66 m); wing area 400 sq ft (37.16 m²)
Armament: one M61 20-mm six-barrel gun with 540 rounds, plus two AIM-9 Sidewinders, or two AIM-7 Sparrows, or two Martin Marietta sensor pods.
Operators: none (aircraft under development)

Northrop's two YF-17 prototypes lost out in the 1974 – 75 evaluation against the F-16, but selection of the same basic design for the Naval Air Combat Fighter (today's F-18) has enabled Northrop to try to promote a new land-based F-18L to many countries.

Northrop YF-17/F-18L

PAF T-610 Cali (AJI Super Pinto)

In the mid-1950s the Temco Aircraft Corporation in the USA produced a private-venture jet primary trainer called the Model 51, which had tandem seats, and a pod-and-boom fuselage with a 920-lb (417-kg) Continental J69 turbojet. This flew for the first time on 26 March 1956, and 14 were later built as TT-1 Pintos for the US Navy, to evaluate the feasibility of providing naval cadets with *ab initio* jet training. One of these aircraft was bought by AJI (American Jet Industries Inc) in the late 1960s and developed into a potential COIN (counter-insurgency) type, by installing a more powerful CJ610 engine, stretching the fuselage by 2 ft 6 in (0.76 m), increasing the standard fuel load by adding wingtip tanks, and adding six underwing attachment points on which the aircraft could carry a variety of armament or additional fuel tanks. In this form, known as the T-610 Super Pinto, it was flown for the first time on 28 June 1968, and subsequently was one of a number of light strike types evaluated at Eglin Air Force Base, Florida, in August 1971 as part of the US Air Force's Pave Coin programme. Unsuccessful in attracting orders on this occasion, the Super Pinto then lay dormant for a number of years while AJI concentrated its efforts to more rewarding effect in the civil general-aviation field. In 1978, however, came news that the Self-Reliance Development Wing of the Philippine air force had purchased the prototype, together with all works drawings and rights in its design and production. The PAF, which has re-christened the aircraft Cali, is participating in endeavours to build up an aircraft manufacturing capability in the Philippines, but up to early 1979 had not taken a decision on whether to put the T-610 into production.

Type: two-seat primary jet trainer or light strike aircraft
Powerplant: one 2,850-lb (1293-kg) General Electric CJ610-4 turbojet
Performance: (without tip-tanks) maximum speed 518 mph (834 km/h); maximum rate of climb at sea level 9,000 ft (2743 m) per minute; absolute ceiling 48,000 ft (14630 m)
Weights: empty 3,233 lb (1466 kg); maximum take-off (without tip-tanks) 5,001 lb (2268 kg)
Dimensions: span (without tip-tanks) 30 ft 0 in (9.14 m); length 31 ft 5 in (9.58 m); height 11 ft 5 in (3.48 m); wing area 150.0 sq ft (13.93 m²)
Armament: six underwing hardpoints for external loads, including drop-tanks; no details of individual ordnance known
Operators: Philippines

PAF T-610 Cali (AJI Super Pinto)

Originally called the TT-1 Pinto, this neat primary jet trainer has reappeared as the T-610 Cali, which the Self-Reliance Wing of the Philippines Air Force hopes to put into production as an armed COIN attack platform (note pylons) and trainer.

Panavia Tornado

The tri-national Panavia Tornado fighter-bomber, previously known as the MRCA (Multi-Role Combat Aircraft), has been developed to equip the air forces of Britain, Germany and Italy, together with the German navy. The manufacuturer, Panavia, was formed in March 1969 and comprises a consortium of British Aerospace, Messerschmitt-Bölkow-Blohm (MBB) and Aeritalia. The complementary engine organisation, Turbo-Union, was set up in September 1969 and consists of Rolls-Royce, Motoren- und Turbinen-Union (MTU) and Fiat.

The Tornado has resulted from the need to replace a wide variety of earlier types used for several roles. These include German and Italian Lockheed F-104G Starfighters, together with the Royal Air Force's HS Vulcans, BAC Canberras and HS Buccaneers. These are all due to be superseded by the Tornado IDS (interdictor/strike) version, called Tornado FG.1 by the RAF. In addition, the Tornado F.2 or ADV (Air-Defence Variant) is being developed to succeed the RAF's BAC Lightning and McDonnell Douglas Phantom interceptors.

The abandonment of earlier studies, such as the AFVG (Anglo-French Variable-Geometry) and joint US-German projects, led to the adoption of Tornado as a tri-national programme in an effort to increase the production run and thus reduce unit costs. Canada, Belgium and the Netherlands also took part in the early studies but subsequently withdrew, leaving the present three sponsoring countries. Development began in mid-1970, following the completion of the feasibility and project-definition phases.

The Tornado is a twin-engined, two-seat aircraft which is intended to perform six major roles covering the requirements of the four initial operating services. These are close air support and battlefield interdiction, interdiction/counter-air operations, air superiority, interception, naval attack and reconnaissance. A dual-control trainer version with secondary combat responsibilities is also in production.

A variable-geometry (swing-wing) layout was adopted to give the Tornado the maximum operating flexibility. This includes the ability to use dispersed semi-prepared airfields, loiter for long periods with the wings swept forwards, cruise for long distances at high and medium altitudes, and fly at high speed just above the ground or sea with its wings swept back for the best gust-response characteristics and a smooth ride. An extremely sophisticated navigation-attack system is installed, but a two-man crew was nevertheless selected to maximize the aircraft's efficiency. The Tornado will perform its attack role at least as well as the much larger General Dynamics F-111 and provide an effective all-weather counter to the build-up of Warsaw Pact forces.

The first of nine prototypes made its maiden flight in August 1974, this series being followed by six pre-production Tornadoes. Four of these are to be refurbished to operational standard and will enter service alongside 805 new production aircraft: 324 for the *Luftwaffe* and German navy, 385 for the RAF (of which 165 will be ADVs) and 100 for the Italian air force. Delays have resulted in the service-entry timetable being put back, but delivery for service test began in February 1977, and the Tri-National Training Unit at Cottesmore began operations in 1979.

The shoulder-mounted wings are swept by 25° when fully forward and 66° when swung completely aft; the angle is controlled manually by the pilot, although a semi-automatic arrangement is likely to be adopted (certainly for the F.2) to relieve the crew's workload in air combat. The navigation-attack system includes a Texas Instruments multi-mode radar for terrain following, ground mapping, air-to-air acquisition and lock-on, navigation fixes and air-to-ground target ranging. The Ferranti-inertial navigator and Decca doppler radar feed navigation information to the main computer, a Litef Spirit 3. Data are communicated to the navigator on his combined radar/projected-map and television displays, and to the pilot on a projected-map repeater. Flight-director and weapon-aiming symbology is presented to the pilot on his head-up display, and any other in-

continued

Panavia Tornado prototype P-09 depicted in the red-white finish adopted by the early test aircraft and with the tri-national insignia on the fin.

Panavia Tornado P-11, the first of the pre-production aircraft, shown in the markings of Erprobungsstelle 61, the Luftwaffe test unit at Manching.

Test-flown with four Kormoran anti-shipping missiles, Tornado P-04 was the second prototype assembled in Germany.

Panavia Tornado 03, seen here high over northern England in its fourth year of flying was the first of the dual trainer versions for which BAe has responsibility. Basically similar aircraft are now with the TTTE (Tornado Tri-national Training Establishment).

formation required by the navigator can be extracted from the central computer using television tabular displays.

This avionic equipment, including a retractable derivative of the Ferranti LRMTS (Laser Ranger and Marked-Target Seeker) also used in the SEPECAT Jaguar and BAe (HS) Harrier, allows the Tornado to carry out single-pass attacks at high speed and deliver its weapons extremely accurately. During low-level trials the aircraft has demonstrated a sustained indicated airspread of 920 mph (1472 km/h), which is well above the limit of almost all other types at present in existence.

The demanding specification laid down for the Tornado called for an advanced new

engine, the RB.199-34R. This three-spool turbofan, two of which are installed, is designed for an economic fuel consumption at maximum dry thrust and a high maximum afterburning thrust. This combination of attributes is necessary if the aircraft is to be able to take off from a short run, have a top speed of more than Mach 2 and good combat manoeuvrability, yet also have a worthwhile range during low-level interdiction missions at transonic speeds with heavy weapon loads. Thrust reversers and anti-skid brakes provide a short-landing capability.

The F.2 Air-Defence Variant, an interceptor designed specifically for the RAF, incorporates a number of modifications for its role of

patrolling the East German border and defending the large sea areas around Britain. Marconi Avionics and Ferranti are collaborating on development of a new air-interception radar, known unofficially as Foxhunter, which will be able to detect intruders at distances of more than 115 miles (185 km). The Tornado F.2 will also be fitted with a Marconi Avionics long-range visual identification system to sort out targets from friendly aircraft, and it will carry British Aerospace Sky Flash air-to-air missiles which, operating in conjunction with the radar, can seek out and destroy intruders at ranges of 25 miles (40 km) or more regardless of their height. In addition to the four Sky Flash missiles mounted in semi-recessed belly

positions, the Tornado F.2 will be armed with two or four AIM-9L Super Sidewinder air-to-air missiles and will carry a single built-in 27-mm Mauser cannon of the same as is installed in the IDS aircraft, which are fitted with two guns.

Despite these changes, the ADV is 80% common with the IDS. The major obvious difference is a 4 ft (1.2 m) extension to the forward fuselage to accommodate the new radar (with a pointed radome), different avionics and extra fuel. Three ADV prototypes are being built, and the first was expected to fly before the end of 1979. The aircraft is due to enter service with the RAF in about 1982.

Panavia Tornado IDS cutaway drawing key

1 Pitot head
2 Radome (AEG-Telefunken)
3 Ground mapping/attack radar scanner (Texas Instruments)
4 Terrain following radar scanner (Texas Instruments)
5 Yaw vane
6 Radar processing unit
7 IFF aerial
8 Windscreen rain-repelling air duct
9 Avionics bay
10 Angle of attack probe
11 Canopy release handle
12 Port cannon port
13 Laser ranger and marked target seeker on starboard side (Ferranti)
14 Windscreen (Lucas-Rotax)
15 Instrument panel shroud
16 Cockpit bulkhead
17 Rudder pedals
18 Avionics bay
19 Cannon barrel
20 Nosewheel door
21 Flight refuelling probe (bolt-on)
22 Pilot's head-up display (Smiths)
23 Instrument panel
24 Control column
25 Engine throttles
26 Wing sweep control
27 Command and Stability Augmentation System (CSAS) controller (Marconi-Elliot)
28 Autopilot control panel (Elliot)
29 Pilot's ejection seat (Martin Baker Mk 10)
30 Port 27-mm cannon (Mauser)
31 One piece canopy, open (Kopperschmidt)
32 Rear-view mirrors
33 Canopy jettison charge
34 Navigator's instrument console
35 Port two-dimensional air intake
36 Ammunition feed to starboard cannon
37 Ammunition tank
38 Oxygen bottle
39 Nose undercarriage leg (Dowty Rotol)
40 Twin nosewheels (Dunlop)
41 Cold air inlet
42 Navigator's rear-view mirrors
43 Navigator's instrument display
44 Starboard air intake
45 Navigator's ejection seat (Martin Baker Mk 10)
46 Canopy jack
47 Air-intake ramp jacks (Liebherr Aerotechnik)
48 Formation light
49 Intake variable-area ramp doors
50 Bleed air louvres
51 Supplementary intake doors
52 Air conditioning plant (Normalair-Garrett)
53 Intake control system (Nord-Micro)
54 Intake trunking
55 Wing-root glove fairing

56 Krüger flap, extended
57 Wing pivot sealing fairing
58 Front fuselage bag fuel tank (Uniroyal)
59 Wing sweep actuator (Microtecnica)
60 Wing sweep hydraulic motor
61 Slat and flap combined motor (Microtecnica)
62 Communications navigation aerials
63 Anti-collision light

64 Starboard wing sweep actuator
65 Wing pivot titanium box carry through structure
66 Starboard wing pivot
67 Upper surface wing seal
68 Inboard pylon pivot point
69 Wing torque box
70 Integral fuel tank
71 Full-span leading-edge slats
72 Outboard pylon pivot point
73 Outboard pylon
74 Starboard navigation light
75 Wing tip antenna
76 Spoilers
77 Spoiler jacks
78 Full-span double-slotted flaps
79 Starboard external fuel tank
80 Wing root pneumatic seal
81 Pressurising air inlet
82 HF notch aerial
83 Tailplane mechanical emergency linkage
84 Air-conditioning supply
85 Primary heat exchanger
86 Air outlet
87 Two spar fin construction
88 Fin fuel tank

89 Communications antenna, VOR
90 Electronic tuning controls
91 Passive ECM housing
92 Fin tip antenna, Tacan and V/UHF aerials
93 Tail warning radar (Elettrotecnica)
94 Tail navigation light
95 Rudder
96 Starboard taileron surface
97 Starboard fully-variable exhaust nozzle
98 Thrust-reverser bucket-doors, open
99 Spine end fairing, "half-Whitcomb" body
100 Port fully-variable exhaust nozzle
101 Thrust-reverser bucket-door, closed
102 Bucket-door actuator
103 Nozzle actuator
104 Port taileron construction

105 Taileron tip fairing
106 Runway arrester hook (Nardi)
107 Taileron actuating link
108 Taileron pivot
109 Port taileron actuator
110 Turbo Union RB.199-34 engine
111 Airbrake jack
112 Port airbrake, extended
113 Vortex generators
114 Rudder actuator (Fairey Hydraulics)
115 Airbrake hinge point
116 Fly-by-wire tailplane control unit

Type: multi-role combat aircraft
Powerplant: two 15,000-lb (6805-kg) Turbo-Union RB.199-34R afterburning turbofans
Performance: maximum level speed at altitude over Mach 2.2 or 1,450 mph (2335 km/h); level speed (clean) at low altitude about Mach 1.2 or 810 mph (1305 km/h); tactical radius at least 870 miles (1390 km) with heavy weapon load; ceiling 50,000 ft (1520 m)
Weights: empty about 25,000 lb (11350 kg); maximum take-off about 60,000 lb (27200 kg)
Dimensions: span (wings swept) 28 ft 2 in (8.60 m); span (wings forward) 45 ft 7 in (13.90 m); length 54 ft 9½ in (16.70 m); height 18 ft 8½ in (5.70 m)
Armament: (IDS) two 27-mm Mauser cannon and up to more than 18,000 lb (8180 kg) of stores, including bombs, Martel air-to-surface missiles Kormoran and P3T anti-ship missiles, Sparrow, Aspide, Sky Flash and Sidewinder air-to-air missiles, MW-1 sub-munition dispensers, BL755 and other cluster bombs, JP233 anti-runway bombs, etc; (ADV) one 27-mm Mauser cannon and four Sky Flash air-to-air missiles, plus up to four AIM-9L Super Sidewinder air-to-air missiles
Operators: on order for Italy, UK, West Germany

The Panavia Tornado IDS in the foreground is carrying eight bombs of 1,000 lb (454 kg), two large tanks and the new Ajax ECM pods outboard.

117 Hydraulic reservoir
118 Hydraulic system accumulator (Dowty)
119 Engine access doors
120 Intake frame
121 APU (KHD) in starboard gearbox bay
122 Rear fuselage bag fuel tank (Uniroyal)
123 Intake ducting
124 Engine-driven auxiliary gearbox (KHD)
125 Wing housing cross-frame
126 Wing-root pneumatic seal
127 Undercarriage frame
128 Main undercarriage retraction jack

129 Flap control shaft
130 Flap screw jacks
131 Port wing pivot bearing
132 Drive shaft gearbox
133 Leading-edge slat drive shaft
134 Main undercarriage door
135 Landing lamp
136 Full-span leading-edge slats, extended
137 Slat control units
138 1,000-lb bomb (454-kg), total of eight

139 Pylon pivot control rod
140 Inboard pylon pivot point
141 Main undercarriage leg (Dowty Rotol)
142 Fuselage bomb rack, port
143 Wing swept position
144 Port mainwheel (Dunlop)
145 Spoilers
146 Spoiler jack (Fairey Hydraulics)
147 Wing box construction
148 Integral fuel tank
149 Port inboard pylon
150 Port external fuel tank
151 Leading-edge slat rails
152 Outboard pylon pivot point
153 Flap track rail
154 Full-span double-slotted flaps, extended
155 Line of wing sweep
156 Wingtip antenna
157 Port navigation light
158 Port outboard pylon
159 Matra rocket launcher

Production Tornadoes have a taileron (the horizontal tail surfaces act as both tailplanes and ailerons) with a kinked leading edge to improve airflow at full sweep with the largest stores. Immediately ahead of the nozzles are the upper clamshells of the engine reversers, which, with non-skid brakes and powerful steering, permit short landings in wet or icy conditions. Further ahead can be seen the large upper-surface airbrakes.

The Texas Instruments main radar operates in seven modes for different parts of each mission. Below and behind is the terrain-following radar and the retractable laser. The Tornado F.2 interceptor has a different radar with smaller aerial array and no terrain-following set, so has a slimmer and more pointed nose for reduced drag. On each side of the nosewheel bay is the new gun armament, the outstanding MK27 cannon by IWKA-Mauser.

The Tornado has fully modulated variable engine inlets for highly supersonic performance. Despite the no-distortion flat windscreen it is the fastest aircraft in the world at low level, cleared for speeds in excess of 800 kt (920 mph), compared with the normal indicated airspeed limit for the Mk 10A seat of 725 mph. Wings are integral tanks and are shown at the sweep limits of 25° and 68°. Note the swivelling pylons.

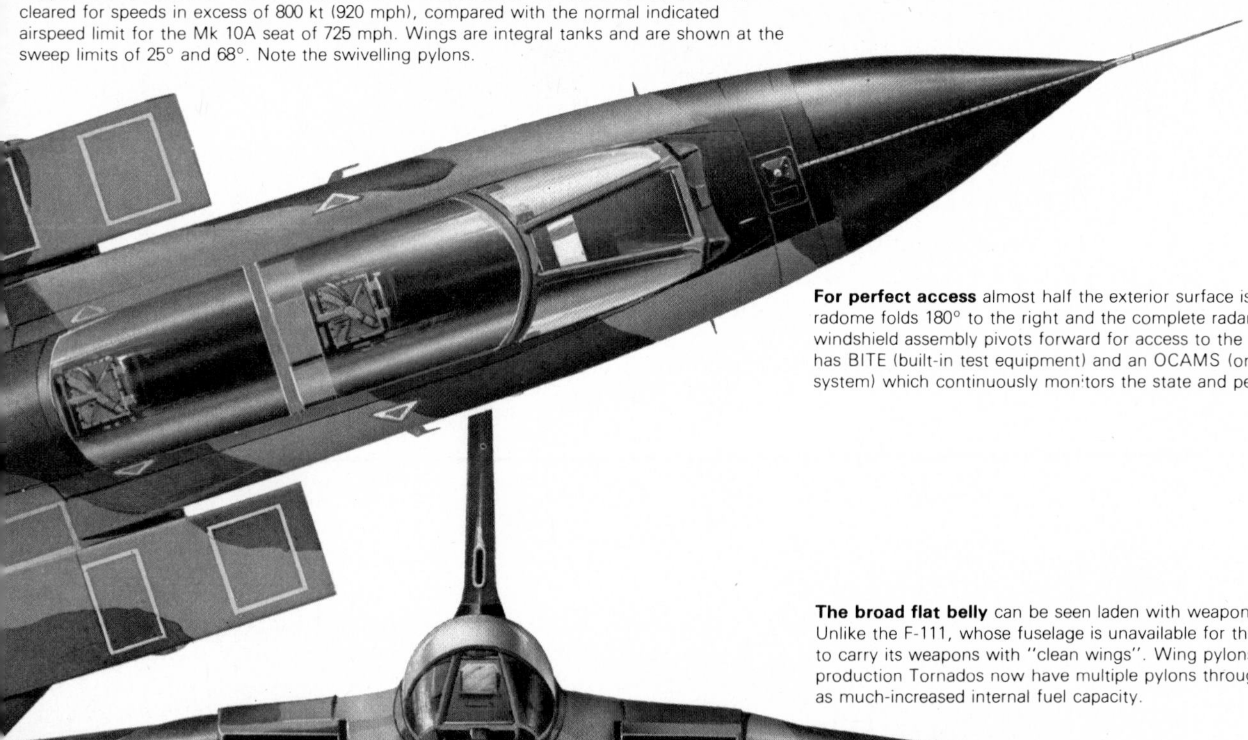

For perfect access almost half the exterior surface is made up of hinged panels. The radome folds 180° to the right and the complete radar package swings round behind it. The windshield assembly pivots forward for access to the pilot's instruments. The entire aircraft has BITE (built-in test equipment) and an OCAMS (on-board checkout and monitoring system) which continuously monitors the state and performance of the systems.

The broad flat belly can be seen laden with weapons, in this case eight bombs of 1,000 lb. Unlike the F-111, whose fuselage is unavailable for this purpose, the Tornado was designed to carry its weapons with "clean wings". Wing pylons were added as an overload, and production Tornados now have multiple pylons throughout both fuselage and wings, as well as much-increased internal fuel capacity.

This example is one of the original nine flight prototypes, P.06 (XX948), assembled at Warton by BAe and used for various stores-separation and gun-firing trials. In addition to the eight 1,000 lb bombs it is shown with two 1500-litre (396 US gal) drop tanks and ECM jammer pods. Defensive electronics are said to include the EL-73 radar warning system, Ajax pods, ALQ-101(V) pods, ARI.18228 fin aerials and various dispensers.

Pazmany PL-1B Chiensou

Originally a two-seat amateur-built aircraft originating in California, the Pazmany PL-1 was selected in 1968 by the Chinese Nationalist air force in Taiwan for production on the island as a first step in creating a local aircraft industry. Construction of the first military prototype, the PL-1A, began in June 1968 under the supervision of Colonel C.Y. Lee of the Nationalist air force. It was built at the Aeronautical Research Laboratory, Taichung. First flight was on 26 October 1968 and the aircraft was demonstrated to Generalissimo Chiang Kai-shek four days later. Two more prototypes were built the following year, and the decision was made to build a series under the designation PL-1B Chienshou for use as primary trainers for Nationalist air cadets.

The PL-1B is a cantilever low-wing monoplane, closely resembling the PL-1A, but with a wider cockpit, larger rudder and more powerful Lycoming O-320-E2A engine in place of the original 125-hp (93-kW) O-290-D. Fuel is carried in wingtip tanks. The wing is an all-metal single-spar structure in one piece with leading-edge torsion box. Piano-hinged ailerons and flaps are also of metal. The undercarriage is of fixed tricycle configuration. The two cockpit seats are side-by-side with dual control under a rearward-sliding one-piece 'bubble' canopy. The angular cantilever tail has a swept-back fin and rudder and a one-piece all-moving horizontal surface with anti-servo tab/trim tab.

Apart from 50 PL-1Bs built for the Nationalist air arm, the very similar PL-2 was ordered by South Korea, South Vietnam and Thailand.

Type: two-seat primary trainer
Powerplant: one 150-hp (112-kW) Lycoming O-320-E3A four-cylinder horizontally-opposed air-cooled piston engine
Performance: maximum speed at sea level at maximum take-off weight 150 mph (241 km/h); economical cruising speed 115 mph (185 km/h) at sea level; stalling speed with flaps down 54 mph (87 km/h); rate of climb at sea level 1,600 ft (488 m) per minute; range with maximum fuel 405 miles (652 km); take-off run 560 ft (171 m); landing run 550 ft (167 m)
Weights: empty equipped 950 lb (431 kg); maximum take off 1,440 lb (653 kg)
Dimensions: span 28 ft 0 in (8.53 m); length 19 ft 8⅛ in (5.98 m); height 7 ft 4 in (2.24 m); wing area 116 sq ft (10.78 m²)
Armament: none
Operators: South Korea, Taiwan

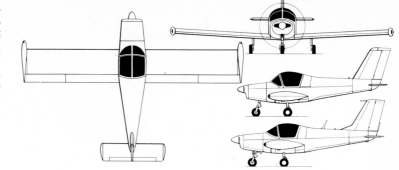

Pazmany PL-1B Chiensou

Primary trainer of Taiwan is the PL-1B Chienshou, of which 55 were built by the Aero Industry Development Centre at Taichung. The design is that of the Pazmany PL-1, a popular US homebuilt two-seater with side-by-side seating. Pupils go on to the T-CH-1.

Piaggio P.148

Designed by Giovanni Casiraghi in less than six months, the first prototype P.148 primary trainer/liaison aircraft flew initially on 12 February 1951. The Italian government ordered 100 series aircraft for the *Aeronautica Militare,* and these were delivered in 1953. They were intended to equip elementary flying schools for initial (1° *periodo*) training, but a radical change in the training programme resulted in their allocation to regional flying centres and the *Scuola Plurimotori* (training school for multi-engined aircraft crews) on liaison duties and to the *Centro Militare di Volo a Vela* (military gliding centre) for glider-towing.

A number of P.148s were disposed of by Italy to Zaire and Somalia, but in 1970 a reversion to previous policy led to the transfer of surviving *Aeronautica Militare* P.148s to the elementary flying schools for the role originally intended in 1953. Only recently have they been phased out and replaced by the new SIAI-Marchetti SF.260.

An all-metal low-wing cantilever monoplane, the P.148 is normally a side-by-side two-seater, but there is provision for an optional third seat in the rear of the cabin. The cockpit was enclosed by a transparent 'bubble' canopy, the rear section of which slides backwards for access. The front windshield frame is reinforced to protect the crew in the event of a nose-over on landing. The wing is a riveted single-spar structure with a section derived from NACA 230/4412. It has square tips, and all-metal slotted ailerons and flaps.

The circular-section fuselage is a riveted stressed-skin monocoque. Wings, fuselage and the angular cantilever tailplane are all of aluminium alloy.

The cantilever main legs of the fixed landing gear are spaced well apart, and have oleo-pneumatic shock absorbers and hydraulically-operated brakes. The tailwheel is steerable.

Two integral wing tanks have a total capacity of 37 gallons (169 litres).

Type: two-seat primary trainer
Powerplant: one 190-hp (142-kW) Lycoming O-435-A six-cylinder horizontally-opposed air-cooled engine
Performance: maximum speed at sea level (with two crew) 145 mph (234 km/h); cruising speed at 2,953 ft (900 m) 127 mph (204 km/h); range 497 miles (800 km); climb to 6,562 ft (2000 m) in 8 minutes 10 seconds; service ceiling 14,436 ft (4400 m); take-off run

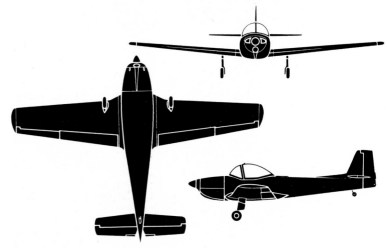

Piaggio P.148

636 ft (194 m); landing run 591 ft (180 m)
Weights: empty 1,931 lb (876 kg); gross (with two crew) 2,645 lb (1200 kg)
Dimensions: span 36 ft 5.8 in (11.12 m); length 27 ft 8.3 in (8.44 m); height 7 ft 10.5 in (2.40 m); wing area 202.5 sq ft (18.81 m²)
Armament: none
Operators: Italy, Somalia, Zaïre

Piaggio P.149D

Giovanni Casiraghi extrapolated his Piaggio P.148 into the P.149 four-seat touring aircraft with increased power and a retractable tricycle landing gear, the new P.149 was flown in prototype form on 19 June 1953 and the type was subsequently built in limited numbers largely for private owners. Many structural components of the P.148 were utilised in manufacturing the P.149.

Two years later the firm converted an aircraft as a demonstrator equipped for the military liaison/training role. Designated P.149D, the type was evaluated by the West German *Luftwaffe,* which subsequently ordered 72 from Piaggio and arranged for a further 190 in due course to be licence-built by the Focke-Wulf company at Bremen. The military version differs from the commercial type in having the 260-hp (194-kW) Lycoming GO-435-C2 engine replaced by a 270-hp (201-kW) GO-480.

The basic construction of the P.149 closely follows that of the P.148 with the exception of the powerplant, landing gear and cabin. The nosewheel retracts backwards into the fuselage, and main legs outwards into the

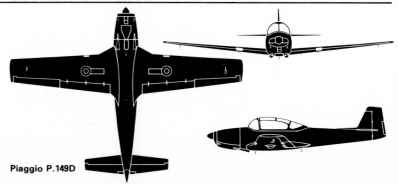

Piaggio P.149D

wings. Oleo-pneumatic shock absorbers and hydraulic wheel brakes are fitted.

The cockpit is covered by a large curved canopy which slides backwards for access and can be jettisoned in an emergency. The two front seats have dual controls, and the rear bench seat can accommodate two or three. The German air force machines have given many years service as the standard basic trainer and liaison machine of the *Luftwaffe*. Complete

blind-flying equipment and navigational radio with D/F loop are carried.

The success of the P.149D has brought a number of export orders for the military version, notably from Nigeria, Tanzania and Uganda. All surviving ex-*Luftwaffe* aircraft have been passed on to other air forces.

Type: basic trainer/liaison aircraft
Powerplant: one 270-hp (201-kW) Lycom-

ing GO-480 six-cylinder horizontally-opposed air-cooled engine
Performance: maximum speed 194 mph (312 km/h) at sea level; cruising speed at 70% power at 8,202 ft (2500 m) 167 mph (268 km/h); range with maximum fuel 609 miles (980 km); climb rate 984 ft (300 m) per minute; service ceiling 19,849 ft (6050 m)
Weights: empty 2,513 lb (1140 kg); loaded 3,700 lb (1680 kg)

Dimensions: span 36 ft 5.8 in (11.12 m); length 28 ft 10.5 in (8.8 m); height 9 ft 4.2 in (2.85 m); wing area 202.5 sq ft (18.81m²)
Armament: none
Operators: Nigeria, Tanzania, Uganda, West Germany

Piaggio P.166

Bearing obvious traces of its development from the P.136 amphibian, the P.166 is a landplane and was designed as a six-to eight-seat executive aircraft, the position of the pusher propellers providing a quieter cabin.

The prototype flew on 26 November 1957, since when more than 120 have been built in various versions as follows: P.166 (32); P.166M (51); P.166B (5); P.166C (2); P.166S (20); P.166DL-2 (5); P.166DL-3 (4). Of these, only the P.166M and P.166S were delivered to military customers.

The P.166M is a military version of the basic P.166, designed to the requirements of the Italian air force for training, ambulance and communications work. A strengthened floor permits the carriage of heavy loads and an enlarged freight door in the left forward fuselage can admit an Orpheus turbojet to support the Fiat G.91 strike and reconnaissance aircraft. A total of 51 P.166Ms was supplied to

the *Aeronautica Militare Italiano*. A number are still in service, some on communications duties with the *Reporti Volo Regionale* and others with the *Reparto Sperimentale Volo* at Pratica di Mare, Rome, an evaluation unit.

The other military user is the South African air force, which received 20 P.166S radar-equipped versions in 1973-74 for short-range coastal patrol and search and rescue duties. In SAAF service the type is named Albatross.

Type: (P.166) twin-engine light transport
Powerplant: two 340-hp (254-kW) Lycoming GSO-480-B1C6 piston engines
Performance: maximum speed at 9,500 ft (2900 m) 222 mph (357 km/h); cruising speed at 75% power at 12,800 ft (3900 m) 207 mph (333 km/h); rate of climb at sea level 1,240 ft (380 m) per minute; service ceiling 25,500 ft (7770 m); take-off to 50 ft (15 m) 1,570 ft (480 m); landing run from 50 ft (15 m) 1,560 ft

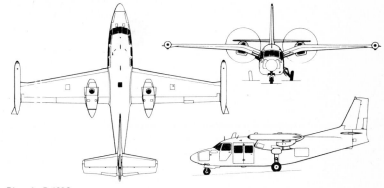

Piaggio P.166C

(475 m); range 1,200 miles (1930 km)
Weights: empty 5,181 lb (2350 kg); loaded 8,115 lb (3680 kg)
Dimensions: span 46 ft 9 in (14.25 m);

length 38 ft 1 in (11.60 m); height 16 ft 5 in (5.0 m); wing area 285.9 sq ft (26.56 m²)
Operators: Italy, South Africa

Piaggio PD-808

The letters in the designation PD-808 indicate that the aircraft was a joint venture. Designed by the El Segundo Division of Douglas Aircraft, the PD-808 was built in Italy by Piaggio, this company being responsible also for detail drawings and tooling. The Italian Ministry of Defence agreed to be responsible for a third of the development cost, buy two prototypes and provide test facilities, and in 1965 placed an order for 25 production aircraft, of which 22 were eventually delivered.

The prototype flew on 29 August 1964, followed by a second in 1965. It was planned that when the type entered quantity production the first 115 would be built by Piaggio with further orders being met from a joint Italian-US production line. However, it was not to be; the aircraft did not attract further orders.

Four versions were built and delivered to the Italian air force. The PD-808 is a six-seater military VIP transport, four of which serve

with the Italian air staff flying unit at Rome; eight PD-808 TA nine-seaters for navigation training and transport are in service; four PD-808 RMs carry out radio and navaid calibration; and the PD-808 ECM is an electronic countermeasures version carrying two pilots and three equipment operators, six of these aircraft operating with 71 *Gruppo Guerra Elettronica* at Pratica de Mare, Rome

Type: twin-jet passenger/utility transport
Powerplant: two 3,000-lb (1361-kg) thrust Rolls-Royce Viper 525 turbojets
Performance: maximum speed at 19,500 ft (5945 m) 529 mph (852 km/h); cruising speed at 41,000 ft (12500 m) 449 mph (722 km/h); rate of climb at sea level 5,400 ft (1650 m) per minute; service ceiling 45,000 ft (13715 m); take-off run to 35 ft (10.7 m) 3,180 ft (970 m); landing run from 50 ft (15 m) 2,990 ft (912 m); range with 45-minute reserve 1,322 miles (2128 km)

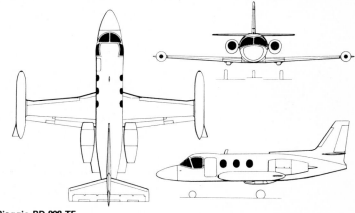

Piaggio PD-808 TF

Weights: empty 10,650 lb (4830 kg); maximum take-off 18,000 lb (8165 kg)
Dimensions: span 37 ft 6 in (11.43 m);

length 42 ft 2 in (12.85 m); height 15 ft 9 in (4.80 m); wing area 225 sq ft (20.9 m²)
Operators: Italy

Pilatus P-2

The Pilatus Flugzeugwerke AG of Stans, near Lucerne, was formed in December 1939 and work on aircraft began in September 1941. The firm is a subsidiary of Oerlikon.

In an attempt to interest the Swiss *Flugwaffe* in a trainer of domestic design, Chief Engineer H. Fierz developed a low-wing cantilever monoplane of mixed construction with an inward-retracting main landing gear. Designated P-2-01, it flew for the first time on 27 April, 1945. Aircraft P 2-02, built concurrently, was used for structural ground testing.

Successful evaluation led to an order for 26 P-2-05 series aircraft, which went into service from 1947. They symbolised the Swiss official policy of economy, since they re-used a number of parts from *Flugwaffe* Messerschmitt Bf 109E fighters which had been scrapped. These included main-undercarriage legs, wheels and brakes; the tailwheel assembly; and the hydraulic pumps.

This first production series was used for liaison as well as for intermediate flying training. In 1968 they were converted for blind-flying instruction.

In 1947–8 two prototypes were built to utilise Hispano-Suiza HS-57 500-hp (373-kW) engines taken from obsolete Dewoitine D27 fighter-trainers, but the P-2-03 and -04 were not successful and the idea of re-cycling old engines was abandoned by the Swiss authorities.

The P-2-06 series of a further 26 machines was ordered in 1948. They differed only in minor detail from the first batch, but were equipped for armament training with a synchronized cowling machine-gun and underwing racks for light practice bombs.

Surviving aircraft were converted for blind-flying training in 1965. The two batches of series machines were initially serialled A-103 to A-128 and U-103 to U-128 respectively.

The P-2 wing is a wooden two-spar structure with a stressed plywood skin. Ailerons are fabric-covered, and the flaps ply-covered. The light alloy fuselage is built up on four main longerons, with two flat side panels and detachable formed top and bottom sections. The cantilever tailplane is all-metal with the exception of the fabric-covered control surfaces. The swivelling tailwheel is non-retractable.

Type: two-seat advanced trainer
Powerplant: one 370-hp (276-kW) Argus As 410 A-2 12-cylinder inverted-vee air-cooled supercharged piston engine
Performance: maximum speed at 8,202 ft (2500 m) 211 mph (340 km/h); cruising speed at 10,827 ft (3300 m) 206 mph (332 km/h); range 348 miles (560 km); maximum rate of climb 1,280 ft (390 m) per minute; service ceiling 21,653 ft (6600 m)
Weights: empty 3,404 lb (1544 kg); loaded

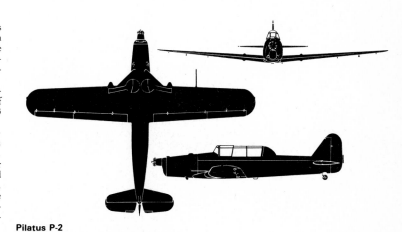

Pilatus P-2

4343 lb (1970 kg)
Dimensions: span 36 ft 1.1 in (11.00 m); length 29 ft 9.1 in (9.07 m); height 8 ft 10.3 in (2.70 m); wing area 183 sq ft (17 m²)
Armament: (combat training configuration) fixed 7.62-mm (0.3-in) machine-gun in cowling, synchronized to fire through propeller arc, and light bombs on six underwing racks
Operators: Switzerland

Pilatus P-3

The Pilatus P-3-01 prototype aerobatic trainer made its first flight on 3 September, 1953. The Swiss *Flugwaffe* considered it underpowered and the company accordingly built the P-3-02 for service evaluation, powered by a 240-hp (179-kW) Lycoming GO-435-C2AS six-cylinder air-cooled inverted-vee engine. Satisfactory tests led to an order for a service test series of 12 machines, serialled A-802 to A-813. Most of the machines were still in first-class condition 20 years after going into service. They were followed by a series of 60 P-3-05 aircraft, serials A-814 to A-873, which were powered by the same engine as the evaluation series. Although the Swiss authorities wanted more power, no suitable powerplant was available. Deliveries began in 1958.

The P-3 is a low-wing cantilever monoplane with NACA Series 649-wing section. The wing is a single-spar aluminium-alloy structure with split flaps and ailerons. The fuselage is an all-metal semi-monocoque. The angular tailplane is a cantilever all-metal structure. The nosewheel of the tricycle landing gear retracts backwards into the fuselage, and the main-wheels retract inwards.

Pupil and instructor are seated in tandem under a large glazed canopy with sliding sections. Dual controls are provided. Equipment can include oxygen apparatus, a 7.62-mm (0.3-in) machine-gun in a pod below the left wing, racks for two light practice bombs below the right wing, a single training rocket launcher under each wing, or a camera gun. An R/T transceiver is standard.

The P-3 has been used for *ab initio* and intermediate training aerobatics (with inverted-flight capability for short periods), night flying, instrument flying, and weapon training.

In order to improve flight characteristics the Swiss air arm has modified all P-3s by the addition of a long vertical fin on the rear underside of the fuselage. As a result a propensity for aircraft to go into a 'flat spin' during training was overcome.

A small batch of P-3s was exported to Brazil.

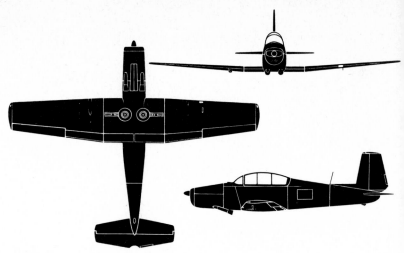
Pilatus P-3

Type: two-seat intermediate trainer
Powerplant: one 260-hp (194-kW) Lycoming GO-435-C2A six-cylinder horizontally opposed air-cooled engine
Performance: maximum speed 193 mph (310 km/h) between sea level and 6,562 ft (2000 m); economic cruising speed 158 mph (255 km/h); range 466 miles (750 km); maximum rate of climb at sea level 1,378 ft (420 m) per minute; service ceiling 18,135 ft (5500 m)
Weights: empty 2,623 lb (1190 kg); maximum take-off 3,373 lb (1530 kg)
Dimensions: span 34 ft 1.4 in (10.4 m); length 28 ft 8.5 in (8.75 m); height 10 ft 0 in (3.05 m); wing area 177.6 sq ft (16.5 m²)
Armament: provision for one 7.62-mm (0.3-in) machine-gun, two practice bombs, or two rocket launchers
Operators: Switzerland, Brazil

Pilatus PC-6 Porter

Developed from the Pilatus P-4 high-wing monoplane, the PC-6 was originally intended for civil use for operation in areas where small airfields difficult of access were the norm. It is a single-engined general utility machine, capable of lifting loads of up to 1,102 lb (500 kg). Its spacious cabin has double doors with a clear width of 5 ft 3 in (1.6 m) when open. As a transport there is accommodation for five passengers, and in ambulance configuration there is room for two stretcher cases plus attendants. The first flight of the prototype took place on 4 May 1959.

The PC-6 is a high-wing monoplane, braced by a single strut on each side. The single-spar, thick-section, narrow, parallel-chord all-metal wing is hinged along the whole length of the trailing edge, the inner sections serving as flaps and the outer sections as ailerons. The fuselage and tall, angular cantilever tailplane are also of all-metal construction. Each main wheel of the fixed landing gear is braced to the fuselage by three struts. Oleo-pneumatic shock absorbers and low-pressure tyres are fitted. The main wheels have brakes and the tailwheel is steerable. The integral wing fuel tanks possess a total capacity of 57 gallons (260 litres).

The pilot's seat is on the left side of the cabin, with one passenger seat alongside it. From the back of the seats to the rear cabin wall is a distance of 7 ft 10 in (2.4 m), while internal width of the cabin is 3 ft 9 in (1.15 m). A loading hatch in the cabin floor measures 1 ft 11.5 in by 2 ft 11.5 in (60 cm by 90 cm), and can be opened from inside the cabin for supply-dropping or alternatively to allow operation of an aerial camera.

The first production model flew initially in August 1960, and a number of Porters were employed by flying doctor services in the less-accessible areas of Germany and Switzerland. By 1964 over 50 aircraft had been sold, comprising various models with piston engines in the 340-hp/350-hp (254-kW/261-kW) class.

The Swiss *Flugwaffe* ordered 12 PC-6/H2Ms powered by 320-hp (239-kW) Lycoming GSO-480-B1A6 engines in 1965, delivery of aircraft serialled V-612 to V-623 taking place two years later. The Swiss authorities have found the type very reliable, although underpowered. It can be fitted with skis for winter operations, and is employed for parachute drops and forest fire-fighting as well as for the tasks already indicated. Ecuador and Colombia have purchased PC-6s for service use from Fairchild, the US licence-holder for the Porter.

Type: general utility STOL transport

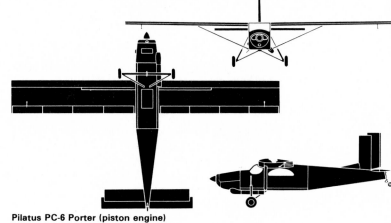
Pilatus PC-6 Porter (piston engine)

Powerplant: one 340-hp (254-kW) Lycoming GSO-480-B1 A6 six-cylinder horizontally opposed air-cooled piston engine
Performance: maximum speed 145 mph (233 km/h); cruising speed 135 mph (217 km/h); stalling speed 44 mph (70 km/h); range with maximum fuel 559 miles (900 km); service ceiling 23,950 ft (7300 m); rate of climb 1,148 ft (350 m) per minute; landing run 256 ft (78 m); take-off run 420 ft (128 m)
Weights: empty equipped 2,959 lb (1340 kg); maximum take-off 4,850 lb (2200 kg)
Dimensions: span 49 ft 7.7 in (15.13 m); length 33 ft 5.8 in (10.20 m); height 10 ft 6 in (3.20 m); wing area 310 sq ft (28.8 m²)
Armament: none
Operators: Colombia, Ecuador, Switzerland

The Swiss Flugwaffe operates seven squadrons of fixed-wing light transport aircraft, numbered among which are 11 locally built piston-engined Pilatus Porters, with excellent STOL capability. They fly general utility and light transport missions, alongside 24 of the much more powerful PC-6/B Turbo-Porters with turboprop engines. Though ungainly in appearance these machines are robust and ideally suited to operation from short unsurfaced airstrips, with skis fitted when appropriate.

Pilatus PC-6 Turbo Porter/Fairchild AU-23A Peacemaker

Pilatus recognised that a turboprop-powered derivative of the Porter would confer a better 'hot and high' performance. The economy and reliability thus obtained was expected to outweigh the increased technology required for servicing. So 2 May 1961 saw the first flight of the Turbo Porter, a standard airframe with a 563-shp (420-kW) Turboméca Astazou. Performance proved superior in all flight regimes. Later several turboprops were offered to customers.

The 700-shp (522-kW) Astazou XII was fitted to the PC6-A1/H2, while the PC-6B1-H2 used a 550-shp (410-kW) Pratt & Whitney PT6A-20 and flew for the first time in May 1966. This variant was built in parallel by Fairchild Industries of the USA. Fairchild was also responsible for the AiResearch TPE331-powered PC-6C1/H2 and C2/H2 Turbo Porters, the former leading to the Fairchild AU-23 Peacemaker.

Fairchild had demonstrated a Porter to the US Air Force in 1970 with an XM-197 manually-operated 20-mm cannon installed to fire laterally from the side door. As a result the USAF placed an initial order for 15 AU-23As, which were evaluated in the Credible Chase programme.

The Peacemaker, as the AU-23A came to be known, was powered by a 650-shp (485-kW) AiResearch T76. A complete military navigation/communications system was installed with VHF, UHF, HF and FM radio. The type was utilized by the USAF on counter-insurgency (COIN), light armed and photo-reconnaissance duties, leaflet dropping and 'psy-war' loudspeaker broadcasting. An underfuselage hardpoint capable of carrying 590 lb (268 kg) was provided, while four underwing stores points could accommodate loads of up to 1,400 lb (636 kg) in total.

Armament included two cabin-mounted 7.62-mm (0.3-in) Miniguns with 2,000-round magazines, Minigun pods on the inner wing points, and rocket pods or 250-lb (113-kg) bombs on the outer hardpoints. For the psy-war role, a broadcasting pod could be carried, while three cameras could be coupled with flares. The USAF passed its 14 remaining

Peacemakers to the Royal Thai Air Force. A further 20 Fairchild-built Porters were supplied to Thailand in 1975-76. Switzerland took delivery of 24 Turbo Porters to serve alongside 11 of their piston-engined forebears. The *Flugwaffe* operated both types for alpine supply and rescue missions, for which the Turbo Porter's good high altitude performance, stability on sloping snowfields and excellent manoeuvrability made it ideal.

The functional-looking Turbo Porter lends itself to many military tasks. Its large rearward-sliding hatch on the right side, complemented by double doors on the left, facilitate parachute training and supply-dropping. A smaller hatch may be used for supply-dropping or cameras. Ski or float landing gear are customer options. Production continues at Stans at the rate of some three aircraft per month.

Type: STOL utility transport
Powerplant: one 550-shp (410-kW) Pratt & Whitney Aircraft of Canada PT6A-27 turboprop
Performance: maximum design speed 174 mph (280 km/h); maximum cruising speed at 10,000 ft (3050 m) 161 mph (259 km/h); range on internal fuel 644 miles (1036 km); service ceiling 30,025 ft (9150 m); rate of climb at sea level 1,580 ft (482 m) per minute; take-off to clear 50-ft (15-m) obstacle 771 ft (235 m); landing from 50 ft (15 m) 722 ft (220 m)
Weights: empty 2,678 lb (1215 kg); loaded 4,850 lb (2200 kg)
Dimensions: span 49 ft 8 in (15.13 m); length 35 ft 9 in (10.9 m); height 10 ft 6 in (3.2 m); wing area 310 sq ft (28.8 m²)
Armament: not usually fitted
Operators: Angola, Australia, Austria, Bolivia, Chad, Ecuador, Israel, Oman, Peru, Sudan, Switzerland, Thailand

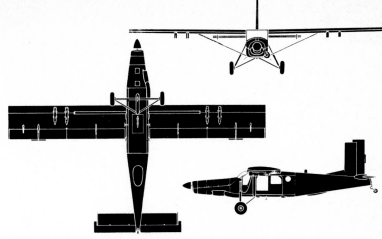

Pilatus PC-6B Turbo Porter/Fairchild AU-23A Peacemaker

The Pilatus PC-6/B Turbo-Porters used by the Australian Army Aviation Corps are powered by the Pratt & Whitney Canada PT6 turboprop (other models have Turbomeca or Garrett engines). The AAAC has 18, serving with units at Oakey and Holsworthy.

Pilatus PC-7 Turbo Trainer

The Pilatus PC-7 Turbo Trainer stems from an aircraft first flown in 1953. This was the P-3, whose immediate predecessor, the P-2, had utilised assemblies salvaged from scrapped Messerschmitt Bf 109 fighters.

Intended to fulfil the roles of both *ab initio* and advanced training, the P-3 was powered by a 240-hp (179-kW) Lycoming GO-235 engine, which conferred a top speed of 193 mph (310 km/h). Major operator was Switzerland's *Flugwaffe*, which flew a total of 72 examples from 1958. The type completed 20 years' continuous incident-free service, although a tendency to flat-spin when handled carelessly had proved troublesome. A large ventral fin was added beneath the rear fuselage to remedy this.

Following its success with the Turbo Porter, Pilatus produced the P-3-06, flown on 12 April 1966, with a Pratt & Whitney PT6A turboprop, flat-rated to 550 shp (410 kW) for improved 'hot-and-high' performance. A lengthy period of development followed. The aircraft's designation was changed to P-3B and finally to PC-7. The frame canopy was replaced by a Plexiglas 'bubble' assembly.

The PC-7, marketed by Dornier of Germany in some areas, can double as a basic and advanced trainer. Equipment options can fit it for instrument and tactical training. The PC-7 was intended to meet many different military requirements and specifications, among these being the FAR-23 Aerobatic and Utility categories; the type also complies with a selected group of US Air Force military specifications in the trainer category. Like the P-3 before it, which carried a single 7.9-mm (0.31-in) machine-gun and a pair of Oerlikon rocket launchers for the armament training role, the PC-7 can carry real or dummy offensive loads.

The inner underwing hardpoints are stressed to accept 551 lb (250 kg), the middle 353 lb (160 kg) and the outer pair 242 lb (110 kg)

each. The maximum external load permissible is 2,293 lb (1040 kg). In COIN operations the aircraft would be flown from the front seat.

First deliveries were scheduled for late 1978, with output of four to five per month achieved by mid-1979. The largest order to date has been placed by Burma, which will take delivery of 18 aircraft in 1979, while Mexico with 12, Bolivia and Jordan complete the order book.

Type: tandem two-seat military trainer
Powerplant: one 550-shp (410-kW) Pratt & Whitney Aircraft of Canada PT6A-25A turboprop
Performance: maximum design speed 310 mph (500 km/h); maximum cruising speed 275 mph (445 km/h); range 685 miles (1100 km); service ceiling 31,175 ft (9500 m); rate of climb at sea level 2,065 ft (630 m) per minute; take-off to clear 50-ft (15-m) obstacle 1,020 ft (310 m); landing from 50 ft (15 m) 605 ft (185 m)
Weights: empty 2,866 lb (1300 kg); normal loaded 4,188 lb (1900 kg); loaded with full military stores 5,952 lb (2700 kg)
Dimensions: span 34 ft 1½ in (10.4 m); length 32 ft 0 in (9.75 m); height 10 ft 6½ in (3.21 m); wing area 178.7 sq ft (16.6 m²)
Armament: a mixed load of practice bombs and flares may be carried in the armament training role on six underwing hard points, up to a maximum external load of 2,293 lb (1040 kg); a machine-gun may also be fitted
Operators: Bolivia, Burma, Jordan, Mexico

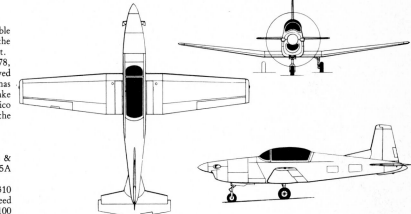

Pilatus PC-7 Turbo Trainer

One of the most attractive propellor-driven trainers, the Swiss Pilatus PC-7 Turbo-Trainer is now being delivered to several overseas customers. The PC-7 in the foreground of this Alpine scene was flown out to the Fuerza Aerea Boliviana in 1979.

Piper L-18/U-17/Piper Cub Series

In 1941 the US Army began the process of selecting a suitable lightplane for artillery spotting and liaison, eventually ordering prototypes for evaluation from Aeronca, Piper and Taylorcraft.

From Piper the US Army ordered four examples of the Cub, a robust tandem-seat high-wing monoplane, which it designated YO-59; 40 O-59 production aircraft were ordered shortly afterwards. All three manufacturers received worthwhile production orders, but Piper had the lion's share with more than 7,000 Cub variants supplied by the mid-1950s, some acquired for other armed forces under the Military Assistance Program. The US Army name for all three makes was Grasshopper.

The O (observation) designation changed to L (liaison) in 1942. YO-59s and O-59s became L-4s (after a brief hiccup as L-59s), and the next version was the L-4A with better all-round visibility. L-4Bs had reduced radio equipment, but most extensively built (1,801 examples) was the L-4H with improved equipment. The L-4J, the last wartime production version, had a controllable-pitch propeller.

After World War II the L-4J was revised for supply under assistance programmes, but this new design, designated L-18A, was not considered suitable. Instead, standard Piper Super Cub 95s were acquired, 105 as L-18Bs for the Turkish army, and 108 of 838 similar L-18Cs to other nations. In 1951 the US Army procured 150 Super Cubs with 125-hp (93-kW) engines as L-21As. A further 568 with 135-hp (101-kW) engines were designated L-21Bs. In 1962 remaining L-21A/Bs were redesignated U-7A and U-7B respectively.

Type: two-seat liaison aircraft
Powerplant: (L-18B) one 90-hp (67-kW) Continental C90-8F flat-four piston engine
Performance: (L-18B) maximum speed 110 mph (177 km/h); cruising speed 100 mph (161 km/h); range 250 miles (402 km)
Weights: (L-18B) empty 800 lb (363 kg); maximum take-off 1,500 lb (680 kg)
Dimensions: (L-18B) span 35 ft 3 in (10.74 m); length 22 ft 4½ in (6.82 m); height 6 ft 8 in (2.03 m); wing area 179 sq ft (16.63 m²)
Armament: none

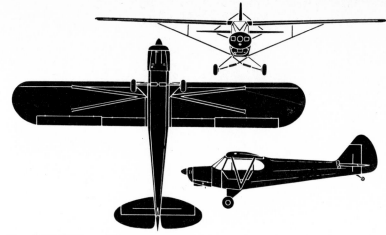

Piper L-18/U-17 Super Cub

Operators: (L-18/U-7) Argentina, Belgium, Denmark, France, Germany, Iran, Israel, Italy, Netherlands, Nicaragua, Norway, Thailand, Turkey, Uganda, Uruguay, US Army, US Navy

---

Piper PA-23 Aztec/U-11A

The Piper Aztec first entered service with the United States Navy in 1960 under the designation UO-1, a designation changed to U-11A in 1962. There had been a need for a light communications aircraft for general duties in the continental United States, and the Navy Department appreciated that the small quantity required could best be obtained by means of an 'off-the-shelf' procurement. This meant looking around the models being produced for business and private owners by America's large General Aviation manufacturers so as to achieve early delivery at the most economical price. It would have been logical for the US Navy to have bought the Cessna 310, because the US Air Force had met a similar need a couple of years before by ordering some 160 Cessna 310As (designated L-27A). However, it was the Aztec which finally won the selection process.

Piper's designation was the PA-23-250, and the aircraft was an all-metal five-seat, low-wing cabin monoplane, powered by two horizontally-opposed six-cylinder engines. The Aztec had its origins in the highly popular Piper Apache which had first entered production in 1952. The Apache was a good example of continuous development, with every year bringing new refinements and modifications, but it became evident with the passing of time that a fairly radical reappraisal of the design was necessary if the PA-23 was to compete with more modern light twins appearing on the market. The type needed full five-seat capacity with commensurate baggage and fuel loads, and the only way of achieving this was to increase the available power. The Apache had two 160-hp (119-kW) Lycomings, and these were replaced by 250-hp (186-kW) Lycoming O-540 engines. At the same time more vertical tail area was needed,

so a swept fin and rudder was designed and all-moving horizontal tail surfaces were introduced. This enabled Piper to increase the maximum take-off gross weight by 1,000 lb (454 kg) and offer one of the most flexible light twins on the market.

The Aztec first reached customers in early 1960, and the US Navy placed an order for 20 early production machines. The US Navy aircraft were essentially standard production models. They were painted in a distinctive white and orange colour scheme and carried a rather more comprehensive array of communications equipment than was to be seen on other Aztecs leaving the Lock Haven factory. They were issued in single units to Naval Air Stations, and performed their role efficiently for many years.

The major demand for military versions of the Aztec came from Piper's export markets where the type was finding ready acceptance among commercial and executive users. The air forces of South America and Africa accumulated a number of Aztecs over the years, and the main variant to find favour was the Aztec D, which was introduced in June 1968. This model benefited from an increase in the certificated gross weight over that of the U-11A and can be distinguished from the earlier model by its long nose, which incorporates a baggage compartment.

The Argentine army ordered a batch of six for communications work, and Peru also received Aztecs, in both cases the aircraft being almost the same as commercial machines from the main production line. Two Aztec Ds were put into service by the French Armée de l'Air in the South Pacific, and these joined the Groupe Aérien Mixte 82 at Tahiti-Faaa, providing support for the French nuclear testing range. In a number of cases, Aztecs were

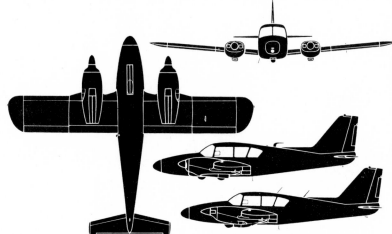

Piper PA-23 Aztec D

taken on charge by African air arms as a consequence of the fighting in the Congo and elsewhere, and the aircraft used by the Armée de l'Air Malagache and by the Uganda air force were former civil machines.

Type: five-seat light communications transport
Powerplant: two 250-hp (186-kW) Lycoming IO-540-C4B5 six cylinder, horizontally-opposed piston engines
Performance: maximum speed 216 mph (348 km/h); normal cruising speed 210 mph (338 km/h); long-range cruising speed at 10,000 ft (3050 m) 195 mph (314 km/h); maximum range at long-range cruising speed 1,210 miles (1947 km); stalling speed (flaps down) 68 mph (109 km/h); rate of climb 1,490 ft (464 m) per minute; service ceiling 21,100 ft (6430 m)

Weights: empty 2,933 lb (1330 kg); maximum take-off 5,200 lb (2360 kg); maximum take-off (UO-1/U-11A) 4,800 lb (2178 kg)
Dimensions: span 37 ft 2½ in (11.34 m); length 30 ft 2⅝ in (9.21 m); height 10 ft 4 in (3.15 m); wing area 207.56 sq ft (19.28 m²)
Operators: Argentina (Army), France, Malagasy Republic, Peru, Spain, Uganda, United States (Navy)

Piper PA-28-140 Cherokee

In early 1964 Piper announced the introduction of a two-seat sport and training aircraft, called the Cherokee 140, to replace the earlier Colt, and deliveries of production aircraft started after FAA certification was received on 14 February 1964. Approximately 18 months later the basic Cherokee 140 was superseded by a new version known as the Cherokee 140-4, which in its basic two-seat form is virtually identical to the Cherokee 140. The subtle difference is that it has provision for conversion to a four-seat layout, and an engine rated at 150 hp (112 kW), but which in the basic model is limited to an output of 140 hp (104 kW) by the propeller. When it is required to convert the Cherokee 140 to four-seat accommodation, there is available a conversion kit which includes two seats for attachment to pre-installed fittings, and a propeller which allows its Lycoming O-320 engine to develop its full 150 hp (112 kW).

The Cherokee is an attractive lightplane of

low-wing configuration. The monoplane wing has pronounced dihedral (7°) providing good inherent stability and which, in conjunction with non-retractable tricycle type landing gear (which incorporates a steerable nosewheel) makes this an excellent training aircraft or an ideal first mount for a newly qualified pilot.

It was these features, in conjunction with good economy in operation, which made Tanzania select the Cherokee 140 as an *ab initio* trainer for military use, and in early 1972 five of the lightplanes were supplied for use by the Tanzanian People's Defence Force Air Wing.

Type: two/four-seat sporting/training lightplane
Powerplant: (140-4) one 150-hp (112-kW) Lycoming O-320 flat-four piston engine
Performance: (140-4) maximum speed at sea level 142 mph (229 km/h) maximum cruising speed at 7,000 ft (2135 m) 135 mph (217

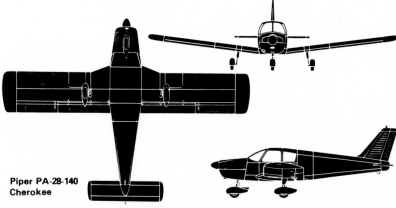

Piper PA-28-140 Cherokee

km/h); maximum range with maximum fuel at 4,000 ft (1220 m) 839 miles (1350 km)
Weights: (140-4) empty 1,233 lb (559 kg); maximum take-off 2,150 lb (975 kg)
Dimensions: span 30 ft 0 in (9.14 m); length

23 ft 6 in (7.16 m); height 7 ft 3½ in (2.22 m); wing area 160 sq ft (14.86 m²)
Armament: none
Operator: Tanzania

Piper PA-31 Navajo

Piper first announced that it was developing a cabin-class light twin aircraft in 1965. Previously, the 5-seat Aztec had been the company's flagship, but the success of Beech with the Queen Air and Cessna with the Model 411 meant that Piper could not afford to ignore the 6/8-passenger business and general utility market. The PA-31 Navajo is a low-wing monoplane of all-metal construction. The prototype first flew from Piper's Lock Haven headquarters on 30 September 1964, and went through numerous detailed changes before receiving its FAA Type Certificate in February 1966. The Navajo was offered with two power options — the standard version with two Lycoming IO-540-M1A5 engines and the Turbo Navajo with two turbocharged Lycoming TIO-540-A1As. In practice, the majority of customers bought the Turbo Navajo and the normally-aspirated version was eventually dropped from production.

The aircraft rapidly became popular because of its large cabin and 'mini-airliner' appearance. Internally, the standard aircraft was equipped with six forward-facing passenger seats or in an executive configuration had a six-seat 'club' arrangement, and the two crew members benefited from a partitioned-off flight deck. The Turbo Navajo was joined in the product line by the Navajo C/R in 1975. Improved performance was offered in this aircraft through the use of 325-hp (242-kW) Lycoming TIO-540-F2BD engines, and these incorporated the counter-rotating concept which allows both propellers to turn inwards thus eliminating many of the torque effects experienced on piston twins. Some 1,430 examples of the Navajo, Turbo Navajo and Navajo C/R had been sold by December 1978.

The Navajo had been designed as the basis for a family of aircraft and the next move was the introduction of pressurization. The PA-31P Pressurized Navajo appeared in 1970, and 248 were sold by the time it was withdrawn in 1978. In its turn, the PA-31P permitted Piper to develop the PA-31T Cheyenne, powered by two Pratt & Whitney PT6A turboprops, which is now available in three separate versions, each offering a different choice of power and seating capacity. The PA-31P and PA-31T have both been commercially successful but military use has been limited. One Pressurized Navajo was used for a time by the *Escuadron* 912 of the Spanish air force, but no Cheyennes

had been delivered to military users by the end of 1978.

The other alternative open to Piper was stretching the Navajo's fuselage, and this came about in September 1972 when the PA-31-350 Chieftain appeared. This proved to be the most successful model, substantially outselling the Turbo Navajo. Engine power increased to 350-hp (261-kW) and two extra passengers could be carried, with baggage accommodated in large nose and rear cabin compartments. Navajos became popular as light transport aircraft with several air arms, although the type was not selected by any of the US military forces. It was generally procured 'off-the-shelf' with either a utility or executive interior, and the largest operator has been the French *Aéronavale* which received 12 aircraft in 1973 and 1974. These replaced the Dassault MD312 Flamants which had given good service since the late-1940s. Navajos were allocated to a number of *escadrilles de servitude* for use on communications within metropolitan France. The aircraft allocated to *Escadrille* 3S have been applied to instrument training duties, and the VIP *Section de Liaison de Dugny* has three Navajos to support the Paris naval headquarters. Other users of the type include the Syrian air force, which bought two Navajos equipped with aerial survey cameras for mapping work, and the

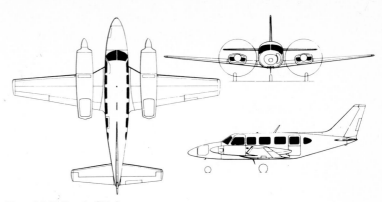

Piper PA-31 Navajo Chieftan

Kenyan and Nigerian air forces which both use Chieftains.

Type: eight-seat light communications aircraft
Powerplant: two Lycoming turbocharged 310-hp (231-kW) TIO-540-A1A six-cylinder horizontally-opposed piston engines
Performance: maximum speed 260 mph (418 km/h); normal cruising speed at 75% power at 23,500 ft (7163 m) 247 mph (398 km/h); long-range cruising speed at 45% power at

24,000 ft (7315 m) 181 mph (291 km/h); maximum range at long-range cruising speed with 45 minutes reserves 1,550 miles (2480 km); rate of climb 1,395 ft (425 m) per minute; service ceiling 26,300 ft (8016 m)
Weights: empty 3,842 lb (1741 kg); maximum take-off 6,500 lb (2945 kg)
Dimensions: span 40 ft 8 in (12.40 m); length 32 ft 7½ in (9.94 m); height, 13 ft 0 in (3.96 m); wing area 229 sq ft (21.3 m²)
Operators: Argentina (Navy), Chile (Navy), France (Navy), Kenya, Nigeria, Spain, Syria

This capable Piper Navajo Chieftain is the VIP executive transport of the Kenya Air Force, operating thoughout East Africa.

Piper PA-34 Seneca (EMBRAER EMB-810)

The Piper Seneca is a six/seven-seat light twin which has earned considerable respect from its users during the eight years of its production life. While its military importance is only now emerging, more than 2,500 had been delivered, largely to civil customers, by the end of 1978.

In the late 1960s Piper realised that a market existed for a light twin-engined aircraft with a gross weight of around 4,000 lb (1814 kg) to fit into their range between the PA-30 Twin Comanche and the PA-23-250 Aztec. The applications of this aircraft would include light freight transport and air-taxi work, together with traditional business executive transport duties. The company already had the single-engined PA-32 Cherokee Six in production and the project team at Vero Beach, Florida, conducted exercises on this aircraft, realising that the large cabin volume and well-tried systems would be a sound basis for development. The Cherokee Six had already been tested in a counter-insurgency role as the PA-32-300M with hardpoints on the wings carrying 1,400 lb (630 kg) of stores and a Minigun pack mounted in the fuselage main door opening, and it was apparent that the twin-engined version could be attractive to military buyers.

Initial design studies included the three-engined XPA-32 — a standard Cherokee Six with two wing-mounted engines in addition to the existing powerplant; but the Twin Cherokee which finally emerged was only superficially similar to the PA-32. The twin-engined layout resulted in a strengthened structure, the fuselage was made deeper, the vertical tail was enlarged and provision was made for a fully retractable undercarriage. The

new PA-34 Seneca was powered by two Lycoming IO-360 engines with counter-rotating propellers. This feature, first introduced on the Twin Comanche, cancels out asymmetric forces in twin-engined flight, resulting in very docile characteristics for the Seneca.

The new aircraft was announced in September 1971 at a basic price of $49,900, and the economy of operation and simplicity of its systems immediately appealed to US general-aviation users. Subsequently, in 1975, Piper brought a number of changes to the PA-34. The Seneca II was fitted with 200-hp (149-kW) turbocharged Continental TSIO-360-E engines (still with the counter-rotating propellers) housed in new streamlined nacelles. The useful load was increased from 1,521 lb (690 kg) to 1,800 lb (817 kg), an additional cabin window was added on either side, and a new external baggage hatch was fitted beside the existing left entrance door to provide access for long loads. The performance of the Seneca II was improved in almost all respects.

At this time, the Brazilian economy was going through great difficulties and the once considerable exports of light aircraft from the United States to Brazil had been restricted to a minimum. There was an opportunity for Piper to enter into an agreement for licence production of its models by Empresa Brasiliera de Aeronautica SA (EMBRAER), with the Seneca being one of the initial types to be built. Under the agreement, Piper was to ship assembly kits to Sao Paulo but EMBRAER would move towards an increasingly large Brazilian content as the time went by. Under this arrangement the Seneca received the type

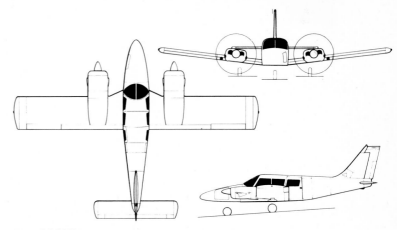

Piper PA-34 Seneca

number EMB-810, and slightly less than 200 had been assembled by December 1978. Of these, 10 aircraft were delivered to the government VIP flight (GTE) as communications aircraft, with the military designation U-7, based at Brasilia. This may be the start of a wider military application for the Seneca in South America. It also seems likely that another licence for Seneca production — by the Polish organisation, Pezetel — may result in the type reaching East European military forces at some future date.

Type: six/seven-seat light communications aircraft
Powerplant: two 200-hp (149-kW) Continental TSIO-360-E turbocharged six-

cylinder horizontally-opposed piston engines
Performance: maximum speed at 14,000 ft (4267 m) 228 mph (367 km/h); cruising speed at 75% power at 20,000 ft (6096 m) 218 mph (349 km/h); long-range cruising speed at 16,000 ft (4877 m) 201 mph (324 km/h); maximum range at long-range cruising speed 775 miles (1248 km); stalling speed (flaps down) 69 mph (111 km/h); rate of climb 1,340 ft (408 m) per minute; service ceiling 25,000 ft (7600 m)
Weights: empty 2,770 lb (1258 kg); maximum take-off 4,570 lb (2075 kg)
Dimensions: span 38 ft 11 in (11.9 m); length 28 ft 6 in (8.7 m); height 9 ft 11 in (3.0 m); wing area 208.7 sq ft (19.4 m²)
Operators: Brazil, Argentina

PZL-104 Wilga/Gelatik

Designed as a successor to the Yakovlev Yak-12 and its Polish version the PZL-101 Gawron, the Wilga 1 prototype all-purpose light aircraft made its maiden flight on 24 April 1962, with a 180-hp (134-kW) WN-6B radial engine. A thoroughgoing redesign of the fuselage and tail was undertaken and the Wilga 2 made its first flight on 1 August 1963, powered by a 195-hp (145-kW) WN-6RB. A further prototype, with a 225-hp (168-kW) Continental O-470, flew on 30 December of that year.

Some 360 of various versions, differing in powerplant and equipment, were built in Poland. Military versions are in service in Poland, the USSR and Venezuela. The main military version in Polish service is the Wilga 32, powered by a 260-hp (194-kW) AI-14R radial engine. Licence production in Indonesia of a version named the Gelatik 32, powered by the Continental O-470, totalled 56. The type serves with the Indonesian air arm. Military variants are used largely for liaison, parachute training and glider-towing.

The wing is an all-metal single-spar structure with leading edge torsion box. Electric single-slotted flaps are in two sections on each wing. The slotted ailerons can be drooped to supplement the flaps, and there are full-span fixed slats. Four wing tanks hold 39.6 Imperial gallons (180 litres). The rounded metal fuselage tapers sharply aft of the cabin to form a boom for the tail. The well-glazed cabin accommodates the pilot plus three passengers or equivalent weight of cargo, and has large doors. Later versions include the Wilga 40 with a detachable freight container and the Wilga 43 with a slab tailplane.

Type: liaison and general-purpose aircraft
Powerplant: (Wilga 32) one 260-hp (194-kW) Ivchenko AI-14R nine-cylinder radial engine; (Gelatik 32) one 230-hp (172-kW) continental O-470-L piston engine
Performance: (Wilga 32) maximum speed at maximum take-off weight (125 mph (201 km/h); economic cruising speed 79 mph (127 km/h); range 423 miles (680 km); service ceiling 15,000 ft (4580 m); rate of climb at sea level 1,250 ft (380 m) per minute; take-off run 410 ft (125 m); landing run 690 ft (210 m)
Weights: (Wilga 32) empty 1,874 lb (850 kg); maximum take-off 2,756 lb (1250 kg)
Dimensions: (Wilga 32) span 36 ft 6.6 in (11.14 m); length 26 ft 6.9 in (8.1 m); height 9 ft 7.8 in (2.94 m); wing area 166.8 sq ft (15.5 m²)
Armament: none
Operators: (Wilga) Poland, Soviet Union, Venezuela; (Gelatik) Indonesia

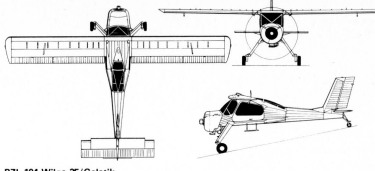
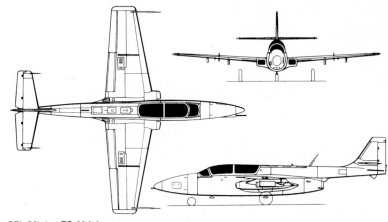

PZL-104 Wilga 35/Gelatik

PZL-Mielec TS-11 Iskra/Iskra 2

The first Polish-designed jet aircraft is the PZL-Mielec TS-11 Iskra (spark) trainer. Surprisingly, in view of the Warsaw Pact's rigid policy of standardization, it was adopted by the Polish air force instead of the Pact's otherwise universal Aero L-29.

Design work on a jet advanced trainer to replace the TS-8 Bies started under the direction of Tadeusz Soltyk. The first TS-11 took to the air in December 1959. In the autumn of 1961 a later TS-11 participated in a 'fly-off' competition with the L-29 and the Soviet Union's Yakovlev Yak-30. The L-29 emerged as the winner, and was duly adopted as standard equipment by the Warsaw Pact.

However, Poland elected to continue development of the TS-11, partially because of performance improvements anticipated from the PZL-Rzeszów SO-1 turbojet. This powerplant was not available for early Iskras, which flew with the 1,720-lb (780-kg) HO-10.

Of conventional, all-metal structure, the TS-11 has an unswept, mid-mounted wing, with manual ailerons, double-slotted flaps and slatted airbrakes inboard of a fence. The pod-and-boom fuselage is built in three sections. An avionics bay and a 23-mm cannon occupy the nose section. Tandem pressurized cockpits have an upward-hingeing canopy and lightweight ejection seats. A tapered boom, beneath which the engine exhausts, carries the manually-controlled tail. The landing gear is of the tricycle type, and designed for rough-field operation.

The engine is mounted under the wing. Later production Iskras have the SO-3 turbojet, which offers a longer period between overhauls. The fuel is housed in a fuselage tank of 110 Imperial gallons (500 litres), a 15.5-Imperial gallon (70-litre) collector tank (between the cockpit section and the engine bay) and two wing tanks each of 69-Imperial gallon (315-litre) capacity.

The Iskra carries its cannon low on the right side, and also has provision for various combinations of underwing stores. Up to 220 lb (100 kg) of bombs, rocket pods or 7.62-mm (0.3-in) machine-gun pods can be carried on each of two pylons (increased to four on later models). A single-seat attack prototype has been tested. This has an uprated engine and a 44-Imperial gallon (200-litre) increase in fuel capacity. A reconnaissance prototype mounts three cameras in the aft cockpit.

Pre-production Iskras, powered by the HO-10, reached the Polish air force in 1964. However, it was not until 1967 that the Iskra entered service in appreciable numbers. The type serves at the Central Flying School in the basic training role and as a weapons trainer.

In 1974 the Indian air force placed an order for 50 Iskras to replace the de Havilland Vampire. These were delivered between October 1975 and March 1976. They serve with the Fighter Training Wing at Hakimpet, whose role is to provide advanced pupils with 180 hours of jet instruction. It is anticipated that the HAL HJT-16 Kiran will eventually oust the Iskra at Hakimpet.

Type: jet trainer
Powerplant: one 2,205-lb (1000-kg) PZL-Rzeszów SO-3 turbojet
Performance: maximum speed at 16,400 ft (5000 m) 447 mph (720 km/h); initial rate of climb 2,756 ft (840 m) per minute; ceiling 36,550 ft (11140 m); range with maximum internal fuel 720 miles (1160 km)
Weights: empty equipped 5,500 lb (2495 kg); loaded 7,020 lb (3185 kg); maximum take-off 8,400 lb (3810 kg)
Dimensions: span 33 ft 0 in (10.06 m); length 36 ft 5 in (11.15 m); height 11 ft 5½ in (3.5 m); wing area 188.37 sq ft (17.5 m²)
Armament: one 23-mm NS-23 cannon; 880 lb (400 kg) of underwing stores, or rocket and gun pods
Operators: India, Poland

Poland's only export sale of the TS-11 Iskra jet trainer was to India, some 50 having been supplied to the Indian Air Force in 1975-76. About 40 are now in use, equipping the Fighter Training Wing at Hakimpet. This is considered a more advanced machine that the locally built HJT-16 Kiran, and with tandem seats is more 'fighter-like'.

RFB ATI-2 Fantrainer

RFB (Rhein-Flugzeugbau GmbH) has been a leading explorer of several new techniques during the past two decades, in particular the use of GRP (glassfibre-reinforced plastics) materials for aeroplane construction and the flight-testing of ducted-fan aircraft propulsion systems. These two techniques are combined in the interesting little Fantrainer (and its civil stablemate, the Fanliner), first projected in 1970. The Fanliner was built first, two prototypes making their maiden flights on 8 October 1973 and 4 September 1976, and subsequently accumulating several hundred successful flying hours. The quieter and more efficient ducted-fan system, mounted behind the cockpit, offers several other advantages (better view from the cockpit, reduced ground hazard from fan blades, etc), and the Fanliner and Fantrainer programmes have otherwise been useful in evaluating alternative means of powering the fan.

Both Fanliner prototypes had single Wankel-type rotating-piston engines (114 and 150 hp/85 and 112 kW), and twin 150-hp (112-kW) Wankel engines powered the first Fantrainer prototype (the AWI-2) for its first flight on 27 October 1977. For comparison,

the second Fantrainer (the ATI-2, to which the specification refers) has a single Allison shaft-turbine, with which it flew for the first time on 31 May 1978. Developed under a Federal Defence Ministry contract of March 1975, the Fantrainer is intended to replace the conventionally-propelled Piaggio P.149D as the *Luftwaffe*'s standard basic trainer, and evaluation by that service began in the spring of 1978. The powerplant is mounted amidships, with wing-root intakes, and drives a seven-blade Dowty Rotol constant-speed fan turning inside an annular duct or shroud. The two seats are tandem-mounted (those in Fanliner being side-by-side); other design features include a slight forward sweep to the wings, and a T-tail.

Type: two-seat basic and IFR trainer
Powerplant: one 420-shp (313-kW) Allison 250-C20B turboshaft engine, driving a ducted fan
Performance: maximum speed 224 mph (360 km/h); maximum cruising speed 199 mph (320 km/h); range with maximum fuel 684 miles (1100 km); maximum rate of climb at sea level 1,969 ft (600 m) per minute; service

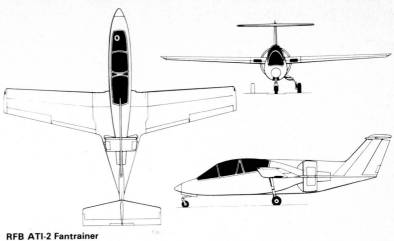

RFB ATI-2 Fantrainer

ceiling 19,685 ft (6000 m)
Weights: empty equipped 1,984 lb (900 kg); maximum take-off (aerobatic) 2,976 lb (1350 kg); maximum take-off (utility) 3,483 lb (1580 kg)
Dimensions: span 31 ft 6 in (9.60 m); length

29 ft 4¼ in (8.95 m); height 9 ft 6 in (2.90 m); wing area 149.6 sq ft (13.90 m²)
Armament: none
Operator: West Germany (under development)

Robin HR 100

Avions Pierre Robin, formed in 1957 as *Centre Est Aéronautique*, assumed its present name in 1969 and is marketing an extensive range of low-wing light aircraft. Employing only about 160 people at its Dijon factory, the company initially concentrated on wooden construction but then switched to metal.

The HR.100 was the first metal type in production, the prototype flying on 3 April 1969. The definitive HR.100/250 (200-hp/149-kW Lycoming) entered production in January 1971 and 20 were built in the first year.

A requirement for a higher powered model was met by using the Tiara-engined prototype HR.100/250TR and installing a Lycoming IO-540-C4B5, and this model was put into production in the second half of 1975 as a trainer for the *Armée de l'Air*. Around 18 were delivered to the *Centre d'Essais en Vol* (CEV) during 1976-77. Two HR.100/250s are

operated by the *Aéronavale* on communications flights from Hyères.

Type: four-seat light aircraft
Powerplant: one 250-hp (187-kW) Lycoming IO-540-C4B5 piston engine
Performance: maximum speed at sea level 196 mph (315 km/h); cruising speed at 65% power at 10,000 ft (3050 m) 177 mph (285 km/h); maximum rate of climb at sea level 1,065 ft (324 m) per minute; stalling speed with wheels and flaps up 82.5 mph (132.5 km/h)
Weights: maximum take-off 3,086 lb (1400 kg)
Dimensions: span 29 ft 9 in (9.08 m); length 24 ft 11 in (7.59 m); height 8 ft 11 in (2.71 m); wing area 163.6 sq ft (15.2 m²)
Operators: France

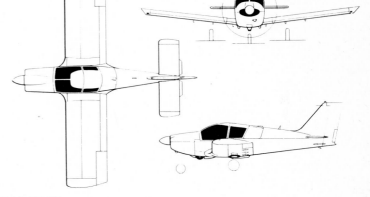

Robin HR 100

Rockwell A-5 Vigilante

In 1955, in response to a US Navy requirement for a high-performance all-weather attack aircraft, North American initiated design of a suitable contender for this competition under the short-lived acronym NAGPAW, signifying North American general purpose attack weapon. The company's design was selected for production in 1956, the US Navy's letter contract confirming selection being received on 29 June 1956, with an order for two prototypes following in August. Initial designation was YA3J-1, but this became changed to A-5 in 1962, by which time the name Vigilante had already been adopted.

In configuration the A-5 showed its typically North American derivation, with a high-set sharply swept wing and swept tail surfaces. The forward fuselage was narrow in section, virtually doubling from the engine intakes aft to accommdate two turbojet engines in the rear fuselage. The A-5 was, however, unique in several respects: it was the largest attack bomber ever built for operation from US Navy aircraft-carriers, and the only one with supersonic speed; it was the first production aircraft to introduce hydraulically-actuated variable-geometry air inlets for its engines; and the first aircraft to have a 'linear' bomb bay, in the form of a tunnel extending along the centre of the fuselage, and from which the bombs were ejected at the aft end. Primary weapon in the original planning was a free-fall nuclear device, this having attached to it aerodynamic stabilizers which carried extra fuel for consumption before the target was reached.

The first of the two prototypes flew for the first time on 31 August 1958, and construction of production A-5As started almost immediately. Initial carrier trials were carried out on board the USS *Saratoga* in July 1960, and the first delivery of production A-5As was made to NAS Sanford, Florida, on 16 June

1961. Subsequently, in early 1962, Navy Squadron VAH-7 was declared operational at this base before joining the carrier USS *Enterprise*. Production of this version totalled 55 examples.

The A-5A was followed by the long-range A-5B, which had additional fuel tankage housed in a hump fairing aft of the cockpit, larger area trailing-edge flaps, and BLC (boundary layer control) blowing over most of the wing upper surface. The prototype flew for the first time on 29 April 1962, but only five more were built before it was decided to abandon use of the Vigilante in the attack role.

It was decided instead to adopt this aircraft for a reconnaissance role under the designation RA-5C, and in this capacity the Vigilante has

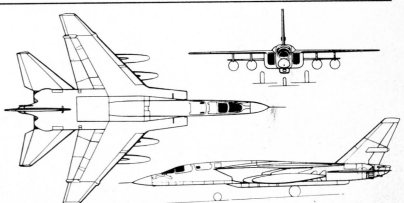

Rockwell RA-5C Vigilante

Departure of an RA-5C Vigilante from the deck of USS *Forrestal*. This sophisticated strategic reconnaissance platform, seen here serving with RVAH-3, is tough to replace; the intention is to try a considerably modified version of the F-14 Tomcat.

given vital sevice. A total of 59 were ordered originally, but these numbers were swelled by the conversion of many A-5As and A-5Bs to RA-5C standard; and because these aircraft were shown to be making an important contribution to reconnaissance operations over Vietnam, an additional 36 new aircraft were built. Retaining an attack capability, the RA-5Cs carried vertical, oblique and horizon-to-horizon reconnaissance cameras, side-looking radar, infra-red sensors, low-light-level TV, and other non-visual sensors. Most importantly, the aircraft comprised the airborne compo-

nent of the Integrated Operational Intelligence System (IOIS), which meant that immediately the Vigilante landed back at its carrier, the total intelligence which it had gathered was fed into the ground-based component of the IOIS, a tactical data system, from which constantly updated intelligence information can be retrieved easily and quickly for tactical planning. One of the interesting features of RA-5C deployment in Vietnam resulted from the fact that these aircraft had an inertial navigation system, which made it possible for each reconnaissance photograph to

have precise co-ordinates of latitude and longitude detailed on each negative, so that subsequent location of interesting 'finds' was virtually 'child's play'. In 1979 the RA-5C has been greatly updated. There is no apparent replacement though, a version of the Grumman F-14 might be an interim answer.

Type: carrier-based reconnaissance/attack aircraft
Powerplant: (RA-5C) two 17,000-lb (7711-kg) afterburning thrust General Electric J79-GE-8 turbojets

Performance: (RA-5C) maximum speed Mach 2.1 or 1,386 mph (2231 km/h); at 40,000 ft (12190 m); long-range cruising speed 560 mph (901 km/h) at 40,000 ft (12190 m); normal range 2,650 miles (4265 km)
Weights: (RA-5C) empty 40,900 lb (18552 kg); maximum take-off 66,800 lb (30300 kg)
Dimensions: span 53 ft 0 in (16.15 m); length 75 ft 10 in (23.11 m); height 19 ft 4¾ in (5.91 m); wing area 700 sq ft (65.03 m²)
Armament: none
Operators: US Navy

Rockwell B-1

The Rockwell B-1 was designed to meet the requirement for a low-altitude penetration bomber to replace the Boeing B-52s of the USAF Strategic Air Command. It was intended to be the third and most flexible component of the US 'triad' defence system, which comprises also land-based and submarine-launched ballistic missiles.

Designed to operate at supersonic speeds at high altitude and at near-sonic speeds at treetop heights, the B-1 bomber embodies a blended wing/body configuration and swing wings. A unique structural mode control system minimises the effect of turbulence on crew and airframe likely to be encountered during prolonged high-speed, low-level missions. The B-1 has a radar-signature about one-twentieth of that of the B-52, and can carry twice the bomb-load over the same range as the older bomber. The bomb load is carried in three internal weapon bays, each 15 ft (4.57 m) long. Each bay was designed to accommodate up to 25,000 lb (11340 kg) of nuclear or conventional weapons.

Among the many innovative features of the bomber is the crew escape capsule embodied on the first three prototypes. This was, however, to be deleted from later aircraft, partly as an economy measure and partly because ejection-seat technology had advanced to the stage when they can accomplish what the escape capsule was designed to do. As an economy measure the variable-geometry engine inlets were also to be deleted.

Four prototypes were built, but the type did not go into production. In June 1977 President Carter announced that production of the bomber would be cancelled and priority given instead to cruise missiles. However, authority was given for the prototype development programme to continue, in order to provide the needed technical base that would be required to update the old B-52 force, or even to resurrect the B-1 should the development of cruise missiles encounter difficulties.

Type: Supersonic, strategic heavy bomber
Powerplant: four 30,000-lb (13608-kg) thrust-class General Electric YF101-GE-100 turbofans

Performance: maximum level speed Mach 1.8 or 1,188 mph (1910 km/h) at 50,000 ft (15240 m); maximum level speed at 500 ft (152 m) 750 mph (1205 km/h); maximum range 6,100 miles (9815 km)
Weights: maximum take-off 389,800 lb (176810 kg); maximum weapon load 115,000 lb (52160 kg)
Dimensions: span (maximum 136 ft 8½ in (41.67 m), (minimum) 78 ft 2½ in (23.84 m); length 150 ft 2½ in (45.78 m); height 33 ft 7 in (10.24 m); wing area 1,950 sq ft (181.2 m²)
Armament: nuclear and conventional weapons, including 24 2,240-lb (1016-kg) Boeing AGM-69A Short Range Attack Missiles (SRAMs), Air-Launched Cruise Missiles (ALCMs), decoy missiles and remotely piloted vehicles
Operators: none

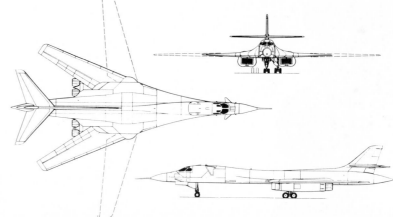

Rockwell B-1A

Flight development of the B-1 was continuing in 1979, more than four years after this picture of the first aircraft was taken over California in January 1975. The fourth aircraft is now flying the vast ECM installation; Nos 1 and 2 are grounded.

Rockwell Commander 500/Shrike Commander

In 1958 the Aero Commander Division of Rockwell Standard Corporation, currently Rockwell International's General Aviation Division, began development of a light transport designated Model 500B, and this received FAA Type Approval on 21 April 1961. This designation was changed subsequently to 500U, the letter U indicating that the Model 500 satisfied the FAA's Part 3 Utility Category Requirements.

This attractive light transport is powered by two Lycoming flat-six piston-engines, driving constant-speed fully-feathering propellers. The high-set wing is of all-metal construction, and has Frise-type ailerons and hydraulic single-slotted flaps. The fuselage is a conventional light-alloy semi-monocoque structure, and to provide easy passenger access is carried on a retractable tricycle landing gear which leaves minimal clearance between the undersurface of the fuselage and the ground. In consequence the main landing gears are long oleo-pneumatic struts which retract aft, the wheels turning through 90° during retraction so that the wheels are stowed horizontally in the rear of the engine nacelles.

Standard seating is for four persons, the two forward seats having dual controls. Alternative seating arrangements can provide for a maximum of seven passengers and a pilot; or all but the pilot's seat can be removed to enable a useful volume of cargo to be carried. In cases where cargo is more important than passengers, a strengthened floor can be provided, and it is possible to have quick-change interiors to carry passengers and/or freight. There is ample space for the installation of a wide range of avionics and equipment, including survey cameras, and the utility value of such an 'off the shelf' aircraft appealed to several air forces. Later versions of the Model 500 are known by the name Shrike Commander.

Type: four/eight-seat light transport
Powerplant: (500U) two 290-hp (216-kW) Lycoming IO-540-EIA5 flat-six piston engines
Performance: maximum cruising speed 218 mph (351 km/h); range with maximum fuel and maximum payload (30 minutes reserves) 1,230 miles (1979 km)
Weights: empty equipped 4,348 lb (1972 kg);

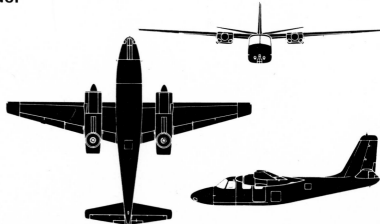

Rockwell Shrike Commander L-26

maximum take-off and landing 6,750 lb (3062 kg)
Dimensions: span 49 ft 0½ in (14.95 m); length 35 ft 1⅛ in (10.70 m); height 14 ft 9½

in (4.51 m); wing area 255 sq ft (23.69 m²)
Armament: none
Operators: Argentina, Iran

Rockwell (North American) OV-10 Bronco

In 1956 Grumman designed a battlefield surveillance aircraft to satisfy a joint US Army and Marine Corps requirement, and in the following year the US Navy, acting as joint programme manager, ordered nine of these aircraft for test and evaluation. The Marine Corps had allocated the designation OF-1 to its version of what became the Grumman G-134 Mohawk, but withdrew from the project before the first prototype was completed.

Experience of limited-warfare engagements, following cancellation of the OF-1, convinced US Marine planners that they had an urgent need for a light multi-purpose aircraft which could, if and when required, be operated in a counter-insurgency (COIN) role. Accordingly, a specification was drawn up for a light armed reconnaissance aircraft (LARA) and Requests For Proposals were issued by the US Navy. Submissions were received from nine US manufacturers, and in August 1964 North America's NAH300 design was announced as the winner. As in the case of the Mohawk, the US Navy was acting both for the US Marines and the US Army, the latter service being anxious to procure an aircraft suitable for light armed reconnaissance, helicopter escort, and forward air control (FAC) duties. This had arisen primarily because of the need to replace the lightweight Cessna O-1 Bird Dog, then used for light observation and FAC missions, and it was believed that the North American NAH300 would provide a light attack capability far more cheaply than the current going rate for attack-bombers in even the lightest 'off the shelf' category. This latter also made the USAF a customer.

Following the selection of North American's design, seven YOV-10A prototypes were ordered for test and evaluation, and the first of these made its maiden flight on 16 July 1965. Features included two crew in tandem with near-perfect view, STOL wing and rough-field landing gear, armament on sponsons on the nacelle-type fuselage, and a rear door for casualties or cargo. The first six prototypes were powered by Garrett AirResearch T76-G-6/8 turboprops, the propellor of the -6 rotating clockwise when viewed from behind, that of -8 anti-clockwise. The seventh prototype was powered by Pratt & Whitney YT74-CP-8/10 similarly 'handed'

engines for comparative evaluation, but the T76 was selected to power production examples, the first of which were ordered in October 1966. Shortcomings in performance were rectified by increasing the short wingspan by one-third, uprating of the engines, replacing the 'straight' sponsons by a new design with pronounced anhedral, plus a number of minor modifications.

Production aircraft began to enter service in 1967 and the USAF's OV-10As, of which they acquired 157, were used operationally in Vietnam at the beginning of 1968. The US Marine Corps received 114 OV-10As, with deliveries to VMA-5 beginning on 23 February 1968. To enhance their capabilities for operations in Vietnam, 15 of the USAF's OV-10As were equipped with special equipment under the Pave Nail programme. This provided a stabilized night periscope, a laser range-finder/target illuminator, a Loran receiver and co-ordinate converter. Such aircraft proved valuable for locating targets at night, which could then be illuminated for attack by laser-seeking missiles.

Other versions of the OV-10 Bronco include six IV-10Bs, similar to the OV-10A, supplied to the German forces for target towing, plus 18 OV-10B(Z) aircraft supplied in 1970 for improved performance in the same mission, these having a 2,950-lb (1338-kg) General Electric J85-GE-4 turbojet pylon-mounted above the wing. The Royal Thai air force received 32 OV-10Cs, similar to the OV-10A, all of which had been delivered by September 1973, and Indonesia and Venezuela have each received 16 similar OV-10Fs and OV-10Es respectively.

Two OV-10As were modified under a 1970 US Navy contract to YOV-10D NOGS (Night Observation/Gunship System) aircraft

to provide the Marine Corps with a new night operational capability. Special equipment included a 20-mm gun turret beneath the aft fuselage, and a forward-looking infra-red (FLIR) sensor and laser target illuminator in a turret beneath an extended nose. Under-wing pylons carry a wide range of stores. Following extensive tests, 17 USMC OV-10As were delivered to Rockwell's Columbus Division in early 1978 for conversion to OV-10D NOS (night observation surveillance) aircraft with developed equipment and avionics as installed in the YOV-10D NOGS prototypes, plus the provision of 1,040-hp (776-kW) T76 engines. Initial deliveries began in early 1979.

Type: multi-purpose counter-insurgency aircraft
Powerplant: (OV-10A) two 715-ehp (533-kW) GarrettAiResearch T76-G-416/417 turboprops
Performance: (OV-10A) maximum speed at sea level without weapons 281 mph (452 km/h); combat radius with maximum weapons 228 miles (367 km); ferry range with maximum auxiliary fuel 1,382 miles (2224 km)
Weights: (OV-10A) empty 6,893 lb (3127 kg); normal take-off 9,908 lb (4494 kg); overload take-off 14,444 lb (6552 kg)
Dimensions: span 40 ft 0 in (12.19 m); length 41 ft 7 in (12.67 m); height 15 ft 2 in (4.62 m); wing area 291 sq ft (27.03 m)
Armament: four weapons attachment points beneath the sponsons and one beneath centre fuselage with combined capacity of 3,600 lb (1633 kg); two 7.62-mm (0.3-in) M60C machine-guns in each sponson; USMC aircraft can carry one AIM-9D Sidewinder beneath each wing
Operators: Germany, Indonesia, Thailand, US Air Force, US Marine Corps, Venezuela

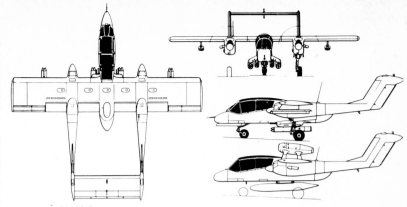

Rockwell OV-10 Bronco

The US Marine Corps uses the Rockwell OV-10A Bronco for observation missions. This example has a low infra-red paint scheme.

This Rockwell International OV-10D Bronco of the US Air Force was photographed on 15 August 1968 on the type's first mission over Vietnam. Designed for multiple roles in 'brushfire' warfare, the Bronco proved popular and versatile — to a point.

Rockwell T-2 Buckeye

In 1956 the US Navy required a jet training aircraft which, once a student had completed his *ab initio* period on a less potent and less costly to operate machine, would be suitable for continuous instruction in stages up to advanced training, fighter tactics, and carrier operation. The winner of the competition was North American Aviation (now North American Aircraft Group of Rockwell International). North American was then producing the T-28 Trojan for both the US Navy and US Air Force, and the fact that the new design included a control system similar to that used in the T-28, plus the utilization of many proven components, may have influenced the US Navy's decision.

In late 1956 North American received a contract for 26 production aircraft under the designation T2J-1, later changed to T-2A, and it was decided to dispense with construction of a prototype. The first T-2A Buckeye flew on 31 January 1958, and initial deliveries went to NAS Pensacola, Florida. Production totalled 217, used mainly by VT-7 and VT-9 at NAS Meridian, Missouri, whose students had already completed 35 hours on the T-34.

The T-2A has a wing in the mid-position, with pupil and instructor in tandem on rocket-powered zero-altitude ejection seats. The single 3,400-lb (1542-kg) Westinghouse J34-WE-36 turbojet is mounted in the belly, and fed by twin intakes.

Under a US Navy contract two T-2As were rebuilt in 1960 with two 3,000-lb (1361-kg) Pratt & Whitney J60-P-6 turbojets. The first of these YT-2Bs flew on 30 August 1962; the first of 10 T-2Bs flew on 21 May 1965, entering service at Meridian in May 1966. A total of 97 T-2Bs were built, the 34th and subsequent aircraft having additional fuel capacity.

Most extensively built was the T-2C, with two 2,950-lb (1338-kg) General Electric J85-GE-4 engines. The first flew on 10 December 1968, and all of 231 had been delivered by 1976. The T-2D has been supplied to the Venezuelan air force; this variant differs in its avionics and in the deletion of the carrier equipment. T-2Es for the Greek air force have six wing stations with a combined capacity of 3,500 lb (1588 kg) of ordnance, plus protection for the fuel tanks from small-arms fire. The standard T-2C has one store station beneath each wing, with a combined capacity of 640 lb (290 kg).

Type: general-purpose jet trainer
Powerplant: (T-2C) two 2,950-lb (1338-kg) General Electric J85-GE-4 turbojets
Performance: (T-2C) maximum level speed 530 mph (853 km/h) at 25,000 ft (7620 m); maximum range 1,070 miles (1722 km)
Weights: (T-2C) empty 8,115 lb (3681 kg); maximum take-off 13,191 lb (5983 kg)
Dimensions: span (over wingtip tanks) 38 ft 1½ in (11.62 m); length 38 ft 3½ in (11.67 m); height 14 ft 9½ in (4.51 m); wing area 255 sq ft (23.69 m²)

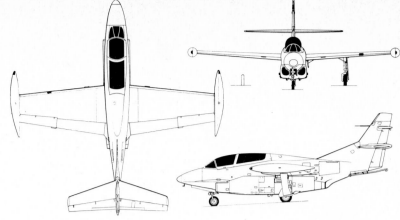

Rockwell T-2C Buckeye

Armament: (T-2C) can include gun packs, target-towing gear, practice bombs and rockets
Operators: Greece, US Navy, Venezuela

In the Greek or Hellenic Air Force (Elliniki Aeroporia) advanced training is flown on 40 Rockwell T-2E Buckeyes of 350 Sqn.

Rockwell (North American) T-39 Sabreliner

In August 1956 the USAF specified a requirement for a general utility/trainer aircraft, then identified as UTX, signifying utility/trainer experimental, and in sending out its requests for proposals stipulated that interested manufacturers would be required to design, build and fly a prototype as a private venture. At that time North American Aviation had more or less completed the design study of a small pressurized jet transport aircraft, and was thus in a position to offer this design to the US Air Force with but few changes to make it capable of meeting their specification. So, on 27 August 1956, the company announced that it was to build a prototype of a small turbine-powered transport under the name Sabreliner.

The original design had placed the engines in the wing roots, but as detail design proceeded during early 1957 the configuration was changed to a rear-engine layout, with two turbojet engines attached to the sides of the rear fuselage. Construction was virtually complete in May 1958, but the first flight was delayed until four months later, as the result of the non-availability of suitable engines. It was with two 2,500-lb (1134-kg) General Electric J85 turbojet engines that the prototype flew on 16 September 1958, and the type completed its USAF flight test evaluation at Edwards AFB, California in December. Early in 1959 North American received an initial production order for seven aircraft.

The first of these, which by then had the USAF designation T-39A, made its initial flight on 30 June 1960. This had two Pratt & Whitney J60-P-3 turbojets of increased power, and some internal changes, and initial deliveries for the Air Training Command, on 4 June 1961, went to Randolph AFB. Subsequent contracts brought total orders for the T-39A to 143, and these were delivered for service with the Air Training Command, Strategic Air Command, Systems Command, and to the Headquarters of the USAF for command duties. From June 1967 the USAF also took delivery of a number of T-39As, which had been modified with strengthened landing gear and provided with seven, instead of four, passenger seats.

In the period February-June 1961, six aircraft designated T-39B were delivered to the Tactical Air Command for training duties at Nellis AFB, Nevada. These were equipped with a doppler navigation system and the NASARR all-weather search and range radar which was installed in the Republic F-105, and were used to train crews who were to fly the Thunderchief.

The designation T3J-1, subsequently T-39D, was allocated to 42 Sabreliners ordered from North American in 1962 by the US Navy. Required for the training of maritime radar operators, these had Magnavox radar systems installed, and delivery to the Naval Air Training Command HQ, at NAS Pensacola, Florida, began in August 1963. The US Navy acquired also seven Series 40 commercial Sabreliners, under the designation CT-39E, for high-priority transport of passengers, ferry pilots and cargo, and since 1973 has procured 12 of the longer-fuselage Sabreliner 60s under the designation CT-39G. These are used by both the US Marine Corps and US Navy for fleet tactical support duties. Under the designation T-39F, a number of USAF T-39As were modified to make them suitable for the training of Wild Weasel ECM operators for service with the USAF's F-105Gs and McDonnell Douglas F-4Gs.

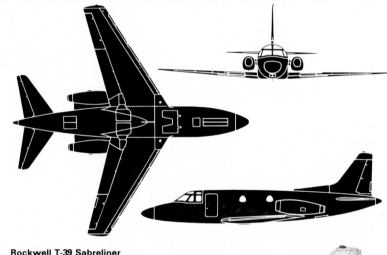

Rockwell T-39 Sabreliner

ft (31.78 m²)
Armaments: none
Operators: US Air Force, US Marine Corps, US Navy

Type: twin-engine utility transport/trainer
Powerplant: (T-39A) two 3,000-lb (1361-kg) thrust Pratt & Whitney J60-P-3 turbojets
Performance: (T-39A) maximum speed 595 mph (958 km/h) at 36,000 ft (10970 m); cruising speed 452 mph (727 km/h) at 40,000 ft (12190 m); design range 1,725 miles (2776 km)
Weights: (T-39A) empty 9,300 lb (4218 kg); maximum take-off 17,760 lb (8056 kg)
Dimensions: span 44 ft 5¼ in (13.54 m); length (T-39A/B/D) 43 ft 9 in (13.34 m); length (CT-39E/G) 46 ft 11 in (14.30 m); height 16 ft 0 in (4.88 m); wing area 342.05 sq

Rockwell T-39 Sabreliner operated by Strategic Air Command, USAF, on VIP and communications duties.

Rockwell's T-39B Sabreliner, seldom in the news, has done a good job for 20 years and is numerically the No 3 type in Military Airlift Command, USAF. These T-39s are from Pacaf, and were pictured in July 1970 starting J60 engines at Tan Son Nhut AB, Vietnam.

Rockwell Turbo Commander 690

North American Rockwell's Aero Commander Division began in late 1963 to develop an improved version of the Commander 500/Shrike Commander. There was a growing market for executive aircraft with more capacity and range, with a pressurized cabin in order to be able to operate fast and economically at high altitudes, and North American decided to produce a turboprop version.

Originally called the Turbo 11 and subsequently renamed Hawk Commander, the prototype flew on 31 December 1964, and had reduced wingspan, a lengthened fuselage to seat up to nine, with the pressurization and air-conditioning systems fed by bleed from the turboprop engines. Deliveries to civil operators began in May 1966.

The Hawk Commander has greater span, a larger tail, more powerful engines with larger propellers, and greater fuel capacity than its predecessor. Further developments, known as the Turbo Commander 690 and 690B, flew in March 1969 and January 1976 respectively. Production aircraft followed in 1971. Standard

seating is for a pilot and six passengers, but 10 passengers can be accommodated. These aircraft proved attractive to armed forces for transport of VIP or high-priority personnel, and continue in service.

Type: light transport
Powerplant: two 715-shp (533-kW) Garrett AiResearch TPE 331-5-251 turboprops
Performance: maximum speed at 12,000 ft (3660 m) 328 mph (528 km/h); maximum cruising speed at 17,500 ft (5335 m) 322 mph (518 km/h); maximum range with maximum fuel, with allowances for start, taxi, take-off, climb to 25,000 ft (7620 m) and 45-minute reserves, with payload of 1,817 lb (824 kg) 1,567 miles (2522 km)
Weights: empty 5,910 lb (2681 kg); maximum take-off 10,250 lb (4649 kg)
Dimensions: span 46 ft 6½ in (14.19 m); length 42 ft 11¾ in (13.10 m); height 14 ft 11½ in (4.56 m); wing area 266.0 sq ft (24.71 m²)
Armament: none
Operators: Argentina, Guatemala, Iran

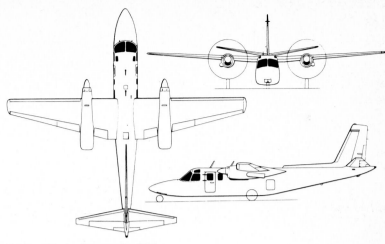

Rockwell Turbo Commander 690A

Saab-32 Lansen

Though designed in the late 1940s, the Saab 32 Lansen (lance) all-swept tandem-seat aircraft combined such good qualities that a few remain in service with the Swedish air force in 1979. The original A32A version was a ground-attack weapon platform to replace the piston-engined Saab 18 bomber, and it was noteworthy in being significantly larger and more capable than otherwise similar 'fighters' then being developed elsewhere. The prototype flew on 3 November 1952, and production aircraft entered service from December 1955. The chosen engine was the British Rolls-Royce Avon turbojet, fitted with a Swedish-developed afterburner and variable nozzle. The A32A had the RM5A2 version of this engine, rated at up to 10,362 lb (4700 kg), while the later J32B night-fighter had the RM6A, derived from the more powerful Avon 200-series and with a new afterburner, with maximum thrust of 15,190 lb (6890 kg). The third version of the Lansen is the S32C reconnaissance aircraft, with RM5A2 engine, originally flown in March 1957 with a basic kit of optical cameras but updated in the past

20 years with ECM, advanced navigation equipment and both inbuilt and podded sensors for multi-spectral reconnaissance. In 1979 the A32A had been replaced by the Saab AJ37 Viggen, and the J32B had been replaced by the Saab J35F Draken and was serving only as a target tug. A few S32Cs, however, remained in use with F11 wing at Nyköping, though being replaced by the SF37 and SH37 versions of the Viggen.

Type: (S32C) multi-sensor reconnaissance aircraft
Powerplant: one 10,362-lb (4700-kg) Svenska Flygmotor RM5A2 afterburning turbojet
Performance: maximum speed 692 mph (1114 km/h) (supersonic in clean condition in a dive); ceiling 49,200 ft (15000 m); range with external reconnaissance pod 1,400 miles (2250 km)
Weights: empty 16,250 lb (7370 kg); maximum loaded 28,660 lb (13600 kg)
Dimensions: span 42 ft 7¾ in (13.0 m); length 48 ft 0¾ in (14.65 m); height 15 ft 3 in (4.65 m)

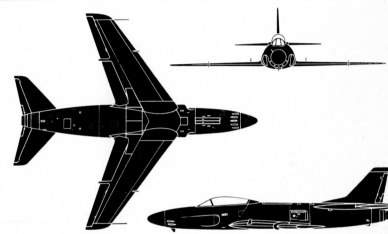

Saab-32 Lansen

Armament: (C) none
Operators: Sweden

Saab-35 Draken

Although designed as a bomber interceptor, the Draken (dragon) has been developed for a wide variety of roles including ground attack and reconnaissance. The radical double-delta wing, designed in the late 1940s for lightness and strength so that supersonic speed could be achieved, was tested on the Saab 210 research aircraft in 1952 and the layout proved practicable. The Draken was designed around this arrangement, with fuel and equipment distributed along the fuselage and long wing-root to compensate for the small volume available within the wing, and the first prototype made its maiden flight in October 1955. The three prototypes, powered by Rolls-Royce Avon 200 turbojets, were followed by the first production aircraft in February 1958. Initial production J35As were powered by RM6Bs — Avons built under licence by Svenska Flygmotor (now Volvo Flygmotor).

The J35A entered service with the Swedish air force in March 1960 and was armed with up to four Sidewinder air-to-air missiles, designated Rb24 in Sweden, together with an Aden 30-mm cannon in each wing. Although designed just to exceed the speed of sound, the Draken reached Mach 2 some two months before the type entered service — and this was under the power of a single Avon, whereas the shorter-ranged English Electric (later BAC) Lightning needed two of these powerplants to achieve a similar performance.

The second version was the J35B, which incorporated Saab's S7 fire-control radar; some were built as J35Bs from scratch, and others were converted from J35As. The J35D, similar to the B model but powered by an RM6C (Avon 300) producing 12,790 lb (5800 kg) of dry thrust and 17,650 lb (8000 kg) with after-

burner compared with the 15,190 lb (6890 kg) achieved by the RM6B, first flew in 1960. The variant built in the largest numbers was the J35F. The first, a converted J35D, took to the air in 1965 and the type will remain in service until the late 1980s. The J35F is fitted with a Hughes weapon system, comprising a pulse-Doppler radar, automatic fire-control system and Falcon air-to-air missiles, built under licence in Sweden by LM Ericsson and other companies. The missiles were constructed by Saab: the radar-guided AIM-26A, known as the RB27 in Swedish service, and the infra-red AIM-4D (Rb28). A J35F normally carries a combination of the two types.

A large number of the original J35As were converted into SK35C two-seat trainers, and the S35E reconnaissance version was developed for overland operations; it has since been replaced by the Saab SF37 Viggen. Nearly 550 Drakens have seen service with the Swedish air force, and the production run was extended by export orders received just as the line was about to be closed. Denmark ordered fighter-bomber, trainer and reconnaissance versions of the Saab 35X export model and designated them F-35, TF-35 and RF-35 respectively. The 35X is similar to the J35F but has a larger internal fuel capacity and can carry up to 9,920 lb (4500 kg) of external armament. The RF-35s are fitted with the FFV Red Baron night reconnaissance pod. Drakens have also been assembled under licence by Valmet in Finland to supply the Finnish air force, bringing the total Draken production run to more than 600.

Type: (35X) single-seat fighter-bomber
Powerplant: one 17,650-lb (8000-kg) Volvo

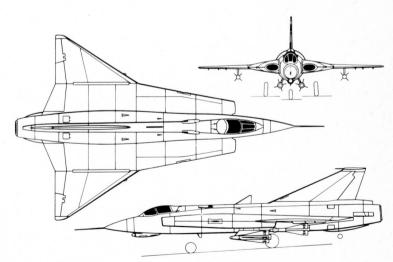

Saab J35F Draken

Flygmotor RM6c (licence-built Rolls-Royce Avon 300) afterburning turbojet
Performance: maximum level speed at 40,000 ft (12190 m) 1,320 mph (2112 km/h) or Mach 2; maximum rate of climb 34,450 ft (10500 m) per minute; time to 49,200 ft (15000 m) 5 minutes; radius of action (hi-lo-hi) with two 1,000-lb (454-kg) bombs and two drop tanks 623 miles (1000 km); ferry range with external fuel 2,020 miles (3250 km)
Weights: take-off (clean) 25,130 lb (11400 kg); maximum take-off 33,070 lb (15000 kg);

overload 35,275 lb (16000 kg); normal landing 19,360 lb (8800 kg)
Dimensions: span 30 ft 10 in (9.40 m); length 50 ft 4 in (15.35 m); height 12 ft 9 in (3.89 m); wing area 538 sq ft (50.0 m²)
Armament: two 30-mm Aden cannon and up to 9,920 lb (4500 kg) of external stores including Rb24 Sidewinder air-to-air missiles, pods containing nineteen 75-mm air-to-air rockets each, twelve 135-mm Bofors air-to-ground rockets, nine 1,000-lb (454-kg) or 14,500-lb (227-kg) bombs, and other weapons
Operators: Denmark, Finland, Sweden

Saab MFI-17 Supporter

The Saab MFI-17 is the latest development of an all-metal two-seat light aircraft designed in 1958 by Bjorn Andreasson. In the hands of AB Malmo Flygindustri, this amateur-market prototype was refined and put into production as the MFI-9 Trainer, and it was also taken by MBB and built for worldwide sale as the Bölkow BO 208 Junior. With further development by MBB it became the BO 209 Monsun, sold to civilian users.

The MFI-9 was a strut-braced shoulder-wing monoplane of very small dimensions having side-by-side accommodation for pupil and instructor under a rear-hinged canopy. A tricycle landing gear or floats were fitted. The powerplant was a 100-hp (75-kW) Rolls-Royce Continental O-200 and the first of 70 production aircraft flew in mid-1962. Two MFI-9s were delivered to the Swedish air force for evaluation as trainers and light armed support aircraft in 1964, but they were subsequently returned to Malmo Flygindustri and no production order was forthcoming. However, MFI was convinced that, in its MFI-9B Mili-Trainer form, the type had a market. Equipped with underwing weapon packs the Mili-Trainer could be used in a light attack role, and it was clearly suitable for artillery spotting and photographic reconnaissance. This application was confirmed when Count Gustav von Rosen used Mili-Trainers in the Biafran war for rocket missions against the Nigerian air force.

It became clear that the MFI-9 would need greater power and load-carrying ability if it was to be successful as a military machine. Under the watchful eye of Saab Aktiebolag (the parent company of MFI) the type was enlarged with provision for a third seat or other payload in a centre fuselage compartment. It was fitted with a T-tail and a 160-hp (119-kW) Lycoming IO-320-B20 engine and stressed to accept either tricycle or tailwheel landing gear. Designated MFI-15, the new model flew in late 1969, named Safari. In production form, fitted with a 200-hp (149-kW) Lycoming, it demonstrated favourable STOL performance, which fully suited its role in isolated locations. The Safari was intended as a trainer, but capable of carrying 661 lb (300 kg) of external load on four underwing hard-

points. This feature was used to advantage by Count von Rosen in mercy supply missions in Ethiopia. Saab also claimed that a casualty stretcher (litter) could be accommodated in the fuselage, and that two 24-man life rafts could be carried under the wings for marine rescue operations.

The main military variant is the MFI-17 Supporter, a close support machine and trainer. It is similar to the MFI-15 plus a comprehensive weapon-delivery system. The six underwing attachment points can carry air-to-ground rockets, Bantam wire-guided missiles, various gun pods or other loads. The two crew have an excellent field of vision. The Supporter is a stable weapons platform, well able to use its low-speed handling and manoeuvrability in combat missions. It is suitable for third-world air arms who require a simple multi-role aircraft but have limited financial resources.

Both the Safari and Supporter are in service. The Zambian air force has 20 Safaris used as basic trainers and Sierra Leone has four. The Pakistan air force has replaced its North American T-6s with 45 Supporters. In Denmark 32 Supporters have taken over artillery observation from the army flying service's ageing Piper L-18s and also replaced the training fleet of DHC Chipmunks.

Type: two/three-seat light training and army support aircraft
Powerplant: one 200-hp (149-kW) Lycoming IO-360-A1B6 four-cylinder piston engine
Performance: maximum speed at sea level 146 mph (236 km/h); cruising speed at 75% power 129 mph (208 km/h); stalling speed (flaps down) 62 mph (99 km/h); rate of climb at sea level 1,050 ft (324 m) per minute; time to climb to 6,560 ft (2000 m) 7 minutes 24 seconds; range at cruising speed, with 10% reserve, 701 miles (1122 km); take-off distance 490 ft (150 m); service ceiling 17,000 ft (5190 m)
Weights: empty equipped 1,378 lb (625 kg); maximum take off 2,205 lb (1000 kg)
Dimensions: span 29 ft 3 in (8.85 m); length 22 ft 11 in (7.00 m); height 8 ft 6 in (2.60 m); wing area 128.1 sq ft (11.90 m^2)
Armament: various light attack stores on

Saab MFI-17 Supporter

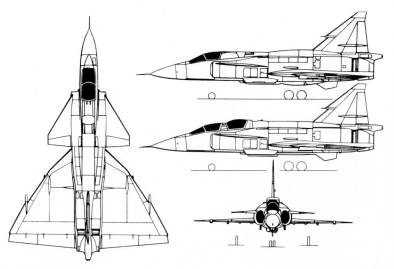

Saab's Supporter is cheap, versatile and supremely useful, being able to fly casevac or liaison missions, carry supply containers (as seen here) or an assortment of tactical weapons.

wing hardpoints
Operators: Denmark, Pakistan, Sierra Leone, Zambia

Saab-37 Viggen

Despite her small population and long-standing policy of neutrality, Sweden has maintained a formidable arms industry and the capability of developing combat aircraft. The Saab 37 Viggen (thunderbolt) is the most potent example of this capability, and because of the high cost of developing new advanced weapon systems, may well be the last Swedish-designed type of this complexity. The Viggen forms part of the Swedish air force's System 37: this is a complete weapon system, including support facilities, which is integrated into the STRIL 60 air-defence network. The Viggen is a true multi-role combat aircraft, having been developed to succeed a variety of earlier types used for attack, interception, reconnaissance and training missions. Other parts of System 37 include the aircraft's engine, avionic equipment, armament, ammunition and reconnaissance sensors, together with supporting items for servicing, maintenance, testing and training.

The first of seven Saab 37 prototypes took to the air in February 1967 and the initial production version, the AJ37, began to replace the Saab A32A Lansen (lance) in mid-1971. The AJ37 is a single-seat attack variant which can carry out interceptor and fighter roles as secondary responsibilities. The combination of a large delta wing and foreplanes fitted with flaps allows the Viggen to operate from short runways and lengths of roadway, thus greatly increasing the flexibility of dispersed operations possible in wartime. This ability is enhanced by the use of a powerful engine: the RM8A, a development of the Pratt & Whitney JT8D-22 turbofan built under licence by Volvo Flygmotor, produces 26,015 lb (11800 kg) of thrust with a Swedish afterburner; the engine is also provided with a Swedish thrust-reverser, which cuts in automatically as the Viggen's nosewheel

strikes the ground. The use of automatic speed-control equipment and an advanced head-up display coupled with the Viggen's other STOL features, allows the aircraft to land on strips only 1,640 ft (500 m) long.

The AJ37's sophisticated navigation and fire-control system is based on a Saab CK-37 miniaturized digital computer, which relieves the pilot of much of the workload and allows this single-seat type to carry out an attack as effectively as more normal two-crew aircraft. The CK-37 takes its inputs from an LM Ericsson search and attack radar, together with the air-data computer, doppler radar, radio altimeter and other sensors, the resulting information being shown on a Marconi Avionics head-up display. The AJ37 carries no built-in armament but can be equipped with a variety of air-to-surface and air-to-air weapons.

Two specialized reconnaissance versions are the SF37 and SH37. The first to enter service was the SH37, in mid-1975. This is a sea-surveillance platform which has replaced the S32C Lansen, using a nose-mounted surveillance radar similar to that in the AJ37 and a pod-mounted forward-looking long-range radar as its main sensors. Other equipment can include the FFV Red Baron infra-red reconnaissance pod or others containing active or passive ECM (electronic countermeasures) equipment. An auxiliary fuel tank may be

Saab JA37 Viggen

mounted beneath the fuselage, and lightweight air-to-air missiles such as the AIM-9 Sidewinder can be carried for self defence.

The SF37, which followed the SH37 into service during the first half of 1977, is replacing the Saab S35E Draken (dragon) for

Royal Swedish Air Force Saab AJ37 Viggen of F15 stationed at Soderhamn in current camouflage.

overland reconnaissance; each reconnaissance squadron operates aircraft of both types. The SF37's nose section and two pods contain a total of nine cameras looking forwards, vertically downwards and sideways, together with an infra-red camera in the nose and illumination equipment for operations at night. All cameras are controlled by the aircraft's central digital computer, and the amount of information which can be recorded is prodigious. When all cameras are working simultaneously they produce 75 photographs per second, which contain as much data as about 50 black-and-white television cameras operating at the same time. The SF37 is operated in conjunction with a System 37 intelligence platoon, which includes a mobile evaluation centre with briefing, processing,

evaluation and interpretation facilities.

The SH37 and SF37, like the SK37 two-seat trainer, are similar to the basic AJ37. The latest version to be developed, the JA37 interceptor, has substantial differences, however. The Volvo Flygmotor RM8B turbofan has a different fan, compressor and afterburner, giving improved climb rates and manoeuvrability, especially at high altitude. An extremely accurate inertial navigator, the Singer Kearfott KT-70L, is one of several new sensors which feeds the same company's central digital computer, built under licence by Saab as Computer 107. Another innovation is the LM Ericsson PS-46 pulse-doppler radar, which allows two JA37s on fighter patrol along the coast to survey as much airspace as required a whole squadron of earlier aircraft.

The new cockpit presentation layout, developed by Saab in collaboration with Svenska Radio, is based on three electronic displays. These can show electronic maps giving the location of air bases and anti-aircraft batteries, together with a tactical plot either received by radio-link from the ground or derived directly from the AJ37's radar. A Smiths Industries head-up display is installed, allowing the pilot to operate his radar and weapon systems while continuing to look outside the aircraft. The HUD also makes for easier transition from fighter to attack missions.

The JA37, unlike earlier versions, carries it own built-in armament. This comprises an underbelly pack containing a 30-mm Oerlikon KCA cannon of enormous power. The gun

fires 0.79 lb (0.36 kg) projectiles at a rate of 1,350 rounds per minute and a velocity of 3,450 ft (1050 m) per second. These shells have as much penetrating power after 4,920 ft (1500 m) of flight as a conventional 30-mm round has as it leaves the muzzle of an Aden or DEFA weapon, and the small drop due to gravity (because the muzzle velocity is so high) eases problems of sighting in tight manoeuvres.

Deliveries of JA37s to the Swedish air force began in late 1978, and the type will eventually replace all J35F Draken interceptors. There is also the possibility of a new attack version, known as the A20, being developed from the JA37 to replace the AJ37 in due course.

continued

First user of the AJ37A attack Viggen was F7 wing at Såtenas whose three squadrons were all fully equipped with the extremely effective new aircraft by the end of 1975. This example is seen carrying four pods of Bofors spin-stabilized rockets (each housing six 135mm projectiles).

Type: (AJ37) single-seat attack aircraft with secondary fighter role (also reconnaissance and two-seat trainer versions); (JA37) single-seat interceptor

Powerplant: (AJ37) one 26,015-lb (11800-kg) Volvo Flygmotor RM8A afterburning turbofan; (JA37) one 28,150-lb (12770-kg) Volvo Flygmotor RM8B afterburning turbofan

Performance: maximum level speed Mach 2.0 or 1,320 mph (2112 km/h) at 39,990 ft (12190 m); maximum level speed at low level at least Mach 1.1 or 835 mph (1335 km/h); tactical radius with external armament (AJ37), hi-lo-hi at least 620 miles (1000 km), lo-lo-lo at least 310 miles (500 km); time to 32,810 ft (10000 m) (AJ37) less than 1 minute 40 seconds; ceiling (AJ37) estimated at 49,870 ft (15200 m)

Weights: empty (AJ37) more than 26,015 lb (11800 kg); maximum take-off (AJ37) more than 45,085 lb (20450 kg); normal operating (JA37) 37,480 lb (17000 kg)

Dimensions: span 34 ft 9 in (10.60 m); length (AJ37 excluding probe) 50 ft 8 in (15.45 m); length (JA37 excluding probe) 51 ft 1½ in (15.58 m); height (AJ37) 19 ft (5.80 m); height (JA37) 19 ft 4 in (5.90 m); wing area 495 sq ft (46 m²)

Armament: (AJ37) up to 13,230 lb (6000 kg), including Saab Rb04E or Rb05A or Rb75 Maverick ASMs, Bofors pod-mounted 135-mm rockets, bombs or Aden 30-mm gun pods; (fighter mission) Rb24 Sidewinder or Rb28 Falcon air-to-air missiles; (JA37) one 30-mm Oerlikon KCA (304K) cannon and Rb71 Sky Flash and/or Rb24 Sidewinder air-to-air missiles

Operators: Sweden

Camouflage is meant to be anything but conspicuous, but on white paper it can look very striking. This AJ37 is assigned to F7 wing at Satenäs, the first unit to equip with the Viggen in 1971. The tail number is that of the individual aircraft. The Flygvapen does not at present use sprayed-on winter camouflage but has conducted extensive research on low-visibility colour schemes. The JA37 fighter will have a different blue/grey scheme.

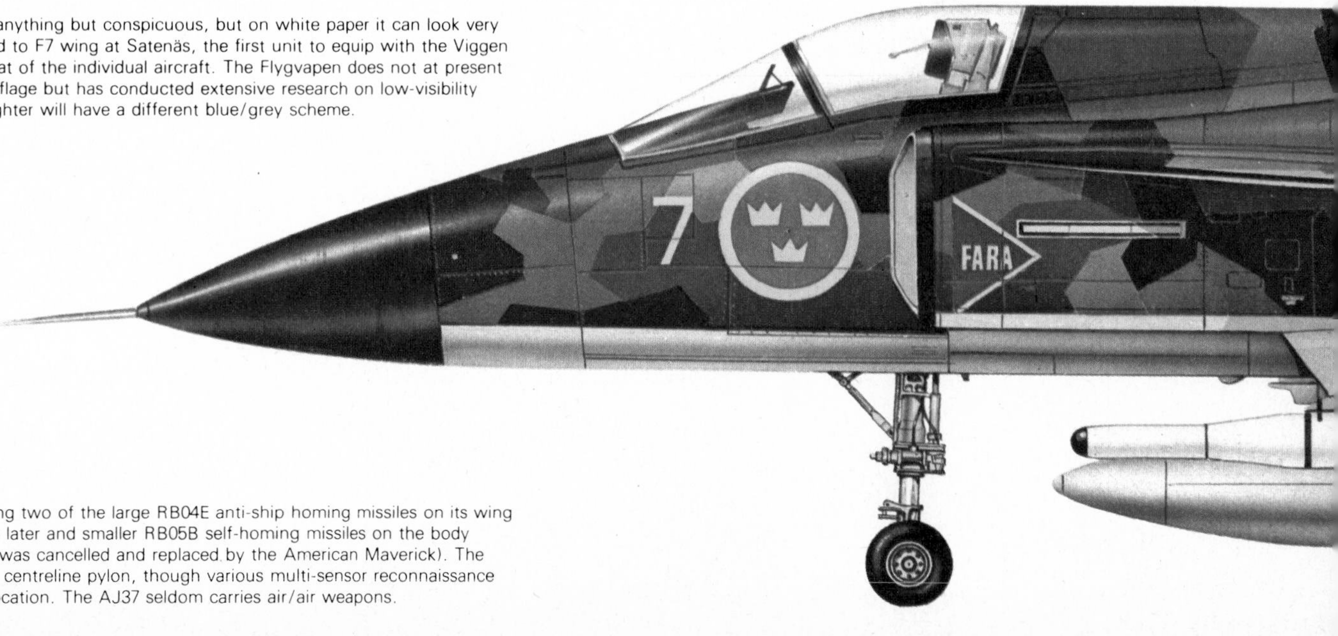

This AJ37 is depicted carrying two of the large RB04E anti-ship homing missiles on its wing pylons, as well as two of the later and smaller RB05B self-homing missiles on the body pylons (this Swedish missile was cancelled and replaced by the American Maverick). The giant drop tank occupies the centreline pylon, though various multi-sensor reconnaissance pods can be carried in this location. The AJ37 seldom carries air/air weapons.

The large silvery aperture seen in front of the jet nozzle is the outlet for the integral reverser, the first to go into service on a supersonic afterburning turbojet or turbofan aircraft and an all-Swedish development. Used at full power immediately after a violent "no flare" landing it allows the Viggen to operate in snow or ice conditions on short stretches of farmland, country roads or other dispersed areas away from vulnerable bases.

Saab-91 Safir

Mass production for six of the world's air forces, within a decade or so after a global war in which Sweden had maintained a strict neutrality, was probably not the thought uppermost in the minds of Saab's designers when this attractive little primary trainer first took shape on the drawing board. World War II was then gradually progressing towards its close, and had been over in Europe for less than six months when the Saab-91 Safir (sapphire) prototype made its initial flight on 20 November 1945, a notable feature of the new design being the extremely short retractable tricycle landing gear. Four basic production models appeared subsequently, the first of these being the three-seat Saab-91A, powered by a 145-hp (108-kW) de Havilland Gipsy Major 10 engine. Initial customer for this version was the Royal Swedish Air Force, which ordered 10 for liaison and communications duties under the designation Tp 91. A further 16 were built for the Ethiopian imperial air force, but were later replaced by a similar quantity of the more powerful Saab-91B. Sweden also ordered 75 of this model for training duties, as the Sk 50B, and 25 were purchased by the Royal Norwegian air force. The

Saab-91C was similar, except that it was a four-seater, and was ordered by Ethiopia (14) and Sweden (14, designated Sk 50C). The final model was the Saab-91D, also a four-seater but with a lower-powered and more modern engine; this was ordered by the air forces of Austria (24), Finland (35) and Tunisia (15), to bring military production of the Safir, excluding prototypes, to 244. Several major airlines also bought Safirs for pilot training, and overall production exceeded 300. Some B, C and D models remain in service with the air forces of Austria, Ethiopia and Sweden, and can be adapted for light attack duties with two 7.9-mm (0.31-in) machine-guns and eight rockets or small bombs under the wings. A few Safirs were used to flight-test various components for the Saab-29 Tunnan and Saab-32 Lansen combat aircraft, one having swept wings.

Type: two/four-seat basic trainer and communications aircraft
Powerplant: (91B and C) one 190-hp (142-kW) Lycoming O-435-A flat-six piston engine; (91D) one 180-hp (134-kW) Lycoming O-360-A1A flat-four piston engine

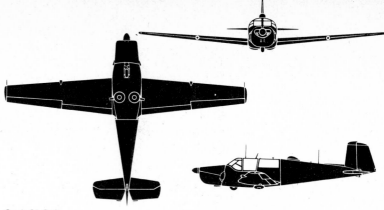

Saab-91 Safir

Performance: (91B) maximum speed 171 mph (275 km/h); maximum cruising speed 152 mph (244 mph); maximum range 670 miles (1078 km); maximum rate of climb at sea level 1,142 ft (348 m) per minute; service ceiling 20,500 ft (6250 m)
Weights: (91B) empty equipped 1,587 lb (720 kg); maximum take-off 2,685 lb

(1218 kg)
Dimensions: (91B) span 34 ft 9¼ in (10.60 m); length 25 ft 11¾ in (7.92 m); height 7 ft 2½ in (2.20 m); wing area 146.39 sq ft (13.60 m²)
Armament: normally none (but see text)
Operators: Austria, Ethiopia, Sweden

Saab-105

The twin-jet Saab-105 was developed as a private venture, primarily as a trainer and light ground-attack aircraft, but with a number of other roles available. These secondary duties include liaison and executive transport (for which the side-by-side ejection seats of the trainer can be removed and four fixed seats substituted), reconnaissance, air survey and air ambulance. The first of two prototypes flew on 29 June 1963, and the following year the Saab-105 was ordered into production for the Royal Swedish Air Force. The initial order was for 130, the first of which flew on 27 August 1965, and a follow-up order for a further 20 was placed in 1964.

The fuselage of the Saab-105 is all-metal, with accommodation for a pupil and instructor side-by-side on ejection seats beneath a rear-ward hingeing canopy. Hydraulically-actuated airbrakes are mounted on the lower fuselage, aft of the mainwheels.

The shoulder-mounted wing is a two-spar cantilever with slight sweepback of 12° 48' at quarter chord and 6° of anhedral. It has manual ailerons and hydraulic single-slotted flaps. The tailplane is on top of the fin, and a small ventral fin is fitted.

The Swedish air force's aircraft are powered by two Turboméca Aubisques mounted in nacelles partially-recessed into the fuselage sides. The Austrian air force's Saab-105Ö and the Saab-105G have the General Electric J85-17B. Fuel is carried in two integral fuselage tanks and two integral wing tanks, total capacity being 310 Imperial gallons (1400 litres). Standard avionics fitted to the Swedish trainers comprise duplicated flight instruments, two VHF sets and a Decca flight log. Armament may be carried on six underwing hardpoints, with a total capacity of 1,543 lb (700 kg). Available combinations of armament include 30-mm gun pods, rocket pods or Saab Rb05 air-to-surface missiles.

In Swedish service the Saab-105 is designated Sk 60, the basic training and liaison version being the Sk 60A. This variant entered service in spring 1966 with F5, the Flying Training School at Ljungbyhed. After delivery most of these aircraft were modified by the addition of armament hardpoints, gunsights and associated equipment, giving them a secondary light ground-attack capability. The Sk 60B has ground-attack as its primary role, and the Sk 60C is equipped for photographic reconnaissance, having a Fairchild KB-18 camera in the nose, while retaining ground-attack capability.

Some 75 Sk 60A, serve in the training role with F5, pupils progressing from the Sk 61 Bulldog and flying some 160 hours on the jet before qualifying. In an emergency, these trainers would comprise the equipment of five light ground-attack squadrons. A squadron of F21 based at Lulea within the Arctic Circle, Sweden's most northerly airbase, operates a mixture of Sk 60B attack and Sk 60C recon-

naissance aircraft. F20, the Air Force College at Uppsala, also operates these variants, and second-line users include a staff liaison flight (who operate the four-seat version) and F13M who undertake target-tug and weapon-testing duties.

A development of the Sk 60B powered by J85 turbojets, the Saab-105XT first flew on 29 April 1967. Fuel capacity was increased to 451 Imperial gallons (2050 litres) to compensate for the higher fuel consumption, two 110-Imperial gallon (500-litre) underwing drop tanks being available. In addition to enhanced performance from the new powerplant, the Saab-105XT has improved avionics, and a strengthened wing enables the underwing load to be increased to 4,410 lb (2000 kg). In addition to training, reconnaissance and ground-attack duties, this version can perform the interception and target-towing roles. Infra-red guided missiles such as Sidewinder are carried for day interceptor duties. Forty aircraft, designated Saab-105Ö were built for the Austrian air force. The Saab-105G is a further refinement of the basic design, with greater improvements in avionics and warload.

The Saab-105Ö is the only jet in Austrian service, equipping four *Staffeln*. The *Uberwachungsgeschwader* (surveillance wing) comprises two *Staffeln* operating in the air-defence role. The Saab-105Ö is ill-suited to this task and a replacement is required. The remaining two *Staffeln* operate in the light-attack role as part of the *Jagdbombergeschwader*, one of the *Staffeln* being a weapon-training unit, and the *Düsenflugstaffel* (jet conversion squadron) also flies the type. It is intended to operate the Saab-105Ö until the end of the 1980s.

Type: trainer and light attack aircraft
Powerplant: (Sk 60 series) two 1,640-lb (743-kg) Turboméca Aubisque turbofans; (Saab-105Ö and Saab-105G) two 2,850-lb (1293-kg) General Electric J85-GE-17B turbojets
Performance: maximum speed at sea level 447 mph (720 km/h) for Sk 60, 603 mph (970 km/h) for Saab-105Ö; maximum permissible diving speed Mach 0.86; climb to 29,525 ft (9000 m) 15 minutes for Sk 60; climb to 32,810 ft (10000 m) 4 minutes 30 seconds for Saab-105Ö; service ceiling 39,400 ft (12000 m) for Sk 60, 42,650 ft (13000 m) for Saab-105G; range at 29,525 ft (9000 m) 1,106 miles (1780 km) for Sk 60; range at 42,980 ft (13100 m) 1,491 miles (2400 km) for Saab-105Ö

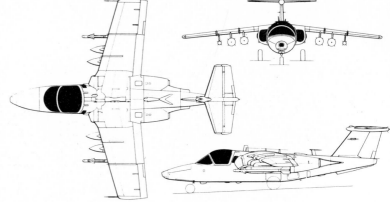

Saab-105G

Weights: empty 5,534 lb (2510 kg) for Sk 60, 5,662 lb (2550 kg) for Saab-105Ö; maximum take-off 9,920 lb (4500 kg) for Sk 60, 14,330 lb (6500 kg) for Saab-105Ö
Dimensions: span 31 ft 2 in (9.5 m); length 34 ft 5 in (10.5 m); height 8 ft 10 in (2.7 m);

wing area 175 sq ft (16.3 m²)
Armament: provision for up to 1,543 lb (700 kg) of underwing stores (Sk 60); up to 4,410 lb (2000 kg) of underwing stores (Saab-105Ö)
Operators: Austria, Sweden

This quartet of Saab-105 twin-jets are of the sub-type designated SK60A by the Swedish *Flygvapen* which uses them as basic trainers to follow the SK 61 Bulldog. These come from F21 Wing at Lulea. Sweden and Austria use several Saab 105 versions.

Saab-105 (designated Sk60 in service) of the Flygvapen (Swedish Air Force), operated by F5 Training School at Ljungbyhed.

SEPECAT Jaguar

Developed jointly by BAC in Britain and Breguet in France, the SEPECAT Jaguar was originally intended as a light tactical attack and training machine with supersonic performance. Development resulted in a machine so capable that it seemed pointless to use it only as a trainer, and the tandem dual-control versions are fully combat-ready (though not fitted with the full spectrum of avionics and weapons as the single-seater). The extremely neat afterburning turbofan engine was developed by Turboméca and Rolls-Royce, two being installed in a manner reminiscent of the McDonnell Douglas F.4 Phantom's arrangement. The wing was mounted high to give good access underneath for large tanks and weapons, and is liberally fitted with leading-edge slats, full-span double-slotted flaps and powered spoilers for roll control. The rudder and slab tailplane are also powered. The twin-wheel main gears retract forwards into the fuselage, ahead of the perforated airbrakes. Much of the structure is covered in honeycomb-stabilized skin, about 40 per cent of the exterior being access panels.

The engines occupy titanium bays in the lower part of the rear fuselage, with the nozzles just ahead of the tail section. The air ducts have plain fixed inlets of square section on each side behind the cockpit and pass inwards and downwards under the one-piece wing. Fuel is housed in four fuselage tanks and the integral tank formed by the fixed portion of wing on each side of the centreline. Single-seat versions are normally equipped with a retractable flight-refuelling probe on the right side, just forward of the cockpit. Three 264-Imperial gallon (1200-litre) drop tanks can be carried on the centreline and inboard wing pylons. Most of the air-conditioning system is grouped along the top of the finely profiled fuselage, the primary heat-exchanger being situated in a large bulge ahead of the fin, a position dictated by area-rule considerations to give minimum drag. Two oblique ventral fins

This SEPECAT Jaguar GR.1 of 54 Sqn, RAF Coltishall, has done a lot of hard flying at low level but seems rarely, if ever, to have fired its very useful twin 30 mm guns. The GP bombs are described as 500 kg, or 1,102 lb, instead of the previous "1,000 lb".
continued

SEPECAT Jaguars have proved extremely popular and effective in RAF service, delivery of 163 single-seat GR.1s and 37 T.2s being completed by the end of 1977. This GR.1. formation was pictured during a low-level training mission across Britain; RAF Germany, where four GR squadrons at Brüggen are backed up by a PR unit at Laarbruch, has fewer hills.

A GR.1 Jaguar from 54 Squadron, based at RAF Coltishall, carrying two 1200 litre fuel tanks and four 1000 lb bombs.

are added below the main engine access doors to increase side area aft. A retractable arrester hook is standard.

A common requirement for the Jaguar was drafted by the British (RAF) and French (*Armée de l'Air*) in 1965, calling for single-seat attack and dual-control trainer versions to enter service with the *Armée de l'Air* in 1972 and RAF in 1973; a single-seat naval model was also specified for the French *Aéronavale* for use from the two French aircraft-carriers. The first prototype flew on 8 September 1968, and all other variants were developed within the allotted time and budget. Unfortunately the *Aéronavale* abandoned the naval Jaguar M after the prototype had completed its development in favour of an all-French aircraft of substantially lower performance and capability delivered five years later. The other four initial versions all entered service on schedule.

The first to fly and enter service was the Jaguar E (*Ecole* or school) trainer which entered the inventory of the *Centre d'Expériences Aériennes Militaires* at Mont de Marsan in May 1972. This has pupil and instructor seated on old Martin-Baker Mk 4 seats which cannot be used safely at speeds below 104 mph (167 km/h). In most other respects, including armament, it is identical to the next version to enter service, the Jaguar A. The Jaguar A (*Appui* or attack) model is the *Armée de l'Air* single-seat version, with a Mk 9 zero/zero seat, pointed nose without sensors, and a simple nav/attack system based on a Doppler radar navigation system and twin-gyro platform. Two DEFA 553 30-mm guns are installed in the centre fuselage, and a total external load of up to 10,000 lb (4535 kg) can be

carried on centreline and four wing pylons. As previously noted, the three inboard pylons are plumbed for tanks. External stores include the AN-52 tactical nuclear bomb of the *Armée de l'Air*, Belouga cluster bombs, AS.37 anti-radar Martel, Durandal runway-piercing missile, retarded bombs, SNEB rocket packs, ECM payloads, and Magic air-to-air missiles. The Martin Marietta/Thomson-CSF Atlis TV target acquisition and laser-designation pod was added in 1978, and a simple reconnaissance pod and Super Cyclope IRLS can also be fitted.

Britain's Jaguars are more sophisticated, and have inertial nav/attack systems, HUD (head-up display), projected map display, radar height, laser ranger (in a 'chisel' nose) and more comprehensive ECM including the ARI.18223 radar warning receiver installation near the top of the fin. Called Jaguar S by SEPECAT, the consortium formed by BAC and Breguet and today a joint venture of British Aerospace and Dassault-Breguet, this version is designated Jaguar GR.1 by the RAF and 165 were delivered by 1978. The guns are 30-mm Adens, and all navigation and weapon-delivery is integrated in a Navwass system controlled by a digital computer. The usual cluster bomb is the BL-755, and a specially designed BAe multi-sensor reconnaissance pod can be carried flush under the centreline, with five optical cameras and IRLS all linked to Navwass. From 1978 all these aircraft are

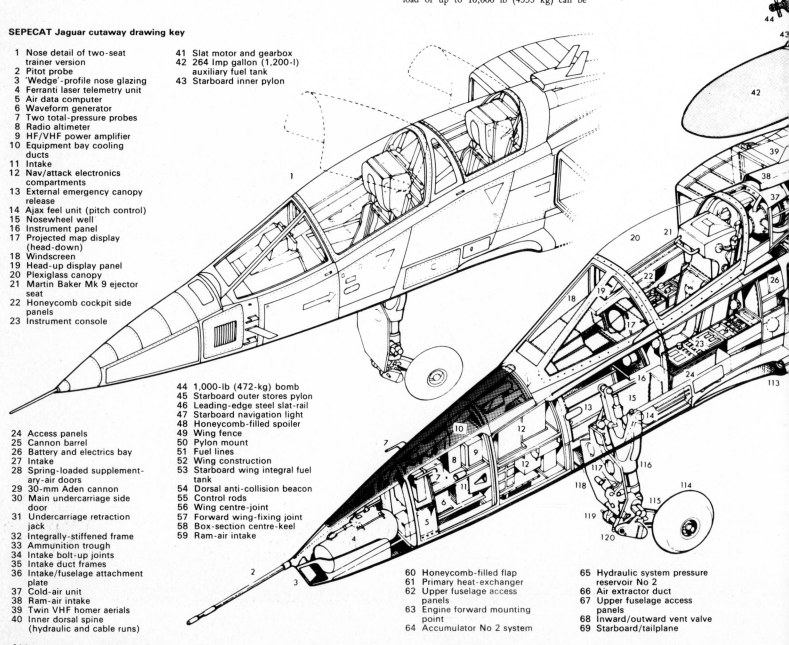

SEPECAT Jaguar cutaway drawing key

1 Nose detail of two-seat trainer version
2 Pitot probe
3 'Wedge'-profile nose glazing
4 Ferranti laser telemetry unit
5 Air data computer
6 Waveform generator
7 Two total-pressure probes
8 Radio altimeter
9 HF/VHF power amplifier
10 Equipment bay cooling ducts
11 Intake
12 Nav/attack electronics compartments
13 External emergency canopy release
14 Ajax feel unit (pitch control)
15 Nosewheel well
16 Instrument panel
17 Projected map display (head-down)
18 Windscreen
19 Head-up display panel
20 Plexiglass canopy
21 Martin Baker Mk 9 ejector seat
22 Honeycomb cockpit side panels
23 Instrument console

24 Access panels
25 Cannon barrel
26 Battery and electrics bay
27 Intake
28 Spring-loaded supplementary-air doors
29 30-mm Aden cannon
30 Main undercarriage side door
31 Undercarriage retraction jack
32 Integrally-stiffened frame
33 Ammunition trough
34 Intake bolt-up joints
35 Intake duct frames
36 Intake/fuselage attachment plate
37 Cold-air unit
38 Ram-air intake
39 Twin VHF homer aerials
40 Inner dorsal spine (hydraulic and cable runs)

41 Slat motor and gearbox
42 264 Imp gallon (1,200-l) auxiliary fuel tank
43 Starboard inner pylon

44 1,000-lb (472-kg) bomb
45 Starboard outer stores pylon
46 Leading-edge steel slat-rail
47 Starboard navigation light
48 Honeycomb-filled spoiler
49 Wing fence
50 Pylon mount
51 Fuel lines
52 Wing construction
53 Starboard wing integral fuel tank
54 Dorsal anti-collision beacon
55 Control rods
56 Wing centre-joint
57 Forward wing-fixing joint
58 Box-section centre-keel
59 Ram-air intake

60 Honeycomb-filled flap
61 Primary heat-exchanger
62 Upper fuselage access panels
63 Engine forward mounting point
64 Accumulator No 2 system

65 Hydraulic system pressure reservoir No 2
66 Air extractor duct
67 Upper fuselage access panels
68 Inward/outward vent valve
69 Starboard/tailplane

being refitted with Adour 104 engines of greater thrust. The RAF trainer is the Jaguar B, called T.2 by the RAF, of which 37 had been delivered by late 1976. This has one gun and no nose laser, but retains Mk 9 seats.

For export various options have been added, including more powerful engines, overwing pylons for Magic, AIM-9L or other dogfight missiles, Agave nose radar with Ferranti 105S laser in a small fairing below the nose, low-light TV and new weapon options including Harpoon and Kormoran for use against ships. One Jaguar was rebuilt by BAe with the Dowty quadruplex fly-by-wire flight control system in 1978. The first two export sales were for aircraft of fairly standard type, though with uprated engines. The third, a very large contract with India involving about £1,200 million and more than 200 aircraft, will take advantage of most of the new options. About 60 Jaguars are to be supplied from the joint production by BAe and Dassault-Breguet, assembly and finally complete licence-manufacture later taking place in India. As 'almost three-quarters of the total requirement' will be made in India this will clearly also include the engines, and also involves a buy-back by Europe of parts made in India.

Type: single-seat attack aircraft and two-seat trainer
Powerplant: two Rolls-Royce/Turboméca Adour afterburning turbofans each rated at (Mk 102) 7,305 lb (3314 kg) or (Mk 104) 8,600 lb (3900 kg)
Performance: maximum speed at altitude (clean) 990 mph (1593 km/h) or Mach 1.5; maximum speed at sea level 840 mph (1350 km/h) or Mach 1.1; take-off run with typical tactical load 1,900 ft (580 m); typical attack radius with weapons and no external fuel 507 miles (815 km); ferry range 2,614 miles (4210 km)

Weights: empty (A) 15,432 lb (7000 kg); maximum loaded 34,000 lb (15500 kg)
Dimensions: span 28 ft 6 in (8.69 m); length (A,S) 55 ft 2½ in (16.83 m); length (B,E) 57 ft 6¼ in (17.53 m); height 16 ft 0½ in (4.89 m); wing area 258.33 sq ft (24.0 m²)
Armament: see text
Operators: Ecuador, France, India, Oman, UK

continued

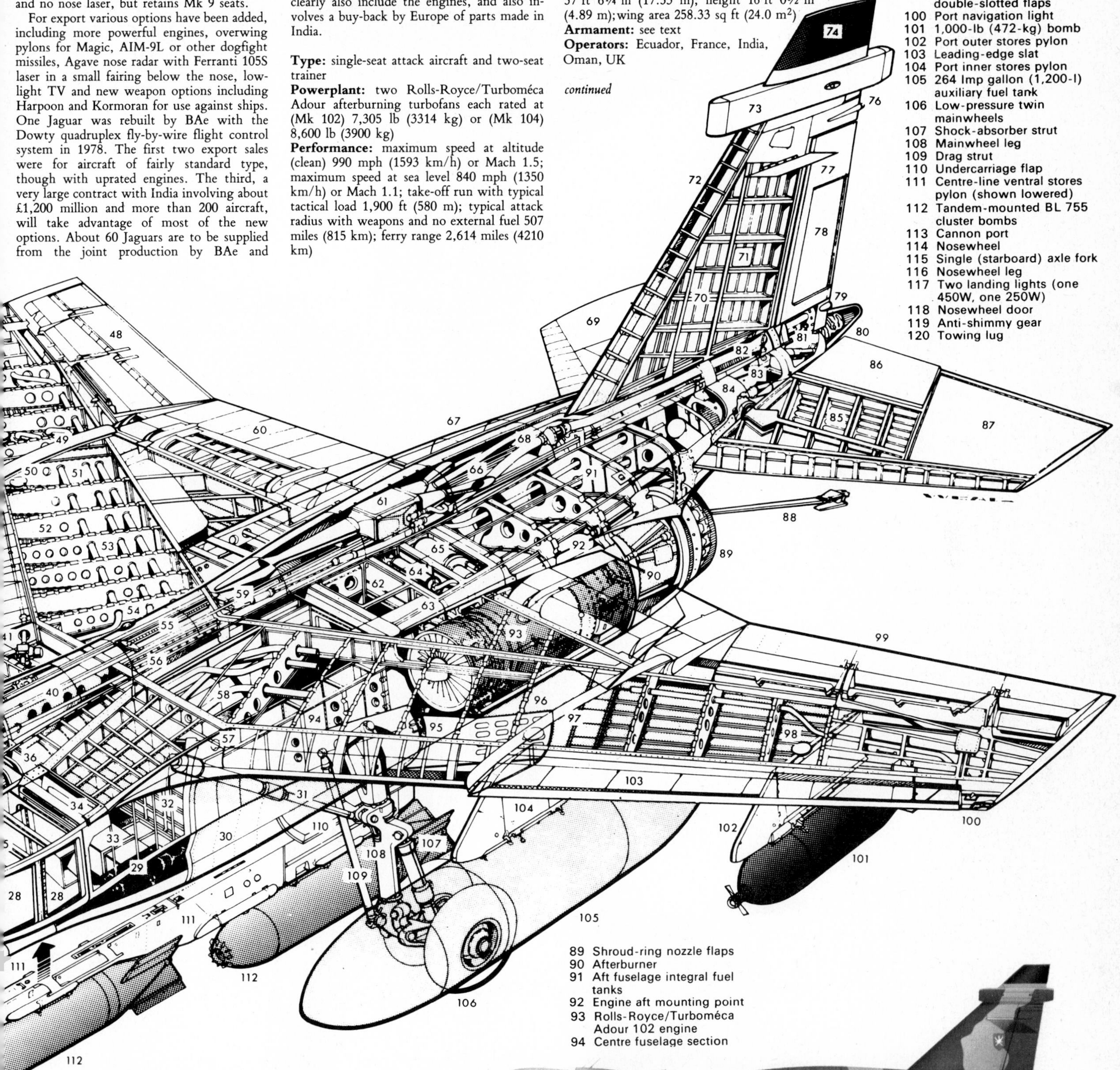

70 Tailfin construction
71 Magnetic detector
72 Tailfin leading-edge
73 Sensor fairing
74 VHF/UHF antenna in fin tip
76 Rear navigation light
77 HF antenna
78 Honeycomb-filled rudder section
79 Fuel dump vent
80 Landing parachute housing
81 Rudder power control unit
82 Control run linkage
83 Tailplane control units
84 Tailplane pivot point
85 Tailplane construction
86 Tailplane longitudinal stability discontinuity
87 Honeycomb-filled outer section
88 Arrester hook (extended)

89 Shroud-ring nozzle flaps
90 Afterburner
91 Aft fuselage integral fuel tanks
92 Engine aft mounting point
93 Rolls-Royce/Turboméca Adour 102 engine
94 Centre fuselage section

95 Air brake actuator
96 Air brake (extended)
97 Wing fence
98 Pylon mount
99 Full-span trailing-edge double-slotted flaps
100 Port navigation light
101 1,000-lb (472-kg) bomb
102 Port outer stores pylon
103 Leading-edge slat
104 Port inner stores pylon
105 264 Imp gallon (1,200-l) auxiliary fuel tank
106 Low-pressure twin mainwheels
107 Shock-absorber strut
108 Mainwheel leg
109 Drag strut
110 Undercarriage flap
111 Centre-line ventral stores pylon (shown lowered)
112 Tandem-mounted BL 755 cluster bombs
113 Cannon port
114 Nosewheel
115 Single (starboard) axle fork
116 Nosewheel leg
117 Two landing lights (one 450W, one 250W)
118 Nosewheel door
119 Anti-shimmy gear
120 Towing lug

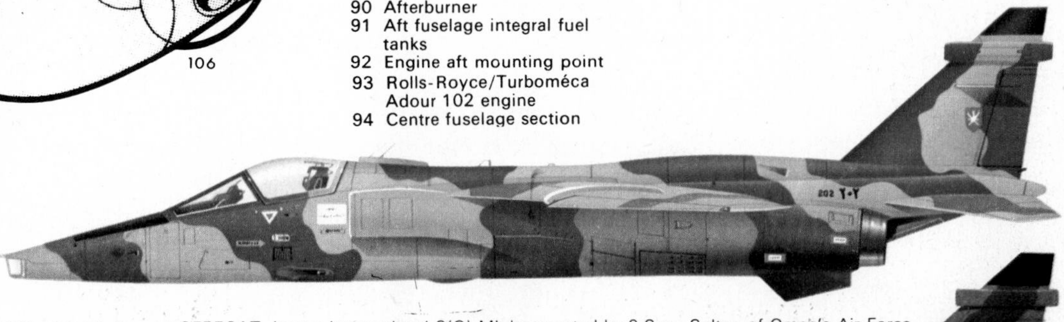

One of the ten single-seat SEPECAT Jaguar International S(O) Mk Is operated by 8 Sqn, Sultan of Oman's Air Force.

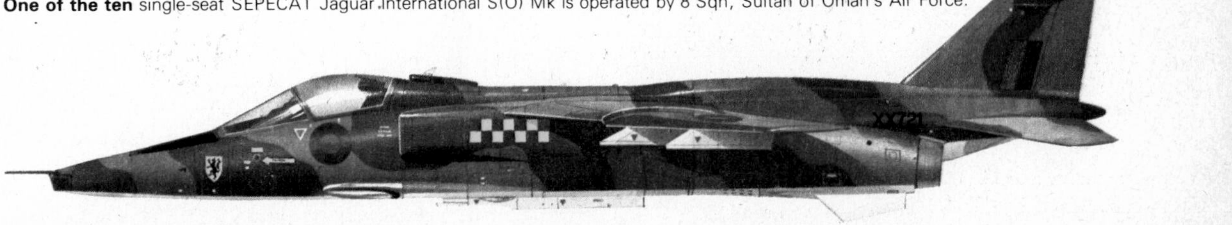

SEPECAT Jaguar GR Mk 1 XX721 of 54 Sqn, RAF, one of three units making up Coltishall's Jaguar Wing.

The compactness of the Jaguar is evident in plan view; span is much less than a Viggen or F-16. The wing has high-lift double-slotted flaps, two-section spoilers (no ailerons) and leading-edge slats outboard.

This is a SEPECAT Jaguar GR.1 of RAF No 20 Sqn (former Harrier unit) at Bruggen. It is shown fitted with Matra Magic AAMs for trials; AIM-9L Sidewinder may become standard.

The robust rough-field landing gear is impressive, as is the ground clearance for carrying large external stores, in this case two 1,000 lb bombs, four BL755 cluster bombs and two 1,200-litre tanks.

The "chisel nose" houses a Ferranti laser ranger and marked-target seeker. Above the mid-fuselage is the cabin-conditioning duct with VHF aerials on top, while the lower body houses two Aden 30 mm cannon.

Among the inbuilt defensive electronics the ARI.18228 analog-controlled radar warning system is evident, with front/rear aerials high on the fin. Anti-skid brakes are backed up by a hook and braking parachute.

XZ389

CN

Shenyang F-4/TF-4

By about 1966 the vast aeronautical complex at Shenyang (formerly called Mukden), in what used to be Manchuria, had completed about 1,000 licence-built Mikoyan-Gurevich MiG-15 and MiG-15UTI fighters and trainers, and was continuing to build the later MiG-17 fighter with various small Chinese modifications. Few single-seat MiG-15s were built, but the MiG-17 sustained a major programme and

it is believed production continued into the 1970s. Large numbers of Chinese-built MiG-17s of at least four sub-types were encountered in the NVAF (US name for the air force of the People's Republic of Vietnam) during the US involvement in South-East Asia up to 1973, and considerable numbers were exported to Albania, Pakistan and, it is believed, Tanzania. The American designation

for the Chinese-built MiG-17 is F-4, and the same codename ('Fresco') is used as for the original Russian aircraft. Considerable numbers of F-4s remain in Chinese service, and since 1977 it has become evident that a proportion are tandem dual trainers. It is not known whether these were built as such or converted from fighters. The designation TF-4 was applied, the Chinese designation being

unknown in early 1979. No dual two-seat MiG-17 ever went into production in the Soviet Union, the MiG-15UTI remaining the chief jet advanced trainer in all Warsaw Pact forces. So far as is known the dual TF-4 has not been exported, except possibly to Vietnam prior to 1976.

Data: basically as for MiG-17

Shenyang F-6

Prior to the political break with the Soviet Union in 1960, the Chinese People's Republic imported a number of Mikoyan-Gurevich MiG-19 'Farmer' fighters of several sub-types, together with spares and support equipment. Without a licence the Chinese Shenyang design offices copied the aircraft and issued engineering drawings, and manufacture of the Shenyang F-6 version began at once. The first flew in December 1961. Subsequently several thousand have been made. The F-6 swiftly became the dominant type in the Chinese air force, and it remains in production in advanced forms in 1979.

Most F-6 fighters are derived from the MiG-19SF, and are configured as day interceptors and air-superiority fighters. Though older in concept than the MiG-21 (also built for a time at Shenyang but soon withdrawn) the F-6 has outstanding manoeuvrability, stemming from relatively low wing-loading and good thrust/weight ratio, combined with cannon of devastating effect, firing ammunition having approximately twice the kinetic energy and explosive power of Western guns of the same calibre. This original F-6 version was first seen by Western observers in Pakistan in 1966, the outstandingly good overall detailing and finish being noted. Pakistan subsequently received 150 of these excellent aircraft.

In the Chinese air force a proportion of F-6 aircraft have only the wing-root guns. Most of

these two-gun machines are night and all-weather interceptors derived from the MiG-19PF, with a Chinese modification of the Izumrud (emerald) radar. In 1978 variations on the radar bullet fairing in the inlet were first seen in photographs. The rest of the two-gun F-6s are photo-reconnaissance fighters with vertical and oblique cameras in the nose. The F-6 was the basis for the F-9

Type: fighter (for variations, see text)
Powerplant: two 7,165-lb (3250-kg) Tumansky-designed RD-9B afterburning turbojets
Performance: maximum speed at high altitude 902 mph (1452 km/h); service ceiling 58,725 ft (17900 m); range with two drop tanks 1,366 miles (2200 km)
Weights: empty 12,700 lb (5760 kg); maximum take-off 19,180 lb (8700 kg)
Dimensions: span 29 ft 6½ in (9.00 m); length (excluding probe) 41 ft 4 in (12.9 m), (PF) 43 ft 2½ in (13.16 m); height 13 ft 2¼ in (4.02 m)
Armament: three 30-mm NR-30 cannon (two on PF and photo versions); two bombs or other stores each of up to 500 lb (227 kg) inboard of drop tanks; two Sidewinder or other close-range air-to-air missiles outboard
Operators: Albania, China, Pakistan, Tanzania

The Chinese Shenyang F-6. This type of tactical fighter/bomber has proved extremely well built and reliable, and Western observers have praised the detailed finish of the airframe. China also builds the engines and NR-30 gun.

Shenyang Type 6bis Fighter (Sinshi Liyu Itsi Chaen Toe) Fantan-A

Derived from the Soviet MiG-19 fighter, which has been in continuous production at the Shenyang (Mukden) aircraft manufacturing complex as the Type 6 Fighter (Sinshi Liyu Chaen To) since February 1959, when production licenses were acquired for the MiG-19SF and MiG-19PF, together with their Tumansky RD-9B turbojets. The Type 6bis Fighter, known by the reporting name Fantan-A, differs from the Type 6 (alias MiG-19) essentially in having a lengthened forward fuselage and lateral air intakes. In addition, the vertical tail surfaces have been revised and enlarged. The Type 6bis Fighter appears to have been optimised for the clear-weather strike role as the new fuselage nose does not house an all-weather radar. In consequence, the purpose of this redesign is unclear as it is unlikely to enhance performance. Armament comprises one 30-mm cannon in each wing root and a gyro gunsight is fitted, no radar ranging being provided. There are two weapons stations aft and slightly inboard of the main undercarriage attachment points and

there are two "wet points" for drop tanks outboard of the undercarriage. External loads include 551-lb (250-kg) bombs and rocket pods. The following data are estimated.

Powerplant: two Shenyang-built Tumanski RD-9B-811 turbojets each rated at 5,730 lb (2600 kg) dry and 7,165 lb (3250 kg) with max reheat
Performance: maximum speed, Mach 1.35, or 900 mph (1450 km/h) at 33,000 ft (10000 m); range cruise, Mach 0.83, or 590 mph (950 km/h); normal range 860 miles (1385 km); maximum range (with external fuel) 1,360 miles (2190 km); initial climb, 22,600 ft/min (115 m/sec)
Weights: empty 13,000 lb (5900 kg); normal loaded 17,000 lb (7700 kg); maximum take-off 19,000 lb (8620 kg)
Dimensions: span 29 ft 6 in (9.00 m); length (without probe), 47 ft 0 in (14.30 m), (with probe) 50 ft 0 in (15.25 m); height 13 ft 0 in (3.95 m); wing area 269 sq ft (25.00 m²)

Shenyang Type 6bis Fighter

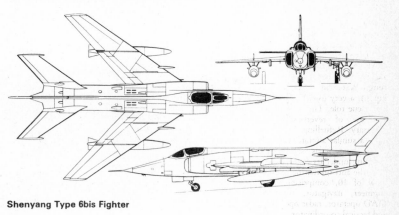

Though derived from the **F-6** (MiG-19SF), the Shenyang fighter/bomber called 'F-6bis Fantan' by the West is much longer, heavier and more capable, and must have engines of increased power. This is one of the versions without radar.

Shenyang F-12

This is the US designation for the completely new fighter and attack aircraft being developed at the Chinese state factory at Shenyang around the Rolls-Royce Spey 200-series afterburning turbofan (maximum rating 20,515 lb/9306 kg), which is to be made under licence at a purpose-built factory in China. Few hard facts about the F-12 have emerged, though following the supply of at least one Mikoyan-Gurevich MiG-23 swing-wing fighter from Egypt in 1976 it has been speculated that the F-12 will owe much to this Russian design, whose engine is of basically similar size. Other reports suggest that the Chinese designers have produced prototypes with tailed-delta and variable-sweep configurations, which are to be subjected to competitive fly-off trials to establish which is superior. Apart from the strong belief that the F-12 will be single-engined, designed for at least Mach 2, have STOL capability and be capable of both air-to-air and air-to-ground operations, all information on this programme is speculative. The licence with Rolls-Royce was signed in December 1975.

Shin Meiwa PS-1/US 1

Only Japan and the USSR have continued to develop the flying boat/amphibian in an operational military role, and the Shin Meiwa PS-1/US-1 represent the most advanced aircraft of this type to be built. Shin Meiwa is better known by its former name Kawanishi, the change being made in 1949 when the company was re-established as a major overhaul centre for US and Japanese aircraft.

Following considerable studies, Shin Meiwa received a contract in January 1966 for development of an anti-submarine flying boat to meet the requirements of the Japanese Maritime Self-Defense Force. Company designations SS-2 and SS-2A were allocated respectively to the anti-submarine flying boat which became the JMSDF PS-1 and the amphibian version which became the US-1.

The first two prototype PS-1s flew in October 1967 and June 1968 and the aircraft was awarded its Type Approval in late 1970, following evaluation by the JMSDF Flight Test Squadron at Iwakuni.

Tests have taken place with the first prototype PS-1 to assess the feasibility of its use as a water bomber, in which form an eventual load of 14 short tons (28,000 lb/12700 kg) of water is visualised; present tests have been limited to just over eight tons (16,000 lb/7258 kg).

A licence-built Ishikawajima/General Electric T58-IHI-10 gas turbine providing 1,250 shp (933 kW) is situated in the upper centre fuselage to provide power for a boundary-layer control system operating on the rudder, flaps and elevators. The resultant 'blowing' of these surfaces together with propeller slipstream deflection for the flaps and an automatic flight control system, give much greater lift control and stability at low speed, and make possible the aircraft's STOL performance.

Take-offs and landings in wave heights up to 10 ft (3 m) have been made, and the PS-1 dips its sonar into the sea by repeated landings and take-offs, being capable of landing on very rough water in winds up to 29 mph (47 km/h), a very useful capability also in its air-sea rescue role. The aircraft can back up with the use of reversible-pitch propellers if necessary. Refuelling at sea is possible either from a similar aircraft or surface vessel. As a flying boat it is self-launching and self-beaching under its own power.

In the anti-submarine role the PS-1 carries a crew of 10, comprising two pilots, flight engineer, navigator, two sonar operators, MAD operator, radar operator, radio operator and tactical co-ordinator, while the US-1 SAR version has a crew of nine and space for 20 seats or 12 stretchers.

Type: anti-submarine flying boat/amphibian
Powerplant: four 3,060-ehp (2283-kW) Ishikawajima-built General Electric T64-IHI-10 turboprops
Performance: maximum speed at 10,000 ft (3050 m) 308 mph (496 km/h); cruising speed at 10,000 ft (3050 m) 265 mph (426 km/h); rate of climb at sea level at maximum take-off weight 2,380 ft (725 m) per minute; service ceiling 27,000 ft (8230 m); take-off run from water to 50 ft (15 m) 1,970 ft (600 m)*; landing run on water from 50 ft (15 m) 950 ft (290 m); range at 10,000 ft (3050 m) 2,614 miles (4207 km) (above performance data are for US-1 at 79,365 lb/36000 kg except*, 94,800 lb/43000 kg)
Weights: (US-1) empty equipped 56,218 lb (25500 kg); maximum take-off from water 94,800 lb (43000 kg); maximum take-off from land 99,200 lb (45000 kg) PS-1 empty 58,000 lb (26300 kg)
Dimensions: span 108 ft 9 in (33.15 m); length 109 ft 9 in (33.46 m); height 32 ft 3 in (9.82 m); wing area 1,462 sq ft (135.8 m²)
Armament: (PS-1) internal weapons-bay storage can accommodate four 330-lb (149-kg) anti-submarine bombs, smoke bombs, AQA-3 Jezebel passive acoustic search equipment and 20 sonobuoys with launchers, and Julie acoustic echo ranging equipment with 12 explosive charges; externally, a pod between the engine nacelles under each wing carries two homing torpedoes; launcher beneath each wing tip carries three 5-in (12.7-cm) air-to-surface rockets; searchlight beneath right wing
Operators: Japan

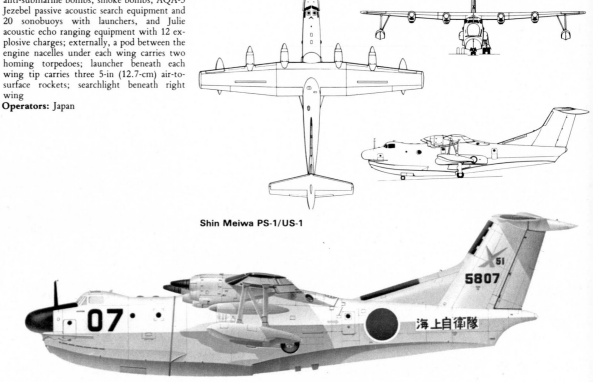

Shin Meiwa PS-1/US-1

The **Japanese Shin Meiwa** PS-1 is the western world's only four-engined amphibious flying-boat in production and currently fulfills patrol duties with the Japanese Maritime Self-Defence Force: the 31st Koku-tai is the main operational unit with the type.

Shin Meiwa's ASR (air/sea rescue) amphibian is called PS-1Kai by the Japanese Maritime Self-Defence Force and SS-2A or US-1 by the company. The first of the batch of six is here seen taxiing on a calm sea.

Short Skyvan 3M

The Short Skyvan, a small but capable airlifter, started life with piston engines (two 390-hp/291-kW Continental GTSIO-520s) and first flew on 17 January 1963. These powerplants were subsequently replaced by 520-shp (388-kW) Turboméca Astazou turboprops, and this re-engined version flew for the first time on 2 October 1963. Designated Srs 1 and 1A, these versions were superseded by the Astazou XII-powered Srs 2, of which 16 production aircraft were built. Current skyvans, Srs 3, are powered by the Garrett AiResearch TPE331 turboprop. The first Srs 3 flew on 15 December 1967, and more than 60 have since been sold to civil operators. Early in 1970 Shorts flew the first military version, the 3M. With a basic layout lending itself to military operation, the Skyvan is used for dropping supplies, evacuating casualties, paratrooping and troop transport, carrying vehicles or ordnance, and assault landings. It is capable of very short take-off and landing (780 ft/238 m and 695 ft/212 m respectively), even under hot and high conditions, and despite its 'workhorse' shape the Skyvan cruises at a useful speed. A large rear-door loading ramp allows carriage of outsize cargo such as light vehicles, and it can be opened in flight for the dropping of supplies up to 4 ft 6 in (1.37 m) in height. Excluding the flight deck, 780 cu ft (22.09 m³) of cabin volume is available on 120 sq ft (11.15 m²) of floor area, entered through the rear door which measures 6 ft 6 in (1.98 m) high by 6 ft 5 in (1.96 m) wide. Usable cabin length is 18 ft 7 in (5.67 m). The 3M can accommodate up to 22 fully equipped troops, or 16 paratroops plus dispatcher, or 12 stretcher cases and two attendants, or normally up to 5,200 lb (2358 kg) of freight. Equipment peculiar to the 3M includes a blister window on the port side for the dispatcher and rollers on the floor for facilitating loading and positioning of heavy cargo. The tail is also fitted with a guard rail to prevent fouling of the control surfaces by static lines during dropping. Parachuting fittings include anchor cables for static lines, inward-facing seats with safety nets and a signal light. Many Skyvan 3Ms have nose radar.

Oman is the largest user of the military Skyvan, the Sultan's Air Force operating 16. They fly with No 2 Sqn based at Seeb, and are part of a largely British-made inventory. The Ghana air force flies six 3Ms. Based at Takoradi, they are used for tactical support, communications, coastal patrol and casualty-evacuation duties. No 121 Sqn of the Singapore air force uses six Skyvans for search-and-rescue and anti-smuggling duties around the island. They are also used for light transport and supply work. The *Comando de Aviación Naval Argentina* assigns five 3Ms to the *Prefectura Naval Argentina*, a small force tasked with coastguard duties, and which also operates six Hughes 500M helicopters. Indonesia's air force flies three of the aircraft on short-range transport work. They are assigned to No 2 Sqn and are equipped to civil standard so that they can also operate for the Ministry of the Interior. Three Skyvan 3Ms are flown by the Royal Thai Border Police. A light transport squadron of the Austrian air force (III *Geschwader* of *Fliegerregiment* I) uses two of the

aircraft for supply duties and also for aerial survey from the base at Tulln. The Mauretanian air force and army operate two aircraft jointly, based at Nouakchott. Two 3Ms are flown by the air wing of the Royal Nepalese Army on light transport duties, and one of them is used also by the Royal Flight. The Yemen Arab Republic's air force flies two for transport work, and the Ecuadorian army uses one. Four more have been sold to undisclosed customers.

Type: light STOL utility transport
Powerplant: two 715-shp (533-kW) Garrett AiResearch TPE331-201 turboprops
Performance: maximum design speed 250 mph (402 km/h); maximum cruising speed at 10,000 ft (3050 m) 203 mph (327 km/h); range with 5,000-lb (2268-kg) payload 240 miles (386 km); range at long-range cruising speed 670 miles (1075 km); rate of climb at sea level 1,530 ft (466 m) per minute
Weights: empty equipped 7,400 lb (3356 kg); take-off (normal) 13,700 lb (6214 kg); take-off (maximum) 14,500 lb (6577 kg)

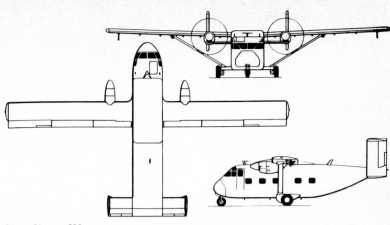

Short Skyvan 3M

Dimensions: span 64 ft 11 in (19.79 m); length 41 ft 4 in (12.6 m); height 15 ft 1 in (4.6 m); wing area 373 sq ft (34.65 m²)
Armament: none

Operators: Argentina, Austria, Ecuador, Ghana, Indonesia, Mauretania, Mexico, Nepal, Oman, Singapore, South Yemen, Thailand

Largest operator of the versatile Short Skyvan 3M is the Sultan of Oman's Air Force, with 15 operational from 16 delivered. Despite extremely high ambient temperatures and a harsh environment these aircraft have flown intensively in the persistent (and now Cuban-backed) Dhofar war. They are operated by 2 Sqn at Seeb and 5 Sqn at Salaah, on multiple duties.

Short Skyvan 3M, one of 15 in transport use with 2 and 5 Sqn, Sultan of Oman's Air Force.

SIAI-Marchetti S.208 M

Evolved from a civil touring aircraft, 44 SIAI-Marchetti S.208Ms are used by the Italian air force for liaison and training. The first flight of the four/five-seat tourer was on 22 May 1967.

The S.208M is a low-wing monoplane identical with the civil S.208 except that the forward-opening right door can be jettisoned in emergency; there is a second door on the left. The wing has a covering of honeycomb panels and the inner leading edge accommodates the electrically retracting main gears. Other features include a baggage compartment accessible from the cabin and two integral wing tanks plus two wingtip auxiliary tanks totalling 98.1 Imperial gallons (446 litres). Deliveries to the Italian air force began in 1971 and were completed the following year. Full blind-flying and navigation systems are standard.

Type: liaison and intermediate training aircraft
Powerplant: one 260-hp (194-kW) Lycoming O-540-E4A5 six-cylinder horizontally-opposed air-cooled engine
Performance: maximum speed at sea level at maximum take-off weight 200 mph (320 km/h); maximum cruising speed 186 mph (300 km/h); range 745 miles (1200 km) with maximum internal fuel; service ceiling 17,806 ft (5400 m)
Weights: empty equipped 1,720 lb (780 kg); maximum take-off 2,976 lb (1350 kg)
Dimensions: span 35 ft 7.6 in (10.86 m); length 26 ft 3 in (8.00 m); height 9 ft 5.8 in (2.89 m); wing area 173.2 sq ft (16.09 m²)
Armament: none
Operator: Italy

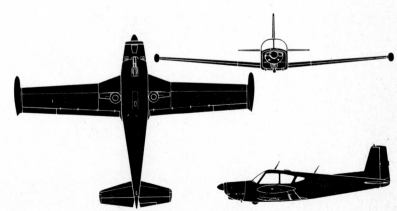

SIAI-Marchetti S.208

SIAI-Marchetti SF.260

Designed by Stelio Frati as a fast, compact and flamboyant private aircraft, the SIAI-Marchetti SF.260 has found favour with a large number of armed forces. The prototype flew on 15 July 1964 and was known as the F.250. It was built by Aviamilano and was powered by a 250-hp (186.5-kW) Lycoming O-540 six-cylinder piston engine. When SIAI-Marchetti took over the project the aircraft was renamed SF.260 and a 260-hp (192.4-kW) Lycoming O-540 installed. To all intents and purposes merely a three-seater, the SF.260 offers an unusually high level of versatility for its size. It is used for such diverse roles as training, light attack, aerobatic tuition, forward air control, fishery protection, search and rescue, liaison and maritime patrol. SIAI-Marchetti is now directing virtually all its production capacity at military orders, although a civil version is still marketed (at $150,000 basic, the price is a deterrent to most civilians). In 1978 the Italian company pulled off a massive order from Libya, by which 250 aircraft would be bought and, for the most part, built in a new plant in the African country.

There are three military variants. The M, a three-seat trainer developed from the civil A, first flew on 10 October 1970 and pioneered a number of important structural modifications which were subsequently adopted for all versions. Among the changes were stronger wings, which on earlier models had relied on external stiffening. Some 150 Ms have been sold to date. May 1972 saw the first flight of the SF.260W Warrior. Equipped with underwing pylons, this is a light strike platform and has become popular with air forces which cannot afford to risk expensive metal on minor skirmishes. The list of mission profiles is almost limitless for this variant, varying from long-duration sorties close to base (5 hours or so at about 50-mile/80-km range) to 5 minutes over a target 350 miles (565 km) away. A recent innovation is the SF.260SW Sea Warrior maritime-patrol variant, which has enlarged tip-tanks housing (left) lightweight Bendix radar and (right) photo-reconnaissance equipment in addition to fuel. This is an overcrowded market, and the order book has not been encouraging.

Of 36 MBs delivered between 1969 and 1971, 33 are still in service with the Belgian air force on elementary training duties from Goetsenhoven. Burma's 10 MBs operate in the dual strike/trainer role. Dubai, a component of the United Emirates air force, operates an almost exclusively Italian-built fleet, including one SF.260WD Warrior for armed training. Ireland has replaced its eight Chipmunks with 10 SF.260WE Warriors. The home market, Italy, operates the type for basic training, but, as mentioned earlier, Libya is the largest customer with an order for 250 WL Warriors. Morocco's two Ms operate alongside North American T-6s and T-28s. Sixteen Warriors

equip the 17th Attack Wing of the Philippine air force, and the Singapore air force's No 150 (Falcon) Sqn flies 14 MSs on basic training duties. Some of the Singapore aircraft have been updated to Warrior standard. Korat Air Base is home for the Royal Thai Air Force's 12 MTs, used for training. Replacing Saab Safirs, 12 WTs train the Tunisian Republic's air force. Zaire's 23 MZs are used for basic training, as are Zambia's eight Ms, although some of the latter are occasionally flown on COIN missions.

Type: three-seat light attack, trainer and maritime reconnaissance aircraft
Powerplant: one 260-hp (192-kW) Avco Lycoming O-540-E4A5 flat-six piston engine
Performance: maximum level speed at sea level (M) 211 mph (340 km/h), (W) 196 mph (315 km/h), (SW) 189 mph (304 km/h); maximum level speed 75% power at 5,000 ft (1524 m) (M) 200 mph (322 km/h), (W) 178 mph (287 km/h), (SW) 171 mph (275 km/h); radius of action (W) single-crew armed patrol mission at 2,564 lb (1163 kg) 6 hours 25 minutes, with 5 hours 35 minutes over target, 57 miles (92 km); (W) ferry 1,066 miles (1716 km); (SW) 5 hours 17 minutes for two-crew surveillance mission, with 3 hours 40 minutes on station at 120 mph (194 km/h) plus reserves 115 miles (185 km); maximum rate of climb at sea level (M) 1,558 ft (475 m) per minute, (W) 1,099 ft (335 m) per minute, (SW) 885 ft (270 m) per minute
Weights: empty equipped (M) 1,761 lb (799 kg), (W) 1,794 lb (814 kg), (SW) 1,889 lb (857 kg); maximum take-off (M) 2,645 lb (1200 kg), (W, SW) 2,866 lb (1300 kg)
Dimensions: span over tips (M, W) 27 ft 4¾ in (8.35 m), (SW) 28 ft 6½ in (8.7 m); length 23 ft 3½ in (7.1 m); height 7 ft 11 in (2.41 m); wing area 108.7 sq ft (10.10 m²)
Armament: (W) two or four underwing hardpoints with maximum total capacity of 661 lb (300 kg); typical ordnance includes (alternatives) one or two SIAI gun pods each with one 500-round 7.62-mm FN machine-gun; two Simpres AL-8-70 launchers each with eight 2.75-in FFAR rockets; two Matra F2 launchers each with six 68-mm SNEB 253 rockets; two Samp EU 32 275.5-lb (125-kg) general-purpose bombs or EU 13 264-lb (120-kg) fragmentation bombs; two Alkan 500B cartridge throwers for Lacroix 74-mm explosive cartridges, F 725 flares or F 130 smoke cartridges; one Alkan 500B cartridge

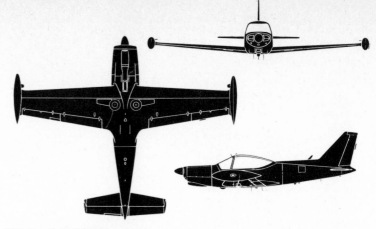

SIAI-Marchetti SF.260

thrower and one photo-reconnaissance pod with two 70-mm automatic cameras; or two 18.25-gallon (83-litre) auxiliary fuel tanks

Operators: Belgium, Burma, Dubai, Ireland, Italy, Libya, Morocco, Philippines, Singapore, Thailand, Tunisia, Zaire, Zambia

Standard primary pilot trainer of the Force Aérienne Belge is the Italian SIAI-Marchetti SF.260M, of which 33 remain out of 36 supplied before 1971. User is the FTS at Goetsenhoven.

SIAI-Marchetti SF.260WT trainer/counter-insurgency aircraft, one of 12 in service with the Tunisian Republican Air Force.

SIAI-Marchetti SM.1019

Replacement of an ageing fleet of army co-operation aircraft is a problem which has faced most European air arms during the early 1970s. Many countries moved towards helicopters, but in Italy a specification was issued for a new fixed-wing aircraft with a wide speed range, STOL performance and the ability to carry weapons. The contenders were the Aermacchi AM-3C and the SIAI-Marchetti SM.1019. The latter won.

SIAI had taken the airframe of the Cessna O-1 Bird Dog and substituted an Allison 250 turboprop for the Continental O-470 piston engine. The Allison engine drives a 90-in (2.29-m) Hartzell propeller and is related to the engine of the Agusta Bell AB 206 helicopter. Because of the power increase, SIAI fitted a larger vertical tail. Standard accommodation is for two crew in tandem. In the training role a rear set of controls is provided.

Airframes for the SM.1019A are completely new. Drawings were made available by Cessna and, apart from redesign of the forward fuselage to accept the new powerplant, SIAI added two additional fuel tanks, a rear entry door on the right, and a rear instrument panel. The aircraft has three hardpoints. The cen-

treline load is usually a battlefield surveillance camera.

Typical wingloads are two AS.12 air-to-surface missiles, two 2.75-in (70-mm) rocket pods, machine-gun pods, anti-personnel bombs, auxiliary fuel tanks, or night reconnaissance equipment.

In Italian army use the aircraft is designated SM.1019EI as a result of the installation of the uprated Allison 250-B17B engine. Over 80 of 100 had been delivered by 1979. Their roles are training, artillery spotting and forward air control, battlefield reconnaissance and protective cover for the helicopter force. The training and general support (utility) version has a lower gross weight and superior performance. With two external tanks the escort/reconnaissance version has a range of up to 840 miles (1352 km), and an endurance of some 8 hours 40 minutes.

To date, the SM.1019 is only in service with the *Aviazione Leggera dell'Esercito*, to whom first deliveries were made in mid-1975. However, it is possible to remanufacture existing Cessna O-1s and many Bird Dog users may be tempted to rejuvenate their aircraft. Under the agreement signed by SIAI, Cessna can build the SM.1019 in the United States.

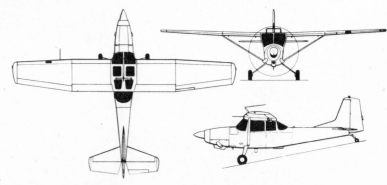

SIAI-Marchetti SM.1019E

Type: (EI) training, observation and light attack aircraft
Powerplant: one 400-shp (298-kW) Allison 250-B17 turboprop
Performance: (utility) maximum cruising speed at sea level 184 mph (296 km/h); economical cruising speed (75% power at 8,200 ft/2,500 m) 175 mph (281 km/h); stalling speed (flaps down) 43 mph (70 km/h); rate of climb 1,810 ft (551 m) per minute; maximum range at sea level (standard tankage) 575 miles (925 km); landing distance at sea level 300 ft (91.5 m); service ceiling 25,00 ft (7620 m)
Weights: empty equipped 1,521 lb (690 kg); maximum take-off 2,866 lb (1300 kg)
Dimensions: span 36 ft 0 in (10.97 m); length 27 ft 11 in (8.52 m); height 9 ft 4 in (2.86 m); wing area 173.95 sq ft (16.16 m²)
Armament: light tactical stores on wing hardpoints
Operators: Italy

Sikorsky S-55/H-19 Chickasaw/Westland Whirlwind (see also Westland Whirlwind)

Continuing the development of rotary-wing aircraft from the R-4 (the first production helicopter to serve with the US armed forces) via the improved R-5, during 1948 the Sikorsky company evolved the design of a large and more useful helicopter. Details of this design were submitted to the USAF, resulting in a contract for five YH-19 prototypes for evaluation, the first making its maiden flight at Bridgeport, Connecticut, on 10 November 1949.

The basic similarity of the S-55 and the S-51 (R-5, later H-5) was easily seen, but the new design included an unusual powerplant installation, with the engine mounted obliquely in the fuselage nose, a long straight drive-shaft between the pilots connecting the engine and main rotor gearbox, which was immediately beneath the rotor hub. To permit easy examination and maintenance of the engine, it was enclosed by large clamshell doors which allowed good all-round access. Other new features included two small fins in the form of an inverted V beneath the tail boom, and the provision of a two-seat enclosed crew compartment above the main cabin, which had accommodation for 8-10 passengers or up to six stretchers and a medical orderly.

Extensively built for a helicopter of its era, with more than a 1,000 examples being supplied to the US armed services alone, these included the original H-19A for the USAF with 600-hp (447-kW) Pratt & Whitney R-1340-57 engine, similar H-19C Chickasaws for the US

Army, and HO4S-1s for the US Navy. With a 700-hp (522-kW) Wright R-1300-3 and increased rotor diameter, the USAF, US Army, US Navy, and US Coast Guard received H-19B, H-19D Chickasaws, HO4S-3s, and HO4S-3Gs respectively. HRS-1s/-2s and -3s, generally similar to the HO4S series, were supplied to the US Marine Corps. H-19B/C/Ds became redesignated UH-19B/C/D respectively in 1962, the US Marines' HRS-3 became CH-19E, and Navy HO4S-3 and Coast Guard HO4S-3G became UH-19F and HH-19G respectively. A few operators have had their machines converted to turbine power with TPE331 or PT6T engines.

In addition to production by Sikorsky for the US armed forces, S-55s were built under licence by SNCASE in France, Misubishi in Japan, and by Westland Helicopters in Great Britain. This last company built a number of variants with US engines but also developed the design and installed the British-built Alvis Leonides Major 14-cylinder engine. Westland-built S-55s had the name Whirlwind and in addition to being supplied to the British armed forces, were exported to France and Yugoslavia, as described separately.

Type: utility helicopter
Powerplant: (H-19B) one 700-hp (522-kW) Wright R-1300-3 radial piston engine
Performance: (H-19B) maximum speed at sea level 112 mph (180 km/h); cruising speed

A handful of these old Sikorsky UH-19 (S-55) helicopters were still operating with the US Army in late 1979, the first having entered service early in the Korean war in 1951.

91 mph (146 km/h); range 360 miles (579 km)
Weights: (H-19B) empty 5,250 lb (2381 kg); maximum take-off 7,900 lb (3583 kg)
Dimensions: main rotor diameter (H-19A) 49 ft 0 in (14.94 m), (H-19B) 53 ft 0 in (16.15 m); tail rotor diameter 8 ft 8 in (2.64 m); length of fuselage 42 ft 3 in (12.88 m); height 13 ft 4 in (4.06 m); main rotor disc area (H-19A) 1,886 sq ft (175.21 m²), (H-19B)

2,206 sq ft (204.94 m²)
Armament: none, but machine-guns and rockets in Korea, Indo-China, Algeria and elsewhere
Operators: have included Chile, France, Japan, Malaya, UK (Navy), US Air Force, US Army, US Coast Guard, US Marine Corps, US Navy

---

Sikorsky S-58/H-34 Choctaw/Seabat/Seahorse/Westland Wessex

Originating from a US Navy requirement of 1951 for an anti-submarine helicopter, Sikorsky built the prototype S-58, and this has proved to be the most extensively built of all Sikorsky helicopters. The prototype flew on 8 March 1954. The origins of the requirement lay in the US Navy's discovery that the S-55 (in service as the HO4S/HRS) had only limited payload and range too limited for anti-submarine missions.

But the S-55 had proved an efficient design, so the S-58 was basically a larger version with an engine of almost three times the power. Landing gear is of the fixed tailwheel type, instead of a quadricycle unit, and there is accommodation for a pilot and co-pilot above the main cabin, which can accommodate up to 18 passengers, or an equivalent weight in equipment or cargo. The main and tail rotors each have four all-metal blades, and it is claimed that the transmission system has 25% fewer components than those of earlier designs. The US Navy had sufficient confidence in this design to order the production HSS-1 before the prototype had flown. After flight trials had begun, orders began to flow in also from the US Army and US Marine Corps.

The first production SH-34G Seabat (formerly HSS-1) for the US Navy flew on 20 September 1954, entering service with HS-3 in August 1955. The US Navy realised that despite a payload increase of some 70%, it was still not possible for these helicopters to operate singly, and decided to 'pair' them into hunter/killer units. The hunter carried dipping sonar, and the killer homing torpedoes. In practice hunters often worked alone, calling in surface vessels when a kill capacity was needed.

The SH-34J Seabat was suitable for day or night operation with Sikorsky autostabilization. US Army versions included the CH-34A Choctaw transport, followed by the CH-34C with autostabilization. First version for the US Marine Corps was the UH-34D Seahorse, followed by the UH-34E equipped with pontoons for emergency amphibious operations. Six examples for the US Coast Guard had the designation HH-34F. A single SH-34H had two General Electric T58 turboshaft engines; the LH-34D was a winterized Seabat; the VH-34D was a VIP transport; and the UH-34G/J were utility conversions.

Sikorsky built many S-58s for other nations under the Military Assistance Program, as well as for direct sale. In addition, Sud-Aviation in France mass-produced S-58s for the French army and navy, plus five for Belgium. Westland Helicopters in Britain

built a turbine-powered development as the Wessex.

Type: general-purpose helicopter
Powerplant: one 1,525-hp (1137-kW) Wright R-1820-84 Cyclone radial air-cooled piston engine
Performance: (CH-34A): maximum level speed 122 mph (196 km/h) at sea level; maximum cruising speed 97 mph (156 km/h); range (with maximum fuel, 10% reserves) 247 miles (398 km)
Weights: empty equipped (CH-34A) 7,750 lb (3515 kg), (UH-34D) 7,900 lb (3583 kg), (SH-34J) 8,275 lb (3753 kg); maximum normal take-off 13,000 lb (5897 kg); maximum permissable 14,000 lb (6350 kg)
Dimensions: main-rotor diameter 56 ft 0 in (17.07 m); tail-rotor diameter 9 ft 6 in (2.90 m); length (rotors turning) 56 ft 8¼ in (17.28 m); height 15 ft 11 in (4.85 m); main-rotor disc area 2,460 sq ft (228.53 m²)
Armament: (SH-34G/J) homing torpedoes

Sikorsky S-58

carried externally in ASW 'killer' role
Operators: Argentina, Belgium, Brazil, Canada, France, Germany, Italy, Japan,

Netherlands, Thailand, US Air Force, US Coast Guard, US Marine Corps, US Navy

Westland Wessex HC Mk 2 XR527 of 28 Sqn, RAF, formerly based at Kai Tak, Hong Kong, but recently moved to Sek Kong.

Sikorsky H-34 (S-58) with special mission equipment as still used in small numbers by the Israeli Heyl Ha'Avir.

Sikorsky S-61A/B/SH-3 Sea King/H-3/Agusta SH-3D (see also Westland Sea King/Command

US Navy operation of fixed-wing aircraft in the ASW hunter/killer role showed that such missions could be carried out more effectively by single aircraft which combined both roles. As the combination of hunter/killer capabilities into one vehicle was just as desirable for a helicopter, at the end of 1957 the US Navy contracted with Sikorsky for such a machine.

Inevitably, the new helicopter needed to be larger than the S-58, for it had to carry the sensors, avionics and weapons accommodated in two HSS-1s. Sikorsky adopted a watertight hull and retractable landing gear to provide amphibious capability, and the reliability of twin turboshaft engines and a five-blade main rotor to take full advantage of their combined power.

For the 'hunter' part of its mission the HSS-2 was equipped with Bendix dipping sonar, the autopilot holding the required constant altitude, controlled by Doppler radar and a radar altimeter. All-weather autostabilization was fitted. For the 'killer' part of its mission, the HSS-2 could carry up to 840 lb (381 kg) of weapons, including homing torpedoes.

Seven YHSS-2 test aircraft were contracted on 23 September 1957, the first flying on 11 March 1959. In September 1961 the first deliveries were made to VHS-3 at Norfolk, Virginia, and VHS-10 at Ream Field, San Diego. Early examples were powered by two 1,250-shp (932-kW) General Electric T58-GE-8B turboshafts, soon replaced by the T58-GE-10 with increased fuel capacity. In 1962 these versions were redesignated SH-3A and -3D Sea King respectively.

The S-61 has had a long life in many variants. These include nine RH-3A minesweepers, able to deploy and recover a variety of MCM (mine countermeasures) equipment to deal with the various types of mines. The HH-3A has Minigun turrets, armour protection, extra fuel capacity, and a high-speed rescue hoist to provide the US Navy with an armed search and rescue helicopter (12 were converted by the US Navy at Quonset Point). The Canadian Armed Forces operate the CH-124; four were delivered by Sikorsky, and 37 assembled in

Canada from 1963. Ten VH-3As of the Executive Flight Detachment in Washington, providing VIP transport for the US President and senior executives, were replaced by 11 VH-3Ds. Under the designation SH-3G, 105 SH-3As were converted as simple utility helicopters, followed by the multi-purpose SH-3H with new ASW equipment, advanced radar and magnetic anomaly detection (MAD) gear. In 1979 a conversion programme was updating earlier variants.

Commercial variants of the SH-3A under the designation S-61A have been supplied to the Royal Danish Air Force for air-sea rescue, and as the S-61A-4 Nuri to the Royal Malaysian Air Force as transport/cargo/rescue aircraft. The SH-3D equivalent is the S-61D-4, of which four were delivered to the Argentine navy.

SH-3As and S-61As are built under licence by Mitsubishi in Japan for the JMSDF, and SH-3Ds built under licence by Agusta in Italy have been manufactured by Sikorsky for the Brazilian and Spanish navies. Developments of the S-61 are built by Westland Helicopters in Britain as the Sea King and Commando.

Type: amphibious all-weather ASW or general purpose/transport helicopter
Powerplant: (SH-3D): two 1,400-shp (1044-kW) General Electric T58-GE-10 turboshafts
Performance: (SH-3D) maximum speed 166 mph (267 km/h); range (with maximum fuel, 10% reserves) 625 miles (1006 km)
Weights: (SH-3D) empty 11,865 lb (5382 kg); maximum take-off 18,626 lb (8449 kg)
Dimensions: main rotor diameter 62 ft 0 in (18.90 m); tail rotor diameter 10 ft 7 in (3.23 m); length (rotors turning) 72 ft 8 in (22.15 m); height 16 ft 10 in (5.13 m); main rotor disc area 3,019 sq ft (280.47 m²)
Armament: (SH-3D) provision to carry up to 840 lb (381 kg) of weapons
Operators: Argentina, Brazil, Canada, Denmark, Iran, Italy, Japan, Malaysia, Spain, US Air Force, US Marine Corps, US Navy

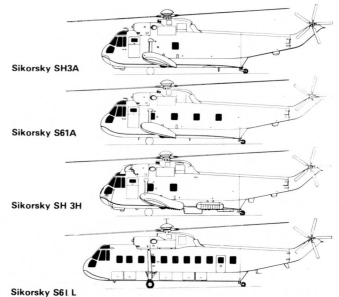

Sikorsky SH-3 Sea King

Sikorsky SH3A

Sikorsky S61A

Sikorsky SH 3H

Sikorsky S61 L

This Sikorsky SH-3D Sea King, of US Navy squadron HS-2, is one of about 80 serving with ten ASW squadrons. Some ASW Sea Kings have been rebuilt to SH-3G and -3H utility and multi-purpose configuration, and the Sikorsky SH-60B will soon arrive.

Sikorsky S-61R/CH-3/HH-3 Jolly Green Giant/Pelican

The undoubted success of the Sikorsky S-61B in US Navy service provided an indication to the USAF as to which company it should approach when a long-range transport helicopter was required in the early 1960s. In fact, the US Air Force had gained a good insight into the potential of this helicopter when, in April 1962, it had borrowed three HSS-2s fom the US Navy in order to carry supplies to radar units based at 'Texas Towers' in the Atlantic: the USAF found them so useful that it borrowed three more. By that time the US Navy's S-61s had become SH-3As, and those in US Air Force use became designated CH-3B.

In November 1962 the decision was made to acquire similar aircraft for use by the USAF, but a number of design changes were requested to make these more suitable for the transport role, which was the US Air Force's specific requirement. Major change was to the rear fuselage, with the provision of a hydraulically-operated rear loading door/ramp at the rear of the cabin, this making possible the straight-in loading of wheeled vehicles without the need for any other support equipment. Landing gear configuration was changed from that of the S-61B, to more conventional tricycle type, with twin wheels on each unit; a pneumatic 'blow-down' system ensured safe extension of the landing gear in the event of hydraulic failure. Though the planing boat hull was not required, the fuselage was made watertight, with sponsons to house the rear wheels. To ensure that, so far as possible, these aircraft would be able to operate quite independently of ground facilities, pressurized rotor blades simplify inspection, both main and tail rotor hubs are self-lubricating, a gas-turbine auxiliary power unit can supply essential electric and hydraulic power, and equipment is carried to make possible the exchange of all major components without recourse to local facilities, even in the most remote areas. New equipment includes a 2,000-lb (907-kg) capacity winch for internal cargo handling, and considerable care was taken to ensure that the landing gear and rear fuselage modifications did not affect the amphibious capability.

Sikorsky's first S-61R flew initially on 17 June 1963, and just over six months later, on 30 December, the first operational CH-3C was delivered to Tyndall AFB, Florida. A total of 41 were built for the USAF, the powerplant comprising two 1,300-shp (969-kW) General Electric T58-GE-1 turboshaft engines, with standard accommodation for a crew of two and 25 fully equipped troops, or 15 stretchers, or up to 5,000 lb (2268 kg) of cargo.

The CH-3E was introduced in 1966, and differed by having uprated T58-GE-5 engines. A total of 42 were built, and all CH-3Cs were converted later to this standard. An important third variant, which entered service with the USAF's Aerospace Rescue and Recovery Service, has the designation HH-3E, and are equipped to fulfil their role in a combat zone. Their additional equipment includes armour, rescue hoist, a retractable flight-refuelling probe, self-sealing fuel tanks, and defensive armament. Some 50 of these were provided for service in south-east Asia by conversion of CH-3Es. In service these aircraft were known as Jolly Green Giants, and were used mainly to rescue pilots who had been forced down in hostile territory. They were used extensively in North Vietnam, making deep penetrations of enemy airspace, and carrying out successful rescue missions despite heavy gunfire being directed at them.

In 1968 the US Coast Guard received the first 40 HH-3Fs, generally similar to the HH-3E except for deletion of armament, armour and self-sealing tanks. These aircraft, which have the name Pelican, have advanced avionics to facilitate their use in the search and rescue role.

Type: amphibious transport helicopter
Powerplant: (CH-3E) two 1,500-shp (1119-kW) General Electric T58-GE-5 turboshafts
Performance: (CH-3E) maximum speed 162 mph (261 km/h); range with maximum fuel and 10% reserves 465 miles (748 km)
Weights: (CH-3E) empty 13,255 lb (6012 kg); normal take-off 21,247 lb (9637 kg); maximum take-off 22,050 lb (10002 kg)
Dimensions: main rotor diameter 62 ft 0 in (18.90 m); tail rotor diameter 10 ft 4 in (3.15 m); length (rotors turning) 73 ft 0 in (22.25 m); height 18 ft 1 in (5.51 m); main rotor disc area 3,019 sq ft (280.47 m²)

Armament: (HH-3E) two 7.62-mm (0.3-in) Miniguns on each side
Operators: US Air Force, US Coast Guard

Sikorsky S-61R

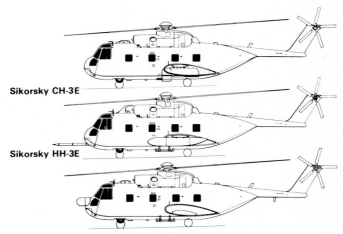

Sikorsky CH-3E

Sikorsky HH-3E

Sikorsky HH-3F Pelican

A Sikorsky HH-3, of the nosewheel/rear-door S-61R species of the USAF Aerospace Rescue & Recovery Service, retrieves a BQM-34C Firebee II supersonic RPV target during the November 1976 William Tell annual Fighter Weapons meet at Tyndall AFB.

Sikorsky S-64 Skycrane/CH-54 Tarhe

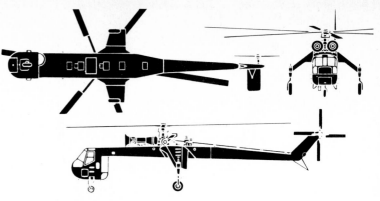

The requirement for a heavy lift helicopter was growing in the late 1950s, as it became clear that improving technology concerned with the design of rotary-wing dynamic systems, combined with lightweight high-powered turboshaft engines, should make it possible to build aircraft in this category with entirely new standards of performance. It was at about this same time that development of the Boeing Vertol Model 115 (CH-47 Chinook) began, and Sikorsky initiated its own design for a 'flying crane' that was very different in conception.

It consisted of a basic prime mover comprising a long fuselage beam. At the forward end was suspended a cab to accommodate a crew of three, plus jump seats for two loaders/technicians; at the aft end was a tail with the anti-torque rotor on the left. Above the fuselage two turboshaft engines, main and intermediate gear boxes, main rotor and drive shafts were mounted, leaving the undersurface clear. The tricycle landing gear consisted of a nosewheel beneath the cab, and main legs on outriggers to allow the fuselage to straddle a bulky load. A cargo hook could be lowered by the third, aft-facing crew member.

Sikorsky's concept did not rely purely on the use of cargo hoists, it being intended that the S-64A would straddle interchangeable pods for a variety of purposes. The fundamental idea was linked closely to the road/ship transit of goods in sealed containers: Sikorsky believed that Skycranes might replace ships over short ranges.

The first of three prototypes made its initial flight on 9 May 1962 and was delivered to the US Army at Fort Benning, Georgia, for test and evaluation. The second and third prototypes were delivered to Germany for evaluation, and VFW-Fokker participated in design and development.

The Army's evaluation was sufficiently successful to gain for Sikorsky a contract for six YCH-54A helicopters for further investigation. The company designed containers for troop transport, field hospital support, anti-submarine warfare, mine-sweeping, and heavy-lift support operations.

Five of the US Army's prototypes were delivered in 1964-5 as production CH-54A

Tarhes. The sixth was retained by Sikorsky to assist FAA certification, which was awarded on 30 July 1965.

Evaluation by the US Army involved deployment in Vietnam with the 478th Aviation Company, where Tarhes performed near-miracles in the retrieval of some 380 damaged aircraft, and the transport of such vehicles as bulldozers and roadgraders, and even armoured vehicles weighing up to 20,000 lb (9072 kg). On one occasion a CH-54A lifted a van containing a total of 90 persons, including 87 combat-equipped troops. Approximately 60 CH-54As were built, powered by two 4,500-shp (3356-kW) Pratt & Witney T73-P-1 engines.

An improved CH54-B was ordered in November 1968, the first two being accepted in 1969. Improvements included more powerful engines, uprated gearbox, structural strengthening, introduction of a high-lift rotor blade, improved flight-control system, and twin wheels added to the main landing gear. In October 1970, such an aircraft lifted a load of 40,780 lb (18497 kg).

Sikorsky built for the US Army a Universal Military Pod, measuring internally 27 ft 5 in × 8 ft 10 in × 6 ft 6 in high (8.36 × 2.69 × 1.98 m), with a maximum weight of 20,000 lb (9072 kg), for the carriage of troops or field conversion as a surgical unit, command post or communications centre.

Type: heavy-lift flying-crane helicopter
Powerplant: (CH-54B) two 4,800-shp (3579-kW) Pratt & Whitney T73-P-700 turboshafts
Performance: (CH-54A) maximum speed 126 mph (203 km/h) at sea level; maximum cruising speed 105 mph (169 km/h); range with maximum fuel (10% reserves) 230 miles (370 km)
Weights: (CH-54A) empty 19,234 lb (8724 kg); maximum take-off 42,000 lb (19051 kg)
Dimensions: main rotor diameter 72 ft 0 in (21.95 m); tail rotor diameter 16 ft 0 in (4.88 m); length (rotors turning) 88 ft 6 in (26.97 m); height 25 ft 5 in (7.75 m); main rotor disc area 4,070 sq ft (378.10 m²)
Armament: none
Operators: US Army

Sikorsky S-64 Skycrane/CH-54A Tarhe

The Sikorsky CH-54 Tarhe, called the S-64 by the manufacturer, is the only heavy-lift crane helicopter in the West — and used only by the US Army, despite its universal applicability. This is an early CH-54A, with single mainwheels and less-powerful engines.

Sikorsky S-65/H-53 Sea Stallion

American interest in heavy-lift helicopters was not confined to the US Army. As early as 1950 a US Marine Corps requirement had first involved Sikorsky in the design and construction of such a helicopter, this having the company designation S-56. With a maximum take-off weight of 31,000 lb (14061 kg), these HR2S-1 helicopters, subsequently designated CH-37C, were easily the largest rotary-wing aircraft in the West when introduced into service in 1956.

In 1960 the US Marine Corps decided that it needed a more advanced assault-transport helicopter, and Sikorsky produced a new design which utilised the dynamic system which had been developed for the S-64A Skycrane (CH-54 Tarhe), as well as many other components. Completely new, of course, was the watertight hull, provided to permit emergency water-landing capability, rather than being intended for amphibious operations. The emphasis was on good load-carrying capabiity, so rear-loading doors were included in the upswept rear fuselage to simplify loading of bulky items, and hydraulically-operated winches were installed at the forward end of the cabin, with a roller-skid track combination in the floor to make it easy for the loading of wheeled vehicles, a 105-mm howitzer and its carriage, or a wide variety of very heavy cargo.

On 27 August 1962 the US Navy announced that it would procure two prototypes and one static-test airframe, and that Sikorsky were required also to construct a mockup of their S-65A design. The first of these prototypes made its maiden flight on 14 October 1964, and following successful evaluation the first production examples, designated CH-53A and named Sea Stallion, were delivered to USMC units in September 1966. By the beginning of 1967 the type was in operational ser-

vice in Vietnam.

These aircraft were able to operate in all weathers, had an external cargo system which made possible in-flight pickup and release without any assistance from the ground, and had hydraulically-folded main-rotor blades and tail pylon for shipboard stowage. The powerplant consisted normally of two 2,850-shp (2125-kW) General Electric T64-GE-6 turboshaft engines.

In September 1966 the USAF ordered eight of these aircraft for use by the Aerospace Rescue and Recovery Service, to be equipped similarly to the HH-3E. In other respects they were similar to the CH-53A, except for a powerplant comprising two 3,080-shp (2297-kW) T64-GE-3 turboshafts. The first of these HH-53B helicopters flew on 15 March 1967. An improved version for the USAF had the designation HH-53C, this having 3,925-shp (2927-kW) T64-GE-7 engines, provision for auxiliary fuel tanks, a flight-refuelling probe, rescue hoist, and a 20,000-lb (9072-kg) external cargo hook. The first of these entered service with the USAF on 30 August 1968. Eight HH-53s are being modified under the USAF'S Pave Low 3 programme to provide night search and rescue capability. Completion of these is scheduled for 1980.

The final twin-engined version for the US Marine Corps is the CH-53D, an improved CH-53A. The type differs in having more powerful engines, a special internal cargo handling system suitable for one-man operation, and the capacity to carry 55 equipped troops. The first of this version entered service in March 1969, and when the last was delivered, on 31 January 1972, combined production of the CH-53 then totalled 265 examples. All but the first 34 were equipped with special gear for minesweeping opera-

tions, but in October 1972 production was initiated of 30 RH-53D special-purpose minesweeping helicopters, designed to operate with all current and foreseeable equipment for the sweeping of accoustic, magnetic and mechanical mines. First delivery of production aircraft, to the US Navy's HM-12 Squadron, was made in September 1973. Powered currently by two T64-GE-413A turboshafts, it is planned to modify these to 4,380-shp (3266-kW) T64-GE-415 standard.

The designation CH-53G applies to 112 aircraft for the German army with 3,925-shp (2927-kW) T64-GE-7 engines. Two were built and delivered by Sikorsky on 31 March 1969. Of the remainder, 20 were assembled by VFW-Fokker in Germany, using American components, and 90 were manufactured by VFW-Fokker with some 50% of the components being of German manufacture.

Two aircraft were supplied by Sikorsky to the Austrian air force for operation as rescue aircraft in the Alpine regions. Delivered in

The USAF Aerospace Rescue and Recovery Service uses the HH-53B and HH-53C, with extensive special mission equipment including a flight refuelling probe. This example was photographed with landing gear extended.

1970, these have the designation S-65-Oe. The three-engined CH-53E is described separately.

Type: heavy assault transport helicopter
Powerplant: (CH-53D) two 3,925-shp (2927-kW) General Electric T64-GE-413 turboshafts
Performance: (CH-53D) maximum speed at sea level 196 mph (315 km/h); cruising speed 173 mph (278 km/h); range (with 4,076-lb (1849-kg) fuel, 2 minutes warm-up, cruising speed, 10% reserves) 257 miles (414 km)
Weights: (CH-53D) empty 23,485 lb (10653 kg); mission take-off 36,400 lb (16511 kg); maximum take-off 42,000 lb (19051 kg)
Dimensions: main rotor diameter 72 ft 3 in (22.02 m); tail rotor diameter 16 ft 0 in (4.88 m); length (rotors turning) 88 ft 3 in (26.90 m); height 24 ft 11 in (7.59 m); main rotor disc area 4,070 sq ft (378.10 m²)
Armament: none
Operators: Austria, Germany, Israel, US Air Force, US Marine Corps, US Navy

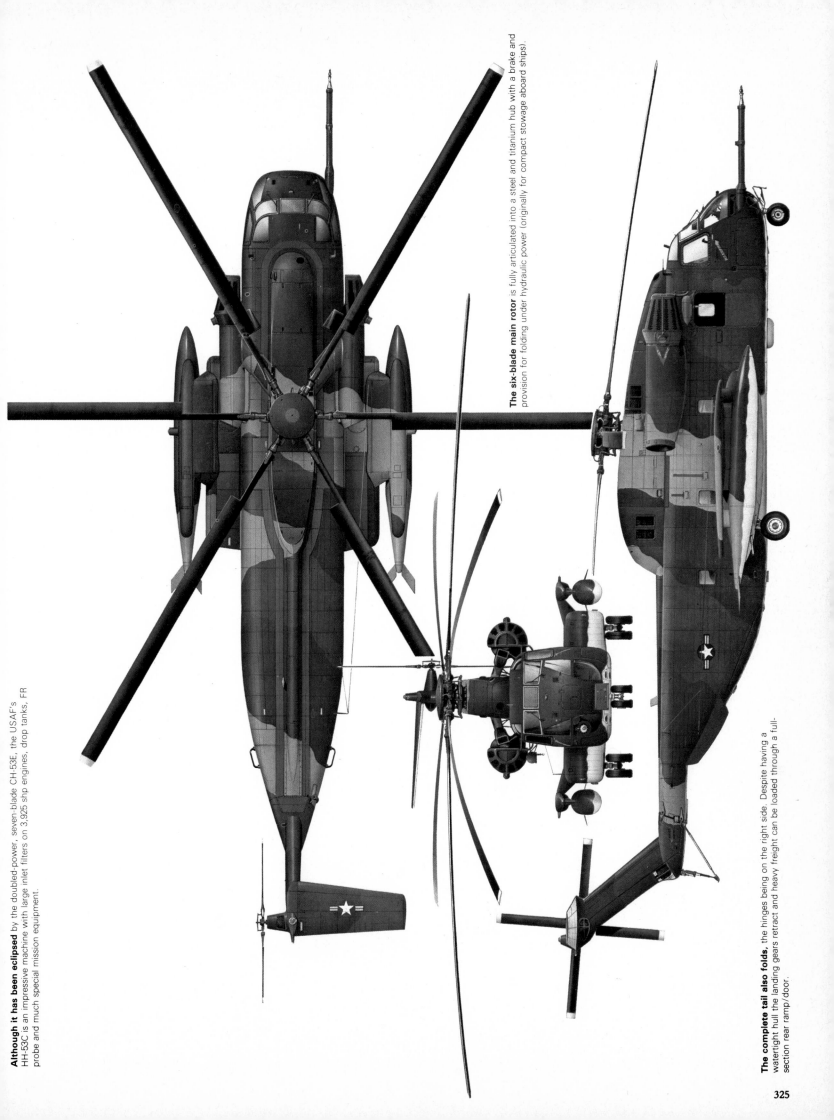

Although it has been eclipsed by the doubled-power, seven-blade CH-53E, the USAF's HH-53C is an impressive machine with large inlet filters on 3,925 shp engines, drop tanks, FR probe and much special mission equipment.

The six-blade main rotor is fully articulated into a steel and titanium hub with a brake and provision for folding under hydraulic power (originally for compact stowage aboard ships).

The complete tail also folds, the hinges being on the right side. Despite having a watertight hull the landing gears retract and heavy freight can be loaded through a full-section rear ramp/door.

Sikorsky S-65/CH-53E Super Stallion

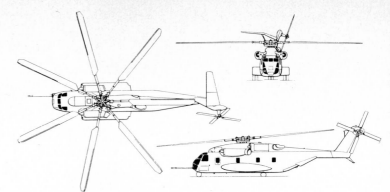

The US Navy and Marine Corps, which had received from Sikorsky the last of the CH-53Ds in early 1972, soon realised the need to procure a multi-purpose helicopter with an even greater lift capability. Consequently, Sikorsky was contracted in May 1973 to design, develop and construct two prototypes of a three-engined version of the S-65A under the designation YCH-53E.

While the airframe is generally similar to that of the CH-53D, a number of changes have been made to cater for the considerable increase in power, as well as to look forward to further development. Thus, a new seven-blade main rotor has been designed for this aircraft, with advanced blades of titanium construction. The anti-torque rail rotor is of increased diameter, and mounted on a pylon canted 20° to port. An uprated transmission has been developed, with a 30-minute rating of 11,570-shp (8628 kW) and an emergency 10-second rating of 13,500 shp (10067 kW).

The US Navy's contract for the prototypes looked forward to a first flight in April 1974, but Sikorsky managed to improve on this and the first YCH-53E flew on 1 March 1974, a month ahead of schedule. Unfortunately this aircraft was lost in a ground accident soon after, and it was not possible to resume the test programme until the second prototype became available in early 1975, making its first flight on 24 January. Used for preliminary test and evaluation, the potential of this helicopter was such that two pre-production aircraft and a static-test airframe were contracted, and the first of the pre-production aircraft flew on 8 December 1975. By May 1978 these two aircraft had completed more than 1,000 flight hours in their test programme, and Sikorsky had received a contract for the manufacture of an initial six production aircraft as CH-53E Super Stallions, their introduction into service with the US Navy and US Marine Corps being due in 1980.

The YCH-53E prototype has demonstrated a lift capability of 70,000 lb (31751 kg), and clearly this new aircraft will be able to fulfil all of its intended missions of vertical on-board delivery, the support of mobile construction battalions, and the removal of damaged aircraft from the decks of aircraft-carriers.

Type: heavy-duty multi-purpose helicopter
Powerplant: three General Electric T64-GE-415 turboshaft engines, each with a maximum 10-minute rating of 4,380 shp (3266 kW), and a maximum continuous rating of 3,670 shp (2737 kW)
Performance: maximum speed at sea level 196 mph (315 km/h); maximum cruising speed at sea level 173 mph (278 km/h); range at optimum cruise condition for maximum range (20 minutes reserves) 306 miles (492 km)
Weights: empty 32,048 lb (14537 kg); maximum take-off 69,750 lb (31638 kg)
Dimensions: main rotor diameter 79 ft 0 in (24.08 m); tail rotor diameter 20 ft 0 in (6.10 m); length (rotors turning) 73 ft 9 in (22.48 m); height 27 ft 9 in (8.46 m); main rotor disc area 4,902 sq ft (455.40 m²)
Armament: none
Operators: (from 1980) US Marine Corps, US Navy

Sikorsky YCH-53E Super Stallion

The Sikorsky YCH-53E, prototype of the new three-engined S-65 family, is in many ways the greatest helicopter in the Western skies, with 13,140 hp (9802 kW) compared with the 5,700 hp (4252 kW) of most versions.

Sikorsky S-70/UH-60 Black Hawk/SH-60B

At the beginning of the 1970s the US Army began the somewhat protracted process of procuring a new helicopter. Identified as the Utility Tactical Transport Aircraft System (UTTAS), this is primarily a combat assault helicopter. In August 1972 it was announced that the US Army had selected the submissions received from Boeing Vertol and Sikorsky, and both were contracted to build three prototypes and a static test vehicle of their design for competitive evaluation.

Boeing Vertol's design, designated YUH-61A, was for a conventional helicopter with four-blade main and anti-torque rotors, tricycle landing gear, and two 1,500-shp (1119-kW) General Electric T700-GE-700 engines. Features included a hingeless main rotor, modularized design, and built-in access platforms. The first flew on 29 November 1974.

Sikorsky's competing YUH-60A was generally similar and powered by the same engines. The most noticeable external differences were the tailwheel landing gear and canted anti-torque rotor. The first flight was made on 17 October 1974, the second and third prototypes flying in January and February 1975. The fly-off evaluation of the competing prototypes occupied seven months of 1976, and on 23 December of that year Sikorsky's design was selected for production. The US Army regards the UH-60A Black Hawk as its primary assault helicopter for the immediate future, and hopes to procure a total of 1,107 by 1985. Production of the first 15 began in late 1977, and initial deliveries were made during 1978.

The main rotor is of advanced design, with aft-swept tips; the rotor is designed to survive hits from 12.7-mm or 23-mm armour-piercing shells; and the main-rotor hub has elastomeric bearings needing no lubrication. The fuel system is regarded as crashworthy, as is the fuselage which is designed to survive hits from armour-piercing rounds of up to 7.62-mm calibre. Accommodation is provided for a crew of three and 11 troops, the pilot and co-pilot having armoured seats. Eight seats can be replaced by four stretchers or internal cargo. An external hook of 8,000-lb (3629-kg) capacity is provided for the airlift of artillery and supplies. Six Black Hawks can be carried by a Lockheed C-5A Galaxy.

The US Navy's continuing search for advanced ASW helicopters resulted in competition for the LAMPS (light airborne multi-purpose system) Mk III configuration, in which Boeing Vertol also contended but again lost to a special version of the S-70 designated SH-60B. These helicopters must not only have an up-to-the-moment ASW capability, but be able to serve also for ASST (anti-ship surveillance and targeting) roles, with capability for search and rescue, medevac sorties, and vertical replenishment to ships at sea. They will serve on board cruisers, destroyers and frigates for sea periods of up to three months. The SH-60B has automatic main rotor and tail pylon folding, shorter wheelbase, and naval avionics, including radar, MAD, sonar

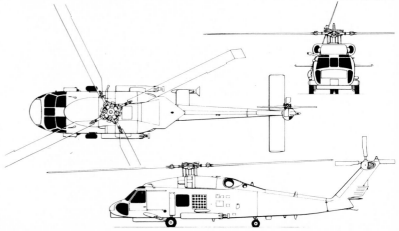

Sikorsky UH-60A Black Hawk

This prototype Black Hawk is distinguished by a long instrument boom carried ahead of the nose. The UH-60A development programme was the largest for any helicopter of the 1970s, the basic engineering task being multiplied by the need to meet severe numerical values for reliability and maintainability in harsh environments.

and ESM. By early 1979 no funding had been allocated for procurement of the SH-60B for the US Navy and, therefore, no estimate can be made for an in-service date.

Type: (UH-60A) combat assault squad transport; (SH-60B) ship-based multi-purpose helicopter
Powerplant: two 1,543-shp (1151-kW) General Electric T700-GE-700 turboshafts
Performance: (UH-60A) maximum speed 184 mph (296 km/h) at sea level; maximum speed at maximum take-off weight 182 mph (293 km/h); maximum cruising speed 169 mph (272 km/h) at 4,000 ft (1220 m); single-engine speed 149 mph (240 km/h); range at maximum take-off weight with 30-minute reserves 373 miles (600 km)
Weights: (UH-60A) empty 10,900 lb (4944 kg); mission take-off 16,450 lb (7462 kg);

Sikorsky UH-60A Black Hawk utility helicopter, destined for large-scale use with the United States Army.

maximum take-off 20,250-lb (9185 kg)
Dimensions: main rotor diameter 53 ft 8 in (16.36 m); tail rotor diameter 11 ft 0 in (3.35 m); length (rotors turning) 64 ft 10 in (19.76 m); height 16 ft 10 in (5.13 m); main-rotor

disc area 2,261 sq ft (210.05 m²)
Armament: (UH-60A) provision for one or two 7.62-mm (0.3-in) M 60 machine-guns firing from opened side doors; (SH-60B) two homing torpedoes

Operators: (UH-60A) US Army; (SH-60B) potentially US Navy

Soko Galeb/Jastreb

Soko was founded in 1951 and its first indigenous production aircraft was the G2-A Galeb (Seagull), a jet trainer of similar appearance and characteristics to the Italian Aermacchi M.B.326, which pre-dated it by about two years.

Galeb design work began in 1957. The first of two prototypes flew in May 1961 and production began in 1963, initially to meet orders from the Yugoslav air force.

Designed to withstand load factors of +8 to −4, the Galeb has a fuel system which allows up to 15 seconds inverted flight for aerobatic training. Lightweight HSA (Folland) fully-automatic ejector seats are fitted, and the jettisonable canopy has separate sideways-hingeing sections for the two crew. There is no pressurization, but air-conditioning is available to special order. The jettisonable wing tip tanks each have a capacity of 375 lb (150 kg); for target towing there is a hook beneath the centre fuselage.

The G2-A is the standard version; the Yugoslav air force has about 60, a few of which are believed to be used in the reconnaissance role. The G2-AE export version was flown in late 1974, and production began in 1975 for the Libyan air force, which has received 20. Prior to this, Zambia bought two Galebs and four Jastrebs in 1971, a rather strange purchase since the Zambian air force also bought about 20 of the rival Aermacchi M.B.326.

The J-1 Jastreb (hawk) is basically a single-seat version with a strengthened airframe and more powerful engine with a built-in starter. The rear canopy is replaced by a metal fairing, and each tip tank houses 485 lb (220 kg) of fuel. The two current production versions are the J-1 attack and RJ-1 tactical reconnaissance models for the Yugoslav air force, which operates about 150 in 12 squadrons, and the equivalent export models, the J-1E and RJ-1E. The former is said to have been ordered, but customers have not been named.

The RJ-1 has a fuselage camera, plus one in the nose of each tip tank.

A Yugoslav air force requirement to provide operational conversion to the Jastreb has been met not by the Galeb but by producing a two-seat trainer version of the Jastreb, the TJ-1. Flying in mid-1974, the variant retains the full operational capability of the ground attack Jastreb and deliveries began in January 1975. At an empty equipped weight of 6,570 lb (2980 kg) the TJ-1 is slightly heavier than its predecessor, and carries only the two tip-tank cameras.

It seems probable that the single- and two-seat versions of the Soko/CIAR Orao will eventually replace the Galebs and Jastrebs.

Type: two-seat trainer/single-seat attack aircraft
Powerplant: (Galeb) one 2,500-lb (1134-kg) Rolls-Royce Viper 22-6 turbojet
(Jastreb) one 3,000-lb (1360-kg) Rolls-Royce Viper 531 turbojet, plus provision for two 1,000-lb (454-kg) ATO rockets
Performance: (Galeb) maximum level speed at sea level 470 mph (756 km/h); maximum speed at 20,350 ft (6200 m) 505 mph (812 km/h); cruising speed at 19,680 ft (6000 m)

453 mph (730 km/h); rate of climb at sea level 4,500 ft (1370 m) per minute; service ceiling 39,375 ft (12000 m); take-off run to 50 ft (15 m) 2,100 ft (640 m); landing run from 50 ft (15 m) 2,330 ft (710 m); range at 29,520 ft (9000 m) with full wing tip tanks 770 miles (1240 km)
(Jastreb) maximum level speed at 19,680 ft (6000 m) 510 mph (820 km/h); cruising speed at 16,400 ft (5000 m) 460 mph (740 km/h); rate of climb at sea level 4,135 ft (1260 m) per minute; service ceiling 39,375 ft (12000 m); take-off run to 50 ft (15 m) 3,150 ft (960 m); landing run from 50 ft (15 m) 3,610 ft (1100 m); range at 29,520 ft (9000 m) with full wing tip tanks 945 miles (1520 km) (performance data at 8,478 lb (3968 kg)
Weights: (Galeb) empty equipped 5,775 lb (2620 kg); maximum take-off aerobatic trainer 7,438 lb (3374 kg), basic trainer 7,690 lb (3488 kg), navigational trainer 8,439 lb (3828 kg), weapons trainer 8,792 lb (3988 kg), strike version 9,480 lb (4300 kg)
(Jastreb) empty equipped 6,217 lb (2820 kg); maximum take-off 11,243 lb (5100 kg)
Dimensions: (Galeb) span 34 ft 4 in (10.47 m); span (over tip tanks) 38 ft 1 in (11.62 m); length 33 ft 11 in (10.34 m); height 10 ft 9 in

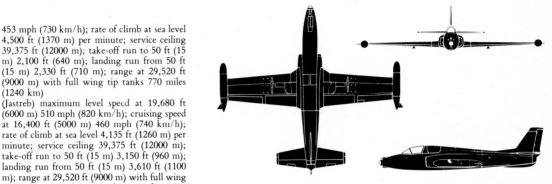
Soko Jastreb

(3.28 m); wing area 209.14 sq ft (19.43 m²)
(Jastreb) span 34 ft 4 in (10.47 m); span (over tip tanks) 38 ft 4 in (11.68 m); length 35 ft 8 in (10.88 m); height 12 ft (3.64 m); wing area 209.14 sq ft (19.43 m²)
Armament: (Galeb) two 0.50-in (12.7-mm) machine-guns in nose, underwing pylons for two 220-lb (100-kg) bombs and four 57-mm rockets or two 127-mm rockets or bomb clusters in containers up to 660 lb (300 kg) total

(Jastreb) three 0.50-in (12.7-mm) machine-guns in nose; eight under wing weapon attachments can carry a wide range of bombs, rockets or photo flares
Operators: Libya, Yugoslavia, Zambia

Yugoslav Air Force Soko Galeb two-seat trainer of the Flying Training Headquarters at Mostar.

Second prototype Soko Jastreb ground-attack aircraft in Yugoslav Air Force markings.

The locally built Soko Jastreb is the chief Yugoslav ground-attack aircraft, though it is planned to be replaced eventually by the Yugoslav/Romanian Orao; powered by a Rolls-Royce Viper, it is based on the Jastreb trainer.

Soko Kraguj

Soko's Galeb (seagull) jet-powered trainer and Jastreb (hawk) ground-attack aircraft have been familiar products of the Yugoslav aviation industry for nearly 20 years, but rather more surprise was evinced at the emergence of the little Kraguj in the middle 1960s. It was cast in the mould of the Fletcher Defender, a US lightplane which, some 15 years earlier, had pioneered the concept of the armed, piston-engined lightplane to perform a useful role in COIN (counter-insurgency) situations and local brushfire wars. The Defender was rejected by the US armed forces, which did not have such a requirement at that time, although the COIN concept was revived later in Vietnam.

The Kraguj, a single-seater, was designed at the Aeronautical Research Establishment in Belgrade, and manufacture was undertaken by the state-owned Soko factory at Mostar. A prototype flew for the first time in 1966, and about 30 were built subsequently for ground-attack units of the Yugoslav air force. The emphasis throughout was on simplicity of both construction and operation, the all-metal low-wing monoplane layout being intended primarily as a launching platform for a range of small but effective weapons, capable of being flown by pilots with only a modest number of hours in their logbooks. Robust construction enables the Kraguj to take off and land on grass fields or unprepared airstrips, the required ground run being 395 ft (120 m) or less. The tailwheel-type landing gear is non-retractable. The Kraguj entered production and service in 1968; with about 100 Jastrebs currently forming the major equipment of the Yugoslav air force ground-attack squadrons, there is some doubt whether the Kraguj is still operated in its original role, but it may continue in service as an elementary weapons trainer.

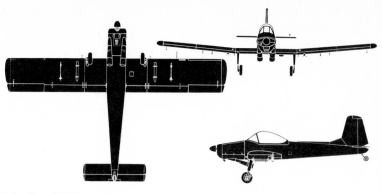

Soko Kraguj (P-2)

Type: single-seat light close-support aircraft
Powerplant: one 340-hp (254-kW) Lycoming GSO-480-B1A6 flat-six piston engine
Performance: maximum speed at sea level 171 mph (275 km/h); maximum speed at 4,925 ft (1500 m) 183 mph (295 km/h); range with maximum fuel 495 miles (800 km); rate of climb at sea level at gross weight of 2,857 lb (1296 kg) 1,575 ft (480 m) per minute
Weights: empty equipped 2,491 lb (1130 kg); maximum take-off 3,580 lb (1624 kg)
Dimensions: span 34 ft 11 in (10.64 m); length 26 ft 0¼ in (7.93 m); height 9 ft 10 in (3.00 m); wing area 183.0 sq ft (17.00 m²)
Armament: one 7.7-mm (0.303-in) machine-gun in each wing, with 650 rounds per gun; two inboard underwing hardpoints, each able to carry a 220-lb (100-kg) bomb, 33-gallon (150-litre) napalm tank or 12-round rocket pack; and four outboard underwing points, each able to carry one 57-mm (2.24-in) or 127-mm (5-in) rocket
Operators: Yugoslavia

Soko/CIAR-93 Orao ("Jurom")

Subject of a joint development programme between Soko in Yugoslavia and CIAR (Centrala Industriala Aeronautica Romana) in Romania, the Orao (eagle) twin-jet fighter and ground attack aircraft is in production in both countries. The designers worked together at the Vazduhoplovno Technical Institute, Zarkovo, near Belgrade, where tunnel testing took place, and simultaneous construction of prototypes began in both countries with Soko having responsibility for assembly and test. The prototype is reported to have flown in August 1974, and its first public appearance was at a display held the following April near Belgrade.

It is thought that three prototypes and nine pre-production examples had flown by 1979. The second prototype is a two-seater, and the third is believed to be a static-test specimen. A production batch of about 40 is reported to be under construction.

UK suppliers include Graviner whose Firewire and BCF fire detection and extinguishing systems are installed, Fairey Hydraulics which supplies filters and sampling valves, Dowty Boulton Paul for the powered flying controls, Rolls-Royce for the engines. French representation appears with the Messier-Hispano landing gear, licence-built by Prva Petoljetka.

Romania, nominally a member of the Warsaw Pact, is expected to require 80 Oraos, and Yugoslavia 200. There have been persistent reports that production aircraft will be re-engined with a single General Electric J79, though these would not be new. To avoid the possibility of a US export embargo, though, a more likely choice would be the Rolls-Royce Spey, with or without afterburner, as selected by Italy for her AM-X.

Type: fighter and strike/trainer
Powerplant: two 4,000-lb (1814-kg) Rolls-Royce Viper 632-41 turbojets (afterburning version planned)
Performance: maximum low level speed 762 mph (1226 km/h); high level speed 1,089 mph (1752 km/h); maximum rate of climb at sea level 39,370 ft (12000 m) per minute; time to 36,000 ft (11000 m) 1 minute 36 seconds; service ceiling 52,500 ft (16000 m); take-off run at maximum weight 3,280 ft (1000 m); landing run same (figures estimated, based on production aircraft using afterburners)
Weights: (estimated) empty equipped 10,360 lb (4700 kg); maximum take-off with external stores 22,700 lb (10300 kg)
Dimensions: span 24 ft 10 in (7.56 m); length (without probe) 40 ft 11 in (12.45 m); height 12 ft 5 in (3.78 m); wing area 193.75 sq ft (18.00 m²)
Armament: two 30-mm fuselage-mounted cannon; four underwing and one under-fuselage hardpoint for maximum of 6,615 lb (3000 kg) external stores
Operators: Romania, Yugoslavia

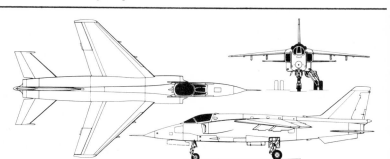

Soko/CIAR-93 Orao ("Jurom")

This Orao is seen in Yugoslav markings and may be the first prototype flown in 1974. It is expected that production aircraft will reach service units in late 1980.

Sud SO 4050 Vautour

The multi-role Sud Vautour (vulture) was France's first jet bomber and also the country's first twin-jet to exceed Mach 1, a feat which it achieved in a shallow dive early in the test programme. Three prototypes were ordered by the French government and the first flew on 16 October 1952. They were followed by six pre-production aircraft: one bomber, two single-seat tactical support aircraft and three all-weather fighters. These six aircraft were fitted with a variety of engines before the final choice of powerplant was made. Refuelling trials were undertaken in January 1958 using an English Electric Canberra as tanker.

Quantity production of all three versions was commenced for the French air force, and the first of 30 Vautour IIA single-seat tactical fighters flew on 30 April 1956; next was the first of 70 IIN two-seat all-weather fighters on 10 October 1956; and the first of 40 Vautour IIB two-seat bombers was flown on 31 July 1957.

A number of Vautour IIAs and IINs were supplied to the Israeli air force, crews being trained at Tours, while in France the IIN entered service initially with the 30e Escadre de Chasse, and the IIB began to replace the Douglas B-26 from 1958.

A handful of Vautours continued in Israeli service as ECM platforms up to 1978, but most of the Armée de l'Air aircraft have been replaced by SEPECAT Jaguars. Among the last units to operate the type were 85e Esc. de Marche with a few IIBs and IINs for air sampling duties from Hao during the French nuclear-tests and 92e Esc. de Bombardement at Bordeaux-Merignac, which used both versions.

Type: (IIB bomber) twin-jet fighter and bomber
Powerplant: two 7,716-lb (3500-kg) thrust SNECMA Atar 101E-3 turbojets
Performance: maximum speed 720 mph (1158 km/h) at sea level; rate of climb 11,800 ft (3600 m) per minute at sea level; service ceiling 50,000 ft (15240 m); take-off run 2,600 ft (792 m); tactical radius (high) 750 miles (1207 km)
Weights: empty 22,046 lb (10000 kg); loaded 44,092 lb (20000 kg)
Dimensions: span 49 ft 6 in (15.08 m); length 51 ft 1 in (15.5 m); height 14 ft 2 in (4.32 m); wing area 484.4 sq ft (45 m²)
Armament: (IIB) four bombs up to 6,000 lb (2721 kg) carried internally, plus underwing pylons for rockets or bombs — see IIN; (IIA) four 30-mm cannon in bomb bay, plus four rocket packs each with 19 rockets, or 24 120-mm rockets, or two 1,000-lb (454-kg) bombs carried on underwing pylons; (IIN) similar to IIA except that four Matra R.511 air-to-air missiles can be carried on underwing pylons
Operators: France, Israel

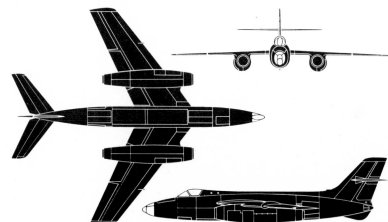

Sud SO 4050 Vautour IIB

Sukhoi Su-7 Fitter

The standard strike fighter of Soviet Air Force Frontal Aviation from the early 1960s to the introduction of the Mikoyan-Gurevich 'Flogger-D' MiG-27 and Sukhoi Su-17 'Fitter-C' and '-D' in the early 1970s, the Sukhoi Su-7 'Fitter-A' has earned a reputation as a reliable and dependable warplane in action in the Middle East and the Indian subcontinent. Its radius of action and warload, however, are not what might be expected of so large an aircraft, and in general it carries fuel or weapons, but not both. The type also relies to a great extent on visual weapon-aiming, which limits its effectiveness.

The Sukhoi bureau had been disbanded for some years before it was re-formed to produce a new supersonic fighter designed around an afterburning version of the Lyulka AL-7 turbojet. The Lyulka bureau had been developing high-powered turbojets based on wartime German research since 1945; the AL-7 was the first of these to enter production.

The Sukhoi and Mikoyan bureaux were each apparently directed by the TsAGI (the Central Hydrodynamic Institute) to develop two alternative fighter designs: one with a wing not dissimilar to that of the MiG-19 'Farmer', then showing great promise, and the other with the newly developed tailed-delta configuration. All four prototype designs shared the mid-wing and circular-section fuselage of earlier Soviet jet fighters, leading to problems for Western intelligence analysts as they tried to determine which of the new types had gone into service.

Both Sukhoi types were ordered in quantity. The Su-7, the swept-wing version, was selected as the strike fighter for Frontal Aviation, and built in large numbers. Points in its favour for this role included reasonable, if not outstanding, field performance; unlike that of the MiG-19, the swept wing of the Su-7 is furnished with area-increasing trailing-edge flaps. Like the definitive MiG-19, the Su-7 has an all-moving tailplane.

The Su-7 was clearly not designed from the same sort of deep interdiction role that was foreseen for contemporary Western strike aircraft, being more of the traditional fighter-bomber. The type has never been seen even with simple air-to-air missiles, indicating that its role is exclusively air-to-ground, using rockets, bombs and its heavy cannon against ground targets. Its endurance is limited, because the general arrangement of a circular-section fuselage and long inlet ducts drastically limits available fuel capacity. In service, Su-7s are seldom seen without their twin ventral fuel tanks, precluding the carriage of weapons on the fuselage pylons.

Operational equipment includes a ranging radar in the intake centre-body. The nose pitot boom carried yaw and pitch sensors, presumably feeding a simple ballistic computer for weapon-aiming.

Early production Su-7Bs, delivered from 1959, probably had early 20,000-lb (9000-kg) versions of the AL-7. The Su-7BM as the more powerful engine described above, while the later BMK versions has low-pressure tyres and twin brake parachutes. Some Su-7BMKs are equipped for take-off rocket boost. Many have been seen operating from rough fields during manoeuvres. Also in service is the Su-7U conversion trainer.

The Su-7BMK is the standard export model, and often mounts two extra pylons aft of the mainwheel wells. Some aircraft of the type have been seen with up to six underwing stations. Egyptian pilots have described their Su-7s as the best aircraft available to them for high-speed combat at low level, where the type is tractable despite the high air loads in such conditions; losses against strong AAA and missile fire in the October 1973 war were remarkably low. The main problems were the lack of efficient navigation and weapon-aiming systems (possibly being rectified by British avionics, though this has yet to be confirmed) and the lack of range and endurance. Just over 1,000 Su-7s were built before production switched to the Su-17 series in 1971-72.

Type: fighter-bomber
Powerplant: one 15,400-lb (7000-kg) dry or 22,000-lb (10000-kg) afterburning Lyulka AL-7F-1 turbojet

Performance: maximum speed at altitude 1,050 mph (1700 km/h), or Mach 1.6; maximum speed (clean) at sea level Mach 1.1; service ceiling 49,700 ft (15150 m); range with two drop tanks 900 miles (1450 km)
Weights: empty 19,000 lb (8620 kg); maximum loaded 30,000 lb (13600 kg)
Dimensions: length (including probe) 57 ft (17.37 m); span 29 ft 3½ in (8.93 m); height 15 ft 5 in (4.7 m)
Armament: two 30 mm NR-30 cannon in wing roots, plus four wing and two ventral stores pylons, all capable of carrying weapons (rocket pods and bombs form main armament)
Operators: Afghanistan, Algeria, Czechoslovakia, Egypt, Hungary, India, Iraq, North Korea, Poland, Romania, Syria, USSR, Vietnam

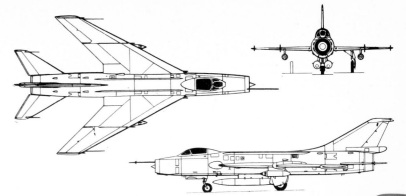

Sukhoi Su-7BM Fitter

Sukhoi Su-7BMK of the Egyptian Air Force. About 100 equip three regiments in ground attack and strike duties.

Striking desert camouflage adorns a Force Aérienne Algerienne Su-7BMK supplied by the Soviet Union.

Indian Air Force Su-7B strike aircraft in crudely-applied camouflage for operations over Pakistan in the December 1971 war.

The Sukhoi Su-7B is still widely used by many Arab air forces. Probably operating from an Egyptian base, this Su-7 is not carrying the twin tanks needed for most missions.

Sukhoi Su-9/11 Fishpot

Never as widely used or as well known as the contemporary Mikoyan-Gurevich MiG-21 'Fishbed' or Su-7 'Fitter-A', the Sukhoi bureau's delta-wing prototype of 1955-56 nevertheless led to the Su-9 'Fishpot-B' the most numerous supersonic interceptor in the PVO (Air Defence Forces) fleet for many years. The type was supplanted by the Su-15 'Flagon' on the production lines in the late 1960s, but some 600 remain in service.

The Su-9 was designed as an all-weather fighter based on the same tailed-delta configuration as the MiG-21. Entering service in 1958-59, it typified Soviet practice in that it combined a new engine and airframe with an existing weapon, the K-5M 'Alkali' air-to-air missile already in service on the MiG-19P 'Farmer'. The small radar fitted quite simply into the nose of the Su-9, which was closely similar to that of the Su-7. However, the all-weather capability of the Su-9 is fairly limited, as this radar lacks search range. In practice, the type presumably operates in close co-operation with ground control.

An Su-9 development aircraft was probably the type which, under the designation T-405, established a 100-km (62-mile) closed-circuit speed record of 1,299 mph (2091 km/h) in May 1960. This was probably close to the ultimate 'clean' maximum speed of the early type, which like early production Su-7s was powered by a 20,000-lb (9000-kg) engine.

The 1961 Tushino air display, however, saw the appearance of a new derivative of the basic type, featuring a longer and less tapered nose.

The inlet diameter was considerably larger, and there was a proportionate increase in the size of the centre-body radome to accommodate a new and more powerful radar know to NATO as 'Skip Spin'. The new type replaced the Su-9 on the production lines, and was designated Su-11, with the codename 'Fishpot-C'; it appears to be Sukhoi practice to apply new designations to reflect relatively minor changes, the Su-11 being no more different from its predecessor than some MiG-21 versions differ from others.

It is possible that the aircraft designated T-431, which established a series of records in 1959-62, was an Su-11 development aircraft. The T-431's performance suggests that Western estimates of the Su-11s performance may be on the conservative side; its records include a sustained altitude of 69,455 ft (21170 m) and a speed of 1,452 mph (2337 km/h) round a 500-km (311-mile) closed circuit. The improved performance of the Su-11 can probably be attributed to greater power and more efficient inlet design.

A measure of the comparative worth of the 'Alkali' and later 'Anab' missiles is the fact that the Soviet air force was prepared to accept two of the more potent later weapons on the Su-11 in place of four 'Alkalis' on the Su-9. It is probable that, like many first-generation missile systems, the performance of the K-5M Izumrud system was barely good enough for operational clearance. The 'Anab' has clearly been more successful, and has remained in service and under development for many years.

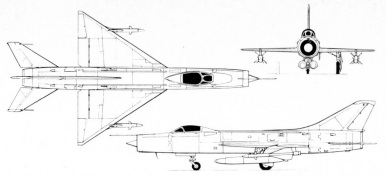

Sukhoi Su-9 Fishpot B

Like most Soviet interceptors, the Su-9/11 series has never been exported, even to the Warsaw Pact. The Su-11 is closely comparable to the British Aerospace Lightning, lacking the British fighter's combat performance but possessing radar-guided missiles. It presented a credible defence against the high-flying bomber armed with free-fall weapons, but is increasingly an anachronism in the age of low-level aircraft armed with stand-off weapons, as it lacks the range for long-range patrols. Its importance in combat units, together with that of the Su-9U trainer variant, is likely to decline rapidly in the late 1970s and early 1980s.

Type: all-weather interceptor
Powerplant: one 22,000-lb (10000-kg) after-burning Lyulka AL-7F turbojet
Performance: maximum (clean) 1,400 mph (2250 km/h), or Mach 2.1; maximum speed with two AAMs and external fuel tanks 1,000 mph (1600 km/h) or Mach 1.5; service ceiling 65,000 ft (20000 m); range about 700 miles (1125 km)
Weights: empty 20,000 lb (9000 kg); maximum loaded 30,000 lb (13500 kg)
Dimensions: span 27 ft 8 in (8.43 m); length (including instrument boom) 60 ft (18.3 m); height 15 ft (4.9 m)
Armament: (Su-9) four K-5M (AA-1 'Alkali') beam-riding air-to-air missiles on wing pylons; (Su-11) two AA-3 'Anab' semi-active bombing (almost certainly) AAMs
Operators: USSR

Sukhoi Su-15 Flagon

The Sukhoi Su-15 'Flagon' interceptor is a demonstration of the Soviet Union's practice of constantly improving a basic design over a period of many years to produce a highly effective definitive production aircraft. It is now the main interceptor in service with the PVO air-defence force, some 850 being reported to be operational. However, PVO re-equipment needs are now being met partly by the Mikoyan-Gurevich MiG-23S, and with the next generation of interceptor likely to enter service in the early 1980s the importance of the Su-15 could soon decline.

The Su-15 traces its origin back to a requirement issued in the early 1960s for a supersonic interceptor with better radar and speed than the Su-11 then under development.

The Mikoyan bureau produced its E-152, which was demonstrated at Tushino is 1961 but not put into service. The Su-15 appears to have evolved rather later, and as flown in 1964-65 appears to have combined the Tumansky R-11 engines, 'Skip Spin' radar and AA-3 'Anab' missiles of the Yakovlev Yak-28P with the delta wing and tail of the Su-9/-11 (almost completely unchanged) and a new fuselage. The two engines were fed by variable-geometry side inlets with auxiliary inlet doors. The Su-15 thus represented a very low-risk development, making use of a large proportion of components from existing aircraft, though it evolved with an uncharacteristically low power-loading and high wing-loading.

A pre-series batch of Su-15s made their appearance at the 1967 Domodedovo air display, but this basic type does not appear to have been built in quantity, probably because it did not represent enough of an advance over the Su-11 to warrant replacement of the single-engined type. Development of the Su-15 was already under way, as indicated by the presence at Domodedovo of an experimental version known to NATO as the 'Flagon-B' (the designation 'Flagon-A' being allotted to the basic aircraft). The 'Flagon-B' was a reduced-take-off-and-landing (RTOL) aircraft similar to the Mikoyan 'Faithless', with three Kolesov lift jets installed in the centre fuselage. The sweep of the outer wing panels was reduced, possibly in order to allow the ailerons to be extended; one of the problems of such RTOL prototypes was the difficulty of control in the partially jetborne flight. Although the Soviet Union abandoned research into such aircraft, the wing planform of the 'Flagon-B' foreshadowed the compound sweep of the later Su-15 variants.

The first major production version of the Su-15 is reported to have been the 'Flagon-D', which entered service in the late 1960s or early 1970s. Retaining the radar and missiles of the 'Flagon-A', the 'Flagon-D' probably introduced more powerful engines and compound sweep on the outer wings, separated by a short unswept section from the inner wing. This curious 'soft dog-tooth' is reminiscent of that fitted to the wing of the Ilyushin Il-62 airliner, the only other type to display such a feature. It is likely that the modification to the Su-15 wing is intended to improve low-speed handling and to reduce landing speeds; these were very high on the earlier sub-types, which are considerably heavier than the Su-11 despite having a similar wing area.

The 'Flagon-E', with more powerful R-13 engines, is said to be the most important production version so far. According to the US Department of Defense, it has improved electronics, but these do not appear to have advanced so far as to make the aircraft useful against low-flying targets; this capability was not credited to any PVO aircraft until the introduction of the MiG-23S. Neither are there any firm reports of Su-15s carrying the AA-7 'Apex' missile which arms the MiG-23S, although any new radar fitted to the later 'Flagons' could be the equal of the MiG-23S equipment.

The latest production version of the Su-15 is identified as the 'Flagon-F' by NATO, and is distinguished by a new radome which may be able to accommodate a larger aerial than the unusual conical radome of versions, although it is possible that the modification has been made for aerodynamic reasons.

Persistent reports that the Su-15 was to be equipped with cannon appear to have been in error. The type seems to be confined to the high-altitude interception role, which it shares with the MiG-25. Like other single-seat Soviet interceptors, it operates under close ground control. There appears, for instance, to be no HUD display, suggesting that the pilot need never see the target except on head-down radar and flight-director displays. In its primary role, the Su-15's attributes include speed and respectable fuel capacity; just how much space there is in the airframe can be judged by the fact that the fuselage of the 'Flagon-B' was little if any wider than standard, despite the battery of lift engines. The engines are tried and proven as is the AAM system. Despite this, however, the Su-15 is likely to see many more years' service with the PVO.

Type: interceptor
Powerplant: two 16,000-lb (7500-kg) Tumansky R-13 afterburning turbojets
Performance: maximum speed Mach 2+ at medium altitude, equivalent to 1,320 mph (2120 km/h) at 36,000 ft (11000 m); maximum speed at sea level 680 mph (1100 km/h) or Mach 0.9; service ceiling 55,000 to 60,000 ft (17000 to 18000 m); combat radius 400 miles (650 km)
Weights: empty 27,500 lb (12500 kg); normal loaded 40,000 lb (18000 kg); maximum loaded 45,000 lb (20000 kg)
Dimensions: span 34 ft 6 in (10.5 m); length 70 ft 6 in (21.5 m); height 16 ft 6 in (5 m); wing area 385 sq ft (35.7 m²)
Armament: two air-to-air missiles, normally AA-3-2 'Advanced Anab'; guns have been reported, but are unconfirmed
Operator: USSR

Characterized by extremely high wing-loading and an abundance of power, the Su-15 is in no sense a dogfighter but an all-weather interceptor. This is an interim variant with new wing but original radar known to NATO as Flagon-D.

The broad box-like fuselage is dominated by the odd outward-inclined engine inlets. Ram inlets at the tail provide cooling and secondary-nozzle air. The belly has twin pylons for drop tanks.

This Sukhoi Su-15 "Flagon-F" is unpainted and serving with the air defence IA-PVO. The radar is later than the "Skip Spin" of earlier versions, and the large antenna occupies a curved radome of lower drag.

Normal armament is two AA-3 "Anab" air-to-air missiles, one IR and the other radar homing. Under the nose are "Odd Rods" IFF and curved ATC/SIF radio antennas; the bulge is caused by the retracted nosewheel.

The top and bottom of the right side, showing the subtly curving inlets leading to Tumansky afterburning turbojets (said to be designated R-25). Anti-flutter masses project ahead of the tailplanes.

Sukhoi Su-17 Fitter D/Su-20/Su-22 Fitter C

The Sukhoi Su-17/-20/-22 'Fitter' family of close-support fighters stems from what was apparently a research aircraft, and the three types are the only examples of production variable-sweep aircraft derived from a fixed-geometry design. They reflect the Soviet industry's traditional reluctance to terminate production of an established design, and its talent for filling an operational requirement in a manner which may appear crude but is nonetheless effective. Pending the emergence of a specialized close-support type, the Su-17 and its derivatives continue to fill an important role in the Soviet armoury.

It appears that the development of the Su-17 was a matter of chance. Soviet designers became absorbed in the study of variable sweep in the early 1960s, and discovered the same fundamental problems as had plagued Western designers. Among them was the tendency for the aerodynamic centre to move aft with increasing sweep, causing trim difficulties. The answer, it was discovered, was to set the pivots outboard, but only in the Soviet Union, however, was this trend continued to produce a 'semi-variable-geometry' layout, in which only the outer panels move. This was adopted by the Tupolev bureau for a supersonic bomber in 1965-66, and a Sukhoi Su-7 was apparently modified as a test-bed. This modified aircraft made its public debut at the Domodedovo air display in 1967, and was condenamed 'Fitter-B' by NATO. However, the improvement over the Su-7 was so great that it was decided to place this testbed in produc-

tion. The first were observed in service in 1970-71.

The basic Su-17 is thought to be powered by the higher-powered AL-21F, while the Su-22 and possibly the Su-20 may have the older AL-7. The Su-17 differs from the Su-7 and the 'Fitter-B' in having a more advanced weapon-aiming system using a complex array of aerodynamic sensors on the nose boom. Control runs are relocated in a dorsal spine, possibly to improve maintainability.

Compared with the Su-7, the Su-17 offers a slight increase in maximum speed in clean condition, but the main advantage comes in weight-lifting and runway capability. The outer wing sections are fitted with slats and trailing-edge flaps, allowing the Su-17 to take off at least 7,500 lb (3500 kg) heavier than the Su-7 from a shorter runway. Two of the pylons, attached to the massive wing fences, are nearly always occupied by large tanks, but even so the Su-17 can still lift more weapons than an Su-7.

The Su-17 is not in the class of the Mikoyan-Gurevich MiG-27, despite its similar thrust, because of its much smaller internal fuel capacity (demanding the carriage of drag-causing external tanks), its less optimized unswept configuration, and its less efficient engine. However, it remains an effective close-support aircraft. At low level with tanks it is probably subsonic, and would use the afterburner only for take-off.

Poland was the first country to take delivery of the Su-20, the initial export model. Some sources suggest that the Su-20 has the AL-7 engine, and it has only two ventral pylons. One possible explanation is that the Poles, lacking MiG-27s, operate their Su-20s as long-range strike aircraft with four tanks, while Russian aircraft are used in the close-support role exclusively, for which wing tanks are adequate.

The second export version is the Su-22, the first Soviet combat aircraft in South America when delivered to Peru in 1977. The Su-22 carries AA-2 'Atoll' missiles, but otherwise is equipped to a very basic standard, lacking radar-warning systems and other items. Peru has had great difficulty in turning the type into an efficient weapon platform.

The Soviet forces, by contrast, are now taking delivery of an even more advanced version, the 'Fitter-D'. First reported in 1977, this appears to have a new weapon-aiming system with an electro-optical device or laser in the centrebody and radar beneath the nose, probably matched with 'smart' weapons similar to those arming the MiG-27. The Su-17 derivatives seem to have proved an unexpected windfall for Soviet close-support units, and a highly successful interim type.

Type: close-support attack
Powerplant: one 24,250-lb (11000-kg) Lyulka AL-21F afterburning turbojet

Performance: maximum speed at 36,000 ft (11000 m) 1,200 mph (1925 km/h) or Mach 1.8: maximum speed at sea level (clean) 830 mph (1340 km/h) or Mach 1.1; maximum speed at sea level with external fuel (almost invariably carried) 650 mph (1050 km/h) or Mach 0.88; service ceiling 55,000 ft (17000 m); tactical radius 300 miles (480 km)
Weights: empty 22,000 lb (10000 kg); maximum external load about 7,500 lb (3500 kg); maximum take-off about 37,500 lb (17000 kg)
Dimensions: span (swept) 34 ft 6 in (10.5 m); span (spread) 45 ft (14 m); length (including probe) 58 ft (17.6 m); height 15 ft (4.6 m)
Armament: two wing-root 30-mm NR-30 cannon, plus a total of six (some Su-17s have eight) hardpoints for rockets, air-to-surface missiles or fuel tanks, although 250-Imperial gallon (1130-litre) auxiliary tanks are nearly always carried on outer pylons; some aircraft are fitted to carry AA-2 'Atoll' air-to-air missiles
Operators: Egypt, Peru, Poland, USSR

Polish Air Force Sukhoi Su-17/20; a regiment of three squadrons is operational with these aircraft.

The swing-wing Su-17 is a vast improvement over the fixed-sweep Su-7 series, but still a basically old and limited design. This Frontal Aviation example is a common 'Fitter-C', but there are several other versions, some better and some (export) worse.

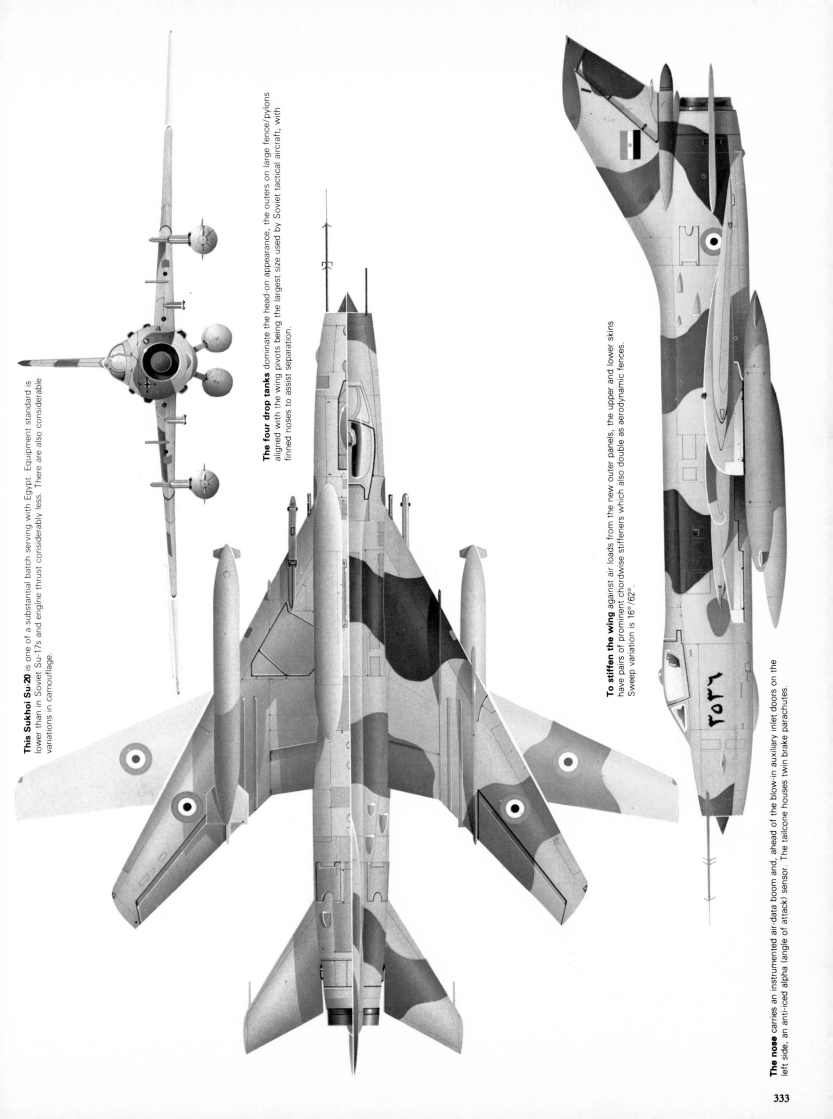

This Sukhoi Su-20 is one of a substantial batch serving with Egypt. Equipment standard is lower than in Soviet Su-17s and engine thrust considerably less. There are also considerable variations in camouflage.

The four drop tanks dominate the head-on appearance, the outers on large fence/pylons aligned with the wing pivots being the largest size used by Soviet tactical aircraft, with finned noses to assist separation.

To stiffen the wing against air loads from the new outer panels, the upper and lower skins have pairs of prominent chordwise stiffeners which also double as aerodynamic fences. Sweep variation is 16°/62°.

The nose carries an instrumented air-data boom and, ahead of the blow-in auxiliary inlet doors on the left side, an anti-iced alpha (angle of attack) sensor. The tailcone houses twin brake parachutes.

Sukhoi Su-19 Fencer

The Sukhoi Su-19 'Fencer' interdiction strike aircraft brings a wholly new capability to Soviet Frontal Aviation: the ability to make night or bad-weather precision strikes throughout the European Central Region. It is the first Soviet aircraft designed specifically for non-strategic air-to-ground strike to be put into production since World War II, and as such represents a very important step forward in the rise in strength and independence of Frontal Aviation.

The Su-19 was first observed in 1971–72. Its development appears to have taken a long time, the first squadrons of the type not working up until mid-1977, and in early 1979 it had still not been deployed in East Germany. Suggestions that the type is so important that its security cannot be compromised by forward basing must be treated as speculation; especially with an aircraft which brings a new concept in crew operation, the advantages of training over the ground which may eventually be fought over must outweigh the risks of a good-quality photograph falling into Western hands. So far, very few illustrations of the 'Fencer' have been available to the West, and the data below are based on what evidence is available.

The Su-19 has been accurately described as a 'mini-F-111', and indeed resembles a slightly smaller version of the US type, even down to the side-by-side seating. It is the first Soviet tactical aircraft to carry a weapons operator, and is probably the first to carry a multi-mode radar for terrain-avoidance and ground attack. The proportions of the airframe and air intakes (the latter similar to those of the Su-15) suggest that the powerplants are afterburning turbofans.

If the Su-19 is to take advantage of its two-crew layout, the avionic systems must be well in advance of anything seen on earlier Soviet tactical aircraft. The radar, for instance, is clearly large and powerful, and would be the first confirmed multi-mode equipment on a Soviet design. Some early aircraft are believed, though, to have been fitted with an interim avionic suite similar to that of the MiG-27. Doppler radar is almost certainly fitted, together with the avionic installations associated with the latest Soviet guided and unguided air-to-surface weapons and an extensive range of active and passive electronic countermeasures.

Armament of the Su-19 is generally assumed to include an internal gun, the most likely weapon being the six-barrel 23-mm weapon fitted to the MiG-27. Apart from gliding 'smart bombs' the Su-19 is also expected to carry the AS-X-9 anti-radiation missile, with a range of about 60 miles (100 km), and the electro-optically guided Advanced TASM and AS-X-10. For some reason NATO estimates of total weapon load are about half of what one would expect from such a variable-geometry aircraft.

The introduction of the Su-19 is likely to lead to some changes in the the Frontal Aviation command structure. The main attribute of the variable-sweep, twin-turbofan configuration is outstanding performance in hi-lo-hi profiles; this will be less significant if the aircraft are to be based in Eastern Germany, because in that event most missions would have to be flown lo-lo-lo to avoid NATO air defences. It would be logical to deploy Su-19s well to the rear of the central region, out of range of most enemy counter-air activities, just as the USAFE's General Dynamics F-111s are based in England. Su-19s based in the Western Soviet Union would normally be attached to the Air Army in the appropriate Military District, which falls under the appropriate regional command. If the aircraft are to operate at the direction of the commander in the battle front, they will have to be attached for operational purposes to the 16th Air Army in East Germany. Thus Su-19 units are probably free from regional command, marking the emergence of the FA as an independent force in its own right rather than a unit in a geographically defined command.

Su-19 units are likely to operate in close conjunction with FA MiG-25R reconnaissance platforms in providing tactical surveillance and strike over much of the NATO central Region. Assuming that the whole of NATO-held Europe is a low-level zone, Su-19s based in the shelter of the Soviet Union can cover the whole of western Germany on non-stop missions; if they can land and refuel in East Germany on the return trip, the radius of action is extended to cover most of England. This capability, like the all-weather strike potential of the fully developed aircraft, is new to Frontal Aviation and a major problem for NATO. NATO's fears that the 'Fencer' might use air refuelling to extend its radius of operations, however, were thought not to have been realised by early 1979.

Future developments of the 'Fencer' with greater weapon loads and combat radii of 1,000 miles (1600 km) are likely, but the type's camera-shyness to date presents something of a puzzle. In early 1979 there was some speculation that the type may have en-

Head-on, the Su-19 closely resembles a MiG-27, and uses similar aerodynamics, but it is larger and has a wider body, broad cockpit with round-topped canopy and a nose radome. Twin ventral fins slope out.

The Su-19 is believed to carry the same six-barrel gun as the MiG-27, as well as at least twice the load of external stores on six fixed and two pivoting pylons. The twin engines may have thrust reversers.

countered difficulties, very little having been heard of progress since a report of three regiments working up in mid-1977.

Type: two-seat all-weather interdiction/strike aircraft

Powerplant: two unidentified afterburning turbofans, each rating about 18,000 lb (8200 kg) with afterburner

Performance: maximum speed at 36,000 ft (11000 m) 1,320 mph (2120 km/h) Mach 2; maximum speed at sea level (clean) 900 mph (1450 km/h), Mach 1.2; cruising speed at sea level 600 mph (980 km/h); ferry range 3,750 miles (6000 km); combat radius 700 miles (1100 km) on hi-lo-hi profile

Weights: empty 35,000 lb (16000 kg); maximum normal external load 10,000 lb (4500 kg); maximum take-off 65,000 lb (30000 kg)

Dimensions: span (spread) 56 ft 10 in (17.3 m); (span swept) 32 ft 8 in (10 m); length 72 ft 10 in (22.2 m); height 18 ft (5.5 m); wing area (swept) 430 sq ft (40 m²)

Armament: one fixed cannon, probably same as on MiG-27; up to 10,000 lb (4500 kg)of guided and unguided weapons on two or four swivelling wing pylons and other hardpoints under wing gloves and fuselage

Operator: USSR

Until 1977 no photograph had been seen in the West of the very important Sukhoi Su-19 all-weather precision attack aircraft. Then this fuzzy picture emerged from West Germany, and in early 1980 it is still the only available photograph (though it has served as the basis for various artists' impressions).

This is believed to be the most accurate illustration yet published in the West of the outstanding Su-19 "Fencer", now widely used by Soviet Frontal Aviation.

The top and bottom of the right half of the Su-19, emphasize the impressive 16°/72° range of sweep of the swing wings, which are fitted with full-span slats and trailing-edge high-lift flaps.

Swearingen Merlin 3A

Swearingen Aircraft gained a high reputation in the early-1960s with their powerplant conversions of Beech Twin Bonanzas and Queen Airs. As a natural development the company rebuilt a Queen Air with a new streamlined, pressurized fuselage and a pair of 400-hp (298-kW) Lycoming TIGO-541 piston engines. As testing advanced, it became clear that this aircraft — the Merlin I — was an ideal mount for turboprop engines. The Merlin I was therefore shelved, and the production version was the SA-26T Merlin IIA powered by two United Aircraft of Canada, Pratt & Whitney PT6A turboprops. The first aircraft flew on 13 April 1965, with FAA certification being granted on 15 July 1966.

In 1971, with brisk Merlin II sales in hand, Swearingen announced the SA-226T Merlin III. The gross weight was increased from 10,000 lb (4536 kg) to 12,500 lb (5670 kg), the engines were changed to Garrett AiResearch TPE331s in redesigned nacelles, the vertical tail surfaces were redesigned and the tailplane was raised to a mounting on the fin. The Merlin III got a new landing gear with forward-retracting nose leg and twin-wheel main units, and an extra starboard cabin

window. Later, after Swearingen had been acquired by Fairchild Industries, the Merlin was further developed as the IIIA with detailed changes and improved performance. By the end of 1978, over 100 of the Merlin III series had been delivered.

First military use of the Merlin IIIA was with the Belgian air force. Their Hunting Pembroke C.51s had been in service for over 20 years and needed costly re-sparring. Accordingly, six Merlins were ordered as replacements and these were delivered in mid-1976, entering service with the 21 *Smaldeel*, a mixed transport squadron based at Brussels-Melsbroek. The second military user of the Merlin is the Argentine army, which started to take delivery of four aircraft at the end of 1978 for use in the communications role.

Type: 11-seat light transport
Powerplant: two 840-shp (626-kW) Garrett AiResearch TPE331-3U-303G turboprops
Performance: maximum cruising speed at 16,000 ft (4877 m) 325 mph (520 km/h); maximum rate of climb at gross weight 2,530 ft (771 m) per minute; maximum standard

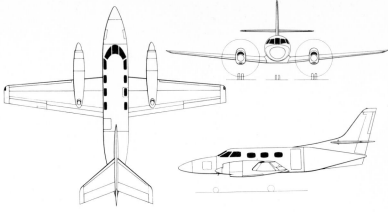

Swearingen Merlin 3

range with 45 minutes reserve 2,860 miles (4576 km); service ceiling 28,900 ft (8809 m); stalling speed (flaps down) 96 mph (154 km/h)
Weights: empty 7,400 lb (3357 kg); maximum take-off 12,500 lb (5670 kg)

Dimensions: span 46 ft 3 in (14.10 m); length 42 ft 2 in (12.85 m); height 16 ft 10 in (5.13 m); wing area 277.5 sq ft (25.78 m²)
Operators: Argentina, Belgium

Swearingen Merlin 4A

The Swearingen Merlin IV is a general transport manufactured by Fairchild-Swearingen for executive and military use, and is derived from the SA-226TC Metro airliner. In its turn, the Metro was the result of stretching the fuselage of Swearingen's Merlin III and fitting it with up to 21 passenger seats for commuter airlines. The Metro first flew on 26 August 1969 and is designed for use in passenger or cargo configuration. Similarly, the SA-226AT Merlin IV can be fitted with a convertible interior but its normal layout provides two passenger cabins with up to 15 seats. There are cargo sections in the nose and tail, and the aircraft has no direct competitor among the light turboprop aircraft in current production. The latest version, the Merlin IVA, is distinguishable by its larger rectangular cabin windows (replacing the round windows previously used) and is powered by two Garrett AiResearch TPE331 turboprops. Some 49 Merlin IVs had been delivered to customers by the end of 1978. The Royal Thai Air Force received two in 1978: these were

luxuriously fitted out for use by the King of Thailand and by the Crown Prince; regrettably, however, one of them crashed in November 1978 following an engine fire and attempted forced landing.

The main user of the Merlin IVA is the South African Air Force which has seven in operation with No 21 Squadron. One aircraft has been equipped for casualty evacuation and two are used as government transports. The remaining four Merlins carry out general VIP and communications missions. The Merlin IVA is also operated by the *Fuerza Aerea Argentina*, which has equipped its two aircraft as mobile hospitals for use in both military and civil emergency work.

Type: SA-226AT Merlin IVA 15-seat light transport
Powerplant: two 840-shp (626-kW) Garrett AiResearch TPE331-3U-303G turboprops
Performance: maximum cruising speed at 16,000 ft (4877m) 310 mph (496 km/h); maximum rate of climb at gross weight 2,400

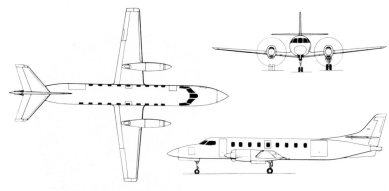

Swearingen Merlin 4 (Metro II)

ft (732 m) per minute; maximum standard range with 45 minutes reserve 2,095 miles (3352 km); service ceiling 27,000 ft (8230 m); stalling speed (flaps down) 99 mph (158 km/h); balanced field length 2,620 ft (799 m)
Weights: Empty 7,700 lb (3493 kg); maxi-

mum take-off 12,500 lb (5670 kg)
Dimensions: span 46 ft 3 in (14.10 m); length 59 ft 5 in (18.11 m); height 16 ft 10 in (5.13 m); wing area 277.5 sq ft (25.78 m²)
Operators: Argentina, South Africa, Thailand

Transall C-160

The Transall (Transporter Allianz or Transport Alliance) group was formed in January 1959 by companies which now form part of Aérospatiale, Messerschmitt-Bölkow-Blohm and VFW-Fokker, with the aim of producing the C-160 military transport for the French and German air forces. The first prototype made its maiden flight in March 1963, and the initial production aircraft took to the air in April 1967. By the time the production line closed in 1972 the consortium had built 179 examples. The *Luftwaffe* has a large number stored in reserve, but despite this, in October 1977 the programme was relaunched to provide additional aircraft for the French air force and for possible export customers, mainly to maintain employment at Aérospatiale.

The C-160 is a twin-turboprop medium transport which can carry troops, casualties, freight, supplies and vehicles from semi-prepared surfaces. The floor is stressed to take large vehicles and is provided with lashing points of 11,025-lb (5000-kg) and 26,455-lb (12000-kg) capacity. A hydraulically operated rear loading ramp is provided, in addition to a front door on the left side and paratroop doors on each side. A winch and roller conveyor allows loads to be taken aboard, and single loads of up to 17,635 lb (8000 kg) can be dropped from the air.

The new batch of aircraft will incorporate some differences. The loss of French bases in Africa has led to a requirement for additional range, which will be met by installing an extra centre-section fuel tank with a capacity of 1,540 gallons (7000 litres) and by fitting a probe so that the aircraft can be refuelled in flight. The new C-160s will additionally have

improved avionic equipment, and the left door, which is rarely used, is to be deleted. The French air force is expected to receive 28 new aircraft, and up to 75 may be built in all. First deliveries are likely to take place between 1981 and 1983.

Type: medium transport aircraft
Powerplant: two 6,100-ehp (4550-kW) Rolls-Royce Tyne 22 turboprops
Performance: maximum level speed at 16,000 ft (4875 m) 368 mph (592 km/h); economical cruising speed at 20,000 ft (6100 m) 282 mph (454 km/h); range with 17,635-lb (8000-kg) payload, 10% reserves and allowances for 30 minutes at 13,125 ft (4000 m) 2,982 miles (4800 km); range as above, but with twice the payload 1,056 miles (1700 km); maximum rate of climb at sea level 1,300 ft (396 m) per minute; service ceiling 25,500 ft (7770 m)
Weights: empty equipped 63,405 lb (28760 kg); maximum take-off 112,435 lb (51000 kg); maximum landing 103,630 lb (47000 kg)
Dimensions: span 131 ft 3 in (40.0 m); length 106 ft 3½ in (32.40 m); height

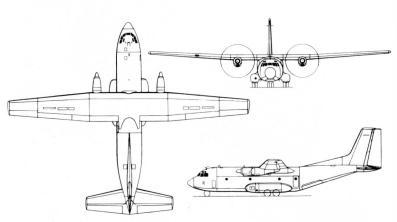

Transall C-160

40 ft 7 in (12.36 m); wing area 1,722 sq ft (160.1 m²)
Payload: up to 35,275 lb (16000 kg), including 93 troops, or 81 paratroops, or 62 stretchers and four attendants
Operators: France, South Africa, Turkey, West Germany

Luftwaffe C.160D Transall of Flugzeugführerschule 'S' at Wunsdorf, one of 90 in service with the German Air Force.

TS-8 Bies

A two-seat trainer in the Harvard tradition, the TS-8 Bies uses Poland's first post-war aero engine, the 320-hp (239-kW) Narkiewicz. Designed by T. Soltyk, the Bies flew for the first time on 23 July 1955. By the time of the Poznan Fair in 1956, the first public appearance of the aircraft, the third prototype had been built. The tricycle landing gear was, for its time, quite an advanced feature for a trainer. Several class speed records were established by the Bies and ratified by the FAI, including 199.06 mph (320.3 km/h) over a 2000-m (1.24-mile) closed circuit on 20 May 1957. Deliveries to the Polish air force began the following year from the Warsaw factory, replacing Yakovlev Yak-11s, and the Bies remained in production for about five years. Final production versions, designated TS-8 B-11, had some changes in equipment and the engine was uprated to 340-hp (254-kW). Equipped for day and night training, the Bies is fully aerobatic, and for gunnery training can be fitted with a fixed machine-gun.

Its replacement, the TS-11 Iskra jet trainer,

began entering service in 1964, and it is thought that only a few Bies are still in service.

Type: two-seat basic trainer
Powerplant: one 320-hp (239-kW) Narkiewicz WN-3 radial piston engine
Performance: maximum speed 192 mph (309 km/h) at sea level; cruising speed at 75% power 168 mph (270 km/h); initial rate of climb at sea level 1,340 ft (408 m) per minute; service ceiling 19,685 ft (6000 m); landing speed 56 mph (90 km/h); range 497 miles (800 km)
Weights: empty 2,359 lb (1070 kg); loaded 3,417 lb (1550 kg)
Dimensions: span 34 ft 5 in (10.5 m); length 28 ft 0 in (8.5 m); height 9 ft 10 in (3.0 m); wing area 205.6 sq ft (19.1 m²)
Armament: underwing racks can carry up to 440 lb (200 kg) of practice bombs
Operators: Poland

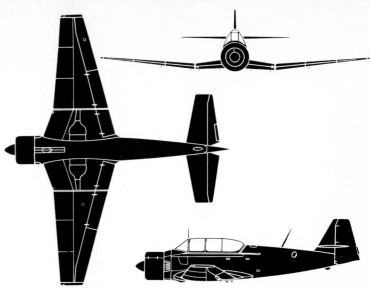

TS-8 Bies

Tupolev Tu-4 Bull

Despite the age of this venerable aircraft, the Tupolev Tu-4 'Bull' may still be in limited service with the Chinese air arm. It was in fact reported to be the carrier for the first Chinese nuclear weapons in the late 1960s.

Faced in 1945 with a series of failures in the Soviet industry's attempts to build a modern heavy bomber, the Soviet leadership decided to produce a carbon copy of the Boeing B-29 Superfortress, several of which had force-landed in Siberia during 1945 after raids on Japan. The Tupolev and Myasishchev bureaux were assigned the task of copying the airframe, while the Shvetsov team worked on producing a copy of the Wright R-3350 Cyclone 18 engine. Other teams copied the many complex systems of the American bomber, including its system of low-drag remotely controlled gun turrets. The formidable task of copying an aircraft so far in advance of anything previously seen in the Soviet Union was accomplished with remarkable speed; the first aircraft of the type to fly, in the

spring of 1948, was not a true prototype but the first of 20 pre-series aircraft, and production deliveries started in 1949. The main difference between the US and Soviet aircraft was the latter's heavier defensive armament, 23-mm cannon replacing the 0.5-in machine-guns of the Boeing B-29.

About 1,200 Tu-4s were built, of which some 400 were supplied to China. The type was replaced as a first-line bomber by the end of the 1950s in the Soviet Union, but continued to be used for the development of flight-refuelling techniques and for maritime reconnaissance.

Type: strategic bomber, tanker and reconnaissance aircraft
Powerplant: four 2,300-hp (1716-kW) Shvetsov ASh-73TK 18-cylinder radial piston engines
Performance: maximum speed 360 mph (580 km/h) at 33,000 ft (10000 m); range with 11,000-lb (5000-kg) bomb load 3,050 miles

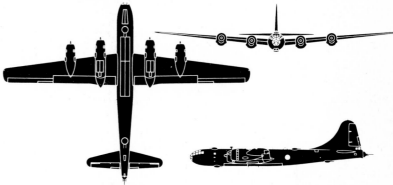

Tupolev Tu-4 (B-29) Bull

(4900 km); ceiling 36,750 ft (11200 m)
Weights: empty 75,000 lb (34000 kg); normal loaded 105,000 lb (47600 kg)
Dimensions: span 141 ft 4 in (43.08 m); length 99 ft 1 in (30.19 m); wing area 1,680 sq ft (156 m²)

Armament: up to 11,000 lb (5000 kg) of bombs in two internal bays; five remote-controlled turrets (tail, two dorsal and two ventral) each mounting two 23-mm NS cannon
Operators: China (and formerly USSR)

Tupolev Tu-16 Badger

The development in the early 1950s of the Mikulin bureau's massive AM-3 turbojet marked the end of the Soviet Union's dependence on Western technology in engines. Rated at 18,000 lb (8200 kg) in its initial version, the AM-3 made possible the design of new bombers with fewer engines than their Western counterparts, being twice as powerful as most contemporary Western engines.

Known as the Tupolev Tu-88 or Samolet N, the prototype of the Tu-16 'Badger' was flown in 1952; it was thus a contemporary of the British V-bombers rather than the American Boeing B-47. Like many Soviet aircraft designs, it was a mixture of the radically new and the conservative in its design philosophy. The fuselage was generally similar to that of the Tu-4, and the defensive armament, structure and systems were all based on the Tu-4. The wing set the pattern for future Tupolev aircraft, with a high degree of sweep and a bogie landing gear retracting rearwards into trailing-edge pods. The layout offered a sturdy and simple gear, left the centre-section free for weapon stowage and offered wide track; in addition, the pods helped to delay the transonic drag-rise. An apparent anomaly was the fixed forward-firing gun, retained to the present day.

The Tu-88 was ordered into production for the DA (Long-Range Aviation) and entered service in 1955. Later versions were equipped with the uprated AM-3M, and most of the type were eventually fitted with flight-refuelling equipment. The system fitted to Tu-16s so far seen is unusual, involving a tip-to-tip connection; other Soviet aircraft have nose probes. Some Tu-16s were completed as specialized tankers with a tip-hose or belly hose-reel.

Soviet production of the Tu-16 probably

gave way to the Tu-20 and Tu-22 in the late 1950s, but in the 1970s the type was put back into production in China, as a replacement for the Tu-4. The Chinese designation of the Tu-16 is unknown. The Tu-16 also formed the basis for the Tu-104, the first Soviet jet airliner.

A new lease of life for the Tu-16 came with the rising power of the Soviet navy in the early 1960s. Tu-16s were steadily transferred from the DA to the AVMF (Soviet Naval Aviation), and became that service's first missile-carriers. The first missile-armed variant, the 'Badger-B', of 1961, carried two turbojet-powered AS-1 'Kennel' missiles under the wings; these aircraft appear to have been converted into 'Badger-Gs' with the more

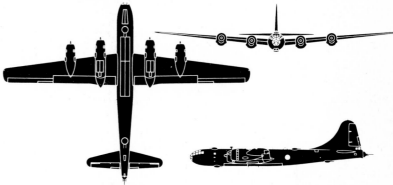

Tupolev Tu-16 Badger F

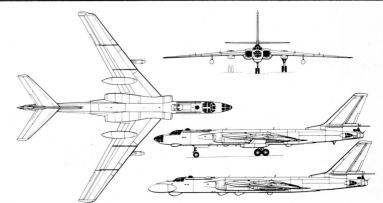

Called 'Badger-F' by NATO, this Tu-16 is an electronics platform probably operated by the AV-MF, the Soviet Union's naval air arm.

One regiment of the Egyptian Air Force still operates the Tu-16 Badger-G, although serviceability is thought to be low.

advanced AS-5 'Kelt' missile, and a number of these were delivered to Egypt in the late 1960s and early 1970s. The 'Badger-C' also seen in 1961, carries a single supersonic AS-2 'Kipper' missile, with a large radar installation replacing the glazed nose. A similar radar is featured by the 'Badger-D' maritime reconnaissance aircraft, together with an array of radomes indicating an electronic surveillance capability. The 'Badger-E' and 'Badger-F' are generally supposed to be specialized electronic intelligence (Elint) aircraft, with glazed noses and a plethora of aerials. The reporting names

'Badger-H' and 'Badger-J' have been quoted for further Elint aircraft.

About 350 Tu-16s are still in service with AVMF, including tankers as well as strike aircraft. The reconnaissance and Elint aircraft are likely to be replaced in first-line service by the better-optimized turboprop Ilyushin Il-38 and Il-18 while the missile-armed variants are being replaced by Tu-26s. However, there is life in the 'Badger' yet, as is shown by the re-equipment of some 'Badger-Gs' with a single AS-6 'Kingfish' missile under one wing.

Type: strategic bomber, missile platform, reconnaissance aircraft, Elint aircraft and flight-refuelling tanker
Powerplant: two 19,200-lb (8700-kg) Mikulin AM-3M turbojets
Performance: maximum speed 620 mph (1000 km/h) or Mach 0.91; cruising speed 530 mph (850 km/h or Mach 0.8; service ceiling 46,000 ft (14000 m); maximum range 4,000 miles (6400 m)
Weights: empty 80,000 lb (36000 kg); maximum take-off 158,500 lb (72000 kg)
Dimensions: span 113 ft 3 in (34.54 m);

length 120 ft (36.5 m); height 35 ft 6 in (10.8 m); wing area 1,820 sq ft (170 m²)
Armament: ('Badger-B') two AS-1 'Kennel' ASMs (no longer in service); ('Badger-C') one AS-2 'Kipper'; ('Badger-G') two AS-5 'Kelt'. Bomber versions have provision for 13,000 lb (6000 kg) of internal stores. All versions have seven 23-mm NR-23 cannon: one fixed in forward fuselage, two in tail turret and two each in ventral and dorsal barbettes
Operators: China, Iraq, Indonesia (in storage), Libya, USSR

Tupolev Tu-20 Bear

Unquestionably the most spectacular of contemporary warplanes, the vast Tupolev Tu-20 'Bear' remains in service with the AVMF (Soviet Naval Aviation) by virtue of its unmatched range. The Tupolev giants are the only turboprop combat aircraft in use, and the only swept-wing turboprop aircraft ever to see service. Their mighty propellers still defy conventional design wisdom, which states that the peak in propeller efficiency has been passed long before the speed of the aircraft is high enough to justify a swept wing.

The design of the Tu-95 (the design bureau designation for the Tu-20) is directly descended from that of the Boeing B-29, copied by Tupolev as the Tu-4 'Bull'. The refined Tu-80 development of the Tu-4 led to the much larger Tu-85, whose speed was inadequate to evade jet fighters. In view of the progress being made on turbine engines, it was decided to abandon the Tu-85 and develop a more advanced design using a similar fuselage.

Design of the Tu-95 started before 1952, in parallel with the Myasishchev M-4 'Bison'. The massive NK-12 turboprop was bench-tested at 12,000 hp (8952-kW) in 1953 and the first prototype Tu-95 flew in the following year. In flight tests without military equipment the Tu-95 attained a speed of 590 mph (950 km/h), equivalent to nearly Mach 0.9, an achievement matched by scarcely any other propeller aircraft, and certainly by none of the Tu-20's size.

Tu-20's superlative range and endurance and replace it in AVMF service, although the Tu-26 offers a close approach to its range performance. According to the US journal *Aviation Week*, a large subsonic aircraft is under development to replace Tu-20s in both these roles. For many years, the force has been dwindling due to accidents (several of the type have been lost on patrol) and even structural reconditioning can only delay the damage caused by vibration from the propulsion system. Apart from the AVMF and DA, the only operator of the Tu-95 has been Aeroflot: a rudimentary passenger and mail version, designated Tu-114D, operated some high-priority services in the early 1960s.

Type: strategic bomber, missile platform and maritime reconnaissance aircraft
Powerplant: four 15,000-shp (11190-kW) Kuznetsov NK-12MV turboprops
Performance: maximum speed 540 mph (870 km/h); economical cruising 465 mph (750 km/h); service ceiling 41,000 ft (12500 m); maximum range 11,000 miles (17500 km)
Weights: empty about 165,000 lb (about 75,000 kg); normal take-off 330,000 lb (150000 kg); maximum overload, 375,000 lb (170000 kg)
Dimensions: span 167 ft 8 in (51.1 m); length 155 ft 10 in (47.5 m); height 38 ft 8 in (11.78 m)
Armament: (original aircraft) six NR-23

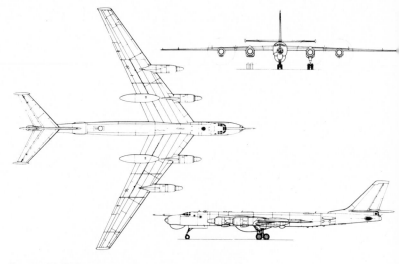

Tupolev Tu-20 Bear

23-mm cannon on dorsal semi-retractable barbette, ventral barbette and manned tail turret, plus a normal bomb load of 22,000 lb (10000 kg); 'Bear-B' converted to carry AS-3 'Kangaroo' stand-off weapon
Operator: USSR

Tu-20 Bear-D long-range strategic bomber. About 45 of these aircraft continue in Soviet maritime reconnaissance service.

The Tu-20 entered service in 1955 with the DA bomber force, and caused something of a panic in US defence circles; at that time most of the all-weather/night fighters in US service were still straight-winged, and would have had trouble intercepting the Soviet bomber. However, with the advent of the surface-to-air guided missiles and radar-controlled, missile-armed interceptors in the late 1950s, the Tu-20 became largely obsolete as a bomber. To maintain a credible deterrent, the massive AS-3 'Kangaroo' missile was developed, measuring 49 ft (15 m) from nose to tail and weighing nearly 10 tons.

About 50 of the DA's became 'Bear-Bs' with the AS-3 missile and a large nose radar. 'Bear-C' is apparently an MR type with the same radar. The 'Bear-E' is similar to the bomber, but equipped for Elint (electronic intelligence) and other reconnaissance duties. The 'Bear-F' is a more recent MR modification, with extended inner engine nacelles, and conversion of Tu-20s to this standard continues. The 'Bear-D' is a highly interesting variant, with a large ventral radar in a bulged radome. One theory is that the 'Bear-D' is a director for over-the-horizon surface-to-surface missiles such as the SS-N-3. Within these types there are many sub-variants, and no two AVMF Tu-20s appear to be exactly alike. Recently, some aircraft have been seen with some or all defensive armament deleted. The 'Bear-F' has a small stores bay in place of the ventral turret.

It is possible that the last 'Bear-Bs' will not be retired until the mid-1980s. Equally, there is no sign of any aircraft which can match the

This Tupolev Tu-20 'Bear-D' was one of those intercepted almost every day near the British Isles by the RAF. Devoid of numbers or unit markings, it is packed with electronics for Elint, missile guidance and other duties. Endurance exceeds 24 hours, and some routine missions must reach close to this figure.

Tupolev Tu-22 Blinder

Often considered a failure, the Tupolev Tu-22 'Blinder' appears in fact to be a workmanlike design, and limited production appears to be a consequence of changing requirements and political factors rather than a technical decision. The figures below reflect the compiler's latest estimate, and in some respects contradict earlier information; the range quoted for the aircraft, for example, has generally been closer to the all-supersonic range capability of the type, rather than reflecting its normal operating profile.

Development of the Tu-22, under the Tupolev bureau designation Tu-105, was initiated in 1955-56. By that time it was clear that the effectiveness of Western air-defence systems was improving rapidly, and that supersonic, missile-armed all-weather interceptors and medium/high-altitude SAMs would be in large-scale service by the end of the decade. The Tu-16, with its modest cruising altitude and defensive gun turrets, was already obsolescent for penetration of hostile territory. The design objectives of the Tu-105 were to produce an aircraft with performance generally comparable with the Tu-16, but with greatly increased penetration altitude and speed.

The Tu-105 was thus designed to incorporate supersonic dash at high altitude without excessively penalizing subsonic efficiency. The engines were mounted high on the rear fuselage in slim cowlings to avoid the weight and drag penalties of long inlet ducts. Sweep was increased relative to that of the Tu-16, but a compound-sweep layout was chosen for minimum subsonic and low speed penalty. The fuselage, wing, landing-gear pods and engine nacelles were positioned and designed in strict accordance with the area rule. The elimination of defensive armament except the tail cannon saved weight and volume and the crew was reduced to three, seated in tandem downward-ejecting seats. For the first time in a Soviet aircraft, bombing/navigation radar displaced the glazed nose.

The source of the engines has long been a mystery, but it appears they are Kolesov VD-7s, similar to the engines fitted to the Myasishchev M-50. The nacelles are fitted with plain inlets; production Tu-22s have narrower inlets than early aircraft, and the lips slide forwards to open an auxiliary annular aperture at low speeds.

The Tu-105 probably flew in 1959, in time for 10 (including one with a missile) to be demonstrated at Tushino in 1961. The type's debut was a complete surprise to Western intelligence, but progress in defence systems had come to the point where a supersonic dash and better cruise altitude were in practice not much of an advantage over the subsonic Tu-16. In addition, the decision to rely solely on missiles for strategic attack had already been taken, leading to the temporary cessation of bomber development, and transfer of many aircraft to the Soviet naval air arm (AVMF).

There was, however, a continuing role for the Tu-22 in the precision strike and missile-carrying role, and about 170 of the type were delivered to Long-Range Aviation (DA) units from about 1964. These were of the variant known to NATO as 'Blinder-B', with a bomb-bay modified to accept the AS-4 'Kitchen' air-to-surface missile, as well as free-fall weapons. The designation 'Blinder-A' was applied to the nine non-missile aircraft seen at Tushino in 1961. The AS-4 is the Soviet equivalent of the defunct British Hawker Siddeley Blue Steel, rocket-powered and with a 200-mile (320-km) range.

The main AVMF variant of the Tu-22 in current service is the maritime-reconnaissance Elint 'Blinder-C'. The 'Blinder-B' and the AS-4 do not appear to be in AVMF service. In the reconnaissance role, the 'Blinder-C' offers payload and flight-refuelled endurance similar to those of the Tu-16, but less space for the crew. Only some 50 are in AVMF service. Both the DA and AVMF operate a few 'Blinder-D' (probably Tu-22U) conversion trainers, with a separate second cockpit above and behind the standard (pupil's) cockpit.

Although the Tu-22 is far from being the failure it has been considered in the West, it has not found an important niche in the Soviet forces. Its main role in the late 1960s and early 1970s was strike in the European region, but its importance in this role has diminished with the introduction of the Sukhoi Su-19 into the FA, and the Tu-26 'Backfire' into the DA and AVMF. The small batches of 'Blinder-Bs' supplied to Libya and Iraq (without AS-4 missiles or nuclear weapons) were probably surplus to DA requirement. The Iraqi aircraft have been used in action against Kurdish insurgents, and one Libyan machine at least against Tanzania, in support of Uganda. The Tu-22 has thus become one of very few large bombers conceived since 1945 to drop bombs in anger.

In 1974 it was reported that Tu-22s were being converted to the interceptor role to replace Tu-28Ps, but this report has not been substantiated.

Type: bomber, reconnaissance and maritime-strike aircraft

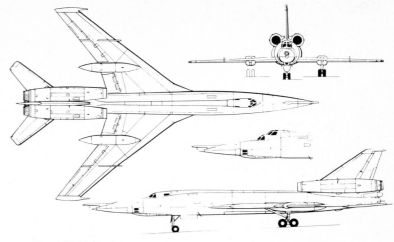

Tupolev Tu-22 Blinder A

Powerplant: probably two 31,000-lb (14000-kg) Kolesov VD-7 afterburning turbojets

Performance: maximum speed at 36,000 ft (11000 m), 1000 mph (1600 km/h) Mach 1.5; cruising speed 36,000 ft (11000 m) 560 mph (900 km/h) or Mach 0.85; service ceiling 60,000 ft (18000 m) with afterburning, 45,000 ft (14000 m) without; maximum range (subsonic) 4,000 miles (6500 km); unrefuelled tactical radius with 250 miles (400 km) supersonic dash 1,750 miles (2800 km)

Weights: empty 90,000 lb (40000 kg); internal fuel 80,000 lb (36000 kg); maximum take-off 190,000 lb (85000 kg)

Dimensions: span 91 ft (27.5 m); length 133 ft (40.5 m); height 35 ft (10.7 m); wing area 1,550 sq ft (145 m²)

Armament: one 23-mm cannon in radar-directed tail barbette, and about 22,000 lb (10000 kg) of internal stores or ('Blinder-B') one AS-4 'Kitchen' cruise missile

Operators: Iraq, Libya, USSR

Though the sub-type cannot be positively identified this Tu-22 is probably of the multi-sensor reconnaissance variety called 'Blinder-C' by NATO, with batteries of cameras (and, since 1973, other sensors) in the fuselage and elsewhere. Surviving examples are believed to operate also in the Elint and ECM roles, with the Soviet ADD and AV-MF.

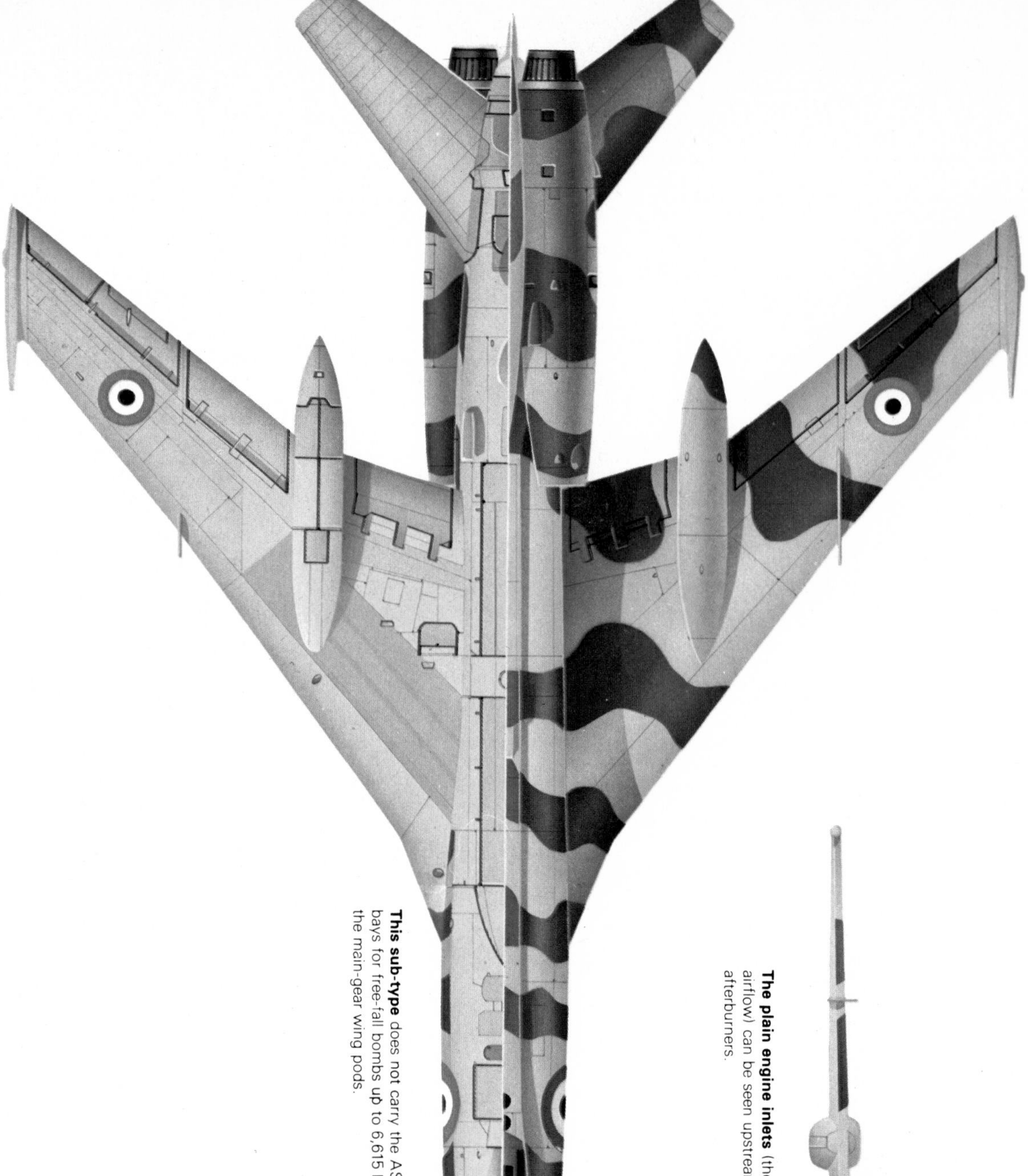

This drawing (below) of a Tupolev Tu-22 "Blinder-A" of the Libyan Arab air force shows the upper and lower sides of the left half of the aircraft. Some original Soviet equipment has probably been removed.

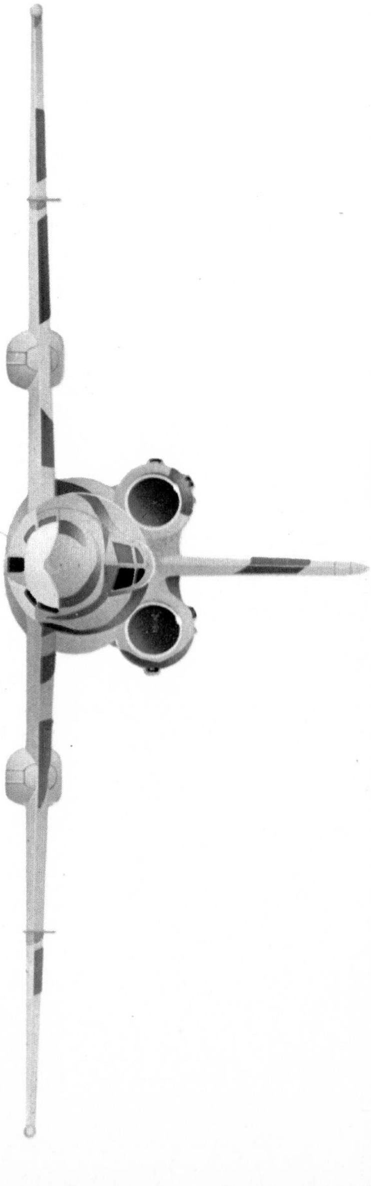

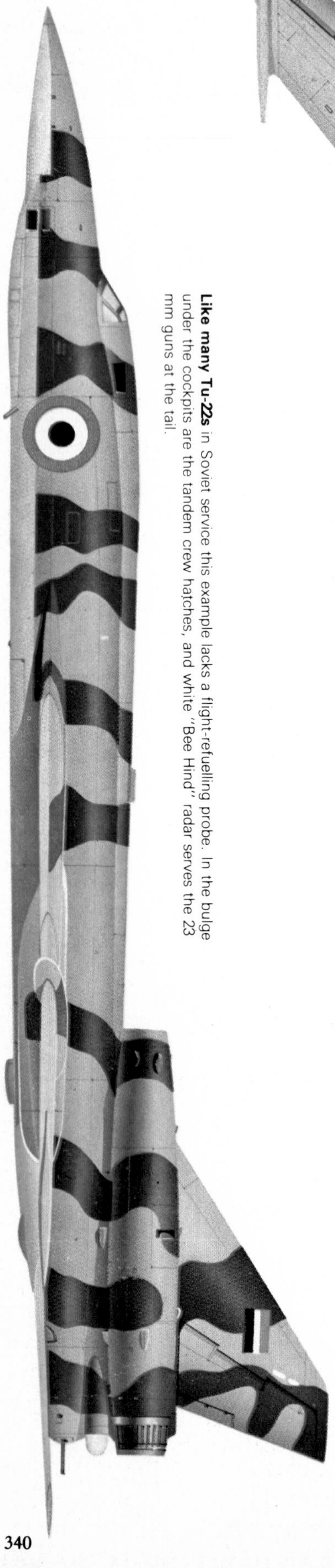

Like many Tu-22s in Soviet service this example lacks a flight-refuelling probe. In the bulge under the cockpits are the tandem crew hatches, and white "Bee Hind" radar serves the 23 mm guns at the tail.

This sub-type does not carry the AS-4 "Kitchen" stand-off missile, but has front and rear bays for free-fall bombs up to 6,615 lb size, with damage-assessment cameras in the tail of the main-gear wing pods.

The plain engine inlets (the front ring of which can translate forwards on take-off for extra airflow) can be seen upstream of the projecting ram inlets to cool the structure round the afterburners.

Tupolev Tu-26 Backfire

Few contemporary combat aircraft have been the subject of as much controversy as the Tupolev bureau's swing-wing bomber, codenamed 'Backfire' by NATO and referred to as the Tu-26 by the US Department of Defense. Throughout the Strategic Arms Limitation Talks (SALT) negotiations, the Soviet Union has maintained that the 'Backfire' is intended for maritime and European strike missions rather than long-range strike against the USA; US negotiators, on the other hand, have consistently argued that the aircraft has strategic range, and there have been accusations that some estimates of 'Backfire' performance have been deliberately suppressed to suit the political line. However, the aircraft is now regarded as a 'peripheral' system, and unless it is equipped with long-range cruise missiles (allowing it to fly its entire mission to the launch point at subsonic speed, while still threatening a large proportion of the USA) it is not seen as a true strategic system. However, it still presents a very serious threat to Western Europe, the North Atlantic and above all to China, which completely lacks the air-defence capability needed to intercept the 'Backfire' at any altitude.

'Backfire' development started in 1964-65, to meet a joint Soviet Naval Aviation (AVMF) and Long-Range Aviation (DA) requirement for a Tu-22/Tu-16 replacement. It is questionable whether or not, by that time, the decision to abandon the bomber as a strategic weapon had been reversed. It was inevitable that any bomber developed with variable sweep and turbofans would have very long subsonic range, and thus some strategic potential, as a corollary of improved low-level and loiter performance.

The design of the 'Backfire' (reported bureau designation is Tu-116, but this is not confirmed) was typically evolutionary, combining elements from a number of designs. The NK-144 engines were already well developed for the Tu-144 supersonic airliner, while the general arrangement of the aircraft was similar to that of the Tu-102/28, with long inlet ducts and a low-set wing. The Tupolev bureau decided to accept the performance penalties of the unique semi-variable-geometry layout, with pivot points at one-third span, rather than take the much greater risks of a fully variable configuration, as used on the Rockwell B-1. In addition, the initial design retained the waisted fuselage and podded landing gear of the Tu-28. High-lift devices were apparently conventional, with slats on the outer wings, Fowler flaps and (possibly) a droop on the glove leading edge.

The first prototype, representative of the aircraft known as 'Backfire-A' to NATO, flew in 1969 and demonstrated a considerable range deficiency as a result of excessive drag, probably affecting low-level performance most severely. It was decided to modify the aircraft radically. The 'Backfire-B' thus features new outer wings of increased span, with a distinctive double-taper on the trailing edge, and a new landing gear, which retracts inwards into the fuselage. There may have been other changes, but the nose and tail were little altered. The first trials unit started working up in 1975. Production is reported to be running at a rate of 35 aircraft af year.

With refuelling, the 'Backfire-B' does sustain a one-way threat to the continental USA, but its main role (particularly in view of the long-range bomber anticipated in early 1979) is in the European and maritime theatres. In Europe, the 'Backfire' remains the only aircraft in the Soviet inventory which can cover the whole of the NATO region at low level from a 'starting line' on the Eastern bloc border, operating on a hi-lo-hi profile from secure bases in the western Soviet Union.

An equally serious threat is posed by AVMF 'Backfires', with their capability to launch long-range strikes from the North Cape area over much of the Atlantic. The 'Backfire' force thus menaces NATO's vital resupply route; NATO's main counter seems to be to close the gap between Scotland and Iceland with AWACS aircraft (BAe Nimrod AEW.3) and long-range interceptors (Panavia Tornado F.2). Another potential use of the 'Backfire' is as a long-range 'air interdictor', armed with a heavy load of air-to-air missiles for use against transatlantic freight aircraft carrying priority reinforcements.

Missile armament of the 'Backfire' is an area of uncertainty. The Mach 3 AS-6 'Kingfish' anti-shipping missile was reported to be under develoment for the 'Backfire', and at one stage it was thought that two of these weapons might be carried. However, as seen in late 1977 the weapon appears to be larger than first reported, and is more suited to a single installation like that of the AS-4, on the Tu-22. Armament of the 'Backfire' on long-range missions is likely to comprise a single AS-4 or AS-6.

In early 1979 the US journal *Aviation Week* reported that a 'Backfire' development with MiG-25-type ramp inlets was under test. Such a version might be marginally faster at medium altitude, but this would make little difference to its effectiveness. It is expected that about 450 'Backfires' will be delivered to the AVMF and DA, and deliveries to date appear to have been shared roughly equally between the two sub-types.

This Tu-26 'Backfire-B' was one of many Soviet aircraft engaged in Elint and photo-reconnaissance missions during Exercise 'Northern Wedding' in early 1978. Intercepted by a Swedish aircraft, it later radioed 'I'm going home now, he's got his pictures.'

Type: medium-range bomber and maritime strike/reconnaissance aircraft
Powerplant: two 45,000-lb (20500-kg) Kuznetsov NK-144 afterburning turbofans
Performance: maximum speed at 36,000 ft (11000 m) 1,200-1,320 mph (1930-2120 km/h) or Mach 1.8-2.0; cruising speed 560 mph (1900 km/h) at 36,000 ft (11000 m); maximum speed at sea level 650 mph (1050 km/h); cruising speed at sea level 500 mph (800 km/h); service ceiling 55,000 ft (17000 m); range 5,000 miles (8000 km); hi-lo-hi combat radius 1,600 miles (2600 km); sea-level combat radius 850 miles (1400 km)
Weights: empty 110,000 lb (50000 kg); internal fuel 105,000 lb (47500 kg); maximum take-off 245,000 lb (11000 kg)
Dimensions: span (unswept) 113 ft (34.5 m); span (swept) 86 ft (26.2 m); length 132 ft (40.2 m); height 30 ft (9.1 m); wing area 1,785 sq ft (166 m²)
Armament: one 30-mm cannon in radar-directed tail barbette, plus one or two AS-4 'Kitchen', or AS-6 'Kingfish' missiles recessed into fuselage or under wings; other stores may be carried in internal weapons bay, for a total stores capacity estimated at 17,500 lb (8000 kg)
Operators: USSR

This drawing was prepared chiefly from photographs of a Soviet naval 'Backfire' secured by a Swedish reconnaissance aircraft in 1978. Colouring is believed to be correct though the pictures were in monochrome.

About half the lift comes from the fuselage, ducts and large inboard wing which is of fixed geometry. Missiles, such as the 'AS-6 Kingfish', are carried on pylons at the outer ends of the fixed wing.

Tupolev Tu-28 Fiddler

Originally developed as the Soviet Union's counter to missile-carrying subsonic bombers in the late 1950s and early 1960s, the Tupolev Tu-28 'Fiddler' remains the largest fighter in the world. Most of the aircraft of this type appear to be deployed along the northern edge of the Soviet Union; in that sense, their opposite numbers are the fighters of the Canadian Armed Forces, with a vast periphery to protect an inhospitable territory beneath them.

The Tu-28P appears to have entered service rather later than the Tu-22, but the design is earlier in origin and carries the bureau designation Tu-102. It represented a development of one of the most publicised but least used of Soviet aircraft, the Tupolev Tu-98 'Backfin'. It is difficult to work out the characteristics of the Tu-98, because in 1956-60 it was the object of a vast amount of speculation in the West, by intelligence and press sources alike. Some of this appears to have been picked up by Eastern European sources and 're-transmitted'. This speculation was aroused by the inclusion of the Tu-98 among a collection of (mostly cancelled) Soviet aircraft demonstrated to the US Air Force in the summer of 1956 at Kubinka near Moscow. The Tu-98 was then ascribed by the West to the Yakovlev bureau, and even designated Yak-42.

In fact the Tu-98 had been flown in 1955, as a light transonic tactical bomber intended as a successor to the Ilyushin Il-28. Like the contemporary Il-54, it was powered by two Lyulka AL-7F afterburning turbojets of 20,000-lb (9000-kg) thrust. Unlike the Tu-16, it had engines mounted inside the rear fuselage, fed by long intake ducts curving over the wing. The crew numbered three, with a navigator in a pointed, glazed nose.

Both the Tu-98 and Il-54 were cancelled in favour of the small Yak-28, but the Tupolev bureau developed the Tu-98 into the refined Tu-102, which was apparently intended to fill the light strike role as well as having potential as an interceptor. The Tu-102 is believed to have made its first flight in 1959, and differed from the Tu-98 in having a more sharply swept wing, adjustable half-cone inlets and podded main bogies.

In the event, the Tu-102 was to be adapted as the carrier for a new long-range air-to-air missile and its powerful 'Big Nose' radar. The intended role of the eventual Tu-28P was to intercept Western subsonic bombers before they came close enough to launch long-range missiles such as the North American Hound Dog, Hawker Siddeley Blue Steel or Douglas Skybolt. This demanded considerable endurance at remote patrol points, and the answer was an aircraft of considerable size.

Development of the radar, avionics and AA-5 'Ash' missile (the largest air-to-air missile in the world until the appearance of the AA-6 'Acrid') appears to have run behind that of the airframe. The Tu-28s demonstrated at Tushino in 1961 carried only two AA-5s (both apparently infra-red homing), a very large ventral fairing and ventral fins.

Production deliveries are believed to have

started in 1963-64, but it was not until 1967 that the production standard aircraft was observed, at the Domodedovo air display. Production Tu-28Ps carry two AA-5s under each wing, and are reported to be armed with a mix of semi-active radar and infra-red homing weapons. The ventral fairing and fins are absent. It is possible that the ventral blister was a 'mission pack' containing stores of avionics, designed for the Tu-102's original multi-role function and deleted when the type was assigned to interception. It is likely that pre-production Tu-102s, like the Tu-98, were powered by AL-7Fs; production aircraft, in this case, would almost certainly have the more powerful AL-21F, which may have been developed for the Tu-28.

The Tu-28 continues to fill a niche in the defensive cordon of the Soviet Union which cannot be catered for adequately by any other type, and it is likely to remain in service until the new air-defence system expected in the early 1980s becomes operational. The aircraft referred to by US sources as the 'Super MiG-25', the main air vehicle in the new system, is the only other two-seat Soviet fighter. It is also likely to match the range and loiter capability of the Tu-28P; the present MiG-25 lacks this by a large margin. The effectiveness of the Tu-28P depends on the degree to which it has been updated, but it is

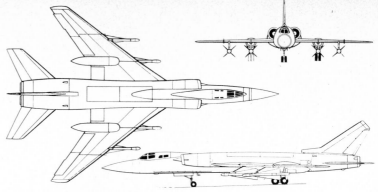

Tupolev Tu-28P Fiddler

likely to fall well short of Western systems such as the AWG-9/Phoenix system carried by the Grumman F-14. Even operating in conjunction with the Tu-126 'Moss', the Tu-28P is unlikely to be effective against low-flying targets. However, its presence will still tend to force them down on to the deck, reducing penetration range; and rebuilding these impressive aircraft with new radar and weapons might be logical.

Type: two-seat long-range interceptor
Powerplant: two Lyulka AL-21F afterburning turbojets

Performance: maximum speed 1,200 mph (1900 km/h) Mach 1.8 at 36,000 ft (11000 m); maximum speed with four missiles 1,000 mph (1600 km/h), or Mach 1.5; service ceiling 60,000 ft (18000 m); range 2,000 miles (3200 km); tactical radius 800 miles (1300 km)
Weights: empty 40,000 lb (18000 kg); maximum take-off 85,000 lb (38500 kg)
Dimensions: span 65 ft (20 m); length 85 ft (26 m); height 23 ft (7 m); wing area 850 sq ft (80 m²)
Armament: four AA-5 'Ash' air-to-air missiles
Operators: USSR

Three of the world's biggest fighters, Tu-28P 'Fiddler' all-weather interceptors of the PVO of the kind still used in remote areas of the Soviet Union. They carry four 'Ash' missiles and almost 40,000 lb (18145 kg) of internal fuel, enough for eight hours.

Tupolev Tu-124 Cookpot

After enjoying limited success in its designed role as an airliner, the Tupolev Tu-124 'Cookpot', a scaled-down version of the Tu-104, has remained in service as a VIP and government transport, for which its small size and relatively good field performance render it suitable.

The Tu-124 was designed in the late 1950s to meet an Aeroflot requirement for an Ilyushin Il-14 replacement, designed to carry 44–56 passengers and to operate from small and unprepared fields. The prototype flew in June 1960, and possessed the distinction of being the first airliner to be designed specifically for turbofan engines. The Tu-124's D-20P turbofans were also the first engines to carry the name of the Soloviev bureau, which since then has powered a number of Soviet transport types.

In general arrangement the Tu-124 is similar to the Tu-104, but smaller in all respects, with a narrower cabin cross-section. The undercarriage is considerably shorter than

that of the Tu-104, to facilitate servicing without inspection platforms, and the wing-loading is lower. The wing is fitted with double-slotted trailing-edge flaps and over-wing spoilers for better short-field performance. Like the later Tu-134, the Tu-124 features a large door-type airbrake beneath the centre section, to steepen the glide-path and thus shorten the field length.

Initial production Tu-124s have 44 seats, but the later Tu-124V seats 56 in a high-density layout. Government and VIP versions are the 36-seat and Tu-124K and the 22-seat Tu-124K2.

Type: twin-engined 44/56-seat airliner and government transport
Powerplant: two 12,000-lb (5400-kg) Soloviev D-20P turbofans
Performance: cruising speed Mach 0.82 or 540 mph (870 km/h); range with maximum payload of 13,200 lb (6000 kg) 775 miles (1250 km); maximum range with 30–35

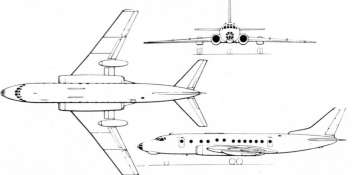

Tupolev Tu-124 Cookpot

passengers 1,300 miles (2100 km); service ceiling 38,400 ft (11700 m); take-off ground roll at maximum take-off weight 3,380 ft (1030 m); landing ground roll 3,050 ft (930 m)
Weights: empty 50,485 lb (22900 kg); maximum payload 13,200 lb (6000 kg); normal

take-off 80,500 lb (36500 kg); maximum take-off 82,500 lb (37500 kg)
Dimensions: span 83 ft 10 in (25.55 m); length 100 ft 4 in (30.58 m); wing area 1,285 sq ft (119.37 m²)
Operators: (governments of) Czecholovakia, East Germany, India, USSR

Tupolev Tu-126 Moss

The existence of a Soviet equivalent to the Western Boeing E-3A Sentry airborne warning and control system (AWACS) was revealed in late 1969, by which time the type had probably been flying for at least two years. The fact that the type was not among those demonstrated at the 1967 Domodedovo air display may be significant: the Soviet Union would hardly have anything to gain from attempting to conceal so large and distinctive a weapon system while at the same time revealing so many smaller aircraft. It is therefore likely that the first flight of a development aircraft took place in late 1967, with the system becoming operational in 1970. In 1971 a single aircraft was detached with its crew to assist the Indian air force in the war with Pakistan, indicating that the type was operational by that time.

Carrying the designation Tu-126 in Soviet service, and codenamed 'Moss' by NATO, the Soviet AWACS resembles the Boeing aircraft in the location of its main radar in a saucer-shaped rotodome on a fuselage. The location is chosen to reduce the interference generated by the wing and propellers while minimizing the effects of the radome and its pylon on stability.

The Tu-126 is based on the airframe of the Tu-114 airliner, and it is probable that aircraft of this type have been converted from Tu-114s surplus to Aeroflot requirements. The advantages of the Tu-114 for this role include its roomy cabin (the comparable E-3A has a crew of 17, including systems operators) and its impressive endurance, especially at reduced patrol speeds. Less favourable aspects of the design probably include high vibration levels at cruising speed, providing a less-than-perfect environment for delicate electronic systems.

In addition to the main radar, the Tu-126 carries a considerable array of smaller aerials, enabling it to communicate with the fighter aircraft it controls and to interrrogate the IFF (identification, friend or foe) systems of radar contacts. Blister fairings around the rear fuselage presumably contain defensive and offensive electronic countermeasures (ECM) equipment.

The Tu-126 programme ran some eight years ahead of the Western AWACS development, and the US Department of Defense has a low opinion of its performance. According to the DoD, the Tu-126 system is 'ineffective' over land and 'only marginally effective' over water. If this unsubstantiated estimate is accurate, it would explain why only a small number of these aircraft have been seen in service: Western estimates are that fewer than 20 are in use.

The ability of the Tu-126 system to look-down on targets in the presence of high sea states or ground clutter depends on the technological standard of its radar and data-processing equipment, and it is thought that the Soviet Union has not progressed as far in these areas as the West. Moreover, the Tu-126 is the first airborne early warning (AEW) aircraft of any sort to enter service with the Soviet air forces. This contrasts with the 35 years of continuous US experience in the field. It would thus be surprising if the Tu-126 did fully match Western standards.

A more capable Soviet AWACS system is expected to be deployed in the early 1980s. It is expected to incorporate important advances in the areas of data processing and radar performance and to have overland look-down capability. A likely carrier aircraft for the new system is the Ilyushin Il-86 wide-body airliner, first flown in December 1976.

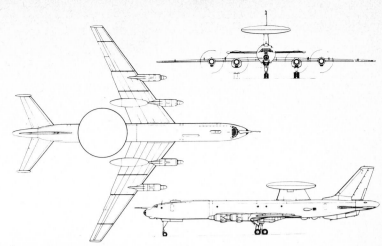

Tupolev Tu-126 Moss

It is still not known whether the Tu-126 'Moss' AWACS-type aircraft of the Soviet air-defence forces were new airframes or rebuilt Tu-114 civil transports retired from Aeroflot. Though used for nine years, only 12 appear to be operational.

Type: airborne warning and control (AWACS) aircraft
Powerplant: four 15,000-shp (1190-kW) Kuznetsov NK-12MV turboprops
Performance: maximum speed at 33,000 ft (10000 m) 460 mph (740 km/h); long-endurance patrol speed 320 mph (520 km/h); service ceiling 33,000 ft (10000 m); endurance more than 20 hours
Weights: empty 200,000 lb (90000 kg); load-ed 365,000 lb (165000 kg)
Dimensions: span 167 ft 8 in (51.1 m); length 188 ft (57.3 m); height 38 ft (11.6 m); wing area 3,350 sq ft (312 m²)
Operator: USSR

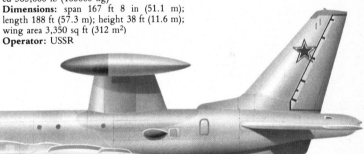

Tu-126 Moss serves with the IAP-VO Strany in the airborne warning and control system role.

Tupolev Tu-134 Crusty

Originally designated Tu-124A, the Tupolev Tu-134 'Crusty' started life as a highly developed version of the Tu-124 incorporating the then-fashionable rear-engined layout. The Tu-134 retains the fuselage section, undercarriage layout and wing design philosophy of the Tu-124, but the later aircraft is substantially larger and heavier than its predecessor.

The Tu-134 made its first flight in 1963 – 64, being contemporary with the BAC One-Eleven and Douglas DC-9. As well as the revised arrangement, the new aircraft had more powerful Soloviev engines than those fitted to the Tu-124. (The designation D-30 is, however, something of a mystery: the Tu-134 powerplants have much more in common with the earlier D-20 than with the much larger and later Soloviev D-30K.)

The Tu-134 was followed into service in 1970 by the Tu-134A, with a fuselage stretched to 124 ft 2 in (37.7 m) and capacity for up to 80 passengers. Gross weight, payload and fuel capacity have been increased, and thrust reversers are fitted. Later Tu-134As were fitted with a solid nose containing weather radar, in place of the glazed nose which had been inherited from the Tu-104 and Tu-16 bomber.

Like the Tu-124, the Tu-134 features a ventral door-type speedbrake, but this has been wired shut on some aircraft because it closes too slowly for safety in case of a missed approach. Featuring a comparatively sharply-swept wing and no leading-edge devices, the Tu-134 has a high approach speed compared with Western types, and thus never completely replaced older turboprop transports in Aeroflot service. The Yakovlev Yak-42 has been expected to replace the Tu-134 in due course. The Tu-134D was a proposed 110-passenger version of the design, but it does not appear to have been proceeded with.

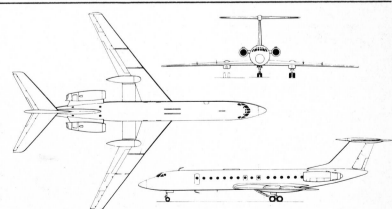

Tupolev Tu-134A Crusty

Type: airliner (72 seats), VIP and government transport
Powerplant: two 15,000-lb (6800-kg) Soloviev D-30 turbofans
Performance: Cruising speed 530 mph (849 km/h) at 36,000 ft (11000 m); range with maximum payload of 16,980 lb (7700 kg), 1,500 miles (2400 km); take-off field length to international standards 7,150 ft (2180 m); landing field length to international standards 6,730 ft (2050 m)
Weights: empty 60,500 lb (27500 kg); maximum landing 88,000 lb (40000 kg); maximum take-off 99,000 lb (45000 kg)
Dimensions: span 95 ft 2 in (29.0 m); length 114 ft 8 in (34.9 m); height 29 ft 7 in (9.0 m); wing area 1,370 sq ft (127 m²)
Operators: Bulgaria, East Germany, Hungary, Poland

UTVA-66/60

Announced in 1968, the UTVA-66 is descended from the 1959 UTVA-56 four-seat utility aircraft, the production development of which was the UTVA-60. This all-metal aircraft, powered by a 270-hp (210-kW) Lycoming GO-480-B1A6 engine, was produced in five versions: the U-60-AT1 basic utility model for air taxi, light freight, liaison or sporting flying; the -AT2, a dual-control version for training; the -AG, an agricultural aircraft; the -AM ambulance variant with accommodation for two stretchers loaded via an upward-hinged rear cabin canopy; and the U-60H, a seaplane with a strengthened fuselage, flown in October 1961 using Edo floats, although production models used Yugoslav-built floats. The seaplane was available in the same versions as the landplane, and examples of both types

served in the Yugoslav air force.

Development continued with the UTVA-66 with the more powerful 320-hp (239-kW) Lycoming engine. The new model was also available in utility and glider-towing configuration (UTVA 66), ambulance (-66AM) and seaplane (-66H), and utilised a number of UTVA 60 components. The wings were the same size but leading-edge slats were added, tail surfaces were enlarged and a servo tab plus a controllable trim tab were fitted to the elevator. Landing-gear shock absorbing was improved, and a larger fuel tank with 55-gallon (250-litre) capacity was fitted. A susbtantial number of UTVA 66s are in service with the Yugoslav air force.

Type: single-engine utility aircraft

Powerplant: one 320-hp (239-kW) Lycoming GSO-480-B1J6 piston engine
Performance: maximum speed at sea level 143 mph (230 km/h); maximum cruising speed 143 mph (230 km/h); initial rate of climb at sea level 885 ft (270 m) per minute; service ceiling 22,000 ft (6700 m); take-off distance to 50 ft (15 m) 1,155 ft (352 m); lan-

ding run from 50 ft (15 m) 594 ft (181 m); range 466 miles (750 km)
Weights: empty 2,756 lb (1250 kg); loaded 4,000 lb (1814 kg)
Dimensions: span 37 ft 5 in (11.40 m); length 27 ft 6 in (8.38 m); height 10 ft 6 in (3.20 m); wing area 194.50 sq ft (18.08 m²)
Operators: Yugoslavia

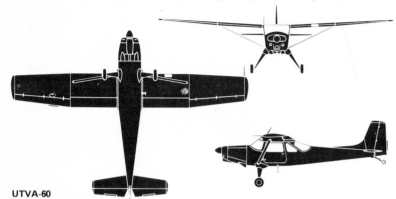

UTVA-60

Derived via the UTVA-60 from the UTVA-56, designed by Nikolic and Petkovic in the 1950s, the UTVA-66 appeared in 1968 and has become the standard STOL utility aircraft and glider tug of the Yugoslavian air force.

UTVA-75

A replacement for the Aero 3 as the Yugoslav air force's basic trainer, the UTVA-75 was designed and built by a partnership consisting of UTVA, Prva Petoletka and two Belgrade institutes. Design work began in 1974 and two prototypes were built the following year, flying respectively on 20 May and 18 December 1976. An initial production order covered 30 aircraft, most of which had been

completed by 1979.

In addition to its use as a basic trainer, with side-by-side seating, the UTVA-75 is also capable of glider towing. Construction is all-metal, and racks beneath the wings can carry light weapon loads, including rockets, for armament training.

Type: two-seat trainer and utility aircraft

Powerplant: one 180-hp (134-kW) Lycoming IO-360-B1F piston engine
Performance: maximum speed 136 mph (220 km/h); cruising speed (75% power) 102 mph (165 km/h); maximum rate of climb at sea level 885 ft (270 m) per minute; service ceiling 14,760 ft (4500 m); take-off run to 50 ft (15 m) 820 ft (250 m); landing run from 50 ft (15 m) 1,150 ft (350 m); range with drop tanks

1,242 miles (2000 km)
Weights: empty 1,433 lb (650 kg); loaded 2,116 lb (960 kg)
Dimensions: span 31 ft 11 in (9.73 m); length 23 ft 4 in (7.11 m); height 10 ft 4 in (3.15 m); wing area 157.5 sq ft (14.63 m²)
Operators: Yugoslavia

Valmet Leko-70 Vinka

In nearly 60 years since its foundation in the early 1920s the Finnish state aircraft industry has manufactured nearly 30 different types of aircraft, 18 of which have been designed in Finland. First new indigenous product for many years is the Leko-70, which emerged from a modern design office set up in 1970 and charged with finding a suitable basic trainer to replace the Swedish-built Saab Safirs of the Finnish air force. Valmet (a multi-faceted state industrial complex which now embodies the former IVL, or State Aircraft Factory) was responsible for manufacture of the prototype, which flew for the first time on 1 July 1975, some 2¼ years after receipt of contract. Valmet is now producing 30 Leko-70s for the Finnish air force, where they are known as the Vinka (blast), ordered in November 1976 and scheduled for delivery between 1979–81.

Configured as a side-by-side two-seater for training, the Vinka is of all-metal low-wing monoplane construction, with a non-retractable tricycle landing gear. (For winter operation, the normal wheeled gear can be replaced by skis.) Dual controls are of course standard, but one control column can be omitted if required, and there are inverted-flight fuel and oil systems for fully-aerobatic manoeuvres. The Vinka's cabin is roomy enough for two more seats to be installed at the rear (for touring), or for a stretcher and one medical attendant in addition to the pilot (for casualty evacuation). Instead of passengers, the aircraft can carry 617 lb (280 kg) of cargo; be fitted with hooks for glider or target towing; dispersal gear for crop-spraying or dusting; carry cameras in the floor of the rear cockpit, for aerial photography; or transport 661 lb (300 kg) of supplies on four underwing pylons.

Type: two-seat basic trainer
Powerplant: one 200-hp (149-kW) Lyco-

ming AEIO-360-A1B6 flat-four piston engine
Performance: maximum speed at sea level 149 mph (240 km/h); cruising speed (75% power) at 5,000 ft (1525 m) 118 mph (190 km/h); range with maximum fuel 630 miles (1015 km); maximum rate of climb at sea level 1,300 ft (400 m) per minute; service ceiling 16,400 ft (5000 m)
Weights: operating weight empty equipped 1,631 lb (740 kg); maximum take-off (two-seat) 2,205 lb (1000 kg); maximum take-off (four-seat) 2,645 lb (1200 kg)
Dimensions: span 32 ft 3¾ in (9.85 m); length 24 ft 7¼ in (7.50 m); height 10 ft 10¼ in (3.31 m); wing area 150.7 sq ft (14.00 m²)
Armament: none
Operator: Finland

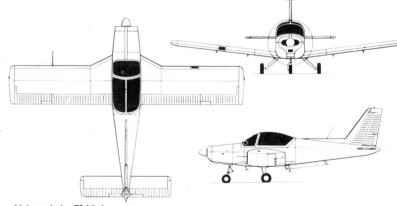

Valmet Leko-70 Vinka

Prototype of the Valmet Leko-70, popularly called the Vinka (blast), 30 of which are being delivered as the standard *ab initio* trainer of the Finnish *Ilmavoimat*. As part of an offset deal British Aerospace may assist marketing, despite its own Bulldog.

VFW-Fokker VFW 614

Ideas for a post-war German airliner began to take shape in the early 1960s and, like many others, the design team at VFW turned their attention to the need for a Douglas DC-3 replacement. Their solution was bold and imaginative. When a model of a 40-seater jet was first shown at the 1963 Paris Air Show it revealed overwing podded engines and a hinged nose which swung sideways to allow easy access to a tubby fuselage. The aircraft was designed to be capable of operating from short grass airfields. Although aimed principally at civil operators, the designers also had military transport roles very much in mind.

In 1968, after years of hesitation (when the swing nose was abandoned and replaced by a door on the right side), the German government gave the aircraft full-scale backing and agreement was also reached with Sabca and Fairey to build parts in Belgium. The prototype made its maiden flight in mid-1971, and the type entered service with Cimber Air in November 1975. In 1976 the VFW 614 was an unsuccessful candidate for a US Coast Guard order for a low-cost, medium-range surveillance aircraft, but the type entered military service as a transport/communications aircraft with the *Luftwaffe* from April 1977. Though 44 seats can be installed, these aircraft seldom have this number and are usually operated in mixed passenger/cargo configuration.

Although a number of airlines and governments had expressed interest in the aircraft and options came and went over the years, it became increasingly clear in 1976 and 1977 that sales had become firmly stuck below the 20 mark. Production officially ceased on 31 December 1977.

Type: medium-range transport/communications aircraft and VIP transport
Powerplant: two 7,280-lb (3302-kg) Rolls-Royce M45H Mk 501 turbofans
Performance: (at maximum take-off weight) maximum level speed 443 mph (713 km/h); maximum cruising speed 438 mph (704 km/h); range with 40 passengers and full

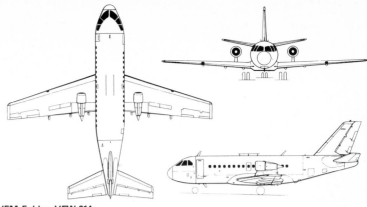

VFM-Fokker VFW 614

reserves 748 miles (1204 km)
Weights: empty 26,850 lb (12180 kg); maximum take-off and landing 44,200 lb (19950 kg); maximum zero fuel 38,580 lb (17500 kg)
Dimensions: span 70 ft 6½in (21.5 m);

length 67 ft 7 in (20.60 m); height 25 ft 8 in (7.84 m); wing area 688.89 sq ft (64.0 m²)
Armament: none
Operator: West Germany

Vickers-Armstrongs Viscount

The world's first turbine airliner, the Vickers Viscount 630 flew in July 1948, offering accommodation for 32 passengers. Subsequent upgrading of the engine power by 50% increased this to 40 passengers in the first production series, the V.700, the prototype of which was flown in April 1950.

British European Airways opened the world's first scheduled turboprop airliner service between London and Rome, Athens and Cyprus with V.701s on 17 April 1953, and from there orders began to flood in from the world's airlines. The Rolls-Royce Dart engine proved to have considerable potential for 'stretch', also the Vickers design team lengthened the Viscount's fuselage, placed the pressure bulkhead farther back and offered a 65-seat cabin in the V.800 series, launched once again by BEA. The last V.700 series new delivery was a batch of four V.794s to Turkish Airlines between July and November 1958, while the very last of 444 Viscounts built, a V.828, went to All Nippon Airways in February 1963.

Comparatively few Viscounts were delivered new for military service; they included a V.723 and V.730 for the Indian air force in December 1955 and January 1956 respectively, a V.734 for the Pakistan air force (for presidential use) in March 1956 and a V.742 for similar work with the Brazilian air force in February 1957. The Sultan of Oman's air force received four ex-airline Viscount V.800 series. The Royal Australian Air Force operated a V.816 and V.836. In Britain, the Empire Test Pilots' School used a pair of former Capital Airlines Viscounts, a V.744 and V.745, for several years for multi-engine conversion. The only ones believed still to be used are three ex-Turkish Airlines V.794s based at Ankara with the Turkish air force for VIP and government use, and a V.781D with No 21 Squadron, South African Air Force, at Zwarkop in the VIP role. The UK Royal Signals and Radar Research Establishment uses an ex-Austrian Airlines V.837 and a former Ghana Airways V.838.

Type: four-turboprop commercial airliner
Powerplant: four 1,740-ehp (1298-kW) Rolls-Royce Dart 506 turboprops
Performance: cruising speed at 53,000 lb (24000 kg) at 20,000 ft (6100 m) 324 mph (518 km/h); rate of climb at 58,500 lb (26560 kg) 1,200 ft (366 m) per minute at sea level and 700 ft (202 m) per minute at 15,000 ft (4575 m); take-off to 50 ft (15 m) at 58,800 lb (26560 kg) 4,290 ft (1307 m); landing distance

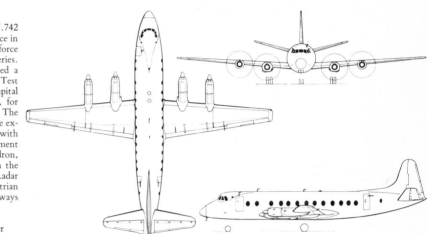

Vickers-Armstrongs Viscount 800

from 50 ft (15 m) at 52,000 lb (23608 kg) 2,850 ft (870 m); range (no reserves and with maximum payload) 1,785 miles (2872 km) at 309 mph (496 km/h)
Weights: Empty operational 38,358 lb (17400 kg); maximum take-off 64,500 lb

(29256 kg); maximum landing 57,500 lb (26081 kg)
Dimensions: span 93 ft 8 in (28.54 m); length 81 ft 10 in (24.93 m); height 36 ft 9 in (11.19 m); wing area 963 sq ft (89.45 m²)
Operators: South Africa, Turkey, UK

Vought A-7 Corsair II

In late 1962 the US Navy was considering the procurement of a supplement for the Douglas A-4 Skyhawk, which had first entered service in 1956. Though aware since July 1954 of the potential of the A-4, the US Navy saw the need for an attack aircraft capable of carrying twice the weight of disposable stores over twice the range. Thus in May 1963 the US Navy initiated a design competition to find a supplement for the A-4 Skyhawk. At this stage it was identified as VAL, signifying a heavier-than-air lightweight attack aircraft, and the specification called for subsonic speed, a maximum weapon load exceeding 10,000 lb (4536 kg), and the ability to fly three differing missions with a reduced weapon load.

In fact, the US Navy regarded the requirement as very urgent, and the ability to achieve an in-service target date in 1967 was an important factor. Four years in which to design, develop and start producing hardware is not very long in terms of the highly sophisticated aircraft needed by major powers in modern times, and it was probably this factor which limited to four the number of design proposals received by the US Navy. They came from Douglas, Grumman, North American and LTV Aerospace, and it was the last which, on 11 February 1964, was named as the winner of the competition; little more than a month later, on 19 March, LTV received a contract for seven test aircraft and the first 35 production aircraft, these having the designation A-7A. LTV bestowed the name Corsair, resurrected from the famous Vought-Sikorsky F4U carrier-based fighter of World War II,

Start of a 'cat shot' of a Vought A-7E Corsair II of 'The Clansmen' — who are not necessarily Scotsmen — from the *JFK*. A big flat-top in action is rather like an American football game; all the crew colours have meanings.

continued

adding the Roman II to ensure that historians would not get them confused.

The A-7A Corsair II was derived from the Chance Vought F-8 Crusader, the last US Navy fighter to emanate from that company before organisational changes brought in the name LTV (Ling-Temco-Vought) Aerospace (today Vought). It was, however, a very different aeroplane, with a less-swept, increased-span, fixed-incidence wing of which the outer panels folded upward, a shorter fuselage, and a more robust wing and fuselage structure to cater for the heavy weapons load. The fact that supersonic performance was not required from the A-7A meant that a non-afterburning engine would suffice, so for the initial version the 11,350-lb (5148-kg) thrust Pratt & Whitney TF30-P-6 was chosen, this being a non-afterburning version of the engine which had been developed for the General Dynamics F-111 variable-geometry aircraft. Internal fuel capacity was approximately 1,513 US gallons (5728 litres), which could be supplemented by up to 1,200 US gallons (4544 litres) in four drop tanks. One of the requirements of the VAL specification had been to provide the A-7 with greater range than the A-4, and two A-7As aptly demonstrated this on 19 May 1967 when they flew non-stop and without flight refuelling from Patuxent River NAS, Maryland, to Evreux Airport, France, a distance of 3,831 miles (6165 km), *en route* to the Paris Air Show.

The first A-7A had flown for the first time on 27 September 1965, and the first deliveries to the US Navy's Air Test Center at Patuxent River NAS were made between 13 and 15 September 1966. Deliveries to squadrons began on 14 October 1966, and the first aircraft involved in combat was an A-7A of Navy Squadron VA-147, which was flown into action off the USS *Ranger* in the Gulf of Tonkin on 3 December 1967. LTV had more than met the 1963 requirement for an in-service date in 1967.

A total of 199 A-7As were built for the US Navy and delivered by the spring of 1968, and these were followed into production by an improved version designated A-7B, the first of which made its first flight on 6 February 1968. These aircraft had the more powerful 12,200-lb (5534-kg) thrust Pratt & Whitney TF30-P-8 turbofan engine, and the first of these were used operationally in Vietnam on 4 March 1969. These engines were modified later to TF30-P-408 configuration, providing 13,400-lb (6078-kg) thrust. The A-7C designation was reserved originally for a two-seat trainer version, but was used retrospectively in late 1971 for the first 67 A-7Es which were powered by the TF30-P-408 engines.

In October 1966 the USAF ordered a tactical attack version which was to be powered by a 14,250-lb (6464-kg) thrust Allison/Rolls-Royce TF41-A-1 turbofan, derived from the Spey, and this version has the designation A-7D. The first two were powered by TF30-P-8 engines, but all of the 457 aircraft built subsequently for the US Air Force had the Allison engine. The first flight with this latter engine was made on 26 September 1968 and the first production aircraft was accepted by the USAF three months later. This version had advanced avionics to provide its pilot with continuous-solution navigation, and a weapon delivery system that could ensure all-weather radar bomb delivery. Under a programme initiated in mid-1978, 383 A-7Ds are being modified to carry a Pave Penny laser target designation pod. The A-7D also introduced a 20-mm M-61 gun in the fuselage. The A-7E was a developed version for the US Navy to fulfil a light attack/close air support/interdiction role, the first 67 of which were powered by TF30-P-408 engines and which were designated subsequently A-7C. From the 68th production aircraft onward, the powerplant consisted of the 15,000-lb (6804-kg) thrust Allison/Rolls-Royce TF41-A-2 turbofan. The first flight of an A-7E was made on 25 November 1968, and this version entered

US Navy service on 14 July 1969. In early 1977 an A-7E FLIR (forward-looking infrared) version entered production, this equipment offering improved night capability.

Other versions of the A-7 Corsair II which have been designated to date include the TA-7C, a tandem two-seat trainer with operational capability, of which 60 are being converted from A-7B/C aircraft (none of which remain active); A-7H, a land-based version of the A-7E of which 60 were built for the Greek air force; TA-7H two-seat trainer for the Greek air force, to be powered by the Allison TF41-A-400 engine, of which five have been ordered for delivery in 1980; and the YA-7E Corsair II$_2$ advanced trainer of which, so far, only a prototype has been built.

During operations in south-east Asia, USAF and USN A-7s flew more than 100,000 sorties, proving that this subsonic aircraft was more than capable of holding its own against supposedly superior aircraft. It seems likely that with improved sensors and equipment it could well be around for some time to come. The Allison/Rolls-Royce TF41 has the remarkable time between overhauls of 1,500 hours.

Type: single-seat subsonic tactical fighter
Powerplant: (A-7E) one 15,000-lb (6804-kg) thrust Allison/Rolls-Royce TF41-A-2 turbofan
Performance: (A-7E) maximum speed at sea level 691 mph (1112 km/h); maximum speed at 5,000 ft (1525 m) clean 685 mph (1102 km/h); ferry range with maximum fuel 2,861 miles (4604 km).
Weights: (A-7E) empty 19,111 lb (8669 kg); maximum take-off 42,000 lb (19051 kg)

Dimensions: span 38 ft 9 in (11.81 m); length 46 ft 1½ in (14.06 m); height 16 ft 0¾ in (4.90 m); wing area 375 sq ft (34.84 m²)
Armament: a wide range of stores totalling more than 15,000 lb (6804 kg) can be carried on two fuselage stations and six underwing pylons, and these can include air-to-air and air-to-surface missiles, TV and laser-guided weapons, general purpose bombs, rockets and gun pods; a 20-mm M61A-1 Vulcan gun is mounted in the fuselage
Operators: Greece, US Air Force, US Navy

Pilots of the "SLUF" (short little ugly fella) climb aboard in a way reminiscent of scaling a cliff-face. In the stubby nose is the APQ-126 radar, with ten modes of operation, but a laser (Pave Penny) has to be hung as an external pod. Low on the left side is the M61A-1 gun (early A-7 versions had two Colt Mk 12 cannon) fed by a drum containing 1,032 rounds of 20 mm ammunition. To the rear of the nose gear is the bulge for doppler radar.

This late-model A-7D is the wing commander's aircraft from the 355th TFW at Davis-Monthan AFB, near Tucson, Arizona. Internal ALR-46(V) digital radar warning is fitted, but a jammer pod (ALQ-101) would have to displace bombs. For self-defence two early-model AIM-9B Sidewinders are carried on the fuselage pylons, high on each side. Just visible under the rear fuselage is the retracted sting hook, identical to that for carrier use.

Vought F-8 Crusader

At the beginning of the 1950s the US Navy had a requirement for an air superiority fighter with supersonic performance. Requests For Proposals resulted in eight submissions from US manufacturers in 1952, and in May 1953 Chance Vought was awarded a contract for two prototypes under the designation XF8U-1 (later XF-8A). The first exceeded Mach 1 in level flight on its initial flight on 25 March 1955. The first F-8A flew on 20 September 1955, and entered operational service with VF-32 in March 1957. A trifle less than four years from contract award to in-squadron service of a highly supersonic carrierborne fighter was no mean achievement.

The high-mounted folding wing is pivoted and can be set to either of two positive angles (these angles varying with sub-type) to keep the fuselage level at low speeds, and to improve the pilot's view. When the wing incidence is raised to its maximum, the ailerons, flaps and 'dog tooth' leading edge all droop 20° automatically.

Initial production F-8As were powered by a Pratt & Whitney J57-P-12 afterburning turbojet, but the majority had the 16,200-lb (7348-kg) afterburning J57-P-4A. Armament comprised four 20-mm cannon and two AIM-9 Sidewinder air-to-air missiles on the sides of the fuselage, plus an underfuselage pack of rockets. Production of F-8As totalled 318, and a small number of these were remanufactured in 1965–70 to extend their operational life, with the redesignation F-8M. More than 400 of different variants were treated similarly, the work involving structural reinforcement, the introduction of boundary layer control (BLC), and the provision of new landing gear and improved avionics.

Variants include the F-8B which has radar to provide limited all-weather capability. First flown on 3 September 1958, a total of 130 were built, 63 being remanufactured as the F-8L, having wing stations for weapons added at that time. The RF-8A is the reconnaissance version of the F-8A, with five cameras in place of weapons; 144 were built and 73 of these

were modified as RF-8Gs. F-8C production totalled 187, with initial deliveries on 28 January 1959. These have the 16,900-lb (7666-kg) J57-P-16, slightly reduced span, two fixed ventral fins, new radar and improved fire-control. 87 were remanufactured as F-8Ks. The 152 F-8Ds, with the 18,000-lb (8165-kg) J57-P-20, has a maximum speed approaching Mach 2. Improvements include advanced avionics, increased fuel capacity, and revised armament of four Sidewinders and no under-fuselage rockets; 138 were remanufactured as F-8Hs. Final version for the US Navy was the F-8E, with improved avionics and detail refinements. Of 286 built, 136 were remanufactured as F-8Js, with aerodynamic and avionics improvements. The F-8E (FN) for the French navy has BLC and two-stage leading-edge flaps to reduce still further the minimum flight-control speed for operation from the relatively small carriers *Clemenceau* and *Foch*. These can be armed with Matra R.530 air-to-air missiles and/or Sidewinders. When the 48th of this model was delivered in January 1965 it concluded the manufacture of new Crusaders.

Special designations have included the DF-8A for control of Regulus missiles, the QF-8A RPV conversion, the TF-8A prototype two-seat armed trainer, and the DF-8F RPV control aircraft.

Type: supersonic single-seat carrier-based fighter
Powerplant: (F-8D/E) one 18,000-lb (8165-kg) Pratt & Whitney J57-P-20 afterburning turbojet
Performance: (F-8D/E) maximum speed about Mach 1.8 or 1,188 mph (1912 km/h) at 40,000 ft (12190 m); combat radius 440 miles (708 km)
Weights: normal take-off (F-8C) 27,550 lb (12496 kg); maximum take-off (F-8E) 34,000 lb (15422 kg)
Dimensions: span (F-8A/B) 35 ft 8 in (10.87 m), (F-8C/D/E) 35 ft 2 in (10.72 m); length (all but F-8E) 54 ft 3 in (16.54 m),

(F-8E) 54 ft 6 in (16.61 m); height 15 ft 9 in (4.80 m); wing area 350 sq ft (35.52 m²)
Armament: four 20-mm Colt-Browning 20-mm cannon in nose, two Sidewinder missiles and underfuselage rocket pack, or four

Sidewinder missiles, and (F-8E) wing racks for two 2,000-lb (907-kg) bombs, or two Bullpup missiles, or 24 Zuni air-to-surface rockets
Operators: France, Philippines, US Marine Corps, US Navy

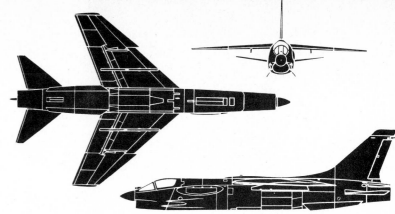

Vought F-8L Crusader

This weatherbeaten Vought F-8E Crusader, since remanufactured into an F-8J, was photographed early in the US involvement in Vietnam taking off from Da Nang AB in April 1966. The only Crusaders still in US service are a few RF-8G of the US Navy.

Westland Sea King/Commando (see also Sikorsky S61)

The Westland Sea King, of which the first example for the Royal Navy made its initial flight on 7 May 1969, is usually dismissed as a licence-built version of the Sikorsky S-61/SH-3 Sea King. This simple and unvarnished statement has not really been acceptable to Westland Helicopters from the first occasion that it was used, because considerable development work was carried out by the British company to produce an advanced antisubmarine helicopter to meet the Royal Navy's requirements. The central factor was the inclusion of a tactical compartment so that ASW operations could proceed with no assistance from a ship or other platform. In addition to its basic ASW role, this aircraft was required also to fulfil such secondary roles as cargo transport, casualty evacuation, search and rescue, and tactical troop transport. Good ferry range was considered essential.

The original HAS.1 version for the Royal Navy was developed from four imported Sikorsky SH-3D airframes. Westland's licence agreement allowed utilisation of the basic airframe and rotor system, and in addition to the installation of two Rolls-Royce Gnome turboshaft engines and specialized avionics and equipment to satisfy the Royal Navy's requirements, numerous improvements have been made to the airframe and systems during 10 years of development. Production of the Sea King was continuing in 1979, and specialized equipment includes an advanced Newmark automatic flight-control system, Plessey 195 long-range sonar, doppler navigation radar, and AW.391 search radar.

The Commando, designed for tactical transport, assault, close support and rescue operations, has a fixed tailwheel landing gear, with the sponsons of the Sea King replaced by small stub wings. The revised fuselage accomodates a flight crew of two and up to 28 troops, and can be equipped to carry a wide range of guns and missiles in a secondary air-to-surface strike role.

Sikorsky S-61A Nuri, Sikorsky-built aircraft of which 38 had been supplied to Malaysia by late 1979 for multiple military and civil duties.

27 Commando Mk 2 versions of the Sea King have been bought by the Egyptian Army.

This Commando Mk 2A is operated by the Qatar Emiri Air Force at Doha.

Type: (Commando) tactical military helicopter

Powerplant: two 1,660-shp (1238-kW) Rolls-Royce Gnome H.1400-1 turboshafts

Performance: (Commando) cruising speed at sea level 129 mph (208 km/h); range with maximum payload (28 troops), allowance for take-off and 30-minute reserves 276 miles (444 km); ferry range with maximum standard and auxiliary fuel 937 miles (1508 km)

Weights: (Commando) operating empty 12,566 lb (5700 kg); maximum take-off 21,000 lb (9525 kg)

Dimensions: (Commando) main-rotor diameter 62 ft 0 in (18.90 m); tail rotor diameter 10 ft 4 in (3.15 m); length (rotors turning) 72 ft 8 in (22.15 m); height 16 ft 10 in (5.13 m); main-rotor disc area 3,019 sq ft (280.5 m²)

Armament: (Commando) can include guns, rocket pods, missiles, and avionics to customer's requirements

Operators: (Commando) Egypt, Qatar, UK; (Sea King) Australia, Belgium, Egypt, India, Norway, Pakistan, UK, West Germany

continued

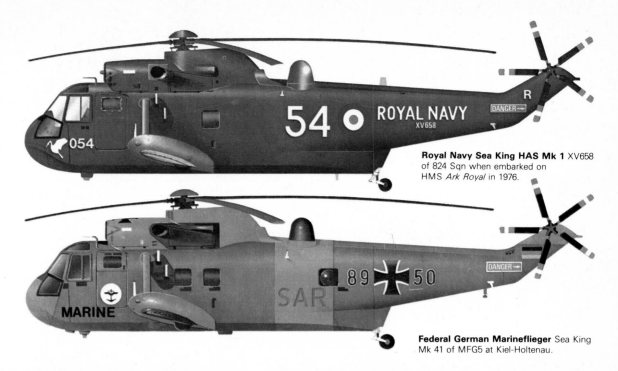

Royal Navy Sea King HAS Mk 1 XV658 of 824 Sqn when embarked on HMS *Ark Royal* in 1976.

Federal German Marineflieger Sea King Mk 41 of MFG5 at Kiel-Holtenau.

The RAF's Sea Kings have multiplied the range and mission capability of Nos 22 and 202 Sqns in the vital search and rescue role. This Sea King HAR.3 was pictured over Elgin, neighbouring community to No 202 Sqn D-Flight at Lossiemouth.

Royal Australian Navy Sea King Mk 50 of 817 Sqn, operating from HMAS *Melbourne*.

Six Sea King Mk 45s were purchased by the Pakistan Navy in 1975.

One of six Sea King Mk 47s equipping an Egyptian Navy squadron for ASW duties.

Indian Navy Sea King Mk 42 of 330 Sqn, shore-based at Cochin Naval Air Base.

1 Static dischargers
2 Fixed tailplane
3 Anti-collision beacon
4 Five-blade tail rotor
5 Tail rotor couplings
6 Hub spider
7 Tail rotor transmission shaft
8 Intermediate gearbox
9 Folding tail pylon
10 Glass-fibre access panels
11 Folding pylon attachment lock
12 Tail pylon hinges
13 Antenna loop
14 Cable/pushrod transition
15 Transmission shaft
16 Spine shaft housing
17 Fuselage "L"-section stringers
18 Fuselage frames
19 Provision for internal walkway
20 ESM (electronic surveillance measurement) housing
21 UHF aerial
22 Thermal barrier bulkhead
23 Crew/freight area
24 Door latch
25 Pull-out emergency window
26 Transmitter/receiver
27 Electronics bays (ASW recorders, amplifiers, etc)
28 Sliding door
29 AQS-13B transmitter
30 ASQ-81 MAD electronics
31 LN-66 power supply
32 IDF-7·5 digital analyser
33 Hydraulic winch motor housing

34 Door rail
35 Fire extinguishers
36 Utility reservoir
37 Generator
38 Main transmission
39 Blade root fitting
40 Rotor head mechanism
41 Rotor head cowling (damper reservoir)
42 Light-alloy blade spars
43 Cooling grilles
44 Turbine exhaust
45 Handhold
46 Tie-down lug
47 Soundproof bulkhead
48 Energy-absorbing bracing strut
49 Pull-out emergency window
50 ASW sonar operators (two)
51 Track-mounted ASW console
52 Heater
53 Fuel control computers
54 Cabin fresh-air inlet
55 General Electric T58-GE-10 turbine
56 Oil tank
57 Turbine intakes
58 Electric starter bullet

Though the transducer is not visible here the dunking sonar of this Royal Navy Sea King is probably a Plessey Type 195, which is also used by other navies.

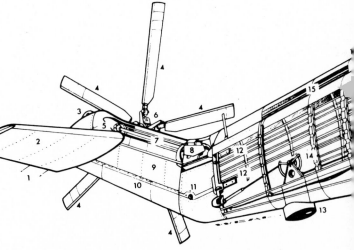

59 Pitot head
60 Intake ice deflection shield
61 Overhead console
62 Pilot's seat
63 Co-pilot's seat
64 Side console

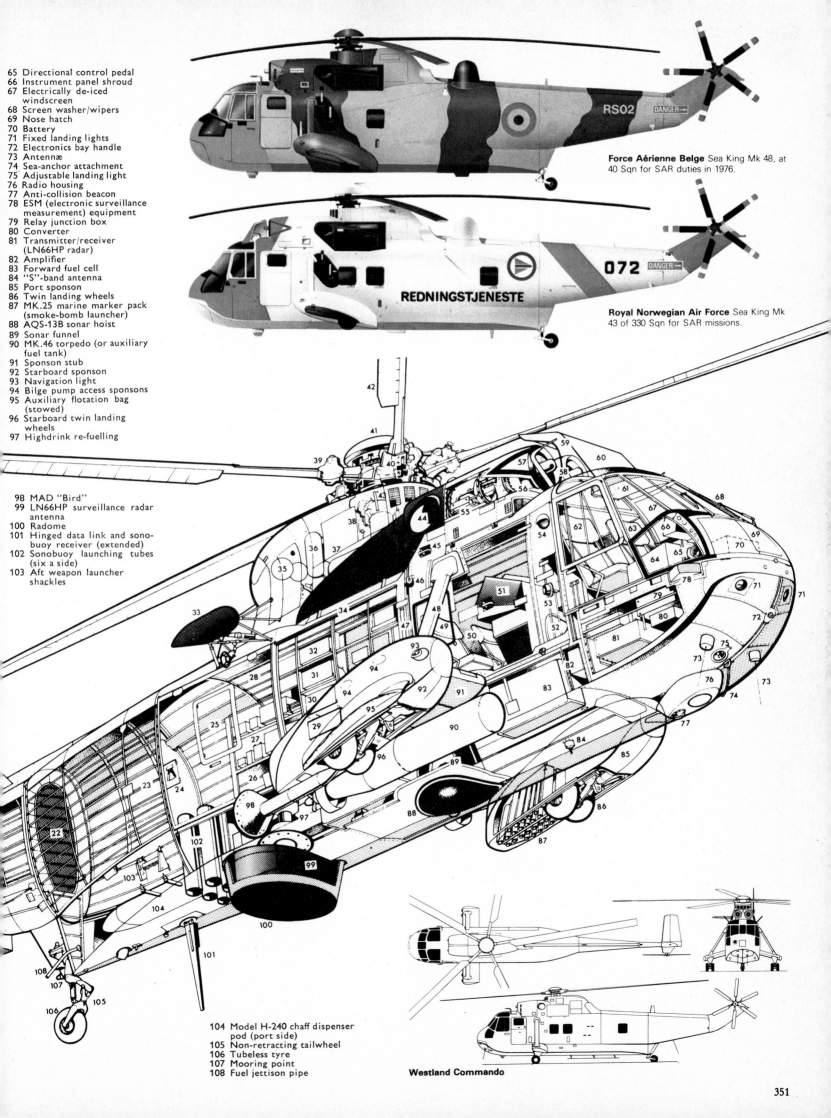

65 Directional control pedal
66 Instrument panel shroud
67 Electrically de-iced windscreen
68 Screen washer/wipers
69 Nose hatch
70 Battery
71 Fixed landing lights
72 Electronics bay handle
73 Antennæ
74 Sea-anchor attachment
75 Adjustable landing light
76 Radio housing
77 Anti-collision beacon
78 ESM (electronic surveillance measurement) equipment
79 Relay junction box
80 Converter
81 Transmitter/receiver (LN66HP radar)
82 Amplifier
83 Forward fuel cell
84 "S"-band antenna
85 Port sponson
86 Twin landing wheels
87 MK.25 marine marker pack (smoke-bomb launcher)
88 AQS-13B sonar hoist
89 Sonar funnel
90 MK.46 torpedo (or auxiliary fuel tank)
91 Sponson stub
92 Starboard sponson
93 Navigation light
94 Bilge pump access sponsons
95 Auxiliary flotation bag (stowed)
96 Starboard twin landing wheels
97 Highdrink re-fuelling

98 MAD "Bird"
99 LN66HP surveillance radar antenna
100 Radome
101 Hinged data link and sono-buoy receiver (extended)
102 Sonobuoy launching tubes (six a side)
103 Aft weapon launcher shackles

Force Aérienne Belge Sea King Mk 48, at 40 Sqn for SAR duties in 1976.

Royal Norwegian Air Force Sea King Mk 43 of 330 Sqn for SAR missions.

104 Model H-240 chaff dispenser pod (port side)
105 Non-retracting tailwheel
106 Tubeless tyre
107 Mooring point
108 Fuel jettison pipe

Westland Commando

Westland Scout

Production of this compact five/six-seat general-purpose helicopter ceased in 1970, but the type remains in service. Its main roles are liaison, casualty evacuation, air/sea rescue (although the Wasp is the truly naval variant), air-to-ground attack, reconnaissance, training and light freight work. Equipped as an air ambulance, the Scout carries two internal stretchers, and a further two can be carried on external panniers. Normal seating is for five, with three on a rear bench seat and two in the front.

Early prototypes were powered by a 325-shp (242-kW) Blackburn-Turboméca Turmo, derated from 400 shp (298 kW), but the production prototype flew with a Bristol Siddeley (now Rolls-Royce) Nimbus, which was derived from the Turmo and adopted for all subsequent examples. Originally a Saunders-Roe design, the Scout first flew on 20 July 1958, followed by the Nimbus-powered variant on 9 August 1959. The helicopter entered service with the British army in the spring of 1963, and some 120 examples are still operated by the Army Air Corps. One hundred Westland/Aérospatiale Lynx AH.1 general-purpose helicopters have supplemented and largely replaced them, and these larger, faster aircraft will carry TOW missiles for the anti-tank role. Forming part of the 400-strong Army Air Corps helicopter fleet, the Scouts have seen extensive duty in Northern Ireland on anti-terrorist duties. The AAC has put the Scout's versatility to wide use, the aircraft having filled almost every role except heavy lift: for anti-tank duty the Scout carries a roof-mounted sight and SS.11 missiles. Distinguishing features of the Scout against the maritime Wasp are a skid undercarriage and a low-set horizontal stabilizer under the tail rotor.

A number of Scouts were sold for export, including two to the Royal Australian Navy for operation from survey ships. Three went to the Jordanian air force, one for the personal use of King Hussein. The government of Uganda bought two for police work; and a further two went to the Bahrain State Police.

Type: (AH.1) five/six-seat general-purpose helicopter
Powerplant: one 685-shp (511-kW) Rolls-Royce Nimbus 102 free-turbine turboshaft
Performance: maximum design speed 132 mph (212 km/h); maximum cruising speed 122 mph (196 km/h); range (four passengers, reserves) 315 miles (510 km); maximum rate of climb 1,670 ft (510 m) per minute; vertical rate of climb at sea level 600 ft (183 m) per minute
Weights: empty equipped 3,232 lb (1465 kg); maximum 5,300 lb (2405 kg)
Dimensions: main rotor diameter 32 ft 3 in (9.83 m); length (rotors turning) 40 ft 4 in (12.29 m); fuselage length 30 ft 4 in (9.24 m); height (tail rotor turning) 11 ft 8 in (3.56 m); main-rotor disc area 816.86 sq ft (75.9 m²)
Armament: manually-controlled guns of up to 20-mm calibre; fixed GPMG or other gun installations; rocket pods or guided missiles such as SS.11 anti-tank
Operators: Australia, Bahrain, Jordan, Uganda, UK

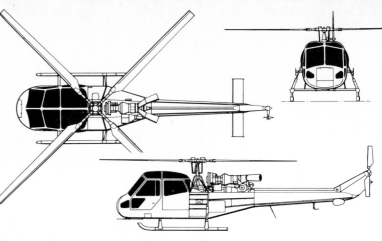

Westland Scout AH.1

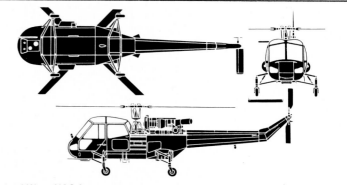

The Westland Scout AH.1, of which 120 were deployed, has been the British army's chief helicopter but is now being replaced by 100 Lynx. This Scout, XP897, has a new paint job and fin insignia, but lacks the pylons and roof sight for missiles.

Westland Wasp

The Westland Wasp general-purpose naval helicopter was developed from the Scout for the Royal Navy. It originated in a Saunders-Roe design and differs from its land-based counterpart in having totally different equipment (for the anti-submarine warfare role), a more powerful engine, folding tail, and special landing gear for deck operations. This last consists of four non-retractable, fully castoring wheels with sprag brakes and special damping. Following an evaluation of three P.531s (the designation of pre-production Scouts), the Royal Navy ordered development and production of the Wasp HAS.1 for shipboard use. The first flew on 28 October 1962, and some 60 were subsequently bought. Their main role is to operate from small platforms on board frigates and destroyers on anti-submarine missions, for which they carry two Mk 44 torpedoes. The aircraft is also used aboard an ice patrol ship for ice reconnaissance and personnel ferrying work, as well as for survey. Deliveries to the Royal Navy began in the second half of 1963, after more than 200 landings had been made in February of that year on board the frigate *Nubian*. They were conducted with the wind coming from all directions, by day and by night, in a rigorous trials programme. Standard equipment fit on the Wasp includes UHF and UHF homing radio, plus a standby set, blind-flying instrumentation, and an autostabilization system/autopilot with radio altimeter. Royal Navy aircraft were later fitted with APX Bézu M.260 gyro-stabilized periscopic weapon sights (for AS.11 or AS.12 missiles), licence-built by the Precision Products Group of BAC's Guided Weapons Division. The Wasp has a crew of two, with provision for three passengers or a stretcher across the rear of the cabin. In place of the two Mk 44 torpedoes, a variety of external stores can be carried. Well over 100 Wasps were built, some 40 for export. The South African air force operates 11 of the type. This country is the subject of an arms ban by several nations, and the country is as far as possible extending the useful lives of its current inventory to maintain an effective military posture. The 11 Wasps are deployed aboard a number of South African navy ships, serving with Maritime Command's 22 Flight in the anti-submarine-warfare and communication roles. Seventeen Wasps were ordered originally. The *Forca Aeronaval*, Brazil's naval air arm, has been a helicopter since the early 1950s, using the Westland Widgeon. This type was succeeded by two Wasps, a number augmented in 1977–78 with the delivery of a further six. They fly with a liaison and general-duties squadron alongside three Westland Whirlwind 3s and 18 Bell 206B JetRangers. The anti-submarine role will be filled by the Westland/Aérospatiale Lynx. Despite being surrounded by water, New Zealand fields a very small truly naval air arm, in the form of two Wasps. When deployed they fly from the frigates HMNZS Canterbury and Waikato, but when shore-based they are operated by No 3 Sqn at Hobsonville. (Maritime patrol work is performed by the air force's five Lockheed P-3B Orions.) After South Africa, the Netherlands' Marine *Luchtvaartdienst* is the largest export operator of the type. Designated AH-12A, 10 are still flown No 860 Sqn, although they will be replaced by the uprated Lynx after 1983.

Type: five/six-seat general-purpose helicopter
Powerplant: one 710-shp (530-kW) Rolls-Royce Nimbus 503 turboshaft
Performance: maximum design speed 126 mph (203 km/h); maximum level speed at sea level 120 mph (193 km/h); maximum cruising speed 110 mph (177 km/h); range with maximum fuel, 5 minutes for take-off and landing, and four passengers 270 miles (435 km); maximum rate of climb at sea level 1,440 ft (439 m) per minute; maximum vertical rate of climb at sea level 600 ft (183 m) per minute
Weights: empty equipped 3,452 lb (1566 kg); maximum take-off and landing 5,500 lb (2495 kg)

Westland Wasp HAS.1

Dimensions: main rotor diameter 32 ft 3 in (9.83 m); length (rotors turning) 40 ft 4 in (12.29 m); height (tail rotor turning) 11 ft 8 in (3.56 m); main rotor disc area 816.86 sq ft (75.9m²)
Armament: two Mk 44 torpedoes
Operators: Brazil, Netherlands, New Zealand, South Africa, UK

This Westland Wasp HAS.1 of the Fleet Air Arm must be draughty with both main doors wide open. It probably belongs to No 829 Sqn, which supplies the aircraft for all Royal Navy frigates. Most Wasps can carry Mk 44 or 46 torpedoes and a few have AS.11s.

Westland Wessex (see Sikorsky S-58)

Westland Whirlwind (see also Sikorsky S-55)

Westland Aircraft Ltd at Yeovil, England acquired licence-rights to build the Sikorsky S-51 in 1947, and this marked the beginning of an association with Sikorsky Aircraft which continues in 1979.

The potential of the larger Sikorsky S-55 was such that Westland lost little time in obtaining licence-rights to build military versions for the British armed forces, and for export within specified geographical areas. The prototype of Westland's Whirlwind HAR.1 (HAR = helicopter, air rescue) for the Royal Navy first flew on 15 August 1953, and initial deliveries of 10 production examples for the Fleet Air Arm began to enter service with No 705 Squadron soon after. The Royal Navy had gained experience of the type at an earlier date however, for some 25 Sikorsky HO4S-3s had been supplied to Britain under the Mutual Defense Assistance Program, to equip the Fleet Air Arm's first operational helicopter squadron (No 848) in November 1952. The initial order was followed by 10 generally similar HAR.2s for the RAF and British army, these aircraft and the ensuing HAR.3s and 4s all being powered by 600-hp (447-kW) Pratt & Whitney R-1340 Wasp engines. The HAR.5 for the Royal Navy was the first Whirlwind to be powered by a British engine (in 1955), the 775-hp (578-kW) Alvis Leonides Major 755/1, as were the RAF's HAR.6 and RN's HAS.7 (HAS = helicopter, anti-submarine). This latter aircraft was the first version to be designed for an operational combatant role, being equipped with radar and dipping sonar, and armed with a homing torpedo for deployment in an ASW capacity. Two communications versions, designated HCC.8, were the last piston-engined Whirlwinds, equipped with VIP interiors for service with The Queen's Flight.

In 1960 Westland designed the uprated Whirlwind Series 3 with turbine power, uprated transmission, increased weights and downward-sloping tail boom to increase main-rotor clearance. First of the Series 3 Whirlwinds entered service with the RAF's No 225 Squadron, at RAF Odiham, on 4 November 1961. These were powered by the Bristol Siddeley (now Rolls-Royce) Gnome, a licence-built version of the General Electric T58 turboshaft, and with this powerplant the Whirlwind gained a new lease of life. Subsequently, piston-engined Whirlwinds were returned to the factory for conversion to turbine power, Royal Navy HAS.7s becoming redesignated HAR.9s.

These Series 3 aircraft in British military service were used primarily for ambulance, rescue, or transport duties. Two HCC.12s were provided for The Queen's Flight, and a number were exported before production ended in 1968.

Type: (HAR.10) light utility helicopter
Powerplant: one 1,050-shp (783-kW) Rolls-Royce Gnome H.1000 turboshaft
Performance: maximum speed 106 mph (171 km/h); cruising speed 104 mph (167 km/h); range 300 miles (483 km)
Weights: empty equipped 4,952 lb (2246 kg); maximum take-off 8,000 lb (3629 kg)
Dimensions: main rotor diameter 53 ft 0 in (16.15 m); tail rotor diameter 8 ft 11 in (2.72 m); length (rotors turning) 62 ft 4 in (19.00

m); height 15 ft 7½ in (4.76 m); main-rotor disc area 2,026 sq ft (188.2 m²)
Armament: can include a homing torpedo or Nord AS.11 anti-tank missiles
Operators: Brazil, Brunei, Ghana, Nigeria, Qatar, UK

Westland Whirlwind HAR.10

The RAF's Westland Whirlwind HAR Mk 10s performed important rescue duties around Britain's coast until replaced by Sea Kings.

The RAF's Whirlwind HAR.10, of which this (XJ726) is a colourful example, is by far the best of all the many versions of the S-55 of 1949. Powered by a Gnome turboshaft, they have many airframe and systems improvements. This one is a trainer at Shawbury.

Westland WG.34

In early 1977 the Ministry of Defence (Navy) completed feasibility studies to decide the features of an SKR (Sea King replacement) helicopter. It was decided that such an aircraft should have very long range, the ability to operate all missions independently of surface vessels, the ability to carry sonobuoys (rather than dipping sonar) and radar/radar intercept equipment/MAD sensors, plus automated data-handling, and general payload greater than that of Westland Sea King in an overall size no larger. Westland announced the WG.34 SKR in spring 1978, and in November of that year gave further details and announced agreements with Agusta and Aéro-

spatiale, and discussions with other possible partners as well as the possibility of developing troop-carrier and other versions.

In mid-1979 the only undecided factor in the basic design was the powerplant, which will probably comprise three engines of 1,000 to 2,500 hp (746 to 1865 kW) (see below). Crew will comprise pilot, observer and acoustic operator, with room for a second pilot. The engines will have side-facing anti-iced inlets, the landing gear will be fully retractable, the weapon bays will be internal and enclosed, and the airframe will of course fit existing Sea King ship platforms. Equipment will include an advanced Ferranti Sea-

spray radar, an advanced development of the AQS-901 acoustic processor, developed Lynx ESM systems, secure voice communications, a JTIDS data link, and probably the American ASQ-81 towed MAD 'bird'. Marconi is handling the acoustic processor and displays, Decca the Doppler radar and Omega navigation and ESM, and Ferranti the radar and tactical data-processing. Westland is responsible for airframe and avionics integration.

Type: ASW and multi-role naval helicopter, with land tactical and transport versions projected
Powerplant: Prototypes, General Electric

T700; production, probably Rolls-Royce Turboméca RTM 321
Performance: range and endurance greater than those of the Sea King
Weights: design gross 24,000 lb (10886 kg); will probably climb with development
Dimensions: main rotor diameter not greater than that of the Sea King; length overall 67 ft 6 in (20.57 m); fuselage length 56 ft 9 in (17.3 m); height overall 17 ft 10 in (5.45 m)
Armament: fullest spectrum of AS weapons
Operator: under development for UK

Westland Lynx (Army)

Design leadership of the Anglo-French Lynx helicopter rests with Westland, from whose WG.13 design the Lynx is developed. It is an extremely capable and fast helicopter, and is being .produced in two basic versions: a general-purpose and utility variant for army use; and a more specialized naval version (described elsewhere). In British army service the Lynx is designated AH.1, and 100 are being delivered to replace the Army Air Corps' 120 Westland Scouts. The first production AH.1 flew on 11 February 1977. In December of that year the Lynx International Trials Unit, established to test the aircraft in the field and centred on Middle Wallop, was disbanded after successful completion of the proving programme. Army Air Corps squadrons in West Germany were the first to put the Lynx into service, each division operating one squadron of Gazelle light observation helicopters and one squadron of Lynx equipped with TOW missiles for the anti-tank role. All the Army Air Corps Lynxes will be so equipped, but they will also be tasked with general duties such as tactical troop transport, armed escort of other troop-carrying rotary-wing aircraft, search and rescue, firefighting and crash rescue, logistic support, reconnaissance, casualty evacuation and command-post work.

The origins of the Lynx stretch back to an agreement between France and the UK in February 1967, signed on 2 April 1968. Under the terms, three helicopters were developed jointly (Lynx, Puma and Gazelle). Westland is responsible for 70% of the Lynx and Aérospatiale for 30%. The first of 13 prototypes flew on 21 March 1971, and in June the following year the fifth aircraft set a speed record over a 25-km (15.5-mile) course also 199.9 mph (321.7 km/h). The helicopter also demonstrated a rate of roll in excess of 100° per second, dived at 230 mph (370 km/h) and flew backwards at 80 mph (130 km/h), all testimony to its outstanding flight performance.

A promising start to exports augurs well for a long and numerous production run. Under a £50 million order announced in January 1978, Egypt and other Arab countries will eventually be flying at least 250 Lynx helicopters, having built most of them under licence. The first 20 are being constructed in the UK, before knocked-down components for a further batch are shipped out for local assembly. Self-sufficiency in manufacturing is envisaged eventually, and the agreement also covers Rolls-Royce Gem engines. The figure of £50 million is likely to cover the costs of tooling.

A great variety of stores and equipment is available, according to role. For search and rescue this can include a waterproof floor, eight 4-in (100-mm) flares and an electric hoist clipped on to the starboard side of the cabin and capable of lifting up to 600 lb (272 kg). On offensive missions such as anti-tank or air-to-surface strike, armament can include a cannon with 1,500 rounds or, mounted in or out of the cabin, a 7.62-mm (0.3-in) Minigun with up to 3,000 rounds. A pylon on each side of the cabin can carry two Miniguns or thirty-six 68-mm (2.68-in) rockets in two launchers. A variety of air-to-surface missiles can be hung on the pylons, such as six Hawkswing or AS.11, or eight HOT or TOW. Up to eight more missiles can be stowed in the cabin for rearming. Detection and guidance is performed with an Avimo-Ferranti 530 stabilized, lightweight sight. If not actually destroying tanks itself, the Lynx can deploy a three-man team complete with anti-tank missiles and associated equipment. For night-time opera-

Westland Lynx AH.1 (Army)

tions low-light TV and infra-red linescan can be carried, as well as searchlights. As in all Lynx versions, all-weather flight and navigation is largely automatic: with automatically controlled twin-engine safety, this maximizes safety and minimizes pilot work-load.

Type: twin-engined multi-purpose helicopter
Powerplant: two 750-shp (560-kW) or 900-shp (671-kW) contingency rating Rolls-Royce BS.360-07-26 Gem turboshafts (uprated versions 1,050 shp/783 kW, later 1,200 shp/895 kW)
Performance: maximum cruising speed 175 mph (282 km/h); maximum endurance speed 81 mph (130 km/h); radius of action, out and return at maximum cruising speed, maximum hover weight 9,500 lb (4309 kg), take-off and landing allowances, 15-minute loiter in search area, 2-minute hover for each of eight survivors, 20-minute loiter at end of mission 154 miles (248 km); maximum forward rate of climb 2,180 ft (664 m) per minute; vertical rate of climb 1,235 ft (376 m) per minute
Weights: empty equipped (troop transport) 6,144 lb (2787 kg); empty equipped (anti-tank strike) 6,772 lb (3072 kg); empty equipped (search and rescue) 6,532 lb (2963 kg); normal take-off 9,500 lb (4309 kg); maximum take-off 10,500 lb (4763 kg)
Dimensions: rotor diameter 42 ft 0 in (12.8 m); length (rotors turning) 49 ft 9 in (15.16 m); height (tail rotor turning) 12 ft 0 in (3.66 m); main rotor disc area 1,385 sq ft (128.7 m²)
Armament: one 20-mm AME 621 cannon (1,500 rounds); 3,000-round Minigun; each external pylon on each side of cabin can take two Miniguns or other self-contained gun pod, thirty-six 68-mm (2.68-in) or fourteen 2.75-in (69.8-mm) rockets, or up to six BAe Hawkswing or Aérospatiale AS.11 or eight Euromissile HOT or Hughes TOW air-to-surface missiles (see text for more details)
Operators: Egypt, UK, Germany, Belgium.

This Westland Lynx AH.1 was photographed during type conversion training with the Lynx Intensive Flying Trials Unit at Middle Wallop. This unit has since disbanded, and Lynx are building up in strength in Germany, with HOT missile sights and pylons.

Westland Lynx (Navy)

A shipborne version of the land-warfare Lynx AH.1, the naval Westland/Aérospatiale Lynx has been ordered by the navies of eight countries. In Royal Navy service the aircraft is designated HAS.2 and is tasked with advanced shipborne anti-submarine duties and other specialised missions. A total of 88 are on order by the British service. In September 1976 the Royal Navy and the Royal Netherlands Navy formed a joint Lynx Intensive Flying Trials Unit, No 700L Naval Air Squadron, at Yeovilton in Somerset. Formed to prove the aircraft operationally, the unit put the Lynx through a rigorous programme which included deck handling trials on board HMS Birmingham, operating from Portland. From the outset, the naval Lynx has been designed to operate in all conditions of sea and weather. To this effect, a different landing gear is fitted. Wheels replace skids, and for retrieval in the roughest seas the main wheels are toed out by 27°, the nose wheels can be castored through 90°, and a harpoon deck-lock system is available as an option. This last aid means that the helicopter is secured the moment contact is made, and allows landings on small decks in otherwise impossible conditions. In the anti-submarine-warfare role, equipment includes two Mk 44 or Mk 46 homing torpedoes mounted externally on single pylons beside the cabin, and six marine marking devices. Alternatively, two Mk 11 depth charges can be carried. The Lynx can attack submarines in two ways: either the parent ship is tasked with detection when only retractable classification equipment is carried on the Lynx, or the helicopter can operate independently with an Alcatel DUAV.4 lightweight dunking sonar, maintaining stability in the hover with the help of an automatic flight-control system. In rough seas and conditions of poor visibility, surface vessels can be sought out and tracked by the lightweight Ferranti Seaspray radar, designed for overwater use. Once identified, surface craft are attacked by four British Aerospace Sea Skua semi-active homing missiles or, until these are available, by up to four AS.12

missiles launched with the aid of a stabilized optical sight. Although specialised for anti-submarine duties, the naval Lynx can be put to work on many of the general-purpose version's tasks. On search and rescue missions up to nine survivors can be winched aboard.

The first Royal Navy Lynx squadron, No 702, was commissioned in January 1978. First ship to be supplied by this unit is HMS Birmingham, and 'Leander' class and Type 42 vessels will be similarly equipped. French naval Lynx helicopters, designated Lynx 2 (FN), are broadly similar to the Royal Navy aircraft but are fitted with different detection equipment, including the OMERA Herculès radar. Twenty-six have been ordered to replace anti-submarine Sikorsky HSS-1s and Aérospatiale Alouette IIIs. Deliveries began in 1978. Brazil's Forca Aeronaval operates nine naval Lynx from six 'Niteroi' class destroyers, and Argentina has ordered three for operation from frigates in the anti-submarine role. Three were delivered to Qatar in 1978 to meet an order placed in 1976. Seven aircraft have been ordered by the Danish navy. Based on frigates and ashore, they will be used for reconnaissance and fishery protection in Greenland, the Faroes and the North Sea. Norway has four on order. Apart from the UK and France, the Netherlands is the largest operator of the type yet, with 24 on order. De Kooy-based No 7 Sqn was the first unit to receive the type, which is designated UH-14A or SH-14B in Marine Luchtvaartdienst service. No 7 Sqn's first six UH-14As replace Agusta-Bell 204s in the search-and-rescue, VIP and ship-to-shore communication roles. The SH-14B, a more powerful anti-submarine version with dunking sonar, will equip frigates. Eight SH-14Cs ordered in January 1978 will be fitted with magnetic-anomaly detection (MAD) gear. A repeat order for a further 12 aircraft is expected to fill the gap left by retiring 10 Westland Wasps in 1983.

Type: twin-engined multi-purpose helicopter
Powerplant: two 750-shp (560-kW) or

The Westland Lynx HAS.2 will soon be the most important helicopter in the navies of NATO, perfectly suited to all-weather multi-role duties on surface vessels. This Lynx, armed with Mk 46 torpedoes, is about to leave HMS Birmingham in a gale.

900-shp (671-kW) maximum contingency (uprated aircraft 1,050-shp/783-kW) Rolls-Royce BS.360-07-26 Gem turboshafts
Performance: maximum cruising speed 167 mph (269 km/h); maximum cruising speed (single-engine) 130 mph (209 km/h); radius of action, out and return at maximum cruising speed, crew of three, maximum hover weight 9,500 lb (4309 kg), take-off and landing allowances, 15-minute loiter in search area, 2-minute hover for each of two survivors, reserves for 20-minute loiter at end of mission 157 miles (253 km); maximum forward rate of climb 2,020 ft (616 m) per minute; maximum vertical rate of climb 1,235 ft (376 m) per minute
Weights: empty equipped (anti-submarine

strike) 6,836 lb (3101 kg); empty equipped (reconnaissance) 6,794 lb (3082 kg); empty equipped (dunking-sonar search and strike) 7,515 lb (3409 kg); take-off (normal) 9,500 lb (4309 kg); take-off (maximum) 10,500 lb (4763 kg)
Dimensions: main rotor diameter 42 ft 0 in (12.8 m); length (rotors turning) 49 ft 9 in (15.16 m); height (tail rotor turning) 11 ft 9¾ in (36 m); main rotor disc area 1,385 sq ft (128.7 m²)
Armament: two Mk 44 or Mk 46 torpedoes; or two Mk 11 depth charges; dunking sonar; Sea Skua or AS.12 air-to-surface missiles (see text for more details)
Operators: UK, Argentina, Brazil, Denmark, Egypt, France, Netherlands, Norway, Qatar

Unquestionably the most important new multi-role military helicopter, already adopted by 13 countries, the Westland-Aerospatiale Lynx is seen here in its naval version with wheel landing gear, nose radar and extensive mission equipment. This is a Lynx HAS.2 of Royal Navy 702 Sqn, probably over the fantail pad of HMS Sheffield.

Yakovlev Yak-11 Moose

Although phased out by the Soviet Union and the more advanced Warsaw Pact forces, the Yakovlev Yak-11 'Moose' continues in service with some users. Designed as an advanced combat trainer, the Yak-11 is the last offshoot of the long line of Yakovlev fighters of the 1939–45 war; the wing platform, and the basic construction of the all-metal wing and metal-and-fabric covered fuselage are similar to the later Yak fighters.

The Yak-11 was flown in 1946 and entered service in the following year. Production in the Soviet Union totalled 3,850 aircraft, and the type was the first aircraft used by the expanding satellite air forces in the 1950s. In 1954 it was put into production in Czechoslovakia, as the C-11, and among the 707 examples of the type produced in Czechoslovakia were a number of C-11Us, a modified version of the type with a nosewheel landing gear and mainwheels mounted farther aft. The C-11U offered handling characteristics more representative of contemporary combat aircraft than the tailwheel version, but was heavier and of slightly lower performance.

Replacement of the Yak-11 in the basic trainer role started in 1963, but the type fulfilled a useful role as a transitional aircraft between the basic trainers of the time and the MiG-15UTI.

Type: two-seat advanced trainer
Powerplant: one 570-hp (425-kW) Shvetsov ASh-21 seven-cylinder radial piston engine
Performance: maximum speed at sea level 263 mph (424 km/h); maximum speed at 7,380 ft (2250 m) 285 mph (460 km/h); ceiling 23,290 ft (7100 m); range 800 miles (1290 km)
Weights: empty 4,190 lb (1900 kg); normal take-off 5,290 lb (2400 kg)
Dimensions: span 30 ft 10 in (9.4 m); length 27 ft 11 in (8.5 m); height 10 ft 9 in (3.28 m); wing area 165.6 sq ft (15.4 m)
Armament: one 12.7-mm UBS machine-gun and two 110-lb (50-kg) practice bombs
Operators: Albania, Austria, Afghanistan, Bulgaria, China, Czechoslovakia, Egypt, Hungary, Poland, Romania, Syria, USSR, Yemen

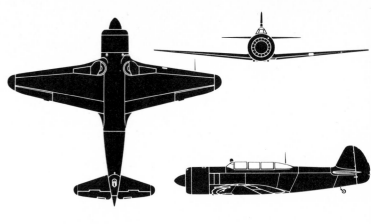

Yakovlev Yak-11 Moose

Yakovlev Yak-18 Max

The Yakovlev Yak-18 'Max' basic trainer has shown extraordinary longevity; itself a development of a pre-war design, the UT-2, it remained under active development into the 1970s and its probable replacement, the Yak-52, bears a close resemblance to its predecessor. The original Yak-18 flew in 1946, with the tailwheel undercarriage of its predecessor and the same 'helmet-type' cowling over the five cylinder M-11FR radial engine. The tricycle undercarriage of later versions was introduced on the Yak-18U of 1954, but the main production version was the Yak-18A, introduced in 1957, which added a more aerodynamically efficient NACA-type cowling and the much more powerful AI-14 engine. The aircraft is of metal construction with fabric covering, in typical Yakovlev style.

The first single-seat version of the Yak-18 was an unsuccessful prototype of 1946, but the concept was revived in 1959 with the first Yak-18P aerobatic aircraft. The prototype Yak-18P had the single cockpit in the aft position, while the initial production aircraft had a forward-set cockpit. The pilot was moved aft

of the wing again in the Yak-18PM of 1965, which was strengthened to accept aerodynamic loadings of plus 9g to minus 6g, and it was this aircraft which started the run of Soviet success in international aerobatics. The Yak-18PS of 1970 reverted to the tailwheel landing gear of the first aircraft, to save weight and led to the development of the Yak-50.

The latest version of the Yak-18 is the four-seat Yak-18T, first seen in 1967 and recently reported to be entering service with the Soviet Union's state flying clubs. The wing span is increased by the installation of a wider centre-section, and a new cabin-type fuselage is fitted. The inwards-retracting landing gear is basically similar to that of the Yak-18PM. About 6,700 Yak-18 trainers have been built, and the Yak-18T is still in production.

Type: (Yak-18A) two-seat basic trainer; (Yak-18PM) single-seat aerobatic aircraft; (Yak-18T) four-seat liaison and training aircraft (specification for Yak-18A).
Powerplant: one 260-hp (194-kW) Ivchenko AI-14R nine-cylinder radial piston engine

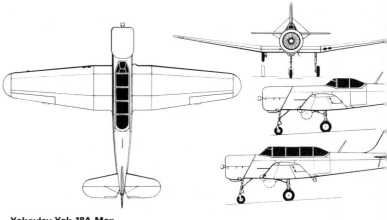

Yakovlev Yak-18A Max

Performance: maximum speed at sea level 163 mph (263 km/h); ceiling 16,600 ft (5060 m); range 440 miles (710 km)
Weights: empty 2,238 lb (1025 kg); normal take-off 2,900 lb (1316 kg); fuel load 210 lb (95 kg)

Dimensions: span 34 ft 9½ in (10.6 m); length 27 ft 5 in (8.354 m); wing area 182.9 sq ft (17m²)
Operators: China, Czechoslovakia, East Germany, Egypt, Hungary, North Korea, Poland, Rumania, USSR

Yakovlev Yak-25 RD Mandrake/Yak-27 Mangrove

The original Yakovlev Yak-25 'Flashlight', flown in 1953, was a twin-engined tandem-seat night and all-weather interceptor, armed with cannon and later modified to carry air-to-air missiles. It had swept wings mounted in the mid position, and bicycle landing gear with small wing-tip outriggers. From this stemmed a prolific range of later tactical aircraft, many of which are still in service. Closest to the original, and possily even rebuilds of Yak-25s, are the Yak-25RD 'Mandrake' long-range reconnaissance platforms, with a mid-high wing without sweep and having span increased from 36 ft (11 m) to just twice as much. Roughly in the class of the long-span Martin B-57 high-altitude platforms, this extremely high-flying machine was usually operated as a single-seater. In the 1970s surviving examples were being converted into radio-controlled targets and RPVs for electronic warfare.

The Yak-26 introduced a wing of greater strength, area and sweepback than the original, with many other changes, and was usually seen with a glazed nose and three seats. The -27 was a diverse family with the same wing but afterburning Tumansky RD-9B engines each rated at 8,820 lb (4000 kg). Most sub-types had a glazed nose and were reconnaissance platforms (NATO name 'Mangrove') though the -27P was a tandem-seat night fighter ('Flashlight-C'). Con-

siderable numbers were built, and though all are thought to have been withdrawn from first-line service the majority appear still to be operational in second-line duties such as advanced trainers, trials platforms, engine test-beds, target tugs and as RPVs of various kinds. Recent photographs also suggest that some Yak-27s are active in the EW (electronic-warfare) role, with additional fuselage-mounted avionic installations.

Type: various (see text)
Powerplant: (27) two 8,820-lb (4000-kg) Tumansky RD-9B afterburning turbojets
Performance: maximum speed at altitude 686 mph (1104 km/h) (-25RD much slower); range very varied, but usually about 1,675 miles (2700 km)
Weights: (typical -27R) empty about 17,640 lb (8000 kg); maximum loaded 24,000 lb (10900 kg)
Dimensions: (-27R) span 38 ft 6 in (11.75 m); length 55 ft 0 in (16.75 m); height 14 ft 6 in (4.4 m)
Armament: today, none
Operators: USSR and possibly other Warsaw Pact air forces

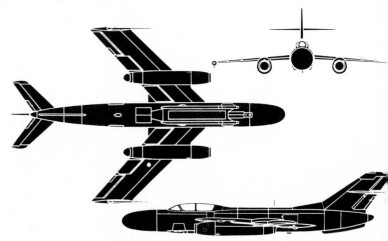

Yakovlev Yak-25 RD Mandrake

Yakovlev Yak-28 Firebar/Brewer/Maestro

Alexander Yakovlev's Yak-28 family of combat aircraft, similar in concept and performance to the French Sud-Ouest Vautour series, continues to fill an important role in the Soviet air arm, although the numbers in service are declining. The last to be retired will be the 'Brewer-E' ECM aircraft, with some Yak-28P 'Firebar-Es' carrying on in less strategically-important areas of the Soviet periphery.

The current Yak-28s are direct descendants of the original Yak-25, developed from 1950 as the Soviet Union's first all-weather jet fighter. The layout of the Yak-25, with engines under the swept wings, was conventional and followed wartime German studies; it was one of the first aircraft to feature a 'zero-track bicycle' undercarriage, with a single twin-wheel main unit on the centre of gravity and single nose and outrigger wheels. Like the Mikoyan-Gurevich MiG-19, the Yak-25 was initially powered by Mikulin AM-5 engines, but most aircraft were fitted with the Tumansky RD-9. Developments of the Yak-25 included the Yak-25RD 'Mandrake', Yak-26 and Yak-27 'Mangrove'.

The Yak-28 series bears little relationship to these earlier aircraft, beyond a general similarity in configurations. Initially, the Yak-28 seems to have been developed as a transonic all-weather fighter using two of the Tumansky R-11 turbojets developed for the MiG-21. The Yak-28's wing is more sharply swept than that of its predecessors and is raised from the mid to the shoulder position. The landing gear has a true bicycle layout, leaving space for a large weapons bay between the main units. On the Yak-28P interceptor this space is used for fuel; the strike version carries stores in the internal bay, and drop tanks on underwing stations.

Deliveries of the Yak-28P 'Firebar' started in 1962, and the type is still widely used by the PVO air-defence force. It offers considerably better endurance than the Sukhoi Su-15, which has similar engines but is lighter and much faster. Later Yak-28Ps, seen from 1967, have sharper and much longer nose radomes and provision for AA-2 'Atoll' short-range missiles on additional underwing pylons.

Developed in parallel with the Yak-28P was a glazed-nose strike version with a second crew member seated ahead of the pilot and a bombing-navigation radar aft of the nose landing gear. Originally codenamed 'Firebar' by NATO, the type was re-christened 'Brassard' when its bomber role became obvious, and the reporting name was then changed to 'Brewer'

to avoid confusion with the French Holste Broussard. Because the designations 'Firebar-A' and 'Firebar-B' has already been allotted, the 'Brewer' series appears to have started as 'Brewer-C'.

The 'Brewer-C' was used as a replacement for the Ilyushin Il-28 in Soviet Frontal Aviation strike units, but was not supplied to any aligned nations. The presence of an internal weapons bay strongly suggests that its primary role was tactical nuclear strike; the small cross-section of the fuselage limits the load that can be carried internally, but the internal bay may have been necessary for the environmental control and arming of a nuclear weapon. The Soviet Union's reluctance to supply the aircraft to its allies is understandable if it is seen as basically a nuclear system. The closest Western equivalent was probably the early BAe (HS) Buccaneer S.1. The type is probably now used mainly in the 'Brewer-D' reconnaissance and 'Brewer-E' ECM versions, many 'Brewer-Cs' having been converted to this configuration. The 'Brewer-E' appears to carry active jamming equipment in the weapons bay for the support of strike formations. The other operational version of the Yak-28 series is the Yak-28U 'Maestro' conversion trainer, which like many Soviet trainers has separate cockpits for instructor and pupil.

Type: Yak-28 'Brewer-C' strike; 'Brewer-D' reconnaissance; 'Brewer-E' electronic countermeasures (ECM); Yak-28P 'Firebar-8' all-weather interceptor; Yak-28U 'Maestro' two-seat conversion trainer
Powerplant: two 13,000-lb (6000-kg) Tumansky R-11 afterburning turbojets
Performance: maximum speed at medium altitude 750 mph (1200 km/h) or Mach 1.13; maximum speed at sea level Mach 0.85; service ceiling 55,000 ft (17000 m)
Weights: empty 30,000 lb (13600 kg); maximum loaded 45,000-50,000 lb (20000-22000 kg)
Dimensions: span 42 ft 6 in (12.95 m); length (except late 'Firebar') 71 ft (21.65 m); length (late 'Firebar') 76 ft (23.17 m); height 13 ft (3.95 m)
Armament: ('Brewer-C') one 30-mm NR-30 cannon plus underwing bombs or rocket pods and 4,500 lb (2000 kg) of internal stores; ('Firebar C') two AA-3 'Anab' air-to-air missiles and, on some aircraft, two AA-2 'Atoll' air-to-air missiles
Operators: USSR

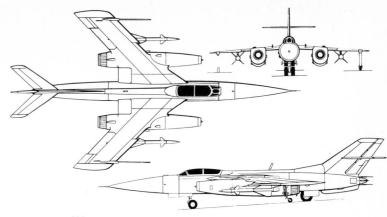

Yakovlev Yak-28P

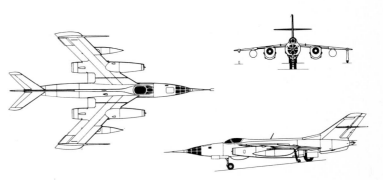

Yakovlev Yak-28 Brewer C

Several Soviet commands, including Frontal Aviation and the 16th Air Army in Germany, use the Yak-28 'Brewer-D' multi-sensor reconnaissance aircraft, which retains a radar.

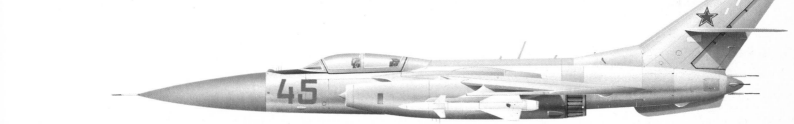

Soviet Air Force Yakovlev Yak-28P Firebar two-seat interceptor of the IAP-VO Strany. The type is now obsolete and is being phased out of use.

Contrasting stripes adorn the 'Anab' air-to-air missiles (possibly inert training rounds) carried by the Yak-28P all-weather interceptor, of which a small number are still in service with the Soviet air defence of the homeland (PVO). This excellent photograph was taken in East Germany and probably shows an aircraft on temporary detachment.

Yakovlev Yak-36 Forger

In the late 1960s US reconnaissance satellites revealed that the Nikolayev shipyards on the Black Sea were starting construction of a warship far bigger than the 'Moskva' class ASW helicopter cruisers. As work progressed, it became clear that the new ship was to be a compound of missile cruiser and aircraft-carrier, with an open angled flight-deck over more than half its length. The new ship, *Kiev*, the first of its class, was obviously designed to carry V/STOL aircraft as well as helicopters, and Western observers waited with interest for the *Kiev*'s first voyage in international waters.

Some indication of progress in V/STOL technology in the Soviet Union had already been given. In the late 1950s, a group of Soviet engineers flew a VTOL test rig called the Turbolet, a simple wingless machine intended, like the similar Rolls-Royce Flying Bedstead, to explore the problems of zero-airspeed reaction control systems. Some years later, the Kolesov engine bureau began to study the design of specialized lift engines.

The Yakovlev bureau became involved in the study of V/STOL airframes, and two examples of a small research aircraft of Yakovlev design were demonstrated at the Domodedovo air display in 1967. Codenamed 'Freehand' by NATO, the type appeared to be crude in comparison with Western designs; the third-generation BAe Harrier was at that time undergoing flight tests before entering RAF service, while the 'Freehand' appeared little more advanced than the Bell X-14 of 1957. The basic layout was awkward, with two engines in the forward fuselage feeding rear

vectoring nozzles, and the type clearly had little space for operational equipment. At the same time, a number of conventional aircraft fitted with lift-jets were demonstrated, showing that considerable progress had been made in this area. One of the 'Freehand' prototypes was reported to be used for sea trials aboard *Moskva*.

A considerable number of V/STOL prototypes appears to have been tested in the Soviet Union before the Yakolev Yak-36 'Forger' design was selected for large-scale evaluation. The configuration is unique, with only two rear vectoring nozzles on the lift-cruise engine and two lift jets forward, and imposes some basic limitations on the design. The most important is that the Yak-36 is apparently unable to make a short take-off. The short take-off is the standard operating mode for the Harrier, and permits substantial increase in payload: the aircraft rolls forward with nozzles aft for 200 ft (60 m), the nozzles are rotated partially down and the aircraft lifts off with a combination of wing and engine lift (with the 'ski jump' ramp the gains are even greater). The Yak-36 cannot emulate this performance because the thrust of its lift jets has to be balanced by full vectoring of the rear nozzles, and is limited to what can be achieved with a vertical lift-off. Other drawbacks of the layout include a far higher risk of engine failure (more than tripled, because the lift engines are started twice as often as the cruise engine), which will usually result in loss of the aircraft. Neither can the Yak-36 take advantage of an incidental benefit of the Harrier's V/STOL technique: the ability to use vec-

tored thrust for air combat (Viffing).

Theoretical advantages of the 'Forger' layout include a cruise-matched main engine, but the improvement in efficiency is at least partly offset by the higher fuel consumption in transition. The 'Forger' is, however, notably stable in transition, and the smoothness of operational approaches to *Kiev* has led to speculation about precision ship-guidance. Other details include large cushion-augmentation strakes under the fuselage.

When *Kiev* sailed into the Mediterranean in the summer of 1976, details of the Yak-36 became quickly apparent. She carried a small trials unit of about 12 Yak-36s, including two or three 'Forger-B' trainers with an ungainly lengthened forward fuselage and a balancing 'stretch' aft. The 'Forger-A' single-seaters were apparently pre-production aircraft, some being equipped with blow-in doors around the inlets and others lacking them. At the time of writing it appears that the aircraft embarked on *Minsk*, the second of the 'Kiev' class ships, are not greatly different from the *Kiev*'s aircraft; *Minsk* made her maiden voyage into the Mediterranean in early 1979.

The avionic systems carried by the Yak-36 limit them to a clear-weather role; the only weapon-aiming system is apparently a small ranging radar in the extreme nose. Although the aircraft on *Kiev* carry AA-8 'Aphid' missiles and gun pods, the unit seems to be concerned mainly with operational trials of VTOL operating techniques and control systems.

When a more effective version of the Yak-36, or a replacement for it, will appear is

hard to tell. *Komsomlec,* the third of the 'Kiev' class ships, was launched in early 1979, and fourth is under construction. In the absence of any consensus on what these ships are intended to do, it is difficult to define the role of the Yak-36. If it is intended for point air defence against, for example, Harpoon-carrying Lockheed P-3s, its present performance may be adequate and the main modification needed would be the addition of air-to-air radar; if it is regarded as a multi-role aircraft in the class of the BAe Sea Harrier, however, it will probably be necessary greatly to increase its payload and offensive capability. However, the Soviet Union may prefer to develop a completely new aircraft which can exploit the angled flight decks of the 'Kiev' class by means of a rolling take-off.

Type: light VTOL shipboard strike fighter
Powerplant: one 16,500-lb (7500-kg) class lift/cruise engine (possibly a relative of the Tumansky R-27/R-29 series) and two 5,500-lb (2500-kg) Kolesov lift jets
Performance: maximum speed at 36,000 ft (11000 m) 800 mph (1280 km/h) or Mach 1.2; maximum speed at sea level 650 mph (1050 km/h) or Mach 0.85; service ceiling 46,000 ft (14000 m); combat radius 150 miles (250 km)
Dimensions: span 23 ft (7.0 m); length 49 ft 2 in (15.0 m); height 10 ft 6 in (3.2 m); wing area 170 sq ft (15.8 m²)
Armament: four external pylons for up to 2,200 lb (1000 kg) of stores, including AA-8 'Aphid' air-to-air missiles and gun pods
Operator: USSR

Clearly an interim type, the Yak-36, called 'Forger-A' in this single-seat version, is deployed aboard the first two large multi-role carriers of the Kuril class, and is expected on the remaining two ships. It cannot make a STOL takeoff, though as a training and indoctrination machine it is useful.

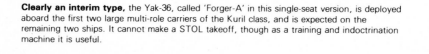

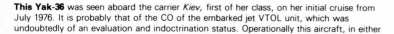

This Yak-36 was seen aboard the carrier *Kiev*, first of her class, on her initial cruise from July 1976. It is probably that of the CO of the embarked jet VTOL unit, which was undoubtedly of an evaluation and indoctrination status. Operationally this aircraft, in either single-seat or dual form, is limited in roles, though it can carry gun pods, rockets and short-range air-to-air missiles.

Yakovlev Yak-40 Codling

The Yakovlev Yak-40 'Codling' has been one of the Soviet Union's most successful commercial aircraft, and as the only small jet transport to emerge in the Soviet Union it fulfils a minor role as a VIP and government transport.

The design of the Yak-40 was started in 1964 to meet an Aeroflot requirement for a modern replacement for the unpressurized, piston-engined Lisunov Li-2, Ilyushin Il-12 and Il-14. For its first transport design, the Yakovlev bureau chose the unusual combination of jet engines and an unswept wing, the aircraft being optimised for good STOL airfield performance rather than speed. Location of the three engines at the rear of the fuselage, close to the centreline, also minimizes engine-out problems and makes the aircraft reasonably easy to fly. Manual controls are employed, and the aircraft has been designed with regard to ease of servicing at primitive fields. The high-aspect-ratio wing is fitted with simple Fowler-type flaps.

The first Yak-40 was flown in October 1966, and by September 1968 the first version was in service with Aeroflot. Later aircraft had

greater payload and passenger capacity than the initial versions, and CSA took delivery of a convertible passenger/freight version of the aircraft. Considerable efforts have been made to export the Yak-40 to the West, and three aircraft of the type are operational in Italy. However, efforts to certificate the type in the UK and Canada have not been successful.

The last of Aeroflots order for more than 800 Yak-40s was delivered in 1978, and in that year it was proposed that the tooling for airframe production should be transferred to the USA. A newly formed company, ICX Aviation, planned to start production of an Americanised Yak-40 in Ohio, with US engines and systems. Deliveries of the new version, called the X-Avia, are expected to begin in 1981 – 82.

Type: light 32-seat transport or VIP/communications aircraft
Powerplant: three 3,300 lb (1500 kg) Ivchenko AI-25 turbofans
Performance: maximum speed 345 mph (560 km/h) at 24,000 ft (7320 m); long-range cruising speed 290 mph (470 km/h); range

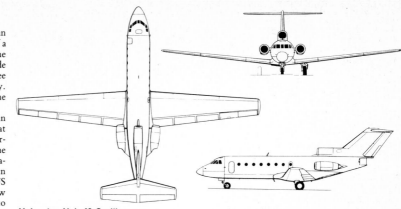

Yakovlev Yak-40 Codling

with 3,750 lb (1700 kg) payload or 19 passengers 1,300 miles (2100 km); range with 30 passengers 900 miles (1450 km); take-off field length at sea level 3,540 ft (1076 m); landing field length 3,100 ft (945 m)
Weights: empty 22,630 lb (10263 kg); maximum take-off 35,280 lb (16000 kg); max-

imum landing 32,410 lb (14700 kg)
Dimensions: span 82 ft (25 m); length 66 ft 9 in (20.3 m); height 21 ft 4 in (6.5 m); wing area 753 sq ft (70 m²)
Operators: (airlines) Aeroflot, Avioligure, Balkan, Bulgarian, CSA, Vietnam; (governments) Poland, probably USSR

Yakovlev Yak-50/52

Whereas the Yak-18P series of aerobatic aircraft was developed from the original trainer, the Yakovlev Yak-52 trainer is a development of the Yak-50 aerobatic type. The Yak-52 may be adopted by many Eastern bloc air forces as a replacement for the Yak-18.

Designed by Sergei Yakovlev and Y. Yankevitch to succeed the Yak-18PM and Yak-18PS, the Yak-50 first competed at the 1976 world aerobatic championships Kiev. Design objectives included better manoeuvrability and inverted-flight characteristics than the Yak-18 series. As the new aircraft was designed to be a single-seater, it could be slightly smaller and

lighter than the Yak-18; combined with a more powerful, fan-cooled version of the Yak-18's Ivchenko engine, this would markedly increase the power/weight ratio of the aircraft. Like the Yak-18PS, the Yak-50 has a rearwards-retracting tailwheel landing gear, although drawings of a version with a fixed, spatted gear have been published. The Yak-50 has a symmetrical aerofoil, for good inverted handling, and a variable-incidence tailplane.

The two-seat Yak-52 appeared in 1977. It is closely similar to the Yak-50 except in its undercarriage layout: the Yak-52 features a very basic semi-retractable tricycle gear, the

wheels being completely exposed even when the legs are folded. The type is heavier and less agile than the single seater, and is stressed to lower 'g' levels (7g positive and 5g negative), compared with 9g positive and 6g negative for the Yak-50).

The Yak-52 is being adopted by the DOSSAF, the network of state-run flying clubs in the Soviet Union which provides basic training for Soviet air force recruits and refresher training for reservists.

Type: (Yak-50) single-seat aerobatic aircraft; (Yak-52) two-seat trainer (specification for Yak-52)

Powerplant: one 360-hp (269-kW) Ivchenko/Vedeenev M-14P nine-cylinder radial engine.
Performance: maximum speed in level flight 175 mph (285 km/h); permissible diving speed 225 mph (360 km/h); ceiling 19,700 ft (6000 m); range 340 miles (550 km)
Weights: empty 2,200 lb (1000 kg); normal take-off 2,845 lb (1290 kg)
Dimensions: span 31 ft 2 in (9.5 m); length 25 ft 2 in (7.676 m); wing area 161.3 sq ft (15 m²)
Operators: USSR

Zlin 42

Following its success with the Z.26 series, in which the two occupants were seated in tandem, Zlin designed and built a side-by-side trainer, the Z.42, the prototype flying on 17 October 1967. It was put into production in 1971 with the 180-hp (134-kW) Avia MI37 engine as the Z.42M. A number, said to be several dozen, were supplied to East Germany. A later version has a revised fin and constant-speed propeller, production of this variant beginning in 1974. Total production to date amounts to around 180 aircraft, and other known military customers are Czechoslovakia and Hungary.

A contemporary of the Z.42M was the Z.43, a slightly larger four-seat aircraft which entered production in 1972.

Type: two-seat training and touring

monoplane
Powerplant: one 180-hp (134-kW) Avia MI37 AZ piston engine
Performance: maximum speed at sea level 140 mph (226 km/h); cruising speed at 1,975 ft (600 m) 134 mph (215 km/h); rate of climb at sea level 1,025 ft (312 m) per minute; service ceiling 13,950 ft (4250 m); take-off to 50 ft (15m) 1,245 ft (380 m); landing from 50 ft (15 m) 1,345 ft (410 m); range 329 miles (530 km)
Weights: empty 1,422 lb (645 kg); normal maximum take-off 2,138 lb (970 kg) or for aerobatics 2,028 lb (920 kg)
Dimensions: span 29 ft 11 in (9.11 m); length 23 ft 2 in (7.07 m); height 8 ft 10 in (2.69 m); wing area 141.5 sq ft (13.15 m²)
Operators: Czechoslovakia, East Germany, Hungary

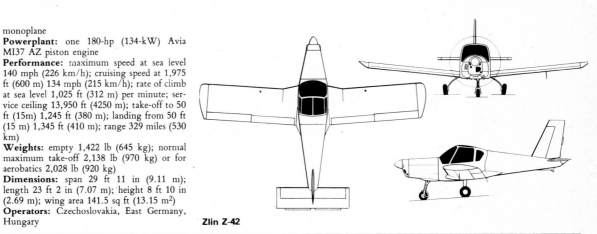

Zlin Z-42

Zlin 326 series

While the name Zlin invariably evokes thoughts of exceptionally agile aerobatic monoplanes, the Z.26 Trener was designed as a two-seat primary trainer to meet specifications for Czech civil and military flying schools, and a prototype flew in 1947, with a 105-hp (78-kW) Walter Minor 4 engine. Following competitive evaluation, the wooden Z.26 entered production and was designated C-5 by the Czech air force.

An all-metal version, the Z.126, replaced the earlier model in production from 1953, and this in turn was supplanted by the Z.226 with the 160-hp (119-kW) Walter Minor 6-III. The Z.226B was a glider-tug which flew in 1955, followed the next year by the Z.226T Trener-6. A fully-aerobatic single-seat version, the Z.226A Akrobat, also flew in 1956 and this name was retained for the similar variant of the Z.326, a derivative of the Z.226T with retractable landing gear and other improvements. Following tests with three prototypes, the Z.326 entered production in 1959 and by 1965 1,540 examples of the family had been built. Development continued with the

Z.526F which appeared in 1966 as the Trener-Master and, in a single-seat version, the name Akrobat was again used; with a one-piece canopy the latter became the Z.526AS Akrobat Special, and for advanced aerobatics the Z.526AFS Akrobat was offered, a special batch being produced for participation in the 1972 World Aerobatic Championships. To provide more power, the Z.526L was fitted with a 200-hp (149-kW) Lycoming AIO-360-B1B engine, and first production examples of this version were available in early 1972. Final development of the series was the Z.726 Universal, similar to the Z.526F but with shorter-span wings and a 180-hp (134-kW) Avia MI37 engine.

Direct military use of the Zlin 26 series seems to have been confined to four countries. The Cuban air force received 60 Z.226/326 aircraft; East Germany uses the same types alongside Soviet trainers; the Forca Popular Aérea da Libertacao de Mocambique has seven Z.326s; and the Czech air force uses the Z.526. Indirect military use includes countries such as Hungary where, although aircraft are

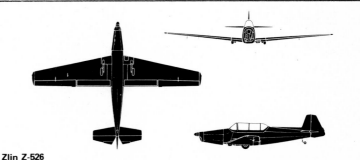

Zlin Z-526

civil registered, they belong to the state and therefore are used to train both civil and military pilots.

Type: two-seat trainer and aerobatic aircraft
Powerplant: one 160-hp (119-kW) Walter Minor 6-III piston engine
Performance: maximum speed at sea level 151 mph (243 km/h); cruising speed at 70% power 132 mph (212 km/h); rate of climb at sea level 866 ft (264 m) per minute; service ceiling 15,585 ft (4750 m); take-off run 820 ft

(250 m); landing run 540 ft (165 m); range 360 miles (580 km); range with tip tanks 610 miles (980 km)
Weights: empty 1,433 lb (650 kg); maximum normal take-off 2,150 lb (975 kg) or for aerobatics 2,006 lb (910 kg)
Dimensions: span 34 ft 9 in (10.60 m); length 25 ft 7 in (7.80 m); height 6 ft 9 in (2.06 m); wing area 166.3 sq ft (15.45 m²)
Operators: Cuba, Czechoslovakia, East Germany, Mozambique

The World's
Air-launched missiles

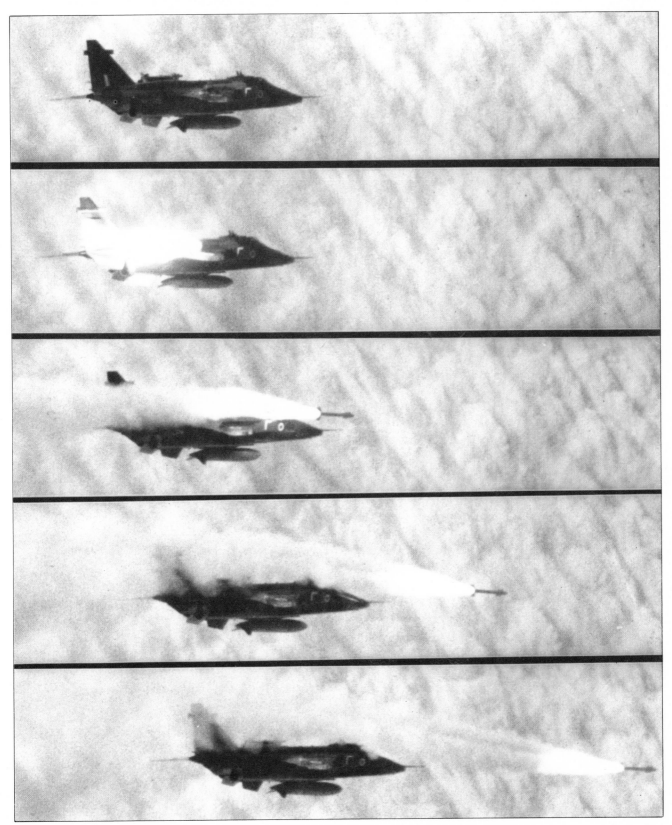

British Aerospace have developed overwing launchers for short-range air-to-air missiles on the Jaguar, leaving the attack payload undiminished. This impressive sequence shows the launch of a Matra 550 Magic, and the AIM-9L Sidewinder is also compatible. An advantage of these heat-seeking weapons is that they have so-called "fire and forget" capability.

Aérospatiale Lasso AM.10

The LASSO (Légèr Anti-Surface Semi-automatique Optique), also known as AM.10, is being developed to meet the French Navy's requirement for a small anti-ship missile with greater range than the Aérospatiale AS.12. The weapon could be launched from any medium-sized naval helicopter, such as the Westland/Aérospatiale Lynx or Aérospatiale SA.365 Dauphin, and can be fired from existing AS.12 rails. Typical targets include attack craft, landing craft, hydrofoils or hovercraft, and objectives on land can also be engaged.

The helicopter is fitted with an APX 397 gyro-stabilized sight, which can incorporate a thermal imager for engagements at night. In this case the imager is mounted on the platform which carries the sight mirror and guidance infra-red localizer, with the night-time image injected into the standard eyepiece. LASSO uses the TCA (télécommande automatique) guidance equipment developed for the Aérospatiale/MBB HOT anti-tank missile. The localizer measures the angle between the target and the missile in flight, with the aid of flares on the round, and a computer in the launch aircraft generates steering instructions to keep the weapon on the desired interception course. These corrections are transmitted down trailing wires, as in HOT, although the

longer-range AS.15 series also being developed by Aérospatiale employs a radio link.

LASSO can additionally be employed for coastal defence, using a ground-based periscopic sight and one or more two-round launchers. The sight has two magnifications, ×3 and ×12, and the same method of guidance is employed. Full development of LASSO depends on money being made available, and the longer-range AS.15 series is thought to have priority. A new type of guidance wire has been developed for LASSO to allow its range to be extended to 6.9 miles (11 km), but further increases are impossible with the existing guidance method.

Type: air-to-surface and surface-to-surface missile
Powerplant: two-stage solid-propellant rocket motor
Performance: average speed 615 mph (275 m/sec); maximum range 6.9 miles (11 km)
Weight: 210 lb (95.7 kg)
Dimensions: span 2 ft 0.4 in (62 cm); length 6 ft 10.7 in (2.10 m); diameter 8.7 in (22 cm)
Warhead: 66-lb (30-kg) high-explosive
Operators: under development

Aérospatiale AM.39 Exocet

The AM.39 air-launched development of the MM.38 Exocet anti-ship missile entered service in the summer of 1977, following the completion of six fully guided development flights. The weapon has been deployed initially on helicopters but will also arm the French Navy's carrier-based Dassault-Breguet Super Etendard attack aircraft and the proposed ANG (Atlantic Nouvelle Génération) maritime-patrol aircraft. Additional potential overseas customers have shown interest in mounting the weapon on a wide variety of fixed- and rotary-wing types.

The AM.39 (AM = Air-Mer or air-to-sea) is based on the ship-launched MM.38 but is shorter and lighter than its predecessor, allowing the maximum range to be increased from 26 miles (42 km) to 47 miles (75 km). Other changes include an increase in the area searched by the Electronique Marcel Dassault Adac active-radar seeker, since the flight time to extreme range is longer and the target could therefore have travelled a greater distance. A high-impulse sustainer motor, with a thin steel casing in place of the aluminium body used in MM.38, has been developed to reduce weight even further while increasing the range, and the boost motor has been shortened since the launch aircraft's forward speed provides some initial velocity.

Targets are detected by the aircraft's search radar and the missile is fed with a heading to steer and a time at which the seeker is to be switched on. Once an AM.39 has been launched it descends to low level under the control of its inertial navigation system and a radio altimeter. When the missile is near the target's predicted position the Adac homing head switches on automatically and sweeps across the horizon until it acquires the enemy vessel. The weapon is then under the control of Adac for the rest of its flight and descends

One of the carriers of AM.39 Exocet is the Super Etendard, the first prototype of which is seen here with a carry-trials AM.39 under the right wing. This large missile is also launched by the Mirage F1, Atlantic and Super Frelon.

to just above the waves in the final seconds before impact. The AM.39 penetrates the side of its target before the warhead explodes, in order to cause the maximum possible damage.

Type: air-launched anti-ship missile
Powerplant: (boost) Société Nationale des Poudres et Explosifs Condor solid-propellant

rocket motor, burning for 2 seconds; (sustain) Société Nationale des Poudres et Explosifs Hélios solid-propellant rocket motor
Performance: speed Mach 0.93 or 702 mph (1130 km/h); maximum range varies from 32.5 miles (52 km) to 47 miles (75 km) depending on launch height
Weight: 1,455 lb (660 kg)

Dimensions: span 3 ft 3.4 in (1.00 m); length 15 ft 4.6 in (4.69 m); diameter 13.8 in (35 cm)
Warhead: GP1 blast/fragmentation weighing 364 lb (165 kg)
Operators: France, Iraq, Pakistan

Aérospatiale AS.11

The AS.11 air-launched version of the SS.11 anti-tank missile is operated by a large number of air arms, equipping both helicopters and fixed-wing aircraft. The round itself is identical to that used in the surface-to-surface role, the main difference in airborne applications being the adoption of a stabilized sight so that the weapon can be controlled from a manoeuvring launch platform. Helicopters such as the Westland Wasp, Aérospatiale Alouette II Astazou and Alouette III can easily be modified for AS.11 operation by attaching launcher arms on each side of the fuselage (the normal number is two rails per side) and installing the roof-mounted sight.

The operator acquires his target in the sight and begins to track it manually, launching a missile once he is in range. He then continues to keep cross-hairs in the sight positioned over the target throughout the round's flight and steers the missile by means of a joystick so that it remains on his line of sight. Movements of the joystick are converted into steering commands which are transmitted down trailing wires to the missile, where they operate deflectors in the sustainer-motor effluxes to manoeuvre the weapon. The AS.11 can carry any one of three types of warhead, according to the target being engaged.

More than 160,000 AS.11/SS.11s had been built by the time the production line closed in the late 1970s, 50,000 of these being con-

structed under licence in the United States, where the weapon was designated AGM-22A. The missile remains in service in many countries, although it is being replaced in France's ALAT (Aviation Légère de l'Armée de Terre) by the Aérospatiale/MBB HOT weapon mounted on Aérospatiale/Westland Gazelle helicopters. The AS.11 also formed the basis for the scaled-up AS.12, which allows even light helicopters to pack a powerful punch, and some forces use AS.11 as a training round for the larger AS.12.

Type: air-launched anti-tank missile
Powerplant: (boost) Simplet solid-propellant rocket motor, burning for 2 seconds; (sustain) Sophie solid-propellant rocket motor, burning for 20 seconds
Performance: cruise speed 335 mph (150 m/sec) average; maximum range 3,300 yds (3000 m)
Weight: 67 lb (30.4 kg)
Dimensions: span 19.7 in (50 cm); length 4 ft (1.21 m); diameter 6.45 in (16.4 cm)
Warhead: three interchangeable types: 140 AC anti-tank, 104 AP 02 high-effect, or 140 AP 95 fragmentation
Operators: Abu Dhabi, Argentina, Brazil, France, Iran, Iraq, Netherlands, Peru, South Africa, United Kingdom & others

Firing an AS.11 from Alouette III, a combination widely used by the French ALAT and several other countries. Replacements for different roles include the anti-tank HOT and the anti-ship AS.15, still under development.

Aérospatiale AS.12

The AS.12, together with the SS.12 land-launched version and the SS.12M naval variant, has more than twice the range of the smaller AS.11 and carries a warhead more than four times as powerful. The warhead has been described by the manufacturer as packing as big a punch as a 6.9 in (175 mm) shell, yet the missile can be launched from comparatively small helicopters and fixed-wing aircraft. The use of a large warhead expands the number of target types which AS.12 can engage to include ships and heavily fortified emplacements, in addition to tanks and other vehicles.

The AS.12 is very similar in operation to AS.11. The missile is fired from rails attached to the side of a helicopter or beneath the wings of a fixed-wing aircraft and is steered by an operator, who tracks his target with the aid of a stabilized sight. Early AS.12 installations required the aimer to control the round throughout its flight by means of a joystick, in the same way as AS.11, but semi-automatic command to line-of-sight guidance has since been introduced as an option. In this sytem, known by the French as TCA (télécommande automatique), the operator merely tracks the target and the missile's position is measured automatically by an infra-red sensor aligned with the sight axis. The sensor detects flares on the missile and a small computer calculates steering corrections which will bring the round back on to the desired flight path. These commands are then transmitted down trailing wires in the normal way.

Aérospatiale is developing a range of weapons, such as the AS.15, to succeed AS.12, but the older weapon is likely to remain in service for many more years.

Type: air-to-surface missile
Powerplant: (boost) SNPE/Aérospatiale Achille solid-propellant rocket motor, burning

Due for replacement by the wire-guided AS.15 in the early 1980s, the obsolescent AS.12 is still in service with French helicopters including the Lynx of the Aéronavale as seen here. TCA guidance is not available on AS.12.

for 1.15 seconds; (sustain) SNPE/Aérospatiale Hermione solid-propellant rocket motor
Performance: speed 580 mph (260 m/sec) at end of flight; maximum range 4.97 miles (8 km) when launched at 230 mph (368 km/h)
Weight: 165 lb (75 kg)
Dimensions: span 25.6 in (65 cm); length 6 ft 1½ in (1.87 m); diameter 8.3 in (21 cm)
Warhead: 63 lb (28.6 kg), of three interchangeable types: 170 AC hollow-charge, OP.3C anti-tank, or anti-personnel fragmentation
Operators: Abu Dhabi, Argentina, Brazil, Egypt, France, Iraq, Iran, Italy, Netherlands, South Africa, United Kingdom & others

Aérospatiale AS.15/AS.15TT

Aérospatiale is developing a series of air-to-surface missiles to meet the requirement for a successor to AS.12. Potential export customers have specified a range of at least 9.4 miles (15 km) for such a weapon, to allow the launch aircraft to remain safe from retaliation by the vessel under attack, so the manufacturer has designed a fair-weather version (AS.15) and the all-weather AS.15TT (TT = Tous Temps).

The basic AS.15 can be fired from existing AS.12 launchers and incorporates a warhead based on that used in the earlier weapon. The aimer acquires his target with the aid of a gyro-stabilized optical sight, which can be fitted with a forward-looking infra-red set for

use at night, and tracks the enemy ship manually. A missile is fired and is controlled throughout its flight by a version of the TCA (télécommande automatique) semi-automatic command to line-of-sight system developed for the Aérospatiale/MBB HOT anti-tank missile. An infra-red sensor aligned with the operator's sight detects flares on the AS.15 and measures the angle by which they are displaced from the sightline, allowing a small computer to calculate appropriate steering commands for transmission to the missile. The AS.15 differs from both AS.12 and HOT, however, in that the corrections are sent over a radio link rather than down wires; this overcomes the problem of wire breakages

associated with earlier weapons.

The AS.15TT operates on a different principle, despite its similar designation. The missile follows a pre-programmed descent after launching until it comes under the control of an on-board radio altimeter, which allows it to fly just above the sea surface. The launch aircraft, normally a helicopter, is fitted with a Thomson-CSF Agrion 15 radar which tracks both the missile and its target. The angle between the two is measured, and steering corrections are automatically transmitted to the round via a radio link. Both the AS.15 and AS.15TT will be operational in the early 1980s if full development funding is made available.

Type: air-launched anti-ship missile
Powerplant: solid-propellant rocket motors
Performance: speed 625 mph (280 m/sec); maximum range 9.4 miles (15 km)
Weight: (AS.15) 212.1 lb (96.2 kg); (AS.15TT) 211.6 lb (96 kg)
Dimensions: span (AS.15) 1 ft 11.6 in (60 cm), (AS.15TT) 1 ft 8.9 in (53 cm); length (AS.15) 7 ft 1.6 in (2.175 m), (AS.15TT) 8 ft 6.8 in (2.61 m); diameter 7.1 in (18 cm)
Warhead: 65.5-lb (29.7-kg) high-explosive
Operators: under development

Aérospatiale AS.20

The AS.20 was developed by Nord-Aviation, now Aérospatiale, as a weapon to allow fighter-bombers to attack ground targets from reasonable stand-off ranges. The missile can be fired from any aircraft capable of sustaining the Mach 0.7 speed needed for launching, and is normally controlled manually by the pilot, who tracks his target visually and generates steering commands by means of a joystick; these instructions are then transmitted over a radio link to the round, where they result in deflection of baffles in the sustainer-motor

nozzle. The missile carries flares to aid visual tracking. The AS.20 can also use TCA (télécommande automatique) guidance, in which steering corrections are computed automatically. In this case the pilot keeps an optical sight aligned with the target and an infra-red sensor measures the angle between the missile and its objective. A small computer in the launch aircraft calculates the amount of exhaust deflection needed to bring the AS.20 back on course and this instruction is transmitted over the normal radio link.

The AS.20 is used by several air forces as a weapon in its own right, and it is also widely employed as a training round for pilots who would normally fire the larger AS.30. More than 1,000 rounds have been built under licence in West Germany for this purpose.

Type: air-to-surface missile
Powerplant: (boost) SNPE/Aérospatiale Aspic solid-propellant rocket motor, burning for 16.3 seconds (sustain) SNPE/Aérospatiale Icaré solid-propellant rocket motor

Performance: speed Mach 1.7 or 1,304 mph (2100 km/h) at low level; maximum range 4.4 miles (7 km) when fired at Mach 0.9 or 683 mph (1100 km/h) at low level
Weight: 315.3 lb (143 kg)
Dimensions: span 2 ft 7½ in (80 cm); length 8 ft 6⅓ in (2.60 m); diameter 9.85 in (25 cm)
Warhead: 66-lb (30-kg) high-explosive
Operators: France, Germany, Italy, South Africa and one other

Aérospatiale AS.30

The AS.30 was developed by scaling up the AS.20 and adding flip-out tail fins, thereby producing a formidable air-to-surface weapon. The specification called for high accuracy: the ability to impact within 33 ft (10 m) of its target when launched from a distance of at least 6.2 miles (10 km), with the aircraft having to approach no closer than 1.8 miles (3 km). The missile can be launched at any aircraft speed above Mach 0.45 and is steered either manually by the pilot, using a joystick in his cockpit, or by the TCA (télécommande automatique) method. In the latter case an infra-red sensor, aligned with the pilot's optical sight, detects flares on the missile and

thus allows the off-boresight angle to be measured. Steering commands are then transmitted over the radio link.

Aérospatiale is now developing the AS.30L, a laser-guided version which is scheduled to arm the French air force's SEPECAT Jaguar attack aircraft from the end of 1981. The new variant carries an electronics pack to compensate for missile roll and is fitted with a Thomson-CSF Ariel laser seeker in the nose. The launch aircraft carries a Thomson-CSF/Martin Marietta Atlis (Airborne Tracking Laser Illumination System) pod containing a CILAS ITAY-71 laser designator; this illuminates the target, and the AS.30L homes

on to reflected radiation. The launch aircraft can turn away after firing the missile. Captive carry trials of the Ariel seeker began in late 1977 and firings of unguided rounds from a Jaguar, to check separation from the aircraft, took place during 1978. The first fully guided AS.30Ls were expected to be launched early in 1979.

The Atlis/AS.30L combination may later arm the French air force's Dassault-Breguet Mirage 2000 strike fighters, and the pod can be used to designate targets for other weapons such as laser-guided bombs.

Type: air-to-surface missile

Powerplant: SNPE/Aérospatiale two-stage solid-propellant rocket motor
Performance: speed up to 1,120 mph (500 m/sec) at impact; maximum range up to 7.5 miles (12 km) when fired at Mach 0.9 or 683 mph (1100 km/h) at low level
Weight: 1,146 lb (520 kg)
Dimensions: span 3 ft 3.4 in (1.00 m); length 12 ft 5 in (3.785 m); diameter 13.4 in (34 cm)
Warhead: 507 lb (230 kg) interchangeable semi-armour-piercing or general-purpose
Operators: France, India, Peru, South Africa, Switzerland

Aérospatiale ASMP

The ASMP (*Air-Sol Moyenne Portée* air-to-surface medium-range) is being developed to arm some of the French air force's Dassault Mirage 2000 strike-fighters from 1985, and will probably also be carried by that service's SEPECAT Jaguar attack aircraft. The weapon is to be used mainly in the tactical role against targets such as tank marshalling areas, bridges, railway depots and military headquarters, but could also have a strategic role, since it will carry a nuclear warhead. The ASMP was originally intended to arm the proposed Dassault Super Mirage, and development was frozen when that project was abandoned. The programme was revived in March 1978 when Aérospatiale, which had been competing with Matra, was awarded a full development contract.

The ASMP will be powered by a ramjet being developed by ONERA (Office National d'Etudes et de Recherches Aéronautiques); a solid-propellant boost charge supplied by SNPE (Société Nationale des Poudres et Explosifs) will be cast inside the ramjet's combustion chamber to accelerate the missile to its cruise speed. Once this charge has burnt out the ramjet comes into operation, burning kerosene oxidized by air drawn through two lateral intakes. Matra's unsuccessful proposal was powered by a turbojet.

The weapon is expected to be launched at medium altitude, then climb to high level for its supersonic cruise phase before descending to hug the ground in its final attack. The maximum range on this type of mission will be about 62.5 miles (100 km), although this would be reduced to 47 miles (75 km) for a completely low-level flight. ASMP will use an inertial navigation system, possibly with some form of terminal homing, and is expected to carry a thermonuclear warhead with a yield of 100–150 kilotons. Development is likely to cost about Fr500 million, and the weapon may also be supplied to the French navy for use on its carrier-based Dassault Super Etendard attack aircraft.

Aérospatiale/MBB HOT

HOT (*Haut-subsonique Optiquement Téléguidé*), developed jointly by Aérospatiale in France and Messerschmitt-Bölkow-Blohm in Germany, has been ordered to arm a variety of helicopters and ground vehicles. At least three export customers have awarded contracts for the weapon to equip Aérospatiale Gazelles, and the French Army's ALAT (*Aviation Légère de l'Armée de Terre*) will itself introduce this missile/helicopter combination in 1980. The German Army is due to receive the first of 212 PAH-1 helicopters (the military designation of the MBB BO-105 used in this role) in September 1979; each PAH-1 carries six rounds, whereas the Gazelle is limited to four under some conditions. The PAH-2 helicopter gunship which the French and German armies are planning to introduce in the late 1980s may also carry HOT, at least as an interim weapon. Firing trials held in August 1978 demonstrated that the missile could be integrated with the Westland/Aérospatiale Lynx with no difficulty, and the aircraft of this type which are to be built in Egypt are expected to carry the Franco-German missile as standard.

HOT uses TCA (*télécommande automatique*) guidance, so the operator has only to keep his gyro-stabilized sight centred on the target for the round to strike its objective. An infra-red sensor aligned with the sight measures the angular difference between the target and the missile, and steering corrections are automatically transmitted to the weapon over a wire link. Night sights for use with HOT are being developed in both France and Germany for service from the early 1980s, and a mid-life improvement programme is being planned to increase the missile's lethality and cruise speed. The manufacturers have already examined the possiblity of providing a range of interchangeable warheads, including one designed specifically for the anti-ship role and another for use against troop concentrations.

Type: anti-tank missile
Powerplant: (boost) Société Nationale des Poudres et Explosifs *Bugéat* solid-propellant rocket motor, burning for 0.9 seconds; (sustain) 52.8 lb (24 kg) Société Nationale des Poudres et Explosifs *Infra* solid-propellant rocket motor, burning for 17.4 seconds
Performance: cruise speed 580 mph (260 m/sec); maximum range 4,375 yards (4000 m)
Weight: 48.5 lb (22 kg)
Dimensions: span 12.2 in (31 cm); length 4 ft 3.2 in (1.30 m); diameter 5.63 in (14.3 cm)
Warhead: 13.2-lb (6-kg) hollow-charge
Operators: Egypt, France, Germany, Iraq, Kuwait, Syria

Standard new anti-tank missile of many countries including the sponsors, France and West Germany, the Euromissile HOT is seen here in a four-barrel installation on a Gazelle of the French ALAT. The German Heer (Army) BO105s carry six rounds.

Anti-Surface Euro Missile ASSM

The ASSM (Anti-Ship Supersonic Missile or Anti-Surface-Ship Missile) is a collaborative NATO project aimed at developing a replacement for first-generation anti-ship missiles such as the Aérospatiale Exocet and MBB Kormoran. A memorandum of understanding signed by France, Germany, Britain, the Netherlands, Norway and the United States in April 1977 led to a feasibility study aimed at defining the most cost-effective way of meeting all the laid-down requirements, which included a supersonic cruise speed, maximum range of some 113 miles (180 km), improved penetration of defences by means of altering the motor thrust during the attack phase, and autonomous operation after launching. The ASSM is intended to arm fixed-wing aircraft and helicopters, in addition to surface vessels and submarines.

The missile, which is unlikely to enter service before 1990, is expected to be powered by a solid-propellant ram-rocket. Inertial mid-course guidance will almost certainly be employed and a dual-mode seeker, with an active-radar homing head backed up by infra-red sensing, has been specified for the attack phase.

If the project proceeds into development and production, it will be organised by the ASEM (Anti-Surface Euro Missile) consortium, comprising British Aerospace, Aérospatiale and Messerschmitt-Bölkow-Blohm. The active-radar seeker is likely to be a collaborative effort by Electronique Marcel Dassault and Marconi Space and Defence Systems, while the contenders for the powerplant contract are the Aérospatiale/ONERA team in France and Bayern Chemie in Germany.

By the beginning of 1979 no firm decisions on the future of ASSM had been announced, although the initial 14-month feasibility study is believed to have been completed successfully.

ASRAAM

The designation ASRAAM (Advanced Short-Range Air-to-Air Missile) covers joint US Navy/Air Force studies of a replacement for the AIM-9 Sidewinder. A common operational requirement was established in January 1978, and guidelines as to the performance required have been provided by the ACEVAL/-AIMVAL series of comparative guidance trials and the Pave Prism programme, which has evaluted infra-red and laser seekers. The ASRAAM has a lower priority than the AMRAAM, since the AIM-9L and newer variants of Sidewinder are expected to remain viable for several more years, and the new weapon is unlikely to enter service before the end of the 1980s.

Boeing AGM-69A SRAM

The Boeing AGM-69A SRAM (Short-Range Attack Missile) is one of the main weapons carried by the Boeing B-52G and B-52H Stratofortress bombers of the USAF's Strategic Air Command, and the weapon also arms SAC's General Dynamics FB-111s. The first operational round was delivered in March 1972 and all 1,500 were in service by July 1975, equipping 17 wings of B-52s and two of FB-111s; the former type can carry eight rounds in an internal rotating dispenser and a further 12 missiles under the wings, while the latter has room for two SRAMs in the weapons bay and four more on swivelling pylons beneath its wings.

The SRAM can be used to attack the bombers' main targets or to destroy defences in their path, even when they are off to one side of the launch aircraft. The weapon's inertial navigation system is fed with its current position and information relating to the target, and is then launched on one of four types of flight path: semi-ballistic, in which it climbs to high altitude before diving on to its objective; terrain-following, using a radio altimeter to help it hug the ground; all-inertial at medium altitudes; or a combination of inertial and terrain-following to make use of natural cover such as mountain ranges.

The SRAM's rocket motor has two stages of operation, boost and sustain, and the interval between the two can be preset for any time between 1.5 seconds and 80 seconds according to the distance to the target and the type of mission to be flown. The proposed AGM-69B SRAM-B, powered by a new motor and carrying an improved thermonuclear warhead, was abandoned following cancellation of the Rockwell B-1 strategic bomber in the summer of 1977, but existing SRAM-As are being upgraded with longer-life motors and more versatile guidance.

Type: strategic air-to-surface missile
Powerplant: one Lockheed SR75-LP-1 (LPC-415) two-pulse solid-propellant rocket motor
Performance: burnt-out speed Mach 3+ or at least 1,980 mph (3187 km/h) at 40,000 ft (12190 m); maximum range 100 miles (161 km); minimum range 37 miles (60 km)
Weight: 2,200 lb (998 kg)
Dimensions: length 14 ft (4.27 m); diameter 1 ft 5½ in (44.5 cm)
Warhead: W69 thermonuclear, 200 kilotons yield
Operators: United States Air Force

Boeing AGM-86B ALCM-B

Flight trials of the Boeing AGM-86B ALCM-B (Air-Launched Cruise Missile model B) are due to begin in the summer of 1979, and the weapon will take part in a fly-off competition with the General Dynamics AGM-109 TALCM (Tomahawk Air-Launched Cruise Missile). The winner is expected to arm the USAF Strategic Air Command's Boeing B-52 Stratofortress bombers, each of which might be modified to carry eight ALCM-Bs in a rotary launcher in the weapons bay and a further 12 on underwing pylons.

The ALCM-B has replaced the AGM-86A ALCM-A programme, the later missile having an extended fuselage and longer wings; internal fuel capacity is increased, thus improving the weapon's maximum range. The greater length means that the missile will not fit the AGM-69 SRAM launcher. Missiles would be launched against strategic targets while the bomber was still at least 230 miles (370 km) from hostile territory, using inertial guidance for the early part of the mission. Once over land, however, ALCM-B can update the navigation computer by means of a program known as Tercom (Terrain Contour Matching). The missile's radio altimeter takes a series of readings, giving a profile of the terrain being flown over, and the computer matches this pattern with a stored map of the planned flight path. This process allows the weapon's course to be corrected so that it remains within 100 ft (30.5 m) or so of the desired flight path throughout the terminal stages of its mission. Last-second corrections are made under the control of a SMAC (Scene-Matching Area Correlator), which compares the missile's view of its target area with a map stored on board.

The fly-off is expected to involve 10 rounds from each contractor, and the selected weapon is planned to be operational by mid-1981. The USAF hopes to buy about 2,300 air-launched cruise missiles and may deploy them on additional types of aircraft, although the whole programme has many hurdles to cross, and could be abandoned if such weapons are prohibited by any new strategic arms limitation agreement.

Type: air-launched cruise missile
Powerplant: one 600-lb (272-kg) Williams Research F107-WR-100 turbofan
Performance: cruising speed Mach 0.7 or 535 mph (861 km/h) at sea level; maximum range at least 1,730 miles (2784 km)
Weight: 2,800 lb (1270 kg)
Dimensions: span 12 ft (3.66 m); length 20 ft 9 in (6.32 m); diameter 2 ft (61 cm)
Warhead: 270-lb (123-kg) W-80 thermonuclear, 200 kilotons yield
Operators: United States (planned)

Inside the Seattle facility of Boeing Aerospace the long-range ALCM-B (AGM-86B) is seen in the foreground packaged for installation in or under a B-52. Beyond is the shorter ALCM-A, with everything for air-breathing cruising flight.

Bofors R653 Bantam

Although deployed primarily with surface forces, the Bofors Rb53 Bantam anti-tank missile has also been mounted on helicopters and fixed-wing aircraft, including the Agusta-Bell AB 204 and Saab Supporter. The operator tracks his target with the aid of an optical sight and steers the round by means of a joystick: movements of the stick result in commands being transmitted down trailing wires to the missile, where they operate spoilers for control. The Bantam has been in service with the Swedish army since 1963.

Type: anti-tank missile
Powerplant: (boost) one 145-lb (66-kg) solid-propellant rocket, burning for 1.2 seconds; (sustain) solid-propellant rocket
Performance: cruising speed 190 mph (305 km/h); maximum range 2,190 yards (2000 m)

Weight: 16.7 lb (7.6 kg)
Dimensions: span 15.7 in (40 cm); length 2 ft 9.8 in (84.8 cm); diameter 4.3 in (11 cm)
Warhead: 2.2-lb (1-kg) high-explosive anti-tank or general-purpose
Operators: Argentina, Sweden, Switzerland

British Aerospace Dynamics Firestreak

The Firestreak, originally code-named Blue Jay, was one of a trio of first-generation air-to-air missiles developed in Britain during the 1950s; the Fairey Fireflash entered service only briefly and the Vickers-Armstrongs Red Dean was cancelled, leaving Firestreak as the only one to become fully operational. The missile entered service in 1958, originally arming Gloster Javelins of the Royal Air Force and the Royal Navy's de Havilland Sea Vixens; each of these types carried four rounds, while the later BAC Lightning was limited to two. The Firestreak was designed when the main threat to Britain came from slow, unmanoeuvrable bombers, yet the missile was still operational more than 20 years after it entered service.

Missile design was still in its infancy when Firestreak was conceived, with the result that the weapon is heavy and has only poor manoeuvrability. Its infra-red seeker is not sufficiently sensitive to detect a target head-on, so Firestreak-armed fighters are limited to engagements from the rear, where the hot engine parts of the opposing aircraft can be detected and tracked by the weapon's homing head. Many of these difficulties were overcome in the Firestreak's successor, the Red Top (originally known as Firestreak Mk IV), and the two missiles remain in limited service as primary armament for the Lightning fighter.

Type: air-to-air missile
Powerplant: boost and sustainer solid-propellant rocket motors
Performance: speed Mach 2+ or at least 1,320 mph (2124 km/h) at 40,000 ft (12190 m); maximum range 4 miles (6 km)
Weight: 300 lb (135 kg)
Dimensions: span 2 ft 6 in (76.2 cm); length 10 ft 5½ in (3.19 m); diameter 8.75 in (22.2 cm)
Warhead: 50-lb (23-kg) high-explosive
Operators: Saudi Arabia, Royal Air Force

British Aerospace Dynamics P3T

The British Aerospace Dynamics P3T is a turbojet-powered derivative of the Matra/BAe Martel, and is being developed to arm the Royal Air Force's anti-ship BAe (HS) Buccaneer and Panavia Tornado aircraft from the early 1980s, replacing the present rocket-powered AJ168 version. The P3T will also be carried by the Royal Navy's BAe Sea Harrier strike-fighters aboard the 'Invincible' class anti-submarine cruisers. The weapon will carry a mid-course guidance package comprising an inertial-navigation system coupled with a radio altimeter, allowing it to cruise just above the sea surface. Terminal homing will be under the control of a Marconi Space and Defence Systems active radar seeker which has been under development in its basic form for many years, the previous projected applications (Ship Martel and Sub-Martel/Under-Sea Guided Weapon) having been cancelled.

Type: air-launched anti-ship missile
Powerplant: one 787-lb (357-kg) Microturbo TRI 60-1-067 turbojet

Performance: cruising speed Mach 0.9 or 685 mph (1102 km/h) at sea level; maximum range approximately 62 miles (100 km)
Other data similar to those of the Martel, though the P3T is heavier and longer

British Aerospace Dynamics Red Top

The Red Top, originally known as the de Havilland Firestreak Mk IV, entered service in 1964 as a complement to and partial replacement for earlier marks of the Firestreak. Unlike its predecessor, the new missile can engage targets from any direction, and both the launch aircraft and its target may be travelling at speeds of up to Mach 2. The Red Top, which carries a larger warhead than the Firestreak and uses semiconductors in place of valves, was designed for use against low-level manoeuvring targets rather than high-level bombers, and may be fired without having to aim the launch aircraft in the exact direction of its objective. The position of the target to be engaged may be supplied by the interceptor's fire-control radar (the Ferranti Airpass in the BAC Lightning, which is the only type still to carry the weapon) or by the pilot.

The Red Top remains in service and will continue to do so as long as the Lightning is retained in service. Hawker Siddeley Dynamics (now BAe), which absorbed de Havilland, designed the QC434 SRAAM (Short-Range Air-to-Air Missile) to succeed Red Top, but this programme was reduced to the status of a technology-demonstration project in January 1974, and the Royal Air Force has since ordered the AIM-9L Sidewinder as its short-range air-to-air missile for the 1980s.

Type: air-to-air missile
Powerplant: one two-stage solid-propellant rocket motor
Performance: cruising speed Mach 3 or 1,980 mph (3186 km/h) at 40,000 ft (12190 m); maximum range 7 miles (11 km)
Weight: 330 lb (150 kg)
Dimensions: span 3 ft (91.4 cm); length 10 ft 9 in (3.276 m); diameter 8.75 in (22.2 cm)
Warhead: 68-lb (31-kg) high-explosive
Operators: Royal Air Force, Kuwait, Saudi Arabia

Red Top, carried by the nearer of these early Lightning interceptors, was the improved IR-homing air-to-air missile that replaced Firestreak (carried by the more distant aircraft) in RAF service. Red Top remains in use at RAF Binbrook.

British Aerospace Dynamics Sea Skua

The Sea Skua, formerly known as CL834, is being developed to arm the Royal Navy's Westland/Aérospatiale Lynx helicopters from the early 1980s, this combination replacing Wasps equipped with Aérospatiale AS.12s. Lynxes carrying the Sea Skua will operate from frigates and destroyers to seek out and destroy small vessels such as fast attack craft, hydrofoils and hovercraft before they can launch their own missiles at the helicopter's parent ship or others in the task force or convoy.

The Lynx would be despatched to intercept such targets while they were still 60 miles (97 km) or more away. As the helicopter approached the enemy craft the crew would identify it by means of visual sightings or cross-bearings taken on its radar transmissions; this information would then be fed into the Lynx's Decca TANS (Tactical Airborne Navigation System) computer so that the target to be attacked can be correlated with its blip on the helicopter's Ferranti Seaspray radar. Seaspray is then switched from its surveillance and navigation role to target tracking and illumination for the Sea Skua's semi-active radar seeker.

The pilot selects which of the four rounds carried by his Lynx is to be fired, and he can instruct the missile to cruise at any one of four heights depending on the sea state. The round is then released and descends to the selected height, just above the waves, with its homing head tracking the target by means of the radar energy which is transmitted by the Seaspray and reflected from the enemy craft. The Sea Skua is a comparatively small missile and its warhead is designed to disable attackers rather than to sink them: once the vessel's anti-ship missiles and radars have been put out of action it is effectively neutralised. This means that small helicopters can carry several 'disabling' missiles rather than perhaps just one 'destroying' missile.

BAC, now British Aerospace, was instructed to proceed with development of Sea Skua in March 1972, but the programme has

Specially designed for compatibility with the naval versions of Westland Lynx helicopter, the BAe Dynamics Sea Skua is the most effective weapon in its class in the world though it relies upon illumination of the target by the helicopter's radar.

several times been delayed by lack of funding and firing of guided rounds had not begun by the end of 1978.

Type: helicopter-launched anti-ship missile

Powerplant: one solid-propellant rocket motor
Performance: maximum range 8.75 miles (14 km)
Weight: 323 lb (147 kg)

Dimensions: span 2 ft (61 cm); length 8 ft 3 in (2.5 m); diameter 10.6 in (26.9 cm)
Warhead: high-explosive, weighing 77 lb (35 kg)
Operators: ordered by Royal Navy

British Aerospace Dynamics Sky Flash

The Sky Flash is a development of the US-designed Raytheon Sparrow air-to-air missile and incorporates a number of new British systems, including a Marconi Space and Defence Systems semi-active radar seeker and an EMI Electronics proximity fuse. The weapon, previously known as XJ521 or UK Sparrow, is based on the AIM-7E2 version of the US missile and uses that type's airframe, rocket motor and warhead. The later AIM-7F has an uprated motor, giving it a much longer range, but this was thought to be unnecessary for the type of air combat normally found in Europe.

The US forces have themselves been searching for an improved version of the Sparrow, and the US Navy has received the results of flight trials in exchange for providing the launch aircraft and facilities. The first round was fired from a McDonnell Douglas F-4J Phantom fighter of the USN at the Pacific Missile Test Center in November 1975, and the Sky Flash performed so effectively that it was adjudged to have proved itself after only 17 of the planned 22 shots. Further firings followed on behalf of the US Navy, and the first production rounds were delivered to the Royal Air Force in July 1977. The missile became operational the following year, arming Phantom interceptors, and will later equip the RAF's Tornado F.2 air-defence interceptors. The Sky Flash can easily be integrated with existing fire-control radars and has additionally been ordered for the Swedish air force's Saab JA37 Viggen fighters. In 1978 the weapon was fired from a General Dynamics F-16 to demonstrate that it was compatible with that type, and a number of F-16 customers have expressed interest in buying the Sky Flash. The initial production run is thought to total 1,350 rounds, and British Aerospace hopes to sell between 6,000 and 8,000 in all.

Type: air-to-air missile
Powerplant: one Rocketdyne Mk 38 single-stage solid-propellant rocket motor

By late 1979 all the Phantom FGR.2's interception duties in the RAF were armed with the BAe Dynamics Sky Flash. Though using many Sparrow airframe and motor parts, this weapon has many times greater lethality, especially under conditions of severe clutter or jamming.

Performance: speed Mach 3.5 or 2,310 mph (3718 km/h) at 40,000 ft (12190 m); maximum range 28 miles (45 km)

Weight: 425 lb (193 kg)
Dimensions: span 3 ft 4 in (1.02 m); length 12 ft (3.66 m); diameter 8 in (20.3 cm)

Warhead: continuous-rod, weighing 66 lb (30 kg)
Operators: Swedish air force, Royal air force

ritish Aerospace Dynamics/Matra Martel

he Martel has been built in two versions, as
name (which is derived from Missile Anti-
adar and Television) suggests. The
levision-guided AJ168 variant was developed
der British control, with the French having
ime responsibility for the radiation-homing
S.37, although the project as a whole was
n on a collaborative basis. The two types
are the same main structure, wings, fins,
wer system, most of the control system and
ost motor, although the sustainer motors
e different (because of varying launch
velopes and flight profiles) and the
arhead/fuse combination is matched to the
ecific type of target which each weapon is
ely to attack.

The AJ168, which arms British Aerospace
IS) Buccaneer attack aircraft of the Royal
r Force, can be launched at any height bet-
en 50 ft (15 m) and 7,000 ft (2134 m). It is
rmally employed in the anti-ship role but
n also be operated over land. The rear-seat
erator in the Buccaneer launches one of his
ree missiles (the fourth underwing pylon is
ed to carry the associated command/video-
k pod) and watches his cockpit display,
nich shows the view as seen by a television
mera in the weapon's nose. He can make the
issile climb, dive or turn to either side dur-
g the mid-course stage by means of a
ystick; the commands are transmitted over a
icrowave link which carries the TV pictures

in the opposite direction. When the Martel
nears its target the operator places the cross-
wires on his display over the desired impact
point, and the missile is automatically steered
to hit that position.

The AS.37 version carries an Electronique
Marcel Dassault AD37 passive radiation seeker
which homes on to transmissions from enemy
radars. The missile can be launched from an
aircraft flying at subsonic or supersonic speed
at any height between 50 ft (15 m) and
45,931 ft (14000 m). the AS.37's warhead is
the same size as that in the AJ168 but is
detonated by a Thomson-CSF proximity fuse
in order to cause the maximum damage,
whereas the AJ168 explosive charge is
detonated on impact.

Type: television-guided or anti-radiation air-
to-surface missile
Powerplant: (boost) Hotchkiss-
Brandt/SNPE Basile solid-propellant rocket
motor, burning for 2.4 seconds; (sustain:
AJ168) SNPE solid-propellant rocket motor;
(sustain: AS.37) SNPE Cassandre solid-
propellant rocket motor, burning for 22.2
seconds.
Performance: speed about Mach 2 or
1,520 mph (2446 km/h) at sea level; maximum range (AJ168) 35 miles (56 km); maximum range (AS.37) 19 miles (30 km) when
launched at Mach 1 or 760 mph (1223 km/h)

Under the right wing of an RAF Buccaneer S.2B can be seen an AS.37 anti-radar Martel
(left) and the British AJ.168 TV-guided version (right). Surprisingly, the French, who
collaborated on both versions, never bought the more versatile 'British' version.

at low level
Weight: AJ168 1,213 lb (550 kg); AS.37
1,170 lb (531 kg)
Dimensions: span 4 ft (1.2 m); length

(AJ168) 12 ft 8 in (3.87 m); length (AS.37)
13 ft 6 in (4.12 m); diameter 15.7 in (40 cm)
Warhead: 331-lb (150-kg) high-explosive
Operators: French air force, Royal Air Force

ord Aerospace/Raytheon Sidewinder

he Sidewinder is one of the world's most
idely operated missiles and has been produ-
d in more variants than almost any other.
he weapon derives its name from a type of
tlesnake which detects its prey by means of
dy heat, in much the same way as the
issile homes on to infra-red radiation. Test
ings began in September 1953 and the
iginal version, now known as AIM-9B,
tered service in mid-1956. More than 60,000
this variant alone had been built by the time
S production ended during 1962, and a fur-
er 9,000 or more were constructed under
ence by a European consortium led by
odenseewerk Gerät Technik.

Although developed for the US Navy, the
dewinder was also adopted by the USAF.
he AIM-9B was lacking in performance, so
provements were soon introduced. The
SN and USAF originally planned to work
gether on this programme, but in the event
ey went their separate ways. Those
veloped for the USN were designated AIM-
C, -9G and -9H, while the USAF's versions
ere the AIM-9D, -9E and -9J. The -9D had
r greater range than the -9B and carried a
arhead more than twice as large; the respon-
veness and performance of its infra-red seeker
ere also much improved. Further refine-
ents were introduced in the -9G and -9H.
he US Air Force retained thermo-electric
oling for the seekers in its new versions, and
e original rocket motor, but made up for
ese deficiencies by introducing im-
rovements in other areas.

The radar-guided AIM-9C (matched to later
odels of the Vought F-8 Crusader) was soon
ithdrawn from service, but the USAF and
SN streams have now rejoined in the form of
IM-9L Super Sidewinder. Although retain-
g some existing features, the AIM-9L is

Though the AIM-9L series is designed to be manufactured by a consortium in Europe for European air forces, most F-16 flying so far has
been done with the earlier AIM-9J series with double-delta cropped-tip flight controls.

almost completely new under the skin and
looks set to remain in production well into the
1980s. It has a completely new infra-red homing head (with some features of the German
BGT weapon cancelled to make way for it)
and long-span pointed control fins. It will be
built by a European consortium including Britain, which cancelled its own (technically
superior) SRAAM. The AIM-9L is expected
to be replaced by the ASRAAM (Advanced
Short-Range Air-to-Air Missile).

Type: (AIM-9L Super Sidewinder) air-to-air
missile
Powerplant: one Rocketdyne Mk 36 solid-
propellant rocket motor
Performance: cruising speed Mach 3 or
1,980 mph (3168 km/h) at 40,000 ft (12190
m); maximum range 11 miles (17.6 km)
Weight: 186 lb (84.5 kg)
Dimensions: span 2 ft 0½ in (63 cm); length
9 ft 4 in (2.85 m); diameter 5 in (12.7 cm)
Warhead: about 25-lb (11.4-kg) high-

explosive with preformed rods
Operators: (all models) Argentina, Australia,
Brazil, Canada, Chile, Denmark, Greece,
Iran, Israel, Japan, Kuwait, Malaysia,
Netherlands, Norway, Philippines, Portugal,
Pakistan, Saudi Arabia, South Korea, Spain,
Singapore, Sweden, Taiwan, Tunisia, Turkey,
UK, US Air Force, US Marine Corps, US
Navy, West Germany

General Dynamics AGM-78/RGM-66D Standard ARM

he Standard ARM (Anti-Radiation Missile)
as developed from 1966, using the RIM-66A
andard surface-to-air missile as its starting
oint, in order to give the US Air Force and
avy a larger, longer-range and generally
ore effective complement to the Texas In-
ruments AGM-45A Shrike for use in
ietnam. In order to save time the original
GM-78A version of the Standard ARM used
much existing equipment as possible, in-
uding the RIM-66A airframe and rocket
otor (which was modified so that the missile
uld be carried at high altitudes for long
riods), together with the Texas Instruments
eker which was already operational in the
hrike.

Flight trials began in 1967 and the weapon
entered service the following year, initially
equipping the US Air Force's Republic
F-105F/G Thunderchief Wild Weasel
(defence-suppression) aircraft and the USN's
equivalent Grumman EA-6A Intruders. The
weapon's performance was found to be only
marginally acceptable, however, so work
began in 1967 on the improved AGM-78B; in
this model a new Maxson Electronics anti-
radiation seeker replaced the Shrike-type homing head. The family has since been extended
to AGM-78C, -78D and -78D2, with the cost
per round rising steadily although performance has increased. The most recent models
are carried by USAF McDonnell Douglas

F-4G Wild Weasels, which are replacing
Thunderchiefs, and by the US Navy's Grumman EA-6B Prowlers.

Aircraft equipped to operate Standard ARM
are fitted with a TIAS (Target Identification
and Acquisition System), which analyses
enemy radar transmissions and computes the
trajectory which a missile should fly to engage
the transmitter to be attacked. The weapon is
then programmed to follow this flight path
even if the enemy radar is switched off after
launching — a trick which North Vietnamese
forces quickly learnt was effective against the
Shrike. If the radar keeps transmitting, the
Standard ARM's seeker will home on to its
emissions to update the missile's trajectory un-

til impact. The RGM-66D is the shipborne
surface-to-surface model of the AGM-78.

Type: anti-radiation missile
Powerplant: one Aerojet Mk 27 solid-
propellant rocket motor
Performance: speed Mach 2 or 1,320 mph
(2124 km/h) at 40,000 ft (12190 m); max-
imum range 15 miles (25 km)
Weight: 1,400 lb (635 kg)
Dimensions: span 3 ft 7 in (1.09 m); length
15 ft (4.57 m); diameter 13.5 in (34.3 cm)
Warhead: high-explosive
Operators: US air force, US navy

General Dynamics AGM-109 Tomahawk

The General Dynamics AGM-109 Tomahawk cruise missile is being developed in a number of versions for both the US Air Force and the US Navy, and for a variety of strategic and tactical roles. The AGM-109 TALCM (Tomahawk Air-Launched Cruise Missile) was due to take part in a competitive fly-off against the Boeing AGM-86B ALCM-B (Air-Launched Cruise Missile) during the spring of 1979 to decide which of these weapons would be ordered to arm the Strategic Air Command's B-52G/H Stratofortress bombers. The US Navy is additionally evaluating an air-launched version of the tactical (anti-ship) variant of Tomahawk.

In its strategic role, TALCM would be launched in large numbers from B-52s patrolling outside the Soviet Union's borders, thus flooding the defences — if enough were bought — and guaranteeing a massively effective strike against military targets such as intercontinental ballistic missile silos. Both the AGM-109 and the competing AGM-86B use an advanced form of guidance, known as Tercom (Terrain Contour Matching), to confer extremely high accuracy — about 100 ft (30.5 m), irrespective of the range. Tercom is fed with signals from a radar altimeter, thus building up a relief map of the terrain over which the missile is flying. This is compared with a map stored in the computer's memory after being prepared from reconnaissance satellite photographs, until a match is found, allowing the Tomahawk's inertial navigator to update its position exactly. Up to 20 such maps can be stored, and the last stages of an attack are carried out with the aid of SMAC (Scene-Matching Area Correlator), which compares a television view of the target with stored film of the surrounding area.

This version is also intended for service with the USAF Tactical Air Command and USAF Europe as a Ground-Launched Cruise Missile (GLCM). This would release tactical aircraft for other duties.

The tactical anti-ship version of Tomahawk uses a modified active-radar seeker of the type developed for the McDonnell Douglas AGM-/RGM-84A Harpoon, combined with mid-course inertial navigation, and is not fitted with Tercom. It also carries less fuel, giving it a shorter range, and employs a convention[al] warhead rather than a thermonuclear payloa[d].

Type: air-launched strategic cruise missile
Powerplant: Williams Research 600 (272-kg) F107-WR-102 turbofan.
Performance: cruising speed Mach 0.7 760 mph (1223 km/h) at sea level; maximu[m] range more than 1,730 miles (2785 km)
Weight: 2,520 lb (1144 kg)
Dimensions: span 8 ft 4 in (2.54 m); leng[th] 18 ft (5.49 m); diameter 1 ft 9 in (53.3 cm)
Warhead: (strategic version) W80 n[uclear, ther]monuclear, 200 kilotons yield
Operators: under evaluation by US [Air] Force, US Navy

Hughes AGM-65 Maverick

The Hughes AGM-65 Maverick has been developed in several versions, fitted with different homing heads, to meet a wide variety of requirements. The first variant was the AGM-65A, for which Hughes was awarded a development and testing contract in July 1968. This model is fitted with a nose-mounted television camera which is locked on to its target before launching. The pilot or second crew member of the parent aircraft has a monitor on which he can see the view from the TV camera, and he steers cross-hairs by means of a joystick, to place them over the object to be attacked. The AGM-65A, which hit a tank during its first guided flight in December 1969 and entered service three years later, was designed to attack hardened point targets such as armoured vehicles, fortifications, bunkers, parked aircraft and radar or missile sites.

Hughes built several thousand AGM-65As to arm the USAF Tactical Air Command's McDonnell Douglas F-4D/E Phantoms, Vought A-7D Corsairs and Fairchild A-10 Thunderbolt IIs before switching to the AGM-65B. This model, known as the Scene Magnification Maverick, entered service in 1976 and is fitted with magnifying optics so that it can be locked on to targets at greater ranges.

Production of 17,000 AGM-65A/Bs was completed in April 1978 but three other variants continued in development. The AGM-65C is fitted with a Rockwell semi-active laser seeker in place of the television guidance, allowing it to home on to low-contrast targets illuminated from the air or by ground-based designators. This Laser Maverick, which was still being tested in 1978, is intended for use in both the interdiction and close-support roles. The AGM-65D is a version fitted with an imaging infra-red (IIR) seeker so that it can attack targets at night or when they are obscured by smoke or haze. Up to 15,000 AGM-65Ds are expected to be built. By the end of 1978 the latest Maverick type to be revealed was AGM-65E, carrying a 250-lb (113-kg) penetration anti-ship warhead in place of the lighter payload employed with earlier types.

Type: air-to-surface missile
Powerplant: one Thiokol TX-481 du[al]-thrust solid-propellant rocket motor
Performance: speed Mach 1.2 or 912 m[ph] (1468 km/h) during boost phase, subso[nic] during glide after burn-out; maximum ra[nge] about 14 miles (22.4 km)
Weight: 465 lb (211 kg)
Dimensions: span 28.3 in (72 cm); leng[th] 8 ft 2 in (2.49 m); diameter 8 in (30 cm)
Warhead: hollow-charge, weighing 130 [lb] (59 kg)
Operators: Greece, Iran, Israel, Korea, Sa[udi] Arabia, Sweden, South Korea, Turkey, [US] Air Force

Hughes AIM-4 Falcon

The Hughes AIM-4 Falcon was the world's first operational guided air-to-air missile, entering service in 1956 as an anti-bomber weapon arming Northrop F-89 Scorpions and then Convair F-102A Delta Daggers of the US Air Force's Aerospace Defense Command. Hughes built 4,000 of these AIM-4As (originally designated GAR-1s), the missile being fitted with a semi-active radar seeker which homed on to energy transmitted by the fighter's fire control radar and reflected from its target. These were followed by 12,000 examples of the GAR-1D (also known later as AIM-4A) and were joined in 1956 by the first of 16,000 GAR-2/AIM-4Cs. This version employed infra-red homing rather than radar seeking and was carried by McDonnell F-101B Voodoo fighters in addition to the F-102As. By fitting a combination of IR and radar Falcons, the interceptors could engage targets at any height, in both fair and bad weather. An additional 9,500 AIM-4Cs were built as GAR-2As, while 4,000 were constructed under licence by Saab in Sweden (3,000 as Rb28s for the Swedish air force, and 1,000 as HM58s for the Swiss air force).

The AIM-4D/GAR-2B was the first mark of Falcon designed for tactical air combat rather than bomber interception and was carried by USAF Tactical Air Command fighters until replaced by late models of the AIM-9 Sidewinder, having proved ineffective in combat. By this time the AIM-4E/GAR-3 was in service, being joined in 1960 by the AIM-4F/GAR-3A (semi-active radar) and AIM-4G/GAR-4A (infra-red) models. The heavier AIM-26 entered production in 1960 and was built in two versions: AIM-26A, with a nuclear warhead; and AIM-26B, carrying a conventional payload. The latter was also built by Saab as the Rb27/HM55. The AIM-26B is the only version of Falcon remaining in US service, some 600 rounds being deployed by Aerospace Defense Command. The AIM-4H, with an active optical seeker, was abandoned during development, as was the Mach 6, 100-mile (160-km) AIM-47A carried by the YF-12A interceptor.

Type: (AIM-26B Falcon) air-to-air missile
Powerplant: one 5,800-lb (2630-kg) Thiok[ol] M60 solid-propellant rocket motor
Performance: burn-out speed Mach 2 1,320 mph (2124 km/h) at 40,000 [ft] (12190 m); maximum range 10 miles (16 k[m])
Weight: 250 lb (113 kg)
Dimensions: span 2 ft (61 cm); leng[th] 6 ft 9 in (2.06 m); diameter 11.5 in (29.2 c[m])
Warhead: high-explosive
Operators: Canada (AIM-4D/AIM-26[B]), Greece (AIM-4D), Sweden (Rb27/Rb2[8]), Switzerland (HM55/HM58), Turkey (AI[M-] 4D), Taiwan (AIM-4D), USAF Aerospa[ce] Defense Command (AIM-26B)

Hughes AIM-54A Phoenix

The Hughes AIM-54A Phoenix was originally developed to arm the US Navy's General Dynamics F-111B fleet air-defence fighter, and guided firing trials from this type began in March 1968. The F-111B was abandoned, however, and its place taken by the Grumman F-14 Tomcat, which inherited both the Phoenix and its associated Hughes AWG-9 fire-control system from its predecessor. A Tomcat launched its first Phoenix in April 1972 and the missile entered service in 1974.

An F-14 can carry six AIM-54s, all of which can be guided simultaneously to intercept different targets. The Tomcat's pulse-doppler search and tracking radar can detect fighter-sized targets at any altitude while they are still at least 133 miles (214 km) away; this coverage extends across a 174 mile (280 km) front, giving a surveillance volume more than 10 times that which can be achieved by the AWG-10 radar in the F-4J Phantom, which the F-14 has replaced. The radar can track 20 targets simultaneously while continuing to search, and six of these can each be attacked with a Phoenix, the targets being illuminated in turn; the semi-active homing head in AIM-54 does not need continuous illumination in order to home on to its objective. In the last 10 miles (16 km) or so of the interception, the Phoenix switches to active radar seeking and is independent of the Tomcat's radar. The missile's main drawback is its high cost.

The Phoenix has proved itself capable of engaging targets at very long ranges, and of

Six Phoenix AAMs are seldom carried at once by F-14A Tomcats on inventory duty, but this photograph was taken during the AIM-15A development programme. Current AIM-54B missiles have cheaper sheet-metal wings and fins, and part-digital guidance.

intercepting low-flying cruise missiles in addition to high-altitude intruders. Aircraft flying in close formation, manoeuvring in an attempt to break the radar seeker's lock, or jamming the Tomcat radar have also been attacked successfully.

In early 1978 Hughes was awarded a contract to develop the improved AIM-54C version, which is intended to counter any threat which might be introduced in the 1990s.

Type: long-range air-to-air missile
Powerplant: one Rocketdyne Mk 47 solid-propellant rocket motor
Performance: cruise speed at least Mach 3.8 or 2,500 mph (4023 km/h) at 40,000 ft (12190 m); maximum range 125 m[iles] (201 km)
Weight: 975 lb (442 kg)
Dimensions: span 3 ft 3 in (99 cm); leng[th] 13 ft (4.26 m); diameter 15 in (38 cm)
Warhead: high-explosive, weighing 132 [lb] (60 kg)
Operators: Iran, US Navy

Hughes TOW

The Hughes BGM-71A TOW (Tube-launched, Optically sighted, Wire-guided missile) has been widely deployed in both the ground-based and air-launched roles. Firings from helicopters began in October 1966, using a Bell UH-1B 'Huey' as the launch platform, and two of these aircraft fitted with the XM26 TOW system were sent into action to help defend Kontum in Vietnam from May 1972. They destroyed 62 targets between them and proved the value of helicopters armed with modern anti-tank missiles.

Development of the UH-1B/XM26 combination had been completed in mid-1968 after a total of 62 firings, this programme overlapping work carried out between mid-1967 and the end of 1972 on fitting TOW to the Lockheed AH-56 Cheyenne attack helicopter. A total of 110 launches from this platform were made, including 16 at night, but the Cheyenne was eventually abandoned and emphasis switched to the new XM65 installation for the AH-1 HueyCobra. Firing trials began in February 1973, and by the early 1980s the US Army will have nearly 1,000 of the uprated AH-1S version equipped with eight TOW launchers each.

The XM65 installation uses a chin-mounted gyro-stabilized sight, with which the gunner in the HueyCobra's front seat tracks his target. A missile is then fired from one of the eight launchers, four on each stub wing, and is automatically gathered on to the gunner's line of sight by means of an infra-red sensor aligned with the sight; this detects radiation from a lamp on the TOW, and a small computer calculates steering corrections which are

Frame from a high-speed cinefilm showing the departure of a Hughes anti-tank missile from an AH-1Q TOWCobra of the US Army.

transmitted down trailing wires to the missile. This process continues until impact.

The TOW/XM65 has also been fitted in other helicopters, including the Hughes 500M-D Defender, the Italian Agusta A 109 and the Westland/Aérospatiale Lynx. The Defender has been ordered by a number of customers; although the A 109 carried TOW for trials, it was for such purposes only and will be succeeded by the A 129 as the Italian army's definitive TOW-armed helicopter.

The British Army will operate TOW from its Lynxes. Total production of all versions of the TOW missile exceeds 200,000 rounds, probably a record for guided missiles.

Type: anti-tank missile
Powerplant: solid-propellant boost and sustain rocket motors
Performance: cruise speed Mach 1.05 or 798 mph (1284 km/h) at sea level; maximum range 12,300 ft (3750 m)

Weight: 46 lb (20.9 kg)
Dimensions: span 13.4 in (34 cm); length 3 ft 10 in (1.17 m); diameter 6 in (15 cm)
Warhead: hollow-charge, weighing 8.6 lb (3.9 kg)
Operators: Canada, Denmark, Germany, Greece, Holland, Iran, Israel, Italy, Jordan, Kenya, Kuwait, Lebanon, Luxembourg, Norway, Oman, Turkey, Morocco, South Korea, Sweden, Saudi Arabia, UK, US Army, US Marine Corp

Hughes/Martin Walleye

The family of AGM-62 Walleye television-guided unpowered glide bombs has been developed by the US Naval Weapons Center at China Lake and built by both Hughes and Martin Marietta. The latter received a production contract for Walleye I in January 1966, with the former starting production as second-source contractor the following year. This original version is operated by both the US Air Force and the US Navy, seeing action during the war in Vietnam, and has additionally been supplied to the Israeli Defence Forces.

The larger Walleye II forms the basis for the latest version, Extended-Range Data-Link Walleye, which has enlarged wings to give it a greater glide range. All Walleyes are fitted with a nose-mounted television camera with the launch-aircraft pilot or weapons operator locks on to its target by means of a cockpit monitor and joystick. Once the camera crosshairs have been placed over the bomb's objective Walleye can be released and will automatically home on to that point. The US Navy favours a two-aircraft collaborative at-

tack with the extended-range version, one dropping the weapon and the other either locking on its TV camera after launch or steering the Walleye all the way to impact, using the data link to carry video signals from the bomb and steering commands in the reverse direction.

Although unpowered, Walleye can glide considerable distances and has been considered by the US Navy as a possible alternative to the powered Condor air-to-surface missile, which was abandoned despite its much greater range.

Type: (Walleye I) glide-bomb
Powerplant: none
Performance: glide speed, subsonic; maximum range 16 miles (25 km)
Weight: 1,100 lb (499 kg)
Dimensions: span 3 ft 9 in (1.14 m); length 11 ft 3 in (3.44 m); diameter 12.5 in (31.7 cm)
Warhead: high-explosive, weighing 850 lb (386 kg)
Operators: Israel, US Air Force, US Navy

Hughes/Raytheon AMRAAM

The US Air Force announced in February 1979 that it had selected Hughes and Raytheon to build prototype AMRAAMs (Advanced Medium-Range Air-to-Air Missiles) for competitive evaluation. The losing contenders were Ford Aerospace, General Dynamics and Northrop. This so-called validation phase will last 33 months, after which the winning design will enter full-scale development. AMRAAM is expected to

enter service in about 1986, arming the US forces' Grumman F-14 Tomcats, McDonnell Douglas F-15 Eagles, General Dynamics F-16s and McDonnell Douglas/Northrop F-18 Hornets, replacing the AIM-7 Sparrow family. The new missile may be built in Europe to equip other NATO air forces.

The AMRAAM will have greater performance than the Sparrow but is intended to cost less to produce and weigh only half as

much. Requirements include the use of an active rather than semi-active radar seeker, allowing the launch aircraft to break away or launch other weapons immediately an AMRAAM has been fired. A high-impulse rocket motor will be used to give a short flight time. All electronic components are to use digital techniques, and a 'strapdown' mid-course inertial guidance unit, in which the assembly is attached directly to the airframe

rather than being gimballed, is specified.

Launch aircraft will need few modifications to adapt them for AMRAAM operations, but improvements in fire-control equipment and long-range target identification will be introduced to complement the new weapon.

Martin Marietta/Maxson Bullpup

The US Navy began development of the Bullpup in 1954 under the designation ASM-N-7, using a USN-designed solid-propellant rocket motor mated to a standard 250-lb (113-kg) bomb; the pilot of the launch aircraft steered the weapon by means of a joystick which generated manoeuvre commands for transmission over a radio link. This version, later redesignated AGM-12A, entered service with the US Navy in 1959, but was soon succeeded by the improved AGM-12B (formerly ASM-N-7A) Bullpup A, with a packaged liquid-propellant rocket motor, extended range and more effective warhead. In 1961 the USAF also adopted AGM-12B, which it designated GAM-83 for a time, incorporating a modified guidance system so that attacks could be made with the launch aircraft flying off to one side of the target. Kongsberg Våpenfabrikk constructed the missile under licence in Norway from 1963. Production totalled 22,100 rounds in the United States, both Martin Marietta and Maxson Electronics setting up assembly lines, plus about 8,000 more constructed by Kongsberg.

The much larger AGM-12C Bullpup B

(originally known as ASM-N-7B by the US Navy and GAM-83B by the USAF) entered service in 1964, production ending in 1969 after 4,600 rounds had been constructed (mostly by Maxson). Some 840 examples of the AGM-12E version with a fragmentation warhead were built for service in Vietnam, but this programme was then abandoned. Other variants which failed to enter service were the AGM-12D with a nuclear warhead, the Martin AGM-79A Bulleye using electro-optical homing, the Chrysler AGM-80A Viper employing inertial guidance, and the laser-guided Texas Instruments AGM-83A Bulldog. Development of the last-named began in 1969 with the intention of fitting new seekers to existing rounds in order to provide the US Marine Corps with an accurate close-support weapon; a number of Bulldogs were built, but this plan has now been abandoned.

Type: (AGM-12B Bullpup A) air-to-surface missile
Powerplant: one 12,000-lb (5433-kg) Thiokol LR-58RM4 packaged liquid-

The four chief members of the Bullpup ASM family are: (thin missile) ATM-12A training weapon without warhead; (largest missile) AGM-12C Bullpup B; (upper left) AGM-12D with option of nuclear warhead; and (lower left) the common AGM-12B Bullpup A.

continued

propellant rocket motor
Performance: speed about Mach 1.8 or 1,370 mph (2205 km/h) at sea level; maximum range 7.5 miles (12 km)
Weight: 571 lb (259 kg)
Dimensions: span 3 ft 1 in (94 cm); length 10 ft 6 in (3.20 m); diameter 1 ft (30.5 cm)

Warhead: high-explosive 250 lb (113 kg)
Operators: Argentina, Australia, Brazil, Chile, Denmark, Greece, Israel, New Zealand, Norway, Philippines, South Korea, Taiwan, Turkey, US Air Force, US Navy, Venezuela

Type: (AGM-12C Bullpup B) air-to-surface missile
Powerplant: one 33,000-lb (14969-kg) Thiokol LR-62RM2 storable liquid-propellant rocket motor
Performance: speed about Mach 2.0 or 1,520 mph (2446 km/h) at sea level; max-

imum range 10 miles (16 km)
Weight: 1,785 lb (810 kg)
Dimensions: span 3 ft 10½ in (1.18 m); length 13 ft 4 in (4.07 m); diameter 17.3 in (44 cm)
Warhead: 1,000 lb high explosive
Operators: US Air Force, US Navy

Matra Super 530

Despite its similar designation, the Matra Super 530 is very different from its predecessor, R.530. It has twice the range of the earlier missile, and its seeker can lock on to targets at double the distance. Whereas the R.530 has interchangeable infra-red or semi-active radar seekers, the Super 530 has only one type: the Electronique Marcel Dassault Super AD26, developed from the SAR head employed in the earlier weapon, and which began airborne captive trials in September 1972. Targets are illuminated by the launch aircraft's fire-control radar, allowing the Super AD26 to home on to reflected radiation.

Flight trials of inert rounds began in 1973, with the first target interception being achieved the following year. The Super 530 is planned to arm the French air force's Dassault Mirage F.1 and Dassault Mirage 2000 interceptors, entering service on the former type in 1980. The project was announced in 1971, and at that time a service-entry date of the late 1970s was announced. The missile will be able

to snap up or down after launching, being capable of intercepting an intruder flying at a height of 75,468 ft (23000 m) after having been fired at 59,054 ft (18000 m).

Type: air-to-air missile
Powerplant: Thomson-Brandt/SNPE Angèle dual-thrust solid-propellant rocket motor with a 2-second boost burn and 4-second sustain burn.
Performance: speed Mach 4.5 or 2,951 mph (4750 km/h) at 40,000 ft (12190 m); maximum range 22 miles (35 km)
Weight: 529 lb (240 kg)
Dimensions: span 35.4 in (90 cm); length 11 ft 7 in (3.54 m); diameter 10.24 in (26 cm)
Warhead: high-explosive
Operators: ordered by French air force

Replacing the unsatisfactory Matra R.530, the Super 530 is a high performance air-to-air missile carried by the Mirage F1, as shown here, and intended for the Mirage 2000.

Matra R.550 Magic

Matra's R.511 and R.530 air-to-air missiles were developed to arm interceptors operating under ground control, with engagements taking place head-on at comparatively long ranges, but many of the company's actual and potential customers wanted a weapon to complement the cannon in the air-superiority role. The requirement was therefore for a highly manoeuvrable weapon which could be fired at short notice and acquire its target over a wide angle, allowing the missile to be effective in dogfights as well as straight-on interceptions.

Matra began full-scale development of the R.550 Magic in April 1969, following completion of a two-year feasibility study, and the first fully guided round made its maiden flight in January 1972. Advances in technology since the R.511 and R.530 were designed have been combined to give Magic an impressive performance. The SAT AD3601 infra-red seeker can acquire targets throughout a 140° cone ahead of the missile, which can be launched from an aircraft manoeuvring at up to 6g. The Magic itself can pull more than 35g, being steered by a set of canard cruciform wings. A similar set of fixed fins mounted just ahead of these surfaces guides the airflow and prevents the wings from stalling at high angles of attack. The R.550 can be mounted on standard Sidewinder attachment points, allowing it to be fitted to a wide variety of existing aircraft, and it may be launched at speeds up to 777 mph (1250 km/h).

The first production rounds were delivered in December 1975, and by the end of 1978 more than 5,000 missiles had been ordered to arm a broad selection of Western and Russian-designed fighters. These include the Dassault Mirage III, 5 and F.1; the SEPECAT Jaguar; the Vought F-8 Crusader; the Dassault Super Etendard; the Northrop F-5E and F-5F; and the Mikoyan-Gurevich MiG-21.

Impressive view taken by a fin-mounted camera of firing of a Matra 550 Magic dogfight missile from the left overwing launcher of a Jaguar International export version at about 20,000 ft (9000 m) in a moderate turn.

Type: air-to-air missile
Powerplant: one Société Nationale des Poudres et Explosifs *Roméo* solid-propellant rocket motor, burning for 1.9 seconds
Performance: speed at least Mach 2 or 1,312 mph (2112 km/h) at 40,000 ft

(12190 m); maximum range 6.25 miles (10 km) at medium altitudes
Weight: 198 lb (90 kg)
Dimensions: span 2 ft 2 in (66 cm); length 8 ft 11 in (2.72 m); diameter 6.2 in (15.7 cm)
Warhead: high-explosive, weighing 27.6 lb

(12.5 kg)
Operators: Abu Dhabi, Egypt, Ecuador, India, Iraq, Oman, Pakistan, Saudi Arabia, South Africa, Syria, French air force, French navy and others

Matra R.530

Matra began development of the R.530 in 1958 as a successor to its first air-to-air missile, the R.511, and the weapon entered service with the French air force five years later. Its design reflects the level of technology available at the time: control is by a combination of cruciform rear fins for manoeuvring in pitch and yaw, combined with ailerons for roll control. The R.530's angle of attack for stable flight is limited to 15°, only marginally better than R.511's 12°, and the Israeli air force — an early customer — soon found that the missile did not live up to its expectations.

The weapon has, however, been ordered by many customers for the Dassault Mirage fighter, more than 4,000 rounds having been built. Alternative seeker heads are available: the SAT AD3501 infra-red homing head or the Electronique Marcel Dassault AD26 semi-active radar seeker. The former can detect and track a target from all angles by means of its heat signature, while the latter senses radar energy transmitted from the launch aircraft and reflected by the target. The R.530 can engage intruders at any height up to 68,897 ft (21000 m). In *Armée de l'Air* service the R.530

is to be replaced by the Super 530.

Type: air-to-air missile
Powerplant: one 18,739-lb (8500-kg) Hotchkiss-Brandt/SNPE *Antoinette* dual-thrust solid-propellant rocket motor with a 2.7-second booster burn and 6.5-second sustain burn.
Performance: speed Mach 2.7 or 1,771 mph (2850 km/h) at 40,000 ft (12190 m); maximum range 11 miles (18 km)
Weight: 423 lb (192 kg)
Dimensions: span 3 ft 7.3 in (1.10 m);

length (radar) 10 ft 9.1 in (3.28 m), (infra-red) 10 ft 5.6 in (3.19 m); diameter 10.35 in (26.3 m)
Warhead: Hotchkiss-Brandt interchangeable fragmentation or continuous rod, weighing 60 lb (27 kg)
Operators: Argentina, Austria, Brazil, Colombia, Egypt, Lebanon, Libya, Pakistan, South Africa, Spain, Venezuela, French air force, French navy

McDonnell Douglas Genie

e McDonnell Douglas AIR-2A Genie, ginally designated MB-1, resulted from the Air Force's Ding Dong and High Card jects, entering service in January 1957 ard interceptors of the US Air Force's rospace Defense Command. The nuclear rhead, with a yield of some 1.5 kilotons, d an effective radius of more than 1,000 ft 5 m) against large aircraft, and rendered y form of precision guidance superfluous; nie was controlled only by a stabilizing roscope and fins to counter the drop caused by gravity.

In July 1957 a Northrop F-89J Scorpion fired a Genie carrying a live nuclear warhead over the Nevada desert in order to test the effect on a group of observers standing beneath. The warhead was detonated at a height of 15,000 ft (4572 m) after the weapon had flown 3 miles (5 km), and no ill effects were reported. More than 10,000 Genies are thought to have been built between 1957 and 1962 to arm USAF Convair F-102A Delta Daggers and the later F-106A Delta Darts.

The weapon is still carried by the latter of these types, as well as by McDonnell Douglas CF-101F Voodoos operated by the Canadian Armed Forces. Plans for a guided version, the AIR-2B, were abandoned in 1963 and a 1966 proposal for an air-to-surface variant similarly failed to come to fruition.

Type: air-to-air unguided rocket
Powerplant: one 36,500-lb (16556-kg) Thiokol TU-289 (SR49-TC-1) solid-propellant rocket motor
Performance: cruise speed Mach 3 or 1,980 mph (3186 km/h) at 40,000 ft (12190 m); maximum range 6 miles (10 km)
Weight: 820 lb (372 kg)
Dimensions: span 3 ft 3 in (99.1 cm); length 9 ft 7 in (2.92 m); diameter 17.35 in (44.1 cm)
Warhead: nuclear, approx 1.5 kilotons yield
Operators: Canada, US Air Force

McDonnell Douglas Harpoon

e McDonnell Douglas Harpoon is the ited States Navy's standard anti-ship ssile, and can be launched from aircraft, sure ships or submarines. The weapon is igned to make as much use as possible of sting equipment such as launchers and fire-trol systems. It entered service in 1976-77 ard the USN's 'Knox'-class frigates, on ich it is fired from normal Asroc launchers, d it is also planned to arm 'Spruance' and)G destroyers, CG cruisers, 'Oliver Hazard ry' class patrol frigates, PHM hydrofoils d nuclear-powered attack submarines. rcraft which are expected to carry the ;M-84A air-launched version include Lockheed P-3C Orion, Lockheed S-3A king, Grumman A-6E Intruder and Vought 7E Corsair.

When mounted on aircraft, Harpoon is at-hed to standard weapon pylons and needs boost motor. Information about the target p's position, course and speed is derived m existing sensors such as radar and is fed the missile via a matching unit tailored for t particular application. On surface ships weapon may be fired from specially design-canisters or from multi-role launchers ich can also handle surface-to-air missiles, ddition to the Asroc equipment. The Har-n is enclosed in a buoyant capsule which fits into standard torpedo tubes when it is carried aboard submarines, the encapsulated round floating to the surface before the missile flies free and begins its mission. A rocket boost motor is used for surface and subsurface launches.

The Harpoon is guided during most of its flight by an inertial navigator working in conjunction with a radar altimeter; these keep it flying just above the sea surface so that it cannot be detected by its target. As it approaches the enemy ship, the Harpoon automatically switches on a radar seeker which searches for the target and locks on to it. This homing head then feeds information into the autopilot so that the weapon steers to intercept its target. The Harpoon can 'pop up' in the final stages of an attack and then dive on to the ship, thus making it more difficult to shoot down.

Type: (RGM-84A) anti-ship missile
Powerplant: one 660-lb (300-kg) Teledyne CAE J402 single-spool turbojet; also one 15,000-lb (6800-kg) Aerojet solid-propellant rocket booster in surface- and submarine-launched versions
Performance: cruising speed Mach 0.85 or 650 mph (1040 km/h) at sea level; maximum range 70 miles (110 km)

One of the most versatile modern missiles is the McDonnell Douglas Harpoon, which can be fired from surface vessels (USS *High Point* shown), submarines and aircraft. By late 1979 Harpoon had been adopted by 13 countries, including Britain.

Weight: 1,460 lb (664 kg) with booster, 1,160 lb (527 kg) without booster
Dimensions: span 3 ft 3 in (91 cm); length 15 ft (4.58 m) with booster, or 12 ft 7 in (3.84 m) without booster; diameter 13½ in (34 cm)
Warhead: 500-lb (227-kg) blast high-explosive
Operators: Australia, Denmark, Iran, Israel, Japan, Netherlands, Saudi Arabia, South Korea, UK, US Navy, West Germany

McDonnell Douglas/Martin ASALM

e supersonic McDonnell Douglas/Martin vanced Strategic Air-Launched Missile SALM) is intended for use against both air-ne and surface targets, including aircraft d for early warning and control, surface-to-missile sites, and ballistic-missile silos. The ASALM could thus replace both the Boeing SRAM and the proposed new generation of subsonic cruise missiles such as the Boeing ALCM-B and General Dynamics Tomahawk. Martin and McDonnell Douglas were expected to receive competitive airframe-development contracts in 1979, leading to six demonstration flights in 1981. The winning contractor could then proceed with engineering development, with service entry in 1986.

The ASALM is to be powered by an integral rocket/ramjet, Martin and McDonnell Douglas being teamed with Marquardt and United Technologies (CSD) respectively as their engine contractors. Raytheon and Rockwell are amongst the companies working on guidance technology which could be applied to the ASALM.

Messerschmitt-Bölkow-Blohm Kormoran

e MBB Kormoran (Cormorant) has been veloped to arm the German navy's ckheed F-104G Starfighters and later its navia Tornado multi-role combat aircraft, owing warships of frigate size and above in Baltic and North Sea to be attacked from tside the range of their defensive weapons. e missile entered service in December 1977, initial production contract covering 56 air-ft installations and 350 rounds for delivery 1981. Starfighters can each carry two Kor-rans and the Tornado will be armed with to four.

The missile has been designed so that it can launched at very low levels, down to 100 ft m). This allows the fighter-bomber to ke its attack without being detected by its get, since at that height it is below the ar horizon from the enemy ship. The radar the launch aircraft supplies information ut the target's position, course and speed ile it is still some 50 miles (80 km) distant, d a final updating is carried out just before missile is launched. The pilot can aim the rmoran with the aid of an optical sight if radar is not operating effectively.

The weapon accelerates off its laun-er and descends to a cruise height of about ft (20 m) under the control of an inertial igator and radar altimeter. During the final ges of an attack the Kormoran drops to -16 ft (3-5 m), depending on how rough the is, and switches on its Thomson-CSF ac-e radar seeker. This locks on to the target d issues steering commands so that the nd hits its objective. The Kormoran carries ecially designed warhead which has a

First air-launch of the German MBB Kormoran anti-ship missile from an IDS Tornado, over the Sardinia test range in July 1978. The first Kormoran-equipped Tornado unit will be Marineflieger wing MFG 1 at Schleswig Jagel in 1981. This missile is active-homing.

devastating effect even on large targets. The missile penetrates the side of the ship before the warhead detonates, and 16 individual charges produce high-speed slugs which penetrate bulkheads and other internal structures.

Type: air-launched anti-ship missile
Powerplant: (boost) two 6,065-lb (2750-kg) Société Nationale des Poudres et Explosifs Prades solid-propellant rocket motors; (sustain) one 630-kg (285-kg) SNPE Eole solid-propellant rocket motor
Performance: cruising speed Mach 0.9 or 685 mph (1095 km/h) at sea level; maximum range 20 miles (30 km)
Weight: 1,320 lb (600 kg)
Dimensions: span 3 ft 3 in (1 m); length 14 ft 6 in (4.4 m); diameter 13½ in (34.4 cm)
Warhead: 365-lb (165-kg) high-explosive
Operator: West Germany

Mitsubishi AAM-1

The Mitsubishi AAM-1 (Air-to-Air Missile No 1) was Japan's first weapon of this type and is thought to have entered limited service in 1970 as a replacement for the AIM-9 Sidewinder on North American F-86 Sabre and Lockheed F-104J Starfighter interceptors. The missile was designed in collaboration with the Japanese Defence Agency's Technical Research and Development Institute and appears to be based on its US counterpart. The initial production run is thought to have totalled 330 rounds, but it is not known whether the planned purchase of 3,000 AAM-1s in all was completed.

In 1968 the Mitsubishi/TRDI team started development of AAM-2, which was planned to replace the Hughes AIM-4D Falcons bought as an interim weapon to arm the Japan Air Self-Defence Force's McDonnell Douglas F-4EJ Phantom fighters. The AAM-2 would have overcome the main drawback of AAM-1, the fact that it can intercept targets only from the rear because its infra-red seeker is relatively insensitive, but development has been abandoned and US weapons are likely to be bought instead.

Type: air-to-air missile
Powerplant: solid-propellant rocket motor
Performance: speed unknown; maximum range 3 miles (5 km)
Weight: 167 lb (76 kg)
Dimensions: span 1 ft 8 in (50 cm); length ft 2½ in (2.5 m); diameter 5.9 in (15 cm)
Warhead: high-explosive
Operator: Japan

Mitsubishi ASM-1

Development of the Mitsubishi ASM-1 air-launched anti-ship missile was begun in 1973, and firings of two unguided prototypes took place from a Mitsubishi F-1 fighter-bomber over Wasaka Bay in December 1977. Trials continued in early 1978, and eight rounds were due to have been fired against static targets from low altitude in the middle of that year. Tests against moving targets were scheduled to follow in the first four months of 1979, with final acceptance testing taking place in the winter of 1979-80.

The ASM-1 was originally planned to be powered by an air-breathing engine, but a solid-propellant rocket motor was adopted for early trials. The designers have since reverted to jet propulsion, however, which will allow operational weapons to have at least double the range achieved by the prototypes. The rocket-powered ASM-1 may still enter service in that form, with the longer-range version being used for surface-launched applications by the Japanese Ground and Maritime Self-Defence Forces.

ASM-1 cruises at a height of between 16 ft (5 m) and 65 ft (20 m), depending on sea state, under the control of an inertial navigator and radio altimeter. The final stage of the attack is made with the aid of an active radar seeker, which locks on to the target and updates the missile's course.

The initial production run is expected to total 150 rounds, with the missile arming F-1 attack aircraft and possibly Lockheed P-3C Orion maritime-patrol aircraft. The eventual requirement could run as high as 800 rounds.

Type: air-launched anti-ship missile
Powerplant: Nissan Motors solid-propellant rocket motor; may be replaced by air breathing engine in production missiles
Performance: cruising speed Mach 0.9 685 mph (1095 km/h) at sea level; maximum range 28 miles (45 km) with rocket motor and at least double this with jet propulsion
Weight: 1,345 lb (610 kg)
Dimensions: span 3 ft 11 in (1.2 m); length 12 ft 11½ in (3.95 m); diameter 13.7 in cm)
Warhead: 441-lb (200-kg) high-explosive
Operator: Japan

Rafael Shafrir

The Mk 1 version of Shafrir (Dragonfly), the first air-to-air missile designed by Israel's Rafael armament development authority, did not live up to expectations and was abandoned in the early 1960s. Work on the Mk 2 began in the middle of that decade, using information published in the West since 1959. The missile was not, according to its designer, copied from the US Sidewinder or Russian AA-2 'Atoll' which it closely resembles in appearance. Rafael is normally responsible for research and development only, leaving production to a commercial company, but an exception was made in the case of the Shafrir in order to save time. Production of the rocket motor, of which the pre-series batch was built by Rafael, has since been handed over to a subcontractor, but assembly of the weapon remains Rafael's responsibility.

The Mk 2 version entered service in time for the October 1973 war with the Arabs, in which it was credited with the destruction of more than 100 aircraft. Overall kill rate is claimed to be as high as 60%, part of this resulting from the great emphasis placed on reliability during production. The Shafrir arms the Israeli air force's Dassault Mirage fighters and the various types of indigenously developed derivatives, including the IAI Kfir. Warning lamps and a tone in his headphones inform the pilot that the Shafrir's infra-red seeker has locked on to its target, and the missile can then be fired. The warhead is comparatively large for the size of the weapon and is said to have an effective radius of 23 – 26 ft (7 – 8 m) against a typical target.

A Mk 3 version of Shafrir is reported to be under development. This will be able to attack targets from all angles, with greater manoeuvrability and a larger firing envelope.

Type: air-to-air missile
Powerplant: solid-propellant rocket motor
Performance: maximum range 3.1 miles (5 km)
Weight: 205 lb (93 kg)
Dimensions: span 1 ft 8½ in (52 cm); length 8 ft 1 in (2.47 m); diameter 6.3 in (16 cm)
Warhead: high-explosive, weighing 24.3 (11 kg)
Operators: Chile, Israel, Taiwan, possibly others

Raytheon Sparrow

The current version of this long-serving US air-to-air missile is the Raytheon AIM-7 Sparrow III, which entered service in August 1958. The earlier AIM-7A Sparrow I, which employed beam-riding guidance, is no longer operational and the active radar AIM-7B Sparrow II was cancelled. The latest variant to enter service is the AIM-7F, incorporating several improvements compared with the AIM-7E and -7E2 which saw extensive service in the Vietnam war. The maximum range of -7F is nearly twice that of its immediate predecessor, and a larger warhead is fitted. Raytheon is now developing a new homing head, the advanced monopulse seeker (AMS), to enter service in 1980; like the monopulse seeker of the British Aerospace Sky Flash, this will have greater resistance to countermeasures than earlier seekers and will allow the Sparrow to intercept targets against a background of clutter.

The Sparrow III employs semi-active radar guidance: the fire-control radar in the launch aircraft illuminates the target, and the missile homes on to reflected energy. Large cruciform wings mounted in the mid-fuselage position are used for steering, with fixed fins at the rear for stability.

The Sparrow is standard armament on the McDonnell Douglas F-4 Phantom fighter operated by the US forces and export customers, and the weapon also arms the

In all configurations, as here with 18 conventional bombs, the F-15 Eagle retains its primary load of four Sparrows.

Aeritalia F-104S version of Lockheed's Starfighter. The AIM-7F will replace earlier models on the USAF's McDonnell Douglas F-15 Eagle fighters and the US Navy's Grumman F-14 Tomcats in addition to the Phantoms, and it will also equip the USN's new McDonnell Douglas F-18s. The Sparrow has been adapted for surface-launched applications in the form of Sea Sparrow and Land Sparrow, and the design forms the basis of both the British Sky Flash and the Italian Selenia Aspide. The missile is due to be replaced from the late 1980s by the AMRAAM (Advanced Medium-Range Air-to-Air Missile).

Type: (AIM-7F Sparrow III) air-to-air missile
Powerplant: one Hercules Mk 48 or Aerojet Mk 65 solid-propellant rocket motor
Performance: cruising speed Mach 4 or 2,640 mph (4224 km/h) at 40,000 ft (12190 m); maximum range 62 miles (100 km), although half this figure is more usual in typical engagements, and the AIM-7E's range is seldom over 20 miles (32 km)
Weight: 500 lb (228 kg)
Dimensions: span 3 ft 3½ in (1 m); length ft 11½ in (3.65 m); diameter 8 in (20 cm)
Warhead: 88-lb (40-kg) continuous-rod
Operators: (7E) Germany, Greece, Iran, Israel, Italy, Japan, RAF, South Korea, Turkey, US Air Force, US Navy, US Marine Corp.
(7F) US Air Force, US Navy, Israel

Rockwell Hellfire

The Rockwell Hellfire is being developed to arm the Hughes AH-64 Advanced Attack Helicopter, of which the US Army plans to buy 536 for delivery from 1982; each will carry up to 16 missiles. Hellfire derives its name from Heliborne Laser Fire-and-Forget, and the first version to be deployed will indeed employ semi-active laser guidance. The seeker being developed by Rockwell for this application is also planned to equip the AGM-65C version of the Hughes Maverick, along with a variant of the GBU-15 glide bomb. Targets will be illuminated by laser designators mounted either in the launch aircraft or on some other platform. In the former case the illuminator forms part of the AH-64's TADS (Target Acquisition and Designation System). Ground-based alternatives may include the Hughes PAQ-1 LTD (Laser Target Designator), TVQ-2 GLLD (Ground Laser Locator Designator) or MULE (Modular Universal Laser Equipment).

Hellfire has been developed from the Hornet test vehicle and may form the basis of other weapons. Alternative television and imaging infra-red terminal seekers have been developed, and the same airframe could be adapted for defence suppression by fitting a dual-mode infra-red/radio-frequency homing head. In this form it becomes ADSM (Air Defence Suppression Missile).

The AH-64 gunner/co-pilot uses TADS to search for, detect and recognise targets to be attacked with Hellfire, employing the system's direct-view optics, television or forward-looking infra-red sensor either singly or in combination. He can then track a target either manually or automatically and, once it is being illuminated by a laser, launch a missile against it. The advantage of using a designator on the ground or in another vehicle is that the AH-64, unlike helicopters armed with the current generation of anti-tank missiles, can escape from the target area as soon as a round has been fired.

Type: air-to-surface missile
Powerplant: solid-propellant rocket motor
Performance: cruising speed subsonic; maximum range 3.75 miles (6 km)
Weight: 80 lb (36 kg)
Dimensions: span 13 in (33 cm); length 5 ft 9 in (1.76 m); diameter 7 in (18 cm)
Warhead: Firestone hollow-charge weighing about 20 lb (9 kg)
Operator: US Army

ockwell/Hughes GBU-15

e GBU-15 MGGB (Modular Guided Glide omb) is a family of weapons which can be ilt up from various combinations of payload varhead), guidance, control systems and ng structures. The family forms part of the S Air Force's Pave Strike defence-ppression programme, which is intended to cain the basic features of the earlier ockwell Hobos (Homing Bomb System) eapons deployed in Vietnam from 1969 nile improving delivery range and conferring e ability to operate in all weathers.

Initial production of the basic version, own as the CWW (cruciform-wing eapon), was authorized in the autumn of 78. This is built round a standard Mk 84 000-lb (907-kg) bomb, with cruciform ngs fitted fore-and-aft for stability and conol. A television seeker is normally fitted, hough this can be replaced by either the iming infra-red seeker of the AGM-65D rsion of Maverick or the semi-active laser ker planned for AGM-65C Maverick and ellfire. Similarly, the Mk 84 bomb can be placed by other payloads such as the SUU-54 omunitions dispenser.

Trials of the GBU-15 CWW have taken ce at heights of between 200 and 1,000 ft) and 300 m), and the bomb will be used for w-level attacks against ships and ground

targets. Total procurement is expected to run to 5,000 rounds, including the PWW (planar-wing weapon) version being developed by Hughes but not likely to be ordered into production before the autumn of 1979. The PWW has flip-out wings to increase its glide range, allowing it to be launched against high-value targets from B-52 bombers or fighters at comparatively long distances. GBU-15 can be launched before its seeker locks on to the target, if desired, being guided by command until the homing head can acquire its objective. The operator may be in the carrier aircraft or in another, giving flexibility in the type of attack.

Type: unpowered glide bomb
Powerplant: none
Performance: cruising speed subsonic; maximum range varies with launch height, but up to about 5 miles (8 km) for CWW
Weight: 2,240 lb (1016 kg) with Mk 84 warhead
Dimensions: varies according to type: typical span 3 ft 8 in (1.12 m); length 12 ft 4 in (3.75 m); diameter 1 ft 6 in (46 cm)
Warhead: interchangeable, including 2,000-lb (907-kg) Mk 84 bomb
Operator: US Air Force

Developed under the USAF Pave Strike defence-suppression programme, this CWW (Cruciform-Wing Weapon) is designated GBU-15 (V) and adds precision electro-optical guidance to a large M118 bomb. Carrier in this case is an F-4E Phantom of TAC.

aab B83

e Saab B83 was planned to arm the pro-ted Saab B3LA light attack aircraft, but ubts about the future of that type could well ult in the missile being cancelled, as has ppened several times to Swedish weapon bjects in the 1970s. The B83 uses an infra-d seeker which benefits from development ork done on another abandoned project, the ab Rb72 air-to-air missile. Targets would be quired by an LM Ericsson Munin pod ounted on the launch aircraft. The Munin,

named after one of the ravens which perched on Odin's shoulder and reported back enemy movements in battle, contains a forward-looking infra-red (FLIR) camera mounted on a stabilized platform. The pilot can select wide or narrow fields of view and steer the camera in azimuth and elevation by means of a joystick. Outputs from the camera are processed digitally and the FLIR will lock on to and track hot objects such as tanks.

The missile's infra-red seeker can then be

automatically locked on to the target being tracked by Munin, thus allowing the pilot of a single-seat aircraft to acquire and attack targets at high speed and low level without detracting from his ability to control the aircraft. B83s would be mounted in tandem on a launch rail, the whole assembly being attached to the launch aircraft as one unit.

Type: air-to-surface missile
Powerplant: solid-propellant rocket

Performance: cruising speed subsonic; maximum range not released
Weight: 154 lb (70 kg)
Dimensions: span not released; length 5 ft 5 in (1.65 m); diameter 7.9 in (20 cm)
Warhead: high-explosive
Operator: under development for Sweden

aab Rb04E

e Saab Rb04E is the latest in a series of anti-p missiles dating back to 1949, when the sic Rb04 reached the design phase. In 1959 e Rb04 entered service as armament for the redish air force's Saab A32 Lansen attack ft. This original model was succeeded by e Rb04C and, from 1971, the Rb04D; in at year Saab was awarded a contract for ies production of the improved Rb04E, ich has modifications to the structure and idance equipment to confer a higher hit pro-pility, better reliability and increased istance to electronic countermeasures, as

main armament for the Saab AJ37 Viggen.
The missile is designed to attack landing craft, transport ships and escorts, and carries a warhead which is focussed downwards so that it disables the target. The Rb04E can be launched at any speed between Mach 0.4 or 264 mph (422 km/h) at sea level and velocities just below the speed of sound. After having been fired the weapon descends to low level, under the control of its autopilot and radio altimeter, until it is within about 4 miles (6 km) of its target. The PEAB active radar seeker then automatically searches for its target and locks

on, providing steering commands for the attack phase of the mission. The warhead is detonated by a proximity fuse as the missile flies over its target.
Production of the basic Rb04E was completed in 1978, but Saab has proposed a version known as the Rb04 Turbo. This would have the wings and fins replaced by a cruciform structure and an air-breathing powerplant. The Rb04 Turbo has been offered to the Swedish navy as possibly armament for its 'Hugin' class fast attack craft.

Type: air-to-surface missile
Powerplant: one Imperial Metal Industries solid-propellant rocket
Performance: cruising speed high subsonic; maximum range 25 miles (40 km)
Weight: 1,325 lb (600 kg)
Dimensions: span 6 ft 8 in (2.04 m); length 14 ft 7 in (4.45 m); diameter 19.7 in (50 cm)
Warhead: 440 to 550-lb (200 to 250-kg) fragmentation
Operator: Sweden

aab Rb05

ab began development of the Rb05 in 1960 a light air-to-surface missile for use against all craft, surfaced submarines, land targets d slow-flying aircraft such as helicopters. e weapon normally arms the Saab AJ37 iggen attack aircraft, although it can also be rried by lighter types such as the Saab 105.

a typical attack the launch aircraft ac-lerates to high speed at a height of only -165 ft (20-50 m) above the sea surface and en climbs to about 1,000-1,300 ft (300-400 . After levelling out into horizontal flight, e pilot searches visually for his target. Once has found it, and closed to within the issile's range, the pilot fires an Rb05. The eapon automatically flies up into his field of ew, ahead of the aircraft, within 1.5 seconds being launched.

The missile is steered by means of a joystick ounted on the cockpit side wall and designed comfortable, efficient operation so that the lot can continue to fly his aircraft effectively hile controlling the weapon. Commands nerated by movements of the stick are ansmitted to the Rb05 over a radio link. ares are mounted on the rear of the weapon help the operator keep it in sight, and the arhead is detonated by a proximity fuse.

The operational version is the Rb05A. A rsion designated Rb05B, in which the anual command to line-of-sight control

Saab's all-Swedish Rb05A is a simple command-guidance air/surface missile, here being mated to an AJ 37 Viggen. A more advanced TV-guided RB 05B was cancelled by the Swedish defence board, which bought the American Hughes AGM-65A Maverick instead.

method was replaced by automatic television homing using the Saab TVT-300 camera mounted in the missile's lengthened nose, was abandoned when the Swedish air force selected the Hughes Maverick in its place.

Type: air-to-surface missile
Powerplant: one Volvo Flygmotor VR35 rocket burning storable liquid propellants: hydyne oxidised by fuming red nitric acid
Performance: cruising speed supersonic; maximum range 5.6 miles (9 km)

Weight: 671 lb (305 kg)
Dimensions: span 2 ft 7½ in (80 cm); length 11 ft 10 in (3.6 m); diameter 11.8 in (30 cm)
Warhead: high-explosive
Operator: Sweden

Selenia Aspide

The Selenia Aspide is a multi-role missile which has been developed to form part of naval and land-based anti-aircraft systems in addition to its air-launched role. The weapon is based on the Raytheon Sparrow, which Selenia has built under licence, but the Italian manufacturer claims that this similarity is limited to general layout and that there are no Sparrow components in the Aspide. Development began in 1969, and airborne captive carry trials preceded the firing programme, which started in May 1975. The initial series of tests were made from ground-based launchers, since this application has been given priority. The Aspide entered service in the autumn of 1978 as part of the Selenia Albatros

naval SAM system, and deliveries of land-based Spada batteries, which also use the weapon, are expected to begin in 1980.

Test launches from aircraft may also start in 1980, but money for this part of the programme had still not been made available by early 1979. The only difference between the air-launched Aspide and its naval and land-based counterparts is that larger wings are fitted for air-to-air operations. The Aspide is scheduled to replace AIM-7E Sparrows as armament for the Italian air force's Aeritalia F-104S Starfighters, and the weapon is also likely to be carried by that service's Panavia Tornadoes. The radome and forward fuselage of the Italian missile have been redesigned to

give more efficient operation at hypersonic speeds than its US counterpart, since the Aspide is both faster than the Sparrow and is claimed to have about one-third more range than even the AIM-7F version. Selenia's guidance equipment is also completely new, and is said to have better resistance to jamming, improved performance at low level and a greater ability to track targets flying in ground clutter.

The Aspide will be able to fit present Sparrow-armed fighters with only minor modifications, however, and the missile will compete with Sparrow itself and the British Aerospace Sky Flash for export orders.

Type: air-to-air and surface-to-air missile
Powerplant: solid-propellant rocket
Performance: cruising speed Mach 4 2,640 mph (4224 km/h) at 40,000 ft (121 m); maximum range at least 32 miles (50 k
Weight: 485 lb (220 kg)
Dimensions: span 3 ft 3 in (1 m); length 12 1½ ft (3.70 m); diameter 8 in (20.3 cm)
Warhead: 77-lb (35-kg) fragmentation
Operator: under development for Italy

Sistel/SMA Marte

The Sistel/SMA Marte is an airborne weapon system using an air-launched derivative of the Sistel Sea Killer Mk 2 anti-ship missile, and has been developed to meet a requirement which the Italian navy issued in 1967, calling for a helicopter-launched weapon which could disable ships from stand-off ranges. SMA (Segnalamento Marittimo ed Aereo) was awarded a contract to develop the APQ-706 radar for navigation, target acquisition and missile guidance.

In the early stages of the project both the Sea Killer Mk 1 and Mk 2 were evaluated, the former being suitable as armament for helicopters in the Agusta AB 204/205 class. The Mk 2 version was adopted as standard,

however, and it is planned to equip the Italian navy's Sikorsky SH-3D Sea Kings. Sistel has repeatedly asserted that Marte is virtually ready for production, but the weapon system may not now be deployed until the early 1980s.

Targets are detected by the APQ-706 radar, using a frequency-agile channel. A typical target ship is acquired at a range of 31 miles (50 km) with the Sea King at medium altitude. The helicopter then descends to 130 ft (50 m) and approaches to within missile range. Finally the SH-3D climbs to 650 ft (200 m), after the missiles have been checked and the radar switched on again, to launch a Sea Killer at a range of about 12.5 miles (20 km).

The round is tracked in flight by the helicopter's radar, which allows steering corrections to be computed and transmitted to the missile over a radio link so that it remains on course. The weapon's height is controlled by an on-board radio altimeter, and it can be steered manually by means of a joystick, with the aid of an optical sight, if the radar is inoperative.

Type: (Sea Killer Mk 2) air-launched anti-ship missile system
Powerplant: (boost) one 9,680-lb (4400-kg) SEP 299 solid-propellant rocket burning for 1.7 seconds before being jettisoned; (sustain) one 220-lb (100-kg) SEP 300 solid-propellant

rocket burning for 70 seconds
Performance: cruising speed 670 mph (10 km/h); maximum range 16 miles (25 km)
Weight: 661 lb (300 kg)
Dimensions: span 3 ft 3 in (1 m); length 15 5 in (4.70 m); diameter 8.1 in (20.6 cm)
Warhead: 154-lb (70-kg) semi-armow piercing
Operator: under development for Italy

Texas Instruments HARM

The Texas Instruments AGM-88A HARM (High-speed Anti-Radiation Missile) is being developed jointly for the US Navy and US Air Force, the former service taking the lead. The weapon was due to begin a new series of flight trials in early 1979, following design changes, and a decision on whether to start production is not expected before 1980.

HARM is, as its name suggests, faster than present anti-radiation missiles and is intended to combine the best attributes of the present NWC Shrike and General Dynamics Standard ARM, which it will augment and replace. These advantages include comparative cheapness, light weight and simplicity, the

ability to arm non-specialized aircraft, use of a sensitive broadband receiver, and a large launch envelope. Ground radars to be attacked with HARM are detected by a radar warning receiver in the launch aircraft or by the missile's own seeker operating in the search mode. Threat priorities are automatically calculated, allowing missiles to be fired against the most dangerous ones, those engaged in guiding surface-to-air missiles, for example. Recent improvements made to the weapon's design include the ability to home on to continuous-wave radars and to manoeuvre rapidly as it approaches the target.

The US Navy and US Marine Corps plan to

carry HARM on Grumman A-6 Intruders, Vought A-7E Corsairs and McDonnell Douglas/Northrop A-18 Hornets, while the US Air Force will arm its McDonnell Douglas F-4G Wild Weasel defence-suppression aircraft with the missile.

Type: (AGM-88A) air-launched anti-radiation missile
Powerplant: Thiokol solid-propellant rocket
Performance: cruising speed more than Mach 2 or 1,520 mph (2432 km/h) at sea level; maximum range 11½ miles (18.5 km)
Weight: 807 lb (367 kg)
Dimensions: span 3 ft 8½ in (1.13 m);

length 13 ft 8 in (4.17 m); diameter 10 in (cm)
Warhead: about 145-lb (66-kg) modifi Shrike fragmentation
Operators: under development for US A Force, US Marine Corps, US Navy

Texas Instruments Paveway

The Texas Instruments Paveway laser guidance kit was developed in the mid-1960s to allow conventional free-fall bombs to be converted into guided weapons, thus greatly increasing their accuracy. Trials began in April 1965 and the weapons were introduced in Vietnam from 1968, permitting small, difficult targets such as bridges to be destroyed with a fraction of the number of attacks needed previously. The kit consists of assemblies which are attached to the nose and tail of standard bombs. The guidance and control units are identical for all weapons, but the sizes of the canard steering surfaces and tail assemblies vary from type to type.

The nose section comprises a laser seeker, small computer and four steerable control surfaces. The seeker head is mounted on a two-

axis gimbal and has a ring mounted at the rear. After the weapon is released, air flowing over this ring causes the seeker assembly to weathercock into the local wind and therefore to point approximately at the target, which is illuminated by a laser designator mounted in an aircraft or operated by ground forces. The laser energy reflected from the target is detected by a silicon quadrant in the seeker head. The on-board computer commands the control surfaces to manoeuvre the weapon until the outputs from the four elements in the quadrant are the same, indicating that the bomb is on course for its target, and this control loop continues until impact.

Weapons in the Paveway family include the GBU-2, -10, -12 and -16, which are laser-guided bombs based respectively on the SUU-

54/B Pave Storm cluster bomb, 2,000-lb (907-kg) Mk 84 demolition bomb, 500-lb (227-kg) Mk 82 demolition bomb, and 1,000-lb (454-kg) Mk 83 demolition bomb used by the US Navy. The Paveway kit can also be fitted to the Mk 20 Mod 2 Rockeye 500-lb (227-kg) anti-tank cluster munition, M117 750-lb (340-kg) demolition bomb, or M118E1 3,000-lb (1361-kg) general-purpose bomb. A modified version of the British Mk 13/18 1,000-lb (454-kg) bomb is being adapted for use by the Royal Air Force.

Type: family of laser-guided bombs
Powerplant: none
Performance: cruising speed depends on launch speed; maximum range depends on launch height

Weight: varies according to weapon: e amples are GBU-2 2,064 lb (938 kg), GBU-2,052 lb (932 kg), M118E1 LGB 3,066 (1394 kg)
Dimensions: varies according to weapo length (GBU-10) 14 ft (4.27 m)
Warhead: varies according to basic weapo
Operators: Australia, Greece, Iran, Neth lands, Saudi Arabia, South Korea, Turke UK, US Air Force, US Navy.

Texas Instruments Shrike

The Texas Instruments AGM-45A Shrike, based partially on the Raytheon Sparrow airframe, was the first US anti-radiation missile (ARM). Development began in 1961 with the aim of countering Russian surface-to-air missiles by destroying their search and tracking radars. The missile entered service with the US Navy's carrier-based attack squadrons in 1964 and has also been deployed by the US Air Force. At least 13 variants have been built, each carrying a passive radiation seeker tailored to counter a different threat or combination of them.

The missile's seeker locks on to the radar to be attacked, and the weapon is then fired. It

can either home directly on to the enemy transmitter, or it may first climb and then dive on to its objective. This latter method allows the missile to arrive at the same time as weapons delivered by other aircraft. The US Navy uses the Shrike on its McDonnell Douglas A-4 Skyhawk, Grumman A-6 Intruder and Vought A-7 Corsair attack aircraft, but the US Air Force has a specialist Shrike-armed defence-suppression force in the form of McDonnell Douglas F-4G Wild Weasels. The F-4Gs, which replace Republic F-105 Thunderchiefs in this role, carry the McDonnell Douglas APR-38 radar homing and warning sytem to find and classify targets which are

to be attacked with the Shrike and other weapons. The APR-38 uses 56 antennas spread over the aircraft to derive its information.

More than 25,000 Shrikes have been built, and those in service are being updated to improve their performance. The missile is due to be replaced eventually by the Texas Instruments HARM.

Type: air-to-surface anti-radiation missile
Powerplant: one Rocketdyne Mk 39 Mod 7 or Aerojet Mk 53 solid-propellant rocket
Performance: cruising speed Mach 2 or 1,520 mph (2432 km/h) at sea level; max-

imum range at least 10 miles (16 km) a possibly up to 25 miles (40 km)
Weight: 390 lb (177 kg)
Dimensions: span 3 ft (91 cm); length 10 (3.05 m); diameter 7.9 in (20 cm)
Warhead: 145-lb (66-kg) fragmentation
Operators: Israel, US Air Force, US Nav

Soviet Missiles

Like Russian aircraft the guided weapons of the Soviet Union are produced by a state industrial organization under the direction of a central government department, and few of the official designations have leaked past the tight security that surrounds most Soviet weapons. For this reason the following entries are listed by their Western (NATO or ASCC, Air Standards Co-ordinating Committee) designation and reporting names: AA is the prefix for air-to-air weapons and AS for air-to-surface missiles.

A point worth emphasizing is that there was no evidence until recently of any precision tactical missile for use by tactical aircraft against surface targets. That such weapons exist was confirmed by a Soviet general in 1976, who said "If a target exists, we can see it; if we can see it, we can destroy it; and we can destroy it with one missile".

Soviet AA-1 Alkali

The first Russian air-to-air missile, the AA-1 'Alkali' supplanted the more traditional armament of cannon in Mikoyan-Gurevich MiG-17 and MiG-19 fighters. The MiG-17PFU 'Fresco-E' version carried four rounds on rails ahead of the main undercarriage wells and was fitted with an Izumrud (Emerald) fire-control radar (known as 'Scan Fix' by NATO). The MiG-19PM 'Farmer-D' likewise carried four AA-1s in place of cannon, and was fitted with 'Scan Odd' radar. The third and last type to be armed with the 'Alkali' was the Sukhoi Su-11 'Fishpot-B', which could also carry four rounds and was fitted with an R1L ('Spin Scan') fire-control radar. The AA-1 is no longer in front-line service.

Type: air-to-air missile
Powerplant: solid-propellant rocket
Performance: cruising speed between Mach 1 and Mach 2 or 660-1,320 mph (1056-2112 km/h) at 40,000 ft (12190 m); maximum range about 5 miles (8 km)
Weight: about 198 lb (90 kg)
Dimensions: span 2 ft (61 cm); length about 6 ft 6 in (2 m); diameter 7 in (18 cm)
Warhead: high-explosive
Operator: USSR (no longer in front-line service)

Called AA-1 'Alkali' by the West, this canard-control AAM formerly used on the MiG-19PF and Su-9 has semi-active radar homing guidance.

Soviet AA-2 Atoll

The Russian AA-2 'Atoll' air-to-air missile closely resembles its US equivalent, the AIM-9 Sidewinder, and may be based at least partly on captured examples of that weapon. Two are carried on underwing pylons on the Mikoyan-Gurevich MiG-21F 'Fishbed-C' fighter and its immediate successors, the maximum load being doubled to four rounds on the MiG-21PFMA 'Fishbed-J' and later models. Early versions of the missile are designated K13A by the Russians and AA-2 'Atoll' by NATO, and those arming variants from the MiG-21PFMA onwards are thought to be of an improved design known as the AA-2-2 'Advanced Atoll'. The AA-2 certainly employed infra-red guidance, although the AA-2-2 may have interchangeable infra-red and semi-active radar seekers: this is not confirmed, however.

The 'Atoll' is standard armament on MiG-21s which have been exported or built under licence in India, and the missile is also carried by the MiG-23 'Flogger-B' export version in place of the more advanced AA-7 and AA-8 which equip Russian-operated versions of this fighter. The Sukhoi Su-22s supplied to Peru are reported also to carry the 'Atoll'. The AA-2 has been used extensively in combat in the Middle East, Vietnam and Indo-Pakistani wars, although its performance is no better than that of early Sidewinder models. The present versions are thought to be capable only of pursuit-course interceptions, although an all-aspect seeker, which would allow attacks to be made from any direction, may be under development.

Type: (K13A) air-to-air missile
Powerplant: solid-propellant rocket
Performance: cruising speed Mach 2.5 or 1,650 mph (2640 km/h) at 40,000 ft (12190 m); maximum range 4 miles (7 km)

Weight: 155 lb (70 kg)
Dimensions: span 1 ft 9 in (53 cm); length 9 ft 2 in (2.8 m); diameter 4.7 in (12 cm)
Warhead: 13.2-lb (6-kg) fragmentation
Operators: Afghanistan, Albania, Algeria, Angola, Bangladesh, Bulgaria, China, Cuba, Czechoslovakia, East Germany, Ethiopia, Egypt, Finland, Hungary, India, Iraq, Laos, Libya, Mozambique, Nigeria, North Korea, Peru, Poland, Romania, Somalia, Sudan, Syria, Tanzania, Uganda, USSR, Vietnam, Yemen, Yugoslavia (in some cases, missile supplied but not operational)

By 1980 the chief carrier of the AA-2 Atoll AAM in Soviet PVO service was probably the MiG-23S all-weather interceptor.

Soviet AA-3 Anab

The AA-3 'Anab' can be fitted with either an infra-red or semi-active radar seeker, the latter homing on to radar energy transmitted from the launch aircraft and reflected from its target. The missile is carried by the Sukhoi Su-11 'Fishpot-C', this model replacing the 'Fishpot-B' armed with the AA-1 'Alkali', and also the Su-15 'Flagon'. Both types carry two rounds, one with each type of guidance. In both cases the fire-control radar is known by NATO as 'Skip Spin', and the same missile/radar combination was also carried by the Yakovlev Yak-28, which is no longer in front-line service. The most modern variant of the missile is known by NATO as AA-3-2 'Advanced Anab', but even this is now obsolescent and the latest versions of the Su-15 carry the AA-6 'Acrid' in place of the 'Anab'.

Type: air-to-air missile
Powerplant: solid-propellant rocket
Performance: cruising speed probably about Mach 2 or 1,320 mph (2112 km/h) at 40,000 ft (12190 m); maximum range at least 10 miles (16 km)
Weight: about 606 lb (275 kg)
Dimensions: span about 4 ft 3 in (1.3 m); length 11 ft 10 in to 13 ft (3.6 to 4.0 m); diameter about 11 in (28 cm)
Warhead: high-explosive
Operator: USSR

Soviet AA-5 Ash

The AA-5 'Ash', like the AA-3, exists in both infra-red and semi-active radar versions. The only type known to be armed with the 'Ash' is the Tupolev Tu-28P 'Fiddler' interceptor, which was developed to patrol the boundaries of the Soviet Union where cover from surface-to-air missiles was not available. The 'Fiddler' probably remains in service, despite reports that it is being replaced by an interceptor version of the Tu-22 'Blinder'. The Tu-28P carries four AA-5s, two of each type (twice the load originally fitted). The radar-guided rounds home on to energy transmitted by the Tu-28P's 'Big Nose' fire-control radar and reflected by the target. A common method of interception is to launch an infra-red missile first, followed by a radar-guided round about a second later. This gives a better chance of destroying the target.

Type: air-to-air missile
Powerplant: solid-propellant rocket
Performance: cruising speed probably about Mach 3 or 1,980 mph (3168 km/h) at 40,000 ft (12190 m); maximum range about 19 miles (30 km)
Weight: about 441 lb (200 kg)
Dimensions: span about 4 ft 3 in (1.3 m); length about 18 ft (5.5 m) for infra-red version, 17 ft (5.2 m) for radar version; diameter about 11.8 in (30 cm)
Warhead: high-explosive
Operator: USSR

Though some have also been seen on early examples of MiG-25 Foxbat the main carrier of the missile known to NATO as AA-5 'Ash' is the Tu-28P long range interceptor. It is still in limited service, each aircraft usually having two IR and two radar homing missiles.

Soviet AA-6 Acrid

The AA-6 'Acrid' is one of the three air-to-air missiles (with the AA-7 and AA-8) developed by the Soviet Union to replace the earlier AA-2 'Atoll', AA-3 'Anab' and AA-5 'Ash'. The 'Acrid' was revealed to the West in 1975, when the Russians released a photograph of a Mikoyan-Gurevich MiG-25 'Foxbat' interceptor carrying four rounds. As in the case of many Russian AAMs, the 'Acrid' is operational in two versions, one with an infra-red seeker and the other a semi-active radar homing head. The MiG-25 normally carries two of each type; a typical interception would involve firing an IR round first, followed by a radar missile about a second later, against the same target, provided that it was within the range of the IR seeker.

The AA-6 is virtually twice the size of the West's largest air-to-air missile and is probably built of titanium. The missile has replaced the AA-3 'Anab' in the most recent versions of the Sukhoi Su-15: the 'Flagon-D' and 'Flagon-E' carry two AA-6 missiles each. It could also arm an interceptor version of the Su-19 'Fencer', but there is no evidence that such a combination has been deployed.

Type: air-to-air missile
Powerplant: solid-propellant rocket
Performance: cruising speed about Mach 4.5 or 2,970 mph (4752 km/h) at 40,000 ft (12190 m); maximum range about 31 miles (50 km) for radar version, 12.5 miles (20 km) for infra-red version
Weights: about 1,655 lb (750 kg) for radar version, 1,545 lb (700 kg) for infra-red version
Dimensions: span about 7 ft 5 in (2.25 m); length about 20 ft 8 in (6.3 m) for radar version, 19 ft 5 in (5.9 m) for infra-red version; diameter about 1 ft 2 in (36 cm)
Warhead: about 132.3 to 220.5-lb (60 to 100 kg) high-explosive
Operator: USSR

Soviet AA-7 Apex

The AA-7 'Apex' is the Soviet Union's new medium-size air-to-air missile and, like its predecessors and contemporaries, exists in both infra-red-guided and semi-active radar homing versions. The Mikoyan-Gurevich MiG-23S 'Flogger-B' fighter carries two rounds (one of each type) on its glove pylons, and some examples of the MiG-25 'Foxbat-A' interceptor are fitted with four AA-7s in place of AA-6s. There is also some evidence that the 'Apex' is intended to replace the AA-2 on late-model MiG-21s.

Type: air-to-air missile
Powerplant: solid-propellant rocket
Performance: cruising speed about Mach 3.5 or 2,310 mph (3696 km/h) at 40,000 ft (12190 m); maximum range about 20 miles (32 km) for radar version, 10 miles (16 km) for infra-red version
Weight: about 705 lb (320 kg)
Dimensions: span about 4 ft 7 in (1.4 m); length about 14 ft 9 in (4.5 m) for radar version, 13 ft 10 in (4.22 m) for infra-red version; diameter about 10.2 in (26 cm)
Warhead: about 88.2-lb (40-kg) high-explosive
Operator: USSR

Soviet AA-8 Aphid

The AA-8 'Aphid' is a replacement for the AA-2 'Atoll' air-to-air missile and may be derived from the earlier weapon. A version using semi-active radar guidance is reported to exist in addition to the variant employing infra-red seeking, but the small diameter of the weapon must have caused difficulty (as it did with the AIM-9 Sidewinder). The 'Aphid' is designed for short-range engagements of highly manoeuvrable targets, and may be fitted with fixed vanes, similar to those installed on the Matra R.550 Magic, to straighten the airflow at high angles of attack before it reaches the canard steering fins. Two 'Aphids' are carried beneath the belly of Mikoyan-Gurevich MiG-23S 'Flogger-B' fighters, and up to four can arm the Yakovlev Yak-36 'Forger' shipboard VTOL fighter. Other types are expected to carry the AA-8, both as a primary weapon and for self-defence.

Type: air-to-air missile
Powerplant: solid-propellant rocket
Performance: cruising speed about Mach 3 or 1,980 mph (3168 km/h) at 40,000 ft (12190 m); maximum range about 4.4 miles (7 km)
Weight: about 121 lb (55 kg)
Dimensions: span about 1 ft 8½ in (52 cm); length about 6 ft 7 in (2 m); diameter about 5.1 in (13 cm)
Warhead: about 13.2-lb (6-kg) high-explosive
Operator: USSR

Soviet AS-3 Kangaroo

The AS-3 'Kangaroo' is the Soviet Union's largest stand-off missile and remains in service, although it has been operational since the early 1960s. The weapon arms Tupolev Tu-95 'Bear-B' bombers of both the Soviet Long-Range Aviation and Naval Aviation, and would be used against large targets such as cities, ports, marshalling yards, convoys or task forces.

The AS-3 is apparently derived from the Sukhoi Su-7 'Fitter-A' fighter-bomber, with the tail redesigned. The dorsal fin is smaller than in the aircraft, allowing the 'Kangaroo' to fit into the Tu-95's bomb bay, and a ventral strake is added to restore directional stability. The air intake in the missile's nose is covered by a fairing while the AS-3 is being carried by its launch aircraft, since the weapon is too large to fit completely inside the bomb bay and drag would otherwise be excessive. This fairing may also supply the missile with high-pressure air from the Tu-95's engines immediately before launch, allowing the missile's own powerplant to be started.

Any description of Russian missile operation must be speculative, but the AS-3 is thought to be launched at a height of 39,090-39,370 ft (11000-12000 m), then climbing to about 59,055 ft (18000 m) at a speed of Mach 1.6 or 1,056 mph (1690 km/h). During these early stages of the mission the 'Kangaroo' is thought to use beam-riding guidance, flying along the centre of a beam transmitted by the launch aircraft's radar. The mid-course guidance is probably under autopilot control (updated by radio commands from the bomber or other aircraft) with the missile beginning its descent towards the

Called AS-3 'Kangaroo' by NATO, this air/surface missile carried by the so-called 'Bear-B and C' versions of the Tu-20 is the largest air-launched weapon ever developed in numbers.

continued 377

et from a distance of about 100 miles (160 and at a speed of Mach 1.8. A low-level ion can also be flown as an alternative. AS-3 is not thought to carry any form of inal homing and is therefore relatively in-

accurate, but this is overcome by the sheer size of its intended targets and the use of a large thermonuclear warhead.

Type: strategic air-to-surface missile

Powerplant: one afterburning turbojet
Performance: cruising speed Mach 1.6-1.8 or 1,056-1,188 mph (1690-1900 km/h) at 40,000 ft (12190 m); maximum range 400 miles (650 km)

Weight: about 24,250 lb (11000 kg)
Dimensions: span 32 ft 10 in (9.15 m); length 49 ft (14.9 m); diameter 6 ft (1.85 m)
Warhead: 5,070-lb (2300-kg) thermonuclear
Operator: USSR

Soviet AS-4 Kitchen

h the AS-4 'Kitchen' the Soviet air force n its move away from air-breathing stand- missiles to types powered by rocket ors. The weapon entered service in the -1960s (various sources quote dates spann- 1962 to 1967) as armament for the olev Tu-22 'Blinder-B' bomber. The AS-4 conventional aircraft-type layout but has a ral fin in place of the more normal dorsal , allowing the missile to be semi-recessed e launch aircraft's weapons bay, the doors hich are shaped so that they can fit round 'Kitchen' when it is being carried yet be ed normally if the weapon is not being car- or has been dropped.

he AS-4 would normally be launched at a ht of about 36,090 ft (11000 m), then er dive or climb depending on the type of ion to be flown. Against targets at max- m range the missile would climb at a speed bout Mach 1.8 or 1,188 mph (1900 km/h) l reaching a height of some 88,580 ft 00 m) at a range of 150 miles (250 km) n its objective, then descend in a shallow at up to Mach 2.5 or 1,650 mph (2640 'h). If the target is less than about 200 s (320 km) distant, however, 'Kitchen' is ght to descend for a low-level cruise at h 1.2 or 912 mph (1460 km/h).

1ost of the flight is carried out with the aid nertial guidance, and some form of ter- al homing is used for attacks on ships. h active radar and infra-red have been ted as the type of terminal seeking, and rnative homing heads could possibly be fit- for different missions. The AS-4 has also a seen arming the Tu-26 'Backfire-B' ber, possibly as an interim weapon before

the AS-6 'Kingfish' became generally available. (All data are approximations.)

Type: air-to-surface missile
Powerplant: one liquid-propellant rocket
Performance: cruising speed up to Mach 2.5 or 1,650 mph (2640 km/h) at 40,000 ft (12190 m); maximum range 450 miles (720 km)
Weight: 13,230 lb (6000 kg)
Dimensions: span 10 ft (3 m); length 37 ft (11.3 m); diameter 3 ft (90 cm)
Warhead: 2,205-lb (1000-kg) high-explosive or thermonuclear
Operators: USSR, Libya (possibly on Tu-22)

In this dramatic but puzzling picture of a Tu-22 of the 'Blinder-B' type the AS-4 'Kitchen' air/surface missile can be seen nestled in the belly, with a pale-coloured airframe and large black nose radome. Operator is the AV-MF.

Soviet AS-5 Kelt

first Soviet second-generation air-to- ace missile, the AS-5 'Kelt' was deployed 966-67 as a replacement for the AS-1 'Ken- . The newer missile is carried by the dger-G' version of the Tupolev Tu-16 nber, whereas the 'Kennel' had armed the dger-B' variant. The 'Kelt' is bigger and vier than its predecessor, employs rocket pulsion rather than an early turbojet, and is only Russian ASM known to have been d in action; up to 25 are thought to have n launched by the Egyptian air force in the n Kippur War of 1973, of which three are eved to have hit their targets.

wo 'Kelts' are normally carried beneath wings of the 'Badger-G'; the missile is of ventional aircraft-type layout, with swept gs and a normal tail arrangement, and it y incorporate the same nose section as the face-launched SS-N-2 Styx anti-ship sile. The AS-5 would normally be launched height of about 29,530 ft (9000 m), before nbing for a long-range mission or diving if target is at a comparatively short distance. the former case the weapon cruises at a ed of about Mach 0.9 or 595 mph (950 /h) until it reaches a height of some 59,055 18000 m) and levels out; it then begins to cend once it is about 100 miles (160 km) n its target. On a low-level mission the

Two AS-5 'Kelt' rocket-powered cruise missiles are carried by the 'Badger-G' version of the widely used Tu-16 strategic platform.

missile descends immediately after launching.
Control during the cruise part of the mis- sion is provided by the missile's autopilot, and an active radar seeker is thought to be used for the last 19-25 miles (30-40 km) of an attack. The 'Kelt' can home on to the transmissions from target radars if they are not switched off.

Type: air-to-surface missile
Powerplant: liquid-propellant rocket
Performance: cruising speed up to Mach 0.9 or 595 mph (950 km/h) at 40,000 ft (12190 m), possibly as high as Mach 1.2; maximum range 110-200 miles (180-320 km), depending on the type of mission, but effective operation

may be limited to about 125 miles (200 km)
Weight: 7,715 lb (3500 kg)
Dimensions: span 15 ft (4.55 m); length 31 ft (9.5 m); diameter 3 ft (90 cm)
Warhead: 2,205-lb (1000-kg) high-explosive
Operators: Egypt, USSR

Soviet AS-6 Kingfish

e definitive version of the Russian AS-6 ingfish' missile is thought to have entered vice in 1975-76 as armament for the polev Tu-26 'Backfire-B' variable-geometry nber and perhaps also some Tu-16 'Badger- , although a weapon designated AS-6 by \TO was reported to be available as early 1970. The 'Kingfish' is thought to have n developed from the AS-4 'Kitchen', but re must be some doubt about this because

the new missile is shorter than AS-4, has a dorsal rather than a ventral fin, is said to be powered by a solid-propellant rather than a liquid-propellant rocket, and probably employs different guidance methods.

The AS-6 can be carried in pairs, one beneath each wing, or as a single missile slung beneath the bomber's fuselage. On a maximum-range mission the 'Kingfish' is thought to be launched at a height of about

36,090 ft (11000 m) from a bomber flying at approximately Mach 0.8 or 528 mph (845 km/h), then accelerating to Mach 1.8 or 1,188 mph (1900 km/h) as it climbs to 59,055 ft (18000 m). The AS-6 is then thought to begin a gradual dive towards its target, reaching a speed of Mach 2.5 or 1,650 mph (2640 km/h) and possibly accelerating to as much as Mach 3.5 before impact. On a low-level mission the weapon is thought to cruise at a speed of

about Mach 1.2.

Mid-course inertial guidance is likely to be used, with an active radar seeker assuming control for the last 30 miles (50 km) or so of the mission. The 'Kingfish' is thought to be intended for attacks on shipping and land targets, possibly including seaboard cities in the United States, although the published estimates of its range disagree wildly and the use of a solid-propellant rocket motor seems

continued

questionable, for an air-breather would be far superior. (All data are approximations).

Type: air-to-surface missile
Powerplant: solid-propellant rocket
Performance: cruising speed possibly as high as Mach 3.5 or 2,660 mph (4250 km/h) in the final stages of an attack, but otherwise probably no more than Mach 2.5 or 1,650 mph (2640 km/h) at 40,000 ft (12190 m); maximum range possibly no more than 135 miles (215 km), although distances of up to 500 miles (800 km) have been quoted
Weight: 10,500 lb (4800 kg)
Dimensions: span 9 ft 6 in (2.9 m); length 33 ft (10 m); diameter 3 ft (90 cm)
Warhead: interchangeable 2,205-lb (1000-kg) high-explosive or 200-kiloton thermonuclear
Operator: USSR

Designated AS-6 'Kingfish' by NATO, the missile under the left wing of this Tu-16 'Badger-H' is a standard weapon of the 'Backfire'.

Soviet AS-7 Kerry

Perhaps the most surprising thing about the Russian AS-7 'Kerry' is that it was not developed 10 years or more earlier than was the case. The Western approximate equivalents, the Martin-Marietta Bullpup and Aérospatiale AS.30, have long been in service but the AS-7 was not deployed until the mid-1970s. It is a visually command-guided weapon which allows targets to be attacked from beyond the ranges possible with unguid-ed rockets and has been installed on attack aircraft including the Sukhoi Su-7B 'Fitter-A' and Su-17 'Fitter-C/D' and Mikoyan-Gurevich MiG-27 'Flogger-D'. The weapon may also be carried by the Yakovlev Yak-36 'Forger' shipboard VTOL fighter and is reported also to arm the Su-19 'Fencer' as an interim missile until more advanced all-weather types are available.

The AS-7 is guided by the pilot or second crew member by means of a joystick, movements of which result in steering corrections being generated and transmitted to the missile over a radio link. Semi-automatic command guidance or semi-active laser homing may be adopted in subsequent variants.

Type: air-to-surface missile
Powerplant: solid-propellant rocket
Performance: cruising speed Mach 0.6 or 456 mph (730 km/h) at sea level; maxim range 6¼ miles (10 km)
Weight: up to 2,650 lb (1200 kg), but p bably less
Dimensions: not known
Warhead: high-explosive
Operator: USSR

Soviet AS-8

The Russian AS-8 air-to-surface missile, which is thought to be fitted with a passive radiation seeker so that it will home on to radar transmissions and is autonomous after being launched, has been developed to arm the Mil Mi-24 'Hind' attack helicopter and its suc-cessors. The weapon could also be carried by fixed-wing aircraft such as the Mikoyan-Gurevich MiG-27 'Flogger-D'. Targets to be attacked with the AS-8 are probably acquired by a receiver in the launch aircraft, allowing the missile's homing head to be locked on.

Type: air-to-surface missile
Powerplant: solid-propellant rocket
Performance: cruising speed between Mach 0.5 and Mach 0.8 or 380-608 mph (608-973 km/h) at sea level; maximum range 5-6 miles (8-10 km)

Weight: not known
Dimensions: not known
Warhead: high-explosive
Operator: USSR

Soviet AS-9

The Russian AS-9 is believed to be an anti-radiation missile which will allow the Sukhoi Su-19 'Fencer' attack aircraft to engage enemy transmitters from comparatively long ranges.

Little else is known about the weapon.

Type: air-to-surface missile
Powerplant: solid-propellant rocket

Performance: cruising speed subsonic; maximum range 53-62 miles (85-100 km)
Weight: not known
Dimensions: not known

Warhead: high-explosive
Operator: USSR

Soviet AS-10

The Russian AS-10 missile, which uses television guidance, is understood to be a complement to the radiation-homing AS-8. It is thought to arm the Mil Mi-24 'Hind' attack helicopter, and is probably locked on to its target before launch with the aid of powerful electro-optical sensors carried by the parent aircraft. The AS-10 would be equally suitable for fixed-wing attack aircraft such as the Mikoyan-Gurevich MiG-27 'Flogger-D'.

Type: air-to-surface missile

Powerplant: solid-propellant rocket
Performance: cruising speed between Mach 0.6 and Mach 0.8 or 456-608 mph (730-973 km/h) at sea level; maximum range 6 miles (10 km)
Weight: not known

Dimensions: not known
Warhead: high-explosive
Operator: USSR

Soviet AS-11

The Russian AS-11, also known as the Advanced TASM (Tactical Air-to-Surface Missile), is thought to use television guidance combined with a data link. This would allow it to be command-guided during the mid-course phase of its mission, either by the launch aircraft or by an operator in another vehicle, and to be locked on to its target for the final stages of an attack. This method of operation is most suitable in a two-seat aircraft, and the AS-11 is assumed to arm the Sukhoi Su-19 'Fencer'.

Type: air-to-surface missile
Powerplant: solid-propellant rocket
Performance: cruising speed subsonic; maximum range 25 miles (40 km)
Weights: not known
Dimensions: not known

Warhead: high-explosive
Operator: USSR

Soviet AT-2 Swatter

The AT-2 'Swatter' is thought to have armed the Russian Mil Mi-24 'Hind' attack helicopter as an interim weapon before introduction of the AT-6 'Spiral'. 'Swatter' is believed to be guided by radio command, possibly with infra-red terminal homing. Early models deployed with ground forces are believed to have been steered completely manually, but a semi-automatic version is reported to have been introduced and it may be this variant which has been adapted for air-launching. The AT-2 is unlikely to be retained in service once the AT-6 is fully operational.

Type: anti-tank missile
Powerplant: solid-propellant rocket
Performance: cruising speed not known; maximum range 2,735 yards (2500 m), possibly more in air-launched role
Weight: about 44 lb (20 kg)
Dimensions: span 2 ft 2 in (66 cm); length 3 ft 9 in (1.14 m); diameter 5.2 in (13.2 cm
Warhead: hollow-charge, capable penetrating 11.8 in (30 cm) of armour
Operator: USSR

Soviet AT-6 Spiral

The AT-6 'Spiral' is a Russian replacement for the AT-2 'Swatter' which was deployed as an interim weapon on Mil Mi-24 'Hind' attack helicopters. 'Spiral' is thought to employ semi-active laser guidance, with targets being illuminated by designators mounted on ground vehicles such as tanks and presumably also by infantry.

Type: air-to-surface missile

Powerplant: solid-propellant rocket
Performance: cruising speed not known; maximum range probably 4.4-6.3 miles (7-10 km)
Weight: not known

Dimensions: not known
Warhead: probably hollow-charge
Operator: USSR

INDEX

PICTURE CREDITS

The Publishers would like to thank the following people and organizations for their help in providing illustrations for this book:

AIDC (Aero Industry Development Center)
AISA (Aeronautica Industrial SA)
Aeritalia SpA
Aeronautica Macchi SpA
Aérospatiale (Société Nationale Industrielle Aérospatiale)
Aerotec (Sociede Aerotec Ltda)
Atlas Aircraft Corporation of South Africa (Pty) Ltd
Beech Aircraft Corporation
Bell Helicopter Textron
The Boeing Company
British Aerospace
British Aircraft Corporation
Britten-Norman (Bembridge) Ltd
CAARP (Coopérative des Ateliers Aéronautiques de la Région Parisienne)
CASA (Construcciones Aeronáuticas SA)
Canadair Ltd
Central Office of Information
Dassault-Breguet Aviation
De Havilland Aircraft of Canada
Dornier GmbH
Douglas Aircraft Company
EMBRAER (Empresa Brasiliera de Aeronáutica SA)
FFA (Flug- und Fahrzeugwerke AG)
FMA (Area de Material Cordoba)
Fairchild Industries Inc
Fokker-VFW BV
Fournier, Avions
Fuji Heavy Industries Ltd
GAF (Government Aircraft Factories)
Gates Learjet Corporation
General Dynamics Corporation
Grumman Corporation
Helio Courier Ltd
Hiller Aviation
Hindustan Aeronautics Ltd
Michael J. Hooks
Hughes Helicopters
Israel Aircraft Industries
Avions Jodel SA
Kaman Aerospace Corporation
Kawasaki Heavy Industries Ltd
Lockheed Aircraft Corporation
McDonnell Douglas Corporation
Messerschmitt-Bölkow-Blohm GmbH

Ministry of Defence
Mitsubishi Heavy Industries Ltd
NAMC (Nihon Kokuki Seizo Kabushiki
    Kaisha)
Neiva Ltda
New Zealand Aerospace Industries Ltd
North American Aircraft Operations
Northrop Corporation
Novosti Press Agency
PAF (Philippine Air Force)
Panavia Aircraft GmbH
Pazmany Aircraft Corporation
Piaggio SpA
Pilatus Flugzeugwerke AG
Piper Aircraft Corporation
Ronald T. Pretty
RFB (Rhein-Flugzeugbau GmbH)
Robin, Avions Pierre
Rockwell International Corporation
SIAI-Marchetti Societa per Azioni
SOCATA (Société de Construction d'Avions
    de Tourisme et d'Affaires)
Saab-Scania Aktiebolag
Shin Meiwa Industry Ltd
Short Brothers Ltd
Sikorsky Aircraft Division of United
    Technologies Corporation
R.W. Simpson
Soko
Swearingen Aviation Corporation
Transall Arbeitsgemeinschaft
United States Air Force Information Service
United States Army
United States Navy
Valmet oy Kuorveden Tehdas
Vought Corporation
Wassmer Aviation Société Nouvelle
Westland Helicopters Ltd

Aviation Letter Photo Service:
    p 20 (Tupolev Tu-134)
    p 273 (Mil Mi-6)
Camera Press Ltd:
    p 29 (McDonnell Douglas F-4 Phantom)
    p 99 (Boeing KC-97)
C.E.V. Cazaux:
    p 370 (Matra Super 530)
Keystone Press Agency:
    p 25 (Mikoyan-Gurevich MiG-21)
    p 29 (Dassault Mirage III)
Klaus Niska:
    p 19 (Mikoyan-Gurevich MiG-21)
    p 206 (Ilyushin Il-18)
    p 261 (Mikoyan-Gurevich MiG-21)
    p 266 (Mikoyan-Gurevich MiG-23)
    p 274 (Mil Mi-8)
    p 344 (Valmet Vinka)
Peter Steinemann:
    p 259 (Mikoyan-Gurevich MiG-15)
    p 266 (Mikoyan-Gurevich MiG-23)
    p 272 (Mil Mi-18)